The SAGE
Handbook of

Comparative
Politics

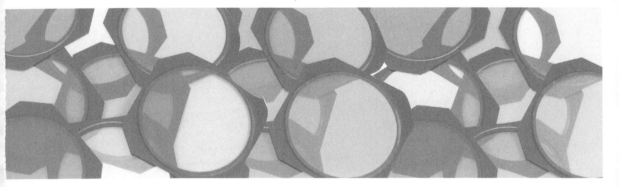

The SAGE
Handbook of

Comparative
Politics

Edited by
Todd Landman and
Neil Robinson

Los Angeles | London | New Delhi
Singapore | Washington DC

February 2011

JF
51
.S24
2009

SAGE Publications Ltd
1 Oliver's Yard
55 City Road
London EC1Y 1SP

SAGE Publications Inc.
2455 Teller Road
Thousand Oaks, California 91320

SAGE Publications India Pvt Ltd
B 1/I 1 Mohan Cooperative Industrial Area
Mathura Road
New Delhi 110 044

SAGE Publications Asia-Pacific Pte Ltd
33 Pekin Street #02-01
Far East Square
Singapore 048763

Library of Congress Control Number: 2008930782

British Library Cataloguing in Publication data

A catalogue record for this book is available from the British Library

ISBN 978-1-4129-1976-0

Typeset by CEPHA Imaging Pvt. Ltd., Bangalore, India
Printed in Great Britain by MPG Books Group, Bodmin, Cornwall
Printed on paper from sustainable resources

Contents

List of Tables and Figures

TABLES

FIGURES

Acknowledgements

We would like to thank all of our contributing authors and the publisher, particularly David Mainwaring, for their patience and perseverance in the preparation of this manuscript. It has taken far longer to put this book together than we had hoped or planned and your forbearance has been much appreciated.

That the book has appeared at all is in no small measure the result of help that we have received along the way. Karen Buckley has on several occasions provided heroic assistance, particularly as we went through the final edit. Financial assistance was provided at the start of the project by the University of Limerick Faculty of Arts, Humanities and Social Sciences Research Board. Tom Lodge also made a crucial intervention that helped move the process along at a critical juncture.

On a personal note we'd like to offer the traditional thanks to our families for their toleration of our absences and complaints about the progress of the work. Neil would like to thank Maura, for listening to the moaning, both general and specific, and for everything else, and Sáoirse and Mani for insisting – quite rightly – that playtime was accorded *at least* equal importance with all of life's other activities, including book editing.

Todd offers thanks to Pavlenka and Stephen Small for being great friends and a super sounding board, and extends his heartfelt thanks to Melissa, Oliver, Sophia and Briony Rose (the newest addition to the Landman clan in the UK) for proving that family life and all that goes with it offers the best lessons for understanding the big questions in life.

Notes on Contributors

Sarah Birch is Reader in Politics at the University of Essex and Co-Editor of the *British Journal of Political Science*. She is author of *Elections and democratization in Ukraine* (Palgrave, 2000), *Electoral systems and political transformation in post-communist Europe* (Palgrave-Macmillan, 2003), and co-author of the companion volume, *Embodying democracy: Electoral system design in post-communist Europe* (Palgrave-Macmillan, 2002). Her most recent book is *Full participation: A comparative study of compulsory voting* (Manchester University Press, 2008). She has also published numerous articles on electoral systems and electoral conduct. Her current research interests include electoral conduct and political ethics.

Vincent Boudreau is Professor of Comparative Politics at the City College of New York and the City University of New York's Graduate Center. Professor Boudreau writes about protest movements, state repression and democratization in Southeast Asia, both comparatively, and with particular focus on the Philippines. His latest book is *Resisting dictatorship: Repression and protest in Southeast Asia* (Cambridge, 2004). His most recent research seeks to explain divergent patterns of post-transition politics in Indonesia and the Philippines, and patterns of collective violence across Southeast Asia. He also serves on the editorial board of *Comparative Politics*.

Shaun Bowler is Professor of Political Science at the University of California, Riverside. His research interests include comparative political behaviour and electoral systems. He is co-author, along with Christopher Anderson, Andres Blais, Todd Donovan, and Ola Listhaug of *Loser's consent* (Oxford, 2005).

James A. Caporaso is Professor of Political Science in the Department of Political Science, University of Washington. He is a former president of the International Studies Association (1997–98), former Chair of the Executive Committee of the European Community Studies Association (1995–97), and the editor of *Comparative Political Studies*. His research interests are in global political economy, regional integration, and comparative institutional analysis. He has published articles in the *American Political Science Review*, *West European Politics*, *Journal of Common Market Studies*, *International Organization*, and *International Studies Quarterly*.

Paola Cesarini teaches in the Department of Political Science at Providence College, specializing in comparative politics and human rights. Previously, she worked for the World Bank, the United Nations, and the Institute of Latin American and Iberian Studies at Columbia University. Her primary research interests are: transitional justice, comparative democratization, and the politics of memory. She is co-editor, with Katherine Hite, of *Authoritarian legacies and democracy in Latin America and Southern Europe* (University of Notre Dame Press, 2004). Her work has appeared in peer-reviewed periodicals – such as the *Journal of Latin American Studies* and *International Studies Review* – and various edited volumes.

Josep M. Colomer is Research Professor in Political Science at the Higher Council of Scientific Research and affiliated professor at Barcelona-Graduate School of Economics. He is elected member of the Academia Europaea and life member of the American Political Science Association. Author of two dozen books, published in five languages, including *Political institutions* (Oxford University Press, 2001), *Handbook of electoral system choice* (Palgrave-Macmillan, 2004) and *Great empires, small nations* (Routledge, 2007).

Jan W. van Deth is Professor of Political Science and International Comparative Social Research at the University of Mannheim (Germany). His main research areas are political culture (especially social capital, political engagement, and citizenship), social change, and comparative research methods. He was Director of the Mannheim Centre for European Social Research (MZES), convenor of the international network Citizenship, Involvement, Democracy (CID), and Book Series Editor of the Studies in European Political Science of the European Consortium for Political Research (ECPR). He is a Corresponding Member of the Royal Netherlands Academy of Arts and Sciences (KNAW) and national coordinator of the German team for the European Social Survey. Recent publications include *Civil society and governance in Europe. From National to international linkages* (edited with William Maloney; Edward Elgar, 2008).

Barbara Geddes has written about the breakdown in authoritarian regimes, bureaucratic reform and corruption, political bargaining over institutional choice and change, and research design. Her publications include *Paradigms and sand castles: Theory building and research design in comparative politics* (2003), *Politician's dilemma: Building state capacity in Latin America* (1994), 'What do we know about democratization after twenty years?' *Annual Review of Political Science* (1999) and 'A game theoretic model of reform in Latin American democracies,' *American Political Science Review* (1991). Her current research focuses on politics inside dictatorships. She teaches Latin American politics, authoritarian politics, and research design at UCLA.

Jack A. Goldstone is Hazel Professor and Director of the Center for Global Policy at George Mason University. He is the author of *Revolution and rebellion in the early modern world* (California, 1991), and editor of *The Encyclopedia of Political Revolutions* (Congressional Quarterly, 1998). He has received the Distinguished Contribution to Scholarship award of the American Sociological Association, the Arnoldo Momigliano Prize of the Historical Society, and fellowships from the ACLS and the MacArthur Foundation.

Stephen E. Hanson is Herbert J. Ellison Professor in the Department of Political Science and the Director of the Ellison Center for Russian, East European, and Central Asian Studies at the Jackson School of International Studies at the University of Washington. He is the author of *Time and revolution: Marxism and the design of Soviet institutions* (University of North Carolina Press, 1997), winner of the 1998 Wayne S. Vucinich book award from the American Association for the Advancement of Slavic Studies. He is also a co-editor of *Capitalism and democracy in Central and Eastern Europe: Assessing the legacy of communist rule*, (Cambridge University Press, 2003), a co-author of *Postcommunism and the theory of democracy* (Princeton University Press, 2001), and the author of numerous journal articles examining postcommunist politics in comparative perspective.

Darren G. Hawkins is Professor of Political Science at Brigham Young University, where he teaches and researches on international relations, human rights, and international organizations. He has coedited a volume of *Delegation and agency in international organizations* (Cambridge University Press) and authored *International human rights and authoritarian rule in Chile*

(Nebraska University Press). He has also published a number of scholarly articles on international human rights, international institutions, and democracy. These have appeared in *International Organization, Journal of Politics, International Studies Quarterly, Comparative Politics, Global Governance, Review of International Studies,* and other journals.

Paul M. Heywood is Sir Francis Hill Professor of European Politics at the University of Nottingham, and Adjunct Professor at Hunan University, China, where he is also Senior Adviser to the Anti-Corruption Research Center. He has published widely on political corruption, as well as on contemporary European politics. Amongst his recent books are *Spain and the European Union* (with Carlos Closa; Palgrave, 2004) and *Developments in European politics* (edited with Erik Jones, Martin Rhodes and Ulrich Sedelmeier; Palgrave, 2006). He is currently working on issues of administrative reform and corruption risks.

John M. Hobson is Professor of Politics and International Relations at the University of Sheffield, and is co-director of the Political Economy Research Centre and a sub-editor of *Political Studies.* His main research interest lies in the critique of Eurocentrism and the reconstruction of a non-Eurocentric account of inter-civilizational relations and globalization, past and present. He has authored/co-authored six books to date, two of which are co-edited volumes. His most recent books are: *The eastern origins of western civilisation* (CUP, 2004); *Everyday politics of the world economy* (CUP, 2007; co-edited with Leonard Seabrooke). He has published over 40 book chapters and journal articles, and is currently working on a book that contains some of John A. Hobson's 1930's lectures, provisionally entitled *The struggle for the international mind.*

Jennifer S. Holmes, is Associate Professor of Political Economy and Political Science at the University of Texas at Dallas. Her major area of research is political violence, terrorism, and political development with an emphasis on Latin America and Southern Europe. She is the author of *Terrorism and democratic stability* (Manchester University Press, 2001, Transaction, 2006), *Terrorism and democratic stability revisited* (Manchester University Press, 2008), and *Guns, drugs, and development: Violence in Colombia* (with Sheila Amin Gutiérrez de Piñeres and Kevin Curtin, University of Texas Press, 2009). She is also the editor of *New approaches to comparative politics: Insights from political theory* (Lexington Books, 2003, 2008), and co-editor of *Latin American democracy: Emerging reality or endangered species?* (Routledge, 2008). Articles by Dr. Holmes have been published in *Terrorism and Political Violence, Latin American Politics & Society, Bulletin of Latin American Research, International Journal of Social Economics, Studies in Conflict and Terrorism, International Journal of Public Administration,* and *Revista de Estudios Colombianos.*

Philip Keefer is Lead Research Economist in the Development Research Group of the World Bank. The focus of his work, based on experience in countries ranging from Bangladesh, Benin, Brazil, and the Dominican Republic to Indonesia, México, Perú and Pakistan, is the determinants of political incentives to pursue economic development. His research, on issues such as the impact of insecure property rights on growth; the effects of political credibility on policy; and the sources of political credibility in democracies and autocracies, has appeared in journals ranging from the *Quarterly Journal of Economics* to the *American Review of Political Science.*

Hans Keman is Professor and Chair in Comparative Political Science at the VU University Amsterdam. He has been editor of the *European Journal of Political Research* and recently *of Acta Politica.* He has published books and articles on Parties and Government in Parliamentary Democracies, Democracy and Social and Economic Performance, Social Democracy and the Welfare State, institutional theory and on Comparative Methods.

Herbert Kitschelt is Professor for Comparative Politics at Duke University, North Carolina. In recent years he has primarily worked on the comparison of parties and party systems in advanced industrial democracies, post-communist Eastern Europe and Latin America. He is the co-editor of *Patrons, clients and policies* (Cambridge University Press, 2007) and co-author of the forthcoming *Latin American party systems* (Cambridge University Press, 2009). He is currently involved in a global comparison of patterns of democratic accountability in electoral democracies.

Jan Kleinnijenhuis is Professor of Communication Science at the VU University Amsterdam since 1998. His research interests include agenda building and agenda setting processes in which both old and new media play their role, as well as methods for content analysis and panel survey analysis to chart these processes in great detail. He has published on these subjects in journals such as *Political Analysis*, the *British Journal of Political Science*, *Journal of Communication*, and the *Harvard International Journal of Press/Politics*. Together with Paul Pennings and Hans Keman he wrote *Doing research in Political Science: An introduction to comparative methods and statistics* (Sage, 1999/2006).

Todd Landman is Reader in the Department of Government and Director of the Centre for Democratic Governance at the University of Essex. He is author of *Studying human rights* (Routledge, 2006), *Protecting human rights* (Georgetown, 2005), and *Issues and methods in comparative politics* (Routledge, 2000, 2003, 2008); co-author of *Measuring human rights* (Routledge, 2009), *Governing Latin America* (Polity, 2003), and *Citizenship rights and social movements* (Oxford, 1997, 2000); and editor of *Human rights*, Volumes I–IV (Sage, 2009). He has published articles in *International Studies Quarterly*, *The British Journal of Political Science*, *Human Rights Quarterly*, *Democratization*, *The British Journal of Politics and International Relations*, and *Political Studies*.

David McKay is Professor of Government at the University of Essex. He is the author of *Federalism and European Union* (Oxford, 1999) and *Designing Europe: Comparative lessons from the federal experience* (Oxford, 2001) which won the W.J.M. Mackenzie prize for the best book published in political science, 2001. His research includes work on the sustainability of federal systems and in particular the links between institutional arrangements and the spatial dimension to political conflict including the political economy of European monetary union.

David S. Meyer is Professor of Sociology, Political Science, and Planning, Policy and Design at the University of California, Irvine. He has published numerous articles on social movements and social change, and is author or coeditor of six books, most recently, *The politics of protest: Social movements in America* (Oxford University Press). He is most interested in the connections among institutional politics, public policy, and social movements, particularly in regard to issues of war and peace.

Wolfgang C. Müller is Professor in Political Science, University of Mannheim and former Director of the Mannheim Centre for European Social Research (MZES). His recent book publications include *Policy, office, or votes? How political parties in Western Europe make hard decisions* (co-edited with Kaare Strøm; Cambridge University Press, 1999), *Coalition governments in Western Europe* (co-edited with Kaare Strøm; Oxford University Press, 2000), *Delegation and accountability in parliamentary democracies* (co-edited with Kaare Strøm and Torbjörn Bergman; Oxford University Press, 2003), *Political parties and electoral change* (co-edited with Peter Mair and Fritz Plasser; Sage, 2004), and *Cabinets and coalition bargaining: The democratic life cycle in Western Europe* (co-edited with Kaare Strøm and Torbjörn Bergman; Oxford University Press, 2008). His research interests include political representation, delegation relationships, government coalitions, political parties, and political institutions in Europe.

Pippa Norris is the McGuire Lecturer in Comparative Politics at the John F. Kennedy School of Government, Harvard University. She has also served as Director of the Democratic Governance Group at UNDP in New York. Her work compares democracy, elections and public opinion, political communications, and gender politics in many countries worldwide. A well-known public speaker and prize-winning author, she has published almost three-dozen books. This includes a series of volumes for Cambridge University Press: *A virtuous circle* (2000, winner of the 2006 Doris A. Graber award), *Digital divide* (2001), *Democratic phoenix* (2002) and *Rising tide* (with Ronald Inglehart, 2003), *Electoral engineering* (2004), *Sacred and secular* (with Ronald Inglehart, 2004, winner of the Virginia Hodgkinson prize), *Radical right* (2005), and *Driving democracy: Do power-sharing institutions work?* (2008), Her most recent books are *Cultural convergence? Cosmopolitan communications and national diversity* (with Ronald Inglehart, CUP, 2009), and an edited volume, *Guardians of the public interest: Strengthening the news media, democratic governance and human development* (The World Bank, 2009).

Paul Pennings is Associate Professor of Political Science at the VU *University Amsterdam*. His research and teaching interests are in the fields of Comparative (European) Politics and Comparative Methods and Statistics. He has publised widely in peer-reviewed academic journals in political science, such as *Acta Politica, Electoral Studies, European Journal of Political Research, European Union Politics, Party Politics, Political Studies* and *Sociological Methods and Research*. His recent publications include *Doing research in Political Science. An introduction to comparative methods and Statistics* (with Hans Keman and Jan Kleinnijenhuis Sage, 2nd edition, 2006) and (with Christine Arnold) 'Is Constitutional Politics like Politics "At Home"? The Case of the EU Constitution', *Political Studies* 56 (4): 789–806, which was a finalist for the Harrison Prize for the best article published in *Political Studies* in 2008.

Thomas Plümper is Professor of Government at the University of Essex and Director of the Essex Summer School in Social Science Data Analysis. He also holds affiliations with the Max Planck Institute of Economics in Jena, the Institute for International Integration Studies, Dublin and the Peace Research Institute in Oslo. He published articles in the *American Journal of Political Science, International Organization, Political Analysis, Annals of the Association of American Geographers, World Development, European Journal of Political Research*, the *British Journal of Political Science, Journal of Conflict Resolution,* and *International Studies Quarterly*.

Charles C. Ragin holds a joint appointment as Professor of Sociology and Political Science at the University of Arizona. His substantive interests include such topics as the welfare state, ethnic political mobilization, and international political economy. However, for the past two decades his work has focused primarily on broad issues in methodology, especially the challenge of bringing some of the logic and spirit of small-N case-oriented research to the study of medium-sized and large Ns. His most recent books are *Redesigning social inquiry: Fuzzy sets and beyond* (University of Chicago Press, 2008) and *Configurational comparative methods: Qualitative comparative analysis and related techniques* (co-edited with Benoit Rihoux; Sage Publications, 2008).

Neil Robinson is Senior Lecturer in the Department of Politics and Public Administration at the University of Limerick, Ireland. He is the author of *Ideology and the collapse of the Soviet system. A critical history of Soviet ideological discourse* (Elgar, 1995), *Post-communist politics* (with Karen Henderson, Prentice Hall, 1997), and *Russia: a state of uncertainty* (Routledge, 2002), and editor of *Institutions and political change in Russia* (Macmillan, 2000), *Reforging the weakest link: global political economy and post-Soviet change in Russia, Ukraine and Belarus* (Ashgate, 2004), and *State-building. Theory and practice* (with Aidan Hehir, Routledge, 2007). He has published in *Soviet Studies, European Journal of Political Research, The Journal of Communist Studies and Transitional Politics, Review of International Political Economy, Communist and Post-Communist Studies* and other journals.

Claude Rubinson is a Ph.D. candidate in the Department of Sociology at the University of Arizona. His interests include globalization and comparative political-economy; art, technology, and culture; social stratification; and research methodology. He uses case-oriented, comparative research methods to study the relationship between political-economic decline and cultural expression. His dissertation examines the changing aesthetics and ideologies of the Arts and Crafts movement, which arose with the decline of British hegemony. In addition to his work on comparative methodology, he has also published work on multi-valued logic and logical ambiguity in ACM's /SIGMOD Record/.

Andreas Schedler is Professor of Political Science at the Centro de Investigación y Docencia Económicas (CIDE) in Mexico City. His recent publications include *Electoral authoritarianism: The dynamics of unfree competition* (Lynne Rienner Publishers, 2006), "The Mexican Standoff: The Mobilization of Distrust," *Journal of Democracy* (January, 2007), "Democrats with Adjectives: Linking Direct and Indirect Measures of Democratic Support" (with Rodolfo Sarsfield), *European Journal of Political Research* (August, 2007), and "The Contingent Power of Authoritarian Elections," *Democratization by elections? A new mode of transition*, ed. Staffan I. Lindberg (Johns Hopkins University Press, 2009). His ongoing comparative research focuses on the internal dynamics of electoral authoritarian regimes worldwide.

Vivien A. Schmidt is Jean Monnet Professor of European Integration and Director of the Center for International Relations at Boston University, and Visiting Professor at Sciences Po, Paris. She has written widely in the areas of European political economy, institutions and democracy, as well as political theory. Recent publications include *Democracy in Europe* (Oxford, 2006), *The futures of European capitalism* (Oxford, 2002), *Welfare and work in the open economy* (2 volumes co-edited with F.W. Scharpf, Oxford, 2000), and "Discursive Institutionalism: The Explanatory Power of Ideas and Discourse" *Annual Review of Political Science* (2008).

Fredrik Söderbaum is Associate Professor of Peace and Development Research at the School of Global Studies, University of Gothenburg, and Senior Associate Research Fellow at the United Nations University-Comparative Regional Integration Studies (UNU-CRIS), Bruges, Belgium. His latest books include *EU and the global South* (co-edited with Patrik Stålgren, Lynne Rienner, 2009, forthcoming); *Afro-regions: The dynamics of cross-border micro-regionalism in Africa* (co-edited with Ian Taylor, Nordic Africa Institute, 2008), *The EU as a global player: The politics of interregionalism* (co-edited with Luk van Langenhove, Routledge, 2006), *The political economy of regionalism: The case of Southern Africa* (Palgrave Macmillan, 2004), *Theories of New Regionalism* (co-edited with Tim Shaw, Palgrave Macmillan, 2003).

Willfried Spohn is Adjunct Professor in sociology at FU Berlin. He was director of an EU research project 'Representations of Europe and the Nation in current and prospective member states – elites, media and civil society' at the European University Viadrina, Frankfurt-Odra. His recent publications are (with Steven Hanson): *Can Europe work? Germany and the reconstruction of postcommunist societies*, Seattle, 1995; 'History and the Social Sciences,'

International Encyclopedia of the Social and Behaviorial Sciences, London, 2001; (with Anna Triandafyllidou): *Europeanization, national identities and migration*, (2002), and 'Multiple Modernity, Nationalism and Religion - A Global Perspective,' in: U. Schuerkens (ed.), *Global forces and local life – Worlds*, (2003).

Christian Welzel is Professor of Political Science at Jacobs University Bremen and Vice-President of the World Values Survey Association. He is also affiliated faculty and a regular visitor of the Center for the Study of Democracy at UC Irvine. His research focuses on the themes of democratization, modernization, human development, as well as human values and cultural change. Christian Welzel has published more than 80 scholarly articles and chapters. His most recent book (with Ronald Inglehart) is *Modernaization, cultural change and democracy: The human development sequence* (New York: Cambridge University Press).

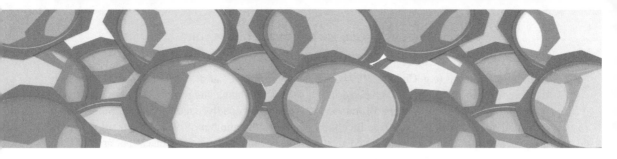

Introduction

Todd Landman and Neil Robinson

Comparative politics has firmly established itself as a significant, vibrant, and definitive tradition and field of inquiry in the discipline of political science. The field, at least as far as research and postgraduate teaching are concerned, has moved well beyond its early 'public law' phase of comparative institutionalism and its more parochial labelling as 'anything that studies countries outside the United States' (see, e.g. Valenzuela, 1988; Landman, 2000, 2003, 2008). It is now one that is at the centre of debates on normative and empirical theory (Lichbach and Zuckerman, 1997), quantitative and qualitative methodology (King et al., 1994; Brady and Collier, 2004; Gerring, 2007), and the ability for political science scholarship to have practical relevance to practitioners and policy makers across a range of significant issues areas in the contemporary world (e.g. Flyvbjerg, 2001; Schram and Caterino, 2006). *The American Political Science Review* (and now *Perspectives on Politics*) has long had a special section devoted to book reviews in comparative politics, the specialized section of the American Political Science Association on Comparative Politics has over 1,500 members and is the largest of the Association's sections, and major political science research meetings such as the European Consortium for Political Research's annual workshops are often dominated by comparative

politics research. There are three main journals dedicated to comparative politics, including *World Politics*, *Comparative Politics*, and *Comparative Political Studies*, while other top-rated journals in the field, such as the *American Journal of Political Science*, *Journal of Politics*, *British Journal of Political Science*, *International Studies Quarterly*, *Government and Opposition*, *Journal of Conflict Resolution*, and *Journal of Peace Research* have a significant and frequent number of articles that can broadly be classified as comparative.

In many ways, the field of comparative politics has been defined by what it does, namely, providing explanation and understanding of important social and political phenomena through the comparison of similarities and differences across different units, where such units are typically, but not exclusively, nation states. The methodological core of comparative politics draws on J. S. Mill's (1843/1961) methods of 'difference' and 'agreement', and allows for some form of 'control' to be introduced in ways that approximate the experimental or quasi-experimental conditions found in the natural sciences (see Faure, 1994; Mahoney and Goertz, 2004; Goertz, 2005). In short, *to compare is to control*. Alongside the methodological identity of comparative politics, some have argued that the field has its own distinctive theoretical traditions (e.g. Chilcote, 1994), but today comparative politics is characterized more through the development of rational, structural, and cultural theories (see Lichbach and Zuckerman, 1997) that are tested using some form of comparative method. Evidence is collected and analyzed in systematic fashion to yield substantive inferences that typically go beyond the confines of the case or cases that have been compared.

From the early comparisons until now, comparative method has advanced considerably, which is a function of greater attention to questions of case selection, the logic of inference and raising the number of observations, data availability, and enhanced computer technology, among others. These new themes and developments are raised repeatedly across the chapters of this volume. Classic 'first generation' comparativists such as Gabriel Almond, Robert Dahl, Barrington Moore, Seymour Martin Lipset, Samuel Huntington, Arend Lijphart, Giovanni Sartori, Ted Gurr, Theda Skocpol, Adam Przeworski, and Henry Teune achieved so much in setting the research agenda of the field across a range of seminal topics such as democracy, political violence, political development, social revolution, institutional design, and many others, while at the same time developing strategies for comparison that were attentive to variation in the outcomes that were to be explained, as well as rules of inquiry that addressed questions of concept development, conceptual stretching, case selection (at least partially), and theory-building. These scholars generally saw a methodological division in the field between those engaged in large-N cross national quantitative analysis on the one hand, and those engaged in either small-N comparative analysis or single-country case studies on the other (Lijphart, 1971).[1] This division has persisted to some degree in the field but was significantly challenged through the publication of *Designing social inquiry* (King et al., 1994), which argued that the same logic of inference that applies to large-N statistical analysis (on individual or aggregate data) should apply to small-N

comparative and single-country analysis. This challenge suggests that all comparative analysis broadly occupies a continuum that trades the number of observations off against the strength of the inferences that are drawn (see Landman, 2000, 2003, 2008). For King et al. (1994), the inferences drawn from small-N comparative analysis and single-country studies could be strengthened only through raising observations, which is achieved through analyzing individual level data within studies that compare few countries, or adding countries and time to the analysis such that variables are given room to vary and comparative studies avoid *indeterminate* research designs. Despite the achievements of the classic comparativists, King et al. (1994) were able to show that many studies still suffered from selection bias and that many of the findings from the existing literature could be called into question on this basis (see also Geddes, 2003).

Since the publication of *Designing Social Inquiry*, there have been many new volumes that respond to, challenge, and modify the main arguments laid out by King et al. (1994). A special symposium on the book appeared in the *American Political Science Review* in which qualitative scholars responded to the challenge. Book-length responses and clarifications most notably include Mahoney and Rueschemeyer's (2003) *Comparative historical analysis in the social sciences*, Brady and Collier's (2004) *Rethinking social inquiry*, George and Bennet's (2005) *Case studies and theory development in the social sciences,* and Gerring's (2007) *Case study research.* Stronger challenges to the position adopted in *Designing social inquiry* came in the form of Bent Flyvjberg's (2001) *Making social science matter* and Schram and Caterino's (2006) *Making political science matter*, which attempt to rescue the substantive role for social (and political) science in studying questions and providing answers to problems in ways that have greater meaning and understanding for the world at large and to avoid the overly scientific and 'technicist' element that had begun to dominate the profession.

These various developments in the field have shown that now, more than ever before, scholars are concerned with how to carry out the best research on the most pertinent topics in ways that provide answers to significant questions that are supported by the best available evidence that is analyzed in the most systematic fashion. The fault lines between different types of practitioners have not been closed through the development of any unified political methodology for comparative politics. Rather, there has been considerable dialogue across the 'separate tables' (Almond, 1990) within the field that recognizes the different ways in which comparative method matters for studying significant social and political phenomena; Comparativists may often work at separate tables but they do so in the same places; they work together, as Stepan (2001: 2) put it, in 'invisible colleges'. Today, comparativists engage in the quantitative comparison of many countries, qualitative and quantitative comparison of few countries and qualitative and quantitative analysis conducted in single countries. These comparisons typically use the nation state and annual observation as the basic unit of analysis, but many studies compare individual level data across and within countries, and analysis of sub-national units, such as states within federal systems have provided new avenues to raise observations within single country studies.

The Sage Handbook of Comparative Politics has been organized in ways that address these larger developments in the field by bringing together leading academics in comparative politics from across many different approaches and many different substantive topics. The volume is organized in three parts. Part I looks at methods and the fields of comparative politics; Part II details research achievements and developments in some of the classic themes of comparative politics research; Part III looks at emerging research themes and issues. Throughout the chapters, the authors have summarized developments within their particular area of interest, discussed challenges relating to the topic, and tried to look toward future developments within the field of comparative politics. The volume should, we hope, provide a primer on how to 'do' or 'think' about comparative politics, and on what the relationship of comparative politics research might be to other areas of political study, and to show the many ways in which the field has responded and is responding to new events and challenges in the political world. The extent to which the book can do this will depend, to a large degree, on how it is used. Books such as this are generally used selectively, that is, the reader dips in the book to read a chapter or two on issues that they have to research, and the rest of the volume goes unread. Such instrumental reading has its place but we would encourage any reader using the book in this way to be a bit less instrumental and to follow themes between chapters and in particular, to follow points made about method and approach from the chapters on substantive research themes to the chapters in Part I of the book on method and the fields of comparative politics and vice versa. Ideally a reader should work their way through all of Part I of the book as well as looking at any of the later chapters on research themes. However since that might be too much for the researcher in a hurry we have sought to assist reading between the chapters of this book by providing brief summaries of the chapters in Part I and by pointing to some (but by no means all) of the connections that exist to later chapters in the course of those summaries. It is unusual to just summarize some chapters of a book rather than all of them. But a handbook is not an edited work where a number of authors seek to explore an issue from a number of different perspectives and the editors draw out the common lessons of their authors' work in an introduction. A handbook presents a much wider selection of topics and approaches and thus any summary of the whole would be little more than an extended contents page for the most part. Many of the substantive issues addressed in Parts II and III of this volume do not relate to one another directly except through comparative method; the best way of having these chapters talk to one another is thus to relate them where possible to the method chapters in Part I. This is particularly important because all areas of comparative politics research, as is apparent in the chapters in Parts II and III are undergoing change. There are many reasons for this. Partly change is driven by intellectual developments within the broad comparative politics research community. Works like King et al. (1994) and the responses to it listed above are one sign of this, but there has also been considerable development of approaches driven by the clash of contrasting theories within comparative politics (for example in comparative political sociology and comparative institutional analysis, as the chapters included here by Willfried Spohn and Vivien Schmidt show). Equally, change is being driven by inter-related changes in global politics and political systems across the globe, not least the spread – no matter that it is uneven and frequently unfinished – of democracy. These changes are generating new research themes, such as electoral authoritarianism and corruption (see the chapters by Andreas Schedler and Sarah Birch in this volume), or allowing them to be studied in a more properly comparative fashion for the first time. They are providing new research data on subjects such as government formation from a wider range of cases (see the chapter by Wolfgang Müller), or public opinion (see the chapter by Pippa Norris), or pose questions about how lessons learnt from longstanding research themes, such as inquiry in to democratization, political economy, and democratic partisan competition, social movements, or corruption (see the chapters by Barbara Geddes, Herbert Kitschelt, Vincent Boudreau and David Meyer, and Paul Heywood) can be exported beyond the boundaries of their original sets of cases. These changes and the new themes and possibilities for research that they raise can only be made sense of through engagement with the methodological issues that comparative political analysis raises and when research

problems are contextualized by reference to other research traditions in political science, most notably area studies and the study of international relations, the two fields that most clearly, explicitly, and sometimes acrimoniously (all sides being guilty) cut across comparative political research. Appreciating methodological problems and the place of comparative research in any substantive research area, whether it be a classic theme such as the study of revolution (here covered by Jack Goldstone) or a new area such as transitional justice or human rights (see the chapters by Paola Cesarini and Todd Landman), requires that we work and think – and therefore read – back and forth between method, theory and data much more rigorously, widely and consistently than might have been the case in the past. This is perhaps particularly important in newer areas of study where there may be a dearth of work or data that can settle conceptual problems inductively, where there are issues about what is being studied (is the topic one that is actually fit to be studied comparatively or is it an international relations issue?), and where there are policy imperatives to provide an answer to a research problem quickly. One or more of these issues pertains at least to the comparative study of terrorism and processes of regionalization as is demonstrated in the chapters by Holmes and Söderbaum.

It is thus important for readers to try and work between the methodological and theoretical points raised in Part I and the ideas about research themes presented in Parts II and III so that issues of change identified in these latter parts of the handbook can be addressed rigorously. There is no consistent answer to how to do comparative research in Part I of this book, rather the chapters within it discuss the status of comparative politics, conceptual specification, large-N versus small-N, and case study methods to highlight the nature of the classic trade-off between 'reliability (which improves with the increase of cases) and validity (which is hampered by a large number of cases)', as Paul Pennings, Hans Keman and Jan Kleinnijenhuis put it in their chapter, and what needs to be done or thought about to work around the trade-off. In the first chapter, Charles Ragin and Claude Rubinson argue for the distinctiveness of comparative politics as a bridge between large-N and case study work and for its formalization as a method using qualitative comparative analysis (QCA). This argument follows Ragin's earlier work (Ragin, 1987; 1994; 2000) and the effort therein to specify how traditional methodological core of comparative politics, Mill's methods of 'difference' and 'agreement', can be augmented to deal with problems of multiple causes for the same phenomenon across a range of cases. Formalization using Ragin's QCA method is a means of dealing rigorously with what he and Rubinson call a 'moderate number of cases (usually around five to fifty)', whilst still being sensitive to the details of each case.

Formalization of comparative method as suggested by Ragin and Rubinson deals with many of the methodological issues associated with smallish (but not really small) N research. However, what if there are a large-N of cases or if there are only a very, very few N, or if cases need to be worked up singly for some reason? The chapters by Paul Pennings, Hans Keman and Jan Kleinnijenhuis, James Caporaso, and Darren Hawkins look at these issues. Pennings et al. give a practical example of how conceptualization is important and underpins large-N comparison. The example that they use to demonstrate the importance of conceptualization and how it influences findings in large-N research should be read in conjunction with Geddes chapter in Part II on the causes of democratization (and vice versa), since Geddes also raises the question of comparability of democratizing systems over time and issues of what needs to be conceptualized to insure comparability and robust conclusions about democratization. The next two chapters by Hawkins and Caporaso deal with problems of case study research and its relationship to small- and large-N research. Broadly, both see qualitative methods as complementary to quantitative methods. Hawkins provides a

general overview of the issues that case study work raises, its use in generating and assessing generalizable hypotheses, the issues that different forms of case study, such as counterfactual and congruence analysis, and process tracing, raise, and the relationship of case studies to different deterministic and probabilistic theories. Caporaso focuses specifically on the benefits of process tracing and the issues raised by that. Process tracing seeks to see if an observed phenomena can be related to a hypothesized cause by a series of intervening variables. Caporaso distinguishes the analytical devices and techniques necessary to distinguish types of process tracing and their relationship to other forms of explanation based on quantitive method or cross-case comparison. The care taken in Hawkins' and Caporaso's chapters to distinguish the different logics at work in case study research should be contrasted with the discussions and comparisons of different case studies in the later chapters of the book.

Finally, the discussion of general methodological issues is rounded off in Jan van Deth's chapter, which puts all of the issues raised above into perspective by reviewing how we establish the ground of comparison by ascertaining equivalence. van Deth surveys the various forms of bias that can hinder the establishment of equivalence and strategies that can be deployed to deal with them. van Deth's chapter highlights the observation made above that to compare is to control. It also confirms the general conclusion of the preceding chapters, namely that no matter what the particular theoretical basis of enquiry or the technique of analysis to be used conceptual development and specification is always the first order priority in comparative analysis.

The other chapters in Part I introduce broad areas of comparative political analysis and relate comparison to area studies and international relations. We start with Willfried Spohn's chapter on comparative political sociology since the development of comparative political sociology mirrors the development of comparative politics more generally. Spohn's chapter therefore sets the scene for the next two chapters on comparative institutional analysis and comparative political economy. This is because the crises of the first major paradigm of comparative politics, modernization, from the 1960s onwards led to the diversification of comparative political sociology research on the one hand, and on the other created the impetus for the development of comparative institutional analysis and comparative political economy.[2] These crises were both intellectual, as it was recognized that the paradigm was failing to account for variation in the development experience, and 'real-world' political, as the template of western industrial democracy, and the modernization experience that went with it, was rejected in large parts of the globe. The modernization paradigm's structural-functionalism, Spohn argues, had allowed the incorporation of the political (government, ideology and ideational factors, social and political movements and parties, policy, etc.) in an overarching framework of social evolution. The collapse of the modernization paradigm as a hegemonic approach to comparative political sociology (and hence too much of comparative politics generally) encouraged developments within comparative political sociology and beyond it. Research in comparative political sociology became more diverse as other traditions that spoke to social evolution, such as Marxism and neo-Marxism, reasserted themselves, and as new paradigms developed, such as post-colonialism and post-modernism, that challenged the positivistic assumptions of all grand theoretical narratives about human development. At the same time, the weakening of the modernization paradigm enabled the assertion of the autonomy of politics, which helped to reinvigorate institutional analysis and encouraged the use of more individualistic research methodologies and theories, which helped the development and spread of political economy approaches. Spohn concentrates on developments within comparative political sociology to show how rational, structural, and cultural theories

have developed in the wake of the modernization paradigm, and how the struggle with that paradigm continues as elements of it reasserted themselves after the collapse of communism in the late 1980s and under the cover of ideas about the globalization as homogenization.

The next two chapters spin off from these themes. Vivien Schmidt examines developments in comparative institutional analysis. This has been one of the most productive areas of comparative research, particularly of small-N research, over the last decade thanks to the emergence of new institutionalism. With Schmidt's chapter we begin to see the tension – sometimes productive, sometimes conflictive, and occasionally both – between rational, structural, and cultural theories since the mainstream varieties of new institutionalism are underpinned by rational, structural/ historical, or cultural/ideational assumptions. Schmidt posits that the three mainstream new institutionalist positions are in dialogue with each other since they, and the scholars working with them, can be placed on a continuum, and argues for a fourth form of new institutionalism,discursive institutionalism. Scholars working from this theoretical position, she argues, draw on the other forms of institutionalism and can see themselves as loyal to a tradition, but are joined together by their efforts at explaining change by demonstrating the causal influence of ideas. Thomas Plümper's chapter provides further discussion of the rational choice version of new institutionalism and places it in the context of the general development of comparative political economy. This, as Plümper notes is different to other fields of comparative political inquiry in that it is 'programmatic'. By programmatic Plümper means that comparative political economy is concerned to develop interdisciplinary research, drawing as it does on insights and methods from economics to try to formulate general theories of political phenomena. Political economy might also be termed programmatic in the sense that this methodological approach and aspiration to develop general theories of politics has developed as a research programme to cover an ever wider number of research topics. Plümper outlines how this has happened, starting with voting and the behaviour of politicians as vote maximizers and interest group behaviour. These areas of research laid the foundations for the expansion of political economy approaches in to new areas: institutional analysis, the macroeconomic consequences of elections and electoral systems, and constitutional political economy (the study of how institutional design influences decision making and the distribution of decision making powers). Plümper gives an overview of each of these areas of research, plus the emerging area of the comparative study of open economies. More detail on these areas, and some discussion of alternative approaches to them can be found in some of the chapters that follow, in particular those by Kitschelt (on political economy and democratic partisan competition in postindustrial democracies), Müller (on government formation), Colomer (on institutional design), Bowler (on comparative political behaviour), McKay (on federalism), and Keefer (on governance and growth).

Part I ends with two chapters on areas that overlap with comparative political analysis, area studies and international relations. Despite this overlap, the relationship between these areas and comparative politics has, as John Hobson puts it at the start of his chapter on international relations and comparative politics, been 'highly complex, fraught and problematic'. Some would say that this is an understatement. The relationship of comparative politics to area studies in particular has bordered on open warfare on a number of occasions as Stephen Hanson's chapter on the relationship between comparative politics and area studies shows. Hanson, however, plots a sensible course between the excessive culturalism of some parts of the area studies community, which argue that there is no point to comparison since the context of local particularities and immersion in language, culture and custom are absolute preconditions

for understanding any society, and some of the claims to superiority of comparative politics researchers based on the assertion that comparison is scientific. The development of area studies and comparative politics, Hanson shows, has in fact often been complementary despite the fiery rhetoric across the 'divide', and many of the charges against area studies are fairly flimsy: area studies have been theoretically diverse, rather than politically constrained by funders, and has lead to generalization as often as not in political science, if not in other disciplinary sections (such as history) of the broader area studies community. Hanson does find some merit with the criticism that the definition of area can frequently be unthinking (a point also raised for the study of regionalization in Söderbaum's chapter), arbitrary and indefensible from the point of view of comparative politics. But the alternatives, comparing by regimes across the globe rather than within regions for example, means defining categories, such as regimes better and more consistently (see also Geddes' chapter on democratization). Finally, there are reasons to keep to traditional area boundaries in some cases because they do share many commonalities and can therefore be made to fit with comparative politics methods.

Hobson defines the gap between international relations (IR) and comparative politics and seeks to correct misunderstandings on both sides. International relations scholars do not recognize comparative politics research as being about international relations because international relations is not interested in variations in states and treats the international as an independent variable. The differences between international relations and comparative politics crystallized for Hobson with the rise of neorealism in international relations and its efforts at developing parsimonious explanation based on a structural theory of international anarchy. This theoretical perspective meant that comparative politics and international relations were forced apart since comparative politics recognized the domestic realm and views states as diverse whilst IR 'accords exclusive ontological weighting to the international system and views states as functionally similar units' with their functions defined by their competition in a continuous anarchic system. There is, Hobson notes, comparison within international relations (between different time periods for example), and recognition that domestic factors can influence state's responses to international phenomena, but this has thus far only served to highlight the outsider status of comparison within IR because these comparisons are used to attack the IR mainstream. The net result is that both sides of the divide IR/comparative politics divide often oversimplify certain aspects of the international in their studies, oversimplification that could be resolved by importing categories from the other or having a better awareness of the theoretical and methodological positions that the other contains. As with Hawkins and Caporaso's chapters, Hanson and Hobson's chapters should be contrasted with the discussions and comparisons of different within region studies and treatments of the international in the later chapters of the book.

Collectively Part I of this handbook shows that there is currently a thorough and ongoing restatement of what comparative politics consists of and what it can do. The descriptions of research developments in classic and emerging areas of comparative politics research in Parts II and III when taken together with his restatement of the nature and possibilities of comparative research open up great opportunities for future research. We hope that this collection is of great value to you as a scholar, who knows that the most solid forms of knowledge are built on the systematic comparison of similarities and differences that you observe.

NOTES

1. Obviously, we are simplifying the history of comparative politics somewhat but the general point being made stands. For more detailed histories of the field, and alternative categorizations of its concerns

and parts, see, Daalder, 1997; Lichbach and Zuckerman, 1997; Mair, 1996; Peters, 1998: 1–27; Ragin, 1987: 1–18. The chapter by Spohn in this volume also provides a detailed history of one major area of comparative politics, comparative political sociology, and many of the others recount the main theoretical and conceptual developments in substrands of comparative politics.

2. For other arguments about how the various crises of the modernization paradigm moved comparative political analysis forward see Mair, 1996 and Geddes, 2003: 6–17.

REFERENCES

Almond, G. (1990) *A discipline divided. Schools and sects in political science*, Newbury Park, CA: Sage.

Brady, H.E. and Collier, D. (eds) (2004) *Rethinking social inquiry: Diverse tools, shared standards*. Lanham, MD: Rowman and Littlefield.

Chilcote, R. (1994) *Theories of comparative politics* (2nd edition). Boulder, CO: Westview Press.

Daalder, H. (ed.) (1997) *Comparative European politics. The story of a profession*. London: Pinter.

Faure, A. (1994) 'Some methodological problems in comparative politics', *Journal of Theoretical Politics*, 6 (3): 307–22.

Flyvbjerg, B. (2001) *Making social science matter*. Cambridge: Cambridge University Press.

Geddes, B. (2003) *Paradigms and sand castles. Theory building and research design in comparative politics*. Ann Arbor: University of Michigan Press.

George, A.L. and Bennett, A. (2005) *Case studies and theory development in the social sciences*. Cambridge, MA: MIT Press.

Gerring, J. (2007) *Case study research: Principles and practices*. New York: Cambridge University Press.

Goertz, G. (2005) *Social science concepts: A user's guide*. Princeton, NJ: Princeton University Press.

King, G., Keohane, R.O., and Verba, S. (1994) *Designing social inquiry: Scientific inference in qualitative research*. Princeton, NJ: Princeton University Press.

Landman, T. (2000) *Issues and methods in comparative politics*. London: Routledge.

Landman, T. (2003) *Issues and Methods in comparative politics* (2nd. edition). London: Routledge.

Landman, T. (2008) *Issues and methods in comparative politics* (3rd. edition). London: Routledge.

Lichbach, M.I. and Zuckerman, A.S. (1997) 'Research traditions and theory in comparative politics: an introduction', in Lichbach, M.I. and Zuckerman, A.S. (eds). *Comparative politics. Rationality, culture, and structure*. Cambridge: Cambridge University Press, pp. 3–16.

Lijphart, A. (1971) 'Comparative politics and the comparative method', *American Political Science Review*, 65 (3): 682–93.

Mahoney, J. and Goertz, G. (2004) 'The possibility principle: Choosing negative cases in comparative research', *American Political Science Review*, 98 (4): 653–69.

Mahoney, J. and Rueschemeyer, D. (eds) (2003) *Comparative historical analysis in the social sciences*. Cambridge: Cambridge University Press.

Mair, P. (1996) 'Comparative politics: an overview', in Goodin, R. and Klingemann, H-D. (eds) *A new handbook of political science*. Oxford: Oxford University Press, pp. 309–35.

Mill, J.S. (1843/1961) *A system of logic, ratiocinative and inductive: being a connected view of the principles of evidence and the methods of scientific investigation*, London: Longman.

Peters, B.G. (1998) *Comparative politics. Theory and methods*. Basingstoke: Macmillan.

Ragin, C.C. (1987) *The comparative method. Moving beyond qualitative and quantitative strategies*. Berkeley: University of California Press.

Ragin, C.C. (1994) *Constructing social research*. Thousand Oaks, CA: Pine Forge Press.

Ragin, C.C. (2000) *Fuzzy-set social science*. Chicago: University of Chicago Press.

Schram, S.F. and Caterino, B. (eds) (2006) *Making political science matter*. New York: New York University Press.

Stepan, A. (2001) *Arguing comparative politics*. Oxford: Oxford University Press.

Valenzuela, A. (1988) 'Political science and the study of Latin America', in Mitchell, C. (ed.) *Changing perspective in Latin American studies. Insights from six disciplines*. Stanford: Stanford University Press, pp. 63–86.

PART I

Methods and Fields of Comparative Politics

The Distinctiveness of Comparative Research

Charles C. Ragin and Claude Rubinson

INTRODUCTION

Social research is inherently comparative (Lieberson, 1985). Researchers compare the relative effects of variables across cases; they compare cases directly with one another; and they compare empirical cases with counterfactual cases. But the *comparative method* – sometimes referred to as 'small-N comparison' – constitutes a distinctive approach to understanding social phenomena. Frequently, comparative methods are portrayed as a 'bridge' between qualitative, case-oriented research and quantitative, variable-oriented research. This interpretation is certainly valid. By embracing aspects of both qualitative and quantitative methods, comparative methods can circumvent some of the limitations of both approaches. But comparative research is not merely a bridge, for it has many distinctive features and strengths.

We begin this chapter by reviewing the conventional view of comparative methods as simultaneously qualitative and quantitative. The moderate number of cases employed by comparative researchers allows them to engage in the development, testing, and revision of theory – traditionally the province of case-oriented research, as well as hypothesis testing and theory adjudication – usually seen as the province of variable-oriented research. But the greatest strengths of comparative methodology arise from its distinctiveness. Fundamentally *set theoretic* in nature, comparative methods presuppose particular epistemological and theoretical perspectives (Ragin, 1987; 2000; Rubinson and Ragin, 2007). Although social researchers conventionally conceive of social reality in terms of tendencies and probabilities, social scientific theory – like comparative research – is predominately set theoretic in nature. Frequently, however, even comparative researchers do not recognize the set theoretic character of their work.

In the second part of this chapter, we explicate the set theoretic nature of a number of classic comparative studies. We identify and illustrate three types of set theoretic relationships and discuss how they form the basis of three forms of comparative analysis: descriptive, constitutive, and causal. Next, we discuss the case-oriented nature of social research.

The set theoretic orientation of comparative research invokes a case-oriented perspective: sets are composed of elements (cases) and comparative research is the analysis of how cases in one set relate to cases in another set. We then discuss the issue of causal complexity. Comparative methods are especially well-suited for the study of how combinations of causal conditions produce particular outcomes. The study of necessary and sufficient conditions – a prominent concern among comparativists – is but one aspect of comparative causal analysis.

We conclude our discussion of comparative research by examining its formal methods. Reviewing two contemporary applications of comparative methodology, we illustrate the construction and analysis of truth tables. Truth tables form the foundation of comparative analysis; whether explicitly or implicitly, most comparative researchers construct truth tables. We demonstrate how Mill's (1875) methods of agreement and difference as well as Ragin's Qualitative Comparative Analysis (QCA) – the two dominant implementations of formal comparative methods – make use of them. QCA builds upon and extends Mill's methods, as we demonstrate through analyses of causal complexity and counterfactual cases.

COMPARATIVE METHODS AS A BRIDGE

In describing the methodological landscape of the social sciences, it is conventional to distinguish between quantitative, variable-oriented analysis and qualitative, case-oriented analysis (Ragin, 1987). There is, of course, no inherent reason that variable-oriented analysis must be quantitative and case-oriented analysis, qualitative (Rubinson and Ragin, 2007). Still, there is a natural affinity, which is a consequence of the way in which the number of cases influences the research process. Quantitative techniques require a large number of cases – the more, the better – so as to meet model assumptions

and enhance statistical power (Cohen, 1988). Faced with hundreds or thousands of cases, however, it is impossible for researchers to know the details of each case. As the cases become obscured and retreat to the background, variables advance to the fore. Large-N analysis, then, tends to focus on variables and their relationships.

The fundamental goal of variable-oriented research is the production of descriptive or explanatory inferences (Brady, 2004). Descriptive inferences are produced by generalizing from patterns found within samples (King et al., 1994). All else being equal, the larger a sample, the greater the researcher's confidence in generalizing to a wider population. Explanatory inferences are produced through hypothesis testing (King et al., 1994). Hypothesis testing requires a well-specified theory of the relationships among variables, which may be confirmed or refuted by comparing the theory's predictions against evidence. Again, all else being equal, the larger the sample, the greater the researcher's confidence that a relationship found in a sample does, in fact, exist in the wider population. As both benefit from a large number of observations, the affinity between variable-oriented research and quantitative methods is mutually reinforcing.

Case-oriented research and qualitative methods, by contrast, are most useful when applied to a small number of cases. Because qualitative techniques leverage the researcher's in-depth knowledge of cases, every additional case requires researchers to further divide their attention. Examination of details highlights the distinctiveness of each case. While imposing limits on generalization and thereby hindering hypothesis testing, this focus facilitates theory development (George and Bennett, 2005). In-depth case knowledge makes it easier to see which case aspects are relevant to the question at hand and how these aspects fit together. This understanding may be used to construct new theory or revise existing theory, thus generating new hypotheses for future testing.

This is not to say that case-oriented researchers cannot engage in hypothesis testing;

indeed, popular examples of case-oriented research include 'crucial,' 'most-likely,' and 'least-likely' case studies that test whether a theory operates as predicted (Eckstein, 1992). In general, however, researchers who want to develop new theory tend to use qualitative, case-oriented techniques to examine small-Ns, while those who want to test theory tend to apply quantitative, variable-oriented methods to large-Ns (Ragin, 1994). A consequence of this bifurcation is that social research is characterized by a large number of studies that examine either small-Ns or large-Ns, but relatively few studies that examine a moderate number of cases (Ragin, 2000: 25).

Comparative research can bridge the divide between qualitative, case-oriented research and quantitative, variable-oriented research. Like case-oriented methods, comparative methods maintain the integrity of cases; like variable-oriented methods, comparative methods examine patterns of relationships among variables. Comparative methods, then, may be used for both theory development and hypothesis testing. With a moderate number of cases (usually around 5–50), it becomes possible to examine cross-case patterns while still attending to the details of each case.

In comparative research, theory development and hypothesis testing interact in two ways. First, comparative methods may be used to develop, test, and revise a particular theory. Second, comparative methods may be used to adjudicate between competing theories.

Developing, testing, and revising theory

Comparative methods encourage a reciprocal relationship between theory development and theory testing. In a strictly qualitative case-oriented study, researchers enter the field armed only with sensitizing concepts, which they use to help them construct new theory as they try to make sense of their cases. In a purely quantitative variable-oriented study,

researchers begin their research armed with a well-specified theoretical model and hypotheses regarding how change in one variable affects changes in others. In contrast to these two extremes, comparativists typically begin their research with a rough idea of the concepts, variables, and cases that are likely to be relevant to their research question. Because comparative researchers typically study a moderate number of cases, it is not feasible to use a purely exploratory approach and conduct an open-ended, in-depth examination of every case. At the same time, conventional hypothesis testing fails due to the limited degrees of freedom available. Instead, comparative researchers seek to answer their research questions by examining the fit between concepts and cases, ideas and evidence. The notion of 'fit' is key. For comparativists, a good theory is a middle-range theory that fits the evidence well (Mjoset and Clausen, 2007). Such a theory will identify which variables are relevant to the question at hand, explain how these variables are related to one another, and, specify the contexts under which they operate.

Through investigation of the fit between theory and data, comparativists discover areas for adjustment and improvement. Ultimately, the resulting theory must be judged on its own merits. Does the theory provide a compelling explanation of the observed cases? Does it explain unobserved or previously anomalous cases? Does it produce observable implications and novel insights? Is it falsifiable? There is always a trade-off between specificity and generality, and theories vary in their explanatory scope. Very specific theories may not generalize beyond the observed cases; very general ones may not add anything new to our understanding. Ultimately, whether any particular theory is successful depends upon striking the proper balance between specificity and generality for the research question at hand. The advantage of using comparative methods to develop, test, and revise theory is that they make these choices, considerations, and decisions explicit.

Adjudicating between theories

A popular use of quantitative methods is to adjudicate between competing theoretical perspectives. Given two or more theories that purport to explain the same phenomenon, researchers identify the variables specified by each theory and estimate a series of models using the same dataset. By examining measures of statistical significance, explained variation, and model fit, researchers can determine which theory best explains the outcome of interest.

Comparative methods may be applied to this purpose as well. While the process tends to differ, the logic is the same. As the goal of hypothesis testing is the generation of explanatory inferences (see above), the construction of the set of relevant cases is crucial. Because comparativists study fewer cases than quantitative researchers, they typically devote much more attention to the task of delineating the set of relevant cases and then constructing their datasets. Of particular concern are scope and possibility conditions. *Scope conditions* specify the conditions under which a theory is relevant (Cohen, 1989). Cases that do not meet a theory's scope conditions are considered irrelevant, regardless of whether they exhibit the outcome of interest. Skocpol (1979), for example, limits her theory of the causes of social revolutions to countries without a recent history of colonial domination and thereby excludes the cases of Mexico and Vietnam. *Possibility conditions* specify the conditions under which an outcome is possible (Goertz, 2005; Mahoney and Goertz, 2004). For example, there are many (in fact, infinite) cases of the *non-occurrence* of social revolutions. When the outcome of interest is clearly impossible, the case is irrelevant for the theory at hand. Irrelevant cases should be excluded from the data set because their inclusion does not benefit hypothesis testing and, indeed, may hinder it (Braumoeller and Goertz, 2002; Clarke, 2002; Mahoney and Goertz, 2004). Mahoney and Goertz (2004) codify the specification of possibility conditions – that is, whether cases are considered relevant or not – as the 'possibility principle.'

Given an initial set of cases, the researcher first examines scope conditions in order to exclude cases to which the theory does not apply. The researcher then applies the possibility principle in order to restrict the sample to relevant cases. Mahoney and Goertz (2004) operationalize the possibility principle as a rule of exclusion and a rule of inclusion. The exclusion rule, which takes priority over the inclusion rule, directs the researcher to develop a list of 'robust eliminatory variables' which predict the absence of the outcome. Cases are excluded as irrelevant 'if their value on any eliminatory independent variable predicts the nonoccurrence of the outcome of interest' (Mahoney and Goertz, 2004: 658). The inclusion rule states that '[cases are relevant if their value on at least one independent variable is positively related to the outcome of interest' (Mahoney and Goertz, 2004: 657). We regard this threshold as a preliminary guideline and recommend that researchers use their theoretical and substantive knowledge when specifying inclusion thresholds.

The proper application of scope conditions and the possibility principle to a population will produce a theoretically and substantively relevant sample of both positive and negative cases. If the resulting sample is too large for comparative analysis, then researchers should select representative cases that maximize the diversity of cases on relevant causal conditions. To adjudicate among competing theories, the comparative researcher examines each case to see if the relationships between causal conditions and outcomes hold as predicted by each theory. Theories are evaluated according to how well they predict both the presence and absence of the outcome. Like conventional quantitative adjudication techniques, comparative techniques of adjudication can indicate opportunities for theory refinement by exposing the ways in which different theories complement one another and might be combined.

Example: Berg-Schlosser and de Meur's (1994) 'Conditions of Democracy'

Social scientists have a longstanding interest in the rise and evolution of democracy and have developed a wide array of theoretical explanations for its emergence, persistence, and breakdown. Observing that there have been few attempts to adjudicate among these theories, Berg-Schlosser and de Meur (1994) test eight of the most prominent models predicting the success or failure of democratization: Dahl (1971, 1989), Hermens (1941), Linz (1978), Lipset (1981), Luebbert (1987), Moore (1966), Sani and Sartori (1983), and Vanhanen (1984). Berg-Schlosser and de Meur (1994) construct their dataset by drawing from the inter-war period in Europe, emphasizing the similarities among the cases:

> For a study of the chances and failures of democracy in a comparative perspective, the interwar period in Europe provides a unique setting, since the cases to be considered share many common socioeconomic and political-cultural characteristics. Their history is relatively well researched and well documented. The time period under consideration is clearly demarcated by common events, the two world wars which significantly altered both the internal and external political landscapes and set them apart from earlier and later developments. All cases can initially be designated as parliamentary democracies, some of them relatively well established, others more recent, and some existing more in form than in substance. They were subsequently affected by a common external stimulus, the world economic crisis of the late 1920s and early 1930s. Some parliamentary regimes survived, while others yielded to authoritarian rule and, in particular, fascism. Prevailing assumptions concerning modernization and progress, whether liberal or Marxist, were severely shattered (1994: 253).

The theories under investigation were developed primarily through the examination of Western European countries, and it is not clear that they should also apply to non-Western societies. In order to satisfy scope conditions, Berg-Schlosser and de Meur (1994), therefore, restrict their sample to 16 Western European countries. The limited time period seeks to satisfy possibility conditions. All of the countries in the sample entered the period as parliamentary democracies and

were subjected to the same historical events. That some emerged as democratic and others as authoritarian suggests that each country possessed the potential for democratic breakdown. Expanding the sample beyond the small handful normally examined in comparative research provides a test of the generalizability of the theories: 'all of the major "breakdown" cases with their specific patterns and the major "survivors," including some of the smaller countries which often tend to be overlooked, are considered' (Berg-Schlosser and de Meur, 1994: 254). At the same time, the moderate sample size permits Berg-Schlosser and de Meur to interrogate the individual cases when seeking to make sense of results. Indeed, to this end, the researchers exclude certain countries from the sample: 'cases like Denmark and Norway have not been included because they were found to add relatively little variation over and above the conditions and relevant factors for a case like Sweden' (Berg-Schlosser and de Meur, 1994: 254). In contrast to conventional quantitative methods, the inclusion of additional cases in comparative research is of no benefit unless they serve to better represent the combinations of conditions present in the population: Berg-Schlosser and de Meur's 1994 sample is representative not of Western European countries during the inter-war period per se but, rather, of the *types* of countries that existed in Western Europe at that time.

For each theoretical model, Berg-Schlosser and de Meur (1994) examine whether the countries in their sample conform to the model's predictions of democratic survival versus breakdown. A model is confirmed when it correctly predicts the survival or breakdown of democracy. The attention to individual cases permits the researchers to identify cases that partially support or contradict a model's hypothesis as well. Comparing the successes and failures of each theory, Berg-Schlosser and de Meur find the strongest support for, first, structural models that emphasize socioeconomic conditions and, second, agency models that emphasize the actions of individual actors. Institutional and meso-level models are only weakly supported. Complex models incorporating nine or more independent variables were more likely to produce mixed results, a consequence of the diversity present among cases. Applying QCA (Ragin, 1987) to simplify their results, Berg-Schlosser and de Meur (1994: 276) find the most parsimonious solutions to emphasize 'basic factors like democratic legitimacy and the political role of the military (as with Dahl) together with some actor-related aspects like interventions by members of the upper class (for Linz)'.

Perhaps the most significant finding, however, is that the emphasis on historically important cases such as Great Britain, Germany, Italy, and Spain has, in fact, hindered understanding of democratic persistence and breakdown:

> But it can also be seen that countries like Finland, Czechoslovakia, Greece, and even France are hardly in line with the expectations of any of the theorists and in several instances provide direct counterfactual examples. This result points to the often rather limited perspective in theory building of some of these authors as far [as] geographical distribution and historical depth are concerned (Berg-Schlosser and de Meur, 1994: 276).

Bridging the worlds of case-oriented and variable-oriented analysis, comparative methods make it possible for Berg-Schlosser and de Meur to adjudicate among competing theories, examine relations among explanatory variables, and identify cases that contradict specific theories.

THE DISTINCTIVENESS OF THE COMPARATIVE METHOD

The greatest strengths of the comparative method arise from its distinctiveness, not from its facility for bridging variable-oriented and case-oriented analysis. Social researchers traditionally conceive of social reality in terms of tendencies and probabilistic relationships. That is, we generally frame

our observations in a contingent manner: 'Given certain conditions, a given effect is *likely* to occur.' In this view, social reality is inherently random and all social processes embody a stochastic component that cannot, even in principle, be identified, much less modeled (Goldthorpe, 2000: chapter 7). The most formal versions of this approach are found in probabilistic models – such as regression analysis – that produce precise predictions of the likely effect of one variable upon another. In contrast to the tendential conception of social reality, comparative methods see the social world in terms of sets and set theoretic relations, especially those that are consistent with arguments of causal necessity or sufficiency. This view motivates a search for invariant or at least highly consistent connections between causal conditions and outcomes.

Set theory in comparative research

Although the tendential view of reality dominates social scientific discourse, most social scientific theory invokes a set theoretic notion of reality. For example, when researchers observe that 'religious fundamentalists are politically conservative' they are arguing that religious fundamentalists form a rough subset of the set of political conservatives. Another example: Esping-Andersen (1990) proposes a set theoretic model of the nation-state. Liberal, corporatist, and social democratic countries are each a subset of the welfare capitalist countries; together, they constitute a complete set: *The Three Worlds of Welfare Capitalism*. Capitalist countries are not necessarily welfare states, however. Esping-Andersen uses the term 'welfare' as a modifier, indicating that welfare states are a subset of capitalist countries. And capitalist countries are, in turn, a subset of *all* countries.

Types of set theoretic connections

The existence of a set theoretic relationship indicates that some type of connection may link distinct phenomena. This connection can take one of three basic forms: descriptive, constitutive, or causal. Consider, for illustration, the opening observation that motivates Weber's investigation of *The Protestant ethic and the spirit of capitalism*: 'the fact that business leaders and owners of capital, as well as the higher grades of skilled labour, and even more the higher technically and commercially trained personnel of modern enterprises are overwhelmingly Protestant' (1958: 35). The puzzle that motivates Weber's analysis is explaining the fact that people in these occupations constituted a rough subset of the set of Protestants. His observation is not simply that there is an 'association' between two variables, but that a specific *connection* – between certain occupations and Protestantism – is remarkably consistent (they are 'overwhelmingly' Protestant). He goes on to query: '[W]hy were the districts of highest economic development at the same time particularly favourable to a revolution in the Church?' (Weber, 1958: 36). Weber notes, in effect, that these highly developed districts constitute a subset of those opposed to the Catholic Church – that again there is a remarkably consistent, almost uniform, connection. As first presented by Weber, these two set theoretic connections are primarily *descriptive* in nature because he says nothing about why these connections exist.

Weber's goal in *The Protestant ethic* is to unravel the puzzle of the set-theoretic connections between capitalism and Protestantism. Defining the spirit of capitalism as the methodical, continuous pursuit of profit, Weber begins by elucidating the relevant characteristics of modern capitalism: rational calculation, entrepreneurs, credit markets, the separation of work and home, and double-entry accounting (Weber, 1958: 17–22).[1] Each of these conditions, however, has existed before and, therefore, cannot be solely responsible for capitalist exchange. It is only with the rise of the labor market – 'the rational capitalistic organization of (formally) free labour' (Weber, 1958: 21) – that these conditions take on a modern, capitalistic character:

> For without the rational capitalistic organization of labour, all this, so far as it was possible at all,

would have nothing like the same significance, above all for the social structure and all the specific problems of the modern Occident connected with it. Exact calculation – the basis of everything else – is only possible on a basis of free labour (1958: 22).

Weber's model of capitalism, then, is a combination of six essential conditions. Such a model is *constitutive*: the elements of the model are closely intertwined and together constitute rational capitalism. For example, double-entry accounting 'is also found in the Far East, the Near East, and in antiquity' (Weber, 1958: 22) but contributes to 'the continual pursuit of profit' only when combined with free labor.

Whenever a set-theoretic connection is interpreted as evidence that something is an 'essential' component, aspect, or part of another, it may be viewed as *constitutive*. Whether a set-theoretic relation is seen as evidence of a *constitutive* versus a *causal* connection is a matter of interpretation. For example, some might interpret the fact that the advanced industrial societies are uniformly democratic as evidence that 'economic development is *causally sufficient* for democratic government.' Others, however, might avoid making a causal argument and interpret this same connection as evidence that having a democratic government is an *essential part* of being an advanced industrial society. The key distinction is in how the connection is understood and interpreted.

Constitutive analysis is central to what Ragin (1992) has referred to as the process of 'casing.' Researchers engage in casing whenever they attempt to delineate the conceptual boundaries of a case or set of cases. Researchers often engage in casing as they attempt to identify conceptually the observations included in their analyses. In *The Protestant ethic*, Weber's primary concern is the casing of rational capitalism. He asks, 'What is rational capitalism? How is it different from other economic systems?' Casing seeks to answer the questions, 'If I see it, how will I know?' 'What are its essential elements?'

An important aspect of casing is that it identifies the theoretically *salient* characteristics of the case. That capitalism involves exchange for gain is not salient because exchange for gain exists everywhere, at all times (Weber, 1958: 17). Exchange for gain may be central to rational capitalism but, theoretically, it is not decisive. The separation of work and home, however, has much greater theoretical salience. Although the 'spatial separation of places of work from those of residence exists elsewhere' (Weber, 1958: 22), it is only under conditions of capitalism that this separation forces workers to seek their livelihood on the labor market: 'The tendency everywhere else was for acquisitive enterprises to arise as parts of a royal or manorial *household* (of the *oikos*), which is, as Rodbertus has perceived, with all its superficial similarity, a fundamentally different, even opposite, development' (Weber, 1958: 22, emphasis in original). Thus, constitutive analysis seeks to identify the interconnected components of a type of case – its essential features. It produces a litmus test for membership in the set of cases under observation. An observation is excluded if it lacks any of the essential features or displays any feature that is prohibited.

Having outlined the characteristics of modern capitalism, Weber observes that modern capitalism first took root in Protestant-dominated regions. That is to say, the set of regions where modern capitalism arose are a subset of the set of Protestant countries. To establish a *causal* connection, Weber seeks to link the rise of Protestantism with the rise of modern capitalism:

> Montesquieu says (*Esprit des Lois*, Book XX, chap.7) of the English that they 'had progressed the farthest of all peoples of the world in three important things: in piety, in commerce, and in freedom'. Is it not possible that their commercial superiority and their adaptation to free political institutions are connected in some way with that record of piety which Montesquieu ascribes to them? (1958: 45)

To establish causality, researchers must specify the mechanism by which membership in

one set is connected to membership in another. Weber does this by linking Luther's conception of the calling to the spirit of capitalism. By describing how the sense of calling combined with a worldly asceticism led Protestants to embrace capitalist production and exchange, Weber details how membership in one set (people possessing the Protestant ethic) connects to membership in another (people possessing the spirit of capitalism). Note that Weber does not claim that all Protestants embraced capitalism, nor does he claim that all those who embraced capitalism were Protestant. That is, Weber does not argue for the existence of a perfect subset relationship at the individual level but rather an affinity between the two. The two rough subset relations described at the outset of this discussion are evidence of this affinity.

Set theory and within-case analysis

Social researchers use the term 'case study' in a variety of ways (Ragin and Becker, 1992). Frequently, comparative research is subsumed under the term (e.g., Gerring, 2007: chapter 2). However, we find it useful to distinguish between within-case analysis (i.e., single case studies) and cross-case analysis (i.e., comparative studies) as each of these forms of analysis entails distinct research methods. Within-case analysis focuses on singular cases. Many researchers feel that because single-case studies lack a comparative element, they are not 'real research.' We disagree. Case studies are particularly useful in interpreting culturally or historically significant phenomenon (Ragin, 1994). Case studies of events such as the storming of the Bastille (Sewell, 1996), the funeral of Abraham Lincoln (Schwartz, 1991), and the rise of the English working class (Thompson, 1966) are valuable because they apply social science theory and concepts to the study of the causes and consequences of important moments of historical transformation or qualitative change.

Moreover, case studies are not necessarily non-comparative. There is a crucial distinction between the unit of analysis and the unit of observation (Denton, 2007). Unfortunately, social researchers often use the term 'case' to refer to both. As King et al. (1994) point out, a single case study may involve many observations. Thompson (1966), for example, uses a variety of methods to examine and synthesize data from a variety of sources in order to explain the emergence of English working class consciousness. Today it is fashionable to refer to such research as 'triangulated' or 'multi-method' (Brewer and Hunter, 2006; Reinharz, 1992), but case study researchers have always leveraged a variety of data sources and analytic techniques in order to confirm their findings and make sense of their cases. As cases exist in space and across time, implicit – if not explicit – comparisons are inevitable. Thompson's study covers 50 years and spans the whole of the country. He invites comparison of the English workers by including separate chapters on field laborers, artisans, and weavers. Likewise, his examination of worker responses compares various forms of resistance, protest, and working-class radicalism. By the conclusion of the text, Thompson has reviewed the cultural and structural transformations between 1780 and 1832 that gave rise to class consciousness among English workers. Thompson's project may be understood as a comparison between the working class of 1780, a class *an sich*, and the working class of 1832, a class *für sich*.

Finally, within-case analysis is an essential component of good cross-case, comparative research. It is for this reason that some researchers subsume comparative research under the moniker of 'case study.' Good cross-case comparison necessarily involves the investigation of individual cases on their own terms. Indeed, a common method of presenting comparative research is exemplified by Barrington Moore, Jr. (1966) in *Social Origins of Dictatorship and Democracy*. Moore spends the bulk of the text reviewing the individual cases (that is, conducting within-case analysis) and offers systematic comparative analysis at the conclusion. It is here that Moore constructs his

three routes to modernity; that is, his three sets of modernizing revolutions. The set of bourgeois revolutions culminating in democracy include the cases of the French Revolution and the English and American civil wars. The set of conservative revolutions culminating in fascism include the cases of Japan's Meiji Restoration and Bismarck's unification of Germany. Finally, the set of peasant revolutions culminating in communism include the Russian and Chinese revolutions. In turn, these three sets of revolutions constitute a subset of what might be termed 'modernizing revolutions.'

Hobsbawm (1967) observes that '[t]he author of a comparative analysis does not compete with the specialists; he exploits them and may have to question them.' (p. 821) Within-case and comparative studies are complementary. The set theoretic nature of comparative research requires the conduct of within-case analysis, as sets are all about cases – the elements contained within sets – and the characterization of cases in terms of set memberships.

Causal complexity in comparative research

Conventionally, researchers do not present their causal arguments in terms of set relations but, rather, in terms of how causes come together to produce outcomes. Moore (1966), for example, speaks of 'three routes to the modern world,' and Skocpol (1979) discusses social revolutions as the product of state breakdowns and peasant revolts. Neither author makes their sets explicit, and frequently it takes some effort to discern the set relations. However, close analysis of most comparative work reveals a conjunctural understanding of causation. In essence, causal conjunctures involve intersections of conditions, which in turn can be understood as set intersections.

Moore (1966), for example, identifies five conditions for the development of democracy.

1. The development of a balance to avoid too strong a crown or too independent a landed aristocracy.
2. A turn toward an appropriate form of commercial agriculture.
3. The weakening of the landed aristocracy.
4. The prevention of an aristocratic-bourgeois coalition against the peasants and workers.
5. A revolutionary break with the past. (pp. 430–31).

Each of these items involves a process of transformation: 'development,' 'turn,' 'weakening,' 'prevention,' 'break.' When these processes are found together, they constitute a 'bourgeois revolution' which is one form of 'modernizing revolutions.' However, Moore's unit of observation is not the modernizing revolution – that is his unit of analysis – but, rather, individual countries. Countries that experienced the combination of these processes, such as England, France, and the United States, are found in the set of countries that experienced bourgeois revolutions. Countries that did not experience each of these processes, such as India which lacked a revolutionary break with the past, are not found in the set of countries that experienced bourgeois revolutions. Moreover, India is not found among the set of countries that experienced modernizing revolutions of any form (bourgeois, conservative, or peasant), which according to Moore explains its long-term stagnation (Moore, 1966: chapter 6).

Skocpol's subtitle – *A Comparative Analysis of France, Russia, and China* – immediately reveals countries as her units of observation. Searching for necessary and sufficient conditions of social revolution, Skocpol uncovers important subset relations. First, countries that experience social revolution are a subset of countries that experience state breakdown *or* peasant revolt. Second, countries that experience state breakdown *combined with* peasant revolt are a subset of countries that experience social revolution. The first relationship – in which the outcome is a subset of the cause – identifies a relationship consistent with necessity; the second relationship – in which the cause is a subset of the outcome – identifies one that is consistent with sufficiency.

The study of necessity and sufficiency is a longstanding interest of comparative researchers (Goertz and Starr, 2003). A cause is necessary when the set of cases exhibiting the cause (e.g., state breakdown) includes the entire set of cases exhibiting the outcome (e.g., social revolution), The presence of state breakdown is a necessary condition for the occurrence of social revolution. A cause is sufficient when the set of cases exhibiting the outcome (e.g., social revolution) includes the entire set of cases exhibiting the cause or, more commonly, a combination of causes (e.g., the combination of state breakdown *and* peasant revolt). The combined presence of state breakdown and peasant revolt is a sufficient condition for the occurrence of social revolution.

Complex conditions of necessity and sufficiency can combine to form what Ragin (1987) calls 'multiple conjunctural causation.' Multiple conjunctural causation exists when a single causal condition is neither necessary nor sufficient to produce the outcome on its own but, rather, only in combination with other causal conditions. Re-examining Gamson's (1990) social protest data, for example, Ragin (1989) finds that challenging groups (social movement organizations) secure new advantages for their constituents if they satisfy any one of the following combinations of causal conditions.

1. No bureaucratic organization, middle or mixed strata constituents, no help from outsiders, and acceptance by antagonists.
2. Middle or mixed strata constituents, non-displacement goals, and help from outsiders.
3. Bureaucratic organization, lower strata constituents, non-displacement goals, and acceptance by antagonists.
4. Non-displacement goals, help from outsiders, and acceptance by antagonists (pp. 392–93).

While any one of these combinations of conditions will result in the challenging group securing new advantages, there is no individual cause common to all combinations. Mackie (1974) refers to such causes as

INUS causes because each is an Insufficient (not sufficient by itself) but Necessary component of a causal combination that is, itself, Unnecessary (due to multiple paths) but Sufficient to bring about the outcome.

METHODS OF COMPARATIVE ANALYSIS

Comparative analysis can be formalized through the construction of truth tables, which show the connections between different combinations of conditions and an outcome (Ragin, 1987, 2000). Although conventional datasets may be used in their construction, the columns of a truth table do not represent variables, per se, nor do the rows represent cases. Rather, the columns of a truth table represent sets and the rows represent relationships among sets, specifically, all logically possible intersections among the relevant sets. These intersections may be understood as representing logically possible combinations of causal conditions. Comparative research is the study of the connections between combinations of conditions and outcomes. Whether implicitly or explicitly, comparative researchers construct truth tables when they examine how causal conditions relate to specific outcomes.

To illustrate the construction of a truth table, we review Brown and Boswell's (1995) analysis of how split labor markets affected interracial strikebreaking and solidarity during the 1919 steel strike. After conducting case studies of 16 northern cities,[2] Brown and Boswell (1995) use comparative methods (specifically, crisp-set QCA) to identify three causal conditions that explain four forms of interracial strikebreaking.[3] To simplify our discussion, we review just one of their outcomes: the presence of black strikebreaking in the face of white worker solidarity.

Brown and Boswell (1995) begin their analysis by constructing a sample of cities that participated in the strike:

> Our unit of analysis is the steel-producing communities where relevant variation in race relations

occurred. Cities in the analysis have the following characteristics in common: the population was over 25,000, the steel industry was an important employer, black workers were a significant part of the steel workforce, and the recruitment efforts of the national committee reached each location during the organizing drive. We selected cases from Foster's (1920) account of the organizing drive and include only those locations that actually participated in the strike. The final group of 16 cases ranges in size from single-industry towns to major multi-industry cities. (1995: 1497–8)

By conducting a case study of each city in the sample, Brown and Boswell produce the data set shown in Table 1.1.[4] 'Recent black migration' is an indicator of whether the city has recently experienced a large increase in its population of young, single, black males. A city is considered to have a weak steel-workers union ('Weak union') if the union had previously suffered a failed strike against US Steel (the primary target of the 1919 steel strike). 'Political repression' exists when local governments align themselves with capital rather than labor.

These three causal conditions were not the only conditions that Brown and Boswell (1995) examined. Their initial truth table included only two conditions, 'Recent black migration' and 'Weak Union.' However, this configuration created a 'contradiction' (Ragin, 1987: 113–18): five cities – Buffalo, Chicago, Gary, Johnstown, and Cleveland – all experienced recent black migration and a history of strong unions; however, the first four cities exhibited black strikebreaking while Cleveland did not. Contradictions indicate an inadequately specified model (Ragin, 1987) because identical conditions should lead to similar outcomes. To resolve contradictions, comparative researchers reexamine both their theory and their cases. It may be that an error was made in the process of casing and that the contradictory case(s) does not properly belong to the population under investigation. More commonly, the researcher uncovers an additional causal condition that explains the contradictory result. In the analysis at hand, Brown and Boswell (1995) considered three variables that they

Table 1.1   Causal conditions and presence of black strikebreaking (from Brown and Boswell, 1995, Table 5)

City	Recent Black migration	Weak union	Political repression	Black strikebreaking
Bethlehem	No	Yes	Yes	No
Buffalo	Yes	No	Yes	Yes
Chicago	Yes	No	Yes	Yes
Cleveland	Yes	No	No	No
Decatur	No	No	Yes	No
East Chicago	Yes	Yes	Yes	Yes
Gary	Yes	No	Yes	Yes
Johnstown	Yes	No	Yes	Yes
Joliet	No	Yes	Yes	No
McKeesport	No	Yes	Yes	No
Milwaukee	No	Yes	Yes	No
New Castle	No	Yes	Yes	No
Pittsburgh	Yes	Yes	Yes	Yes
Reading	No	Yes	Yes	No
Wheeling	No	No	No	No
Youngstown	Yes	Yes	Yes	Yes

suspected might affect the connection between black migration and strong unions, on the one hand, and black strikebreaking, on the other: city size, whether the city was dominated by US Steel or Bethlehem Steel, and local government repression. The addition of the third condition, local government repression, yielded a truth table free of contradictions and also was confirmed as causally relevant in their case studies.

A truth table consists of one row per logically possible combination of conditions. A truth table, then, has 2^k rows, where k equals the number of causal conditions. As the number of causal conditions increases, and the size of the truth table grows exponentially, analysis become increasingly complex. Software packages such as fsQCA (Ragin et al., 2006a) can help to manage this complexity; nevertheless, most practitioners examine between five and ten causal conditions. To construct the truth table, the researcher refers to the previously specified dataset and records which combinations of causal conditions are associated with the presence of the outcome and which are associated with its absence.[5] Brown and Boswell's (1995) final truth table is presented in Table 1.2.

Brown and Boswell (1995) find that all but one of the possible combinations is represented by at least one city; of those, two combinations are associated with the emergence of black strikebreaking. The causal combination that is not represented in the sample is referred to as a 'remainder' (Ragin et al., 2006b) and is identified by marking the outcome with a dash (−). Remainders are common because social phenomena are

Table 1.2   Truth table for the presence of black strikebreaking, derived from Brown and Boswell (1995: 1505, Table 5)

	M	U	R	Y	Cases
1	1	1	1	1	East Chicago, Pittsburgh, Youngstown
2	1	1	0	−	
3	1	0	1	1	Buffalo, Chicago, Gary, Johnstown
4	1	0	0	0	Cleveland
5	0	1	1	0	Bethlehem, Joliet, McKeesport, New Castle, Reading
6	0	1	0	0	Milwaukee
7	0	0	1	0	Decatur
8	0	0	0	0	Wheeling

Note: M = recent black migration, U = weak union, R = political repression, Y = black strikebreaking characterized by limited diversity (Ragin, 1987: 104–13, 2000). That is, many of the logically possible combinations of causal conditions simply do not exist in reality. (We address the issue of limited diversity, especially its relation to counterfactual analysis, in greater detail below).

Mill's methods of agreement and difference

The classic techniques of comparative methodology are those proposed by Mill (1875). The simplest of all comparative logics, the method of agreement is also the most likely to lead to faulty conclusions. The logic behind the method of agreement holds that any given outcome will, inevitably, have a single cause. By examining a sample of cases exhibiting the same outcome, a researcher seeks to identify the single cause that all cases have in common. Ragin (1987: 36) extends this logic to encompass combinations of conditions, arguing that the successful identification of a shared combination of causally relevant conditions would also satisfy the method of agreement. Applying the method of agreement to Brown and Boswell's (1995) truth table (Table 1.2), reveals that all instances of black strikebreaking occurred in cities characterized by recent black migration and political repression. According to Mill's method of agreement, then, the research will conclude that the combined presence of recent black migration and political repression caused black strikebreaking. The process by which the cause produces the outcome remains to be explained. In the absence of a well-specified theory, such explanations are generally best developed through the application of within-case methods such as process tracing.

Mill's indirect method of difference – what Ragin (1987: 39) refers to as 'a double application of the method of agreement' – leverages negative cases (that is, cases that do not exhibit the outcome) in order to strengthen the researcher's conclusions.

The researcher first applies the method of agreement to the positive cases exhibiting the outcome. Upon identifying a causal condition (or causal combination) associated with the outcome, the researcher examines the negative cases to see if the absence of the outcome is associated with the absence of the cause. Referring again to Brown and Boswell's (1995) truth table (Table 1.2), the method of difference reconfirms the initial conclusion that black strikebreaking is a product of recent black migration and political repression. Of the five configurations that exhibit the absence of strikebreaking, none exhibits the presence of both recent black migration and political repression.

As the indirect method of difference comprises two applications of the method of agreement, the same two limitations apply to both methods. The first – the threat of an omitted variable – is common to all comparative research methods and, indeed, all social research methods. Researchers may draw the wrong conclusion when important causes are omitted. If the identified causal condition is, itself, caused by an antecedent condition, the researcher's explanation will be incomplete. Spurious relationships raise a similar type of issue. If both the identified causal condition and the outcome are caused by an omitted third condition, the researcher may identify the wrong condition as causing the outcome. In this latter situation, one hopes that the error will be uncovered as the researcher examines his or her cases and when attempting to elucidate how the condition causes the outcome. The second and more significant limitation of the method of agreement is that it is incapable of addressing multiple conjunctural causation. As Mill (1875), himself, emphasized, when an outcome has more than one cause, the method of agreement will not be able to identify any of them:

> That some one antecedent is the cause of a given effect because all other antecedents have been found capable of being eliminated, is a just inference only if the effect can have but one cause. If it admits of several, nothing is more natural than that each of these should separately admit of being eliminated. (1875: 474–5)

Qualitative Comparative Analysis

Qualitative Comparative Analysis (QCA, see Ragin, 1987, 2000) builds upon Mill's methods in two fundamental ways. Most significantly, QCA permits the analysis of multiple conjunctural causation, addressing the greatest limitation of Mill's methods. Moreover, by employing counterfactual analysis, QCA permits a more nuanced analysis of the relationship between causal conditions and the presence and absence of outcomes.

Rooted in set theory, QCA uses set algebra – also known as Boolean algebra – to analyze causal configurations. Boolean algebra provides operations for analyzing and manipulating sets. The most useful of these operations for comparative research are discussed in Ragin (2000: 171–80) and include set *union* (logical *or*, represented as addition) and set *intersection* (logical *and*, represented as multiplication). Truth table configurations are represented as Boolean equations in which an uppercase letter represents the presence of a condition while a lowercase letter represents its absence. In Boolean notation, Row 1 of Table 1.2 is represented as:

$$M \cdot U \cdot R \xrightarrow{s} Y$$

which indicates that 'The presence of black migration in combination with a weak union and political repression is sufficient for black strikebreaking.' Just as with linear algebra, a shortened notation may be used for multiplicative terms, and the above equation also may be represented as:

$$MUR \xrightarrow{s} Y$$

Row 5, which is read as 'The absence of recent black migration in combination with a weak union and political repression is sufficient for the absence of black strikebreaking,' is represented as:

$$mUR \xrightarrow{s} y$$

Truth table reduction

The analysis of multiple conjunctural causation involves a process known as 'truth table reduction' or 'Boolean minimization.' A reduced or simplified truth table results in a Boolean equation that expresses the various causal combinations that are associated with the presence of the outcome. Ragin (1987) details the complete minimization process; here, we provide only an overview.[6] The basic process of Boolean minimization is derived from the proposition that invariant, or close to invariant, connections exist between explanatory conditions and outcomes. Each row of the truth table represents a logically possible combination of causal conditions. For each combination that is associated with the presence of the outcome, the truth table reduction process seeks to eliminate logically redundant terms. In Table 1.2, the first and third configurations are represented by the equations:

$$MUR \xrightarrow{s} Y$$

$$MuR \xrightarrow{s} Y$$

When a pair of equations is identical except for a *single* causal condition, the distinguishing term may be considered irrelevant and can be eliminated. The minimization of these two equations, therefore, produces:

$$MR \xrightarrow{s} Y$$

which is the same result as was obtained through the application of Mill's method of agreement: the presence of recent black migration and political repression resulted in black strikebreaking. QCA's methods are a superset of Mill's methods.

A more complex example is provided by Stokke's (2007) analysis of 'shaming' as an attempt to secure compliance with international fishing agreements. Shaming involves an attempt to change a party's behavior by exposing their violations to others (in this case, the international community). Having conducted a series of case studies of shaming attempts, Stokke (2007) identifies five causal conditions that affect whether shaming attempts are successful.

1. Advice (A): Whether the shamers can substantiate their criticism by reference to explicit advice by the regime's scientific body.
2. Commitment (C): Whether the target behavior violates explicit commitments.
3. Shadow of the future (S): The target's perceived need to strike future deals and whether ignoring the criticism will jeopardize such beneficial arrangements.

4. Inconvenience (I): The inconvenience to the target of the behavioral change that the shamers seek to elicit.
5. Reverberation (R): Domestic-level political costs if shamers scandalize the target as a culprit. (p. 503)

Having conducted his case studies and identified his causal conditions, Stokke (2007) produces a truth table which we have reproduced as Table 1.3.[7] With five causal conditions, the corresponding truth table has 32 logically possible combinations. The ten cases are distributed among eight configurations, resulting in 24 remainders (two

Table 1.3   Truth table for the presence of shaming, with counterfactual conditions (based on Stokke, 2007, Table 1)

	A	C	S	I	R	Y	Cases
1	1	1	1	1	1	1	Compliance
2	1	1	1	1	0	0	EC unilat. 1
3	1	1	1	0	1	–	
4	1	1	1	0	0	1	EC unilat. 2
5	1	1	0	1	1	–	
6	1	1	0	1	0	–	
7	1	1	0	0	1	–	
8	1	1	0	0	0	–	
9	1	0	1	1	1	1	Overfishing
10	1	0	1	1	0	–	
11	1	0	1	0	1	–	
12	1	0	1	0	0	–	
13	1	0	0	1	1	0	Mesh-size 2
14	1	0	0	1	0	0	Mesh-size 1
15	1	0	0	0	1	–	
16	1	0	0	0	0	1	Krill report, Krill cap2
17	0	1	1	1	1	–	
18	0	1	1	1	0	–	
19	0	1	1	0	1	–	
20	0	1	1	0	0	–	
21	0	1	0	1	1	–	
22	0	1	0	1	0	–	
23	0	1	0	0	1	–	
24	0	1	0	0	0	–	
25	0	0	1	1	1	–	
26	0	0	1	1	0	–	
27	0	0	1	0	1	–	
28	0	0	1	0	0	–	
29	0	0	0	1	1	–	
30	0	0	0	1	0	0	Loophole, Krill cap 1
31	0	0	0	0	1	–	
32	0	0	0	0	0	–	

Note: A = advice, C = commitment, S = shadow of the future, I = inconvenience, R = reverberation configurations, Acsir and acsIr, characterize two cases each).

Half of the represented configurations are examples of successful shaming:

$$ACSIR \xrightarrow{\text{ s }} Y$$

$$ACSir \xrightarrow{\text{ s }} Y$$

$$AcSIR \xrightarrow{\text{ s }} Y$$

$$Acsir \xrightarrow{\text{ s }} Y$$

As the first and third equations differ only with regard to the presence of commitment, that causal condition may be eliminated from those configurations. The resulting minimized Boolean equation:

$$ASIR + ACSir + Acsir \xrightarrow{\text{ s }} Y$$

states that there are three combinations of conditions that result in successful attempts at shaming. Observe that this solution is far more complex and nuanced than that produced by Mill's method of agreement. The method of agreement would identify only condition A (the presence of explicit advice from the scientific community) as common to all events of successful shaming. The method of agreement, therefore, produces:

$$A \xrightarrow{\text{ s }} Y$$

This equation is too simplistic a solution to be convincing: surely the process of successfully shaming a regime is more complicated than simply having the support of the scientific community. And, indeed, application of Mill's indirect method of difference confirms this assertion. An examination of Table 1.3 rejects the hypothesis that it is exclusively the scientific community that determines whether attempts at shaming will be successful. Configurations 2, 13, and 14 are all instances of unsuccessful shaming over the objections of the scientific community. In this instance, Mill's methods are incapable

of determining the cause of successful shaming.

Complexity, parsimony, and counterfactual analysis

In developing explanations of social life, in 'telling about society' (Becker, 1986), social researchers seek to balance complexity and parsimony. The avoidance of crude, vulgar accounts demands that researchers recognize the possibility of multiple conjunctural causation, that there may exist a variety of explanations, across cases, for the same outcome. Indeed, Mill (1875) observes that, in the social world, multiple conjunctural causation is not the exception but the rule:

> Now, in the case of political phenomena, the supposition of unity of cause is not only wide of the truth, but at an immeasurable distance from it. The causes of every social phenomenon which we are particularly interested about, security, wealth, freedom, good government, public virtue, general intelligence, or their opposites, are infinitely numerous, especially the external or remote causes, which alone are, for the most part, accessible to direct observation. No one cause suffices of itself to produce any of these phenomena. (1875: 475)

And yet an explanation that is too particular, too qualified, can be as unsatisfying as one that is too general.

> This tension between particularization and generalization – between literal and abstract representation – comes with the territory, I think, when you're transmitting vicarious experience. A simple chronicle of details, however graphic, locks you into a particular time and place. You move beyond it by abstracting, but abstracting is an artificial exercise, involving an oversimplification of complex realities (Gaddis, 2002: 14).

This tension is particularly acute in comparative research which studies both similarity and difference (Ragin, 1994). To establish set membership and identify explicit relations among sets, comparative researchers must maintain the integrity and distinctiveness of their cases while demonstrating what they do and do not have in common. The more that a researcher emphasizes the particular circumstances and experiences of a case, the more that a researcher restricts their scope and possibility conditions, the less portable the argument becomes.

Counterfactual analysis provides a means by which comparativists can balance particularity and generality. Exploring how the hypothetical presence or absence of a causal condition would affect the outcome under investigation, counterfactual analysis is predominantly associated with case-oriented research. In fact, all social research involves counterfactual analysis in some way (Lieberson, 1985) but case-oriented researchers tend to make their counterfactual theorizing explicit (Fearon, 1991). In comparative research, counterfactual cases form the basis of thought experiments through which researchers assess a theory's plausibility (Weber, 1905).

Counterfactual analysis is particularly useful as a theory development tool (McKeown, 2004). Recognizing the complexity of the social world, researchers tend to be conservative when constructing theories. Preferring to claim too little rather than too much, social researchers are more likely to make errors of omission rather than commission. Counterfactual analysis provides a means by which to test the implications of a theory (McKeown, 2004) and thereby assess the viability of more parsimonious variants. For any given analysis a researcher may construct a variety of counterfactual cases. Frequently, just a single causal condition is altered; more complex analyses examine a range of hypothetical conditions.

Truth tables permit a systematic approach to counterfactual analysis, one which encompasses both simple and complex counterfactuals. As previously discussed, the social world is characterized by limited diversity. In truth tables, limited diversity manifests itself as 'remainders' – the logically possible configurations of causal conditions that lack empirical instances. Representing 'events that did not happen' (Lieberson, 1985: 45), remainders serve as counterfactual cases in comparative research (Ragin and Sonnett, 2004).

Counterfactual analysis using remainders is straightforward: the researcher asks 'How would my conclusions change if the counterfactual existed?' Instead of running a thought experiment, however, the comparative researcher need only include the remainder in the analysis. Whether to incorporate a particular counterfactual case is a determination that must be made upon the basis of substantive and theoretical knowledge (Ragin and Sonnett, 2004). Two criteria must be evaluated. Is the counterfactual case plausible? And, if so, is it reasonable to think that it would produce the outcome in question? Depending upon how it affects the set relations within the truth table, the inclusion of remainders may result in a Boolean equation that is more parsimonious, more complex, or the equivalent of the original solution. Researchers must use their substantive and theoretical knowledge to evaluate the feasibility of any solution resulting from the inclusion of counterfactuals.

Software packages such as fsQCA (Ragin et al., 2006a) simplify the process of conducting counterfactual analysis. For example, by incorporating all remainders that produce a simpler result, fsQCA can be used to identify the most parsimonious solution possible for any truth table. Applying this procedure to Stokke's truth table (Table 1.3) produces a dramatically simpler solution:

$$i + SR \xrightarrow{\text{ s }} Y$$

which indicates that shaming will be successful when (a) it is not inconvenient for the targets of the shaming to change their behavior or (b) when future considerations and present political costs are high.

This solution and the previous solution of the same truth table can be considered two endpoints on a continuum that runs from complexity to parsimony. Observe that the complex solution (Acsir + ACSir + ASIR) is a subset of the parsimonious solution (i + SR). Cases of shaming that involve the absence of inconvenience to the target – that is, members of set i include members of sets Acsir and ACSir. Likewise, cases of shaming that invoke a shadow of the future and reverberations – members of set SR – include members of set ASIR. The presence of this subset relationship indicates that it is possible to select counterfactual cases to produce intermediate solutions, between the parsimonious and the complex.

One way to derive an intermediate solution is to use the technique described in Ragin and Sonnett (2004). Examining the term ASIR, Ragin and Sonnett (2004) observe that 'Causal conditions S and R cannot be removed because they appear in the corresponding parsimonious term (SR) at the other end of the continuum' (p.16). To remove S or R would violate the subset relationship and, therefore, the only candidates for removal are A and I. To discern whether either of these conditions may be removed, the researcher must rely upon theoretical and substantive knowledge. The fact that the support of the regime's scientific advisory board is the only condition present in all cases of successful shaming suggests that it may be a necessary condition and should be retained. However, it does not make sense that shaming would be more likely to be successful when it is inconvenient (I) for a target to change its behavior than when it is convenient (i). The causal condition I, therefore, may be dropped to produce the causal combination ASR.

The same logic applies to the sets Acsir and ACSir. Conditions i, S, and R cannot be removed because it would violate the subset relationship. Nor should conditions A, C, and S be removed as each should contribute to the success of shaming. Removing conditions c, s, and r produces the terms Ai and ACSi. As the latter causal combination is a subset of the former, it may be removed, leaving Ai. The reduced terms, ASR and Ai, yield the intermediate Boolean equation:

$$Ai + ASR \xrightarrow{\ s\ } Y$$

which is a superset of the complex solution (Acsir + ACSir + ASIR) and a subset of the parsimonious solution (i + SR).

As long as the subset principle – that more complex solutions must be a subset of more parsimonious solutions – is maintained, researchers can produce a series of such intermediate solutions using counterfactual analysis.[8] The researcher can then adjudicate among the various solutions, selecting that one that best balances specificity and generalizability given the current state of theory and what is known about the cases.

CONCLUSION

Comparative research is frequently seen as a bridge connecting the worlds of qualitative, case-oriented research and quantitative, variable-oriented research. Focusing on a moderate number of cases, comparativists are able to engage in both theory development (usually the province of qualitative researchers) and hypothesis testing (usually the province of quantitative researchers). While comparative research can certainly be seen as a bridge, its greatest strengths arise from its distinctiveness. In common with the bulk of social science theorizing, comparative methods are fundamentally set theoretic.

In contrast to conventional variable-oriented researchers, comparativists do not seek mere associations but, rather, seek to establish explicit connections among social phenomena, conceived in set-theoretic terms. To do this, comparativists maintain the integrity of cases so as to identify sets that share members. Set relationships take three basic forms. A *descriptive set relation* articulates connections among sets but stops short of explanation. A *constitutive set relation* identifies essential aspects or components of wholes and may be used to constitute theoretically based populations (e.g., the set of modernizing revolutions). A *causal set relation* goes beyond establishing an empirical connection and details the causal mechanisms that explain how and why membership in one set (the cause) is empirically linked to membership in another (the outcome). Causal set relations often address conditions of necessity and/or sufficiency, with a special concern for causal heterogeneity and INUS causation (Mackie, 1974).

The core of causal analysis in comparative research is the truth table, just as the core of variable-oriented causal research is the linear additive regression equation. These are fundamentally different ways of understanding the social world. The configurational perspective of comparative research emphasizes the search for highly consistent relationships linking combinations of causes to outcomes. The truth table models these relationships. Considering that comparativists typically trace their lineage to the likes of Durkheim and Weber, the introduction of truth table analysis to comparative research is relatively recent (Ragin, 1987). We have argued, however, that most comparative analysis involves truth tables, either explicitly or implicitly. Contemporary methodological developments – specifically, the formalization of the comparative method as Qualitative Comparative Analysis (QCA) – aim to improve comparative research by making explicit its assumptions, algorithms, and techniques. This formalization has allowed the development of software packages to facilitate technical aspects of comparative analysis, which in turn frees researchers to concentrate on their most important task: getting to know their cases (Rubinson and Ragin, 2007).

If there is a downside to this formalization and the associated development of software packages for comparative analysis, it is the fear – as others have speculated (Shalev, 2007) – that lowering the bar to entry will encourage the rote application of comparative methods. In fact, we expect the opposite. Truth table analysis simultaneously eliminates the most banal analytic tasks while permitting a more sophisticated analysis of more cases in more depth. The investigation of necessary and sufficient conditions, causal complexity, and counterfactuals all become increasingly feasible through the application of QCA, which directly implements the set theoretic logic of comparative analysis. Comparative research can, indeed, be done with or without formal techniques; however, it is best done with an appreciation of its distinctiveness.

NOTES

1. We recognize that Weber also postulated more complex models of capitalism. See, for example, Collins (1980), Giddens (1958), and Weber (1920). Here, we restrict our discussion to Weber's model as presented in *The Protestant Ethic* for illustrative purposes.

2. The cities that Brown and Boswell (1995) include in the analysis are: Bethlehem, Buffalo, Chicago, Cleveland, Decatur, East Chicago, Gary, Johnstown, Joliet, McKeesport, Milwaukee, New Castle, Pittsburg, Reading, Wheeling, and Youngstown.

3. The four outcomes that Brown and Boswell (1995) examine are: (1) black strikebreaking (whites support union), (2) white strikebreaking (blacks support union), (3) biracial strikebreaking (low overall compliance with union), and (4) biracial labor coalition (high overall compliance with union).

4. Brown and Boswell (1995) do not actually present this dataset in their article. Rather, it is derived from the truth table that they present as Table 5 on page 1505. We are able to derive the original dataset from the truth table only because the researchers include a column listing which cities correspond to which causal configurations. This is one reason that we strongly recommend that comparative researchers explicitly identify which cases correspond to which truth table configurations. (The primary reason being so that cases remain in the foreground of the analysis.)

5. Based upon substantive and theoretical knowledge, the researcher may specify a threshold indicating the outcome's presence. For example, in a large dataset the researcher may specify that the outcome must be present in at least three (or five or ten) cases to be recognized whereas in a small dataset the researcher may specify a minimum threshold of one case. Threshold specification relies upon the researcher's in-depth knowledge of the population. For the present discussion, we rely upon Brown and Boswell (1995) threshold of one case, which is reasonable for an N of 16 cases. For additional discussion of threshold specifications, see Ragin (2005) and von Eye (1990).

6. Specifically, we omit a discussion of prime implicant minimization (see Ragin, 1987: 95–8). Prime implicant minimization does not apply to the examples we review and does not affect our results.

7. There is an inconsistency in Stokke's (2007: 507) reported truth table: rows 4 and 8 share the same configuration of causal conditions and outcomes. Our Table 1.3 reflects this correction.

8. The software package fsQCA (Ragin et al., 2006a) includes procedures to facilitate such analyses.

REFERENCES

Becker, H.S. (1986) 'Telling about society', in H.S. Becker (ed.) *Doing things together: Selected papers*. Evanston, IL: Northwestern University Press, pp. 121–36.

Berg-Schlosser, D. and de Meur, G. (1994) 'Conditions of democracy in interwar Europe: A Boolean test of major hypotheses', *Comparative Politics*, 26 (3): 253–79.

Brady, H.E. (2004) 'Doing good and doing better: How far does the quantitative template get us?', in H. Brady and D. Collier (eds), *Rethinking social inquiry: Diverse tools, shared standards*. Lanham, MD: Rowman and Littlefield, pp. 53–67.

Braumoeller, B.F. and Goertz, G. (2002) 'Watching your posterior: Comment on Seawright', *Political Analysis*, 10 (2): 198–203.

Brewer, J. and Hunter, A. (2006) *Foundations of multimethod research: Synthesizing styles*. Thousand Oaks, CA: Sage.

Brown, C. and Boswell, T. (1995) 'Strikebreaking or solidarity in the great steel strike of 1919: A split labor market, game-theoretic, and QCA analysis', *American Journal of Sociology*, 100 (6): 1479–519.

Clarke, K.A. (2002) 'The Reverend and the ravens: Comment on Seawright', *Political Analysis*, 10 (2): 194–7.

Cohen, B.P. (1989) *Developing sociological knowledge: Theory and method*. Chicago: Nelson-Hall.

Cohen, J. (1988) *Statistical power analysis for the behavioral sciences*. New York: Lawrence Erlbaum.

Collins, R. (1980) 'Weber's last theory of capitalism: A systematization', *American Sociological Review*, 45 (6): 925–42.

Dahl, R.A. (1971) *Polyarchy: Participation and opposition*. New Haven, CT: Yale University Press.

Dahl, R.A. (1989) *Democracy and its critics*. New Haven, CT: Yale University Press.

Denton, T. (2007) 'Unit of observation in cross-cultural research: Implications for sampling and aggregated data analysis', *Cross-Cultural Research*, 41 (3): 3–31.

Eckstein, H. (1992) 'Case study and theory in political science', in *Regarding politics: Essays on political theory, stability, and change*. Berkeley: University of California Press, pp. 117–73.

Esping-Andersen, G. (1990) *The three worlds of welfare capitalism*. Princeton, NJ: Princeton University Press.

Fearon, J.D. (1991) 'Counterfactuals and hypothesis testing in political science', *World Politics*, 43 (2): 169–95.

Foster, W.Z. (1920) *The great steel strike and its lessons*. New York: Huebsch.

Gaddis, J.L. (2002) *The landscape of history: How historians map the past*. Oxford: Oxford University Press.

Gamson, W. (1990) *The strategy of social protest*. Belmont, CA: Wadsworth.

George, A.L. and Bennett, A. (2005) *Case studies and theory development in the social sciences*. Cambridge, MA: MIT Press.

Gerring, J. (2007) *Case study research: Principles and practices*. New York: Cambridge University Press.

Giddens, A. (1958) 'Introduction', in M. Weber (ed.), *The Protestant ethic and the spirit of capitalism*. New Jersey: Prentice Hall, pp. 1–12.

Goertz, G. (2005) *Social science concepts: A user's guide*. Princeton, NJ: Princeton University Press.

Goertz, G. and Starr, H. (eds) (2003) *Necessary conditions: Theory, methodology, and applications*. Lanham, MD: Rowman and Littlefield.

Goldthorpe, J.H. (2000) *On sociology: Numbers, narratives, and the integration of research and theory*. Oxford: Oxford University Press.

Hermens, F.A. (1941) *Democracy of anarchy? A study of proportional representation*. Notre Dame, IN: University of Notre Dame.

Hobsbawm, E.J. (1967) 'Review of *Social origins of dictatorship and democracy*', *American Sociological Review*, 32 (5): 821–2.

King, G., Keohane, R. and Verba, S. (1994) *Designing social inquiry: Scientific inference in qualitative research*. Princeton, NJ: Princeton University Press.

Lieberson, S. (1985) *Making it count: The improvement of social research and theory*. Berkeley: University of California Press.

Linz, J.J. (1978) *Crisis, breakdown, and reequilibration*. Baltimore, MD: Johns Hopkins University Press.

Lipset, S.M. (1981) *Political man: The social bases of politics*. Baltimore, MD: Johns Hopkins University Press.

Luebbert, G.M. (1987) 'Social foundations of political order in interwar Europe', *World Politics*, 39 (4): 449–78.

Mackie, J.L. (1974) *The cement of the universe: A study of causation*. Oxford: Clarendon.

Mahoney, J. and Goertz, G. (2004) 'The possibility principle: Choosing negative cases in comparative research', *American Political Science Review*, 98 (4): 653–69.

McKeown, T.J. (2004) 'Case studies and the limits of the quantitative worldview', in H.E. Brady and D. Collier (eds), *Rethinking social inquiry: Diverse tools, shared standards*. Lanham, MD: Rowman and Littlefield, pp. 139–67.

Mill, J.S. (1875) *A system of logic, ratiocinative and inductive: Being a connected view of the principles of evidence and the methods of scientific investigation*, Vol. 2. London: Longmans, Green, Reader, and Dyer.

Mjoset, L. and Clausen, T.H. (eds) (2007) *Capitalisms compared*, Oxford: Elsevier.

Moore, B., Jr. (1966) *Social origins of dictatorship and democracy: Lord and peasant in the making of the modern world*. Boston, MA: Beacon Press.

Ragin, C.C. (1987) *The comparative method: Moving beyond qualitative and Quantitative Strategies*. Berkeley, CA: University of California Press.

Ragin, C.C. (1989) 'The logic of the comparative method and the algebra of logic', *Journal of Quantitative Anthropology*, 1 (2): 373–98.

Ragin, C.C. (1992) '"Casing" and the process of social inquiry', in C.C. Ragin and H.S. Becker (eds), *What is a case? Exploring the foundations of social inquiry*. Cambridge: Cambridge University Press, pp. 217–26.

Ragin, C.C. (1994) *Constructing social research*. Thousand Oaks, CA: Pine Forge Press.

Ragin, C.C. (2000) *Fuzzy-set social science*. Chicago: University of Chicago Press.

Ragin, C.C. (2005, April) *From fuzzy sets to crisp truth tables* (COMPASS working Paper 2004: 28) Retrieved January 21, 2008, from http://www.compasss.org/Raginfztt_April05.pdf.

Ragin, C.C. and Becker, H. S. (eds) (1992) *What is a case? Exploring the foundations of social inquiry*. Cambridge: Cambridge University Press.

Ragin, C.C., Drass, K.A. and Davey, S. (2006a) *Fuzzy-set/qualitative comparative analysis 2.0* [computer software]. Tucson, Az: Department of Sociology, University of Arizona.

Ragin, C.C., Rubinson, C., Schaefer, D., Anderson, S., Williams, E. and Geisel, H. (2006b) *User's guide to fuzzy-set/qualitative comparative analysis* [computer manual]. Tucson, AZ: Department of Sociology, University of Arizona.

Ragin, C.C. and Sonnett, J. (2004) 'Between complexity and parsimony: Limited diversity, counterfactual cases, and comparative analysis', in S. Kropp and M. Minkenberg (eds), *Vergleichen in der politikwissenschaft*. Wiesbaden: VS Verlag für Sozialwissenschaften.

Reinharz, S. (1992) *Feminist methods in social research*. Oxford: Oxford University Press.

Rubinson, C. and Ragin, C.C. (2007) 'New methods for comparative research?', in L. Mjoset and T. H. Clausen (eds), *Capitalisms compared*. Oxford: Elsevier, pp. 373–89.

Sani, G. and Sartori, G. (1983) 'Polarization, Fragmentation and Competition in Western Democracies', in Hans Daalder and Peter Mair (eds), *Western European party systems: Continuity and change*. London: Sage.

Schwartz, B. (1991) 'Mourning and the making of a sacred symbol: Durkheim and the Lincoln assassination', *Social Forces*, 70 (2): 343–64.

Sewell, W.H., Jr. (1996) 'Historical events as transformation of structures: Inventing revolution at the Bastille', *Theory and Society*, 25 (6): 841–81.

Shalev, M. (2007) 'Rejoinder: Affirming limits and defending alternatives to multiple regression', in L. Mjoset and T.H. Clausen (eds), *Capitalisms compared*. Oxford: Elsevier, pp. 391–409.

Skocpol, T. (1979) *States and social revolutions: A comparative analysis of France, Russia, and China*. Cambridge: Cambridge University Press.

Stokke, O.S. (2007) 'Qualitative comparative analysis, shaming, and international regime effectiveness', *Journal of Business Research*, 60 (5): 501–11.

Stoll, R.R. (1979) *Set theory and logic*. New York: Dover.

Thompson, E.P. (1966) *The making of the English working class*. New York: Vintage Books.

Vanhanen, T. (1984) *The emergence of democracy: A comparative study of 119 states,*

1850–1979. Helsinki: Societas Scientiarum Fennica.

von Eye, A. (1990) *Introduction to configural frequency analysis: The search for types and antitypes in cross-classifications*. New York: Cambridge University Press.

Weber, M. (1905) 'Objective possibility and adequate causation in historical explanation', in E.A. Shils and H.A. Finch (eds), *The methodology of the social sciences*. Glencoe, IL: The Free Press, pp. 164–88.

Weber, M. (1920) 'The origin of modern capitalism', in R. Collins (ed.) *Four sociological traditions: Selected readings*. Oxford: Oxford University Press, pp. 36–57.

Weber, M. (1958) *The Protestant ethic and the spirit of capitalism*. New Jersey: Prentice Hall.

2

Global Comparative Methods

Paul Pennings, Hans Keman and Jan Kleinnijenhuis

INTRODUCTION

Comparative research is generally defined either at the level of systems (often national), or as a process by assessing politics over time (often yearly). Both descriptions are generally considered to differentiate the comparative approach from other approaches within social science such as rational choice. In line with this definition of comparative research, this chapter focuses on comparative studies in which the nation-state is the unit of analysis and countries are researched at one point in time or over time.

Both time and space are important dimensions in most research designs. Depending on the units of variation and the causal relationship under review, inter-temporal and/or cross-sectional variation will define the type of cases that are needed to organize the comparative data. This chapter discusses the strengths and weaknesses of two types of comparative research designs whose logic is closely related to the dimensions of time and/ or space: synchronic cross-sectional comparisons and diachronic (pooled) cross-time comparisons. We make an important restriction by focusing on quantitative research, in particular time series analysis and the use of pooled cross-section time series data sets.

Global comparative methods enable us to compare many countries by using abstract concepts that can travel in order to discover universal factors that account for the phenomenon to be explained. These types of analyses are often characterized by a trade-off between the level of abstraction and the scope (or number) of countries so that they have per definition both strengths and weaknesses attached to them.

The focus on quantitative analysis might give the impression that theory is not considered to be important for comparative research. But the contrary is true. Theory, considered as a set of plausible research answers to a research question, always precedes comparative research. Often it consists of a number of causal relations that are to be confirmed by means of empirical evidence, which refute or confirm the tenability of the proposed relations. Without theory or by using flawed theory, quantitative comparative research becomes meaningless and cannot lead to valid results and insights.

The restriction to quantitative methods does not imply that these provide better means for a comparative study of social reality than qualitative methods. Neither of these approaches is better suited for comparative research by themselves: all depends on how they are used given the research question and the research design. The discussion will focus on methodological problems associated with this form of analysis and makes explicit which problems and pitfalls need to be taken into account in order to arrive at valid results.

The discussion is divided into two main parts. The first part focuses on the measurement of democracy and democratization on a global scale using a synchronic large-N design. This theme is among the most prominent examples of global research. The second part is explanatory and examines factors that account for democratization, such as economic development. In this part the emphasis is diachronic analysis within a large-N design by taking time into account.

CONCEPTS AND MEASUREMENT OF DEMOCRACY AND DEMOCRATIZATION: SYNCHRONIC ANALYSIS WITHIN A LARGE-N DESIGN

Doing research on many countries confronts us with the problem of conceptualization. A classic example from comparative politics is the research on democracy and democratization. The concept of democracy may seem unproblematic, but it is highly complex and multi-dimensional which means it is not self-evident how to apply this concept within a large-N design. Below, various ways of conceptualizing, measuring and transforming democracy into a valid and reliable cross-national variable are explored. We adopt Keman's (2002) view on democracy which distinguishes two dimensions:

- pluralism – representing the possibilities of organizing as a group on the societal level free from the state; and

- polyarchy – indicating the positive conditions for the population to participate in national decision-making.

The combination of both variables presents the degree of 'democraticness' in a society from a comparative perspective. Keman's study is based on 172 countries in the world (40% non-democracies; 10% old democracies; 50% recent (established after 1945) or new (after 1988) democracies). The starting point is the well-known conceptualization of democracy by Dahl as polyarchal democracy, being a political system with the six institutions listed below (Dahl, 1984, 1998).

1. Universal suffrage and the right to run for public office.
2. Free and fairly conducted elections.
3. Availability and observance of the right to free speech and protection to do so.
4. The existence and free access to alternative (and often competing) information (not controlled by government).
5. The undisputed right to form and to join relatively autonomous organizations, in particular political parties (and crucially: parties in opposition).
6. The responsiveness of government (and parties) to voters and accountability of government (and parties) to election outcomes and parliament.

It is this combined set of institutions that distinguishes polyarchic regimes from other regime types. The coming about of these institutions can then be seen as the process towards democratization. The persistence of the whole set is the hallmark of an established democracy (see also Keman, 2002; Schmidt, 2000: 393–5).

Among many comparativists Tatu Vanhanen can be counted as a prime example who has attempted to describe and analyze the process of democratization (Vanhanen, 1990, 1997, 2003). His index of polyarchy is based on two measures representing 'participation' and 'competition' that together form an Index of Democratization (ID). The degree of legal competition (in a democracy there will be at least two equal groups which are free to compete for power) is operationalized as 100 minus the percentage of the votes won by the largest party (a high score indicates a high degree of competition). The degree of participation is operationalized as the number of voters as a percentage of the total population (a high score indicates a high degree of participation). From his analysis it appears that on average the countries score higher today than in the 1980s (1980 = 8.96; 1990 = 13.9) on the Index of Democratization. Indeed, the world has changed towards more democratization and now contains a growing number of countries that have taken the road to greater polyarchy.

Coppedge and Reinicke (1990) have developed a scale that examines the available institutions that promote a pluralist organization of society. In addition to examining the requirements for free and fair elections, they have developed indicators to measure the degree of freedom of organization, of speech and information and of access to government sources of information. This operationalization is quite close to Dahl's idea of polyarchy. Coppedge and Reinicke measure the extent to which groups in society can organize themselves and are capable of conducting a viable opposition. As Schmidt (2000: 402) rightly observes, this kind of operationalization tends to ignore the formal institutions (i.e., Rule of Law) that restrict the powers of government and the state. To some extent this defect has been solved by Jaggers and Gurr (1995), who within the research programme 'Polity III', have collected data across most nation-states on:

- those institutions that facilitate and promote political choice by citizens;
- the availability of basic civil and political rights for all citizens; and
- the existence of constitutional requirements that limit the executive powers.

Jaggers and Gurr have developed a scale that enables them not only to differentiate between 'autocracy' and 'democracy', but also the level of democracy available. What do these cross-national variables tell us about the level of democratization?

First of all, it appears that the dissimilar conceptualizations and operationalizations lead to different results. The number of non-democratic countries is proportionally twice as high according to Coppedge and Reinicke than that found by Jagger and Gurr (the difference is 30 cases). Yet, Keman has found that the differences are less if one controls the results for regime types such as the ones developed by Alvarez et al. (1996): Presidentialism, parliamentarism, dictatorships and autocracies. It should be noted that on the level of individual cases the differences are – again – not large, but certain cases appear to be odd or even out of place (partly due to fact that the data used are more often than not supplied by public authorities or derived from constitutional documents).

Contrary to the indicators and scales discussed here, there is also research that focuses explicitly on the execution of individual rights not interfered with by the state (and its agencies). An example is the Freedom House index of political and civil rights (Freedom House, 2007) which has been established since 1972. This scale runs from 1 to 7, where a low value implies actual availability and observation for these rights. Taken together these two scales provide information on the extent to which a nation is not only formally democratic, but can also be considered as truly liberal democratic in practice and therefore, as close as can be to Dahl's polyarchy. Studies that apply this scale show that the prevalence and observance of political and civil rights do make a difference. What is striking is the marked difference between parliamentarism and presidentialism in this respect. The latter regime type consistently shows a worse record in observing civil and political rights, notwithstanding its rule of law (Riggs, 1998).

Are these scales satisfactory as truly comparative variables? According to Bollen and Paxton (2000) this is not the case, mainly due to the (ab)use of 'subjective' measures (such as, for instance, those of Coppedge and Reinicke and of the Freedom House). Subjective measures often contain judge-specific errors that may produce reliable (whilst measured consistently and dependably), but not valid ratings of democracy due to bias that comes from the inclusion of extraneous factors. A combination by means of grouped panel rating on the basis of judges with diverse orientations or experiences could reduce this bias (Bollen and Paxton, 2000: 79). In Keman's approach objective measures are combined with subjective ones. To this end he collected a number of scales and indexes that have been developed both subjectively and objectively and grouped these variables as being productive for creating pluralistic conditions or promoting polyarchic institutions (see Bollen, 1993; Bollen and Paxton, 2000; Keman 2002; Schmidt, 2000). By ex ante dividing the measures into more pluralistic and polyarchic the *validity* of the variables in use is improved. A statistical procedure to combine variables on pluralism and polyarchy is factor analysis that can be used to merge several variables into one or two that indicate the extent of democracy and degree of democraticness across the world. Of the 127 nations that have positive scores on both dimensions – pluralism and polyarchy – about one-third (N = 43) of the countries included can be considered – according to this operationalization – as genuinely democratic (i.e., the score is >1.0). This is a relatively high number of countries. The 'older' and the 'richer' the countries are the stronger their democraticness appears to be. In addition, the parliamentary types of democracy score consistently higher than any other type of regime, including presidentialism. Finally, Latin-American countries do fare better than postcommunist ones. This supports the idea that 'ageing' is an important factor in developing higher levels of democraticness.

Doing causal analysis in large-N designs: Synchronic designs

In this section we shall employ these three indexes of democracy to (re)consider a

number of associations with the other variables that can be seen as explaining the cross-national variation in democraticness as well as possibly accounting for certain societal performances. We shall employ the 'variable oriented' approach for a global universe of discourse because this type of analysis with a high number of cases and few variables is crucial for the development of a 'middle-range' theory regarding the democraticness of political systems (see Lane and Ersson, 1999).

Surveying the literature on explaining democracy as a system and its development (i.e., the process) the following answers have been offered.

- Economic development and socio-economic circumstances influence both its development and working (e.g., Berg-Schlosser and de Meur, 1996).
- Modernization of society and the extension of public welfare are conducive to (further) democratization of the national state (e.g., Dahl, 1998).
- Institutionalization of democracy as a regime in relation to its viability which over time enhances the level of democraticness (e.g., Diamond and Plattner, 1994).
- Organized political action in terms of participation and opposition, which 'makes democracy work' (in whatever fashion or way) is an important and often neglected facet of democratic politics (e.g., Norris, 1999).

To what extent do these factors account for the cross-national variation regarding the extent of pluralism and polyarchy? Table 2.1 reports four regression models incorporating explanatory variables for occurrence and viability of democracy. The four models are all, but for two factors, statistically significant (the rate of urbanization and the size of the public sector appear irrelevant in this context) and thus all lend support to the answer as to why democracies are dependent on certain factors to develop and remain viable as democracies. Most of the results are unsurprising and underwrite extant knowledge (Landman, 2003). Yet, it is also clear

Table 2.1 Regression analysis of factors explaining democracy

Independent variables		Dependent variables			
		Pluralism		Polyarchy	
Economics	α	−14.1		−25.8	
GNP per Capita	β	0.45	(3.95)	0.42	(3.91)
Government expenditures per Capita	β	0.12*	(1.08)	0.25	(2.33)
	R^2	25.5%		33.1%	
Society	α	−17.7		−18.6	
Urbanization	β	−0.12*	(−1.13*)	0.07*	(0.70)
Human Development Index	β	0.66	(6.49)	0.56	(5.64)
	R^2	32.4%		36.9%	
Institutions	α	−7.3		−7.2	
Presidentialism	β	0.34	(4.48)	0.34	(4.51)
Parliamentarism	β	0.74	(10.49)	0.73	(9.76)
	R^2	40.3%		39.3%	
Politics	α	−16.5		−19.44	
Electoral turnout	β	0.35	(3.37)	0.38	(3.84)
Central government expenditures	β	0.19	(1.81)	0.24	(2.39)
	R^2	16.8%		22.9%	

Note: OLS procedure has been employed; number of cases is 82 and 110; t-values are in parentheses; insignifcant results are flagged*. Source: Keman, 2002 (adapted).

that none of the models is superior to the others: neither in terms of explained variance (adjusted R^2), nor in the magnitude of influence.

The first model, depicting the working of the market as well as the state, demonstrates that the 'wealth of a nation' is certainly an incentive for democratization. However, this is not the case for the size of the public sector. Yet, at the same time it is also clear that this is an insufficient condition per se. There are many outliers that prove the contrary. For example, many non-democratic nations have also considerable levels of public expenditure. Likewise, a number of states with aggregated economic riches spring to mind that are close to dictatorship or autocracy (e.g., some of the Arabian countries). In short, we hold the view that

economic wealth certainly can help to foster democracy and is more often than not associated with higher level of democraticness, but is not the driving force as many political scientists and economists in the period directly after the World War II claimed (Castles, 1998).

The same can be said of the societal forces (the second model). Although much of the literature claims that the composition of society and its consequences for inter-class rivalry are important for understanding the process of democratization as well as the stability of a democratic regime, this hypothesis is not supported by our analysis. From our analysis it appears that urbanization – used as a proxy for modernization – is unrelated to the indicators for democracy. Hence, it is either an invalid proxy indicator or the modernization thesis is not valid. We think both explanations are plausible (and this is supported in much of the literature; see: Landman, 2003; Rueschemeyer et al., 1992).

Conversely, the quality of life as expressed by the Human Development Index (http://hdr.undp.org/) is an important asset for developing and sustaining democracy. Yet, again as with economic factors, we can only go along with this claim as far as it implies a necessary condition; but – judging by an explained variance of approximately 36.8% – it is an insufficient condition for improving the level of democraticness of a nation. In addition, it should be noted that both explanations – the economy and society – tend to become functional ones. If so, and we think this is correct, the causality of the argument is weak if not absent. Rather we would go along with those who advocate a more 'case oriented' approach that enables researchers to disentangle the subtle variations within a society and to develop 'path dependent' explanations (e.g., Putnam, 1993).

The third model concerns the impact on the level of democraticness of the organization of the democratic polity. Too often the institutional fabric of democracy has been considered as the end-result of democratization. We think this view is biased if not wrong because institutions are not static, but are continuously modified by actors. The coming about of a democracy, whether it is 'old' (and now established, as in the OECD-world) or 'new' (hence recently established, as in Central and Eastern Europe), the struggle for more democracy is mainly fought out over institutions which explains why they are not constants (in the long run).

The last model reported in Table 2.1 concerns the active use of designated powers by the people and by the state. On the one hand, we examined the use of the ballot box, and on the other hand, we scrutinized the idea that central government is strongly associated with democraticness: a democratic state will be conducive to greater state intervention (by popular demand). Both contentions are only weakly supported, and – as was the case with economics and society – we can only repeat our observation that, although there is a relationship, it is not convincing and cannot be considered as a major factor for democratization and democraticness as such (Keman, 2002).

In summary: the cross-national analysis of factors promoting pluralism and polyarchy demonstrates (*ceteris paribus*) that favourable economic conditions and high(er) levels of human development are incentives for achieving higher levels of democraticness. However, like political factors, they are not crucial per se, nor functional under all circumstances. It appears rather that the interplay of these factors benefits further democratization and may well enhance the level of democraticness of a nation. Hence there is not a definitive set of factors, conditions or prerequisites (although their absence may certainly harm the level of democraticness attained!) that allows for a successful development and extension of democracy.

TIME SERIES ANALYSIS

Until now we have discussed synchronic research designs. By introducing the element of time one can analyze more cases and study developments over time. In doing so, the problem of 'too many variables and too few cases' becomes less, but it also introduces a new problem, namely that the cases are not independent. This problem may invoke a large number of statistical complications of which the most important ones are discussed below. The discussion and examples are derived from Pennings et al. (2006).

Time series analysis is discussed here only in the sense of ordinary regression analysis with points or periods in time as the units of analysis. The dependent variable y_t is measured at point t. Since it takes some time before effects come into place, the independent variables in time series analysis are often measured in earlier points in time than the dependent variable. Time series regression analysis is a powerful tool for causal analysis, since the timely order of a cause and its consequence can be expressed with a time lag between the independent variables and the dependent variable. A time lag is the difference k between a time t in a series and a time $t-k$ in the same or another series. Often this means that the current Y-values are due to changes in X in the previous period. The introduction of this time element is an important added value compared to the cross-sectional analysis that we discussed before.

The availability of time series data allows one to construct an autoregressive model. In an autoregressive process the current value depends on one or more of the (usually immediately) preceding values. The basic idea of an autoregressive model is that the current state of affairs y_t is dependent primarily on the state of affairs in the immediate past (y_{t-1}), although external influences (effects of x_t and z_t) and random shocks (ε_t) together with an autonomous trend (b_0) may sum up to a change. The resulting R^2 from an autoregressive model is not to be compared with the R^2 in an 'ordinary' model. Especially when almost nothing changes as compared to the previous point in time the R^2 of an autoregressive model will be high, since a lack of changes (due to slowness of social changes and rigidities in social structures) will result by definition in a close correspondence between y_t and y_{t-1}. This contradicts the intuitive meaning of 'explained variance' of many social scientists.

Autocorrelation is defined as serial correlation between residuals. It occurs when the residuals in a given time period carry over into a later time period. *First-order* serial correlation is correlation between immediately successive points in time (between observations at time points t and $t-1$), for example, when an overestimate in one year is likely to lead to an overestimate in the next year. False predictions for one point in time will result in false predictions for the next points in time. If autocorrelation is present, then it is misleading to think of the consecutive time points as *independent* observations. Autocorrelation implies that the number of independent observations is smaller than the number of time points. Whereas the computation of standard errors of regression estimates in ordinary least squares (OLS) is based on the available number of time points, this computation should be based – less optimistically – on the (unknown) number of independent observations. In the presence of autocorrelation OLS estimates of regression coefficients in non-autoregressive models are *inefficient*, although still *unbiased*. Autocorrelation in autoregressive models makes things even worse. Estimates will not only be inefficient but also biased.

A straightforward diagnostic of first-order serial correlation would be the correlation coefficient $r_{t,\,t-1}$ between residuals in successive points in time. The *Durbin-Watson statistic DW* is based on this serial correlation coefficient between residuals. It is roughly equal to $2 - 2r_{t,\,t-1}$; it thus takes values between 0 and 4 rather than between –1 and +1. Since DW is roughly equal to $2 - 2\,r_{t,\,t-1}$; it thus takes values between 0 and 4 rather than between –1 and +1. $DW = 2$ corresponds with $r = 0$, $DW = 0$ with $r = +1$, and $DW = 4$ with $r = -1$. DW-values in the neighbourhood of 2 indicate the absence of autocorrelation. Values near 0 indicate the presence of autocorrelation: it is likely that a deviation from the regression line at time t will be followed at time $t + 1$ by a deviation in the same direction. If errors are positively correlated, as they usually are, standard errors are underestimated and the R^2 and t-values have an upward bias so that they present an overly optimistic view about the accuracy of the coefficients. This bias makes us reject the null hypothesis of no relationship far more often than we should. Values of DW between 2 and 4 indicate an oscillating pattern: if the actual value at time t is higher than one would expect on the basis of the regression equation, then it is likely that the actual value at time $t + 1$ is lower than one would expect on the basis of the regression equation.

Negatively correlated errors ($DW = 4$) are associated with overestimated standard errors.

Durbin-Watson-values are computed by most statistical packages, but usually it is still necessary to consult a table with DW-values to find out whether a specific DW-value indicates autocorrelation, no autocorrelation, or doubt given a specific number of time points as units of analysis and a given number of independent variables. Regrettably the DW-tables have a region of doubt, depending on the number of independent variables and the number of observations, in which it is undecided from a statistical point of view whether autocorrelation is present or not.

The Durbin-Watson test (DW-test) applies to non-autoregressive time series regression models, but should not be applied to autoregressive models. To indicate whether autocorrelation in the residuals from an autoregressive equation is absent, one should not use the ordinary Durbin-Watson-test, but for example the Durbin's h-test. If the usual 5% criterion is used, the assumption that serial autocorrelation is absent is tenable when $h < 1.645$. If Durbin's h-test indicates that autocorrelation is present in an autoregressive regression equation estimated with OLS, then the OLS conclusion should be that should not have been used. One must resort to generalized least squares estimation procedures which are implemented in most statistical packages. OLS estimates of regression coefficients can be used in autoregressive models, however, when Durbin's h-test indicates the absence of autocorrelation.

An often used, rather intuitive solution to obtain independent observations would be to diminish the number of time points in the regression analysis, for example by aggregating quarterly data to yearly data, or by aggregating yearly data to five years data, or by aggregating all time points before and after important historical events (e.g., World War II, the 1973 oil crisis, the 1989 velvet revolution). Two procedures may be used: simply pick out one time point per period or smooth the data within each time period (for example by computing average values for each time period). This intuitive solution is flawed, however. Meaningful variation within the aggregated time spans is easily ignored. Moreover the periodization is often arbitrary, because each variable tends to have its own periodicity, its own rhythm of change. Here we will stick to solutions which retain all data points in the regression equation.

Let us first consider a non-autoregressive model which exhibits autocorrelation according the DW-test (DW far lower than 2). This indicates that the process being studied remains by and large in the same state as in the previous point in time. It may still be possible to explain changes, however. To explain changes relative to the status quo either a simple first-order-difference regression model or a more advanced autoregressive model should be used.

In the first-order-difference model the dependent variable is the change $Dy_t = y_t - y_{t-1}$ in Y (the zero-order-dependent variable) as compared to the previous point in time. Regardless of the previous level y_{t-1} of the dependent variable Dy_t will become zero whenever $y_t = y_{t-1}$. The difference model $Dy_t = b_0 + b_2 x_{t-1} + b_3 z_{t-1} + \varepsilon_t$ is equivalent to a model $y_t = b_0 + b_1 y_{t-1} + b_2 x_{t-1} + b_3 z_{t-1} + \varepsilon_t$ with y_t as the dependent and the lagged dependent variable y_{t-1} as an independent variable with b_1 constrained to 1. In a first-order-difference model the *motion* of an object is the dependent variable, whereas in a zero-order model the *position* of an object is the dependent variable.

In an autoregressive model $y_t = b_0 + b_1 y_{t-1} + b_2 x_t + b_3 z_t + \varepsilon_t$ the regression coefficient for the lagged dependent variable y_{t-1} is not constrained to 1, but empirically estimated. The autoregression coefficient b_1 gives information about what exactly is being influenced by the remaining independent variables. An estimate of $b_1 = 0$ is equivalent to an ordinary regression model with y_t as the dependent variable. An estimate of $b_1 = 1$ is equivalent to the first-order-difference model. Empirical estimates of b_1 will often result in between 0 and 1. An estimate of $b_1 = 1/2$ would indicate that the remaining independent variables in the model have an influence on $y_t - 1/2 y_{t-1}$.

To compare a non-autoregressive model ($b_1 = 0$), a first difference model ($b_1 = 1$) and an autoregressive model (say, with $b_1 = 1/2$) it is helpful to think of the 'shocks' required from the remaining independent variables to keep y at an extreme high (or low) level. In a first-order-difference model a continuation of the shocks which brought about today's level of y_t is superfluous to preserve the status quo. For this reason a first-order-difference model is also known as the *random walk* (RW) which is the most well-known non-stationary process. This process resembles a walker who time and again takes a step so as to keep a tail wind from the independent variables, regardless of where he came from or where he wants to go. He will stay where he is when it is dead calm. In a non-autoregressive model our walker will return home immediately once there is not a breath of wind. This property of non-autoregressive model is known as regression towards the mean, which means that without continued external shocks the mean will be restored. An autoregressive model with an autoregressive parameter of 0.5 resembles a walker who returns half way home when the wind drops.

The solution for autocorrelation in an autoregressive regression equation (as indicated by Durbin's h) or in a first-order-difference model (as indicated by the ordinary DW-test) is subject to debate, both from a theoretical as from a statistical point of view. One solution would be to develop a second-order-difference model, which has as the dependent variable the rate of the change of the change of the original dependent variable. A second-order model from physics would be a model with the acceleration of an object – rather than its position (zero-order) or its motion (first-order) – as the dependent variable.

Time series data are a perfect means to assess causality because of their timely order and therefore might be superior to cross-sectional models. However, this is only the case when they are handled properly given a large number of statistical complications that are likely to impact on the results.

The regression models based on the original variables typically suffer from the autocorrelation defect. Difference models and/or autoregressive models will usually cure the autocorrelation disease, but difference models and autoregressive are usually not robust. At least three origins of this lack of robustness can be mentioned.

Autoregressive models will usually leave only a small portion of the variance in the dependent variable unexplained. Exogenous influences are hard to verify when the remaining unexplained variance is small, especially when measurement errors are present. A second reason why autoregressive models and difference models often fail to retrieve the obvious is their fixation on short term changes. Long term shocks in exogenous variables which have already influenced the lagged dependent variable will not be attributed to exogenous variables but to the endogenous lagged dependent variable. In the last decades error correction models or co-integration models have been developed to account for long-term effects of exogenous variables, without introducing autocorrelation once more. These models will be left aside here.

The third, and most important reason, is simply the limited number of time points. Data on 25 consecutive years is almost nothing, especially when autocorrelation is present. Twenty-five years may shrink to five 'independent' years when most years are almost perfect copies of their predecessors. Data on short time series cursed with autocorrelation are compatible with many simplistic rivalling theories, but they are simply insufficient to estimate the parameters of any complex theory.

Pooled time series analysis

One way out of this difficulty in time series analysis is to test elaborated theories for many time series simultaneously, which brings us to pooled time series analysis. The advantage of time series analysis is its ability to assess the time dependency of causal relationships. Often the data available do mount up to short time series only (e.g., 40 points in time or even less). More often than not various plausible models will account for the data on such a short time series. One way out is to increase the quantity of the data used for testing.

Pooled time series analysis (or panel analysis) combines time series for several cross-sections. The data are stacked by cross-section and time points. A classical example is a pooled time series database of 828 units stacked by 18 OECD countries over 46 years (1960–2006). Instead of studying the effects of various variables on public expenditures in each country through time, these effects may be studied for a number of countries simultaneously. Instead of testing a time series model for one country using time series data, or testing a cross-sectional model for all countries at one point in time, a pooled time series model is tested for all countries through time. Much more refined tests of theories will become possible, since the available units of analysis increase from T (number of time points) to NT (number of cross-sections times number of time points). Pooled time series analysis captures not only variation that emerges through time, but variation across different cross-sections as well. Note that not all global methods are necessarily highly complex. Most available studies can be situated between the advanced statistical analysis of Przeworksi et al. (2000) on the relationship between democracy and development (1950–1990) and the more descriptive approach of Lane and Ersson (2002) who study the size of government in all countries on the basis of aggregated data.

Regrettably pooled time series analysis also has a serious drawback. Since pooled time series analysis is still time series analysis, the problem of autocorrelation must still be dealt with. But in addition to autocorrelation per cross-section heteroscedasticity between cross-sections comes in. Heteroscedasticity is the unequal distribu-tion or variance of the error term which invalidates significance tests. It is a common problem in cross-sectional analyses, especially in aggregate data. Heteroscedasticity will usually arise because the appropriate models for the various cross-sections will not be precisely identical. Therefore, a model to explain all cross-sections will usually do better for some than for others, which amounts to unequal variances of the residuals for the cross-sections. In our example on expenditures heteroscedasticity means the following. The tendencies which led to higher public expenditures in the seventies manifested themselves in all capitalist countries. Nevertheless, the precise effect of an increasing percentage of elderly on public expenditures may depend on polity variables such as the electoral system, and on policy and legislation with respect to health care technology, health care insurances and pensions for the elderly. If one model is tested for all cross-sections at all time points, then heteroscedasticity comes in since the residuals for 'extreme' countries will be large as compared to the residuals for mainstream countries.

The combination of autocorrelation and heteroscedasticity in sample data may result in extremely inefficient, although unbiased, estimates of the true population parameters. The diagnosis of autocorrelation and heteroscedasticity in pooled time series analysis is fairly straightforward, although statistical software packages are usually not ideally suited for its implementation. The degree of heteroscedasticity due to pooling is to be obtained by examining the residual variances of the pooled model per cross-section. A sequence plot of the residuals for the various cross-sections will give a first visual impression. Ideally the average of the residuals within each cross-section should be equal to zero. If an inspection of the sequence plot suggests that the mean residual varies from cross-section to cross-section then the conclusion should be that crucial variables that explain the differences between cross-sections (regardless of the precise time point being looked at) are still lacking.

A simple diagnostic test on the robustness of the pooled model is to run the same model on its residuals for each cross-section through time and on its residuals for each time unit over cross-sections. If the same model holds for all cross-sections and all time points, then the pooled model will not be able to explain its own residuals split up by cross-section and time unit. Thus, for a regression model tested on 80 units stacked by 8 cross-sections over 10 years, 8 + 10 = 18 regressions should be performed on the residuals from the pooled model. The model should not be able to explain significant proportions of the variance within its own residuals in more than 5% of the cases. Thus, the pooled model from our example should not be able to produce significant regression estimates within its own residuals in more than four time units or cross-sections. If the model is able to explain additional variance in its own residuals for a large number of time units or cross-sections (more than 4 in our example) then the suspicion should be that the original model does not hold for all cross-sections and time units equally well.

A proper diagnosis of autocorrelation in pooled time series analysis is cumbersome, because of its statistical relatedness with cross-sectional heteroscedasticity. If there is cross-sectional heteroscedasticity there will be autocorrelation almost by definition: if the predictions for the complete cross-section are wrong, then the mispredictions for each of its successive time points will be serially correlated. Model improvements to reduce the cross-sectional heteroscedasticity will therefore usually also diminish autocorrelation. The formulas of the Durbin-Watson statistic and Durbin's h allow for a computation over time series for several cross-sections. One technical warning is probably not superfluous: the lag of the first time point for a specific cross-section is missing (and not equal to the last time point for the preceding cross-section in the data file). It is a pitfall to rely on autocorrelation diagnostics per time series. Precisely because the separate time series in pooled time series analysis are too short, Durbin-Watson-tests per cross-section produce chaotic results.

The solutions to the problems raised by pooled time series analysis might be divided in two groups. The first group of solutions is directed at the improvement of the models to fit pooled time series data. The second group of solutions is directed at the development of statistical estimation procedures to improve on OLS deficiencies when a combination of autocorrelation and heteroscedasticity is present.

Let us start with model improvements to get rid of heteroscedasticity between cross-sections. When the mean of the residuals for one or more specific cross-sections is unequal to zero, then one should add variables to the model so as to explain these cross-sectional differences better. A non-theoretical model to get rid of heteroscedasticity between cross-sections completely would be to add one dummy variable to the model for each cross-section, except one. This model is called the least squares dummy variable (LSDV) model in the jargon of pooled time series analysis. The LSDV-model accounts for different Y levels by estimating different intercepts for each cross-section. A more advanced variant would be to assume that each cross-section has a randomly distributed intercept associated with it (the random coefficients model). We would advise against these non-theoretical solutions, since a-theoretical dummies and random intercepts that are added to a regression model will usually be collinear with some variables of theoretical interest. The explanatory power of the variables of theoretical interest will easily get obscured. It is far better to include a few variables which account for the major differences between the cross-sections, than to include every separate cross-section (except one) as a dummy-variable. The LSDV model and the random coefficients model should only be used when the available theory gives no cues at all with respect to differences between processes in the cross-sections being studied.

To get rid of serial autocorrelation the same model ramifications (first-order-difference model, autoregressive model) should be considered as in ordinary time series analysis. A rather different question is which estimation technique should be used when autocorrelation and heteroscedasticity have not been banned completely. How should we deal with the fact that OLS estimates will be inefficient and therefore usually underestimate the standard errors of the regression estimates? Econometricians have proposed various estimation techniques for this purpose. The most widely applied is the Parks-Kmenta method, a specimen of the generalized least squares (GLS) family of estimation techniques (White, 1994: 245–54). These estimation techniques guarantee that the estimates asymptotically hit the mark. They are unbiased when sample sizes draw near infinity. Recently Beck and Katz (1995) have shown that the Parks-Kmenta estimation technique produces quite chaotic results when time series are as short as in comparative political science (usually less then 50 years per cross-section). Katz and Beck showed also that OLS estimates of regression coefficients are more robust than Parks-Kmenta estimates when sample sizes are small. Katz and Beck have developed a formula to compute panel corrected standard errors (PCSEs) which encompass autocorrelation and heteroscedasticity in the computation of the standard errors of the OLS-regression estimates.

The use of panel data has become quite common in quantitative comparative research. Unfortunately this is accompanied by a number of problems and pitfalls. These are discussed by Kittel and Winner (2005) and Plümper et al. (2005) in their critique on the study of Garrett and Mitchell (2001) on the relationship between total government expenditure and the partisan composition of government as well as economic internationalization. In their discussion on PCSE they argue that autoregressive models with panel corrected standard errors should not be used as a universal remedy for problems in panel data analysis. If the assumption on the error terms are not tested before PCSEs are calculated and/or problems with non-stationary data are not recognized, the conclusions will always be highly problematic (Plümper and

Troeger, 2007). In addition, both the size and the sign of the estimates may strongly depend on the exclusion of particular countries.

From this overview of the problems and pitfalls of pooled analysis follows that purely cross-sectional analyses are still necessary and useful since they are not disturbed by the problems inherent in time series. They can be used to validate the results of pooled time series analysis. If an analysis includes institutional and political variables that hardly vary over time, there is not much use for pooling repeated observations over time, unless efficient estimation techniques can be utilised (Plümper and Troeger, 2007). Pooling data is especially useful if an effect is assumed to be equal across space and time or when the research focuses on short term effects. When these conditions are not fulfilled, statistical problems are likely to make the results meaningless.

We end our discussion with the same example as in a previous section on synchronic analysis, but we now introduce the element of time. Burkhart and Lewis-Beck (1994) have analysed the economic factors that may boost democratization. Their data set is an adapted and extended version of the Freedom House democracy indicators. Burkhart and Lewis-Beck added to this data dummies for the position of countries (c = core, m = semiperiphery, p = periphery). They also employ the energy consumption per capita (logged) as an economic development measure (that correlates 0.9 with gross national product per capita). Burkhart and Lewis-Beck test the 'economic development thesis' with the following model:

$$D_t = a + bD_{t-1} + cE_t + d(M \times E_t) + e(P \times E_t) + u$$

where

  D_t is the democracy index at time t;
  D_{t-1} is the democracy index from the year before;
  E_t is energy consumption per capita (logged to the base 10) at time t; and
  ($M \times E_t$) is the dummy variable for semiperiphery status multiplied by E_t.

The Burkhart and Lewis-Beck's model is an autoregressive model having the lagged dependent variable at the right hand side of the equation (like in $Y_t = Y_{t-1} + X_t$). This type of modelling is not without complications as it may well boost the R^2 and Beta-weight. D_{t-1} acts to control for omitted independent variables: as the other forces acting on democracy are uncertain, they will be essentially summarized in the democratic performance of the nation during its previous year. Their estimation procedure is GLS-ARMA which avoids first-order autocorrelation and cross-sectional heteroscedasticity. Their model throws up a pseudo-R^2 of 0.71 and the b-scores are 2.49 (for E_t), -1.33 (for $M \times E_t$) and -1.54 (for $P \times E_t$). Their conclusion is that economic development matters most for nations in the core, it still matters, but about half as much, in the semi-periphery. For nations in the periphery, the economic effect is just a bit less. Taken together, economic factors, both international and domestic, appear decisive in shaping a nation's democratic future.

In order to show the complications of this type of diachronic analysis, we will replicate the analysis synchronically, using OLS regression on a 1988 cross-section. The results of our analysis match with that of Burkhart and Lewis-Beck, be it that our estimates indicate moderate effects. This outcome confirms our suspicion that the autoregressive model might not throw up a reliable R^2, namely an adjusted R^2 of 0.36 (compared to 0.71 in the original analysis). A theoretical, instead of statistical, explanation of the moderate performance of the Burkhart and Lewis-Beck model is provided by Vanhanen (1990). He proposed an alternative for the socio-economic hypothesis of democratization, by hypothesizing that democratization takes place under conditions in which power resources have become so widely distributed that no group is any longer able to suppress its competitors or to maintain its hegemony (Vanhanen, 1990: 66). The main difference with Burkhart and Lewis-Beck is that Vanhanen not only looks at the level of welfare but also, and more importantly, at the distribution of a wider range of power resources. Vanhanen's conceptualization and operationalization of the index of power resources indeed results in a much higher explained variance of 0.71.

This example shows us that a high explained variance is only to be trusted when both the theoretical and statistical specifications of the model are correct. The diachronic Burkhart and Lewis-Beck model is far more complicated than our synchronic replication. But by reducing its complexity and by comparing its results with other research outcomes, it becomes clear what the weaknesses of this model are. In that sense we can conclude that, although diachronic methods are more advanced, they cannot replace synchronic methods.

CONCLUSION

Global comparative methods are potentially capable to incorporate many countries and extensive time series in the analysis. The strengths and weaknesses are closely related to those of quantitative methods in general. Their main strength is that the scope of comparison is widened across time and space. This opens up new possibilities for strong inferences and theory-building and the identification of deviant cases. Their main weakness is that they may easily lead up to misleading results due to their complexity. In addition, global methods are often applied in a case-blind manner by focusing on the interrelationships between the variables which are included in the statistical models.

These pitfalls or weaknesses do not make 'global methods' worse or better equipped for comparative studies than other approaches in social science since their usefulness for comparative research depends on how they are applied. Anyone applying 'global methods' should be aware of the methodological trade-offs which are involved in doing this type of research. In particular, there is a trade-off between reliability (which improves with the increase of cases) and validity (which is hampered by a large number of cases).

During the last 20 years several new techniques have been introduced which enable the statistical analysis on data relating to many countries and time points that are integrated into a single pooled data set (also referred to as panel data). The main problem with panel analysis is the lack of robustness, since the estimates are highly dependent on the model specification. For this reason it is often necessary to compare the results of panel analysis with those of cross-sectional analysis in order to determine whether they point into the same direction. This brings us to the conclusion that, although pooled time series analysis is often seen as a methodological advancement compared to cross-sectional regression analysis, it does not make the latter useless. In addition, cross-sectional analysis is still to be preferred to panel analysis if the variables vary little over time, as is often the case with institutional variables.

REFERENCES

Alvarez, M., Cheibub, J. A., Limongi, F. and Przeworski, A. (1996) *Classifying political regimes*. Unpublished manuscript. University of Chicago.

Beck, N. and Katz, J. (1995) 'What to do – and not to do – with time-series cross-section data in comparative politics', *American Political Science Review*, 89 (3): 634–47.

Berg-Schlosser, D. and de Meur, G. (1996) 'Conditions of authoritarianism, fascism, and democracy in interwar Europe: Systematic matching and contrasting of cases for "small N" analysis', *Comparative Political Studies*, 29 (4): 423–68.

Bollen, K.A. (1993) 'Liberal democracy: validity and method factors in cross-national measures', *American Journal of Political Science*, 37 (4): 1207–30.

Bollen, K.A. and Paxton, P. (2000) 'Subjective measures of liberal democracy', *Comparative Political Studies*, 33 (1): 58–86.

Burkhart, R.E. and Lewis-Beck, M.S. (1994) 'Comparative democracy: The economic development thesis', *American Political Science Review*, 88 (4): 903–10.

Castles, F.G. (1998) *Comparative public policy. Patterns of post-war transformation.* Cheltenham: Edward Elgar.

Coppedge, M. and Reinicke, W.H. (1990) 'Measuring polyarchy', *Studies in Comparative International Development*, 25 (1): 51–72.

Dahl, R.A. (1984) 'Polyarchy, pluralism, and scale', *Scandinavian Political Studies*, 7 (4): 225–40.

Dahl, R.A. (1998) *On democracy*. New Haven, CT: Yale University.

Diamond, L. and Plattner, M.F. (eds) (1994) *Nationalism, ethnic conflict, and democracy*. Baltimore, MD: Johns Hopkins University Press.

Freedom House (2007) *Freedom in the World 2006. The Annual Survey of Political Rights and Civic Liberties*. Retrieved June 6, 2007, from www.freedomhouse.org

Garrett, G. and Mitchell, D. (2001) 'Globalization, government spending and taxation in the OECD', *European Journal of Political Research*, 39 (2): 145–77.

Jaggers, K. and Gurr, T.R. (1995) 'Tracking democracy's third wave with the Polity III data', *Journal of Peace Research*, 32 (4): 469–82.

Keman, H. (ed.) (2002) *Comparative democratic politics. A guide to contemporary theory and research*. London: Sage.

Kittel, B. and Winner, H. (2005) 'How reliable is pooled analysis in political economy? The globalization-welfare state nexus revisited', *European Journal of Political Research*, 44 (2): 269–93.

Landman, T. (2003) *Issues and methods in comparative politics. An introduction* (2nd edition) Oxford: Oxford University Press.

Lane, J.E. and Ersson, S. (1999) *Politics and society in Western Europe*. London: Sage.

Lane, J.E. and Ersson, S. (2002) *Government and the economy. A global perspective*. London: Continuum.

Norris, P. (ed.) (1999) *Critical citizens: Global support for democratic government*. New York: Oxford University Press.

Pennings, P., Keman, H. and Kleinnijenhuis, J. (2006) *Doing research in political science. An introduction to comparative methods and statistics*. London: Sage.

Plümper, T. and Troeger, V. (2007) 'Efficient estimation of time-invariant and rarely changing variables in finite sample panel analyses with unit fixed effects', *Political Analysis*, 15 (2): 124–39.

Plümper, T., Troeger, V. E. and Manow, P. (2005) 'Panel data analysis in comparative politics: Linking method to theory', *European Journal of Political Research*, 44 (2): 327–54.

Przeworski, A., Alvarez, M.E., Cheibub, J.A. and Limongi, F. (2000) *Democracy and development. Political institutions and well-being in the world, 1950–1990*. Cambridge: Cambridge University Press.

Putnam, R.D. (1993) *Making democracy work: Civic traditions in modern Italy*. Princeton, NJ: Princeton University Press.

Riggs, F.W. (1998) 'Presidentialism vs. parliamentarism: Implications for representativeness and legitimacy', *International Political Science Review*, 18 (3): 253–78.

Rueschemeyer, D., Huber, E. and Stephens, J.D. (1992) *Capitalist development and democracy*. Cambridge: Polity Press.

Schmidt, M.G. (2000) *Demokratietheorien* (3rd edition) Opladen: Leske and Budrich.

Vanhanen, T. (1990) *The process of democratization. A comparative study of 147 states, 1980–1988*. New York: Crane Russak.

Vanhanen, T. (1997) *Prospects of democracy: A study of 172 countries*. London: Routledge.

Vanhanen, T. (2003) *Democratization. A comparative analysis of 170 countries*. London: Routledge.

White, L.G. (1994) *Political analysis: Technique and practice*. Belmont, CA: Wadsworth.

3

Case Studies

Darren Hawkins

INTRODUCTION

A case study is among the oldest and most widely used methods available to comparative scholars. While many concepts in widespread usage come to mean different things to different people and even lose meaning and coherence, scholarly understandings of the nature, purpose, strengths, and weaknesses of a case study have actually experienced relative convergence over the past decade. Scholars who utilize different methods also tend to agree on the importance of methodological pluralism, arguing that while case studies can stand on their own, they can also complement, improve, check, and deepen other methods, especially large-N quantitative studies. Much of the scholarly dialogue on methods has also converged on the view that case studies should adhere to rigorous scientific standards similar to those that govern quantitative analysis, thereby discarding interpretivist or postmodern relativist positions on case studies (Brady and Collier, 2004; George and Bennett, 2005; Gerring, 2004; King et al., 1994).

This is not to say that case study practice or quality is uniform or that no conceptual confusion exists. Indeed, scholars continue to debate best practices and relative advantages of different methods and to use the term 'case study' in confusing ways, especially in informal conversation. Some of the largest disagreements concern whether case studies, and especially process tracing techniques, involve fundamentally different forms of scientific processes and inference than quantitative methods. This debate has large consequences for how scholars conceptualize and carry out case studies.

Unlike some debates in political science, however, this discussion has generated more light than heat and has been unusually productive. In this chapter, I argue that important differences do indeed exist between case study and quantitative methods, or more specifically, between process tracing and correlational methods. These differences concern the extent to which underlying observations are independent of each other and the extent to which temporal sequencing is used to identify causation. Case studies embrace and utilize the spatial and especially temporal connections between observations while quantitative methods assume the independence of observations, often viewing connections among observations and temporal sequencing as problems to be solved (e.g., when scholars insert autoregressive terms as a problem-solving procedure without a substantive interest in those terms). Whether these differences require fundamentally different scientific logics is a much murkier question that may not ultimately prove productive.

What is clear is that case studies offer particular advantages to scholars that are frequently complementary to the advantages from large-N quantitative research. These include depth of analysis, construct validity, the identification of causal mechanisms, asymmetric theoretical arguments (related to necessary and sufficient conditions), and theory generation. Once those advantages are understood, scholars can design their research to improve their methodological choices, produce more insightful analyses, and reach more defensible conclusions. Without such progress, case studies may become relatively undervalued and under-utilized, a development that some fear has already come to pass.

This chapter consists of three parts. It first examines the definitions and scope of case studies as well as their prominence in the comparative literature. The second elaborates three key case study techniques: counterfactual analysis, congruence analysis, and process tracing, with an emphasis on this last technique. The third explores the trade-offs inherent in case study analysis along a series of dimensions. In the spirit of case study methods, I illustrate many abstract points throughout this essay by referring to Elisabeth Jean Wood's book (2003), *Insurgent Collective Action and Civil War in El Salvador*. To clarify my selection procedure, the book is one of only two single case study books to win the best book award from the Comparative Politics section of the American Political Science Association from 1993–2005 (the remainder are all comparative case studies and the other case study award winner on imperial Japan is much farther from my substantive expertise). Wood's book deals with classic questions of comparative politics involving collective action, social activism, rebellion, class, social values, and material interests and hence should be relevant to a wide array of scholars.

PROMINENCE, DEFINITIONS, AND SCOPE

Discussion of case study methods has increased substantially in recent years, with a number of important books and articles published, as evidenced by the bibliography for this chapter. This discussion has increased at the same time as, or a little after, a decline in the actual use of case studies in articles published in many top journals. First glancing at the related sub-discipline of international relations, a study of top journals in the field found that case studies and qualitative studies lacking an explicit methodology (which many would also label case studies) fell steadily from 1980–2000 with a commensurate rise in quantitative methods and a small rise in cross-method studies (Sprinz and Wolinski-Nahmias, 2004: 5–8). In fact, a causal relationship between the two seems likely. As case studies have been squeezed out of journals and threatened by increasingly sophisticated quantitative methods, scholars trained in and committed to qualitative case methods have fought back by becoming more self-conscious about their methodologies and engaging in debates with their quantitative colleagues. These efforts have been institutionalized through a qualitative methods section of the American Political Science Association, annual workshops, and similar efforts.

Similar data on the use of case study methods over time in comparative politics are more difficult to find, but some scattered evidence suggests that the pattern is similar to that of international relations. Munck and Snyder (2007) conducted the most comprehensive survey of methods used in comparative research, but did not examine trends over time and restricted their analysis to three top-ranked comparative politics journals, *Comparative Politics, Comparative Political Studies,* and *World Politics,* thereby ignoring comparative politics research published elsewhere. They found 63% of the articles in those journals (using sample years from 1989 to 2004) were mainly qualitative, a category that suggests some type of case study (Munck and Snyder, 2007: 13). Mahoney's (2007a: 33) critique of this study examined the three leading general journals in political science, *American Journal of Political Science, Journal of Politics,* and *American Political Science Review,* finding that only 8% of the comparative politics research published there was qualitative. Perhaps more importantly, Mahoney reported that from 2001–2005, only 40% of the articles in *Comparative Political Studies* were qualitative, and that about half of the comparative articles in *World Politics* in recent years have been qualitative, suggesting a trend to quantitative analysis. Once again, as the proportion of articles in top journals utilizing case studies has declined, the scholarly conversation on case study methods has ramped up. Unfortunately, no studies examining case study methods in books or other types of (geographically or topically bounded) journals have appeared.

The contemporary scholarly conversation on qualitative case study methods began in earnest with the publication of King et al.'s *Designing Social Inquiry* in 1994. A variety of scholars immediately engaged and challenged the work and some then spent the next several years formulating more systematic responses. Whether conceptualized as direct responses or not, most subsequent qualitative methods pieces have at least addressed King et al.'s arguments and some engage those arguments at considerable length. The most prominent examples are the book-length treatments in 2004 by Brady and Collier (who most often write as Collier, Brady and Seawright) and in 2005 by George and Bennett.

While scholars quarrel about a wide variety of arguments put forward in King et al.,

there is also a remarkably strong level of agreement that methodological pluralism can and should be valued. Brady, Collier, and Seawright (2004), among King et al.'s most well-known, energetic and persistent critics, have argued that 'scholars should carefully evaluate the strengths and weaknesses of these diverse [methodological] tools. ... This eclectic approach is the most promising avenue for productive decisions about research design' (pp. 19–20). Of equal importance, they argue that this methodological eclecticism should take place under an umbrella of 'shared standards for the application of these tools' (p. 19). The debate, in other words, is not a relativistic one in which all points of view are equally valued and no grounds for discrimination are tolerated. King et al.'s critics go to great lengths to articulate rigorous methodological standards that utilize sound logic and careful nuances. The main thrust for the critics is that King et al. treat qualitative research as derivative of the logic governing quantitative research. The critics argue, in contrast, that qualitative research is often quite distinctive and governed by a separate, though equally rigorous logic (George and Bennett, 2005: 10–16; McKeown, 1999).

Moreover, both King et al., and their critics largely agree that quantitative and qualitative work are complementary and often improve each other when used jointly. King et al. argued (in a follow-up article to their book) that 'much of the best social science research can combine quantitative and qualitative data, precisely because there is no contradiction between the fundamental processes of inference involved in each' (King et al., 2004: 183). While many critics argue that the inferential processes underlying case study and statistical work are different, they tend to agree that the two methods are fundamentally complementary. Tarrow (2004) offered six different bridges or ways of putting them together. Collier et al. (2004a) discussed case study and statistical research in terms of trade-offs, a useful metaphor employed by a number of scholars and invoked in this chapter.

As a result of this conversation, basic definitions of case studies have become more precise and delimited in recent years. One fairly typical definition is offered by Gerring (2004: 342): 'An intensive study of a single unit for the purpose of understanding a larger class of (similar) units.' Units, in turn, refer to 'spatially bounded phenomenon – e.g., a nation-state, revolution, political party, election, or person – observed at a single point in time or over some delimited period of time.' Seawright and Collier (2004: 275) suggest much the same thing when they say that a case study is a 'research design focused on one (N = 1) or a few cases' where cases are defined as 'the units of analysis of a given study.' Similar definitions can be found in Sprinz and Wolinsky-Nahmias (2004) and in George and Bennett (2005). Since comparative cases are taken up elsewhere in this volume, this chapter focuses on the single case study. By way of example to illustrate Gerring's various levels at which the unit of analysis might be situated, a case study might concern the examination of El Salvador during the period of Civil War, the Christian Democratic Party, the military, the resistance movement known as the Frente Farabundo Martí para La Liberación Nacional (Farabundo Martí Front for National Liberation, or FMLN), the October 1979 coup, social inequality, or Roberto d'Aubuisson, the death squad director. The nature of the unit to be studied is the choice of the researcher, as informed by theory and previous studies. Wood's (2003: 2, 17) unit of analysis is the 'powerful insurgent movement' that formed in El Salvador in the 1980s, with a particular focus on 'insurgent campesinos' or peasants who actively supported the insurgency by providing information and supplies but were not themselves combatants. The question motivating the selection of this unit of analysis is a classic one in comparative politics: Given the high risks and uncertain outcomes of collective action, how and why do collective movements develop?

While at first glance these definitions may seem overly expansive or painfully obvious, they are not at all in comparison with prior definitions. In Yin's (1990) book on case study methods for the well-known Sage methods series, he defined a case study in negative fashion by arguing that it was almost any qualitative method that did not involve experiments, surveys, histories, and analyses of archival information. Yet this definition confuses different methodological techniques with overall methodological purpose and design implicit in the definition endorsed here. In fact, historical and archival research or quantitative surveys can form an important part of a case study.

In a different vein, Eckstein's (1975: 85) classic article on case studies defines a case as a 'phenomenon for which we report and interpret only a single measure on any pertinent variable'. If Wood had used this definition, she would have been able to report only on a single measure of the underlying variables of interest. The key dependent variable for Wood consists of the level of peasant support for guerrillas, but this varied by area of the country and over time in the 1980s. It would be far too restrictive to report a single value for this variable and it would not be helpful to label each locality and time period a discrete case, thereby creating thousands of cases within a time span of several years. In fact, Eckstein's definition calls into question whether a single 'case study' could actually exist in any context because it seems likely that all case studies involve some kind of variation along some important dimension.

Rather, it is more productive to think of a case study as the study of a particular temporally and spatially bound unit (whose scope can vary substantially depending on the research question), which can itself be decomposed into more discrete periods of time, subunits and variables (Gerring, 2004: 342). The nature of a particular unit, time period and variable depends on the scholar's choices and objectives. For Wood, the El Salvadoran civil war constitutes a spatially and temporally delimited unit that can be broken down further. Temporally, scholars could examine each month or some other discrete time period within the war.

Spatially, scholars can examine different actors, processes, or geographical areas within El Salvador. These are sometimes referred to as 'within-case' variations. At each of those points in time and space, many variables can be observed. In her study, Wood interviewed approximately 200 peasants, many repeatedly, from 1987 to 1996 in two different areas of the country.

While this definition of a case study defined as a unit is fairly elastic, it is not infinitely so. When choosing a given case, the researcher is essentially asserting that the various components of that case interact with each other in important ways and that the internal cohesion of the moving parts within the case is greater than the cohesion between that case and other examples of a similar phenomenon. In Wood's book, the social movement supporting the guerrillas ebbed and flowed across space and time, yet can be treated as a cohesive whole because these internal dynamics fed off and responded to each other more than they responded to, for example, the ebb and flow of Peru's guerrilla movement in the 1980s. Wood (2003: 171–2, 189–90) argues, for example, that the successful establishment of peasant land cooperatives in one area produced similar efforts in nearby areas – though by way of critique, Wood does not provide interview evidence that peasants were learning from or inspired by nearby examples. This notion of moving parts within a comparatively cohesive unit marks a fundamental distinction with Eckstein's (1975) classic definition, which focuses on a much more discrete observation of a particular unit at a particular point in time; for example, an individual peasant in the year 1990. Eckstein's conceptualization is more consistent with the concept of a case advanced by King et al.

'Observations' is also a term that seems straightforward but can become rather complicated. In quantitative analysis, an observation is often conceptualized as a single measure on each of a number of different variables pertaining to a particular unit at a particular point in time (and is thus similar to Eckstein's definition of a 'case'). In a traditional quantitative matrix dataset with units in the rows and variables in the columns, an observation consists of the set of measures of each variable found for a given unit along its row. King et al. (1994) utilized this definition of observation and repeatedly argued that increasing the number of observations is one of the most important measures that qualitative scholars could take to produce better research. Increasing the number of observations makes it easier to identify patterns and to sort out which variables change in predicted directions and which do not. They help solve the many variables, small-N problem that plagues case study research.

As Collier et al. (2004b: 252) have pointed out, however, the application of this advice to a case study can create confusion because observations can also refer to a single piece of information (rather than a group of observations about a set of variables for one unit). Moreover, that piece of information may not pertain to any of the existing variables for which the scholar already has data or it might be a fairly unique piece of information that cannot be replicated for other units and thus cannot be included in a traditional matrix dataset.

Hence, the term 'observation' can mean two different things, which necessarily complicate King et al.'s seemingly straightforward advice to increase the number of observations. The first general strategy, most consistent with King et al. (1994: 219–28), is to add observations in one of three ways:

(a) observe additional units similar to the unit under study or subdivide the unit under study into more discrete units or periods of time, or both;

(b) identify additional observable implications of the theory by identifying other hypotheses that account for variation in the dependent variables within the same unit; or

(c) combine a and b.

These strategies are generally familiar to quantitative analysts who might, for example, break years down into months in order to increase observations and obtain greater variation. They are also generally well-known and practiced in case studies. Where scholars retain the same unit of analysis and break it into smaller parts, this is often labeled 'within-case analysis.'

Wood utilizes this strategy by disaggregating the El Salvador civil war into different areas, smaller time periods and 200 individuals, though she does not formalize it as a quantitative analyst would by creating actual rows and columns of data. She then identifies informal correlations, or their absence, among the variables. For example, when assessing the issue of whether social class contributed to collective action, Wood reports that support for the guerrillas occurred in areas where land was distributed more widely as well as in areas where it was held by very few and that insurgent peasants were drawn from all walks of life and classes (Wood, 2003: 198–9). The lack of correlation, perceived intuitively, leads her to conclude that social class was not an important factor in the emergence of collective action. Recent scholarship stressing the complementarity of methods suggests that Wood could have utilized statistical analyses to investigate these correlations more rigorously.

The second strategy for increasing observations, advocated by Collier et al., is to treat 'causal-process' observations differently from 'data-set' observations. A causal-process observation refers to any information that 'provides information about context or mechanism and contributes to a different kind of leverage in causal inference' (Collier et al., 2004: 252). The leverage used by quantitative scholars is that of correlation. The leverage used in causal process observations, in contrast, is 'generative' or 'ontic'; that is, it offers direct information about how causes generate effects by focusing on the connection between the two (McKeown, 1999: 171–2; also see the discussion below on process tracing).

To illustrate, Wood's most important causal-process observations came from her detailed interviews in which peasants offered reasons for acting as they did. The interviews suggested that most peasants did not fight due to class consciousness, material benefits or pre-existing social networks, but rather because they wanted to express their dignity and pride

in the face of oppression and violence. As one peasant put it, 'There were so many deaths of cooperative promoters – half a battalion of dead for the simple crime of lending help to the cooperatives. But I would say that this 'crime' has been, simply, my accomplishment' (Wood, 2003: 204). Peasants who did not join the insurgency, on the other hand, spoke only of loss and never of pride as in this passage: 'We have suffered and we continue suffering. We can't hold either side responsible; it is the system of war that has brought us these losses' (Wood, 2003: 212). It is important to note that correlational and generative inferences are not mutually exclusive. Wood finds correlational patterns where those who joined the collective action nearly always mentioned pride, dignity, and the virtue of standing up for something. Yet it is the fact that these interviews shed light on motives, on how and why some peasants translated poverty and oppression into collective action that makes them valuable causal-process observations.

CASE STUDY TECHNIQUES

Just as quantitative researchers have a variety of techniques at their disposal, so do case study scholars. Those techniques may be grouped into three main categories: counterfactual analysis, congruence analysis, and process tracing (Bennett, 2004: 22–6).

Counterfactual analysis typically seeks to test the proposition that A was necessary for Y to occur by asking what would happen if A were not present (Fearon, 1991; Tetlock and Belkin, 1996). Because it is relatively simple to imagine a different outcome in the absence of any A, thereby confirming its importance, scholars have articulated some important checks on counterfactual reasoning. Tetlock and Belkin (1996: 18) identify six:

1. clearly specified and circumscribed antecedents and consequents;
2. consistent causal logic that links antecedents and consequents;

3. alterations to as few historical facts as possible;
4. articulating principles that are consistent with existing theory;
5. articulating principles that are consistent with existing statistical generalizations; and
6. the identification of testable implications in the case under study or a related case.

For many, this final check is crucial because it involves non-counterfactual data. A useful example relates to speculation about the causes of the extinction of dinosaurs, where the counterfactual is that a large asteroid impacted the earth 65 million years ago (Tetlock and Belkin, 1996: 10). This counterfactual is particularly amenable to empirical investigation because scientists have been able to draw a number of related observable implications about its impact and find evidence for those implications.

Congruence analysis refers to the basic idea that the presence and strength of independent and dependent variables should be correlated (Van Evera, 1997: 56–63). Scholars utilize theories to make predictions about the nature of that correlation and then observe the presence and strength of independent and dependent variables to determine the extent to which the theoretical predictions seem to hold. This fundamental idea lies at the heart of some of the most well-known and venerable methodological discussions in social science and comparative politics: Mill's (1875) 'method of agreement' and 'method of difference,' Przeworski and Tenue's (1970) 'least similar cases' and 'most similar cases,' George's (1979) 'structured focused case comparisons' and Ragin's (1987) 'qualitative comparative analysis.' While George and Bennett (2005: 151–92) go to great lengths to demonstrate differences between their 'congruence method' and these other congruence analyses, their similarities are more striking than their differences. All are based on the same underlying logic of identifying correlational patterns in the presence and strength of independent and dependent variables.

All forms of congruence analysis also face similar problems. Similar to quantitative analysis, they focus on correlation between variables and so care should be used in making causal inferences. Correlational patterns between independent and dependent variables might be spurious or might seem more prominent than they are because other relevant variables have been omitted from the pattern-matching effort. The units and time periods selected for observation might be biased in some way, producing a stronger or weaker sense of correlation than would exist if more observations were added. Because congruence analysis has so much in common with statistical regression analysis and is subject to many of the same problems and pitfalls, Collier et al. (2004c: 94) even refer to it as 'intuitive regression.' As mentioned, Wood relied on such intuitive patterns in assessing the strength of key variables (see pp. 227–8 for one example); in some of those cases, quantitative methods would have been feasible and increased the transparency of her reasoning and confidence in her results.

Perhaps an even larger problem is that for probabilistic rather than deterministic theories, correlations offer uncertain insights. If A is likely to produce Y, and A is present while Y is absent, the argument cannot be infirmed since the relationship is only probable. Repeated observations can give more confidence in the results (if A is present and Y absent in ten different observations, we have stronger evidence against the proposition), but the number of observations required to produce high levels of confidence may also require quantitative analysis. Congruence analysis can produce, on the other hand, more definitive results for deterministic theories, such as those that invoke the language of necessary and sufficient conditions. Where A is posited as a necessary condition to produce Y, for example, and A is absent while Y is present, we can with this single observation infirm the argument that A is a necessary condition. Many scholars, however, are understandably reluctant to utilize deterministic theories in the social sciences (see discussion below). A related problem is that different independent variables can produce similar results, a process known as equifinality. Where several different paths can produce the same result, the number of observations needed to identify such correlations will increase substantially. To see if A or B or C produce Y, scholars would need to observe A without B or C, B without C or A, and so forth.

While problems undoubtedly exist with congruence procedures, they still mark an important and useful method in almost any case study (George and Bennet, 2005: 181–185; King et al., 1994: 206). Some variables can be discounted while others gain more credibility. The absence of A in the presence of Y does not rule out the theoretical proposition that A is likely to produce Y, but it does mean that A does not produce Y *in that case*. Hence, this can lead to the identification of new variables that are also likely to produce Y and it can lead to ideas about the conditions under which A produces Y. If A is widely perceived to be an important variable and the case is significant, it can cast some doubt on A's importance. Because it offers initial insights into how the independent variables map onto the dependent variable, congruence analysis is almost always helpful and productive. At the same time, it is less useful for identifying causal mechanisms.

As a result, a wide variety of scholars endorse process tracing as the third key technique, and perhaps the most important, in case study research. For King et al., process tracing is simply a way of increasing the number of observations by redefining the unit of analysis to a lower level of aggregation. For critics, this is precisely the point where King et al. go astray. In the critics' view, process tracing is a fundamentally different technique that requires different kinds of observations and that allows scholars to go beyond correlation and to identify causation with greater certainty (Collier et al., 2004b: 252–8; George and Bennett,

2005: 176–8). Causality can be identified with greater certainty because of the time sequencing inherent in process tracing that unravels the ways in which one small event triggers another and how the chain of events results in the overall whole.

Process tracing 'focuses on whether the intervening variables between a hypothesized cause and observed effect move as predicted by theories under investigation' (Bennett, 2004: 22). Similar techniques are also labeled 'within-case analysis' (Mahoney, 2007b: 131) 'causal process observations' (Collier et al., 2004b: 252–8). In essence, the investigator asks: What chain of events should we observe if this casual mechanism is correct? Different causal logics should suggest different paths from the independent to the dependent variable. Those paths should have different observable implications that can be broken down into relatively discrete moments of time applicable to different actors and processes. George and Bennett (2005) describe the nature of process tracing in the following terms:

> Process tracing is an indispensable tool for theory testing and theory development not only because it generates numerous observations within a case, but because these observations must be linked in particular ways to constitute an explanation of the case. It is the very lack of independence among these observations that makes them a powerful tool for inference. ... Process-tracing is fundamentally different from methods based on covariance or comparisons across cases. In using theories to develop explanations of cases through process-tracing, *all* the intervening steps in a case must be as predicted by a hypothesis ... or else that hypothesis must be amended – perhaps trivially or perhaps fundamentally – to explain the case. It is not sufficient that a hypothesis be consistent with a statistically significant number of intervening steps. (p. 207)

Process tracing holds out two great promises to researchers: it can distinguish between spurious correlations and cause and effect, and it can identify which of many possible causal mechanisms is the most likely or the most important. The possibility of establishing strong evidence for causation leads many scholars to remark on the complementarity between process tracing and statistical methods, which address issues of causal process either not at all or only with great difficulty (Collier et al., 2004b, 255; George and Bennett, 2005: 207–8, 224). Ideally, statistical methods can establish patterns of covariation while process tracing can identify the causal mechanisms that demonstrate the linkages underlying these patterns.

The most easily accessible illustration of process tracing is that of falling dominoes in a chain (George and Bennett, 2005: 206–7). Where quantitative approaches might examine the first domino and last domino in a chain and observe that they were both upright at time t1, and then that they both fell in the same direction at t2 and t3, process tracing requires that scholars document the fall of the intermediate dominoes. The observable implication is that an intermediate domino was struck by the one ahead of it and in turn struck the one behind it at some point between the fall of the first and the fall of the last.

At least two problems arise. The first is that process tracing may reveal a variety of causal mechanisms at work, perhaps simultaneously, and it is difficult or impossible to sort them all out, even at close range. Requiring *all* of the intervening steps to be consistent with the hypothesis (as George and Bennett do in the above quote, emphasis in the original) could be a recipe for frustration in the social sciences where people often operate with mixed motives, behavior often cannot be observed but must be reconstructed, random events intervene, or various factors combine in unexpected ways. In the social sciences, we would rarely be able to capture the dominoes on camera but rather have to interview them later and deal with all of the psychological phenomena and effects of human agency that the social world encompasses. Some would undoubtedly claim they wanted to fall while others would say they were forced to do so. The wind was probably gusting while the dominoes were falling, creating doubts about the relative importance of the chain reaction versus the wind. And, exercising their agency,

some probably responded to the wind and the chain reaction by standing more resolutely in place while others eagerly joined in the process, with the result that there were several chain reactions that stopped and started at various places in the longer chain.

All of this is 'documentable' using process tracing (hence, its advantage), but the notion that a single hypothesis will be consistent with the multitude of observed behavior seems less realistic. In the end, we have improved our analysis because we now know that the fall of the first domino did not in fact cause the fall of the last, but the cause of the last's fall remains a mix of different causal processes focused on the wind, the chain reaction, and the last domino's weak-willed reaction to external forces. The point is not that process tracing is useless. Rather, the point is that isolating causal mechanisms is very difficult, even with process tracing methods. Wood (2003) grapples with these sorts of issues in her study (see pp. 208–12 for one example). Some affected by government violence responded by supporting the rebels while others withdrew into themselves. Some who believed in social justice supported the rebels while others argued violence was not justified. Wood aptly and honestly summed up the evidence: 'Those who did not support the insurgency were a heterogenous group, yet some patterns are evident' (p. 212). One such pattern is that government violence generally increased peasant action except in areas where government forces were particularly strong. This sort of interactive effect is the product of careful process tracing, but Wood's broader difficulty in identifying patterns may illustrate the inherent limitations in social science research.

The second problem is meshing this process tracing with the observed correlations (Beck, 2006). If a causal mechanism is identified in one case, is it generalizable to other cases? For many social phenomena, there may of course be multiple paths toward the outcome in question (equifinality). Not only do different combinations of variables stimulate the same outcome, but the same cause may produce the same effect through different causal pathways. Understanding general cause-effect relationships thus requires a back-and-forth process between identifying causal mechanisms and identifying correlations among variables. A given correlation is likely to be consistent, in theory, with a variety of causal mechanisms. Process tracing that identifies a particular causal mechanism in a given case should then suggest new correlations to explore quantitatively.

TRADE-OFFS

One important trend among scholars is to consciously consider the trade-offs involved in the choice of any given methodology. Case studies provide several benefits but also incur some important costs. Generally speaking, case studies are, *in abstraction*, better at depth (rather than breadth) of arguments, internal, and construct validity (rather than generalizability), causal mechanisms (rather than causal effects), deterministic (rather than probabilistic) arguments, and the generation of new theories (rather than theory-testing) (Gerring, 2004: 346–52). Not all scholars would agree with this list, of course, but many recent qualitative studies have endorsed a subset of these costs and benefits (Bennett, 2004: 34–45; Collier et al., 2004a: 195–227), and thus the list identifies various possible trade-offs rather than a consensus of opinion. Each of these trade-offs is considered in turn, an organizational device that I borrow from Gerring (2004).

Depth versus breadth

As Gerring (2004, p. 348) put it, 'Research designs invariably face a choice between knowing more about less and knowing less about more.' While this is an intuitive and widely accepted claim, it is worth considering the normative dimensions of this trade-off for a moment. Many of the classical questions of political science are often framed

as searches for generalizable causal laws: Why do individuals engage in collective action? Why does democracy arise? Why does poverty persist?

These are certainly important questions; perhaps so important they can sometimes blind scholars to the pursuit of other important and perhaps more tractable questions. Such questions might include: How unified or fractured is the anti-globalization movement and how is it evolving? What is the current quality of democracy in Mexico? How bad is poverty in Britain; is it worse some places than others and has it changed at all over recent years? These sorts of questions often have clearer policy relevance: international trading rules might become more responsive to their critics; problems in Mexico might be identified and addressed; and future recruits to the ranks of terrorism might be deterred. Scholars should at least consider the possibility that the quest for broad causal statements may get in the way of worthy and valuable case-specific information. Again, since both seem necessary the language of 'trade-off' seems quite applicable.

Construct validity versus generalizability

Relatedly, the second trade-off involves construct validity versus generalizability. Construct validity refers to the ability to measure the theoretical concepts that scholars intend to measure. The difficulty is that scholars frequently wish to measure abstract concepts whose meaning and practice can vary substantially across different cultural and historical contexts. As Bennett (2004) summarized the issue:

This requires detailed consideration of contextual variables, which is extremely difficult to carry out in statistical studies but common in case studies. Whereas statistical studies run the risk of 'conceptual stretching' if they lump together dissimilar cases to get a higher sample size (Sartori 1970), case studies move in the opposite direction, refining concepts with a higher level of validity but doing so at the cost of producing generalizations applicable only over a smaller number of cases. (p. 34)

The generalizability problems with case studies are well-known. Geddes (1990) and Achen and Snidal (1989) are often credited with first bringing sustained attention to the problem of drawing theoretical inferences from single cases. King et al. (1994: 149) are well-known for their advice to minimize selection bias by selecting cases so that variation is achieved on the explanatory variables while allowing the possibility of variation in the dependent variable (where the selection should ideally be blind). Geddes examined three prominent causal arguments for broad and important phenomena in comparative politics: economic growth, revolution, and inflation. In each case, she showed how answers about the causes of these phenomena would vary widely depending on which countries and time periods the analyst examined. In most cases, the factors thought to create the outcomes in question also existed in cases where the outcomes did not occur, leading her to articulate the oft-repeated wisdom that scholars should not select cases by examining just one outcome on the dependent variable.

For Geddes (1990: 54–8), however, these selection problems went even deeper than attempting to confirm causal connections. Unwarranted assumptions about generalizability also infected efforts to create new theories, one of the strengths of case study analysis (see below). In her view, modernization and dependency theory – the classic paradigms of comparative politics in developing countries – both arose from selective readings of readily available case study evidence. If so, there is little mystery about why both paradigms wound up in the discard pile after too much inconvenient evidence accumulated around them. Their history is certainly a useful reminder to comparativists to be careful about generalizing too much from specific cases, even in the name of developing new theory.

Case study scholars have developed a large supply of responses to these generalizability issues and the related question of case selection (Collier et al., 2004c). If generalizability is such a problem, why engage in case studies at all? One relatively simple response is that some phenomena are rare enough that they cannot be subjected to statistical methods, with social revolutions as an oft-cited example (Gerring, 2004: 351; Skocpol, 1979). Even when events are not so rare, they may be normatively important because of their large effects on others or their status as important reference points in policy debates. The Spanish transition to democracy, for example, is but one of dozens of democratic transitions since 1974, but received enormous attention because of its smooth, peaceful nature, and the model it provided for Latin American countries in the 1980s (Colomer, 1991). Similarly, democratic transitions in large, important countries like Mexico, Brazil, and Argentina attracted numerous case studies justified on normative grounds that it is simply worth knowing in some detail how their tens of millions of citizens accomplished such desirable outcomes with wide-ranging implications for them and for numerous other people and states.

These responses answer the generalizability challenge by focusing on the importance of the cases at hand. Other responses meet the challenge in a head-on fashion. Numerous scholars have pointed out that selecting cases on the dependent variable is helpful if the theory in question posits necessary causes. If causes are necessary for an outcome, then selecting only positive outcomes provides the most demanding way for telling analysts if those causes are in fact always present (Dion, 1998; Harvey, 2003; Ragin, 2000). Alternatively, if identifying causal mechanisms that produce the outcomes in question is the goal of the research (see discussion in next section), then it is a viable strategy to select the dependent variable and examine the process by which the desired outcomes occurred. Such cases could then generate new hypotheses that could be tested on a wider range of cases (see discussion of theory generation below).

Case study scholars have long defended selection procedures by invoking the notion of a 'crucial case' (Eckstein, 1975), though recent research calls that argument into question

(Gerring, 2007). A crucial case is one that is most (least) likely to produce the outcome in question on a range of criteria but fails to do so (and does so). Where these unexpected outcomes occur, runs the typical argument, scholars can have higher levels of confidence in their results (Hawkins, 2001). The difficulty, Gerring argues (2007: 236), is that few social science theories make 'risky' predictions about outcomes that are subject to being falsified by a single case. Most theories are probabilistic; are thought to be true only under certain (often underspecified) conditions; identify interaction effects that can alter the outcomes; and/or posit a variety of causal mechanisms by which the outcomes may occur. Hence, a predicted outcome that does not occur may simply be the result of chance or may be the result of an underspecified, unclear theory. In this view, the more precise the theory (the riskier its predictions), the more it can be subjected to a 'crucial case' logic.

As an alternative to the crucial case, Gerring (2007: 238–46) suggests a 'pathway case' approach in which the general correlational patterns between causes and outcomes are known, but the causal pathway or mechanisms are unknown. In these circumstances, researchers can select cases in which the cause (established in correlational statistical studies) and effect are both present and other established causes are either missing or present in lower quantities. In other words, the case is one in which the hypothesized cause should be exerting a large influence on the outcome. In such a case, scholars can more clearly identify the causal mechanisms that lead from cause to effect (see next section). While generalizability would still be an issue, it is less of a concern because correlational studies establish the existence of a relationship between the cause and effect.

Causal mechanisms versus causal effects

Quantitative researchers are often interested in estimating the causal effects of independent variables; that is, in calculating the average effect of various causes on the outcome, taking all other effects into account (Mahoney and Goertz, 2006: 230) As Gerring points out, multiple cases, and statistical methods are required to estimate these causal weights.

> Assuming that the causal relationship is probabilistic in nature … the researcher must examine several instances of this phenomenon to gauge the average causal effect of X on Y and the random element of that variation. The calculation of a causal effect presumes the investigation of cross-unit variation precisely because, for a probabilistic cause, one cannot assume that the behavior of one unit will be indicative of the behavior of other units. Units may behave differently. Thus, the example of a single unit, even if subjected to iterated testing, is not a good way to estimate casual effects and is certainly inadequate to the task of estimating probabilities. (2004: 348)

Calculating average causal weights is impossible in case studies, though it is sometimes possible to obtain an ordinal ranking of the importance of various causes. Rather, case studies focus on careful explication of causal mechanisms in particular cases, or in delimited sets of cases. In particular, case study researchers often set out to identify the multiple pathways or combinations of factors that produce the outcome of interest (Mahoney and Goertz, 2006: 232). They are often interested in equifinality, or the variety of paths that can produce similar outcomes.

Mackie (1980: 62) refers to these factors as INUS conditions – '*insufficient* but *nonredundant* part of an *unnecessary* but *sufficient*' combination of conditions. While this formulation at first appears unwieldy, it appears upon reflection to capture the tenor of much case study research and could actually be quite helpful in organizing and presenting conclusions. Mahoney and Goertz (2006: 232) point out, 'Research findings with INUS causes can often be formally expressed through Boolean equations such as Y=(A AND B AND C) OR (C AND D AND E).' In this abstraction, all of the factors from A to E are INUS conditions. They are insufficient on their own yet an important part of the explanation (nonredundant). When combined together with each other in particular ways, they jointly become unnecessary (because multiple causal paths are available) but sufficient conditions to explain the outcome. This detailing of different causal pathways or mechanisms is a clear strength of qualitative research that makes it a valuable complement to quantitative methods (Ragin, 1987; 2000).

Wood's book may have been strengthened by a greater effort to incorporate this sort of analysis. Rather than identifying the different ways in which the underlying factors combine into causal pathways, she tends to treat the factors in isolation from each other. The main variable of peasant values is not an important part of the analysis until late in the book (p. 226) and its interaction with other factors is only briefly discussed (pp. 237–40). That discussion refers to local state violence and proximity of insurgent forces as necessary factors for rebellion, but the evidence for that claim is lacking. If instead of seeking to show how some factors were more important than others, Wood had first sought to identify and sort out the multiplicity of causal pathways, her analysis may have offered even more insights.

Once several causal pathways have been charted through varying combinations of underlying factors, scholars might even begin to analyze the relative importance (causal weights) of those individual factors. If C is found in 90% of the causal pathways, for example, it could be considered a more important influence on the outcome than the other factors. In emphasizing the values of peasants and the meanings they ascribed to their actions, Wood (2003: 231–41) essentially utilized an intuitive form of this INUS/Boolean analysis. Her claim that those values constitute the most significant part of the explanation would be strengthened by demonstrating that they are present in most of the causal pathways, each of which combines multiple factors.

Deterministic versus probabilistic arguments

Case studies have often been associated with deterministic rather than probabilistic arguments, with determinism taking the form of necessary and/or sufficient conditions (Dion, 1998; Gerring, 2004: 349). Although there are no clear measures of how many case studies employ these concepts, Goertz (2003: 76–94) demonstrated that the practice is at least not terribly rare by compiling a sample of 150 necessary condition hypotheses in the social sciences. The underlying logic is straightforward: in necessary conditions, an outcome Y cannot occur without the presence of X; and in sufficient conditions the presence of X ensures the presence of Y. Yet a large debate has erupted over whether necessary and sufficient conditions are in fact deterministic. The wording and logic appear to be inherently deterministic, or more precisely, invariant – because multiple sufficient conditions might exist (equifinality) and hence the notion of 'determinism' is misleading. Still, on its face, a condition that is necessary for an outcome or that ensures a particular outcome appears to suggest a worldview inconsistent with probabilistic views of political outcomes.

The difficulty is that many proponents of necessary and sufficient conditions seem unwilling to defend the proposition that the social world is invariant (Braumoeller and Goertz, 2000; Dion, 1998; Mahoney and Goertz, 2006). They argue, common-sensically, that we all inhabit a probabilistic world. Efforts to square the circle by making deterministic theories work in a probabilistic world, however, have run into a variety of problems. One of the most obvious is the semantic illogic of the claims, as in this example from Dion (1998, p. 136): 'deterministic necessary conditions are perfectly compatible with a probabilistic world.' He explains that even if condition X occurs, this does not determine whether Y will occur. While true by definition, this claim glosses over the fact that the relationship is still invariant with respect to Y, which cannot exist without X. Braumoeller and Goertz (2000) have argued that invariant claims can be evaluated by using evidence probabilistically. In their view, counter-examples (where Y is present without X) may be due to some kind of error in measurement or conceptualization, and the likelihood that negative cases are errors can be evaluated using statistical probability. This approach, like that of Dion, preserves the invariant nature of the underlying theoretical relationship between X and Y and by using observed frequencies to assess the likelihood that they are invariant.

The difficulty is that these arguments do not completely square the circle. They introduce some element of probability, but the underlying hypothesized relationship remains essentially invariant. Case study scholars thus still face an unpalatable option between accepting the invariant nature of necessary and sufficient claims or abandoning the logic altogether. Clark et al. (2006) have offered one potential way out of the conundrum by dropping the notion of necessary and sufficient conditions for that of asymmetrical causes and conditions. A condition is asymmetrical, in their view, if it exhibits relatively small levels of variance in the associated outcomes: If Y is present, X is *nearly always* present. Necessary conditions are thus 'near-necessary' and the entire problematic language is abandoned in favor of asymmetry. This approach is more clearly probabilistic; the logic asserts that the presence of Y dramatically increases the probability that X is also present, but does not guarantee it.

A related issue concerns the relationship between qualitative methods and asymmetrical (necessary and sufficient) theories. Mahoney and Goertz (2006: 232–4) draw a fairly sharp line between qualitative and quantitative conceptions of causation, arguing that the former deals with the logic of necessary and sufficient conditions while the latter deals with the logic of probability. Yet further examination suggests the pairing between approaches and logics is not so clear. While qualitative research certainly seems better suited to dealing with asymmetrical hypotheses, Clark et al. (2006) have developed a quantitative method for dealing with these kinds of arguments. On the flip side, any argument identifying sufficient causal mechanisms in a particular case can easily be turned into a probabilistic argument for multiple cases. Mainwaring and Pérez-Liñán (2005: 21–5) do precisely that when surveying much of the qualitative literature on Latin American democratization and drawing probability-oriented hypotheses from it.

Moreover, case studies can be used to provide systematic evidence for probabilistic arguments by utilizing within-case analysis. This is precisely what Wood achieves in her account of insurgent collective action in El Salvador. She found that peasants who joined the rebellion were far more likely to refer to deeply held values of participation, defiance, and pleasure in agency (Wood, 2003: 229–36). The correlation between values and participation was not invariant, and Wood repeatedly refers to 'many' (rather than all) who felt this way. Hence, these values were neither necessary nor sufficient, but they did constitute 'principal reasons' (Wood, 2003: 18) for engaging in collective action. In short, qualitative research and common arguments associated with them are quite compatible with probabilistic views of political outcomes and can be used to both generate and test probabilistic arguments.

Theory generation versus theory testing

Case study methods can be rich sources of new theoretical propositions and insights (Van Evera, 1997: 21–7). Uncovering the causal mechanism in one particular case can lead scholars to develop new ideas about how other cases might work. Mahoney (2007b) notes three particular techniques that can be used to generate new hypotheses. The first is the exploration of deviant case studies, or cases where outcomes do not conform to theoretical expectations (Eckstein, 1975; Lijphart, 1971). The second involves careful involvement in the details of the cases to identify overlooked patterns that crop up in interviews, archival records, and the like. The third consists of particular attention to the temporal dimension of the phenomena to identify turning points or the conjunction of different factors. None of these theory-generating mechanisms is likely to be utilized in quantitative research unless scholars are involved in gathering and coding their own data, a procedural step that has much in common with case study analyses. The close relationship between case studies and theory generation is brought into striking relief by Munck and Snyder (2007: 13), who found that 80% of the articles in their study combined qualitative methods and inductive theorizing.

While few would contest the claim that case studies are useful for generating new theoretical insights, the ability to test theories using case studies is much debated. One potential impediment to using case studies in theory testing is data mining, or using the same data to both generate and test hypotheses. While case study practitioners could of course use data from one case to generate hypotheses that are examined in other cases and thereby avoid the problem, the amount of time and effort put into a case study and the need to publish results often means that data are used to both generate and test (or, perhaps more often, 'illustrate') theories. As Mahoney (2007a: 37) points out, however, data mining is not unique to case study methods. Quantitative researchers can also (and perhaps routinely do) look for patterns in the data, generate hypotheses to fit those patterns, and then 'test' them on the same data set. Mahoney and Goertz (2006) argue that such data mining is far more harmful in quantitative analyses because the goal is to estimate the average effects of independent variables and such effects can change dramatically through changes in model specification that occur through data mining. In case study research, on the other hand, the goal often consists of explaining outcomes in particular cases. Hence, a careful examination of the evidence is an integral part of producing that explanation. For this reason, case studies are quite frequently inductive in nature.

CONCLUSION

Scholars have engaged in a sophisticated and productive debate about case study methods that has produced a wealth of insights. Case studies are widely viewed as useful complements to large-N statistical methods with particular strengths in depth of analysis, construct validity, the identification of causal mechanisms, asymmetric theoretical arguments (related to necessary and sufficient conditions), and theory generation. While case studies seem to possess these 'natural' strengths and trade-offs undoubtedly exist, it is also important not to overstate case study limitations. Case studies can also be useful in causal inference, probabilistic theories, and theory testing. Some of the most important advances in case study methods involve insights into appropriate case selection, process tracing and causal-process observations, and the role of necessary and sufficient conditions. Whether scholarly research will incorporate all of these 'lessons learned' remains an open question, but case study methodologists have certainly done much to carefully consider the uses of case studies and to make available the necessary analytical tools and procedures.

ACKNOWLEDGEMENTS

I would like to thank Kirk Hawkins, Jay Goodliffe, Kelly Patterson, and participants in the research seminar in Brigham Young University's political science department for their insights and comments on this piece.

REFERENCES

Achen, C.H. and Snidal, D. (1989) 'Rational deterrence theory and comparative case studies', *World Politics*, 41 (2): 143–69.

Beck, N. (2006) Is causal-process observation an oxymoron? *Political Analysis*, 14 (3): 347–52.

Bennett, A. (2004) 'Case study methods: Design, use, and comparative advantages', in D.F. Sprinz and Y. Wolinsky-Nahmias (eds), *Models, numbers and cases: Methods for studying international relations*. Ann Arbor: University of Michigan Press, pp. 19–55.

Brady, H.E. and Collier, D. (2004) *Rethinking social inquiry: Diverse tools, shared standards*. Lanham, MD: Rowman and Littlefield.

Brady, H.E., Collier, D., and Seawright, J. (2004) 'Refocusing the discussion of methodology', in H.E. Brady and D. Collier (eds), *Rethinking social inquiry: Diverse tools, shared standards*. Lanham, MD: Rowman and Littlefield, pp. 3–20.

Braumoeller, B.F. and Goertz, G. (2000) 'The methodology of necessary conditions', *American Journal of Political Science*, 44 (4): 844–58.

Clark, W.R, Gilligan, M.J., and Golder, M. (2006) 'A simple multivariate test for asymmetric hypotheses', *Political Analysis*, 14 (3): 311–31.

Collier, D., Brady, H.E., and Seawright, J. (2004a) 'Critiques, responses, and trade-offs: Drawing together the debate', in H.E. Brady and D. Collier (eds), *Rethinking Social Inquiry: Diverse Tools, Shared Standards*. New York: Cambridge University Press, pp. 195–228.

Collier, D., Brady, H.E., and Seawright, J. (2004b) 'Sources of leverage in causal inference: Toward an alternative view of methodology', in H.E. Brady and D. Collier (eds), *Rethinking Social Inquiry: Diverse Tools, Shared Standards*. New York: Cambridge University Press, pp. 229–66.

Collier, D., Mahoney, J., and Seawright, J. (2004c) 'Claiming too much: Warnings about selection bias', in H.E. Brady and D. Collier (eds), *Rethinking Social Inquiry: Diverse Tools, Shared Standards*. New York: Cambridge University Press, pp. 229–66.

Colomer, J.M. (1991) 'Transitions by agreement: Modeling the Spanish way', *American Political Science Review*, 85 (4): 1293–302.

Dion, D. (1998) 'Evidence and inference in the comparative case study', *Comparative Politics*, 30 (January): 127–45.

Eckstein, H. (1975) 'Case study and theory in political science', in F.I. Greenstein and N.W. Polsby (eds), *Handbook of Political Science: Strategies of Inquiry*. Reading, MA: Addison-Wesley.

Fearon, J. (1991) 'Counterfactuals and hypothesis testing in political science', *World Politics*, 43 (2): 169–95.

Geddes, B. (1990) 'How the cases you choose affect the answers you get: Selection bias in comparative politics', *Political Analysis*, 2: 131–50.

George, A. (1979) 'Case study and theory development: The method of structured, focused comparison', in P. Gordon (ed.), *Diplomacy: New approaches in history, theory and policy*. New York: Free Press, pp. 43–68.

George, A. and Bennett, A. (2005) *Case Study and Theory Development in the Social Sciences*. Cambridge, MA: MIT Press.

George, A. and McKeown, T. J. (1985) 'Case studies and theories of organizational decision making', in R.F. Coulam and R.A. Smith (eds), *Advances in information processing in organizations*. Greenwich, CT: Jai Press, pp. 21–58.

Gerring, J. (2004) 'What is a case study and what is it good for?', *American Political Science Review*, 98 (2): 341–54.

Gerring, J. (2007) 'Is there a (viable) crucial-case method?', *Comparative Political Studies*, 40 (3): 231–53.

Goertz, G. (2003) 'The substantive importance of necessary conditions hypotheses', in G. Goertz and H. Starr (eds), *Necessary Conditions: Theory, Methodology and Applications*. New York: Rowman and Littlefield, pp. 65–94.

Harvey, F.P. (2003) 'Practicing coercion: Revisiting successes and failures using Boolean logic and comparative methods', in

G. Goertz and H. Starr (eds), *Necessary Conditions: Theory, Methodology, and Applications*. New York: Rowman and Littlefield.

Hawkins, D. (2001) 'Democratization theory and nontransitions: Insights from Cuba', *Comparative Politics*, 33 (4): 441–61.

King, G., Keohane, R., and Verba, S. (1994) *Designing social inquiry: Scientific inference in qualitative research*. Princeton, NJ: Princeton University Press.

King, G., Keohane, R., and Verba, S. (2004) 'The importance of research design', in H.E. Brady and D. Collier (eds), *Rethinking social inquiry: Diverse tools, shared standards*. Lanham, MD: Rowman and Littlefield, pp. 181–92.

Lijphart, A. (1971) 'Comparative politics and the comparative method', *American Political Science Review*, 65: 682–93.

Mackie, J.L. (1980) *The cement of the universe: A study of causation*. Oxford: Oxford University Press.

Mahoney, J. (2007a) 'Debating the state of comparative politics: Views from qualitative research', *Comparative Political Studies*, 40 (2): 32–38.

Mahoney, J. (2007b) 'Qualitative methodology and comparative politics', *Comparative Political Studies*, 40 (1): 122–44.

Mahoney, J. and Goertz, G. (2006) 'A tale of two cultures: Contrasting quantitative and qualitative research', *Political Analysis*, 14 (3): 227–49.

Mainwaring, S. and Pérez-Liñán, A. (2005) 'Latin American democratization since 1978: Democratic transitions, breakdowns, and erosions', in F. Hagopian and S.P. Mainwaring (eds), *The third wave of democratization in Latin America: Advances and setbacks*. Cambridge: Cambridge University Press, pp. 14–59.

McKeown, T. (1999) 'Case studies and the statistical worldview: Review of King, Keohane, and Verba's *Designing social inquiry: Scientific inference in qualitative research*', *International Organization*, 53 (1): 161–90.

Mill, J.S. (1875) *A system of logic, ratiocinative and inductive: Being a connected view of the principles of evidence and the methods of scientific investigation*, Vol. 2. London: Longmans, Green, Reader, and Dyer.

Munck, G. and Snyder, R. (2007) 'Debating the direction of comparative politics: An analysis of leading journals', *Comparative Political Studies*, 40 (1): 5–31.

Przeworski, A. and Tenue, H. (1970) *The logic of comparative social inquiry*. New York: Wiley.

Ragin, C.C. (1987) *The comparative method: Moving beyond qualitative and quantitative strategies*. Berkeley: University of California Press.

Ragin, C.C. (2000) *Fuzzy-set social science*. Chicago: University of Chicago Press.

Sartori, G. (1970) 'Concept misformation in comparative politics', *American Political Science Review*, 64 (4): 1033–53.

Seawright, J. and Collier, D. (2004) 'Glossary', in H.E. Brady and D. Collier (eds.), *Rethinking social inquiry: Diverse tools, shared standards*. New York: Cambridge University Press, pp. 273–313.

Skocpol, T. (1979) *States and social revolutions: A comparative analysis of France, Russia, and China*. New York: Cambridge University Press.

Sprinz, D.F., and Wolinsky-Nahmias, Y. (2004) 'Introduction: Methdology in international relations research', in D.F. Sprinz and Y. Wolinsky-Nahmias (eds) *Models, numbers and cases: Methods for studying international relations*. Ann Arbor: University of Michigan Press, pp. 1–16.

Tarrow, S. (2004) 'Bridging the quantitative-qualitative divide', in H.E. Brady and D. Collier (eds), *Rethinking social inquiry: Diverse tools, shared standards*. Lanham, MD: Rowman and Littlefield, pp. 171–80.

Tetlock, P.E. and Belkin, A. (1996) 'Counterfactual thought experiments in world politics: logical, methodological, and psychological perspectives', in P. E. Tetlock and A. Belkin (eds), *Counterfactual thought experiments in world politics: Logical, methodological, and psychological perspectives*. Princeton, NJ: Princeton University Press, pp. 1–38.

Van Evera, S. (1997) *Guide to methods for students of political science*. Ithaca, NY: Cornell University Press.

Wood, E.J. (2003) *Insurgent collective action and civil war in El Salvador*. New York: Cambridge University Press.

Yin, R.K. (1990) *Case study research: Design and methods*. Newbury Park, CA: Sage Publications.

4

Is there a Quantitative-Qualitative Divide in Comparative Politics? The Case of Process Tracing

James A. Caporaso

MEANINGS OF QUALITATIVE AND QUANTITATIVE

The discipline of political science is said to be divided between those who pursue a qualitative approach and those who study politics quantitatively. As Pierson (2007) has shown, this division is uneven across sub-fields, with American politics the most quantitative and international relations the least. Comparative politics has a history in which knowledge of particular countries, their cultures, institutions, and behavior, are thought of as very important components of research, whether as context for more detailed empirical generalizations, or as objects of study themselves. As such, comparative politics has had to grapple with the qualitative/quantitative issue in a particularly intensified fashion. Yet, without a clear idea of what is meant by the qualitative/quantitative distinction, it is impossible to know what is at stake. Below is a brief inventory of meanings of this term.

Quality as the property itself

Quantity as variation in degree of that quality. This is the most basic distinction of qualitative and quantitative. A quality is the property itself, such as democracy, alienation, or integration while a quantity refers to measurable variation in that property. So 'democracy' is qualitatively different from 'party government' but perhaps different in degree (in quantity in other words) from authoritarianism. Some qualities do not vary. They exist only as types, for example, pregnancy, sovereignty (some say you are sovereign or not), and party affiliation (Democrat or Republican), though not party loyalty. Most qualities do vary, so that one can say there is more or less alienation, more or less democracy, more or less party fragmentation and so on. I do not think that it is a major claim of qualitative analysis that most political science properties do not vary and therefore do not, at bottom, have a quantitative aspect.

Even when qualitative analysis is called for, as in Ragin's (2000) analysis based on Boolean algebra, there is a practical recognition that the qualitative categories are often truncated versions of underlying continua. If one accepts this reasoning, it is a logical mistake to treat qualitative and quantitative as alternatives to one another. They are mutually implicated categories.

Qualitative analysis is analysis that is verbal

It relies on words, imagery, and ordinary language, or a modified (jargon) extension of ordinary language. It is opposed to numerical analysis where numbers carry the message, even if the numbers are themselves representative of concepts in a theory. Qualitative analysis in this sense could use a rich repertoire associated with ordinary language, including metaphor, analogy, relationships, sequences, stories (narratives, about which more later), ambiguity, irony, and so on. While this usage of qualitative is central to how many think of the qualitative-quantitative divide, we should note that it is not congruent with the distinction made above. In short, one can easily use ordinary language to express quantitative relationships and numbers to represent qualities. 'The more I ignore him, the more he tries to engage me in conversation'. Think of the underlying quantitative nature of this statement in contrast to 'code Republicans as 0 and Democrats as 1', where the numbers indicate membership or non-membership.

Qualitative analysis as interpretive or hermeneutic

The term 'qualitative' can refer to a style of research, one that aims at understanding rather than explanation and prediction. Qualitative becomes an aspect of an approach rather than a property of a concept. The goal is to place oneself in the position of the other person, in order to understand the context (historical, cultural, sociological, class) and meanings, and to be able to reconstruct the symbols and worldviews so that it becomes comprehensible that others act as they do. Herbert Gans' *Urban Villager* (1982), Ann Cornelisen's *Women of the Shadows* (1976) and Paul Willis' *Learning to Labor* (1981), are representative of this category of work.

Qualitative as case study

Sometimes scholars in comparative politics use the term 'qualitative' to refer to detailed studies of single cases, where a case can be a country, region, political party, peasant movement, land tenure system, and so forth. Often such studies are contrasted with large-N statistical work. While this use of qualitative can be useful, case studies are often statistical and rely on extensive use of within-case observations to provide variation and the basis for generalization. If many studies are not formally cross-country, informally most of them are. Scholars are constantly asking 'what is this an instance of?' and 'how does this compare to other cases I am not studying?'

CLAIMS OF QUALITATIVE RESEARCH

In this chapter, by qualitative I mean an approach which relies on verbal reasoning and representation, limits itself to a single case (though this can be relaxed), and attempts to understand within-system relationships either through comparisons over time, across sub-system units, or by the nesting of intra-systemic relationships within the overall political and social system.[1]

Given this definition of qualitative, what are some of its claims? I discern four claims about the distinctive strengths of the qualitative approach of which I will address only one. First, deviant case analysis: qualitative researchers argue that they are well equipped to deal with cases that do not conform to a general pattern, whether that pattern is produced by statistical analysis or simply by theoretical expectation. Deviant case analysis turns out to be a particular expression of the broader problem of causal heterogeneity. Large-N researchers frequently address deviant cases by statistical methods which attempt to reduce the distance between outliers and the regression line. Qualitative researchers argue that the problem is best approached through attempts to reduce heterogeneity of cases. A homogenous population will have less confusion between independent and dependent variables. Second, the qualitative approach is better equipped to discover new concepts and to elaborate these concepts in a theoretically fruitful way (Coppedge, 1999). Its typical strengths are present more in the context of discovery rather than the context of verification. Third, qualitative research, because of its ties to categorical logic, is better equipped to uncover the combinatorial logic of causality underlying many relationships central to comparative politics (Mahoney, 2001; Ragin, 1987, 2000). And fourth, the qualitative approach is said to be more adept at uncovering causal mechanisms, in contrast to the quantitative approach which relies on identifying controlled covariance structures to elucidate causality.

All four claims are important and raise complex issues that are clearly too complex for a single chapter to manage. I will focus on only the last of these four claims, the dispute about causality. The basic dispute revolves around the exact meaning of a causal relation and which of two approaches provides the more satisfying account. The two approaches are the covariance model of causality drawing first upon Hume (1748/1955) and later refined in the Simon-Blalock (Simon, 1957a, b; Blalock, 1961) model and second, the qualitative model which provides a mechanistic account of the process that characterizes a causal relation. Both approaches provide a definition of a causal relation, suggest appropriate methods to study these relations, and are supported by distinctive philosophies of science. It is therefore difficult, if not impossible, to resolve the dispute by using a neutral

philosophy of science as a third-party arbiter. The most one can do is to point out the implications of the approaches and look for places where their logics converge or diverge.

QUALITATIVE ANALYSIS AND CAUSAL MECHANISMS

In this section, I will restate the claim that qualitative analysis is superior in terms of its ability to demonstrate causal relations. Since this claim runs counter to the standard view of causality, I will briefly describe the latter. The qualitative approach has a formidable foe to address; one that finds its philosophic roots in Hume and that has been updated by modern technologies associated with time series analysis and recursive structures. For convenience, I refer to the standard view as the Simon-Blalock model of causality.

After stating the claims of qualitative analysis regarding causality, I attempt three things. First, I elaborate the causal model relying on a mechanistic account. In so doing, I set out the elementary logic of mechanistic thinking and show why, according to its adherents, it constitutes a different and superior way of thinking of causality. Second, I compare one variant (the theoretical narrative) of this account of causality to the standard Simon-Blalock view and argue that there is no *necessary* incompatibility between both accounts. Indeed, the two approaches seem to require one another for a full understanding of causality (Seawright, 2005). Third, I consider a second variant and reach a conclusion that is not so accommodating. Recasting the logic of the mechanistic account into one called the historical narrative leads to a way of thinking about temporal processes that cannot be assimilated into the standard model.

The main claim

The main claim of the qualitative approach is that quantitative research, based on large-Ns, is very good at identifying statistical associations and covariance structures, but not so good at uncovering specific causal mechanisms.[2] While these associations fit well with the Humean idea of causality as constant conjunction (or succession of events), they do not provide for a critical component of causal arguments, namely a mechanism (Bunge, 1997; Elster, 1998; Hedstrom and Swedberg, 1998). In its strongest form, the claim is that qualitative research is best equipped to make causal inferences because it is well suited to discover mechanisms. Since discovering causal mechanisms requires a close-up qualitative examination of processes that can only be imperfectly glimpsed from the large-N vantage point, extended analysis of single cases (process tracing in the most popular version) offers the best opportunity to study mechanisms. Causality, mechanisms, single cases, and process tracing are linked in this approach.

At first glance, this claim to grasp causality through direct examination of the mechanisms seems to be based on a naïve empiricism. One of the legacies of Hume was the banishment of necessary forcings and all mechanisms that claim to have such powers in favor of a strict empiricist view of causality that relies on associations among observable events. Necessary relations, causal forcings, and generative relations are not observed. True, as we learn early in graduate school, correlation does not mean causation, and as should be added, 'at least not by itself'. Nevertheless, demonstration of a connection between X and Y would seem to be the first-cut requirement on which additional causal investigation rests. In this sense, evidence of association establishes candidacy for causal status.

To qualitative analysts, extended discussion of causality as covariance is beside the point. Qualitative researchers argue that mere correlations, even when embedded within a theory that has asymmetric (recursive) properties with controls for confounding variables, still falls short in terms of causal theory. To demonstrate causality, one must uncover a causal mechanism and show how this mechanism is connected to outcomes. If this claim is true, there is a considerable gap between the qualitative and quantitative approaches to causal explanation.

Reliance on mechanisms has a longstanding tradition in post-Humean philosophy of science and is increasingly the favored stance among practicing social scientists and philosophers of science. Harré (1972), for example, argues that the two great metaphysical theories of causality are the generative theory and the succession theory.

> In the generative theory the cause is supposed to have the power to generate the effect and is connected to it. In the succession theory a cause is just what usually comes before the event or state, and which comes to be called its cause because we have acquired a psychological propensity to expect that kind of effect after the cause. (p. 116)

In case there is any doubt as to which view is preferred, Harré observes:

> For the believer in generative causality the existence of the statistics is but the first step in a long process of investigation which ends only when the nature of the things involved has been found out and the reasons for the statistics thus elicited. Science follows the generative rather than the successionist theory of causality (p. 118).[3]

In the rest of this section, I link mechanisms to the methodology of process tracing and show that this method can go in two quite different directions. The first version of process tracing is decidedly explanatory and cannot avoid covariance. Each successive link in the extended causal chain rests, if only implicitly, on another covariance structure. The second version of the process-tracing methodology is more idiosyncratic. It rests on the discovery of a chain of events, rather than a distribution of values of variables, that leads to certain outcomes. While these two approaches share some features – the observations in both are temporally ordered, steps in the sequence of events link background conditions with outcomes – there are many important differences too. However, since the idea of mechanism plays such a big role in what follows, I briefly discuss this concept.

The idea of mechanism has become very popular in modern social research and philosophy of science (see Bunge, 1997 and Hedstrom and Swedberg, 1998, for general discussions of the role of this concept in social research and philosophy of science). The term has been used in quite different ways, sometimes to refer to observables and sometimes to unobservables, at times to events that have a general theoretical status as opposed to specific events that have no general counterpart. Sometimes the use of mechanism is limited to the micro level while macro theory is deprived of the term while others (e.g., Boudon, 1998) see mechanisms as potentially operating at any level. I bypass these controversies to define a mechanism as an intervening factor[4] that occurs between some background variable and an outcome. Mechanisms seek to connect background factors (often structural) with a definite but more remote outcome. If a series of mechanisms is linked together in some kind of temporal order, we can refer to that structure as a causal pathway or process. Several different causal pathways might exist, linking background conditions to outcomes, in which case we can speak of equifinality.

The device of mechanism is useful for giving coherence to temporally extended causal chains, especially where any particular link may not be crucial in bringing about the outcome. In this sense, a mechanism cannot be exogenous or the point of departure of a causal chain just as it cannot be the final outcome. A mechanism is by definition intermediate. It provides the connective tissue that links temporally ordered events. Indeed, its function is to give coherence to these connections and to provide this temporal order. If the connections are made rigorously, a causal process can be the result. If mechanisms do not refer to variables but instead refer to particular events and actors without theoretical status, the result can be a historical narrative or simply a story. I will illustrate the two types of processes below. The first process model is fully compatible with the covariance view of causality and can be seen as complementing it (Gerring, 2005, 2006). I call it the theoretical narrative. The second model, which relies on specific events of a non-theoretical sort, is more particular and leads to the historical narrative.

(a) Mechanism and covariance, the theoretical narrative

The qualitative approach argues that a focus on single cases and the isolation of mechanisms is the best way to go in order to understand causality. Sometimes, it is implied that the exploration of a causal mechanism is sufficient, on its own, to prove a causal relationship. That is, the relationship between X and Y can be proven through the identification of a causal pathway stretching from X to Y. The relationship can be diagrammed as follows:

$$X1 \rightarrow X2 \rightarrow X3 \rightarrow X4 \rightarrow Y$$

The argument is that the above account is superior to one based on the demonstration of the covariation of X1 and Y. The specification of mechanisms (X2, X3, and X4) fills in the temporal and spatial gaps between X1 and Y and increases our confidence that this is how the causal process works. A statistical correlation between X1 and Y might group together instances where X1 was followed by these three intervening variables with instances where no such succession of events occurred. A coefficient could then rest on an unidentified mixture of different causal processes: some where the above process holds, some where no relationship at all exists, and some where X1 does 'lead to' Y but via a different causal path, that is, with different intervening factors. Because the process approach gives us a purer view of the causal process that does not rely on mixing heterogeneous causal relations, it is preferred to the covariance view.

While elaboration of intervening mechanisms may be desirable, a nagging question still remains. Is the identification of the process leading from X1 to Y *ipso facto* evidence of causality? Sometimes advocates of the qualitative mechanistic view of causality treat this as a non-problem, as if the analyst directly grasps the causal connection by direct intuition. Once the intervening mechanisms have been delineated, the causal relation has been demonstrated and epistemological inquiry can cease. This seems unsatisfying and in need of further examination. How can we be certain that a causal relation has been demonstrated? If David Hume (and Alexander George) (George and Bennett, 2005) watch someone flip a light switch, followed by light, which one has witnessed a causal relation? Presumably, Hume would be satisfied by the before-after relationship so long as it proved stable (a constant conjunction) while George might be bewildered by the magic involved in the joining of these two events, since no intervening mechanisms were provided. George would have to press for a more detailed account, perhaps even learning something about electricity.

I accept the proposition that the more we know about the land in between, the more confident we can be about a causal relation. Yet the critical question, perhaps obscured by the light switch example, is this: how do we know that the intervening factors identified are the ones that truly cause the outcome? It is a legitimate question because the qualitative view claims to focus on generative relations, that is, those where the identified factors produce the outcomes. This is a decidedly anti-Humean position (consciously so) but this is precisely where the qualitative view of causality has its distinctive appeal. How do we know that the intervening factors are not irrelevant or spuriously related to the outcome? The constant conjunction model of causality must identify not only a stable association between X and Y but must demonstrate that this pattern is non-spurious, that is, not the result of association with a third variable. By what logic should the qualitative view be exempt from demonstrating non-spuriousness?

Once we have asked this question we can see that the mechanistic approach does not provide a satisfying stand-alone account of causality. If a mechanism is a link in a causal chain, it can only be shown to be a valid link to the extent that it is non-spurious. Repeated associations between X and Y (covariance) as well as the elimination of third variables as common causes are required to demonstrate the relationship. Seen in this light, a mechanism does not have a distinct ontological status compared to a variable and therefore mechanisms do not have special dispensation from the task of explaining covariation between X and Y.

To understand this better, let us pursue the logic of the mechanistic approach. Suppose we observe a relationship between X and Y. The accuracy of our measures is not at issue. We are sure that X and Y occurred. How could we know that X in fact had causal force in bringing about Y? What basis would we have for knowing that the joint occurrence of X and Y was not utterly contingent, that is, that they co-occurred completely by chance? Further, even if the relationship was not due to chance (which we could not know with only one observation), how would we know that the relationship was not spurious? In any snapshot or pairing of temporally adjacent events, there is an impossibly large number of other events that also fit the co-occurrence of X and Y. How do we know one of these events (or several in conjunction) is not the true cause? We don't. In order to establish some basis for the causal inference, we would have to repeatedly observe the temporal ordering of X and Y and we would have to go to some lengths to rule out other causal mechanisms that might be at work. In short, this would take us back to the standards of stable association (covariance) and non-spuriousness characteristic of the quantitative approach.

Yet, the reasons for adopting a process-based model of causality are greater than the light switch example suggests. In that example, we are fairly certain that the association between flipping the switch and the light going on is not a spurious relation. We may not know what happens 'inside the wall' beyond the switch (the black box in this case), but the relation is stable and when exceptions occur (an old light bulb, overtaxed fuse box, or faulty wiring) we can generally detect the culprit. In cases such as this, we might think it fastidious rather than scientific to peer inside the black box. Why, after all multiply entities against the advice of William of Occam? The answer is easily given if we utilize examples more akin to the social sciences.

Take the relationship between levels of inequality and public policies aiming at the reduction of inequality. A high level of inequality is a background factor (with respect to some outcome such as political demands for greater equality) while the mobilization of sentiment against this inequality would be closer to the outcome. Closer yet would be party strategy to use this inequality as a campaign issue while a particular speech or television advertisement would be even more proximally related to the outcome (e.g., an election). In turn, the election could be seen as an event which leads to a public policy that aims to reduce inequality. The basic idea is clear enough. Background factors are related to outcomes via extended causal chains, series of events and intervening conditions which mediate the remote and proximal conditions. Now suppose there are two different research studies. The first one shows the reader an impeccable state of the art regression connecting macro inequality in a society with public policies aiming to reduce these inequalities. The second shows the same beginning and ending conditions but elaborates numerous intervening conditions which connect inequality with public policies. The second study would be more credible than the first because there is more connective tissue. While we can never be certain, we have more confidence if the main episodes of the intervening process are established and if the links in the chain do seamlessly lead to the outcome. A gross pattern of inequality need not lead to remedial policies and a macro correlation between inequality and public policies would be difficult to interpret with confidence. Someone who can show that such inequality works through the system by illustrating its class composition, and demonstrate how the inequality is mobilized by political actors who manage a campaign on this issue will have produced a more convincing study.

In this section, I have argued that one type of qualitative model of causality, the theoretical narrative, joins mechanisms to the idea of covariance essential to Humean approaches to causality. It is not mechanism versus covariance but rather mechanism and covariance. In this approach, neither mechanism nor covariance by itself is sufficient for an adequate account of causality. Covariance by itself may blend heterogeneous causal processes into one set of coefficients (e.g., a correlation coefficient representing a variety of causal pathways connecting background factors to outcomes). A mechanistic account might identify a set of temporally related events with no underlying causal connections, in the sense that the identified relations are contingent and spurious. Subjecting mechanisms to the covariance requirement and subjecting covariance to the mechanism requirement enriches both.

(b) Mechanisms and stories, the historical narrative

In the theoretical narrative, I argued that mechanism and covariance are best seen as complementary to one another and that a more satisfying explanation can be obtained by joining them in a unified account. In this view, mechanism and covariance are not fundamentally at odds with one another. Indeed, the two ideas are worth more together than separately. Considered as such, there is no barrier between qualitative and quantitative approaches. The qualitative aspect urges us to uncover the mechanisms lying between variables temporally and spatially removed from one another. The quantitative aspect urges us to think of these mechanisms as variables which must be viewed as covariance structures in their relations with one another. Neither can be disregarded without loss of information.

In this section, I present an alternate view that is not nearly so conciliatory. This view holds that mechanistic accounts need not rest on variables at all but rather on arrays of events/actors/actions viewed in particularistic ways. This particularity can be achieved in two ways. The historical narrative can be made up of terms that represent specific events which are not presented as instances of more general categories. What are joined are events that do not have broad conceptual status and are not treated as variables, even qualitative ones. The second form of particularity occurs when the narrative assumes the form of a story in which rare events and conjunctures made up of independent streams of low probability events, influence outcomes. This is sometimes called conjunctural history. In both cases, elements of the story resist quantification, though with more force in the former than the latter.[5] In what follows I focus on the former meaning of historical narrative.

The significance of stories, or historical narratives, is downplayed, even degraded, in social science. Stories have connotations of being ad-hoc, descriptive, and cobbled together sequences of events designed (even tailored) to account for an outcome without offering a general explanation. The critic argues that the narrative essentially describes what has happened but does not recognize the event as an instance of a general category, thus working against accumulation and integration of knowledge. The contrast between the theoretical and historical narrative is stark. On the one hand, we have abstract concepts where events must submit to the question 'of what is this an instance?' The United States and Canada are members of a democratic dyad. Italy is an example of a fragmented party system and Amnesty International is an international non-governmental organization. Each of these conceptual umbrellas carries a theoretical message. On the other hand we have concrete events with proper names, and specific information about time and place attached. 'The Austrian Archduke Franz Ferdinand was assassinated by a Serbian nationalist, Gavrilo Princip, in the summer of 1914', and the Soviet representative in the Security Council (Andrei Vyshinsky) was absent in late June 1950 when the United Nations undertook collective security measures to respond to the North Korean invasion of South Korea. No attempt is made to describe these events as elements of a more general class of events (assassinations of political leaders) or to assign them scores on some underlying continuum.

What is sometimes difficult for the quantitative approach to accept is that the use of proper names is not just for the purpose of describing, rather than explaining, an event such as the outbreak of World War I. According to some accounts (Lebow, 2000–2001), the assassination of the Archduke Franz Ferdinand by Gavrilo Princip was not a superfluous and substitutable event in the inevitable march toward war. Few would deny that the assassination had consequences. Rather, the argument is made that if it had not been for the assassination in the summer of 1914, another event would surely have triggered war. Europe was a dry forest ready to burn. Any number of events could have initiated the fire. Against the 'streetcar' view that catalysts come along often (Thompson, 2003), one can place the view that rare and unpredictable events sometimes have big consequences that would not have otherwise occurred. If the Serbian nationalist had been apprehended, delayed, thrown off balance by the policeman who tried to interfere with his shot, or if the carriage holding the archduke had not stopped to allow another touring car to back up because of a wrong turn (Lebow, 2000–2001: 592–3), the immediate crisis and perhaps the war itself would have been averted. To be sure, WWI had underlying structural causes but even structural causes do not last forever. Striking as the counterfactual is, if the crisis of the summer of 1914 had been averted, time would have been bought. According to Lebow (2000–2001: 601), the window of opportunity for war was probably only several years long.

Without the twin assassinations at Sarajevo, Europe might have remained at peace for another several years. In even that short a time, there is good reason to believe that many of the pressures making Austrian, German, and Russian leaders risk-prone would have abated ... In Austria ... the death of Franz Joseph in 1916 would have brought Franz Ferdinand to the throne, and he was committed to introducing the universal franchise into Hungary. Internal turmoil in Austria-Hungary would have made it less, not more, war-prone. It is possible that Europe would have evolved in very different ways, and without the Great War many of the horrors of the twentieth century could have been averted. (Lebow, 2003: 476)

The above example suggests that specific events, narrated properly, can be interpreted causally. But I am getting ahead of myself since I have not discussed what narration, properly construed, means. In what follows, I attempt to identify the historical narrative structure, provide a simple schematic to distinguish it from the theoretical narrative, and make arguments as to why we might consider such a narrative as explanatory in the broad sense. In doing this, I hope to show the continuities as well as discontinuities between qualitative and quantitative approaches.

Let me start by acknowledging a debt to A. R. Louch's 'History as Narrative' (1969) as well as to the work of Howard Becker more generally.[6] The former is a historian and the latter a sociologist, yet both arrive at similar conceptions of the logical form of a narrative explanation.

Becker (1998) asks us to imagine that what we 'want to study has, not causes but a history, a story, a narrative' (pp. 60–61). Continuing, he suggests that a narrative account, in contrast to correlational studies, depicts the thing to be explained '... as something that comes about through a series of steps.' (p. 208). Instead of asking about the necessary (and perhaps sufficient) conditions for X, we ask how X came to be the way it is. This way of looking at things pushes us to discover X's history, that is, the sequences and links that are part of the process that brought X about. What makes a narrative interpretation possible is the temporal and spatial adjacency of different events and the

significance of these events in terms of some larger story.

Once the question is formulated in this way, the major research task is to focus on the discovery of the steps and their sequences. A 'step' is not a value of a variable. It has no distribution and it is not necessarily treated as an instance of a larger distribution.[7] Narrative structure may go as follows: first we had these conditions, which led to Y, and that served to stimulate m, n, and o (mechanisms), which in turn led to Z. As Becker puts it, the process (the connection of events over time) is taken to be important for the result, 'perhaps even constitutive of it' (Becker, 1992: 209). So temporal ordering (sequence), conjunctures (the coming together of independent events), and time-sensitive influences are all central to good story telling.

The historical narrative is deceptively similar in structure to the theoretical narrative, though it has some important differences. We can think of the theoretical narrative as follows:

$$X \rightarrow Y \rightarrow Z$$

where X, Y, and Z refer to distributions of time-ordered variables, which implies a lagged data matrix where X and Y are paired with later observations of Y and Z respectively.

$Xt1$	$Yt2$	$Zt3$
:	:	:
:	:	:
:	:	::
Xtn	$Ytn +1$	$Ztn +2$

This in turn implies that r X.Y and rY.Z (correlation of X with Y and Y with Z). The results of the data analysis of this matrix is a set of coefficients (correlation coefficients, regression coefficients) describing the relations between X, Y, and Z. The larger the n (number of observations) and the smaller the number of coefficients, the more parsimonious the theory.

Now consider the case of the historical narrative with intermediate mechanisms:

$$X \rightarrow Y \rightarrow Z$$

Where X, Y, and Z are specific events (not variables), which implies:

$$X \rightarrow m, n, o \rightarrow Y \rightarrow p, q, r \rightarrow Z$$

Where m, n, o and p, q, and r are intervening mechanisms. The role of detailed process tracing becomes critical here with the burden on the analyst to identify the factors that lie in between X, Y, and Z. Notice that covariance (constant conjunction) is not an issue here because there is no distribution (so means, and variances, and covariances cannot be calculated). If causality is to be established, the steps in the process leading from X to Z must be made convincingly. This in turn requires that the intervening mechanisms must be supplied in such a way as to leave little doubt that the larger events in question are actually (non-spuriously) connected. The historical narrative satisfies the requirement that a series of mechanisms is identified which connects X to Y.

Let us carefully consider the idea of the historical narrative as put forth by Louch (1969). His basic idea is that a narrative is a way of accounting for something as the outgrowth or result of a series of prior steps. Though Louch does not emphasize the role of mechanism, his account is fully consistent with it, indeed, it even depends on it. Yet it is clear in his argument that the steps in the sequence are not variables. The Xs and Ys are actors and specific events whose actions are told at an increasingly fine level of granularity. Louch's narrative is clearly a version of the historical narrative diagrammed above.

But if the connections are made in terms of specific events, it means we cannot observe a pattern in the succession of events. All we can say is that B followed A in this case. The light switch can't be repeatedly thrown. The archduke has either been assassinated or he has not. So two questions immediately arise. The first is what grounds do we have for believing that the relationship between A and B is causal and not spurious? Presumably, there are lots of other events that might interpose themselves between A and B. What standards do we use for including A in the chain along with B and not some other event? The second concerns explanation. Do these sequences of events qualify as explanation? The first question is answered in terms of 'narrative smoothness'. The second is answered in terms of explanatory logics outside the covering law model.

What basis do we have for believing that later events came about because of earlier ones? Clearly this is a more demanding question than the descriptive one that asks if certain events follow or precede others. We have already seen that one of the claims of qualitative research is that it can identify causal patterns and it can do this on the basis of a generative idea of causality whereby later forms result from earlier ones. In one sense, this claim is circular. It amounts to saying that a chain of causality can be shown by observing a chain of causality. In a certain sense, this is true. Belief in the causal chain depends to a large extent on the not so simple act of seeing or observing the sequence of events. But if this is true, it is no more circular than the covering law model of explanation in which the occurrence of X is 'explained' by telling us that X occurred because Y occurred and X always occurs when Y occurs. Everything interesting in the covering law model is a part of the auxiliary action (is this an instance of X? and is the relationship between X and Y really invariant?) What makes the historical narrative interesting is the extent to which the narrator can give a seamless account of the sequence of events leading to the outcome. In pulling this off, the idea of narrative smoothness is crucial (Louch, 1969).

The task of the historian, according to Louch (1969), is to lay out the thing to be explained on a continuum, and to trace the temporal process which led to the final result in great detail. The gaps may be filled in by visual observation of that which occurs between background events and the outcome. The historian Roberts (1996) speaks of the necessity of microcorrelation.[8] Historical sociology deals with broad macro forces: social unrest, inequality of wealth, remoteness of political institutions, and class conflict. There is much explanatory room between these background factors, which predispose people toward mobilization, and actual mobilization for a specific cause. The greater the reliance on mechanisms for intermediate information, the fewer the gaps between distal and proximal terms, the greater the confidence we have in the story. Louch's idea is that if we look carefully, we can literally see the process by which the event in question comes about. A detailed account in terms of mechanisms provides the semiotic glue that gives meaning to the narrative. The process of carefully observing the chronology of events, if disciplined and fine-grained enough, is explanation. The final result, the thing we want to explain, comes about as a natural result of the process leading up to it.

The task of the historian is to focus on the apparent dissimilarities in an object or process, and through a form of observational arbitrage, to show how later forms emerge out of earlier ones. Filling in the gaps, ironing out the differences, and demonstrating continuity help to achieve narrative smoothness. For example, one could look at the French Revolution (1789), France in 1848, the birth of the Fourth Republic in France (1946), and the appearance of the Fifth Republic in 1958. Despite the many important differences, the historian would fill in the considerable gaps in such a way as to smooth out the differences between France in these different periods and to show how later periods were somehow extensions or modifications of earlier ones. That this would be a mighty task, given this example, may be one reason historians are inclined to focus on shorter time periods. As Louch (1969) argues, the task of the historian is to 'make[s] continuity visible; he [the historian] fills in the gaps' (p. 56).

The attempt to achieve narrative smoothness blurs the line between a close description and explanation. This is why within-case analysis is often favored by the qualitative researcher. Any event that might intrude into the process to affect the outcome is either made part of the process (endogenized in a different sense) or argued to be irrelevant. Irrelevancy would have to be argued on exactly the inverse grounds of narrative smoothness.[9] It is in this sense that the historical narrative controls irrelevant considerations. While this is quite different from partial correlations and stratified research designs of the quantitative researcher, it fits in with the overall qualitative approach. Anything that cannot be shown to be part of a tight sequence of events, does not qualify to be part of the narrative.

From the standpoint of historical narrative, a small number of cases (one is the limit) is a strength rather than a weakness, largely because it minimizes the problem of causal heterogeneity. Since the case is pure (unmixed with heterogeneous cases), its causes are likely to be more homogeneous. The large-N researcher must attempt to deal with disjointed findings by introducing new variables and specifications, by using dummy variables to account for group differences, by assigning time-varying parameters, or by assigning unexplained cases to an error vector (Ragin, 2000: 50). Adding cases has benefits, in terms of both internal and external validity, but it makes a single satisfactory theory less likely.

To strengthen the case that narrative smoothness gives us greater inferential leverage, let me provide an example of a powerful theory where narrative smoothness does not exist. I illustrate with a strong theory to avoid the straw man charge. The Stolper-Samuelson (1941) theorem, as told by Rogowski (1989), predicts that exogenous shifts in international economic openness lead to electoral realignments. Increasing (decreasing) exposure to trade will benefit (harm) holders of relatively abundant (scarce) factors of production and this will lead to changes in domestic political alignments. Such a spare story, based only on background economic information (relative factor profiles) and its relationship to political coalitions, would not give us as much inferential confidence as one in which background conditions were tied to the electoral outcomes via an elaborate specification of mediating mechanisms. If the theory specified not only how trade affects factor incomes, but also how these incomes are perceived by real social classes, how these objective interests are mobilized (or not) by political entrepreneurs, and the way in which these classes are or are not organized into electoral constellations where they could make their votes count, this would greatly add to the story. Indeed, one of the main goals of the *Analytic Narrratives* book is to '... focus on the mechanisms that translate ... macrohistorical forces into specific political outcomes.' (Bates et al., 1998: 13) To the extent that the gaps are filled in, the account is all the more plausible, even convincing. So there is a sense, more than intuitive, that a detailed tracing of the process helps us understand the outcome.

The second question has to do with whether the historical narrative is explanatory. This is a difficult question to answer, not least because there are different models of explanation. Perhaps some would argue that the historical narrative provides description but not a general law. Hence there is no explanation. I argue that the historical narrative is more than mere description but different from a general covering law in the Hempel (1965) and Nagel (1961) sense. Broader significance of the historical narrative is realized not by subsuming particulars under covering laws but through the relationship between the particulars of the story and interpretive frameworks, metaphor and myth (Lakoff, 2003). The story parts may cohere in

some fashion, but not necessarily because of explicit causal connections of the sort that X caused Y. However, coherence may be supplied through analogies or by interpretive reference to a larger narrative template in the mind of the reader or historian. The Vietnam War has been debated in light of the Munich analogy, the domino 'theory', and the quagmire metaphor. One could tell a story of the first Gulf War of 1990–1991 using nothing but proper names and specific time-place information (Bush, Baker, Glaspie, Sununu, Hussein, the United Nations, and the Gulf Cooperation Council). Still, the reader could very well understand these specific events in light of a larger morality play emphasizing a villain (Hussein), a victim (Kuwait), and a hero or rescuer such as the United States, United Nations (Lakoff, 2003: 3). These stories, or narrative templates, are deeply embedded in our memories. Thus, Alker (1987) suggests that we take seriously 'alternative scripts', 'plot possibilities', and 'context-sensitive story grammars' that lie behind historical processes we study (pp. 1–5). There are metaphors of birth, growth and decay, of the virtuous person gone astray (sin) and cleansing himself (penance, redemption and renewal), of innocence and loss of innocence, and of humility and hubris. There is considerable evidence that people orient themselves to the world in terms of metaphors (Lakoff and Johnson, 1980).

Let us take as a time-tested example the story of Ulysses and the Sirens, the subject of a great literary epic. One reason that this theme has been so appealing across the ages is that it is so widely useful and evocative for both theoretical and interpretive accounts. This theme (of Ulysses having himself tied to the mast) has been invoked to describe the daily pre-commitments by which the recovering alcoholic tries to pre-commit (empty the liquor cabinet in the morning), the institutional devices 'invented' by politicians and bankers to avoid inflation (place banks outside the line of executive and legislative authority), and the behavior of the military commander who wants to send costly signals to the enemy (by burning bridges). The Ulysses metaphor brings together a wide array of examples and integrates them within a common interpretive framework. It is by the assimilation of these examples to the master framework that the particulars acquire significance. The tale of Ulysses is not a causal story, though surely it could be re-expressed as such.

In this section I have attempted to explicate the underlying logic of the theoretical and historical narratives. Both rely on time-ordered information and both attempt to achieve a meaning that goes well beyond the data at hand. In the theoretical narrative, the introduction of mechanisms does not make for challenges that are qualitatively new. Mechanisms are just 'in-between variables'. In addition, quantitative expression is not only compatible with the theoretical narrative; it goes naturally with it.

The historical narrative is based on a different logic. To demonstrate causality, the theoretical narrative relies on regular ties (constant conjunction) between temporally adjacent but lagged observations. Extraneous causes are eliminated through statistical controls or research design strategies. The explanatory model is one based on a fit between the particulars to be explained and a general covering law. The historical narrative relies on filling in the gaps between events that are temporally removed from one another and achieving a narrative smoothness. It is the closing of the gap between background conditions and outcomes, along with placement of the story within a larger interpretive framework that lends cogency to the account.

A focus on mechanisms involves a shift away from abstract general laws with no spatial-temporal parameters to the operation of factors in specific social and political contexts. Since narratives are by definition processes which transpire over time, these mechanisms will of necessity be tailored to limited temporal orders such as episodes (Tilly, 2001), conjunctures, and sequences (Pierson, 2004). The term mechanism often carries the connotation of limited generalizability (see Boudon, 1998; Elster, 1989). The particularity of such accounts is best (though not exclusively) addressed by qualitative approaches.

CONCLUSION

In this chapter I have focused on the role of causal process tracing in single cases within the context of comparative politics. While admittedly different from cross-country comparisons, single cases offer ample opportunities for within-case comparison and analysis. I have addressed a main claim of qualitative researchers, which is that the qualitative approach is better positioned to make causal inferences in a single case narrative study. Quantitative approaches are well designed to detect structures of covariance in large-N studies and thus have an affinity with Humean (and Simon-Blalock) models of causality, while qualitative approaches have an affinity with mechanistic models of causality. In what sense is this claim true? In what sense can small N studies, even single cases using detailed process tracing, provide a convincing model of causality?

In answering this question, I confronted a prior issue about the nature of mechanism. Depending on the conception of mechanism, two quite different views of causal process analysis are possible, leading inescapably to two distinct versions of within-case analysis. The first view of mechanism leads to the theoretical narrative and relies on variables and their connections. The causal process is not substantially different from the Humean model. What is required to demonstrate causality are still constant conjunction, asymmetry (temporal ordering is the most common kind), and non-spuriousness. As such, there is no barrier to quantitative expression. Indeed, it is hard to see how causal inferences could be supported in the absence of quantitative expression. In the second case, the historical narrative, the logic is different.

Here the terms of the narrative are either particular (not instances of general variables) or a combination of general variables and particular events. The historical narrative follows the causal flow and can mix actions of specific actors with statements about general theoretical variables (Abbott, 2001: 142). Specific mechanisms and historical detail are filled in to supply narrative smoothness and coherence without much attention to the ontological status of the connections. There are few formal models of the structure of explanation outside of the Hempel (1965) or Nagel (1961) variety.[10] Instead, practitioners of the historical narrative appeal to more intuitive and everyday standards such as 'does the story make sense?', 'is it followable?', and 'can one understand how later events flowed out of prior ones?'

With all the talk of history, we may have to remind ourselves that this is a chapter about comparative politics. Are not comparative and historical approaches usually alternatives to one another? My underlying assumption is that the answer to this question is no, and that much of the power of small-N studies in comparative politics lies in teasing out the temporal structure of single cases or small-N comparisons. Research in comparative politics does not imply the absence of history, especially in small-N settings. I point to the work of Pierson (2004); Collier and Collier (1991); Moore (1966); and Luebbert (1991) as examples of comparative research that is sensitive to the temporal dimension.

What are some of the implications of this analysis of the quantitative theoretical narrative and the qualitative historical narrative? First, it makes less sense to think of a dichotomy between qualitative and quantitative approaches, and more to accept a continuum running from the abstract language of variables to completely idiosyncratic stories which have no generalizability. Variable-based accounts are quantifiable in principle while particularistic stories are not. In the middle we can think of contingent theories, not so much as probabilistic theories but rather as situations described by the possibility of

going in different directions, depending on the options given by a prior state, that is, more the idea of a stage or phase. As Becker (1998: 32–3) might put it, if A occurs (say I graduate high school), then I could learn a trade, go into the army, or become a fly fishing guide in the Rockies in the following years. This agentic, or case-oriented view, gives us a different perspective than the variable-centered view of the world where probability transition matrices and Markov processes might describe the life courses of large numbers of individuals.

Second, there is nothing inherently qualitative about mechanism and mechanism-based explanation. We have seen (or I have tried to show) that a mechanism can operate as a special kind of variable, one with an in-between location. As such, mechanisms can be used to produce correlation and regression coefficients in the normal ways. As a result, a static, cross-sectional account based on a large sample can be enriched by stretching out the time period and examining the process, that is, the way the variables relate over time.

Third, mechanism-based accounts become qualitative when the terms in the account are particular, that is, when they are proper names. Since these terms do not refer to properties which vary (increase or decrease), they cannot be quantified. Still, coherent stories can be told incorporating idiosyncratic terms and actions of individuals. The worth and meaning of a narrative account is not exhausted by a descriptive summary of the terms in the story. The assassination of the Archduke Ferdinand by Gavrilo Princip could be understood as the action of a Serbian nationalist (agent of a frustrated nation) or as a catalyst in a tragic play (unintended consequences, the war no one wanted). Strangely absent from most accounts of World War I are references to villains, victims, and heroes. In the qualitative account, much more depends on meaning than on correlations and regressions. And the semiotic glue is provided by the mechanisms in the story.

Fourth, and finally, there are opportunities where the two approaches can be complementary. As Mahoney (2007: 132) and

Sambanis (2003: 2) forcefully argue, there are numerous studies in which a macro (large-N) correlation holds, but where the process by which the outcome occurred is not the one specified by the theory. This points to a place where quantitative and qualitative approaches can be helpful to one another. The quantitative approach can be responsible for establishing the correlations; the qualitative process approach (either theoretical or historical narrative) can examine the pathways to see if they conform to the theory. Perhaps a single outcome, say an advanced welfare state or a democratic peace, can be achieved via a number of different causal paths. If so, a judicious mix of qualitative and quantitative approaches would be best equipped to demonstrate that 'why?' and 'how?' are different questions that connect at a higher level.

ACKNOWLEDGEMENT

I am indebted to John Gerring for several of his articles on causality and mechanism, particularly Gerring (2006). I am also grateful for his ongoing conversations with me on these subjects. I am also grateful for a seminar organized by my colleague Aseem Prakash in which two of my colleagues – Margaret Levi and Susan Whiting – served as critical and helpful discussants.

NOTES

1. While there is no logically necessary reason why verbal expression, detailed case studies and avoidance of statistical relationships have to come together, in this chapter I combine them to dramatize the differences between qualitative and quantitative research. In practice, quite often researchers combine statistical analysis with detailed analysis of single cases.

2. For an extended treatment of this subject, and a careful comparison of the covariance and mechanismic approaches to causality, see Gerring (2006).

3. This formulation would seem to remove causality from the empirical realm, at least insofar as demonstration of the link between cause and effect is concerned. Instead of demonstrating a pattern of covariance, the absence of feedback (no endogeneity), and the absence of symptomatic covariation due to confounding influences (perhaps a third variable causing both X and Y, with these two variables showing symptomatic correlation), the attention of the analyst turns toward internal relations and discovery of 'the nature of things'.

4. I use the term 'factor' advisedly here, since the logical status of mechanism is controversial. If a mechanism is really a variable taking up a particular position between background facts and outcomes, then it is easy to assimilate mechanistic accounts into the standard view of causality. The term 'factor' allows us to keep the logical status of mechanism open.

5. See Braumoeller (2003) for an attempt to quantify complex conjunctural phenomena.

6. By Becker, see especially *Tricks of the Trade* (1998) and 'Cases, causes, conjunctures, stories, and imagery' in Ragin and Becker, *What is a Case?* (1992).

7. This does not mean that the terms in the historical narrative are completely idiosyncratic. I will return to this point later.

8. The argument about microcorrelation in narrative history is analogous to the posited need for microfoundations in rational choice theory. In both cases, there is a perceived gap between a background condition (macroincentives and background causes) and some observable outcome. The outcome is not explainable on the basis of macro data. What is needed is the information that comes from the individual and his choices or from the chain of events that lead up to, and in a sense, cause the outcome.

9. Narrative irrelevance would have to be established on the basis of the absence of smooth connections among events in the story. If a term in the narrative overlapped with others in meaningless ways, if it created sequences that did not make sense, or if it enlarged the discontinuities rather than minimized them, it would be difficult to justify inclusion.

10. There are attempts at formal models by Roberts (1996), especially chapter 2 'The Explanatory Power of Colligation'; by Danto (1985); and by Stinchcombe (1968).

REFERENCES

Abbott, A. (2001) *Time matters: On theory and method*. Chicago, IL: University of Chicago Press.

Alker, H.R., Jr. (1987) 'Fairy tales, tragedies and world histories', *Behaviormetrika*, 21: 1–28.

Bates, R.H., Greif, A., Levi, M., Rosenthal, J.-L. and Weingast, B. R. (1998) *Analytic Narratives*. NJ: Princeton University Press.

Becker, H.S. (1992) 'Cases, causes, conjunctures, stories, and imagery', in C.C. Ragin and H.S. Becker (eds), *What is a Case?* Cambridge: Cambridge University Press, pp. 205–216.

Becker, H.S. (1998) *Tricks of the trade*. Chicago, IL: University of Chicago Press.

Blalock, H.M., Jr. (1961) *Causal inference in nonexperimental research*. Chapel Hill, NC: University of North Carolina Press.

Boudon, R. (1998) 'Social mechanisms without black boxes', in P. Hedstrom and R. Swedberg (eds), *Social Mechanisms*. Cambridge: Cambridge University Press, pp. 172–203.

Braumoeller, B.F. (2003) 'Causal complexity and the study of politics', *Political Analysis*, 3 (3): 209–233.

Bunge, M. (1997) 'Mechanism and explanation', *Philosophy of the Social Sciences*, 27 (4): 410–65.

Collier, R. B. and Collier, D. (1991) *Shaping the political arena: Critical junctures, the labor movement, and regime dynamics in Latin America*. Princeton, NJ: Princeton University Press.

Coppedge, M. (1999) 'Thickening thin concepts and theories; Combining large n and small n in comparative politics', *Comparative Politics*, 31 (4): 465–476.

Cornelisen, A. (1976) *Women of the shadows*. Boston: Little, Brown.

Danto, A. C. (1985) *Narration and knowledge*. New York: Columbia University Press.

Elster, J. (1989) *Nuts and bolts for the social sciences*. Cambridge: Cambridge University Press.

Elster, J. (1998) 'A plea for mechanisms', in P. Hedstrom and R. Swedberg (eds), *Social mechanisms: An analytical approach to social theory*. Cambridge: Cambridge University Press, pp. 45–73.

Gans, H.J. (1982) *The urban villagers: Groups and class in the life of Italian–Americans*. New York: Free Press.

George, A.L., and Bennett, A. (2005) *Case studies and theory development in the social sciences*. Cambridge: MIT Press.

Gerring, J. (2005) 'Causation: A unified framework for the social sciences', *Journal of Theoretical Politics*, 17 (2): 163–98.

Gerring, J. (2006, May) The mechamismic worldview: Unpacking the box. Manuscript (pp. 1–19) Boston University.

Harré, R. (1972) *The philosophies of science: An introductory survey*. Oxford: Oxford University Press.

Hedstrom, P. and Swedberg, R. (eds) (1998) *Social mechanisms: An analytical approach to social theory*. Cambridge: Cambridge University Press.

Hempel, C.G. (1965) *Aspects of scientific explanation and other essays in the philosophy of science*. New York: Free Press.

Hume, D. (1748/1955) *An inquiry concerning human understanding*. USA: Liberal Arts Press.

Lakoff, G. (2003, March 18) Metaphor and war, again. *Alter Net*. Retrieved February 4, 2008, from http://www.alternet.org/story/15414.

Lakoff, G. and Johnson, M. (1980) *Metaphors we live by*. IL: University of Chicago Press.

Lebow, R.N. (2000–2001) 'Contingency, catalysts, and international system change', *Political Science Quarterly*, 115 (4): 591–616.

Lebow, R.N. (2003) 'A data set named desire: a reply to William R. Thompson', *International Studies Quarterly*, 47 (4): 475–478.

Louch, A.R. (1969) 'History as narrative', *History and Theory*, 8 (1): 54–70.

Luebbert, G.M. (1991) *Liberalism, fascism, or social democracy: Social classes and the political origins of regimes in interwar Europe*. New York: Oxford University Press.

Mahoney, J. (2001) 'Beyond correlational analysis: Recent innovations in theory and method', *Sociological Forum*, 16 (3): 575–93.

Mahoney, J. (2007) 'Qualitative methodology and comparative politics', *Comparative Political Studies*, 40 (2): 122–144.

Moore, B. (1966) *Social origins of dictatorship and democracy: Lord and peasant in the making of the modern world*. Boston: Beacon Press.

Nagel, E. (1961) *The structure of science: Problems in the logic of scientific explanation*. New York: Harcourt Brace.

Pierson, P. (2004) *Politics in Time*. Princeton, N.J.: Princeton University Press

Pierson, P. (2007) 'The costs of marginalization: Qualitative methods in the study of American politics', *Comparative Political Studies*, 40 (2): 145–169.

Ragin, C.C. (1987) *The comparative method*. Berkeley: University of California Press.

Ragin, C.C. (2000) *Fuzzy set social science*. Chicago, IL: University of Chicago Press.

Ragin, C.C., and Becker, H.S. (eds), (1992) *What is a Case?* Cambridge: Cambridge University Press.

Roberts, C. (1996) *The logic of historical explanation*. College Park: Pennsylvania State University Press.

Rogowski, R. (1989) *Commerce and coalitions: How trade affects domestic political alignments*. Princeton, NJ: Princeton University Press.

Sambanis, N. (2003) *Using case studies to expand the theory of civil war* (Conflict prevention and reconstruction working papers, no. 5: 1–62) Washington, DC: Social Development Department, World Bank.

Seawright, J. (2005) 'Qualitative comparative analysis vis-à-vis regression', *Studies in Comparative International Development*, 40 (1): 3–26.

Simon, H.A. (1957a) 'Causal ordering and identifiability', in *Models of man, social and rational*. New York: John Wiley, pp. 10–36.

Simon, H.A. (1957b) 'Spurious correlation: a causal interpretation', in *Models of man, social and rational*. New York: John Wiley, pp. 37–49

Stinchcombe, A.L. (1968) *Constructing social theories*. Chicago, IL: University of Chicago Press.

Stinchcombe, A.L. (1991) 'The conditions of fruitfulness of theorizing about mechanisms in social science', *Philosophy of the Social Sciences*, 21 (3): 367–88.

Stolper, W.F. and Samuelson, P.A. (1941) 'Protection and real wages', *Review of Economic Studies*, 9 (1): 58–73.

Thompson, W.R. (2003) 'A streetcar named Sarajevo: Catalysts, multiple causal chains, and rivalry structures', *International Studies Quarterly*, 47 (4): 453–474.

Tilly, C. (1997) 'Means and ends of comparison in macrosociology', *Comparative Social Research*, 16 (1): 43–53.

Tilly, C. (2001) 'Mechanisms in political processes', *Annual Review of Political Science*, 4: 21–41.

Willis, P.E. (1981) *Learning to labor: How working class kids get working class jobs*. New York: Columbia University Press.

5

Establishing Equivalence

Jan W. van Deth

INTRODUCTION

An Austrian businessman embarrassed his French colleagues by insisting on concluding their negotiations before they went to dinner. An Italian in Sweden could not find a religious association that would provide him with social support and was sent to the town hall to fill out a number of forms. A French politician appeared in a crisp white dress on the Chinese Wall and did not know that white indicates grief and mourning in that part of Asia. A Dutch couple decided to spend much money on a 'deftig' meal to celebrate their wedding anniversary in a German sea resort and were very disappointed to be served a very simple farmer's meal. An American fundraiser visited several European cities only to find out that in many languages no translation of the word 'fundraising' exists. This list of misunderstandings, embarrassments, and confusions can be easily made longer. They all share the basic pattern that specific ideas and phenomena can have different meanings in different circumstances. Finishing negotiations before dinner, approaching religious organizations, wearing white clothes, dining in a formal environment, or looking for opportunities to collect financial support is generally unproblematic – it is the particular context which makes these behaviours unusual or odd. As a consequence,

intentions are misinterpreted and goals are seldom reached.

With the burgeoning of comparative research in the last few decades, contexts increasingly attracted attention. Many comparativists started their career by studying such topics as voting behaviour, marriage patterns, or religious norms in a single context, and their need for comparisons is usually based on the assumption that similar phenomena can be found in other groups, cultures, regions, or countries. The basic design of comparative research is simple and straightforward. In order to reach insights not attainable in single-case studies, one examines either the same phenomena in different contexts or different phenomena in similar contexts (cf., Przeworski and Teune, 1970: 31–46). For many purposes, a comparative approach is preferred to single-observation studies and reasoning by analogy,[1] although case studies clearly have their own merits and advantages (cf., Feagin et al., 1991; Rueschemeyer, 2003) and strong arguments have been offered for so-called 'small-N' analyses (cf., Ebbinghaus, 2005; Hall, 2003: 395–8; Ragin, 2004) as well as ingenious strategies for middle-of-the-road positions (cf., McKeon, 2004; Ragin, 2000; Schneider and Wagemann, 2006). In comparative approaches, difficult questions arise once we examine the terms 'same phenomena' or 'similar contexts' somewhat closer. Is a Swedish community agency for social caring 'the same' as a religious social association in Italy because they perform similar tasks? Is collecting financial support in a German village 'the same' as 'fundraising' in Scotland although the last phrase cannot even be translated into German? When then, is a phenomenon 'the same' in different contexts, or is it allowed to speak of 'similar' contexts?

Ironically, the very core of the comparative approach – to trace differences and similarities by looking at two or more objects, or phenomena – seems to lead directly to a number of nasty complications. If we use only culture- or nation-specific terms and concepts, it will be difficult to make any cross-cultural or cross-national comparisons at all. But if we simply use identical concepts for various settings, we are unlikely to obtain appropriate information about national or culture-bound phenomena. This dilemma is a more restrictive formulation of the fundamental problem of comparative research in finding generalizations, whereas the 'uniqueness' of every setting is immediately apparent and historic and idiographic factors usually cannot be neglected. The heart of the problem is that in comparative research '... reality seems to demand a configurative approach; generalizability seems to demand a more analytical approach' (Verba, 1967: 117). How then, are we to sail between the Scylla of losing national or cultural validity by looking for generalizations, and the Charibdis of endangering cross-cultural or cross-national comparability by focusing on specific features only?

In this chapter the problems of establishing equivalence in comparative research are discussed. The next section presents a brief overview of several aspects of identity and equivalence as well as an overview of several types of equivalence and bias. The third section addresses the practical complications of studying similar phenomena in different settings and offers options for empirical research by focusing on functional equivalence. This implies that in the practical part of this chapter approaches are emphasized that can be applied by comparativists, and that the epistemological complications of 'travelling' theories are not a major concern here.

TYPES OF EQUIVALENCE

Identity, equivalence, bias

The problem of equivalence is not restricted to the use of particular terms or concepts in different contexts. In fact the problem is evident in each type of comparative research irrespective of the particular field, irrespective of the particular methodology applied and irrespective of the phase of the comparative research process considered. It is this almost universal relevance that gives the debate about equivalence its prominent status.

Problems of equivalence in comparative research become clear when we start with the notion of identical terms or concepts. Two things are considered to be *identical* when they agree or are exactly the same in every detail or are similar in appearance. The term *identity*, however, refers to absolute sameness or equality of two values. Ever since the development of traditional logic in the Middle Ages, the *Principle of Identity* ('A = A'; 'Whatever is, is') has been a cornerstone of reasoning. The common version of the idea of identity states that two things are identical when they share all their qualities: that is when all of their properties are the same. In other words, two objects, or phenomena are identical if for every class, one object belongs to the class if, and only if, the other does.[2] Leibniz used this line of reasoning to formulate an important conclusion based on a nontrivial version of the so-called principle of *Identity of Indiscernibles* ('principium identitatis indiscernibilium'). If two objects differ in some intrinsic, non-relational property, reasoned Leibniz, they must be two. The paradoxical nature of the identity problem has been formulated by Wittgenstein

(1921/1963) succinctly and conclusively: 'Roughly speaking, to say of *two* things that they are identical is nonsense, and to say of *one* thing that it is identical with itself is to say nothing at all' (p. 83, emphasis in original).

Comparative research, then, must start from the idea that even similar phenomena or objects are never identical. The question is whether we can restrict the differences between two phenomena or objects to intrinsic, non-relational properties irrelevant to the goal of our research. For instance, the fact that Scottish and German voluntary associations differ in the way they acquire financial resources does not have to bother us in comparative studies on the role of these organizations in community politics. Another example concerns the field of currencies and exchange rates. In order to see whether exchange rates are 'correct', one can use the so-called *Hamburger Standard* or *Big Mac Currency*. It is based on the idea that a Big Mac hamburger is made according to the same recipe in some 80 countries. The purchasing-power parity of the product can be computed by comparing its price in local currency to its price in dollars in the US. The result is an assessment of the under- or over-valuation of the local currency. This assessment is based on the fact that all disturbing or irrelevant factors are controlled for (ingredients, weight, production, sales conditions, etc.), while the relevant property (local value) varies across nations.[3] In other words, comparisons become meaningful if one distinguishes between relevant and irrelevant properties.

The search for (ir)relevant properties of distinct phenomena or objects suggests a move from the idea of identity towards that of equivalence. The concept of equivalence appears in fields as divergent as logic, informatics, physics, psychology, mathematics, electronics, finance, and civil and criminal law. Although the term has specific meanings in each discipline, broadly speaking we refer to the *equivalence* of two objects or phenomena if they have the same value, importance, use, function, or result. Although the etymological origin of the term points in the direction of similarities,[4] the important aspect is the restriction of similarity to one or more specifically defined properties. We are willing to accept conclusions about the role of clearly differently financed voluntary associations in different cities if these organizations manage to hold similar positions in communal networks for many decades. Likewise, we are willing to assess the different purchasing powers of local currencies if we can be sure that the appearance and taste of hamburgers are 'identical' in various countries. It is the *similarity of relevant properties of different phenomena or objects* that lies at the centre of the idea of equivalence in comparative research.

Mainly based on psychological research Van de Vijver and Leung (1997; Harkness et al., 2003: 13–15; Van de Vijver, 2003a) propose to stress a *lack of equivalence* to characterize the problematic aspects of comparisons in cross-cultural research. In this way, the complications attached to the idea of equivalence become much clearer than by focusing on the idea itself, and, as a consequence, strategies to deal with non-equivalence can be developed more systematically and applied more efficiently. In order to search for the causes of equivalence problems, the term *bias* is introduced defined as '... the presence of nuisance factors that challenge the comparability of scores across cultural groups' (Van de Vijver, 2003a: 144; cf., Van de Vijver, 1998: 43). Obviously, bias and equivalence are closely related, but they are distinct concepts focusing the attention on the sources of the problems of comparability on the one hand, and the problems as such on the other. In other words: if we can locate and analyze the bias in our concepts and indicators, appropriate procedures can be developed and applied to establish equivalence. Since using the concept bias directly leads to possible causes of equivalence problems, the two terms are used here.

Types of bias and equivalence

The concepts of equivalence and bias offer the opportunity to depict the specific problems and solutions at each phase of comparative research processes. Especially in the field of cross-cultural and cross-national survey methods interest for these problems has been rising rapidly in the last two decades (cf., Braun, 2006; Harkness, 1998; Hoffmeyer-Zlotnik and Harkness, 2005; Hoffmeyer-Zlotnik and Wolf, 2003a; van Deth, 1998). In this area a number of large scale comparative projects have been successfully carried out and many strategies to deal with comparability and validity are based on the experiences accumulated here.[5] Yet the concepts and terminology developed in survey research can easily be generalized and transferred to applications of other social science methods.

Equivalence problems usually become apparent as translation problems at the outset. Even seemingly straightforward translations of single words provide complications due to different meanings of the words in different contexts. As mentioned, no German word exists for the English term 'fundraising'. Similarly, the term 'Bürgerinitiative' is closely related to, but certainly not identical with, the Dutch phrase 'inspraak'. But even if the translation appears to be unproblematic, phrases can have very different meanings. A German prosecutor was cited by an American newspaper after he had called a Holocaust denier a 'rat catcher'. This is a perfect translation of the German word 'Rattenfänger' that the prosecutor had used, but fails to make clear that the accused Nazi defender was not a specialized animal exterminator, but somebody who misled his followers with propaganda and humbug. The English language depiction would be a 'pied piper'. For identifying errors in translations, a number of procedures are available now.[6]

Although translations in comparative research are vital, we will not discuss them here as a separate strategy to deal with equivalence problems. Instead, we will emphasize the complications of actual comparative research confronted with the problem of equivalence. Several proposals have been presented to characterize equivalence problems systematically. In order to summarize the various types of these problems and

the respective strategies to handle them, three categorizations are used here. First, equivalence problems can be discerned on the basis of the *source of the complications*. In his elaboration of the different types of bias Van de Vijver (2003a: 145–8) proposes to distinguish between three main sources of bias: construct bias (occurs when a construct is not identical across groups), method bias (occurs when methods applied are not identical across groups), and item bias (occurs when item measures do not have the same average across groups). Method bias is further specified as sample bias, instrument bias, and administration bias. This classification of three main possible sources of bias and the subdivision of the second category are used here as a first step to distinguish equivalence problems and the respective strategies to handle them.

A second distinction is based on the question whether the problems are dealt with *in advance* or that procedures are developed *to handle existing information* (cf. Ehling, 2003; Hoffmeyer-Zlotnik and Harkness, 2005). In case of *ex-ante* strategies, concepts and procedures are developed to maximize chances that the final measures will be equivalent. The precautions are considered before the actual collection of data starts and can include, for example, guidelines for translations or detailed instructions on how to construct an index. *Ex-post* strategies, on the other hand, focus on the establishment of equivalence after the data have been collected and usually contain such strategies as, for example, weighting and selecting of cases or an increase of the level of abstraction of the concepts used. Ex-post strategies are typically part of secondary analyses research strategies (cf. van Deth, 2003: 302–3) and include corrections and selection of available information.

Partly overlapping with ex-ante and ex-post characterisations is the third distinction between input and output harmonization (cf. Ehling, 2003; Hoffmeyer-Zlotnik and Harkness, 2005; Hoffmeyer-Zlotnik and Wolf, 2003b). *Input harmonization* requires the specification of common concepts and procedures that have to be used in each group in similar ways. Context-specific deviations from these prescriptions are only permissible when they are indispensable. Equivalence of the final measures is obtained on the basis of the fact that common concepts and procedures have been defined for each group from the outset. From this characterization it is clear that input harmonization can only be part of ex-ante strategies. *Output harmonization* focuses on the common aim to obtain equivalent measures by specifying the goals to be reached and by offering the opportunity to apply appropriate concepts and procedures for each group separately. Usually, context-specific deviations are required here in order to establish equivalence. Output harmonization can be included in both ex-ante and in ex-post strategies. Large scale international projects normally use a mixture of input and

output harmonization strategies by specifying, for instance, the data collection and translation procedures in detail (input harmonization) and urging for the use of adequate measures for the level of education in each country (output harmonization).

The three categorizations can be combined to characterize the various strategies to handle equivalence problems. The rows in Table 5.1 are defined by the five distinct sources of bias as proposed by Van de Vijver and Lueng (1997), whereas the columns distinguish between ex-ante and ex-post strategies. Furthermore, ex-ante strategies can be divided into input and output harmonization. In this way, a total of 15 different types of bias and equivalence in comparative research can be discerned. Ex-ante input harmonization strategies all aim at establishing equivalence by defining concepts and prescribing procedures to be implemented. For instance,

Table 5.1 Different types of equivalence problems and strategies

		Ex-ante strategies		Ex-post strategies
		Input harmonization	Output harmonization	Output harmonization
Construct bias		Define concepts – translation procedures – intercultural teams	Specify concepts – intercultural teams	Specify and correct concepts – reassessment/reinterpretation – 'conceptual stretching'
Method bias	Sample bias	Define population and sample – population definition for each group	Specify sample – instructions for sampling and quotas	Specify and correct sample – weighting procedures – selection procedures
	Instrument bias	Define instruments – concept definition	Specify instruments – specification of dimensions, structure, or aspects	Specify and correct instruments – index construction – dimensional analyses; scaling
	Administration bias	Define administration rules – procedures for organization of fieldwork	Specify administration rules – specification of goals to be attained	Specify and correct administration rules – weighting procedures – selection procedures
Item bias		Define items – translation procedures – intercultural teams – linguistic analyses	Specify items – specification of indicators	Specify and correct items – psychometric scaling techniques

Search for specific
measures:
Definition and rules

Search for common
measures:
Specification

Establish common
measures:
Correction

a clear definition of the concepts to be used and unambiguous rules for the translation process can reduce construct bias and item bias from the very beginning. In a similar way, sample bias can be reduced if a detailed description of the sampling procedures to be applied is available. Usually, ex-ante input harmonization strategies are based on the idea of convergence: the development of a measure for each group according to specific rules will finally result in an equivalent measure for the set of groups.

Whereas the common characteristic of ex-ante input harmonization strategies is that definitions and specifications of rules are of imminent importance, ex-ante output harmonization strategies focus on common measures and their conceptual specifications for each group from the very beginning. In this approach, for instance sample bias can be reduced by specifying the population to be included in the study clearly and leaving it to experts to develop appropriate sampling procedures to reach these populations in different settings (cf. Häder and Gabler, 2003: 119). Another example is provided by the use of a common concept that is operationalized in different ways for different groups by intercultural teams of researchers in order to reduce construct bias.

The final group of strategies distinguished consists of ex-post output harmonization approaches. Here the question is irrelevant whether the information available is obtained by using ex-ante input or ex-ante output procedures – or by using no procedure at all. Ex-post strategies try to establish equivalence by selecting and correcting information. For example, instrument bias (and item bias) can be reduced by searching for a set of items that can be used to construct an appropriate index for each group. As in the case of ex-ante output harmonization strategies, ex-post strategies presume that a clear-cut specification of the concept to be measured is available.

With the development of teams of experts from several countries to study such topics as voting behaviour, party platforms, value orientations, or social mobility ex-ante strategies have become increasingly important. Furthermore, many international projects such as the European Social Survey have made high-quality data available that can be used to reassess equivalence systematically. Detailed instructions for both input and output harmonization procedures are available now (cf. Ehling, 2003; Harkness, 1999; Hoffmeyer-Zlotnik and Wolf, 2003b; Lynn, 2001; Van de Vijver, 2003a: 149–52). However, even the strict implementation of all these instructions does not guarantee that the final constructs are equivalent. Here, too, the proof of the pudding is in the eating: that is, equivalence can only be assessed on the basis of empirical information. For that reason, ex-post strategies to reduce bias and to establish equivalence will be further elaborated here.[7]

EX-POST EQUIVALENCE STRATEGIES

Ex-post equivalence strategies can be specified by looking at the main sources of potential bias: construct bias, method bias, and item bias. Construct bias seems to be a distinct category here, while the border line between method bias – especially instrument bias – and item bias is not always easy to draw when dealing with ex-post approaches.

Construct bias and construct equivalence

As every child knows, apples and pears can be easily compared if they are considered to be specimen of 'fruit'. In a similar way, Catholic and Muslim practices can be compared as being particular instances of the more general concept 'religious behaviour'. In this way, a reinterpretation or reassessment of available information can be used to establish construct equivalence: not the specific measures or indicators (apples, Catholic prayers), but the more abstract concepts (fruit, religion) are equivalent. Information, then, does not have to be similar at the operational level as long as we succeed in constructing measures indicating similar concepts at a higher level of abstraction. Construct equivalence is established by eliminating features that are relevant for specific groups only.

This line of reasoning suggests a direct way of dealing with equivalence problems among different groups: increase the level of abstraction until group-specific differences become irrelevant and can be ignored. This strategy requires extensive auxiliary information about the settings being compared as well as a sophisticated way of developing and demarcating constructs. Although the intelligent use of auxiliary information is a *conditio sine qua non* for every type of comparative research and although a high level of abstraction is always desirable from a theoretical point of view, the risks involved in increasing the level of abstraction are evident. First, we risk the fallacy so nicely presented by Sartori (1970, 1994) that concepts easily can be 'stretched' in such a way that they lose virtually all of their analytical and heuristic power.[8] If, for instance, the concept 'constitutional states' is stretched to 'any state form', we have no way of testing the proposition 'constitutions obstruct tyranny'. The second risk in increasing the level of abstraction is, of course, the neglect of 'real' differences and the establishment of 'pseudo equivalence'. For example, an explanation of the role of 'social associations' in Italy and Sweden can be highly misleading if the term 'associations' is not differentiated between the two countries. Finally, it is clear that increasing the level of abstraction could come down to nothing more than a move of the equivalence problem from one level to another. Not much is gained if we have to assess the equivalence of the concept 'social support' instead of that of the stimulus 'being a member of an association'.[9]

By increasing the level of abstraction of our concepts irrelevant or group-specific properties are removed from our analyses. In other words, we establish construct equivalence by ignoring specific properties and we accept two constructs to be equivalent exactly because these properties are ignored. As mentioned, this strategy requires a high level of auxiliary information about the systems being compared in order to avoid the fallacies of 'conceptual stretching', 'pseudo equivalence', or simply shifting the problem from one level to another. Yet it is clear that the explicit neglect of specific characteristics certainly increases the opportunities for comparative research by improving construct equivalence.

Sample bias and sample equivalence

Sample bias exists when the information available is obtained from groups that differ in relevant aspects. For instance, cross-national survey research usually focuses on sampling 'inhabitants of age 15 and higher'. Even if the resulting samples are evidently representative of the populations defined accordingly, it is not appropriate to use these samples for a comparison of, for instance, 'eligible voters' since voting requirements (minimum age, citizenship, etc.) vary between countries. In a similar way, a comparison of welfare payments in various countries can be clearly biased if the information available is restricted to statistics made available by the OECD.[10] The OECD provides high-quality information for the major industrial countries – limiting any comparison to this specific group of countries. Especially, experiences with multiple sampling frames in international projects have stimulated the attention for the problems of sample equivalence (cf. Lynn et al., 2004).

Ex-post strategies to deal with sample bias consist, first of all, of selection procedures. If the minimum age to be eligible to cast a vote is 18 years in one country and 21 in another, the non-eligible voters in each country can be easily deleted in order to establish sample equivalence. Selection procedures, however, can also include extensions of the information available. Adding information about welfare payments in several central European countries and restricting the information available from the OECD to the European member states of this organization, results in a dataset that enables a comparison of welfare state payments across Europe and avoids the limitation of analyzing developed European countries only. An elaborate example of reducing sample bias is presented by Schäfer (2006) who compares political orientations among 'young adolescents' in a number of German youth studies – each of which using a different definition of the exact age group questioned.

A second strategy to deal with sample bias is to weight the samples in order to obtain a more representative image of the statistical populations (cf. Häder and Gabler, 2003: 123–4). By now, weighting procedures are common practice in survey research and most datasets include weight coefficients to correct the under- and overrepresentation of specific groups. Obviously, weighting procedures correct the samples for specific features (usually groups defined according to their level of education, sex, and age), and the impact of these corrections on the relevant variables remain unclear frequently.

As these examples of selection and weighting strategies make clear, sample bias shares an important characteristic with all other ex-post equivalence strategies: meaningful corrections can be implied only if an unambiguous specification of the groups to be compared is available.

Instrument bias, item bias, and functional equivalence

In order to examine the equivalence of concepts systematically specific ex-post procedures have been developed. Many of these procedures rely on the idea of an indissoluble connection between the meaning of particular concepts, on the one hand, and their relationships with other concepts, on the other. Two concepts, then, are considered to be equivalent if they fit in similar ways in similar structures within each groups. This approach stresses the position of, or the function of, a concept in specific structures and is usually called *functional equivalence*.[11] Strategies based on the idea of functional equivalence are especially suitable to deal with instrument bias and item bias.

Functional equivalence stresses the relevance of relationships instead of intrinsic properties of concepts. Especially in system theories as proposed by Luhmann (1970), relationships provide the core and backbone of the argument. In this perspective, any comparison of systems will be confronted by the question of identity and functional equivalence:

> Every comparison of a system presupposes a preceding theoretical analysis of the systems involved, which clarifies its relational problem and possible solutions. Under these circumstances the comparison yields several variants of solutions for one and the same relational problem. In this way the hypothesis of its functional equivalence is verified. The question why single systems opt for different variants is then converted into concrete historical research, which always presupposes the determination of equivalences in case it should not be limited to the detection of facts only. (Luhmann, 1970:25)

Although very critical of traditional (American) functionalism, Luhmann's analyses show the opportunities for using the idea of functional equivalence in comparative research. His suggestion to study the historical development of existing systems helps us answer the question of why different systems opt for different solutions. These measures do not have to belong to a common set of measures or indicators but can be attuned to the specific circumstances in each system.[12] It is this 'belonging' to a specific part of a system which makes concepts equivalent in comparative research. This suggestion can be rephrased as a general plea to rely on interpretations (or hypotheses) and auxiliary information in the course of assessing the equivalence of (different) concepts or indicators used in different settings.

Functional equivalence refers to the requirement that concepts should be related to other concepts in other settings in more or less the same way. It is based on the notion that comparability '... cannot be conceived as an attribute of elements but as an *attribute of the elements' relationships to a more general point of reference*' (Nießen, 1982: 86, emphasis in original). Stated in this way, functional equivalence has much in common with reasoning by analogy. An analogy is based on the recognition or suggestion of similarity between two objects or two sets of objects. However, while analogies are based on similar relationships between different objects (i.e., A:B therefore C:D), functional equivalence refers to similar relationships between similar objects in different settings (i.e., A[i]:B[i] therefore A[j]:B[j]). It is this last type of similarity between the theoretical or operational contexts ([i] and [j]) which provides clues for answering the question about which properties are considered relevant in our comparisons.

The seminal work of Przeworski and Teune (1966; 1970) contains a precise depiction of the basic structure of comparative analyses as well as a clear definition of the equivalence concept based on the idea that inference should guide attempts to solve the problems. Their concept of equivalence:

> ... does not refer to observations but only to the results of inferences made from those observations, that is, the inferred measurement statements. An instrument is equivalent across systems to the extent that the results provided by the instrument reliably describe with (nearly) the same validity a particular phenomenon in different social systems. *Stimulus equivalence is an important problem only if measurement does not involve inference.* (Przeworski and Teune, 1970: 108, emphasis in original)

Przeworski and Teune argue within a framework of classical test and measurement theory and rely heavily on the distinction between direct and indirect measurement. But 'inference' can also be observed when we use some directly measured indicator in a wider theoretical setting and study its relationships with other factors. Some type of inference is always required in order to establish equivalence, whether in the form of constructing an instrument with a set of items

(and dealing with instrument bias) or in the form of relating different items to each other in various settings (and dealing with item bias). The concept under consideration has to be integrated into some structure (pattern, model, network, theory), and equivalence is established by assessing the degree to which these similar concepts have the same position or play the same role within these structures. In empirical-analytical approaches in comparative research, the idea of functional equivalence is operationalized as instrument validity: that is, as the satisfactory performance of indicators within some theoretical and operational context to which they refer.

From this depiction of functional equivalence it is clear that relationships (structures) are at the centre of the problem of comparability. Apparently, by developing this strategy we return immediately to the position taken by Przeworski and Teune (1970): that the ultimate test of concepts and instruments is not to be found in a meticulous search for identical measures, but in '... *the similarity of the structure of indicators ... Equivalence is a matter of inference, not of direct observations*' (pp. 117–18, emphasis in original). Sophisticated approaches to deal with this search for structures have become available through techniques like confirmatory factor analysis or (full) structural equation models (cf. Braun, 2006; Harkness, 1998; Hoffmeyer-Zlotnik and Harkness, 2005; Van de Vijver, 2003b; Van de Vijver and Leung, 1997: 99–106). Equivalence is certainly not to be considered an intrinsic property of some indicator or construct, but, as Van de Vijver and Leung (1997) put it: '*Equivalence should be established and cannot be assumed*' (p. 144, emphasis in original). And Hoffmeyer-Zlotnik and Wolf (2003b) phrase the same idea even more clearly for cross-national comparisons: "Functional equivalence in this respect cannot be attained by a process of 'translation'. Instead functional equivalence can only be attained by identifying the overall similarities between the national concepts and national structures that relate to the background variables of interest." (p. 391)

From this repeated emphasis on inference in assessing the degree of instrument bias and equivalence, three important conclusions can be drawn about research strategies in comparative politics. First, if we wish to establish equivalence as the functional equivalence of some concept by analyzing relationships in terms of underlying patterns, we must use at least two indicators for each concept in each setting, since the minimum requirement for any relationship is the existence of two objects or phenomena. It is the relationship between items which will provide information about the equivalence of the concepts obtained. Second, we do not have to restrict our analyses to inferences based on a common set of stimuli, items, or indicators. Inference can be based on different stimuli, items, or indicators in various settings, and equivalence once again becomes a question of relationships. Third, if inference is stressed, we must distinguish between internal and external ways to infer conclusions about relational aspects of our observations or indicators. Internal consistency means that the stimuli, indicators or items used should show more or less the same structure in different environments; external consistency means that indicators are related in the same way to an element not belonging to the initial set of indicators. For example, the question of whether a construct like fundraising is equivalent in various settings has no meaning. Only if we introduce relationships between two or more items to measure the collection of financial resources of voluntary associations (internal consistency) or linkages between fundraising and another concept (external consistency) we can try to establish equivalence. These relationships can be conceptualized among a common set of stimuli or indicators, but different measures can be used in different settings.

By focusing on functional equivalence to deal with instrument and item bias, opportunities for comparative research are substantially expanded. Concepts and measures do not have to be similar at the operational level as long as we succeed in depicting similar structures which encompass these concepts and measures. If we want to reduce instrument bias and item bias, four different strategies for constructing functional equivalence are available based on the question whether we focus on internal or external structures, on the one hand, and whether we use a common set of items or specific items for each group, on the other (cf. van Deth, 1998: 9–14). In all four cases the logic of the strategy is straightforward: the equivalence of an instrument (and its containing items) is based on the consistency of its structural relationships.

Using a common set of indicators; internal consistency

If we use a common set of items, the question is how to assess the equivalence of an instrument based on these items. The strategy of using a common set of indicators and the criterion of internal consistency is meant to resolve this problem by analyzing the structure among similar items in various settings. Sophisticated methodological applications of this type of strategy have been proposed by Mokken (1971: 224–53); Saris and Münnich (1995); Saris (1997); and others (cf. Hoffmeyer-Zlotnik and Harkness, 2005).

A traditional example of this strategy is Rokkan's emphasis on so-called 'second-order comparisons' and its application in Almond and Verba's (1963) work on political culture in five countries. In that work, nations are compared by emphasizing patterns between indicators within different countries. Even if the cross-national validity of the indicators is questionable, the results obtained from the analyses of the relationships between the indicators provide the basis for accepting the equivalence of the phenomena (cf. Verba, 1969). An identical position is taken by Inglehart in his analyses of the rise of postmaterialist value orientations in 11 countries in the early 1970s. He explicitly avoids discussions about different levels of postmaterialism between the countries and focuses on comparisons within given samples (Inglehart, 1997: 37–8). Methodologically more sophisticated examples are the use of a multi-trait–multi-method approach in the field of cross-national research on stereotype effects of the characterizations of nations (Hunyady and Münnich, 1995) or the cross-national measurement of life satisfaction (Saris and Scherpenzeel, 1995). Van de Vijver and Leung (1997: 55) point to mono-trait–multi-method approaches involving the use of multiple diverse measures to capture the same construct (so called 'triangulation').

Using a common set of indicators; external consistency

As the examples of Almond and Verba, Inglehart, and others indicate, functional equivalence can be established by referring to relationships between the construct considered and one or more other concepts. In this strategy, a similar structure in different settings is accepted as evidence of the equivalence of the concepts. This line of reasoning can be found in several areas of comparative research. Gabriel (1998: 46–8) evaluated differences in the degree of national pride of West European countries by looking at the correlations with other indicators of attachment to the political system.[13] In order to deal with both longitudinal and cross-sectional comparisons, Clausen (1967) introduced the method of 'differential correlations' for establishing the equivalence of measures of voting behaviour in different sessions of the American Congress.

The complications of analyses involving levels of education illustrate an example from another area of comparative research. Since national educational systems are very different, a straightforward cross-national comparison of levels of education is highly problematic. An attempt to resolve these problems uses directly-related concepts like income, occupational status, or social mobility and labour market chances as 'criterion variables'. If nation-specific measures of the level of education appear related in a similar way to the other indicators, the functional equivalence of the indicator for education is established (Brauns et al., 2003; Treiman, 1975; Treiman and Terrel, 1975). This example provides a clear strategy for basing equivalence on the idea of structural similarity and the use of inference. However, it also shows the weakness of the approach. As Müller (1997: 130) argues, the complications of establishing equivalence are simply moved from the concept of education to the concepts of income and occupational status and differences in the impact of background factors may well modify the structure in different countries.[14]

A sophisticated variant of this strategy is a two-step strategy transforming instruments to a similar level in the first phase in order to perform intra-level comparisons in the second phase. An example of this strategy lies in the analyses of Kuechler (1991) who suggests using so-called 'contingency patterns' in his work on political support in Western Europe. In order to avoid the pitfalls in a comparison of the marginal distributions of survey questions (like the degree of satisfaction with democracy), he relates the developments of these marginals to the development of macro-economic indicators like inflation and unemployment rates in different countries. In this way, he is able to test several ideas about the relationships between the state of the economy and the level of mass support without relying on the assumption that the instrument applied has the same meaning in different countries. In other words, the macro-economic indicators serve as external points of reference to establish the equivalence of the instruments used in the questionnaires.

Using a non-common set of indicators; internal consistency

The use of internal consistency as the central criterion for equivalence among a set of non-common indicators is illustrated by looking at two applications of a method proposed by

Przeworski and Teune (1966). The so-called *Identity-Equivalence Method* relies explicitly on the idea that constraint among items or indicators does not imply using the same set of stimuli or items in each setting. The method starts with the search for a core set of identical stimuli or items which provide an anchor for evaluating the constraints of each measurement instrument. The next step is to add culture- or nation-specific indicators or items in order to reduce instrument bias in a specific context. Finally, the instruments are applied in each setting and comparisons are based on the results obtained with these distinct instruments.[15]

An example of this strategy is the construction of equivalent measures for the concept 'political participation'. The level of political participation can be measured in several countries by constructing nation-specific instruments (van Deth, 1986). On the basis of the 'identity-equivalence method', a common structure emerges in eight West European countries. This set appears to be a cumulative, one-dimensional scale in each country. The next step is the search for nation-specific additions to the common scale and the construction of non-identical, equivalent measures.

The strategy of relying on the structure between different sets of stimuli in different settings as a means of establishing equivalence avoids 'conceptual stretching' as well as moving the problem of equivalence from one area to another. In this way, a fruitful strategy is obtained to deal with instrument bias and item bias in comparative research.

Using a non-common set of indicators; external consistency

It is hard to find empirical examples of strategies based on a non-common set of indicators and the criterion of external consistency. In a study of role conflict, Ehrlich et al. (1962) collected data from two distinct populations and from the fact that different stimuli showed a high degree of association and

resulted in consistent predictions, the authors concluded that different questions were measuring the same dimensions (pp. 91, 93). More recently interesting proposals have been developed to rely more heavily on historical and qualitative information for comparative research. Locke and Thelen (1998) point at the relevance of 'national institutional arrangements' for any cross-national comparison of conflicts between labour and management. They suggest a strategy called 'contextualized comparison' which '... self-consciously seeks to address the issue of equivalence by searching for analytically equivalent phenomena – even if expressed in substantively different terms – across different contexts' (Locke and Thelen, 1998: 11). The various contributions presented in the publication edited by Mahoney and Rueschemeyer (2003) can be seen as examples of this strategy of 'contextualized comparison'.

CONCLUSION

Establishing equivalence is one of the nastiest problems facing comparativists. On the one hand, specific features of each group, culture, or nation have to be taken into account, because they establish the objects and phenomena that lead to the research interests and curiosity in the first place. On the other hand, meaningful comparisons can only be carried out if the objects or phenomena have at least one feature in common. Phrased in this way, it is clear that establishing equivalence is at the very heart of each comparison. Although especially survey researchers increasingly pay attention to this problem, the simplistic idea that identity would imply equivalence still seems to be widely spread.

Several strategies are available to deal with equivalence problems. The idea to start with a distinction between the sources of non-equivalence (bias) and actual attempts to establish equivalence proved to be very helpful to systemize various approaches available. Bias can be located in the constructs, methods, or items applied. The rapidly increasing recommendations to avoid equivalence problems (ex-ante strategies) have already resulted in a number of high-quality datasets available for comparative research. Scholars developing comparative research can rely on the experiences collected in other projects and follow the recommendations presented.[16] Furthermore, important constructs, such as the level of education have been standardized and made comparable by international groups of experts. This work has been expanded to include many other demographic and socio-economic 'background' variables (cf. Hoffmeyer-Zlotnik and Wolf, 2003a).

The depiction of distinct types of bias appears to be very helpful for a discussion about the various ex-post strategies to deal with equivalence problems. Attempts to increase the level of abstraction can be very helpful to improve the equivalence of our constructs, but run the risk of 'conceptual stretching' and the accompanying loss of analytical power. Sample bias can be reduced by selecting or expanding the cases selected, or by applying weighting procedures. Many authors have suggested procedures to deal with instrument bias and item bias by relying on the idea of functional equivalence. In these approaches structural relationships among the items considered (internal consistency), or between the items and some other measures (external consistency) are used to construct instrument equivalence.

None of the procedures suggested for dealing with equivalence problems can be recommended in general or can be praised as the 'best' procedure. Establishing equivalence in comparative research requires a careful location of the sources of bias as well as an attentive exploration of the opportunities to reduce this bias without losing crucial information about the phenomena to be studied. Any equivalence procedure, however, can only be implemented successfully if an unambiguous specification of the concept to be compared is available.

Establishing equivalence is, first of all, a theoretical and conceptual problem. In other words: vague and ambivalent concepts require careful theoretical reconsiderations from the outset; not the application of sophisticated procedures to establish equivalence.

ACKNOWLEDGEMENT

Parts of this overview are based on an earlier publication on the same topic (van Deth, 1998).

NOTES

1. This does not deny, of course, the specific value of single-observation studies or the opportunities for combining case studies in a comparative design. The obligatory quotation here, however, is taken from Durkheim (1937/1981): 'La sociologie comparée n'est pas une branche particulière de la sociologie; c'est la sociologie même, en tant qu'elle cesse d'être purement descriptive et aspire à rendre compte des faits' (p. 137).

2. This statement becomes a tautology when the property of 'being identical with an object' is allowed to be a property of that very same object. Proof of this trivial version is given by Honderich (1995: 391). See for a different approach Lowe (1989).

3. The Big Mac index was introduced by The Economist and is published every year since 1986 (cf., www.economist.com/markets/Bigmac/Index.cfm). Obviously, other 'identical' products like a pair of Levi 501 jeans or a bottle of Coca-Cola can perform the same function in comparisons of the purchasing power of currencies.

4. The word equivalence is a combination of the Latin words 'aequus' (equal) and 'valere' (to be strong; to be worth). See for an extensive overview of the use of this concept Johnson (1998) who presents a list of no less than 52 (!) different types of equivalence – ranging from 'Calibration Equivalence' to 'Vocabulary Equivalence' – mentioned in the literature.

5. Examples are the International Social Survey Programme (ISSP) or the European Social Survey (ESS). See van Deth (2003: 305, 309) for an overview of these projects and their web site addresses or the contributions presented by Hoffmeyer-Zlotnik and Wolf (2003b); Hoffmeyer-Zlotnik and Harkness (2005).

6. See Osgood (1967) for an early example of evaluating linguistic differences on the basis of cross-national consistency or Van de Vijver and Leung (1997: 35–51) for a list of guidelines for translation and adaptation of instruments in comparative research. Harkness (2003) presents overviews of linguistic problems in cross-cultural survey research and available procedures to deal with these complications.

7. Ehling's (2003) remark that 'Ex-post output harmonisation is associated in general with the greatest quality losses in terms of international comparability, since subsequent adjustment of the data is frequently only possible within certain limits' (p. 28), clearly underestimates the opportunities to deal with bias systematically as explained in the next section below. See for an impressive application of exactly this strategy to the field of gender-specific concepts: Braun (2006).

8. In a discussion of the opportunities to reach comparability by increasing the level of abstraction of the concept 'democracy' Collier and Levitsky (1997) show the advantages and limitations of this approach.

9. The 'general tension between easy operationalizability and comparative adequacy' is discussed by Smelser (1973; cf., Van de Vijver and Leung, 1997), but the most elegant presentation of the problem is clearly Sartori's 'Ladder of Abstraction' that can be climbed and descended in actual research (1970: 1041). For an application of this idea to coups d'état in Africa, see O'Kane (1993).

10. See for access to these data: www.oecd.org/statsportal.

11. For this reason the term 'structural equivalence' is used as a synonym for 'functional equivalence' (Van de Vijver, 2003a: 153).

12. For a similar line of reasoning based on clear functionalist notions, see the analyses presented by Patterson and Wahlke (1972) and Arter (2006) in the field of legislative behaviour or the proposals of Helms (1995) to study political parties.

13. This example once again shows that the line between strategies using external and internal consistency among a common set of indicators is not always very clear. If Gabriel had started with the aim of measuring the construct 'attachment to the political system' and had used his two questions as different indicators of this construct, his approach would have been an example of a mono-trait–multi-method strategy as indicated by Van de Vijver and Lueng (1997: 55).

14. In addition, Müller (1997: 130) states that the argument becomes circular if we want to explain income and status on the basis of education if the relationships between these indicators are already used to establish equivalence. Although the implicit warning is important, this criticism seems to be based on a confusion of the phases of concept formation and measurement, on the one hand, and

testing hypotheses or causal interpretations, on the other. As Jackman (1985) states, '... to identify and measure a variable is not to assume that it influences a second variable. Indeed, any such assumption would beg the question' (p. 171). For this distinction, see also the concept 'structural equivalence' discussed by Esser (1996: 433–4).

15. A formal definition of this procedure is presented by Przeworski and Teune (1966: 557). See Westle (1998) for a more extensive discussion and application of their approach.

16. See for instance documentation of the European Social Survey (www.europeansocialsurvey.org) or the 'rules' summarized by Hoffmeyer-Zlotnik and Wolf (2003b: 404–5); Harkness (1999); or Lynn (2001).

REFERENCES

Almond, G.A. and Verba, S. (1963) *The civic culture. Political attitudes and democracy in five nations*. Princeton, NJ: Princeton University Press.

Arter, D. (2006) 'Conclusion. Questioning the 'mezey question': An interrogatory framework for the comparative study of legislatures', *The Journal of Legislative Studies*, 12 (3–4): 462–82.

Braun, M. (2006) *Funktionale äquivalenz in interkulturell vergleichenden umfragen. Mythos und Realität*. Mannheim: ZUMA.

Brauns, H., Scherer, S., and Steinmann, S. (2003) 'The CASMIN educational classification in international comparative research', in J.H.P. Hoffmeyer-Zlotnik and C. Wolf (eds), *Advances in cross-national comparison. A European working book for demographic and socio-economic variables*. New York: Kluwer/Plenum, pp. 221–44.

Clausen, A.R. (1967) 'Measurement identity in the longitudinal analysis of legislative voting', *American Political Science Review*, 64 (4): 1020–35.

Collier, D. and Levitsky, S. (1997) 'Democracy with adjectives. Conceptual innovation in comparative research', *World Politics*, 49 (3): 430–51.

Durkheim, E. (1937/1981) *Les règles de la méthode sociologique*. Paris: Presses Universitaires de France.

Ebbinghaus, B. (2005) 'When less is more: selection problems in large-N and small-N cross-national comparisons', *International Sociology*, 20 (2): 133–52.

Ehling, M. (2003) 'Harmonising data in official statistics', in J. H. P. Hoffmeyer-Zlotnik and C. Wolf (eds), *Advances in cross–national comparison. A European working book for demographic and socio–economic variables*. New York: Kluwer/Plenum, pp. 17–31.

Ehrlich, H.J., Rinehart, J.W. and Howell, J.C. (1962) 'The study of role conflict: Explorations in methodology', *Sociometry*, 25 (1): 85–97.

Esser, H. (1996) *Soziologie*. Allgemeine Grundlagen. Frankfurt a. M: Campus.

Feagin, J.R., Orum, A.M., and Sjoberg, G. (1991) *A case for the case study*. Chapel Hill, NC: University of North Carolina Press.

Gabriel, O.W. (1998) 'Fragen an einen europäischen vergleich', in R. Köcher and J. Schild (eds), *Wertewandel in Deutschland und Frankreich. Nationale Unterschiede und europäische Gemeinsamkeiten*. Opladen: Leske & Budrich, pp. 29–51.

Häder, S. and Gabler, S. (2003) 'Sampling and estimation', in J.A. Harkness, F.J.R. Van de Vijver and P.Ph. Mohler (eds), *Cross-cultural survey methods*. Hoboken, NJ: Wiley, pp. 117–42.

Hall, P.A. (2003) 'Aligning ontology and methodology in comparative research', in J. Mahoney and D. Rueschemeyer (eds), *Comparative historical analysis in the social sciences*. Cambridge: Cambridge University Press, pp. 373–404.

Harkness, J.A. (ed.) (1998) *Cross-cultural survey equivalence* Mannheim: ZUMA.

Harkness, J.A. (1999) 'In pursuit of quality: Issues for cross-national survey research', *Social Research Methodology*, 2 (2): 125–40.

Harkness, J.A. (2003) 'Questionnaire translation', in J.A. Harkness, F.J.R. Van de Vijver and P. Ph. Mohler (eds), *Cross-cultural survey methods*. Hoboken, NJ: Wiley, pp. 35–56.

Harkness, J.A., Mohler, P. Ph. and Van de Vijver, F.J.R. (2003) 'Comparative research', in J.A. Harkness, F.J.R. Van de Vijver and P. Ph. Mohler (eds), *Cross-cultural survey methods*. Hoboken, NJ: Wiley, pp. 3–16.

Helms, L. (1995) 'Parteiensysteme als systemstruktur. Zur methodisch-analytisch konzeption der funktional vergleichenden parteiensystemanalyse', *Zeitschrift für Parlamentsfragen*, 26 (4): 642–57.

Hoffmeyer-Zlotnik, J.H.P. and Harkness, J.A. (2005) 'Methodological aspects in cross-national research: Foreword', in J.H.P. Hoffmeyer-Zlotnik and J.A. Harkness (eds), *Methodological aspects in cross-national research*. Mannheim, Germany: ZUMA. 11, pp. 5–10.

Hoffmeyer-Zlotnik, J.H.P. and Wolf, C. (eds) (2003a) *Advances in cross-national comparison. A European working book for demographic and socio-economic variables*. New York: Kluwer/Plenum.

Hoffmeyer-Zlotnik, J.H.P. and Wolf, C. (2003b) 'Comparing demographic and socio-economic variables across nations', in J.H.P. Hoffmeyer-Zlotnik and C. Wolf (eds), *Advances in cross-national comparison. A European working book for demographic and socio-economic variables*. New York: Kluwer/Plenum, pp. 389–406.

Honderich, T. (1995) *The Oxford companion to philosophy*. Oxford: Oxford University Press.

Hunyady, G. and Münnich, Á. (1995) 'A modified true score MTMM model for analysing stereotype effects of characterizations of nations', in W.E. Saris and Á. Münnich (eds), *The multitrait-multimethod approach to evaluate measurement instruments*. Budapest: Eötvös University Press, pp. 173–84.

Inglehart, R. (1977) *The silent revolution. Changing values and political styles among Western publics*. Princeton: Princeton University Press.

Jackman, R.W. (1985) 'Cross-national statistical research and the study of comparative politics', *American Journal of Political Science*, 29 (1), 161–82.

Johnson, T.P. (1998) 'Approaches to equivalence in cross-cultural and cross-national survey research', in J.A. Harkness (ed), *Cross-cultural survey equivalence*. Mannheim: ZUMA, pp. 1–40.

Kuechler, M. (1991) 'The dynamics of mass political support in Western Europe: Methodological problems and preliminary findings', in K. Reif and R. Inglehart (eds), *Eurobarometer: The dynamics of European public opinion*. Houndmills, Basingstoke: Macmillan, pp. 275–93.

Locke, R. and Thelen, K. (1998) 'Problems of equivalence in comparative politics: Apples and oranges, again', *APSA–CP: Newsletter* of the APSA Organized Section in Comparative Politics, 9 (1): 9–12.

Lowe, E.J. (1989) 'What is a criterion of identity?', The Philosophical Quarterly, 39 (154): 1–21.

Luhmann, N. (1970) Soziologische aufklärung. Aufsätze zur theorie sozialer systeme. Opladen: Westdeutscher verlag.

Lynn, P. (2001) Developing quality standards for cross-national survey research: Five approaches (ISER Paper 2001–21) Essex, UK. Working papers of the Institute for Social and Economic Research.

Lynn, P., Häder, S., Gabler, S., and Laaksonen, S. (2004) Methods for achieving equivalence of samples in cross–national surveys: The European social survey experience. (ISER Paper 2004–09) Essex, UK: Working Papers of the Institute for Social and Economic Research.

Mahoney, J. and Rueschemeyer, D. (eds) (2003) Comparative historical analysis in the social sciences. Cambridge: Cambridge University Press.

McKeon, T.J. (2004) 'Case studies and the limits of the quantitative worldview', in H.E. Brady and D. Collier (eds), Rethinking social inquiry. Diverse tools, shared standards. Lanham, MD: Rowman and Littlefield, pp. 139–67.

Mokken, R.J. (1971) A theory and procedure of scale analyis. With applications in political research. The Hague: Mouton.

Müller, W. (1997) 'Vergleichende sozialstrukturforschung', in D. Berg-Schlosser and F. Müller-Rommel (eds), Vergleichende politikwissenschaft. Ein einführendes studienhandbuch (3rd edition). Opladen: Leske & Budrich, pp. 121–41.

Nießen, M. (1982) 'Qualitative aspects in cross-national comparative research and the problem of functional equivalence', in M. Nießen and J. Peschar (eds), International comparative research. Problems of theory, methodology and organisation in Eastern and Western Europe. Oxford: Pergamon Press, pp. 83–104.

O'Kane, R.H.T. (1993) 'The ladder of abstraction. The purpose of comparison and the practice of comparing African coups d'etat', Journal of Theoretical Politics, 5 (2): 169–93.

Osgood, C.E. (1967) 'On the strategy of cross-national research into subjective culture', Social Science Information, 6 (1): 5–37.

Patterson, S.C. and Wahlke, J.C. (1972) 'Trends and prospects in legislative behavior research', in S.C. Patterson and J.C. Wahlke (eds), Comparative legislative behavior: Frontiers of research. New York: Wiley, pp. 289–303.

Przeworski, A. and Teune, H. (1966) 'Equivalence in cross-national research', Public Opinion Quarterly, 30 (4): 551–68.

Przeworski, A. and Teune, H. (1970) The logic of comparative social inquiry. New York: Wiley.

Ragin, C.C. (2000) Fuzzy-set social science. Chicago: University of Chicago Press.

Ragin, C.C. (2004) 'Turning the tables: How case-oriented research challenges variable-oriented research', in H.E. Brady and D. Collier (eds), Rethinking social inquiry. Diverse tools, shared standards. Lanham, MD: Rowman and Littlefield, pp. 123–38.

Rueschemeyer, D. (2003) 'Can one or a few cases yield theoretical gains?', in J. Mahoney and D. Rueschemeyer (eds), Comparative historical analysis in the social sciences. Cambridge: Cambridge University Press, pp. 305–36.

Saris, W.E. (1997) 'Comparability across mode and country', in W.E. Saris and M. Kaase (eds), Eurobarometer. Measurement instruments for opinions in Europe. Mannheim: ZUMA, pp. 125–39.

Saris, W.E. and Münnich, Á. (eds) (1995) The multitrait-multimethod approach to evaluate measurement instruments. Budapest: Eötvös University Press.

Saris, W.E. and Scherpenzeel, A. (1995) 'Correction for measurement error in life satisfaction research', in W.E. Saris and Á. Münnich (eds), The multitrait-multimethod approach to evaluate measurement instruments. Budapest: Eötvös University Press, pp. 243–67.

Sartori, G. (1970) 'Concept misformation in comparative politics', American Political Science Review, 64 (4): 1033–53.

Sartori, G. (1994) 'Compare why and how. Comparing, miscomparing and the comparative method', in M. Dogan and A. Kazancigil (eds), Comparing nations. Concepts, strategies, substance. Oxford: Blackwell, pp. 13–34.

Schäfer, J. (2006) Sozialkapital und politische Orientierungen von jugendlichen in Deutschland. Wiesbaden: VS Verlag.

Schneider, C.Q. and Wagemann, C. (2006) 'Reducing complexity in qualitative analyses (QCA): Remote and proximate factors and the consolidation of democracy', *European Journal of Political Science*, 45 (5): 751–86.

Smelser, N.J. (1973) 'The methodology of comparative analysis', in D.P. Warwick and S. Osherson (eds), *Comparative research methods*. Englewood Cliffs: Prentice-Hall, pp. 42–86.

Treiman, D.J. (1975) 'Problems of concept and measurement in the comparative study of occupational mobility', *Social Science Research*, 4 (3), 183–230.

Treiman, D.J. and Terrel, K. (1975) 'Status attainment in the United States and Great Britain', *American Journal of Sociology*, 81 (3), 568–83.

Van de Vijver, F.J.R. (1998) 'Towards a theory of bias and equivalence', in J.A. Harkness (ed.), *Cross-cultural survey equivalence*. Mannheim: ZUMA, pp. 41–65.

Van de Vijver, F.J.R. (2003a) 'Bias and equivalence: Cross-cultural perspectives', in J.A. Harkness, F.J.R. Van de Vijver and P. Ph. Mohler. (eds), *Cross-cultural survey methods*. Hoboken, NJ: Wiley, pp. 143–55.

Van de Vijver, F.J.R. (2003b) 'Bias and substantive analyses', in J.A. Harkness, F.J.R. Van de Vijver and P. Ph. Mohler (eds), *Cross-cultural survey methods*. Hoboken, NJ: Wiley, pp. 207–33.

Van de Vijver, F.J.R. and Leung, K. (1997) *Methods and data analysis for cross-cultural research*. Thousand Oaks, CA: Sage.

van Deth, J.W. (1986) 'A note on measuring political participation in comparative research', *Quality and Quantity*, 20 (2–3): 261–72.

van Deth, J.W. (ed.) (1998) *Comparative politics. The problem of equivalence*. London: Routledge.

van Deth, J.W. (2003) 'Using published survey data', in J.A. Harkness, F.J.R. Van de Vijver, and P. Ph. Mohler. (eds), *Cross-cultural survey methods*. Hoboken, NJ: Wiley, pp. 291–309.

Verba, S. (1967) 'Some dilemmas in comparative research', *World Politics*, 20 (1): 111–27.

Verba, S. (1969) 'The uses of survey research in the study of comparative politics: Issues and strategies', in S. Rokkan, S. Verba, J. Viet and E. Almasy (eds), *Comparative survey analysis*. The Hague: Mouton, pp. 56–105.

Westle, B. (1998) 'Tolerance', in J.W. van Deth (ed), *Comparative politics. The problem of equivalence*. London: Routledge, pp. 20–60.

Wittgenstein, L. (1921/1963) *Tractatus logico-philosophicus. Logisch-philosophische abhandlung*. Frankfurt a. M: Suhrkamp.

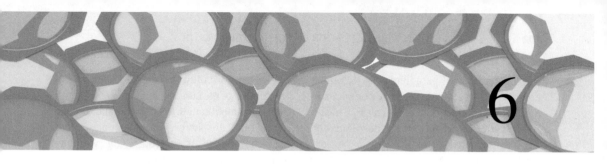

6

Comparative Political Sociology

Willlfried Spohn

THE CHANGING CONTOURS OF COMPARATIVE POLITICAL SOCIOLOGY

Sociology and political science have a complex relationship and against the backdrop of the two disciplines political sociology can be defined as an interdisciplinary field of inquiry developed by both sociologists and political scientists to study the interrelations and interactions between the socio-cultural life-world and the political sphere: between society and state, between social and political institutions, groups and behaviour. Political sociology in short, looks at 'the social bases of politics' (see *inter alia*, Braungart and Braungart, 2000; Janoski et al., 2004; Kimmerling, 1996; Lipset, 1959; Nash, 2000; Orum, 1983, 1996).[1] Comparative political sociology relates to those parts of political sociology that use explicitly a comparative methodology and related comparative methods. Whereas comparative politics concentrates on the comparative analysis and explanation of political phenomena, comparative political sociology as an interdisciplinary field of inquiry combines comparative politics and comparative sociology, focusing on socio-cultural phenomena and their interconnections with the political sphere. As a consequence, the range of comparative methods used in comparative political sociology differs to some extent to those used in comparative politics and sociology. However, because political science and comparative politics are also involved in the investigation of relationships between the political and social spheres, there is a considerable overlap between comparative political sociology and comparative politics (Landman, 2003).

Modern political sociology only emerged as a distinct field of specialization after World War II, building on the different intellectual and academic traditions of political science and sociology that had developed in the first half of the twentieth century, and combining European and American legacies (Bendix, 1973; Eckstein, 1971; Eisenstadt, 1971). A common theoretical background for the interdisciplinary development of political sociology was the modernization paradigm. This integrated classical sociological traditions and in its structural-functional version provided a way of integrating the political into a multi-dimensional framework of socio-political evolution (Knöbl, 2001; Kumar, 2000; Tipps, 1973). This also allowed it to integrate the specific aspects of traditional political science: government, political institutions, public law and related political behaviour (Almond and Bingham, 1966; Apter, 1965; Dahl, 1971; Easton, 1953).

The modernization paradigm was accompanied by a fast-growing field of comparative research that extended classical European-American comparisons to the decolonizing, newly developing states in the non-Western world (Lerner, 1965; Weiner, 1966). As a result, political sociology became essentially defined by comparative political modernization research on the globally varying formation of modern political systems as a crucial part of societal modernization processes.

The modernization paradigm grounded comparative political sociology in a macro-sociological Western-centric evolutionist framework. This served not only as a value-free analytical frame of reference but also as a self-legitimising ideology of the Western, and particularly US-American, developmental models. Increasingly this has been questioned by critical counter-trends in political sociology (Latham, 1997; Yack, 1997). A first counter-trend questioning the mainstream affirmative positivism was developed by conflict theory on the basis of renewed forms of critical theory orienting political sociology to issues of political power and social inequality (Coser, 1967). Second, in a renewal of Marxist traditions, neo-Marxism developed a critical analysis of political power and its foundation in capitalist development and class conflict (Bottomore, 1979). A third counter-trend evolved in the form of post-modernist and post-structural perspectives based on the 'cultural turn' that questioned not only the Western-centric modernization paradigm but also the economism of most neo-Marxist approaches and hence the positivistic mode of comparative political macro-sociology (Nash, 2001). Finally, a fourth counter-trend has extended the post-modernist-cultural orientation to the non-Western world in the form of post-colonial studies (Chaturvedi, 2000). These counter-trends have been accompanied by a general movement from social-scientific approaches seeking causal explanation through the identification of invariant laws or regularities between social and political variables to cultural-scientific approaches concerned with cultural meaning and cognitive construction in their impacts on the social and political spheres. These counter-trends also questioned the predominant variable-oriented quantitative methods used in comparative political macro-sociology and resulted in the development of case-oriented qualitative and interpretive comparative methods. Though comparative political macro-sociology with its theoretical focus on political modernization and methodological orientation to quantitative methods has remained the defining core of political sociology, there emerged a strong tendency towards the search for the micro-sociological foundation of politics and case-oriented comparisons. On the social-scientific side, historical-sociological approaches focused on the micro-sociological foundations of political processes (Skocpol, 1984; Tilly, 1984); institutionalist approaches tried to specify the institutional environments of politics (Mahoney and Rueschemeyer, 2003); and rational-choice approaches analysed the rational action orientation involved in political individual and collective action (Kiser and Hechter, 1998). On the cultural-scientific side, the post-modernist and post-structuralist 'cultural turn' renewed a hermeneutic-interpretive and cultural-historical tradition in sociology and political science, and hence also in political sociology (Adams et al., 2005); this was often radicalized by constructivist epistemological perspectives that directed research to the deconstruction of cultural archaeologies or frames of political power, institutions and actions (Nash, 2000).

These traditional and counter currents continue to shape the present state of comparative political sociology. The liberal-capitalist modernization paradigm in the form of transition and transformation research experienced a conspicuous revival with the breakdown of communism as an alternative form of modernization as well as an ideology (Grancelli, 1995). Once again, renewed macro-modernization analysis in political sociology has been contested in two directions. On the one hand, the comparative-civilizational approach argues for a multiple modernities perspective because of the persistence of many different forms of modern societies (Eisenstadt, 2002). This has been augmented by the intensification of globalization and the trend towards examining the impact of various globalization processes on national and international politics that it has produced (Held et al., 1999; Robertson, 1992; Scholte, 2002). On the other hand, critical alternatives to the liberal-capitalist modernization paradigm in the form of neo-Marxism, post-modernism and post-colonialism remain, and are complemented by micro-sociological perspectives calling for the comparative analysis of the sociological foundations of multiple modernities and globalization.

The resulting current epistemological, theoretical, methodological and analytical pluralism in comparative political sociology demarcates the space of comparative methodology and research involved. On the social-scientific pole of this methodological space, the comparative enterprise in political sociology continues through the application of large-scale, global quantitative variable-oriented research methods and through comparative qualitative, case-oriented research on the micro-foundations of politics and political processes. On the cultural-scientific pole of this methodological space, comparative qualitative, case-oriented methods combine with interpretive and deconstructive research orientations, often in tension with quantitative, variable-oriented approaches and seldom complementing them (Ragin, 1987). In the following, I will outline the changing contours of comparative political sociology in its different currents and waves, concentrating on exemplary comparative studies, and summarizing the resulting pluralistic – though compartmentalized – space of comparative methodology in comparative political sociology.

COMPARATIVE MACRO-SOCIOLOGY OF POLITICS: POLITICAL MODERNIZATION AND SOCIAL CHANGE

Modern political sociology as the systematic study of the relationships between the political and social spheres emerged with the experience of the social and political changes in Western Europe and the Americas in the late-eighteenth and early-nineteenth centuries. Although the roots of political sociology can be traced back to Greek philosophy and its impact on medieval, early modern and enlightenment political thought, emerging modern political sociology as a combination of political science and sociology wanted to understand the formation of modern absolutist nation-states, how political revolutions produced change, and the impact of the social changes created by the industrial revolution on politics (Eisenstadt, 1963, 1971). Whereas early political science concentrated more on political governance and public law (Eckstein, 1971), early political sociology focused more on the socio-economic changes related to capitalist development, industrialization and social structure and their impact on the political realm (Kumar, 2005). Early political sociology was on the one hand macro-sociological, in that it studied macro-trends in political and social evolution, and on the other hand explicitly or implicitly comparative in contrasting Western European and North American processes of political and socio-economic modernization to each other and to Eastern or Oriental experiences. At the same time, the founding fathers of comparative political sociology – among whom we can count Charles Montesquieu and Alexis de Tocqueville in France; Adam Smith and John Stuart Mill in Great Britain; and Karl Marx and Lorenz von Stein in Germany – reflected both their particular intellectual traditions of philosophical and political thought as well as the specific social and political experiences of their countries.

On these foundations, the classical phase of comparative political sociology started with the institutionalization of sociology as a specific academic discipline at European universities in the late-nineteenth and early-twentieth centuries. It was connected with new political experiences such as the formation of new nation-states in Italy and Germany, the importance of nationalism and democratization, as well as the rise of communism and fascism after World War I. In this context, the traditional evolutionist and optimistic approaches of the founding fathers became contested by more ambiguous and pessimistic perspectives and at the same time new topics became relevant. French sociology founded by Emile Durkheim and Maurice Halbwachs (Lukes, 1972) emphasized social integration, national consciousness or *conscience collective* as the basis and cement of national politics (Aron, 1967; Duverger, 1972). German political sociology, in close contact with Austria and developed particularly by Ferdinand Tönnies, Ludwig Gumplowicz, Max Weber, Werner Sombart, Otto Hintze, Robert Michels and Karl Mannheim (for an overview see Mommsen and Osterhammel, 1987), concentrated on topics such as nation, ethnicity and nationalism; state bureaucracy and state agencies, democratization, political parties and charismatic political leaders Nedelmann 1997. Italian political sociology by Gaetano Mosca and Vilfredo Pareto and particularly influenced by Weber and Michels focused on the role of political elites (Linz, 2006). In contrast, British and American scholars such as Henry Maine, Thomas Marshall, Harold Lasswell and Harold Laski were rather concerned with the political development of constitutional democracy, political parties and political/social pressure groups in Britain and the US (Eckstein, 1971). Whatever the topical emphasis, all these approaches in political sociology remained comparative macro-sociological, contrasting the tendencies of the modern political realm with the European traditional order and with the non-European world, as well as with some attempts to compare the individual countries with each other.

The different national traditions of European political sociology came together only with the synthesis of American and European sociology, enabled by the forced emigration of many of its representatives, in post-World War II American sociology. Structural-functional system theory and the related modernization paradigm developed by Talcott Parsons, Edward Shils and others played a central role (Alexander, 1994; Knöbl, 2001; Zapf, 1971). Societal development was conceptualized according to basic social-evolutionary processes such as social differentiation and individualization, capitalist industrialization and social stratification, nation-state formation and democratization, as well as value generalization and secularization. This multi-dimensional bundle comprised the major evolutionary processes from traditional to modern society and simultaneously claimed the functional co-evolution of these processes. Within this frame of reference, the realm of politics was seen as one sub-system of the social system, and political modernization as one functional component of overall societal modernization. Characteristically, modern American society and polity formed the *telos* of these evolutionary processes and accordingly served as a comparative model not only for the reconstruction of European societies but also for the many post-colonial societies in the non-European world (*inter alia* Black, 1966; Finkle and Gable, 1966; Geertz, 1963; Lerner, 1965; Parsons, 1977; Shils, 1977).

Guided by this universal framework, a rapidly expanding field of comparative research on modernization and particularly political modernization developed. One cornerstone of systematic-comparative analysis of components of political modernization such as social communication, bureaucracy, education, national culture and political culture were the influential 'Studies in Political Development' organized by the Committee on Comparative Politics of the Social Science Research Council (Almond and Verba 1963; Binder et al., 1971; Grew, 1978; LaPalombara, 1963; Pye and Verba, 1965; Weiner, 1966; also Deutsch, 1953). Another cornerstone was Seymour Martin Lipset's democratization thesis and Stein Rokkan's social cleavage thesis. Lipset's (1959) democratization thesis, originally formulated in his *Political Man*, stated that democracy as a political system with constitutional government, citizens' rights and free elections goes generally hand in hand with economic development, the formation of a middle class, the rise of cultural education and social welfare and a resulting pluralist political culture (Bollen, 1980; Lipset, 1984; Marks and Lipset, 1998). The social cleavage thesis developed by Stein Rokkan (Lipset and Rokkan, 1967) tried to explain the post-World War II voter alignment patterns in Western Europe as a result of varying cleavage structures evolving between state and church, aristocracy and bourgeoisie as well as bourgeoisie and working class during the course of political modernization (Rokkan et al., 1999). Whereas Lipset particularly focused on American exceptionalism in contrast to Western Europe, Rokkan concentrated more on the varieties of political modernization in Western Europe; but both also initiated broadly comparative research on political modernization in the new states in the non-Western regions of Asia, Africa and Latin America. A current summary of this continuing research agenda, although there have been some revisions of the original modernization framework, can be seen in many volumes on democracy in Western and non-Western states (Diamond, 1999; Diamond and Plattner, 2002; Lipset, 1998).

The refinement and revision of the original modernization framework as it related particularly to the evolutionary, functional and macro-sociological premises of comparative political modernization research had three major aspects.[2] First, modernization was questioned as an evolutionary progressive process and instead seen as fragile and full of contradictions and breakdowns (Eisenstadt, 1966). Second, modernization was questioned as a functionally interdependent multidimensional process and instead conceptualized as two distinct dimensions of economic and political modernization. In

particular, Samuel Huntington (1968/2003) pointed out that political modernization was not necessarily promoted by economic modernization, but was also influenced by the interconnection of state stability and democratization, a linkage that was particularly in jeopardy in new post-colonial states. Third, the tendency for macro-sociological research cum quantitative research methods was questioned by in-depth historical-comparative research that highlighted the path-dependent specific causal configurations of dimensions and factors of political modernization. For instance, Barrington Moore (1966) highlighted the crucial importance of pre-industrial landlords and peasants for the different types of capitalist-democratic, conservative-fascist and communist-autocratic paths of modernization; Reinhard Bendix (1977) focused on the historically varying legitimacy pattern of political power related to different concepts of nationhood and citizenship; and Charles Tilly (1975) emphasized the historical contingency of the formation of nation-states in Europe. These refinements and revisions of comparative research on political modernization also had consequences for the comparative methods used. The predominant search for general or functional laws between a few independent and dependent variables across a large number of cases pursued in macro-sociological, quantitative cross-national comparative research on political modernization became contested and complemented by comparative research methods that concentrated more on causal configurations in a few cases on the basis of qualitative-historical research. The resulting methodological space for comparative analysis was summarized by Tilly (1984) who distinguished generalising comparisons with many variables and cases, individualizing comparisons with few variables and cases, encompassing comparisons with cases and variables embedded in a larger system, and variation-finding comparisons with a systematic search for varying causal relations of variables in few, well researched cases; or in a more qualitative direction by Theda Skocpol (1984) who emphasized model-theoretical, causal and interpretive comparative methods.

CRITICAL ALTERNATIVES: CONFLICT THEORY, NEO-MARXISM, POST-PODERNISM AND POST-COLONIALISM

The modernization paradigm and the related comparative research on political modernization represented not only an analytical framework for comparative investigation but also, in a sense, an ideological base for American foreign policy. At its core, much of political modernization theory and research took for granted that the American model of modern society, its capitalism, social structure and democracy, was the highest stage of socio-political evolution. This went hand in hand with a missionary democratic orientation to the development of the Third World, a strong anti-communist sentiment against the Second World and a conservative-affirmative attitude regarding the existing democratic regimes in the First World (Latham, 1997; Yack, 1997). As a consequence, the modernization paradigm became the target of a variety of critical countermoves against and within the Western model of modernity in search of more democracy that were particularly fuelled by the political and cultural revolt of 1968 in most Western, and some non-Western, societies. These critical countermoves against the predominant modernization paradigm revolved around four main currents that have had a lasting impact on political sociology and related comparative research. Conflict theories based on traditions of critical theory challenged the affirmative functions of modernization theory *vis-à-vis* Western modernity. More specifically within this critical tradition, neo-Marxism renewed and developed Marxist political economy as a key to understanding power structures in Western and between Western and non-Western societies. Post-modernist approaches emerged as a critical move against the grand narratives not only of modernization theory but also of neo-Marxism. And post-colonial approaches, which are often married with post-modernism, criticized the Euro-centrism not only of modernization theory but also of neo-Marxism from the perspective of the post-colonial world.

Broadly, the critical countermovement against the mainstream modernization paradigm in political sociology started with the perception of the negative features of advanced liberal-capitalist societies and was accompanied by a renewal of critical-theoretical currents within classical sociology. An influential strand was the critical analysis of the political and social power structures of Western societies as developed, for instance, in C. Wright Mills (1956, 1963) and George W. Domhoff's (1967, 2001) investigation of the American power elite and replicated by John Scott (1991) in the United Kingdom, Raymond Aron (1950) in France, and Ralf Dahrendorf's (1965) and W. Zapf's (1965) studies of German elites. Characteristically, the core concept of power was less seen in its positive aspects of national sovereignty, responsible government and rational authority and more in its negative aspects of hierarchical power structures, limited democratic participation, and social inequality. A second strand of this renewal of critical-theoretical currents in sociology developed a variety of critical concepts with the purpose to expand the democratic spaces in Western societies. Particularly important were the concepts of participatory democracy, social protest and social movements, industrial democracy, welfare state, civil society and public sphere. Here, of lasting influence were Jürgen Habermas's (1989) study of the transformation of the public sphere in Germany, Pierre Bourdieu's (1984, 1987) concepts of social, political and cultural capital, Marshall's (1964) category of citizenship, and the concept of civil society re-imported from East-Central Europe (Keane, 1988). Related to this critical orientation was the general criticism of the static, functional and evolutionist premises of the modernization paradigm and the inverse emphasis on the tensions, contradictions, conflicts and social change at the centre of political sociology. This was connected to a general renewal of critical theory in political sociology, reinvigorating the critical-reflexive potential of classical sociology, Marxism and psychoanalysis for the study of modern societies and politics (Bottomore, 1979).

A second critical countermove against comparative political modernization research can be classified as neo-Marxism. Though neo-Marxism shared the general motivations and orientations of critical theory in many respects, it was oriented more specifically to the Marxist legacy of political-economic analysis rather than to the Marxist philosophical heritage (Bottomore, 1979). At the core of neo-Marxist analysis was the relationship between the economic structure of capitalism and the capitalist state (Giddens, 1973; Offe, 1972; Poulantzas, 1973); the impact of class structures and interrelations on political power (Miliband, 1977; Therborn, 1978); and following Antonio Gramsci (1971) the changing forms of the state and functioning of capitalist hegemony (Laclau and Mouffe, 2001). Neo-Marxism was primarily oriented to the social inequalities, social conflicts and political power structures in advanced Western capitalism, though it was limited – like modernization theory and comparative political modernization research – by its inbuilt Euro-centrism, economism, and evolutionism. In the long run, more influential for comparative political sociology were the more historical-comparative approaches to state formation and class conflicts in the transition from feudalism to capitalism (Anderson, 1979) as well as the origins and development of the modern world system concentrating on the changing global economic hierarchy between core, semiperipheries and peripheries (Chase-Dunn, 1991; Wallerstein, 1999).

The third countermove against comparative modernization research developed against the limits of the neo-Marxist alternative and thus can be seen also as a post-Marxist phenomenon (Anderson, 1991). Both modernization and neo-Marxist theories shared a Eurocentric tendency to structuralism, functionalism and evolutionism, and were fixated on economic development, social-structure and class-based power politics. Against this, post-modernism emphasized, on the one hand, new structural developments and phenomena of Western/global capitalism, such as post-industrialism, post-Fordism, new communication technologies, consumer culture, new social movements, feminism and multiculturalism and a related cultural pluralism that had a crucial impact on postmodern attitudes, political culture (for a cultural-scientific interpretation, see Kumar, 2005), and new patterns of political party formation (for a political-scientific explanation see Inglehardt, 1990; 2006). On the other, post-modernism went hand in hand with the emergence of new collective actors in the social and political spheres, particularly feminist and ecological orientations in the context of the many new social movements that shifted the analytical attention from structures to culture and agency (Archer, 2000; Lister, 2002; Squire, 2004). In parallel, there developed new post-modernist theories and methodologies that criticised the grand narratives of modernization theory and neo-Marxism and shifted to the 'micro-physics' and cultural-epistemological construction of power (Foucault, 1972; Nash, 2000). Against this background, a post-modern political sociology emerged that focused particularly on the deconstruction of the power relations built into state structures and agencies in relation to various social and political actors and movements under the post-modern condition (Owen, 2000).

The fourth countermove against comparative modernization research represents a parallel post-modern development in the relationship between the advanced capitalist countries and the post-colonial Third World. Primarily developed by non-Western intellectuals in contact with the Western academia, post-colonialism reflected the post-modernist disenchantment not only with modernization theory but also with neo-Marxism. Particularly influential was Edward Said's *Orientalism* (1979) and the following post-colonial and subaltern studies redirecting the structural power analysis of the Third World towards the cultural construction of colonial and post-colonial societies, and from elites to the lower, oppressed and silenced classes, groups and individuals (Chaturvedi, 2000; Conrad and Randeria, 2002). Since post-colonial and subaltern studies were primarily developed in literary criticism, comparative literature, anthropology and ethnography, there is also a hitherto unresolved tension, but also emerging debate on their relation to a political sociology of post-colonial societies (Bartolovich and Lazarus, 2001). Here, in contradistinction to the political modernization approaches in the sociology of development (So, 1990), three currents developed: the political economy of the Third World (Hoogvelt, 1997; McMichael, 2004; Menzel, 2000); the political analysis of the third-world state (e.g., Bayart, 1993; Kamrava, 2002); and the analysis of political culture (Comaroff and Comaroff, 1991; Cooper, 2003; Ferguson, 2006).

These four counter-currents against the predominant political modernization paradigm also had important consequences for the use of comparative methods. Generally speaking, the critique of liberal-capitalist modernity profoundly weakened the systematic comparative study of processes of political modernization and promoted critical, but rarely comparative, research. The only exception was neo-Marxism, where the historical-sociological move to compare political-social configurations with qualitative case-oriented methods remained influential. But critical theory and conflict theory were generally more interested in the re-examination of individual cases and only rarely and in a few cases engaged in systematic comparative research. Even more so, post-modern approaches generally discouraged systematic comparative work, since the individualized, decentred, fragmented and chaotic world these approaches depicted emphasized differences but not

similarities. As a result, post-colonial studies in political sociology were also mostly interested in qualitative-deconstructive work rather than systematic comparisons between the various types of post-colonial political regimes and societies. Nevertheless, the main effect of these various critical alternatives on comparative political sociology was to strengthen qualitative case-oriented against quantitative variables-oriented methods of comparison (Adams et al., 2005).

COMPARATIVE MICRO-FOUNDATIONS OF POLITICS: SOCIAL-SCIENTIFIC AND CULTURAL-CONSTRUCTIVIST APPROACHES

The common denominator of the various critical counter-currents against the predominant modernization paradigm and related comparative research in political modernization has been a broad critique of its Eurocentric universalistic, evolutionary and normative premises. The major impacts on comparative political sociology have been the questioning of the self-explanatory validity of macro-structural causal correlations; the movement from structure to agency and culture; the shift from researching system stability to conflict and change; as well as the movement from an affirmative normative attitude to a more pluralistic value orientation in politics. However, it would be misleading to state that the critical countermoves brought the predominance of the comparative macro-sociology of politics to an end. Rather, the comparative macro-sociology of politics has lost its original capability of defining the sub-discipline of political sociology, being forced to revise the structural-functionalist assumptions of modernization theory by integrating many components of the critical counter-currents. These critical counter-currents, however, did not converge in a common counter-paradigm. Instead, they developed and institutionalized in various currents, thus pluralizing but also compartmentalizing the interdisciplinary enterprise of political sociology. At the same time, the common effect of the critical revisions has been a general movement towards the search for the micro-foundations of politics. This search has developed in two principled directions of social-scientific and cultural-constructivist approaches, thereby increasingly making complex the macro-micro research agenda and strategies in comparative political sociology.

A first redirection of the comparative macro-sociology of politics motivated by the critique of the structural-functional and evolutionary modernization framework developed as a corollary to the rise of historical sociology. Instead of taking the unfolding self-propelling causality of social and political modernization macro-processes for granted, a general methodological thrust became directed towards the historicization and contextualization of the macro-process of political modernization, focusing on particular trajectories and sequences of political modernization. Of special influence here was Moore's *Social Origins* (1966), which provided an in-depth analysis of four different trajectories of political modernization and their specific class constellations. He was followed in a similar vein by Skocpol's *States and Social Revolutions* (1979), Anderson's *Passages from Antiquity to Feudalism* (1979) and *Lineages of the Absolutist State* (1980). This approach was further developed by Michael Mann's *Sources of Social Power* (1986/ 1993; see Hall and Schroeder, 2006), and Dietrich Rueschemeyer, Evelyn Huber-Stephen and John Stephen's *Democracy and Capitalist Development* (1992). At the same time, there developed more specialized topics of research that looked comparatively at particular historical phases and topical dimensions of political modernization, particularly in the historical sociology of the state (e.g., Ertmann, 1997; Evans et al., 1985 or Poggi, 1978, 2001); of nations and nationalism (e.g., Anderson, 1983; Bendix, 1977; Gellner, 1983; Marx, 1998; Smith, 1986, 2001); the historical sociology of revolutions (Goldstone, 1991; McDaniel, 1989, 1991); and of social classes, social movements, social protest and political mobilization (e.g., Katznelson and Zolberg, 1986; Moore, 1981; Tilly, 1978; Thompson, 1963). The comparative methods used in these historical orientations in political sociology are either constellative-causal (analysing causal connections and regularities in political-social macro-configurations) or variation-finding (identifying varying meso- and micro-causal mechanisms of political processes) in the social-scientific direction; and qualitative-interpretive (understanding and comparing different kinds of meaning and action orientations) or deconstructive (analysing and comparing hidden cognitive structures) in a cultural-scientific direction (Ragin, 1987; Sewell, 2005; Skocpol, 1984; Tilly, 1984).

The second redirection of the macro-sociology of politics has concerned the analytical differentiation of the macro-unity of the state. With the aim of 'bringing the state back in' (Evans et al., 1985) – a demand against liberal-utilitarian and neo-Marxist orientations alike – political-sociological analysis turned to the social basis of specific state functions, agencies and actors. In the social-scientific direction, particularly influential has been the comparative analysis of social policy (Charrad, 2001; de Swaan, 1998; Esping-Anderson, 1990; Orloff, 1993; Skocpol, 1992; Weir et al., 1988), but also other state domains, such as economic policy (Carruthers, 2005), administration (Kiser and Kane, 2001), police (Knöbl, 1998) and military (Tilly, 1990) were of interest. In the cultural and constructivist orientation, there have been investigations of the cultural frameworks of the state (Steinmetz, 1999); the impact of religion on state-formation and political culture (Bellah, 1981; Gorski, 2003; Zaret, 1985); the relationships between state, nation and nationalism (Giddens, 1985; Greenfeld, 1993); nationalism and religion (Casanova, 1994; Spohn, 2003); nationalism and language (Laitin, 1992); ethnicity and citizenship (Brubaker, 1992; Joppke, 1999;

Soysal, 1994), or power and legitimacy (Chirot, 1996).

The third trend in comparative political sociology has attempted to analyze the complex intermediary space between the political realm and society in terms of civil society and public sphere, or meso-level social and political institutions (Bryant and Hall, 1994; Rueschemeyer and Rueschemeyer 1998). In addition to the classical topics of political society such as political parties and pressure groups, interest has focused on the political impact of business associations or trade unions, the political role of city or regional governments; and the various forms of new social movements such as women's, environmental, anti-nuclear or civil rights movements in their cultural repertoires, organizational structure and mobilization patterns (Rucht, 1990); also important here is the analysis of social capital and its impact on politics and political culture (Putnam, 1993). In a cultural and constructivist direction increasing attention has been focused on social institutions such as prisons or asylums, which were analyzed as part of the 'micro-physics' of power (Foucault, 1972; Nash, 2001). Culture, language, discourse and identity of collective actors have also been investigated, particularly, following Thompson (1963), class languages and identities (e.g., Sewell, 2005) or following Bourdieu (1977) cultural capital and discourse patterns (e.g., Wuthnow, 1989). More recently, the media as a medium and an actor alike in the public sphere has increasingly become a focus (Schudson and Waisbrod, 2004). Connected to the analysis of these various institutions as meso-level foundations of politics different kinds of institutionalist approaches developed:

(a) a historical institutionalism oriented to the institutional frameworks of path-dependent developments;
(b) a rational choice institutionalism concentrating on the interplay of institutional frameworks and rational choices of actors; and
(c) a cultural institutionalism that concentrated on the institutionalized cultural frames or the cultural construction of institutions (Hall and Taylor,

1996; Thelen, 1999; see also Chapter 6 of this volume).

The fourth trend in comparative political sociology is connected to these different kinds of institutionalism, but has gone even further in the direction of individual and collective agency and related forms of a renewed methodological individualism. On the social-scientific side, the rational choice approach became increasingly influential in comparative political sociology. Here, the big categories of socio-political analysis such as state, bureaucracy, nation and nationalism are strategically explained by reference to rational choices of actors in specific institutional contexts. Examples of this rational choice approach in political sociology are Michael Hechter's *Internal Colonialism* (1975) or Margaret Levi's *Of Rule and Revenue* (1988). The comparative method used here attempts to establish general law-like causal statements about action choice patterns. Another micro-sociological approach represents the idea of social mechanism that tries to explain context-specific political processes by reference to general causal interaction or network patterns. This approach has been developed generally by Hedström and Swedberg (1998) and used by McAdams et al. (2003, also Tarrow and Tilly, 2007) regarding different issues of political contention. The comparative method used here tries to identify and explain variations of political processes. On the cultural-constructivist side, there is a revival of Max Weber's recourse to action orientations and corresponding ideal-types as components of political institutions and behaviour and the related hermeneutic method of *Verstehen* and interpretive types of comparisons (Matthes, 1992). Sometimes overlapping with hermeneutic-interpretive approaches, but often based on a constructivist epistemology, cultural-constructivist approaches attempt to understand the microphysics of political power by deconstructing the epistemological and cultural frameworks of political actors. Important examples here are in particular in the area of post-colonial studies (e.g., Comaroff and Comaroff, 1991; Cooper, 2003; or Ferguson, 2006). This deconstructivist method, however, is primarily oriented to uncover the cultural frames of individual and collective behaviour and seldom used for systematic comparisons.

In comparison to variable-oriented comparative methods in cross-cultural political modernization research, the trend in political sociology to examine the micro-foundations of politics clearly advances qualitative, context-bound case-oriented methods of comparison. In social-scientific approaches there is continuity towards generalizing comparisons. But with the search for context-bound or case-specific causality, the thrust of comparative analysis favours case study-oriented comparisons, be it in the form of model-theoretical, configurational-causal, or variation-finding analysis (Ragin, 1997; Skocpol, 1984; Tilly, 1984). In cultural-constructivist approaches, even if there is a methodological continuum from configurational-causal and interpretive methods, comparative methods are mostly oriented to qualitative, interpretive, individualizing and contrasting methods in order to understand cultural specificities (Matthes, 1992). As a result, the generalizing orientations in comparative political sociology are weakened in favour of individualizing methods of comparison.

THE RENEWED COMPARATIVE MACRO-SOCIOLOGY OF POLITICS: NEO-MODERNIZATION ANALYSIS, MULTIPLE MODERNITIES, EUROPEANIZATION AND GLOBALIZATION

The main counter trend to a macro-sociology of politics based on a revised modernization paradigm and complemented by neo-Marxist macro-approaches was thus a move to a meso- and micro-sociology of politics (Adams et al., 2005; Mahoney and Rueschemeyer, 2003). In turn, this trend became reversed with a new instance of macro-political change: the

breakdown of communism as a system as well as a political ideology. This *caesura* was followed by attempts to catch-up to Western modernity through political transition and social transformation processes in the post-communist Second World, but with repercussions also for socialist and communist states and movements in the non-Western Third World. As a corollary to this there has been a decisive renewal of comparative political macro-sociology in the form of transition and transformation research on the foundations of a revised modernization framework or neo-modernization analysis (Bönker et al., 2002). At the same time, with the diversification of modernization processes in Western and non-Western societies, there has developed also a new multiple modernities perspective that has criticized the modernist premise of a converging Westernization of the world and instead analyzed the dynamics of a variety of different modernities (Eisenstadt, 2002; Spohn, 2001; Therborn, 1995). In addition to these two macro-sociological approaches, a third macro-sociological direction has developed around the new area of transnational comparative political sociology looking particularly to the process of European integration and enlargement (Bach, 2000; Wallace and Wallace, 2004) as well as the overarching processes of globalization and its impacts on national politics (Albrow, 1996; Held, 2005; Held et al., 1999; Lechner and Boli, 2001; Scholte, 2002).

The renewal of a revised modernization approach has been particularly connected to transition and transformation research on post-communist countries. Where explicitly stated, this research has been based on a neo-modernization analysis that emphasizes not only objective structures, institutions and functions but also the subjective modernizing action orientations directing the transition and transformation of post-communist societies and polities (Alexander, 1994; Tiryakian, 1995). Transition research concentrated on the various transition paths from authoritarian, post-totalitarian or totalitarian rule to democratic-constitutional regimes, their consolidation, fragility or reversal to authoritarianism (Bremmer and Tarras, 1997; Dawisha and Parrot, 1997; Linz and Stepan, 1996). It has explicitly compared not only the various post-communist experiences in East-Central Europe, South-Eastern Europe, Russia and the Commonwealth of Independent States with each other, but also compared them to the earlier transitions from authoritarian to democratic rule in Southern Europe and South America as constitutive parts of the third wave of democratization (Huntington, 1991; Linz and Stepan, 1996). Transformation research has also looked at the socio-economic processes of emerging capitalist market economies in the form of the shock therapies, privatization strategies and other economic policies, their relation to the political transition processes as well as their variations (Grancelli, 1995). In a similar direction, the political sociology of third-world countries, divided between modernization research and world-system or dependence approaches and confronted with the widespread weakening of socialist or communist developmental strategies moved to a neo-modernist mode of transformation and transition research (So, 1990).

Although the neo-modernist renewal of political macro-sociology used a more open theoretical framework and produced a rapidly growing comparative research (Andrain and Apter, 1995; Plattner, 2003; Vanhannen, 1997), it once again was questioned by the many cases which did not follow prescribed Western paths to capitalism and democracy and instead preserved the communist framework or moved in authoritarian or totalitarian directions (Centeno and Lopez-Alves, 2001). Against this background, the multiple modernities perspective in the tradition of comparative political macro-sociology has been developed, particularly by Shmuel Eisenstadt and his collaborators, and become increasingly influential (Arnason et al., 2005; Arjomand and Tiryakian, 2004; Arnason, 2003; Eisenstadt, 2002). In a nut-shell, this approach assumes that there are differing kinds and dynamics of world civilisations on the bases of core institutions and core religions, related political and cultural programmes of modernity and crystallizing in multiple modernities and paths of modernization. Of particular importance here are the different kinds of world religions and different ways and strengths of transcendental orientations that generate tensions and contradictions between pragmatic and fundamentalist forms of politics or paradoxes of democracy (Eisenstadt, 1999a, 1999b). This research programme has been realized in several studies on Europe (Eisenstadt, 1987; Sachsenmaier and Riedel, 2002), North and South America (Roniger and Waisman, 2002; Whitehead, 2005), Judaism and Israel (Eisenstadt, 1992), India and Japan (Dornbos and Kaviraj, 1997; Eisenstadt, 1996), but opens also approaches to Russia, China, the Islamic civilisation, North and sub-Saharian Africa (Eisenstadt, 1989).

A third form of comparative political macro-sociology looks at the intensification of transnational and global forces following the collapse or transformation of the communist second world. Against the background of the formation of the EU and its enlargement to the East an important field of comparative-transnational studies in political sociology has become the analysis of the Europeanization of national societies (Bach, 2000; Beichelt et al., 2006; Graziano and Vink, 2007). Historically, the study of European integration was a subject in political science and its sub-discipline of international relations concentrating primarily on the macro-unit of the state in order to explain the formation and dynamics of a transnational institutional order (Loth and Wessels, 2001). After the reunification of Europe following the collapse of Soviet communism, the foundation of the EU after Maastricht in 1992 and the developing eastern enlargement, and as a consequence the increasing impact of the enlarging European integration process on individual societies, sociology, and particularly political sociology, brought in perspectives from below on the social and cultural bases of European integration and enlargement. In contrast to political science approaches that concentrate primarily on the political, legal and institutional impacts on European societies, the political sociology of Europe has looked at the impacts of European integration particularly on national economies, social policies, public spheres and civil societies (Eder and Giesen, 2002; Lehmbruch and Scharpf, 2000; Marginson and Sisson, 2006). In its comparative orientation, it concentrates on the varying forms of Europeanization not only on old member-states but combines with post-communist transformation research to examine the new and prospective member-states (e.g., Eder and Spohn, 2005; Grabbe, 2006; Ichijo and Spohn, 2005; Katzenstein and Byrnes, 2004; Spohn and Triandafyllidou, 2003).

Finally, a growing field of political macro-sociological research looks increasingly beyond Europe to the impact of globalization and the emerging world order on nation-states and the transformation of the interrelationships between the national political sphere and national society, economy and culture. Globalization has three general meanings:

- the growing interconnection of the world by transnational economic, social and cultural, particularly communicative forces;
- the growing dominance of transnational spaces over national societies; the formation of a world order; and
- a related cognitive dimension of a growing global consciousness or globality (Held et al., 1999; Lechner and Boli, 2002; Martinelli, 2005; Robertson, 1992; Scholte, 2002; Waters, 1995).

Whereas political science approaches concentrate on the interrelation between global political and legal institutions and nation-states and national politics, the political sociology of globalization looks at the economic, social and cultural global forces and their impact on the nation-state and national political order (Fobden and Hobson, 2002). Comparative political sociology then has two main foci in analysing globalization: a historical-diachronic orientation comparing differing degrees of globalization in relation to nation-state societies (Mann, 1997; Osterhammel and Petersson, 2003); and a

contemporary-synchronic direction comparing structural and cultural variations in the multiple forms of globalization in global-national and global-local links (Berger and Huntington, 2002; Haynes, 1998; Robertson, 1992). At the same time, there is an increasing tendency not only to concentrate on the impact of globalization on Western, but also on non-Western politics and societies (Hoogvelt, 1997; McMichael, 2004; Menzel, 2000). As well, the issues analyzed take up the whole range of dimensions and components of macro- and micro-analysis in comparative political sociology (e.g. Huber and Stephens, 2001; Janoski and Wang, 2004; Weiss, 2005, 2007).

The renaissance of neo-modernization political macro-sociology has thus gone hand in hand with a re-emphasis of variable-oriented, survey-based and multivariate comparative methods (Barnes and Simon, 1998; Inglehardt, 2006). At the same time, this come-back of macro-sociology of politics cum quantitative methods has not been able to dominate the overall trends in comparative political sociology. Rather, it combined in different ways with comparative research methods more appropriate for the analysis of individual cases. Accordingly, qualitative case-oriented, comparative-historical as well as interpretive-comparative methods have remained in place, either as distinct modes of comparison or in combination with quantitative variable-oriented comparative methods (Abbott, 2001; Ragin, 1997, 2000; Rueschemeyer, 2003).

CONCLUSION: THE SPACE OF COMPARATIVE METHODOLOGY IN POLITICAL SOCIOLOGY

Political sociology can be characterized as an inter-disciplinary research field between political science and sociology, moving from the synthesis of classical foundations in the form of macro-sociological political modernization research through the challenges of critical alternatives to political meso- and micro-sociological approaches and to renewed macro-approaches in the form of neo-modernization analysis, the multiple modernities perspective and transnational/global orientations. This inter-disciplinary development of political sociology where it involved comparison included a widening and pluralizing of comparative methodology, encompassing social-scientific generalizing to cultural-scientific individualizing methods of comparison on macro-, meso- and micro-levels of political-sociological analysis. This final section attempts to summarize the widening, pluralizing, but also compartmentalizing, space of comparative methodology and methods in political sociology and concludes with a plea for a more energetic intra- and inter-disciplinary methodological cooperation in comparative political-sociological research.

Political sociology – like sociology more generally – from its classical phase onwards, has oscillated between generalizing nomothetic and individualizing idiographic research orientations (Chilcote, 1994; Collier, 1991; Collins, 1968; Goldstone, 1997; Smelser, 1976; Vallier, 1971; Spohn, 1998, 2001). In a parallel, comparative methodology has been characterized by tensions between social-scientific positions attempting like John Stuart Mill (1872) or Emile Durkheim (1982) to establish through comparative methods general causal laws, on the one hand, and, on the other, cultural-scientific positions insisting, like German historicism, on the uniqueness of the human condition allowing only for comprehension through individualizing contrasts, as well as few attempts to mediate like Max Weber in his Wissenschaftslehre (1951) between both positions (Hall, 1999; Ragin, 1987). With the crystallization of modern political sociology in the framework of the modernization paradigm, however, the predominating mode became a generalizing comparative methodology using particularly quantitative multivariate statistical techniques (Dogan and Pelassy, 1984; Przeworksi and Teune, 1970). As Kohn (1989) summarizes,

comparisons in this tradition refer particularly to four aspects:

1. nation-state societies as units for comparisons;
2. the relations between components or variables within different national contexts;
3. national configurations of components; and
4. national configurations within the global system.

The emergence of critical alternatives against the structural-functional modernization paradigm, however, has been accompanied by a general tendency towards qualitative-comparative orientations and sometimes even further to a reproduction of a historicist position of the uniqueness, and thus incomparability, of human experiences. Critical theory and conflict theory were more interested in reflecting and analysing the contradictory and conflictive nature of Western modernity rather than developing a systematic orientation in comparative research on these conflicts and contradictions. Also neo-Marxist approaches, by continuing the social-scientific mode of analysis, were more interested in investigating the contradictory nature of modern capitalism, class structure and political power rather than applying a rigorous comparative methodology. Post-modernism and post-colonialism as part of the 'cultural turn' in the social sciences, sociology and also political sociology renewed cultural-critical analysis and often historicist positions on the uniqueness and authenticity of decentred, fragmented and individualized 'worlds'. In various ways, therefore, critical alternatives against mainstream comparative political macro-sociology also implied a move away from macro-sociological, cross-cultural and quantitative methods towards qualitative, hermeneutic and deconstructive ones.

Against this background of critical moves against modernist political macro-sociology, comparative political sociology increasingly looked to the analysis of the micro-foundation of politics. This trend towards context-specific, time/space-bound or grounded comparisons continued in social-scientific as well as cultural-scientific modes of analysis. On the social-scientific side, there developed particularly three types of causal analysis.

1. The comparative macro-analysis of specific path-dependent configurations (in contrast to the application of theoretical models or interpretive analysis, see Skocpol, 1984, also Rueschemeyer et al., 1992: 12–39);
2. Comparisons of the social mechanisms of political processes that sought variation (in contrast to generalizing, individualizing or encompassing comparisons, eg., Tilly, 1984); and
3. General models of rational choices as basis of social actions in institutional contexts.

On the cultural-scientific side, there can be distinguished individualising comparisons between a few cases (Skocpol, 1984); contrasting deconstructive comparisons of different cultural institutions, symbolic systems, meaning structures or discourses (Sewell, 1998; 2005); as well as intercultural or transcultural comparisons of mutual communication, perception, definition of self and the other and understanding (Matthes, 1992). A few attempts have been also made to combine quantitative and qualitative methods of comparative inquiry, particularly Charles Ragin (1987, 2000) or Andrew Abbott (2001), but these have been rarely applied in actual political-sociological studies.

The renewal of political macro-sociology has meant continued comparative research characterized by the use of quantitative multivariate methods in cross-cultural comparisons (Dogan and Pelassy, 1984). The scope of international comparisons has decisively expanded with the third wave of democratization and related transition and transformation research. At the same time, the renewal of political macro-sociology has included also cultural-constructive approaches, such as the multiple modernities perspective, thus requiring configurative, cultural and individualising comparative methods on the macro-level, particularly in the form of inter-civilizational comparisons. In addition, the intensifying globalization processes in the context of a developing global system require new methods of relational comparisons, starting from the premise of entangled rather than independent units of analysis (Kaelble and Schwierer, 2003). Regarding the analysis of general patterns of globalization, generalizing, data-based, multivariate comparisons are generally used, but the analysis of different forms of globalizations or 'glocalizations' (interconnecting the global and the local) require again context-bound, variation-finding or cultural comparative methods (cf., Landman, 2003).

The complex space of comparative methodology in political sociology is thus characterized by an increasing methodical pluralism, but at the same time there is also, under the pressures of academic specialization, a tendency towards intra- and interdisciplinary compartmentalisation and segmentation. The challenging task therefore is to combine more strategically than often done the different comparative methods on the levels of epistemologies, theoretical approaches, research strategies and research agendas. This would particularly require to link comparisons of socio-political macro-configurations with comparisons of institutional meso-settings as well as micro-levels of individual and collective action; to bring together social-scientific quantitative and cultural-scientific case-oriented comparisons; to make systematic use of historical comparative analyses; and to concentrate, under the conditions of an increasingly globalizing world, on the varying entanglements between the global, the national and the local. A crucial academic precondition for attacking this task would be to enhance considerably intra-, inter-disciplinary and trans-disciplinary cooperation in political sociology and its reference disciplines of sociology and political science (Hall, 1999).

NOTES

1. There is no generally agreed definition of political sociology; it changes with the contours of this interdisciplinary undertaking in the context of its

changing subject. On the one hand, the meaning of the 'social' creates problems: in many definitions it is identical with society, but with the questioning of the boundaries of the nation-state by transnational and global processes, it is seen as complex social network not necessarily coextensive with national boundaries (e.g., Braungart and Braungart, 2000: 197). Moreover, the concentration on the social basis of politics often implies the exclusion of the 'cultural'. On the other, the meaning of 'politics' delineates the political to state, governmental and political institutions instead of taking also into account the pervasive role of power relations through the whole socio-political space. As well, it tends to abstract from the cultural frames and components of the political and power (cf., Nash, 2000: 1ff., calling for a new political sociology).

2. In contrast to Francis Fukuyama (2006) in his preface to the new edition of Samuel Huntington (1968, 2003), I hold the view that the self-critical revision of modernization theory by giving up the structural-functionalist and evolutionary framework does not mean the end of modernization theory as such. Rather, the basic categories of modernization remain in place, now conceived of as analytical tools in search for causal explanations; as a set of normative-ideal-typical orientations instead of universal real types of socio-political evolution; and as political developments based on agency and culture rather than objective processes of structural evolution (Tiryakian, 1990). In this sense, mainstream modernization theory has moved from structural-functional system theory of socio-political evolution to a historical-contextual and agency based analytical framework. At the same time, this revisionism does not prevent the predominant mainstream projection of Western modernity to the political development in European history as well as non-Western societies.

REFERENCES

Abbott, A. (2001) *Time matters: On theory and method*. Chicago: Chicago University Press.

Adams, J., Clemens, E. and Orloff, A. (eds) (2005) *Remaking modernity. Politics, history, and sociology*. Durham, London: Duke University Press.

Albrow, M. (1996) *The global age*. CA: Stanford University Press.

Alexander, J. (1994) 'Modern, anti, post, and neo: How social theories tried to understand the 'new world' of 'our time'', *Zeitschrift für Soziologie*, 23 (1): 165–97.

Almond, G. and Bingham Powell G. (1966) *Comparative politics: a developmental approach*. Boston: Little, Brown.

Almond, G. and Verba, S. (1963) *The civic culture. Political attitudes and democracy in five nations*. Newbury Park, CA: Sage.

Anderson, B. (1983) *Imagined communities*. London: Verso.

Anderson, P. (1979) *Passages from antiquity to feudalism*. London: Verso.

Anderson, P. (1980) *Lineages of the absolutist state*. London: Verso.

Anderson, P. (1991) *The origins of postmodernism*. London: Verso.

Andrain, C.F. and Apter, D.E. (1995) *Political protest and social change. Analyzing politics*. London: Macmillan.

Apter, D. (1965) *The politics of modernization*. Chicago: The Chicago University Press.

Archer, M. (2000) *Being human: The problem of agency*. Cambridge: Cambridge University Press.

Arjomand, S. and Tiryakian, E. (2004) *Rethinking civilizational analysis*. Leiden: Brill.

Arnason, J. (2003) *Civilizations in dispute: Historical questions and theoretical questions*. Leiden: Brill

Arnason, J., Eisenstadt, S. and Wittrock, B. (2005) *Axial age civilizations and world history*. Leiden: Brill.

Aron, R. (1950) 'Social Structure and the Ruling Class', *British Journal of Sociology*, 1(1) 1–16 and 1(2)126–143.

Aron, R. (1967) *Eighteen lectures on industrial society*. London: Weidenfeld and Nicolson.

Bach, M. (ed.) (2000) *Europäisierung nationaler gesellschaften*. Opladen: Westdeutscher Verlag.

Barnes, S.H. and Simon, J. (eds) (1998) *The postcommunist citizen*. Budapest: Erasmus Foundation.

Bartolovich, C. and Lazarus, N. (eds) (2002) *Marxism, modernity and postcolonial studies*. Cambridge, UK: Cambridge University Press.

Bayart, J.-F. (1993) *The state in Africa*. Oxford: Oxford University Press.

Beichelt, T., Chotuj, B., Rowe, G. and Wagner, H.-J. (2006) *Europastudien*. Eine Einführung, Wiesbaden: Verlag für Sozialwissenschaften.

Bellah, R. (1981) *Varieties of civil religion*. New York.

Bendix, R. (ed.) (1973) *State and society. A reader in comparative political sociology*. Berkeley: University of California Press.

Bendix, R. (1977) *Nation-building and citizenship*. Berkeley: University of California Press.

Bendix, R. (1978) *Kings and people*. Berkeley: University of California Press.

Bendix, R. and Lipset, S.M. (1967) 'The field of political sociology', in L. Coser (ed.), *Political sociology*. New York: Harper and Row, pp. 9–47.

Berger, P. and Huntington, S. (2002) *Globalizations*. Princeton, NJ: Princeton University Press.

Binder, L., Coleman, J. S., LaPalombara, J., Pye, L.W., Verba, S. and Weiner, M. (eds) (1971) *Crises and sequences in political development*. NJ: Princeton University Press.

Black, C. (1966) *Dynamics of modernization*. New York: Harper & Row.

Bollen, K.A. (1980) 'Issues in the comparative measurement of political democracy', *American Sociological Review*, 45 (2): 370–90.

Bönker, F., Müller, K. and Pickel, A. (eds) (2002) *Postcommunist transformation in the social sciences*. Lanham, RI: Roweman & Littlefield.

Bottomore, T. (1979) *Political sociology*. New York: Harper and Row.

Bourdieu, P. (1984) *Distinction: A social critique of the judgement of taste*. Trans. R. Nice. London: Routledge.

Bourdieu, P. (1987) *Outline of a theory of practice*. Cambridge: Cambridge University Press.

Braungart, R.G. and Braungart, M.M. (2000) 'International political sociology', *Current Sociology*, 50 (2): 197–217.

Bremmer, I. and Taras, R. (Eds.) (1997) *New states, new politics: Building the post–soviet nations*. New York: Cambridge University Press.

Brubaker, R. (1992) *Citizenship and nationhood in France and Germany*. Cambridge, MA: Harvard University Press.

Bryant, C. and Hall, J.A. (eds) (1994) *Civil society. Theoretical, historical and comparative perspectives*. Cambridge, MA: Cambridge University Press.

Carruthers, B.G. (2005) 'The sociology of money and credit', in N. Smelser and R. Swedberg (eds), *The handbook of economic sociology* (2nd edition). Princeton, NJ: Princeton University Press, pp. 355–78.

Casanova, J. (1994) *Public religions in the modern world*. Chicago: Chicago University Press.

Centeno, M. and Alves–Lopez, J. (2001) *The other mirror. Grand theory in the lens of Latin–America*. NJ: Princeton University Press.

Charrad, M. (2001) *States and women's rights: The making of postcolonial Tunisia, Algeria, and Morocco*. Berkeley: University of California Press.

Chase-Dunn, C. (1991) *Global formations*. Cambridge, MA: Cambridge University Press.

Chaturvedi, V. (ed.) (2000) *Mapping subaltern studies and the postcolonial*. London: Verso.

Chilcote, R. (1994) *Theories of comparative politics* (2nd ed.) Boulder, CO: Westview Press.

Chirot, D. (1996) *Modern tyrants*. Berkeley: University of California Press.

Collier, D. (1991) 'The comparative method: Two decades of change', in D. Rustow and K. Erickson (eds.), *Comparative political dynamics*. New York: HarperCollins.

Collins, R. (1968) 'A comparative approach to political sociology', in R. Bendix (ed.), *State and Society*. Berkeley: University of California Press.

Comaroff, J. and Comaroff, J. (1991) *Of revelation and revolution*. Chicago: Chicago University Press.

Conrad, S. and Randeria, S. (eds) (2002) *Jenseits des eurozentrismus. Postkoloniale perspektiven in den geschichts - und kulturwissenschaften*. Frankfurt/M.: Campus.

Cooper, F. (2003) *Colonialism in question. Theory, knowledge, history*. Berkeley: University of California Press.

Coser, L.A. (ed.) (1967) *Political sociology*. New York: Harper & Row.

Dahl, R.A. (1971) *Polyarchy: Participation and opposition*. New Haven, CT: Yale University Press.

Dahrendorf, R. (1965) *Gesellschaft und freiheit in deutschland*. München: Piper.

Dawisha, K. and Parrot, B. (eds) (1997) *The consolidation of democracy in east–central Europe*. MA: Cambridge University Press.

De Swaan, A. (1988) *In care of the state: Health care, education and welfare in Europe and the USA*, Cambridge: Polity Press.

Deutsch, K. (1966) *Nationalism and social communication. An inquiry in the foundations of nationality*. Cambridge, MA: MIT Press. (Original work published 1953).

Diamond, L. (1999) *Developing democracy*. Baltimore, MD: The Johns Hopkins University Press.

Diamond, L. and Plattner, M. (2002) *Democracy after communism*. Baltimore, MD: The John Hopkins University Press.

Diamond, L., Linz, J. and Lipset, S.M. (1995) *Politics in developing countries: comparing experiences with democracy*. Boulder, CO: Rienner Publishers.

Dogan, M. and Pelassy, D. (1984) *How to compare nations: Strategies in comparative politics*. Chatham, NJ: Chatham House.

Domhoff, G.W. (1967) *Who rules America?* Englewood Cliffs, NJ: Prentice Hall.

Domhoff, G.W. (2001) *Who rules America? Power and politics*. Boston: McGraw-Hill.

Dornbos, M. and Kaviraj, S. (eds) (1997) *Dynamics of state formation. India and Europe*. New York: Sage.

Durkheim, E. (1982) *The rules of sociological method*. New York: The Free Press.

Duverger, M. (1972) *The study of politics*. London: Nelson.

Easton, D. (1953) *The political system: An inquiry into the state of political science*. New York: A. Knopf.

Eckstein, H. (1971) A perspective on comparative politics, past and present. In H. Eckstein, H. and D. Apter (eds), *Comparative politics. A reader*. New York: The Free Press, pp. 1–33.

Eder, K. and Giesen, B. (2002) *European citizenship*. Oxford: Oxford University Press.

Eder, K. and Spohn, W. (2005) *European identity and collective memory. The effects of integration and enlargement*. Aldershot: Ashgate.

Eisenstadt, S.N. (1963) *Political systems of empire*. New Brunswick, NJ: Transaction Publisher.

Eisenstadt, S.N. (1966) *Modernization. Protest and change*. Englewood, NJ: Prentice-Hall.

Eisenstadt, S.N. (1971) 'General introduction: The scope and development of political sociology', in S.N. Eisenstadt (ed.), *Political sociology. A reader*. New York: Basic Books, pp. 3–23.

Eisenstadt, S.N. (ed.) (1971) *Political sociology. A reader*. New York: Basic Books.

Eisenstadt, S.N. (1987) *The European civilization in comparative perspective*. Oslo: Scandinavian University Press.

Eisenstadt, S.N. (ed.) (1989) *Patterns of modernization* (2 vols.) Leiden: Brill.

Eisenstadt, S.N. (1992) *Jewish civilization. The Jewish historical experience in comparative perspective*. New York: State University of New York Press.

Eisenstadt, S.N. (1996) *The Japanese civilization. A Comparative View*. Chicago: Chicago University Press.

Eisenstadt, S.N. (1999a) *Paradoxes of democracy*. Baltimore, MD: The Johns Hopkins University Press.

Eisenstadt, S.N. (1999b) *Fundamentalism, sectarianism and revolution: The Jacobin Dimension of Modernity*. Cambridge: Cambridge University Press.

Eisenstadt, S.N. (ed.) (2002) *Multiple modernities*. New Brunswick: Transaction Publishers.

Eisenstadt, S.N. and Rokkan, S. (eds) (1973) *Building states and nations*. Beverly Hills: Sage.

Eisenstadt, S.N., Roniger, L. and Seligman, A. (1987) *Centre formation, protest movements and class structure in Europe and the United States*. Leiden: Brill.

Ertmann, T. (1997) *Birth of the Leviathan. Building states and regimes in early modern Europe*. Cambridge, MA: Cambridge University Press.

Esping-Andersson, G. (1990) *Three worlds of welfare capitalism*. Princeton, NJ: Princeton University Press.

Evans, P., Rueschemeyer, D. and Skocpol, T. (1985) *Bringing the state back in*. Cambridge, UK: Cambridge University Press

Ferguson, J. (2006) *Global shadows. Africa in the neo-liberal world order*. Durham, NC: Duke University Press.

Finkle, J. and Gable, R. (eds.) (1966) *Political development and social change*. New York: John Wiley.

Fobden, S. and Hobson, J.M. (2002) *Historical sociology and international relations*. Cambridge: Cambridge University Press.

Foucault, M. (1972) *The archaeology of knowledge*. London: Tavistock.

Fukuyama, F. (2006) 'Foreword', in S.P. Huntington, *Political Order in Changing Societies*. Yale: Yale University Press.

Geertz, C. (1963) *Old societies and new states. The quest for modernity in Asia and Africa*. London: Free Press.

Gellner, E. (1983) *Nations and nationalism*. London: Verso.

Giddens, A. (1973) *The class structure of the advanced societies*. London: Hutchinson.

Giddens, A. (1985) *Nation-state and violence*. Berkeley: University of California Press.

Goldstone, J. (1991) *Revolution and rebellion in the early modern world*. Berkeley: University of California Press.

Goldstone, J. (1997) 'Methodological issues in comparative macro-sociology', *Comparative Social Research*, 16: 107–20.

Gorski, P. (2003) *The disciplinary revolution. Calvinism, confessionalism and the growth of state power in early modern Europe*. Chicago: Chicago University Press.

Grabbe, H. (2006) *The EU's transformative power. Europeanization through conditionality in Central and Eastern Europe*. Palgrave, Macmillan.

Gramsci, A. (1971) *Selections from prison notebooks*. London: Lawrence and Wishart.

Grancelli. B. (ed.) (1995) *Social change and modernization. Lessons from eastern Europe*. Berlin: Gruyter.

Graziano, P. and Vink, M. (eds) (2007) *Europeanization: New research agendas*. Basingstoke: Palgrave Macmillan.

Greenfield, L. (1993) *Nationalism. Five roads to modernity*. Cambridge, MA: Harvard University Press.

Grew, R. (1978) *Crisis of political development in Europe and the United States*. Princeton, NJ: Princeton University Press.

Habermas, J. (1989) *The structural transformation of the public sphere. An inquiry into a category of bourgeois society*. Cambridge, MA: MIT Press.

Hall, J.A. (1986) *International orders*. Oxford: Polity Press.

Hall, J.A. and Schroeder, R. (Eds.) (2006) *An anatomy of power. The social theory of Michael Mann*. Cambridge: Cambridge University Press.

Hall, J.R. (1999) *Cultures of inquiry. From epistemology to discourse in sociohistorical research*. Cambridge: Cambridge University Press.

Hall, P. and Taylor, R. (1996) 'Political science and the three institutionalisms', *Political Studies*, 44 (3): 936–57.

Haynes, J. (1998) *Religion in global politics*. New York: Longman.

Haynes, J. (2005) *Comparative politics in a globalizing world*. Oxford: Polity Press.

Hechter, M. (1975) *Internal colonialism. The Celtic fringe in British national development, 1536–1966*. London: Routledge.

Hedström, P. and Swedberg, R. (eds) (1998) *Social mechanism: An analytical approach to social theory*. New York: Cambridge University Press.

Held, D. (2005) *Democracy and the global order*. Cambridge, UK: Polity.

Held, D., McGrew, A., Goldblatt, D. and Perraton, J. (1999) *Global transformations: Politics, economics and culture*. Oxford: Polity Press.

Hoogvelt, A. (1997) *Globalization and the postcolonial world*. London: McMillan.

Huber, E. and Stephens, J. (2001) *Development and crisis of the welfare state. Parties and policies in global markets*. Chicago, IL: University of Chicago Press.

Huntington, S.P. (1968/2003) *Political order in changing societies*. New Haven: Yale University Press.

Huntington, S.P. (1991) *The third wave: Democratization in the late twentieth century*. Norman, OK: University of Oklahoma Press.

Huntington, S.P. (1996) *The clash of civilizations*. Princeton, NJ: Princeton University Press.

Ichijo, A. and Spohn, W. (Eds.) (2005) *Entangled identities. Europe and the nation*. Aldershot: Ashgate.

Inglehardt, R. (1990) *Culture shift in advanced industrial society*. Princeton, NJ: Princeton University Press.

Inglehardt, R. (1997) *Modernization and postmodernization*. Princeton, NJ: Princeton University Press.

Inglehardt, R. (2006) *Modernization, postmodernization and democracy*. Cambridge, UK: Cambridge University Press.

Janoski, T., Alford, R., Hicks, A. and Schwartz, M. (Eds.) (2004) *The handbook of political* sociology. *States, civil society and globalization*. Cambridge, MA: Cambridge University Press.

Janoski, T. and Wang, F. (2004) 'The politics of immigration and national integration', in T. Janoski, R.R. Alford, A.M. Hicks, and M.A. Schwartz (eds), *The handbook of political sociology*. Cambridge, MA: Cambridge University Press, pp. 630–54.

Joppke, C. (1999) *Immigration and the nation–state, the United States, Germany and Great Britain*. Oxford, UK: Oxford University Press.

Kaelble, H. and Schwierer, J. (eds) (2003) *Transfer und vergleich. Komparatistik in den sozial-, geschichts – und kulturwissenschaften*. Frankfurt/M: Campus.

Kamrava, M. (1993) *Politics and society in the third world*. London: Routledge.

Katzenstein, P. and Byrnes, T. (eds) (2004) *Religion in an expanding Europe*. Cambridge: Cambridge University Press.

Katznelson, I. and Zolberg, A. (eds) (1986) *Working-class formation*. Princeton, NJ: Princeton University Press.

Keane, J. (ed.) (1988) *Civil society and the state: New European Perspectives*. London: Verso.

Keane, J. (1998) *Civil society*. Cambridge: Polity Press.

Kimmerling, B. (ed.) (1996) Trend report: Political sociology at the crossroads?, *Current Sociology*, 44 (3), 152–76.

Kiser, E. and Hechter, M. (1998) 'The debate on historical sociology, rational choice and its critics', *American Journal of Sociology*, 104: 785–816.

Kiser, E. and Kane, J. (2001) 'Revolution and State Structure: The Bureaucratization of Tax Administration in Early Modern England and France', *American Journal of Sociology*, 107 (1): 183–22.

Knöbl, W. (1998) *Polizei und herrschaft im modernisierungsprozess. Staatsbildung und innere sicherheit in Deutschland, England und Amerika, 1770–1914*. Frankfurt/M.: Campus.

Knöbl, W. (2001) *Spielräume der modernisierung. Das ende der eindeutigkeit*. Weilerswist: Vielbrück.

Knoke, D., Pappi, U., Broadbent, J. and Tsujinaka, M. (1996) *Comparing policy networks*. New York: Cambridge University Press.

Kohn, M. (ed) (1989) *Cross-national research in sociology*. Newbury Press.

Kumar, K. (2000) 'Industrialization and modernization', in M. Waters (ed.), *Modernity. Critical concepts*. London: Routledge.

Kumar, K. (2005) *From post-industrial to post-modern society*. London: Routledge.

Laclau, E. and Mouffe, C. (2001) *Hegemony and socialist strategy. Towards a radical democratic politics* (2nd edition) London: Verso.

Laitin, D. (1992) *Language repertoires and state construction in Africa*. Cambridge: Cambridge University Press.

Landman, T. (2003) *Issues and methods in comparative politics. An introduction* (2nd edition) London: Routledge.

LaPalombara, J. (ed.) (1963) *Bureaucracy and political development*. Princeton, NJ: Princeton University Press.

Latham, M. (1997) *Modernization as ideology. American social science and 'nation–building' in the Kennedy era*. Duke, NC: University of North Carolina Press.

Lazarus, N. (2001) 'Unsystematic fingers at the conditions of the times: "Afropop" and the paradoxes of imperialism', in G. Castle (ed.), *Postcolonial Discourses*. Oxford, Blackwell, pp. 232–50.

Lechner, F. and Boli, J. (2001) *Globalization. A reader*. London: Sage.

Lehmbruch, G. and Scharpf, F. (2000) *Europäische sozialpolitik*. Frankfurt/M: Suhrkamp.

Lerner, D. (1965) *The passing of traditional society. Modernizing the Middle East*. New York: Freedom.

Levi, M. (1988) *Of rule and revenue*. Berkley, CA: University of California Press.

Linz, J. (2006) *Robert Michels, political sociology, and the future of democracy*. New Brunswick, NJ: Transaction Publisher.

Linz, J. and Stepan, A. (1996) *Problems of transition and consolidation of democracy. Southern Europe, South America and postcommunist Eastern Europe*. Baltimore, MD: The Johns Hopkins University Press.

Lipset, S.M. (1959) *Political man: The social bases of politics*. Garden City, NY: Doubleday.

Lipset, S.M. (1984) 'Social conflict, legitimacy and democracy', in W. Connolly (ed.),

Legitimacy and the state. New York: New York University Press, pp. 88–103.

Lipset, S.M. (1994) 'The social requisites of democracy revisited', *American Sociological Review*, 59 (1): 1–22.

Lipset, S.M. (ed.) (1998) *Democracy in Europe and the Americas*. Washington, DC: Congressional Quarterly.

Lipset, S.M. and Rokkan, S. (1967) *Party systems and voter alignments: Cross–national perspectives*. New York: Free Press.

Lister, R. (2002) 'Citizenship and gender', in K. Nash and A. Scott (eds), *The Blackwell companion to political sociology*. Cambridge, UK: Blackwell, pp. 323–32.

Loth, W. and Wessels, W. (eds) (2001) *Theorien europäischer integration*. Opladen: Westdeutscher Verlag.

Lukes. S. (1972) *Emile Durkheim: His life and work*. New York: Harper & Row.

Mahoney, J. and Rueschemeyer, D. (2003) *Historical analysis in the social sciences*. Cambridge: Cambridge University Press.

Mann, M. (1986/1993) *The sources of social power* (2 vols.) Cambridge. MA: Cambridge University Press.

Mann M. (1997) 'Has globalization ended the rise and rise of the nation-state?', *Review of International Political Economy*, 4 (3): 472–96.

Marginson, P. and Sisson, K. (2006) *European integration and industrial relations. Multi-level governance in the making*. New York: Palgrave.

Marks, G. and Lipset, S. (1998) *Reexamining democracy*. Newbury Park, CA: Sage.

Marshall, T. (1964) *Class, citizenship and social development*. Garden City, NY: Doubleday.

Martinelli, A. (2005) *Global modernization. Rethinking the project of modernity*. London: Sage.

Marx, A. (1998) *Making race and nation. A comparison of Brazil. South Africa and the United States*. Cambridge, MA: Cambridge University Press.

Matthes, J. (1992) 'The operation called verstehen', in J. Matthes (ed.), *Zwischen den kulturen?* Göttingen: Vandenhoek & Ruprecht. pp. 75–99.

McAdam, D., Tarrow, S. and Tilly, C. (2003) 'Dynamics of contention', *Social Movement Studies*, 2 (1), 99–102.

McDaniel, T. (1989) *Autocracy, modernization and revolution in Russia*. Princeton, NJ: Princeton University Press.

McDaniel, T. (1991) *Autocracy, modernization and revolution in Russia and Iran*. Princeton, NJ: Princeton University Press.

McMichael, P. (2004) *Development and social change* (3rd edition) Thousand Oaks, CA: Pine Forge.

Menzel, U. (2000) *Globalisierung und fragmentierung*. Frankfurt/M: Suhrkamp.

Meyer, J., Boli, J., Thomas, G. and Ramirez, F. (1997) 'World society and the nation-state', *American Journal of Sociology*, 103: 144–81.

Miliband, R. (1977) *Marxism and politics*. Oxford: Oxford University Press.

Mill, J. S. (1872) *On Liberty*. Boston: James R. Osgood.

Mills, C. W. (1956) *The power elite*. New York: Oxford University Press.

Mommsen, W. and Osterhammel, J. (1987) *Max Weber and his contemporaries*. London: Hyman.

Moore, B. (1966) *Social Origins of Dictatorship and Democracy. Lord and peasant in the making of the modern world*. Boston: Beacon Press.

Moore, B. (1981) *Social injustice. The social bases of obedience and revolt*. Cambridge, MA: Cambridge University Press.

Nash, K. (2000) *Contemporary political sociology. Globalization, politics and power*. Oxford: Blackwell.

Nash, K. (2001) 'The cultural turn in social theory: towards a theory of cultural politics', *Sociology*, 35 (1): 77–92.

Nash, K. and Scott, A. (2004) *The Blackwell companion to political sociology*. Oxford: Blackwell.

Nedelmann, B. (1997) 'Between national socialism and real socialism: Political sociology in the federal republic of Germany', *Current Sociology*, 45: 157–86.

Offe, C. (1972) *Strukturprobleme des kapitalistischen Staates; Aufsätze zur politischen Soziologie*. Frankfurt am Main: Suhrkamp.

Offe, C. and Keane, J. (1984) *Contradictions of the welfare state*. Cambridge, MA: MIT Press.

Orloff, A. (1993) *The politics of pensions: A comparative analysis of Britain, Canada and the United States, 1880s–1940*. Madison: The University of Wisconsin Press.

Orum, A.M. (1983) 'Political sociology', in N. Smelser (ed.), *Handbook of sociology*. Newbury Park: Sage.

Orum, A.M. (1996) 'Almost a half century of political sociology: Trends in the United States', *Current Sociology*, 44: 132–51.

Osterhammel, J. and Petersson, N. (2003) *History of globalization. Dimension, processes, epochs*. Princeton, NJ: Princeton University Press.

Owen, D. (2000) 'Postmodern political sociology', in K. Nash and A. Scott (eds), *The Blackwell companion to political sociology*. Oxford: Cambridge University Press, pp. 71–81.

Parsons, T. (1977) *Societies. Evolutionary and comparative perspectives*. Englewood Cliffs, NJ: Prentice Hall.

Poggi, G. (1978) *The development of the modern state: A sociological introduction*. Stanford: Stanford University Press.

Poggi, G. (1990) *The state: Its nature, development and prospect*. Stanford, CA: Stanford California Press.

Poggi, G. (2001) *Forms of power*. Malden, MA: Polity Press.

Poulantzas, N. (1973) *Political power and social classes*. London: Verso.

Przeworski, A. and Teune, H. (1970) *The Logic of comparative social inquiry*. New York: Wiley-Interscience.

Putnam, R. (1993) *Making democracy work: Civic traditions in modern Italy*. Princeton, NJ: Princeton University Press.

Pye, L. and Verba, S. (1965) *Political culture and political development*. Princeton, NJ: Princeton University Press.

Ragin, C. (1987) *The comparative method. Moving beyond qualitative and quantitative strategies*. Berkeley, CA: University of California Press.

Ragin, C. (2000) *Fuzzy-set social science*. Chicago: Chicago University Press.

Robertson, R. (1992) *Globalization. Social theory and global culture*. London: Routledge.

Rokkan, S., Flora, P., Kuhnle, S. and Urwin, D.W. (Eds) (1999) *State formation, nation-building and mass politics in Europe: The theory of Stein Rokkan*. Oxford, UK: Oxford University Press.

Roniger, L. and Waisman, C. (eds) (2002) *Globality and multiple modernities. North and Latin America in comparative perspective*. Brighton, UK: Sussex Academic Press.

Rucht, D. (1990) *Modernisierung und soziale bewegung, Deutschland, Frankreich und USA Im Vergleich*. Frankfurt/M: Campus.

Rueschemeyer, D. (2003) 'Comparative historical analysis and knowledge accumulation in the social sciences', in J. Mahoney and D. Rueschemeyer (eds), *Comparative historical analysis in the social sciences*. Cambridge: Cambridge University Press, pp. 3–39.

Rueschemeyer, D., Huber-Stephens, E. and Stephens, J. (1992) *Democracy and capitalist development*. Chicago: Chicago University Press.

Rueschemeyer, D. and Rueschemeyer, M. (eds) (1998) *Participation and democracy East and West. Comparisons and Interpretations*. Amonk, NY: Sharpe.

Sachsenmeyer. D. and Riedel, J. (eds) (2002) *Reflections on multiple modernities, European, Chinese and other interpretations*. Brill: Leiden.

Said, E. (1979) Orientalism. New York: Vintage.

Scholte, J-A. (2000) *Globalization. A critical introduction*. New York: Palgrave

Scholte, J-A. (2002) *Governing global finance*. Coventry: University of Warwick.

Schudson, M. and Waisbrod, S. (2004) 'Toward a political sociology of the new Media', in T. Janoski, R.R. Alford, A.M. Hicks, and M.A. Schwartz (eds), *The Handbook of political sociology*. Cambridge: Polity, pp. 350–365.

Schwinn, T. (ed.) (2006) *Vielfalt und einheit der moderne*. Wiesbaden: Verlag für Sozialwissenschaften.

Scott, J. (1991) *Who Rules Britain?* Cambridge: Polity

Sewell, W. (1998) 'Are cultural history and comparative method compatible?', in W. Spohn (ed.), *Kulturanalyse und vergleichende forschung. Comparativ* 8 (1): 89–93.

Sewell, W. (2005) *Logics of history. Social theory and social transformation*. Chicago: Chicago University Press.

Shils, E. (1977) *Center and periphery. Essays in macro-sociology*. Chicago: Chicago University Press.

Skocpol, T. (1979) *States and social revolutions*. Cambridge, MA: Harvard University Press.

Skocpol, T. (ed.) (1984) *Vision and method in historical sociology*. Cambridge: Cambridge University Press.

Skocpol, T. (1992) *Protecting soldiers and mothers: The political origins of social policy in the United States.* MA: Belknap Press of Harvard University Press.

Smelser, N. (1976) *Comparative methods in the social sciences.* Englewood Cliffs

Smith, A. (1986) *Ethnic origins of nations.* Cambridge: Cambridge University Press.

Smith, A. (2001) *Nationalism.* Oxford: Oxford University Press.

So, A. (1990) *Social change and development. Modernization, dependency and world-system theories.* London: Sage.

Soysal, Y. (1994) *Limits of Citizenship. Migrants and post-national membership in Europe.* Berkeley, CA: University of California Press.

Spohn, W. (1998) 'Cultural analysis and comparison in historical sociology', in W. Spohn (ed.), *Kulturanalyse und vergleichende forschung.* Comparativ, pp. 94–120.

Spohn, W. (2001) 'History and the social sciences', in L. Baltes and N. Smelser (eds), *International encyclopaedia of the social and behavioral sciences* (vol. X) London: Elsivier, pp. 6829–35.

Spohn, W. (2003) 'Nationalismus und religion in West- und Osteuropa. Ein historisch-soziologischer ansatz', in M. Minkenberg and U. Willems (eds), *Politik und religion,* Politische Vierteljahresschrift 33.

Spohn, W. and Triandafyllidou, A. (2003) *Europeanization, national identities and migration. Changes in boundary constructions between Western and Eastern Europe.* London: Routledge.

Squire, J. (2004) 'Feminism and democracy', in K. Nash and A. Scott (eds), *The Blackwell companion to political sociology.* Cambridge, UK: Blackwell, pp. 366–74.

Steinmetz, G. (ed.) (1999) *State/culture: State formation after the cultural turn.* Ithaca, NY: Cornell University Press.

Stompka, P. (1994) *The sociology of social change.* Chicago: University of Chicago Press.

Tarrow, S. and Tilly, C. (2007) *Contentious politics.* Boulder, CO: Paradigm.

Thelen, K. (1999) 'Historical institutionalism in comparative politics', *Annual Review of Political Science,* 2: 369–404.

Therborn, G. (1978) *What does the ruling class do when it rules? State apparatuses and state power under feudalism, capitalism and socialism.* London: New Left Books.

Therborn, G. (1995) *European modernity and beyond. The trajectory of European societies, 1945–2000.* London: Sage.

Thompson, E.P. (1963) *The making of the English working class.* Harmondsworth: Penguin.

Tilly, C. (1968) *The vendée.* Cambridge, MA: Harvard University Press.

Tilly, C. (ed.) (1975) *The formation of national states in Western Europe.* Princeton, NJ: Princeton University Press.

Tilly, C. (1978) *From mobilization to revolution.* Reading, MA: Addison-Wesley.

Tilly, C. (1984) *Big structures, large processes, huge comparisons.* New York: Russell Sage Foundation.

Tilly, C. (1990) *Coercion, capital and European states, AD 990–1990.* Oxford: Blackwell.

Tipps, D. (1973) 'Modernization theory and the comparative study of societies: A critical perspective', *Comparative Studies in Society and History,* 15 (2): 199–226.

Tiryakian, E. (1990) 'Modernization. Exhumetur in pace. Rethinking macro-sociology in the 1990s', *International Sociology,* 6 (2): 165–80.

Tiryakian, E.A. (1995) 'Collective effervescence, social change and charisma: Durkheim, Weber and 1989', *International Sociology: Journal of the International Sociological Association,* 10 (3): 269.

Vallier, I. (ed.) (1971) *Comparative methods in sociology.* Berkeley, CA: University of California Press.

Vanhanen, T. (1997) *Prospects of democracy: A study of 172 countries.* London: Routledge.

Wallace, H. and Wallace, W. (2004) *Policymaking in the European Union.* Oxford: Oxford University Press.

Wallerstein, I. (1999) *The essential Wallerstein.* Cambridge: Cambridge University Press.

Waters, M. (1995) *Globalization.* London: Routledge.

Weber, M. (1951) *The methodology of the social sciences.* New York: Free Press.

Wiener, A. and Diez, T. (2004) *European integration theory.* Oxford: Oxford University Press.

Weiner, M. (1966) *Modernization. The dynamics of growth.* New York: Basic Books.

Weir, M., Orloff, A.S. and Skocpol, T. (1988) *The politics of social policy in the United States.* Studies from the project on the federal social role. Princeton, NJ: Princeton University Press.

Weiss, L. (2005) *States in the global economy. Bringing domestic institutions back in.* Cambridge: Cambridge University Press.

Weiss, L. (2007) *The myth of the powerless state*. Hong Kong: UP Publications.

Whitehead, L. (2005) *Latin America. A new interpretation*. Princeton, NJ: Princeton University Press.

Wuthnow, R. (1989) *Communities of discourse: Ideology and social structure in the reformation, enlightenment and European socialism*. Cambridge, MA: Cambridge University Press.

Yack, B. (1997) *The fetishism of modernities: Epochal self-consciousness in contemporary social and political thought*. Notre Dame: Indiana University Press.

Zapf, W. (1965) *Wandlungen der deutschen eliten*. München: Piper.

Zapf, W. (1971) *Die theorien der modernisierung*, Köln: Athenäum.

Zaret, D. (1985) *The heavenly contract: Ideology and organisation in pre–revolutionary puritanism*. Chicago: Chicago University Press.

7

Comparative Institutional Analysis

Vivien A. Schmidt[1]

INTRODUCTION

In recent years, the 'new institutionalism' has become central to the methodological debates in political science. What political scientists mean by new institutionalism, however, beyond the basic tenet that political institutions are key to the study of political action, is often very different. There are, in fact, a variety of 'new institutionalisms' which focus on different objects of study, with different logics of explanation, and with very different ways of conceptualizing not just institutions but also interests, causes, norms, and ideas. Such differing institutionalisms also deal with the question of institutional change in very different ways. It is only very recently, moreover, that scholars within the different institutionalisms have made serious attempts to bridge these differences, mainly on the borderline between approaches.

'New institutionalism' began in the late 1970s and early 1980s with the desire of a wide range of scholars to bring institutions back into the explanation of political action. It was less focused on rejecting the

'old institutionalism' prevalent until the early 1950s, which studied the formal institutions of government, than in countering the behaviorism that had subsequently largely eclipsed the old institutionalism with the study of political behavior (on this history, see Somit and Tanenhaus, 1982; see also Schmidt, 2005). 'New institutionalism' was a response to the absence of institutional analysis in political science, and maintained the importance of considering collective action as collective – through composite or institutional actors – as opposed to reducing political action to its methodological individualist parts. The theoretical core uniting the very disparate kinds of institutionalisms that emerged rejected the proposition that observable behavior was the basic datum of number of different, readily identifiable approaches, divided along continua ranging from universalistic to particularistic generalizations, from positivism to constructivism, and from static to more dynamic explanations of political action.

From the one 'new institutionalism' originally defined in the mid 1980s by James March and Johan Olsen (1984) and the three 'new institutionalisms' elaborated in the mid 1990s by Peter Hall and Rosemary Taylor (1996), we can now identify four main new institutionalist approaches: the three older 'new institutionalisms' – rational choice, historical, and sociological institutionalism – plus a fourth newer 'new institutionalism' – discursive institutionalism. Rational choice institutionalism focuses on rational actors who pursue their preferences following a 'logic of calculation' within political institutions, defined as structures of incentives. Historical institutionalism instead details the development of political institutions, described as regularized patterns and routine practices, which are the (often unintended) outcomes of purposeful choices and historically unique initial conditions in a 'logic of path-dependence.' Sociological institutionalism sees political institutions as socially constituted and culturally framed, with political agents acting according to a 'logic of appropriateness' that follows from culturally-specific rules and norms. Finally, discursive institutionalism considers the ideas and discourse that actors use to devise, deliberate, and/or legitimize political action in institutional context – whether seen as incentive structures, regularized practices, or social constructions – according to a 'logic of communication.'

This chapter analyzes each of the four 'new institutionalisms' in turn in terms of their basic characteristics, their epistemological and ontological presuppositions, their approaches to institutional change, and their benefits and drawbacks. In addition, it considers the ways in which these different approaches have in recent years sought to bridge their differences, in particular in the growing dialogues between rational choice and historical institutionalism on the one hand, historical and sociological institutionalism on the other. Importantly, however, it also shows that the recent turn to ideas and discourse which is in large part responsible for the rise of discursive institutionalism has roots in all three other institutionalist traditions, and represents a natural progression in these three traditions.

RATIONAL CHOICE INSTITUTIONALISM

Rational choice institutionalism emerged from the need to bring institutions back in as a way of explaining outcomes that could not be explained by universal theories of rational action without reference to their institutional context. This began with those interested in American congressional behavior who found that conventional rational choice analyses which predicted instability in congressional decision-making due to uncertainties resulting from the multiplicity of individual preferences and issues (e.g., Riker, 1980) could not explain the unexpected stability of outcomes. They found the answer in the institutional context, in particular, in congressional rules of procedure that lowered the transaction costs of making deals (Shepsle, 1986; Weingast and Marshall, 1988).

Their main object of inquiry, however, was not the institutional context itself but rather the nature of rational action within such institutions. For their methods of explaining such action, moreover, rational choice institutionalists owe much to the 'new economics of organization' focused on property rights, rent-seeking, and transaction costs with regard to the operation and development of institutions (Moe, 1984; Weingast and Marshall, 1988; Williamson, 1975). Thus, they posit rational actors with fixed preferences who calculate strategically to maximize those preferences and who, in the absence of institutions that promote complementary behavior through coordination, confront collective action problems. Such collective action problems include the 'prisoners' dilemma' and the 'tragedy of the commons,' where individual actors' choices can only lead to sub-optimal solutions (Elster and Hylland, 1986; Hardin, 1982; Ostrom, 1990). And they have been elaborated through a variety of theoretical approaches. These include principal agent theories about how 'principals' in national governments maintain control or gain compliance from the 'agents' to which they delegate power, whether in the US (e.g., Cox and McCubbins, 1993; McCubbins and Sullivan, 1987) or in the European Union (Pollack, 1997); and theories about delegation in international organizations (Martin, 2000) or about the collective decision-making traps of supranational regional organizations, such as the European Union (Scharpf, 1999). Moreover, they may explore game-theoretic approaches to democratic transitions (Przeworski, 1991) or offer 'analytic narratives' of individual historical events (Bates et al., 1998).

Rational choice institutionalism focuses on the interests and motivations behind rational actors' behavior within given institutional settings. Its deductive approach to explanation makes it good at capturing the range of reasons actors would normally have for any action, at identifying the institutional incentive structures, at predicting likely outcomes, and at bringing out anomalies or actions that are unexpected given the general theory. However, it has difficulty explaining any anomalies that depart radically from interest-motivated action. And problems with over-generalization abound where the push is toward universalistic generalizations (Scharpf, 1997). Only an approach like 'actor-centered institutionalism' has largely managed to avoid this problem, by developing 'bounded generalizations' about the outcomes of actors' institutionally-constituted strategic interactions through the identification of subsets of cases in which variance in policy outcomes can be explained by variances in the same set of factor constellations (i.e., problems, policy legacies, actors' attributes, and institutional interactions) (Scharpf, 1997). But however 'bounded' the generalizations, rational choice institutionalism's very deductiveness, along with its theoretical generality that starts from universal claims about rationality, make it difficult if not impossible for it to explain any one individual's reasons for action or any particular set of real political events (Green and Shapiro,

1994). Because rational choice institutionalist explanation works at such a high level of abstraction, it offers a very 'thin' definition of rationality in which individuals *qua* individuals are not considered. Moreover, because it has a rather simplistic understanding of human motivation as interest-based, it misses out on the subtleties of human reasons for action (see Mansbridge, 1990).

The rational choice institutionalist approach also has difficulty explaining institutional change over time, given its assumptions about fixed preferences and its focus on equilibrium conditions (see Blyth, 1997; Green and Shapiro, 1994). In addition to being static, it can be highly functionalist, because it tends to explain the origins of an institution largely in terms of its effects; highly intentionalist, because it assumes that rational actors not only perceive the effects of the institutions that affect them but can also create and control them; and highly voluntarist because they see institutional creation as a quasi-contractual process rather than affected by asymmetries of power (see Bates, 1988; Hall and Taylor, 1996: 952).

Moreover, rational choice institutionalists' emphasis on the self-interested nature of human motivation, especially where it is assumed to be economic self-interest, is value-laden, and can appear economically deterministic. Its normativity results from its assumptions that political action is motivated by instrumental rationality alone and that a utilitarian calculus serves as the universal arbiter of justice (e.g., Elster and Hylland, 1986: 22 – see the critique by Immergut, 1998: 14). Moreover, rational choice institutionalists generally tend to see institutions in a positive light (Moe, 2003: 3), and rarely question the institutional rules within which rational actors seek to maximize their utility, either in terms of the justness of the institutional rules, the exercise of institutional power (see Immergut, 1998: 13), or even in terms of efficiency (e.g., North, 1990). A notable exception is Margaret Levi's (1989) Marxian rationalist analysis of the 'predatory' state with regard to tax collection. But mostly, institutions are assumed to be good things that create greater stability for rational actors' utility maximization.

HISTORICAL INSTITUTIONALISM

Historical institutionalism has been much more focused than rational choice institutionalism on the actual institutions, or 'macro-structures,' in which political action occurs. It began in the late-1970s and early- to mid-1980s by 'bringing the state back in' (Evans et al., 1985; Skocpol, 1979; Katzenstein, 1978), with a focus on how the state structured action and on how state capacity and policy legacies structured outcomes. Very quickly, however, historical institutionalists began to disaggregate the state into its component institutional parts (see Blyth and Vargwese, 1999). Their studies included accounts of how structural constraints implicit in France and Britain's socio-economic organization affected their political economic development (Hall, 1986); of how small European states' combination of economic openness with strong welfare states could be explained by historically-developed, corporatist institutional structures (Katzenstein, 1985); and of how past welfare state policies set the conditions for future policies in a comparison of the US and Britain (Pierson, 1994).

Institutions, for the historical institutionalist, are understood not as rationalist structures of incentives but rather as sets of regularized practices with rule-like qualities that structure action and outcomes (see Hall and Thelen, 2006). Historical institutionalists, moreover, are primarily concerned with sequences in development, timing of events, and phases of political change. They examine not just the asymmetries of power related to the operation and development of institutions but also the path-dependencies and unintended consequences that result from such historical development (Hall and Taylor, 1996: 938; Steinmo

et al., 1992; Thelen, 1999). Path-dependency itself ensures that rationality in the strict rational choice sense is present only insofar as institutions are the intended consequences of actors' choices. But this is often not the case, given the unintended consequences of intentional action and the unpredictability of intervening events. As a result, the institutional structures of the historical institutionalists are not as efficient as they appear to rational choice institutionalists.

Moreover, historical institutionalism tends to be less universalistic in its generalizations than rational choice institutionalism while interests are contextual rather than universally defined (Thelen, 1999; Zysman, 1994). The result is less general, more 'mid-range' theory, which tends to focus on changes in a limited number of countries unified in space and/or time or on a specific kind of phenomenon that occurs in or affects a range of countries at one time or across time (Thelen, 1999). But although more particular in its generalizations, the 'new' historical institutionalism rarely stays at the level of the 'mere story-telling' of which it is sometimes accused by rational choice institutionalists. Noticeably absent is the focus on 'great men' or 'great moments' characteristic of more traditional historical approaches in the old institutionalism. In fact, the macro-historical approach prevalent in most accounts tends to emphasize structures and processes much more than the events out of which they are constructed, let alone the individuals whose actions and interests spurred those events. Here, too, then, there are no individual actors as such. What is more, any 'micro-foundational logic' related to strategic action and rationalist calculation is generally missing. Instead, historical institutionalist explanation tends to follow the logic of path-dependency.

In the logic of path dependency, development begins with 'configurative' moments (e.g., Collier and Collier, 1991), 'punctuated equilibrium' (Krasner, 1988), or critical junctures which 'set into motion institutional patterns or event chains (with) deterministic properties' (Mahoney, 2000: 507). Path dependence is a self-reinforcing sequence of events which, through positive feedback or self-reinforcing mechanisms, ensure increasing returns that, if lasting over a very long time, make for a 'deep equilibrium' which is highly resistant to change (Pierson, 2000, 2004). But as a result, historical institutionalism can appear historically deterministic or even mechanistic given the focus on continuities and the assumption that change comes only in bursts, with stasis in between.

A corrective to this problem can be found in the work of Kathleen Thelen (2002, 2004) and Wolfgang Streeck (Streeck and Thelen, 2005), who theorize about the process of incremental change. They argue that the (many) evolutionary changes over time may be as if not more transformative than the (rarer) revolutionary moments, and they therefore replace path dependence with various processes of path renewal, revision, or replacement. They show that institutional evolution results from certain mechanisms of change such as 'displacement' when actors 'defect' from one set of institutions to another; 'layering' in which institutions are amended or added to by reformers; 'drift,' in which institutions increasingly fail to do what had been intended as a result of deliberate neglect; 'conversion' in which institutions are reinterpreted or redirected to new goals, functions, or purposes; 'exhaustion' in which institutions are depleted, and break down (Streeck and Thelen, 2005; Thelen, 2002, 2004). But although this approach effectively put the history back into historical institutionalism, by detailing the full panoply of changes that may occur, and by abandoning historical determinism in favor of historical indeterminacy, it mainly *describes* institutional change. It does not *explain* it. How change is instigated remains unclear, and cannot be adequately explained without adding elements from other analytic approaches (for a fuller discussion, see Schmidt, 2006b).

The main problem for the historical institutionalists, given their emphasis on structures, is how to account for human agency. For this, historical institutionalists mostly turn to analyses that add what Peter Hall and Rosemary Taylor (1996: 940–41) term either a 'calculus' approach – which puts the historical institutionalists closer to the rational choice institutionalists, albeit still with a primacy to historical structures that shape actors' interests – or a 'culture' approach – which puts them closer to the sociological institutionalists, although here historical structures add to norms to give meaning to actors' interests and worldview.

Examples abound in particular on the combination of historical institutionalism with rational choice institutionalism. Ellen Immergut's (1992) comparative study of healthcare reform explains cross-national differences in physicians' calculations of their interests in terms of the way in which governing structures – as veto-points – affect their expectations of future success in limiting (or not) reform efforts. Thelen's (2004) study of institutional change in skills regimes in Britain, Germany, Japan and the United States turns to rationalist accounts of ongoing political negotiation focusing on political coalitions and political conflicts to explain change through layering and conversion. Peter Hall in a collaborative project with David Soskice (2001) embedded a rationalist analysis of firm-centered coordination in a historical institutionalist analysis of the binary division of capitalism into liberal market economies (e.g., Britain) and coordinated market economies (e.g., Germany), in seeking micro-foundations for historical institutionalism. Paul Pierson (2004), finally, in his study of the dimension of time in political analysis has used historical institutionalism to provide a temporal dimension to rational choice institutionalism.

The main question for historical institutionalists who seek to combine their approaches with rational choice institutionalism in an effort to provide micro-foundations is how to reconcile historically evolving institutional rules and shifting actor preferences with rationalist expectations of fixed preferences and stable institutions. Most often, where the rationalist elements in any given analysis become predominant, historical development gives way to rationalist logics of coordinated games and systemic equilibria. Thus, for example, one of the main criticisms of Hall and Soskice's account of the varieties of capitalism is that its emphasis on complementarity and positive feed-back effects from coordination makes for an explanation which is largely static, overly functionalist and path-dependent, and unable to account for change (see Crouch, 2005; Morgan et al., 2005; Schmidt, 2002a; Chapter 3). By the same token, where the historical institutionalist is predominant, as in Streeck and Thelen's (2005) emphasis on incremental change, the rationalist elements remain rather thin. This is because where macro institutions change all the time, it becomes difficult to theorize how they structure individual actors' incentives. Moreover, if some individual actors accept the institutions while others are seeking to redirect or reinterpret them, then actors' preferences are differentially affected by the institutions, and it is impossible a priori to know which ones. Rational choice institutionalist theorizing within the context of incrementalist historical institutionalism is therefore difficult if not impossible, and we are left only with empirical investigation of actors' motivations, their interests, and their ideas within macroinstitutional context (see Schmidt, 2006b).

Although the problems of integrating historical institutionalism and rational choice institutionalism are great, research at the borders of these two institutionalisms remains arguably the most vibrant in political science today. Rational choice institutionalists themselves have sought to bridge the gap as well, as evident from the increasing numbers of collaborative volumes bringing together top rationalist and historical institutionalist scholars (e.g., Katznelson and Weingast, 2005). The main problem with regard to integrating approaches is that historical institutionalist analyses that take on rational institutionalist elements tend to get taken over by them, largely because the very process of translation from historical to rationalist terms leads many to end up speaking a different, primarily rationalist, language (e.g., Pierson, 2004).

SOCIOLOGICAL INSTITUTIONALISM

Sociological institutionalism, much like historical institutionalism, began in the late 1970s, mainly in the sociological sub-field of organizational theory. Sociological institutionalists rejected rationalist assumptions about the rationality and efficiency of organizations in particular, to focus instead on the forms and procedures of organizational life stemming from culturally-specific practices. Although sociological institutionalism has its origins in the writings of organizational theorists (e.g., Meyer and Rowan, 1977; DiMaggio and Powell, 1991), in political science, the seminal work is by James March and Johan Olsen (1989), who argued that cultural as well as historical structures matter, and who have therefore been claimed as often by historical institutionalists as by sociological institutionalists. Sociological institutionalist analyses that are particularly significant for political scientists include Frank Dobbin's (1994) study of nineteenth century railways policy, where reasonably similar policies were 'concealed' as state actions in the United States but 'revealed' as state actions in France; Neil Fligstein's (1990) account of the transformation of corporate control as resulting from change not just in economic environments but also in corporate leaders' perceptual lenses; and Yasemin Soysal's (1994) contrast of immigration policy in Europe and America, which showed the importance of distinctive 'incorporation regimes' for absorbing immigrants based on differing models of citizenship. The field of international relations, when not rationalist, has been particularly affected by sociological institutionalism (see Finnemore, 1996), although it goes under the rubric of 'constructivism.' Most notable has been Peter Katzenstein's (1996) edited volume which focuses on how interests develop from state identities, with norms acting as collective expectations about the proper behavior for a given identity, and with state identities structuring national perceptions of defense and security issues.

Institutions, for the sociological institutionalist, are cast neither as rationalist incentive structures nor path-dependent macrostructures but rather as the norms, cognitive frames, and meaning systems that guide human action as well as the cultural scripts and schema diffused through organizational environments, serving symbolic and ceremonial purposes rather than just utilitarian ones. Rationality, moreover, is socially constructed and culturally and historically contingent. It is defined by cultural institutions which set the limits of the imagination, create shared understandings and norms that frame actions, establish basic preferences, shape identity, and influence interests. Moreover, such institutions constitute the setting within which purposive, goal-oriented action is deemed acceptable according to a 'logic of appropriateness' (see March and Olsen, 1989; Meyer and Rowan, 1977; DiMaggio and Powell, 1991; see also Campbell, 2004).

Sociological institutionalism is thus in direct contradiction to rationalists' views of human behavior as following a 'logic of calculation' which is prior to institutions, by which individuals may be affected but not defined. Instead, it assumes that norms, identities, and culture constitute interests, and are therefore *endogenous* because they are embedded in culture, as opposed to *exogenous* (see Ruggie, 1998; Wendt, 1987). As a result of the cultural embeddedness of rationality, however, sociological institutionalism is sometimes accused by rational choice institutionalists of not allowing for general enough explanations, with the 'cultural knowledge' it provides useful mainly as preliminary to rational choice universalization. But when the objects of sociological institutionalism are subsumed under rational choice explanation, often the very essence of sociological institutionalism – the norms, rules, and reasons which are culturally unique or

anomalous because they do not fit generally expected interest-motivations – get lost. Because such explanations are arrived at inductively rather than deductively, they can lend insight into individuals' reasons for action in ways that rational choice institutionalism cannot, whether they fit the norm or depart from it. Moreover, because such explanations account contextually for individuals' reasons for action, sociological institutionalism is better able to explain the events out of which historical institutional explanations are constructed. And because sociological institutional explanations emphasize the role that collective processes of interpretation and legitimacy play in the creation and development of institutions, they can account for the inefficiencies in institutions that rational choice institutionalism cannot (Meyer and Rowan, 1977; see discussion in Hall and Taylor, 1996: 953).

By the same token, however, because sociological institutionalism makes no universalistic claims about rationality and is generally focused on explanation within rather than across cultures, it risks an implicit relativism which leads one to question whether sociological institutionalism allows for any cross-national generalizations at all. In fact, generalizations are possible here too, by invoking similarities as well as differences in cultural norms and identities, much in the way of historical institutionalism with country-specific institutional structures and processes. The resulting explanation, however, involves a lower level of generality and less parsimonious, 'thicker description' than in historical institutionalism, let alone rational choice institutionalism.

Finally, rather than appearing either economically or historically deterministic, sociological institutionalism can appear culturally deterministic where it emphasizes the cultural routines and rituals to the exclusion of individual action which breaks out of the cultural norm, that is, rule-creating action as opposed to rule-following action. Moreover, its emphasis on macro-patterns may make it appear like 'action without agents' (Hall and Taylor, 1996: 954) or, worse, structures without agents (see the critique by Checkel, 1998: 335). And like the rational choice approach, it too can be too static or equilibrium-focused, and unable to account for change over time – although where it adds a historical perspective, it can also show how norms are institutionalized, as in the case of the police and military in postwar Japan and Germany (Katzenstein, 1996) or how state identities can change and pull interests along with them, as in the case of anti-militarism in Germany and Japan (Berger, 1998).

While the boundaries between rational choice and sociological institutionalism tend to be clearly demarcated, the boundaries between historical and sociological institutionalism have never been, especially since historical institutionalists who did not turn for agency to the strategic action of rational choice institutionalism turned instead to the cultural norms and ideas of sociological institutionalism. In recent years, however, the boundaries between rational choice and sociological institutionalism have also been softening, as increasing numbers of scholars have been seeking to engage a dialogue between the approaches (e.g., Jupille et al., 2003). For the moment, though, the gap remains quite large, with the greatest advances mainly by rational choice institutionalists who have used the results of sociological institutionalist studies for rationalist purposes, as in the 'analytic narratives' approach of Robert Bates and colleagues (Bates et al., 1998).

DISCURSIVE INSTITUTIONALISM

Discursive institutionalism is the term we will use for the fourth and newest of the 'new institutionalisms' (see Campbell and Pederson, 2001; Kjaer and Pederson, 2001; Schmidt, 2002a: Chapter 5; Schmidt, 2008; Schmidt and Radaelli, 2004) – although other terms abound, such as ideational institutionalism (Hay, 2001), constructivist

institutionalism (Hay, 2006), and economic constructivism (Abdelal et al., in press). But these other terms tend to highlight primarily the substantive content of ideas in discourse, whereas our term also encompasses the inter-active processes that serve to generate those ideas and communicate them to the public. The 'institutionalism' in the term, moreover, suggests that this is not only about the communication of ideas or 'text' but also about the institutional context in which and through which ideas are communicated.

Discursive institutionalism tends to offer an analysis of political reality which, although very different from the other three new institutionalisms, nonetheless builds on the others in a complementary manner. Institutions – whether understood in 'new institutionalist' terms as socially constituted, historically evolving, or interest-based rules of interaction that represent incentives, opportunities, and/or constraints for individual and collective actors – frame the discourse, serving to define repertoires of more or less acceptable (and expectable) ideas and discursive interactions (see Schmidt, 2002a: Chapter 5). However, discursive institutionalism also offers a framework within which to theorize about how and when ideas in discursive interactions may enable actors to overcome constraints that explanations in terms of rational behavior and interests, historical rules and regularities, and/or cultural norms and frames present as overwhelming impediments to action. Discursive institutionalism itself has its sources in the turn to ideas of scholars immersed in the other three new institutionalisms, who looked to ideas as a way to enable them to explain the dynamics of institutional change within their own preferred institutionalism. But while for some, turning to ideas meant staying within the initial constructs of their own institutionalist approach, others moved beyond, into discursive institutionalism, and a primary concern with ideas and how they are communicated through discourse (for a fuller account see Schmidt, 2008).

Rational choice institutionalism and the turn to ideas

Among rational choice institutionalists, the foray into the realm of ideas has remained rather circumscribed. For the most part, ideas have been cast as mechanisms for choosing among interests, behaving like switches (or 'road maps') that funnel interests down specific policy directions, serving as filters, focal points, or lenses that provide policy-makers with strategies (see also Bates et al., 1998; Goldstein and Keohane, 1993; Weingast, 1995). Douglass North (1990) went farther, by casting ideas as 'shared mental modes.' But if this is the case, then there is nothing to stop ideas from having an effect on the content of interests, and not just on the order of interests – which would make it impossible for rationalists to continue to maintain the artificial separation of 'objective' interests from 'subjective' ideas about interests, that is, beliefs and desires (see critique in Blyth, 2003: 696–7; also Blyth, 2002: Chapter 2). What is more, taking ideas seriously would force rational choice institutionalists to abandon a whole range of assumptions, in particular, about fixed preferences and neutral institutional incentive structures, that make for the parsimony of the approach and everything that follows from it, including the ability to mathematically model games rational actors play as opposed to those 'real actors play' (see Rothstein, 2005: Chapter 1; Scharpf, 1997). This helps explain why most rational choice institutionalists quickly abandoned the pursuit of ideas.

For the relatively few rational choice institutionalists who nonetheless persisted, and thereby flipped over into discursive institutionalism, some of the most knotty problems could be addressed, such as assumptions about institutions as inherently good (or bad) and actors as instrumental. If one takes ideas seriously, as Bo Rothstein argues, institutions need no longer be treated as neutral structures of incentives or (worse) the immutable products of 'culture' that lead to inescapable 'social traps.' Instead, institutions are better understood as the carriers of ideas or 'collective memories,' which make them objects of trust or mistrust and changeable over time as actors' ideas and discourse about them change in tandem with changes in their performance (Rothstein, 2005: Chapters 1 and 7). Moreover, if one sees ideas as constitutive of interests, then, as Paul Sabatier demonstrates, the dynamics of policymaking can be better cast in terms of the advocacy coalitions that are differentiable not just in terms of cognitive ideas – meaning perceptions of objective interests – but also in their normative ideas – meaning perceptions of which interests are appropriately pursued (Sabatier and Jenkins-Smith, 1993).

Discursive institutionalists who follow in the rational choice institutionalist tradition do not ignore the material interests, economic in particular, which are at the basis of much of the institutional incentive structures in the rational choice institutionalist literature. But they separate analytically the very concept of material interests into material reality and interests. Whereas they posit interests as constituted by ideas and discourse, such that interests cannot be separated from ideas about interests, they see material reality mostly as separate from interests, and best understood as the setting within which or in response to which agents conceive of their interests. Thus, they problematize the rationalists' whole notion of 'objective' material interests by theorizing interests as subjective responses to material conditions (see Blyth, 2002 and discussion in Hay, 2006). Moreover, although they would not deny that a certain range of responses to material realities can be expected, given what we know about human rationality (and irrationality), they do deny the validity of rational choice institutionalists' extrapolation of predictions about rational actors' 'objective' and fixed preferences from such expected responses. Instead, discursive institutionalists take the actual responses to material reality as their subject of inquiry.

Historical institutionalism and the turn to ideas

In the historical institutionalist tradition, the move into ideas has been more significant. Here, the question is really where the tipping point is between historical institutionalists who continue to see institutions as constitutive of ideas and those who might better be called discursive institutionalists within a historical institutionalist tradition because they see ideas as constitutive of institutions even if shaped by them. Interestingly enough, even in the book that gave historical institutionalism its name (Steinmo et al., 1992), the few chapters that were focused on ideas – those of Peter Hall, Desmond King, and Margaret Weir – take us beyond historical institutionalism. But whereas Peter Hall's (1989) earlier edited volume on the adoption of Keynesianism ideas remained largely historical institutionalist because historical structures come prior to ideas, influencing their adoptability, his later article (Hall, 1993) on the introduction of monetarist ideas in Thatcher's Britain crossed the line to discursive institutionalism, since ideas are central to change and constitutive of new institutions. Desmond King (1999) in his book on illiberal social policy in Britain and the US makes this move quite explicit through the focus on the role of ideas and knowledge in the making of policy, although historical institutionalism remains in the emphasis on how institutional arrangements facilitated British reform efforts and hindered US ones.

What defines work that is clearly discursive institutionalist within the historical institutionalist tradition is the focus on ideas as explanatory of change, often with a demonstration that such ideas do not fit predictable 'rationalist' interests, are underdetermined by structural factors, and/or represent a break with historical paths. Examples include Sheri Berman's (1998) historical contrast between the German Social Democrat capitulation before Nazism and the Swedish Social Democrats' success in reinventing socialism; Kate McNamara's (1998) account of the learning process that led to a neo-liberal consensus on European Monetary Union following the German exemplar; Craig Parsons' (2003) detailed history of the ways in which French ideas about constructing EU institutions became institutionalized; and my own elaboration of the ideas and discourse that help explain the different dynamics of change in the three (rather than just two) varieties of capitalism of Britain, Germany, and France (Schmidt, 2002a: Chapters 5 and 6).

For discursive institutionalists in the historical institutionalist tradition, then, while the macro-structures and regularized practices that are the subject of historical institutionalist analysis are significant for shaping ideas, ideas can also serve to reshape the macro-structures and regularized practices. This suggests another avenue for historical institutionalists who seek to go beyond description to explanation of 'what happens.' Instead of turning to rational choice or sociological institutionalism for human agency, both of which are still quite static, as we have already seen, they could turn to discursive institutionalism to help explain the dynamics of institutional change, with ideas and discourse providing another kind of micro-foundational logic to institutional development.

Sociological institutionalism and the turn to ideas

In the sociological institutionalist tradition, one cannot talk about a move into ideas as such, since ideas have always been at the basis of the approach – as norms, cognitive frames, and meaning systems. However, there is also a tipping point here, On the one side are those 'constructivist' scholars who see ideas more as static ideational structures, as norms and identities constituted by culture, and who therefore remain largely sociological institutionalist as per the earlier definition. These include constructivists like Peter Katzenstein and his colleagues who show how interests developed from state identities structure national perceptions of defense and security issues (Katzenstein, 1996). On the other side are those constructivists who more clearly fit under the rubric of discursive institutionalism. These are the constructivists who, in addition to putting ideas into cultural context, also put them into their 'meaning' context (e.g., Hay, 2006; Kjaer and Pederson, 2001). They tend to present ideas as more dynamic, that is, as norms, frames, and narratives that not only establish how actors conceptualize the world but also enable them to reconceptualize the world, serving as a resource to promote change through 'structuration' (Wendt, 1987: 359–60), through the diffusion of international norms in developing countries (e.g., Finnemore, 1996), through the reconstruction of state identities and ideas about European integration (Risse, 2001), through the dissemination of neo-liberal ideas in Britain (Hay, 2001) or through the continuity and changes in ideas and values in the politics of welfare state adjustment (Schmidt, 2000).

Constructivist discursive institutionalists, in short, add a focus on values, culture, and norms to the emphasis on the construction of interests of the more 'positivist' discursive institutionalists of the rationalist or historical institutionalist traditions. But importantly, the ideas in discourse do not only reflect cultural norms; the discourse through which they are conveyed, if persuasive, can also serve to reframe such norms and recreate new cultural mores.

Discursive interactions

Most of the discursive institutionalists just discussed tend to deal mainly with ideas, leaving the interactive processes of discourse implicit as they discuss the ideas generated, accepted, and legitimized by the various actors. Some scholars, however, have gone farther to formalize the interactive processes of idea generation, acceptance, and legitimization, and to clarify how they are structured. They tend to see discourse not only as a set of ideas bringing new rules, values, and

practices but also as a resource used by entrepreneurial actors to produce and legitimate those ideas. Their approaches can be divided into those focused on the 'coordinative' discourse among policy actors and those more interested in the 'communicative' discourse between political actors and the public (see Schmidt, 2002: Chapter 5).

In the coordinative sphere, discursive institutionalists tend to emphasize primarily the individuals and groups at the center of policy construction who generate the ideas that form the bases for collective action and identity. Some of these scholars focus on the loosely connected individuals united by a common set of ideas in 'epistemic communities' in the international arena (Haas, 1992). Others target more closely connected individuals united by the attempt to put those ideas into action through 'advocacy coalitions' in localized policy contexts (Sabatier and Jenkins-Smith, 1993) or through 'advocacy networks' of activists in international politics (Keck and Sikkink, 1998). Yet others single out the individuals who, as 'entrepreneurs' (Finnemore and Sikkink, 1998; Fligstein and Mara-Drita, 1996) or 'mediators' (Jobert, 1992; Muller, 1995) draw on and articulate the ideas of discursive communities and coalitions in particular policy domains in domestic or international arenas.

In the communicative sphere, discursive institutionalists emphasize the use of ideas in the mass process of public persuasion in the political sphere. Some of these scholars focus on electoral politics and mass opinion (Mutz et al., 1996), when politicians translate the ideas developed by policy elites into the political platforms that are put to the test through voting and elections; others are more concerned with the 'communicative action' (Habermas, 1996) that frames national political understandings; yet others, focus on the more specific deliberations in the 'policy forums' of informed publics (Rein and Schön, 1991) about the on-going policy initiatives of governments. Exemplary of this is David Art's (2006) investigation of the elite-led public debates about the Nazi past in Germany and Austria in the 1980s that engendered very different political cultures and partisan politics by the 1990s, and highly contrasting results with regard to the rise of the far right.

In all of these approaches, the empirical analysis of institutions and the process of institutional change is very different from that found in rationalist, historical, or sociological institutionalism, since it is focused on who talks to whom about what when how and why, in order to show how ideas are generated, debated, adopted, and changed as policymakers, political leaders, and the public are persuaded, or not, of the cognitive necessity and normative appropriateness of ideas. Institutional context clearly also matters here, affecting *where* who talks to whom about what. For example, in 'simple' polities (or single-actor constellations) where governing activity tends to be channeled through a single authority, mainly the executive – countries like Britain and France – the communicative discourse to the general public tends to be much more elaborate than the coordinative discourse among policy actors, since without it governments face sanctions ranging from interest group protest to loss of public confidence and loss of elections. By contrast, in 'compound' polities where governing activity tends to be dispersed among multiple authorities – countries like Germany and Italy – the coordinative discourse among policy actors tends to be much more elaborate than the communicative discourse to the public, since it is crucial for reaching agreement on policy among the many actors involved (see Schmidt, 2002a, 2006a).

The limits of discursive institutionalism

Discursive institutionalism, in short, explains the dynamics of change (but also continuity) through ideas and discursive interactions. As such, it largely avoids the static determinism of the other three 'new institutionalisms'. By the same token, however, it risks appearing highly voluntaristic unless the structural

constraints derived from the three newer institutionalisms are included – whether rationalist interests, historical paths, or cultural norms. The appearance of voluntarism is especially problematic for scholars who focus only on ideas, where 'text' appears without context, occasionally in postmodernist approaches. But even where the context is considered, other problems may arise.

In discursive approaches that follow in the sociological institutionalist tradition, there is always the danger that social construction goes too far, and that material interests qua material interests are ignored in favor of seeing everything as socially constructed within a given culture (see the critique of Sikkink, 1991, by Jacobsen, 1995). This leads one to question whether there is anything 'out there' at all, mutually recognizable across cultures. But while discursive approaches in the sociological institutionalist tradition may suffer from too much constructivism, those in the rational choice or historical institutionalist tradition may suffer from too much positivism, with political action assumed to be motivated by instrumental rationality alone, such that cognitive ideas about interests over-determine the choice of ideas, crowding out the normative values which also color any conceptualization of interest.

But all discursive institutionalist approaches, whether positivist or constructivist, may also be overly deterministic with regard to the role of ideas, seeing the influence of ideas everywhere in the way that rational choice institutionalists see instrumental rationality everywhere or sociological institutionalists, cultural rationality. Most importantly, 'stuff happens'. As the historical institutionalists remind us, processes of change are often unconscious – as people may act without any clear sense of what they are doing, creating new practices as a result of 'bricolage' and destroying old ones as a result of 'drift' (Thelen, 2004; Streeck and Thelen, 2005; see also Campbell, 2004: 69–74). But even when there is conscious action, when people do have ideas about what they are doing, what they do most often has unintended consequences, not only in an historical institutionalist sense because the outcomes may be unanticipated but also in a discursive institutionalist sense because ideas may be reinterpreted or misunderstood.

Thus, the big question for discursive institutionalism in explaining change, once we have established that ideas and discourse do matter and how they matter, is: *When* do ideas and discourse matter, that is, when do they exert a causal influence? And when don't they?

Establishing causality with regard to ideas and discourse can be problematic. The very question itself may seem inappropriate to constructivist discursive institutionalists who see causal logics of explanation as operating in a different domain from a constructivist logic of interpretation (e.g., Bevir and Rhodes, 2003; Wendt, 1999). Other constructivists, however, argue that bracketing off questions of causality and explanation from those of meaning and interpretation is unnecessary (see Hay, 2004: 145). In fact, whether constructivist or positivist, most discursive institutionalists see their main explanatory task as that of demonstrating the causal influence of ideas and discourse (e.g., Blyth, 2003; Hay, 2001; Parsons, 2003; Schmidt, 2002a: Chapters 5 and 6).

Discourse, just as any other factor, sometimes matters, sometimes does not in the explanation of change. The question is *when* does it matter, say, by redefining interests as opposed to merely reflecting them in rationalist calculations, by reshaping historical paths as opposed to being shaped by them, or by recreating cultural norms as opposed to reifying them (see Schmidt, 2002a: 250–6). And when are other factors more significant, say, where the creation of new institutional paths or cultural norms may be better captured by historical or sociological institutionalist analysis, because actors don't have any clear idea about what they are doing when they are doing it. Part of the reason many political scientists avoid explanations related to discourse is that it is difficult to separate it

from other variables, to identify it as *the* independent variable. But instead of ignoring discourse because of the difficulties, because it may not be *the* cause, it is much better to ask when is discourse *a* cause, that is, when does discourse serve to reconceptualize interests, to chart new institutional paths, and to reframe cultural norms. But for this, more work needs to be done on establishing what general criteria to use in evaluating what represents 'good' ideas in a discourse (but see Schmidt and Radaelli, 2004) and in establishing when discourse is 'transformative,' and when not.

Even in the absence of general criteria of evaluation, empirical investigations have gone a long way to demonstrate how and when ideas and discourse have been transformative. This has been done through process-tracing of ideas held by different actors that led to different policy choices (Berman, 1998); through matched pairs of country cases where everything is controlled for except the discourse to show the impact of discourse on welfare adjustment (see Schmidt, 2002b); through speeches and debates of political elites that then lead to political action (Dobbin, 1994); through opinion polls and surveys to measure the impact of the communicative discourse (Koopmans, 2004); through interviews and network analysis to gauge the significance of the coordinative discourse, and more.

Institutional context also needs to be taken into consideration, however. For example, in 'simple' polities (or 'single-actor' systems) where the communicative discourse is most elaborate, the causal influence of discourse is most likely to be ascertainable in the responses of the general public over time, as discovered through protests and election results, opinion polls, and surveys. By contrast, in 'compound' polities (or 'multi-actor' systems) in which the coordinative discourse is most elaborate, the causal influence is more likely to be seen in whether or not there is any agreed policy, with empirical investigation focused on interviews and reports of policy actors (Schmidt, 2002a).

CONCLUSION

Thus, the four new institutionalisms – rational choice, historical, sociological, and discursive institutionalism – differ greatly from one another (see Table 7.1). Each has a different object of explanation – whether rational behavior and interests, historical rules and regularities, cultural norms and frames, or ideas and discourse; a different logic of explanation – whether calculation, path-dependency, appropriateness, or communication; different emphases on continuity or change – whether on continuity through fixed preferences, through path dependency, or through cultural norms, or on change through ideas and discursive interactions. And they also have different problems of explanation: economic determinism for rational choice institutionalism; historical determinism for historical institutionalism; cultural determinism or relativism for sociological institutionalism; and ideational determinism or relativism for discursive institutionalism. Adding confusion to all of this is that concepts may be shared across institutionalisms, although they have different uses and functions in the different institutionalisms. Interest is a concept that has currency across institutionalisms, even though only rational choice institutionalism gives it priority over institutions. Ideas also appear across institutionalisms, but whereas they come second to interests in rational choice institutionalism, to history in historical institutionalism, and to culture in sociological institutionalism, they are constitutive of interests, history, and culture in discursive institutionalism. Moreover, scholars have increasingly been exploring commonalities along the borders of their approaches. The most significant such exploration has been that between the older new institutionalisms and the newest, discursive institutionalism.

To get a sense of how all of this fits together in a very general way, I present a chart that situates scholars' work cited above within each of the four institutionalisms while arraying the four institutionalisms along a horizontal continuum from positivism to constructivism and from interests to culture, with history in between, and along a vertical continuum from static to dynamic, with culture, history, and interests at the static end, ideas and discourse at the dynamic end (see Figure 7.1). I put historical institutionalism between rational choice and sociological institutionalism, mainly because rational choice and sociological institutionalism are largely incompatible, whereas historical institutionalism can go either to the positivist or the constructivist side when it adds agency. I put discursive institutionalism underneath all three because, although it is distinctive, it can rest upon the insights of any one of the three and because scholars often see themselves as continuing to fit in one or another of the traditions even as they fit best in discursive institutionalism.

But although discursive institutionalism thus appears at the bottom of the explanatory

Table 7.1　The four new institutionalisms

	Rational choice institutionalism	Historical institutionalism	Sociological institutionalism	Discursive institutionalism
Object of explanation	Rational behavior and interests	Historical rules and regularities	Cultural norms and frames	Ideas and discourse
Logic of explanation	Calculation	Path-dependency	Appropriateness	Communication
Ability to explain change	Static continuity through fixed preferences, stable institutions	Static continuity through path dependence (except where incremental change)	Static continuity through cultural norms, ideational frames	Dynamic change and continuity through ideas and discursive interaction
Problems of explanation	Economic determinism	Historical determinism	Cultural determinism or relativism	Ideational determinism or relativism

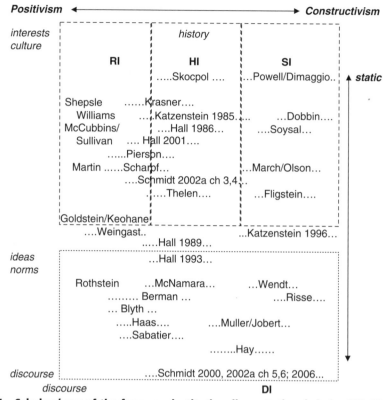

Figure 7.1   Scholars' use of the four new institutionalisms: Rational choice (RI), Historical (HI), Sociological (SI), and Discursive (DI)

hierarchy in this figure, lending new insights into the reconceptualization of rationalist interests, the reshaping of historical paths, and the reframing of cultural norms, it would be a mistake to therefore think of it as something that is secondary to the other three new institutionalisms, to be dismissed as not 'parsimonious' enough or too micro-foundational (as would dyed-in-the-wool rational choice institutionalists) or not a distinctive institutionalism of its own (Campbell, 2004). Rather, it is better to see it as in a natural progression from the three older new institutionalisms, or as progress over them. As such, we could flip the hierarchy over, to present the other three new institutionalisms as background knowledge to the discursive institutionalist approach, providing useful insights into the crystallized

ideas about rationalist interests and cultural norms or the frozen landscapes of macro-structures and routinized actions prior to our investigation into the dynamics of change. But what this in fact illustrates is that rather than speaking of explanatory hierarchies, we do best to see each of the four new institutionalisms as eminently worthwhile methodological approaches in their own right, as all engaged in the theoretically and empirically worthwhile enterprise of explaining different parts of political reality. And most important for ensuring future progress in political science, therefore, would be to continue to explore commonalities at the boundaries of the various approaches, in an effort to build as complete a picture of politics, economics, and society as we can.

NOTE

1. For an earlier discussion of institutionalism, with a focus on the state, see Schmidt (2005). For a much fuller discussion of 'discursive institutionalism,' see Schmidt, 2008.

REFERENCES

Abdelal, R., Blyth, M., and Parsons, C. (in press) *The case for economic constructivism*.

Art, D. (2006) *The politics of the Nazi past in Germany and Austria*. New York: Cambridge University Press.

Bates, R. (1988) 'Contra contractarianism: Some reflections on the new institutionalism', *Politics and Society*, 16 (2–3): 387–401.

Bates, R., Greif, A., Levi, M., Rosenthal, J.-L. and Weingast, B. (1998) *Analytic narratives*. Princeton: Princeton University Press.

Berger, T.U. (1998) *Cultures of antimilitarism: National security in Germany and Japan*. Baltimore: Johns Hopkins University Press.

Berman, S. (1998) *The social democratic moment: Ideas and politics in the making of interwar Europe*. Cambridge: Harvard University Press.

Bevir, M. and Rhodes, R.A.W. (2003) *Interpreting British governance*. London: Routledge.

Blyth, M.M. (1997) '"Any more bright ideas?" The ideational turn in comparative political economy', *Comparative Politics*, 29 (2): 229–50.

Blyth, M.M. (2002) *Great transformations: Economic ideas and institutional change in the twentieth century*. New York: Cambridge University Press.

Blyth, M.M. (2003) 'Structures do not come with an instruction sheet: Interests, ideas, and progress in political science', *Perspectives on Politics*, 1 (4): 695–706.

Blyth, M.M. and Vargwese, R. (1999) 'The state of the discipline in American political science: Be careful what you wish for?', *British Journal of Politics and International Relations*, 1 (3): 345–65.

Campbell, J.L. (2004) *Institutional change and globalization*. Princeton, NJ: Princeton University Press.

Campbell, J.L. and Pedersen, O. (2001) *The rise of neoliberalism and institutional analysis*. Princeton, NJ: Princeton University Press.

Checkel, J. (1998) 'The constructivist turn in international relations theory', *World Politics*, 50 (2): 324–48.

Collier, D. and Collier, R. (1991) *Shaping the political arena*. Princeton: Princeton University Press.

Cox, G. and McCubbins, M. (1993) *Legislative Leviathan: Party Government in the House*, Berkeley: University of California Press.

Crouch, C. (2005) *Capitalist diversity and change: Recombinant governance and institutional entrepreneurs*. Oxford: New York: Oxford University Press.

DiMaggio, P.J. and Powell, W.W. (1991) 'Introduction', in W.W. Powell and P.J. DiMaggio (eds), *The new institutionalism in organizational analysis*. Chicago: University of Chicago Press, pp. 1–38.

Dobbin, F. (1994) *Forging industrial policy*. Cambridge: Cambridge University Press.

Elster, J. and Hylland, A. (eds) (1986) *Foundations of social choice theory*. Cambridge: Cambridge University Press.

Evans, P., Rueschemeyer, D. and Skocpol, T. (1985) *Bringing the state back in*. New York: Cambridge University Press.

Finnemore, M. (1996) 'Norms, culture, and world politics: Insights from sociology's institutionalism', *International Organization*, 50 (2): 325–47.

Finnemore, M. and Sikkink, K. (1998) 'International norm dynamics and political change', *International Organization*, 52 (2): 887–917.

Fligstein, N. (1990) *The transformation of corporate control*. Cambridge, MA: Harvard University Press.

Fligstein, N. and Mara-Drita, I. (1996) 'How to make a market: Reflections on the attempt to create a single market in the European Union', *American Journal of Sociology*, 102 (1): 1–32.

Goldstein, J. and Keohane, R. (1993) *Ideas and foreign policy: Beliefs, institutions and political change*. Ithaca: Cornell University Press.

Green, D. and Shapiro, I. (1994) *The pathologies of rational choice*. New Haven: Yale University Press.

Haas, P.M. (1992) 'Introduction: Epistemic communities and international policy coordination', *International Organization*, 46 (1): 1–35.

Habermas, J. (1996) *Between facts and norms: Contributions to a discourse theory*. London: Polity Press.

Hall, P. (1986) *Governing the economy: The politics of state intervention in Britain and France*. New York: Oxford University Press.

Hall, P. (1989) 'Conclusion', in P.A. Hall (ed.), *The political power of economic ideas: Keynesianism across nations*. Princeton, NJ: Princeton University Press, pp. 361–91.

Hall, P. (1993) 'Policy paradigms, social learning and the state: The case of economic policy-making in Britain', *Comparative Politics*, 25 (3): 275–96.

Hall, P. and Soskice, D. (2001) 'Introduction', in P.A. Hall and D. Soskice (eds), *Varieties of capitalism: The institutional foundations of comparative advantage*. Oxford: Oxford University Press, pp. 1–71.

Hall, P. and Taylor, R. (1996) 'Political science and the three new institutionalisms', *Political Studies*, 44 (4): 952–73.

Hall, P. and Thelen, K. (2006) Varieties of Capitalism and Institutional Change, *European Politics and Society Newsletter* (Spring).

Hardin, R. (1982) *Collective action*. Baltimore, MD: Johns Hopkins.

Hay, C. (2001) 'The "crisis" of Keynesianism and the rise of neoliberalism in Britain: An ideational institutionalist approach', in J.L. Campbell and O. Pedersen (eds), *The rise of neoliberalism and institutional analysis*. Princeton, NJ: Princeton University Press, pp.193–218.

Hay, C. (2004) 'Taking ideas seriously in explanatory political analysis', *British Journal of Politics and International Relations*, 6 (2): 142–9.

Hay, C. (2006) 'Constructivist institutionalism', in R. A. W. Rhodes, S. Binder, and B. Rockman (eds), *The Oxford handbook of political institutions*. Oxford: Oxford University Press, pp. 56–74.

Immergut, E. (1992) *Health politics: Interests and institutions in Western Europe*. New York: Cambridge University Press.

Immergut, E. (1998) 'The theoretical core of the new institutionalism', *Politics and Society*, 26 (1): 5–34.

Jacobsen, J.K. (1995) 'Much ado about ideas: The cognitive factor in economic policy', *World Politics*, 47 (2): 283–310.

Jobert, B. (1992) 'Représentations sociales, controverses et débats dans la conduite des politiques publiques', *Revue Française de Science Politique*, 42 (2): 219–34.

Jupille, J., Caporaso, J.A. and Checkel, J.T. (eds) (2003) 'Integrating institutions: Rationalism, constructivism, and the study of the European Union', *Comparative Political Studies*, 36 (1–2): 1–2.

Katzenstein, P.J. (ed.) (1978) *Between power and plenty*. Madison: University of Wisconsin Press.

Katzenstein, P. (1985) *Small States in World Markets: Industrial Policy in Europe* Ithaca, N.Y.: Cornell University Press.

Katzenstein, P.J. (ed.) (1996) *The culture of national security: Norms and identity in world politics*. New York: Columbia University Press.

Katznelson, I. and Weingast, B.R. (eds) (2005) *Preferences and situations: Points of intersection between historical and rational choice institutionalism*. New York: Russell Sage Foundation.

Keck, M.E. and Sikkink, K. (1998) *Activists beyond borders: Advocacy networks in international politics*. Ithaca, NY: Cornell University Press.

King, D. (1999) *In the name of liberalism: Illiberal social policy in the United States and Britain*. Oxford: Oxford University Press.

Kjaer, P. and Pederson, O. (2001) 'Translating Liberalization: Neoliberalism in the Danish Negotiated Economy', in J. L. Campbell and O. Pedersen (eds), *The Rise of Neoliberalism and Institutional Analysis*. Princeton: Princeton University Press, pp. 191–248.

Koopmans, R. (2004) The Transformation of Political Mobilisation and Communication in European Public Spheres. *5th Fifth Framework Programme of the European Commission*. http://europub.wz–berlin.de

Krasner, S. (1988) 'Sovereignty: An institutional perspective', *Comparative Political Studies*, 21 (1): 66–94.

Levi, M. (1989) *Of rule and revenue*. Berkeley, CA: University of California Press.

Mahoney, J. (2000) 'Path Dependence in Historical Sociology', *Theory and Society*, 29: 507–48.

Mansbridge, J. (ed.) (1990) *Beyond self-interest*. Chicago: University of Chicago Press.

March, J.G. and Olsen, J.P. (1984) 'The new institutionalism: Organisation factors in political life', *American Political Science Review*, 78 (3): 734–49.

March, J.G. and Olsen, J.P. (1989) *Rediscovering institutions: The organizational basis of politics*. New York: Free Press.

Martin, L. (2000) *Democratic commitments*. Princeton: Princeton University Press.

McCubbins, M. and Sullivan, T. (eds) (1987) *Congress: Structure and Policy*. New York: Cambridge University Press, 1987.

McNamara, K. (1998) *The currency of ideas: Monetary politics in the European Union*. Ithaca, NY: Cornell University Press.

Meyer, J.W. and Rowan, B. (1977) 'Institutionalized organizations: Formal structure as myth and ceremony', *American Journal of Sociology*, 83 (2): 340–63.

Moe, T. (1984) 'The new economics of organization', *American Journal of Political Science*, 28 (4): 739–77.

Moe, T. (2003, April) *Power and political institutions*. Paper presented at conference on Crafting and Operating Institutions, Yale University, New Haven, CT.

Morgan, G., Whitley, R., and Moen, E. (eds) (2005) *Changing capitalisms? Internationalization, institutional change, and systems of economic organization*. New York, Oxford: Oxford University Press.

Muller, P. (1995) 'Les politiques publiques comme construction d'un rapport au monde', in A. Faure, G. Pollet and P. Warin (eds), *La construction du sens dans les politiques publiques: Débats autour de la notion de référentiel*. Paris: L'Harmattan.

Mutz, D.C., Sniderman, P.M., and Brody, R.A. (1996) *Political Persuasion and Attitude Change*. Ann Arbor: University of Michigan Press.

North, D.C. (1990) *Institutions, institutional change, and economic performance*. Cambridge: Cambridge University Press.

Ostrum, E. (1990) *Governing the commons*. New York: Cambridge.

Parsons, Craig (2003) *A Certain Idea of Europe*. Ithaca, NY: Cornell University Press.

Pierson, P. (1994) *Dismantling the welfare state?* Cambridge: Cambridge University Press.

Pierson, P. (2004) *Politics in time: History, institutions, and social analysis*. Princeton, NJ: Princeton University Press.

Pollack, M. (1997) 'Delegation, agency, and agenda setting in the European Community', *International Organization*, 51 (1): 99–134.

Przeworski, A. (1991) *Democracy and the market*. Cambridge: Cambridge University Press.

Rein, M. and Schön, D.A. (1991) 'Frame-reflective policy discourse', in P. Wagner, C.H. Weiss, B. Wittrock and H. Wollmann (eds), *Social sciences, modern states, national experiences, and theoretical crossroads*. Cambridge: Cambridge University Press, 262–89.

Riker, W. (1980) 'Implications from the disequilibrium of majority rule for the study of institutions', *American Political Science Review*, 75: 432–47.

Risse, T. (2001) 'Who are we? A Europeanization of national identities?', in M. Green Cowles, J. Caporaso, and T. Risse (eds), *Transforming Europeanization and domestic change*. Ithaca, NY: Cornell University Press.

Rothstein, B. (2005) *Social Traps and the Problem of Trust*. Cambridge University Press, Cambridge.

Ruggie, J. (1998) 'What makes the world hang together? Neo-utilitarianism and the social constructivist challenge', *International Organization*, 52 (4): 855–85.

Sabatier, P. and Jenkins-Smith, H.C. (eds) (1993) *Policy change and learning: An advocacy coalition approach*. Boulder, CO: Westview.

Scharpf, F.W. (1997) *Games real actors play. Actor-centered institutionalism in policy research*. Boulder, CO: Westview Press.

Scharpf, F.W. (1999) *Governing in Europe*. Oxford: Oxford University Press.

Schmidt, V.A. (2000) 'Values and discourse in the politics of adjustment', in F.W. Scharpf and V.A. Schmidt (eds), *Welfare and work in the open economy: Vol 1. From vulnerability to competitiveness*. Oxford: Oxford University Press, 229–310.

Schmidt, V.A. (2002a) *The futures of European capitalism*. Oxford: Oxford University Press.

Schmidt, V.A. (2002b) 'Does discourse matter in the politics of welfare state adjustment?', *Comparative Political Studies*, 35 (2): 168–93.

Schmidt, V.A. (2005) 'Institutionalism and the state', in C. Hay, D. Marsh and M. Lister (eds), *The state: Theories and issues*. Basingstoke: Palgrave.

Schmidt, V.A. (2006a) *Democracy in Europe*. Oxford: Oxford University Press.

Schmidt, V.A. (2006b, August) *Bringing the state back into the varieties of capitalism and discourse into the explanation of institutional change*. Paper prepared for presentation for the Annual Meetings of the American Political Science Association, Philadelphia, PA.

Schmidt, V.A. (2008) "Discursive Institutionalism: The Explanatory Power of Ideas and Discourse," *Annual Review of Political Science*. 11: 303–26.

Schmidt, V.A. and Radaelli, C. (2004) 'Conceptual and methodological issues in policy change in Europe', *West European Politics*, 27 (4): 1–28.

Shepsle, K. (1986) 'Institutional equilibrium and equilibrium institutions', in H.F. Weisburg (ed.), *Political science: The science of politics*. New York: Agathon, pp. 51–82.

Skocpol, T. (1979) *States and revolutions*. New York: Cambridge University Press.

Somit, A. and Tanenhaus, J. (1982) *The development of American political science from Burgess to behavioralism*. New York: Irvington.

Soysal, Y. (1994) *Limits of citizenship*. Chicago: University of Chicago Press.

Steinmo, S., Thelen, K., and Longstreh, F. (eds) (1992) *Structuring Politics: Historical Institutionalism in Comparative Analysis*, Cambridge: Cambridge University Press.

Streeck, W. and Thelen, K. (eds) (2005) *Beyond Continuity*. Oxford: Oxford University Press.

Thelen, K. (1999) 'Historical institutionalism in comparative politics', in *The Annual Review of Political Science*. Palo Alto: Annual Reviews Inc., pp. 369–404.

Thelen, K. (2002) 'How Institutions Evolve: Insights from Comparative-Historical Analysis', in J. Mahoney and D. Rueschemeyer (eds.), *Comparative Historical Analysis in the Social Sciences*. New York: Cambridge University Press.

Thelen, K. (2004) *How institutions evolve: The political economy of skills in Germany, Britain, the United States, and Japan*. New York: Cambridge University Press.

Weingast, B. (1995) 'A rational choice perspective on the role of ideas: Shared belief systems, state sovereignty, and international cooperation', *Politics and Society*, 23 (4): 449–64.

Weingast, B. and Marshall, W. (1988) 'The industrial organization of Congress', *Journal of Political Economy*, 96 (1): 132–63.

Wendt, A. (1987) 'The agent-structure problem in international relations theory', *International Organization*, 41 (3): 335–70.

Wendt, A. (1999) *Social theory of international relations theory*. Cambridge: Cambridge University Press.

Williamson, O. (1975) *Markets and hierarchies*. New York: Free Press.

Zysman, J. (1994) 'How institutions create historically rooted trajectories of growth', *Industrial and Corporate Change*, 3 (1): 243–83.

8

Comparative Political Economy

Thomas Plümper

INTRODUCTION

In many research areas interdisciplinary research constitutes the rule rather than the exception. In the social sciences, one research area exists in which interdisciplinary research is programmatic: *political economy*. Over the last three decades, political economy has been one of the fastest growing approaches in the social sciences. Political economic reasoning has infiltrated virtually all disciplines and fields of research across the social sciences. Theories first formulated by political economists have improved our understanding of social interactions and social order, political behavior and choice and even market mechanisms in general.

In comparative politics, political economists have participated in three major theoretical developments: First, they helped establish an analytical perspective to politics in which uncovering regularities, patterns and causal mechanisms stand are of primary interest rather than person, single events or unique political orders. The functioning of institutions, the interplay between institutions and actors, and the interdependencies between different, perhaps seemingly unrelated political institutions attracted the most attention. By now, almost all students of political science learn about the median-voter theorem (Downs, 1957), the logic of collective action (Olson, 1965), and the tragedy of the commons (Hardin, 1968). Even less commonly known ideas such as log-rolling (Buchanan and Tullock, 1962), political institutions and veto-players (Tsebelis, 1995), and the political business cycle (Hibbs, 1977; Tufte, 1975) are increasingly commonplace on the syllabi of postgraduate courses in political economy.

Second, political economists provided path-breaking insights into the interaction between corporations and governments. The theory of 'special interest politics' (Grossman and Helpman, 2001) explains why opportunistic governments, which are solely interested in their political survival, implement policies that deviate from the interest of the median voter. Clearly, the interaction between various types of actors is mediated by the institutional setting in which political decisions are being made. Policies in autocracies tend to differ from policies in democracies, government spending is usually higher in countries with proportional electoral systems than in countries with majoritarian electoral systems, and presidential democracies are more likely to become autocracies than parliamentary democracies – to mention just a few predictions of political economic models.

Third and more recently, political economists are at the forefront of explaining how government decisions are altered by the increase in global economic integration. Due to these models, comparative politics stands at the brink of relaxing the assumption that policies in one country are independent of policies in other countries.

This review discusses the contribution of political economy to comparative politics. In particular, I discuss the institutional and the comparative turns in political economy and the more recent development toward an 'open economy' political economy – one in which policy choices of government partly depends on policies in other countries. I will also argue here that the institutional turn fuelled a subsequent comparative turn in political economy. Since institutions do not change much over time, a comparative perspective helps in identifying institutional influences on political behavior as well as on social and economic outcomes.

WHAT IS POLITICAL ECONOMY AND WHAT DO POLITICAL ECONOMISTS DO?

Broadly speaking, political economists deal with market failure, suboptimal political outcomes and trade-offs between various political goals – among many other issues. Covering a diverse range of problems, the various different meanings the umbrella term 'political economy' has had during its long history hardly comes as a surprise. Perhaps beginning with Adam Smith's *Wealth of Nations* some authors define political economy simply as the analysis of how, why, and with what consequences governments intervene in markets.

Writing almost a century later, Karl Marx further broadened the concept to also include the 'production' of political, economic and social order. In *Critique of Political Economy* and in *Das Kapital* Marx perceives the class structure as exogenously given and discusses how this class structure simultaneously determines the organization of both the economy and the state. In a Marxian perspective, economics, political science, and sociology all deal with the same logic. As a consequence, economic, political and social phenomena may well be analyzed by the same approach.

Rapidly moving on through history, the early 20th century marked the decisive break-up of the social sciences into a variety of subdisciplines. To gain legitimacy, proponents of various subdisciplines were concerned about becoming distinguishable from what had been called 'Staatswissenschaft' in Germany – and political economy in the Anglo-Saxon countries. Yet, the postwar period witnessed a slow re-appearance of political economic approaches. By then, most political economists treated 'states and markets' as equally important and partly independent systems. Charles Lindblom, for example, discusses politics as a struggle over authority (Lindblom, 1977: 17f.) and markets as institutions which distribute scarce means in the absence of political authority. In this perspective, the state and the market become equally relevant principles according to which resources are distributed within a society.

All these distinct perspectives have their own shortcomings: Smith's perspective appears too narrow, Marx' framework fails to explain the huge differences across 'capitalist societies', and Lindblom's approach has a few blind spots as modern societies are not only about the distribution of authority but also about non-hierarchical relations and about efficient production. We nevertheless still find elements of all three broad perspectives in modern political economy. Many political economists explain governments' intervention into markets by the necessity to constrain market forces, others explain how individuals differ and how these differences affect and bias political decisions. For example, some interests find it easier to organize, some organizations are more influential and better organized than others, and more powerful interest groups have (this borders a tautology) a larger influence on political decisions than less well organized interests and unorganized interests.

True, these dichotomies are partly misleading and largely simplifying. Governments do not just interfere into market policies; they also guarantee the proper functioning of markets by guaranteeing ownership rights and by securing contracts. Moreover, a free-market economic order is consistent with varying levels of political participation of workers and with different degrees of political intervention into 'free markets'. And finally, neither does the market exist free of authority, nor does the state always use its monopoly of power.

Due to this messy interaction between politics and markets, the state and the economy, and politics and economics, recent attempts to define the nature of the beast political economy gave up a clear dominant dichotomy. Most recent authors define political economy by describing what political economists do. Weingast and Wittman (2006) state:

> Political economy is the methodology of economics applied to the analysis of political behavior and institutions. As such, it is not a single, unified framework, but a family of approaches. Because institutions are no longer ignored, but instead are often the subject matter of investigations, this approach incorporates many of the issues of concern to political sociologists. Because political behavior and institutions are themselves a subject of study, politics also becomes the subject of political economy. All of this is tied together by a set of methodologies, typically associated with economics, but now part and parcel of political science itself. (pp. 3–4)[1]

According to Weingast and Wittman, what political economists do defines the nature and boundaries of political economy, but what about the current work of political economists? Without trying to be exhaustive, I would like to give three answers: First, political economists analyze political responses to market failure. The provision (or underprovision) of public goods, cooperation (and the lack thereof) in the face of common dilemmas, and principal/agent problems are frequently studied phenomena in this area of political economy. Second, political economists study political failure. As Allen Drazen (2000: 7) has put it, political economy 'begins with the observation that actual policies are often quite different from optimal policies.' Third and finally, political economists explore political trade-offs. Here, the trade-off between the efficient organization of markets and approximately equal outcomes of market processes (the efficiency-equality trade-off) may be the most famous but hardly the sole trade-off.

INGREDIENTS FROM THE POLITICAL ECONOMISTS' COOKBOOK

The aforementioned definitions hardly explain why political economy became important for theoretical and empirical advancements in comparative politics. To understand the influence of political economy, we have to dig deeper and look into the political economists' 'cookbook'. Only this perspective allows us to observe the significance of political economy for establishing an analytical perspective in political science.[2]

Opportunistic and ideological parties and politicians

Modern political economy has its roots in a discussion of how voters vote and whether partisan or opportunistic models explain political outcomes best. Partisan models assume that parties have a political platform which varies relatively little over time and which makes parties easily distinguishable from each other (Bartels, 2000; Wittman, 1977). In contrast, opportunistic models suppose that (all) parties seek maximizing votes or the probability of being in power (Alesina, 1989; Alesina et al., 1997). If winning elections is the only goal of politicians, then they do not have an ideology. They will support the policy proposal that maximizes their political support.

Both set of assumptions seem not entirely unrealistic, but the truth certainly lies somewhere in the middle. Even ideological parties make concessions if they gain cabinet seats in return. Parties cannot afford to have strict ideologies if they have to compete with purely opportunistic parties. In turn, even opportunistic parties may have ideological positions in some policy dimension, especially since the political market does not immediately punish strong and unpopular views on a relatively unimportant policy. Yet, researchers do not have to formulate complicated models and assume a weighted function which includes both ideology and opportunism. Rather, the choice of the model often depends on the analytical intention.

Some researchers perceive opportunistic models as having a peculiar feature – a feature which sometimes turned them into vigorous critics of these models: if parties are purely opportunistic then there seems no space for stable and diverse partisan preferences. Again, the Downsian median-voter theorem seems to predict this outcome. In fact, however, opportunistic models predict convergence only in the case of a two-party system without entry, without ideology-driven party members, without uncertainty about the position of the voters and so on (Adams, 1999; Plümper and Martin, 2007). If more than two parties populate the political system and the parliament, party positions do not converge. Thus, 'polarized' party systems and differences in partisan platforms can be consistent with the assumption of purely opportunistic models.

Over the last decades, political economists have learned not to consider opportunistic and partisan models as mutually exclusive. They use both types of models as flexible, equally possible tools. The variety of assumptions allows researchers to develop flexible albeit parsimonious models.

Voters

At first glance, how voters vote seems to be a simple question. Anthony Downs (1957), one of the founding fathers of modern political economy, suggested that voters develop rational expectations about their utility from different parties being in power and then vote for the party that maximizes their utility: 'To ignore the future when deciding how to vote (…) would obviously be irrational, since the purpose of voting is to select a future government.' (p. 40) This conception of voting behavior translates nicely into a spatial voting theory: each voter knows his or her individual preferences and the position of the parties in all relevant policy dimensions (often, the number of relevant policy dimensions equals 1 by assumption) and vote for the party closest to their own position. In other words, if voters minimize the distance between their position and the government's position, they maximize their utility.[3]

While Downs provides a convincing answer, an equally plausible argument was formulated by V.O. Key, who stressed the element of punishment. Voters can only force governments to implement 'good' policies, when they punish a poor performance of the incumbent. He writes:

> The patterns of flow of the major streams of shifting voters graphically reflect the electorate in its great, and perhaps principal, role as an appraiser of past events, past performance, and past actions. It judges retrospectively; it commands prospectively only insofar as it expresses either approval or disapproval of what has happened before. (Key, 1966: 61)

Yet, the past performance of a government does not necessarily predict future performances. The influence of government's activities on the business cycle seems to be moderate at best: Not even the most skilled government can isolate their country from the effects of an exogenous shock such as an oil crisis. One has to keep in mind, however, that Key does not necessarily assume fair[4] or fully informed retrospective voters. His retrospective voters just evaluate past performance of governments and generalize from their appraisal – whether fair or unfair, justified or unjustified, whether correct or incorrect.

Both prospective and retrospective voting assumptions contain an element of truth to them. Yet, while both arguments can in principle easily be unified, political economists are interested in parsimonious models and rarely make models more complicated than necessary. Accordingly, political economists prefer to use pure assumption than a combination of positions.

Interest groups

Interest groups provide the perhaps most important reason why political outcomes deviate from the preferences held by the median vote. In fact, most political economists believe that interest groups are founded with the intention to shift policies away from the median voter's preference. In a world without interest-groups, the median voter gets what she wants. With well-organized and influential interest groups, however, the outcome of the political decision-making process deviates from the preferences of the median voter (Grossman and Helpman, 2001).

Mancur Olson in his seminal book on collective action convincingly argued that not all interests are equally likely to organize (Olson, 1965). In his view, small groups will find it easier to overcome the collective action problem associated with establishing an interest representation. The same holds true for groups which find it easier to observe and punish free-riding behavior.

If these assumptions hold true, the median voter and individuals with preferences close to the median voter's preference are least likely to join an interest group. Quite the contrary, bearing the costs of interest groups pays off for individuals with relatively radical preferences in important policy dimensions. However, once radical interest groups gain influence on the policy formation

process, the incentive for individuals with moderate interests to get organized increases. In other words, the presence of interest groups trying to pull policies in their favored direction provides an incentive for others to establish a competing group which prevents this from happening. If all individuals had the same influence on interest groups and if all contributed the same amount of resources to interest groups, then a situation in which no interest group exists and a situation in which all individuals have joined interest groups would lead to the same policy outcome. However, since membership in interest groups is costly, the average level of welfare for each individual is lower in a society where interest groups must spring up to compete with one another than one in which voters did not have to organize.

However, this result does not necessarily hold. Political economists also investigate *how* interest groups influence the government, and this research casts doubt on too 'lobby-sceptical' approaches such as Olson's theory of the 'rise and decline of nations' (Olson, 1982). Interest groups have an ability to provide four not mutually exclusive instruments: First, they can buy policies by giving resources to parties. Second, they can share private information with the government. Third, they can try to change the preferences of voters by providing the public with information, and finally they can buy time from politicians and direct their attention to a particular problem.

The sheer existence of influential interest groups does not necessarily reduce the aggregate welfare of their country, even though information asymmetries between interest groups and the government exist. When interest groups endow the public and the government with valuable information – information which helps the government to improve policies – the aggregate welfare effect of interest groups may even be positive. This holds even if interest groups do not spread information because its members could lose from the potentially induced policy changes.

Lessons learned: The role of assumptions in modern political economy

Political economy brought an analytical perspective into political science. Political economists did not seek to 'explain' particular political events – they tried to formulate general theories of political phenomena. The analytical perspective requires simplifying assumptions.

But how much abstraction provides the most promising research strategy? The answer is: it depends. Neither abstract nor complex theories are per se more valuable. First, researchers have to keep the purpose of their theories in mind. And holding the purpose of the theory constant, they have to find the optimal ratio between abstraction and explanatory power. If more complicated assumptions lead to a more realistic theory, but the explanatory power does not increase, then the simpler theory is superior despite its less realistic assumptions. If, however, a further simplification of a theory leads to a severe decline in explanatory power, researchers should prefer the more complex theory. If one theory is more complex and explains a certain phenomenon better than a second theory, both have their value.

Over the last decades, political economists have learned the principle of parsimony. Competing simplifying assumptions are no longer a matter of intense debates and eitherors. The debates of the 1960s and 1970s centered on the correct set of assumptions might rumble on – but different point of views nowadays rarely lead to heated controversies. Over the last decades, political economists have learned their lessons: different and seemingly competing assumptions enrich the political economy toolbox.

THE INSTITUTIONAL AND COMPARATIVE TURNS IN POLITICAL ECONOMY

Political institutions have only fairly recently been given central attention by political economists. Though research on corporatist bargaining structures in advanced capitalist societies became more central in the 1970s (Schmitter and Lehmbruch, 1979), it almost took another ten years until political economists begun to explore the impact of political institutions more thoroughly. Research on central bank independence (Cukierman, 1992; Grilli et al., 1991), wage bargaining structures (Calmfors and Driffill, 1988; Przeworski and Wallerstein, 1982), and electoral systems (Besley and Case, 1995) more or less simultaneously opened political economy to rigorous research on political institutions. Of course, political economists also became increasingly influenced by developments in mainstream comparative politics, where the institutional turn (March and Olson, 1984) preceded the institutional turn in political economy by at least 10 years. Nevertheless, political economists found their niche within the emerging institutional paradigm.

Due to space constraints, this section can only survey a small faction of the results of two decades of institutional political economic research. Before I do so, however, let me first explain how political economists make a conceptual distinction between institutions and actors. Though such a distinction cannot always be made easily, the political economic perspective is admirably clear: Actors are defined by their independent utility functions and by choices. Institutions are typically modeled as incentive or constraint in the choice set. Thus, researchers may model institutions either as actors or as political constraint. For example, political economists can model independent central banks as institutions, which constrain government decisions, or as actors which have independent utility functions and act strategically (Ferejohn and Weingast, 1992a; 1992b).

Macroeconomic consequences of elections

If parties are (partly) interested in winning elections and if governments have (some) political autonomy, then governments will misuse political power to win elections and to stay in power. As many political economists have shown (Hibbs, 1987; Tufte, 1978), incumbents benefit from favorable economic conditions. Creating favorable conditions thus seems to be a viable strategy for winning elections.

In the 1970s, the Philips curve suggested governments could easily create an increasing demand for labor by reducing the interest rate, increasing money supply, and by rising government deficit spending. This being true, an incumbent could create a political business cycle with lower unemployment rates before and higher unemployment rates after elections which fosters its electoral chances (Nordhaus, 1975). A reduction in the interest rate before the election reduces the price of money and thus stimulates consumption and investment, and in consequence the unemployment rate declines. Similarly, a deficit-financed increase in government spending allows the government to provide benefits to potentially pivotal voters. Hence, if used correctly both policies should significantly increase the incumbent's chances of getting reelected (Hibbs, 1977; Nordhaus, 1975; Tufte, 1978).

In practice, however, this theory has some serious flaws. First, cheap money has, at best, a fairly short effect. As economic subjects learn that the increase in demand originates in unsustainable government policies, they adjust their expectations to the prospect of rising interest rates and cut down consumption and investment despite the low interest rates. If the economic subjects fully anticipate the attempt of the government to manipulate the state of the economy, both the inflation rate and the unemployment rate remain about constant (assuming a closed economy). In the worst case, the economic subjects initially respond to the decline in interest rates but overshoot in their adjustment to learning that governments manipulated the interest rates for electoral purposes. As a consequence, the reduction in the interest rate causes a short term increase in

consumption and investment – the unemployment rate declines. Once the economic subjects correct their expectations, however, the stimulating effect evaporates. Yet, the interest rate cut increases the inflation rate leading an election inducted short-term stimulus package to have long term adverse economic consequences.

Therefore, contrary to the assumptions of early political economists, governments are not likely to misuse monetary policy for electoral purposes. This does not mean, however, that governments never and under no circumstance manipulate the economy. As Robert Franzese repeatedly has argued, not all governments actually need to fuel the economy. If unemployment is already low and economic growth high, a further interest cut would not only look inappropriate, its effect would also be likely to be small. Likewise, the incumbent may not need the help of a politically induced business boom in competition with a weak challenger (Franzese, 2002; Franzese and Long Jusko, 2006).

The mixed empirical results for the political business cycle theory do not come as a surprise. By ignoring what Franzese and Long Jusko have dubbed 'context conditionality', the empirical analyses suffer from severe specification errors. As they have concluded: 'The empirical evidence surveyed here clearly supports models of political-economic cycles that are context conditional' (Franzese and Long Jusko, 2006: 560).

Many 'context conditions' are indeed institutional influences. Trivially enough, independent central banks provide an effective obstacle for the opportunistic use of monetary policies. Less obvious, but almost equally effective, a fixed exchange-rate regime reduces monetary policy autonomy of governments even without independent central banks. Since monetary policy must be used to stabilize the exchange-rate, the political room for manipulating the business cycle declines, but it does not diminish. Rather, the government's room for maneuverability depends on the country's current exchange-rate to the base currency, the parity, the bands within which the exchange-rate may move without intervention, and the elasticity of the exchange-rate to changes in the interest-rate differential.

After 30 years of research into the political business cycle, political economists have a much improved understanding of the mutual dependencies of policies and institutions. In addition, the political business cycle literature not only brought the political economic approach closer to mainstream political science, the political business cycle also constituted the first political economic research agenda, on which political scientists worked alongside economists. The unhealthy division of labor had collapsed and has since then not been re-established.

Macroeconomic consequences of electoral systems

Variation across electoral systems offers one of the most compelling explanations for observed heterogeneities within the group of democracies. Electoral systems vary in many respects, but much of the explanatory power of electoral system results from the seemingly simple distinction between majoritarian and proportional electoral systems.

In proportional systems, each party is awarded with a share of the total number of parliamentary seats which by-and-large resembles its vote shares. Small deviations from this rule result from additional institutional features such as Germany's 5 per cent hurdle, which bans parties below a vote share of 5 per cent from parliament. As a result, parties which win more than 5 per cent and make it into parliament get a slightly larger seat share than vote share.

Majoritarian systems split the electorate up into different districts. Each district represents a defined number of seats in parliament. These seat(s) are won by the party which attracts the simple or a qualified majority of the votes in the district. Majoritarian systems have a relatively low correlation between seat shares and vote shares.

The political consequences of electoral systems can be significant and important. Even at a first glance it becomes obvious that the number of parties actually entering into parliament crucially depends on the electoral system. Majoritarian systems typically lead to 2-party or 3-party systems. In proportional systems the number of represented parties tends to be much larger. For example, 12 parties entered into the Polish Sejm after the 1991 elections and up to 17 parties fragmented the Italian parliament in the 1970s, when parties only had to win 300,000 votes (instead of plus 60,000 votes in one of 27 electoral regions) for one parliament seat.

As a consequence, a single party is not very likely to win a stable majority in proportional systems, while single party governments dominate majoritarian systems. Hence, coalition governments, minority governments and oversized coalitions are by far more frequent in proportional systems.

Both the number of parties and the existence of coalition governments affect the behavior of parties and eventually policies. For example, the larger the number of parties, the more parties spread out in the policy space. In two-party systems, parties formulate positions relatively close to the medianvoter's preferences. In multiparty systems, parties spread out over the entire policy space. As a result, the average distance between voters and their nearest party declines, but the party close to the voter may be small and not very influential. Proportional systems thus bring about radical parties, which at times win seats in the parliament (Lijphart, 1994a, 1994b). In majoritarian systems, radical parties have little chance of winning parliamentary seats. The British National Party, for example, has not won a single seat in the British parliament to date.

The tendency toward radical parties in proportional systems is moderated by the formation of coalition governments. Relatively moderate parties not only tend to win more seats than radical parties, but they also do not like to share political responsibilities with radical parties. In many countries, a consensus between moderate parties ensures that radical parties are not allowed to join a coalition – a strategy which aims at reducing radical parties to mere protest parties. But these mediating forces do not fully remove the political differences between majoritarian and proportional systems.

Another important difference between majoritarian and proportional systems results from the higher importance of parties in proportional systems. In majoritarian systems, the political career of each member of the parliament depends foremost on his constituency. Candidates that do not win their district do not make it into the parliament. In proportional systems, the parties typically rank their candidates before the elections. In this case, the candidate's expected utility depends on his position on the party-list, which gives party leaders a strategic instrument with which they can influence the position of members of parliament.

In subsequent research, political economists build on these institutional differences to explain why policies vary. Persson and Tabellini (2003; 2004), for example, find that government spending is higher under proportional rules. Majoritarian elections concentrate power, which 'tends to favor the wealthy' (Persson and Tabellini, 2006: 733). In majoritarian systems, radical parties are not only unlikely to win parliamentary seats, the influence of lobbies also tends to be higher as the electorate is less influential and power more concentrated.

Constitutional political economy 1: Presidentialism

Before public choice and political economy influenced the discussion of political institutions in political science, scholarly work on presidential systems dominantly dealt with the personality of the presidents. The political economy approach to presidentialism 'shifted the analytical focus from the personality or psychology of individual presidents

to the institutional character of presidency.' (Cameron, 2006: 253). This shift in perspective has advanced political scientists understanding of presidential systems.

In parliamentary systems, the members of parliament elect the chief executive, while in presidential systems the voters elect the president directly. As a consequence, the executive in presidential systems enjoys greater independence from the members of parliament and therefore also from the parties. In most cases, the president also has more competencies in presidential systems. She appoints the prime minister and may also dissolve the government (for a broader discussion, see Lijphart, 1994a, 1994b; Sartori, 1997).

In comparison, the parliament elects the prime minister in parliamentary systems. Often, the largest party of the ruling coalition nominates the prime minister. Given this constellation, conflict of interest between the executive and the legislative is rare.

Presidential systems, to the contrary, often lead to the emergence of divided government – a situation which occurs when the president belongs to another party than the majority of the parliament. In these cases and in other cases in which the president's policy preference differs from the policy preference of the parliament's majority, the president and the parliament interact strategically (Cameron, 2000).

The political economic discussion of the strategic logic of presidentialism draws from the Romer-Rosenthal model (Romer and Rosenthal, 1978). This model assumes that the legislative majority proposes a bill and the president can accept or reject the proposal. If he rejects, the status quo remains in effect. In this type of model, the agenda-setters make an assumption on the preference of the veto actor and maximize their utility by taking the veto-player's position as a constraint into consideration. The veto player will never use his veto unless the agenda-setter miscalculates his policy preferences. Yet, the two actors may find themselves in a war of attrition-like situation in which many pareto-efficient compromises exist. In such a situation, decisions are typically delayed because both actors seek to maximize their individual utility. Usually the actor for whom the strategic delay costs less or who has more resources wins the 'war of attrition' (Cameron, 2000).

Recent variants of the Romer-Rosenthal model treat the game between the legislature and the president as a sequence of connected decisions. These 'sequential veto bargaining' (Groseclose and McCarty, 2001) models assume imperfect information on both sides and are strategically complex. For example, the president can veto even pareto-efficient initial proposals to extract further concessions from the parliament. However, the parliament may prefer not to suggest an updated version of the bill to the president, in order to get more goodwill for other proposals from the president. In other words, a sequential game does not need to be more realistic than single shot games, they all add an important meta-level to the analysis. In sequential bargaining, the legislature and the president fight for dominance over the legislative process rather than for single bills and concessions.

Some authors add a pre-stage to the bargaining game, in which president and legislature signal their preferences or even send a veto threat to the other actor. These models have large empirical significance for the United States (but unknown significance in other presidential systems). As Cameron (2000) shows, in the US post-war history, presidents almost never vetoed a bill without signaling that they intended to do so and the legislature has almost always responded by making concessions. Taking all these into consideration, the direct election of the president gives her more political autonomy than prime ministers typically have. As a consequence, Linz claims, the stakes of the presidential system rise, leading to political polarization and antagonisms and ultimately making presidential systems more prone to becoming authoritarian systems (Linz, 1993).

Constitutional political economy 2: Federalism and bicameralism

In Germany, the classical example for a federal and bicameral country, unified government with one party dominating both chambers (the Bundestag where the population is represented and Bundesrat where the Länder are represented) to create unified government is rare. Thus, many researchers analyzing divided government in bicameral systems compare them utilizing the same framework used to study divided governments in presidential systems. In this perspective, the majority in the upper house strategically interacts with the majority in the lower house (Cutrone and McCarty, 2006; Tsebelis and Money, 1997).

However, federalism is more than bicameralism and divided government. First, federal political systems typically use the subsidiarity principle to distribute political responsibilities across the various political levels. The European Union, which wholeheartedly supports the principle of subsidiarity (presumably because the EU believes subsidiarity increases its political responsibility), claims:

> The subsidiarity principle is intended to ensure that decisions are taken as closely as possible to the citizen and that constant checks are made as towhether action at Community level is justified in the light of the possibilitiesavailable at national, regional or local level. (Europa Glossary, n.d.)

In practice, however, the subsidiarity principle often leads to conflicts and deadlock between overlapping jurisdictions and into a 'joint decision trap' (Scharpf, 1988). Thus, federal systems reduce the autonomy of governments on each level unless responsibilities are clearly defined and fully divided between the various levels of government. If political responsibilities overlap, political authorities find themselves in a veto bargaining game which, at best, delays decisions and, at worst, render a change of the status quo impossible unless a pareto-efficient solution exists.

Under certain conditions federal systems lead to regulatory competition. Without obstacles to the mobility of goods, services, capital and labor, but with different jurisdictions within one country, competition for mobile capital and jobs becomes likely. This situation may cause a downward spiral of regulations and taxation as jurisdictions aim at attracting as much of the mobile factors as possible. As the burgeoning literature on fiscal federalism has demonstrated, federalism may lead to lower overall government spending if the horizontally disintegrated political units (the states) assume authority over the tax rates. However, federalism likely leads to a higher overall level of taxation if the central government maintains the right to set taxes or if states coordinate their tax rates effectively.

Toward a comparative political economy

For early political economists, the United States provided the only relevant test case. Political economy has not entirely overcome an unfortunate degree of US-centrism. The discussion of political institutions in the 'Oxford Handbook of Political Economy' focuses almost exclusively on the US political system and a US style of institutions. But is the USA a well-chosen case? The odds are that it is not if researchers are interested in generalization across space. In many respects, the USA resembles an outlier: the country is too large, too powerful, culturally too diverse, too rich, has only two parties that regularly compete and consistently win elections at the federal and state level, and the subtle system of checks and balances remains unique. Moreover, American interest groups are far too powerful and parties too weak, the country fights far too many wars, has too much influence on international organizations and they in turn have little influence on the American government. In short, the USA looks like one of the least likely cases for generalizations and valid inferences.

With the institutionalist turn in the late 1980s political economists begun to use larger samples. Yet, this shift to comparative research designs was not caused by methodological concerns but by the lack of sufficient institutional variation over time in single countries. For instance, constitutions in postwar OECD countries are very stable and durable. Switzerland maintains many of the same institutions and rules put into place in the late 13th century and the US has had a presidential system since the late 1700s. Electoral rules, central bank autonomy, or federalism – to mention just a few – do not change often even in relatively long time-series datasets. Single case studies and time series analyses simply do not find enough variation for reliable estimates and inferences. The lower the variation over time becomes, the more cases are needed for a reliable analysis. The institutional turn has shifted the political scientists' research interests from merely describing institutions to a more sophisticated analysis of the causes and consequences of institutions.

As a consequence, the 1990s saw a steep increase in comparative research designs in political science. Interestingly, many of the early comparative studies were conducted by non-American scholars who had studied or worked in American political science departments. These scholars brought a fresh comparative perspective to the systematic study of political institutions, and they saw very early on the need for broadening the perspective to make political systems which do not look much like the US system analyzable within the same standard framework.

At the same time, quantitative approaches to analyzing empirical evidence became the dominating methodology at least in American political science. True, European political science lagged behind, but during the last decade European political science began to converge toward the American standard. Again, political economy can be found at the forefront of these developments. Perhaps better trained than mainstream political scientists (the influence of economics!), political economists found it easier to employ more sophisticated methods for analyzing politics and policies in comparative perspective.

Finally, one also should not underestimate the importance of new methodologies and better datasets. Since countries are often fairly heterogeneous, a simple quantitative cross sectional analysis likely suffers from omitted variable bias. In the 1990s, researchers learned to deal with some forms of omitted variable bias when they moved to panel designs, which allowed them to control for time-invariant unit heterogeneity (Beck and Katz, 1995; Plümper and Troeger, 2007).

PERHAPS NOT A CONCLUSION, BUT 'THE NEXT BIG THING': THE POLITICAL ECONOMY OF OPEN ECONOMIES

This chapter discussed the contribution of political economy to comparative politics. I have shown that political economy which was at the core of the development of an analytical perspective to political science and also contributed to (though rather delayed) the institutional turn in comparative politics. Keeping this influential past in mind, we may ask: Where does comparative political economy go from here?

Though, of course, the future remains open, it seems fair to say that the next big thing will be the analysis of spatial effects in economic policy decisions. As yet, comparative political economists have implicitly or explicitly assumed that economic policies are the consequences of a domestic game, in which the government takes its own preferences, the interests of voters and interest groups, domestic political institutions and the state of the economy into consideration. This already complex picture overlooks the fact that policies are not necessarily independent of policies in other countries. Governments respond to changes in active labor market policies in neighboring

countries (Franzese and Hays, 2006, 2007), adjust their monetary policy if the Federal Reserve Bank or the European Central Bank changes its main interest rate (Plümper and Troeger, 2006a, 2006b), and so on. Hence, it seems fair to argue policy choices are increasingly influenced by policy choices in other countries. If this is the case, than a large share of recent empirical studies in comparative politics and comparative political economy are likely to suffer from omitted variable bias.

Of course, theories on policy spill-over between countries can at least be traced back to the globalization literature (Garrett, 1995, 1998). However, the globalization literature lacked a consistent technique for analyzing policy spill-overs. If one country's regulation partly depends on other countries' regulations, then the other country's regulation is also not be independent of the first country's regulation. This constellation leads to a severe endogeneity problem. The endogeneity problem can be solved, but appropriate techniques are not easy to use and their properties have been known for only a short time. If, however, spatial lags are ignored, than regression analyses likely overestimate the effects of domestic influences (Franzese and Hays, 2006, 2007). Accordingly, political economists have to re-examine some old and well-established empirical findings in the light of new theories of policy diffusion (Simmons and Elkins, 2004) and employ on newly developed spatial models with substantive lags (Beck et al., 2006; Franzese and Hays, 2006, 2007).

NOTES

1. This definition sounds remarkably similar to the editorial statement of *Public Choice*, a journal loosely associated with the Public Choice society: 'Public Choice deals with the intersection between economics and political science. It started when economists and political scientists became interested in the application of essentially economic methods to problems normally dealt with by political scientists. It has

retained strong traces of economic methodology, but new and fruitful techniques have been developed which are not recognizable by economists.' Retrieved February 18, 2008 from http://www.thelockeinstitute.org/publicchoice.html

2. Stephen Hanson's contribution to this volume tells the same story of the analytical turn from a different perspective, when he explains how scholars working on area studies developed an interest in generalizations.

3. Over the last 50 years, the Downsian model has been modified to more closely resemble reality and to make better predictions of electoral outcomes. For example, according to probabilistic models (Adams, 1999; Ordeshook, 1986) voters do not know the position of parties perfectly (or parties do not know the distribution of voter preferences perfectly). Other authors have argued that voters are 'biased' toward a certain party and underestimate the distance between their preferences and the party's position while perhaps over estimating their ideological distance to other parties (Converse, 1976).

4. 'Fair' here means that voters hold candidates responsible for policy outcomes that the government could actually influence. Accordingly, an exogenous shock should not influence vote choices, but how the government deals with this shock should.

REFERENCES

Adams, J. (1999) 'Policy divergence in multi-candidate probabilistic spatial voting', *Public Choice*, 100 (1–2): 103–22.

Alesina, A. (1989) 'Politics and business cycles in industrial democracies', *Economic Policy*, 4 (8): 55–98.

Alesina, A., Roubini, N. and Cohen, G.D. (1997) *Political cycles and the macroeconomy*. Cambridge: MIT Press.

Bartels, L. (2000) 'Partisanship and voting behavior, 1952–1996', *American Journal of Political Science*, 44 (1): 35–50.

Beck, N. and Katz, J. (1995) 'What to do (and not to do) with time-series cross-section data', *American Political Science Review*, 89 (3): 634–47.

Beck, N., Gleditsch, K. and Beardsley, K. (2006) 'Space is more than geography. Using spatial econometrics in the study of political economy', *International Studies Quarterly*, 50 (1): 27–44.

Besley, T. and Case, A. (1995) 'Does electoral accountability affect economic-policy choices. Evidence from gubernatorial term limits', *Quarterly Journal of Economics*, 110 (3): 769–98.

Buchanan, J.M. and Tullock, G. (1962) *The calculus of consent. Logical foundations of constitutional democracy*. Ann Arbor: University of Michigan Press.

Calmfors, L. and Driffill, J. (1988) 'Centralization of wage bargaining', *Economic Policy*, 6 (1): 14–61.

Cameron, C.M. (2000) *Veto bargaining. Presidents and the politics of negative power*. Cambridge: Cambridge University Press.

Cameron, C.M. (2006) 'The political economy of US presidency', in B. Weingast and D. Wittman (eds), *The Oxford handbook of political economy*. Oxford: Oxford University Press. pp. 241–55.

Converse, P.E. (1976) *The dynamics of party support. Cohort–analyzing party identification*. Beverly Hills: Sage.

Cukierman, A. (1992) 'Measuring the independence of central banks and its effect on policy outcomes', *World Bank Economic Review*, 6 (3): 353–98.

Cutrone, M. and McCarty, N. (2006) 'Does bicameralism matter?', in B. Weingast and D. Wittman (eds.), *The Oxford handbook of political economy*. Oxford: Oxford University Press. pp. 180–95.

Downs, A. (1957) *An economic theory of democracy*. New York: Harper & Row.

Drazen, A. (2000) *Political economy in macroeconomics*. Princeton, NJ: Princeton University Press.

Europa Glossary (n.d.) Subsidiarity. Retrieved February 18, 2008 from http://europa.eu/scadplus/glossary/subsidiarity_en.htm

Ferejohn, J. and Weingast, B. (1992a) 'Limitation of statutes. Strategic statutory interpretation', *Georgetown Law Journal*, 80 (3): 565–82.

Ferejohn, J. and Weingast, B. (1992b) 'A positive theory of statutory interpretation', *International Review of Law and Economics*, 12 (3): 263–79.

Franzese, R.J. (2002) 'Electoral and partisan cycles in economic policies and outcomes', *Annual Reviews of Political Science*, 5: 369–421.

Franzese, R.J. and Hays, J.C. (2006) 'Strategic Interaction among EU Governments in Active

Labor Market Policy-making', *European Union Politics*, 7 (2): 167–89.

Franzese, R.J. and Hays, J.C. (2007) 'Spatial econometric models of cross-sectional interdependence in political science panel and time-series-cross-section data. *Political Analysis*, 15 (2): 140–64.

Franzese, R.J. and Long Jusko, K. (2006) 'Political-economic cycles', in B. Weingast and D. Wittman (eds), *The Oxford handbook of political economy*. Oxford: Oxford University Press. pp. 554–64.

Garrett, G. (1995) 'Capital mobility, trade, and the domestic politics of economic policy', *International Organization*, 49, 657–87.

Garrett, G. (1998) *Partisan politics in the global economy*. Cambridge: Cambridge University Press.

Grilli, V., Masciandaro, D. and Tabellini, G. (1991) 'Political and monetary institutions and public finance', *Economic Policy*, 13 (12): 342–92.

Groseclose, T. and McCarty, N. (2001) 'The politics of blame. Bargaining before an audience', *American Journal of Political Science*, 45 (1): 100–19.

Grossman, G.M. and Helpman, E. (2001) *Special-interest politics*. Cambridge: MIT Press.

Hardin, G. (1968) 'The tragedy of the commons', *Science*, 162 (3859): 1243–8.

Hibbs, D. (1977) 'Political parties and macroeconomic policy', *American Political Science Review*, 71 (4): 261–75.

Hibbs, D. (1987) *The political economy of industrial democracies*. Cambridge: Harvard University Press.

Key, V.O. (1966) *The responsible electorate. Rationality in presidential voting 1930–1966*. New York: Vintage.

Lijphart, A. (1994a) 'Democracies: Forms, performance and constitutional engineering', *European Journal of Political Research*, 25 (1): 1–17.

Lijphart, A. (1994b) *Electoral systems and party systems. A study of 27 democracies, 1945–1990*. Oxford: Oxford University Press.

Lindblom, C. (1977) *Politics and markets. The world's political economic systems*. New York: Basic Books.

Linz, J. (1993) 'Presidentialism, multipartism, and democracy. The difficult combination', *Comparative Political Studies*, 26 (2): 198–228.

March, J.G. and Olson, J.P. (1984) 'The new institutionalism. Organizational factors in political life', *American Political Science Review*, 78 (2): 734–49.

Nordhaus, W. (1975) 'The political business cycle', *Review of Economic Studies*, 42 (2): 160–90.

Olson, M. (1965) *The logic of collective action: Public goods and the theory of groups*. Cambridge: Harvard University Press.

Olson, M. (1982) *The rise and decline of nations*. New Haven: Yale University Press.

Ordeshook, P.C. (1986) *Game theory and political theory*. Cambridge: Cambridge University Press.

Persson, T. and Tabellini, G. (2003) *Economic effects of constitutions*. Cambridge: MIT Press.

Persson, T. and Tabellini, G. (2004) 'Constitutions and economic policy', *Journal of Economic Perspectives*, 18 (1): 75–98.

Persson, T. and Tabellini, G. (2006) 'Electoral systems and economic policy', in B. Weingast and D. Wittman (eds), *The Oxford handbook of political economy*. Oxford: Oxford University Press. pp. 723–38.

Plümper, T. and Martin, C.W. (2007) *Multiparty competition. A computational model with abstention and memory*. Unpublished manuscript, University of Essex, UK.

Plümper, T. and Troeger, V.E. (2006a) 'Monetary policy autonomy in European non-Euro countries, 1980–2005', *European Union Politics*, 7 (2): 213–34.

Plümper, T. and Troeger, V.E. (2006b) *Fear of floating and the external effects of currency unions* (IIIS discussion papers no. 181), Trinity College, Dublin.

Plümper, T. and Troeger, V.E. (2007) 'Efficient estimation of time invariant and rarely changing variables in finite sample panel analysis with unit fixed effects', *Political Analysis*, 15 (2): 124–39.

Przeworski, A. and Wallerstein, M. (1982) 'Structural dependence of the state on capital', *American Political Science Review*, 82 (2): 11–29.

Romer, T. and Rosenthal, H. (1978) 'Political Resource Allocation, controlled agendas, and the status quo', *Public Choice*, 33 (4): 27–44.

Sartori, G. (1997) *Comparative Constitutional engineering. An inquiry into structures, incentives, and outcomes.* New York: New York University Press.

Scharpf, F.W. (1988) 'The joint-decision trap. Lessons from German federalism and European integration', *Public Administration*, 66 (3): 239–78.

Schmitter, P.C. and Lehmbruch, G. (eds) (1979) *Trends toward corporatist intermediation.* Beverly Hills: Sage.

Simmons, B.A. and Elkins, Z. (2004) 'The globalization of liberalization. Policy diffussion in the international political economy', *American Political Science Review*, 98 (1): 171–89.

Tsebelis, G. (1995) 'Decision-making in political systems. Veto players in presidentialism, parliamentarism, bicameralism and multipartyism', *British Journal of Political Science*, 25 (3): 289–325.

Tsebelis, G. and Money, J. (1997) *Bicameralism.* Cambridge: Cambridge University Press.

Tufte, E. (1975) 'Determinants of the outcomes if midterm congressional elections', *American Political Science Review*, 69 (3): 812–26.

Tufte, E. (1978) *Political control of the economy.* Princeton: Princeton University Press.

Weingast, B. and Wittman, D. (2006) 'The reach of political economy', in B. Weingast and D. Wittman (eds), *Oxford handbook of political economy.* Oxford: Oxford University Press. pp. 3–25.

Wittman, D. (1977) 'Candidates with policy preferences: A dynamic model', *Journal of Economic Theory*, 14 (1): 180–9.

9

The Contribution of Area Studies

Stephen E. Hanson

INTRODUCTION

The role of 'area studies' in the comparative politics subfield of political science has been the subject of a prolonged and often acrimonious debate. On one hand, advocates of a more deductive approach to social science inference have railed against area specialists for their presumed hostility to both generalizable theory and quantitative methodology. As Robert Bates warned in 1996 in his initial 'Letter from the President' in the American Political Science Association (APSA) Comparative Politics Newsletter:

Within the academy, the consensus has formed that area studies has failed to generate scientific knowledge. Many see area specialists as having defected from the social sciences to the camp of the humanists ... They tend to lag behind others in terms of their knowledge of statistics, their commitment to theory, and their familiarity with mathematical approaches to the study of politics. (Bates, 1996)

Area studies centers, Bates argues, thus represent something of an institutional 'problem for political science,' given their ability to attract sufficient outside funding and administrative support to allow area specialists to operate independently of departmental constraints. Bates does concede the continuing relevance of the work of area specialists, but only insofar as they continue to 'record the data from which political inferences [might] be drawn by social scientists residing in political science departments' (Bates, 1996). Some supporters of Bates' position even suggested that this proposed division of labor could become an international one, since 'the area expertise of natives working in their own countries is likely to be deeper and richer than what those of us working in the US can generate anyway,' while more theoretically sophisticated and methodologically rigorous scholars in the US might increasingly focus on 'non-specific, increasingly abstract "theory"' (Golden, 1998: 6).

On the other hand, defenders of area studies have insisted that political analysis should always be grounded in a thorough knowledge of regional context, without which, in their view, a deeper understanding of the dynamics of political order and political change is impossible. Attacks on area studies, according to this camp, reflect the ascendance of narrowly economic approaches to politics that reflect a parochial misunderstanding of human motivation.

Thus Chalmers Johnson excoriates Bates for assuming that 'rational choice theory contains a unique capacity to transcend culture and reduce all human behavior to a few individual motivational uniformities' (Johnson, 2001: 60). As for Bates' and Golden's idea that area specialists might play a useful role as purveyors of regional data useful for more general theoretical analysis, Johnson replies acidly: 'One problem with this proposed division of labor is that these social scientists do not produce beautiful objects but junk and real area specialists have a much better record of producing theory than their self-proclaimed theoretical rivals' (Johnson, 2001: 62).

Given the invidious tenor of this debate, one might think that the crisis over the role of area studies in the comparative politics subfield was truly unprecedented. Certainly, the immediate professional stakes involved are very high, affecting everything from the priorities of private and public funding agencies to future standards for tenure decisions. Not surprisingly, the struggle between area specialists and deductive generalists has frequently devolved into a zero-sum struggle between warring camps.

When one steps back to examine the entire history of the interaction between area studies and the political science discipline, however, one quickly discovers that the basic contours of this debate are very old indeed. Note, for example, the characterization of the area studies controversy contained in the 1973 APSA Presidential Address of prominent Japan specialist Robert E. Ward of Stanford University:

> Many behavioralists allege that something called the 'Area Approach' lacks rigor and scientific potentiality. It is viewed as descriptive and relativistic, often historical or institutional rather than behavioral in focus, and normally idiosyncratic in terms of its findings. In current professional parlance these are not terms of praise.
>
> A few so-called 'area types' respond with countercharges of cultural illiteracy, gross ethnocentrism, uncritical scientism, and scornful characterizations of those members of the opposition who venture abroad as 'itinerant methodologists' or worse. (Ward, 1975: 27)

With only a few minor terminological updates – the word 'behavioral,' which used to signify scientific rigor, would now be changed to 'analytical'; the word 'institutional' would now be claimed by the champions of deductive theory – the same speech could be delivered again today, over three decades later, practically verbatim.

This is quite remarkable, given that Ward's speech emphasized that this fruitless debate had already been raging in the discipline for many decades, and that some way to transcend it should therefore be urgently sought. Indeed, Ward began his presentation by quoting Jasper Shannon's 1950 presidential address to the Southern Political Science Association, which detailed with ironic humor how, in the history of political science since the era of Woodrow Wilson, initial optimism about the discovery of 'laws of politics as clear and definite as those of physics' – knowledge of which would enable the spread of good institutions across the world – had gradually given way in the face of the twin disasters of the Great Depression and World War II to increasing skepticism about the possibility of arriving at a single neutral science of politics (Shannon, quoted in Ward, 1975: 24–26). Historians of the political science discipline confirm the broad outlines of Shannon's account. The 'first behavioral revolution' of the 1920s, led by figures like Charles Merriam, called for a higher level of scientific rigor through the use of modern methods such as public opinion surveys, psychological experiments, and economic approaches to history (Farr and Seidelman, 1993). By the 1930s, however, optimism about this 'rationalist' approach to social science had largely broken down as a result of attacks by émigré scholars fleeing totalitarian rule such as Hannah Arendt, Leo Strauss, and Eric Voegelin – who, in their own way, provided a continental European 'area studies' perspective on the prevailing orthodoxies of American political science (Gunnell, 1993).

Thus, with some slight thematic and stylistic variations, the political science debate about the contribution of area studies has raged in much the same form for nearly a century now. Under such circumstances, one might ask what purpose is served by writing yet another essay on the topic! It is my contention here, however, that the puzzling longevity of the area studies controversy itself provides an important clue as to its nature and possible resolution. Specifically, I argue that the area studies debate reflects a deeper confusion among political scientists of all stripes about how to combine deductive and inductive reasoning in social research. To transcend this debate will require scholarly agreement on some difficult and fundamental questions about how to develop scientifically fruitful typologies of regime type – agreement that is highly unlikely in the absence of mutual intellectual respect between self-professed area specialists and comparative politics generalists.

The chapter will be organized as follows. I will begin by showing how a careful examination of the long history of the area studies controversy helps to invalidate several common stereotypes about area studies in the political science discipline: first, they are not merely a product of Cold War policy concerns; second, they are unlikely to disappear as a result of increasing political and economic globalization; and finally, they are more frequently the source of new general theory than an obstacle to it. I will then turn to a critique of area studies that has substantially greater merit: namely, that the conventional definitions of world 'areas' are arbitrary in ways that inhibit, rather than promote, theoretical cumulation. While there is some truth to this claim, I argue that rival 'theoretical' categorizations of regime types are at least as arbitrary. Indeed, as I show in the subsequent section, the typical geographic divisions utilized in contemporary area studies programs do tend to highlight many important structural, institutional, and cultural variables that are shared among countries within various world regions. Hence area studies tend to sensitize political scientists to the limited scope conditions of supposedly 'universal' models and theories developed in the context of a single world region such as North America. I conclude by showing how heightened awareness of the deeper theoretical complexities of the area studies controversy – by advocates of deductive theory and defenders of regional expertise alike – might promote a more tolerant and fruitful interrelationship between the two camps.

STEREOTYPES ABOUT AREA STUDIES

Before we can assess the contribution of area studies to the subfield of comparative politics, we need to understand precisely how 'area studies' as a distinct approach to the analysis of world politics emerged in the first place. In this respect, several common criticisms of the area studies approach appear to rest on faulty historical premises.

Thus, one common criticism of area studies is that its particular orientations and choice of material were directly influenced by the Cold War priorities of the United States government – in particular, the global struggle against communism (Cohen, 1985; Farish, 2005). Advocates of this viewpoint point out that the initial push to expand area studies training in the postwar era by the Rockefeller, Ford, and Carnegie Foundations focused primarily on Russia and East Asia – the early sites of conflict between the United States and its communist adversaries. The National Defense Education Act of 1958, which initiated the Title VI National Resource Centers of the Department of Education that provide the basic infrastructure for area studies training in most major US universities to this day, was launched as a direct response to the Soviet launch of the *sputnik* satellite the year before.[1] Many leading area specialists in political science departments spent time in the US military during World War II, and many more lent their expertise to various government security agencies, including the Central Intelligence Agency and the Department of Defense, throughout the Cold War period (Lambert et al., 1984: 2–10). Surely the dominant role of Cold War concerns among area studies funders must have hindered the search for objective scientific knowledge among area specialists?

Of course, the connection between the funding of area studies programs and the strategic priorities of the US government cannot be denied.[2] However, the further argument that US and private funding of area studies centers undermined their scholarly objectivity assumes that the divide between political science generalists and area studies practitioners overlaps substantially with an ideological divide between critics and defenders of US foreign policy. Closer examination of the issue calls such an assumption into question. From Herman Kahn to Steven Krasner, social scientists explicitly oriented toward general theorizing have been just as likely to be engaged in the formulation of US foreign policy as have prominent area specialists. Among the latter, too, one finds any number of critics of US policymaking, ranging from the neo-Marxist Barrington Moore (who began his career as a Soviet specialist) to reformist liberals like Albert Hirschman (who made his name as a Latin Americanist). Even within the area specialization most closely connected to Cold War concerns – Sovietology itself – there is no discernable ideological pattern linking an area studies orientation to support of US policy. Indeed, after the collapse of the Soviet Union, one could find both conservatives like Frances Fukuyama and leftists like Jerry Hough criticizing Sovietologists for their failure to apply general political science theory to the USSR – and, on the other hand, both conservatives like Martin Malia and leftists like Stephen Cohen blaming Sovietology for its *overreliance* on abstract social science models (Fukuyama, 1993; Hough, 1997; Malia, 1993; Cohen, 1999). Finally, if the argument that area studies was dominated by inveterate Cold Warriors fails to hold for the Cold War era itself, it fails completely to explain why there was an 'area studies' controversy concerning American foreign policy long before World War II – between proponents of Wilsonian universalism, based on Woodrow Wilson's deeply held convictions about the possibility of expert political science knowledge of the principles ensuring stable democracy and peace, and 'unilateralists' skeptical of the relevance of Wilsonian ideals to non-Western contexts (Knock, 1992; Thorsen, 1998).[3] Nor does the presumed pro-American foreign policy bias of area studies appear to hold after the collapse of the Soviet Union – as any reader of Chalmers Johnson's recent works on US foreign policy can attest (Johnson, 2000).

Even if the accusation that area specialists were unduly affected by Cold War priorities seems unwarranted, however, many analysts would insist that the mission of area studies has nevertheless become anachronistic in the post-Cold War context. Thus one of the most common critiques of area studies research since 1991 has been the argument that it fails to take into account new social, technological, and cultural trends in an era of increasing 'globalization' (Prewitt, 1996). From this point of view, area studies must be reinvented to account for the rise in influence of non-state actors ranging from democratic advocacy groups to terrorist cells; the erosion of state boundaries as a result of cross-border trade, migration, epidemics, and media; and the invention of new international communication technologies such as the Internet and the cellular phone. Indeed, precisely these sorts of concerns led both the Ford Foundation and the Social Science Research Council – historically both key funders of area studies programs – to cut their support for 'traditional' region-based research in the 1990s (Ford Foundation, 1999; Prewitt, 1996).

If this second line of critique is correct, we should expect to find that area specialists prior to 1991 paid little attention in their research to social influences that flow across formal political jurisdictions, to social movements below the level of the nation-state, or to the impact of modern technology on social interaction. Again, however, even a cursory familiarity with the work of leading area specialists throughout the twentieth century makes such claims impossible to sustain.

To begin with, area studies as a whole has arguably been *more*, not less, attuned to international influences on national politics than advocates of quantitative political science approaches, who have often of necessity taken the nation-state as the basic unit of analysis in large-N multi-country databases. Indeed, the earliest area specialists in Western academia were scholars of ancient religions and their long-term cultural effects on 'civilizations'; for them, mere national boundaries were seen as artificial modern divisions that would fail to reroute the deeper allegiances uniting, say, the Muslim, Western Christian, Orthodox, or Confucian 'worlds' (Lambert, 2001). Area specialists working within the paradigm of modernization theory, too, hardly took the nation-state for granted; rather, they took it upon themselves to explain precisely why this form of political organization had emerged out of earlier, more parochial forms of political allegiance (Gellner, 1983; E. Weber, 1976). Others, such as the Western Europeanist Ernst Haas, examined how the nation-state itself might be transcended through the emergence of supranational systems of interest and loyalty in specific regional contexts (Haas, 1958, 1964). Nor did area specialists ever tend to neglect the influence of what today would be called 'non-state actors' – as is clear from an examination of classic works on the peasant village and peasant rebellion in Mexico, China, and Malaysia (Foster, 1965; Johnson, 1962; Scott, 1985) or on revolutionary movements and ideologies in France and Russia (Sewell, 1980; Tucker, 1969). As for the impact of technology, this was always one of the central variables in area studies research, which tended to take for granted the importance of increasing urbanization, industrialization, education, and access to media for understanding social change in various regions of the world (Apter, 1955, 1963; Lerner, 1958; Lowenthal, 1970). Indeed, the typical finding from this body of work was that technological change generally tends to disrupt traditional communities and identities, to facilitate the emergence of modern forms of individualism, and to enable new possibilities for collective action among previously marginalized groups – precisely the sorts of social

challenges and opportunities now highlighted in more recent paeans to the 'unprecedented' impact of globalization (Friedman, 1999, 2005).

This brings us to the third, and by far most widespread, stereotype about area studies research: that it has historically been carried out primarily by scholars resistant to general theoretical concepts and innovative methodologies. Taking into account the entire history of the area studies controversy, however, forces us to re-evaluate this accusation as well. Specifically, while it is true that the original area specialists of the pre-World War II era were primarily humanists interested in topics such as philology, theology, and development of 'ancient civilizations' – a tradition now pejoratively labeled 'Orientalism' (Said, 1978) – one is hard pressed to find representatives of this approach in the comparative politics subfield in any major political science department over the past five decades or so.[4] Indeed, in the immediate post-war period, area studies within the American university system was utterly transformed by its close association with Parsonian structural-functionalism and other variants of modernization theory into an integral part of social science theory-building. Given the widespread acceptance of modernization theory's parsing of the 'necessary' stages of social evolution from agricultural 'traditional society' based on communalism and personal loyalties to industrial 'modern society' based on individualism and impersonal proceduralism, it became possible to conceive of area studies as an arena for scientific investigation of the specific manifestations of 'universal' social processes (Parsons, 1951; Rostow, 1960). Parsons himself articulated such a goal for area studies explicitly as early as 1948, claiming that just as the study of the human body required collaboration among sciences as diverse as 'anatomy, physiology, biochemistry, bacteriology, and even psychology and some of the social sciences,' the study of world regions would provide 'a concrete focus for the disciplines of the social sciences and related fields of the humanities and natural sciences' (quoted in Mitchell, 2004: 86).

From the 1950s on, it is hard to find respected comparativists arguing that their countries of specialization are simply 'unique' and thus not amenable to comparative theorizing. Instead, the goal of most area specialists working in the broad modernization theory tradition was to chart the specific ways in which local 'traditional cultures' in their region had interacted with the inescapable forces of urbanization, industrialization, education, and the spread of mass media to produce either successful, stalled, or failed political modernization and economic development. From this perspective, too, it is not surprising that many social scientists who began as specialists on the effects of modernization in a particular region or country later began to engage in more explicit comparative theorizing – as in the cases of Daniel Lerner, David Apter, Barrington Moore, Lucian Pye, Robert Putnam, and countless other leading comparativists of the period.

It was only when modernization theory began to lose its hegemonic position in the 1970s and 1980s that studies of 'political culture' began to be widely seen as atheoretical, rather than theory-driven. Erstwhile students of Parsons himself, such as Clifford Geertz, became increasingly skeptical of their mentor's claims that human social evolution followed a single universal pattern, leading them to distance themselves from the project of 'general social science theory.' Indeed, Geertz's essay on 'thick description,' which is probably the work most widely cited by critics interested in demonstrating the resistance of area studies to general theory, hardly represented the mainstream area studies viewpoint; rather, it was written in rebellion against the overly-deductive forms of 'cultural theorizing' that had been dominant in the social sciences for most of Geertz's early career (Geertz, 1973).[5] At the same time, the search for a new overarching theoretical paradigm began, and this propelled several prominent former area specialists to convert to ascendant approaches

ranging from neo-Marxism – as in the case of Barrington Moore, whose first books analyzed the impact of modernization on the Soviet dictatorship (Moore, 1950, 1954) – to rational choice theory, as in the case of David Laitin, whose first book dealt with the effects of language policy in the single case of post-independence Somalia (Laitin, 1977).

By the end of the 1980s, modernization theory had fully lost its erstwhile hegemony in the political science discipline, and rational choice theory was quickly emerging as the most influential new approach to comparative politics research. As older modernization theorists retired and younger scholars trained in rational choice modeling entered the field during the 1990s, then, the idea that one could build a 'general theory' by examining global patterns of political culture fell out of favor – and many distinguished scholars who had built their careers pursuing this goal were implicitly recast as traditional 'area specialists.' In the 1970s, for example, the prominent modernization theorist Harry Eckstein firmly declared himself to be a skeptic about 'area studies approaches,' arguing that 'the ultimate (perhaps only) task of comparative politics is to find general solutions of general problems that cut across both geographic areas and periods of history' (Eckstein, 1975: 200). Yet two decades later, two prominent defenders of area studies could cite the very same Eckstein as someone who 'developed a powerful theory about how authority relations in the family influence forms of democracy, based on an intensive study of Norway' – demonstrating the scientific value of the single-country studies (Hall and Tarrow, 2001: 100)! Thus we see that much of the contemporary debate about whether area studies are 'theoretical' enough is, on a deeper level, a struggle over the validity of rival theoretical paradigms.

The myth that area specialists on the whole resist generalizable theory likely persists for three reasons. First, area studies may suffer from 'guilt by association' with the Orientalist scholarship of the pre-World War II period, which truly did insist on the uniqueness of non-Western 'civilizations' – although those who see such ideas as the core of area studies research are by now at least a half-century out of date. Second, since area studies programs are typically broadly inter-disciplinary, it is relatively easy to find histo-rians, anthropologists, and specialists in the humanities who do object to generalizable theory in the social sciences – but this tells us nothing about the intellectual orientations of the political scientists associated with such programs, who, ironically, are frequently seen by their more humanities-oriented col-leagues as being overly deductive in their analytic approaches. Third, and perhaps most importantly, changing political science para-digms have shifted our understandings of what counts as truly 'theoretical,' making it appear that area studies work explicitly ori-ented toward testing hypotheses derived from older theories lacked any theoretical orienta-tion at all. In fact, from the 1950s until con-temporary times, area specialists have continuously been very much in the center of debates about comparative politics theory.

WHAT IS AN 'AREA'?

We have seen that critiques of area studies as driven by Cold War concerns, as irrelevant in an era of globalization, or as inimical to gen-eralizable theory – however, persistent and pervasive – are fundamentally without merit. There is, however, a fourth common criticism of area studies approaches that is rather more difficult to discard: namely, that the typical definitions of 'areas' utilized to demarcate the area studies programs at major US uni-versities are arbitrary, and are therefore likely to hinder scientific progress on topics requir-ing conceptualization and research that tran-scends regional borders. Indeed, one finds this complaint about area studies included in nearly all of the critical literature examined above – even though authors differ as to whether the arbitrariness of defini-tions of the 'areas' in area studies reflects

outmoded Cold War priorities, an insufficient appreciation of social influences that cross existing political jurisdictions, or a simple lack of theoretical imagination. Now that we have stripped away prejudices along all these lines, however, we are in a position to con-front the problem of defining 'areas' directly and theoretically. Simply put: does organiz-ing comparative politics research in distinct regional clusters make any scientific sense? If not, then even the most dispassio-nate, dynamic, and theoretically innova-tive area studies research is built on a faulty foundation.

Ironically, it was Harry Eckstein himself who initially put this theoretical challenge to area studies most clearly. Area studies pro-grams, he noted, might have been formed for any one of four reasons: to fill voids in our factual knowledge about various parts of the world; to provide 'rubrics for interdiscipli-nary collaboration' among scholars with sim-ilar linguistic and historical knowledge; to highlight distinctive problems that arise with particular urgency in particular regions; or because '*the societies and polities of different regions constitute distinctive types*' (Eckstein, 1975: 202, emphasis in original). Eckstein argues that only the last of these four reasons can justify the maintenance of separate area studies programs for political science research in the long term, from a purely scientific point of view. Once sufficient empirical knowledge about the various polities and societies of the world is gathered, and the causes of urgent political problems in various regions isolated, only an assumption of typo-logical commonality at some level can justify principles of case selection that usually gen-erate comparisons within a particular 'area studies' region (say, India with Pakistan) rather than comparisons that ignore such regional designations (say, India with Brazil). Eckstein's own conclusion was that the most up-to-date research on regime types showed no real justification for distinguishing the study of 'Africa,' 'South Asia,' 'South-east Asia,' 'East Asia,' and so on. At best, only three 'clusters' of regimes – European,

'Afro-Asian,' and Latin American – might be justified empirically, based on a comprehensive survey of their typical patterns of state authority (Gurr, 1974). Ironically, Eckstein noted, 'West Europe,' which was one of the last parts of the world to be organized as a separate 'area studies' region in American academia, is actually one of the few geographic zones that might actually merit designation as a 'area' from a scientific point of view (Eckstein, 1975).

Eckstein's point is a powerful one. Clearly, there is an unavoidable element of arbitrariness in grouping world polities and societies in distinct regional clusters. While perhaps world geography seems at first glance to justify the separate study of, say, 'Africa' or 'Latin America' – although even in these cases one finds sharp intraregional divisions such as those between Mediterranean North Africa and the sub-Saharan countries, or between Spanish-speaking and Portuguese-speaking South America – one is hard pressed to find purely geographic reasons for distinguishing among the 'Middle East,' 'South Asia,' 'Southeast Asia,' and 'East Asia.' Indeed, certain geographical zones that appear to be 'regions' in one historical period can suddenly lose their apparent cohesiveness in another. Thus it is not intuitively obvious why, for example, Tajikistan and Slovenia should still be grouped in the same 'postcommunist' regional category, now that the Soviet bloc has disintegrated (Rupnik, 1999). In the face of such difficulties, does it not make more sense to discard the notion of coherent 'areas' in world politics altogether – perhaps searching instead for ways to categorize countries that do not depend on the use of 'proper nouns' at all (Przeworksi and Teune, 1970)?

If political scientists already possessed a consensual typology of political regimes as well as a widely accepted general theory of how such regimes develop, rise, and fall, such a line of criticism would, I think, be devastating. Scientific consensus of this sort might, in principle, render the study of arbitrarily-defined 'world regions' quite anachronistic.

In the absence of such scientific consensus, however, the case for abandoning area studies becomes much less clear cut – and this is a point generally missed by critics of area studies research. Indeed, given the lack of a widely-accepted theory of regime evolution in the field, we cannot in principle develop any clear-cut tests of whether particular polities 'belong together' in a single regional grouping or not – since only such a theory would allow us to identify precisely those empirical factors that might be decisive for arriving at a scientific judgment in this respect. If so, then any provisional 'theoretical' categorization of regimes may ultimately turn out to be just as arbitrary as 'traditional' area studies divides – if not more so.

Note, for instance, that the tests of regional commonality developed by Eckstein and Gurr depend directly on the theoretical notion that 'structures of political authority' (understood in Eckstein's sense as built around five key dimensions: modes of recruitment, constraints on decision-making, levels of participation, intensity of regulation, and complexity) are the central defining feature of all political systems (Eckstein and Gurr, 1975; Gurr, 1974). If one rejects this theoretical approach – as would most political scientists today – their subsequent grouping of world polities into European, Latin American, and 'Afro-Asian' clusters based on indicators of authority structures no longer has any theoretical or empirical justification. Indeed, choosing another theoretical criterion to generate an empirical categorization of regime types must necessarily generate an entirely different set of 'world regions.' Perhaps such alternative theoretical approaches might reveal distinct differences among African, Middle Eastern, and Asian 'clusters' of countries after all – in which case, defenders of traditional 'area studies' centers would turn out to have been on the right track, while supporters of 'grand theory' might inadvertently have missed crucial regional variables affecting the fate of global political development.

Critics of the arbitrariness of area studies programs might reply to this point by suggesting that even if many grand theories of regime-types fail, there is at least a chance that *some* general theoretical approach to regime evolution may eventually succeed. Sticking with established regional groupings of countries, in contrast, cannot possibly generate any grand theory. Thus it is still scientifically preferable to reject area studies approaches a priori.

This argument, however, assumes that the degree of scientific arbitrariness in the groupings of countries typical of traditional area studies programs approaches 100 per cent: that is, were we to possess a scientific consensus about the general reasons for the emergence, maintenance, and disappearance of political regimes, we would find zero theoretical justification for any of the groupings of countries we find in such programs at present. If we hypothesize that existing area studies groupings are only arbitrary to a degree, however – in other words, that there might turn out to be some justification for traditional area studies boundaries, even after the development of a consensual grand theory of regime change – the case for tossing aside area studies research entirely in favor of newly-developed theoretical categorizations is substantially weakened. The scientific decision to embrace or to break with area studies should ultimately turn, therefore, on one's assessment of just *how* arbitrary the various boundaries of regional studies programs in Western academia actually are, relative to one's confidence in the ability of new grand theories to categorize polities in more scientifically fruitful ways.

INSTITUTIONAL LEGACIES, DIFFUSION, AND VERSTEHEN

In fact, based on our current state of knowledge, there are actually many good social scientific reasons to embrace many of the traditional area studies groupings now institutionalized on campuses throughout North America and Europe. In particular, area studies programs actually tend to capture quite well the effects of three causal factors that are attracting greater attention among theorists of comparative political and institutional change. First, such programs implicitly accept the importance of 'legacies of the past' for structuring contemporary political and social issues. Second, the regional groupings of traditional area studies programs do a reasonably good job of capturing the effects of institutional and social diffusion among neighboring regimes. Third, area studies scholars are generally well suited to take into account the causal effects of powerful interpretations of the world – ideological, religious, and cultural – that can shape regional development in ways often poorly predicted by structural and institutional factors alone. I will deal with each of these points in turn.

If there is one obvious reason for the persistence over time of traditional area studies boundaries among 'African Studies,' 'Middle East Studies,' 'South Asian Studies,' and so on, it is a shared conviction among area specialists concerning the crucial importance of history. This is true in myriad ways. To begin with, most fundamentally, the vast majority of contemporary area studies programs are defined in large part by the history of expansion of one or more empires covering much of the territory they examine. Thus it is not much of an exaggeration to describe contemporary 'Middle East Studies' as analyzing the territory of the former Ottoman and Persian Empires; 'East Asian Studies' as examining the territory of the Chinese and Japanese Empires; and 'Latin American Studies' as covering the territory of the Spanish and Portuguese Empires. The 'former Soviet region' is, of course, the most clear-cut case of all in this respect. Other traditionally-defined world areas, such as Africa, South Asia, and Southeast Asia, are more notable for the great diversity of empires that occupied their territories in different historical eras. Yet even in these cases, the direct impacts of foreign conquests by various northern peoples are still at the core of regional self-definition. Of course, most area specialists would also insist that their regional programs are justified even more directly by their coverage of distinct linguistic, religious, and cultural contexts. Yet shared languages and belief systems in different parts of the contemporary world, too, can ultimately be traced to the history of regime change in ancient times.

As contemporary political scientists probe more deeply into the causal effects of structural and institutional legacies inherited from the past, the designation of various regional studies programs to cover geographical zones shaped profoundly by similar experiences of colonial conquest seems to make increasingly good sense. That the legacies of imperial law, bureaucracy, modes of socioeconomic organization, and official cultures might have profound effects on the options available to contemporary state builders is, of course, no surprise for analysts in the historical institutionalist school of comparative politics (Evans et al., 1985; Mahoney and Rueschemeyer, 2003; Skocpol, 1979; Steinmo et al., 1992). More recently, however, comparativists from the rational choice tradition have also begun to investigate the causal sequences that lead from previous institutional arrangements bequeathed by past regimes to contemporary incentives structuring individual decisionmaking – leading some to conclude that a reconciliation between historical institutionalism and rational choice institutionalism may soon be in the offing (Bates et al., 1998; Thelen, 1999; see also Chapter 6 of this volume). If so, general comparative theorists of both persuasions may soon develop a renewed interest in area studies work on postimperial development and postcolonial state building (Wilkinson, submitted).

A second reason why area studies specialists tend to group themselves in distinct research communities that accept traditional regional boundaries is their often implicit understanding that the countries they study tend greatly to influence each other. What happens in Japan, after all, clearly shapes what happens in South Korea – and vice versa – in ways that are clearly not as significant or salient for nations far from the Asian-Pacific region. Similarly, the prospect of accession to the European Union alike had a profound impact on the political and economic institutions of the countries of Eastern and Central Europe; the *acquis communautaire* cannot be said to have had such a dramatic impact on political change in Brazil or Argentina (Ekiert and Hanson, 2003; Vachudova, 2005). True, area studies programs may sometimes overemphasize the interactions among polities within traditional regional borders at the expense of examination of the influence of neighboring states located in 'different' regions; thus the influence of Russia on Japan, or of China on post-Soviet Central Asia, sometimes receives short shrift in area studies research. Yet even in these cases, area studies specialists may intuitively grasp social limits on cross-border influences in ways that general theorists of 'globalization' miss. The social and political impact of South Asia on the Central Asia states since 1991, for example, has arguably been rather marginal compared to that of the longstanding imperial hegemon in the region, Russia – contrary to the assertions of journalistic accounts about the potential for 'radical Islam' to spread north from Afghanistan (Rashid, 2002).

Again, the typical intuitions of area specialists about the impact and limits of diffusion across regional borders are backed up by new theories and methodologies about the mechanisms of institutional diffusion in international politics. Of course, theorists of economic development have long highlighted the ways in which proximity to the developed capitalist 'core' provides structural advantages largely unavailable to countries in the underdeveloped 'periphery' (Evans, 1979; Wallerstein, 1974). Even those who reject dependency theory, however, increasingly accept that geography plays a key role in the global political economy. We now know, more clearly than ever before, just how important geographic 'neighbor effects' can be for successful democratization and marketization: in a nutshell, being surrounded by impoverished autocracies makes liberal capitalism extremely difficult, while bordering the European Union in the 1990s nearly guaranteed democracy and wealth (Collier, 2007; Gallup et al., 1999; Kopstein and Reilly, 2000). And where states break down entirely, non-state networks operating in neighboring states may become the principal conduits of both resources and ideas to would-be revolutionary elites – as we are now discovering in post-invasion Iraq.

This brings us to the third reason why area studies programs tend to maintain their traditional boundaries: namely, despite all of the trends toward cultural globalization over the past two centuries, powerful new ideas about politics must always initially be expressed in some local idiom. Interpretative understanding of such ideas – what Max Weber called the *verstehen* approach – requires a fair degree of contextual knowledge of particular languages and cultures (M. Weber, 1978). Language groupings alone thus provide one clear rationale for traditional area studies programs, since notwithstanding the enormous linguistic diversity of all world regions, there are still major languages in each region that are widely shared among elites – and new political ideas formulated in these languages therefore tend to diffuse quickly along the lines of dominant linguistic communities. Thus fluency in Chinese, Japanese, or Korean is crucial for East Asianists but not for Africanists; fluency in Swahili is a big advantage for a specialist on East Africa but not for a South Asianist. Beyond these obvious linguistic reasons for grouping major world regions, however, is a more subtle cultural one: namely, that shared historical legacies and geographic experiences make particular forms of communication more symbolically meaningful in some regions than others. To understand the political power of ideas like those of Sayyid Qutb in the contemporary Middle East, for example, one needs not only fluency in Arabic, but also enough historical knowledge to see how the common Muslim Arab experience of geopolitical and cultural marginalization since the fall of the Ottoman Empire makes credible a comprehensive theory of global redemption through Islamic jihad against the West (Musallam, 2005).

As with the impacts of historical legacies and geographic diffusion, these traditional concerns of 'area studies' are largely in tune with cutting edge approaches in the political science discipline. On one hand, historical institutionalists are increasingly interested in charting how the impact of 'ideas' may systematically affect the later course of institutional development among countries in a given region (Berman, 1998; Blyth, 2002; Hanson, 1997). On the other hand, rational choice theorists are actively seeking to incorporate the role of 'culture' – understood as shared belief systems – into formal models of strategic interaction, and thus accounting for divergent paths of political and economic change among neighboring peoples in otherwise comparable environments (Greif, 2006). Of course, even Bates (1996) admits that area studies specialists have a strategic advantage over deductive theorists concerning the issue of *verstehen*. As contemporary political science theory illustrates just how much can turn on the cultural meanings attached to particular modes of conduct in different parts of the world, however, that strategic advantage may well begin to count for a great deal more than advocates of deductive theory in the political science discipline initially recognized.

Thus we see that the traditional divisions among major area studies programs, while obviously arbitrary in the sense that their initial organization does not reflect any clear theoretical principle, nevertheless can be justified in ways that are remarkably consistent with emerging theories and methodologies in contemporary comparative politics. Area studies specialists tend to group together polities and societies that have common historical origins in imperial conquest and postcolonial liberation, that geographically occupy the same zones of the world economy and are in a position to influence each other profoundly through institutional diffusion, and that have enough linguistic and cultural commonality to generate distinctive shared responses to new political ideas. Given what we are learning about the importance of past regime legacies, geographical proximity, and cultural interpretations for the course of institutional development in human history, these rough-and-ready principles for the training of future comparativists utilized in most area studies programs may actually serve the comparative politics subfield rather well. At a minimum, discarding the hard-won expertise in regional histories, patterns of economic interaction, languages and cultures that has been built up in area studies programs over the past several decades in favor of newly-proposed theoretical categorizations of regimes seems like a very risky bet.

CONCLUSION

The thrust of this chapter has been to provide a defense of the contribution of area studies to comparative politics. As we have seen, most of the common critiques of area studies are based on incorrect and/or outdated understandings of work in this tradition. And even the strongest theoretical critique of area studies research – that it is built around regional groupings of countries that are in some basic sense arbitrary – can be countered by noting cutting-edge theoretical breakthroughs in comparative politics that re-emphasize the importance of history, geography, and culture for explaining institutional change.

Returning to the vituperative debate with which this chapter began: does this mean that Johnson is right and Bates is wrong? Not entirely. As we have seen, the issues involved in judging the contribution of area studies from a social scientific point of view are extremely complex, and neither side in this longstanding debate has the right to dismiss the contributions of the other out of hand. Indeed, one reason that the debate between area specialists and their critics has continued

in much the same form for many decades now is the lack of intellectual respect shown by partisans on both sides, which tends to perpetuate longstanding stereotypes of the 'enemy.'

More specifically, despite the reasonably large degree of overlap between the criteria for defining 'areas' in most area studies programs and the factors now increasingly thought to be vital for explaining patterns of institutional evolution in time and space, there is clearly still some truth to the claim that traditional area studies boundaries are defined in ways that are theoretically and empirically arbitrary. Even if we accept the importance of past legacies of Soviet rule for structuring post-Soviet politics and societies, does the impact of Leninism still justify grouping Tajikistan and Slovenia in the same typological category – two decades after the collapse of communism in East-Central Europe? Or does the divide between the European Union and post-Soviet 'Eurasia' now provide a more logical point of departure for comparative political analysis? Similarly, is there really any theoretical reason to study Australia and Burma as common members of 'Southeast Asia'? Or should we study Australia and New Zealand as 'former British settler states' and thus as decisively different from other postcolonial settings in that region? Concerning such questions, 'the facts' will never speak for themselves. Only deductive theory, in the end, can provide clear conceptual criteria for deciding which comparisons will be fruitful for examining particular social scientific hypotheses.

Seen in this light, knowledge of current trends in deductive, general social science theory can play a crucial intellectual role for specialists in area studies, provoking them constantly to reexamine their understandings of the 'regions' on which they claim expertise, and undermining implicitly static characterizations of the nature of regional politics, economics, and cultures. In some cases, longstanding institutional divisions among different area studies centers on American campuses might even be fruitfully rethought in light of critiques developed by more general theories of political and social change. On the other hand, purely deductive analysis, unaccompanied by inductive research into the distinct empirical patterns of human interaction typical of particular parts of the world, will frequently be blind to the ways in which existing historical legacies and geographical diffusion generate the 'scope conditions' that limit the generalizability of most (if not all) political science theories (Hanson and Kopstein, 2005). Indeed, a strong training in area studies tends to arm political scientists with precisely the tools they need to see just where 'universal' theories of human behavior break down when applied outside the social contexts in which they were first developed. Thus, an open-minded and mutually respectful dialogue between scholars with a preference for deductive models and highly abstract theories, and those who prefer to chart the mechanisms of political and social change that are distinct to particular world areas, might greatly advance our collective understanding of the human condition.

NOTES

1. Similar developments took place in Western Europe. For example, African, Asian and Soviet area studies centres were set up in the UK in the 1960s as a response to geopolitical developments and inspired by the 1958 US act (Hayter, 1975).

2. Indeed, in an era when the world's sole superpower could find only six fluent speakers of Arabic to hire for work in the US Embassy in post-invasion Iraq, one might argue for much greater support for and utilization of area studies expertise in the formulation of U.S. foreign policy (Baker et al., 2006: 92).

3. Note, for example, Theodore Roosevelt's critique of Wilson's proposals for the League of Nations as requiring the United States to declare war 'every time a Jugoslav wishes to slap a Czechoslav in the face.' (Quoted in Ruggie, 1997).

4. Perhaps the only prominent exception is Samuel Huntington (1996) – who, ironically, is certainly not known in the field as an 'area specialist.'

5. One might also point out that Geertz was an anthropologist, rather than a political scientist; hence it hardly makes sense to cite his work as an example of 'area studies' methodology in the latter discipline.

REFERENCES

Apter, D.E. (1955) *The gold coast in transition*. Princeton, NJ: Princeton University Press.

Apter, D.E. (1963) *Ghana in transition*. New York: Atheneum.

Baker, J.A. (III.), Hamilton, L.H., et al. (2006) *The Iraq study group report*. New York: Vintage Books; Washington, D.C., United States Institute of Peace.

Bates, R.H. (1996, Winter) 'Letter from the president: Area studies and the discipline', *Newsletter of the APSA Comparative Politics Section*, 7 (1): 1.

Bates, R., Greif, A., Levi, M., Rosenthal, J.-L., and Weingast, B. (1998) *Analytic narratives*. Princeton, NJ: Princeton University Press.

Berman, S. (1998) *The social democratic moment: Ideas and politics in the making of interwar Europe*. Cambridge, MA: Harvard University Press.

Blyth, M. (2002) *Great transformations: Economic ideas and institutional change in the twentieth century*. Cambridge: Cambridge University Press.

Cohen, S. (1985) *Rethinking the soviet experience: Politics and history since 1917*. Oxford: Oxford University Press.

Cohen, S. (1999) 'Russian studies without Russia', *Post-Soviet Affairs*, 15 (1): 37–55.

Collier, P. (2007) *The bottom billion: Why the poorest countries are failing and what can be done about it*. Oxford: Oxford University Press.

Eckstein, H. (1975) 'A critique of area studies from a west European perspective', in L.W. Pye (ed.), *Political science and area studies: Rivals or partners?* Bloomington: Indiana University Press, pp. 199–217.

Eckstein, H. and Gurr, T.R. (1975) *Patterns of authority: A structural basis for comparative inquiry*. New York: Wiley.

Ekiert, G. and Hanson, S.E. (2003) 'Time, space, and institutional change in central and eastern Europe', in G. Ekiert and S.E. Hanson (eds), *Capitalism and democracy in* central and eastern Europe: Assessing the legacy of communist rule. Cambridge: Cambridge University Press, pp. 15–48.

Evans, P.B. (1979) Dependent development: The alliance of multinational, state, and local capital in Brazil. Princeton, NJ: Princeton University Press.

Evans, P.B., Rueschemeyer, D. and Skocpol, T. (eds) (1985) Bringing the state back in. Cambridge: Cambridge University Press.

Farish, M. (2005) 'Archiving areas: The ethnogeographic board and the second world war', Annals of the Association of American Geographers, 95: 663–79.

Farr, J. and Seidelman, R. (Eds.) (1993) Discipline and history: Political science in the United States. Ann Arbor: University of Michigan Press.

Ford Foundation (1999) Crossing borders: Revitalizing area studies. New York: Ford Foundation.

Foster, G.M. (1965) 'Peasant society and the image of limited good', American Anthropologist, 67 (2): 293–315.

Friedman, T.L. (1999) The lexus and the olive tree. New York: Farrar, Straus, and Giroux.

Friedman, T.L. (2005) The world is flat: A brief history of the twenty-first century. New York: Farrar, Straus, and Giroux.

Fukuyama, F. (1993) 'The modernizing imperative: The USSR as an ordinary country', National Interest, 31: 10–18.

Gallup, J.L., Sachs, J.D. and Mellinger A.D. (1999) 'Geography and Economic Development', International Regional Science Review, 22 (2): 179–232.

Geertz, C. (1973) 'Thick description: Toward an interpretive theory of culture', in The interpretations of cultures: Selected essays. New York: Basic Books, pp. 3–30.

Gellner, E. (1983) Nations and nationalism. Oxford: Blackwell.

Golden, M. (1998, Summer) 'Is there an international division of labor in contemporary political science: Editor's introduction', Newsletter of the APSA Comparative Politics Section, 9 (2): 6.

Greif, A. (2006) Institutions and the path to the modern economy: Lessons from medieval trade. Cambridge: Cambridge University Press.

Gunnell, J.G. (1993) 'American political science, liberalism, and the invention of political theory', in J. Farr and R. Seidelman (eds), Discipline and history: Political science in the United States. Ann Arbor: University of Michigan Press, pp.179–97.

Gurr, T.R. (1974) 'Persistence and change in political systems, 1800–1971', American Political Science Review, 68 (4): 1478–81.

Haas, E.B. (1958) The uniting of Europe: Political, social, and economic forces, 1950–1957. Stanford, CA: Stanford University Press.

Haas, E.B. (1964) Beyond the nation–state: Functionalism and international organization. Stanford, CA: Stanford University Press.

Hall, P.A. and Tarrow, S. (2001) 'Globalization and area studies: When is too broad too narrow?', in P. O'Meara, H.D. Mehlinger and R. Ma Newman (eds), Changing perspectives on international education (2nd edition). Bloomington: Indiana University Press, pp. 96–100.

Hanson, S.E. (1997) Time and revolution: Marxism and the design of soviet institutions. Chapel Hill: University of North Carolina Press.

Hanson, S.E. and Kopstein, J.S. (2005) 'Regime type and diffusion in comparative politics methodology', Canadian Journal of Political Science, 38 (March), 69–99.

Hayter, W. (1975) 'The Hayter report and after', Oxford Review of Education, 1: 169–72.

Hough, J.F. (1997) Democratization and revolution in the USSR. Washington, DC: Brookings.

Huntington, S.P. (1996) The clash of civilizations and the remaking of world order. New York: Simon and Schuster.

Johnson, C. (2001) 'Preconception vs. observation, or the contributions of rational choice theory and area studies to contemporary political science', in P. O'Meara, H.D. Mehlinger and R. Ma Newman (eds), Changing perspectives on international education. Bloomington: Indiana University Press, pp. 58–66.

Johnson, C. (2000) *Blowback: The costs and consequences of American empire*. New York: Metropolitan Books.

Johnson, C. (1962) *Peasant nationalism and communist power: The emergence of revolutionary China, 1937–1945*. Stanford, CA: Stanford University Press.

Knock, T.J. (1992) *To end all wars: Woodrow Wilson and the quest for a new world order*. New York: Oxford University Press.

Kopstein, J. and Reilly, D. (2000) 'Geographic diffusion and the transformation of the post-communist world', *World Politics*, 53 (October): 1–37.

Laitin, D.D. (1977) *Politics, language, and thought: The Somali experience*. Chicago: University of Chicago Press.

Lambert, R.D., Barber, E.G., Merrill, M.B., Jorden, E., and Twarog, L.I. (1984) *Beyond growth: The next stage in language and area studies*. Washington DC: Association of American Universities.

Lambert, R.D. (2001) 'Domains and issues in international studies', in P. O'Meara, H.D. Mehlinger and R. Ma Newman (eds), *Changing perspectives on international education*. Bloomington: Indiana University Press, pp. 30–48.

Lerner, D. (1958) *The passing of traditional society: Modernizing the Middle East*. Glencoe, IL: Free Press.

Lowenthal, R. (1970) 'Development v. utopia in communist policy', in C. Johnson (ed.), *Change in communist systems*. Stanford: Stanford University Press, pp. 33–116.

Mahoney, J. and Rueschemeyer, D. (eds) (2003) *Comparative historical analysis in the social sciences*. Cambridge: Cambridge University Press.

Malia, M. (1993) 'A fatal logic', *National Interest*, 31: 80–90.

Mitchell, T. (2004) 'The Middle East in the past and future of social science', in D. Szanton (ed.) *The politics of knowledge: Area studies and the disciplines*. Berkeley: University of California Press, pp. 74–118.

Moore, B. (1950) *Soviet politics: The dilemma of power*. Cambridge, MA: Harvard University Press.

Moore, B. (1954) *Terror and progress USSR: Some sources of change and stability in the soviet dictatorship*. Cambridge, MA: Harvard University Press.

Musallam, A. (2005) *From secularism to jihad: Sayyid Qutb and the foundations of radical Islamism*. Westport, CT: Praeger.

Parsons, T. (1951) *The social system*. Glencoe, IL: Free Press.

Prewitt, K. (1996) 'Presidential items', *Items*, 50 (1); 15–18.

Przeworski, A. and Teune, H. (1970) *The logic of comparative social inquiry*. New York: Wiley-Interscience.

Rashid, A. (2002) *Jihad: The rise of militant Islam in Central Asia*. New Haven: Yale University Press.

Rostow, W.W. (1960) *The stages of economic growth: A non–communist manifesto*. Cambridge: Cambridge University Press.

Ruggie, J.G. (1997) 'The past as prologue?: Interests, identity, and American foreign policy', *International Security*, 21 (4): 89–125.

Rupnik, J. (1999) 'The postcommunist divide', *Journal of Democracy*, 10: 57–62.

Said, E.W. (1978) *Orientalism*. New York: Vintage Books.

Scott, J.C. (1985) *Weapons of the weak: Everyday forms of peasant resistance*. New Haven: Yale University Press.

Sewell, W. (1980) *Work and revolution in France: The language of labor from the old regime through 1848*. Cambridge: Cambridge University Press.

Skocpol, T. (1979) *States and social revolutions*. Cambridge: Cambridge University Press.

Steinmo, S., Thelen, K. and Longstreth, F. (eds) (1992) *Structuring politics: Historical institutionalism in comparative analysis*. Cambridge: Cambridge University Press.

Thelen, K. (1999) 'Historical institutionalism in comparative politics', *Annual Review of Political Science*, 2: 369–404.

Thorsen, N. (1998) *The political thought of Woodrow Wilson, 1875–1910*. Princeton, NJ: Princeton University Press.

Tucker, R.C. (1969) *The Marxian revolutionary idea*. New York: Norton.

Vachudova, M.A. (2005) *Europe undivided: Democracy, leverage, and integration after communism*. Cambridge: Cambridge University Press.

Wallerstein, I. (1974) 'The rise and future demise of the world capitalist system: Concepts for comparative analysis', *Comparative Studies in Society and History*, 16 (4): 387–415.

Ward, R.E. (1975) 'Culture and the comparative study of politics', in L.W. Pye (ed.), *Political science and area studies: Rivals or partners?* Bloomington: Indiana University Press, pp. 23–47.

Weber, E.J. (1976) *Peasants into Frenchmen: The modernization of rural France, 1870–1914*. Stanford, CA: Stanford University Press.

Weber, M. (1978) *Economy and society: An outline of interpretive sociology*. Berkeley: University of California Press.

Wilkinson, S.I. (submitted) *Colonization, institutions and conflict*. Cambridge: Cambridge University Press.

10

Comparative Politics and International Relations

John M. Hobson

INTRODUCTION

The relationship between the disciplines of International Relations (IR) and Comparative Politics (CP) – as well as Comparative Political Economy (CPE) and Comparative Sociology (CS) – despite a *prima facie* or intuitive appearance of natural or inherent overlap, turns out to be highly complex, fraught and problematic. For given that CP scholars often assume that they work broadly within IR, it is naturally perplexing to be told by many IR scholars that their disciplines share very little in common: that 'CP is not IR'. It is indeed perplexing, of course, because so many CP scholars frame their analyses within an international context. One need only think of scholars such as Theda Skocpol (1979) or Michael Mann (1993) who not only factor in the role of the international into their theories but go yet further by seeking to break down what Ian Clark (1999) usefully calls the 'great divide' between theories of the international and national realms. How could such comparative scholarship be characterized as 'not IR'?

I know just how perplexing, if not bewildering, this can be for I was once on the receiving end of such a dismissal, even though I had begun teaching and working in IR. I began in my PhD by developing a comparative historical-sociological perspective on the shift from free trade to tariff protectionism in Europe in the late nineteenth century. The dissertation was essentially a critique of Marxist and liberal conceptions of trade policy and sought not just to theorize the role of the international as it impacted upon different states, but simultaneously reveal how the domestic realm impacted on the international (thereby fundamentally breaking down the 'great divide' between the two realms). At the time I assumed that my comparative historical-sociological perspective overlapped with IR and that, in effect, I had already paid the high start-up costs that would ease my transition from a sociology doctoral student to a lecturer in IR. But having joined a politics department in order to do just this (at La Trobe University, Melbourne in 1992), I quickly learned how little I really knew about IR and how my work up to that point did not fit well within the discipline. Having battled through my initial bewilderment, and not infrequent bouts of perplexing difficulties over a considerable period of time, I then prepared the dissertation for publication by adding in a critique of neorealism and, in the process, completely recast the argument to provide a comparative historical-sociology not simply of trade policy but of IR more generally (Hobson, 1997). Even so, it was not until I wrote my book *The State and International Relations* (Hobson, 2000) that I came to fully understand why IR scholars dismiss CP as 'not IR'. Accordingly, I seek in the first section to relay my own learning experience undertaken between 1992 and 2000 so as to provide a potted, 'pain-free' explanation for those CP scholars who experience bewilderment or puzzlement in the face of this dismissal. And this will simultaneously provide an introduction to the *problematique* and study of IR.

However, while I now fully appreciate why IR dismisses CP as 'not IR', I do not accept its wholesale rejection within an IR context, as I believe that ignoring comparative insight limits the study of IR. The irony is that the two disciplines should be 'bedfellows', working together to explore the many issues and problems that confront the world today. And so what should be a fruitful dialogue between like-minded scholars has degenerated into a dialogue of the deaf, which, I argue, comes to the detriment of *both* disciplines. The issue then becomes, therefore, how we can resolve this problem so as to render the two disciplines commensurable in the first instance so that we may then consider how each can benefit through mutual dialogue (which will be considered in the conclusion). And finally, the second section acts as a bridge between the first section and the conclusion, relaying how comparative analysis has been conducted within IR. Above all, outlining the *problematique* and study of IR conducted in the first two sections is a vital pre-requisite for promoting bicultural or bi-disciplinary understanding so that a productive dialogue can be developed in order to enhance both disciplines.

THE PROBLEMATIQUE OF IR: OR, WHY 'COMPARATIVE POLITICS IS NOT IR'

It helps to begin by highlighting the point that for many CP/CPE or CS analyses the key methodological approach deployed examines how international forces or pressures are responded to in a variety of ways across national societies. Thus, for example, Peter Gourevitch's book, *Politics in Hard Times*, examines how various states responded differently to international economic recession in the late-nineteenth century (Gourevitch, 1986). Specifically, he opens up the 'black box' to reveal how domestic actor preferences came to shape national trade policy. Similarly, Theda Skocpol's *States and Social Revolutions* argues that various states fared differently under the challenges posed by the geopolitical inter-state system (Skocpol, 1979). Thus revolutions occurred in France (1789), Russia (1917) and China (1949) because the respective states were unable to overcome domestic fetters to the enhancement of its fiscal-military capacity. By contrast, the Prussian and Meiji Japanese states were able to overcome domestic fetters and were accordingly able to remain militarily competitive, thereby avoiding the fate of social revolution. Many other examples could, of course, be marshalled here – for example, Gerschenkron's analysis of late industrialisation (Gerschenkron, 1962), or Tilly's and Mann's analysis of state formation (Tilly, 1990; Mann, 1993). But this is sufficient to establish the key point at stake here: that the comparative methodology is one that holds the international realm constant and examines how domestic forces – usually state-society relations – differ across national states and lead to different outcomes on the ground. That is, uniform international pressures are refracted in different ways at the national level owing to specific constellations of domestic forces. This is, to borrow Gourevitch's well-known phrase, a 'second-image reversed' approach (Gourevitch, 1978). And ultimately this boils down to the point that varying state-society relations are treated as the independent variable.

IR can be differentiated from CP in two immediate ways. First, and most obviously, IR is interested primarily in explaining occurrences within the international, rather than the domestic, realm. Second, and more importantly, for mainstream IR the international is treated as the independent variable such that national variations are ignored (ie., state-society relations are black-boxed). How and why has this particular spatial ontology emerged as the defining aspect of mainstream IR? In answering this question I shall delve into a sociology of knowledge through relating the construction of contemporary IR, the sub-text of which is that the present definition of the discipline is highly contingent and problematic. And this in turn fits into my argument made in the conclusion where I suggest that the discipline can and should, I believe, be reconstructed so as to allow for inter-disciplinary dialogical learning.

As I personally entered the discipline of IR I came to realize that the key that unlocks its door is the 'W-word' – Waltz. In 1979 Kenneth Waltz published his seminal text, *Theory of International Politics* (Waltz, 1979). In the present context, there are two inter-related achievements that marked the book. First, it brought neorealism onto the IR agenda in no uncertain terms. Second, it was important because it sought to redefine or reconstruct the discipline of IR in highly exclusive or parsimonious ways that entailed banishing CP and comparative insight from that which constitutes 'legitimate IR research'. And here it is vital to realize that Waltz's 1979 book is *the* foundationalist text for all of modern IR; so much so that intimate familiarity with it probably marks the litmus test for whether someone is conversant with modern IR – a test that my CP readership might want to apply to itself. Waltz's approach was defined as 'neo-realist'

in contradistinction to classical realism. Significantly, while earlier classical realists – E.H. Carr (1939) and especially Hans Morgenthau (1948/1978) – had become famous in the discipline because they sought to lay out a 'science' of international politics, Waltz took this enterprise one step further. And he did so in large part by constructing a great divide between the national and international realms on the one hand and banishing comparative analysis from the study of IR on the other. But to understand this, it is worth providing the background context that underpins these various moves that culminated in the placing of the present goalposts between which the gatekeeper of 'legitimate IR' stands on guard.

While it would be wrong to assume that IR as a discipline began after 1919 as most IR scholars problematically assume (Schmidt, 1998), it has nevertheless become a trope that IR, conceived as a separate 'scientific' discipline within the social sciences, had to await the arrival of Carr and Morgenthau around the time of World War II. IR is, perhaps more than any other discipline, defined by a certain insecurity. It is assumed by most IR scholars (notwithstanding Schmidt's pioneering insights) that it began later than most other disciplines. The insecurity emerged as a function of the perception that IR was a derivative late-comer discipline that comprised an awkward amalgam of a variety of different disciplines and, therefore, had no autonomous integrity. Crucially, it has been the quest for such exclusive disciplinary integrity that has obsessed IR theorists in the latter half of the last century – an obsession that is probably unique to IR. And it is this obsession that gave Carr and Morgenthau their privileged status within the discipline. However, as we shall see shortly, this was governed by a fundamental irony. Indeed, the whole process of constructing the discipline is replete with ironies. And I shall spend a good deal of time considering these ironies because they point up the manufactured process through which the discipline has been defined in its present exclusionary form.

Both Carr's and Morgenthau's prominent status emerged through their calling for a 'science of International Politics' (IP) that would at last deliver to IR its disciplinary autonomous integrity. The key contribution here lies with the first chapter of Morgenthau's seminal text, *Politics Among Nations* (Morgenthau, 1948/1978). There he set out the 'six principles of political realism' that served to lay the foundations for this 'science of IP'. Moreover, the book's 'legitimacy' was enhanced further because it provided a kind of manual or handbook for American statesmen in their pursuit of great power politics after 1947 (Hoffmann, 1977; Smith, 2000). The key principles here are the second and sixth, which effectively assert that the sphere of politics must be separated out from all others, whether these be economic, legalistic, moralist, social, etc. Moreover, his argument was that for foreign policy to be effective statesmen must ignore domestic social forces completely. Furthermore, his approach advanced a positivism that transcends time and space. This was realized in his famous claims that 'the struggle for power [between states] is universal in time and space' (Morgenthau, 1948/1978: 36), and that 'all history shows that nations active in international politics are continuously preparing for, actually involved in, or recovering from organized violence in the form of war' (Morgenthau, 1948/1978: 42). All in all, then, in this conventional reading of Morgenthau we can see the (tentative) origins of the claim that the international realm must be analytically separated out from the domestic, that international politics must be separated out from all non-political factors, and that the processes that govern international politics are universal in time and space.

And yet the deep irony here lies in the point that the following 32 chapters in many ways contradicted these positivistic and spatial-ontological claims for which he had become famous. Perhaps more surprising still is that there has been very little recognition of this point among IR scholars, with

students still taught that the key to Morgenthau lies in the first chapter and its six principles of political realism (so that students very rarely read beyond the first chapter). Yet more surprising is that even in the first chapter there is a hint of an alternative formulation that is outlined in his third principle which asserts that

> the contemporary connection between interest and the nation state is a product of history, and is therefore bound to disappear in the course of history. Nothing in the realist position militates against the assumption that the present division of the political world into nation states will be replaced by larger units of a quite different character, more in keeping with the technical potentialities and the moral requirements of the contemporary world. (Morgenthau, 1948/1978: 10)

And the following 32 chapters lay out a relatively complex 'comparative historical' approach to the study and analysis of IR that in effect extrapolates on the third principle (see Hobson, 2000: 47–55; Griffiths, 1992). In short, it is as if the vast majority of the book elaborates on the third principle which, in contrast to the other five, rejects a positivist/ scientific epistemology. And it is the desire of IR scholars to preserve a constructed view of IR as having its own autonomous and scientific (positivist) integrity that, I believe, accounts for why this alternative reading has gone largely unnoticed. That is, this alternative comparative historical sociological reading has gone largely unnoticed because it would disturb the preferred construction of the discipline that has been embraced by mainstream, positivist IR scholars and gatekeepers in the last three decades.

Nevertheless, a yet more profound irony quickly emerges for it was Kenneth Waltz in his 1979 book who forcefully took issue with classical realism. And in considering this critique, so we necessarily move closer to understanding how and why the break or divide between IR and CP has occurred. As signalled earlier, Waltz's major task was to redefine the discipline in ways that fundamentally separated it out from all others in the social sciences. And here he took to task the classical realism of Carr and especially Morgenthau in order to achieve this objective. Hic criticism was simple but powerful. He claimed that classical realism was not after all a scientific theory of IP because, despite all popular perceptions to the contrary, it failed to separate the international ontologically from the domestic. Carr and Morgenthau erred, he argued, because they had in fact 'merely' created a 'theory of foreign policy' rather than a proper, positivistic theory of the international. That is, they had looked at the domestic origins of foreign policy – something that rendered their theories more commensurate with comparative analysis rather than IR. And in the process yet another irony emerges. For to fully understand Waltz's disciplinary and theoretical move here requires us to entirely rethink the conventional positivistic reading of Carr and Morgenthau (as alluded to above and to which I shall return more fully in the second section). But while it is certainly true that a minority of scholars have reinterpreted Carr and Morgenthau in ways that in effect take Waltz's claim much further (eg., Griffiths, 1992; Hobson, 2000: 45–61; Howe, 1994), it is telling that students for the most part are still taught that classical realism developed a 'science of IP' that echoes much of what Waltz (1979) stands for (eg., Burchill, 1996).

It helps to contextualize all this within Waltz's three-fold typology of theories of international conflict that was systematically laid out in his equally famous book, *Man, the State, and War* (Waltz, 1959). There he labelled those theories that locate the causes of international conflict in the nature of individuals as 'first image' conceptions. 'Second image' theories focus on state-society relations that exist at the national, domestic level. By contrast, 'third image' theories locate the causes of international conflict at the international level. Beaming forward to 1979, Waltz returned to this conception and argued that a 'scientific theory' of IR/IP could only be achieved by developing a third image approach, which grants the international

realm – what he terms the anarchic international political structure – an ontological primacy such that it is deemed to be entirely autonomous of influences emanating from the domestic-national realm.

Crucially, it was this Waltzian conception that led to a rapid narrowing of the discipline's mainstream boundaries (though this process had begun under the influence of behaviourism in the 1960s). Indeed, Waltz's theory sought explicitly to banish the study of CP or equally Comparative Sociology/ Economics from the definition of that which constitutes 'legitimate IR enquiry' (eg., Waltz, 1979: 43–9). Above all, his central analytical focus upon which he constructed his own theory, rested on the assumption that the key aspect that governs the international realm is 'continuity'. By continuity he means that the international realm has always remained the same: that international politics has always comprised conflict between political units, whether these be empires, city-states or nation-states (Waltz, 1979: 66). To explain this *uniformity* of international outcomes, Waltz established four major points, all of which sought to banish comparative political/economic/sociological enquiry from the mainstream IR research agenda.

First, conceiving international anarchy (defined as the absence of a higher authority above states) as an autonomous *structure*, ensures that states have no choice but to adapt or conform to the structuralist logic of anarchic competition. Accordingly, the politics of 'agency' drops out (and is thereby consigned or banished to the discipline of CP). Second, Waltz posits a strict dividing line between the autonomous or self-constituting international realm and the residual national/domestic realm, in order to retain the ontological primacy of international anarchy (again banishing the analysis of domestic politics to Comparative Politics/Political Economy/Sociology). Third, he insists on the omission of social process and identity – again so as to preserve the centrality of the structural/materialist logic of anarchy, as is consistent with his positivist, asociological and ahistorical epistemology – thereby, once more banishing CP/CPE/CS from view.

And fourth, as noted above, he dismisses the study of international change by arguing that the international realm is and always has been marked by a dismaying persistence of recurring events. Indeed, according to one prominent IR scholar, Waltz's theory contains only a reproductive rather than a transformationist logic (Ruggie, 1986). And it does so because by conforming to the competitive logic of anarchy, so states unintentionally reproduce the structure of international anarchy. Thus as states are required to emulate the leading powers and, above all, to engage in balance of power politics in order to ensure individual survival (thereby conforming to the 'logic of anarchy'), so it becomes impossible for any one state to take over the system and transform the anarchic multi-state system into an imperial hierarchy. But to understand this vital aspect of the argument we need to delve more deeply.

Waltz argued that there are two types of political structure – domestic and international – with each being defined by various levels or tiers. The first tier is the 'ordering principle'; the second tier is the 'character of the units'; and the third tier is the 'distribution of capabilities'. For the purposes of this discussion it is only the first two tiers that require consideration. At the domestic level, political structures are hierarchical, whereas the international political structure is anarchic. The critical point is that in the domestic political structure the 'second tier' (the character of the units) stays in, whereas at the international level the second tier 'drops out'. Understanding why this difference emerges, which he explains in Chapter 5, takes us to the very heart of the issue that is at stake here. In the domestic system, which entails a hierarchic political structure, the first tier ('ordering principle') requires that the units 'specialize'. That is, the units (individuals) 'specialize' in that activity in which each does best. Some become lecturers, others butchers, others bakers and others chefs, etc.

And by each specializing in a particular all individuals become *interdependent* since the lecturer relies on the butcher, the baker or the chef for his meals. Crucially, this interdependence/specialization nexus only becomes possible because the problem of security has been solved by the presence of a hierarchy (ie., a state) that stands above the individuals. And the ordering principle that instructs individuals to specialize means that the domestic system is characterized by 'unlike units' (since they all perform different functions or tasks).

By contrast, precisely because the international system is anarchic given that there is no higher authority that can guarantee security among states, so states (as the units) are necessarily insecure and must conform to a different ordering principle: that of 'self-help'. That is, each state must be self-sufficient and must not rely on others for its reproduction. Thus *independence* rather than interdependence ensues so that states become 'like units' (ie., they become undifferentiated in that they are *functionally* alike). That is, states are socialized entirely by an exogenous variable as they conform to the competitive logic of international anarchy. And so it is here where we move to the final piece of the jigsaw. The crux is that only in the international political structure does the second tier (the nature or characteristics of the units) 'drop out'; that is, 'the second [tier] is not needed in defining [the] international political structure, because so long as anarchy endures, states remain like units' (Waltz, 1979: 93, 101). Why then does the second tier drop out of the definition of the international political structure?

There are two main reasons why the character of the units must not be allowed to enter into the definition of the international structure. First, the internal properties of states – social, economic, political, ideational – are always changing. Moreover, their properties vary (eg., some are democratic others authoritarian, some are capitalist others communist, some are Christian others Islamic). It is this reason in particular why states cannot enter into defining the international precisely because the international political structure never changes – it always remains anarchic. Put differently, if we allowed ever-changing states an ontological primitivism, then the international would appear to be changing all the time; something that would offend the very basis of Waltz's 'continuity' assumption. Second, although the properties of states do indeed change over time, nevertheless states are a by-product of the international system rather than vice versa. And paradoxically, while their properties vary their *primary function* becomes uniform – to maintain security against other states in a hostile, anarchic world. It is this homogeneity of function that leads onto the famous 'billiard ball metaphor'. States are likened to billiard balls not simply because they constantly clash, but because billiard balls are solid such that their internal *functional* properties do not vary. And it is this assumption of functional homogeneity that leads Waltz to characterize states as 'like-units'. Accordingly, because they are all product and not at all productive they cannot play a causal role in shaping and determining the international political structure. For these two reasons then, the second tier drops out of the analysis or causal determination of the international system.

The upshot of this is that the international and national realms necessarily become ontologically separated out, such that the former is enshrined with ontological primacy/primitivism. Accordingly, this manoeuvre means that CP and IR are necessarily divorced from each other precisely because CP grants ontological weighting to the domestic realm and views states as unlike units, whereas mainstream IR accords exclusive ontological weighting to the international system and views states as functionally similar units.

Crucially, Waltzian neorealism has probably done most to mark out the borders of the discipline so as to explicitly exclude and marginalize CP from that which constitutes 'real international relations'. Indeed it has

been the determined quest for scientific certainty, and a celebration of positivism which views 'legitimate international relations enquiry' as defined *only* by the acquisition of objective knowledge, that prompted Waltz and others to find in international politics 'law-like patterns' of recurrence and continuity. As noted above, by definition such a linear pattern could not be revealed through a comparative analysis of any sort precisely because this entails treating states as ontologically important on the one hand and functionally differentiated on the other. And to reiterate the most important point: such law-like patterns of international recurrence and continuity could not be revealed were we to treat states (or the national realm) as ever-changing, unlike units that shape the international structure because this would necessarily lead to a picture of constant international change. This is why for Waltz, states must be black boxed and held constant. And in noting this, so we arrive at the terminus of our quest not simply as to why CP is 'not IR' but why CP *must not* be IR.

All this, however, is not without various ironies, which are useful to consider so as to reveal the arbitrary 'construction' of an autonomous IR that stands separate to CP and other comparative disciplines. First, in his 1959 book Waltz argued in the final chapter that an adequate account of IR had to combine insights from each of the three image theorists of international conflict (Waltz, 1959: Chap. 8). And second, he wrote a somewhat lesser-known book in the intervening period, *Foreign Policy and Democratic Politics* (Waltz, 1967), where he argued that the nature of domestic politics is vital to understanding the foreign policies of states. But by 1979 Waltz had turned his back on these potentially inclusive-disciplinary insights to embrace a highly parsimonious and narrow conception of legitimate IR theoretical enquiry. Does this contradict his earlier position? Answering this takes us to the very heart of his exclusionary conception of legitimate IR enquiry. For where he and the classical realists had 'gone wrong', he now insisted, was in developing a 'theory of foreign policy' (Waltz, 1979: 63–4, 121–3), which requires all manner of domestic and comparative political insight. So by 1979 his central claim was that a 'theory of foreign policy' might well tell us about how different states respond differently in the international system, but a *scientific theory* of international politics is necessarily uninterested in such complexities or particularities. Rather, a scientific theory of IP is concerned to explain only a 'small number of big and important things' (Waltz, 1979: Chap. 1, 70–2, 121–3; 1986: 329, 344–5). And this entails revealing the law-like tendencies of the international system, which define or govern the essential and common strategies that all states will necessarily undertake regardless of their domestic characteristics or properties. All in all, then, a scientific (international) systemic theory eschews the complexities that comparative insight necessarily entails.

Still, what sealed the centrality of international systemic analysis (as opposed to comparative analysis) in defining that which constitutes 'legitimate IR' was the publication of Robert Keohane's seminal book, *After Hegemony* (Keohane, 1984). By accepting Waltz's systemic structuralist premise while simultaneously moving away from his earlier work on global interdependence (Keohane and Nye, 1977), domestic and comparative politics were effectively dismissed from his purview. Moreover, Keohane's book was crucial because it was this that set up the neoliberal institutionalist research agenda, which soon played a central role in the mainstream American IR agenda. And given that in the US – the 'home of IR' (Crawford and Jarvis, 2001; Hoffmann, 1977; Smith, 2000) – the mainstream IR research agenda was defined by the neorealist-neoliberal debate during the 1980s and 1990s, so the divorce of CP from IR, or the *decree nisi*, became finalized.

This is reflected by the way in which constructivist IR has been inserted into the discipline. Thus what could have seen a fundamental challenge to the identity of the discipline became, at least in its leading figures, a reinforcement of the systemic modality of IR (eg., Finnemore, 1996; Wendt, 1999). Moreover, while in recent years the English School of IR – building on *inter alia* the work of Hedley Bull (1977) – has witnessed a resurgence, it nevertheless produces an approach which black-boxes the state and state-society relations, thereby once more reinforcing the present identity of IR (eg., Dunne, 1998; Wheeler, 2000).

Thus by the late-1980s, to many IR scholars the new construction of a narrowly defined discipline unconcerned with comparative insight appeared as entirely natural. But by revisiting the genealogy of the discipline, we can now see that the present positioning of the discipline's boundaries is not natural but the product of an extremely recent intellectual construction. This is important to establish as a prerequisite for the argument of the Conclusion below. Still, it is instructive to note that not all IR scholars ignore comparative insight. But perhaps the greatest significance of this lies in the point that their analyses constitute in effect a radical challenge to the present construction of the discipline. How then has this been affected?

COMPARATIVE INTERNATIONAL RELATIONS: A NON-SEQUITUR?

I suggest that at least two broad comparative analytical variants can be discerned in the IR literature. My aim here is to provide a sketch of these approaches before considering in the Conclusion how we might begin the task of reconciling CP and IR so that both disciplines might be reconstructed in mutually beneficial ways. But before we proceed here it needs to be asked, in the light of the argument of the previous section, whether a comparative IR is a non-sequitur. There are two responses. First, what makes the following analyses part of the IR field is ultimately the point that they are all seeking to explain developments or changes in the international system (as opposed to CP/CPE/CS analyses which ultimately seek to explain developments or changes at the domestic/national level). And second, many of these analyses seek to provide – often explicitly – a challenge to mainstream 'systemic' approaches.

The comparative-sociological method in IR

It is possible for analytical purposes to discern two sub-sets within this variant; one that makes historical comparisons between international systems or regions across time and one that compares them within one temporal context. I shall take each in turn. As indicated earlier, one of the ironies here lies in the point that while conventionally regarded as proponents of a positivistic, exclusive IR, Carr and Morgenthau in fact developed a theory of IR that was based on a comparative historical sociological analysis. Here the essential mode of comparison is not between states in a similar time period but between international systems in different historical epochs. In *Politics Among Nations*, Morgenthau differentiated two key historical epochs, which he labelled the 'aristocratic international' and 'nationalistic universalism'. The former epoch that existed between approximately 1648 and the nineteenth century was characterized by relative peace and cooperation between states. It was so because rulers had a high institutional autonomy from the masses and were able to pursue interstate policies that were based on feudal norms of politeness and honour. However, the rise of democratic nation-states in the nineteenth century witnessed a fundamental change or transformation in the international system. Now states became embedded within their societies, such that the mass of citizens exercised an influence in foreign policy. In the process the moral boundary contracted from the international to the national level. Thus international aristocratic morality was replaced by a nationalistic ethic of 'Right or wrong – my country' (Morgenthau,

1948/1978: 253). Accordingly, the extant restraint of states was replaced by a crusading 'nationalistic universalism' in which democratic national states looked to impose their own ethics on all other countries through war. This, he argued, was responsible for the era of total war that characterized the first half of the twentieth century (the war of all against all).

Thus in fundamental contrast to Waltz, Morgenthau prioritized the study of international change, which is explained by transformations within the units through the extension of citizenship rights. No less significantly, this schema is very similar to that produced by E.H. Carr, not in his famous 1939 book but in two lesser-known volumes, *The New Society* (Carr, 1951) and *Nationalism and After* (Carr, 1945). Indeed the essential argument is almost identical, with the main difference comprising in the point that Carr singles out four historical epochs rather than two (for a full discussion see Hobson, 2000: 55–61).

Importantly, this kind of comparative-historical research is returning to IR, not surprisingly as a means to challenge mainstream, and especially neorealist, positivist analysis. Indeed since the end of the Cold War mainstream (Waltzian) neorealism has come under sustained attack from a range of sociological approaches, some of which deploy a comparative-historical sociological methodology (for a full discussion see Hobson, 2002). One of the more easily identifiable versions in terms of CP understanding can be found in the recent work of Chris Reus-Smit in his book, *The Moral Purpose of the State* (Reus-Smit, 1999). He develops a constructivist comparative historical sociology by comparing three regional international systems in world history – specifically the Ancient Greek city-state system, the medieval Italian city-state system and the modern sovereign state system. His principal focus is to reveal how each system was governed by different international/regional institutional frameworks, with each being differentiated by the unique normative environments that characterized the relevant constituent units. Through such a comparative historical socio-logical framework he is able to reveal why multilateralism has become a unique prop-erty of the modern sovereign state system.

A more well-known example is found in the pioneering article by John Ruggie in which he challenged neorealism's ontology by revealing how the European feudal 'heter-onomous' system differed fundamentally from its modern Westphalian successor (Ruggie, 1986). And it is noteworthy that others have produced a range of comparative historical-sociological analyses that reveal differences in international systems through time (eg., Buzan and Little, 2000), usually as a function of different state-society relations, whether these be based on class forces (eg., Rosenberg, 1994), or purely normative fac-tors (eg., Hall, 1999), or an amalgam of materialist and non-materialist social forces (cf. Buzan and Little, 2000; Ruggie, 1986).

The second sub-set of this variant com-pares regions in the same temporal context, usually that of the present. One instructive example here is found in Georg Sørenson's book, *Changes in Statehood* (Sørenson, 2001). Sørenson seeks to break down the great divide between CP and IR where the national-domestic and international realms become co-constitutive. Crucially he argues that domestic structures can resist interna-tional pressures towards homogenization and, in contrast to Waltz, argues that the world is characterized by the presence of states as unlike units. He specifies the existence of three forms of state – the *modern* state (which conforms to the Weberian definition and is found in large parts of Asia); the *postcolonial* state (which does not have a monopoly of the means of violence as found in Africa); and the *postmodern* state (where there are multi-level layers of governance, found especially in the EU). Most importantly, he argues that each region undergoes specific domestic and international security dilemmas (Sørenson, 2001, Chapters 7–9). Thus, postcolonial states enjoy limited external threat owing to the structure of international law, which supports

their external sovereignty. Paradoxically, this opens up a domestic space for such states to implement repressive domestic policies. Their security dilemma leads to intra-state wars (derived from their inability to secure domestic order and legitimacy). By contrast, postmodern states, while having solved their external security challenge, face other exter-nal challenges connected with globalization and the democratic deficit problem. And, of course, modern states face the traditional security dilemma. More generally, this type of comparative approach is receiving consid-erable attention within IR as regionalism is increasingly viewed as a major feature of the contemporary global system.

Comparative politics/ economics in IR

The second major variant of comparative analysis conducted within IR has perhaps the most in common with traditional CP/CPE/CS. This approach opens up the black box of state-society relations and examines the ways in which national variations impact on the inter-state system/international economy and sometimes vice versa. One such example lies in my own work that was set out in *The Wealth of States* (Hobson, 1997). As noted earlier, my task here was to provide a com-parative historical sociology of international change, using the transition from free trade to protectionism in late-nineteenth century Europe as a case study. The central claim lies in the point that international trade regime change is significantly informed by the nature of internal relations within European states. The principal states chosen were Russia, Germany and Britain where the 'most differ-ent' comparative method is deployed. Thus unitary democratic Britain is compared with federal authoritarian Germany and unitary autocratic Russia.

The argument begins by noting that the shift to protectionism was significantly dependent upon the fiscal choices of states given that tariffs are (regressive) indirect taxes.

As states faced fiscal crisis after 1870, given the escalation of the costs of war at the same time that international recession reduced the tax take, so governments looked for new sources of tax revenues. The key claim is that where states were disembedded from the mass of the population (which meant that they suffered from low governing capacity), so they resorted to regressive indirect taxes and therefore chose to shift to tariff protectionism (as in Germany and Russia). But in addition, a state's level of institutional centralization was a further important variable, with federal states relying on indirect taxes (and hence protectionism) while unitary states had greater capacity to resort to progressive income taxation. Thus the more robust unitary British state, which was also more embedded within the newly enfranchised masses, chose to enhance progressive income taxes in order to pay for new spending prerogatives, thereby avoiding the shift back to protectionism. The British example is also significant because it pre-empted the later shift to an international free trade regime after 1945 as first world states developed more deeply embedded relations with their societies. Hence national trade policy responses and changes in international trade regimes were based on specific configurations of domestic state-society relations as they responded to external and domestic challenges. No less importantly, while the international system constrained states in certain ways, it was also a 'resource pool' into which states dipped in order to push through various domestic changes. Accordingly, *The Wealth of States* simultaneously deploys a 'second image' (inside-out) and 'second image-reversed' (outside-in) approach.

Finally, while other IR scholars have produced comparative studies that examine the domestic origins of international change (eg., Seabrooke, 2006), others have invoked a comparative domestic institutional approach that reveals how different nexuses of state-society relations lead to different policy outcomes, in response to globalization and other external economic and non-economic challenges (cf. Keohane and Milner, 1996; Katzenstein, 1996; Risse-Kappen, 1995). And interestingly, these complement the analyses of various prominent comparativist scholars (eg., Garrett, 1998; Gourevitch, 1986; Weiss, 1998, 2003).

CONCLUSION: RECONCILING CP AND IR FOR THEIR MUTUAL BENEFIT

The upshot of the previous section is that comparative analysis is certainly re-emerging within IR, which in turn might appear to contradict the argument of the first section. But we can resolve this potential confusion by pointing out that the majority of those IR scholars who deploy comparative insight do so in order to challenge the present mainstream identity of the discipline (even if this is sometimes only implicit). And this in turn implies that comparative insight still occupies an *outsider* position within the discipline. But while such extra-disciplinary insight has, paradoxically, produced much richer analyses of IR, I think it highly unlikely that the growing cumulative weight of such comparative analyses will spontaneously tip the scales away from the discipline's current international systemic identity at some point in the future. For this thrust will remain stymied until the discipline's identity is explicitly reconstructed so as to become more inclusive. But by the same token, I do not believe that IR should simply import CP as it is presently constructed because the latter also suffers various problems that can be resolved by a more open and constructive engagement with IR.

Most generally, I want to argue that CP and IR, as they are presently constructed, both suffer major blind spots that limit their utility. The essential limitations are summed up by their propensity to lop-sided analysis. Thus while CP/CPE/CS black boxes the international or holds it constant so that the domestic realm is invested with ontological primacy, mainstream IR suffers the inverse problem, investing the international with ontological primacy and treating the national-domestic level as an analytical residual. The implication of this is of course that both sides of the great divide need to develop thick analyses of the international/global *and* domestic realms that focus on their co-constitutive relations if these disciplines are to progress beyond their present confines. But this is easier said than done, and would in any case be resisted by their respective gatekeepers, largely on the grounds that it would supposedly expand almost infinitely the boundaries of each discipline, thereby rendering them so unwieldy that they would be impossible to teach to students. Noteworthy too would be Waltz's response: that it would serve merely to replace 'theory' with 'thick description'. As he put it, 'Elegant [ie., parsimonious] definitions of [international political] structure enable one to fashion an explanatory system having only a few variables. If we add more variables, the explanatory system becomes more complicated … [such that] theoretical acuity gives way to rich and dense description' (Waltz, 1986: 330). Clearly then there is a great deal of ground-clearing that needs to be undertaken before we can begin the task of creating a dialogical community between IR and CP scholars.

And yet for all this a profound irony emerges here. For one of the significant points that Waltz made in the well-known response to his critics was that: '[s]omeone may one day fashion a unified theory of internal and external politics … [Nevertheless] students of international politics will do well to concentrate on separate theories of internal and external politics until someone figures out a way to unite them' (Waltz, 1986: 340). I suggest that the time has surely come to develop such an 'integrationist theory', which effectively links up the domestic and international realms without reducing or collapsing one to the other. My aim here is not to begin this task in the limited space that remains,

but rather to point to some of the problems that each discipline necessarily faces by ignoring the other.

Perhaps the most poignant example here can be found in neo-Weberian comparative sociological analyses. The irony is that while neo-Weberian analyses claim to 'bring the state back in' (eg., Evans et al., 1985; Skocpol, 1979; Tilly, 1990), their analyses in effect end up by 'kicking the state back out' (Hobson, 2000: 174–91). This is because they (unwittingly) deploy a neorealist analysis of the international. And as was noted in the first section of this chapter, such a conception of international structure inevitably renders obsolete a thick conception of the state that has agency in the international system. In the work of Skocpol and Tilly, ultimately domestic factors are envisaged as intervening variables given that they are salient only to the extent that they enable or prevent a state from conforming to the primary logic of international anarchy/geopolitical competition. Put simply, in bringing the international geopolitical structure back in, they unwittingly kick the state back out as an independent variable. But the deepest irony here is that in deploying a neorealist conception of the international, neo-Weberian historical sociologists end up by producing an asociological and ahistorical analysis (Hobden, 1998; Hobson, 2000: Chap. 6; Hobson, 2006). Critically, therefore, had these prominent scholars been conversant with IR theory these perplexing contradictions could have been avoided. And so it is a particular irony that it is historical sociologists working within IR who have revealed this problem. Accordingly, neo-Weberians can ignore this extra-disciplinary IR insight only at their peril.

Inter-relatedly, when comparative scholars think of the international, they usually do so along implicitly neorealist lines. That is, they assume that the international realm is in effect a geopolitical realm of competing or warring states. But this is merely one conception of the international. Constructivist, English School and various liberal approaches all treat the international realm as imbued with social properties of one sort or another that can promote cooperation between states. Paradoxically, therefore, it is to IR scholars that we must often look in order to gain a proper sociological understanding of the international. Still, the key point is that as the analysis of globalization increasingly embeds itself in many of the disciplines across the social sciences, so comparative scholars can ignore IR theory only at their peril.

But by the same token, the systemic focus of IR precludes various factors that could enable a much richer analysis of the international or global realms. Thus in ignoring state-society and social relations so the whole issue of *social agency* is often lost. Accordingly, this promotes a structuralist or elitist, top-down conception of the world, which provides no space or voice for more everyday actors especially, though not exclusively, at the sub-national level, whether these be class-based, gender-based or ethnic-based (see Hobson and Seabrooke, 2007). One of the costs here is that we end up with a highly limited, if not parochial, Eurocentric conception of the international system which is shaped and governed by American hegemony, Western-based international institutions, or globalization as Western capitalism *writ large*. And the paradox here is that this Eurocentric trap is one that many critical theories of IR fall into as much as do the more mainstream approaches (Hobson, 2007). Of course, this is not to say that CP/CS necessarily escapes such a trap. But it is to say that the typical top-down approaches found in IR can be challenged by more comparatively sensitive analyses that are able to point to bottom-up social forces that are expressive of non-elite interests and identities in both the West and the East (Hobson, 2004).

More generally, though, without a thick conception of state-society and social relations, IR remains caught within a systemic international/global reductionist ontology that often banishes the possibility of social politics, as is apparent within so much of the IR literature on globalization. And such a structuralist ontology leads on to an ahistorical and asociological approach in which the issue of change becomes obscured. Thus opening IR up to CP/CPE and comparative historical sociology can paradoxically yield a much richer or thicker conception of the international or global systems as socially complex and immanent orders of social change. In short, therefore, opening up both disciplines to mutual dialogue is vital to promoting the study and research of CP/CPE/CS and IR, the success of which will be measured by the extent to which the 'great disciplinary divide' becomes reconstructed as a two-way permeable boundary.

REFERENCES

Bull, H. (1977) *The anarchical society*. London: Macmillan.

Burchill, S. (1996) 'Realism and neorealism', in S. Burchill and A. Linklater (eds), *Theories of international relations*. London: Macmillan.

Buzan, B. and Little, R. (2000) *International systems in world history*. Oxford: Oxford University Press.

Campbell, D. (1992) *Writing security*. Manchester: Manchester University Press.

Carr, E.H. (1939) *The twenty years' crisis 1919–1939*. London: Macmillan.

Carr, E.H. (1945) *Nationalism and after*. London: Macmillan.

Carr, E.H. (1951) *The new society*. London: Macmillan.

Clark, I. (1999) *Globalization and international relations theory*. Oxford: Oxford University Press.

Crawford, R.A. and Jarvis, D.S.L. (eds) (2001) *International relations – still an American social science?* NY: SUNY Press.

Dunne, T.J. (1998) *Inventing international society*. Basingstoke: Macmillan.

Evans, P.B., Reuschemeyer, D. and Skocpol, T. (eds.) (1985) *Bringing the state back in*. Cambridge: Cambridge University Press.

Finnemore, M. (1996) *National interests in international society*. Ithaca: Cornell University Press.

Garrett, G. (1998) *Partisan politics in the global economy*. Cambridge: Cambridge University Press.

Gerschenkron, A. (1962) *Economic backwardness in historical perspective*. Cambridge, MA: Harvard University Press.

Gourevitch, P.A. (1978) 'The second image reversed: the international sources of domestic politics', *International Organization*, 32 (4): 281–313.

Gourevitch, P.A. (1986) *Politics in hard times*. Ithaca: Cornell University Press.

Griffiths, M. (1992) *Realism, idealism and international relations*. London: Routledge.

Hall, R.B. (1999) *National collective identity*. New York: Columbia University Press.

Hobden, S. (1998) *International relations and historical sociology*. London: Routledge.

Hobson, J.M. (1997) *The wealth of states*. Cambridge: Cambridge University Press.

Hobson, J.M. (2000) *The state and international relations*. Cambridge: Cambridge University Press.

Hobson, J.M. (2002) 'What's at stake in bringing historical sociology *back* into international relations? Transcending 'chronofetishism' and 'tempocentrism' in international relations', in S. Hobden and J.M. Hobson (eds), *Historical sociology of international relations*. Cambridge: Cambridge University Press, pp. 3–41.

Hobson, J.M. (2004) *The eastern origins of western civilisation*. Cambridge: Cambridge University Press.

Hobson, J. M. (2006) 'Mann, the state and war', in J.A. Hall and R. Schroeder (eds), *An anatomy of power*. Cambridge: Cambridge University Press, pp. 150–66.

Hobson, J.M. (2007) 'Is critical theory always *for* the white west and *for* western imperialism? Beyond Westphalian, towards a post-racist, critical international relations', *Review of International Studies*, 33 (SI): 91–116.

Hobson, J.M. and Seabrooke, L. (eds) (2007) *Everyday politics of the world economy*. Cambridge: Cambridge University Press.

Hoffmann, S. (1977) 'An American social science: international relations', *Daedalus*, 106 (3): 41–60.

Howe, P. (1994) 'The utopian theory of E.H. Carr', *Review of International Studies*, 20 (3): 277–97.

Katzenstein, P.J. (1996) *Cultural norms and national security*. Ithaca: Cornell University Press.

Keohane, R.O. (1984) *After hegemony*. Princeton, NJ: Princeton University Press.

Keohane, R.O. and Milner, H. (eds) (1996) *Internationalization and domestic politics*. Cambridge: Cambridge University Press.

Keohane, R.O. and Nye, J.S. (1977) *Power and interdependence*. Boston: Little, Brown.

Mann, M. (1993) *The sources of social power* (Vol. 2) Cambridge: Cambridge University Press.

Morgenthau, H. (1948/1978) *Politics among nations*. New York: Alfred Knopf.

Reus-Smit, C. (1999) *The moral purpose of the state*. Princeton, NJ: Princeton University Press.

Risse-Kappen, T. (ed.) (1995) *Bringing transnational relations back in*. Cambridge: Cambridge University Press.

Rosenberg, J. (1994) *The empire of civil society*. London: Verso.

Ruggie, J.G. (1986) 'Continuity and transformation in the world polity: Toward a neorealist synthesis', in R.O. Keohane (ed.), *Neorealism and its critics*. New York: Columbia University Press, pp. 131–57.

Schmidt, B.C. (1998) *The political discourse of anarchy*. New York: SUNY Press.

Seabrooke, L. (2006) *The social sources of financial power*. Ithaca: Cornell University Press.

Skocpol, T. (1979) *States and social revolutions*. Cambridge: Cambridge University Press.

Smith, S. (2000) 'The discipline of international relations: Still an American social science?', *British Journal of Politics and International Relations*, 2 (3): 374–402.

Sørenson, G. (2001) *Changes in statehood*. Basingstoke: Macmillan.

Tilly, C. (1990) *Coercion, capital and European states, AD 990–1990*. Oxford: Blackwell.

Waltz, K.N. (1959) *Man, the state, and war*. New York: Columbia University Press.

Waltz, K.N. (1967) *Foreign policy and democratic politics*. Boston: Little, Brown.

Waltz, K.N. (1979) *Theory of international politics*. New York: McGraw Hill.

Waltz, K.N. (1986) 'Reflections on *Theory of international politics*: A response to my critics', in R.O. Keohane (ed.), *Neorealism and its critics*. New York: Columbia University Press, pp. 322–45.

Weiss, L. (1998) *The myth of the powerless state*. Cambridge: Polity.

Weiss, L. (ed.) (2003) *States in the global economy*. Cambridge: Cambridge University Press.

Wendt, A. (1999) *Social theory of international politics*. Cambridge: Cambridge University Press.

Wheeler, N.J. (2000) *Saving strangers*. Oxford: Oxford University Press.

PART II

Classic Issues in Comparative Politics

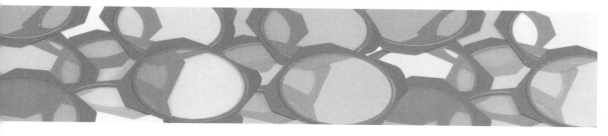

11

Post-Industrial Democracies: Political Economy and Democratic Partisan Competition

Herbert Kitschelt

INTRODUCTION

There is no other region of the world that has attracted as much systematic theory-guided comparative research in political science as today's set of affluent, post-industrial, politically, and economically stable democracies (abbreviated: PI-democracies). Except Japan, all of them are Western European or derivatively European as British settler democracies. Internationally, after World War II, this group of countries, crystallized around a network of military alliances with the United States as its hub, was the main antagonist of the communist bloc.

Comparative political science has pursued primarily four broad subjects of research with regard to PI-democracies. First, a great deal of attention has been devoted to their democratic institutions, especially their electoral systems, the relationship between legislative representation and executive power, and the centralization, or decentralization of authoritative

decision-making between national and subnational governments. Second, a huge number of studies have examined political participation and electoral behavior, as well as the strategic conduct of organized intermediaries that bring about collective action and bundle political preferences – social movements, interest associations and political parties (cf. Kitschelt and Rehm, 2007). Third, comparative politics has tried to account for the outputs and outcomes of the political process, that is, the authoritative allocation of benefits and costs through 'policies' and the consequences of such policies for citizens' quality of life. This research most prominently features the field of 'comparative political economy' that has devoted itself to two major questions: How do democratic political institutions and processes affect the macroeconomic performance of democratic polities (growth, unemployment, inflation, balance of accounts)? And to what extent do democracies protect citizens from the risks that wage earners run in the capitalist market place (unemployment, illness, old age) and correct the spontaneous market-based in-equality of incomes through public policy (taxes, transfers, public services)? Fourth, with the increasing policy integration of the European Union particularly since the Single European Act of 1986, the Maastricht Treaty of 1992, the introduction of the Euro, and the expansion of the EU to 27 members, research has focused on the multi-level governance of democratic polities that cede some decision-making authority, particularly in the realm of market-regulatory policies (competition, product standards, non-discrimination, environmental and safety regulations, etc.), to the supra-national, regional level.

As a result of research on democratic institutions, processes of interest mobilization, and policy formation, comparativists have tried to identify coherent 'types' of PI-democracies, each characterized by distinct institutions, processes and policy results. The best-known proposal is that of Arend Lijphart (1999) who distinguishes majoritarian and consensual democracies (see also Powell, 2000). This distinction empirically overlaps to a large extent with the political-economic distinction between 'liberal market economies' (LME) and 'coordinated market economies' (CME) proposed by David Soskice (1999). Beyond the comparative-static analysis of polity types, scholars have also devoted a great deal of research to the dynamic change of such types of democratic polities and political economies over time. How do polities respond to the 'shocks' of technological innovation, demographic change, as well as increasing incorporation of national polities in the global economic and political-military system?

In this overview I focus on the political economics of PI-democracies and bring in political institutions, democratic processes of interest articulation and aggregation, and multi-level governance only in as much as they affect political economic arrangements and outcomes in PI-democracies. In the first section, I identify basic attributes that set PI democracies apart from non-PI democracies

and (semi-)authoritarian regimes elsewhere around the globe. PI-democracies are a highly restricted set of the worlds' polities sharing social, economic, political and cultural traits that vary across the full global set of countries. As a consequence, causal mechanisms identified to account for political-economic variance *among* PI-democracies may be irrelevant for an account of political-economic variance *between* such democracies and all the rest of non-PI-democracies and authoritarian regimes. The second section turns to the explanation of macro-economic policy-making among PI-democracies. My focus is on two closely intertwined performance indicators, economic growth and employment, with some glances at inflation. In the third section, I give an overview of theories of the welfare state and how they account for different patterns, changes, and new challenges of social policy in PI-democracies.

THE GROUP OF POST-INDUSTRIAL DEMOCRACIES

All current PI-democracies embarked on the transition from agrarian to capitalist industrial market economies in the nineteenth century. With some major exceptions (Austria, Germany, Italy, Japan, and, for very different reasons, colonial Ireland), in the late nineteenth century these countries were more or less inclusive competitive oligarchies with restricted suffrage (property/ethnic restrictions and/or no women's suffrage until 1918 and 1945, respectively), but open and intensely competitive contestation of legislative and executive office, a fairly firm entrenchment of civic and political rights, and a robust entrenchment of the rule of law. In the four 'axis powers' Austria, Germany, Italy, and Japan, the onset of industrialization was supported by an authoritarian state, although also here capitalist economies resulted, albeit of a non-competitive, trust- and association-based kind. This model was partially broken up only in the aftermath of World War II, once totalitarian rulers in these countries were defeated. Nevertheless, the types of capitalism prevailing in these four countries continued to diverge from market liberal arrangements.

In the post-World War II reconstruction era, all of today's PI-democracies entered what Seymour Martin Lipset (1961) termed the 'democratic class compromise.' They built mixed economies that pacified the class struggle and endowed governments with considerable leverage in manipulating the market economies for a variety of short-term and long-term political objectives (win elections by demonstrating economic competence, entrench partisan support of electoral constituencies by providing them with club goods through policy legislation, etc.). The emergence of the 'mixed' economy with durable democracy coincided with an unprecedented period of prolonged economic growth between 1949 and 1973 when the first world oil crisis disrupted economic stability. Since that time, capitalist PI-democracies have experienced less spectacular, but still quite respectable, though more volatile, economic growth rates when measured by standards of long-term historical and global averages for the region. They achieved about 2 per cent/per capita growth in the 1980s, slightly less in the 1990s and again a touch less since 2000.

While PI-democracies economically fared worse after 1973 than in previous decades, the variance and volatility of their performance pales compared to that of the less affluent polities, whether democratic or not. Some of them, particularly in South and South-east Asia, performed spectacularly and are on their way to join the tier of affluent countries in the first quarter of the twenty-first century. Others, particularly in Sub-Saharan Africa and Latin America, have done badly and delivered negative or just marginal economic growth over the past thirty years. By global standards, growth rates in PI-democracies have been neither exceptionally high nor exceptionally low, and the same applies to inflation and unemployment. Among other things, this may be due to the economic

structure and institutions the configuration of which is unique to PI-democracies:

- They all have agricultural employment below 5 per cent of the labor force and agricultural value added to GDP of less than 3 per cent. This applies even to important agricultural exporters such as Australia, the Netherlands, or the United States.
- More than 65 per cent of all gainfully employed are in services, with the major growth areas being social services (particularly health and education), financial services and private personal services, at the expense of conventional clerical and sales-distributive services that are progressively displaced by machinery and information technology.
- The proportion of jobs in the occupational structure that require sophisticated skills and long-term training has increased dramatically, as simple task structures are taken over by computerized machinery. The bulk of the entire wealth stock of PI-democracies is therefore in human capital, while only small amounts are in fixed capital investments, let alone land and natural resources that dominate the picture in poorer non-PI-polities (cf. World Bank, 2005).
- PI democracies are by far the greatest investors in tertiary higher education (between 1 and 3 per cent of GDP) and in research and development (1.0–4.6 per cent of GDP).
- All of the PI-countries are affluent. They have a purchasing power parity (PPP) corrected per capita gross national income (GNI)[1] of at least $ 25,000 in 2005.
- Average gross capital formation in PI-democracies tends to be somewhat lower than in the rest of the world, particularly lower than in South and Southeast Asia. The average is in the vicinity of 20 per cent of GDP, with lows near 16 per cent in the United States (followed by Britain with 17.0 per cent and Germany with 17.2 per cent) and highs at 25 per cent (Australia, followed by Japan at 24 per cent) in 2005, compared to greater global variance, reaching from 39 per cent in China and 30 per cent in India to only 10 per cent in Côte d'Ivoire and 12 per cent in Bosnia.

All PI-democracies are currently caught up in a demographic transition in which life expectancy is gradually rising while fertility rate has fallen below replacement (albeit to a varying extent, see below). Because of the rapid rise in the number of retirees, the share of the working age population is falling, even though the proportion of children is falling as well.

In terms of basic political-economic institutions, PI-democracies offer relatively cheap and expedient facilities to enforce contracts, protect investors' rights, open or close a business and register property, and conduct business across national borders (cf. World Bank, 2006a). They provide an exceptional quality of the rule of law, governmental effectiveness, and impartial administration with little propensity to corruption (World Bank Global Governance Indicators, 2004). They top the ranks of economic (market) freedom and global competitiveness in business leaders' perceptions (World Economic Forum, 2006). Also economic policy-making has features that set PI-democracies apart from all other countries. PI-countries have budget and external account balances that typically vary between moderate deficits and balanced budget, but rarely approach public debts triggering fiscal crisis (yet consider Belgium and Italy in the 1980s and 1990s and Japan since 2000). Nevertheless, social policy expenditure, and public expenditure more generally, are very high by global standards (35–55 per cent of GDP), based on an exceptional capacity to tax the domestic economies.

Finally, in terms of politics, PI-democracies are looking back on political regime stability for at least 30 years. They have institutionalized full civic and political freedoms and have developed dense associational networks and a diverse landscape of mass media. Political parties mostly compete on broad policy appeals rather than on narrow geographically targeted benefits to specific individuals and groups contingent upon their vote preference ('clientelism'). Nevertheless, clientelistic politics eroded in several countries only after momentous political-economic difficulties in the public or publically regulated and subsidized sectors in the 1990s (cf. Kitschelt, 2007a).

Just about all electorally attractive parties support liberal democracy and basic economic institutions of capitalist market economies and therefore articulate programmatic alternatives within a more or less narrow range. Parties disperse over one, two or at most three dimensions of programmatic politics (cf. Benoit and Laver, 2007; Kitschelt, 1994; Kriesi et al., 2006; Warwick, 2002), and the major parties may line up on a left-right super dimension that combines positions on the policy dimensions in predictable fashion. Parties disagree over the extent to which governments regulate the economy and redistribute resources in favor of the worse off ('redistribution'). A second dimension concerns the extent to which citizens and parties endorse a socio-culturally libertarian conception of individual freedom to choose life styles and participate in collective decision making or a more authoritarian view of immutable collectively binding compliance with norms and cultural standards as well as deference to higher political authorities. This dimension is also often associated with positions on immigration and multiculturalism in society, with the more authoritarian view rejecting immigrants and insisting on cultural norms embraced by the indigenous population. Sometimes a third separate dimension concerns ecology/environmental protection and societal decentralization.

In practice, among the larger parties, and at least at the elite level of political leaders who communicate their parties' issue profile to the mass media, there is a fairly high, though not perfect, association between positions taken on these dimensions. The 'left' tends to be in favor of redistribution, libertarian conceptions of life style, immigration and multiculturalism, as well as priority for ecology and societal decentralization. The 'right' calls for acceptance of market allocation and market-based inequality in the economic sphere, endorses more authoritarian views of collective culture and national collective identity, and subordinates ecological protection to economic performance. Party systems then run from a 'new' left crystallized around left-socialist and ecology parties, via social democrats as center-left, Christian/confessional parties as center-right, liberal parties with distinct market liberal, yet often also mildly socio-culturally liberal positions to radical right parties that emphasize exclusionary and authoritarian socio-cultural conceptions, yet tacitly or explicitly also support a range of market liberal views on economic policy.[2]

In PI-democracies, political conflict, and competition certainly cannot be reduced to economic-distributive conflict. Yet at the same time, prophecies that economic conflict would wither away in favor of controversies over quality of life (cf. Inglehart, 1997) have been empirically disproved. The critical issue is to illuminate how economic and socio-political governance issues are intertwined in party appeals and popular preference distributions and underlying economic market positions of the actors. In post-industrial society the electoral constituency with the on average most 'leftist' policy and partisan preferences, both in the economic-distributive as well as the socio-cultural sense, are no longer blue collar manual workers, regardless of skill level, but the category of socio-cultural professionals employed by not-for-profit social service organizations and symbol producing culture and media companies (Kitschelt and Rehm, 2005, 2006).

Overall, in PI-democracies there is a broad consensus around the merits of democracy in principle, but at the same time citizens voice a generally high, though variable, level of mistrust in existing democratic institutions and politicians who govern them. It is often people inclined to be politically active and fully supportive of democracy in principle who embrace the most critical positions vis-à-vis the empirical performance of democracy in their own country (Dalton, 2004). This mistrust in parties and politicians goes together with a propensity to seek participatory involvement outside parties in social movements and interest groups independent of partisan divides. In the first half of the twentieth century powerful political parties were often closely aligned with subordinated interest groups and movement organizations and encapsulated them through broad membership overlap. Since the 1960s and 1970s, mass party membership has

declined in most PI-democracies and citizens have in greater numbers joined interest groups and became mobilized around social movements that keep parties at arms-length. A differentiation of vehicles of political preference mobilization over parties, interest groups and social movements has taken place (cf. Kitschelt, 2003).

As empirical referents for the cohort of PI-democracies, consider Table 11.1, listing all countries on earth with a per capita income of more than US $10,000 in purchasing power parity (PPP) in 2005, as listed in the World Bank's 2007 development report.[3] They are ranked from 1 through 45, with no ranks assigned to a couple of very small countries (Iceland, Luxembourg) and two entrepôt cities that are difficult to compare to large territorial countries (Hong Kong and Singapore).[4] Membership in the PI-democracy cohort is dependent on:

1. per capita gross national income (> $25,000 in 2005 at purchasing power parity);
2. share of employment in services above 65 per cent, as opposed to extractive industries (agriculture, mining) and manufacturing; and
3. a persistence of stable democracy for at least 30 years before 2005 (i.e., since 1975).

The first column in the table shows countries that meet all three criteria. Those in italic are countries that are usually included in cross-national macro-economic studies of contemporary capitalist democracies. Among countries that meet at least two PI-criteria, Norway and Ireland, the most recent arrival in the tier of the most affluent polities, most clearly belong to the PI group. The same can be said also for New Zealand, a British settler democracy with very old political institutions. More arguably, Greece and Portugal, both countries that had authoritarian rulers until 1974, may be included in the group of PI-democracies. In the most inclusive delineation of PI-democracies, then, we would find 22 countries in this group, not counting Iceland and Luxembourg because of size.

All other countries in Table 11.1 fail to meet at least two criteria to count as PI-democracies.

Table 11.1　Post-industrial democracies and the next tier of countries

Country meets all three criteria*	Country meets two criteria*	Country meets one criterion*	Country meets none of the criteria*	Excluded polities (entrepots, small countries)
1. *United States* (41.9 K; 77% S)	2. Norway (40.5 K; 59% S)	28. Hungary (16.9 K; 65% S)	20. United Arab Emirates (24.1 K; n.d.)	Luxembourg (65.4 K; n.d.)
3. *Switzerland* (37.1 K; n.d. S)	4. Ireland (34.7 K; 56% S)	29. Slovakia (15.8 K; 67% S)	21. Kuwait (24.0 K; 47% S)	Iceland (34.7 K; n.d.)
5. *Denmark* (33.6 K; 73% S)	22. Greece (23.6 K; 70% S)	30. Estonia (15.4 K; n.d.)	24. Slovenia (22.2 K; 62% S)	Hong Kong (34.7 K; 90% S)
6. *Austria* (33.1 K; 67% S)	23. *New Zealand* (23.1 K; n.d. S)	35. Latvia (13.5 K; 73% S)	25. Rep. Korea (21.9 K; 55% S)	Singapore (29.7 K; 66% S)
7. *United Kingdom* (32.7 K; 73% S)	27. Portugal (19.7 K; 70%)	37. Trinidad and Tobago (13.2 K; n.d.)	26. Czech Rep. (20.1 K; 58% S)	Cyprus (22.2 K; n.d. S)
8. *Belgium* (32.6 K; 73% S)		39. Mauritius (12.4 K; n.d.)	31. Saudi Arabia (14.7 K; 37% S)	Malta (19.0 K; n.d. S)
9. *Netherlands* (32.5 K; 72% S)		40. South Africa (12.1 K; 66% S)	32. Oman (14.7 K; 42% S)	
10. *Canada* (32.2 K; n.d.)		43. Botswana (10.3 K; n.d.)	33. Lithuania (14.3 K; 63% S)	
11. *Sweden* (31.4 K; 69% S)		45. Mexico (10.0 K; 70% S)	34. Argentina (13.9 K; 54% S)	
12. *Japan* (31.4 K; 68% S)			36. Poland (13.5 K; 65% S)	
13. *Finland* (31.2 K; 66% S)			38. Croatia (12.8 K; 64%)	
14. *Australia* (30.6 K; 71% S)			41. Chile (11.5 K; 48% S)	
15. *France* (30.5 K; 76%)			42. Russia (10.6 K; 56% S)	
16. *Germany* (29.3 K; 70% S)			44. Malaysia (10.3 K; 40% S)	
17. *Italy* (28.8 K; 70% S)				
18. *Spain* (25.9 K; 67% S)				
19. *Israel* (25.3 K; n.d.)				

*Criteria: (1) GNI per capita > $25 K at PPP in 2005; (2) service sector >65% value added in GDP; (3) democracy older than 30 years; only countries with more than one million inhabitants scored (except Luxembourg, Iceland).

All except the entrepôt city states of Hong Kong and Singapore tend to be too poor to qualify. Moreover, most, but not all of them, have service sectors falling below 65 per cent of employment (exceptions are Slovakia, Latvia, South Africa and Mexico). Most countries between US $10,000 and US $25,000 per capita GNI do not even meet a single criterion to qualify them as PI-democracies. On average, the 23 countries in that income class have a per capita GNP of not even one half of the average prevailing in the lead group of 22 PI-democracies (US $31,000/per capita at PPP in 2005 in the lead group compared to US $15,300) in the trailing group.

The delineation of the set of PI-democracies is thus not akin to drawing an arbitrary line among closely clustered observations. In the early twenty-first century there is, indeed, a real gulf in affluence and institutions between a top tier of more than 20 democracies and the rest of the world in both economic and political-democratic regards. This gulf would come into even starker relief, were we to present a broader set of indicators including questions of governance and rule of law or of global economic competitiveness. In the two major sections of this article, however, I will focus on the dynamics of macro-economic policy-making and performance, as well as the development of welfare states, both policy areas in which PI-democracies created unique and globally unparalleled institutions and policies.

MACRO-POLITICAL ECONOMY: EXPLAINING ECONOMIC PERFORMANCE

The political-economic analysis of PI-capitalism may trace back its origins to Marxist and non-Marxist theorists of 'organized capitalism' in the interwar period, advancing the idea that the self-organization of capital in trusts and industrial groups, in combination with state intervention, would create productive economic systems that counterbalance the tendency of market economies to evolve in cycles with violent up and downswings. The boldest and simultaneously most pessimistic statement of this perspective was probably Schumpeter's (1950) *Capitalism, Socialism and Democracy*. Whereas theorists of organized capitalism focused on common changes in the interaction between markets and politics, contemporary political economy really began to take off with a work that focused on the institutional and procedural differences within the group of affluent capitalist democracies.

The fountain of insight at the origin of the research field is without doubt Andrew Shonfield's *Modern Capitalism* (1965). Here, a business economist for the center-left *Guardian* tried to account for the astounding success of post-World War II capitalism when compared to the interwar period, particularly the achievement of full employment and sustained, accelerated technological innovation (Shonfield, 1965: 63). He argues that there are common trends in all OECD countries toward mixed economies involving some element of political-organizational 'planning' that corrects and displaces spontaneous market contracting. The main point, however, is that different countries achieve this common result in very different, yet causally equivalent ways. What the French achieved by indicative planning through allocation of capital and industrial reorganization of enterprises by governments, the Americans and British did through macro-economic fiscal policies, whereas the Germans resorted to the self-organization of industrial businesses and financial institutions to counteract volatility in market behavior. Whereas much of the scholarship following Shonfield over the next twenty years focused on industrial relations, Shonfield had the foresight to emphasize the corporate governance and organization of private business itself as a component of capitalist economies that varies systematically across national political contexts.

After Shonfield, macro-political economy of economic performance in the 1970s focused on employment and inflation exploring two major lines of reasoning, one centered on interest group mobilization and the other on party governance. With regard to the former, scholars established a relationship between the organization of economic interest groups and economic performance. Schmitter's (1974; 1981) distinction between pluralist and corporatist interest intermediation was most influential. Whereas in pluralism multiple competing associations represent the same functional interests, in corporatism each economic interest is represented by a single group and officially partakes in authoritative decision-making under the leadership of a single monopoly association. Corporatism facilitates the achievement of inter-elite consensus among other reasons because the associational leaders can quell internal protest by radical dissenters, respectively exclude them from the organization without having to fear that such challengers could form their own alternative associations. Over the decades, scholars have developed multiple measures of corporatism (cf. Kenworthy, 2001; Siaroff, 1999). In all of them, the critical ingredients are (1) centralization of associational representation and industrial bargaining above the firm level, all the way up to the national level; and (2) monopoly representation of functional interests by a single associational entity. Whereas this conceptualization homes in on structural properties of political mobilization, some have advocated a more behavioral conception of corporatism, placing (3) a consensus-oriented predisposition of the bargaining parties representing different functional interests at the center of analysis.

In the late 1970s and 1980s, a wealth of studies showed that corporatist political economies have enjoyed particular advantages. Hibbs (1976, 1977) found that centralized labor unions engage in fewer strikes, as business and labor can anticipate and evade the costs of industrial action. Cameron (1978; 1984) shows that it is particularly trade-open, smaller democratic polities where corporatist interest intermediation prevails and improves economic performance. In such polities, both inflation and unemployment tend to be lower than elsewhere, thus defying the Keynesian idea of an inflation/unemployment trade-off. In a similar vein, for small European democracies Katzenstein (1985) analyzed the origins and virtues of different modes of corporatism that boosted the countries' capacity to adapt to new economic challenges. Among economists speaking to political science, the most influential political economy contribution was probably Olson's (1982) thesis that a proliferation of special interest groups promotes rent-seeking and reduces economic growth, as the provision of group advantages leads to an undersupply of collective goods, unless this proliferation is counteracted by the authority of encompassing interest organizations ('corporatism') that internalize the externalities of special group advantages and prioritize collective goods provision. In the more technical economics literature on industrial relations and wage bargaining, this argument was further elaborated in an influential article by Calmfors and Driffill (1988). Economic outcomes are good (low inflation, low nominal wage increases) where interest groups are too weak to affect market pricing or where business and unions are organized in a highly centralized fashion. Economic outcomes are worse, where intermediate organizational capacity and centralization of unions makes them pursue advantages in individual firms or industries that accelerate inflation.

Parallel to the interest group literature, a second line of reasoning in comparative political economy focused on party competition and partisan governance of the economy. Key is the incentives of vote- and office-seeking politicians to manipulate the economy through political resource allocation in order to advance their electoral objectives. In the short-run, parties incumbent in executive office may boost fiscal expenditure and run deficits before elections to boost earnings power and dispose voters favorably to the governing party, as the costs of fiscal profligacy translate into higher inflation only after the elections (cf. Alt and Crystal, 1983: Chapter 5; Nordhaus, 1975; Tufte, 1978). As voters anticipate political business cycles, however, parties are no longer capable of partisan cycles before elections, but are rather likely to deliver partisan-biased fiscal and monetary policies, with left incumbents boosting spending, after electoral victories (cf. Alesina and Rosenthal, 1995). Nevertheless, politicians may not think of voters as particularly far-sighted and therefore engage in both pre- and post-election budget cycles (Franzese, 2002). The critique of the original business cycle literature is consistent with partisan models of long-run government policy that assert the ideological impact of left (social democratic) and right (conservative, market-liberal) governments on the size of the public sector and the propensity of different governments to prioritize fights against inflation or unemployment (cf. Hibbs, 1977, 1987).

When it comes to fiscal deficits that boost public debts and ultimately inflation, however, a rather different partisan logic may prevail. Multi-party coalition governments deliver more deficits, as each coalition partner is preoccupied with negotiating tangible advantages for its own constituency, thus discounting the externalities detrimental effects of losing the collective externalities of large budget deficits out of sight (cf. Alesina and Perotti, 1995; qualified also Franzese, 2002: chapter 3). No single coalition partner can incorporate these externalities in its bargaining strategy and not pay an electoral penalty. Recent research has shown that budget restraint is delivered by powerful finance ministers in single-party or small-N coalition governments or by ex-ante compacts among the coalition partners in large-N coalition governments where no party is willing to cede too much authority to the finance minister (Hallerberg, 2004; Hallerberg et al., 2009). Large-N coalitions without compacts, however, are likely to generate large deficits and inflation. The original claim, however, that left-wing partisan governments or greater ideological diversity within governing coalitions produce higher deficits, has been by and large set aside (cf. Franzese, 2002: chapter 3; Hallerberg et al., 2009).[5]

Since the mid-1980s, a series of papers by Lange and Garrett (1985) and the ensuing research (see especially Alvarez et al., 1991 and Garrett, 1998) then attempted to combine the logics of interest group bargaining with that of partisan governance by highlighting the interdependence of interest group (union) strategies of wage bargaining and government strategies of fiscal policy-making. This interaction yields two favorable equilibria with low inflation, low unemployment, and robust growth. The first is where conservative, market-liberal partisan government imposes fiscal restraint and weak, decentralized labor unions are incapable of boosting nominal wages. The second presupposes strong centralized labor unions that exercise wage restraint in exchange for a left government delivering fiscal expansion to maintain or restore full employment. Scharpf (1991), however, pointed out at least two flaws of this model. First, labor unions have no incentive to cooperate with social democratic governments, as social democrats could not retaliate against unions as a core element of their electoral support base. Second, under conditions of a 'classical' economic crisis, driven by low profits and lack of incentives to invest, fiscal government expansion is unlikely to stimulate the economy. The fiscally expansionary left government strategy worked only in the 1970s during a 'Keynesian' crisis, when the oil shock drained consumer purchasing power out of the Western economies so that public deficit spending could fill the hole. This strategy no longer worked in the 1980s when firms suffered from a classical low profitability crisis. A fiscal macroeconomic stimulus was bound to make things only worse (Scharpf, 1991: 36).

Scharpf then draws on observations that an independent central bank, put in charge of monetary stability and not controlled by partisan government, may operate as a check on the actions of governments and industrial relations partners. Such central banks are wont to raise real interest rates, if governments and industrial relations partners engage in 'irresponsible' wage increases. Knowing the Central Bank's independence and propensity to punish inflationary policies, political actors opt for fiscal and wage restraint in anticipation of monetary sanctions. Thus, social democratic governments can count on union cooperation not only because of organizational and ideological links between labor movements and left parties, but also because of the anticipation that a strong central bank is ready to sanction fiscal profligacy in government spending and industrial relations bargaining.

A synthesis of theoretical insights in the fields of partisan fiscal policy, industrial relations wage bargaining, and central bank-led monetary policy has been most systematically achieved in Torben Iversen's *Contested Economic Institutions* (1999). As a special twist of his argument, powerful central banks are beneficial to price stability and employment particularly under conditions of sectorally centralized industrial relations systems, yet not in nationally centralized systems. In the latter, centralized labor unions can maintain all-encompassing unity only by favoring unskilled workers and thus promoting progressive wage compression. As this strategy is detrimental to skill investment, employers pay skilled workers more than union wages, thus triggering 'wage drift' and inflation. Central banks would fight such drift, but therewith undercut employment.

Empirically, Iversen finds support for the expected pattern, but there are reasons to question the mechanism driving his theoretical argument. If diverse labor union groups under the umbrella of a single national bargaining unit anticipate that a strong central bank will react to policies of wage compression and wage drift with tight monetary policy causing a loss of employment, wouldn't they seek a different wage compact allowing for more wage inequality that would eliminate wage drift? Building on the same empirical observations as Iversen, Franzese (2002: Chapter 4, especially pp. 243–45) offers a different rationale and interpretation of the reasons that make central bank autonomy trigger higher unemployment in nationally centralized industrial relations systems. This result occurs, depending on whether private or public sector unions dominate the national union federation. Where private sector unions are dominant, they bargain in anticipation of the central bank's capacity to punish excessive wage deals and wage drift. But where centralized unions are dominated by public sector unions whose members' employment is not endangered by high real interest rates and losses of their companies' international competitiveness, the centralization of industrial relations may lead to job losses in the private sector, when central banks punish undisciplined wage bargaining.

Franzese not only proposes a sectoral disaggregation of union power, but also makes a move from a closed to an open economy model. A systematic treatment of international openness constitutes the next stage of macro-political economic analysis.[6] Theoretically this brings in complications that prevent the emergence of unique equilibria, induced by institutional arrangements only. Instead, assuming open economies makes possible a whole range of equilibria, contingent upon the nature and extent of international exposure (Soskice, 2000). If prices are no longer set by local wages, but also by wages and monetary policies elsewhere, even under conditions of wage restraint no full employment equilibrium may occur. Lower wages may restore an industry's international competitiveness, but they also drain domestic demand, domestic wage bargaining may be unable to restore full employment, in addition to accelerating domestic inflation to world levels. Empirically,

Garrett's (1998) work for the 1980s and early 1990s showed that international embeddedness of an economy has only a limited influence on the extent to which domestic industrial relations systems and governments achieve favorable macro-economic outcomes. Yet at the same time, his investigation also shows that institutions (wage bargaining arrangements, central bank autonomy) have only preciously limited capacity to affect macroeconomic performance altogether.

Two more recent extensions of the macro-political economic literature are worth reporting in this overview. The first pushes the scope of analysis, the second the depth of causal analysis. Isabela Mares (2004, 2006) has recently observed that the most advanced comparative political economy literature, represented by Iversen (1999), explains cross-national divergence of unemployment and inflation until the 1990s, but cannot account for rising unemployment over time in countries such as Germany and other corporatist economies, where the theory would predict good economic performance. She argues that governments could induce unions to comply with wage restraint in the past by offering additional social policy benefits for wage earners. More recently, however, increasing shares of social policy benefits have gone to working age permanent labor market outsiders (homemakers, the structurally unemployed, early retirees) so that unions have lost the incentive to moderate wage demands, with the consequence of rising unemployment. Hence, 'the process of welfare state maturation gradually undermines the political exchange among trade unions and governments based on wage restraint in exchange for social policy expansion.' (Mares, 2004: 115). While her model is logically consistent, Mares provides only a weak test of her argument, regressing unemployment on a range of variables that includes effective tax rates and transfers to labor market outsiders (ages 18–64).

But both the concept as well as the empirical measure of outsider benefits are hazardous: When is someone a permanent outsider, rather than a temporary drop-out of labor markets and thus not potentially a member of the union constituency? And how does Mares arrive at the very high estimate of expenses for labor market outsiders?[7] Moreover, is the large number of labor market outsiders, particularly early retirees, just an exogenous constraint on wage bargaining imposed by the 'mature' welfare state or is it itself a consequence of certain wage bargaining systems, where unions insist on sticky wage contracts and high wages, even at the loss of jobs, so long as unemployment of older workers can be financially buffered and concealed by pensioning them off into quite generous early retirement deals? The real explanation of high unemployment and low job creation, then, would lead entirely out of the realm of wage bargaining. It may have more to do with labor market inflexibility due to high job protection and short weekly work time in continental Europe, the (semi-)corporatist countries that saw low job creation and rising unemployment in the 1990s where the conventional political economy literature would have expected continued good performance. Mares study asks pertinent questions, but her answer may be only one of several that deserve close examination.

The second extension of the comparative political economy literature turns away from pure macro-aggregates, such as factors of production and economic sectors, and instead considers how firms and employees respond to economic incentives. It seeks to provide the actions of market participants as micro-foundations to the macro-political economy of corporatism and monetary authority. Moreover, it seeks to go beyond the focus on wage earners as key actors and also examine the decisions firms make when calibrating their production function. Based on this bottom-up analysis, it distinguishes different 'varieties of capitalism' (VoC) (Hall and Soskice, 2001; Soskice, 1999) that consist of clustered, complementary sets of institutions configured around firm-level decision-making in at least four realms:

1. corporate governance and financing;
2. industrial relations and wage contracting;
3. employee skill formation; and
4. technological innovation.

Soskice distinguishes between two clusters of institutional conditions that structure the environment and internal organization of the firm he terms 'coordinated market economies' (CMEs) and 'competitive/liberal market economies' (LMEs).

CMEs have firms with concentrated ownership structures (family ownership or few large individual or corporate equity holders, often involving cross-ownership and bank ownership) with active owners who supervize company management. This is often paired with a financing of firms through internal funds and bank debt rather than bonds or dispersed equity ownership held by individuals and institutional investors. The quality of a company and its worth as a trading partner for upstream and downstream business is assessed based on private, 'insider' information, generated through informal networks of communication, relational banking, and important industry-wide associations that provide membership services. Company management is recruited from its internal labor force cultivated by a prolonged process of intra-organizational socialization and specific skill upgrading. There is neither a market for companies (hostile takeovers) nor a market for managers. This structure of corporate governance and interfirm cooperation nurtures 'patient' capital in which principals are interested in the long-run performance of company management, not short-term profit objectives. This also makes firms more inclined to opt for a system of labor market governance in which long-term wage contracts prevail. This increases unions' receptivity to wage moderation and to participate in a 'stakeholder' structure of corporate governance, alongside the company's equity owners. Long-term capital and wage relations thus feed into a consensus-oriented system of industrial relations where wage earners are willing to embrace wage moderation in exchange for long-term job security and an incremental improvement of earnings (e.g., through seniority).

Employers, in turn, are willing to negotiate with powerful centralized labor unions and incorporate employees' and union representatives into company management (works councils or co-determination).

Because in CME capitalism capital is patient and oriented to long-term profit goals, firms can credibly commit to long-term wage contracts. Such contracts reduce work force turnover. Durability of employment relations, in turn, make it attractive to firms to invest in the specific human capital of employees that improves company performance, whether at the beginning of employment relations (vocational training) or later through continuous retraining and upgrading of skills. Corporate governance, skill formation, and labor relations shape a specific style of technological innovation. It is concentrated in large firms, as venture capital is difficult to raise in underdeveloped public equity capital markets and relationship banking based on established reputations continues to prevail. Large firms favor incremental product and process innovations that can be brought online with the gradual reskilling and upskilling of their labor force, often after collaborative research with other firms in the same industry. For those firms, it is unimportant in the product cycle of an innovation to be first, but to be a solid second or third that can produce the new widget more reliably, efficiently, with marginally improved features, and great after-sale service.

Liberal market economies, by contrast, rely on public, transparent capital markets where firms raise equity capital through stock offerings and bond issues. Ownership structures tend to be dispersed, giving senior management extraordinary control over firms with large numbers of passive owners, even though corporate law imposes more 'anti-director' rules on companies to respect the rights and participation of minority owners. There are both markets for firms and senior managers who are often recruited from outside the firm. Rather than production engineers who worked their way into management (in CMEs), corporate leaders in LMEs have

a background in business administration, accounting, or law. Publicly traded companies that report quarterly earnings results are not wont to honor long-term wage relations and – with some exceptions – prefer a flexible labor force the size of which can be adjusted to demand. Therefore firms and employees invest little in specific skills pertinent to the business or the industry and instead focus on general skills wage earners can deploy in different companies. General skill formation and high labor mobility resulting from short-term contracts are also inhospitable to centralized wage bargaining, employees' representation on company boards and job security. Industrial relations systems tend to be decentralized, with unions playing only a minor role.

In LMEs, innovation takes place not only in large corporations, but to a substantial extent also in small start-up companies founded by entrepreneurs emerging from the non-profit sector of universities and research laboratories and raising capital initially through venture capitalist funds and later through equity offerings. Such research is focused on revolutionary product innovations and successful particularly in areas where innovation is the main challenge, while production and after-sale service are easily arranged or irrelevant. Examples may be parts of the IT and the biotechnology industries, but also design, fashion, music and film production and a broad array of financial and personal services all of which thrive under LME arrangements. This stands in contrast to manufacturing industries for consumer durables or investment goods (heavy machinery, turnkey production plants, etc.) whose production challenges predispose them to work better where CME institutions are prevalent.

PI-polities that feature institutionally different varieties of capitalism therefore specialize in industries and companies where their institutions give them a competitive advantage. Where global companies organize complex production chains, they place bits and pieces in polities that have comparative institutional advantages for coping with the specific production challenge posed by that link in the chain. The co-existence of different varieties of CME and LME capitalism, therefore, is compatible with globalization of production, as long as there are multiple institutional equilibria to achieve comparative advantage. Worst off are countries that cannot take advantage of the complementarities between different institutional components in each type, such as corporate governance, industrial relations, human skill formation and technological innovation. Such 'incoherent' arrangements thus are expected to translate into weak macro-economic performance. Hall and Gingerich (2004) find in a cross-national study of economic growth that indeed 'pure' incarnations of varieties of capitalism deliver better economic growth.

The varieties of capitalism approach constitutes a definite advance over macro-economic political economy models that do not flesh out the micro-economic relations between employers and wage earners or the relations among firms and between firms and financial markets. But there are also formidable conceptual, theoretical and empirical challenges this intellectual framework is beginning to face.

In conceptual terms, are two varieties of capitalism enough? There are the usual complaints that the postulate of national patterns hides variance at the level of sectors or firms (Allen, 2004), but even if we admit that the country (polity) level of institutions influences trajectories of economic growth and performance (employment, inflation), there may be problems with a binary division between LME and CME. For one thing, the divisions may not be fine enough to capture differential economic performance rates. Thus, the Scandinavian variety of CME is substantially different in institutional terms from continental European CMEs and it also exhibits a different performance profile. For another thing, in addition to market contracting (LME) and horizontal relational contracting (CME), is there not hierarchical planning within firms and initiated by states at the origin of many industrial innovations? And are hierarchical arrangements not sometimes prominent enough to shape a polity's capitalist economy (its 'variety' of capitalism) or at least to introduce critical heterogeneities in its variety that need to be conceptually accommodated? One might think of the role of state funded research and development in the LME political economy of the United States with its wide array of public or non-profit funding agencies for innovation in bio- and information technologies, aerospace and energy production, often linked to the military-industrial complex. Also 'mixed' varieties of capitalism such as France and to a lesser extent Italy have had powerful cores of state-owned or state–nurtured companies at the heart of political-economic development strategies (consider Airbus). LME and CME arrangements do not exhaust the range of institutional forms deployed to promote economic production and growth.

Second, in theoretical-explanatory terms, the varieties of capitalism literature has a functionalist ring. If complementarities are arrangements in which the benefits obtained from each component are improved by the presence of the other components, are these interfaces brought about by intentional design, by evolutionary selection, or by unintended actions that accidentally created high yield production functions in specific historical circumstances only? The origins of different capitalisms appear to have to do a great deal with the extent to which European polities and their colonial settler spinoffs dismantled guilds in the early nineteenth century and the timing of the first wave of industrialization (cf. Crouch, 1993). Where guilds were only incompletely removed and where industrialization took off comparatively late in the second half or last quarter of the nineteenth century during a time when very heavy fixed capital investments fuelled the growth of the lead industries (heavy industry, railroads, later chemical and electromechanical engineering industries), market actors built economic institutions around CME-type arrangements.

More research is needed on the origins and trajectories of different capitalist varieties.

The account of varieties of capitalism, as initially presented, is entirely divorced from a consideration of politics in terms of parties and political conflict (Pontusson, 2005a). We are dealing with a micro-logic of interaction between firms, wage earners, and customers. Institutional frameworks provided by the state, and the political actors that bring about such institutions either do not matter or are seen as executors of a logic of economic comparative institutional advantage. Most recently Iversen and Soskice (2006a, 2006b) have tried to remedy the political lacunae in the varieties of capitalism literature by arguing that historically varieties of capitalism shaped party system alignments which, in turn, affected the electoral strength and opportunities for left parties to dominate governments and affect production and welfare systems. CME capitalism promotes systems of proportional representation in countries, where remnants of the guild system precipitated differences of interest between companies employing workers with lesser or greater skill specificity, a line of conflict cross-cutting the class divide and thus translating into party system fragmentation that eventually induced strategic politicians in a variety of parties to opt for a replacement of plurality electoral systems. The presence of proportional representation, in turn, makes center-left governments more likely, as lower thresholds of legislative representation facilitates party system fragmentation. By supporting centrist parties and depriving socialists of outright electoral majorities, this, in turn, enables voters to force office-seeking socialist parties into coalition agreements with non-socialist parties in order to reduce the risk that a left government could engineer a dramatic reversal of the political-economic status quo. Center-left governments, finally, reinforce CME institutional arrangements. Whether or not this theoretically elegant account of the emergence of party systems, electoral systems, and political economic outcomes is historically

accurate, however, is open to debate and requires a great deal of research. For now, Iversen and Soskice have made an interesting, provocative proposal to construct a link between production systems and democratic politics.

Third, it is questionable whether coherent models of capitalism perform better than mixed models, and whether different coherent models have equivalent performance. Both of these propositions can be always true, always wrong, or true at times contingent upon certain boundary conditions (e.g., technological innovation frontiers). Empirically, the performance postulates in the VoC literature are controversial. The VoC theorists' claim that good economic performance can be achieved by functionally equivalent, yet different institutions is most plausible for the era from about 1950 to 1990, but not before and unlikely thereafter. Starting in the 1990s, some of the continental CME systems, above all Germany, have performed badly in terms of growth and employment. If anything, a branching of different subtypes of CMEs has taken place, with the small Scandinavian branch doing well economically and the bigger continental European branch performing weakly over extended periods of time. In a reanalysis of Hall and Gingerich's (2004) study of economic growth with data covering OECD countries until the beginning of the new millennium, Kenworthy (2006) could not find a growth advantage to countries having a 'pure' rather than a 'mixed' variety of capitalism. The other 'congruence' hypothesis that precedes and stimulated the VoC literature has run into similar empirical difficulties. Lange and Garrett's (1985) proposition that left (right) wing governments when paired with centralized (decentralized) industrial relations systems, perform better than 'incongruent' alignments (left governments + decentralized industrial relations, and right governments + centralized industrial relations), appears to hold PI-democracies up to the 1980s, but hardly after the early 1980s (Scruggs, 2001).

Many of the productivity advantages of CME capitalism may have eroded in the 1990s and beyond, as the lead economic growth sectors involve technologies and contractual relations that are difficult to accommodate in a CME world. Innovative industries thrive where there are flexible, open and transparent capital markets and where labor contracts are short-term, permitting the frequent reconfiguration of the wage force. It is therefore not surprising that previously pure incarnations of CME capitalism are fraying at the margins. This applies particularly to corporate governance, where both the 'pure' CME capitalism in Germany (Beyer and Höpner, 2003) as well as the 'mixed' CME capitalism in France (Goyer, 2006) has undergone momentous change toward a liberal corporate governance model. And the relative success of the Scandinavian economies since the mid-1990s may have more to do with their excellent general educational systems that produce a versatile, flexible work force than their asset-specific vocational education. More generally, technological change has reduced the promise of vocational education as an avenue to successful occupational careers in all but a very limited set of manufacturing industries. It is the lack of emphasis on higher general education that contributes to the economic crisis of continental European CMEs where governments spend little on the tertiary educational sector and private universities are marginal.

THE POLITICAL ECONOMY OF WELFARE STATES: SOCIAL PROTECTION AND REDISTRIBUTION

The notion 'welfare state' encompasses authoritative policies enacted to 'hedge' wage earners and their dependents from the risks of losing their market income and to 'redistribute' income from those with higher market incomes to those with low or no market incomes. Social protection and redistribution are analytically distinct activities. Hedging takes place when people contribute to an insurance pool and premiums are based on actuarial risks. Ex ante, everyone expects to derive benefits proportional to contributions and risks covered. No one knows who will benefit from the insurance more than others. Ex post, the distribution of payouts is unequal, as some contributors received benefits under the terms of the contract while others did not. Hedging does create winners and losers, but only ex post, behind a veil of ex-ante ignorance. Public, compulsory insurance, such as pension plans, can be based on a pure principle of hedging and social protection, without redistribution, just as any private insurance. 'Redistributive' social policy, by contrast, involves both *ex ante knowledge* and *ex post realization* of benefit allocations that require some to pay more than others per unit of benefit. Examples are compulsory health insurance plans that offer exactly the same coverage to all members, even if contributions are set differentially by income. The same redistributive impact occurs, if social services (e.g., childcare) or unemployment benefits are paid out of general tax revenue that has been collected based on earnings and capital assets.

In a highly stylized way, we can distinguish three 'types' of welfare states that closely follow Gøsta Esping-Andersen's (1990) famous tripartition, but use the language of social protection (risk hedging) and redistribution. First, there are residual 'liberal' welfare states that limit redistribution and leave most insurance protection to market participants. Public programs provide protection and some redistribution for a residual group of 'needy' citizens who cannot take advantage of insurance markets. Examples are minimum income support and welfare, public health benefits to the poor, and unemployment benefits covered out of general taxes poor recipients of social benefits may have never paid. Second, there are 'conservative' or Christian Democratic welfare states that organize comprehensive, universalistic and compulsory social protection, but contributions are more or less proportional to benefits thus limiting the redistributive effect of social policy. This third 'social democratic' type of universalistic welfare state both hedges all citizens against market risks, but its universalistic coverage schemes with flat benefits and services also redistributes a substantial amount of income to the advantage of the worst-off.

In substantive policy terms, the historical core of social protection and redistribution concern (1) old age insurance; (2) health and accident insurance; and (3) unemployment insurance. Whereas better paid wage earners could hedge against risks of old age and illness through private and voluntary insurance (typically in unions and non-profit 'friendly societies') before government programs stepped in, in the realm of unemployment insurance problems of adverse selection (only those facing high risk to become unemployed will voluntarily insure themselves) and moral hazard (people covered by insurance may perform badly in their jobs and willfully become unemployed) made this liability strictly a matter of public coverage. Since World War II, the core programs have dramatically increased in generosity and coverage. Moreover, social policy got involved in a range of additional activities such as (1) support for raising children (financial transfers and public childcare); (2) provision of low-income housing; and (3) a variety of new means-tested measures to maintain incomes of the poor and disabled not covered by other programs.

Public education, as the public effort to turn citizens into competent participants in labor markets and politics, may be considered part of the 'hedging' and 'redistributive' role of the welfare state. But whereas high-quality public primary and secondary education redistribute mostly toward the less well-off, public university funding redistributes toward the affluent whose offspring is more likely to take advantage of tertiary education. Active labor market policy that provides retraining to those unemployed whose skills have become obsolete, by contrast, delivers redistribution toward low-income households. Together with parts of health care services and family support for children, education constitutes a category of public 'social investments' in the human capital

of future labor market participants, as opposed to social policies that are primarily 'social consumption' expenditures benefiting those who are outside labor markets or have left them for good (pensions, much of health care, some means-tested income maintenance programs). Knowing the 'type' of welfare state (residual, conservative, social democratic) does not help us much to predict the 'age bias' of the welfare state, conceived as its relative emphasis on social investment or social consumption programs (Lynch, 2006).

There are at least four grey areas that make it difficult to delineate the welfare state. First, are private, but legally compulsory insurance programs, common in Switzerland, part of the welfare state or not? Functionally, such programs operate in a fashion very similar to some publicly run insurance programs and therefore should be included in the welfare state. Second, are publicly funded social policies whose administration and implementation has been delegated to quasi-private, non-profit institutions part of the welfare state? Consider Australia, where a wide array of benefits was part of national wage bargaining agreements, but not administered by governmental agencies. Third, legislation to make it difficult for employers to hire and fire workers (security of the wage contract, labor market 'rigidity') certainly constitutes a form of governmental social protection and in some ways even of redistribution, if consumers keep paying for workers' wages who would have been made redundant, had it not been for labor laws preventing employers from laying them off.

Fourth, and most importantly, does it make sense to focus on the welfare state, as the government-initiated programs enabling people to hedge against market risk and imposing a redistributive scheme on them, or is it more accurate to focus on the broader category of 'welfare regimes' that include non-governmental communal (family) and associational institutions achieving social protection and redistribution? Especially the feminist critique of the welfare state literature has pointed to the intimate linkage between women's unpaid labor in the family and social networks, on the one hand, and public provisions, on the other (cf. Sainsbury, 1999; also Esping-Andersen, 1999). The absence of public social investment and consumption payments (e.g., for child care, elder care, unemployment payment for young labor market participants) keeps women bound to the home. Where a large portion of women are still homemakers, social policy makers may not offer public services that would supplant those delivered already in the family.

Why have today's PI-countries historically developed different kinds of welfare states since the late nineteenth century? How do they now cope with the new challenges facing the welfare state, particularly changing labor markets, the demographic revolution involving low birthrates and a growing share of retirees in the population? Whereas the retrospective research question primarily focuses on the causes of social protection and redistribution, the forward-looking analysis of ways to cope with new challenges focuses on trade-off between social investment and social consumption.

Why have governments been involved in risk hedging and redistribution at all? With regard to *risk hedging (social protection)*, some liabilities are uninsurable in markets because of *adverse selection and moral hazard*. In addition to unemployment insurance, this applies to family services and health care to a considerable extent. In other instances, the non-provision of compulsory public insurance policies would yield *collective externalities* (destitution, crime), that reduce everyone's quality of life. Weakness of will may make people shun voluntary insurance against future risk and rather consume resources that would have to be sacrificed for social protection. Myopic current selves 'free ride' on the well-being of their future selves and produce externalities also for others. Finally, for physical and/or mental reasons, some individuals cannot effectively participate in a market society. Here humanitarian motivations, as well as concerns about externalities generated by a poverty sector, may lead to the adoption of public policy.

With regard to *redistribution*, the best starting point is the by now famous Meltzer and Richards (1981) hypothesis that since the less well-off are more numerous than the well-off (i.e., the median voter earns less than the mean voter), in democracies there will always be demand for redistribution, and that demand will be more intense, where inequality is starker. Because democracies require a larger share of the population to pass a winning policy than authoritarian governments, democracies are likely to produce more redistributive social policies than authoritarian regimes.[8] But the extent to which this is true depends on the ability of the poor to overcome collective action problems and organize effectively to press for their interests. Moreover, with increasing income the propensity to buy insurance increases so that moderately affluent people may embrace social policy, provided it is not targeted to non-labor market participants (Moene and Wallerstein, 2001, 2003). In as much as insurance and redistributive mechanisms are intertwined, even under conditions of relatively low inequality support for some kinds of redistributive policies may therefore be widespread.

At least four different arguments explain the historical trajectory of welfare states in contemporary PI-democracies. The first, sometimes named 'logic of industrialism,' a derivate of modernization theory, postulates that welfare states grow with increasing societal aggregate affluence. The transition to industrial and then PI-societies reduces the role of the family as a social protective and human capital forming institution, along with traditional voluntary associations, such as churches. Public policy is burdened with the task of filling the void. Development also comes with a continuous increase in life expectancy that expands the population of retirees and their social insurance needs (retirement, health care). Indeed, in global comparison, affluence and demographics may be the most powerful factors that account for cross-national differences in scope and social policy effort, as Wilensky (1975) showed long ago. But when we probe into finer social policy distinctions among PI-democracies today, economic development drops out as a causal engine of social policy variance. In a similar vein, a second theory which postulates that it is democratization, i.e., political regime form that boosts social policy, may explain variance among welfare states in global comparison, but not among already democratic PI-countries. More promise to explain welfare state differences among PI-democracies is an argument that builds on social class mobilization through unions and parties ('power resource theory,' PRT). It has been challenged recently by an argument that Iversen calls 'welfare production regime theory,' WPRT). It sees social policies as the result of a positive-sum game in which workers and employers agree on policies that meet their respective preferences, even though they maintain some conflicting distributive interests. Both PRT and WPRT go a considerable way to account for different past trajectories of welfare states in contemporary PI-democracies. But they are both relatively uninformative, when employed to explain how PI-democracies respond to new challenges that force them to address the trade-off between social investment and social consumption as priorities of social policy making.

According to PRT, it is the mobilization of wage laborers in unions and employers' associations and the crystallization of redistributive struggles around political parties that determines the shape of the welfare state. Because it is impossible here to render the subtleties of this research program, I will confine myself to a stylized account that is not identical with any one of the major statements of this perspective.[9] The critical engine to build welfare states is the mobilization of the industrial working class through socialist labor unions and socialist parties all of which call for social protection and redistribution in favor of their constituencies. But these claims do not go unopposed. Business developed its own associations and employed its resources to strengthen anti-welfare state parties and

associations. In some polities, associations (such as churches) and parties with a socio-cultural cross-class appeal, based on religion and/or national identity attracted support from different classes. In order to compete with the socialist movement, cross-class parties adopted the social protectionist agenda without endorsing far-reaching redistribution.

The balance of power among associations and parties organizing different classes or cross-class coalitions then determines social policy outcomes, mediated by institutional rules of democratic political decision-making. Where a simple majority in unicameral legislatures with parliamentary government decided on policy, social policy innovations could be adopted most speedily. The presence of additional decision-making arenas – such as a second chamber of parliament, an independently elected presidency, federal decision-making, a constitutional court with rights to review the constitutionality of legislation, and plebiscitarian policy approval – tended to slow down social policy legislation, wherever interests defeated in one arena of decision making could reemerge as veto players in another arena.[10]

Wage earners come closest to realizing their social protectionist and redistributive objectives under conditions of social *corporatism*, where large portions of the work force are organized in centralized unions that bargain with corresponding employers associations, and/or where *unified left party representation* voices their interests in legislatures and governments, while confronting a fragmented, internally divided non-socialist party camp (e.g., Castles, 1978). Corporatism and left party hegemony are not identical, but moderately strongly related (Hicks, 1999).

Workers might initially demand means-tested social policy programs bestowing health care, pension and unemployment benefits just on them, as the most vulnerable wage earners in society, but excluding white collar professionals and all self-employed. Socialist politicians, however, realized in the 1940s and thereafter that they could entice at least some non-socialist parties and their supporters in the salariat and small business to back a broad-based welfare state consensus, if socialists agreed to encompassing, universalistic benefits schemes that also covered non-working class claimants (cf. Baldwin, 1990). By doing so, socialist politicians put social policy gains onto much firmer political footing, while still achieving a substantial amount of social protection and even some redistribution in favor of their own constituency.

Universalistic social policy schemes enabled left governments to go beyond narrow industrial working class interests in search of securing median voter support. In the last third of the twentieth century, in universalistic social democratic welfare states a whole range of social policy innovations evidences the same strategy of political incorporation. By expanding family and child care benefits as well as women's labor market opportunities, especially through public service employment, social democrats reinforced their cross-class appeal. Such policies were nevertheless consistent with redistributive objectives, as they made services available in a universalistic fashion even to very poor beneficiaries who had not paid taxes that financed such services. A similar dual logic of social protection and marginal redistribution applies to educational reform, and even to the expansion of higher education. Although it most benefits the middle and upper income professions and business whose offspring enjoys the greatest chances to attend university, social democrats pushed it with the idea that broad-based public university education would also give access to working class youths, in addition to drawing non-working class voters to support the party.

In contrast to countries with labor corporatism and strong leftist parties, countries with a powerful united non-socialist right and a weaker, only intermittently governing labor party produced a rather different welfare state. Here liberal residual welfare states emerged with very modest universalistic flat-rate benefits, complemented by narrow, targeted, and means-tested programs for the poor. In the Anglo-Saxon polities, where this partisan configuration prevailed, broad universalistic and

redistributive social policies could be adopted only during major general crises, such as the Great Depression (US Social Security Act) or the immediate aftermath of World War II (British National Health Service). Family benefits remained marginal in liberal-residual welfare states and the equalization of women's economic opportunities meant the removal of barriers to labor market entry more than the extension of public child care facilities.

In countries where Catholic confessional or ecumenical ('Christian Democratic') religious parties or nationalist parties (such as the French Gaullists) became politically dominant in the 1950s and 1960s, legislators developed conservative welfare states with encompassing social protection, but limited redistribution, held back by the fragmentation of insurance systems along occupational, geographic, and even ideological lines. At the same time, the doctrine of 'subsidiarity' and reverence for traditional gender-roles in the family made politicians stay away from or go slow on social policies that would have enabled women to leave home and hearth and give them access to higher education, childcare, gender-neutral pay, etc. An exception is France with its long-standing pro-natalist policies. Exercising restraint in terms of promoting economic redistribution and emphasizing subsidiarity rather than government activism with regard to the family, as a core institution of human capital formation, conservative welfare states also have neglected educational reform and expansion of high-quality higher education after a brief burst in the 1960s and 1970s.

PRT theories of social policy reform emerging from class-based political party competition have a great deal of plausibility, but also encounter a number of anomalies. While countries with strong left or even cross-class parties in government undoubtedly deliver more redistribution than countries dominated by market-liberal conservatives (cf. Bradley et al., 2003; Kenworthy, 2004; Pontusson, 2005b), this redistribution takes place *within* the class of wage earners – from higher earners to lower earners and from those active in the labor force to retirees – rather than from capitalists to workers (cf. Cusak and Beramendi, 2006; Kato, 2003; Timmons, 2005). Larger welfare states are typically financed through payroll taxes on labor and indirect taxes on consumption all of which are proportional and even sometimes regressive and to a much lesser extent by progressive taxes on income and capital gains (cf. Beramendi and Rueda, 2007).

Even if political parties represent socio-economic classes with different redistributive desires, the logic of partisan competition and government policy-making is not identical with a politics of class conflict and redistribution. As I suggested above in what may be already my own 'amendment' to PRT theory, social democrats may embrace universalistic cross-class benefits packages for reasons of a class-transcending logic of electoral office-seeking in order to attract support by the median voter and beyond. And one should add here: For the same reason, they will structure tax schemes for such reforms that widely dissipate tax burdens rather than 'fleece the rich.' This sometimes may entice employers to agree with unions on social reform strategies (cf. Swenson, 2002).

A second anomaly of PRT is that social policy conflict often did not unfold along class, but sectoral lines, with sectors characterized by differential risk profiles, foreign trade exposure, and organizational capabilities (small versus large firms). A whole phalanx of historical studies has demonstrated how accident, unemployment or retirement insurance schemes have emerged from such cross-class alignments, with compromises between conflicting positions often crafted by pragmatic, office-seeking politicians in both socialist or conservative parties (cf. Baldwin, 1990; Swenson, 1989; Mares, 2003).

A third problem of PRT is not so much a failure of causal analysis, but a lack of capacity to see the limitations of social policy success in social democratic or conservative welfare states. While redistribution among wage earners does not directly slow down economic growth in contemporary capitalist economies (Kenworthy, 2004: Chapter 4), high payroll taxes, high unemployment benefits, and extensive employment regulation create rigid labor markets that have discouraged employment growth (Kenworthy, 2004: Chapter 5). This, in turn, contributes to a new insider/outsider divide in which social policy pushed by left parties protects those who are in labor markets, but does not benefit the neediest people without capacity to obtain work (Rueda, 2005). Whereas at least activism in educational and training policies counteracts the exclusionary quality in social democratic welfare states, conservative welfare states lack such counterweight and create a particularly severe insider/outsider divide.

A recent alternative to PRT is the new 'welfare production regime' theory (WPRT) advanced by Torben Iversen in a number of publications and closely associated with the 'varieties of capitalism' theory.[11] Similar to PRT, the new theory accounts for social policy outcomes in terms of preferences over social protection and redistribution held by *factors of production* (wage earners and capital owners) in a polity, not by conditions and interests specific to firms or sectors. Unlike PRT, WPRT argues that employers agree to social policies that are in their own interest to boost the productive deployment of the factors of production in their firms. Where exactly employers' interests overlap with those of workers in social protection and even redistribution, as long as it is confined to redistribution among wage earners, depends on whether the prevailing production regime is of the CME or LME type.

Coordinated market economies (CME) rely on skill formation that is 'specific' to industries or firms. For employees it is risky to invest in such skills, as no alternative employment outside the firm or industry in which they currently work would allow them to amortize their skill investment. What makes wage earners shoulder such risk? If skill specificity limits employment options to a single economic sector, generous unemployment insurance with high wage replacement rates over a long period of time may encourage workers to invest in risky skills by compensating them for the extra effort it would take to find a new job, were they to lose the existing one (Iversen, 2005: 41–5). If skill-specificity limits employment to a single firm, workers would make such risky investments only if they enjoy high job protection.

Hence, one would surmise that countries which already have an array of institutions that promote CME production – such as encompassing, unified labor unions, strong business associations and networks, and incremental technological innovation configured around large companies and networks among companies – witness energetic efforts by employers and workers to craft social policies that encourage investment in specific skills. And, indeed, Iversen (2005: 53–8) can demonstrate empirically that CME countries with strong vocational (i.e. specific skill) training have much higher levels of job protection and/or more generous unemployment insurance schemes. In cross-national comparison, CME economies such as Austria, Belgium, Germany and Sweden score high on both job security and unemployment insurance, whereas the Anglo-Saxon LMEs score low on both. Japan and Italy have strong job protection (with 'life time' employment) and Denmark, Switzerland, and the Netherlands have generous unemployment insurance, but low job protection, to enable flexible medium-sized companies to adjust their labor force without great transaction costs.

Interestingly, at the individual level of public opinion, Iversen (2005: Chapter 3) finds that citizens with asset-specific skills have a greater propensity to support social spending on income maintenance and social policy. As a further implication of the theory, Iversen and Rosenbluth (2006) can show that women are much more in favor of social policy and left parties, when they are employed in countries where demand is strong for specific skills. Because prevailing cultural practices of child rearing force women to leave the labor force intermittently, in CMEs they have thus great difficulties in maintaining specific skills and reentering labor markets successfully.

Women are relatively less concerned about income-maintaining social protection and less supportive of left parties in LMEs, where they can (re)enter labor markets easily because of the prevalence of general skills. As a consequence of differential labor market opportunities, in CMEs marriages tend to allocate a greater share of housework to women and discourage divorce, as women have less promising prospects to find gainful employment.

WPRT, based on the postulate of complementarity between social policy and production regimes, is highly suggestive as a theoretical account of different levels of unemployment insurance and job protection, although only detailed process tracing could determine, whether the hypothesized constellations of interests indeed brought about the resulting policies of social protection or whether other political forces were at work. It is more difficult, however, to argue that the generosity and distributive schemes of health care and pension insurance – the two financially biggest components of modern welfare states – or policies to support families causally and functionally depend on production regimes. How would a more generous pension plan or more comprehensive public health insurance provide incentives to invest in specific skills? Conversely, should not a rather restrictive, occupationally specific and non-redistributive health and pension scheme give wage earners the greatest incentive to invest in specific skills, provided such jobs come with life time employment or generous unemployment benefits proportional to previous wage earnings and with ongoing health coverage? Universal health and pension plans that redistribute toward the least skilled workers, but exist for example in Scandinavian CMEs as well as to a lesser extent in some continental CMEs, certainly are not functionally complementary to the acquisition of specific skills.

WPRT invites us to make the leap of faith and to surmise that skill-specific workers, once sensitized to their particular labor market vulnerabilities, endorse not only job security and unemployment insurance, but social protection and redistribution in general. But the generalization to other insurance programs (health, pensions) or need-based subsidies (family benefits) does not follow from the production regime argument. Moreover, it is unclear why a desire for insurance (social protection) would also imply a desire for redistribution on the part of skill-specific workers, at least not when in comes to health care and pension benefits.[12] It is one thing to endorse insurance with ex post redistributive consequences and quite another to call for social programs that ex-ante redistribute benefits across social categories. Because insurance is not the same thing as redistribution and because redistribution is not functionally required by CMEs, WPRT theory cannot explain the distinction between less redistributive continental and the more redistributive Scandinavian welfare states both of which have CME production regimes. The partisan-based argument of PRT may be more convincing in this regard, even though it misses that employers sometimes consented to universalistic social security systems (cf. Swenson, 2002), especially if they were funded out of wages by payroll taxes.

Just as with PRT theory, WPRT theory may also retrospectively explain social policy arrangements that are now manifestly becoming fetters on economic growth and job creations. In the case of WPRT theory, new challenges of technology, demographics and globalization may render the equilibrium unviable that matches labor markets based on specific skills to generous, encompassing welfare states. As employment in manufacturing sectors has dramatically shrunk over the past thirty years in all PI-democracies, the bulk of new job creation comes from general low-skill or general high-skill service employment (cf. Iversen, 2005: 67–75). To stimulate employment in these sectors, there may be no way around 'selective deregulation' and/or government employment in the future (Iversen, 2005: 272–4).

We come to the surprising interim result that both the PRT and the WPRT theories may explain substantial aspects of past social policy, although each has its own limitations, but that both theories earmark non-liberal welfare states and production regimes as equilibria compatible with robust economic growth and employment that appear to vanish in the early twenty-first century because of new exogenous parameters (technology, demographics, global competition). Does this imply that only the market liberal option of residual welfare states with low unemployment insurance and job protection remains viable? Or are there driving forces of social policy not emphasized in both theories that allow us to reach different conclusions? In order to provide a tentative and somewhat speculative answer to this question, let us briefly review the challenges and patterns of social policy reform that have emerged in PI-democracies.

The first challenge is that of *technology*, especially the penetration of information technologies (IT) as 'general purpose' technology into all spheres of production and service delivery. Recent econometric work once again confirms that IT technology probably has had the biggest impact on wages and jobs, particularly for unskilled workers (IMF, 2007: Chapter 5). The penetration of IT may promote the progressive obsolescence of specific skills in manufacturing, with many of the remaining jobs requiring a high quality scientific education. At the same time, the changing demand for occupational skills makes rigid labor markets with high job protection inhospitable to investment and economic growth. While there is some disagreement on the precise calibration of the causes that bring about low employment growth, there is no one who would claim that CME regimes have an advantage over LME countries. Nevertheless labor market rigidities may not doom CME institutions in the short or medium run. The good news for CMEs is that the changing demographics of PI-democracies with small age cohorts entering labor markets and large baby boomer cohorts exiting might render unemployment irrelevant even in the presence of rigid labor markets. Add on to this the boom in Asian demand for capital goods, a sector in which CME countries have a huge institutional advantage, and job creation may be less of a problem than labor scarcity, particularly for high-skill professions.

The new technological challenges in PI democracies, however, call for a continuous upgrading of education to deliver the skill profile demanded by changing labor markets. It is currently not clear which institutional arrangements are most conducive to delivering a profile of qualifications congruent with a post-industrial economy and there is next to no comparative research on the political economy of human capital investments (but see Iversen and Stephens, 2008). In LME residual welfare states, low public investment in education, complemented by private educational investments by the upper middle class, generates a skill and qualification profile that may restrain economic growth and international competitiveness. The weak performance of most LMEs in comparative literacy and school achievement tests suggests that a solid broad middle of well-trained general-skill professionals is missing. The economic competitiveness of LMEs may depend increasingly on global 'skimming' of foreign high-skill students having received superior primary and secondary education elsewhere on earth, but then being lured to PI-economies by access to outstanding tertiary educational facilities and access to high-paying jobs thereafter.

As explained above, an office-seeking electoral logic embraced by strong Social Democratic parties vying for the median voter and government control may induce party strategists to win marginal voter groups by providing collective goods or club goods that actually do not primarily benefit the working class. Higher education reform and expansion is a case in point. Scandinavian CMEs now spend more on their public university systems than any other set of countries on earth.[13] As their economic growth performance since the mid-1990s suggests, high-quality tertiary education may facilitate expansion into entirely new industries and avert unemployment, even in the face of labor market rigidities. It is not the skill-specificity of the Scandinavian labor force that boosts the region's growth, but the investment in general skill higher education.

Continental CME economies that have not invested much in higher education and that still rely to a considerable extent on traditionally skill-specific training trajectories, have performed much worse in terms of economic growth and job creation, a result particularly visible in France, Germany, and Italy. Not by accident, it is in such countries that reform of higher education has become a key political issue, although it is unclear whether politics can deliver. Improved higher education would financially require that the beneficiaries, mostly middle class offspring, pay for reforms through higher tuition, or that governments could extract more taxes to pay for such services, both prospects likely to provoke intense opposition. Overall, when it comes to the challenge of technology and education, continental European CMEs appear to be least prepared, whereas LMEs and Scandinavian CMEs each have strengths and weaknesses.

The second challenge is the *demographic transition* due to declining fertility and increasing life expectancy. It reduces the population share that works and finances social security and health care programs. Again we witness a divide that sets LMEs with residual welfare states and Scandinavian CME universalistic welfare states apart from continental CMEs with conservative welfare states. Whereas fertility rates in Anglo-Saxon LMEs have hovered slightly below the replacement rate of 2.1 (US: 2.0; Australia: 1.8; UK: 1.7; Canada: 1.5), continental European CMEs have seen very low birth rates (1.3 or 1.4 in Austria, Germany and Italy), with the recent exception of France (1.9). Scandinavia claims an intermediate position (between 1.6 in Sweden and 1.8 in Denmark and Finland), as do Belgium and the Netherlands (1.7) with welfare states that combine conservative continental and universalistic redistributive features.

In LMEs relatively cheap private childcare services as well as possibly the fear of poverty in old age without support by children may encourage families to have more children, whereas in Scandinavian CMEs and France the availability of public child care lowers the burden of child rearing. In contrast, in continental Europe the high cost of private services and the absence of public child care depress fertility (cf. Esping-Andersen, 1999, 2002). Economists would add the generosity of public pension schemes as another fertility-depressing constraint because it makes people less likely to treat children as an investment in their own future (Boldrin et al., 2005).

Add on to this that continental European social security systems have been exclusively financed by pay-go public pension plans, in which current pensions for retirees are paid directly out of current receipts in payroll tax, whereas LME residual welfare states, as well as CME Scandinavia, and the Netherlands have strong complementary capitalized, funded public, or private pension plans. Hence the emerging fiscal crisis of social protection induced by demographics tends to be much more intense in the continental CMEs than elsewhere. Once again, it is not divergence from market-liberalism in general, but the specific institutional architecture of continental European CMEs with conservative welfare states that generates major economically detrimental incentives.

The differential attention to education also affects the capacity of PI-democracies to cope with the third challenge, that of *globalization of production, capital flows and labor*. There is clear evidence that the globalization of trade and capital has contributed to a reduction of low-skilled employees' wage levels, though its effect is probably less pronounced than that of technological innovation (IMF, 2007). Nevertheless, there is little evidence that countries with rapid increases in globalization also are compelled to cut social expenditure to make the price of labor more competitive. Ironically, only in the least well-funded, liberal-residual welfare states with already low payroll taxes by

standards of PI-democracies economic openness appears to have induced expenditure retrenchment (cf. Swank, 2003). With regard to labor mobility, there is some evidence that immigration reduces public spending on social policy (cf. Soroka et al., 2006). Causal mechanisms bringing about this result, however, are not entirely obvious (indirect influence of radical right parties?), as there is little statistical association between rates of immigration at the national level, mobilization of xenophobic political parties, and public policy.

The challenges of technology, demographics, and globalization call less for a reduction in social expenditure than a recalibration that targets different groups and provides incentives for different social behavior.[14] Social protection and redistribution primarily fund 'social consumption' (pensions, health care, income support), even though the WPRT approach points out that minor expenses of the welfare state – such as unemployment insurance and job protection – can sometimes be considered a component of 'social investment,' insofar as they encourage specific skill acquisition. With traditional specific skills becoming obsolete in many places, however, the targets of social investment in PI-democracies, regardless of whether they have LME or CME institutions, has moved on to broad investments in general skills (higher education) and larger cohorts of competent labor market entrants (higher fertility rates and more immigrants, if properly trained to participate in PI economies). Taken together, these efforts may cope with technological innovation, demography, and globalization.

In order to mobilize resources for new social investments, however, private capital investment, public social consumption, or private consumption must be cut. The former would imply higher taxes on capital income, something difficult to achieve in a world of open capital markets and probably detrimental to economic growth prospects. This leaves the alternatives of doing nothing, cutting private consumption (higher taxes on consumption and/or wages) and/or reducing public consumption ('welfare state retrenchment') in the hope that some of the funds made available to private consumers actually end up in social investment (private schools and universities, for example).

Table 11.2 gives an overview of investment, private consumption and public consumption as shares of GDP in PI-democracies, plus the share of net foreign trade balance, disaggregated by country groups: LMEs with residual welfare states, CMEs with universalistic/redistributive welfare states (Scandinavia,

Table 11.2 Functional Division of the Gross Domestic Product 2005 (in percent of GDP)

Country groups	Capital investment	Private consumtion	Public consumtion	Total domestic allocation	Net balance of exports minus imports
1. ANGLO-SAXON COUNTRIES					
Australia	25.0	61.4	18.2	104.4	−4.4
Canada	19.3	55.9	19.3	94.5	+4.3
New Zealand	24.0	58.7	17.8	100.5	−0.5
United Kingdom	17.0	65.1	21.3	103.4	−3.3
United States	16.4	70.1	18.6	105.1	−5.1
Unweighted average, group 1	20.5	62.2	19.0	101.5	−1.5
2. SCANDINAVIA					
Denmark	20.0	47.9	26.5	94.4	+5.0
Finland	18.5	52.4	22.3	93.6	+6.6
Norway	19.0	44.8	22.0	85.8	+14.2
Sweden	17.7	47.8	26.9	92.4	+7.6
Unweighted average group 2	18.8	48.2	24.4	91.4	+8.6
3. LOW COUNTRIES					
Belgium	16.7	54.0	22.7	93.4	+3.0
Netherlands	19.7	49.4	23.5	92.6	+7.2
Unweighted average group 3	18.2	51.7	23.1	93.1	+6.9
4. CONTINENTAL EUROPE GROUP					
Austria	21.2	55.8	17.8	94.8	+5.2
France	19.5	55.3	24.2	99.0	+0.5
Germany	17.2	59.2	18.6	95.0	+4.9
Italy	19.5	59.8	19.7	100.0	0.0
Switzerland	20.1	60.5	11.9	92.6	+7.4
Unweighted average group 4	19.5	58.1	18.4	96.0	+4.0
Japan	23.9	56.5	17.6	98.0	+1.9
RESIDUAL GROUP: LATE CATCH-UP					
Greece	25.8	66.8	16.4	109.0	−8.9
Ireland	25.1	45.4	14.4	84.9	+15.1
Israel	17.7	59.2	28.6	105.5	−5.3
Portugal	23.0	64.1	20.7	107.8	−7.8
Spain	28.3	57.7	17.8	103.8	−3.8

SOURCE: Calculated from OECD, *Quarterly National Accounts*.

and as marginal cases Belgium and the Netherlands), CMEs with continental social protectionist welfare states, and a residual group of latecomers to the PI-democracy group or outliers (Israel with low private investment and high public consumption, in part due to military expenses). The OECD's category of 'final public consumption' should not be confused with the contrast between social consumption and social investment proposed here. In the OECD categorization, 'public consumption' includes all social services, including public educational expenditure and child care that I have termed here 'social investment.'

Interestingly, the share of GDP devoted to investments is about the same in all LMEs and CMEs, regardless of overall size of the public sector and tax rates. Some countries with low tax rates have also very low investment rates (United States!). Higher investments in human capital show up either in high public sector consumption (Scandinavia and Low Countries), or in high private consumption (LME countries with residual welfare states, private educational and family services). The continental European CMEs, by contrast, have neither very high private consumption nor high public consumption. In order to stimulate human capital generating expenditure, resources would have to be diverted from private consumption to private investment (e.g., private child care and private universities) or public investment (tuition for public universities, higher taxes on consumption and/or wage income), each implying a highly unpopular reduction of private final consumption.[15] Add onto this that the demographic transition increases pressures to spend on social consumption, and the intensity of the ongoing distributive conflict between private and social consumption, on one side, and social investment, on the other, comes into sharp relief.

Let us address here only the question of the extent to which PI-democracies have begun to reign in on social and/or private consumption as a step toward recalibrating expenditures and making room for social investment. The factual question of whether or not PI-democracies have reduced social consumption over the past decades depends on the measures employed. As a share of GDP, social expenditure has stayed high or even slowly increased over the past decade just about anywhere in the OECD. But growing numbers of claimants, whether as unemployed or pensioners, may conceal the at times substantial entitlement cutbacks per claimant (cf. Allan and Scruggs, 2004; Korpi and Palme, 2003; Pontusson, 2005: Chapter 8). Several different arguments have been made to account for the timing, size and program structure of these cutbacks, but it may be too early to judge the relative importance of each.

First, there are theories that hold responsible objective economic exigencies for the decline of social expenditure. While Huber and Stephens (2001) subscribe to a partisan theory of welfare state expansion, they argue that recent cuts cannot be accounted for in partisan terms, but result from increasing claims made on social programs by unemployment. PRT has no prospective applicability. A similar exigencies based argument could be teased out of Iversen's (2005) work. Social expenditure declines when the occupational structure changes such that specific skills become less relevant, rendering high unemployment payments and job protection less productive. Similarly, picking up on Iversen and Cusak (2000), one might also surmise that as the speed of change in the occupational structure, particularly the loss of jobs requiring specific skills, declines with the shrinking share of manufacturing in overall employment, social policy expenditures, as a way to compensate losers in the labor market, will contract as well. WPRT, however, has not yet developed or tested an explicit theory of welfare state retrenchment in PI-democracies.

Second, some research sees partisan politics consistent with PRT at work in the political retrenchment process (Allen and

Scruggs, 2004; Korpi and Palme, 2003; Pontusson, 2005). This research is based on a careful analysis of changes in entitlement levels in social insurance schemes (unemployment payments, sickness pay), based on standardized need profiles of claimants (say, a single wage earner in a family with two under-age children). Consistent with PRT, such entitlement levels appear to have fallen most in liberal-residual welfare states.

A different measure of social policy retrenchment would not look at current payouts and benefit levels, but at fundamental changes in the operation of social insurance. Most important here is the partial transition from a 'pay-go' pension system that ploughs current payroll tax receipts into current pensions to a partially capitalized insurance that makes the magnitude of a contributor's pension dependent on that individual's choice of funds and levels of contribution to a personalized pension savings account. Fundamental structural reform of national pension systems may not be the exclusive reserve of market liberal conservative governing parties. Governments led by social democratic or labor parties may be willing to embrace such long-term reforms, but also sometimes short-term benefits reductions contingent upon the configuration of party competition.

Left party governments may go ahead and reduce public social protection and income maintenance, where their major competitors have a reputation of being more fiercely committed to financial retrenchment of the welfare state. When compared to their partisan competitors, social democrats then present themselves as the "lesser evil" from the vantage point of all those who defend the status quo of generous pension systems that become unsustainable, when compared to their partisan competitors (cf. Green-Pedersen, 2002; Kitschelt, 2001; Schludi, 2005). In polities with strong cross-class Christian Democratic parties or nationalist parties, like the Gaullists in France, however, social democrats are not the only party with a reputation of having expanded the welfare state. Here they risk losing large blocs of voters to the opposition in elections after painful social policy reforms, as voters see their social-protectionist demands better represented with an opposition party.

Thus, in party systems where social democrats encounter strong, market-liberal conservative parties or alliances of parties waiting to replace a center-left government – e.g. in Scandinavia, Belgium, or the Netherlands – left parties in government are more likely to embrace social policy retrenchment, particularly when they can conceal reductions of entitlements behind complicated long-term incremental changes of contribution and benefits schemes. Conversely, center-left governments dare less reform, where the main opposition is not a market-liberal party, as in continental Europe with very weak market-liberal parties, particularly in France, Germany, and Italy. The electoral costs of retrenchment reform may be too high for either center-left or center-right governments. Where in such competitive configurations governing parties risk painful social policy reform anyway, they face heavy electoral losses subsequently, as long as some competitors can credibly preserve its reputation as a stalwart of the welfare state.

Third, a further line of reasoning about welfare state retrenchment rejects both a partisan politics-based account of retrenchment as well as an argument concerning objective social and economic circumstances. According to Pierson's (2001) 'new politics' thesis, many welfare state programs have created so broad a favorable electoral constituency that politicians, regardless of partisan stripes, can engage in cutbacks only if they somehow can avoid the blame for the reform. Hence, politicians can usually make cuts in universalistic, encompassing social insurance programs only through all-party coalitions or if the program is caught up in an acute fiscal crisis.

An interesting idea directly speaking to the social consumption/social investment trade-off has recently been made by Silja

Häusermann (2007). Based on continental European polities with Bismarckian paygo pension plans, she argues that issue linkage and logrolling can help reform. Retrenchment proposals have more promise to be implemented, if they counterbalance social consumption at least in part by stimulating social investments. In the realm of pensions, parties could offer higher pension entitlements for times spent by women staying outside labor markets in order to raise small children in exchange for cutbacks of the standard pensions earned after a lifetime of payroll contributions as a wage earner.

Continental European CMEs face not only the greatest urgency to change their welfare states due to low investments in general education that exacerbate the problems of technological innovation and globalization as well as due to the extent of demographic transformation. They also have the least political capacity to engineer unpopular reforms, as they are lacking powerful market-liberal parties. Both on the side of problem pressure as well as problem-solving abilities, continental European CMEs trail behind LMEs with liberal-residual welfare states and CMEs with universalistic-redistributive welfare states.

CONCLUSION

What are future prospects of research on the comparative macro-political economy and welfare state development of post-industrial democracies? It appears that the basic categories organizing institutional differences between national economies – whether in terms of 'varieties of capitalism' or 'worlds of welfare states' – are in the process of becoming inadequate to capture the empirical realities of political economic changes in individual PI-democracies and the global political economy. This may also reduce their value as causal mechanisms to account for cross-national variance in economic growth or patterns of inequality.

With regard to varieties of capitalism, over the past decade coordinated market economies have witnessed the beginnings of profound change in their practices of corporate governance, industrial relations, guarantees for job security, systems of skill formation, and technological innovation. In that process, they have adopted elements of LME arrangements to overcome rigid labor markets, low profitability, and weak innovativeness (few new technology start-ups). This does not imply, however, that LME type arrangements 'win' the competition of institutional models. LMEs have generated a whole range of growth inhibiting features of their own, such as corporate governance scandals, perverse effects of managerial compensation, the cost and inefficiency of private health care systems such that even in America a bipartisan consensus appears to emerge that holds universalistic compulsory coverage to be indispensable, and a weak primary and secondary education system for which LME countries compensate by encouraging the immigration of highly skilled professionals attracted by an intensely competitive tertiary education system. Also the sharp rise in inequality and poverty in LMEs places a considerable population share at risk of permanently losing the capacity to function competently in the market economy and polity of PI-democracies.

The ideal types whose institutional features were postulated to create efficiency-enhancing complementarities empirically give way to mixed arrangements or hybridization. And where reality still approximates a pure type, such arrangements do not deliver distinct economic payoffs (cf. Kenworthy, 2006). New challenges become prominent with which neither the market liberal variety of capitalism with residual welfare states nor the coordinated market economies with conservative or social democratic welfare states can fully cope. This concerns the political economy of (higher) education and the social consequences of demographic change. Both are intertwined insofar as they place a new distributive question on the agenda, one between social investments in current and future labor market participants and social consumption by past or soon retiring labor market participants.

The new priorities reveal lacunae in the comparative study of production systems and welfare states that need to be addressed in future research. Two of such lacunae appear to me to be particularly important. The first concerns the comparative political-economic analysis of education systems and particularly institutions of higher education, including their interface with technological innovation pursued by market entities. Little systematic comparative research has addressed the causes of differential education systems nor the forces that hasten or resist reform. The second concerns the empirical comparative study of tax systems and their consequences for efficient resource allocation and distribution. Economics has been better at identifying normative criteria of efficient tax systems than empirically studying the diversity of such systems. In comparative political economy, most of the varieties of capitalism as well as the worlds of welfare state literatures have just about ignored systems of taxation, except with regard to corporate taxation, a source of government revenue that pales in all PI-democracies when compared to the flow of resources furnished by income, payroll, and consumption taxes. Tax systems, however, play critical roles in shaping incentives for citizens' and firms' market strategies (and thus ultimately economic growth) as well as for social protection and inequality. As political economy begins to ponder the reconfiguration of systems of production and welfare states, it may be critical to incorporate close analysis of taxation and education.

NOTES

1. Gross domestic product (GDP) plus net receipts of primary income from foreign sources (World Bank 2006b: 300).

2. This claim is controversial in the literature on the radical right, but academic experts rate anti-immigrant and authoritarian radical right parties typically also on the pro-market liberal right, except on trade. At the mass level, the parties combine constituencies with somewhat different propensities on distributive politics around authoritarian and xenophobic appeals. In a highly simplistic way, radical right parties in Western Europe that have been electorally on the ascent in a number of countries (such as Austria, Belgium, Denmark, France, Italy, Norway, and Switzerland) have drawn over-proportionally on working class voters with authoritarian and xenophobic appeals and centrist to center-right economic-distributive propensities, but they also tap small business strata with vigorous anti-tax and anti-welfare inclinations. On the controversy about the association between market liberal and xenophobic-authoritarian appeals on the radical right, see Mudde (2007) arguing against and Kitschelt (2007a) arguing in favor.

3. In other words, the cut-off is slightly above the world's weighted average GNI per capita in 2005, $9,400 at PPP.

4. Counting these cities as countries would be equivalent to counting New York, London, Paris, or Los Angeles as separate countries. Each of their per capita GDP is higher than Luxembourg's, and that of Luxembourg, as a city state, is already substantially greater than that of Hong Kong or Singapore.

5. The exception is Iversen and Wren (1998) who argue that full employment and low wage inequality require very high public employment implying high budget deficits. One might argue, however, that high payroll and consumption taxes may close these loopholes, yet displace the problem to low private sector job formation and investment.

6. Curiously, Franzese's (2002: Chapter 4) otherwise technically much more sophisticated treatment than Garrett's completely brackets international variables, with the exception of the sectoral composition of the economy.

7. Mares (2006): 'I divide the number of persons aged between 18 and 65 who are neither employed nor unemployed to the working age population, and I multiply the resulting number by the level of expenditures on unemployment benefits' (pp. 69–70).

8. On the importance of regime and suffrage, see recently Lindert (2004).

9. The main contributors to this train of thinking are Castles (1978), Esping-Andersen (1990), Hicks (1999), Huber and Stephens (2001), Korpi (1983; 2006), and Stephens (1979).

10. On institutional modifications of the PRT argument, see especially Huber et al. (1993).

11. I am drawing on Estevez et al. (2001), Iversen (2005: Chapters 1–4), Iversen and Rosenbluth (2006) and Iversen and Soskice (2001, 2006).

12. Unemployment insurance may be the exception to that rule. If unskilled workers have a higher risk of becoming unemployed than skill-specific

workers and accumulate more days in unemployment per year per unskilled worker, but all workers pay the same insurance premiums and draw benefits according to the same schedule, risk pooling will redistribute resources in favor of unskilled workers.

13. According to OECD statistics, in 2001, LME countries spent between 0.9 per cent/GDP (UK, US) and 1.5 per cent/GDP (Canada) on public higher education, while all four Scandinavian countries dedicated about 1.5 per cent/GDP to that purpose. The continental European CMEs spent only between 0.7 per cent/GDP (Italy) and 1.1 per cent/GDP (Austria) on higher education. But unlike the LMEs, they did not supplement this expenditure with generous private investment, bringing the US total to no less then 2.7 per cent of GDP and that of other LME countries to 2.5 (Canada), 1.5 (Australia) and 1.1 (Britain), (see OECD, 2006).

14. For an interesting analysis of recalibration in social policy, see Häussermann (2007).

15. Of course, continental Europeans could try to reduce their export surplus and consume more of what they produce. A large trade deficit is clearly one major reason why U.S. consumption is exorbitantly high as share of GDP. But Scandinavia has an even higher export surplus than continental Europe and still manages to devote more to social investment and restrict private consumption.

REFERENCES

Alesina, A. and Perotti, R. (1995) 'Fiscal expansions and adjustments in OECD countries', *Economic Policy*, 10: 207–48.

Alesina, A. and Rosenthal, H. (1995) *Partisan politics, divided government, and the economy*. Cambridge: Cambridge University Press.

Allan, J.P. and Scruggs, L. (2004) 'Political Partisanship and Welfare State Reform in Advanced Industrial Societies,' *American Journal of Political Science*, 48 (3): 496–512.

Allen, M. (2004) 'The varieties of capitalism paradigm: Not enough variety?', *Socio-Economic Review*, 2 (1): 87–108.

Alt, J.E. and Crystal, K.A. (1983) *Political economics*. Berkeley: University of California Press.

Alvarez, R.M., Garrett, G. and Lange, P. (1991) 'Government partisanship, labor organization, and macroeconomic performance', *American Political Science Review*, 85 (2): 541–56.

Baldwin, P. (1990) *The politics of social solidarity. Class bases of the European welfare state 1875–1975*. Cambridge: Cambridge University Press.

Benoit, K. and Laver, M. (2007) *Party policy in modern democracies*. London: Routledge.

Beramendi, P. and Rueda, D. (2007) 'Social democracy constrained: Indirect taxation in industrialized democracies', *British Journal of Political Science*, 37 (4): 619–41.

Beyer, J. and Höpner, M. (2003) 'Corporate governance and the disintegration of organized capitalism in the 1990s', *West European Politics*, 26 (4): 179–98.

Boldrin, M., De Nardi, M., and Jones, L.E. (2005) *Fertility and social security*. (National Bureau of Economic Research working paper, no. 11146).

Bradley, D., Huber, E., Moller, S., Nielsen, F., and Stephens, J. D. (2003) 'Distribution and redistribution in post-industrial democracies', *World Politics*, 55 (2): 193–229.

Calmfors, L. and Driffill, J. (1988) 'Coordination of wage bargaining', *Economic Policy*, 6 (1): 14–61.

Cameron, D. (1978) 'The expansion of the public economy: A comparative analysis', *American Political Science Review*, 72 (4): 1243–61.

Cameron, D. (1984) 'Social democracy, corporatism, labor quiescence, and the representation of economic interest in advanced capitalist society', in J. H. Goldthorpe (ed.), *Order and conflict in contemporary capitalism. Studies in the political economy of Western European nations*. Oxford: Oxford University Press, pp. 143–78.

Castles, F.G. (1978) *The social democratic image of society*. London: Routledge.

Castles, F.G. (2002) *The future of the welfare state. crisis myths and crisis realities*. Oxford: Oxford University Press.

Crouch, C. (1993) *Industrial relations and European state traditions*. Oxford: Oxford University Press.

Cusack, T.R. and Beramendi, P. (2006) 'Taxing work', *European Journal of Political Research*, 45 (1): 43–73.

Dalton, R.J. (2004) *Democratic challenges. Democratic choices. The erosion of political support in advanced industrial democracies*. Oxford: Oxford University Press.

Esping-Andersen, G. (1990) *The three worlds of welfare*. Princeton, NJ: Princeton University Press.

Esping-Andersen, G. (1999) *Social foundations of post-industrial economies*. Oxford: Oxford University Press.

Esping-Andersen, G. (2002) *Why we need a new welfare state*. Oxford: Oxford University Press.

Estevez, M., Iversen, T., and Soskice, D. (2001) 'Social protection and the formation of skills: a reinterpretation of the welfare state', in P. Hall and D. Soskice (eds), *Varieties of Capitalism. The institutional foundations of comparative advantage*. Oxford: Oxford University Press, pp. 145–83.

Flora, P. and Heidenheimer, A. (eds) (1981) *The development of welfare states in Europe and America*. New Brunswick: Transaction Books.

Franzese, R. (2002) *Macro-economic policies in developed democracies*. Cambridge: Cambridge University Press.

Garrett, G. (1998) *Partisan politics and the global economy*. Cambridge: Cambridge University Press.

Goyer, M. (2006) 'The transformation of corporate governance in France', in P. D. Culpepper, P. A. Hall and B. Palier (eds), *Changing France. The politics that markets make*. New York: Palgrave MacMillan, pp. 80–104.

Hall, P.A. and Gingerich, D.W. (2004) *Varieties of capitalism and institutional complementarities in the macroeconomy. An empirical analysis* (MPI Cologne Discussion Paper 04/5).

Hall, P.A. and Soskice, D. (eds) (2001) *Varieties of capitalism. The institutional foundations of comparative advantage*. Oxford: Oxford University Press.

Hall, P.A. and Soskice, D. (2001) 'An introduction to varieties of capitalism', in P.A. Hall and D. Soskice (eds), *Varieties of capitalism, the institutional foundations of comparative advantage*. Oxford, Oxford University Press, pp. 1–70.

Hallerberg, M. (2004) *Domestic budgets in a United Europe*. Ithaca, NY: Cornell University Press.

Hallerberg, M., Strauch, R., and von Hagen, J. (2009) *Domestic budgets in a United Europe. Fiscal governance from the end of Bretton woods to EMU*. Ithaca, NY: Cornell University Press.

Häusermann, S. (2007) *Modernization in hard times. Post-industrial pension politics in France, Germany and Switzerland*. (Dissertation, Department of Political Science, University of Zurich).

Hibbs, D. (1976) 'Industrial conflict in advanced industrial societies', *American Political Science Review*, 70 (4): 1033–58.

Hibbs, D. (1977) 'Political parties and macroeconomic policy', *American Political Science Review*, 71 (4): 1467–87.

Hibbs, D.A. (1987) *The international political economy of industrial democracies*. Cambridge, MA: Harvard University Press.

Hicks, A. (1999) *Social democracy and welfare capitalism. A century of income security politics*. Ithaca: Cornell University Press.

Huber, E., Ragin, C., and Stephens, J.D. (1993) 'Social Democracy, Christian Democracy, constitutional structure, and the welfare state', *American Journal of Sociology*, 99 (3): 711–49.

Huber, E. and Stephens, J.D. (2001) *Development and crisis of the welfare state*. Chicago: University of Chicago Press.

IMF (2007) *World economic outlook. Spillovers and cycles in the global economy*. Washington, D.C.

Inglehart, R. (1997) *Modernization and post-modernization: Cultural, economic, and political change in 43 societies*. Princeton, NJ: Princeton University Press.

Iversen, T. (1999) *Contested economic institutions. The politics of macroeconomics and wage bargaining in advanced democracies*. Cambridge: Cambridge University Press.

Iversen, T. (2005) *Capitalism, democracy and welfare*. Cambridge: Cambridge University Press.

Iversen, T. and Cusak T.R. (2000) 'The Causes of welfare State Expansion: Deindustrialization or Globalization?' *World Politics*, 52 (3): 313–49.

Iversen, T. and Rosenbluth, F. (2006) 'The political economy of gender: Explaining cross-national variation in the gender division of labor and the gender voting gap', *American Journal of Political Science*, 50 (1): 1–19.

Iversen, T. and Soskice, D. (2006a) 'New macroeconomics and political science', *Annual Review of Political Science*, 9: 425–53.

Iversen, T. and Soskice, D. (2006b) 'Electoral institutions and the politics of coalitions: Why some democracies redistribute more than others', *American Political Science Review*, 100 (2): 165–82.

Iversen, T. and Stephens, J. (2008) 'Partisan Politics, the Welfare State, and the Three Worlds of Human Capital Formation', *Comparative Political Studies*, 41 (4–5): 600–37.

Iversen, T. and Wren, A. (1998) 'Equality, employment, and budgetary restraint: The trilemma of the service economy', *World Politics*, 50: 507–46.

Kato, J. (2003) *Regressive taxation and the welfare state*. New York: Cambridge University Press.

Katzenstein, P. (1985) *Small states in world markets*. Ithaca, NY: Cornell University Press.

Kenworthy, L. (2001) 'Wage-setting measures: A survey and assessment', *World Politics*, 54 (1): 57–98.

Kenworthy, L. (2004) *Egalitarian capitalism. jobs, incomes, and growth in affluent countries*. New York: Russell Sage Foundation.

Kenworthy, L. (2006) 'Institutional coherence and macro-economic performance', *Socioeconomic Review*, 4 (1): 69–91.

Kitschelt, H. (1994) *Rationale Verfassungswahl?: Zum Design von Regierungssystemen in neuen Konkurrenzdemokratien; Antrittsvorlesung, 2. Mai 1994, Department of Political Science, Duke University, North Carolina und Humboldt-Universität zu Berlin, Philosophische Fakultät III, Institut für Politikwissenschaft*. Berlin: Humboldt–Univ.

Kitschelt, H. (2003) 'Landscapes of political interest intermediation. Social movements, interest groups, and parties in the early twenty-first century', in P. Ibarra, (ed.), *Social movements and democracy*. Basingstoke: Palgrave MacMillan, pp. 81–104.

Kitschelt, H. (2007a) 'Party systems', in C. Boix and S. Stokes (eds), *Handbook of comparative politics*. Oxford: Oxford University Press, pp. 522–54.

Kitschelt, H. (2007b) 'Growth and persistence of the radical right in post-industrial democracies. Advances and challenges in comparative research', *West European Politics*, 30 (5): 1176–207.

Kitschelt, H. and Rehm, P. (2005) *Family, and politics. Foundations of electoral partisan alignments in post-industrial democracies*. Paper prepared for delivery at the 2005 Annual Meeting of the American Political Science Association, Washington, DC.

Kitschelt, H. and Rehm, P. (2006) 'New Social Risks and Political Preferences', in K. Armingeon and G. Bonoli (eds) *The Politics of Post-Industrial Welfare States. Adapting postwar social policies to new social risks*. London: Routledge, pp. 52–82.

Kitschelt, H. and Rehm, P. (2007) 'Political participation', in D. Caramani (ed.), *Comparative politics*. Oxford: Oxford University Press.

Korpi, W. (1983) *The democratic class struggle*. London: Routledge and Kegan Paul.

Korpi, W. (2006) 'Power resources and employer–centered approaches in explanations of welfare states and varieties of capitalism. Protagonists, consenters, and antagonists', *World Politics*, 58 (2): 167–206.

Korpi, W. and Joakim P. (2003) 'New Politics and Class Politics in the Context of Austerity and Globalization. Welfare State Regress in 18 Countries', 1975–1995. *American Political Science Review,* 97 (3): 425–46.

Kriesi, H., Grande, E., Lachat, R., Dolezal, M., Bornschier, S., and Frey, T. (2006) 'Globalization and the transformation of the national political space: Six European countries compared', *European Journal of Political Research*, 45: 921–56.

Lange, P. and Garrett, G. (1985) 'The politics of growth. strategic interaction and economic performance in the advanced industrial democracies, 1974–1980', *Journal of Politics*, 47 (3): 792–827.

Lijphart, A. (1999) *Patterns of democracy: Government formation and performance in thirty-six countries*. New Haven: Yale University Press.

Lindert, P.H. (2004) *Growing public. social spending and economic growth since the eighteenth century* (Vol. 1, The Story) Cambridge: Cambridge University Press.

Lipset, S.M. (1961) *Party systems and the representation of social groups*. Berkeley: University of California.

Lynch, J. (2006) *Age in the welfare state. The origins of social spending on pensioners, workers, and children*. Cambridge: Cambridge University Press.

Mares, I. (2003) *The politics of social risk*. Cambridge: Cambridge University Press.

Mares, I. (2004) 'Wage bargaining in the presence of social services and transfers', *World Politics*, 57 (1): 99–142.

Mares, I. (2006) *Taxation, wage bargaining, and unemployment*. Cambridge: Cambridge University Press.

Meltzer, A.H. and Richards, S.F. (1981) 'A rational theory of the size of government', *Journal of Political Economy*, 89 (5): 914–27.

Moene, K.O. and Wallerstein, M. (2001) 'Inequality, social insurance and redistribution', *American Political Science Review*, 95 (4): 859–74.

Moene, K.O. and Wallerstein, M. (2003) 'Earnings Inequality and Welfare Spending: A disaggregated analysis', *World Politics*, 55 (4): 485–516.

Mudde, C. (2007) *Populist radical right parties in Europe*. Cambridge: Cambridge University Press.

Nordhaus, W. (1975) 'The political business cycle', *Review of Economic Studies*, 42 (2): 169–90.

OECD (2001) *Literacy in the information age*. Paris.

OECD (2004) *Learning for tomorrow's world. First results of PISA 2003*. Paris.

OECD (2006) *Education policy analysis. Focus on higher education*. Paris.

Olson, M.J. (1982) *The rise and decline of nations*. New Haven: Yale University Press.

Pontusson, J. (2005a) 'Varieties and commonalities of Capitalism', in D. Coates (ed.), *Varieties of capitalism, varieties of approaches*. New York: Palgrave-Macmillan, pp. 163–88.

Pontusson, J. (2005b) *Inequality and prosperity. Social Europe vs. liberal America*. Ithaca, NY: Cornell University Press.

Powell, G.B. (2000) *Elections as instruments of democracy*. New Haven: Yale University Press.

Rueda, D. (2005) 'Insider-outsider politics in industrialized democracies: The challenge to social democratic parties', *American Political Science Review*, 99 (1): 61–74.

Sainsbury, D. (1999) 'Gender policy regimes, and politic', in D. Sainsbury (ed.), *Gender and welfare states regimes*. Oxford: Oxford University Press.

Scharpf, F. (1991) *Crisis and choice in European social democracy*. Ithaca, New York: Cornell University Press.

Schludi, M. (2005) *The Reform of Bismarckian Pension Systems. A Comparison of Pension Politics in Austria, France, Germany, Italy and Sweden*. Amsterdam: Amsterdam University Press.

Schmitter, P. (1974) 'Still the century of corporatism?', *Review of Politics*, 36: 85–131.

Schmitter, P. (1981) 'Interest intermediation and regime governability in contemporary Western Europe and North America', in S. Berger (ed.), *Organizing interests in Western Europe. Pluralism, corporatism, and the transformation of politics*. Cambridge: Cambridge University Press, pp. 287–330.

Schumpeter, J. (1950) *Capitalism, socialism, and democracy*. New York: Harper.

Scruggs, L. (2001) 'The politics of growth revisited', *Journal of Politics*, 63 (1): 120–40.

Shonfield, A. (1965) *Modern capitalism*. Oxford: Oxford University Press.

Siaroff, A. (1999) 'Corporatism in 24 industrial democracies: Meaning and measurement', *European Journal of Political Research*, 36 (2): 175–205.

Soroka, S., Banting, K., and Jonston, R. (2006) 'Immigration and redistribution in the global era', in P. Bardhan, S. Bowles and M. Wallerstein, (eds), *Globalization and Egalitarian Redistribution*. Princeton, NJ: Princeton University Press, pp. 261–88.

Soskice, D. (1999) 'Divergent Production Regimes. Coordinated and uncoordinated market economies in the 1980s and 1990s', in H. Kitschelt, P. Lange, G. Marks and J.D. Stephens (eds), *Continuity and change in contemporary capitalism*. New York: Cambridge University Press, pp. 101–34.

Soskice, D. (2000) 'Macroeconomic analysis and the political economy of unemployment', in T. Iversen et al. (eds) *Unions, employers and central banks*. Cambridge: Cambridge University Press, pp. 38–74.

Stephens, J. (1979) *The transition for capitalism to socialism*. London: MacMillan.

Swank, D. (2003) *Global capital, political institutions, and policy change in developed welfare states*. Cambridge: Cambridge University Press.

Swenson, P. (1989) *Fair shares. Unions, pay, and politics in Sweden and West Germany*. Ithaca, NY: Cornell University Press.

Swenson, P. (2002) *Capitalists against markets: The making of labor markets and welfare states in the United States and Sweden*. Oxford: Oxford University Press.

Timmons, J. (2005) 'The fiscal contract: States, taxes, and public services', *World Politics*, 57 (4): 530–68.

Tufte, E. (1978) *Political control of the economy*. Princeton, NJ: Princeton University Press.

Warwick, P.V. (2002) 'Toward a common dimensionality in West European policy spaces', *Party Politics*, 8 (1): 101–22.

Wilensky, H. (1975) *The welfare state and equality: The roots of public expenditure*. Berkeley, CA: University of California Press.

World Bank (2005) *Where is the Wealth of Nations? Measuring capital for the 21st century*. Washington DC, The World Bank.

World Bank (2006a) *World development report. Development and the next generation*. Washington, DC: World Bank.

World Bank (2006b) *Doing business in 2007. How to reform*. Washington, DC: World Bank.

World Bank Global Governance Indicators (2004) World Bank Global Governance Indicators (n.d.) Retrieved February 22, 2008, from refe-http://info.worldbank.org/governance/wgi2007/faq.htmpaper

World Economic Forum (2006) *The global competitiveness report 2006–07*. New York: Palgrave Macmillan.

12

Government Formation

Wolfgang C. Müller

INTRODUCTION

According to Schumpeter's (1942) 'realistic' theory of democracy, competition for government office is at the heart of modern democracy. Because governments are the central actors in most political systems politically ambitious individuals aim at government office and government participation is also a central goal for most political parties. In democracies such competition for government office ultimately is tied to elections. Either the people elect the government directly or their elected agents do so, or the government is appointed by the head of state but responsible to a parliament resulting from general elections. In the first case – in presidential systems – only the chief executive (and possible a vice-president as part of a 'package') is directly elected. Government formation is nevertheless an interesting process that is worthwhile studying as appointments can indicate a more or less partisan policy and can indicate the relative weight of the various tendencies in the president's party. Presidential regimes in multi-party systems may even require building multi-party cabinets, though this is only one of the options available to presidents (Amorim, 2006; Cheibub et al., 2004; Cox and Morgenstern, 2006).

Notwithstanding the relevance of government formation in presidential regimes the present chapter concentrates on parliamentary democracies. Certainly cabinet formation in parliamentary regimes with a two-party system often resembles government formation in presidential regimes with a Congress majority of the president's party. The leader of the winning party assumes a role similar to that of the president. Yet, unlike the president, the prime minister remains dependent on their party for survival in office. And they may be constrained by intra-party rules, for instance a commitment to confine the choice of the government team to the party's shadow cabinet, as is the case in the British Labour Party when coming to government from opposition. If anything, over time the similarities between presidential and parliamentary systems with regard to the powers of the chief executive in government formation seem to have increased, even in multi-party systems (Poguntke and Webb, 2005). While interestingly, not much research has focused on the politics of cabinet appointments. This chapter, therefore, will focus on the more structural features of government composition: government type and the various types of coalitions. The relationship between elections and government formation is not straightforward. While most parties commanding a parliamentary majority form single-party governments this is not universally the case.

Likewise, the outcome of government formation in minority situations is not always majority-based coalition government. And elections in many cases do not determine the government's party composition. Rather they provide the initial endowment of politicians with bargaining power.[1] This allows for flexibility, but potentially also weakens political accountability.

There is a long history of writing about organizing government as either based on single-party majorities or coalitions. Although some of the early comparative studies including those of A. Lawrence Lowell and James Bryce, were not shy of making generalizations for instance about the instability of coalition government (see Dodd, 1976: 6–10), the scientific study of the phenomena of interest in this chapter is closely tied to the invention of game theory. The first game-theoretic treatments of government formation plus the behavioural revolution in the social sciences have inspired empirical work that is completely different from earlier considerations of government. It is this research tradition, often labelled 'coalition studies' (despite the fact that it is also concerned with non-coalition outcomes), that is at the heart of the present chapter.

Research on government formation in parliamentary democracies can be classified along two dimensions. The first dimension distinguishes theoretical and empirical work. The former aims at developing theoretical arguments that help us to understand government formation. Such studies theorize on the effects factors such as actor preferences, their endowment with resources, institutions, and random events have on government formation. Empirical work aims at describing and explaining government formation in real-world situations. This is not to say that empirical studies are not based on theory and that theoretical work is completely separated from confrontation with the real world. While we can see the divide between theoretical and empirical studies as a continuum, in practice the focus of most studies allows them to be placed clearly on one side. Theoretical work typically highlights a limited number of variables, but specifies the theoretical propositions very clearly, often in the form of mathematical equations. Empirical work is much wider in its scope. Ideally, it includes all variables that potentially help explain the variance in coalition formation. We should thus expect a more complete account of coalition formations from well-crafted empirical studies than from those that aim at testing specific theories. Thus, if we are interested in accounting for the factors that explain government formations in, for instance, post-war Western Europe, a specific country, or any specific situation, empirical accounts will provide us with a richer explanation: a greater amount of explained variance in quantitative studies, or a more plausible account of individual cases of cabinet formation. Yet, the explanation is fitted to the cases and is often theoretically underspecified. It is not so clear what we have gained in terms of understanding government formation in different continents, countries, periods, or situations.

The second dimension relates to the number of cases employed in empirical work: one, a few, or many. This dimension is one of the organizing principles of this volume and with regard to coalition formation can be translated into the archetypical case study of individual episodes of government formation, the country study covering all such episodes in a given period, and the quantitative comparative study of government formations maximizing both countries and formation situations. Certainly a few studies place themselves somewhere in-between these categories, for instance by studying several episodes in different countries (Jungar, 2000).

In this chapter, I will review these traditions in two main sections: one for the work that is first and foremost of a theoretical nature and the second for studies that place a premium on providing the best account of the real world of coalition politics. Thus, the next section presents and discusses the theoretical advances in understanding coalition formation. The subsequent one discusses how cross-national quantitative studies, country studies, and case studies of individual government formations have contributed to our understanding of government formation and how these approaches can help making further progress. A brief conclusion, highlighting particular promising avenues for future research, follows.[2]

COALITION THEORIES

Office-seeking and its limits

Theorists start from more or less plausible assumptions that are rooted in credible beliefs about human predispositions, such as greed, or – more nobly expressed – utility maximization. While the main body of literature focuses on 'structural' factors (resources, preferences, institutions) alternative approaches focus on various dimensions of the formation process (Adrian and Press, 1968; Grofman, 1982). All the first generation of coalition theorists additionally needed were minimal assumptions about a stylized world of politics. According to Riker's path-breaking study *The Theory of Political Coalitions* (1962) the world of government formation is a zero-sum game, governed by majority rule, with all actors having perfect information. Consequently, the theory predicts 'minimum winning' governments. That is single-party cabinets whenever a single party masters the 'winning' criterion, or, in minority situations (i.e., when no single party commands a majority), the majority coalition that has fewer parliamentary seats than any alternative winning coalition.[3] Without claiming to derive his predictions from game theory, Gamson (1961) had already theorized the formation of the 'cheapest winning coalition', a concept equivalent to Riker's 'minimum winning' solution.

The underlying zero-sum assumption in Riker's work is that the pay-offs from government participation (i.e., cabinet offices) are fixed and so have to be shared among the smallest number of players (in this case MPs), allowing a bigger share for each of them. Political parties in this theory are implicitly treated as coalitions of MPs. We can think of the frontbenchers taking over government office, some of the backbenchers moving to the frontbench (taking leadership positions in parliament), and the remaining backbenchers being rewarded otherwise (e.g., by government resources that help them get re-elected). However, early empirical tests of coalition theories based on office-seeking political parties have found their predictive power disappointing. Browne's (1970) empirical test showed that the Riker-Gamson theory only predicted eight per cent of the coalitions actually formed in 13 Western European countries (1945–1970). Two other office-seeking theories did better. Von Neumann and Morgenstern's (1953) 'minimal winning' theory, predicting the formation of coalitions that would no longer win if any of its members (i.e., parties) left, was supported in 50.4 per cent of the actually formed coalitions. Leiserson's (1966) 'bargaining proposition' theory, predicting the coalition with the minimum number of parties, was correct in 37.8 per cent of the government formations. Yet, these theories often predict not a single government but a set of equally likely outcomes. Once Browne calculated the theories' probability for correct predictions, 'minimum number of parties' ('bargaining proposition') was the best theory, followed by 'minimal winning', with 'minimum winning' last. While all three theories did better than random, most observers were not satisfied with probabilities for correct predictions in 12 per cent of the cases (for the 'minimum number of parties' theory) or less. Yet perhaps the problem is less in the predictive power of these theories than in the originally inflated expectations. A theory that does 17 times better than chance while requiring only a minimum amount of information – the distrbution of seats among parties – can definitively count as scientific progress. As Laver and Schofield (1990: 97) put it, it is a different matter that 'it does not tell us everything that we would like to know about the process of coalition formation'. Multivariate tests of coalition theories generally have confirmed that office-seeking assumptions have considerable explanatory power (Franklin and Mackie, 1984; Martin and Stevenson, 2001; Mitchell and Nyblade, 2008; Warwick, 1996).

Yet, the fact remains that office-seeking is not the whole story. Perhaps it is intuitive to mention that such theories can neither account for the occurrence of minority governments nor oversized cabinets. In the former case the opposition parties would unnecessarily leave office perks to the government parties and in the latter case government spoils would be divided among too many parties or among parties comprising too many greedy MPs (resulting in disappointingly small shares for the individual politicians). In practice, both types of governments exist and they are not infrequent. Several studies have shown that oversized cabinets (i.e., cabinets containing more parties than necessary for a bare majority) are about as frequent as minimal or minimum winning ones (e.g., Lijphart, 1999: 98). And the work of Kaare Strøm (1984, 1990a) has powerfully brought to the discipline's attention that minority cabinets are not rare exceptions. Nor do they typically indicate political crises. Indeed, it is possible to explain their occurrence as the outcome of rational party strategies. Empirical accounts show that roughly a third of all cabinets are of minority status (Müller and Strøm, 2000; Strøm, 1990a).

Early coalition theorists have recognized that their size-based predictions do conflict with at least some observed behaviour. Riker himself resorted to introducing incomplete information about the actual size of the coalition as explanation for such deviations (1962: 48, see also 78). In order to secure winning, actors resort to forming coalitions that command 'working majorities', that is coalitions with a safety net of a few extra seats (Riker and Ordeshook, 1973). If correct, this idea could also explain the formation of minority governments, as parties may recognize that they can win with less than a majority. Yet it seems impossible to identify 'working majority' requirements *a priori*. Browne's (1970: 29–30) test of Riker's theory in a revised form, considering majority coalitions with up to 55 per cent of the seats as 'minimum winning', indicated that while improving the prediction rate of actual coalitions to 16.8 per cent, it did so at the price of reducing the probability to predict the coalition correctly

to random level (because of the increase in the number of predicted outcomes).

Another possible reason for deviation at least from the minimum winning outcome is payoff sensitivity. A few seats more may not really matter with regard to payoff distribution among the coalition's members. The question then is how big the difference between alternative majorities must be to make a difference in practice. Moreover, office payoffs are not really fixed (zero-sum) in practice: cabinets can be increased or decreased in size, as can the number of parliamentary committees (and hence committee chairs), and government resources can also be increased by borrowing. Adding cabinet posts may decrease their value but as with all position goods the question is *when* exactly the devaluation sets in. Is one cabinet position out of 15 indeed worth more than one out of 18 and if yes, is the decrease in the value of individual positions proportional to the increase in their number? And although public borrowing may have detrimental long-term consequences on the availability of government resources, the short-term constraints on such a strategy may be soft, allowing for the considerable expansion of government funds. Indeed, as Verzichelli (2008) shows, an increase in the number of cabinet parties often leads to an increase in the number of portfolios.

The literature provides several other factors that can explain why office-seeking parties form coalitions deviating from the expected minimum or minimal outcomes (see de Swaan, 1973: 81–7): the requirement of qualified majorities, the distribution of societal power deviating from that of parliamentary power, transaction costs (Adrian and Press, 1968), the strategy of sharing the costs of governing among a larger group of actors, or the strategy of avoiding the costs of government (Mershon, 2002; Müller and Strøm, 2000; Strøm, 1990b), the existence of anti-system parties, and situations where democracy is under threat (Budge and Herman, 1978; Budge and Keman, 1990: 44; von Beyme, 1983). Most of these explanations typically have an ad hoc character. Integrating them in theory-building and, perhaps even more so, measurement constitute challenges. Budge and Herman (1978) have undertaken the most systematic early attempt at formulating an 'empirically relevant' theory of coalition formation including such factors. They theorize that a number of hierarchically ordered criteria (threat to system survival, absolute single-party majority, existence of anti-system parties, etc.) can explain government formation. In their empirical application they claim to explain 85 per cent of post-war governments in 12 democracies. Typically, this theory is also very efficient in predicting a single outcome only. This research cumulates in Budge and Keman (1990), a work that aims to also explain portfolio allocation, party policy influence, and the causes for government termination.

Michael Laver (1995) has criticised this 'semi-deductive' approach (Budge and Keman, 1990: 3) by stressing the inherent danger of circular reasoning: On the one hand a threat to democracy and the saliency of socialist–bourgeois differences are theorized to exercise influence on government formation, on the other hand actual government formations are likely to influence whether a threat to democracy is considered real and how salient the socialist–bourgeois differences are. And while Budge and Keman (1990) claim that their theory explains more than 80 per cent of past government formations in 20 democracies, Laver highlights that it clearly failed with regard to three predictions the authors themselves singled out to illustrate the prognostic capacity of their approach. Indeed, Budge and Keman's (1990: 190) predictions that the *pentapartito* in Italy will continue to the end of the 1990s, that the Dutch Christian Democratic Appeal will continue to dictate the composition of government coalitions and that the Irish Fianna Fàil will continue to avoid coalitions have not faired particularly well. Yet, perhaps making these predictions in the first place was overstretching what the approach can deliver. The work of Budge and Keman (1990) of course is no office-seeking approach. Indeed, no one has done more for

providing empirical data for the cross-national measurement of party policy positions than Ian Budge (see Budge et al., 2001; Budge et al., 1987; Klingemann et al., 2006). And it is this version of coalition theory to which we turn next.

Policy-seeking and associated problems

Coalition theories based on policy-seeking political parties constitute the main alternative to the office-seeking assumption of early coalition theories. While some early theories included policy motivations as an add-on to the parties' office-seeking motivation (Axelrod, 1970; Leiserson, 1966), it was Abram de Swaan (1973) who formulated the first pure *policy-seeking* coalition theory (Laver and Schofield, 1990: 97–103). In his words: 'Coalitions emerge from the interaction among actors, each of which strives to bring about and join a coalition that he expects to adopt a policy which is as close as possible to his own most preferred policy' (de Swaan, 1973: 82).

Departing from exclusively office-seeking parties means taking issue with the constant-sum assumption in early coalition theory. This assumption makes the formation of a government akin to a bank robbery. In this business the individual shares are handed out once the money is counted. What the partners in this wealth-creating operation do thereafter, does not affect the individual payoffs of the others (unless delivering them to the police). Although some taxpayers will be at ease with this analogy, it is not exactly what is at the heart of many government formations. Rather, to a large extent the rewards from government office still need to be *produced*. In this perspective government policy is the driving force behind government formation. And once the focus shifts to government outputs, the coalition's ability to agree on policies becomes central. Such agreement requires that the government parties share policy preferences, or, at least, have policy preferences that are compatible (i.e., do not conflict). Government formation hence is a positive-sum game and the gains from government participation increase the more the government parties agree on the policies they want to pursue. The analogy to government formation hence is not a bank robbery but the founding of a business firm, with the payoffs resulting from conducting regular business over some time.

Why, then, are political parties considered policy-seekers? Real-world politicians with serious chances for public office are typically recruited from party activists. Party activists, in turn, are those who are primarily motivated by ideological incentives and typically hold more extreme policy positions than party voters (save activists in pure patronage parties). This relationship is covered in May's law (see May, 1973) and in economic theories of party organization. Although politicians may become less radical and trustful in ideologically derived quick-fix solutions on their way up the career ladder due to contacts with other elites and experience, some of their initial motivation is likely to remain. Moreover, typically career politicians need the approval of their rank-and-file for renomination as candidates for public office and hence need to please them (Luebbert, 1986). At the same time, politicians know that voters normally do not care about them having well-paid and otherwise attractive jobs but about the policy outputs of government. As Laver (1997) argues, 'even politicians who personally have no interest whatsoever in the policy packages they promote for purely entrepreneurial reasons do have some incentive to honour such promises when they have the opportunity to do so' (p. 136). And politicians have an incentive to implement these packages, 'almost as if they really do care about them, when they become incumbents' (Laver, 1997: 136). The emerging consensus in coalition studies thus is that policy is indeed important, either because politicians genuinely care or because they are aware that the voters will sanction them if they do not live up to their promises.

Another body of literature assumes *complex motivations*, that is, the co-existence of different goals such as policy and office (Budge and Laver, 1986; Laver and Schofield, 1990), or a combination of either or both of these goals with the parties' electoral concerns (Lupia and Strøm, 1995; Müller and Strøm, 1999; Schofield, 1993, 1995; Schofield and Sened, 2006; Sened, 1996; Strøm, 1990a, 1990b). Under favourable circumstances politicians may be able to achieve their multiple goals simultaneously. Under less favourable circumstances, they may have to abandon one or more goals to achieve another. In most situations, however, politicians will aim for some mix of political 'rewards'. Rather than prioritizing one goal over all others (i.e., displaying lexicographic preferences) they will make decisions about what a gain in office positions is worth in terms of policy concessions, and vice versa. Policy and office are party goals that are typically at stake in government formation situations. Yet, such negotiations also occur in the shadow of future elections, and past elections provide cues as to how the voters will react to party moves. Hence, party leaders try to anticipate whether their actions will be rewarded or punished by the voters. The empirical record suggests that most parties are punished for being in government (Narud and Valen, 2008). Thus, leaders taking their party to government are either ready to suffer some electoral losses as a price for government office, or they are overly optimistic that their skills will help them avoid this fate. Indeed, some parties maintain or even increase their electoral base while in government. Of course, electoral results are also influenced by other factors that can neither be anticipated nor influenced by serving in government. Knowing that the future is uncertain, party leaders may go for immediate rewards (Lupia and Strøm, 2008).

While the introduction of policy as a driving force of coalition formation has made the basic assumptions of coalition theory more realistic, it also has added considerable theoretical and empirical challenges. If we were able to locate each party's policy preferences precisely on some metric, and if we leave aside other party goals, it is only in the one-dimensional policy space that we can predict the outcome of government formation processes precisely. Once we move to two or more relevant policy dimensions, a weighting problem emerges. If, for instance, economic and foreign policy issues divide the parties, how do they weigh in? And, to make things more complicated, the answers may differ from party to party and over time. Assuming that all policy dimensions are equally important to all parties does not really help, as we then face a situation in which coalition formation becomes unpredictable (and coalitions unstable) once a minimum of three dimensions are involved (McKelvey, 1979).

Notwithstanding these difficulties, coalition theorists have formulated a number of specific policy-based theories of government formation. In one dimensional policy space the powerful median voter theorem (Black, 1958) leads us to expect the median party in parliament to play a dominant role (de Swaan, 1973; Laver and Schofield, 1990: 110–3). If political parties were motivated by policy exclusively the median party could form a minority cabinet and still be a 'policy dictator' (Budge and Laver, 1993: 501). A more realistic assumption is that median parties play a crucial role in government formation. This means that they will typically participate in government and do well with regard to portfolio allocation and government policy. The assumption of a special role of the median party is indeed supported by all empirical analyses (see, e.g., Laver and Schofield, 1990; Martin and Stevenson, 2001; Mitchell and Nyblade, 2008; Müller and Strøm, 2000; Warwick, 1996; for a similar concept see van Roozendaal, 1990).

A number of theories are based on the idea that coalition building aims at minimizing the policy distance between the government parties. One prominent case is the 'minimal connected winning' coalition that is composed of adjacent parties that collectively cover the smallest policy range of all potential 'connected winning' coalitions (Axelrod, 1970). In de Swaan's (1973) terms, this is almost identical with the 'closed minimal range' theory. According to de Swaan (1985: 249), who satisfied himself with ordinal policy scales, the 'closed minimal winning' (or 'minimal connected winning') theory is the best one. It did not perform so well, however, in the eight-country study of Laver and Budge (1992).

Most recently, Warwick (2000, 2006) has introduced the idea that political parties work with distinct policy thresholds. They are willing to engage in coalitions only until their 'policy horizon' is reached, that is the point where the policy costs from making concessions to the coalition partners become too large. As Warwick (2006: 175) puts it, the paradox of the policy horizon hypothesis is that it 'is so simple to state and yet so difficult to test'. Indeed, his test using party manifesto data to derive both the party and the government positions seems to involve a good dose of circularity. To be sure, Warwick (2006) also draws on an expert survey and simulations and marshals evidence 'that is consistent with the existence of horizons'. For the time being, however, we are left with a plausible hypothesis and enough supporting evidence that suggests that further investigation may be worth the effort. Yet, even in the best of all worlds, policy horizons will only help us understand which coalitions are unfeasible and not which ones will be formed.

Finally, Laver and Shepsle (1990, 1996) have theorized that institutional constraints force political parties to consider their coalition options as an 'all or nothing' choice of government policy in each policy dimension. This means that cabinet parties will get 100 per cent of their policy preferences in the domain of the government portfolios occupied by their leaders but at the price of conceding the same to their coalition partners with regard to the other domains. This theory will also be discussed below. Here it is sufficient to say that a thorough cross-national test is still beyond the means available to empirical coalition researchers. Although portfolio allocation theory certainly contains a kernel of truth, the overwhelming tenor is that the underlying assumption of 'coalitions that cannot coalesce' (Dunleavy with Bastow, 2001) is too radical and does not meet the experience of coalition governance in Western Europe (see the contributions of country experts in Laver and Shepsle, 1994; Müller and Strøm, 2000).

Notwithstanding the differences between the specific policy-based coalition theories and the precise dependent variable, multivariate tests generally show that policy outperforms office (size) in explaining government formation (Franklin and Mackie, 1984; Martin and Stevenson, 2001).

Finally, unlike size-based theories, the testing of coalition theories based on policy preferences involves considerable measurement problems. In recent years the comparative literature has employed party documents, in particular electoral manifestos (Laver and Budge, 1992), and expert surveys (Benoit and Laver, 2006; Laver and Hunt, 1992; Warwick, 2006). Both methods are certainly better than the party family and literature extraction approaches that were characteristic of early attempts to place political parties on policy scales. Yet, both have their own pitfalls. On the practical side, the identification, location, and coding of relevant party documents requires country knowledge and language skills. In practice, the most similar documents, the parties' electoral manifestos, vary considerable in comprehensiveness. Much of the party placements depends on the coding scheme and the actual coding, and concerns have been raised over both issues (Laver, 2001; Benoit and Laver, 2007). Expert surveys delegate the 'coding decisions' to the experts who fill in the questionnaires and thus replace the explicit and traceable choices that characterize content analysis by undocumented processes in the brains of the respondents. While sufficient numbers of respondents allow the calculation of statistical error terms, the fact remains that in the context of

coalition research expert surveys involve the danger of circular reasoning: when actual coalition behaviour influences the perception of party distances then these results cannot be used for predicting coalition behaviour (Budge, 2000). These are just a few of the problems associated with the two most important methods employed in the generation of party positions (see Laver, 2001 and Marks, 2007 for a fuller discussion). Of course, the solution is not to abandon these methods, but to improve on their practice, combine them, and check their results with other evidence where it is available (e.g., political elites surveys). And while we have better data now than the pioneers of policy-based coalition theory, we should be aware that our measures of party policy positions are approximations only, and at times very rough ones.

Non-cooperative game theory and institutions

Coalition theory started out as a branch of cooperative game theory. In a cooperative game the inherent logic is to create the coalition that provides the biggest reward for its members *collectively*. For that purpose they communicate and can make agreements that are binding and enforceable (i.e., a non-specified third power is assumed to enforce the deal on its partners). Most important coalition studies discussed above employ cooperative game theory. Yet, cooperative game theory has largely given way to non-cooperative game theory. Rather than assuming that actors cooperate in the production of the maximum total payoff, non-cooperative game theory focuses on the strategies of *individual* actors and the payoffs they receive. A coalition thus forms when it provides the best outcome each of its partners can achieve individually, acting unilaterally. Agreements between the players are not considered enforceable a priori. Rather the enforcement mechanism itself is part of the game (Morrow, 1994: 75–6; Ritzberger, 2002: 7–8). What is enforceable in coalition formations strongly depends on the institutions regulating the government taking office. Consequently, analyses employing non-cooperative game theory explicitly model the impact of institutions. Coalition formation studies in this tradition are explicit about the consequences of, for instance, recognition rules (the choice of formateur), the sequence in which parties assume this role, the existence of investiture votes, and government accountability to second chambers (Austen-Smith and Banks, 1988; Baron, 1991, 1993; Diermeier et al., 2003; 2006). Actors base their strategies on the calculation of the reversion outcome (i.e., what will happen if a bargain fails). In the words of Baron (1991), 'whether a bargain will be struck depends on the expectations that all parties have about what will happen if they fail to reach an agreement on the present attempt' (p. 139). Several of the studies cited here do not just focus on the legislative game at government formation stage but also integrate electoral politics, while Baron (1998) extends his analysis to the life-time of coalitions in an infinitely repeated game.

While the bulk of the formal coalition literature considers coalition formation as a legislative bargaining game, Laver and Shepsle (1990; 1996) build their approach on the insight that government coalitions are very distinct from legislative voting alliances.[4] They assume that cabinet ministers have monopolistic control over their portfolios. Hence, as noted above, the policy in each policy domain will fully represent the ideal policy of the minister's party. While in legislative bargaining there is an infinite number of policy points, in the portfolio allocation approach of Laver and Shepsle the number of possible policy points is reduced to those represented by the parties in the game. And rational parties, of course, chose the government that allows them to maximize their gains.

Coalition theories based on non-cooperative game theory have the virtue that the theory is very precisely formulated. This precision is not free of costs, however. First, such theories tend to be 'very complicated', to quote one of the foremost formal theorists in political science, Norman Schofield (1993: 13). One of the consequences of great modelling complexity is that thus far only games in systems with three parties have been modelled which often do not constitute the most thrilling environment for coalition theory. Second, 'predictions from such institutionally rich models tend to be highly sensitive to the institutional detail' (Austen-Smith, 1996: 235). This has two consequences: (a) small changes in the model often have large consequences for predictions; and (b) small deviations of real institutions from those assumed in the model often render the model irrelevant for the empirical case. For these reasons it is problematic to generalize the results derived from such models beyond their precise specification. Third, some of the common assumptions in these theories are at odds with the reality of coalition politics, for instance that the players in this game have full and perfect information (e.g., Austen-Smith and Banks, 1988; Baron, 1991, 1993; Baron and Diermeier, 2001). Fourth, progress in game-theoretic modelling has remained relatively divorced from empirical research. This is partly due to the fact that many game-theoretic models require empirical data that is hard (if not impossible) to provide. Moreover, many game theorists fail to confront their models with empirical data. The work of Daniel Diermeier and colleagues is a notable exception to this rule (see Diermeier and Merlo, 2004; Diermeier et al., 2003; 2006).

All this is not to say that formal modelling of government formation should be abandoned. On the contrary, this approach has great potential and it would be wrong to overlook the impressive progress coalition theories based on non-cooperative game theory have made in the few years since this tradition was established. Yet, because of the limitations of even the most sophisticated non-cooperative game theoretic models our understanding of coalition formation has greatly benefited from empirical studies of institutional factors in government formation without explicit game-theoretic foundations.

Examples constitute the work of Torbjörn Bergman (1993) on cabinet formation rules and 'negative' versus 'positive' parliamentarism, and Strøm, Budge, and Laver's (1994) seminal article on (mostly institutional) constraints on government formation. More recently, the impact of second chambers on government formation has been empirically scrutinized (Druckman et al., 2005; Druckman and Thies, 2002). The most comprehensive survey of the relevance of institutional factors in coalition politics can be found in Strøm et al. (2003, 2008).

EMPIRICAL RESEARCH ON COALITION FORMATION

Quantitative comparative studies

The dominant line in empirical coalition studies assembles cross-national datasets and employs increasingly sophisticated inference statistics. All specific empirical results that were referred to in the preceding section emerged from this research tradition. The relevant studies differ in their relative emphasis on testing coalition theory and explaining the outcome of government formations. Typically, authors who conduct empirical analysis to test their own theory put a premium on the former.

Quantitative studies aim at maximizing the number of roughly comparable observations in order to control for as many factors as possible. The number of stable parliamentary democracies and years of observation were relatively small when the first studies were conducted in the 1970s. Browne (1970) had to satisfy himself with 125 coalitions in 13 countries while Taylor and Laver (1973) were confined to data from 132 coalitions in 12 countries. More recent researchers have benefited from the ceaseless march of time that has multiplied the number of formation situations. Thus, Martin and Stevenson (2001: 34) could base their study on 220 coalition bargaining situations in 14 post-war democracies

(including Israel). Warwick (1996: 478) drew on 310 cabinets in 16 post-war West European democracies and Mitchell and Nyblade (2008) worked with data from 424 cabinets in 17 post-war West European democracies (including systems that have no experience with coalition government). Volden and Carrubba (2004) used annual data to increase the number of cases. The breakdown of Communism in Eastern Europe has greatly increased the number of stable parliamentary democracies and hence the number of cases relevant to coalition formation studies. As yet, this potential has hardly been used.

Studying government formation, however, is no straightforward task as several dependent variables can be at the centre stage. *Government type* is the most basic choice. We can distinguish cabinets based on political parties and non-partisan ones, majority and minority cabinets, single-party governments and coalitions, and various types of coalitions (minimal winning and surplus, etc.) (Mitchell and Nyblade, 2008). *Cabinet composition* in many cases is a more demanding dependent variable, as it requires predicting the precise party composition of government (Martin and Stevenson, 2001). Finally, the analysis can settle with predicting the *cabinet membership of individual parties*. Warwick (1996) aims at identifying both successful formateur parties and mere cabinet membership. Another line of research focuses on the formation process, in particular its duration and the number of formation attempts (De Winter and Dumont, 2008; Diermeier and van Roozendaal, 1998; Golder, 2006; Martin and Vanberg, 2003).

Without doubt the quantitative cross-national study of coalition formation displays virtues any academic discipline is searching for: steady progress and cumulation, thus each generation could build on the achievements of the previous ones rather than starting anew. At the same time it is clear that a considerable agenda still lies ahead. And, indeed, impatient observers see 'major shortcomings' (De Winter and Dumont, 2006: 180). As De Winter and Dumont (2006) put it, 'existing theories do not predict and therefore suffi-ciently explain a significant proportion of cabinet compositions formed in the real world' (p. 180). These authors are not at ease with the best result – Martin and Stevenson (2001) predicting close to half of the real-world coalitions correctly – because 'this is done by lumping together two dozen variables drawn from three main schools', with the consequence of lacking 'parsimony and inter-nal consistency'. While this judgement may be too harsh, it makes clear that quantitative comparative studies have their limits and should be supplemented with studies from other traditions.

Single country studies

Single country studies constitute the second major genre of the coalition literature.[5] In the first comprehensive attempt at country-specific analysis of coalition politics – coalition forma-tions, the distribution of portfolios, and the end of coalition cabinets – Browne and Dreijmanis (1982) explain that it was motivated by the gap between game theoretical and cross-national empirical studies of coalitions, with the 'repeated failure' of the latter 'to provide con-vincing support for the derived implications of formal coalition theories' (p. 356). In providing single-country studies they aimed at adding 'a 'flesh and blood' dimension to coalition stud-ies' (p. 1). In the Conclusion, Browne (1982) claims 'what is needed is to orient theoretical work more directly towards the contexts in which they are applied' (p. 356). This tradition of research thus aims at a configurative under-standing of coalition politics. The underlying assumption is that history, the specific configu-ration of political institutions (rather than indi-vidual institutional features), and perhaps the personalities of key actors are crucial for a full explanation of coalition politics. While many of these factors can be coded and quantified, little but important differences (e.g., in institu-tional rules) and their great number makes the translation of 'country' into analytical categories a hopeless task. A configurative

explanation thus requires country-knowledge and in-depth studies. The more peculiar an outcome is, the greater the advantage of such studies (Gerring, 2006).

Quantitative coalition studies, regardless of their independent variable, indeed have regu-larly identified substantial country effects. According to Franklin and Mackie (1984), size and ideology perform very differently across countries in predicting coalition formation. Estimating their regressions separately for each of three groups of countries, these authors almost doubled the explained variance. Similarly, Grofman (1989) concluded that some of the best-supported results in coalition research do not apply *within* most countries, but stem from the composition of the cross-national samples (with countries being repre-sented by substantially different numbers of cabinets). Proper explanations should work both between and within countries. From the high country-sensitivity of such results Michael Laver, writing in the mid-1980s, arrived at a radical conclusion: 'at this stage in our under-standing of the coalitional process, to conduct anything other than a country-specific analysis of the phenomena involved is to do great vio-lence to reality' (Laver, 1986: 33).

For all these reasons single-country stud-ies have remained important in coalition research. They make at least four important contributions to the development of coalition research. First, country studies with a uni-form format are an important means for generating data that can also be employed in comparative analyses. For one thing there are practical reasons that suggest such a strategy, as no single researcher can ever hope to master the complexities of coming to grips with national sources as a team of country specialists (see Strøm et al., 2008).

Data rarely speaks for itself. Therefore, it is often equally important that country specialists interpret the data and employ it in configurative analysis, drawing on all kinds of other informa-tion (that may exist for no other country). Such country-specific analysis has proved useful even in the case of a very standardized overall research design, such as the Comparative

Manifesto Project's inquiry into the world of coalition politics (Laver and Budge, 1992). While it is not possible to translate all the insights from in-depth country analysis into variables employed in comparative quantitative studies, the country studies remain a treasure trove for understanding 'anomalies' and outliers in cross-national analysis. This is the second contribution of country studies towards the development of the coalition studies field.

Third, identifying outliers and forces that are behind such placement in a comparative mapping can serve the refinement of the initial theoretical argument. Interesting cases are countries that routinely appoint non-minimal and non-minimum cabinets – such as Austria and Italy (Mershon, 2002; Müller, 2000; Pridham, 1988) – and countries that tend to have minority cabinets – such as the Scandinavian countries (Strøm, 1986). Another way country studies can contribute to the refinement of theory is checking their underlying assumptions. Laver and Shepsle's portfolio allocation theory, for instance, was first presented in a radical version (1990). These authors then assembled a group of country specialists who discussed the plausibility of their major assumption – that of ministers as policy dictators within their portfolio – on the basis of all evidence available for the respective country (see the country chapters in Laver and Shepsle, 1994). While Laver and Shepsle (1996) in their final version of the portfolio allocation theory tended to give more weight to the country evidence that supported their theorizing, they made good use of the country experts' input in somewhat deradicalizing their claim. For instance, the minister as 'policy dictator' (1990: 888) has given way to a more nuanced treatment (1996: 30–33).

The fourth vital contribution of country studies lies in their role in pushing forward the research agenda. Often novel ideas emerge from the close scrutiny of individual cases. The relevance of the institutional rules of government formation, for instance, emerged from the study of the Swedish case (Bergman, 1993, 1995). And the full menu of coalition governance mechanisms that is detailed in Müller and Strøm (2000) and used in comparative analysis in Strøm, et al. (2008) represents the collective experience of country specialists who spent some time on identifying and defining the relevant mechanisms.

Case studies

Case studies of specific government formations push the idea of an intensive research design one step further. Episodes of government formation are often crucial pathways in the life of a nation and for that reason merit close study. Yet, to be useful for coalition theory, such studies need to be theoretically informed and they should be explicit about their contribution towards evaluating and, perhaps, refining, theoretical claims. A case study, of course, is confined to what typically is just one data point (observation) in quantitative coalition studies. The genuine contribution it can make is providing a mechanism-based explanation of the case. Quantitative studies typically are 'black-box explanations' in the sense that the link between *explanans* and *explanandum* is theoretically stated and proven by (statistically controlled) co-variation (Hedström and Swedberg, 1998). Good case studies can show whether the theorized mechanism indeed works. In other words, it can check whether the theorized 'intermediary process' by which a causal relationship links inputs and outputs indeed takes place and, if not, what an alternative mechanism may be (cf. Gerring, 2005, 2007). To achieve that case studies must typically draw on primary data such as interviews with key actors, position papers, letters exchanged in negotiations, and perhaps minutes of inter- or intra-party meetings. Such sources do not always exist, if they exist it requires skill to locate them, and even then access often is hard to achieve. To be sure, even the best qualitative research may never be able to identify the most inner motivations of individuals. Yet, resource-rich and well-executed case studies can move us sufficiently close to understanding the true causal mechanisms at work in government formation situations.

Such accounts can also take the form of analytical narratives, which by employing game-theoretic models marry the narrative account with 'parsimony, refinement, and (in the sense used by mathematicians) elegance' (Bates et al., 1998: 11). As Bates (2007) argues, game-theoretic modelling itself 'should be shaped by the understandings achieved through fieldwork and by the materials mobilized in thick descriptions' (p. 175). Thus, on the one hand game-theoretic modelling can only benefit from 'intimate knowledge of the key players and the strategic environment that they inhabit' (p. 175). In the terms of Bates (2007) such knowledge provides a 'bullshit meter', that allows the analyst to distinguish arguments 'that offer traction from those that are merely clever' (p. 174). On the other hand, carefully executed case studies can serve as tests of game-theoretic models by exposing the mechanisms at work in decision-making processes. Case studies are an excellent tool to check arguments about the sequence of moves (Büthe, 2002), signalling, and the relevance of nested games (Tsebelis, 1990).

The rich potential of case study research has not yet been fully used in coalition studies. Hardly anything has been published in international journals and only two efforts have been made to assemble relevant case studies for some analytic purpose. The studies in Müller and Strøm (1999) focus on cases involving trade-offs of party goals and hence force political parties to chose. While the relevant cases here are overwhelmingly, but not exclusively, government formations, the case studies assembled by Andeweg et al. (2009) focus on complex government formation processes, that is processes that are characterized by long duration and/or failed attempts. Interesting as these studies are, they represent no more than a beginning. There are plausible reasons for this underdevelopment of a potentially very fruitful angle of coalition research. One is that those scholars who are most familiar with the relevant primary sources are often not interested in and knowledgeable of general theories, and vice versa. Another reason is that the incentives in the publication and citation business are at odds with the production of case studies. Yet, all those capable of producing such studies should remind themselves that even a study of what might be considered a 'non-event' – a failed attempt to unseat a government in a small country – can be published in the discipline's most prestigious journal when it is masterly done (Strøm, 1994).

While case studies can fulfil these tasks standing alone, it is perhaps most rewarding to include them in a 'nested' research design (Lieberman, 2005), meaning that the analysis moves back and forth between quantitative and case analysis. Bäck and Dumont (2007) have produced the first such analysis in coalition research.

CONCLUSION

This chapter has reviewed the literature of government formation in systems that are parliamentary and multi-party. In such systems elections typically result in minority situations. Then inter-party bargaining decides on government formation and often, though not invariably, the outcome is coalition government. Among social science research fields, the study of government coalition is certainly a showpiece. Since the beginning of political science research into that subject in the early 1960s important and steady progress has been made. This chapter has also shown that this progress results from the interplay of game-theoretic work, quantitative comparative analyses, and single-country studies. Yet, the review has demonstrated that we still have to travel quite a distance to make the state of the art truly satisfying. In the remainder of this chapter, I will suggest a few avenues that seem particularly promising for a better understanding of government formation. These relate to extensions of the scope of analyses, improvements of research methods, and innovations in terms of new or refined research questions.

As noted above, coalition research has been constrained by the fact that government formations are not that numerous. While the situation has improved though the ceaseless march of time, the third wave of democratization has provided a huge and as yet hardly used range of new democracies to which coalition research should be extended. These systems would not only increase the N of coalition studies but also add historical, institutional, and behavioural variance that can be fruitfully exploited in statistical analysis. Bringing in new cases, of course, also raises the demand for country studies for all the reasons given above.

Throughout its history coalition research was good at adopting and at times encouraging improvements in methods and data. As noted above, coalition studies – as all other research fields working with party positions data – must rely on data that is less precise than we ideally would want to. While the method that would merit redoing the huge amount of work that has gone into the CMP data is yet to emerge, attempts at developing such measures and first applying them to small samples clearly should be encouraged. Government formation constitutes a natural testing ground for alternative preference measures. Another issue is the choice of research strategy. As noted above, the potential of case study research currently is underused in the discipline's attempts at understanding government formation. Yet, the passing of time since the inception of coalition studies not only provides new cases but also opens the gates of archives. We can expose those government formations to close scrutiny based on primary sources that perhaps have influenced the reasoning of early coalition theorists and that have figured in quantitative analysis since ever. It would be a pity, if political science would leave this opportunity to professional historians, who are unlikely to ask the questions relevant to coalition theory.

Finally, what novel perspectives should be taken up in research on government formation? It is the very nature of true innovation that it is more difficult to foreshadow than it is to make extensions and improvements. Yet, there are two analytical perspectives that have been around as ideas and desiderata for a long time but which may now be attracting serious efforts to translate them into rigorous theorizing and empirical research. One is the insight that coalition formation ought to be understood dynamically (Laver, 1974, 1986). Rather than treating each government formation as an isolated event, it should be viewed as part of two cycles. One is the 'big' cycle that connects one government with its predecessor and successor (cf. Franklin and Mackie, 1983). The other one is the 'smaller' cycle that connects the various stages coalitions go through – formation, governance, and termination. These phenomena are typically researched in mutual isolation rather than understood in their mutual causality. This is the perspective advanced in Strøm et al. (2008), but much remains to be done.

Another long-term critique of coalition research is its exclusive focus on *inter*-party relations. While this choice can be defended (see Laver and Schofield, 1990, Chapter 2), it does considerable violence to reality (see Luebbert, 1986; Müller and Strøm, 1999). Renewed interest in the role of *intra*-party politics in coalitions (Giannetti and Benoit, 2008) may indicate that what is ahead of us is the nested analysis of intra- and inter-party politics in government formation (and probably even more so at other stages of the coalition life cycle).

NOTES

1. The initial endowment normally is equated with the 'mechanical' bargaining power of parties – as measured by voting power indices. Alternatively, we could think about 'directional' bargaining power of parties, resulting from their belonging to the winners or losers of the elections (see Mattila and Raunio, 2004).

2. Other surveys of coalition studies, not always confined to government formation, include Bandyopadhyay and Chatterjee (2006), De Winter and Dumont (2006), Diermeier (2006), Laver (1998), Laver and Schofield (1990), Strøm et al. (2008), Strøm and Nyblade (2007).

3. Volden and Carrubba (2004: 521) interpret Riker's 'minimum winning' criterion as meaning the minimum number of parties. To the best of my knowledge this is the only interpretation of Riker's size principle; 'coalitions just as large as they [the participants] believe will ensure winning and no larger' (Riker, 1962: 47) as referring to parties rather than parliamentary seats. After all, parliamentary seats are the decisive resource for winning in government formation games. Nevertheless, the number of parties in a coalition is a powerful predictor that was introduced by Leiserson (1966: 313; 1968: 775).

4. Austen-Smith and Banks (1990) have developed a model that builds on essentially the same basic idea.

5. The volumes of Bogdanor (1983), Browne and Dreijmanis (1982), Groennings et al. (1970), Laver and Budge (1992), Laver and Shepsle (1994), Müller and Strøm (2000) and Pridham (1986), contain more or less standardized country studies.

REFERENCES

Adrian, C.R. and Press, C. (1968) 'Decision costs in coalition formation', *American Political Science Review*, 62 (2): 556–63.

Amorim Neto, O. (2006) 'The presidential calculus: Executive policy making and cabinet formation in the Americas', *Comparative Political Studies*, 39 (4): 415–40.

Andeweg, R.B., De Winter, L., and Dumont, P. (eds) (2009) *Puzzles of government formation*. London: Routledge.

Austen-Smith, D. (1996) 'Refinements of the heart', in N. Schofield (ed.), *Collective decision-making: Social choice and political economy*. Boston, MA: Kluwer, pp. 221–36.

Austen-Smith, D. and Banks, J. (1988) 'Elections, coalitions and legislative outcomes', *American Political Science Review*, 82 (2): 405–22.

Austen-Smith, D. and Banks, J. (1990) 'Stable governments and the allocation of policy portfolios', *American Political Science Review*, 84 (3): 891–906.

Axelrod, R. (1970) *Conflict of interest*. Chicago: Markham.

Bäck, H. and Dumont, P. (2007) 'Combining large-n and small-n strategies: The way forward in coalition research', *West European Politics*, 30 (3): 467–501.

Bandyopadhyay, S. and Chatterjee, K. (2006) 'Coalition theory and its applications: A survey', *Economic Journal*, 116 (509): F136–F155.

Baron, D.P. (1991) 'A spatial bargaining theory of government formation in a parliamentary system', *American Political Science Review*, 85 (1): 137–64.

Baron, D.P. (1993) 'Government formation and endogenous parties', *American Political Science Review*, 87 (1): 33–47.

Baron, D.P. (1998) 'Comparative dynamics of parliamentary governments', *American Political Science Review*, 92 (3): 593–609.

Baron, D.P. and Diermeier, D. (2001) 'Elections, governments, and parliaments in proportional representation systems', *Quarterly Journal of Economics*, 116 (3): 933–67.

Bates, R.H. (2007) 'From case studies to social science: A strategy for political research', in C. Boix and S. C. Stokes (eds), *The Oxford handbook of comparative politics*. Oxford: Oxford University Press, pp. 172–85.

Bates, R.H., Greif, A., Levi, M., Rosenthal, J.-L., and Weingast, B.R. (1998) *Analytical narratives*. Princeton, NJ: Princeton University Press.

Benoit, K. and Laver, M. (2006) *Party policy in modern democracies*. London: Routlege.

Benoit, K. and Laver, M. (2007) 'Estimating party policy positions: Comparing expert surveys and hand-coded content analysis', *Electoral Studies*, 26 (1): 90–107.

Bergman, T. (1993) 'Formation rules and minority governments', *European Journal of Political Research*, 23 (1): 55–66.

Bergman, T. (1995) *Constitutional rules and party goals in coalition formation*. Umeå: Umeå University.

Black, D. (1958) *The theory of committees and elections*. Cambridge: Cambridge University Press.

Bogdanor, V. (ed.) (1983) *Coalition government in Western Europe*. London: Heineman.

Browne, E.C. (1970) *Coalition theories: A logical and empirical critique*. Beverly Hills: Sage.

Browne, E.C. (1982) 'Conclusion: considerations on the construction of a theory of cabinet coalition behavior', in Browne, E.C. Browne, and J. Dreijmanis, (eds) *Government coalitions in Western democracies*. New York: Longman, pp. 335–57.

Browne, E.C. and Dreijmanis, J. (eds) (1982) *Government coalitions in Western democracies*. New York: Longman.

Budge, I. (2000) 'Expert judgements of party policy positions: Uses and limitations in political research', *European Journal of Political Research*, 37 (1): 103–13.

Budge, I. and Herman, V. (1978) 'Coalitions and government formation: An empirically relevant theory', *British Journal of Political Science*, 8 (4): 459–77.

Budge, I. and Keman, H. (1990) *Parties and democracy: Coalition formation and government functioning in twenty states*. Oxford: Oxford University Press.

Budge, I., Klingemann, H.-D., Volkens, A., Bara, J., and Tannenbaum, E. (2001) *Mapping policy preferences. Estimates for parties, electors, and governments 1945–1998*. Oxford: Oxford University Press.

Budge, I. and Laver, M. (1986) 'Office seeking and policy pursuit in coalition theory', *Legislative Studies Quarterly*, 11 (4): 485–506.

Budge, I. and Laver, M. (1993) 'The policy basis of government coalitions: A comparative investigation', *British Journal of Political Science*, 23 (4): 499–519.

Budge, I., Robertson, D., and Hearl, D. (1987) *Ideology, strategy, and party change: Spatial analyses of post-war election programmes in 19 democracies*. Cambridge: Cambridge University Press.

Büthe, T. (2002) 'Taking temporality serious: Modeling history and the use of narratives as evidence', *American Political Science Review*, 96 (3): 481–93.

Cheibub, J.A., Przeworski, A., and Saiegh, S. (2004) 'Government coalitions under parliamentarism and presidentialism', *British Journal of Political Science*, 34: 565–87.

Cox, G.W. and Morgensten, C. (2002) 'Epilogue: Latin America's reactive assemblies and proactive presidents', in C. Morgenstern, and N. Benito, (eds) *Legislative politics in Latin America*. Cambridge: Cambridge University Press, pp. 446–68.

de Swaan, A. (1973) *Coalition theories and cabinet formations*. Amsterdam: Elsevier.

de Swaan, A. (1985) 'Coalition theory and multi-party systems', in H.A.M. Wilke (ed.), *Coalition formation*. Amsterdam: North-Holland, 229–60.

De Winter, L. and Dumont, P. (2006) 'Parties into government: Still many puzzler', in R.S. Katz and W. Crotty (eds), *Handbook of party politics*. London: Sage, pp. 175–88.

De Winter, L. and Dumont, P. (2008) 'Uncertainty and complexity in cabinet formation', in K. Strøm, W.C. Müller, and T. Bergman (eds), *Cabinets and coalition bargaining: The democratic life cycle in Western Europe*. Oxford: Oxford University Press, pp. 123–57.

Diermeier, D. (2006) 'Coalition government', in B.R. Weingast and D.A. Wittman (eds), *The Oxford handbook of political economy*. Oxford: Oxford University Press, pp. 162–79.

Diermeier, D. and Merlo, A. (2004) 'An empirical investigation of coalition bargaining procedures', *Journal of Public Economics*, 88 (4–5): 783–97.

Diermeier, D., Merlo, A., and Eraslan, H. (2002) 'Coalition government and comparative constitutional design', *European Economic Review*, 46 (4–5): 893–907.

Diermeier, D., Merlo, A., and Eraslan, H. (2003) 'A structural model of government formation', *Econometrica*, 71 (1): 27–70.

Diermeier, D., Merlo, A., and Eraslan, H. (2006) 'The effects of constitutions on coalition governments in parliamentary democracies', in R.C. Congleton and B. Swedenborg (eds), *Democratic constitutional design and public policy*. Cambridge, MA: MIT Press, pp.133–61.

Diermeier, D. and van Roozendaal, P. (1998) 'The duration of cabinet formation processes in Western multi-party democracies', *British Journal of Political Science*, 28 (4): 609–26.

Dodd, L.C. (1976) *Coalitions in parliamentary government*. Princeton, NJ: Princeton University Press.

Druckman, J.N., Martin, L., and Thies, M. (2005) 'Influence without confidence: upper chambers and government formation', *Legislative Studies Quarterly*, 30 (4): 529–48.

Druckman, J.N. and Thies, M.F. (2002) 'The importance of concurrence: The impact of bicameralism on government formation and duration', *American Journal of Political Science*, 46 (4): 760–71.

Dunleavy, P. with Bastow, S. (2001) 'Modelling coalitions that cannot coalesce: A critique of the Laver-Shepsle approach', *West European Politics*, 24 (1): 1–26.

Franklin, M.N. and Mackie, T.T. (1983) 'Familiarity and inertia in the formation of governing coalitions in parliamentary democracies', *British Journal of Political Science*, 13 (3): 275–98.

Franklin, M.N. and Mackie, T.T. (1984) 'Reassessing the importance of size and ideology for the formation of government coalitions in parliamentary democracies', *American Journal of Political Science*, 28 (4): 671–92.

Gamson, W.A. (1961) 'A theory of coalition formation', *American Sociological Review*, 26: 373–82.

Gerring, J. (2005) 'Causation: A unified framework for the social sciences', *Journal of Theoretical Politics*, 17 (2): 163–98.

Gerring, J. (2006) 'Single-outcome studies', *International Sociology*, 21 (5): 707–34.

Gerring, J. (2007) 'The case study: What it is and what it does', in C. Boix and S.C. Stokes (eds), *The Oxford handbook of comparative politics*. Oxford: Oxford University Press, pp. 90–122.

Giannetti, D. and Benoit, K. (eds) (2008) *Intraparty politics and coalition governments in parliamentary democracies*. London: Routledge.

Golder, S.N. (2006) *The logic of pre-electoral coalition formation*. Columbus, OH: Ohio State University Press.

Groennings, S., Kelley, E.W., and Leiserson, M. (Eds.) (1970) *The study of coalition behavior*. New York: Holt, Rinehart and Winston.

Grofman, B. (1982) 'A dynamic model of protocoalition formation in ideological *n*-space', *Behavioral Science*, 27 (1): 77–90.

Grofman, B. (1989) 'The comparative analysis of coalition formation and duration: distinguishing between-country and within-country effects', *British Journal of Political Science*, 19 (2): 291–302.

Hedström, P. and Swedberg, R. (eds) (1998) *Social mechanisms*. Cambridge: Cambridge University Press.

Jungar, A.-C. (2000) *Surplus majority government. A comparative study of Italy and Finland*. Uppsala: Uppsla Universitet.

Klingemann, H.-D., Volkens, A., Bara, J., Budge, I., and McDonald, M.D. (2006) *Mapping policy preferences II*. Oxford: Oxford University Press.

Laver, M. (1974) 'Dynamic factors in government coalition formation', *European Journal of Political Research*, 2 (3): 259–70.

Laver, M. (1986) 'Between theoretical elegance and political reality: Deductive models and cabinet coalitions in Europe', in G. Pridham (ed.), *Coalition behaviour in theory and practice*. Cambridge: Cambridge University Press, pp. 32–44.

Laver, M. (1995) 'Review of Ian Budge and Hans Keman, Parties and democracy: Coalition formation and government functioning in twenty states', *Party Politics*, 1 (2): 290–93.

Laver, M. (1997) *Private desires, political action*. London: Sage.

Laver, M. (1998) 'Models of government formation', *Annual Review of Political Science*, 1: 1–25.

Laver, M. (ed.) (2001) *Estimating the policy positions of political actors*. London: Routledge.

Laver, M. and Budge, I. (eds) (1992) *Party policy and coalition government*. London: Macmillan.

Laver, M. and Hunt, B.W. (1992) *Policy and party competition*. New York, NY: Routledge.

Laver, M. and Schofield, N. (1990) *Multiparty government*. Oxford: Oxford University Press.

Laver, M. and Shepsle, K.A. (1990) 'Coalitions and cabinet government', *American Political Science Review*, 84 (3): 873–90.

Laver, M. and Shepsle, K.A. (eds) (1994) *Cabinet ministers and parliamentary government*. Cambridge: Cambridge University Press.

Laver, M. and Shepsle, K.A. (1996) *Making and breaking governments: Cabinets and legislatures in parliamentary democracies*. Cambridge: Cambridge University Press.

Leiserson, M. (1966) *Coalitions in politics: A theoretical and empirical study*. (Ph.D. dissertation, Yale University).

Leiserson, M. (1968) 'Factions and coalitions in one-party Japan: An interpretation based on the theory of games', *American Political Science Review*, 62 (1): 70–87.

Lieberman, E.S. (2005) 'Nested analysis as a mixed-method strategy for comparative research', *American Political Science Review*, 99: 435–52.

Lijphart, A. (1999) *Patterns of democracy*. New Haven, CN: Yale University Press.

Luebbert, G.M. (1986) *Comparative democracy. Policymaking and governing coalitions in Europe and Israel*. New York: Columbia University Press.

Lupia, A. and Strøm, K. (1995) 'Coalition termination and the strategic timing of parlimentary elections', *American Political Science Review*, 89 (3): 648–65.

Lupia, A. and Strøm, K. (2008) 'Bargaining, transaction costs, and coalition governance', in K. Strøm, W. C. Müller and T. Bergman (eds), *Cabinets and coalition bargaining: The democratic life cycle in Western Europe*. Oxford: Oxford University Press, pp. 51–83.

Marks, G. (ed.) (2007) 'Special symposium: Comparing measures of party positioning: Expert, manifesto, and survey data', *Electoral Studies*, 26 (1).

Martin, L.W. and Stevenson, R.T. (2001) 'Government formation in parliamentary democracies', *American Journal of Political Science*, 45 (1): 33–50.

Martin, L.W. and Vanberg, G. (2003) 'Wasting time? The impact of ideology and size on delay in coalition formation', *British Journal of Political Science*, 33 (2): 323–44.

Mattila, M. and Raunio, T. (2004) 'Does winning pay? Electoral success and government formation in 15 west European countries', *European Journal of Political Research*, 43 (2): 263–85.

May, J.D. (1973) 'Opinion structure of political parties: The special law of curvilinear disparity', *Political Studies*, 21 (2): 135–51.

McKelvey, R.D. (1979) 'General conditions for global intransitives in formal voting models', *Econometrica*, 47 (5): 1085–111.

Mershon, C. (2002) *The costs of coalition*. Stanford, CA: Stanford University Press.

Mitchell, P.L. and Nyblade, B. (2008) 'Government formation and cabinet type in parliamentary democracies', in K. Strøm, W. C. Müller, and T. Bergman (eds), *Cabinets and coalition bargaining: The democratic life cycle in Western Europe*. Oxford: Oxford University Press, pp. 782–802.

Morrow, J.D. (1994) *Game theory for political scientists*. Princeton, NJ: Princeton University Press.

Müller, W.C. (2000) 'Austria: Tight coalitions and stable government', lin W.C. Müller and K. Strøm (eds), *Coalition governments in Western Europe*. Oxford: Oxford University Press, pp. 86–125.

Müller, W.C. and Strøm, K. (eds) (1999) *Policy, office, or votes? How political parties in Western Europe make hard decisions*. Cambridge: Cambridge University Press.

Müller, W.C. and Strøm, K. (eds) (2000) *Coalition governments in Western Europe*. Oxford: Oxford University Press.

Narud, H.M. and Valen, H. (2008) 'Coalition membership and electoral performance in Western Europe', in K. Strøm, W.C. Müller and T. Bergmann (eds), *Cabinets and coalition bargaining. The democratic life cycle in Western Europe*. Oxford: Oxford University Press, pp. 369–402.

Poguntke, T. and Webb, P. (eds) (2005) *The presidentialization of politics*. Oxford: Oxford University Press.

Pridham, G. (ed.) (1986) *Coalition behaviour in theory and practice: An inductive model for Western Europe*. Cambridge: Cambridge University Press.

Pridham, G. (1988) *Political parties and coalitional behaviour in Italy*. London: Routledge.

Riker, W.H. (1962) *The theory of political coalitions*. New Haven, CN: Yale University Press.

Riker, W.H. and Ordeshook, P.C. (1973) *An introduction to positive political theory*. Englewood Cliffs, NJ: Prentice-Hall.

Ritzberger, K. (2002) *Foundations of noncooperative game theory*. Oxford: Oxford University Press.

Schofield, N. (1993) 'Political competition in multiparty coalition governments', *European Journal of Political Research*, 23 (1): 1–33.

Schofield, N. (1995) 'Coalition politics: A formal model and empirical analysis', *Journal of Theoretical Politics*, 7 (3): 245–81.

Schofield, N. and Sened, I. (2006) *Multiparty democracy. Elections and legislative politics*. Cambridge: Cambridge University Press.

Schumpeter, J.A. (1942) *Capitalism, socialism and democracy*. New York: Harper & Brothers.

Sened, I. (1996) 'A model of coalition formation: Theory and evidence', *Journal of Politics*, 58 (2): 350–72.

Strøm, K. (1984) 'Minority governments in parliamentary democracies: The rationality of nonwinning cabinet solutions', *Comparative Political Studies*, 17 (2): 199–227.

Strøm, K. (1986) 'Deferred gratification and minority governments in Scandinavia', *Legislative Studies Quarterly*, 11 (4): 583–605.

Strøm, K. (1990a) *Minority government and majority rule*. Cambridge: Cambridge University Press.

Strøm, K (1990b) 'A behavioral theory of competitive political parties', *American Journal of Political Science*, 34 (2): 565–98.

Strøm, K. (1994) 'The Presthus debacle: Intraparty politics and bargaining failure in Norway', *American Political Science Review*, 88 (1): 112–27.

Strøm, K., Budge, I. and Laver, M.J. (1994) 'Constraints on cabinet formation in parliamentary democracies', *American Journal of Political Science*, 38 (2): 303–35.

Strøm, K., Müller, W.C. and Bergman, T. (eds) (2003) *Delegation and accountability in parliamentary democracies*. Oxford: Oxford University Press.

Strøm, K., Müller, W.C. and Bergman, T. (eds) (2008) *Cabinets and coalition bargaining: The democratic life cycle in Western Europe*. Oxford: Oxford University Press, pp. 782–802.

Strøm, K. and Nyblade, B. (2007) 'Coalition theory and government formation', in C. Boix and S.C. Stokes (eds), *The Oxford handbook of comparative politics*. Oxford: Oxford University Press.

Taylor, M. and Laver, M. (1973) 'Government coalitions in Western Europe', *European Journal of Political Research*, 1 (3): 205–48.

Tsebelis, G. (1990) *Nested games: Rational choice in comparative politics*. Berkeley: University of California Press.

van Roozendaal, P. (1990) 'Centre parties and coalition cabinet formation: A game theoretic approach', *European Journal of Political Research*, 18 (3): 324–48.

Verzichelli, L. (2008) 'Portfolio allocation', in K. Strøm, W.C. Müller, and T. Bergman (eds), *Cabinets and coalition bargaining: The democratic life cycle in Western Europe*. Oxford: Oxford University Press, pp. 237–67.

Volden, C. and Carrubba, C.J. (2004) 'The formation of oversized coalitions in parliamentary democracies', *American Journal of Political Science*, 43 (3): 521–37.

von Beyme, K. (1983) 'Governments, parliaments and the structure of power in political parties', in H. Daalder and P. Mair (eds), *Western European party systems*. London: Sage, pp. 341–67.

von Neumann, J. and Morgenstern, O. (1953) *Theory of games and economic behavior*. Princeton, NJ: Princeton University Press.

Warwick, P.V. (1996) 'Coalition government membership in west European parliamentary democracies', *British Journal of Political Science*, 26 (4): 471–99.

Warwick, P.V. (2000) 'Policy horizons in west European parliamentary systems', *European Journal of Political Research*, 38 (1): 37–61.

Warwick, P.V. (2006) *Policy horizons and parliamentary government*. Basingstoke: Palgrave Macmillan.

13

Institutional Design

Josep M. Colomer

INTRODUCTION

Institutional design is the choice of rules for collective decision-making. At the moment of designing institutions, two main questions have to be addressed: who is entitled to participate? and how will decisions be made? The first question points to the design of the community. Collective decisions can be enforceable if people within some boundaries think or accept they share enough with the others to abide by the outcomes, even if they find themselves to be losers or in a minority on some issues, or if the costs of not complying are too high. The Western European model of nation-state building has been too often taken as the only reference and interesting path for building a political community. Political science is still very state-centered. However, recent and current developments, in both Europe and the rest of the world, demand for a more diversified menu, as we will discuss in the following pages. The second question – how decisions are made – implies at least to major issues: what can be decided on each occasion, which refers to how decision powers are divided among different bodies or branches of government, and how people's preferences are transformed into collective outcomes, which

basically involves choices on voting and electoral rules. Many years ago, David Hume advised institutional designers with these words:

> In contriving any system of government, and fixing the several checks and controls of the constitution, every man ought to be supposed a knave, and to have no other end, in all his actions, but private interest. By this interest we must govern him and, by means of it, make him cooperate to public good, notwithstanding his insatiable avarice and ambition. (Hume, 1741 [1994])

In this chapter, we will prove that the assumption that people seek their own interest not only in making private or public policy decisions, but also when choosing the institutional rules for making those decisions, is broadly shared and analytically fruitful. Institutional designers, while tending to deploy their 'ambition', often aim at putting levers of rule at their easy disposal in order to concentrate, rather than check power. However, an efficient institutional design – that is, one making rulers 'cooperate to public good', in Hume's terms – can result from circumstances in which no actor has sufficient influence to impose its own project and diverse ambitions counterweight each other. Not surprisingly, this is a relatively frequent situation in a complex world, which may explain why major institutional choices are increasingly made in favour of formulas able to produce power-sharing and to satisfy broad groups of people, which is just another way to refer to 'public good'.

The following review shows that, in the current world, the number of small, sufficiently homogeneous communities to make consensual and enforceable collective decisions is increasing; the number of democracies is also increasing; institutional choices tend to favour division of powers rather than concentration in a single body or party; and electoral rules are increasingly chosen to permit multiple parties to participate and share government. As actors' self-interested behavior leads to broadly efficient and satisfactory institutional choices, it seems that a kind of 'invisible hand' in the field can be identified – actually in a not very dissimilar way as a pattern of unintended consequences for private decisions was also identified by Adam Smith, in truth David Hume's favourite disciple.

The chapter is divided in two parts. In the first, the problems of building a community are addressed with the help of the categories of 'state', 'nation' and 'empire'. In the second part, we review the state of the art regarding the choice of institutional rules for division of powers and elections. A few remarks conclude.

COMMUNITY-BUILDING

The design of institutions may involve the building of a large nation-state under the modern West European model. But it may entail the building of other types of community, such as 'empires' or 'cities', as very large and small communities, respectively, were called in classical studies in the field. After having lost the 'state' and brought it back in, a more diversified categorization of polities or structures of governments is opening its way in recent political studies.

Decline and failure of the sovereign state

About a generation ago, a claim was made to 'bring the state back in' the social sciences, as in Peter Evans, Dietrich Rueschmeyer and Theda Skocpol (1985) and, especially, Skocpol (1985). This claim was initially addressed to correct 'too society-centered' ways of explaining politics and governmental processes that had prevailed during a previous period starting in the 1950s and 1960s. Bringing the 'state' back in brought about much more attention to formal rules and institutions, governmental activities, and the impact of authorities on societal processes, including economic interests and social movements. New knowledge and science have indeed developed from that impulse and the subsequent turn in methodological approaches.

However, in a number of further scholarly studies, the 'state' was conceived not only as an institutional and organizational structure for different actor's strategies and decisions, but as a unitary actor, especially in the field of international or transnational relations. The 'explanatory centrality' given to the state as a potent and autonomous actor somehow neglected the role of both larger and smaller political units, especially as the scale of politics has been changing during the most recent period.

The promoters of the newly 'state-centered' approach remarked that it derived in part from analytical developments and problems in previous 'society-centered' approaches, since the explanation of many societal processes required to ascertain the impact of the political system and the state itself. Analogously, the development of studies directly or indirectly inspired on the assumption of state centrality has contributed to pay attention to alternative political units with an impact on states. In recent times scholars of the state have realized that the state cannot be taken for granted; its very existence is problematic; processes of state-building and nation-building show that there are different degrees of 'statehood' or 'stateness'; there are strong and weak states, as well as numerous failed 'states'; and the future of the national state in the current world is questioned by new issues of scale, space and territoriality.

'State' is in fact a category that has become decreasingly able to account for many polities in the current world. Apparently, the current world is organized in almost 200 'states'. But only a relatively limited number of these political units can be considered to be successful 'states' in a strict sense of the word. Sovereign states succeeded in Europe within a historical period that began about 300 years ago and is today essentially finished. In fact the Western European model of state has either not been applied or has mostly failed elsewhere in the world. Now, as a consequence of the creation, successive enlargements and strengthening of the European Union, the validity of the traditional Western European model of sovereign nation-state has weakened further because it is in decline even in the original experience.

Elsewhere, the Western European model of the sovereign state has been much less successful. The US was created from the beginning, rather than as a nation-state, as a 'compound republic' formed by previously existing units retaining their constituent powers, as elaborated, among others, by Vincent Ostrom (1987). In Asia, a few very large, overpopulated empires have also escaped from the project of statization: China, the compound India-Pakistan-Bangladesh, as well as Indonesia and Japan, have maintained certain traditional imperial characteristics of internal complexity, not adopting the homogenizing features typical of modern European states.

Unlike in either North America or Asia, attempts to replicate the typical European 'state' form of government were made in Hispanic America, Africa and the Middle East as a consequence of the colonial expansion of European states and the further independence of their colonies. The experience has been much less successful than it was in the metropolis – in many cases, a failure indeed. Often the very idea of 'state' was frustrated since the new political units achieved neither internal monopoly nor external sovereignty.

There are several accounts of failed states in the current world. The World Bank holds a permanently revised list of 'fragile states', called LICUS (for 'low income countries under stress'), to be given priority, but in most cases impotent foreign aid. There are between 30 and 40 of these countries, including 'collapsed or failing states', others in permanent internal conflict, encompassing all together between five and ten per cent of the world's population. In another comparable report, Britain's Department for International Development has named 46 'fragile states' of concern (Cabinet Office, 2005). Other periodical reports on fragile or failed states are produced by the OECD, the CIA (2000), and Fund for Peace and Foreign Policy (2005). The failure of statehood as an explanation for social disorder and economic stagnation is not, however, very frequent and, when used, it is typically within a teleological framework by which state-building is presented as the only possible model for non-European countries (as in Fukuyama, 2004).

Small is democratic

In recent worldwide developments, classical state-building under the Western European model has been largely replaced with a proliferation of small countries, most of which do not brandish some essential elements of 'sovereignty'. While there were only about 50 independent countries in the world at the beginning of the twentieth century, there are about 200 members of the United Nations in the early twenty-first century. They include about 70 mini-states with a population between one and ten million inhabitants and 40 microstates with less than one million inhabitants (among them most members of the European Union). In addition, there are more than

500 non-state political units with governments and legislative powers located within a couple of dozen vast federations or decentralized 'empires'. There are also about 20 'territories' formally linked but physically non-contiguous to some large empire or state and in fact quite independent, and about 15 other territories de facto seceded from recognized states. Helpful data are provided by Kristian S. Gleditsch and Michael D. Ward (2007) and by the Correlates of War project at the University of Michigan. A good collection of cases of states in process of separation can be found in Bahcheli et al. (2004).

The increase in the number of independent countries and the corresponding decrease in their size, as well as the concurrent decentralization of large states and empires, have accompanied the recent spread of democracy in the world. Contrary to some conventional knowledge, democracy does not require sovereign statehood. It can be argued that some lively forms of 'democracy' in the sense of open elections and control of rulers by broad layers of citizens existed in old small communities, cities, nations and republics not invested with the attribute of sovereignty, long before the notion of state was even invented. Likewise, there are also nowadays several hundred democratic, but non-sovereign local and regional governments within large states or empires.

As discussed in the seminal work by Robert A. Dahl and Edward R. Tufte (1973), small communities can be more appropriate than large and populous territories for democratic forms of self-government. Their advantages can be found in each of the three stages of the decision process: deliberation, aggregation, and enforcement. In a small community, people have more opportunities to gain knowledge for collective decisions by direct observation and experience; thanks to territorial proximity, people can also deal more directly with political leaders; the latter can easily gain information about people's demands and expectations by direct communication. Since a small community tends, in general, to be relatively homogeneous in terms of both economic and ethnic variables, people may also

have relatively harmonious interests, shared values and a common culture, which may make it easier to identify priority public goods and make collective decisions that are generally acceptable. Finally, small communities are more likely to generate loyalty; people will tend to comply with collective rules and decisions, while leaders may be more responsive regarding their own decisions and activity.

Looking at the question from the other side, the disadvantages large unitary states have in establishing a democracy able to satisfy the preferences of a large majority of its citizens are not difficult to identify. Within a large political unit, different interests, values and opinions are likely to exist among the citizens. A collective decision made on a set of different policy issues in bloc is likely to produce a high number of losers. Local majorities may become state-wide minorities and see their preferences rejected from binding collective decisions. In large and heterogeneous communities, there is likely to be a group of absolute winners, whose endurance may induce the losers either to resist the enforceability of collective decisions, not comply with them, rebel, secede or emigrate. In the extreme, dictatorships are more likely to emerge and triumph in very large political units or in highly heterogeneous ones.

The correlation between small size and democracy is empirically consistent, since the creation of increasingly numerous, smaller countries has accompanied the spread of democratic regimes. At the beginning of the twenty-first century, there is democracy in all recognized micro-countries with less than 300,000 inhabitants, in more than two thirds of those with less than one million inhabitants (including the former group), and in more than one half of all small countries with less than 10 million inhabitants (including the two former groups), while only one third of large countries with more than 10 million inhabitants enjoy democratic regimes (specifically, there is democracy in 59 of the 112 smaller countries, but in only 30 of the 86 larger countries). In other words, the number of small democracies is twice the number of large democracies.

The rates of success in democratization are even higher for small communities within large federations. Nowadays, of all the large countries in the world with more than 10 million inhabitants, those with a federal structure are democratic in almost three-fourths of the cases, while in large centralized and unitary states, democracy only exists in one-fourth of the cases (specifically, there is democracy in 13 of 18 large federal countries, but in only 17 of 68 large centralized states).

Bringing the empire back in

The increase in the number of viable small democratic governments seems to rely upon membership to very large areas of 'imperial' size, which provide public goods such as defense, security, trade agreements, common currencies, and communication networks. Precisely because they do not have to pay the heavy burdens of classical statehood and sovereignty, including a costly army and a single currency, small countries in an open international environment can benefit from their internal homogeneity and inclination to democracy. Within efficient, internally varied vast empires, small nations are now viable and, at the same time, better fit than large, heterogeneous states for democratic self-government.

A few vast empires do exist in the current world, including democratic and market-oriented empires, such as the USA, the European Union, India and Japan, as well as China and Russia, just to mention the most prominent ones. An 'empire' can be conceived as a very large size polity with a government formed by multiple institutional levels and overlapping jurisdictions. In this sense, 'empire' is an alternative formula to 'state', which can also be dictatorial or democratic or something in between, but is founded on fixed boundaries, external sovereignty and the aim of internal homogenization. Empires typically encompass a high number of small political units, including states, but also regions, cities and other communities, with different institutional formulas across the territory.

Empire-wide political and institutional processes indeed disappeared from the field of academic political studies after the Second World War. A search in the *American Political Science Review* (APSR) since its foundation gives the following results. In the first period, from 1903–1949, as many as seven articles and 74 books reviewed included the words 'empire' or 'imperial' in the title. Most of them dealt with the 'problems and possibilities' (as titled in one of the reviews) of the British empire, followed by the German empire, as well as the American, Chinese, Japanese and Ottoman empires. Articles and books approached such suggestive subjects as empire's unity, nationalism, federalism, government and politics, political system, governance, constitution and laws, legislative jurisdiction, administrative system, civil service or civil code – that is, the same kind of subjects that can be studied under the alternative framework of 'state'.

In contrast, not a single piece of work published in the APSR between 1950–1967 included the words 'empire' or 'imperial' in the title. This suggests that 'society-centered' approaches which were prevalent during that period, at the same time that they neglected the study of states also forgot the study of empires. Since 1968, the words 'empire' or 'imperial' reappear, although only in 40 book reviews, not in the titles of full-fledged articles. Most of the reviews in this period focus on history of past colonial empires, while only eight address imperial relations in the current world (mainly regarding American foreign affairs).

A new source of interest in the concept of empire can be derived, however, from state-centered studies in state-building and nation-building. Two generations of political scientists ago, some fundamental discussion was collected by S.N. Eisendstadt and Stein Rokkan (1973). As they were embedded in the 'modernization' paradigm, the editors acknowledged they had not been capable of 'developing a general theoretical structure for comparisons across all regions of the world', but remarked on 'the uniqueness of the Western experience of state formation and nation-building' and its inappropriateness for the 'Third World'. Specifically for Africa, for instance, 'nation-building in the European style was a luxury when not a catastrophe'.

Somehow following or paralleling this intuition, a number of historians have identified spatial and temporal limits for the validity of the concept of 'state': basically Western Europe and a few of its colonies since mid-seventeenth century to late twentieth century. A masterful survey of the modern states in this perspective is given, for example, by Martin L. Van Creveld (1999). Other enlightening studies on the formation of early states include William Doyle (1978), Charles Tilly (1975), Hendrik Spruyt (1994) and Philip Bobbitt (2002). The importance of initial violence, force and coercion in building a state has been particularly highlighted by social historian Charles Tilly, who went so far as to present both war-making and state-making as forms of 'organized crime' (Tilly, 1985). In the academic headquarters of political science more strictly defined, the role of violence and coercion in the formation of states has also been stressed by Margaret Levi (1988, 1997) and Robert H. Bates (2001). Bertrand Badie and Pierre Birnbaum (1983) remarked that the state is but one possible institutional formula in complex societies in the modern world. The failure of the state model beyond Europe was subsequently analyzed also by Bertrand Badie (1992).

States, nations, and empires

A few works dealing more directly with political and governmental processes in empires can also be mentioned. Specifically, 'the concept of empire' and its potential in the analysis of long-term historical periods was discussed in an excellent book co-authored by an outstanding selection of historians and political scientists at the initiative of Maurice Duverger (1980a).

More recently, Samuel E. Finer provided the only political science-oriented history of

government in the world that goes beyond the last 200 years (Finer, 1997). Finer states at the very first page of his impressive, indispensable and irregular three volume study that his 'concern is with states'. However, he immediately acknowledges that most 'pre-modern' polities did not fulfill the basic characteristics of 'state', namely the notion of territorial sovereignty (and far less that of 'a self-consciousness of nationality'). Actually in his own 'conceptual prologue', Finer goes to provide a three-fold typology of structures of government based on the distinction between city, state and empire. In his extensive survey, the category of city-republics includes a number of cases in Mesopotamia, the poleis of Greece, and medieval Europe. The 'formation of the "modern European state"', in turn, 'starts effectively with, and is built around, the erection of known frontiers … States were the product either of aggregation from small territorial units or of the disaggregation of large territorial units', according to Finer (1997: 9, 35). But it can also be argued that, in the current world, the states themselves are suffering processes of both disaggregation into small polities (along the revived tradition of city-republics) and aggregation into large territorial units of imperial size.

In fact, most of Finer's work deals with empires, using regularly and explicitly the word. Specifically his analysis includes Assyria, 'the first empire in our modern sense'; Persia, 'the first secular-minded empire'; China, in fact a series of 'multi-state empires'; Rome, which ruled through 'imperial agents' like the provincial governors; the Byzantine empire; the Arab empire of the Caliphate; the Ottoman empire; and the Indian empires. Finer's work provides, thus, highly valuable material for political science analysis of polities or structures of government through history, although his initial emphasis on 'states' is dismissed by his own substantive analysis of really existing governments. Other interesting suggestion for further work from Finer's materials can be found in George E. Von der Muhll (2003).

Regarding current configurations, the European Union has also been analyzed as an 'empire' or at least as an empire under construction. The European Union is indeed a very large political unit (the third in population in the current world), it has expanded continuously outward without previously established territorial limits, it is organized diversely across the territory and has multiple, overlapping institutional levels of governance. The point that the European Union may not be 'unique', 'exceptional' or 'unprecedented', as frequently asserted in certain journalistic literature and political speech, was addressed, for instance, by Caporaso et al. (1997). For a social scientist this only means that we are not using a sufficiently broad analytical concept capable of including this case among those with common relevant characteristics, such as that of 'empire'. A comparison between the processes of constitutional building of the European Union and of the US was sketched by Richard Bellamy (2005). The war motives in building large empires like the European one were remarked by William H. Riker (1987, 1996). The vision of the European Union as a new kind of empire was suggested by Robert Cooper (2003). Europe 'as an empire' has been elaborated in parallel works by Jan Zielonka (2006) and Josep M. Colomer (2006, 2007a).

In the long-term there has been an ever-continuing historical trend toward larger empires. The size and evolution of empires have been studied in four illuminating articles by Rein Taagepera (1978a, 1978b, 1979, 1997), which are partly based on data in Colin McEvedy and Richard Jones (1978). According to these data, there is no evidence of empires larger than 10,000 km^2 much before 3000 BC. The largest ancient empires, in Egypt and Mesopotamia, with about one million km^2, were still tiny compared to the present ones. The largest ones at the beginning of our era, in China and Rome, were already much larger, with about five million km^2. But modern empires, including Russia and the colonial empires of Spain and Britain, have encompassed double-digit millions of km^2.

Another historical trend is toward an increasing number of simultaneous empires,

so that the imperial form of government includes increasingly higher proportions of the world's population. Virtually none of the territories of the currently existing states in the world has been alien or outside some large modern empire. Among the very few exceptions are Thailand (which emerged from the old kingdom of Siam without Western colonization) and Israel (which was created from scratch in 1948). But a world's single-government is not foreseeable from historical developments. If the tendency toward increasingly larger sizes of empire, as measured by territory, is extrapolated, we find only a 50 per cent probability of a single world empire by a date placed between 2200 and 3800 (depending on the author making the calculation). If the extrapolation is based on the proportion of the world's population within the largest empire, that expectation should be deferred to nothing less than the year 4300.

A relevant implication of all this discussion is that, contrary to a still common assumption inspiring the US and other great empires' foreign policy, especially regarding the Arab region and the Middle East, democracy does not require nation-state building. In ethnically highly heterogeneous countries, federal-type structures and the establishment of large-size areas of free trade and military and security cooperation, can work rather well. Even more: if sovereign units were strengthened in isolation from each other, a higher degree of stateness could, paradoxically, jeopardize the chances of freedom and democracy, since it might revive or foster inter-state rivalries and mutually hostile relations.

THE CHOICE OF INSTITUTIONS

Within established communities, the designers of institutions will aim at anticipating collective decisions on government and policy. Two types of decisions on institutions are reviewed in the following. First, those to regulate the division of powers among the various branches of government, and second, those to define the relationships between these and the public, which in democracy are based on elections (Colomer, 2001b).

Division of powers

In the old legalistic approach to institutional design, democratic regimes were basically distinguished as 'parliamentary' or 'presidential' depending on the relations between the legislative and the executive, as shown, for example, in the compilation by Arend Lijphart (1992). In parliamentary regimes there is fusion of powers between the parliament's political majority and the cabinet. But by the early twentieth century, the development of political parties was usually interpreted as a force eroding the central role of the parliament, up to the point to label the British model rather than 'parliamentary', a 'cabinet' regime. However, it has more recently been remarked that the growth of party was instrumental to reduce the influence of the monarch but not necessarily that of the parliament. With the reduction of the monarch to a figurehead, the prime minister has indeed become the new one-person relevant figure, but the position of the cabinet has weakened. In contrast, the role of parliament has survived, and even, in a modest way, thrived. At least regarding Britain, despite long-standing concerns regarding the balance of power, 'parliament has always remained the primary institution of the polity', according to Matthew Flinders (2002; see also Bogdanor, 2003).

In the so-called 'presidential' regime, originated with the 1787 constitution of the US, there are separate elections for the assembly and the presidency and a complex system of 'checks and balances' or mutual controls between institutions. They include term limits for the president, limited presidential veto of congressional legislation, senate rules permitting a qualified minority to block decisions, senatorial ratification of presidential appointments, congressional appointment of officers and control of administrative agencies, congressional impeachment of the president, and judicial revision of legislation.

Recent analyses have formally shown how these counter-weighting mechanisms play in favor of power sharing between institutions and as equivalent devices to super-majority rules for decision-making. The obstacles introduced by the numerous institutional checks may stabilize socially inefficient status-quo policies, but they also guarantee that the most important decisions are made by broad majorities able to prevent the imposition of a small or minority group's will. With similar analytical insight but a different evaluation, other analyses have remarked that separate elections and divided governments create a 'dual legitimacy' prone to 'deadlock', that is, legislative paralysis and inter-institutional conflict. A seminal contribution, based on a formal model for the United States constitution, showed how the interaction of separate institutional bodies is likely to produce stable policy outcomes, as by Thomas Hammond and Gary Miller (1987). Further discussion includes contributions by Fred Riggs (1988), Juan J. Linz (1990a, b), William H. Riker (1992), Kenneth Krehbiel (1996, 1998), Robert A. Dahl (2002), José A. Cheibub and Fernando Limongi (2002), Josep M. Colomer (2005b).

A variant of political regime with separate elections for the presidency and the assembly, better called 'presidentialism', was established in almost all republics in Latin America since the mid- or late- nineteenth century. Some founding constitution-makers in these countries claimed to be imitating the US constitution, but, in contrast to the preventions against one-person's expedient decisions introduced in the US, some of them looked farther back to the absolutist monarchies preceding division of powers and mixed regimes and aimed at having 'elected kings with the name of presidents' (in Simón Bolívar's words). The distinction between US-style checks-and-balances, unified government in presidential regimes, and the more concentrated formula of 'presidentialism' can be referred to Madison, Jefferson, and Hamilton, respectively, according to James Burns (1965).

Presidential dominance has been attempted in Latin American countries through the president's veto power over legislation and his control of the army, which also exist in the US, supplemented with long presidential terms and re-elections, unconstrained powers to appoint and remove members of cabinet and other high officers, legislative initiative, capacity to dictate legislative decrees, fiscal and administrative authority, discretionary emergency powers, suspension of constitutional guarantees, and, in formally federal countries, the right to intervene in state affairs. The other side of this same coin is weak congresses, which are not usually given control over the cabinet and are frequently constrained by short session periods and lack of resources. Recent discussion includes Matthew S. Shugart and John M. Carey (1992), Juan J. Linz and Arturo Valenzuela (1994), Scott Morgenstern and Benito Nacif (2002). Actually the Latin American model of presidential dominance has gained the lowest reputation among scholars and has been proposed to be replaced with all the other regime types, including semi-parliamentarism by Carlos S. Nino (1992), Westminster features by Scott Mainwairing and Matthew S. Shugart (1997), US-style checks and balances by Bruce Ackerman (2000), and multiparty parliamentarism by Josep M. Colomer and Gabriel L. Negretto (2005).

Another variant, usually called 'semi-presidential' regime, but also 'semi-parliamentary', 'premier-presidential' or 'dual-executive', was consistently shaped with the 1958 constitution of France. With this formula, the presidency and the assembly are elected separately, like in a checks-and-balances regime, but it is the assembly that appoints and can dismiss a prime minister, like in a parliamentary regime. The president and the prime minister share the executive powers in a 'governmental diarchy', as early stated by Maurice Duverger (1965, 1970, 1978, 1980b).

At the beginning of the French experience, Duverger speculated that this constitutional model would produce an alternation between presidential and parliamentary phases, respectively favoring the president and the prime minister as dominant figure. The first phase of the alternation was indeed confirmed with presidents enjoying a compact party majority in the assembly. In these situations, 'the president can become more powerful than in the classical presidential regimes', as well as more powerful than the British-style prime minister because he accumulates the latter's powers plus those of the monarch.

The second, parliamentary phase was, in contrast, not confirmed, since, even if the president faces a prime minister, a cabinet and an assembly majority with a different political orientation, he usually retains significant powers, including the dissolution of the assembly, as well as partial vetoes over legislation and executive appointments, among others, depending on specific rules in each country. This makes the president certainly more powerful than any monarch or republican president in a parliamentary regime, as acknowledged by Duverger himself (1986, 1996, 1998). The French call this 'cohabitation'. There can, thus, be indeed two 'phases', depending on whether the president's party has a majority in the assembly and can appoint the primer minister or not; however, the two phases are not properly presidential and parliamentary, but they rather produce an even higher concentration of power than in a presidential regime and a dual executive, respectively. See also discussion in Bahro et al. (1998), Giovanni Sartori (1994), Robert Elgie (1999).

Political regime performances

The introduction of a second dimension, the electoral system, makes the problems for institutional design of democratic regimes more complex. In particular, within parliamentary regimes one can choose either majoritarian electoral rules, which typically imply that a single party will be able to win an assembly majority and appoint the prime minister, or proportional representation rules, which correspond to multi-party systems and coalition cabinets. Presidential regimes and their variants, in contrast, are less affected by the electoral system dimension since at least one of the systems, the one for the election of the president, must be majoritarian and produce a single absolute winner.

Different institutional choices have been linked to different rates of success in attempts of democratization and in the duration of democratic regimes. In order to understand some results, it may be convenient to think again about the stylized assumption that strategic choices of different institutional formulas tend to be driven by actors' relative bargaining strength, electoral expectations, and attitudes to risk. It is logical to expect that citizens and political leaders will tend to support those formulas producing satisfactory results for themselves and reject those making them permanently excluded and defeated. As a consequence, institutional formulas producing widely distributed satisfactory outcomes can be more able to develop endogenous support and endure. Widely representative and effective political outcomes can feed social support for the corresponding institutions, while exclusionary, biased, arbitrary, or ineffective outcomes might foster citizens' and leaders' rejection of the institutions producing such results.

Generally, constitutional democracies favoring power-sharing and inclusiveness should, thus, be able to obtain higher endogenous support and have greater longevity than those favoring the concentration of power. Empirical accounts show that democratic regimes are the most peaceful ones, while semi-democratic or transitional regimes are most prone to conflict, even more than exclusionary dictatorships (basically because the latter increase the costs of rebellion). Among democracies, parliamentary regimes are more resilient to crises and more able to endure than presidential ones (Stepan and Skach, 1993). But parliamentary regimes with majoritarian electoral systems appear to be associated to higher frequency of ethnic and civil wars than presidential regimes, while parliamentary regimes with proportional representation are the most peaceful ones (Reynal-Querol, 2002). Updated calculations show that of all attempts to establish a democratic regime in countries with more than one million inhabitants since the nineteenth century, those having initially adopted the British model of parliamentarism with majoritarian electoral rule have survived only in 37 per cent of the cases, while the rate of success for presidential and semi-presidential regimes is 54 per cent (with high variance in duration), and for parliamentarism with proportional representation, of 72 per cent (Colomer, 1995, 2001a, 2007b).

Electoral rules

Electoral system design requires major choices between indirect elections, direct elections by majority rule, mixed systems, and proportional representation. Regarding the strategies of political parties to design electoral systems, in general the 'Micro-mega rule' applies: the large prefer the small and the small prefer the large ('Micro-mega' is the title of Voltaire's tale in which dwarfs and giants dialogue). Specifically, dominant and large parties prefer single-member districts with majoritarian rules able to exclude others from competition, while multiple small parties prefer large districts with proportional representation rules able to include them. Thus, political configurations in which there is a single dominant party or two rather balanced parties tend to produce choices in favor of rather restrictive or exclusionary electoral systems, such as those based on the majority principle, while pluralistic settings with multiple parties tend to favor choices in favor of more inclusive electoral formulas, such as those using rules of proportional representation.

Maurice Duverger (1951) already noted that 'the first effect of proportionality is to maintain an already existing multiplicity … On the whole, proportional representation maintains virtually without change the party system existing at the time of its adoption', although he did not elaborate. Precisely in a book review of Duverger, John G. Grumm remarked:

> the generally-held conclusions regarding the causal relationships between electoral systems and party systems might well be revised. ... it may be more accurate to conclude that proportional representation is a result rather than a cause of the party system in a given country (Grumm, 1958: 375).

Seymour M. Lipset and Stein Rokkan also suggested that electoral systems should be treated as the result of institutional choices by political actors: 'In most cases it makes little sense to treat electoral systems as independent variables. The party strategists will generally have decisive influence on electoral legislation and opt for the system of aggregation most likely to consolidate their position' (Lipset and Rokkan, 1967). More recently, analytical models, surveys, and discussion on electoral system design and choice have been provided by Arend Lijphart and Bernard Grofman (1988), Carles Boix (1999), Josep M. Colomer (2004), Pippa Norris (2004), Michael Gallagher and Paul Mitchell (2005), and Kenneth Benoit (2007).

It seems reasonable to assume that, under restrictive formulas such as majority rule, political actors facing the effects of their own failure at coordinating themselves into a small number of candidacies and the emergence of new issues and new contenders for seats and offices, may shift to prefer electoral institutions able to reduce the risks of competing by giving all participants higher opportunities to obtain or share power. When there are only a few parties, they can be satisfied with majoritarian electoral systems, but when the number and the size of new parties increase, the incumbent parties may begin to fear the risk of becoming absolute losers and try to shift to more inclusive electoral formulas. Electoral system changes indeed tend to move overwhelmingly in favor of increasingly inclusive, less risky formulas: from indirect to direct elections, from unanimity to majority rules, and from the latter to mixed systems, and to proportional representation (Colomer, 2004; see also Blais and Massicotte, 1997; Lijphart, 1994).

Existing parties tend, thus, to choose electoral systems able to crystallize or consolidate the previously existing party configurations and systems. Only in large countries with large assemblies, limited voters' participation, and successful coordination in two large parties, single-member districts and plurality rule remain stable as an equilibrium institutional formula. In the US, in particular, in spite of being a very large and heterogeneous country, each representative is elected by the rather homogeneous population of a small territory in a way that the two main nation-wide parties become large-tents or umbrellas of varied representation.

Since the nineteenth century, we can count 82 major changes of assembly electoral system in 41 countries with more than one million inhabitants. In consistency with the discussion above, we observe that more than 80 per cent of these changes have been in the direction toward more inclusive formulas. Specifically, indirect assembly elections decreased and virtually disappeared in the early twentieth century. Majority rule, which was the basic formula in the few democratic countries existing in the late nineteenth and early twentieth centuries, was replaced in its appeal by proportional representation, especially after the First World War. This trend has intensified in recent processes of democratization. Mixed systems have spread widely in the most recent period, mostly as a result of changes from non-democratic regimes or plurality rule. Nowadays, most democratic countries with more than one million inhabitants use electoral systems with proportional representation rules.

Likewise, we can count 28 major changes of presidential electoral rules in 14 countries, mostly moving from electoral college to simple plurality rule and to second-round formulas based on qualified-plurality or absolute majority rules, the latter permitting multiparty competition at the first round. This trend is stronger during present democratic periods.

More specifically, it has been proven that while dominant and large parties are likely to choose simple plurality rule, small parties are likely to choose variants of majority rule with second round runoff, a system which permits broader participation and coalition formation in support of the two leading candidates. This hypothesis has been supported by a statistical analysis of the determinants of electoral choice in 49 cases of major and minor constitutional changes in Latin American countries by Gabriel L. Negretto (2006).

Large (small) assemblies, small (large) districts

An example of how the analysis of inter-institutional relations and institutional choices can be operationalized for quantitatively measurable variables and further empirical test is the following. Rein Taagepera (2001, 2007), by deductive reasoning, has presented a formula between basic elements of the electoral system, the district magnitude, M, the number of seats or size of the assembly, S, and the number of parliamentary parties, P, by which: $P = (MS)^{1/4}$. His initial intention was to explain the number of parties as derived from the electoral system. But his own formula also permits to analyze the relation the other way round, that is, the electoral system as derived from the number of parties. More clearly, it is: $M = P^4/S$.

In a previous work, Rein Taagepera and Mathew S. Shugart had established that the size of the assembly, S, depends on the size of the country in terms of population, C, approaching $S = C^{1/3}$ (Taagepera and Shugart, 1989). Now we can see in the above formula that the larger the country, and hence the larger the assembly, S, the smaller the expected district magnitude, M. Very large countries, precisely because they have large assemblies, can stay associated to small single-member districts. With similar number of parties, the institutional designers in India, for example, are likely to choose single-member districts, while the institutional

designers in Estonia are likely to choose multimember districts, typically associated to proportional representation rules.

In separate work, I myself hypothesized that electoral systems based on single-member districts and majority rule would be established and maintained when the effective number of parties lies between one and four, that is, when a single party may have or expect to have an absolute majority. Beyond four effective parties, the parties may want to change the electoral system to introduce multimember electoral districts with proportional representation rules. The hypothesis was supported with empirical data for 70 countries showing that only when the number of effective parties increases to four, the probability of an electoral system change in favor of proportional representation rises above half (Colomer, 2005a).

There is, thus, a great coincidence between the results of both the deductive and the inductive analyses just reported. The stylized approach focusing just on a few clearly defined, well measurable variables makes us realize that the pressures from multiparty systems to adopt inclusive electoral rules work differently in countries of different sizes. In large countries, a large assembly, whose number of seats is positively correlated to the country's population, can be elected in small, single-member districts. In small countries, by contrast, the size of the assembly is small and, as a consequence, the development of multiple parties favors more strongly the adoption of inclusive, large multimember districts with rules of proportional representation. Thus we tend to see *large assemblies with small districts*, and *small assemblies with large districts*.

This may seem counter-intuitive, since apparently small countries should have more 'simple' party configurations and less problems to identify a majority winner, so that they could work by simple electoral systems such as those with single-member districts and majority rule in acceptable ways (actually this tends to happen in very small and micro-countries with only a few hundred thousand inhabitants in which no more than two parties emerge). If the relation between variables is clearly established and measured, we can have an answer to the intriguing question of why large countries, including the US and other former British colonies, in spite of the fact that large size is typically associated to high heterogeneity, keep single-member districts and have not adopted proportional representation.

A relevant implication for institutional design is that if the size of the assembly is rather stable and depends on the country's size, for a small country with a small assembly, just a few parties are necessary to produce a change of electoral system in favor of proportional representation. In contrast, for a large country and a large assembly, many parties would be necessary to produce such a result, as discussed for the UK, after some failed attempts to reform the electoral rules, by Patrick Dunleavy (2005).

In the long-term, as we have seen in the first part of this chapter, both the number of countries and the number of democracies in the world are increasing, leading to an overall decrease in the size of the democratic countries. The size of democratic assemblies also decreases, since it is positively correlated to the country's population. As the number of parties increases within each democracy, more and more countries tend, thus, to adopt electoral systems with proportional representation rules.

In large countries and empires, such as Australia, Canada, France, India, the UK, and the US, a large assembly can be sufficiently inclusive, even if it is elected in small, single-member districts, due to territorial variety of the representatives. In small countries, by contrast, the size of the assembly is small and, as a consequence, the enlargement of voting rights, the broadening of the public agenda and development of multiple parties favors more strongly the adoption of more inclusive, large multi-member districts with proportional representation rules. Indeed, proportional representation began to be adopted for parliamentary elections in a few relatively small Western European countries in the early twentieth-century, as analyzed in several of the studies previously cited, and has widely spread among new democracies during the last decades.

CONCLUSION

It is not unfounded to assume that the design of political institutions is usually driven by politicians' and would-be rulers' ambition, the pursuit of power, and calculations, estimates or expectations about the likely consequences of different institutional formulas to favor designers' self-interest. However, as we have seen in the previous pages, the outcomes of such endeavors tend to be relatively favorable to formulas restricting the opportunities for high concentration of power and permitting broad satisfaction of people's preferences and demands. Specifically, institutional choices during the last decades tend to produce *small countries, more democracies, division of powers, and electoral rules favoring multiparty representation*. In spite of, or precisely through actors' self-interested behavior, institutional choices seem to be guided by an 'invisible hand' favouring relatively acceptable solutions.

Of course, all of this is based on long-term tendencies and positively tested with only average values for large numbers of cases. For single-case analyses, several possible situations faced by self-interested political actors can be identified. If the distribution of power in a community is such that one single group is institutionally dominant and expects to be secure winner with the existing institutional rules, these will not likely be changed – institutional stability can be expected. In contrast, situations more prone to institutional change include those in which there is high uncertainty regarding the different groups' relative strength and those in which new groups are emerging and gaining increasing support among voters. For anticipated losers or threatened winners, institutional change can be a rational strategy if the expected advantages of alternative formulas balance the risks of keeping playing by the existing rules.

We should take into account that many specific decisions and reforms are embedded in larger sets of institutional choices. Most prominently, the introduction of universal suffrage and processes of democratization have been, already since the late nineteenth century and in further waves through the twentieth century, paramount occasions for incumbent rulers and challenging opposition groups to decrease the global costs of changing political institutions and deal with innovative rules and formulas. In general, self-interested actors may try to enlarge the opportunities to compete for power positions by creating multiple institutional levels submitted to elections, such as the separation of the presidency from the assembly, the embodiment of regional governments or the creation of newly independent units.

But institutional decisions may entail some trade-offs between different levels and sets of rules. As we have seen, federalism or territorial representation in large countries and empires with diverse population may work as a substitute for proportional representation by giving different homogeneous, territorially-based groups opportunities to enter institutions and, thus, preventing a major electoral reform. As another example, the introduction of direct presidential election may open a new opportunity for electoral contest, but it may also constrain the degree of multipartism in the assembly because it is always submitted to majority rule and thus fosters polarization. Specific analyses of institutional design processes need, thus, to place the question in the context of the global relationship of forces among the relevant political actors and take into account the exchanges in which they can enter on parallel settings for multiple choices.

REFERENCES

Ackerman, B. (2000) 'The new separation of powers', *Harvard Law Review*, 113: 633–729.

Badie, B. (1992) *L'état importé. Essai sur l'occidentalisation de l'ordre politique*. Paris: Fayard.

Badie, B. and Birnbaum, P. (1983) *The sociology of the state*. Chicago: The University of Chicago Press.

Bahcheli, T., Bartmann, B., and Srebrnik, H. (eds) (2004) *De facto states. The quest for sovereignty*. London and New York: Routledge.

Bahro, H., Bayerlein, B. and Veser, E. (1998) 'Duverger's concept: Semi-presidential government revisited', *European Journal of Political Research*, 34: 201–24.

Bates, R.H. (2001) *Prosperity and violence: The political economy of development*. New York: W. W. Norton.

Bellamy, R. (Ed.) (2005) 'Symposium: A united states of Europe? (with Alberta Sbragia, Sergio Fabbrini, Glyn Morgan, Paul Magnette and Justine Lacroix)', *European Political Science*, 4 (2): 175–8.

Benoit, K. (2007) 'Electoral laws as political consequences: Explaining the origins and change of electoral institutions', *Annual Review of Political Science*, 10: 363–90.

Blais, A. and Massicotte, L. (1997) 'Electoral formulas: A macroscopic perspective', *European Journal of Political Research*, 32: 107–29.

Bobbitt, P. (2002) *The shield of achilles. War, peace, and the course of history*. New York: Alfred Knopf.

Bogdanor, V. (ed.) (2003) *The British constitution in the twentieth century*. Oxford: Oxford University Press.

Boix, C. (1999) 'Setting the rules of the game: the choice of electoral systems in advanced democracies', *American Political Science Review*, 93: 609–24.

Cabinet Office (2005) *Investing in prevention: An international strategy to manage risks of instability and improve crisis response*. London: Prime Minister's Strategy Unit. Available: http://www.cabinetoffice.gov.uk/strategy/work_areas/countries_at_risk.aspx

Burns, J. (1965) *Presidential government*. Boston: Houghton Mifflin.

Caporaso, J., Marks, G., Moravcsik, A., and Pollack, M. (1997) 'Does the European Union represent an N of 1?', *European Community Studies Association Review*, 10 (3): 1–5.

Cheibub, J.A. and Limongi, F. (2002) 'Modes of government formation and the survival of presidential regimes', *Annual Review of Political Science*, 5: 151–75.

CIA (2000) *State failure task force reports* (Daniel C. Esty, Jack A. Goldstone, Ted Robert Gurr et al.), *Phase III Findings*. Directorate of Intelligence.

Colomer, J.M. (2001a) *Political institutions*. Oxford: Oxford University Press.

Colomer, J.M. (ed.) (2001b) 'The strategy of institutional change', *Journal of Theoretical Politics*, 13: 235–48.

Colomer, J.M. (ed.) (2004) *Handbook of electoral system choice*. New York: Palgrave–Macmillan.

Colomer, J.M. (2005a) 'It's the parties that choose electoral systems (or Duverger's laws upside down)', *Political Studies*, 53 (1): 1–21.

Colomer, J.M. (2005b) 'Policy making in divided government', *Public Choice*, 37: 1.

Colomer, J.M. (2006) *Grans imperis, petites nacions*, Barcelona: Proa; (Spanish trans. *Grandes imperios, pequeñas naciones*. Barcelona: Anagrama)

Colomer, J.M. (2007a) *Great empires, small nations. The uncertain future of the sovereign state*. London: Routledge.

Colomer, J.M. (2007b) *Instituciones políticas* (2nd edition) Barcelona: Ariel.

Colomer, J.M. and Negretto, G.L. (2005) 'Can presidentialism work like parliamentarism?', *Government and Opposition*, 40 (1): 60–89.

Cooper, R. (2003) *The breaking of nations. Order and chaos in the twenty-first century*. New York: Atlantic Monthly Press.

Correlates of War project (n. d.) University of Michigan. Retrieved February 28, 2008, from www.correlatesofwar.org.

Dahl, R.A. (2002) *How democratic is the American constitution?* New Haven: Yale University Press.

Dahl, R.A. and Tufte, E.R. (1973) *Size and democracy*. Stanford, CA: Stanford University Press.

Doyle, W. (1978) *The old European order 1660–1800*. Oxford-New York: Oxford University Press.

Dunleavy, P. (2005) 'Facing up to multi-party politics: How partisan dealignment and PR voting have fundamentally changed Britain's party systems', *Parliamentary Affairs*, 58: 503–32.

Duverger, M. (1951) *Les parties politiques*. Paris: Seuil (English trans. *Political Parties*. New York: Wiley, 1954).

Duverger, M. (1955/1970) *Institutions politiques et droit constitutionnel* (11th ed.) Paris: Presses Universitaires de France.

Duverger, M. (1978) *Échec au roi*. Paris: Albin Michel.

Duverger, M. (ed.) (1980a) *Le concept d'empire*. Paris: Presses Universitaires de France.

Duverger, M. (1980a) 'A new political system model: Semi-presidential government', *European Journal of Political Research*, 8 (2): 168–83.

Duverger, M. (ed.) (1986) *Les régimes semi–présidentiels*. Paris: Presses Universitaires de France.

Duverger, M. (1996) *Le système politique français* (21st edition). Paris: Presses Universitaires de France.

Duverger, M. (1998) *La constitution de la France*. Presses Universitaires de France.

Eisendstadt, S.N. and Rokkan, S. (eds.) (1973) *Building states and nations* (2 vols). Beverly Hills-London: Sage.

Elgie, R. (ed.) (1999) *Semi-presidentialism in Europe*. Oxford: Oxford University Press.

Evans, P.B., Rueschmeyer, D. and Skocpol, T. (eds) (1985) *Bringing the state back in*. New York: Cambridge University Press.

Finer, S.E. (1997) *The history of government from the earliest times* (3 vols) Oxford: Oxford University Press.

Flinders, M. (2002) 'Shifting the balance? Parliament, the executive and the British constitution', *Political Studies*, 50 (1): 23–42.

Fukuyama, F. (2004) *State-building: Governance and world order in the 21st century*. Ithaca, NY: Cornell University Press.

Fund for Peace and Foreign Policy (2005) The failed states index. *Foreign Policy*, July–August.

Gallagher, M. and Mitchell, P. (eds.) (2005) *The politics of electoral systems*. Oxford: Oxford University Press.

Gleditsch, K.S. and Ward, M.D. (2007) Expanded war data. Retrieved February 28, 2008, from http://privatewww.essex.ac.uk/~ksg/expwar.html

Grumm, J.G. (1958) 'Theories of electoral systems', *Midwest Journal of Political Science*, 2 (4): 357–76.

Hammond, T. and Miller, G. (1987) 'The core of the constitution', *American Political Science Review*, 81: 1155–74.

Hume, D. (1741/1994) 'Of the independence of parliament', in K. Haakonssen (ed.), *Political essays*. Cambridge: Cambridge University Press, pp. 24–7.

Krehbiel, K. (1996) 'Institutional and partisan sources of gridlock: A theory of divided and unified government', *Journal of Theoretical Politics*, 8: 7–40.

Krehbiel, K. (1998) *Pivotal politics*. Chicago: University of Chicago Press.

Levi, M. (1988) *Of rule and revenue*. Berkeley: University of California Press.

Levi, M. (1997) *Consent, dissent and patriotism*. New York: Cambridge University Press.

Lijphart, A. (Ed.) (1992) *Parliamentary versus presidential government*. Oxford: Oxford University Press.

Lijphart, A. (1994) *Electoral systems and party systems*. Oxford: Oxford University Press.

Lijphart, A. and Grofman, B. (Eds.) (1988) *Choosing an electoral system*. New York: Praeger.

Linz, J.J. (1990a) 'The perils of presidentialism', *Journal of Democracy*, 1 (1): 51–69.

Linz, J.J. (1990b) 'The virtues of parliamentarism', *Journal of Democracy*, 1 (2): 84–91.

Linz, J.J. and Valenzuela, A. (eds.) (1994) *The failure of presidential democracy*. Baltimore: Johns Hopkins University Press.

Lipset, S.M. and Rokkan, S. (eds.) (1967) *Party systems and voter alignments: Cross-national perspectives*. London: Collier–Macmillan–Free Press.

Mainwaring, S. and Shugart, M.S. (eds.) (1997) *Presidentialism and democracy in Latin America*. Cambridge: Cambridge University Press.

McEvedy, C. and Jones, R. (eds.) (1978) *Atlas of world population history*. Harmondsworth: Penguin.

Morgenstern, S. and Nacif, B. (eds.) (2002) *Legislative politics in Latin America*. Cambridge: Cambridge University Press.

Negretto, G.L. (2006) 'Choosing how to choose presidents', *Journal of Politics*, 68: 421–33.

Nino, C. (1992) *El presidencialismo puesto a prueba*. Madrid: Centro de Estudios Constitucionales.

Norris, P. (2004) *Electoral engineering: Voting rules and political behavior*. Cambridge: Cambridge University Press.

OECD *The Fragile States Group*. Retrieved February 27, 2008, from www.oecd.org/dac/fragilestates.

Ostrom, V. (1987) *The political theory of a compound republic: Designing the American experiment*. Lincoln: University of Nebraska Press.

Reynal-Querol, M. (2002) 'Ethnicity, political systems and civil wars', *Journal of Conflict Resolution*, 46 (1): 29–54.

Riggs, F. (1988) 'The survival of presidentialism in America', *International Political Science Review*, 9 (4): 247–78.

Riker, W.H. (1987) *The development of American federalism*. Boston: Kluwer.

Riker, W.H. (1992) 'The Justification of Bicameralism', *International Political Science Review*, 13 (1): 101–16.

Riker, W.H. (1996) 'European federalism: The lessons of past experience', in J.J. Hesse and V. Wright (eds), *Federalizing Europe? The costs, benefits, and preconditions of federal political systems*. Oxford: Oxford University Press, pp. 9–24.

Rokkan, S. and Urwin, D.W. (eds.) (1983) *Economy, territory, identity: Politics of West European peripheries*. London: Sage.

Sartori, G. (1994) *Comparative constitutional engineering*. London: Macmillan.

Shugart, M.S. and Carey, J.M. (1992) *Presidents and assemblies*. Cambridge: Cambridge University Press.

Skocpol, T. (1985) 'Bringing the state back in: Strategies of analysis in current research', in P.B. Evans, D. Rueschmeyer and T. Skocpol (eds), *Bringing the state back in*. New York: Cambridge University Press, pp. 3–37.

Spruyt, H. (1994) *The sovereign state and its competitors*. Princeton, NJ: Princeton University Press.

Stepan, A. and Skach, C. (1993) 'Constitutional frameworks and democratic consolidation: Parliamentarianism versus presidentialism', *World Politics*, 46 (1): 1–22.

Taagepera, R. (1978a) 'Size and duration of empires: Systematics of size', *Social Science Research*, 7: 108–27.

Taagepera, R. (1978b) 'Size and duration of empires: Growth-decline curves, 3000 to 600 BC', *Social Science Research*, 7: 180–96.

Taagepera, R. (1979) 'Size and duration of empires: Growth-decline curves, 600 BC to 600 AD', *Social Science History*, 3 (4): 115–38.

Taagepera, R. (1997) 'Expansion and contraction patterns of large polities: Context for Russia', *International Studies Quarterly*, 41: 475–504.

Taagepera, R. (2001) 'Party size baselines imposed by institutional constraints', *Journal of Theoretical Politics*, 13 (4): 331–54.

Taagepera, R. (2007) *Predicting party sizes: The logic of simple electoral systems*. Oxford: Oxford University Press.

Taagepera, R. and Shugart, M.S. (1989) *Seats and votes*. New Haven: Yale University Press.

Tilly, C. (ed.) (1975) *The formation of national states in Western Europe*. Princeton, NJ: Princeton University Press.

Tilly, C. (1985) 'War making and state making as organized crime', in P.B. Evans, D. Rueschmeyer and T. Skocpol (eds), *Bringing the state back in*. New York: Cambridge University Press, pp. 169–87.

Van Creveld, M.L. (1999). *The rise and decline of the state*. Cambridge: Cambridge University Press.

Von der Muhll, G.E. (2003) 'Ancient empires, modern states, and the study of government', *Annual Review of Political Science*, 6: 345–76.

Zielonka, J. (2006) *Europe as empire: the nature of the enlarged European Union*. Oxford: Oxford University Press.

14

Comparative Political Behaviour: What is being Compared?

Shaun Bowler

INTRODUCTION

The literature on electoral studies and electoral behaviour is vast, and growing. Any review of the literature must therefore necessarily be limited, and this chapter is no exception in picking out only a few elements from that vast literature. In what follows we are concerned not so much with the specific part of political behaviour being modelled so much as the implications and limitations of the kinds of comparisons being made. That is, there are a large number of studies of political behaviour – of turnout or of vote choice and so on but in this chapter the focus is not just on the kinds of political behaviour under view but also the kinds of comparisons being made.

For a considerable period the intellectual history of electoral studies was driven by American experience and examples. While there are important intellectual strands that still derive from American theoretical development – the intellectual shift has been away from seeing the electoral world through an American lens as we begin to see American experience as one of a class of problems from within a broader theoretical perspective. What has helped this shift in perspective is a combination of a growth in the number of democratic states (i.e., cases) coupled with the development of large scale cross national data collection efforts. These two trends have provided the basis for the comparative study of mass behaviour and allowed the literature to move from making inferences about how a particular case differs from or is similar to US experience and to being talking about comparative political behaviour.

In what follows we distinguish between two broad approaches within this overarching category of comparative political behaviour. One approach focuses on similarities of social trends across nations, the other on crossnational institutional comparison and the consequent differences between nations. Both of these approaches have helped to make great strides in the development of a comparative approach to political behaviour, but each of them has a series of strengths and weaknesses that are tied to the kinds of comparisons they make and the kinds of theoretical claims which interest them.

THE 'FIRST' GENERATION: THE TWIN BUILDING BLOCKS OF A MODEL OF VOTE CHOICE – PARTY IDENTIFICATION AND ECONOMIC VOTING

With relatively few exceptions initial attempts at electoral studies outside the US were built around a series of national election studies and were developed in light of insights taken from the American context and typically by American researchers. Thus much of the very early work on voting and voting behaviour considered vote choice as a major object of study and examined the role of party identification, leader assessments and issue positions as drivers of vote choice. Party identification was – as in the American context – a central focus and discussions of its antecedents and/or its stability occupied considerable attention. Gradually, following developments in the US literature, the set of topics and questions addressed broadened and work began to examine the impact of economic factors on vote choice in which incumbent performance on key economic indicators was seen to drive vote choice over and above party identification.

In general this strand of work saw a series of high-quality studies of individual countries and the development of national election studies in the mould of the American National Election Study and conducted for example in Britain, Canada and Germany.

But the multi-party nature of politics outside the US limited the applicability of models derived in the American two party setting. At the very least, American models could not be applied 'off the shelf'. For example, in models of party identification it became commonplace to represent party identification on a single continuum ranging from strongly identifying leftists via weakly identifying leftists through to weakly identifying rightists and on to strongly identifying rightists. One of the major advantages of this measurement approach was that it meant that, as a variable, partisanship could be represented by a single dimension and, further, that this dimension

could be treated more or less as if it were an interval scale. The mapping of this psychological model to a single left-right policy dimension was an added bonus. In party systems that were dominated by two large parties this did not present too many problems. Where politics was defined by a predominantly two-party system such a model was acceptable. The examples of Britain in the 1960s and 1970s, Germany in the 1970s and, for a while at least, Canada outside of Quebec in the same period all seemed to have elements that made them ripe for analysis using American centred models. There were some difficulties but since these only concerned minor parties or relatively small fractions of the political system they could be sidestepped. But genuinely multi-party systems would seem to inherently challenge the idea of a single dimension. In the 1980s the German party system began to change in new ways. Where, for example, should one place 'weakly identifying' German Greens on the party identification scale – to the 'left' of the SPD or to the right of them? These problems became even more pressing in nations such as the Netherlands or Italy with many viable parties. Party identification could either be seen to be represented by one measure per party or require at least two dimensions – one measuring intensity and another reflecting the 'left-right' policy position. Regardless of challenges to a 'single dimension' of politics posed by debates over post-materialism (see below), the concept of party identification seemed to have to be treated as multi-dimensional outside the US.

Multi-partyism poses a similar challenge to the simple but extremely powerful argument of retrospective voting.[1] The retrospection involved voters judging the performance of the incumbent on economic issues and, if that performance was seen to be lacking the voter would cast a vote for the challenger. A standard approach was to use aggregate data to model the popularity function of an incumbent party, prime minister or president: vote shares and/or popularity would go up when economic times were good and down when economic times were bad.

Again, multi-partyism necessarily implies that the simple version of the argument needs to be revised: in a three party system with one party in power the voter still has to choose which party to vote for; in a four or five party system and coalition government the voter also has to decide whether all partners to the government are to be voted against or whether one coalition member may nevertheless be worthwhile. Thus, while it is possible within say a popularity function approach to quite readily see a prime minister's popularity dip in response to economic downturns it can be harder to predict which party will pick up votes in consequence.

Certainly the problems posed by multi-partyism for the two-party ('American') model are not insurmountable. For example, more sophisticated estimation techniques (multi-nomial logit/probit) can handle the question of the impact of multi-partyism in a choice framework (e.g., Alvarez and Nagler, 1998). But the point here is simply that while the early theoretical running of comparative electoral studies was made by American models they could not be applied wholesale and 'off the shelf' into other experiences. This point mattered because the 'comparative' part of comparative political behaviour often meant a series of case studies and pairwise comparisons with the US typically being the benchmark country of comparison. More ambitious work examined data from across several different countries, but the overarching theoretical models remained the familiar ones of partisanship, economics and – to some extent – the social underpinnings of both those factors. For example, one strand of work considered the class basis of partisanship and whether it was withering or not. A related strand considered class differences in the kinds of economic factors of interest in which, say, working class voters being more concerned with unemployment than inflation while the more job secure middle class voters were more concerned with inflation than unemployment. Even in these more sociological flavoured studies intellectual anchors would be typically provided by one or the other of the twin pillars of voting studies – party identification or issue-voting based on economic indicators of some kind.

These kinds of studies took us a great way along the road to understanding representative democracy in various nations around the world. But the comparisons were limited by the use of the US as a benchmark. That is, the framing of research questions was implicitly in terms of how well or poorly the US model worked rather than an attempt to fold US experience into a more general model of voter behaviour. That is findings were often couched in terms such as 'by contrast to American experience, the experience of country X shows …'. Glimpses of a more sustained and more forcefully comparative approach to voting behaviour could be seen in two influential sets of studies: one set of studies concerned 'political culture' and the second concerned voter turnout. We will address the political culture literature in more detail below. For the moment we will consider the literature on turnout.

While models of partisanship or of economic voting took as their main objects of inquiry who the voter would choose – either to identify with or to vote for – models of turnout took an even more basic question as its starting point: would the voter cast a ballot at all? Work in this area took an expressly comparative approach – whether comparing across US states or across nations – to include institutional factors in the analysis. For example, variations in electoral rules were seen as a major driver in variations in the motivations of voters to turnout (e.g., Blais and Dobryzynska, 1998; Franklin, 2004; Jackman, 1987). Unsurprisingly, compulsory voting is an important determinant of turnout. More surprisingly, perhaps, proportionality of the electoral system was also seen as a major positive force in prompting people to go out to vote. This literature thus began to locate individual behaviours within a context defined by institutions. But the expressly comparative approach of these turnout studies was largely restricted to explaining the one variable – turnout.

A SECOND GENERATION OF STUDIES: NEW DATA TO ADDRESS OLD AND NEW ISSUES

Beginning in the 1990s, however, a number of developments meant a step forward in the range of topics and theoretical approaches that could be addressed from within a genuinely comparative framework. One important step was the gradual cumulation of cross-national data collections. A series of major data collection projects meant the collection of data across a number of countries at the same time. One prominent example is the Euro-barometer series of public opinion polls which are conducted at the same time across all EU member states. Other examples include the World values surveys, the Latinobarometer and the CSES effort to co-ordinate across national election surveys.[2]

It is difficult to imagine now, but the early post-WWII studies were conducted in an era when public opinion polling was relatively new and, since it relied on face-to-face interviews, very labour intensive. Extensive public opinion polling in the early years was therefore restricted to a few, richer, states (Britain, Canada, Australia) and ones of particular concern for historical reasons (Germany). But it meant that in some senses the study of opinion was – to borrow a term – 'frozen' by historical circumstance. The only new democracies from 1945 to 1989 were essentially the cases of Germany, India, Italy and Japan. If these countries were not surveyed at the time of democratic formation it became extremely difficult to draw firm conclusions about democratic values and democratization in retrospect. For example, even if one interviewed the elderly in 1980 it would be difficult to draw conclusions about what went on in the 1950s in those nations for obvious reasons of memory and memory-loss. It seemed that the chance to study the democratic moment had gone. By 1989, however, when a new set of countries became democracies, researchers were ready with a range of survey tools to examine the transitions in Eastern Europe and elsewhere brought about by the fall of the Berlin wall. Not only did the fall of the wall bring about a second chance to examine democratization it also brought about an increase in the number of cases that scholars could examine.[3] It also helped generate a series of studies on democratization that were expressly comparative and allowed scholars to assess the relative impacts of, for example, economic factors on support for democracy as opposed to more political or value laden factors (e.g., Duch, 1995; Evans and Whitefield, 1995; Rose et al., 1998). This was only possible because surveys were fielded across these new democratic nations more or less in 'real time' as democratization unfolded.

Cross-national work of this kind raises issues of translation across languages that are themselves worth further study and affect our ability to conduct cross-national work sensibly (Blais et al., 2001; Sinnott 1998). But the availability of properly conducted opinion polls which asked the same questions of citizens in may different states and often at the same time meant that the literature as a whole could begin to address more comparative questions of interest. Furthermore, these surveys allowed researchers to go beyond the simple behavioural comparison of variation in turnout to examine affective and cognitive underpinnings of mass behaviour across a newer and wider range of cases than before in an explicitly comparative approach. These more explicitly comparative approaches can be loosely categorized into two broad groups. The first of these can be loosely termed as ones that are interested in 'socio-cultural' approaches to citizen politics and in particular the use of political culture as an explanation. The second, newer group, is more institutional in outlook and much less interested in cultural explanations. We examine each in turn.

SOCIO-CULTURAL APPROACHES TO THE STUDY OF COMPARATIVE MASS BEHAVIOUR: SIMILARITIES ACROSS NATIONS

Above we noted that many of the early electoral studies were largely pair-wise comparisons in which one country was compared to another – usually the US. A major exception to the single country case study approach in the early years of electoral studies was Almond and Verba's study of civic culture (1963). This was one of the first systematic and sustained attempts to move beyond a single country study to establish a comparative framework for the study of public opinion and attitudes. The study was of five countries – Britain, the US, Germany, Italy and Mexico – and it sought to establish a 'culture' or way of doing politics in those nations. Among the conclusions of the study was that Britain and the US had a 'participant' culture in which citizens were engaged in democracy and, hence, supportive of it. This kind of culture contrasted with that of the 'subject' political culture of Mexico in which citizens did not expect to take part in politics and consequently helped non-democratic forms of government persist (Almond and Verba, 1963).

Since its publication the study has come in for sustained criticism. But the study remains a landmark in conceptualizing democracy at the mass level and attempted to do so within a comparative framework. Nevertheless, doubts remain about a cultural approach to mass behaviour. Perhaps the most straightforward criticism is the observation that the attitudes of voters could be a product of the political system, rather than a cause and so cultural arguments often muddle cause and effect. In addition the 'political culture' argument of Almond and Verba was subject to a series of criticisms that apply to attempts to apply labels to nations, that is, that they are imprecise in defining the mechanisms at work, they are definitionally blurred and often assign a level of homogeneity to nationalities that is, at best, over-stated and, at worst, inconsistent with the main thesis.

Two subsequent research programmes have sought to address some of these criticism by seeking to be more specific about the mechanisms at work and, also, by being more specific about the behaviours that are affected and so have breathed new life into the idea of civic culture.

One of these research programmes has been to cast an understanding of politics in generational terms. In a series of works Inglehart advanced the argument that different generations come with different political outlooks (Inglehart, 1977, 1990). In casual conversation one might, as a passing generalization, refer to the 'Depression era baby' or 'boomers' as a short-hand for a group of people of a certain age. For Inglehart such generational markers often come with a meaningful package of political attitudes and predispositions. This is a more subtle analysis than one in which shifting trends in demographics are identified and their consequences teased out. To be sure, the changing class composition of societies have electoral fortunes of parties: as the blue collar working class shrank over the twentieth century so, too, did the 'natural' constituency of traditional socialist parties (see for example, Franklin et al., 1992 for an excellent extended discussion of these kinds of trends). Inglehart's argument, however, is not that the composition of the electorate changes in terms of who is a member – although that does play its part – so much as that what the electorate wants changes.

The big change, for Inglehart, is the shift to a new politics of 'post-materialism' driven by the accumulation of material wealth and resources.[4] There have been more elaborate examples of what is meant by the term post-materialism since then but the original survey instrument (question) gives a straightforward means of understanding the difference in attitudes being identified:

If you had to choose among the following things, which are the two that seem the most desirable to you?

- Maintaining order in the nation.
- Giving people more say in important political decisions.
- Fighting rising prices.
- Protecting freedom of speech.

Affirmative responses to options 2 and 4 in that list are taken as signs of post-materialism. Inglehart anticipated that younger, more affluent, voters who no longer experience worries over economic scarcity should be more ready to support those two responses. He further expected that these responses should become more and more prevalent over time.

Unfortunately, those expectations were not quite borne out. While significant portions of the electorate can be said to be 'post-materialist' they do not seem to have produced a wholly new way of conducting politics. 'Materialist' concerns persist in a number of ways, either the responses to these survey questions are seen to fluctuate in response to economic circumstances that suggests that attitudes may not be so much a cultural shift more a short-term response to circumstances (see for example, Duch and Taylor, 1993 and subsequent debate). More worryingly still, the share of post-materialists seems not to have grown very much despite a generation of economic prosperity (and the generational replacement of older 'materialist' voters by younger post-materialist ones): 'post-materialists' do not seem to have become the dominant cultural or generational force.

One area in which identifying generational shifts has had more success than others has been in discussing the changing attitudes towards government and governing. The 1990s saw a wave of concern about declining regard for politics and politicians. When one looked at the time series of public sentiment on trust in government or satisfaction with democracy the trends seemed in a secular trend downwards in the post-war period. In and of themselves these trends worried many as an erosion of regard for democratic governance. In the work of Norris and Dalton we see painted – in very broad-brush terms – a generational model of what drives trust in government grounded in careful analysis of cross-national data series. Both authors develop broadly similar themes to document the rise of what Norris calls the 'critical citizen' (Norris, 1999). Dalton's approach, for example, is carefully grounded in a social-psychological model of cognitive resources

(Dalton, 2004, 2007). That is, voters develop higher expectations of government and of politics and seek more avenues for participation. Thus newer generations of citizens are at the same time less trusting of government and traditional means of participation but are often more participatory in general (see Dalton, 2007). While clearly related to the arguments of post-materialism this approach is more specific both in its object of explanation (trust in government) and also in identifying some of the mechanisms at work to produce the trends.

Another, but ultimately somewhat less successful, way in which cultural explanations have been revived is through a series of arguments about 'social capital' which comprises the second of the research programmes that essentially modernize and update the sociocultural arguments typified by Almond and Verba. These social capital arguments have a long intellectual history but in the modern period became highly influential due to the work of Robert Putnam (Putnam, 2000; Putnam et al., 1993). Putnam's is a much more specific version of a cultural argument than the ones seen in earlier work of Almond and Verba but very much in the same theme: individuals who engage in social groups, sports groups, civic associations, choirs and the like are expected to be much more participatory and, also, have a set of values that aid democratic governance. An even more specific version of this argument is found in Verba et al. (1995) who argue that engagement in social organizations builds specific skill sets of organizational ability among individuals. That is, learning how to manage a mailing list for a child's soccer team is little different from managing a mailing list for a candidate or lobby group and, hence, in building organizational skills informal social organizations such as children's soccer teams or charities also build the human capital that makes democratic participation easier. To some extent, we could see the effect of the lack of social capital in the immediate post-wall period in Eastern Europe. While the scope for democratic action expanded very quickly ordinary citizens were unaccustomed to such freedom after a generation (or more) of one party rule. It is not clear that people did at first understand the limits of democratic practice. If they went on a protest march could they shout slogans? Were they allowed to wave banners? Could they challenge any onlookers verbally? People did not know how to behave.[5]

The literature on social capital has taken full advantage of the range of cross-national survey evidence now available, most notably in the work of van Deth and Hooghe, to examine the implications of the argument beyond a single country or, even, a small set of groups. Despite, and in some instances because of, the considerable body of work on this topic it has not been widely influential as an intellectual project (see Newton, 2001 and van Deth, 2003 for a thorough conceptual assessment: Hooghe and Stolle, 2003 for a cross-national application). Some of van Deth's work, for example, in part confirms some of Weber's conjectures to the effect that heavy social engagement can lead to political disengagement (van Deth, 2000). Other work notes that even groups that are hostile to democratic values invest heavily in various bonding kinds of social capital. Indeed, it may be precisely these sorts of groups – extremist, revolutionary and possibly even violent – who invest most heavily in building social capital among their members. While the literature on social capital is extensive, and discussions of it tap very readily into popular discussions of 'what's wrong with society today?' the evidence in support of the effects of social capital is more equivocal and less certain than many proponents would care to admit.

One of the concerns about over time comparisons of course is the time period taken as a starting point. For example, if one of the concerns is that regard for democracy has declined since the 1960s one might wonder what would happen if the 1930s were chosen as the start point since that period saw widespread support for both fascism and communism among voters across the democratic world – including the US and Britain.[6] Again, then, the conclusions being drawn depend in part on the implicit comparison being made.

The growing series of opinion data and the growing number of democratic countries have, over time, provided the means by which scholars can begin to understand social changes and democratic politics. Early work on cultural or socio-cultural trends have been re-cast and re-worked into more concrete and more focused examples of 'cultural' underpinnings to politics both in terms of becoming more specific about the objects of interest (the set of dependent variables) and also the mechanisms that produce the changes (the independent variables). Nevertheless, and despite the successes, these literatures do have some limitations. At the risk of some generalization, by focusing on generational trends in attitudes and widely shared sets of values or opinions these analyses typically see democratic politics as being caused by or brought about by social change.

In a sense, this is a theme that has remained within socio-cultural approaches since the days of Almond and Verba. Democratic institutions – while not exactly a 'black box' – tend not to be dealt with in any sustained way. There are, of course, exceptions to that statement but in general socio-cultural approaches tend to assume the trends should be seen across institutional environments and not to develop detailed discussion of the kinds of institutions that may be brought about by cultural change. The socio-cultural approach seeks similar trends across many nations and so resembles a 'most different' systems research design. This approach is of course important if the goal is to identify and trace similar trends across different countries but it does give short shrift to differences between countries; differences which persist even if one accepts that the time trends are similar and driven by similar processes.

Socio-cultural approaches also invest voters with a great deal of agency. That is, at least in the sense that voters in their aggregate have agency because political consequences follow on from changes in the electorate or changes among voters. What voters do or how electorates change shape political institutions and the process of democracy but the institutions do not, in turn, shape voters. It is not, however, entirely clear that voters do have such agency. Nor is it clear that the causal arrow flows from citizens to institutions but not vice versa. Buried within socio-cultural approaches, then, is an implied argument on the limitations of democratic institutions. At a very general level variation in institutional form simply does not seem to matter very much; what matters in this literature are general trends at the level of citizens. A more recent literature has developed a very different understanding of comparative electoral studies by seeking to embed studies of voting behaviour within its institutional context. In doing so they have developed a different set of research concerns from those that underpin socio-cultural approaches.

THE 'DECISION DEPENDENCE' OF VOTING: AN INSTITUTIONAL APPROACH TO CROSS-NATIONAL VARIATION

In focusing on the institutional context of voters, vote choice and voter behaviour it is not only possible to begin to build a more general model of voter behaviour it is also possible to begin to understand some of the more fundamental mechanisms of representative democracy. That is, there is a strong component of 'decision dependence' when it comes to understanding voters; both their decisions and decision making processes are dependent upon the institutional context in which they are embedded.

It thus becomes not just possible but also necessary to examine the 'decision dependence' of voters when we begin to frame questions of interest in terms of cross-national variation in political institutions rather than cross-national similarity in social processes. Important examples of work in this area have been a series of books and papers by Chris Anderson (2000, 2007) Anderson and

Wlezien (1997) and Bingham Powell (2000) who take as a central concern the accountability of governments, a key feature of democratic governance and one that is closely tied to the literature on economics and voting. While that literature assumed the institutional context of a two party (US) system subsequent scholars began to model those assumptions more explicitly.

One key underpinning to the idea of accountability is that voters be able to identify the government responsible for policy action. In fact, in democratic politics, voters *have* to be able to hold governments accountable for their actions in systematic ways. For representative democracy to work voters need to be able to 'throw the rascals out' of office and put the competent people into office. But it is much easier for voters to identify who is responsible for the conduct of policy in some systems than in others. In particular, voters find it far easier to hold single party governments accountable than to assign responsibility for actions in coalition systems. In this way, the literature tying shifts in economic variables to government popularity can be made richer. It is not simply that economic factors inform voter assessments, but how they manage those assessments and indeed whether they can act upon them depends on institutional context.

Powell's (2000) work goes a step further to consider the ways in which governments are not just accountable but also representative. In doing so, he can begin to make comparisons across systems about important normative concepts. Powell compares the left-right (policy) positions of voters to the left-right positions of governments arguing that the closer the government position is to the position of the median voter then the closer the government is to being representative. On average, coalition governments are closer to the median voter than are single party governments. In which case, coalition governments may be more representative kinds of governments even as they may be less accountable, thus revealing an underlying trade-off in the nature of representative democracy – at least so far as parliamentary democracy is concerned.

There are a series of questions one could raise about this general approach – and especially in relation to the topic of representation. For example while the median voter is an important figure in rational choice theory it is less clear that they are well suited to normative evaluations of democracy. Furthermore even assuming that a single left/right scale is appropriate to use across all polities, there may be problems in matching this across governments and mass publics. Powell (2000) himself is very careful to try a series of measures in looking for the gap between median voter and government position, but while public opinion surveys are extremely useful at establishing where voters may fall on a left right scale finding a properly commensurable scale for where governments fall is much harder if – as is often the case – the voters are not asked to place the government on the same scale. One solution used is to rely on expert surveys of party placements which, as Powell is careful to demonstrate, do provide consistent measures.[7]

Nevertheless, what the work of Powell and others does is to follow along a similar path to the literature on turnout: it advances a theory of individual political action that is embedded within a theory of institutions – and seeks to test it. Furthermore, the range of opinions and attitudes that are assessed by these cross-national surveys opens up the possibility to test more or less any kind of model of voter choice, voter behaviour or opinion formation with regard to institutional and political variations.

Perhaps the most sustained example of this approach comes in the Comparative Study of Electoral Systems project. In this project members of national election survey teams agree to ask a common set of questions and the data from these surveys are made available. In addition a number of questions about the nation's political institutions are also collected and made available.[8]

This combination allows the marrying of individual and institutional level variables in a number of ways. One example of work using these data is a look at the prevalence of tactical or strategic voting. In principle all electoral systems should see some form of strategic voting (see Shiveley, 2005). Most famously, perhaps, is the tactical voting that underlies (and is caused by) the bias against smaller parties in first past the post systems. But by comparing across systems it is possible to examine which electoral systems encourage or allow more strategic voting than others (see also Gschwend, 2007). Similarly it is possible to examine the motivations of voters across different systems: do voters weigh the personal characteristics of candidates more heavily in some systems than others? We know, for example, that some electoral systems provide incentives for candidates to seek a personal vote (Carey and Shugart, 1995; Farrell and Scully, 2007) but is it the case voters depend more heavily on assessments of individual candidate attributes to arrive at a decision in some systems than others? More generally still, the model of vote decision making with its various components of partisanship, issue and candidate assessment, may have varying weights across different electoral systems. Thus the model of individual vote choice can be informed by institutional context that is more or less permissive of tactical concerns and that values or discounts certain kinds of information.

A similar set of institutional questions tying institutions to attitudes can relate to at least some of the questions studied from within a socio-cultural framework. Take, for instance, the example of an understanding of satisfaction with or trust in democracy. Leaving aside the question of trends over time and whether the trends are shared or not, persistent differences in levels of trust exist across nations. These differences may be rooted in different institutional arrangements. Shiveley (2005), for example, notes that satisfaction with democracy may vary with the decentralization and concentration of political power. Alienation from government may be determined by the 'nationalization' of politics. As more decisions are made at the national level – and fewer at the local level – then politics may seem more remote from citizens and, hence, less trustworthy. Mistrust of government may reflect a sense of perceived distance from government – in which case decentralization of power may help re-engage citizens. Evidence consistent with this argument comes from the literature on 'second order' elections in which voter turnout is, in part, driven by how consequential the election is to voters (Marsh, 1998; Percival et al., 2007; Reif and Schmitt, 1980). If elections simply do not matter very much to voters – if not very much is at stake – voters will not turn out and vote. Again, then, the kinds of voter decision-making we see – over turnout and affect towards the political process – are shaped in fundamental ways by the type of decision they are asked to make at election time.

Even after the election we may see consequences of the kinds of decisions voters are asked to make in terms of how citizens feel about the government in power. Anderson and Guillory (1997) and Anderson et al. (2005) also address how different institutional arrangements shape satisfaction with democracy. Politics – and elections in particular – sort citizens into 'winners' and 'losers' but different political systems make the loss and the sense of loss greater than others. So, for example, single party 'winner take all' systems make citizens from the 'out' parties feel a greater sense of loss than multiparty coalition systems that build broad bases of support.

The institutional approach thus considers a different set of questions than the sociocultural approach. It has also developed a series of successes in understanding how and why elections vary across nations. As the research programme on the institutional effects is worked out, however, several issues remain to be worked on.

First, while the focus to date is often on cross-national comparison there is a great deal of value to making comparisons across sub-national units – states, provinces or even cities. But the emphasis on national politics often overshadows the sub-national dimension. There are several reasons for a greater appreciation for sub-national studies. Cross-national comparisons can still invite criticism from a cultural perspective: if people are also embedded in cultural 'institutions' that are not appropriately measured then the models (of turnout, trust or accountability) will be under-specified and may provide omitted variable bias. Within-country comparisons should reduce the number of omissions while at the same time allowing a focus on institutional effects.

Furthermore, if the election of interest is a national level general election then these are – more or less by definition – atypical: they are high profile, high spending, and high stakes elections. US Presidential elections, for example, are probably the most studied elections, yet they are the least typical elections. The more usual kind of elections are local ones – low information and low-engagement elections. The comparison across regions or political units within a single country, then, should provide scope for work on whether institutions do, in fact, make a difference (see e.g., Hoffmann-Martinot et al., 1996).

Second, the study of the institutional bases of mass behaviour and public opinion has helped generate over-confidence in our ability to bring about changes in voter opinions and behaviours. Take, for example, this statement made by IDEA (Institute for Democracy and Electoral Assistance – http://idea.int/elections/index.cfm) – an international think tank on electoral design:

> The choice of electoral system is one of the most important institutional decisions for any democracy. Electoral systems define and structure the rules of the political game; they help determine who is elected, how a campaign is fought, the role of political parties, and most importantly, who governs. Furthermore, the choice of an electoral system can help to 'engineer' specific outcomes, such as to encourage cooperation and accommodation in a divided society. (IDEA, 2008)

This is a fairly typical kind of statement in part because the tie between electoral systems and electoral behaviour appears to be both clear-cut and well understood. But it is far from clear how precisely we can engineer outcomes. Much of our confidence in the ability to engineer outcomes comes from the results of cross-sectional models – but it is not always clear that we have established appropriate causal relations. There are very few examples of being able to track changes among the public in light of institutional changes. New Zealand may be one of the few cases for which we have the data available to track these kinds of concerns.[9]

Our over-confidence in our ability to engineer is related, in part, to a third issue: there is a need for greater theoretical work on institutions and their effects. Certainly, some work on socio-cultural patterns does not seem to be terribly theoretically sophisticated either. In fact in some instances early work on social trends seems to involve identifying trends in data post hoc. By contrast to such work the institutional approach seems to be much more theoretically driven. Nevertheless, there is some scope for greater theoretical development within the institutional approach. While the guiding impulse is to examine mass behaviour embedded within the context of institutions the theories of institutions we examine often involve very large-scale differences. Much of the work on electoral systems in the vein of Duverger's Law considers different effects of 'first past the post' and list PR systems. These differences seem to be real and persistent. But these two electoral systems are very different from each other; ranged in-between these two extreme points are a series of electoral systems that may or may not have such stark effects. Our confidence seems to be a product more of our understanding of the more extreme examples of electoral systems rather than the range of ground in between. A better understanding of institutions might help better ground our confidence in our ability to engineer.[10]

Relatedly, it is not always clear that the literature shares a common definition of what constitutes an institution. The de facto choice of institutions included in analysis often seems to gravitate towards the formal and constitutional rather than the less formal, but this need not be the only kind of institution to consider. While it is true that political parties may be seen as organizations rather than institutions one would think that – even as organizations – their actions are likely to have as much impact on election outcomes as less formal associations and organizations that build social capital. Yet political parties and their actions are often absent from models looking at political behaviour in this institutional sense.

Similarly, some institutional effects really compare not just one institution to another but bundles of institutions to other bundles of institutions. For example the distinction between consensus and majoritarian democracies is due to Lijphart, who has formed a major conceptualization of democratic institutions taken up by the literature to date (e.g., Lijphart 1984, 1994). It is hard to understate Lijphart's contribution in 'bringing institutions' back in to the comparative study of representative democracy. Yet his categories are not simply one institution but bundles of institutions – some of which are related to each other in obvious ways (coalition governments and PR for example), but other aspects of which are not (central bank independence and federalism). Furthermore, these categories seem not so much to be theories in themselves as inductively arrived at ideal types (grounded in the contrast between British/New Zealand experience on the one hand and Dutch experience on the other) that operate in different ways. To be sure, there are consequences and hypotheses that can be drawn from his models. And the influence of his work in many different areas shows just how important his categorization has been. Nevertheless, the differences he discusses are broad ranging and broad brush. It is not entirely clear which institutional arrangement within a given bundle is the most important one, or whether its effects are contingent on or interactive with the effects of other institutions. The comparison across bundles of institutions, then, can still leave a degree of uncertainty about what is doing the work.

In part because institutional approaches are sometimes somewhat under-theorized beyond the general belief that we should see institutional effects it might, therefore, be worth exercising more caution about our collective capacity to engineer before investing too heavily in an institutional approach. After all, if only large-scale differences in institutional arrangements make a difference to mass behaviours and attitudes then perhaps there is only limited scope for institutional arguments?

Finally, experimental methods have remained relatively under-utilized to date but would seem especially appropriate to use to explore institutional arguments. The ability to conduct comparative work has been supported by the range of available survey data and the range of statistical tools available to analyze those data. For example, hierarchical or multi-level models now mean there is a way to appropriately combine 'country level' institutional factors and individual level data. But experimental methods have a great deal of promise to allow scholars to focus on the micro-mechanisms of opinion and attitude formation across different institutional contexts. Heaney and Hanson (2006) note the contributions of the Chicago based scholars Gosnell, Merriam and others in the 1920s and 1930s in using experimental techniques. The advent of large scale public opinion polls seemed to have pushed aside this kind of experimental work until their re-popularization in the American context (e.g., Druckman, 2004; Gerber and Green, 2000: Lupia and McCubbins, 1998). Some work outside the US setting has been conducted using experiments. Bochel and Denver (1971) for example is a fore-runner of the Gerber and Green experiments on inducing voter turnout from the British case, while other experimental work has proved especially valuable in developing societies where survey work may be difficult to conduct (e.g., Duch and Palmer, 2004; Wantchekon, 2003; Whitt and Wilson, 2007). The scope for more work of this kind seems especially promising. As with other techniques, however, the value of the results depends on strong theory.

CONCLUSION

As we noted at the outset, any review of such a vast literature as that on electoral studies cannot pretend to be encyclopaedic. In this review large sections of the literature have simply been put to one side in order to focus more on the kinds of comparisons that are being made by different kinds of work in comparative electoral studies.

What we have termed a socio-cultural approach is often genuinely comparative in scope. But the framing of these studies is such that the work is often aimed more at identifying similarities across nations than in exploring differences between them. This seems to be especially the case when it comes to identifying whether political institutions have an effect, and if so how. By contrast the institutional approach suggests that political institutions are seen to have a great deal of impact over the way that citizens feel and act within representative democracy. It is an approach that emphasizes the differences and de-emphasizes similarities, and it is this approach that seems to be the more vigorous one at present as the consequence of an institutional perspective are worked out.

This chapter has, then, identified two broad categories of work within the literature on comparative electoral studies that have different theoretical and substantive concerns that are tied, in part, to the kinds of comparisons they make. The growing sophistication of statistical and experimental tools and the ever-growing collection of data means that the capacity to make meaningful comparisons is better now than at any previous time. To the extent there are limitations in the kinds of comparisons that may be drawn they seem to be based in theoretical constraints rather than practical ones such as data availability. In many ways the theoretical impetus given by ideas on social capital and on an institutional process have either run their course or, at least in the case of institutional studies, are gradually being worked out. One other possible source of new theoretical energy may be for more empirically minded scholars to reengage with normative political theory. Many of the earliest studies of voting were often heavily influenced by normative concerns over the ideal citizen grounded in the work of theorists such as John Stuart Mill (Berelson, 1952).

To some extent the work of Dalton and others has already begun the process of re-engagement with newer normative concerns such as those over deliberation and revised definitions of citizenship. Similarly, current concerns about the relationship between Islam and democracy will give an impetus to inter and intra national comparisons concerning the relationship between religious values and democracy. Even so, it may be an appropriate point to attempt a more systematic re-engagement.

NOTES

1. A major impetus for this attention to economic factors came from outside the voting studies literature itself and more from the late 1970s and early 1980s literature on the political business cycle, that is, the argument that governments manipulated macro-economic levers for electoral advantage. While issue positions had been a big part of voting studies the heavy emphasis on economics and the subsequent debates over 'retrospective' versus 'prospective' and 'pocket book' versus 'socio-tropic' voting did not occur until after the political business cycle literature.

2. As something of an aside we should note that in recent years, too, data collection for some single country cases have surpassed, and often far surpassed, the example of the American National Election Study in terms of the kinds of questions that may be investigated. The Australian, British, Canadian and New Zealand election studies have especially well-developed 'value-added' components compared to their American counter-parts. These national surveys may include candidate surveys, rolling cross-sections, media analysis or combinations. The data are also readily available.

3. The main effects of the post 1989 changes, however, remain the dramatic improvements in the lives and well-being of millions of people as well as a series of traumas suffered by large numbers of people in the transitions.

4. Ingelhart's work also marks a major conceptual improvement over some socio-cultural approaches in that he does develop an explicit theory and a set of predictions; some socio-cultural approaches that are content to describe demographic patterns after the event.

5. The 'skill set' argument is not something to take on board without questioning. Some of the skills being discussed would not seem to require too steep a learning curve and – hence – not require a long apprenticeship in non-profits or other informal groups. Similarly, it is not clear what makes someone volunteer as an organizer in an informal group to begin with. Perhaps these skills are just markers for socio-economic status, for example, being a stay-at-home parent or grandparent who used to work in an office with PCs.

6. See, for example, footage of the Cable Street Riots in London in 1936 http://www.youtube.com/watch?v=-AQDOjQGZuA. Similarly, some of the discussion of social capital seems to suggest that things have become 'worse' in a social capital sense from some idealized 'good old days' in which people got along with their neighbours and volunteered a lot more. Given that the 'good old days' of the 1950s and 1960s were also associated with high levels of racism, sexism and homophobia coupled with lower levels of education, wealth and home ownership one could be forgiven for wondering whether the good old days were really that good.

7. More vigorous critiques of some aspects of the Lijphart-Powell conjectures and a flavour of some of the debates may be found in Pinto-Duchinksy (1999).

8. There is an extensive web presence of the CSES project see http://www.cses.org/resources/results/results.htm

9. Saideman et al. (2002) are an exception – they use a pooled time series analysis to look at ethnic conflict and electoral institutions.

10. Newer theoretical work on institutions – for example Tsebelis' work on veto players – may help address some of these issues. Tsebelis' argument, for example, can easily be seen as a way to ground at least some studies of comparative electoral behaviour such as those relating to accountability or efficacy (Tsebelis, 2002).

REFERENCES

Almond, G. and Verba, S. (1963) *The civic culture: Political attitudes and democracy in five nations*. Princeton, NJ: Princeton University Press.

Alvarez, R.M. and Nagler, J. (1998) 'When politics and models collide: Estimating models of multiparty elections', *American Journal of Political Science*, 42: 55–96.

Anderson, C.J. (2000) 'Economic voting and political context: A comparative perspective', *Electoral Studies*, 19 (2–3): 151–70.

Anderson, C.J. (2007) 'The end of economic voting? Contingency dilemmas and the limits of democratic accountability', *Annual Review of Political Science*, 10: 271–96.

Anderson, C.J. and Guillory, C.A. (1997) 'Political institutions and satisfaction with democracy: A cross-national analysis of consensus and majoritarian systems', *American Political Science Review*, 91: 66–81.

Anderson, C.J. and Wlezien, C. (1997) 'The economics of politics in comparative perspective revisited', *Political Behavior*, 19 (1): 1–6.

Anderson, C.J., Blais, A., Bowler, S., Donovan, T., and Listhaug, O. (2005). *Losers' consent: Elections and democratic legitimacy*. Oxford: Oxford University Press.

Berelson, B. (1952) 'Democratic theory and public opinion', *The Public Opinion Quarterly*, 16: 313–30.

Blais, A. and Dobrzynska, A. (1998) 'Turnout in electoral democracies', *European Journal of Political Research*, 33 (2): 239–62.

Blais, A., Gidengil, E., Nadeau, R., and Nevitte, N. (2001) 'Measuring party identification: Britain, Canada, and the United States', *Political Behavior*, 23: 5–22.

Bochel J.M. and Denver, D.T. (1971) 'Canvassing, turnout and party support: An experiment', *British Journal of Political Science*, 1: 257–69.

Carey, J. and Shugart, M.S. (1995) 'Incentives to cultivate a personal vote', *Electoral Studies*, 14: 417–39.

Dalton, R.J. (2004). *Democratic challenges, democratic choices: The erosion in political support in advanced industrial democracies*. Oxford: Oxford University Press.

Dalton, R.J. (2007) *The good citizen: How a younger generation is reshaping American politics*. Washington DC: Congressional Quarterly Press.

Druckman, J. (2004) 'Political preference formation: Competition, deliberation, and the (ir)relevance of framing effects', *American Political Science Review*, 98: 671–86.

Duch, R.M. (1995) 'Economic chaos and the fragility of democratic transition in former communist regimes', *The Journal of Politics*, 57: 121–58.

Duch, R.M. and Palmer, H. (2004) 'It's not whether you win or lose, but how you play the game: self-interest, social justice, and mass attitudes toward market transition', *American Political Science Review*, 98: 437–52.

Duch, R.M. and Taylor, M. (1993) 'Post-materialism and the economic condition', *American Journal of Political Science*, 37: 747–78.

Evans, G. and Whitefield, S. (1995) 'The politics and economics of democratic commitment: Support for democracy in transition societies', *British Journal of Political Science*, 25: 485–514.

Farrell, D. and Scully, R. (2007) *Representing Europe's citizens: Electoral institutions and the failure of parliamentary representation*. Oxford: Oxford University Press.

Franklin, M.N. (2004) *Voter turnout and the dynamics of electoral competition in established democracies since 1945*. Cambridge: Cambridge University Press.

Franklin, M., Mackie, T., and Valen, H. (1992) *Electoral change: Responses to evolving social and attitudinal structures in Western nations*. Cambridge: Cambridge University Press.

Gerber, A.S. and Green, D.P. (2000) 'The effects of canvassing, telephone calls, and direct mail on voter turnout: A field experiment', *The American Political Science Review*, 94: 653–63.

Gschwend, T. (2007) 'Ticket-splitting and strategic voting under mixed electoral rules: Evidence from Germany', *European Journal of Political Research*, 46: 1–23.

Heaney, M.T. and Hansen, J.M. (2006) 'Building the Chicago School', *American Political Science Review*, 100: 589–96.

Hoffham-Martinot, V., Rallings, C., and Thrasher, M. (1996) 'Comparing local electoral turnout in Great Britain and France: More similarities than differences?', *European Journal of Political Research*, 30: 241–57.

Hooghe, M. and Stolle, D. (2003) *Generating social capital*. London: Palgrave.

IDEA (2008). *Electoral system design*. Retrieved February 27, 2008, from http://www.idea.int/esd/

Ingelhart, R. (1977) *The silent revolution*. Princeton, NJ: Princeton University Press.

Ingelhart, R. (1990) *Culture shift in advanced industrial society*. Princeton, NJ: Princeton University Press.

Jackman, R.W. (1987) 'Political institutions and voter turnout in the industrial democracies', *The American Political Science Review*, 81: 405–23.

Karp, J.A. and Banducci, S.A. (2008) 'Political efficacy and participation in twenty seven democracies: How electoral systems shape political behavior', *British Journal of Political Science,* 38 (2): 311–34.

Lijphart, A. (1984) *Democracies: Patterns of majoritarian and consensus government in twenty-one countries*. New Haven: Yale University Press.

Lijphart, A. (1994) *Electoral systems and party systems*. Oxford: Oxford University Press.

Lijphart, A. (1999) *Patterns of democracy: Government forms and performance in thirty-six countries*. New Haven: Yale University Press.

Lupia, A. and McCubbins, M.D. (1998) *The democratic dilemma: Can citizens learn what they need to know?* New York: Cambridge University Press.

Marsh, M. (1998) 'Testing the second-order election model after four European elections', *British Journal of Political Science*, 28: 591–607.

Newton, K. (2001) 'Trust, social capital, civil society, and democracy', *International Political Science Review*, 22 (2): 201–14.

Norris, P. (ed.) (1999) *Critical citizens: Global support for democratic government*. Oxford: Oxford University Press.

Percival, G., Currin-Percival, M., Bowler, S., and van der Kolk, H. (2007) 'Taxing, spending, and voting: voter turnout rates in statewide elections in comparative perspective', *State and Local Government Review*, 39 (3): 131–43.

Pinto-Duschinsky, M. (1999) 'A reply to the critics', *Representation*, 36 (2): 148–55.

Powell, Bingham G. (2000) *Elections as instruments of democracy: Majoritarian and proportional visions*. New Haven, CT: Yale University Press.

Putnam, R., Leonardi, R., and Nannetti, R. (1993) *Making democracy work: Civic traditions in modern Italy*. Princeton, NJ: Princeton University Press.

Putnam, R. (2000) *Bowling alone: The collapse and revival of American community*. New York: Simon and Schuster.

Reif, K. and Schmitt, H.H. (1980) 'Nine second-order national elections: A conceptual framework for the analysis of European election results', *European Journal of Political Research*, 8: 3–44.

Rose, R., Mishler, W., and Haerpfer, C. (1998) *Democracy and its Alternatives: Understanding post-communist societies*. Baltimore, MD: Johns Hokins Press.

Saideman, S.M., Lanoue, D., Campenni, M., and Stanton, S. (2002) 'Democratization, political institutions, and ethnic conflict: A pooled, cross-sectional time series analysis from 1985–1998', *Comparative Political Studies*, 35: 103–29.

Shiveley, W.P. (2005) 'Democratic Design: The Comparative Study of Electoral Systems Project', *Public Opinion Pros*. Retrieved March 26, 2008, from http://www.publicopinionpros.com/from_field/2005/oct/shively.asp

Sinnott, R. (1998) 'Party attachment in Europe: Methodological critique and substantive implications', *British Journal of Political Science*, 28: 627–50.

Tsebelis, G. (2002) *Veto players: How political institutions work*. Princeton, NJ: Princeton University Press.

van Deth, J. (2000) 'Interesting but irrelevant: Social capital and the saliency of politics', *Western Europe European Journal of Political Research*, 37 (2): 115–47.

van Deth, J. (2003) 'Measuring social capital: orthodoxies and continuing controversies', *International Journal of Social Research Methodology*, 6: 79–89.

Verba, S., Lehman Schlozman, K., and Brady, H.E. (1995) *Voice and equality: Civic voluntarism in American politics*. Cambridge, MA: Harvard University Press.

Wantchekon, L. (2003) 'Clientelism and voting behavior: Evidence from a field experiment in Benin', *World Politics*, 55: 399–422.

Whitt, S. and Wilson, R. (2007) 'The dictator game, fairness and ethnicity in postwar Bosnia', *American Journal of Political Science*, 51: 655–68.

15

Changes in the Causes of Democratization through Time

Barbara Geddes

INTRODUCTION

What do we now know about the causes of democratization that we did not know nearly 50 years ago when Seymour Martin Lipset (1959) wrote his famous article linking development with democracy? The answer is: surprisingly little. Indeed, some of the things we thought we knew decades ago have been challenged by recent research. Very fine minds have worked on explaining democratization. They have used multiple methodological tools, including in-depth case studies, small-N research designs comparing events in several countries, large-N statistical tests using sophisticated specifications and newly available data sets, economic models, and game theory. And yet, we have accumulated only a small store of knowledge about which most scholars agree. Instead, serious, carefully done research challenges nearly all theories and findings, and they remain contested.

In this chapter, I suggest that one of the main reasons for the inability of careful researchers to arrive at consensus about the causes of democratization is that causes differ systematically depending on features of the economy of the old regime, the kind of

authoritarian government that marks the starting point of the transition, and characteristics of the international political economy at the time of the transition. Since different kinds of autocracy dependent on different kinds of economic systems have clustered in time and space (Gleditsch and Ward, 2006), and the international political economy has also changed over time, the causes of early transitions tend to differ from later ones. If these observations are correct, they suggest the need for explanations of democratization that take these differences into account. In this chapter, I suggest several such arguments. I also suggest ways to interpret a number of empirical findings about the causes of democratization that makes sense of apparent inconsistencies.

The chapter proceeds as follows. The next section summarizes the current state of research on democratization in three parts: empirical findings; measurement issues; and theoretical models. The following one articulates in greater detail the starting characteristics that I believe systematically affect the democratization process. It also summarizes evidence supporting and challenging these interpretations. Finally, it discusses the usefulness of various theoretical arguments for explaining particular trajectories of democratization. The last section suggests a future research agenda and some new ways of testing arguments about democratization.

THINGS WE USED TO KNOW BUT NOW AREN'T SO SURE ABOUT

As Lipset (1959) showed, more developed countries are more likely to be democratic than the less developed. The correlation between democracy and development has been demonstrated repeatedly in the ensuing decades in increasingly sophisticated large-N studies (Barro, 1999; Bollen and Jackman, 1985; Burkhart and Lewis-Beck, 1994; Gasiorworski, 1995; Przeworski et al., 2000). Lipset's (1959) argument that various consequences of economic development *cause* democracy provoked controversy from the beginning, however, and that controversy continues. During the first ten or so years of what Samuel Huntington (1991) labeled the Third Wave of democratization, as the last West European holdouts and most of the more developed countries of Latin America[1] joined the democratic club, the argument that development causes democratization seemed confirmed, especially when the collapse of the Soviet Union brought most of the rest of the 'misplaced' countries into the club (Diamond et al., 1988). At about the same time as the Soviet collapse, however, a large number of poor, less developed countries in Africa, South Asia, and Latin America democratized, raising new doubts.

In seeming confirmation of these doubts, the very sophisticated large-N study by Przeworski and colleagues (2000) claims forcefully that development has no effect on democratization. Instead, they argue, it is the tendency of democratic governments in poorer countries to break down that leads to the correlation, not the greater likelihood that dictatorships in more developed countries will democratize. Using a different measure of democracy and a data set covering a much

longer period of time, Gleditsch and Choung (2004) and Pevehouse (2002) also found no relationship between development and transitions to democracy after controlling for characteristics of countries' neighbors.

Other analysts, however, challenge these arguments. In a very careful reanalysis that extends the time period back to 1850, Boix and Stokes (2003) show that development does contribute to democratic transitions, though the average effect for the whole period is small relative to the effect of development on maintaining democracy. Boix and Stokes (2003) show that when the data set is divided by time periods, however, economic development is an extremely important predictor of transition prior to 1950, but has only a small (though statistically significant) effect in the post-1950 period. In short, we still know that democracy is correlated with development, but the causal reasons for the correlation remain contested.

Several other empirical associations have also achieved the status of stylized facts, though all have also been challenged. Multiple studies show that oil wealth is associated with autocratic government (Barro, 1999; Fish, 2002; Ross, 2001). Countries with large Muslim populations are less likely to be democratic (Fish, 2002). As with the relationship between development and democracy, controversy continues about whether these are causal relationships or correlations explained by something else. Among those who believe relationships are causal, there are disagreements about the processes through which the causes produce the outcome.

Many Middle East experts explain the correlation between oil wealth and dictatorship as a consequence of the ability of 'rentier states' to use revenues derived from the sale of natural resources to distribute subsidies to large parts of the population and thus to maintain popular compliance with authoritarian government (Anderson, 1987; Crystal, 1995). In a parallel argument, Dunning (2006) claims that oil rents can in some circumstances be used to sustain democracy, though Karl has claimed the opposite (1997).

In contrast to the various arguments about the effects of oil on regime type, Herb (2005) shows that when a measure of development that excludes the effect of oil is used in place of GDP per capita in statistical analyses, oil rich countries fit the same patterns as other countries. Development, as Herb measures it, has a strong positive effect on changes in democracy scores, whereas rent dependence, measured separately, has no effect. In short, he challenges the existence of a relationship between oil wealth and regime type, as well as the rentier state argument per se.

Some observers have explained the correlation between adherence to Islam and autocracy as caused by an affinity between Muslim doctrine or the attitudes of believers and authoritarianism, but public opinion research done in countries with substantial Muslim populations shows that individual Muslims support democratic values (Sarkissian, 2006; Tessler, 2002). Fish (2002) suggests that Muslim countries tend to be authoritarian not for the reasons usually mentioned but because of the suppression of women's rights.

DISAGREEMENTS ABOUT MEASUREMENT

The waters have been further muddied by disagreements about the appropriate measurement of democracy. The main disagreement is over whether dichotomous categorical or polychotomous[2] measures are 'better' (Alvarez et al., 1996; Elkins, 2000). The answer to this question need not detain us: which is 'better' depends on what question the analyst seeks to answer. In studies of democratization, in which the measure is generally used as the dependent variable, if the analyst seeks to explain incremental movement toward democracy, then a polychotomous ordinal scale is better.[3] If the dependent variable to be explained is completed transitions, then a categorical or dichotomized measure is useful. Likewise, if

the analyst wants to use a measure to establish the universe within which to test an argument expected to hold only in one kind of regime, a dichotomous measure is required.

These measurement differences are one of the sources of contending claims about the causes of democratization, as analysts sometimes produce different results depending on whether they have measured 'democratization' as incremental steps toward democracy (using polychotomous measures) or as completed transitions (using categorical or dichotomized measures). For example, Epstein et al. (2006) show that using a trichotomous measure of democracy instead of the dichotomous indicator Przeworski et al. (2000) used changes their results; development does appear to cause democratization. Development seems to affect movement into and out of their intermediate category, which might be labeled mild authoritarianism, but not transitions from full dictatorship to full democracy. Since the word democratization can mean either steps toward the democratic endpoint or completed transition, neither measure is obviously right or wrong, but claims to have identified causes of democratization without specifying which meaning is captured by the measure used contribute to the plethora of claims and counterclaims.

Democratization can take place either in incremental steps or in a rapid leap from harsh dictatorship to fully competitive democracy. Since incremental steps in one direction can be followed by steps in the other, however, we cannot assume that reductions in repression or other changes that are reflected in incremental differences in democracy scales will lead to completed regime transitions – though they may. At the same time, citizens' lives can be much affected by these incremental changes, and there is certainly reason to explain them. Referring to incremental changes on democracy scales as democratization, however, causes confusion.

WHAT CAUSES THE CORRELATION BETWEEN DEVELOPMENT AND DEMOCRACY?

Moving beyond empirical correlations to explain why the correlations exist requires tests of arguments about the causal processes that have been suggested. Economic development is correlated with many other trends, and one or more of those may be the causal mechanism that accounts for the relationship between development and democracy. Lipset (1959) and other modernization theorists suggested that increasing education, equality, urbanization, experience working in factories, and the weakening of traditional loyalties to tribe and village – all correlates of economic development – would lead to more tolerant and participatory attitudes among citizens, who would then demand a say in government. Many of these arguments have been tested. A correlation between education, especially primary education, and democracy is well established (Barro, 1999). The results on urbanization are mixed. Working in factories contributes to more democratic attitudes (Inkeles and Smith, 1974). These studies test the implications of arguments linking individual traits to demand for democracy. They do not consider the interests that might oppose democratization (since the arguments they seek to test did not). They seem to assume that if citizens want democracy, they can achieve it, without giving much attention to the possible reluctance of elites to give up power.

Scholars influenced by Marx expect the middle class – which tends to grow as the economy develops – to be the carrier of the demand for democracy: 'no bourgeoisie, no democracy.'[4] Zak and Feng (2003) have modeled a process through which this relationship might unfold. Though Zak and Feng do not test their model, Barro (1999) shows a relationship between the income share of the middle class and democracy.

The development of theoretical models of democratization is an alternative response

to the need to explain the correlation. In 1999, Barro noted: 'Given the strength of the Lipset/Aristotle hypothesis as an empirical regularity, it is surprising that convincing theoretical models of the relation do not exist. Thus development of such a theory is a priority for future research' (S182). That has changed. Several scholars have proposed plausible deductive arguments that identify underlying causes of democratization. They model interactions between elites, who want to monopolize power, and citizens, who want to influence policy and therefore demand to share power. The advantage of explicit deductive models of the democratization process, besides clarity, is that they usually have many implications that can be tested against real-world experience. The next section discusses recent models of the process of democratization and the evidence supporting them.

MODELS OF DEMOCRATIZATION AS STRATEGIC INTERACTIONS BETWEEN ELITES AND CITIZENS

Models of the interactions between ruling elites and others that may lead to democratization can be divided into two categories depending on their basic assumptions about who the relevant actors are and what their goals are. Some models assume that the most important division within society is between rich and poor, and that the rich form and maintain dictatorships in order to protect their assets. They also assume, as do many other economic models of politics, that the key policy decision that determines redistribution is the level of taxation on domestic capital. It is assumed that the median voter, who is poor, prefers high taxes in order to redistribute wealth. The more unequal the income distribution, the poorer the median voter and thus the more confiscatory the tax rate is expected to be in a democracy. (The median voter in these models has never met 'Homer.'[5]) Autocratic elites only democratize because of the threat of violence or revolution. In these models political leaders are perfect agents of societal interests; they do not maximize their own revenue distinct from the revenue of the elite group they represent.

An alternative conception of autocracy assumes that the most important division in society is between the rulers (sometimes simplified to a single dictator) and the ruled. They assume that rulers maximize their own income from tax revenue at the expense of both rich and poor ruled. Rulers thus set taxes at the highest rate that does not deter economic effort by citizens. In these models, rulers offer increments of democracy when doing so can increase the credibility of their promises to provide public goods and other policies that will increase economic growth and thus benefit both rulers and ruled (Escribà Folch, 2003; North and Weingast, 1989; Weingast, 1997). Alternatively, rulers may offer democratic institutions as a means of directly increasing revenues (Bates and Lien, 1985; Levi, 1988; Rogowski, 1998). In these models, the ruled care about growth and the share of their own production they are allowed to keep. Taxation is not seen as a means to redistribute to the poor, but rather as a means of enriching rulers. Rulers become rich by ruling; they do not rule because they were rich before achieving power. They cling to power in order to continue collecting revenue from the productive population under their control, not to protect themselves from redistribution. The main constraint on rulers' pursuit of wealth is the threat of capital flight or reduction in economic effort.

Rich rulers versus poor ruled

Boix (2003), Acemoglu and Robinson (2001, 2005), and Zak and Feng (2003) argue that democratization is more likely when income distribution – which tends to even out as countries reach high levels of development – is more equal. Boix and Acemoglu/Robinson argue that elites fear redistribution, which they expect to result from democratization. But when income distribution is relatively equal,

they fear it less because the median voter's tax preferences will then be less confiscatory. Elites are willing to cede some power rather than risk revolution when they expect democracy to lead only to moderate redistribution.

Boix (2003) also argues that capital mobility, which, like income equality, tends to rise with development, contributes to democratization. When capital is mobile, it can flee in response to high taxes. Knowing that, democratic governments are expected to refrain from heavy taxation; so elites need not fear democracy. Thus elites' interests can be protected by either a relatively equal income distribution or capital mobility. Where capital mobility is low and income unequal, however, elites should be unwilling to negotiate democratization.

Boix's book (2003) is a seminal contribution to the literature on democratization because it provides plausible micro-foundations for the observed correlation between development and democracy. The analysis covers nineteenth and early twentieth century democratizations as well as more recent ones, and it includes a serious effort to test the argument. Nearly all other quantitative studies of democratization have looked only at the post-World War II period because of data limitations. Boix has made a huge effort to overcome those limitations. His study has not resolved all debates, however, because the empirical support for the argument is somewhat ambiguous. Although he finds that income inequality has a substantial effect on the likelihood of democratization in a data set that covers 1950–1990, some of the other evidence either fails to confirm expectations or can be interpreted in more than one way. In short, although Boix's argument is plausible and attractively simple, empirical support for it is modest.

Furthermore, it does not take into account the capacity of rulers to limit capital mobility, especially capital outflows. It treats capital mobility as exogenous, but governments in fact have substantial capacity to regulate capital outflows (Wong, 2007). If elites are more likely to acquiesce in democratization if they can protect themselves by sending their capital abroad, then why would dictators not limit capital outflows in order to prevent elite defections? The Boix argument fits well with the stylized facts of West European democratization, however, and redistributive changes followed democratization there, as the argument would predict (Lindert, 1994). Further tests of this argument deserve to be important items on the democratization research agenda.

Acemoglu and Robinson's (2001) argument begins with many of the same basic assumptions about the way the world works. It also gives a central role in resistance to democratization to elites' fear of redistribution when the starting income distribution is unequal. They limit the threat of revolution to periods of recession, however, which complicates predictions. In this argument, when the rich are threatened by revolution (which only occurs during recession), they can grant redistribution without changing the political system, grant democracy as a way of making the commitment to redistribution credible, or repress. Redistribution without regime change is not credible to the poor because they know that they cannot maintain the threat of revolution after the recession is over. According to Acemoglu and Robinson, democratization is a more credible commitment to maintaining redistribution over a longer time period. (Why the poor should accept democratization as credible when the model – conforming to reality – allows the rich to stage coups if they are dissatisfied by the later tax rate is unclear.)

In contrast to the Boix argument, Acemoglu and Robinson expect income inequality to lead to unstable regime changes, not continued authoritarianism. One of the attractive features of the Acemoglu and Robinson model is that it explains repeated transitions between democracy and dictatorship, a phenomenon that has characterized some parts of the developing world since the middle of the twentieth century. The model seems to be a plausible simplification of events in much of Latin America and in a few other developing countries. Acemoglu and Robinson (2005) provide some suggestive evidence to support their arguments, but do not carry out systematic

empirical tests so we cannot assess their fit with the real world.

Models linking democratization to inequality seem highly plausible, but the empirical investigation of the relationship between regime type and income inequality does not support their basic assumptions nor does empirical investigation of the relationship between democracy and redistribution outside Europe. If these arguments were correct, we would expect to find the remaining dictatorships in the world more unequal on average than democracies, but there is little evidence that the current set of recalcitrant dictatorships is made up of countries with especially unequal income distributions (Bollen and Jackman, 1985). In fact, in the post-World War II period, longer lived dictatorships (excluding monarchies) have more equal income distributions than brief ones. Przeworski et al. (2000) find a positive relationship between only one of three measures of inequality and transitions to democracy. They find a stronger relationship between inequality in democracies and democratic breakdown, which might explain any relationship that exists between democracy and equality (if one does exist), but does not support the idea that equality makes democratization more likely.

The models also assume that the main reasons elites fear democracy and ordinary citizens want it is that they expect it to lead to redistribution. Lindert (1994) has shown that the expected redistribution occurred in Western Europe after the first steps toward democratization were taken, but Mulligan et al. (2004) show that contemporary democracies do not on average redistribute more than dictatorships.[6] We should not be surprised by this result. Income distribution varied greatly among late twentieth century dictatorships. Many, both communist and non-communist, expropriated traditional elites and redistributed income and opportunities through land reform, much increased public education, and industrialization policies that led to the movement of large numbers of people out of agriculture and into factories. It is hard to imagine that ruling elites in these kinds of authoritarian regimes would be motivated by fear of greater redistribution. They would fear loss of their own power and wealth, but not via redistributive taxation. Income equality would not reassure them because their power and wealth are tied to holding office, not to ownership of private resources protected by stable property rights.

Thus, neither of these models fit many of the struggles over democratization in ex-communist and developing countries, where fear of redistributive taxation is not a plausible reason for resistance to democratization since substantial portions of productive assets were state or foreign owned for much of the late twentieth century. State elites who control a large portion of productive assets may certainly fear loss of power since their access to wealth depends on control of the state, but they will not suffer less dispossession with a more equal income distribution.

Revenue maximizing rulers versus politically powerless citizens

In this approach to the study of democratization, which owes much to seminal articles by North and Weingast (1989) and Olson (1993), rulers maximize their own individual revenue via taxation, and citizens prefer low taxes and share a desire for productivity-enhancing policies and public goods, regardless of their income. In this image of politics, taxes redistribute wealth from citizens to rulers, not from rich to poor. Rulers may want revenue in order to pursue wars, to buy support in order to stay in power, to pay for repression, or for personal consumption; their reason does not affect the logic of the argument. Rulers are motivated by their desire for revenue to offer public goods that increase productivity and to impose a tax rate that does not reduce investment or effort. Citizens demand regime change if they are taxed too heavily or dissatisfied with current leaders' provision of public goods and economic performance.

In some versions of this approach, societal elites or holders of private capital can do most to destabilize the regime if they are dissatisfied. Consequently, they are the ones most likely to be accommodated when the ruler offers an institutionalized form of participation in return for their cooperation. Rulers may offer representative institutions as a credible commitment to supply desired public goods (Escribà Folch, 2003; Levi, 1988; North and Weingast, 1989) or simply in exchange for wealth holders' contingent consent to the taxation of mobile capital (Bates and Lien, 1985). As in the Boix (2003) argument, democratization becomes more likely as capital becomes more mobile, but the reason for the relationship is different. The more mobile capital, according to Bates and Lien (1985), the harder it is to tax without contingent consent, and thus the more likely the ruler will offer representative institutions as a way of obtaining consent. Rogowski (1998) suggests a more general form of this logic in which citizens' ability to move away increases the likelihood that rulers will offer them representative institutions or good government in order to induce them, along with their productive capacity, to remain within the ruler's territory.[7] Thus these models explain the first small steps toward democratization from absolutist monarchy.

Bueno de Mesquita et al. (2003) suggest a more complicated general framework that extends these models to cover more contemporary transitions. Their model includes: a ruler supported by a winning coalition; a 'selectorate,' meaning those citizens who have some influence on who can join the winning coalition; and residents who play no role in selecting rulers. Rulers maximize personal revenue via taxation constrained by the need to provide private and public goods in order to maintain the support of the winning coalition. If members of the ruling coalition defect because they are dissatisfied with their share, the ruler loses office. Citizens outside the winning coalition benefit only from the public goods provided when the winning coalition is too large to be maintained by private goods alone.

Residents and members of the selectorate may hold demonstrations or join rebellions to challenge rulers who tax them too heavily or provide insufficient public goods, but rulers in this model always respond with repression. If revolutionary challengers win despite repression, the new rulers face the same incentives that other rulers have to narrow the winning coalition and keep resources for themselves. In other words, revolutions and popular uprisings in this model do not threaten redistribution or lead to democracy. Instead, they lead to a seizure of power by a new leader and winning coalition, who maximize their own wealth at the expense of those they exclude. One of the most useful and empirically realistic points made by Bueno de Mesquita et al. (2003) is that participation in a coup, uprising, or revolution does not guarantee the participant an improved share of power or wealth after the fall of the old regime because those who lead such movements have incentives to renege on earlier promises after they win.

Thus democracy cannot arise as a response to popular uprising in this model. This result is reasonably consistent with reality. Rebellions and revolutions rarely lead to democracy; instead, they lead to new dictatorships, some of which are redistributive.

Democratization, in the Bueno de Mesquita et al. (2003) model, arises when the members of the winning coalition can improve their own welfare by expanding the coalition's size. This model, like those described above, portrays democratization as elite led. In the Bueno de Mesquita et al. model, however, winning coalition elites are motivated simply by wanting to improve their own welfare relative to that of the ruler. They are not responding either to a challenge from the excluded or the threat of capital strike.

In these models, democracy is given by leaders or other elites, not demanded or taken by ordinary citizens. The political mobilization

of citizens can challenge rulers, but does not lead to democratization. This image is consistent with the many real world elite-led democratizations, but offers no insight into the transitions of the late twentieth century in which reluctant elites were pushed into democratization by popular upheaval.

INTERNATIONAL INFLUENCES ON DEMOCRATIZATION

Although models of democratization and most large-N empirical investigations have focused on domestic causes, many observers of late twentieth century transitions have emphasized the importance of international influences, especially the diffusion of democratic ideas and pressure from international financial institutions (e.g., Bratton and van de Walle, 1997; Dunning, 2004; Whitehead, 1996). If international forces have a major effect on democratization, and especially if there is an interaction between international and domestic factors, their exclusion from statistical tests may explain some of the limited and contradictory results obtained in these tests.

International factors have begun to be included in empirical investigations. Gasiorworski (1995), Gleditsch and Ward (2006) and Gleditsch and Choung (2004) show that the proportion of democratic neighbors increases the likelihood of transitions to democracy in the countries they surround, lending some support to the diffusion argument. Pevehouse (2002) shows that membership in regional international organizations in which most other members are democratic increases the likelihood of democratization. Since membership in democratic regional organizations is likely to be correlated with having democratic neighbors, however, we cannot be sure whether organizations have an independent effect beyond the effect of living in a 'good' neighborhood. Bueno de Mesquita and Siverson (1995), and Bueno de

Mesquita et al. (1992) show that war affects the survival of both political leaders and regimes. Gleditsch and Choung (2004) show that wars increase the likelihood of transition from one authoritarian government to another, but neither Gleditsch and Choung (2004) nor Pevehouse (2002) shows strong evidence that war in the neighborhood decrease the likelihood of democratization. Marinov (2005) shows that although sanctions are effective at bringing down democratic leaders, they have little effect on the survival of dictators and therefore, we can infer, little effect on authoritarian breakdown.[8] These findings suggest that international influences should be included in explanations of democratization, especially post-World War II since international influences – both economic and political – have probably become more pronounced over time.

HOW DEMOCRATIZATION HAS CHANGED

In this section, I describe ways that authoritarian government and the context within which it exists have changed during the last two centuries in order to identify changes in the causes of democratization. Autocracies vary in terms of the most basic characteristics of leaders and the organizations through which they cooperate with each other, the economies from which they draw sustenance, the distribution of ability to influence political outcomes within the citizenry, and the international forces that buffet them. These differences, as I show below, affect the likelihood of transition and how it occurs. Nevertheless, we lump these disparate processes of regime change together for explanation because the end state for all is democratic government.

Assuming that there is one explanation of democratization despite these differences may be the reason that scholars continue to disagree about its causes. The findings of large-N studies differ from each other depending on specification, time period included, and cases used. Such varying results should be expected if single statistical models are being imposed on a set of disparate processes without efforts to model how the processes might differ over time or in different kinds of transitions. If quite different processes, involving different actors with different interests, can lead to democracy, more than one theory is needed. If we are trying to use the same simple statistical model, verbal argument, or game theoretic model to explain multiple disparate processes, we should not be surprised if only the most basic features can be clearly identified or if studies that focus on different regions, time periods, or samples produce different answers, since different processes predominate in different time periods and regions.[9]

Many of the difficulties in theorizing the process of democratization stem from the under-theorized residual-category status of authoritarianism, which has led to the usually implicit assumption that characteristics of the old regime have no effect on transitions.[10] If instead we classify democratization processes in terms of a few basic characteristics of the autocracy and setting prior to democratization, we can then see that a number of the arguments currently contending for preeminence fit one of the processes but not all of them. Others are more useful for explaining democratizations that began at other starting points.

In the following sections, I discuss three issues that affect autocratic elites and other political actors as they make choices that may or may not lead to democratization: the extent of state ownership and intervention in the economy; changes in the international economy and geopolitical world that alter the costs and benefits of autocrats' domestic economic and political strategies; and differences in autocratic institutions that affect both their vulnerability to challenges and the costs of leaving office, which in turn influences their willingness to negotiate.

Market economy versus state ownership and regulation

In countries with predominately market economies, dictatorships have usually served the interests of the rich, consistent with the Boix (2003) and Acemoglu and Robinson (2001, 2005) arguments. The relationship is endogenous, however. Dictatorships with other goals have used expropriation, state investment, and extensive intervention in the economy to reduce both the predominance of market forces and the political influence of wealthy interests. The most common form of autocracy in market-dominated economies has been oligarchy, with or without monarchy, though military governments have also arisen in these contexts. Though levels of state ownership and regulation are determined by governments, oligarchies, as representatives of the owners of private wealth, have no incentive to expropriate and thus usually maintain private ownership. Historically, such regimes tended to fade away as economies developed. This may have occurred through the kinds of processes identified by Lipset and other modernization theorists; as more citizens became educated, joined the middle class, and went to work in factories, they demanded the vote, and in many countries of Latin America and Western Europe, eventually got it. The process may also have been aided by the mechanisms identified by Boix and Acemoglu/Robinson. Elites may have been more willing to extend the franchise where income distribution was more equal and capital more mobile.

In the period from the end of World War II until about 1980, however, most authoritarian regimes governed countries in which increasingly important parts of the economy were state-owned. In fact, dictatorships carried out much of the expropriation and state investment that resulted in these high levels of state ownership. Such strategies helped them consolidate political power. Dictators who rose to power via the military or leadership of a nationalist or revolutionary party

had strong incentives to seize the assets of private wealth holders who might have become sources of opposition, and many of them did. In communist countries, of course, governments owned all large firms and important resources, but nearly all developing countries began pursuing state interventionist development strategies in the mid-twentieth century. Oil and other key natural resources were either state-owned or foreign-owned and heavily taxed in virtually all. In countries endowed with natural resources, government revenues came primarily from either the export of state-owned resources or taxes on foreign-owned ones. These revenues could be used to reward supporters, and additional intervention in markets created many more opportunities for trading benefits for support.

State ownership makes possible both the accumulation of wealth by political leaders and also the distribution of benefits to supporters, and in some cases ordinary citizens, without high taxation of private wealth. Rulers who have *acquired* wealth through access to state resources, in contrast to those who hold political power because they own private wealth, have to fear losing most of their assets if they are deposed, regardless of the income distribution or other factors that might affect future taxation.

As long as the state interventionist development strategy remained feasible, these regimes were not challenged by development. In fact, those that provided good long-term economic performance have been remarkably stable (cf. Przeworski et al., 2000). Some of these regimes increased equality through the expropriation of traditional elites, land reform, the spread of education, and rapid industrialization, which made it possible for many poor rural workers to obtain better paying factory jobs. Others, however, worsened income distribution; they left traditional unequal land-owning patterns intact, and urban bias inherent in import-substitution industrialization strategies increased the wealth gap between rural and urban areas (Bates, 1981). Citizens who became better educated, got jobs in factories, or moved into the middle class were not formally excluded from politics in these regimes, however; most of them held regular universal suffrage elections. In many, upward mobility was available to the talented, who were co-opted into dominant parties. Thus, educated, ambitious citizens who might have led the demand for democratization according to modernization theory were often accommodated by mid-twentieth century autocracies.

The loss of the ability to intervene profitably in their economies, rather than factors linked to development, challenged autocracies reliant on state ownership and other forms of state intervention. As they were forced by changes in the international economy to reduce regulation, end subsidies, and sell state-owned assets, they lost the ability to continue delivering benefits to their supporters, whether elite or mass. To the extent that these economic reforms gave ruling elites the opportunity to transform state assets into private property – as for example, during the economic reforms in Hungary before the collapse of communism – elites feared the loss of office less since their wealth was secured. They were thus more willing to go along with democratization. Fears of losing office may also be allayed by enforceable bargains not to prosecute for corruption and human rights abuses (i.e., amnesties, allowing outgoing rulers to take their ill-gotten gains into friendly exile) or institutional bargains that give them a good chance of returning to office in competitive elections in the future.

Most transitions from oligarchic rule to democracy in market-dominated economies occurred during the nineteenth and first half of the twentieth centuries. Most transitions in the second half of the twentieth century involved autocracies that intervened heavily in their economies, owned significant productive assets, and regulated capital outflows. A number of the empirical disagreements described above make sense if we take these differences into account. The strongest

empirical support for the idea that the causes of democratization might differ depending on levels of state ownership of the economy comes from the very careful Boix and Stokes (2003) study showing a strong relationship between development and democratization before 1950 and a very weak relationship from 1950 to 1990. The Przeworski et al. study (2000), based on a sample drawn entirely from the period of heavy state intervention, shows almost no effect of development on democratization. Although the evidence on the effects of income inequality is not conclusive, in my judgment the bulk of it suggests that less equal income distributions did not hinder democratization during the second half of the twentieth century. Capital outflows in the very late twentieth and early twenty-first centuries seem to have no effect on the likelihood of democratization, as would be expected if dictators regulate capital outflows (Wong, 2007).

International influences

International forces have always influenced domestic politics through trade, international prices, diffusion, and conquest. Big changes in both the international economy and world politics occurred in the late twentieth century, and there are theoretical reasons to think these changes influenced democratizations. Globalization increased the weight of international economic forces on national decision making. Changes in the international economy following the debt crisis of the 1980s undermined the survival strategies of a number of autocratic governments.

Several geopolitical changes have also affected the likelihood of democratization. Although it is rarely mentioned in studies of democratization, during the nineteenth and early twentieth centuries, authoritarianism was maintained in large parts of the world through conquest. Empirical studies of democratization exclude these areas because colonial possessions are not included in standard data sets, but many decolonizations resulted in democratic government (often brief). The Cold War contributed to the maintenance of dictatorships, and its end seems to have contributed both to democratization and to transitions to milder forms of authoritarianism.

Changes in the international economy

During the period of state interventionist development strategies, governments' control over economic assets provided the resources that held coalitions supporting autocracy together. State ownership provided jobs for party cadres. Ruling families and their close allies became rich from the creation of monopolies, subsidies, privileged access to restricted imports, and other regulatory interventions. In a strategy reminiscent of Henry VIII's treatment of the monasteries, the expropriation of traditional and foreign wealth holders made possible the use of these resources to create new elites beholden to the dictatorship. The debt crisis undermined this political strategy because it challenged the economic strategy upon which it depended.

To understand how the debt crisis forced changes in the state interventionist development strategy, we need to think about how the strategy worked in practice. State interventionist development strategies typically included high tariffs to protect domestically produced goods from foreign competition; overvalued exchange rates to shift resources from the export sector (agriculture and minerals) to the industrial; and high state spending on investment, subsidies, social programs, and public employment. Since state spending outran tax collection, budget deficits were very common, as were trade deficits caused by the overvalued exchange rates. An inflow of foreign capital in the form of investment, loans, and/or aid was routinely needed to balance these deficits. During the 1970s, the sharp rise in the price of oil increased the availability and lowered the cost of international borrowing, as capital rich oil exporters put their excess into developed country banks. The banks then lent it to developing countries at low but variable interest rates. With interest rates so low, most developing countries borrowed heavily so that by the late 1970s, borrowing covered the need for capital inflows in most countries. When, in response to the second oil price shock in 1979, northern policy makers raised the interest rates to which developing country debt was linked, debt repayment became unmanageable. When Mexico declared itself unable to meet its debt obligations in 1982, the lending bubble burst. Both lenders and investors fled developing countries.

Without these inflows, the state interventionist economic strategy caused hyperinflation and recession. Many governments resisted economic reform because rulers understood the political difficulties it would create, but failure to change caused economic crises, which also challenges regime survival. Crisis and the neoliberal reforms undertaken in response to it reduced dictators' ability to continue buying support and thus contributed to the fall of many of them, as erstwhile supporters deserted them and ordinary citizens mobilized against them.

When foreign lending dried up, developing country governments faced intense economic pressure to adopt policies conducive to attracting private investment. Prior to the debt crisis, governments had a choice between relying primarily on state investment or private investment. Those that chose state investment did not have to offer credible commitments to provide public goods, predictable economic policy, or policies favorable to private investors in order to secure revenue flows, and thus the economic pressure to initiate institutional constraints on rulers' arbitrary powers was low. Since the 1980s, the state investment strategy has become unworkable except possibly in countries reliant on the export of oil or other high priced natural resources. Consequently, governments have sought to attract private investment. In short, changes in the international economy changed the costs and benefits associated with choices made by dictators, political elites, and ordinary citizens.

Attracting investment depends on credible policy commitments and secure property rights. As noted by North and Weingast (1989), Acemoglu and Robinson (2001), Escribà Folch (2003), and others, policy promises made by dictators inherently lack credibility. Dictators can increase the credibility of these promises by creating institutions that give capital holders a say in policy-making and that increase the constraints on the dictator's arbitrary power. Democratic institutions such as legislatures and multiparty electoral competition can create those constraints if the commitment to the institutional change is itself considered credible (Roberts, 2006). If the institutions benefit both the ruler, by increasing revenues, and the ruled, by increasing productivity or welfare, then the institutional bargain is self-enforcing and thus credible.[11] The need to attract private investment suggests why democratization and economic liberalization tended to vary together in the late twentieth century (Hellman, 1998).[12]

The political effects of the economic crisis of the 1980s and subsequent economic reforms are described and analyzed in numerous country studies, notably Magaloni's (2006) analysis of the effect of economic crisis on the fall of the PRI in Mexico. A number of multi-country comparisons of democratization experiences also emphasize the importance of economic crises in the 1980s and 1990s (Bratton and van de Walle, 1997; Haggard and Kaufman, 1995). In large-N studies, the effect of the economic dislocations of the 1980s and 1990s is captured by coefficients for the effect of growth on the likelihood of transition. Most empirical studies have found that autocratic governments are destabilized by poor economic performance (e.g., Gandhi and Reuter, 2007; Geddes, 2003), though Przeworski et al. (2000) are an exception.

Geopolitical changes

During the Cold War, one superpower or the other provided resources to help many autocrats survive in power. With the Soviet collapse in 1990, the Soviet threat to invade nearby countries that took steps toward democratization ended, and aid to dictatorships from both sides fell. For recipient countries, the drop in aid further reduced the resources available for distribution to the dictator's supporters, compounding the problems caused by the debt crisis and its aftermath.

For countries in the former Soviet sphere of influence, the desire to enter the European Union increased incentives to democratize. Developing countries have been more influenced by international financial institutions (IFIs), which have pressured dictatorships that need their help to adopt democratic political institutions along with neoliberal economic reforms. Many autocrats did follow at least some of the IFIs' prescriptions, though – as with economic reforms – rulers have strong incentives to undermine in practice the reforms they adopt on paper. In response to this pressure, many African autocrats agreed to hold multiparty elections for the first time since achieving office. Some were defeated in those elections, which ushered in democratic governments. Others managed through various means to hang onto power despite multiparty elections and thus avoid transitions.

So far, the effects of these geopolitical changes have been tested only in limited ways. In a sample of hegemonic party regimes, Levitsky and Way (2005) find that since 1990 alliance with the US or Western Europe leads autocrats to adopt democratic-seeming institutions, but not to democratization. Gibson and Hoffman (2007) show that fungible aid, that is, aid that is not earmarked or monitored by donors contributes toward the survival of African dictators. Dunning (2004) shows that foreign aid contributed to democratization in Africa after the end of the Cold War but not before.

Many scholars focused primarily on the domestic causes of regime change have discussed and tried to assess the importance of the international influences and changes described above. The scholars most interested in international influences on transitions, however, have focused on other issues, especially the effects of war, civil war, sanctions, international organizations, and diffusion from neighbors. These topics reflect the core interests of international relations scholars and data availability. Gleditsch and Choung (2004) and Gleditsch and Ward (2006) interpret their finding that having democratic neighbors reduces the coefficient on level of development to insignificance as a challenge to arguments linking development to democracy. Without an explanation of why there are more democratic neighbors in some times and places than others, however, their results add little to explanations of democratization. Other international influence findings do not challenge the predominance of domestic explanations of regime change, though they make the picture more complete.

What has been lacking in most of the efforts to link international causes to regime transition are theoretical arguments about the interaction between international factors and the behavior of domestic political actors. Empirical tests of the effects of international factors have treated domestic politics as a black box that might be shoved this way or that by neighbors, sanctions, or whatever.[13] Instead, domestic political leaders should be modeled as strategic actors who respond to price changes and other international trends that change the costs associated with various choices they can make, as well as to the equally strategic actors in other countries who seek to influence them. The elaboration of such theories, along with tests of them, could potentially transform the study of democratization.

Characteristics of the old regime

If authoritarian regimes with different kinds of leadership tend to have different institutional structures and different relationships with supporters and ordinary citizens, then we would expect them to break down differently because different institutions privilege and disadvantage different groups. A simple and intuitive way to categorize the kinds of autocracy most common since

World War II is as rule by the military as an institution,[14] hegemonic party rule, personalistic dictatorship,[15] and monarchy. Defining regime characteristics emerge from struggles among elite contenders with different backgrounds, support bases, and resources, often after seizures of power. They do not derive in an obvious way from underlying social or political structures, and all have been compatible with a wide range of economic ideologies. These types were common in the late twentieth century while oligarchy was not, which might help to explain why post 1950 democratizations have been different from those that came before.[16]

I have argued elsewhere that these different kinds of autocracy break down in different ways (Geddes, 1999, 2003). To summarize, rule by the military as an institution is more fragile than other forms of authoritarianism because officers' dread of factional strife causes them to prefer returning to the barracks to remaining in power when factionalization threatens to destroy military unity. Consequently, the first moves toward liberalization often arise within the military elite, as noted by O'Donnell and Schmitter (1986). Furthermore, stepping down is relatively costless for intact militaries because they can usually return to their military careers unpunished.

In contrast to the military, several scholars have noted the robustness of hegemonic party regimes (Gandhi and Przeworski, 2006; Geddes, 2003; Magaloni, 2007). Rule by hegemonic party regimes tends to be stable and long-lived because party institutions encompass a broad range of citizens and also create strong incentives for the continued cooperation of both elites and masses.[17] The loss of their monopoly over office is costly to dominant parties but not disastrous, since most of them can transform themselves into successful competitors in democratic systems.

In personalist dictatorships, the autocrat trades private goods for the support of a relatively small group of allies. The loss of resources to distribute to supporters can destabilize such regimes, as can the leader's death, since personalist rulers resist creating institutions that might dilute their personal control. Loss of office, however, can be catastrophic for personalist dictators and their closest allies. Many of them have suffered exile, prosecution for corruption and human rights violations, or assassination (Kaminski et al., 2006), though a few of them have transformed themselves into successful democratic politicians.

Less systematic research has been done on regime change from monarchies. The stability of the authoritarian monarchies that currently exist is often attributed to possession of oil, but in fact not all monarchies export oil, and some that had oil were overthrown decades ago. Herb (1999) shows that monarchies that include the whole extended royal family in decision making and distribution last longer than those in which power is concentrated. His argument thus explains why a number of monarchies were overthrown within a decade or two of independence while others have persisted for a very long time. Lust-Okar and Jamal (2002) argue that monarchs are more likely to take initial steps toward democratization, such as agreeing to multiparty elections, than single-party leaders because their own rule is less threatened by these institutional changes.

These basic characteristics of different kinds of autocracy affect the likelihood of democratization. Poor economic performance more quickly destabilizes military regimes than other forms of autocracy because disagreements over how to respond to economic crisis lead to factionalism and thus back to the barracks (Geddes, 2003). Regime leaders who face relatively low exit costs (i.e., military and dominant-party leaders) are more willing to negotiate transitions than are personalist dictators who risk losing their lives and fortunes if they step down (cf. Bratton and van de Walle, 1997). Democracy is a second-best political outcome for monarchs, military rulers, and dominant-party leaders who face serious challenges to their rule. Military rulers prefer

negotiated democratization to revolution, popular uprising or civil war. Dominant parties prefer democracy, in which they have a good chance of competing successfully, to autocracy that excludes them. Monarchs prefer constitutional monarchy to ouster. Most personalist dictators, however, care little about what kind of regime follows them; if they negotiate their exit, it is usually with foreign leaders who can offer them safe exile.

These differences in willingness to negotiate and second-best choices affect the likelihood that democracy will emerge from authoritarian collapse. Negotiated transitions lead to democracy more often than violent ones. Because they refuse to negotiate or renege on agreements made earlier, personalist dictatorships more often end in revolution, popular uprising, civil war, invasion, or assassination than do other kinds of dictatorship. The new rulers brought to power by these means are less likely to opt for democratic institutions than are those who negotiate transitions.

These observations are consistent with the model of regime change proposed by Bueno de Mesquita et al. (2003). They expect dictators supported by small coalitions to respond to challenges with repression and by further narrowing their support base, as personalist dictators tend to do. When rebellions overthrow dictators, Bueno de Mesquita et al. expect the new regime to become autocratic regardless of earlier promises its leaders may have made to supporters. In contrast, they expect dictators supported by large coalitions to further increase coalition size when challenged. In the real world, we see negotiated transitions from hegemonic to multiparty government. In short, the Bueno de Mesquita et al. (2003) model seems to fit the experience of late twentieth century transitions from personalist and hegemonic party rule, though it fits older transitions and contemporary transitions from military rule less well.

These arguments have a reasonable amount of empirical support, though they have also been challenged. The finding that military regimes are relatively fragile has been confirmed by Smith (2004) and Gasiorworski (1995).[18] Geddes (2003) shows that regimes ruled by dominant parties last substantially longer than other non-monarchic forms of autocracy, though this finding is challenged by Smith (2004).[19] Gandhi and Przeworski (2006) show that dictators supported by single parties survive longer. Bratton and van de Walle (1997) find that dictatorships that allow more political competition, a category that overlaps what I label hegemonic party regimes, are more likely to democratize than those that do not.

Regimes in which power has been personalized under one individual are more likely to be replaced by a new dictatorship than by a democracy (Hadenius and Teorell, 2007). Transitions from personalist dictatorship are seldom initiated by regime insiders; instead, popular opposition, strikes, pressure from IFIs, and demonstrations often force dictators to allow multiparty elections (Bratton and van de Walle, 1997). Personalistic dictators are more likely to be overthrown in revolutions, civil wars, popular uprisings, or invasions (Geddes, 2003; Goodwin and Skocpol, 1989). Linz and Chehabi (1998) have described the difficulties of democratization following what they call sultanistic regimes. Wright (2007) shows that aid contingent on steps toward democratization persuades the leaders of single-party regimes to hold multiparty elections, but that contingent aid has no effect on personalist leaders, as would be expected if personalist dictators have much more to fear from loss of office than do dominant-party rulers.

CONCLUSION

Nearly all arguments about the causes of democratization are contested. No store of knowledge accepted by most analysts has accumulated during the decades of research on the subject. In the discussion above, I suggest that one of the reasons for this continuing disagreement is that democratization occurs through several different processes, depending on basic features of the economy from which the autocracy draws resources, international economic and political pressures that have varied over time, and characteristics of the old regime itself.

A number of the theoretical arguments and empirical findings summarized above fit some of these processes quite well, but do not apply to all democratizations. Of course, no theory ever explains all outcomes, but I argue that there are systematic reasons why these theories explain only some democratizations. Consequently, I suggest that the domains of theories of democratization should be limited to cases that fit their basic assumptions about conditions in the old regime. If a model assumes that the central actors in the struggle over democratization are rulers endowed with private wealth and relatively poor citizens, then the domain of the argument should be defined by old regimes that fit those assumptions. Since many modern autocracies do not, the model should not be expected to explain democratization in them.

Models that emphasize the conflict of interest between rich rulers and poor ruled, such as those proposed by Boix (2003) and Acemoglu and Robinson (2001) are plausible simplifications of reality during pre-World War II transitions from oligarchy to democracy. These transitions occurred in market-oriented economies at a time when international economic and political forces were probably less intrusive than they have since become. In short, these early democratizations fit the implicit assumptions on which these models rely as well as the explicit.

Models that emphasize conflict between revenue-maximizing rulers and their support coalitions (for example, Bueno de Mesquita et al., 2003) capture elements of reality in many recent transitions in developing countries. Their focus on redistribution from the ruled to rulers as a central feature of dictatorship fits well with what we know about many of the autocracies labeled personalistic, sultanistic, or patrimonial by different authors.

Similarly, some of the differences in empirical findings can be explained by differences in samples used. Since democratization processes have tended to vary over time, and types of autocracy have been somewhat regionally concentrated, samples drawn from different time periods or different regions can yield different results.[20]

Nearly all empirical research on democratization has focused on post-1950 experiences because data for earlier periods requires great effort to gather. During the post-war period, no single kind of autocracy was the most common starting point for democratization; state intervention in the economy rose for the first thirty years and then fell rapidly; and international influences not only increased over time but reversed directions. These important influences on democratization have not been included in most large-N studies.

The failure to include them may explain why so few uncontested findings have emerged from this research. The Boix and Stokes (2003) finding that development has a big influence on democratization before 1950 but little after 1950 provides strong evidence that the modal transition process prior to 1950 differed from that after 1950. Scattered empirical evidence suggests that early democratizations may well be explained by the arguments proposed by modernization theorists and the modelers who emphasize the importance of income equality and capital mobility (i.e., Acemoglu and Robinson, 2001; Bates and Lien, 1985; Boix, 2003; Rogowski, 1998). For the post-1950 period, however, empirical findings are either negative or inconclusive. That is, Przeworski et al. (2000) and Boix and Stokes (2003) show little effect of development on democratization, but this finding does not take us very far toward explaining what does cause democratization. Other results remain contested.

If there are theoretically relevant differences among authoritarian governments themselves and in the ways that they interact with their economies, the international context, and the ruled, then progress explaining

democratization will require theoretical arguments and empirical studies that either incorporate these differences or limit what they claim to explain to particular kinds of processes. As Diamond (2002) notes, 'if we are to understand the contemporary dynamics, causes, limits, and possibilities of regime change (including future democratization), we must understand the different, and in some respects new, types of authoritarian rule' (p. 33). If we have fairly well developed theoretical reasons to expect the economy, the international context, and institutional characteristics of the old regime to affect both the likelihood of democratization and how it takes place, then the research frontier for the study of democratization should include: the development of theories of democratization that explicitly identify the contextual domain to which they apply; the development of theories of how particular kinds of contextual and regime characteristics affect democratization; empirical investigations of implications of these models; and the incorporation of more nuanced model specifications to accommodate contextual and regime-type differences into large-N statistical tests.

NOTES

1. Along with several less developed Latin American countries (the Dominican Republic in 1978, Ecuador in 1979, Honduras in 1981, Bolivia in 1982, El Salvador in 1984), to which less attention was paid.

2. Polychotomous measures include multiple discrete categories. I use this term because the most commonly used democracy scales are made up of scores that are not equidistant from each other (as in interval scales) and may not even be ranked ordinally in the middle areas of the scales. See Gleditsch and Ward (2000) for a demonstration.

3. Though serious questions can and have been raised about what the numbers between the end points of the most commonly used scales really mean. One of the issues is that the same scores can be achieved in multiple ways, and it seems reasonable to doubt that one combination of yes answers to questions about political characteristics is equivalent to other combinations that yield the same score.

Another issue is that many users of these scales implicitly assume that every one-unit change in the scores is equal in effect to every other one, which is empirically implausible. Gleditsch and Ward (2000) have shown that nearly all the explanatory power of the Polity scale, the one most commonly used, resides in one component, Executive Constraint. Little explanatory power is added by using the full ten or twenty point scales. This result is what we would expect if the intermediate scores are made up of varying combinations of characteristics, the individual importance of which is unknown.

4. This is Barrington Moore's summary of Marx (1966: 416).

5. Larry Bartels (2005) has christened the real life low-income voter who favors more social spending but who nevertheless opposes the estate tax Homer after the famous Homer Simpson.

6. Boix (2003) challenges this result.

7. But see Bravo (2006) for evidence that the exit of those citizens most dissatisfied with a ruler's policies may increase the probability that he survives in office – thus giving the ruler a reason to provide policies that induce the exit of those citizens most likely to join the opposition.

8. He does not test the effect of sanctions on economic performance and growth is included as a control variable in the test of the effect of sanctions, so it is quite possible that sanctions do affect authoritarian survival through their effect on growth. In democracies, though, sanctions affect leadership survival even with growth controlled for.

9. See, for example, Mainwaring and Pérez-Liñán (2003) for evidence that Latin American democratizations do not fit generalizations made by Przeworski et al. (2000).

10. Bueno de Mesquita et al. (2003) are a partial exception in that they expect the likelihood of democratization to be affected by the size of the winning coalition in the pre-existing authoritarian regime. This is a step in the right direction, though in my view, size is not the most important characteristic of the autocratic support coalition that affects the likelihood of democratization.

11. This logic, in other words, provides a reason for expecting institutional bargains to be more credible than offers to provide desired policies in the absence of institutional change, which the Acemoglu and Robinson (2001) model does not.

12. Milner and Kubota (2005) argue that the causal arrow points in the other direction, that is, that the median voter in new democracies demands economic liberalization, but empirical research on public opinion in these settings does not support this view.

13. Gleditsch and Ward (2006) are a partial exception in that they catalog a number of ways that international forces can influence the relative power and preferences of domestic political actors. They do not test any of these specific arguments, however.

14. As defined by O'Donnell (1973).

15. Hadenius and Teorell (2007) argue that personalism should be seen as a characteristic that varies independently of regime type. They have a point since personalism results from struggles to monopolize power and resources within the ruling elite. See Svolik (2007) for a very insightful model of this struggle between the dictator and ruling elite. Personalist dictatorship, as I use the term here, refers to the set of institutions that are created by the dictator to maintain his dominance as he wins this struggle.

16. Linz and Stepan (1996) offer an alternative though somewhat similar theoretically based classification that might help explain differences in democratization processes. They expect the usual characteristics of the different kinds of autocracy they identify to have systematic effects on different aspects of democratic consolidation, but their expectations have not been tested.

17. For detailed discussions of how this works in practice, see Lust-Okar (2005a, 2005b) and Magaloni (2006, 2007).

18. Gandhi and Przeworski fail to find a relationship between military rule and regime survival because their definition of military rule is different from that used by most others. They code any ruler who ever wore a uniform as a military ruler, regardless of whether the military institution supports or participates in ruling.

19. Hadenius and Teorell (2007) find different survival rates than do most other scholars because their coding rules do not distinguish between what most other analysts would identify as regime changes and smaller institutional changes that occur while a regime, in the usual sense, survives.

20. Mainwaring and Pérez-Liñán (2003) show, for example, that democratization in Latin America differs from the general path shown by Przeworski et al. (2000). Stokes (2004) provides a thoughtful discussion of why regional differences in democratization processes might occur.

REFERENCES

Acemoglu, D. and Robinson, J. (2001) 'A theory of political transitions', *American Economic Review*, 91 (4): 938–63.

Acemoglu, D. and Robinson, J. (2005) *Economic origins of dictatorship and democracy*. New York: Cambridge University Press.

Alvarez, M., Cheibub, J., Limongi, F., and Przeworski, A. (1996) 'Classifying political regimes', *Studies in Comparative International Development*, 31 (2): 3–36.

Anderson, L. (1987) 'The state in the Middle East and North Africa', *Comparative Politics*, 20 (1): 1–18.

Barro, R. (1999) 'Determinants of democracy', *Journal of Political Economy*, 107 (6): S158–S183.

Bartels, L. (2005) 'Homer gets a tax cut: Inequality and public policy in the American mind', *Perspectives on Politics*, 3 (1): 15–31.

Bates, R. (1981) *States and markets in tropical Africa: The political basis of agricultural policy*. Berkeley: University of California Press.

Bates, R. and Lien, D. (1985) 'A note on taxation, development, and representative government', *Politics and Society*, 14 (1): 1–15.

Boix, C. (2003) *Democracy and redistribution*. Cambridge: Cambridge University Press.

Boix, C. and Stokes, S. (2003) 'Endogenous democratization', *World Politics*, 55 (4): 517–49.

Bollen, K. and Jackman, R. (1985) 'Economic and non-economic determinants of political democracy in the 1960s', in R.G. Braungart and M.M. Braungart (eds), *Research in political sociology*. Greenwich, CT: JAI Press. pp. 27–48.

Bratton, M. and van de Walle, N. (1997) *Democratic experiments in Africa: Regime transitions in comparative perspective*. Cambridge: Cambridge University Press.

Bravo, J. (2006) *The Political Economy of Recent Mexico–U.S. Migration: A view into Mexican sub-national politics*. PhD dissertation. Duke University.

Bueno de Mesquita, B. and Siverson, R. (1995) 'War and the survival of political leaders: A comparative study of regime types and political accountability', *American Political Science Review*, 89 (4): 841–55.

Bueno de Mesquita, B., Siverson, R., and Woller, G. (1992) 'War and the fate of regimes: A comparative analysis', *American Political Science Review*, 86 (3): 638–46.

Bueno de Mesquita, B., Smith, A., Siverson, R., and Morrow, J. (2003) *The logic of political survival*. Cambridge, MA: MIT Press.

Burkhart, R. and Lewis–Beck, M. (1994) 'Comparative democracy: The economic development thesis', *American Political Science Review*, 88 (4): 903–10.

Crystal, J. (1995) *Oil and politics in the Gulf: Rulers and merchants in Kuwait and Qatar*. Cambridge: Cambridge University Press.

Diamond, L. (2002) 'Thinking about hybrid regimes', *Journal of Democracy*, 13 (2): 21–35.

Diamond, L., Linz, J. and Lipset, S.M. (edss) (1988) *Democracy in developing countries*. Boulder: Lynne Rienner.

Dunning, T. (2004) 'Conditioning the effect of aid: Cold war politics, donor credibility, and democracy in Africa', *International Organization*, 58 (2): 409–23.

Dunning, T. (2006) 'Does oil promote democracy? Regime change in rentier states', Paper presented to the International Society for New Institutional Economics, Boulder.

Elkins, Z. (2000) 'Gradations of democracy? Empirical tests of alternative conceptualizations', *American Journal of Political Science*, 44 (2): 292–300.

Epstein, D., Bates, R., Goldstone, J., Kristensen, I., and O'Halloran, S. (2006) 'Democratic transitions', *American Journal of Political Science*, 50 (3): 551–69.

Escribà Folch, A. (2003) *Legislatures in authoritarian regimes* (Working Paper 196) Instituto Juan March de Estudios e Investigaciones.

Fish, M.S. (2002) 'Islam and authoritarianism', *World Politics*, 55 (1): 4–37.

Gandhi, J. and Przeworski, A. (2006) 'Cooperation, cooptation, and rebellion under dictatorships', *Economics and Politics*, 18 (1): 1–18.

Gandhi, J. and Reuter, O.J. (2007) *Dictatorial institutions and their impact on economic performance*. Paper presented at the American Political Science Association (APSA), Chicago.

Gasiorowski, M. (1995) 'Economic crisis and political regime change: An event history analysis', *American Political Science Review*, 89 (4): 882–97.

Geddes, B. (1999) 'What do we know about democratization after twenty years?', *Annual Review of Political Science*, 2: 115–44.

Geddes, B. (2003) *Paradigms and sand castles: Theory building and research design in comparative politics*. Ann Arbor: University of Michigan Press.

Gibson, C. and Hoffman, B. (2007) *Can foreign aid help produce democracy? A political concessions model of Africa's transition period*. Unpublished manuscript. UC San Diego.

Gleditsch, K. and Choung, J.L. (2004) *Autocratic transitions and democratization*. Paper presented at the International Studies Association, Montreal.

Gleditsch, K. and Ward, M. (1997) 'Double take: A reexamination of democracy and autocracy in modern polities', *Journal of Conflict Resolution*, 41 (3): 361–83.

Gleditsch, K. and Ward, M. (2000) 'Peace and war in time and space: The role of democratization', *International Studies Quarterly*, 43: 1–29.

Gleditsch, K. and Ward, M. (2006) 'Diffusion and the international context of democratization', *International Organization*, 60 (4): 911–33.

Goodwin, J. and Skocpol, T. (1989) 'Explaining revolutions in the contemporary third world', *Politics and Society*, 17 (4): 489–509.

Hadenius, A. and Teorell, J. (2007) 'Pathways from authoritarianism', *Journal of Democracy*, 18 (1): 143–56.

Haggard, S. and Kaufman, R. (1995) *The political economy of democratic transitions*. Princeton, NJ: Princeton University Press.

Hellman, J. (1998) 'Winner take all: The politics of partial reform in postcommunist transitions', *World Politics*, 50 (2): 203–34.

Herb, M. (1999) *All in the family: Absolutism, revolution, and democracy in the Middle Eastern monarchies*. Albany: SUNY Press.

Herb, M. (2005) 'No representation without taxation? Rents, development and democracy', *Comparative Politics*, 37 (3): 297–317.

Huntington, S. (1991) *The third wave: Democratization in the late twentieth century*. Norman, OK: Oklahoma University Press.

Inkeles, A. and Smith, D.H. (1974) *Becoming modern: Individual change in six developing countries*. Cambridge, MA: Harvard University Press.

Kaminski, M., Nalepa, M., and O'Neill, B. (2006) 'Normative and strategic aspects of transitional justice', *Journal of Conflict Resolution*, 50 (3): 292–302.

Karl, T. (1997) *The paradox of plenty: Oil booms and petro–states*. Berkeley: University of California Press.

Levi, M. (1988) *Of rule and revenue*. Berkeley: University of California Press.

Levitsky, S. and Way, L. (2005) 'International linkage and democratization', *Journal of Democracy*, 16 (3): 20–34.

Lindert, P. (1994) 'The rise of social spending, 1880–1930', *Explorations in Economic History*, 31 (1): 1–37.

Linz, J. and Chehabi, H.E. (eds) (1998) *Sultanistic regimes*. Baltimore: The Johns Hopkins University Press.

Linz, J. and Stepan, A. (1996) *Problems of democratic transition and consolidation: Southern Europe, South America, and Post–Communist Europe*. Baltimore: The Johns Hopkins University Press.

Lipset, S.M. (1959) 'Some social requisites of democracy: Economic development and political legitimacy', *American Political Science Review*, 53 (1): 69–105.

Lust-Okar, E. (2005a) *Structuring conflict in the Arab world: Incumbents, opponents and institutions*. Cambridge: Cambridge University Press.

Lust-Okar, E. (2005b) *Elections under authoritarianism: Preliminary lessons from Jordan*. Paper presented at the APSA. Washington, DC.

Lust-Okar, E. and Jamal, A. (2002) 'Rulers and rules', *Comparative Political Studies*, 35 (3): 337–66.

Magaloni, B. (2006) *Voting for autocracy: The politics of party hegemony and its decline.* Cambridge: Cambridge University Press.

Magaloni, B. (2007) *Elections under autocracy and the strategic game of fraud*. Paper presented at the APSA, Chicago.

Mainwaring, S. and Pérez–Liñán, A. (2003) 'Levels of development and democracy: Latin American exceptionalism, 1945–1996', *Comparative Political Studies*, 36 (9): 1031–67.

Marinov, N. (2005) 'Do economic sanctions destabilize country leaders?', *American Journal of Political Science*, 49 (3): 564–76.

Milner, H. and Kubota, K. (2005) 'Why the move to free trade? Democracy and trade policy in the developing countries', *International Organization*, 59 (4): 107–43.

Moore, B. (1966) *Social origins of dictatorship and democracy: Lord and peasant in the making of the modern world*. Boston: Beacon Press.

Mulligan, C., Gil, R., and Sala-i-Martin, X. (2004) 'Do democracies have different public policies than non-democracies?', *Journal of Economic Perspectives*, 18 (1): 51–74.

North, D. and Weingast, B. (1989) 'Constitutions and commitment: Evolution of the institutions governing public choice in 17th century England', *Journal of Economic History*, 49 (4): 803–32.

O'Donnell, G. (1973) *Modernization and bureaucratic-authoritarianism: Studies in South American politics*. Berkeley: Institute of International Studies.

O'Donnell, G. and Schmitter, P. (1986) *Transitions from authoritarian rule: Tentative conclusions about uncertain democracies*. Baltimore: The Johns Hopkins University Press.

Olson, M. (1993) 'Dictatorship, democracy, and development', *American Political Science Review*, 87 (3): 567–76.

Pevehouse, J. (2002) 'Democracy from the outside-in? International organizations and democratization', *International Organization*, 56 (3): 515–49.

Przeworski, A., Alvarez, M.E., Cheibub, J.-A., and Limongi, F. (2000) *Democracy and development: Political institutions and well–being in the world, 1950–1990*. Princeton, NJ: Princeton University Press.

Roberts, T. (2006) *An international political economy theory of democratic transition*. Unpublished manuscript. UCLA.

Rogowski, R. (1998) 'Democracy, capital, skill, and country size: Effects of asset mobility and regime monopoly on the odds of democratic rule', in P. Drake and M. McCubbins (eds), *The origins of liberty: Political and economic liberalization in the modern world*. Princeton, NJ: Princeton University Press. pp. 48–69.

Ross, M. (2001) 'Does oil hinder democracy?', *World Politics*, 53 (3): 325–61.

Sarkissian, A. (2006) *An unholy alliance? Religion and democratization in Christian and Islamic societies*. PhD dissertation. UCLA.

Smith, B. (2004) 'Oil wealth and regime survival in the developing world', *American Journal of Political Science*, 48 (2): 232–46.

Stokes, S. (2004) *Region, contingency, and democratization*. Paper presented at a Conference on Contingency in the Study of Politics, Yale University.

Svolik, M. (2007) Power-sharing and leadership dynamics in authoritarian regimes. Paper presented at APSA, Chicago.

Tessler, M. (2002) 'Islam and democracy in the Middle East: The impact of religious orientations on attitudes toward democracy in four Arab countries', *Comparative Politics*, 34 (3): 337–54.

Weingast, B. (1997) 'The political foundations of democracy and the rule of law', *American Political Science Review*, 91 (2): 245–63.

Whitehead, L. (1996) 'Three international dimensions of democratization', in L. Whitehead (ed.), *International dimensions of democratization: Europe and the Americas*. Oxford: Oxford University Press.

Wong, S.H. (2007) *Endogenous capital mobility and regime transitions*. Ph.D. dissertation. UCLA.

Wright, J. (2007) *Political regimes and foreign aid: How aid affects growth and democratization*. Ph.D. dissertation. UCLA.

Zak, P. and Feng, Y. (2003) 'A dynamic theory of the transition to democracy', *Journal of Economic Behavior and Organization*, 52 (1): 1–25.

16

Political Culture

Christian Welzel

A stable and effective democratic government … depends upon the orientations that people have to the political process – upon the political culture.

(Almond and Verba, 1963: 498)

INTRODUCTION

This chapter describes the place of the political culture paradigm in comparative politics. It outlines the paradigm's fundamental premises and assumptions and sketches how research in this field has developed. Special emphasis will be placed on where I see the greatest contribution of the political culture approach: understanding the societal fundaments of democracy and how these are transforming in the process of cultural change. In thinking about the driving forces behind democracy, the most basic assumptions of the political culture approach will be juxtaposed to those of the political economy approach. The chapter closes with some thoughts about the future research agenda of the political culture paradigm.

DEFINITION

Going back to Almond and Verba (1963: 13) the term *political culture* is usually understood 'as the particular distribution of patterns of orientation toward political objects among the members of a nation.' Thus, political culture is about the psychological dimension of political systems, including all politically relevant beliefs, values, and attitudes. Depending on what is the reference population one can distinguish elite and mass cultures, local, regional and national cultures, as well as the subcultures of specific groups. Usually one would refer the concept to collective units of which people are aware and have some feeling of belongingness.

To what extent actual political behavior is to be included in the notion of political culture is not always perfectly clear. Insofar, however, as certain patterns of behavior become habitualized, they manifest beliefs in the legitimacy of this behavior. In that sense, political habits can be considered as behavioral manifestations of political culture.

Because individuals are the carriers of political orientations, adherents of the political culture approach gather data from surveying individuals. But the unit of interest in political culture studies is a given population (which can be defined by spatial, organizational or identification boundaries), so individual-level data are aggregated to arrive at descriptions of entire populations. Since these descriptions should be representative of the respective population, the political culture approach has an inbuilt tendency to focus on representative population surveys as its major analytical tool.

THE ROOTS OF THE CONCEPT

The most basic assumption of the political culture paradigm suggests that the orientations, beliefs, and values prevailing among a population constitute a crucial determinant of the type of political system by which a given population is governed. This axiom has been formulated more than 2300 years ago by Aristotle (ca. 350 BC/1984) in Book IV of *The Politics*. In this opus, Aristotle argued that democracies are typically found in middle-class dominated societies in which an egalitarian worldview is predominant among the citizens.

Here we find the classical formulation of a two-step causal process in which (1) the social structures characterizing a given population make certain beliefs predominant among its members; and then (2) these beliefs make specific types of political systems accepted and considered legitimate. Thus, there is a sequence from social structures to subjective beliefs to the legitimacy of political institutions. This sequence provides an early theory to explain the origins of dictatorship and democracy: hierarchical social structures lead to authoritarian beliefs under which dictatorship becomes the legitimate form of government; horizontal social structures lead to egalitarian beliefs under which democracy becomes the legitimate form of

government (Nolan and Lenski, 1999). In a modern version we find this model outlined in more detail in the work of Huntington (1991: 69).

Aristotle's idea that the citizens' beliefs determine the fate of political systems was plausible in the world of the Greek city states. In the history of the Greek *poleis*, the citizenry itself appeared several times as an agent in engineering political institutions, for instance when democracy movements were formed to chase away rulers considered as illegitimate tyrants (Finer, 1999: Book II). But the idea of civic agency became unrealistic in the eras of Roman imperialism and medieval feudalism, falling into oblivion for centuries. A belief in civic agency returned with a vengeance only when the liberal revolutions of early modern times and the first political mass movements brought the people back in, in mobilizing wider parts of the public for political goals. Thus, some 2000 years after Aristotle, Montesquieu et al. (1748/1989) argued in *De L'Esprit des Lois* that whether a nation is constituted as a tyranny, a monarchy or a republic depends on the prevalence of servile, honest, or egalitarian orientations among the people. Likewise, de Tocqueville (1837/1994) reasoned in *De la Démocratie en Amérique* that the flourishing of democracy in the United States reflects the liberal, egalitarian, and participatory orientations among the American people.

In modern times the most flagrant illustration of the fact that people's orientations influence a regime's chances to survive was the failure of democracy in Weimar Germany. Because this failure had such catastrophic consequences as the Holocaust and World War II, it troubled social scientists, psychologists, and public opinion researchers alike. Much of the research inspired by this break in civilization shared the premise that democracy is fragile when it is a 'democracy without democrats' (Bracher, 1971).

In this vein, Lasswell (1951) claimed that democratic regimes emerge and survive where a majority of the people share orientations that are compatible with the operation of democracy. In Lasswell's eyes these orientations are rooted in 'freedom from anxiety' which he saw nurturing a general 'belief in human potentialities,' a sense of 'self-esteem' as well as a sense of 'respect for others.' Similarly, when Lipset (1959: 85–9) reasoned why modernization is conducive to democracy he concluded that this is so because modernization changes mass orientations in ways that make them more compatible with the operation of democracy, by increasing people's appreciation of opposition, criticism, and political pluralism.

Most explicit on this topic, Almond and Verba (1963) and Eckstein (1966) introduced the term 'congruence,' claiming that in order to be stable political institutions must correspond to people's legitimacy beliefs. This is all the more true for democratic institutions, for democracies cannot survive on the basis of suppression (at least not without corrupting their own principles). The congruence theorem has since then been the political culture school's most paradigmatic assumption.

THE QUESTION OF CITIZENS' CIVIC COMPETENCE

Almond and Verba's (1963) *Civic Culture* study is the founding piece of work of the political culture paradigm, especially in its cross-national comparative orientation. Comparing two old democracies (UK, US), two at the time young democracies (Italy, Germany), and a developing nation (Mexico), this study aimed to identify the psychological attributes of a culture that is able to sustain democracy. In identifying these attributes, the authors emphasized two concepts: civic competence and civic allegiance.

Like most scholars of democracy Almond and Verba assumed that democracies put higher demands on the citizens than authoritarian forms of government. For democracy requires voluntary participation in the political process, at least in elections to fill positions of power. Even in a purely representative

type of democracy in which mass participation is limited to elections, citizens must be able to understand the electoral process. They must be capable to evaluate what the parties in power have done and what opposition parties are proposing as alternatives, should they make reasonable choices in an election. If these conditions are not met, the electoral process will be irrational and democracy itself will not make sense. Thus, civic competence is a fundamental precondition for a rational democratic process.

Since then the field has explored the citizens' political competence both in cognitive and perceptive terms. To capture cognitive competence scholars issue survey studies asking people about their political understanding and their political knowledge in an attempt to evaluate an electorate's sophistication, and hence its ripeness for democracy (Zaller, 1992). Inspired by an early study of Converse (1964) emphasizing the inconsistency of most voters' political attitudes, other studies followed, demonstrating a fundamental lack of political knowledge and understanding, even among the electorates of the most advanced democracies (McClosky and Brill, 1983). Quite often it was concluded from such studies that one should not project too high expectations into democracy because in general the democratic process overwhelms most people's cognitive capacities. These conclusions then served as a justification of elite-guided, strictly representative versions of democracy. This position rejected any attempt at extending democracy into a more mass-participative version. Indeed, mass apathy was considered a stabilizing feature of democracy (Crozier et al., 1975; Dye and Ziegler, 1970).

The description of modern mass publics as insufficiently competent has not remained unopposed, of course (Delli Carpini and Keeter, 1996; Lupia and McCubbins, 1998). Invoking the theory of informational shortcuts scholars argue that the demands for voter competence are more modest than the critics of insufficient voter sophistication suggest. Politics is a remote area that ranks low in most people's daily priorities, so people economize the time they invest to obtain the information needed to make reasonable judgments. Instead of studying given policy proposals in all detail, most people pay attention to how the representatives of various social and political groups position themselves to a proposal. From this they draw conclusions on whether or not the proposal is in their own interest, saving the time to study the proposal by themselves. What is important then for people to make reasonable choices is to have easy access to a diversity of views on an issue.

The theory of informational shortcuts shifts the burden of reasonable choice from the expertise of the citizens to the quality of the intermediary system. To be capable to make reasonable choices, the citizens do not have themselves to become political experts. What is needed is political pluralism involving a diversity of group representatives who provide informational shortcuts in identifiable ways (Dalton, 2006: 20–31).

Still another approach opposing the criticism of incompetent citizens refers to the phenomenon of cognitive mobilization in postindustrial societies (Dalton, 2004: 20–31). It is argued that rising levels of education, the expansion of intellectual tasks in the growing knowledge sector, and the increasing exposure to informational diversity, have each contributed to expand people's ability to arrive at independent judgments of given matters. People's factual political knowledge might not have significantly increased in postindustrial societies (Wattenberg, 2006), but their skills to acquire information and to process it have certainly increased through cognitive mobilization, enabling people to make independent judgments.

Civic competence has not only an objective cognition component. It also has a subjective perception component. Subjective political competence has been defined by Almond and Verba (1963: Chapter 8) as people's feeling to understand the political process and the belief that they can participate in meaningful ways, and when they do so, that

it helps to change things to the better. Certainly, citizens can heavily misperceive their political competence. But whether misperceived or not, subjective competence is at any rate a consequential political orientation. For people who feel competent and efficacious about what they can contribute are more likely to participate in politics. They have a stronger sense of agency, which generally motivates action (Verba et al., 1995).[1]

THE ALLEGIANCE MODEL OF DEMOCRATIC CITIZENSHIP

As much as Almond and Verba's (1963) *Civic Culture* study emphasized civic competence, it also emphasized the importance of civic allegiance. In contrast to competence, allegiance is an entirely affective mode of orientation. A minimum of civic competence is thought to be necessary to make the democratic process rational. A basic dose of civic allegiance to the norms, institutions, and actors of democracy is supposed to be necessary to stabilize democracy as a form of government.

The emphasis on allegiance was strongly inspired by Easton's (1965) concept of political support. Easton thought that because modern polities involve the broader masses into politics they need mass support to be stable. This is all the more true for democracies. They allow collective actors to compete for power and this always involves the possibility to vote anti-democratic actors into office, actors who might abandon democracy. To minimize this possibility, mass support for democracy must be so widespread that anti-democratic forces have no real chance to receive sufficient electoral support. In a stable democracy citizen disaffection must be limited to particular policies and specific actors and must not spill over to dissatisfaction with the democratic process and the basic principles of democracy, especially representation. Democracy is designed to digest lacking 'specific' support for concrete policies and actors but it cannot cope with lacking 'diffuse' support for its basic norms, principles, and institutions (Klingemann, 1999).

More recently a new twist has been given to this theme by Anderson and Tverdova's (2003) work on 'losers' consent.' The authors argue that the requirement of preserving diffuse support applies in particular to the supporters of the losing party in an election. Quite naturally, voters of losing parties show less specific support for incumbent governments. It is important, however, that this lack of specific support does not translate into a lack of diffuse support of the democratic process writ large. Accordingly, a democracy is thought to be more stable not only when diffuse support is high on average but also when the *gap* in diffuse support between the winning and the losing camps of the electorate remains small.

At any rate, among scholars concerned with the concept of political support, the ideal democratic citizen is usually seen as a person who participates in elections but is not active outside the institutional channels of representation. This is so because representation is the constitutive principle of modern democracies. To retain legitimacy this principle needs reliable party–voter alignments. This requires voters to be loyal to representatives once these representatives have been voted into office and bestowed with legitimate decision making power. Allegiant democratic citizen do not disobey or oppose decisions made by democratically elected representatives. They accept the leadership role of their representatives and when they are not in line with their policies, they respond by changing their political alignment, giving the vote to another party. The allegiant democratic citizen is supposed to operate strictly within party–voter alignments. They can change their alignment but not operate in a free floating space outside alignments. In the allegiant model, specific support for particular actors and parties is allowed to erode but it must be compensated by re-alignments to new actors and parties, should the principle of representation continue to work (Jennings and van Deth, 1989; Kaase and Newton, 1995).

As a consequence, the allegiance model is in danger when party–voter alignments decrease in general. Three decades of amounting evidence from cross-national survey data seem to suggest that exactly this is about to happen, throughout postindustrial societies (Dalton and Wattenberg, 2000).

PARTY–VOTER DEALIGNMENT

The allegiance model of citizenship came under strain with the emergence of protest politics and new social movements in the late 1960s. Scholars sharing the view that democracy suffers from mass mobilization outside institutionalized channels, saw this development very critically, fearing an overload of government with excessive demands by too highly mobilized publics. It was stated that civic mobilization outside the channels of representative institutions will render governments unable to fulfill inflated demands. This will disappoint the citizens and democratic institutions will fall in disfavor. Thus, a legitimacy crisis and a governability crisis have been predicted as the consequence of increasingly elite-challenging masses (Crozier et al., 1975).

The first comparative empirical study of protest politics came to different conclusions, however (Barnes and Kaase, 1979). Based on surveys among representative samples of the US, Great Britain, Germany, The Netherlands, and other countries the study found that

1. protest participants had higher levels of formal education, better political skills, and felt more efficacious than non-participants;
2. that protest participants emphasized democratic norms more, not less, than non-participants; and
3. that protest participants were in general more engaged and active than non-participants.

Follow-up studies on new social movements in fields of environmental protection, gender equality, human rights, fair trade, and equal opportunities confirmed these findings (McAdam et al., 2001). This line of research helped reshape our understanding of protest behavior and its role in democratic politics.

The predominant view in explanations of elite-challenging mass activities was for a long time influenced by deprivation theories whose object of explanation were in most cases violent mass upheavals (Gurr, 1970). But this is a form of expressing dissent categorically different from the peaceful forms of mass dissent observed in postindustrial societies since the late 1960s. Still, under the impression that some sort of grievance and frustration is motivating protest behavior, the emphasis of revolution theories on deprivation influenced the initial views on the rising protest movements in postindustrial societies. But what is true for the supporters of violent activities – that frustration about social marginalization is a prime motivation – is not true for peaceful forms of dissent in advanced societies. It is not marginalized parts of the population and people most deprived of basic resources that constitute the support basis of elite-challenging activities. Rather it is those who are rich in participatory resources and who have the skills and education enabling them to initiate and join in various campaign activities (Dalton and Kuechler, 1990; Verba et al., 1995).

The transition to postindustrial societies has been linked with rising levels of formal education, more easily accessible information, improved means of communication and mobility, and wider opportunities to connect people across the boundaries of locality, ethnicity, religion, or class. These processes have increased the part of the population possessing the participatory resources that are critical for the campaign activities needed to nurture social movements and mass pressures on elites. As paradoxical as it may seem, societies that are most advanced in providing their populations long, secure, and prosperous lives show the highest rates of protest activity. In other words, people complain the most in societies in which they have the least to complain by means of their objective living conditions. And within these societies it is mostly those being privileged

rather than deprived in resources who organize and express complaints most effectively and vigorously (Welzel et al., 2005).

This is a paradox only if one believes that protest results from misery. In fact, people do not raise their voice when they are the most deprived. People raise their voice when they have the capability to do so and the critical attitude that motivates the expression of dissent. As argued by Inglehart (1990), the transition from industrial to postindustrial societies increases both factors, enabling as well as motivating citizens to put elites under increasingly effective mass pressures.

THE SELF-EXPRESSION MODEL OF DEMOCRATIC CITIZENSHIP

The rise of postindustrial societies nurtures elite-challenging mass activities in two ways. On one hand, it increases the participatory resources that make people capable to initiate and sustain the kinds of activities that put pressure on elites. On the other hand, it nurtures value changes that give rise to the sort of expressive attitude that motivates people to make their voices heard.

This process has first been described in Inglehart's (1977) *Silent Revolution* where he argues that the 'existential security' and 'cognitive mobilization' coming along with postindustrial society nurture post-materialist value priorities. These priorities emphasize people power and freedom of expression.

In his later work Inglehart (1997) embeds rising post-materialist priorities in the wider context of self-expression values, which is a whole syndrome of orientations intertwining five components. As shown in Table 16.1, it comprises

1. *democratic orientations* that aim at giving more power to the people;
2. *liberal orientations* that tolerate diverse and non-conform lifestyle choices, including the practice of homosexuality;

Table 16.1   The concept of self-expression values

DIRECTION of orientation	WVS measurement INSTRUMENT	LOADING on common dimension: aggregate (individual) level	COMMON over-arching orientation
Democratic Orientation (i.e., an emphasis on people power)	Priority on giving people more say in 'government decisions,' 'jobs and communities' and 'freedom of speech'.	0.890 (0.566)	
Liberal Orientation (i.e., tolerance of nonconform lifestyle choices)	Respondent's rating on a 1 to 10 scale indicating the justifiability of 'homosexuality'.	0.841 (0.575)	
Activist Orientation (i.e., inclination to actively voice one's opinion)	Readiness (coded 0.15) or actual participation (coded 1.0) in petitions, demonstrations, and boycotts.	0.837 (0.598)	*EMANCIPATIVE* Orientation ('self-expression values')
Efficacious Orientation (i.e., belief in having control over one's life)	Rating on 1 to 10 scale indicating one's sense of freedom of choice and control in shaping life.	0.596 (0.566)	
Trusting Orientation (i.e., belief in others' trustworthiness)	Belief that 'most people can be trusted' instead of that 'once cannot be too careful enough in dealing with other people.'	0.627 (0.366)	

Data Source: World Values Surveys I–V (1981–2006, www.worldvaluessurvey.org) N (aggregate level) = 237 country-year units, N (individual level) = 320,000 respondents. Loadings on first and only principal component reported.

3. *activist orientations* that make people inclined to make their voices heard in such elite-challenging actions as petitions, boycotts, and demonstrations;
4. *efficacious orientations* that give people the feeling of having control in shaping their lives; and
5. *trusting orientations* that make people believe that others can in general be trusted.[2]

These five orientations show a large overlap, reflecting an overarching emancipative orientation that emphasizes human self-expression. Appreciating and tolerating human self-expression involves a belief in people's positive potential, for which reason generalized trust is part of the syndrome.

As Flanagan and Lee (2003) show self-expression values take shape and grow stronger with the rise of postindustrial societies. This type of society satisfies most people's fundamental survival needs, such that freedom of expression becomes more important to make people satisfied with their lives. Also the growth of material means, intellectual skills, and social opportunities resulting from postindustrial society makes people more capable to

practice basic freedoms. As a consequence, people strive to actualize these capabilities, for self-actualization makes people feel fulfilled, satisfied, and happy (Inglehart and Welzel, 2005: 140–1).

Based on prior work by Welzel (2002), Inglehart and Welzel (2005) theorize in a 'human empowerment framework' the close connection that ties self-expression values to socioeconomic development, on one hand, and effective democracy, on the other hand. In this framework (see Figure 16.1), socio-economic development is thought to empower people on the level of *capabilities*, by widening the means, skills, and opportunities that enable people to pursue self-chosen activities and to practice democratic freedoms. Self-expression values are thought to empower people on the level of *motivations*, by increasing their willingness to pursue self-chosen activities and to practice democratic freedoms. Effective democracy, then, empowers people on the level of *entitlements*, by giving them the rights that allow one to pursue self-chosen activities and practice freedoms.

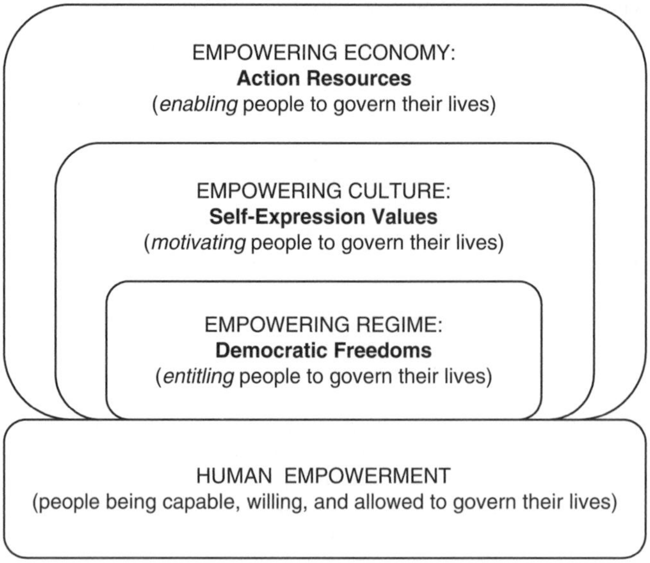

Figure 16.1 The human empowerment framework

The common focus on human empowerment holds these three elements together, such that democracy becomes increasingly effective in response to people's growing willingness to practice freedoms, which in turn arises in response to people's capability to do so.

Rising self-expressive publics emphasize new citizenship norms, as Dalton (2008) notes in the *Good Citizen*. The allegiance model according to which the good citizen is a follower of elected elites does not attract self-expressive citizens. This is the reason why Putnam (2000) observes in *Bowling Alone* a decline in various sorts of civic activities, including participation in elections and voluntary work in a number of formal associations. Most of these activities are linked with the allegiance model of citizenship in which citizens are supposed to function as followers. But this is only one flip side of the coin. The other side is an increase in activities linked to the new, expressive model of citizenship. Citizens are less attracted by those parts of the democratic process that are designed to legitimize elites. They are more attracted to activities in which they express themselves and challenge elites. This is part of the explanation why Norris (2002) in

Democratic Phoenix finds various forms of self-initiated and elite-challenging activities to be on a long-term rise.

The self-expression model of citizenship has various consequences, some of which are outlined below. These consequences are strikingly evident from the temporally and spatially widest exploration into political culture ever, the World Values Surveys (www.worldvaluessurvey.org).

CRITICALITY AND DISAFFECTION

As outlined in Nevitte's (1996) *Decline of Deference* and Norris's (1999) *Critical Citizens*, the value changes proceeding in the wake of the postindustrial transformation of modern societies make people increasingly critical of institutionalized authority over people. Indeed all societies for which survey data are available in considerable time series show a decline of people's confidence in hierarchically structured mass organizations and in institutions that exert authority over people, as Dalton (2004) illustrates in *Democratic Choices – Democratic Challenges*.

This tendency affects representative institutions directly, for the principle of representation is designed to transfer authority from the people to institutions. Accordingly, rates of confidence in parliaments and identification with political parties are on a constant decline (Dalton and Wattenberg, 2000). These tendencies seem to be most pronounced in societies in which self-expression values have grown strong.

EFFICACIOUS AND ELITE-CHALLENGING PUBLICS

At the same time as people tend to become more dissatisfied about politics in representative channels, they are feeling more efficacious about their possibilities to shape their lives by themselves. This rising sense of civic agency seems to be a consequence of the emancipative tendencies coming along with post-industrialization and rising self-expression values. Throughout postindustrial societies, people have come to feel more efficacious, as Figure 16.2 illustrates.

This is important in the context of a society's capacity to initiate and sustain elite-challenging actions, and thus for democratic mass power. It is known from protest mobilization research that dissatisfaction provides an important motivation for the mass actions that challenge elites (Klandermans, 1997). But dissatisfaction is only a necessary and

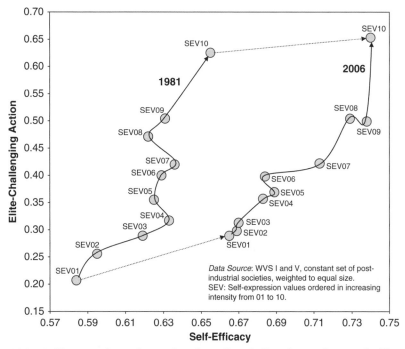

Figure 16.2   Self-expression values related to elite-challenging actions and efficacious orientations

Note: Reduced version of self-expression values measuring the intersection of democratic, liberal, and trusting orientations, as indicated in Table 16.1. Scale is collapsed into an ordinal index with rank 1 representing the weakest and 10 the strongest emphasis on self-expression. *Elite-challenging Activities* measure readiness to participate (coded .10) or actual participation (coded .33) in three elite-challenging actions (petitions, demonstrations, boycotts), yielding a maximum of 1.0. *Self-Efficacy* is the feeling of having control over one's life, transformed into a scale of minimum 0 and maximum 1.0. Countries included at both points in time (weighted to equal sample size): Australia, Canada, Finland, France, Germany (West), Italy, Japan, Netherlands, Spain, Sweden, the UK and the USA.

not a sufficient condition to motivate people to elite-challenging actions. When dissatisfaction goes together with low feelings of agency, it results in resignation and passivity. Only when dissatisfaction goes together with strong feelings of agency do people feel encouraged to actively express their dissatisfaction in public. Hence the combination of rising dissatisfaction with a growing sense of agency is a powerful engine in increasing a public's tendency to initiate and sustain elite-challenging activities.

Both people's sense of agency and their participation in elite-challenging activities are part of self-expression values. As Figure 16.2 illustrates for a group of post-industrial societies, both components have been increasing from 1981 to 2006 and at both points in time they are being stronger along a sequence ordering self-expression values from weak to strong over the other three components of this syndrome.

DEMOCRACY: STRONGER DEMAND, BETTER UNDERSTANDING, MORE ACCURATE ASSESSMENT

With rising self-expression values, the democratic idea that power has to rest among the people resonates stronger in a society. This has three consequences. First, it becomes more important for people to live in a democratic society, so the public demand for democracy is increasing. Second, people's understanding of democracy becomes more liberal: people base their definition of democracy more on the freedoms that empower people and less on strong leadership and popular policy outcomes such as order and prosperity. This becomes obvious from Figure 16.3, mapping self-expression values in a space constituted by people's demands for democracy and the liberalness of their understanding of democracy. With stronger self-expression values people's demand for democracy becomes stronger and their definition of it more liberal.

Third, people's assessment of their society's actual level of democracy becomes more accurate, when one uses the expert democracy ratings of Freedom House as a benchmark. In the new round of the World Values Surveys people are asked to rate their country's level of democracy on a scale from 1 ('not at all democratic') to 10 ('fully democratic'). After having equalized scale polarities and ranges, one can compare people's democracy ratings of their own country with the expert ratings of Freedom House. Doing so it turns out that some people overrate and others underrate their country's level of democracy, these overratings and underratings varying greatly in extent. As is obvious from Figure 16.4, stronger self-expression values make people assess their country's level of democracy more accurately: among people underrating democracy, stronger self-expression diminish the extent of underrating; among people overrating democracy, stronger self-expression values diminish the extent of overrating.

WIDER CIRCLES OF SOLIDARITY

The most surprising result perhaps is that rising self-expression values do not bring greater selfishness, as Flanagan and Lee (2003) assume. On the contrary, the evidence seems to be clear by now that stronger self-expression values widen the circle of others with whom people build up solidarities (Inglehart and Welzel, 2005: 285–98).

Self-expression values are weak when pressing socioeconomic conditions force people into group bonding behavior. Bonding behavior means that people ally with members of their in-group while discriminating members of out-groups (Tajfel, 1970). When more permissive socioeconomic conditions give rise to self-expression values, group boundaries become more variegated, porous, and permeable (Simmel, 1908/1984). This diminishes both the forcefulness of intra-group harmony and the fierceness of inter-group conflict, allowing people to overcome group bonding

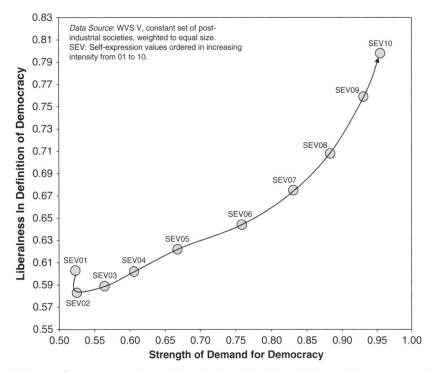

Figure 16.3   Self-expression values related to individual's definition of democracy and their demand for democracy

Note: Self-expression values measure the intersection of democratic, liberal, activist, efficacious, and trusting orientations, as indicated in Table 16.1. Scale is collapsed into an ordinal index with rank 1 indicating the weakest and 10 the strongest emphasis on self-expression. *Strength of Demand for Democracy* relates to a question asking people how important it is for them to live in a democratic society (minimum is 0, maximum is 1.0). *Liberalness in Definition of Democracy* reaches a maximum of 1.0 when respondents rate on 10 ('definitional element of democracy') items referring to free elections, civil rights, referenda votes and gender equality and when they rate at the same time on 1 ('not a definitional element of democracy') items referring to military coups, religious rule, a prosperous economy and a punishing state. Same countries included as in Figure 16.1.

and to engage in group bridging. This process places human solidarity on a different basis. Familiarity, belongingness, and alikeness with others are becoming less important while mutually agreed interests as well as empathy with the situation of others are becoming more important for creating solidarities. Solidarities are becoming more chosen and less enforced.

Evidence supporting these claims is available from the newest round of the World Values Surveys which uses for the first time a value-item battery designed by Schwartz and Ros (1995). This battery allows one to distinguish between collectivist and individualistic values, on one hand, and between selfish and

unselfish values, on the other hand.[3] Related to these distinctions, it is interesting to note that, in postindustrial societies, stronger self-expression values do not only go together with stronger individualistic values (which is not surprising) but also with stronger unselfish values (Deutsch et al., 2008). Apparently, self-expression values merge individualism and altruism into what one might call humanism.

These findings seem paradoxical if one equates individualism with selfishness, which is indeed a widespread misconception. Scholars often think of collectivism as the basis of human solidarity and of individualism as its destructor (Triandis, 1995). In fact,

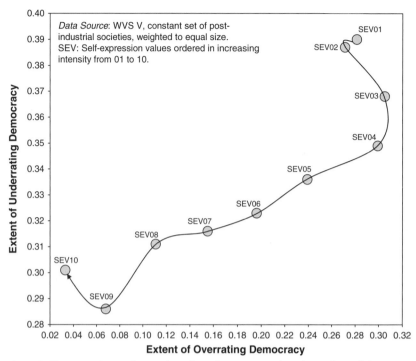

Figure 16.4 Self-expression values related to the over- and underrating of democracy

Note: Self-expression values measured as indicated in the note of Figure 16.2. Citizens have been asked to rate their country's level of democracy. Citizens' ratings of their country's democracy levels are related to the expert ratings of Freedom House (after having standardized both ratings into the same scale range), such that (a) when a citizen's rating exceeds the expert rating the *Extent of Overrating* has been measured and (b) when the citizen's rating falls short of the expert rating the *Extent of Underrating* has been measured. Same countries included as in Figures 16.2 and 16.3.

however, individualism does not destroy solidarity but places it on a different basis. This was recognized early on by sociologists Durkheim (1893/1988) and Tönnies (1887/1955). They described the individualization trend of modernity as bringing a transition from 'mechanical' solidarity to 'organic' solidarity, or from 'community' to 'association.' Both descriptions refer to a transition from externally imposed to internally chosen forms of solidarity. Beck (2002) describes the solidarity effects of individualization in similar terms, speaking of a transition from 'communities of necessity' to 'elective affinities.' Empirical research of interpersonal networks supports the view that modern individualized societies integrate people into more widespread and more diverse solidarity networks (Wellman and Frank, 2001).

Collectivism means that people see others not as autonomous individuals but as group-members in the first place (Triandis, 1995). When group categorization dominates people's views of others, people almost automatically start privileging members of their own group and discriminating members of other groups (Tajfel, 1970). Collectivism in this sense is a form of group-egoism that hinders the creation of solidarities across group boundaries. Individualism, by contrast, means that one does not consider others as members of groups but as autonomous individuals in the first place. This mode of orientation provides a common ground – human individuality – on which one can place all people equally. This is why individualism and altruism go together with stronger self-expression values (Deutsch et al., 2008).

SELF-EXPRESSION VALUES AS A DEMOCRATIZING MOTIVATIONAL FORCE

If one looks at entire societies' aggregate levels of self-expression values, these values appear to be a first-rate indicator of a society's quality of life. On one hand, this is obvious from these values very close association with any indicator of socioeconomic development, as demonstrated by Inglehart and Welzel (2005: 150). As these authors argue, this relationship exists because more comfortable socioeconomic conditions on a mass level tend to give rise to self-expression values.

An equally strong relationship exists between self-expression values and indicators of the quality of a society's institutions. Measures of democracy and of 'good governance,' including rule of law, absence of corruption, and accountable governance, all correlate strongly positively with mass self-expression values (Inglehart and Welzel, 2005: 151). Here the causal relationship seems to operate in a different direction. Self-expression values are not growing stronger because more democratic and accountable governance nurture these values. Instead, it is stronger self-expression values that motivate elite-challenging mass actions, and these mass actions help to remove authoritarian elites from power and to make democratic elites behave in a more responsive manner (Welzel, 2007: 417–8). Thus, mass self-expression values constitute a decisive motivational force in bringing about democracy where it not yet exists and in strengthening it where it is already in place.

IMPLICIT REGIME DISPOSITIONS AND EXPLICIT REGIME PREFERENCES

Self-expression values resemble the attributes that Lasswell (1951) described as a 'democratic character,' which is composed of a 'sense of security,' a 'belief in human potentials,' 'self-esteem,' and 'respecting others.' The assembly of democratic, liberal, efficacious, activist, and trusting orientations that constitute self-expression values comes indeed close to Lasswell's democratic character.

What gives self-expression values an inherently democratic thrust is the fact that they place authority into the people themselves. This implies a rejection of uncontrolled and unlimited authority over people, making authoritarian systems appear illegitimate. Because of these implications, self-expression values constitute an inherently pro-democratic regime predisposition. The civil and political freedoms defining democracy intuitively resonate with these values.

Because they are anchored in people's values, regime dispositions have strong motivational power, even though these predispositions are only implicit. Regime preferences, by contrast, are explicit but their motivational effects are unsure. In surveys, people express a preference for democracy for many reasons (Bratton and Mattes, 2001; Mishler and Rose, 2001; Bratton et al., 2005; Shin and Wells, 2005). It might be that they feel attracted by the fashionableness of the term or that social desirability guides their responses or that they prefer democracy simply because they associate other desirable things, such as prosperity, peace, and low corruption, with it (Inglehart, 2003). In none of these cases is the motivation to prefer democracy based on an inner valuation of the civil and political freedoms defining democracy. Hence, it is unlikely that these preferences motivate people strongly to struggle for democratic freedoms, be it to defend them when they are challenged or to attain them when they are denied. When, however, people have an inner valuation for freedom, which they do when they emphasize self-expression, then there is a strong motivation to struggle for democratic freedoms. In this case the emergence of effective mass pressures in support of these freedoms is more likely.

Accordingly, Inglehart and Welzel (2005) find that predispositions for democracy implied in self-expression values provide a stronger force in sustaining and attaining democracy than do explicit preferences for democracy.

Self-expression values motivate people to initiate and sustain elite-challenging actions that put effective pressure on power holders, even if the political system is undemocratic and confronts people with the risk of suppression (Welzel, 2007).

From the perspective of this research, the mainstream in political culture research has been too obsessed with measuring explicit regime preferences, rather than implicit regime dispositions based on given values. This is a legacy of the *Civic Culture* study. In this study, Almond and Verba (1963: 10) explicitly dissociated themselves from Lasswell's measures of attitudinal predispositions for democracy because they could not see anything specifically political in orientations such as freedom from anxiety, self-esteem, and openness to other people. What is true is that orientations such as these provide no direct measure of regime preferences. Yet, they constitute predispositions with strong motivational implications because these predispositions are anchored in people's values. When a self-expressive worldview arises, it is hardly imaginable how this view can be compatible with political systems exerting uncontrolled and unlimited authority over people. If this worldview emerges, the legitimacy of authoritarianism erodes and the democratic idea of power to the people resonates more strongly among the masses.

TRUST, CONFIDENCE, AND SOCIAL CAPITAL

Putnam's (1993) *Making Democracy Work* gave the political culture approach greater attention in comparative politics. In stark contrast to neo-institutional approaches, this study seemed to demonstrate that differences in the design of institutions can be ignored and that to explain a community's political performance civic traditions account for most of the differences. This study brought an emphasis on civic orientations back in.

In contrast to scholars who insist that the definition of social capital has to be limited to social networks, Putnam's understanding of social capital emphasizes psychological orientations that facilitate human interaction. The orientation supposed to be most effective in this respect is social trust (Gibson, 2001). Trust is understood to overcome collective action dilemmas, for people who trust others do not see themselves playing in prisoner's dilemma games when interacting with people (Uslaner, 2001). Hence, social trust shapes the collective action capacity of a society. It enables the masses to initiate and sustain the actions that put elites under popular pressure and make them responsive.

Social trust certainly increases a society's collective action capacity. But it does not tell us for which ends this capacity will be used because purely by itself trust is not directed toward a particular end, such as democratic freedoms. This is often overlooked in theories of trust or implicitly it is assumed that people anyways strive for liberty and democracy, so the only thing that matters in making this strive effective is social trust. Research in the context of the World Values Surveys, however, shows that trust matters mostly as a component within the broader syndrome of self-expression values. In other words, trust matters for democracy in connection with democratic, liberal, activist, and efficacious orientations that let people strive for democratic freedoms. In isolation from orientations that give trust a direction, it does not show a strongly pro-democratic effect, neither in helping to attain democracy nor to sustain it (Welzel, 2007: 405).

Another aspect of trust that has been considered important for democracy is political trust, usually measured as confidence in a set of basic societal institutions, including the national parliament, the civil service and the like (Newton, 2001). Inspired by the allegiance model of democratic citizenship scholars still think that in order to flourish, democracy needs people who have trust in basic institutions. However, evidence that a society's democratic performance depends on how much political trust its citizens express is non-existent. To the contrary,

Welzel (2007: 405) finds that higher political trust affects a society's democratic performance negatively, even controlling for a society's democratic tradition and various other factors.

When social capital is understood to include orientations that motivate people to initiate and sustain collective actions, self-expression values should certainly be included into the notion of social capital. For these values do motivate people to collective actions, especially the elite-challenging actions that have been found to help bringing about and strengthening democracy. In that sense, self-expression values constitute a particularly pro-democratic form of social capital.

ON THE COHERENCE OF SELF-EXPRESSION VALUES

The concept of self-expression values has been criticized on two accounts. On one hand, it has been shown that the democratic, liberal, activist, efficacious, and trusting tendencies representing this concept do not cluster into a coherent syndrome at the individual level within populations. The claim that trusting, liberal, efficacious, democratic, and activist orientations merge into a robust generic attitude, called self-expression values, has thus been disqualified as a fallacious inference, drawn from ecological correlations (Muller and Seligson, 1994; Seligson, 2002).

More substantively it has been argued that when these attitudes do not strongly correlate at the individual level within populations, this means that the high scorers in these attitudes fall into different social circles with only a small overlap between them (Teorell and Hadenius, 2006). Thus, the social circle of people that can be mobilized on the basis of a consistent set of self-expression values remains always small. This questions the theoretical status of self-expression values as a motivational basis on which to mobilize wider parts of a public for elite-challenging actions.

As Welzel et al. (2003) outline, this criticism overlooks an important point: the five components constituting self-expression values show weak individual-level correlations only if one looks at each country separately, ignoring the massive between-country differences in these components. As soon, however, as one merges the data from various countries into a pooled dataset, the syndrome of self-expression values appears to be as consistent at the individual level as at the aggregate level. What does this mean?

For instance, Swedes who are more activist in their orientations than the Swedish average are not necessarily more trusting than the Swedish average. More generally, the correlation between trusting and activist orientations (or any other pair of self-expressive orientations) tends to be weak when country-specific averages are taken as the reference line. But this is the wrong reference line when most variation is between persons from different countries, not between persons from the same country. Many Swedes might be above the Swedish average in one self-expressive attitude and below the Swedish average in another self-expressive attitude, which makes these attitudes appear inconsistent. However, on a global scale Swedish averages are exceptionally high in all five self-expressive attitudes, so Swedes who are less expressive according to Swedish standards are still very expressive on the global standard. Under the global standard, the five self-expressive attitudes are highly consistent. They do not constitute different social circles.

Another point of criticism that has been raised is that the concept of self-expression values is not theoretically deduced but instead has been discovered inductively by means of factor analyses (Haller, 2002). It appears then that self-expression is just a label tagged on a bewildering assembly of different attitudes, not each of which is actually a measure of values.

However serious one takes this criticism, it does not do away with the finding that human populations tend to score consistently high or low in all five components of self-expression values. This finding is so robust that it must have some meaning. Hence, one should try to make sense of it rather than ignoring it simply because it has not been theoretically deduced. The fact that a finding has not been fully anticipated by a ready-made theory does not make it less important.

It is true that the five components of self-expression values cover a diversity of domains, from efficacy to activity to trust. But the point is that these components cluster into a coherent syndrome *despite* this diversity. The diversity of domains just underlines that self-expression values constitute a pervasive phenomenon that radiates into many spheres. To be sure, not each component is by itself a direct and perfect indication of the generic syndrome of self-expression values. Participating in elite-challenging actions, for example, is not a value. It is not even an attitude but a behavior. But the fact that each component is related to all others implies that none of the components can just be taken by itself. It has to be seen in connection with the other components, which changes the interpretation. Merely by itself, partaking in elite-challenging actions is not necessarily an indication of a self-expressive orientation. But insofar as it is linked with democratic, liberal, efficacious, and trusting attitudes it certainly is a reflection of a self-expressive orientation, or at least a behavioral manifestation of it.

It makes sense to consider participation in elite-challenging actions as a valid indication of self-expression values, insofar as such participation overlaps with the other components of self-expression values. The way in which these values are measured extracts exactly that overlap. At any rate, self-expression values seem to be a real, meaningful, and consequential syndrome of orientations.

POLITICAL ECONOMY AND POLITICAL CULTURE

Both political economy approaches and political culture approaches claim to have identified the reasons why modernization works in favor of democracy. These claims are in direct contradiction to each other. From the point of view of political economists Acemoglu and Robinson (2006), modernization operates in favor of democracy because it makes the idea of democracy more acceptable in the eyes of elites. From the viewpoint of political culturalists Inglehart and Welzel (2005), modernization operates in favor of democracy because it confronts elites with masses that are more capable and willing to struggle for democratic freedoms and to practice them.

These opposing views reflect different understandings of democracy and its driving forces. In political economy it is thought that the driving force behind democracy is a redistributive interest of the impoverished masses in universal suffrage. It is argued that the masses always profit from universal suffrage because it enables them to impose redistributive policies, so the masses always prefer democracy. The privileged elites, by contrast, fear it for exactly the same reason. Authoritarian regimes thus do not survive because majorities would not prefer democracy: Majorities prefer democracies anyways. Instead, authoritarian regimes survive because elites are capable to repress dissenting majorities. Consequently, the only way how democracy can be established is to make elites accept it so that they concede it to the masses. This is where political economists see the impact of modernization. If it proceeds, it tends to equalize the income distribution to an extent that makes democracy appear less threatening to the elites because if the median income comes closer to them, it becomes unlikely that majorities can be rallied around extensive redistributive policies. If this moment comes elites will start to see the costs of repressing the masses' desire for democracy as more costly than the option to concede democracy.

From a political culture perspective various doubts can be cast on these assumptions. To begin with, most authoritarian regimes did not survive because of an impressive capacity to suppress dissenting majorities but because they never had been confronted with dissenting majorities, reflecting the fact that throughout most of pre-modern history the wider masses had neither the capacities nor the will to express and organize political dissent (Gat, 2006: 570–661; Nolan and Lenski, 1999: 233–55). The major effect of modernization is not that it makes democracy more acceptable in the eyes of the elites but, instead, that it confronts elites with increasingly efficacious and ambitious masses. When the masses are becoming capable and willing to struggle for democratic freedoms, the elites are left with little choice in the matter. It is also not true that the masses always invariantly prefer democracy. Quite the contrary, how strongly the people aspire for democracy depends heavily on their values: The desire for democracy is the stronger, the more people value human freedom and self-expression. Where these values are weak, people emphasize authority and strong leadership instead. This might not prevent people from expressing a preference for democracy, yet these preferences are groundless as they are inconsistent with people's deep-seated values.

While in the eyes of political economists the driving force behind democracy is a redistributive interest of the impoverished masses in universal suffrage, from the political culture point of view it is an emancipative striving for freedom by increasingly capable and ambitious masses. It is up to future research to clarify in how far these opposing views are reconcilable.

THE RESEARCH AGENDA

It belongs perhaps to the more important discoveries of the political culture paradigm that there is a coherent syndrome of democratic, liberal, activist, efficacious, and trusting orientations, called self-expression values, that takes shape and grows stronger with the rise of postindustrial societies and which is linked with a comprehensive array of major societal transformations, from increasingly equal opportunities for women and other previously under-privileged groups to the strengthening of democracy.

What seems to be clear then is that the syndrome of self-expression values is of major importance. What is not exactly clear, though, is how these values translate into behavior. The precise micro-level mechanism of how self-expression values create certain forms of elite-challenging activities is unobserved so far and it is also not known how these activities aggregate into the mass-level patterns that have been shown to work so strongly in favor of democracy. Future research should work on these research gaps. An obvious way to do this is to connect the survey method with experimental methods targeted at actual behavior, something that is done far too little so far in the empirical social sciences.

NOTES

1. Scholars distinguish 'internal' and 'external' efficacy but there are two versions of this distinction. One version defines internal efficacy as the feeling of being capable to shape one's own life and external efficacy as the feeling of being capable to shape one's environment. The other version defines internal efficacy as the feeling that one's own participation in a collective activity is a significant contribution to this activity's success, whereas external efficacy is the feeling that authorities are responsive to one's participation. Wherever the dividing line between internal and external efficacy is drawn, both tend to go closely together as they have a common ground in reflecting people's sense of human agency.

2. In a factor analysis these five orientations load on the one and only principal component, representing a common underlying dimension, labeled self-expression values or emancipative values. To measure this dimension each orientation is standardized into a similar scale range and then an average is calculated over all five orientations (in such a way that each orientation is weighted for its loading on the common dimension).

3. Schwartz (1992) himself uses other labels: collectivist versus individualistic values are conservative versus openness to change values in

Schwartz's language. And selfish versus unselfish values are self-enhancement versus self-transcendence values in his terminology.

REFERENCES

Acemoglu, D. and Robinson, J.A. (2006) *Economic origins of dictatorship and democracy*. New York: Cambridge University Press.

Almond, G.A. and Verba, S. (1963) *The civic culture: Political attitudes in five Western democracies*. Princeton, NJ: Princeton University Press.

Anderson, C.J. and Tverdova, Y.V. (2003) 'Corruption, political allegiances, and attitudes towards government in contemporary democracies', *American Journal of Political Science*, 47: 91–109.

Aristotle (1984) *The politics* (C. Lord, Trans. and Intro.) Chicago: Chicago University Press.

Barnes, S.H. and Kaase, M. (1979) *Political action: Mass participation in five Western democracies*. Beverly Hills: Sage.

Beck, U. (2002) 'Losing the traditional: Individualization and "precarious freedoms"', in U. Beck and E. Beck-Gernsheim (eds), *Individualization*. London: Sage, pp. 1–21.

Bracher, K.D. (1971) 'Problems of parliamentary democracy in Europe', in H. Hirsch and M.D. Hancock (eds), *Comparative legislative systems: A reader in theory and research*. New York: The Free Press.

Bratton, M. and Mattes, R. (2001) 'Support for democracy in Africa: Intrinsic or instrumental?', *British Journal of Political Science*, 31: 447–74.

Bratton, M., Mattes, R. and Gymiah-Boadi, E. (2005) *Public opinion, democracy, and market reform in Africa*. New York: Cambridge University Press.

Converse, P. (1964) 'The nature of belief systems in mass politics', in D. Apter (ed.), *Ideology and discontent*. New York: Free Press.

Crozier, M., Huntington, S.H. and Watanuki, J. (1975) *The crisis of democracy*. New York: New York University Press.

Dalton, R.J. (2004) *Democratic challenges, democratic choices*. Oxford: Oxford University Press.

Dalton, R.J. (2006) *Citizen politics*. Washington, DC: CQ Press.

Dalton, R.J. (2008) *The good citizen*. Washington, DC: CQ Press.

Dalton, R.J. and Kuechler, M. (1990) *Challenging the political order*. Oxford: Oxford University Press.

Dalton, R.J. and Wattenberg, M. (2000) *Parties without partisans*. Oxford: Oxford University Press.

Delli Carpini, M.X. and Keeter, S. (1996) *What Americans know about politics and why it matters*. New Haven: Yale University Press.

Deutsch, F., Grzechnik, E., Held, M., Mueller, J. and Welzel, C. (2008) 'On the dimensionality of human values', *World Values Surveys Paper Series*, 1 (1): http://www.worldvaluessurvey.org/

de Tocqueville, A. (1837/1994) *Democracy in America*. New York: Knopf.

Durkheim, É. (1988) *Über soziale arbeitsteilung* [On social division of labor]. Frankfurt a. M., Germany: Suhrkamp. (Original work published 1893)

Dye, T. and Ziegler, H. (1970) *The irony of democracy*. Belmont: Duxbury.

Easton, D. (1965) *A system's analysis of political life*. New York: Wiley.

Eckstein, H. (1966) *A theory of stable democracy*. Princeton, NJ: Princeton University Press.

Finer, S. (1999) *The History of Government I. Ancient Monarchies and Empires*, Oxford: Oxford University Press.

Flanagan, S. and Lee, A.-R. (2003) 'The new politics, culture wars, and the authoritarian-libertarian value change in advanced industrial societies', *Comparative Political Studies*, 36 (3): 235–70.

Gat, A. (2006) *War in human civilization*. New York: Oxford University Press.

Gibson, J.L. (2001) 'Social Networks, civil society, and the prospects for consolidating Russia's democratic transition', *American Journal of Political Science*, 45: 51–69.

Gurr, T.R. (1970) *Why men rebel*. Princeton, NJ: Princeton University Press.

Haller, M. (2002) 'Theory and method in the comparative study of values: critique and alternative to Inglehart', *European Sociological Review*, 18: 139–58.

Huntington, S.P. (1991) *The third wave*. Norman: University of Oklahoma Press.

Inglehart, R. (1977) *The silent revolution*. Princeton, NJ: Princeton University Press.

Inglehart, R. (1990) *Culture shift in advanced industrial societies*. Princeton, NJ: Princeton University Press.

Inglehart, R. (1997) *Modernization and post-modernization*. Princeton, NJ: Princeton University Press.

Inglehart, R. (2003) 'How solid is mass support for democracy – and how do we measure it?', *PS Political Science and Politics*, 36: 51–7.

Inglehart, R. and Welzel, C. (2005) *Modernization, cultural change, and democracy*. New York: Cambridge University Press.

Jennings, M.K. and van Deth, J. (eds) (1989) *Continuities in political action*. Berlin: deGruyter.

Kaase, M. and Newton, K. (eds) (1995) *Beliefs in government* (Vols. 1–4) Oxford: Oxford University Press.

Klandermans, B. (1997) *The social psychology of protest*. Oxford: Blackwell Publishers.

Klingemann, H.-D. (1999) 'Mapping political support in the 1990s: A global analysis', in P. Norris (ed.), *Critical citizens: Global support for democratic governance*. New York: Oxford University Press, pp. 31–56.

Lasswell, H.D. (1951) *Democratic character*. Glencoe: The Free Press.

Lipset, S.M. (1959) 'Some social requisites of democracy: Economic development and political legitimacy', *American Political Science Review*, 53: 69–105.

Lupia, A. and McCubbins, M. (1998) *The democratic dilemma*. New York: Cambridge University Press.

McAdam, D., Tarrow, S. and Tilly, C. (2001) *Dynamics of contention*. New York: Cambridge University Press.

McClosky, H. and Brill, A. (1983) *Dimensions of tolerance*. New York: Russell Sage.

Mishler, W. and Rose, R. (2001) 'Political support for incomplete democracies: Realist vs. idealist theories and measures', *International Political Science Review*, 22: 303–20.

Montesquieu, C.d.S., Cohler, A.M., Miller, B.C., and Stone, H. (1748/1989) *The spirit of the laws*. Cambridge: Cambridge University Press.

Muller, E.N. and Seligson, M.A. (1994) 'Civic culture and democracy: The question of causal relationships', *American Political Science Review*, 88: 635–52.

Nevitte, N. (1996) *The decline of deference*. Ontario: Broadview Press.

Newton, K. (2001) 'Trust, social capital, civil society, and democracy', *International Political Science Review*, 22: 201–14.

Nolan, P. and Lenski, G. (1999) *Human societies*. New York: McGraw-Hill.

Norris, P. (1999) *Critical citizens*. Oxford: Oxford University Press.

Norris, P. (2002) *Democratic phoenix*. Cambridge: Cambridge University Press.

Putnam, R.D. (1993) *Making democracy work*. Princeton, NJ: Princeton University Press.

Putnam, R.D. (2000) *Bowling alone*. New York: Simon & Schuster.

Schwartz, S.H. and Ros, M. (1995) 'Values in the West: A theoretical and empirical challenge to the individualism–collectivism cultural dimension. *World Psychology*, 1 (2): 91–122.

Seligson, M. (2002) 'The renaissance of political culture or the renaissance of the ecological fallacy', *Comparative Politics*, 34 (April): 273–92.

Shin, D.C. and Wells, J. (2005) 'Is democracy the only game in town?', *Journal of Democracy*, 16 (2): 88–101.

Simmel, G. (1984) *Das individuum und die freiheit* [The individual and freedom]. Berlin: Duncker and Humblodt. (Original work published 1908).

Tajfel, H. (1970) 'Experiments in intergroup discrimination', *Scientific American*, 223: 96–102.

Teorell, J. and Hadenius, A. (2006) 'Democracy without democratic values', *Studies in Comparative International Development*, 41 (3): 95–111.

Tönnies, F. (1955) *Community and association*. London: Routledge and Kegan Paul. (Original work published 1887).

Triandis, H.C. (1995) *Individualism and collectivism*. Boulder, CO: West View Press.

Uslaner, E. (2001) 'Producing and consuming trust', *Political Science Quarterly*, 115: 569–90.

Verba, S., Schlozman, K.L., and Brady, H.E. (1995) *Voice and equality*. Cambridge: Harvard University Press.

Wattenberg, M. (2006) *Is voting for the young?* London: Longman.

Wellman, B. and Frank, K. (2001) 'Network capital in a multi-level world', in N. Lin, K. Cook, and R. Burt (eds), *Social capital*. Chicago: Aldine DeGruyter.

Welzel, C. (2002) *Fluchtpunkt humanentwicklung* (Focal point human development) Opladen, Germany: Westdeutscher Verlag.

Welzel, C. (2007) 'Are levels of democracy influenced by mass attitudes?', *International Political Science Review*, 28 (4): 397–424.

Welzel, C., Inglehart, R., and Deutsch, F. (2005) 'Social capital, voluntary associations, and collective action: Which aspects of social capital have the greatest civic payoff?', *Journal of Civil Society*, 1 (2): 121–46.

Welzel, C., Inglehart, R. and Klingemann, H.-D. (2003) 'The theory of human development: A cross-cultural analysis', *European Journal of Political Research*, 42: 341–80.

Zaller, J. (1992) *The nature and origin of mass opinion*. New York: Cambridge University Press.

17

Revolution

Jack A. Goldstone

INTRODUCTION

Revolutions are rapid changes in the institutions of government, carried out by non-institutional means, and usually with the support of popular groups mobilized for demonstrations, local revolts, guerilla warfare, civil war, mass strikes, or other revolutionary actions. Until the 1960s, revolutions were viewed as major turning points in history, ending traditional systems of government and ushering in modern political organization. However, the proliferation of revolutionary movements and of rapid shifts in governments throughout the twentieth century has led to a more open and ambiguous view. Revolutions – even 'great social revolutions' such as the French Revolution of 1789 and the Russian Revolution of 1917 – are now seen as bringing a mixture of change and continuity.

Revolutions include many different kinds of social change, including anti-colonial independence revolts, anti-dictatorial revolutions, and anti-communist revolutions. These brought political and social changes of varying degrees, some of which were lasting and some of which were not. Revolutions are still considered to mark major, sudden, discontinuities in political organization within states. Yet they also need to be seen as part of long-term processes of social and political change, rather than as self-contained episodes of permanent transformation.

WHAT EVENTS ARE CONSIDERED REVOLUTIONS?

Definitions of revolution

For most of the twentieth century, studies of revolution focused on explaining the causes and outcomes of a handful of great revolutions in Europe and Asia, including the British Revolution (1640), the American Revolution (1776), the French Revolution (1789), the Russian Revolution (1917), and the Chinese Communist Revolution (1949). In the 1970s and 1980s, the dominant approach to explaining these revolutions was structural analysis, rooted in Marxist historical perspectives in which the action of capitalist competition on class and state structures produced class-based conflicts that transformed society. Skocpol's (1979: 4) definition of social revolutions, which stressed class conflicts – 'rapid, basic transformations of a society's state and class structures; accompanied and in part carried through by class-based revolts from below' – was taken as standard.

Skocpol's work led what I have called the 'third generation' of theories of revolution (Goldstone, 1980). Those theories, developed by Skocpol and other scholars including Moore (1966), Paige (1975), and Eisenstadt (1978) attributed revolutions to a conjunction of multiple conflicts involving states, elites, and the lower classes, exacerbated by international economic and military pressures. This was a major improvement on simple descriptive generalizations, such as those of Brinton (1938), or of analyses that rested on such broad single factors as modernization (Huntington, 1968) or relative deprivation (Davies, 1962; Gurr, 1970).

From the 1970s through the 1990s, however, the world saw a host of revolutions that challenged the class-based understanding of revolutions. In Iran and Nicaragua in 1979 and in the Philippines in 1986, multi-class coalitions toppled dictators who had long enjoyed strong support from the world's leading superpower, the United States (Farhi, 1990; Parsa, 2000). In Eastern Europe and the Soviet Union in 1989–1991, socialist and totalitarian societies that were supposed to be impervious to class conflict collapsed amid popular demonstrations and mass strikes (Banac, 1992; Beissinger, 1998; Oberschall, 1994a; Stokes, 1993). The Iranian Revolution and the Afghan Revolution of 1979 proudly proclaimed themselves as religious struggles, not based primarily on class issues (Arjomand, 1988; Moaddel, 1993; Moghadam, 1989). And the host of anticolonial and antidictatorial revolutions in the Third World, ranging from Angola to Zaire, became so numerous and affected so many people that the parochial practice of defining revolutions in terms of a few cases in European history plus China became untenable (Foran, 2003, 2005; Zartmann, 1995). In addition, whereas the great revolutions had all led fairly directly to populist dictatorship and civil wars, a number of the more recent revolutions – including that of the Philippines, the revolutionary struggle in South Africa, and several of the anticommunist revolutions of the Soviet Union and Eastern Europe – seemed to offer

a new model in which the revolutionary collapse of the old regime led either to relatively nonviolent transitions to democracy or to cyclic movements between unstable democracy and moderate authoritarianism (Bunce and Wolchik, 2006; Diamond and Plattner, 1993; Hale, 2005).

In response to these events, theories of revolution evolved in three directions. First, researchers sought to modify the structural theory of revolution to suit an increasingly diverse set of cases. These included studies of guerrilla wars and popular mobilization in Latin America (Eckstein, 1989b; McClintock, 1998; Wickham-Crowley, 1991, 1992; Wood, 2000); studies of anticolonial and antidictatorial revolutions in developing nations (Dunn, 1989; Foran, 2005; Goldstone et al., 1991; Goodwin, 2001; Kim, 1991); studies of revolutions and rebellions in Eurasia from 1500 to 1850 (Goldstone, 1991; Tilly, 1993); studies of the Islamic revolution against the Shah in Iran (Keddie, 1995; McDaniel, 1991; Moaddel, 1993; Parsa, 1989; Skocpol, 1982); and studies of the collapse of communism in the Soviet Union and Eastern Europe (Beissinger, 2002; Chirot, 1991; Fenger, 2007; Goldstone, 1998a).

Second, scholars called for greater attention to conscious agency, to the role of ideology and culture in shaping revolutionary mobilization and objectives, and to contingency in the course and outcome of revolutions (Eisenstadt, 1992, 2006; Emirbayer and Goodwin, 1996, Foran, 1997a, 2005; Goodwin, 1994a, 1997; Kimmel, 1990; Parsa, 2000; Rule, 1988, 1989; Selbin, 1993, 1997; Sewell, 1985).

Third, analysts of both revolutions and social movements realized that many of the processes underlying revolutions – for example, mass mobilization, ideological conflicts, confrontation with authorities – have been well studied in the analysis of social movements. Indeed, some of the more extensive and radical social movements that involved major changes to the distribution of power, such as the international movement for women's rights, the labor movement, and the

US civil rights movement, were revolutionary in the risks taken by activists and the institutional restructurings produced by their efforts. Thus, a new literature on 'contentious politics' has developed that attempts to combine insights from the literature on social movements and revolutions to better understand both phenomena (Aminzade et al., 2001; Goldstone, 1998b; McAdam et al., 2001; Tarrow, 1998).

The class-based conception of revolutions advanced by Skocpol, therefore, no longer seems adequate. A huge range of events now claim our attention as examples of revolution, ranging from the fascist, Nazi, and communist transformations of nations in the first part of the twentieth century to the collapses of communist regimes at its end; from the idealistic revolutions of America and France at the end of the eighteenth century to the chaotic revolutionary wars in Africa at the end of the twentieth. Two major surveys of revolution (Goldstone, 1998c; Tilly, 1993) list literally hundreds of events as revolutionary in character. Nonetheless, these events still have a common set of elements at their core: (a) efforts to change the political regime that draw on a competing vision (or visions) of a just order, (b) a notable degree of informal or formal mass mobilization, and (c) efforts to force change through non-institutionalized actions such as mass demonstrations, protests, strikes, or violence.

These elements can be combined to provide a broader and more contemporary definition of revolution: an effort to transform the political institutions and the justifications for political authority in a society, accompanied by formal or informal mass mobilization and non-institutionalized actions that undermine existing authorities or seek to change prior political, social, or economic relationships. This definition is broad enough to encompass events ranging from the relatively peaceful revolutions that overthrew communist regimes to the violent Islamic revolution in Afghanistan. At the same time, this definition is strong enough to exclude coups, revolts, civil wars, and rebellions that make no effort to transform institutions or the justification for authority. It also excludes peaceful transitions to democracy through institutional arrangements such as plebiscites and free elections, as occurred in Chile under Pinochet or in Spain after Franco.

Types of revolutions

Revolutions are distinguished sometimes by outcomes, sometimes by actors. Other typologies distinguish revolutions according to how they unfold, or the goals they seek.

Revolutions that transform economic and social structures as well as political institutions, such as the French Revolution of 1789, are called great revolutions; those that change only state institutions are called political revolutions. Revolutions that involve autonomous lower-class revolts are labeled social revolutions (Skocpol, 1979), whereas sweeping reforms carried out by elites who directly control mass mobilization are sometimes called elite revolutions or revolutions from above (Trimberger, 1978). Revolutions that fail to secure power after temporary victories or large-scale mobilization are often called failed or abortive revolutions (Foran, 2005); oppositional movements that either do not aim to take power (such as peasant or worker protests) or focus on a particular region or subpopulation are usually called rebellions (if violent) or protests (if predominantly peaceful).

Revolutions do not always feature the same set of key actors, nor do they all unfold in the same way. Popular mobilization may be primarily urban (as in Iran and Eastern Europe), feature extensive peasant revolts (Wolf, 1969), or involve organized guerrilla war. Huntington (1968) pointed out that major revolutions show at least two distinct patterns of mobilization and development. If military and most civilian elites initially are actively supportive of the government, popular mobilization must take place from a secure, often remote, base. In the course of a guerrilla or civil war in which revolutionary leaders gradually extend their control of the countryside, they need to build popular support while waiting for the regime to be weakened by events – such as military defeats, affronts to national pride and identity, or its own ill-directed repression or acts of corruption – that cost it domestic elite and foreign support. Eventually, if the regime suffers elite or military defections, the revolutionary movement can advance or begin urban insurrections and seize the national capital. Revolutions of this type, which we may call peripheral revolutions, occurred in Cuba, Vietnam, Nicaragua, Zaire, Afghanistan, and Mozambique.

In contrast, revolutions may start with the dramatic collapse of the regime at the center (Huntington, 1968). If domestic elites are seeking to reform or replace the regime, they may encourage or tolerate large popular demonstrations in the capital and other cities, and then withdraw their support from the government, leading to a sudden collapse of the old regime's authority. In such cases, although the revolutionaries take power quickly, they then need to spread their revolution to the rest of the country, often through a reign of terror or civil war against new regional and national rivals or remnants of the old regime. Revolutions of this type, which we may call central revolutions, occurred in France, Russia, Iran, the Philippines, and Indonesia.

Recent events suggest yet a third pattern of revolution, a general collapse of the government, as occurred in the totalitarian states of Eastern Europe and the Soviet Union. In these countries, the state socialist regimes maintained firm control of rural and urban society through the party apparatus. When a combination of elite-led reform efforts, changing international alignments (the economic advance of capitalist countries, the Soviet Union's peace talks with the United States, and Hungary's open borders allowing mass German emigration), and popular strikes and demonstrations undermined the resolve of communist leaders, the entire national state apparatus rapidly degenerated (Hough, 1997; Karklins, 1994; Lane and Ross, 1999). Although there were

sometimes major confrontations in the capital cities (as in Moscow, Prague, and Bucharest), the critical popular actions in several cases were taken by workers far from the capital – such as coal miners in the Soviet Union and Yugoslavia and shipyard workers in Gdansk in Poland – or by urban protestors in other cities, such as Leipzig in East Germany. There was thus no need for the revolutionary leaders taking power in the capital to spread their revolution by force throughout the country; the very breadth of the prior totalitarian regimes ensured that when they collapsed there were few or no competing power centers, except for the centrifugal forces lurking in autonomous and ethnically distinctive provincial governments (Bunce, 1999). The main problem facing the new post-socialist regimes was not spreading the revolution but rather building new national institutions that could cope with the emergent private, criminal, and bureaucratic entrepreneurs rushing to fill the vacuum of power (McFaul, 2005; Stark and Bruszt, 1998).

Another typology rests on the guiding ideology of revolutionary movements. It distinguishes liberal or constitutional revolutions, which dominated the eighteenth and nineteenth centuries and seem to be reappearing with the revolutions in the Philippines and Eastern Europe (Parker, 2000; Sohrabi, 1995); communist revolutions, which became prominent in the twentieth century; and Islamic revolutions, which appeared in the last quarter of the twentieth century.

Modern studies of revolution thus embrace a wide variety of events. This essay examines what we know (or think we know) about the causes, processes, and outcomes of revolutions.

CAUSES OF REVOLUTIONS

The international system

Skocpol (1979) was crucial in pointing out the effects that international military and economic competition can have on domestic political stability. The costs of war or economic shifts can undermine elite and popular support for a government and put state finances in disarray. Yet this only begins to suggest how international influences can shape revolutions.

Ideological influences can spread across state boundaries, with both the example and the content of revolutionary movements in one nation influencing others (Colburn, 1994; Fenger, 2007; Halliday, 1999; Katz, 1997). Revolutionary texts often carry revolutionary messages across borders, and revolutionary heroes in one country can inspire similar efforts elsewhere.

Direct military and diplomatic intervention by other countries can also shape revolutions, although often not as the interveners might have wished. Intervention by the Soviet Union could not defeat the Islamic Afghan Revolution, and interventions by the United States not only failed to prevent, but probably helped radicalize, the revolutions in Cuba, Nicaragua, Vietnam, and Iran by supporting the prerevolutionary regimes (Halliday, 1999; Snyder, 1999; Wickham-Crowley, 1992). On the other hand, US intervention did head off attempted revolutions in El Salvador and Guatemala, and Soviet support did encourage Marxist revolutions around the globe (Foran, 2005).

In some cases, it is the absence of intervention or the withdrawal (or threatened withdrawal) of ongoing support for a regime that allows a revolutionary movement to grow. Goldfrank (1979) and other scholars (Goodwin and Skopol, 1989; Wickham-Crowley, 1992) have labeled this a permissive or favorable world context. US preoccupation with World War I helped create an interval for Mexican revolutionary movements to spread; the exhaustion of European states and the defeat of Japan provided openings for multiple anticolonial revolutions after World War II; US concern for global human rights under President Carter spread the perception that support of the Shah of Iran and the Somoza regime in Nicaragua

was diminishing; and the reduction of cold war tensions between the United States and the Soviet Union under Gorbachev provided an opening for dissidents, workers, and urban protestors to test the resolve of communist regimes.

Given the many ways in which revolutions can influence, or be influenced by, international trends and events, it is not surprising that revolutions are rarely isolated, but generally cluster in waves of similar events. One can point to several such waves of revolutions in history, including the Atlantic revolutions of the United States (1776), Holland (1787), and France (1789), propelled by antimonarchical sentiment; the European Revolutions of 1830 and 1848, propelled by liberalism; and the anticolonial revolutions of the 1950s through 1970s, propelled by nationalism. Other waves include the communist revolutions of 1945–1979 in Eastern Europe, China, Cuba, Vietnam, and other developing countries; the Arab nationalist revolutions in the Middle East and North Africa in 1952–1969; the Islamic revolutions in Iran, Sudan, and Afghanistan in the 1970s and 1980s; and the anticommunist revolutions in the Soviet Union and Eastern Europe in 1989–1991. In each of these waves, international influences powerfully shaped the onset and outcomes of the revolutionary movements (Johnson, 1993; Katz, 1997).

Relationships among states, elites, and popular groups

International pressures can create challenges for states, or in the extreme case of total military defeat destroy a state's power. Yet it is the reaction of state officials, military forces, elites, and popular groups to such pressures that determine whether or not the result is a revolution, rather than merely state reform or conservative reconstruction.

Skocpol (1979) specified two structural conditions that, when combined with military and economic pressures from the international system, make a state vulnerable to social revolution: autonomous elites able to hamper state actions and organized peasant communities capable of autonomous resistance to landlord rule. However, her analysis underestimated the role of urban workers, as in the Russian Revolution of 1917 (Bonnell, 1983); her scheme thus misses the overwhelming impact of urban protests by workers and students in shaping such events as the Iranian Revolution, the Nicaraguan Revolution, the Philippines Revolution and the Great Cultural Revolution and Tiananmen revolts in China (Calhoun, 1994b; Farhi, 1990; Parsa, 2000; Perry and Li, 1997; Wasserstrom and Perry, 1994). In addition, her treatment of ideologies simply as elite blueprints for political change leads her to overlook the key role that ideologies play in popular mobilization by shaping perceptions of state weakness and injustice and forging a sense of identity among revolutionary actors. Although these omissions indicate the weakness of Skocpol's structuralist approach, the richness of her overall analysis has spurred a deeper understanding of how shifting state/elite/popular relationships lead to state breakdown and upheavals.

The key issues in the relationships among states, elites, and popular groups that govern political stability are (a) whether states have the financial and cultural resources to carry out the tasks they set for themselves and are expected to carry out by elites and popular groups; (b) whether elites are largely united or deeply divided and polarized; and (c) whether elites opposing the state spur mass mobilization and link up with protests by popular groups.

The tasks that rulers set for themselves vary enormously from state to state. Large states may have imperial ambitions, whereas small states may seek merely to survive in peace. Personalist rulers need to maintain flexible resources to support extensive patronage; democratic states need to manage party competition while still maintaining an effective bureaucratic and judicial government. Almost all states are also expected to uphold national pride and traditions; modern states are also

expected to promote economic growth (Goodwin and Skocpol, 1989; Tilly, 1993).

States have a wide range of resources on which to draw to meet these goals and expectations. Domestic revenues in the form of taxation and exploitation of natural resources may be complemented by revenues from foreign aid and direct foreign investment. Funds may be borrowed and resources sold or mortgaged against future expectations of increased tax or other revenues. Some governments may also gain revenue from nationalized enterprises – although these often fail to yield projected profits.

Trouble arises when revenues no longer meet state expenses, whether because of an enlargement of state goals or a reduction in income. The ways in which trouble can arise are so many as to defy brief listing. Overambitious military and/or development adventures can strain state finances; so can a failure to adjust revenues to keep pace with inflation and growing national populations. Overestimates of future revenues can lead to reckless borrowing; corruption can drain funds away from useful purposes and leave state coffers bare. Small but growing deficits can gradually eat away at state fiscal strength; military debacles or deadlocks with elites over fiscal matters can precipitate loss of fiscal control and either runaway inflation or sudden state bankruptcies. In some cases, price shifts in key commodities in the economy can adversely affect economic growth and state revenues. Symptoms of fiscal illness can thus range from a slow depletion of state credit to ballooning debts to rapid price inflation to military incapacity to unanticipated shortfalls and bankruptcies.

Still, state rulers can usually cope with adversity if elites will contribute their efforts and resources to state reorganization. The threat of revolution appears when fiscal weakness arises while elites are reluctant to support the regime or are severely divided over whether and how to do so (Higley and Burton, 2006).

Such reluctance may reflect the financial difficulties of elites themselves. Elites who are struggling to maintain their wealth, or who see themselves being arbitrarily or unfairly fleeced by their rulers, will not readily support a weak and needy regime. Elites may also be alienated by exclusion from power or by assaults on their privileges or control of elite positions. But just as often elite (and popular) allegiance is lost through squandering or neglect of cultural resources.

State rulers operate within a cultural framework involving religious beliefs, nationalist aspirations, and notions of justice and status. Rulers violate these at their peril. Rulers who sell offices or appoint favorites to high positions may win their loyalty but incur the resentment of those left out. Rulers who seek to overturn traditional religious and cultural habits had better be sure of strong military and bureaucratic support to withstand the popular and elite protests that will ensue (Oberschall and Kim, 1996). Rulers who appear too dependent on the whims of foreign powers may also lose the faith and support of their own peoples.

The joint need to manage state tasks and cultural standing can be summed up in two words: effectiveness and justice. States and rulers that are perceived as ineffective may still gain elite support for reform and restructuring if they are perceived as just. States that are considered unjust may be tolerated as long as they are perceived to be effective in pursuing economic or nationalist goals, or just too effective to challenge. However, states that appear both ineffective and unjust will forfeit the elite and popular support they need to survive.

Three social changes or conditions, though neither necessary nor sufficient to bring about revolution, nevertheless so commonly undermine both effectiveness and justice that they deserve special mention. First is defeat in war – or even overextension, when a state attempts military tasks beyond its fiscal and logistic capacity. Particularly galling is the waste of lives and resources for a losing cause. Bueno de Mesquita et al. (1992) found a weak association between war and ensuing revolution but found this relationship much stronger among countries that initiated wars and then lost them. It is this combination that produces the greatest joint loss of both effectiveness and cultural standing for the state.

Second, sustained population growth in excess of economic growth frequently alters the relationships among states, elites, and popular groups in ways that undermine stability. If increased demand produces inflation, real revenues to the government will fall unless taxes are raised; but that may be seen as highly unreasonable if peasants have less land and workers are finding jobs scarce and their pay declining due to increased competition for jobs and resources. Youth cohorts will rapidly grow larger, creating problems of the demand for jobs growing faster than the population as a whole. Urban population may increase disproportionately – and faster than urban administrations can increase housing, health, and police services – if the agricultural sector cannot absorb the population increase. Moreover, as the price of land or other scarce resources rises, those elites or aspiring elites who control those resources will benefit disproportionately to other elite groups, upsetting the normal processes of elite recruitment and social mobility. If the state demands higher taxes while popular living conditions are declining, and if elite patterns of hierarchy and mobility are being upset while the state is demanding more resources or more authority, then perceptions of both effectiveness and justice may be severely damaged. Although some states may find the means, through economic growth or making favorable elite alliances, to cope with rapid population increase, it is not surprising that rebellions and revolutions have been exceptionally widespread during periods when population has grown exceptionally fast – for example, in the late sixteenth and early seventeenth century, the late eighteenth and early nineteenth century, and in parts of the developing world in the twentieth century (Goldstone, 1991, 2002a).

Third, colonial regimes and personalist dictatorships are particularly prone to the dual faults that lead to revolution (Goodwin, 2001).

Colonial regimes, by their nature, are an affront to the nationalist aspirations and power aspirations of native elites. While effective, they may be able to co-opt local elites; however, should the balance of power shift between the colonial regime and the domestic elites with their potential popular support, colonial regimes will degenerate into revolutionary confrontations. Similarly, personalist dictatorships, because they exclude all but a tiny proportion of the elites from sharing in the fruits of power, have far less justice in the eyes of elites than more broadly based authoritarian regimes, such as military juntas, or regimes with a clear ethnic, regional, or class base. Personalist regimes may support themselves by claiming to offer exceptional nationalist achievements or by being ruthless and effective in managing domestic affairs. However, economic reverses, loss of foreign support, or loss of nationalist credentials through corruption or excessive subordination to foreign powers can fatally undermine their effectiveness and spur a multi-class coalition against their narrow base (Dix, 1983; Foran, 1997b; Goldstone, 2003; Goodwin, 1994b; Goodwin and Skocpol, 1989; Snyder, 1998; Wickham-Crowley, 1992).

Of course, even if elites are divided and sharply opposed to the state, the result may merely be coups d'état (Jenkins and Kposowa, 1990) or reforms. In order for a revolutionary situation to develop, there must also be mass mobilization. This may be traditional, informal, elite-directed, or some combination of these types.

Traditional mobilization occurs within the context of local communities to which individuals have long-standing commitments, such as peasant villages or urban craft guilds (Magagna, 1991). Usually triggered by some news of political change, such as plans for state reforms, elections, or news or even rumors of war or local attacks [as Markoff (1996) has shown in the case of the French Revolution of 1789], much peasant mobilization is defensive, even reactionary, aimed at calling attention to economic distress or high levels of taxation. Direct attacks on landlords are less common and are usually prompted by news that the state's authority has been challenged or broken down. Traditional mobilization may also take place in cities through traditional workers' guilds, or through religious communities, and it too is often defensive and conservative in intent (Calhoun, 1983).

Informal mobilization occurs when individuals' decisions to engage in protest actions are made not through communal organizations to which they have long-standing formal ties but instead through loosely connected networks based on personal friendship, shared workplace, or neighborhood. Such informal organization generally occurs in response to a crisis; neighborhoods or friends then mobilize themselves to take unconventional actions. Gould (1995) demonstrated the role of neighborhood ties in popular mobilization during the French commune of 1870; Opp et al. (1995) and Pfaff (1996) have shown that informal organization lay behind the spontaneous Leipzig protests that brought down the East German communist regime; Denoeux (1993) detailed the role played by informal networks in urban protest in the Middle East. Proximity and friendships among students helped mobilize protest in the Tiananmen revolt in China (Zhao, 2001) and in the revolutions of 1979 in Iran and of 1986 in the Philippines (Parsa, 2000).

Traditional and informal organization are not inherently revolutionary in themselves and usually lead only to abortive rural rebellions and urban protest. They become effective in creating revolutionary change when they link up with elite opposition to the regime. In some cases, as in the rural revolts of the French and Russian Revolutions and the Irish revolts of 1640, their impact is to frighten authorities into taking radical steps, shattering efforts by elites to move slowly or wrangle indefinitely. In other cases, dissident elites place themselves at the head of popular revolts, linking up varied local movements and giving them direction and coherence, as the Bolsheviks did with workers' revolts in 1917, or as the radical clerical leader Ayatollah Khomeini did with protests based in the mosques, universities, and bazaars of Iran.

A third way for elites to link up with popular mobilization is to create and direct the organizations through which mobilization takes place. Although it would be too much to say that the Communist Party fully controlled rural revolt in China in the 1940s, the Chinese Communist Party nonetheless played a key role in organizing peasants to redistribute land, curb landlord influence, and undertake armed struggle against the Nationalist regime (Friedman et al., 1991; Selden, 1995). In Latin America in the 1970s, most effectively in Nicaragua, priests established Christian base communities to mobilize opposition to the existing economic and political regimes (Levine and Manwaring, 1989; Van Vugt, 1991). At the same time, radical students and politicians, following the model of Fidel Castro in Cuba, sought to mobilize Latin American peasantries through communist guerrilla movements (Wickham-Crowley, 1992). In the 1980s, church leaders in Poland, the Philippines, and East Germany played a critical role in creating formal and informal linkages between workers, intellectuals, and professionals in opposition to the regime (Osa, 2003; Parsa, 2000; Stokes, 1993).

Given this enormous range of modes of popular organization, there is no easy way to predict the form or direction that popular mobilization will take simply from structural factors. Although there is a substantial literature on peasants in revolutions (Migdal, 1974; Paige, 1975; Popkin, 1979; Scott, 1976; Skocpol, 1994; Wickham-Crowley, 1991; Wolf, 1969), and an ongoing debate about the degree to which inequality leads to revolutionary unrest (Lichbach, 1989; Macculloch, 2005; Midlarsky, 1986; 1999; Muller, 1985; Muller and Seligson, 1987; Weede, 1987), none of these literatures has produced consensus. As Zamosc (1989) argues, it appears that peasants are not inherently conservative or revolutionary; rather, their aspirations take different forms depending on

the state and elite responses and alliances they encounter. The single constant that one can derive from experience is that successful revolutions occur only where there is some linkage or coalition between popular mobilization and elite anti-regime movements (Dix, 1983; Eckstein, 1989a; Farhi, 1990; Foran, 1997b; Goldstone et al., 1991; Goodwin and Skocpol, 1989; Liu, 1988; Wickham-Crowley, 1992).

PROCESSES OF REVOLUTIONS: NETWORKS, IDEOLOGY, LEADERSHIP, AND GENDER

Networks, organizations, and identities

The varied and contingent patterns of revolutionary mobilization have led scholars to place far more emphasis on the processes by which revolutions develop. Structural conditions may set the stage for conflict, but the shape and outcome of that struggle is often determined only in the course of the revolutionary conflict itself. How do elites link up with popular movements of protest? How do individuals come together to act collectively, often in the face of great risk of repression or even death? How are diverse groups with distinct interests brought together to form wide-ranging coalitions? And how do particular leaders and groups emerge to dominate and set the course of a revolution? These questions can only be addressed by attention to the organizational and ideological elements of revolutionary action.

One key finding is that revolutionary actors do not act, or even think of themselves as acting, alone. They are recruited through pre-existing networks of residence, occupation, community, and friendship. They are set in motion by organizations that range from small and informal bands of activists, such as the Charter 77 group in the Czechoslovak Revolution, to the highly disciplined, centralized, and bureaucratic revolutionary parties of China and the Soviet Union. They identify themselves with broader causes and groups and make sacrifices in their name (Calhoun, 1994a; Cohen, 1985; Somers and Gibson, 1994). This is even true of revolutionary terrorists and suicide bombers (Pape, 2006; Sageman, 2004).

Identities, however, are not inherent – particularly protest identities (Abrams and Hogg, 1990). In order to create and maintain identities relevant to revolutionary action, elites and states must produce and cement novel identifications for people who normally just think of themselves as workers or peasants, friends or neighbors. Making certain identities more salient, indeed creating protest identities – that is, a sense of being part of a group with shared and justified grievances, with the ability to remedy those grievances by collective action – is a considerable project (Snow and Benford, 1988; Snow et al., 1986).

For many years, resource mobilization theorists argued that mobilizing people for collective action revolved around building organizations, such as unions, revolutionary parties, and grass-roots movement organizations such as the National Organization for Women or the Southern Christian Leadership Conference (McCarthy and Zald, 1977; Tilly, 1978). Such social movement organizations were held to be at the heart of sustained collective actions. However, recent studies of recruitment and of the experience of movement participants has shown that formal organization is neither necessary nor sufficient to create the sense of commitment and energy needed for risky collective action to occur (Calhoun, 1994b; Gould, 1995; McAdam, 1988; Pfaff, 1996). Instead, the formation of protest identities seems to be critical. Although formal organizations can often help choose tactics for protest and sustain a movement through reverses and lean times, informal organization – as shown in the 1989–1991 revolutions in Eastern Europe – can also bring people together for large-scale, risky, and effective challenges to state authority.

In recent years, much attention has focused on the construction of terrorist networks (Sageman, 2004, 2007). Here too, it is evident that loose and informal networks can function effectively as alternatives or complements to more formal organizations. Moreover, it is striking that the international jihadist movement has flourished in large part by recruiting individuals and groups drawn to specific nationalist liberation struggles, and infusing them with an identity focused on a global revolutionary movement of Islamism against Western powers as well as local regimes (Goldstone, 2002b).

Protest identities – feelings of attachment and affection for a protest group – appear to have three sources. First, the group helps to justify and validate the individual's grievances and anger against the status quo. Second, the group – if it provides concrete benefits or takes actions that seem effective in defending its members and pursuing change – gives a sense of empowerment, autonomy, and efficacy to its members, earning their affective allegiance (Knoke, 1988; Lawler, 1992). Third, the state itself may create or reinforce a sense of oppositional identity by labeling a group as its enemies or by acting against the group, thus demonstrating that the group is now outside the protection and justice of the state. Members then are forced to look to the group for justice and protection (Oberschall and Seidman, 2005). The protest group, in other words, gains commitment through giving followers their own sense of justice and effectiveness.

Indeed, it is precisely because the protest group fulfils these functions in ways that the state has failed to do, or in a way deemed superior to that of the state, that individuals are willing to transfer their allegiance from the state to the protest or revolutionary group (Finkel et al., 1989). In some cases, the revolutionary movement literally becomes the state in the areas under its control, as did the Communist Party in the 1940s in rural China and many guerrilla movements in Latin America, taking over functions of law enforcement, justice, and even taxation

(McClintock, 1998; Selden, 1995; Wickham-Crowley, 1991). In other cases, the revolutionary movement gains allegiance by validating the grievances and aspirations of its members through solidarity rituals and by taking actions against the state that may be largely symbolic (Melucci, 1989).

The darkest side of protest identity appears when revolutionary movements see themselves as surrounded by enemies, and treat opponents to their rule or outsiders to their group as targets to be eliminated. In such cases, revolutionary movements can lead not only to terror and civil war, but to ethnic cleansing and genocide, as in Cambodia, Rwanda, and the former Yugoslavia (Harff, 1991, 1995).

The creation and maintenance of protest identities is a substantial task that depends on cultural frameworks, ideologies, and powerful leadership.

Ideology and cultural frameworks

The perception that the state is ineffective and unjust whereas revolutionary movements of opposition are virtuous and efficacious is rarely a direct outcome of structural conditions (Gamson, 1988; Gamson and Meyer, 1996). Material deprivations and threats need to be seen not merely as miserable conditions but as a direct result of the injustice and the moral and political failings of the state, in sharp contrast to the virtue and justice of the opposition (Martin et al., 1990). Even defeat in war, famine, or fiscal collapse may be seen as natural or unavoidable catastrophes rather than as the handiwork of incompetent or morally bankrupt regimes. Similarly, acts of state repression against protesters may be seen as necessary peacekeeping or conversely as unjustified repression; kidnappings, arson, and bombings may be painted as reprehensible and cowardly terrorist acts or as patriotic measures for liberation of the oppressed. Which interpretation prevails depends on the ability of states and revolutionary leaders to manipulate perceptions by relating their actions and current conditions to existing cultural frameworks and to carefully constructed ideologies (Berejikian, 1992; Chong, 1991; DeNardo, 1985).

Analysts of revolution use the term cultural frameworks or discourses to denote the long-standing background assumptions, values, myths, stories, and symbols that are widespread and actively recounted in the population (Foran, 2005). Naturally, the frameworks of elites and popular groups may differ, and those of different regional, ethnic, and occupational groups may vary. Thus, we find a set of roughly overlapping frameworks rather than a homogenous set of beliefs. Ideologies, in contrast, are consciously constructed, perhaps eclectic but more coherent beliefs, arguments, and value judgments that are promulgated by those advocating a particular course of action. In the early twentieth century, Christianity, German patriotism, and a belief in the virtues of the Frankish tribes and pioneers who conquered the forests of central Europe were part of the cultural framework of Germany; Nazism in contrast was an ideology (Skocpol, 1994).

As this example shows, those ideologies that are most effective are those that strike roots in prevailing cultural frameworks, appropriating older stories and images and retooling them to resonate with the issues of the present day (Nash, 1989; Shin, 1996). The Chinese Communists initially linked their justification for ruling China to restoring the patriarchal order of the traditional Chinese family, which had been undone by the economic chaos and military defeats suffered under the Nationalist regime (Stacey, 1983). Similarly, Communist organizers in Vietnam had no success until they incorporated ethnic Vietnamese content and cultural themes into their appeals (Popkin, 1988).

Foran (2005) has argued that revolution is impossible without drawing on a 'culture of rebellion' from widely remembered prior conflicts. For example, the 1970s Sandinista revolt in Nicaragua drew its name and its claim to virtue from the peasant leader

Sandino, who fought against US domination of Nicaragua at the beginning of the century. Similarly, the Zapatista rebellion in Chiapas, Mexico in the 1980s drew its name and identified its ideals with the peasant leader Zapata of the Mexican Revolution of 1910. However, these examples do not imply that only countries that have actively recalled rebellions in their recent past have the cultural foundation for later uprisings. Revolutionary entrepreneurs have proved quite nimble at appropriating cultural foundations for revolt from the distant past, or even the imagined past or future. Millennial beliefs dating back to Native American legends were appropriated and reconfigured to draw popular support for the Mexican Revolution; similarly, the millennial beliefs of Chinese Buddhist sects undergirded some of the revolutionary imagery of the Chinese Communists (Rinehart, 1997). In the English Revolution of 1640, regicides drew on the myth of the Norman yoke (though they were of ancient Norman lineage themselves), in which the English royal line planted in 1066 by the invasion of William of Normandy was decried as a foreign oppressor that enslaved free Anglo-Saxon Englishmen. In their revolt against Spain in the sixteenth and seventeenth centuries, the Dutch presented themselves as descendants of the ancient Helvetian tribes who had fought Roman imperial rule; in the French Revolution, in an ironic turnaround, the French revolutionaries liked to identify with the Roman founders of the Republic and their struggle against the Tarquin kings.

Any cultural framework may provide the basis for revolutionary or anti-revolutionary ideologies. Christianity and Islam have long been the bastion of conservative established church organizations; but in recent years Islamic fundamentalists and Christian base communities seem as radical as the English Puritans of the seventeenth century. Communism has been both a revolutionary ideology and the cloak for a conservative and privileged elite that was overthrown by liberal intellectuals and nationalist workers.

Whether or not a revolutionary ideology emerges from a given cultural framework seems to depend entirely on how elements of that framework are adapted to particular circumstances or combined with new elements and adopted by particular groups.

Ideologies, in addition to providing value judgments and clothing of virtue for revolutionaries, may accelerate revolutionary momentum in two other, reinforcing ways. First, revolutionary ideologies usually present their struggle as destined to succeed; having history or God on their side will ensure the triumph of their followers (Martin et al., 1990). Second, revolutionary ideologies aim to bridge the varied cultural frameworks of different groups and provide a basis for the multi-group and cross-class coalitions so important for challenging state power (Chong, 1993). These functions reinforce each other. As a revolutionary group attracts a broader range of followers, it begins to seem destined to succeed; at the same time, the more likely a movement's success appears, the more followers it will attract.

Constructing an ideology that will

(a) inspire a broad range of followers by resonating with existing cultural guideposts;
(b) provide a sense of inevitability and destiny about its followers' success; and
(c) persuade people that the existing authorities are unjust and weak

is no simple task. Neither is planning a strategic and tactical campaign of opposition or skillfully taking advantage of spontaneous uprisings and chance events. Thus, the course and outcomes of revolutions depend to a considerable degree on the skills and actions of state and revolutionary leaders.

Leadership

Popular histories of revolutions are filled with accounts of larger-than-life personalities: Cromwell, Washington, Robespierre, Napoleon, Lenin, Stalin, Mao, Castro, Guevarra, Cabral, Mandela, Aquino.

Sometimes it seems that the origins and outcome of the revolutions are inseparable from the will and fate of these revolutionary leaders. Yet collective biographies of revolutionary leaders have shown that although many are exceptionally charismatic, many are not, and indeed as a whole the background and personality profiles of revolutionary leaders do not markedly differ from those of conventional political leaders (Rejai and Phillips, 1988). Moreover, in structural theories of revolution, these leaders hardly ever appear, or if mentioned, they seem to be unwitting dupes of history whose best intentions are always frustrated by deeper social, political, or economic forces.

This disconnect can be understood by focusing on the skills of revolutionary leaders themselves. Successful leaders excel at taking advantage of favorable political and economic circumstances. Poor leaders generally act when circumstances are highly unfavorable to success. The resulting pattern – leaders appear to succeed only when conditions favor them and to fail otherwise – makes revolutionary success appear to be strictly a matter of background conditions and obscures the role of leadership in actually making a revolution out of merely potentially favorable circumstances. The importance of leadership is clear in fairly extreme cases such as the 'New Jewel' Revolution in Grenada, where poor leadership led an apparently successful revolution to self-destruct (Selbin, 1993), or cases such as the Chinese Communist Revolution, where outstanding leadership was able to sustain a revolutionary movement through apparently crushing defeat and to plan for circumstances that would allow victory (Selden, 1995).

The failure of revolutionary leaders to achieve their proclaimed aims – liberty, equality, prosperity – is also taken as evidence of the minor impact of leadership. Yet it is not that simple; after a revolution, its supporters often divide and fall out among themselves, military confrontations test and reshape revolutionary regimes, and once they attain absolute power, many leaders are blinded by it and indulge in megalomaniac fantasies. Thus it is no surprise that revolutions often fail to achieve their pre-revolutionary aims. However, this does not mean leadership is insignificant, only that its impact is complex. It requires varied kinds of leadership not only to build a revolutionary movement that can help topple an old regime, but also to win the internecine struggles that follow the collapse of the old order, and to withstand the military blows that often rain down on a new regime. Sometimes, ruthless manipulation of vital resources such as food supplies is critical to revolutionaries depriving their enemies of support, and keeping control over their own supporters (Oberschall and Seidman, 2005). If a revolutionary leadership survives all this and falls into megalomaniac excess, the suffering that follows only underlines the impact of revolutionary leaders on the fate of ordinary people and of nations (Chirot, 1994; Friedman et al., 1991).

Studies of leadership have found that there are two distinct types and that they usually must be combined – either in one person or through the cooperation of two or more – for an enterprise to succeed. Interestingly, these two types of leadership, 'people-oriented' and 'task-oriented' (Aminzade et al., 2001; Selbin, 1993), mirror the two dimensions of successful governance or mobilization, namely justice and effectiveness. People-oriented leaders are those who inspire people, give them a sense of identity and power, and provide a vision of a new and just order around which their followers unite their energies and their purposes. Task-oriented leaders are those who can plot a strategy suitable to resources and circumstances, set the timetables for people and supplies to reach specific ends, manage money effectively, and respond to shifting circumstances with appropriate strategies and tactics. The purely people-oriented leader is personified by the religious prophet; the purely task-oriented leader is figured by the brilliant military general. Movements with only strong people-oriented leadership may end up as devoted but tiny cults (Hall et al., 2000); movements that have strong task-oriented leadership but no vision often fail to consolidate themselves in popular consciousness, and their revolutionary character will soon fade away (Selbin, 1993).

It generally seems to require two or more people or groups to fulfill the roles of visionaries and organizers of a revolution, even though the division of tasks is not always clear-cut. Puritan preachers and Oliver Cromwell's generalship combined to inspire and effect the Puritan Revolution in Britain; Jefferson and Adams were firebrands of the American Revolution, but it would have failed without Washington's generalship and power brokering at the Constitutional Convention; the Jacobins' vision for France might have failed sooner if not for Napoleon's military victories; Lenin had Trotsky to lead the uprising of the workers and to build the Red Army; Fidel Castro had Ché Guevarra and his brother Raul to fuel and organize the Cuban Revolution; the Ortega brothers had complementary ideological and military roles in leading the Nicaraguan Revolution; and Ayatollah Khomeini relied on the liberal professional Bani-Sadr to help institutionalize the Iranian Revolution and ward off the military attack from Iraq.

In many cases, the visionary and practical leaders clash in the course of the revolution, and one side takes over. In China, Mao and his initial successors, the Gang of Four, clearly leaned toward the visionary side regardless of the practical costs; in Russia, the dull and practical party-builders under Brezhnev won out a little over a decade after Stalin's death. Interestingly, in both these cases, the result was a counterthrust – in China the ultrapragmatic Deng regime, in the Soviet Union the attempt to reinspire the nation with an infusion of more liberal ideas under Gorbachev. In Iran, the more extreme ideological clerical groups initially won out over liberal pragmatists, as did the communist-leaning Sandinistas in Nicaragua over their more liberal allies. In the Iranian case, US pressure actually reinforced the extreme

visionaries, and the current counterthrust of moderates remains weak; in Nicaragua, US pressure weakened the visionaries and allowed a pragmatic coalition under Violetta Chamorro to rise to power. Thus, there is no guarantee that the right balance of people-oriented and task-oriented leadership will be sustained, and the course of a revolution can veer in different directions accordingly.

Gender relations and revolutionary movements

Numerous studies have now documented the extensive role played by women in revolutions, from the English and French Revolutions (Davies, 1998; Hufton, 1992) to recent Third World revolutions (Diamond, 1998; Tétreault, 1994; Wasserstrom, 1994). Women have been active in street demonstrations, guerrilla warfare, provision of food and supplies, and local leadership. However, despite this massive participation, there is often less connection than one would expect between female participation in revolutions and the gender character of the movement or the emergence of women as autonomous leaders.

Moghadam (1997) and Taylor (1999) have pointed out that protest and revolutionary movements always, whether implicitly or explicitly, have a gender agenda in their own organization and goals. Since almost all societies in history have been patriarchal, protest movements and revolutions generally oppose patriarchal regimes and institutions. They therefore must make a choice. While opposing the existing political institutions, do they nonetheless adopt and reproduce the patriarchal character dominant in society in their own movement? Or do they seek to overturn that character in their movement and in their vision of a new society?

Often, there is a significant divergence between rhetoric and practice. The Russian and Cuban revolutions consciously aimed to create a gender-equal society, and they did succeed in bringing many more women into the workplace and the professions (Goldman, 1993; Smith and Padula, 1996). However, they recruited few women to major leadership roles and did not alter the basically male-biased values of their societies. The English, French, and American Revolutions inspired many women to play critical grassroots roles and even included female ideals in their revolutionary iconography (Hunt, 1992). However, they took no action to change the traditional role of women in society. The Iranian Revolution involved many westernized, educated women who consciously adopted traditional Islamic female dress as a symbol of their opposition to Western cultural imperialism and their support for the revolution. Yet these women were surprised to find that they were excluded from further efforts to shape the revolution, and that the very anti-western Islamist modes of self-representation they adopted to help make the revolution became part of their enhanced repression afterward (Fantasia and Hirsch, 1995; Moghadam, 1994).

The key question about engendering revolutionary movements is whether in patriarchal societies women can ever be sufficiently persuasive and powerful to become visionary or effective leaders in their own right. The major female revolutionary leaders – Aquino in the Philippines, Chamorro in Nicaragua, Aung San Suu Ki in Burma – all acquired a leadership mantle from martyred husbands or fathers. This pattern also appears among democratic female leaders in Asia, such as India's Indira Ghandi, Pakistan's Benazir Bhutto, and Sri Lanka's Sirimavo Bandaranaike. To date, despite the widespread participation of women in revolutionary movements and their crucial contributions as bridge leaders, they have yet to play an independently dominant leadership role (except in the movement for women's political equality, if one treats it as revolutionary). Nor have revolutions, even where they have brought women full participation in voting and workplace opportunities, brought rapid

transformations in the household and leadership status of women in their societies.

A PARADOX OF REVOLUTIONARY PROCESSES: IS REPRESSION A BARRIER OR SPUR TO REVOLUTIONS?

The perception that structural conditions are the main, if not the sole, determinant of revolutions is strengthened by the fact that revolutions sometimes seem to come about despite all efforts of the state to appease or repress them. Often, paradoxically, fierce repression is unable to daunt, or even inflames, revolutionary opposition (Davenport, 2007; Khawaja, 1993; Kurzman, 1996; Lichbach, 1987; Moore, 1998; Olivier, 1991; Rasler, 1996; Weede, 1987). In many cases, state reforms only encourage revolutionaries to demand more. Yet in other cases, most recently in the democracy movements in Burma and in China, apparently highly favorable conditions and considerable mass mobilization were crushed by state repression (Brook, 1998; Carey, 1997; Walder, 1989). When do repression and reform work to halt the progress of revolution, and when do they fail or even backfire and provoke or inflame revolutionary action?

While perceptions of state injustice and ineffectiveness may lead to opposition, the development of such conflicts has a contingent and metamorphic character. The actions and reactions of regimes, regime opponents, counter-movements, and the broader public all reshape the processes of group identification, perceptions of the efficacy and justice of the regime and its opponents, and estimates of what changes are possible (Gartner and Regan, 1996; Kurzman, 1996; Rasler, 1996; Zhao, 2001). Movements of reform may become radicalized and revolutionary, initially small confrontations may spiral into mass uprisings, or large popular movements may be crushed.

It is well known that many revolutions and rebellions, from the English and French Revolutions to the Kenyan Mau-Mau revolt and Colombia's *La Violencia*, grew out of efforts to reform, not overthrow, the ruling regimes (Speck, 1990; Walton, 1984). A combination of unexpected popular pressures from below, conflicts between conservative and radical factions of the reform movement, reactions to international interventions, and temporizing or provocative actions by the regime, gave precedence to both more radical leadership and more revolutionary policies (Furet, 1981). In fact, the structural conditions that give rise to social protest movements, unsuccessful rebellions, and revolutions are generally quite similar. The transformation of social movements into rebellions or revolutions depends on how regimes, elites, and publics respond to the conflict situation (Goldstone, 1998b).

When facing demands for change, ruling regimes may employ any combination of concessions and repression to defuse the opposition (Davenport, 1995). Choosing the right combination is not an easy task. If a regime that has already lost its perceived effectiveness and justice offers concessions, these may be seen as 'too little, too late,' and simply increase the popular demands for large-scale change. This is why Machiavelli advised rulers to undertake reforms only from a position of strength; if undertaken from a position of weakness, they will further undermine support for the regime. The efforts of the Dowager Empress in late Imperial China, and of Gorbachev in the waning days of the Soviet Union, to encourage westernizing reforms led to escalating criticism of the old regimes and ultimately to their complete rejection and overthrow (Teitzel and Weber, 1994).

Repression is also a matter of degree and of context. Repression that is powerful, or that is focused on a small and deviant group, may be seen as evidence of state effectiveness and cow the opposition. However, repression that is not strong enough to suppress opponents, or that is so diffuse and erratic that innocents are persecuted, or that is aimed at groups that the public considers representative and justified in their protest, can quickly undermine perceptions of the regime's effectiveness and justice (Goldstone and Tilly, 2001; White, 1989). Thus, the deaths of Pedro Chamorro in Nicaragua and of Benigno Aquino in the Philippines, the diffuse persecution of ordinary citizens by Batista in Cuba, and the deaths inflicted on protestors in Iran by the forces of the Shah in 1978 spurred accelerations of popular protest. In contrast, the overwhelming force used against the Tiananmen Square protestors, who were publicly labeled as counterrevolutionary traitors, broke public resistance to communist rule in China for at least two decades (Zhao, 2001).

Perception of the vulnerability of rulers also makes a difference to the effect of repression. When the regime is judged to be losing support and capable of being overthrown, protestors may bear great risks, and great regime violence may simply further persuade people that the regime has got to go; yet when a regime is seen as unshakeable, indiscriminate violence and terror may simply reduce the opposition to silence (Brockett, 1995; Mason and Krane, 1989; Opp, 1994).

Rulers, however, have few guideposts to help them determine in advance whether a given level of concession or repression is sufficient. Lack of information and overconfidence further conspire to produce inappropriate responses. Worse yet, rulers often veer back and forth between concessions and repression, appearing inconsistent and therefore both ineffective and unjust (Goldstone and Tilly, 2001). For example, both Marcos in the Philippines and Milosevic in Serbia believed they could rig victory in elections, and therefore they made the apparent concession of calling elections to justify their authoritarian rule. When, despite their efforts, it was widely perceived that they lost the elections, they then had to fall back on repression to maintain their rule. But because of the perceived electoral losses, military and police resolve to defend the regime was weakened, and repression of popular protests failed, leading to the collapse of the regime.

An apparently strong regime that represses weakly or inconsistently, or that offers concessions deemed inadequate, can quickly undermine its own position (Kurzman, 1996). Because authoritarian regimes are often so distant from understanding their own subjects, or so overconfident in their estimation of their own power, errors by such regimes are common, and often an apparently secure regime that has lasted many years suddenly unravels in the face of a rapidly expanding opposition that in prior years no one had anticipated – Iran in 1979, the Philippines in 1986, and the Eastern European and Soviet communist regimes in 1989–1991. In contrast, regimes that appear structurally weak, such as the personal rule of Mobutu in Zaire, can persist for many years if the use of concessions and repression is skillful in dividing and neutralizing, rather than uniting and inflaming, the opposition (Snyder, 1998).

MICRO-LEVEL FOUNDATIONS AND QUALITATIVE ANALYSIS

The study of revolutions has been dominated in the past two decades by scholars using the case-study approach with national trajectories as cases. However, political science in general has moved strongly in the direction of micro-level analysis of the motivations of individuals involved in political actions, using rational choice modeling. A number of scholars have applied rational choice analysis to the study of revolutionary origins and dynamics.

Micro-level foundations: The rationality of revolution

Revolution is described by rational-choice theorists as a 'collective action problem.' This is because individuals, making their own decisions, would logically choose not to join in revolutionary action. Since all individuals face some risks and costs if they participate in revolutionary actions, but will reap the same benefits if a revolution succeeds whether they participated or not, individuals who are rational will spare themselves the risks and let others act (Olson, 1965; Tullock, 1971). However, scholars have now demonstrated that in practice, this collective action problem for individuals can be resolved in many ways, and that revolutionary action can indeed have solid micro-level foundations in rational behavior.

Lichbach (1995) has shown that there are four main families of solutions to the collective action problem, each offering a way to motivate individuals to join in protest – changing incentives, using community obligations, arranging contracts, and using authority. In practice, they appear in various combinations and provide a plethora of ways to create collective action. Thus, the research agenda of rational-choice theory in regard to revolutions is no longer one of posing obstacles to collective action; instead rational-choice analysis has joined with other approaches in seeking to identify the processes by which collective action solutions are achieved, and the general characteristics of those solutions.

The general character of these solutions is to change the decision to engage in revolutionary action from an individual decision to a group decision, relying on prior network ties or forging group identities. People who strongly identify with a group generally feel an obligation to act if the group acts, and believe that other group members will act with them (Oliver, 1984). The main check on protest activity then is not the collective action problem but whether people believe that the group will succeed if action is taken (Chong, 1991; Goldstone, 1994; Hardin, 1995; Macy, 1990, 1991; Moore, 1995; Oberschall, 1994b; Opp, 1989; Taylor, 1988).

Rational choice models also demonstrate why revolutionary mobilization is prone to rapid and often surprising spirals of escalation.

If the key to protest mobilization is convincing groups that their actions will be effective against the regime, then two bits of information are crucial: the relative weakness or resolve of the regime and the number of other groups that support the action. Shifts in perception or information can suddenly make groups that long harbored concerns about regime injustice or effectiveness believe that now their action can make a difference. Single events or crises that provide new information can thus precipitate sudden mobilization based on previously concealed preferences and beliefs, producing a bandwagon effect as more groups add their actions to what appears to be an increasingly favorable juncture for action (Chong, 1991; Karklins and Peterson, 1993; Kuran, 1989; Lichbach, 1995; Lohmann, 1993). These models provide a framework for understanding the explosive mobilization seen in events such as the sudden collapse of communist control in the Soviet Union and Eastern Europe (Kuran, 1991).

Finally, recent rational choice models of regime survival and transformation also stress the pivotal role of elites. In these models, it is the ability of elites to maintain unity and respond to popular demands with reasonable concessions, or shifts in elite/popular coalitions, that determine the fate of regimes (Acemoglu and Robinson, 2005; Bueno de Mesquita et al., 2004).

The past decade of rational choice research on revolutions has thus underlined the same topics – group identity, network ties, and elite/popular relationships – emphasized in recent comparative historical studies.

OUTCOMES OF REVOLUTIONS

The outcomes of revolutions have generated far less scholarly inquiry than the causes, with the possible exception of outcomes regarding gender. This may be because the outcomes of revolutions are assumed to follow straightforwardly if the revolutionaries succeed. However, such research as we

have on outcomes contradicts this assumption, for revolutionary outcomes often take unexpected twists and turns.

Stinchcombe (1999) offered the reasonable argument that a revolution is over when the stability and survival of the institutions imposed by the new regime are no longer in doubt. Yet even this definition is ambiguous, as it can take weak and strong forms. By the weak definition, a revolution is over when the basic institutions of the new regime are no longer being actively challenged by revolutionary or counterrevolutionary forces. By this standard, the French Revolution ended in Thermidor 1799 when Napoleon took power, the Russian Revolution of 1917 ended in 1921 with the Bolshevik victory over the White armies, and the Mexican Revolution of 1910 ended in 1920 with Obregon's presidency. Yet a strong definition, by which a revolution has ended only when key political and economic institutions have settled down into forms that will remain basically intact for a substantial period, say 20 years, gives far different results. By this definition, as Furet (1981) has argued, the French Revolution ended only with the start of the French Third Republic in 1871. The Russian Revolution of 1917 would not be considered over until after Stalin's purges of the 1930s; and the Mexican Revolution of 1910 would be dated as lasting through the Cárdenas reforms, to 1940. For that matter, the Chinese Revolution that began in 1910 has yet to end, as none of the Republican, Nationalist, Communist, or Great Proletarian Cultural Revolutions produced a lasting socioeconomic order. Goldstone and Becker (2005), using the strong definition, found that it generally takes quite a long time to restore stability after a revolution. Across 47 cases of revolution from the sixteenth to the twentieth century, the average time to restore order was 12 years, or 18 years if only major social revolutions were considered. Only revolutions that avoided major civil wars were able to restore order in a relatively short period, five years or less.

Sadly, there is no scholarly consensus on what constitutes the end of a revolution, and different analysts use weak, strong, or

idiosyncratic definitions to determine when a revolution has ended. Yet although it is difficult to say precisely when a revolution is over, it is nonetheless possible to discuss the consequences that most commonly unfold after the fall of the old regime.

Domestic outcomes

Revolutionaries frequently claim that they will reduce inequality, establish democracy, and provide economic prosperity. In fact, the record of actual revolutions is rather poor in regard to all of these claims (Weede and Muller, 1997).

Although many revolutions engage in some initial redistribution of assets (particularly land), no revolutionary regime has been able to maintain more than a symbolic equality. Rewards to administrators and top economic producers quickly lead to differentiation of incomes (Kelley and Klein, 1977). This has been true in both capitalist and communist revolutionary regimes. In addition, many regimes that begin with radical and populist economic schemes eventually revert to bourgeois and capitalist economic organization, such as Mexico, Egypt, and most recently China (Katz, 1999).

Until very recently, revolutions have invariably failed to produce democracy. The need to consolidate a new regime in the face of struggles with domestic and foreign foes has instead produced authoritarian regimes, often in the guise of populist dictatorships such as those of Napoleon, Castro, and Mao, or of one-party states such as the PRI state in Mexico or the Communist Party-led states of the Soviet Union and Eastern Europe. Indeed, the struggle required to take and hold power in revolutions generally leaves its mark in the militarized and coercive character of new revolutionary regimes (Gurr, 1988). It is therefore striking that in several recent revolutions – in the Philippines in 1986, in South Africa in 1990, in Eastern European nations in 1989–1991 – the sudden collapse of the old regime has led directly to new democracies, often

against strong expectations of reversion to dictatorship (Foran and Goodwin, 1993; Pastor, 2001; Weitman, 1992). The factors that allowed democracy to emerge in these cases appear to be several: a lack of external military threat, a strong personal commitment to democracy by revolutionary leaders, and consistent external support of the new democratic regimes by foreign powers.

Economic performance is more puzzling. One might expect revolutions to unleash great energy for rebuilding economic systems, just as they lead to rebuilding of political institutions. Yet in fact this rarely if ever takes place. For the most part, long-term economic performance in revolutionary regimes lags that of comparable countries that have not experienced revolutions (Eckstein, 1982, 1986). This may be in part because the elite divisions and conflicts that both precede and often follow revolution are inimical to economic progress (Haggard and Kaufman, 1995).

It appears that the very effort that goes into rebuilding political institutions throttles economic growth (Zimmermann, 1990). Revolutionary regimes are generally more centralized and more bureaucratic than the ones they replace (Skocpol, 1979). In addition, to secure their authority, revolutionary leaders are often quite restrictive in regard to entrepreneurial activity; five-year plans and state supervision or ownership of major economic enterprises place economic activity in narrow channels.

Revolutionary regimes can often focus resources and create hothouse growth in selected industries. The Soviet Union and China were fairly successful in creating nineteenth-century-style heavy industrial complexes. Yet neither of them, nor Iran, nor Nicaragua, nor any other revolutionary regime, has succeeded in generating the broad-based economic innovation and entrepreneurship required to generate sustained rapid economic advance (Chirot, 1991).

It may be, however, that the new democratizing revolutions will prove an exception. They appear to be less economically

restrictive and less heavily bureaucratic than the regimes they replaced. Poland, the Czech Republic, and the former East Germany have all shown strong economic gains. Nonetheless, most revolutionary states even recently have either been so rigid as to continue to restrain economic activity (e.g., Belarus and the Central Asian post-soviet republics), or so weak and disorganized as to be unable to promote and secure a broad economic advance (e.g., Russia, Georgia, South Africa). The general tendency of revolutions to produce poor economic performance thus seems intact, although with a few hopeful exceptions.

As noted above, another area in which revolutionary outcomes usually fall short of expectations is the social emancipation of women and their elevation to leadership roles. Although modern socialist revolutions have generally brought women into the professions and the labor force, they have not changed their essentially secondary status (Lapidus, 1978). Despite women's extensive participation and grass-roots leadership in most of the revolutions in history, gender equality has remained absent, or if articulated, still illusory, in the outcome of revolutionary struggles (Foran et al., 1997; Lobao, 1990; Randall, 1993).

Religious and ethnic minorities often do worse, rather than better, under revolutionary regimes. While revolutions often promise equality in the abstract to all followers, when counterrevolution or external interventions threaten the revolutionary regime, any groups not bound by ethnic and religious solidarity to the new government become suspect in their loyalties and may be singled out for persecution. Such has been the fate of the Bahai under the Islamic revolution in Iran, the Miskito Indians in Nicaragua, and those Croats, Muslims, and Serbs who found themselves on the wrong sides of borders in the revolutionary breakup of Yugoslavia.

With so many disappointments in the outcomes of revolutions, why have they nonetheless been so vigorously pursued? To answer that question, we need to recall one causal factor – the role of leadership – and the one area in which revolutionary outcomes have generally met or even exceeded expectations, namely the augmentation of state power.

The major objectives of revolutionary leaders are to restructure the bases of political power, to leave their mark on the political and/or economic and social organization of society, and to alter the status of their nation in the international system. Whatever their other failings, revolutions have been remarkably successful in mobilizing populations and utilizing that mobilization for political and military power (Skocpol, 1994). Although the eventual goals of democratization or equality or prosperity have often been elusive, for the immediate aims of seizing and expanding state authority, changing the rules for access to political power, improving standing in the international system, and restructuring beliefs and institutions, revolutions have been wildly successful for leaders from Napoleon to Hitler to Lenin to Castro.

The ability of successful revolutionary leaders to reshape their societies (if not always with the expected ultimate results) thus continues to inspire revolutionary entrepreneurs. As we have seen, a major feature of revolutionary mobilization is the effort of a committed core or vanguard to mobilize a mass following based on ideological depictions of the present regime as fundamentally ineffective and unjust. The continued appeal of revolution, despite a lengthy history of frustration of mass aspirations, must be understood in the context of leadership dynamics and mobilization processes that focus attention on present injustices rather than future results (Martin et al., 1990).

Outcomes in the international system

Walt (1996) has demonstrated why one of the first results of revolutions is often external war. The sudden appearance of a new regime upsets old alliances and creates

new uncertainties. Foreign powers may judge the new regime as either vulnerable or dangerous; either judgment can lead to war. New revolutionary regimes, inexperienced in foreign affairs, may make similar errors of judgment regarding their neighbors (Conge, 1996).

Aside from these miscalculations, revolutionary regimes may take actions that precipitate or exacerbate military strife. Many revolutions, from the Puritan Revolution in England and the liberal French Revolution to the communist revolutions in Russia, China, and Cuba and the Islamic revolution in Iran, explicitly made changing the world part of their revolutionary program. Armstrong (1993) has shown how these efforts upset the existing international balance of power. Moreover, we have noted that revolutions are made by coalitions and involve both visionary and pragmatic wings of leadership. Foreign threats may give leverage to the more visionary and radical elements in the revolutionary coalitions, who deliberately seek combat and missionary adventures (Blanning, 1986; Sadri, 1997). In contrast, where more moderate and pragmatic leaders remain in charge, and foreign powers support rather than threaten the new regime, internal impetus for war is likely to be weak, as was the case following the revolutions in the United States, Bolivia, and Zimbabwe (Snyder, 1999).

Eventually, even revolutionary regimes must accommodate to the reality of the international states system and assume a position in the constellation of international powers (Armstrong, 1993). Revolutions can produce long-lasting shifts in national standing and alignments in the international system. Some revolutions provide new aggressive energy to older nations, leading them to become regional or global threats to older powers. Thus, Japan after the Meiji Restoration, Germany after the Nazi revolution, and Russia after Stalin's consolidation of the communist revolution became expansionary states. The outcome of World War II, arguably a product of both the communist revolution in Russia and the Nazi revolution, brought Soviet expansionism into Eastern Europe and split the German nation, shaping the major cleavages in the international system for 50 years. Anti-colonial revolutions, of course, add new states to the international system and reduce the influence of colonial powers in the regions they formerly ruled. Many other revolutions occur in defiance of foreign patrons who supported the old regime; in Afghanistan, Vietnam, Nicaragua, Cuba, and Iran, such revolutions led to extended hostilities between the old patron power and the new regime. Both kinds of revolution satisfy revolutionary elites' strong yearnings for nationalist assertiveness and autonomy while reinforcing the general population's sense of power. Even in Mexico and the Philippines, where the revolutionaries did not assume a strongly hostile stance toward the United States (which had supported their prevolutionary regimes), the eruption of nationalist sentiment accompanying the revolutions led to nationalizing of assets in Mexico and expulsion of the United States from its Philippine military bases. Thus, in ways subtle as well as dramatic, the outcomes of revolutions reshape international relations for many decades, often giving new initiative and autonomy to states in which revolutions took place (Siverson and Starr, 1994).

CONCLUSION

Theories of revolution are moving away from a predominantly structural view, in which a set of economic or political conditions generate revolutions, in favor of a more process-oriented view. In this approach, revolutionary situations emerge from a combination of structural background factors that present challenges to states or that increase conflicts among states, elites, and popular groups, along with contingent decisions and interactions among key actors. Those decisions and interactions in turn are shaped by state rulers and revolutionary leaders, networks of mobilization and multi-class alliances, and state and revolutionary ideologies.

Revolutions continue to reshape both domestic regimes and the international order. As authoritarian and semi-authoritarian regimes continue to evolve in the Middle East, central and south Asia, North Korea, China, Africa, and parts of Latin America, the potential for clashes among rulers seeking to hold power and revolutionary opponents remains. The relatively peaceful and democratic 'color' revolutions in the Philippines, Ukraine, Georgia, and other countries has provided an attractive model for overturning semi-authoritarian regimes (Bunce and Wolchik, 2006). At the same time, the 'internationalization' of revolutionary fundamentalist Islamism, and its use of terror tactics, has captured the attention of the world and shaped the foreign relations and domestic policies of dozens of nations. Whether those clashes lead to further violence or to more peaceful transformations of states and authorities will depend on the actions of leaders, the clash of ideologies and perceptions, and the patterns of mobilization and elite responses that emerge.

REFERENCES

Abrams, D. and Hogg, M.A. (1990) *Social identity theory: Constructive and critical advances*. London: Harvester-Wheatsheaf.

Acemoglu, D. and Robinson, J.A. (2005) *Economic origins of dictatorship and democracy*. Cambridge: Cambridge University Press.

Aminzade, R., Goldstone, J.A., and Perry, E.J. (2001) 'Leadership dynamics and dynamics of contention', in R. Aminzade, J.A. Goldstone, D. McAdam, E.J. Perry, W. Sewell Jr., S. Tarrow and C. Tilly (eds), *Silence and voice in contentious politics*. Cambridge: Cambridge University Press.

Aminzade R., Goldstone J.A., McAdam D., Perry E.J., Sewell W. Jr., Tarrow, S., and Tilly, C. (2001) *Silence and voice in contentious politics*. Cambridge: Cambridge University Press.

Arjomand, S.A. (1988) *The turban for the crown: The Islamic revolution in Iran*. New York: Oxford University Press.

Armstrong, D. (1993) *Revolution and world order: The revolutionary state in international society*. Oxford: Oxford University Press.

Banac, I. (ed.) (1992) *Eastern Europe in revolution*. Ithaca, NY: Cornell University Press.

Beissinger, M. (1998) 'Event analysis in transitional societies: Protest mobilization in the former Soviet Union', in D. Rucht, R. Koopmans and F. Neidhardt (eds), *Acts of dissent. New developments in the study of protest*. Berlin: Sigma, pp. 284–316.

Beissinger, M. (2002) *Nationalist mobilization and the collapse of the soviet state*. Cambridge: Cambridge University Press.

Berejikian, J. (1992) 'Revolutionary collective action and the agent-structure problem', *American Political Science Review*, 86: 647–57.

Blanning, T.C.W. (1986) *The origins of the French revolutionary wars*. London: Longman.

Bonnell, V.E. (1983) *Roots of rebellion: Workers, politics and organizations in St. Petersburg and Moscow, 1900–1914*. Berkeley: University of California Press.

Brinton, C. (1938) *The anatomy of revolution*. New York: Norton.

Brockett, C. (1995) 'A protest–cycle resolution of the repression/popular protest paradox', in M. Traugott (ed.), *Repertoires and cycles of collective action*. Durham, NC: Duke University Press, pp. 117–44.

Brook, T. (1998) *Quelling the people*. Stanford, CA: Stanford University Press.

Bueno de Mesquita, B., Siverson, R.M., and Woller, G. (1992) 'War and the fate of regimes: a comparative analysis', *American Political Science Review*, 86 (3): 638–45.

Bueno de Mesquita, B., Smith, A., Siverson, R.M., and Morrow, J.D. (2004) *The logic of political survival*. Cambridge, MA: MIT Press.

Bunce, V. (1999) *Subversive institutions: the design and the destruction of socialism and the state*. Cambridge: Cambridge University Press.

Bunce, V. and Wolchik, S. (2006) 'Favorable conditions and electoral revolutions', *Journal of Democracy*, 17 (4): 5–18.

Calhoun, C. (1983) 'The radicalism of tradition', *American Journal of Sociology*, 88 (5): 886–914.

Calhoun, C. (1994a) 'The problem of identity in collective action', in J. Huber (ed.), *Macro-micro linkages in sociology*. Newbury Park, CA: Sage, pp. 51–75.

Calhoun, C. (1994b) *Neither gods nor emperors: Students and the struggle for democracy in China*. Berkeley: University of California Press.

Carey, P. (1997) *From Burma to Myanmar: military rule and the struggle for democracy*. London: Research Institute for the Study of Conflict and Terrorism.

Chirot, D. (ed.) (1991) *The crisis of Leninism and the decline of the left: the revolutions of 1989*. Seattle: University of Washington Press.

Chirot, D. (1994) *Modern tyrants*. New York: Free Press.

Chong, D. (1991) *Collective action and the civil rights movement*. Chicago: University of Chicago Press.

Chong, D. (1993) 'Coordinating demands for social change', *The Annals of the American Academy of Political and Social Science*, 2 (1): 126–41.

Cohen, J. (1985) 'Strategy or identity: New theoretical paradigms and contemporary social movements', *Sociological Research*, 52 (4): 663–716.

Colburn, F.D. (1994) *The vogue of revolution in poor countries*. Princeton, NJ: Princeton University Press.

Conge, P.J. (1996) *From revolution to war: State relations in a world of change*. Ann Arbor: University of Michigan Press.

Davenport, C. (1995) 'Multi-dimensional threat perception and state repression: An inquiry into why states apply negative sanctions', *American Journal of Political Science*, 39 (3): 683–713.

Davenport, C. (2007) 'State repression and political order', *Annual Review of Political Science*, 10 (1): 1–23.

Davies, J.C. (1962) 'Toward a theory of revolution', *American Sociological Review*, 27 (1): 5–19.

Davies, S. (1998) *Unbridled spirits: Women of the English revolution, 1640–1660*. London: Women's Press.

DeNardo, J. (1985) *Power in numbers*. Princeton, NJ: Princeton University Press.

Denoeux, G. (1993) *Urban unrest in the Middle East: A comparative study of informal networks in Egypt, Iran, and Lebanon*. Albany, NY: SUNY Press.

Diamond, M.J. (ed.) (1998) *Women and revolution: Global expressions*. Dordrecht and Boston: Kluwer.

Diamond, L.J. and Plattner, M.F. (eds) (1993) *Capitalism, socialism and democracy*. Baltimore: The Johns Hopkins University Press.

Dix, R. (1983) 'The varieties of revolution', *Comparative Politics*, 15 (3): 281–95.

Dunn, J. (1989) *Modern revolutions: An introduction to the analysis of a political phenomenon* (2nd edition) Cambridge: Cambridge University Press.

Eckstein, S. (1982) 'The impact of revolution on social welfare in Latin America', *Theory and Society*, 11 (1): 43–94.

Eckstein, S. (1986) 'The impact of the Cuban revolution: A comparative perspective', *Comparative Studies in Sociology and History*, 28: 503–34.

Eckstein, S. (1989a) 'Power and popular protests in Latin America', in S. Eckstein (ed.), *Power and popular protest: Latin American social movements*. Berkeley: University of California Press, pp. 1–60.

Eckstein, S. (ed.) (1989b) *Power and popular protest: Latin American social movements*. Berkeley: University of California Press.

Eisenstadt, S.N. (1978) *Revolution and the transformation of societies*. New York: Free Press.

Eisenstadt, S.N. (1992) 'Frameworks of the great revolutions: culture, social structure, history, and human agency', *International Social Science Journal*, 133 (3): 385–401.

Eisenstadt, S.N. (2006) *The great revolutions and the civilizations of modernity*. Leiden: Brill.

Emirbayer, M.E. and Goodwin, J. (1996) 'Symbols, positions, objects: Toward a new theory of revolutions and collective action', *History and Theory*, 35 (3): 358–74.

Fantasia, R. and Hirsch, E.L. (1995) 'Culture in rebellion: The appropriation and transformation of the veil in the Algerian Revolution', in H. Johnston and B. Klandermans (eds), *Social movements and culture*. University of Minnesota Press.

Farhi, F. (1990) *States and urban-based revolution: Iran and Nicaragua*. Urbana and Chicago: University of Illinois Press.

Fenger, M. (2007) 'The diffusion of revolutions: Comparing recent regime turnovers in five post-communist countries', *Demokratizatsiya*, 15 (1): 5–28.

Finkel, S.E., Muller, E.N., and Opp, K.-D. (1989) 'Personal influence, collective rationality, and mass political action', *American Political Science Review*, 83 (3): 885–903.

Foran, J. (1997a) 'Discourses and social forces: the role of culture and cultural studies in understanding revolutions', in J. Foran (ed.), *Theorizing revolutions*. London: Routledge, pp. 203–26.

Foran, J. (ed.) (1997b) *Theorizing revolutions*. London: Routledge.

Foran, J. (ed.) (2003) *The future of revolutions: Radical change in an age of globalization*. London: Zed.

Foran, J. (2005) *Taking power: On the origins of third world revolutions*. Cambridge: Cambridge University Press.

Foran, J. and Goodwin, J. (1993) 'Revolutionary outcomes in Iran and Nicaragua: coalition fragmentation, war, and the limits of social transformation', *Theory and Society*, 22 (2): 209– 47.

Foran, J., Klouzal, L., and Rivera, J.-P. (1997) 'Who makes revolutions? Class, gender and race in the Mexican, Cuban, and Nicaraguan Revolutions', *Research in Social Movements, Conflict, and Change*, 20 (1): 1–60.

Friedman, E., Pickowicz, P.G., and Selden, M.J. (1991) *Chinese village, socialist state*. New Haven: Yale University Press.

Furet, F. (1981) *Interpreting the French Revolution*. Cambridge: Cambridge University Press.

Gamson, W.A. (1988) 'Political discourse and collective action', in B. Klandermas, H. Jriesi and S. Tarrow (eds), *International social movement research, Vol 1. From Structure to Action*. Greenwich, CT: JAI Press, pp. 219–44.

Gamson, W.A. and Meyer, D.S. (1996) 'Framing political opportunity', in D. McAdam, J.D. McCarthy and M. Zald (eds), *Comparative perspectives on social movements*. Cambridge: Cambridge University Press, pp. 275–90.

Gartner, S.S. and Regan, P.M. (1996) 'Threat and repression: the non-linear relationship between government and opposition violence', *Journal of Peace Research*, 33 (3): 273–88.

Goldfrank, W.L. (1979) 'Theories of revolution and revolution without theory: The case of Mexico', *Theory and Society*, 7 (1–2): 135–65.

Goldman, W.Z. (1993) *Women, the state, and revolution: Soviet family policy and social life, 1917–1936*. Cambridge: Cambridge University Press.

Goldstone, J.A. (1980) 'Theories of revolution: the third generation', *World Politics*, 32 (3): 425–53.

Goldstone, J.A. (1991) *Revolution and rebellion in the early modern world*. Berkeley: University of California Press.

Goldstone, J.A. (1994) 'Is revolution individually rational?', *Rationality and Society*, 6 (1): 139–66.

Goldstone, J.A. (1998a) 'The Soviet Union: revolution and transformation', in M. Dogan and J Higley (ed.), *Elites, crises, and the origins of regimes*. Boulder, CO: Rowman & Littlefield, pp. 95–123.

Goldstone, J.A. (1998b) 'Social movements or revolutions? On the evolution and outcomes of collective action', in M. Guigni, D. McAdam and C. Tilly (eds), *Democracy and contention*. Boulder, CO: Rowman & Littlefield, pp. 125–45.

Goldstone, J.A. (ed.) (1998c) *The encyclopedia of political revolutions*. Washington, DC: Congressional Quarterly.

Goldstone, J.A. (2002a) 'Population and security: How demographic change can lead to violent conflict', *Journal of International Affairs*, 56 (1): 245–63.

Goldstone, J.A. (2002b) 'States, terrorists, and the clash of civilizations', in C. Calhoun, P. Price and A. Timmer (eds), *September 11: Context and consequences*. New York: New Press, pp. 139–58.

Goldstone, J.A. (2003) 'Revolution in modern dictatorships', in J.A. Goldstone (eds), *Revolutions: Theoretical, comparative, and historical studies*. Belmont, CA: Wadsworth, pp. 70–77.

Goldstone, J.A. and Becker, J. (2005) 'How fast can you build a state? – State building in revolutions', in M. Lange and D. Rueschemeyer (eds), *States and development*. New York: Palgrave-Macmillan, pp. 183–210.

Goldstone, J.A. and Tilly, C. (2001) 'Threat (and opportunity): popular action and state response in the dynamics of contentious action', in R. Aminzade, J.A. Goldstone, D. McAdam, E.J. Perry, W. Sewell Jr., S. Tarrow, and C. Tilly (eds), *Silence and voice in contentious politics*. Cambridge: Cambridge University Press, pp. 179–94.

Goldstone, J.A., Gurr, T.R., and Moshiri, F. (eds) (1991) *Revolutions of the late twentieth century*. Boulder, CO: Westview.

Goodwin, J. (1994a) 'Toward a new sociology of revolutions', *Theory and Society*, 23 (6): 731–66.

Goodwin, J. (1994b) 'Old regimes and revolutions in the Second and Third Worlds: A comparative perspective', *Social Science History*, 18 (4): 575–604.

Goodwin, J. (1997) 'State-centered approaches to social revolutions: strengths and limitations of a theoretical tradition', in J. Foran (ed.), *Theorizing revolutions*. London: Routledge, pp. 11–37.

Goodwin, J. (2001) *No other way out: States and revolutionary movements 1945–1991*. Cambridge: Cambridge University Press.

Goodwin, J. and Skocpol, T. (1989) 'Explaining revolutions in the contemporary Third World', *Politics and. Society*, 17 (4): 489–507.

Gould, R.V. (1995) *Insurgent identities: Class, community, and protest in Paris from 1848 to the commune*. Chicago: University of Chicago Press.

Gurr, T.R. (1970) *Why men rebel*. Princeton, NJ: Princeton University Press.

Gurr, T.R. (1988) 'War, revolution, and the growth of the coercive state', *Comparative Political Studies*, 21 (1): 45–65.

Haggard, S. and Kaufman, R.R. (1995) *The political economy of democratic transitions*. Princeton, NJ: Princeton University Press.

Hale, H. (2005) 'Regime cycles: Democracy, autocracy, and revolution in post-Soviet Eurasia', *World Politics*, 58 (1): 133–65.

Hall, J.R., Schuyler, P.D., and Trinh, S. (2000) *Apocalypse observed: Religious movements and violence in North America, Europe, and Japan*. New York: Routledge.

Halliday, F. (1999) *Revolution and world politics*. London: Macmillan.

Hardin, R. (1995) *One for all*. Princeton, NJ: Princeton University Press.

Harff, B. (1991) 'Cambodia: revolution, genocide, intervention', in J.A. Goldstone, T.R. Gurr and F. Moshiri (eds) *Revolutions of the late twentieth century*. Boulder, CO: Westview, pp. 218–34.

Harff, B. (1995) 'Rescuing endangered peoples: missed opportunities', *Sociological Research*, 62 (1): 23–40.

Higley, J. and Burton, M. (2006) *Elite foundations of liberal democracy*. Lanham, MD: Rowman & Littlefield.

Hough, J. (1997) *Democratization and revolution in the USSR 1985–1991*. Washington, DC: Brookings Institute.

Hufton, O.H. (1992) *Women and the limits of citizenship in the French Revolution*. Toronto: University of Toronto Press.

Hunt, L. (1992) *The family romance of the French Revolution*. Berkeley: University of California Press.

Huntington, S.P. (1968) *Political order in changing societies*. New Haven, CT: Yale University Press.

Jenkins, J.C. and Kposowa, A.J. (1990) 'Explaining military coups d'état: Black Africa, 1957–1984', *American Sociological Review*, 55 (6): 861–75.

Johnson, V. (1993) 'The structural causes of anticolonial revolutions in Africa', *Alternatives*, 18 (2): 201–27.

Karklins, R. (1994) 'Explaining regime change in the Soviet Union', *Europe–Asia Studies*, 46 (1): 29–45.

Karklins, R. and Petersen, R. (1993) 'Decision calculus of protesters and regimes: Eastern Europe 1989', *Journal of Politics*, 55 (3): 588–614.

Katz, M. (1997) *Revolutions and revolutionary waves*. New York: St. Martin's.

Katz, M. (1999) *Reflections on revolutions*. New York: St. Martin's.

Keddie, N.R. (1995) *Iran and the Muslim world: Resistance and revolution*. New York: New York University Press.

Kelley, J. and Klein, H.S. (1977) 'Revolution and the rebirth of inequality: A theory of stratification in post-revolutionary society', *American Journal of Sociology*, 83 (1): 78–99.

Khawaja, M. (1993) 'Repression and popular collective action: Evidence from the West Bank', *Sociological Forum*, 8: 47–71.

Kim, Q.-Y. (ed.) (1991) *Revolutions in the Third World*. Leiden, the Netherlands: Brill.

Kimmel, M.S. (1990) *Revolution: A sociological interpretation*. Cambridge: Polity.

Klosko, G. (1987) 'Rebellious collective action revisited', *American Political Science Review*, 81 (2): 557–61.

Knoke, D. (1988) 'Incentives in collective action organizations', *American Sociological Review*, 53 (3): 311–29.

Kuran, T. (1989) 'Sparks and prairie fires: A theory of unanticipated political revolution', *Public Choice*, 61 (1): 41–74.

Kuran, T. (1991) 'Now out of never: The element of surprise in the Eastern European Revolution of 1989', *World Politics*, 44 (1): 7–48.

Kurzman, C. (1996) 'Structural opportunity and perceived opportunity in social-movement theory', *American Sociological Review*, 61 (1): 153–70.

Lachmann, R. (1997) 'Agents of revolution: elite conflicts and mass mobilization from the Medici to Yeltsin', in J. Foran (ed.), *Theorizing revolutions*. London: Routledge, pp. 73–101.

Lane, D. and Ross, C. (1999) *The transition from communism to capitalism*. New York: St. Martin's.

Lapidus, G.W. (1978) *Women in Soviet society: Equality, development, and social change*. Berkeley: University of California Press.

Lawler, E.J. (1992) 'Affective attachments to nested groups: A choice-process theory', *American Sociological Review*, 57 (3): 327–39.

Levine, D.H. and Manwaring, S. (1989) 'Religion and popular protest in Latin America: Contrasting experiences', in S. Eckstein (ed.), *Power and popular protest: Latin American Social Movements*. Berkeley: University of California Press, pp. 203–34.

Lichbach, M.I. (1987) 'Deterrence or escalation? The puzzle of aggregate studies of repression and dissent', *Journal of Conflict Resolution*, 31 (2): 266–97.

Lichbach, M.I. (1989) 'An evaluation of "Does economic inequality breed political conflict?" studies', *World Politics*, 41 (4): 431–70.

Lichbach, M.I. (1995) *The rebel's dilemma*. Ann Arbor: University of Michigan Press.

Liu, M.T. (1988) 'States and urban revolutions: Explaining the revolutionary outcomes in Iran and Poland', *Theory and Society*, 17 (2): 179–210.

Lobao, L. (1990) 'Women in revolutionary movements: changing patterns of Latin American guerrilla struggles', in G. West, and R.L. Blumberg (eds), *Women and social protest*. Oxford: Oxford University Press, pp. 180–204.

Lohmann, S. (1993) 'A signaling model of information and manipulative political action', *American Political Science Review*, 86: 319–33.

Macculloch, R. (2005) 'Income inequality and the taste for revolution', *Journal of Law and Economics*, 48 (1): 93–123.

Macy, M. (1990) 'Learning theory and the logic of the critical mass', *American Sociological Review*, 55 (6): 809–26.

Macy, M. (1991) 'Chains of cooperation: threshold effects in collective action', *American Sociological Review*, 56 (6): 730–47.

Magagna, V.V. (1991) *Communities of grain: Rural rebellion in comparative perspective*. Ithaca, NY: Cornell University Press.

Markoff, J. (1996) *The abolition of feudalism: Peasants, lords, and legislators in the French Revolution*. University Park, PA: Pennsylvania State University Press.

Martin, J., Scully, M., and Levitt, B. (1990) 'Injustice and the legitimation of revolution: damning the past, excusing the present, and neglecting the future', *Journal of Personality and Social Psychology*, 59 (2): 281–90.

Mason, T.D. and Krane, D.A. (1989) 'The political economy of death squads: Toward a theory of the impact of state-sanctioned terror', *International Studies Quarterly*, 33 (2): 175–98.

McAdam, D. (1988) *Freedom summer*. New York: Oxford University Press.

McAdam, D. (1995) 'Recruitment to high-risk activism: The case of freedom summer', *American Journal of Sociology*, 92 (1): 64–90.

McAdam, D., Tarrow, S., and Tilly, C. (2001) *Dynamics of contention*. Cambridge: Cambridge University Press.

McCarthy, J.D., and Zald, M.N. (1977) 'Resource mobilization and social movements', *American Journal of Sociology*, 82 (6): 1112–41.

McClintock, C. (1998) *Revolutionary movements in Latin America: El Salvador's FMLN and Peru's shining path*. Washington, DC: US Institute of Peace.

McDaniel, T. (1991) *Autocracy, modernization, and revolution in Russia and Iran*. Princeton, NJ: Princeton University Press.

McFaul, M. (2005) 'Transitions from post-communism', *Journal of Democracy*, 16 (3): 5–19.

Melucci, A. (1989) *Nomads of the present: Social movements and individual needs in contemporary society*. Philadelphia: Temple University Press.

Midlarsky, M.I. (ed.) (1986) *Inequality and contemporary revolutions*. Denver, CO: University Denver Press.

Midlarsky, M.I. (1999) *The evolution of inequality*. Stanford, CA: Stanford University Press.

Migdal, J.S. (1974) *Peasant politics and revolution*. Princeton, NJ: Princeton University Press.

Moaddel, M. (1993) *Class, politics, and ideology in the Iranian revolution*. New York: Columbia University Press.

Moghadam, V.M. (1989) 'Populist revolution and the Islamic states in Iran', in T. Boswell (ed.), *Revolution in the world-system*. New York: Greenwood, pp. 147–63.

Moghadam, V.M. (1994) 'Islamic populism, class, and gender in post-revolutionary Iran', in J. Foran (ed.), *A Century of Revolution: Social Movements in Iran*. Minneapolis: University of Minnesota Press, pp. 189–222.

Moghadam, V.M. (1997) 'Gender and revolutions', in J. Foran (ed.), *Theorizing revolutions*. London: Routledge, pp. 137–67.

Moore, B., Jr. (1966) *Social origins of dictatorship and democracy*. Boston: Beacon.

Moore, W.H. (1995) 'Rational rebels: Overcoming the free-rider problem', *Political Research Quarterly*, 48 (2): 417–54.

Moore, W.H. (1998) 'Repression and dissent: Substitution, context, and timing', *American Journal of Political Science*, 42 (3): 851–73.

Muller, E.N. (1985) 'Income inequality, regime repressiveness, and political violence', *American Sociological Review*, 50 (1): 47–61.

Muller, E.N. and Seligson, M.S. (1987) 'Inequality and insurgency', *American Political Science Review*, 81 (2): 425–51.

Nash, J. (1989) 'Cultural resistance and class consciousness in Bolivian tin-mining communities', in S. Eckstein (ed.), *Power and popular protest: Latin American Social Movements*. Berkeley: University of California Press, pp. 182–202.

Oberschall, A. (1994a) 'Protest demonstrations and the end of communist regimes in 1989', *Research in Social Movements, Conflicts and Change*, 17 (1): 1–24.

Oberschall, A. (1994b) 'Rational choice in collective protests', *Rationality and Society*, 6 (1): 79–100.

Oberschall, A. and Kim, H.-J. (1996) 'Identity and action', *Mobilization*, 1 (1): 63–86.

Oberschall, A. and Seidman, M. (2005) 'Food coercion in revolution and civil war: Who wins and how they do it', *Comparative Studies in Sociology and History*, 47 (2): 372–402.

Oliver, P. (1984) 'If you don't do it, nobody will', *American Sociological Review*, 49 (5): 601–10.

Olivier, J. (1991) 'State repression and collective action in South Africa, 1970–84', *South African Journal of Sociology*, 22: 109–17.

Olson, M., Jr. (1965) *The logic of collective action: Public goods and the theory of groups*. Cambridge, MA: Harvard University Press.

Opp, K.-D. (1989) *The rationality of political protest*. Boulder, CO: Westview.

Opp, K.-D. (1994) 'Repression and revolutionary action: East Germany in 1989', *Rationality and Society*, 6 (1): 101–38.

Opp, K.-D., Voss, P., and Gern, C. (1995) *Origins of a spontaneous revolution: East Germany, 1989*. Ann Arbor: University of Michigan Press.

Osa, M. (2003) *Solidarity and contention: Networks of Polish opposition*. Minneapolis, MN: University of Minnesota Press.

Paige, J.M. (1975) *Agrarian revolution*. New York: Free Press.

Pape, R. (2006) *Dying to win: The strategic logic of suicide terrorism*. New York: Random House.

Parker, D. (2000) *Revolutions and revolutionary tradition in the West 1560–1991*. London: Routledge.

Parsa, M. (1989) *The social origins of the Iranian revolution*. New Brunswick, NJ: Rutgers University Press.

Parsa, M. (2000) *States, ideologies, and social revolutions: A comparative analysis of Iran, Nicaragua, and the Philippines*. Cambridge: Cambridge University Press.

Pastor, R. (2001) 'Preempting revolutions: the boundaries of U.S. influence', in M. Katz (ed.), *Revolution: International dimensions*. Washington, DC: Congressional Quarterly, pp. 169–97.

Perry, E.J. and Li, X. (1997) *Proletarian power: Shanghai in the cultural revolution*. Boulder, CO: Westview.

Pfaff, S. (1996) 'Collective identity and informal groups in revolutionary mobilization: East Germany in 1989', *Social Forces*, 75 (1): 91–10.

Popkin, S. (1979) *The rational peasant: The political economy of rural society in Vietnam.* Berkeley: University of California Press.

Popkin, S. (1988) 'Political entrepreneurs and peasant movements in Vietnam', in M. Taylor (ed.), *Rationality and revolution.* Cambridge: Cambridge University Press.

Randall, M. (1993) *Gathering rage: The failure of twentieth century revolutions to develop a feminist agenda.* New York: Monthly Review.

Rasler, K. (1996) 'Concessions, repression, and political protest in the Iranian Revolution', *American Sociological Review,* 61 (1): 132–52.

Rejai, M. and Phillips, K. (1988) 'Loyalists and revolutionaries', *International Political Science Review,* 9 (2): 107–18.

Rinehart, J. (1997) *Revolution and the millennium: China, Mexico, and Iran.* Westport, CT: Praeger.

Rule, J. (1988) *Theories of civil violence.* Berkeley: University of California Press.

Rule, J. (1989) 'Rationality and non-rationality in militant collective action', *Sociological Theory,* 7 (2): 145–60.

Sadri, H.A. (1997) *Revolutionary states, leaders, and foreign relations: A comparative study of China, Cuba, and Iran.* Westport, CT: Praeger.

Sageman, M. (2004) *Understanding terror networks.* Philadelphia, PA: University of Pennsylvania Press.

Sageman, M. (2007) *Leaderless Jihad: Terror networks in the twenty–first century.* Philadelphia, PA: University of Pennsylvania Press.

Scott, J.C. (1976) *The moral economy of the peasant: Rebellion and subsistence in South East Asia.* New Haven, CT: Yale University Press.

Scott, J.C. (1985) *Weapons of the weak: Everyday forms of peasant resistance.* New Haven, CT: Yale University Press.

Selbin, E. (1993) *Modern Latin American revolutions.* Boulder, CO: Westview.

Selbin, E. (1997) 'Revolution in the real world: Bringing agency back in', in J. Foran (ed.), *Theorizing revolutions.* London: Routledge, pp. 123–36.

Selden, M. (1995) *China in revolution: The Yenan way revisited.* Armonk, NY: Sharpe.

Sewell, W., Jr. (1985) 'Ideologies and social revolutions: Reflections on the French case'. *Journal of Modern History,* 57 (1): 57–85.

Shin, G.-W. (1996) *Peasant protest and social change in colonial Korea.* Seattle: University of Washington Press.

Siverson, R.M. and Starr, H. (1994) 'Regime change and the restructuring of alliances', *American Journal of Political Science,* 38: 145–61.

Skocpol, T. (1979) *States and social revolutions.* Cambridge: Cambridge University Press.

Skocpol, T. (1982) 'Rentier state and Shi'a Islam in the Iranian Revolution', *Theory and Society,* 11 (3): 265–303.

Skocpol, T. (1994) *Social revolutions in the modern world.* Cambridge: Cambridge University Press.

Smith, L.M. and Padula, A. (1996) *Sex and revolution: Women in socialist Cuba.* New York: Oxford University Press.

Snow, D.A. and Benford, R.D. (1988) 'Ideology, frame resonance, and participant mobilization', *International Social Movement Research,* 1: 197–217.

Snow, D.A., Rochford, E.B., Jr., Worden, S.K., and Benford, R.D. (1986) 'Frame alignment processes, micromobilization, and movement participation', *American Sociological Review,* 51 (4): 464–81.

Snyder, R. (1998) 'Paths out of sultanistic regimes: combining structural and voluntarist perspectives', in H.E. Chehabi and J.J. Linz (eds), *Sultanistic Regimes.* Baltimore, MD: Johns Hopkins University Press, pp. 49–81.

Snyder, R.S. (1999) 'The U.S. and third world revolutionary states: understanding the breakdown in relations', *International Studies Quarterly,* 43 (2): 265–90.

Sohrabi, J. (1995) 'Historicizing revolutions: constitutional revolutions in the Ottoman Empire, Iran, and Russia 1905–1908', *American Journal of Sociology,* 100 (6): 1383–447.

Somers, M. and Gibson, G. (1994) 'Reclaiming the epistemological "other": Narrative and the social constitution of identity', in C. Calhoun (ed.), *Social theory and the politics of identity.* Oxford: Blackwell, pp. 37–99.

Speck, W.A. (1990) *Reluctant revolutionaries: Englishmen and the revolution of 1688.* New York: Oxford University Press.

Stacey, J. (1983) *Patriarchy and socialist revolution in China.* Berkeley: University of California Press.

Stark, D.C. and Bruszt, L. (1998) *Postsocialist pathways: Transforming politics and property in East Central Europe*. New York: Cambridge University Press.

Stinchcombe, A.L. (1999) 'Ending revolutions and building new governments', *Annual Review of Political Science*, 2 (1): 49–73.

Stokes, G. (1993) *The walls came tumbling down: The collapse of communism in Eastern Europe*. New York: Oxford University Press.

Tarrow, S. (1998) *Power in movement: Social movements and contentious politics* (2nd ed.) Cambridge: Cambridge University Press.

Taylor M. (ed.) (1988) *Rationality and revolution*. Cambridge: Cambridge University Press.

Taylor, V. (1999) 'Gender and social movements', *Gender and Society*, 13 (1): 8–33.

Teitzel, M. and Weber, M. (1994) 'The economics of the Iron Curtain and the Berlin Wall', *Rationality and Society*, 6: 58–78.

Tétreault, M.A. (ed.) (1994) *Women and revolution in Africa, Asia, and the new world*. Columbia: University of South Carolina Press.

Tilly, C. (1978) *From mobilization to revolution*. Reading, MA: Addison-Wesley.

Tilly, C. (1993) *European revolutions 1492–1992*. Oxford: Blackwell.

Tilly, C. (1995) 'To explain political processes', *American Journal of Sociology*, 100 (6): 1594–610.

Trimberger, E.K. (1978) *Revolution from above: Military bureaucrats and development in Japan, Turkey, Egypt, and Peru*. New Brunswick, NJ: Transaction Books.

Tullock, G. (1971) 'The paradox of revolution', *Public Choice*, 11 (1): 89–99.

Van Vugt, J.P. (1991) *Democratic organization for social change: Latin American Christian base communities and literary campaigns*. New York: Bergin and Garvey.

Walder, A.G. (1989) 'The political sociology of the Beijing Upheaval of 1989', *Problems of Communism*, 38 (5): 41–48.

Walt, S.M. (1996) *Revolution and war*. Ithaca, NY: Cornell University Press.

Walton, J. (1984) *Reluctant rebels*. New York: Columbia University Press.

Wasserstrom, J.N. (1994) 'Gender and revolution in Europe and Asia', *Journal of Women's History*, 6 (1): 109–20.

Wasserstrom J.N. and Perry, E.J. (Eds.) (1994) *Popular protest and political culture in modern China* (2nd ed.) Boulder, CO: Westview.

Weede, E. (1987) 'Some new evidence on correlates of political violence: Income inequality, regime repressiveness, and economic development', *European Sociology Review*, 3 (2): 97–108.

Weede, E. and Muller, E.N. (1997) 'Consequences of revolutions', *Rationality and Society*, 9 (3): 327–50.

Weitman, S. (1992) 'Thinking the revolutions of 1989', *British Journal of Sociology*, 43 (1): 13–24.

White, R. (1989) 'From peaceful protest to guerrilla war: micromobilization of the Provisional Irish Republican Army', *American Journal of Sociology*, 94 (6): 1277–302.

Wickham-Crowley, T. (1991) *Exploring revolution: Essays on Latin American insurgency and revolutionary theory*. Armonk, NY: Sharpe.

Wickham-Crowley, T. (1992) *Guerrillas and revolution in Latin America*. Princeton, NJ: Princeton University Press.

Wolf, E.R. (1969) *Peasant wars of the twentieth century*. New York: Harper & Row.

Wood, E. (2000) *Forging democracy from below*. Cambridge: Cambridge University Press.

Zamosc, L. (1989) 'Peasant struggles of the 1970s in Columbia', in S. Eckstein (ed.), *Power and popular protest: Latin American Social Movements*. Berkeley: University of California Press, pp. 102–31.

Zartman, W.I. (1995) *Collapsed states: The disintegration and restoration of legitimate authority*. Boulder, CO: Lynne Rienner.

Zhao, D. (2001) *The power of Tiananmen: State-society relations and the 1989 Beijing student movement*. Chicago: University of Chicago Press.

Zimmermann, E. (1990) 'On the outcomes of revolutions: Some preliminary considerations', *Sociological Theory*, 8 (1): 33–47.

18

Social Movements

Vincent Boudreau and David S. Meyer

INTRODUCTION

Comparative politics has often been a little unsure about what exactly needed to be compared when it comes to social movements. In some studies, the operational definition of a *social movement* shifts to fit the empirical case or cases at hand, while in others, the term does not appear at all, replaced by non-governmental organizations, democratization campaigns, labor movements, agrarian mobilization, and revolutions – among other terms. As with other subjects, comparative politics has produced a large number of single country case studies, informed by explicitly comparative theoretical concerns, which often address larger theoretical questions. And, as with other subjects, the field has produced a number of explicitly comparative studies that sacrifice some amount of detail for theoretical parsimony. Also, again as in other areas of comparative politics, there has been broad recognition that the international context offers constraints and opportunities for both authorities and their challengers, such that we need not see states as autonomous ecological units.

The raft of research on a range of (potentially) related phenomena is greater than the theoretical sum of its parts – a result of discrepancies in subject matter and the theoretical barriers between those who study different

parts of the world. Particularly, studies of movements that press for political reform in the global North generally bear little resemblance to studies of social movements that seek to hold state power in the global South.

Within the thus far distinct literatures on protest movements, scholars have made substantial progress in identifying the proximate causes and consequences of social movements. Broader comparisons have been slower to emerge, presenting a continuing challenge for synthetically minded scholars of comparative politics. It is quite likely that such broader synthesis will reveal relationships within social movement theory similar to those between Einsteinian and Newtonian physics. While the latter is perfectly adequate for making predictions within certain circumstances, the former offers a deeper and more comprehensive understanding that contextualizes and unifies apparent anomalies. Einstein's broader compass revealed Newton's physics as particular cases of more universal laws, and set the key variables for a more unified science as residing in contextual factors like gravity and speed. Not only does Einstein tell us that things work differently outside the Newtonian world, he also suggests that earlier understandings of familiar conditions were incomplete. In a similar vein, we argue that the way forward for the comparative study of social movements lies in the development of a broader and more synthetic analysis. Recently some scholars have suggested a broader theoretical framework, sometimes termed 'contentious politics,' (McAdam et al., 2001; Tarrow and Tilly, 2006) which promises to provide greater synthesis and conceptual unity.

Here, we review some of the major contributions from comparative politics to the study of social movements, noting significantly different areas of inquiry in the North and in the South. We focus on the range of independent variables that scholars use to explain the origins, emergence, development, organization, and ultimate impact of social movements. By situating our review in a systematic retracing of major differences in the organization of political authority, we mean to suggest grounds for a larger, contextual, understanding of how social movements relate to other political phenomena, enabling the development of broader comparisons across different political contexts. We begin by offering a brief history of the field of social movements within comparative politics, then turn to review major issues in studies of unrest in the North, then in the South. We consider the influence of international context on social movement development, and conclude with suggestions for further research.

PROTEST POLITICS AND SOCIAL MOVEMENTS

The term, 'social movements' is inclusive, perhaps overly so, referring to a wide range of political phenomena. Indeed, scholars frequently offer a specific definition that applies to the case at hand, and talk past other work on the topic. For our purposes, we appreciate Tarrow's (1998: 4) handy definition of social movements as 'collective challenges by people with common purposes and solidarity in sustained interaction with elites, opponents, and authorities.' This definition locates social movements firmly as political phenomena, but

allows considerable flexibility in the range of political formations and sequences of events that might be included in an analysis. Despite this flexibility – or perhaps because of it – scholars with a range of relevant concerns have often ignored the broader connections that were possible in their findings.

Most generally, political scientists have struggled to consider whether protest politics and social movements were an extension of more conventional political participation or a rejection of more conventional politics. Classic comparative literature of the 1960s (e.g., Huntington, 1968; Lipset, 1960) saw the emergence of protest politics as a failing of established political institutions to integrate and process grievances and constituencies. Indeed, scholars contended that the forms, claims, and ultimate influence of social movements emerged as an almost direct reflection of state structures and governing coalitions. The premise underlying this work was that the social movement was a temporary, transitional phenomenon, which would fade when established institutions responded to it.

In the wake of the social movements of the 1960s, political scientists emphasized the policy payoff of protest. For Lipsky (1968) and then for Piven and Cloward (1977), protest was the best strategy for affecting influence for poor people and minorities, unlikely to be able to make political gains in other ways. Although protestors need not come to their strategic decisions through rational calculations, their choice of strategy nonetheless was, strictly speaking, rational. This approach dovetailed with an emerging rational choice perspective within political science that focused on the problem of collective action and group size (e.g., Olson, 1967), and which was applied to some of the emerging social movements of the time (e.g., McCarthy and Zald, 1977).

The resource mobilization tradition was later challenged by 'new social movement' scholars who noted that the causes around which contemporary movements organized, particularly peace, the environment, gay and lesbian rights, and feminism, were poorly explained by a narrow rational choice account (e.g., Melucci, 1989; Offe, 1985). These scholars emphasized the context of relative affluence in West Europe and the US, and the relatively advantaged status of those engaged in protest, and questioned whether tactics of mobilization reflected only instrumental concerns. They suggested, instead, that new social movement politics contained expressive elements whose justification was not based on likely efficacy (e.g., Cohen, 1985). Ultimately, they came to argue that social movements were an alternative and additional mode of democratization, characteristic of the advanced industrialized world and 'post-industrial society.' Buechler (1999) has persuasively argued that the so-called new movements did not represent as dramatic break with the past as earlier scholars had argued, but did reflect the significant issues and opportunities of the contemporary period.

Starting at about the same time as the resource mobilization perspective emerged, other scholars examined the development and outcome of social and political rebellions and revolutions. Research focused on the circumstances under which revolutions took place, and the factors affecting the eventual outcomes of those revolutions. Barrington Moore's (1968) classic treatment of historical revolutions traced the outcomes of those revolutions to the composition of the coalitions seeking to replace authorities. Gurr (1969) argued that revolutionary campaigns emerged when the economy's capacity to deliver benefits was outstripped by growing expectations. Skocpol (1979) attributed the success or failure of a revolutionary movement in seeking power to the weight of exogenous challenges on the state.

For the most part, despite potential connections which seem obvious in retrospect, these literatures developed in isolation from each other. Charles Tilly (e.g., 1978), however, contended that the same processes were at work in both smaller scale social movements and large scale social revolutions, with differential outcomes as contingent upon a large number of factors, including both political structures and activist tactics. Later, he would catalog all 'revolutionary situations' in Europe over a 500 year period, noting that only a tiny fraction resulted in regime change (Tilly, 1993b). Tilly (1993a) would also trace the development of a 'repertoire of contention' through which actors made claims and authorities responded; he contended that this repertoire provided an empirical and theoretical link between revolutions and social movements.

Tilly's efforts to provide an overarching framework for understanding what he would call 'contentious politics,' that is, the links between a spectrum of political claims making that ranges from activity centered mostly within conventional political institutions toward violent revolutionary movements, has developed in specificity through collaborative efforts (McAdam et al., 2001; Tarrow and Tilly, 2006); it includes a new emphasis on identifying a large number of mechanisms surrounding the interaction between claim makers and authorities, but the initial theoretical separation between scholarship on revolutions and on reform-oriented social movements has largely continued. This separation, we argue, is supported by the geographic separation of the locations of different movements, and the attendant questions that follow from different forms of contentious politics.

Thus, those who studied revolutions concentrated on the challenges confronting state efforts to build, consolidate, or merely retain power (Goldstone, 2003; Huntington, 1968; Skocpol, 1979). Those who examined transitions to democracy looked at the realignment of political elites, and the rise of moderate coalitions that displaced hardliners (Karl, 1990; Linz and Stepan, 1996; O'Donnell et al., 1986). Those who studied reform-oriented social movements paid particular attention to changes that encouraged individuals to move from routine to non-routine forms of participation – focusing on the question of mobilization over other considerations (McCarthy and Zald, 1977; Tarrow, 1989). Comparativists compared the differential outcomes of similar movements, again, focusing on the connections between movements and more conventional politics. In these pursuits, comparative analysts employed a broad range of research methods, ranging from large sample comparisons of individuals or nations to detailed single case studies of particular movements in particular settings. We believe that there is the potential for a richer theoretical framework to connect ostensibly distinct phenomena and literatures. We will review the distinctions, and then point to potential connections.

SOCIAL MOVEMENTS IN ADVANCED INDUSTRIALIZED COUNTRIES

Many authors who would offer general statements on protest and social movements studied political unrest in the United States and Europe, mostly Western Europe. Scholars of the wealthy world studied, mostly, campaigns for such things as civil rights, women's rights, the environment, and peace – very much like contemporary social movements in the United States and Europe. They borrowed literature from political sociology and opinion research conducted in both political science and sociology. Cross-sectional comparisons, often of similar movements in different countries, emphasized the origins, forms, and outcomes of movements in relation to their political context, which analysts treated as a constant. In contrast, longitudinal studies of particular movements – or sets of movements – generally limited the context to one country and focused on the iterative development of social movements, institutional politics, and public policy, in response to one another.

Much of this work focuses on political context. Looking at the 1960s riots in American cities, Peter Eisinger (1973) was concerned with why some cities experienced violent unrest while others did not. He found that the nature of the political system in each city explained the occurrence of riots: cities with extremely open political structures preempted riots by inviting conventional political participation, and others without room for political input, repressed unrest and robbed dissatisfied people of the organizational space and political hope necessary to stage unrest. Tilly (1978) expanded this concept of a 'political opportunity structure' to a larger field, arguing that the same patterns could be found in mobilization at the national level. This political opportunity approach has been developed in a variety of different ways (see Meyer, 2004 for review), including single country case studies (e.g., Costain, 1992; McAdam, 1982; Meyer, 1990; Schurman, 2004; Tarrow, 1989) and cross-national comparisons (e.g., Kitschelt, 1986; Kriesi et al., 1995).

Particularly important and frutiful is Tarrow's (1989) study of unrest in Italy over a contentious decade, 1965–1975. Offering a more dynamic analysis of Italian politics inside and outside institutions, Tarrow focused on changes in political opportunities to explain a very broad range of protest politics over the decade. Offering the concept of a 'cycle of protest,' which includes decline, and by considering institutional politics, including elections and policy initiatives, as both responses and sources for protest, Tarrow placed social movements firmly within a political context.

In the Italian case, Tarrow contends that government openings and efforts at democratization in the 1960s reduced the costs and increased the promise of political mobilization. The initial mobiliation of one constituency encouraged others to emulate potentially successful actions, leading to a cascade of protest. Workers, students, religious reformers, and leftist factions within parties all took to the streets. As newly mobilized groups sought to gain political attention in a suddenly crowded field, they sometimes experimented with violent action. The government responded to violence with harsh repression, raising the costs of collective action, and diminishing protest. At the same time, some of the social movement actors turned their attention to more conventional political activity, reducing their claims and moderating their tactics, effectively *institutionalizing dissent* (Meyer and Tarrow, 1998). Beyond the empirical case, Tarrow's work was particularly important because it made methodological and theoretical advances.

Methodologically, Tarrow (1989) developed 'events data' analysis, imported from sociology (see McAdam, 1982), as a means of deriving information about the peaks and troughs of social movements, as well as their claims from coded newspaper accounts. European political scientists would extend this analysis further through largescale collaborative efforts to compile large data sets on comparative collective action (see especially Rucht et al., 1999). Events data analysis would develop to compare political tactics over time and across contexts (e.g., Kriesi et al., 1995; Rucht, 1990), the claims of various social movement actors made (e.g., Koopmans and Statham, 1999a, 1999b), and social movements policy outcomes (e.g., Giugni, 2004).

Both here (Tarrow, 1989) and in his expressly theoretical work (Tarrow, 1998), Tarrow stresses the connections between mainstream politics and protest movements. He argues that movements are best understood when studied in the context of a wide range of other political phenomena, which may sometimes spill over into movement actions. The structure of available political opportunities can provide incentives for particular kinds of mobilization strategies as well as cues the savvy activist can read in making decisions about claims, tactics, and potential allies. Activists, authorities, opponents – sometimes in movement forms themselves (Meyer and Staggenborg, 1996), and allies all operate in response to each other and their own perceptions of their interests, changing the field of opportunities for all concerned. In this way, activists, by provoking response from authorities, can generate subsequent opportunities for themselves and for other activists. The focus on the interaction of social movement opposition and political opportunties provides a useful focus for analysts, but in the midst of a wide range of contingencies, it is hard to tease

out generalizations that would apply to other movements in other contexts.

In contrast, scholars embarking on explicit comparisons across states simplify the range of political opportunities to make translation across contexts possible, following Eisinger's (1973) model study. As a key example, Herbert Kitschelt's (1986) study of antinuclear movements in four democracies, France, Sweden, the United States, and West Germany, used political opportunity theory to explain the style and development of social movement politics, as well as their ultimate influence. Although he explicitly recognizes broad conceptions of opportunities, including resources, institutions, and historical precedents, for the purposes of the analysis Kitschelt provides a much narrower specification. He sorts the four states along two dimensions: input structures (open or closed) and output capacity (strong or weak), and argues that this simple classification explains the strategies challengers employed in all four states, as well as their ultimate influence. The available options for participation comprise a menu for collective action from which activists choose. In Kitschelt's terms, activists choose *confrontational* strategies in response to institutional blockages – as the best available approach for expression; in contrast, activists employ *assimilative* strategies when opennings appear. He contends that state capacity determines influence – greater procedural innovation or substantive change in response to pressures in weaker states. This sparse model offers an advantage of clarity, but at the cost of simplifying and flattening a broad range of factors critical to the development of a social movement over time.

On occasion, teams of scholars have worked to combine the virtues of cross-sectional comparison with over-time observation. Kriesi and his colleagues (Kriesi et al., 1995) combine the complexity and nuance of the longitudinal studies with the analytical leverage of cross-sectional studies, comparing 'new social movements' [the 'family' of left-libertarian movements in advanced industrialized states (see della Porta and Rucht, 1995)] across four

European states (France, Germany, the Netherlands and Switzerland) over time. They see opportunity structures as including the nature of political cleavages, institutional structures, alliance structures (for these movements, the openness and political position of left parties), and prevailing strategies of social movements. By focusing on the effects of two factors, the configuration of power on the left and its presence or absence in government, they offer a fuller picture of citizen mobilization as it responds to political opportunity.

Thinking of movement participation as including less disruptive and confrontational tactics such as petitions and peaceful demonstrations, Kriesi et al. (1995) examine the full range of activist mobilization. Their analysis focuses on the role of the state in facilitating some kinds of access, and also in setting the agenda for challengers through the policies it adopts – sometimes raising the threat of inaction.

State action affects the volume, form, and location of protest. Surprisingly, they find the highest per capita level of activism in Switzerland, but it is predominantly expressed through conventional political participation and membership in social movement organizations. In contrast, France demonstrates lower levels of participation, but events are frequently dramatic and disruptive. Kriesi et al.'s (1995) explanation is far more nuanced and comprehensive than Kitschelt's (1986), but also harder to translate easily to other cases.

Drawing from insights in a number of single case studies, however, we can discern general patterns in the development of social movements in advanced industrialized countries. Koopmans' (1995) analysis of 'new' social movements in West Germany, for example, traces the development of movement politics to particular elements of the German political system. Focusing on the interplay of social movements and the political system, he identifies discrete policy opportunities, which he describes 'concrete opportunities' which have direct motivational consequences for movements. In other words, activists are most likely to mobilize when they have reason to

view their efforts as potentially successful or particularly necessary to avoid a bad outcome (also see Meyer, 2007).

Donatella della Porta and Herbert Reiter (1998) focus on the development of the actual conduct of protest by focusing on police behavior in Western democracies. In effect, police and courts present an extremely proximate element in the structure of political opportunities that would-be activists face. Demonstrators and authorities (in this case, police) seek to minimize the costs and disruption of protest by adhering to familiar routines. Della Porta and Reiter contend that the national styles of policing reflect larger patterns of authority and policy making in the polity. Importantly, they contend that opportunities for protesters are not simply 'open' or 'closed,' but instead are specific to particular groups and constituencies and their relationship to the political mainstream (see Meyer and Minkoff, 2004). This emergent and increasingly common style over the past few decades, however, is one in which protest is facilitated to minimize disruption and uncertainty for all concerned; this is likely to limit political influence as well (see McCarthy and McPhail, 1998; Piven and Cloward, 1977).

Giugni (2004) focuses on the influence of the total impact of the range of movement activity on public policy. Considering the intervening effects of public opinion and political structures, he assesses the comparative impact of the environmental, peace, and antinuclear movements in three different countries. He finds that movements matter, but only when deployed in conjunction with a favorable political climate, including supportive public opinion and available political allies. Following a similar track, other scholars have traced an interactive relationship between social movements and public policy (e.g., Banaszak, 1996; Meyer et al., 2005) and assessed the impact of public policy on social movements (e.g., Mettler, 2005). It is clear that social movements can help affect public policies, building state action, which in turn, creates the conditions for subsequent social movements.

More generally, scholars have observed a modal pattern of political mobilization in advanced industrialized states, in which protest as a viable political tactic diffuses broadly throughout the populace, such that it is used by a broader range of constituencies (see Dalton, 2005). As this diffusion takes place, however, citizens increasingly employ *less* disruptive forms of protest, and states adapt to facilitate this kind of participation. Protest is no longer a tool employed by those unlikely to affect influence in other ways, but has become a strategic *component* of a broad range of political actors and causes. The ultimate impact of this kind of 'institutionalization of dissent' remains an open question for scholars (Meyer and Tarrow, 1998). In the global South, we will see that the nature of existing governmental institutions dramatically affects the nature of protest and the nature of comparative analysis.

REVOLUTION, REPRESSION, AND DEMOCRATIZATION IN THE GLOBAL SOUTH

The empirical material scholars address understandably affects the theoretical literatures with which they engage. In the global south, both activists and authorities are less certain that existing political institutions will survive a movement challenge intact. The stakes generally appear higher for all involved, challengers can rely far less on the protection of national laws and authorities' tolerance, and outside actors can exert more influence. As a result, the nature of claims, organizations, and tactics differ accordingly.

When we turn our analysis to include studies of contention under weak states, we see shifts in the nature of the political contest. In such settings, normal politics may include systems of repression or patronage that keep claim makers at arms length, distant from any meaningful access to political institutions; further, authorities may lean very heavily on a narrow band of supporters, addressing claims

through personalistic and discretionary allocations of resources, in conjunction with more or less selective repression (Bratton and Van de Walle, 1997). Here, representative structures or shifting access to government probably influence mobilization patterns less than patterns of political alliance, repression, or exclusion. Social movements may seek (and sometimes win) substantial institutional restructuring rather than more limited reforms. To make sense of movements in the global South, we will pay particular attention to these distinct, but interrelated topics: revolution, repression, and democratization.

Revolution

The extraordinary occasion of a social revolution has spurred a great deal of research, and scholars differ on whether such occurrences reflect a relatively infrequent and distinct phenomenon (e.g., Skocpol, 1979) or a relatively infrequent outcome of a rather common set of processes (Tilly, 1993b). The latter course of analysis underscores the relationship of revolutionary outcomes to the development of politically oriented movements.

Jack Goldstone (2003) argues that the emergence and location of successful revolutionary movements can best be explained by considering the stability and nature of state structures and their relationship to challengers. Structural theories show that revolutions 'begin from some combination of state weakness, conflicts between states and elites, and popular uprisings' (Goldstone, 2003: 6). Revolutionary movements are critical, but they do not make history in the circumstances they choose; a state with weakened capacity to buy off or repress insurgents will be more vulnerable to revolution.

The opposition is still viewed as a key component of revolution, but it is recognized that a state with weakened structural capabilities and a predilection for conflict between the state and the elites will be vulnerable to revolution. When the grievances of peasants or urban dwellers meet with 'conducive structural conditions,' such as landlord vulnerability or weakly policed cities, there is the possibility of effective revolutionary action (Goldstone, 2003: 10–11). Further, when conflict between the state and powerful elites coincides and connects with the structural conditions and popular uprisings, revolution becomes possible.

Building on Huntington (1968), Goldstone adopts a focus on political institutions and particularly their decay, in the makings of a revolution. He writes:

> A marked imbalance between the demands of a changing population on the economy and the government, and the ability of the government to respond creates a situation of declining political stability. Whenever such imbalances become widespread, so too does the risk of revolutions (Goldstone, 2003: 18).

In short, social movements emerge to present claims to a state; when that state is incapable of responding effectively to either the claims or the activities of its challengers, a social movement may become revolutionary. Essentially, when an insurgent movement lines up with a 'revolutionary situation' (Tilly, 1993b), that is, a large opportunity, social revolutions are possible. As Skocpol (1979) pointed out, the international system and the challenges it offers are critical influences on state vulnerability. The organization and claims of challengers, responding to the strengths, weaknesses and openings in the state, shape the development of social movements.

Weak or patrimonial states often cannot address social concerns via formal public policy processes, relying instead on a mix of repression and selective patronage (e.g., Eckstein, 1989). Even where ideas about democratic policy making (often popularized following transitions from authoritarian rule) convince authorities to adopt policies that promise public services or protections, administrative capacity may not be up to the task, creating a disconnect between written policy and government action. Eckstein's analysis of popular protest in Mexico, for instance, demonstrates how government action may require private petitions, off-stage from public political processes that depend on the discretion of a less than ideal-type

bureaucracy (Eckstein, 1990). In this regard, as Suh (2001) has argued in relation to Korean labor movements, activists' policy demands can best be seen as targeted at mobilizing broad constituencies, rather than provoking actual reforms.

Those shut out of meaningful politics are likely to think less about petitioning government, and more about replacing it, in order to produce a system to which they have more access, or carving out autonomous spaces for local community self governance (Ramos, 2002): both tendencies move the politics of protest away from policy issues and more toward issues of governance and (potentially) state control (Davis, 1994). Absent state crisis, activists can still make claims to bureaucratic line agencies, or denounce government development projects, repression, or corruption (Loveman, 1998; Navarro, 1989; O'Brien and Li, 2006).

Paradoxically, the loss of local control, primarily to waves of neoliberal economic reform, reinforces and politicizes ethnic identities, making different sorts of mobilization possible (Yashar, 2005). Episodic mobilizations (Almeida, 2007) can produce modest reforms or somewhat improved positioning of challengers, but often the most significant effect is the development of a history of contention, and the enhanced will to challenge government in the future (Almeida, 2007). When central authority falters, protest can escalate precipitously to regime changing programs (Boudreau, 2004; Kim, 1996).

Most theorists acknowledge that authoritarian regimes do not fall apart simply because they encounter mass opposition, but rather that protest and resistance encourages or accelerates nascent splits in the regime, and encourages processes of dissonance and decay that might have already been underway (Bermeo, 1999; Wood, 2000). Movement outcomes reflect the interaction between structural features favoring (respectively) policy or regime change, and pressure from a political movement. Still, how authorities respond to protest will also have a great deal to do with the choices that activists make.

Repression

Although explicitly theoretical work (e.g., Coleman, 1990), has specifically linked repression of protest in authoritarian settings to the same sorts of factors that expand movement opportunities in democratic settings, only recently have scholars offered empirical illustrations of these links, offering a more variegated analysis of repression that links to challengers' mobilization strategies (e.g., Boudreau, 2004; Ray, 1999).

In such settings, key political opportunities, primarily located in the strength of a regime rather than in the nature of routine political processes, can activate networks of challengers differentially, and result in mobilizing better-positioned cosmopolitan actors first (DeNardo, 1985; Oliver et al., 1985). The critical issues that determine the extent of a challenge and the key mechanisms for mobilization may exist in new connections between sociologically different populations – as, for instance, between residents of towns and rural villages. Other substantial opportunities may be found in processes that undermine authorities' coercive capacities (Wood, 2000) – such as exogenous economic or political pressures. Such pressures can weaken regime alliances or strengthen opposition coalitions against the state or regime, rather than in those that provide easier access to policy making or regime officials. The mechanisms associated with political mobilization are likely to differ across subgroups within a polity, such as residents of cities versus those in rural areas.

In settings where government is less able or inclined to redress broad popular grievances, mainstream politics becomes less representative, often less institutionalized and more brutal. Social movements may regularly fail to secure policy reform and wider representation (Brockett, 1991), but that failure may contribute to the emergence of broader and more fundamental challenges to state power (Almeida, 2007). Kim (1996), for instance, explains the mobilization of a regime-displacing uprising in Korea in terms of state

repression against a more limited student movement. Misagh Parsa (2000) concentrates on middle class entrepreneurs during regime transitions in Iran and the Philippines, noting that the exclusionary nature of the two states pushed middle class entrepreneurs in each setting to adopt regime displacing politics that gathered steam when authorities suddenly grew weaker. Elizabeth Wood's (2000) account of anti-regime insurgencies in South Africa and El Salvador locates the resistance in military formations designed to fight, rather than appeal to, the state. Boudreau's (2004) analysis of protest in Southeast Asia describes how different forms of state repression shaped movements, both by eliminating some political forms, and forcing activists to seek out each regime's weak flank. In these treatments, movement forms are shaped by the need to confront state authorities, and to survive that confrontation – rather than to directly influence state policy or to take advantage of access to the state.

Just as activists may turn to broader claims and more aggressive strategies, states under pressure are also likely to turn to harsher responses, producing a cycle of escalation that may end in revolution (Goldstone, 2003; Mason, 1998). While we might expect more general social support for radicalization in poorer settings, an increasing number of analysts are advising that social movement trajectories treat the opportunity for more modest political institutionalization as movement-specific; some issues have greater potential to evolve into more moderate policy based struggles (Kowalchuk, 2005). For example, Trevizo (2006) describes the crucial difference between Mexican student protests that ended in mass murder and those that produced policy reform as a function of whether activists framed their protest in terms of revolution or policy reform, but his analysis also emphasizes the willingness of the Mexican state at the time to use violence.

Over time, both authorities and movements can alter the conditions of protest. State repression may eliminate some movement forms, or impose new and serious threats to proscribed modes of activity (Boudreau, 2004), while accepted groups and claims can work to navigate new relationships with authorities. Further, repression that produces strong social dissent may also encourage learning and strategic adjustment among security forces, and efforts to make the expression of dissent less dangerous, and ultimately, more routine (della Porta and Rieter, 1998). Still, whether claim making produces greater openness or closure depends on the character of interactions between authorities and challengers. Harsher repression and democratization represent different futures.

Democratization

Interestingly, most of the literature that deals with social movements and state repression focuses on the (potential) outcome of democratization, attending less to an analysis of process and more to an evaluation of outcome. Further, the democratization literature tends to focus on top-down, elite initiated transitions and authors often issue warnings about too much citizen mobilization during a transition from authoritarian rule. Democratic transitions are particularly vulnerable to the threats posed by violent action. Most analysts see moderation, or the rejection of radical mass mobilization, as the preferable choice during the untenable transition process; these authors promote temperate progress: negotiations, pacts, and peace agreements. In this view, protest, political violence, and radical mobilization are obstacles to democratization; disruption is a threat rather than a subject of inquiry.

Others suggest, however, that a heated political process can provide the cauldron for making democracy. Bermeo (1999), for example, criticizes analysts' 'fear of the masses' and their insistence on moderating threats from below. Acknowledging that violence can disrupt democratic transitions, she contends that 'these negative cases do not in themselves make an argument for moderation' (Bermeo, 1999: 127). In contrast, she cites the cases of Spain, Portugal, Peru, and South Korea, where instances of political violence did not derail the transition to democracy. Indeed, the mobilization of violence may have promoted these transitions.

Bermeo contends that the threat of violence can also encourage authorities to pursue reforms, depending upon their perception of the difficulties and costs of repression and their likely fates in a new setting. Given the presence of challengers threatening violent disruption, authorities calculate both the difficulties of repression *and* the likely fortunes of their challengers under a new regime. If key elites predict that their opponents will not win in a new democratic setting, they are likely to allow democratic transitions to progress; they may even welcome democratic elections to legitimate their claims to state power.

Elisabeth Jean Wood (2000) also formulates a democratization argument based on elite perception of mass mobilization. She examines El Salvador and South Africa as examples of successful democracy movements forged from below by the insurgency of poor people. These insurgencies, she argues, reshaped economic interests and opportunities and forced economic, and then political, elites to share power and/or wealth. Focusing on the economic impact of protest, Wood shows how civil war transformed the political economy of El Salvador, directly reshaping elite interests. Sustained unrest led to a structural transformation characterized by declining economic production and export agriculture, as well as capital flight. Repression and resistance became costly strategies for economic elites, less promising than adopting neo-liberal economic reforms and a market economy. The market would provide more effective discipline for workers than state repression.

Similar processes occurred in South Africa, Wood (2000) argues. Again, she focuses on the link between mass mobilization and elites' changing perception of their economic interests. Increased strikes, township unrest, and growing labor militancy all produced domestic instability – as well as an extremely negative international image. Domestic pressures were intensified by international economic sanctions, all undermining the viability of an economic model based on apartheid. As neo-liberal market alternatives grew comparatively more attractive, business elites began negotiating with Nelson Mandela's African National Congress, seeking to limit their losses. Like Bermeo (1999), Wood (2000) sees the power of mass mobilization in a democratic transition less in its force than in its capacity to alter authorities' perceptions of their own prospects. Elites undertake democratic reforms in response to social movements when they begin to think it is in *their own* best interest to do so. Disruptive action affects their calculations about their interests.

Ruth Berins Collier (1999) explicitly challenges the notion that a particular set of actors, either elites or masses, is generically critical to the process of democratization. Comparing 27 cases across Latin America and Europe, over a period of roughly 100 years, she emphasizes the contingencies inherent in the process of democratization. Elites may initiate democratization efforts, as Wood suggests, when they see it in their interests to do so, but change is *sometimes* spurred by collective action from below, particularly when organized labor is able to find potential allies among the elite. For Collier, the particular path of democratization reflects the available coalition partners for would-be reformers.

Boudreau (2004) also focuses on contingencies, unpacking repression to understand the dynamics of social movement challenges in Burma, Indonesia, and the Philippines. He compares the repressive strategies of these states and the subsequent modes of collective action and resistance that arose in response. Boudreau identifies a range of responsive strategies available to state authorities and the choices they made in each setting. He contends that repressive strategies don't just stoke or dampen mass mobilization, but actually sculpt it over a long period of time through sustained interaction. In the Philippines, he contends, the regime's social control strategies became increasingly ineffective as Ferdinand Marcos lost the capacity to buy off substantial

portions of the economic elite. In Indonesia, *keterbukaan* (political reforms akin to *glasnost*) in the 1980s relaxed restrictions on activists and allowed for more institutionalized resistance activity. Finally, Burma's military leaders have not yet reached a position where the social challengers couldn't be contained, and repression not only continued, but it intensified.

Writing directly in response to developing social movement literature (especially, McAdam et al., 2001), Boudreau adopts the focus on the interactions of challengers and authorities, particularly resistance and repression. He argues the particular modes of coercion pattern the resistance. His work suggests the kinds of analytical syntheses available through focused comparisons of state structures and challengers' choices.

CONCLUSION

In this chapter, we have attempted to think in the broadest terms possible about a comparative politics of social movements and political contention. We have concentrated on variations in states' capacities and policy processes, and the ways in which variations in these factors influence the emergence, forms, processes and outcomes of political contention. The review reveals some substantial foundations for a broader comparative analysis than has frequently been attempted heretofore. Processes of political change and democratization make it more likely that reform movements targeting policy processes will emerge in all corners of the world, including places where movements with displacement or separatist goals had been more common. In analyzing these movements, there is much that we can learn from examining protest movements in wealthier settings, with particular attention to variations in the openness of the policy making process. While weaker state capacities in poorer settings will probably make policy reform less likely, this is increasingly an empirical matter, particularly as both democratic procedures and social movement techniques diffuse across the globe. Similarly, processes of insurgent mobilization in the global south have much to teach those interested in advocacy on the part of systematically excluded populations in all settings. Focusing on the capacity and the willingness of authorities to resolve movement grievances, the existence and salience of unresolved grievances in different societies, and the extent to which movements advocate specific policy reforms rather than broader displacement goals, provides the basis for some of these broader comparisons.

REFERENCES

Almeida, P.D. (2007) *Waves of protest: Popular struggle in El Salvador, 1925–2005.* Minneapolis: University of Minnesota Press.

Banaszak, L.A. (1996). *Why movements succeed or fail: Opportunity, culture, and the struggle for woman suffrage.* Princeton, NJ: Princeton University Press.

Bermeo, N. (1999) 'Myths of moderation', in L. Anderson (ed.), *Transitions to democracy.* New York: Columbia University Press, pp. 120–39.

Boudreau, V. (2004) *Resisting dictatorship: Repression and protest in Southeast Asia.* Cambridge: Cambridge University Press.

Bratton, M. and Van de Walle, K. (1997) *Democratic experiments in Africa: Regime transition in comparative perspective.* Cambridge, UK: Cambridge University Press.

Brockett, C. (1991) 'The structure of political opportunities Central America', *Comparative Politics,* 23 (3): 253–74.

Buechler, S. (1999) *Social movements in advanced capitalism.* New York: Oxford University Press.

Cohen, J.L. (1985) 'Strategy or identity: New theoretical paradigms and contemporary social movements', *Social Research,* 52: 663–716.

Coleman, J.S. (1990) *Foundations of social theory.* Cambridge, MA: Harvard University Press.

Collier, R.B. (1999) *Paths toward democracy: The working class and elites in Western Europe and South America.* New York: Cambridge University Press.

Costain A. (1992) *Inviting women's rebellion: A political process interpretation of the women's movement.* Baltimore, MD: Johns Hopkins University Press.

Dalton, R.J. (2005) *Citizen politics: Public opinion and political parties in advanced industrial democracies* (fourth edition) Washington, DC: CQ Press.

Davis, D.E. (1994) 'Failed democratic reform in contemporary Mexico: From social movements to the state and back again', *Journal of Latin American Studies,* 26 (2): 375–408.

della Porta, D. and Reiter, H. (eds) (1998) *Policing protest: The control of mass demonstrations in western democracies.* Minneapolis: University of Minnesota Press.

della Porta, D. and Rucht, D. (1995) 'Left-libertarian movements in context: A comparison of Italy and West Germany, 1965–1990', in J.C. Jenkins, and B. Klandermans (eds), *The politics of social protest.* Minneapolis: University of Minnesota Press, pp. 229–72.

DeNardo, J. (1985) *Power in numbers: The political strategy of protest and rebellion.* Princeton, NJ: Princeton University Press.

Eckstein, S. (1989) 'Power and popular protest in Latin America', in S. Eckstein (ed.), *Power and popular protest: Latin American social movements.* Berkeley: University of California Press, pp. 1–60.

Eckstein, S. (1990) 'Formal vs. substantive democracy', *Mexican Studies/Studios Mexicanos,* 6 (2): 213–39.

Eisinger, P.K. (1973) 'The conditions of protest behavior in American cities', *The American Political Science Review,* 67: 11–28.

Giugni, M. (2004) *Social protest and policy change: Ecology, antinuclear, and peace movements in comparative perspective.* Lanham, MD: Rowman & Littlefield.

Goldstone, J. (ed.) (2003) *Revolutions: Theoretical, comparative, and historical studies.* Belmont, CA: Wadsworth/Thomson Learning.

Gurr, T.R. (1969) *Why men rebel.* Princeton, NJ: Princeton University Press.

Huntington, S.P. (1968) *Political order in changing societies.* New Haven: Yale University.

Karl, T. (1990) 'Dilemmas of democratization in Latin America', *Comparative Politics*, 23: 1–21.

Kim, Q.Y. (1996) 'From protest to change of regime: The 4-11 revolt and the fall of the Rhee regime in South Korea', *Social Forces*, 74 (4): 1179–208.

Kitschelt, H.P. (1986) 'Political opportunity structures and political protest: Anti-nuclear movements in four democracies', *British Journal of Political Science*, 16 (1): 57–85.

Koopmans, R. (1995) *Democracy from below: New social movements and the political system in West Germany*. Boulder: Westview Press.

Koopmans, R. and Statham, P. (1999a) 'Challenging the liberal nation-state? Postnationalism, multiculturalism, and the collective claims making of migrants and ethnic minorities in Britain and Germany', *American Journal of Sociology*, 105 (2): 652–96.

Koopmans, R. and Statham, P. (1999b) 'Political claims analysis: Integrating protest event and political discourse approaches', *Mobilization*, 4 (2): 40–51.

Kowalchuk, L. (2005) 'The discourse of demobilization: Shifts in activists' priorities and the framing of political opportunities in a peasant land struggle', *The Sociological Quarterly*, 46 (2): 237–61.

Kriesi, H., Koopmans, R., Duvydenak, J.W., and Giugni, M.G. (1995) *New social movements in Western Europe: A comparative analysis*. Minneapolis: University of Minnesota Press.

Linz, J. and Stepan, A. (1996) *Problems of democratic transition and consolidation*. Baltimore, MD: Johns Hopkins University Press.

Lipset, S.M. (1960) *Political man*. New York: Anchor.

Lipsky, M. (1968) 'Protest as a political resource', *American Political Science Review*, 62 (4): 1144–58.

Loveman, M. (1998) 'High-risk collective action: Defending human rights in Chile, Uruguay, and Argentina', *American Journal of Sociology*, 104 (2): 477–525.

Mason, T.D. (1998) 'Take two acres and call me in the morning: Is land reform a prescription for agrarian unrest?', *The Journal of Politics*, 60: 199–230.

McAdam, D. (1982) *Political process and the development of black insurgency, 1930–1970*. Chicago, IL: University Chicago Press.

McAdam, D., Tarrow, S., and Tilly, C. (2001) *Dynamics of contention*. New York: Cambridge University Press.

McCarthy, J.D. and McPhail, C. (1998) 'The institutionalization of protest in the United States', in D.S. Meyer, and S. Tarrow (eds), *The social movement society*. Lanham, MD: Rowman & Littlefield, pp. 83–110.

McCarthy, J.D. and Zald, M.N. (1977) 'Resource mobilization and social movements: A partial theory', *American Journal of Sociology*, 82 (6): 1212–41.

Melucci, A. (1989) *Nomads of the present: Social movements and individual needs in contemporary society*. Philadelphia: Temple University Press.

Mettler, S. (2005) 'Policy feedback effects for collective action: Lessons from veterans' programs', in D.S. Meyer, V. Jenness, and H. Ingram (eds), *Routing the opposition: Social movements, public policy, and democracy*. Minneapolis: University of Minnesota Press, pp. 211–35.

Meyer, D.S. (1990) *A winter of discontent: The nuclear freeze and American politics*. New York: Praeger.

Meyer, D.S. (2004) 'Protest and political opportunity', *Annual Review of Sociology*, 30: 125–45.

Meyer, D.S. (2007) *The politics of protest: Social movements in America*. New York: Oxford University Press.

Meyer, D.S., Jenness, V., and Ingram, H. (eds) (2005) *Routing the opposition: Social movements, public policy, and democracy*. Minneapolis: University of Minnesota Press.

Meyer D.S. and Minkoff, D.C. (2004) 'Conceptualizing political opportunity', *Social Forces*, 82 (4): 1457–92.

Meyer, D.S. and Staggenborg, S. (1996) 'Movements, countermovements, and the structure of political opportunity', *American Journal of Sociology*, 101 (6): 1628–60.

Meyer D.S. and Tarrow, S. (eds) (1998) *The social movement society: Contentious politics for a new century*. Lanham, MD: Rowman and Littlefield.

Moore, B. (1968) *Social origins of dictatorship and democracy*. Boston: Beacon.

Navarro, M. (1989) 'The personal is political: Las madres de la Plaza de Mayo', in Eckstein, S. (ed.), *Power and popular protest: Latin American social movements*. Berkeley: University of California Press, pp. 241–58.

O'Brien, K.J. and Li, L. (2006) *Rightful resistance in rural China*. New York: Cambridge University Press.

O'Donnell, G., Schmitter, P.C., and Whitehead, L. (1986) *Transitions from authoritarian rule* (Vols. 1–4) Baltimore: Johns Hopkins University Press.

Offe, C. (1985) 'New social movements: Challenging the boundaries of institutional politics', *Social Research*, 59: 817–68.

Oliver, P., Marwell, G. and Teixeira, R. (1985) 'A theory of critical mass I: Interdependence, group heterogeneity and the production of collective action', *American Journal of Sociology*, 91 (3): 522–56.

Olson, M. (1967) *The logic of collective action*. Cambridge, MA: Harvard University Press.

Parsa, M. (1996) 'Entrepreneurs and democratization: Iran and the Philippines', *Comparative Studies in Society and History*, 37 (4): 803–30.

Parsa, M. (2000) *States, Ideologies, and Social Revolutions: A Comparative Analysis of Iran, Nicaragua, and the Philippines*. Cambridge: Cambridge University Press.

Piven, F.F. and Cloward, R.A. (1977) *Poor people's movements*. New York: Vintage.

Ramos, A. (2002) 'Cutting through state and class: Sources and strategies of self-representation in Latin America', in K.B. Warren and J.E. Jackson (eds), *Indigenous Movements, Self-Representation, and the State in Latin America*. Austin, Texas: University of Texas Press, pp. 251–79.

Ray, R. (1999) *Fields of protest: Women's movements in India*. Minneapolis: University of Minnesota Press.

Rojas, F. (2006) 'Social movement tactics, organizational change, and the spread of African American studies', *Social Forces*, 84 (4): 2147–66.

Rucht, D. (1990) 'The strategies and action repertoires of new movements', in R.J. Dalton and M. Kuechler (eds), *Challenging the political order: New social and political movements in Western democracies*. New York: Oxford University Press, pp. 156–75.

Rucht, D., Koopmans, R., and Neidhardt, F. (1999) *Acts of dissent: New developments in the study of protest*. Berlin: Sigma.

Schurman, R. (2004) 'Fighting frankenfoods: Industry structures and the efficacy of the anti-biotech movement in Western Europe', *Social Problems*, 51 (2): 243–68.

Scott, J.C. (1985) *Weapons of the weak: Everyday forms of peasant resistance*. New Haven, CT: Yale University Press.

Skocpol, T. (1979) *States and social revolutions: A comparative analysis of France, Russia, and China*. New York: Cambridge University Press.

Suh, D. (2001) 'How do political opportunities matter for social movements?: Political opportunity, misframing, pseudosuccess, and pseudofailure', *Sociological Quarterly*, 42 (3): 437–60.

Tarrow, S. (1989) *Democracy and disorder: Protest and politics in Italy, 1965–1975*. Cambridge: Cambridge University Press.

Tarrow, S. (1998) *Power in movement: Social movements and contentious politics* (second edition) Cambridge: Cambridge University Press.

Tarrow, S. and Tilly, C. (2006) *Contentious politics*. Boulder, CO: Paradigm.

Tilly, C. (1978) *From mobilization to revolution*. Reading, MA: Addison-Wesley.

Tilly, C. (1993a) 'Contentious repertoires in Great Britain, 1758–1834', *Social Science History*, 17 (2): 253–80.

Tilly, C. (1993b) *European revolutions*. Cambridge, MA: Blackwell, pp. *1492–1992*.

Trevizo, D. (2006) 'Between Zapata and Che: A comparison of social movement success and failure in Mexico', *Social Science History*, 30 (2): 197–229.

Wood, E.J. (2000) *Forging democracy from below: Insurgent transitions in South Africa and El Salvador*. Cambridge: Cambridge University Press.

Yashar, D.J. (2005) *Contesting citizenship: Indigenous movements and democracy in Latin America*. New York: Cambridge University Press.

19

Corruption

Paul Heywood

INTRODUCTION

After decades during which corruption received relatively little attention from academics and political practitioners alike, there was a veritable explosion of interest in the issue after the end of the Cold War. Not only did corruption scandals become major news stories in both the developed and developing worlds, but a consensus began to emerge amongst both anti-corruption activists and western governments alike that corruption represented a major risk to socio-economic progress and development. Indeed, there is a sense in which corruption replaced another 'c-word' as the major threat facing western democracies, a view most explicitly expressed by the controversial former governor of the World Bank, Paul Wolfowitz, when he called corruption the 'greatest evil facing the world since communism' (Wintour and Leigh, 2005). Certainly, a range of international organizations, including the World Bank, the International Monetary Fund, and the Organization for Economic Co-operation and Development (OECD), as well as the European Union (EU) and many national governments, began in the 1990s to devote major attention to the issue of corruption, which was almost universally seen as an impediment to economic growth.

The obvious question is why there has been such a dramatic increase in concern about corruption. After all, corruption is hardly a new phenomenon in politics: from the accusations against Socrates, through Livy's lament on the decadence and moral decline of Rome, to the endemic 'Old Corruption' evident throughout much of eighteenth and nineteenth century Europe, the charge of corruption has been a constant motif in political life. Indeed, corruption has existed in all societies and at all times, so the current concern requires some explanation. However, in order to provide such an explanation, we first of all need to understand what we mean by corruption. This chapter opens with a discussion of how to define corruption, before addressing the issue of why it is seen as so important in contemporary politics. It then turns to the question of what causes corruption, before looking at the problems associated with attempts to measure how much corruption takes place across the world. There then follows an assessment of the impact of corruption, and the chapter concludes with an overview of the key strategies employed to combat corruption.

WHAT DO WE MEAN BY CORRUPTION?

Corruption is not easy to define. There is a considerable literature, stretching back over several decades, which seeks to identify the core characteristics of the concept – but, as yet, there is no universally agreed definition. Until the post-Cold War resurgence of interest in the topic, much of the literature followed Arnold J. Heidenheimer (1970) in distinguishing between definitions based respectively on public office (violation of trust placed in the office), public interest (officials engineer private benefit at the expense of the public interest), and the market (maximization of personal gains through dispensing public goods). In more recent years, the most commonly cited definition has been that developed and refined by the anti-corruption non-governmental agency, Transparency International (TI), which states that corruption is 'the misuse of entrusted power for private gain', further differentiated between 'according to the rule' and 'against the rule' variants (Transparency International, 2008). The former refers to situations in which, for instance, facilitation payments ('speed money') are given to a public official in order to secure preferential treatment in an area where the official is legally entitled to act; the latter involve bribes paid to secure services which the official is not entitled to provide.

While the TI definition has the virtue of parsimony, it seems to imply that all corruption is characterized by the search for private pecuniary gain. Corruption, though, involves much more than simply securing private profit through the breaking of rules. In reality, it is probably fruitless to try to identify one generic catch-all definition of corruption which captures the complexity of the concept in such a way that it can inform research into why it takes place and how to combat it. One reason for that fruitlessness is that in order to judge whether something has been corrupted, we need an understanding of its proper or un-corrupt state – and in the case of 'politics' that is almost impossible. Logically, any definition of political corruption entails an implicit notion of '*un*-corrupt' politics, and therefore our definition of politics itself will affect our understanding of political corruption (Philip, 1997). It therefore follows that the meaning of corruption in political life

will vary with the nature of the political system itself, and any definition will inevitably depend upon normative – and therefore inevitably contestable – judgements.

A wide-ranging, generic definition of corruption can at best provide a starting point for identifying and analyzing a range of different *types* of corruption, which would need to be broken down according to a number of different dimensions. These more taxonomical approaches run the risk of becoming overly descriptive, but they are probably an essential first step in developing a basis for meaningful comparison. A good example of such an approach is that by Alatas (1990), who distinguishes between 'transactive' and 'extortive' corruption. The former refers to situations in which there is a mutually entered into arrangement between the donor and recipient of a corrupt exchange, and can be further broken down into a variety of subtypes, including 'investive' (where goods and favours are offered with a view to future returns), 'nepotistic' (the unjustified appointment of friends and relatives to positions of authority), 'autogenic' (where one person benefits from misuse of privileged information), and 'supportive' (action to protect existing corruption networks, such as machine politics). Extortive corruption, meanwhile, involves some form of compulsion, often through the threat of violence. More recently, Johnston (2005) has drawn a distinction between different 'syndromes' of corruption, according to the political and economic opportunities provided by different regime types. Thus, he identifies 'influence markets' (mature democracies), 'elite cartels' (consolidating or reforming democracies), 'oligarchs and clans' (transitional regimes), and 'official moguls' (undemocratic regimes).

A further important distinction referred to in the literature is that between 'low-level' corruption and 'high-level' corruption. Low-level corruption, which is often also labelled bureaucratic corruption or petty corruption, refers to corruption by state officials in their interaction with the public. For instance, when traffic police or doctors accept bribes in the day-to-day performance of their duties, we talk about petty corruption. Low level corruption can be both particularly widespread and also hugely damaging to the functioning of a state, and is arguably the most difficult to root out since it often takes place in contexts where corrupt exchanges are effectively embedded into the daily fabric of social existence. In many poor or developing countries where corruption is endemic, such exchanges have become simply a way of life, usually met with resignation rather than outrage.

By contrast, high-level corruption refers to corrupt acts performed by politicians and other top state officials. High level corruption is sometimes also labelled as 'grand corruption' or 'political corruption', though this form of corruption is not limited to political office-holders but may also concern top officials in – at least nominally – administrative positions. Consistent with the Alatas and Johnston approaches, high level corruption also entails different forms (see Rose-Ackerman, 1999, 2006). It may refer to the organization of entire state sectors into corrupt rent-seeking machines, whereby institutions such as the police force are organized as corrupt networks from top to bottom (Warburton, 2007). It may also refer to forms of illegal campaign financing and to the payment of kickbacks and other private benefits for the award of public contracts and positions.

In its most damaging form, however, high-level corruption refers to the purchase of laws and regulations, since senior public officials are in a position to influence the formulation and adoption of laws and regulations, which can subsequently work in favour of specific client groups. This form of high-level corruption has also been labelled 'state capture' (Hellman et al., 2003; World Bank, 2000) in order to indicate that the law-making process is biased and that the regulatory output tends to work to the advantage of particular groups of captors. A key point is that 'state capture' as a form of high-level corruption does not automatically entail the direct exchange of money between politicians or senior officials on the one hand and some client firm or organization on the other. Corrupt transactions can also be more indirect. For instance, corrupt client actors can donate funds to political parties, which can subsequently be used for the financing of electoral campaigns (as has happened in many established democracies). Benefits may also be handed out at some future stage when politicians or top officials are given jobs or other rewards for loyalty and favourable behaviour in the past, or even more indirectly, when these benefits are handed out to third parties at a later point in time. Corruption is therefore not just about paying bribes.

There is some disagreement as to whether corruption necessarily entails illegal activity. It could be argued that the most sinister forms of corruption in a democracy are those which 'betray the democratic transcript' by undermining mechanisms of accountability – that is, by failing to keep citizens fully informed or by not operating in a transparent manner. For instance, a privatization process may take place formally according to prevailing legal requirements, but if the valuation of the state assets being sold is deliberately kept low without the public being informed (perhaps to ensure more bids) then that could be seen as a form of corruption. This means that corruption is sometimes hard to distinguish from other, legitimate, political activities – especially in the arena of winning votes or securing support. Party patronage for instance, which essentially refers to public sector appointments made by political parties (Kopecky and Mair, 2006), is seen by some as corrupt but by many others as just a normal part of the political process.

Rent-seeking and pork-barrel politics are other forms of behaviour which to some seem corrupt, but they do not in themselves necessarily entail corruption. Rent-seeking (Tullock, 1987) refers to situations where firms or other economic actors are able to secure benefits without compensatory costs as a result of public policy decisions which work in their favour (for instance, the granting of monopoly rights over the import or export of certain goods). Since public officials are often able to grant monopoly rights, there is suspicion that firms lobby to secure such rent-seeking opportunities. Whilst rent-seeking may be seen as improper and immoral in many social and cultural settings, it can really be considered corrupt only if accompanied by some breaking of rules by public officials in exchange for private benefit. The term pork-barrel politics (Ferejohn, 1974), meanwhile, was originally coined in the US and refers to the attempt by politicians to channel public resources to their constituencies. Pork-barrel politics may be criticized using economic efficiency arguments. However, as long as this form of biased distribution of public resources takes place within a formal legal framework of law-making and is subject to public debate and scrutiny, it can hardly be considered as corrupt.

Corruption is thus a difficult concept to pin down. It does not always imply formal breaches of rules (even though it usually does), and interpretations of corruption are also influenced by public reactions to different forms of behaviour. There is thus an inescapably normative dimension to the concept: what is deemed acceptable in one context may not be in another. Moreover, we need to be careful not to confuse arguments about the economic efficiency of public policies with judgements on corrupt *processes* of policy making, especially since judgements on efficiency are themselves influenced by underlying value assumptions.

WHAT IS THE IMPACT OF CORRUPTION?

Concern about corruption is driven not just (or even mainly) by moral repugnance. Recent literature on corruption (see World Bank, 2000: 18–24) has reached several conclusions about the direct and indirect impacts of corruption on the economic well-being of society, using both theoretical arguments and empirical case studies.

First, corruption hurts economic growth. It does so by undermining investments and by distorting the allocation of resources towards inefficient ends, driven more by corrupt rent-seeking opportunities than by any rationale based on economic productivity or growth – hence the existence of so-called 'white elephant' projects, often associated with poor standards in construction and safety (Cartier-Bresson, 2000). Corruption also means that the rules of economic activity are arbitrarily enforced, that property rights are insecure, and that the administrative capacity to provide services is diminished, all of which translates into a highly uncertain business environment (World Bank, 1997: 18–20). Uncertainty in turn raises the costs of private investment and damages the growth of productive capacity. At the same time, corruption undermines the effectiveness of public investment (Tanzi and Davoodi, 1997) – it leads not just to higher public investment expenditure, but also to lower productivity of such investment. Corruption also hurts prospects for foreign direct investment, put off by concern at the misappropriation of funds (World Bank, 2000: 23, note 2). In addition, corruption decreases the efficiency of resource allocation by introducing severe distortions into the price system (Shleifer and Vishny, 1993: 599–617) and, by creating incentives for lower budget revenues and higher budget expenditures, generates unsustainable fiscal positions (Tanzi and Davoodi, 1997; World Bank, 2000: 21–22) which result in high inflation and again in lower effectiveness of the price system. The impact on the price system results in a misallocation of resources towards sub-optimal uses. Ultimately, low investments and poor allocation of resources spell low growth in the long run.

Second, corruption not only hurts citizens' long-term welfare, but it does so in an unfair way. The costs associated with corruption fall primarily on the weakest and most vulnerable groups in society. Societies in which corruption is widespread experience more poverty and higher inequality than those where there is only limited corruption. This is due not only to lower growth, but to the fact that corrupt governments are effectively financed through regressive, rather than progressive taxes, that they cannot successfully establish and maintain social safety nets, and that they divert resources away from investment in human and social capital, both of which are important for reducing poverty and inequality (Gupta et al., 1998; World Bank, 2000: 20–21).

Third, corruption is a key factor in the erosion of trust in institutions, and therefore damages the social fabric more generally. That corruption leads to lower revenues and higher expenditure justifies people in thinking that they are paying more for less. Moreover, those who foot the bill – mainly the poor and the disadvantaged – get almost nothing from the services they are in fact financing. Logically, this leads to a very low level of public trust in state organs and in political leaders, thereby further reducing the capacity of the state to provide welfare enhancing services (Gupta et al., 1998; Tanzi, 1998; Tanzi and Davoodi, 1997; Shleifer and Vishny, 1993; World Bank, 2000: 21–22).

Fourth, as della Porta (2000) has persuasively argued, the spread of corruption over time generates a vicious circle in which widespread corruption undermines confidence in the government and public officials and thereby encourages the search for ways to by-pass or short-circuit the official state machinery; in turn, the readiness to pay for privileged access to services which should by rights be provided free of charge, or at least without favour or discrimination, generates further incentives for public officials to engage in corrupt activity and thereby further undermines trust and confidence in the political process. As in post-war Italy, public officials may wish to be seen as inefficient, since that will increase their scope for charging a premium price to perform what should be routine duties. In this way, corruption and poor governance feed off each other in a self-sustaining manner.

WHY HAS CORRUPTION BECOME SO SALIENT?

Despite the difficulties in defining corruption, the issue has none the less attracted major attention since the early 1990s. How can we explain this surge of interest in an age-old phenomenon? It is tempting to point to the extraordinary events surrounding the *Tangentopoli* scandal in Italy, when the entire body politic was shaken by revelations of endemic deep-rooted corruption, as the starting point. The scale of Italian corruption was massive, and implicated politicians at the very highest level from all the major parties (della Porta and Vannucci, 1999). In the wake of events in Italy, a series of further scandals were revealed in a number of European states – notably Belgium, France, Germany and Spain. However, if the scale of corruption in Italy had not been fully appreciated, the fact of its existence was hardly news: indeed, it had long been widely recognized that corruption was widespread in the country. So, in a sense, the scandal surrounding corruption in Italy simply adds force to the question of why the issue emerged in the early 1990s, rather than at some earlier point. Whilst it is impossible to provide a definitive answer, we can identify four main factors which have contributed to the increased visibility and salience of corruption.

First, the end of the Cold War was itself an unanticipated stimulus. Following the collapse of the Soviet Union, there was no longer any reason for Western democracies to support corrupt dictators who had sought to use anti-communism as a legitimizing rationale: it was neither necessary nor credible to continue turning a blind eye to corruption under the pretext of security issues. The end of the Cold War also effectively ended the great ideological confrontation between capitalism and communism in both the developed and developing world. When asked to explain the success of the operation *Mani Pulite* ('Clean hands') in Italy, Romano Prodi, the Italian premier and former President of the EU Commission, simply answered 'Yalta'. What he meant was that the end of the geo-strategic political framework established by Yalta helped convince Italian businesses that paying the 'party tax' to lock out the communists was no longer legitimate.

In fact, the end of communism gave rise to an unanticipated challenge to the very legitimacy of the democratic states which had 'won' the Cold War. Deprived of this great ideological clash, citizens in the established democracies were able increasingly to focus their attention on the integrity of the political class (Heywood and Krastev, 2006). Debate about moral values and the personal integrity of political leaders became increasingly widespread, and general elections in particular saw ever more references to the personal attributes of the candidates for top office as a key factor in appealing for votes. Any scandals involving the party in government prompted opposition leaders to emphasize their own trustworthiness as a marked contrast to the alleged dishonesty of the incumbent governments (especially as regards financial matters), a pattern repeated throughout many of the world's democracies and one which maintained the visibility of corruption as a political issue.

A second factor relates to changes in global communication technologies. In a world where 'infotainment' has become a major growth industry, and in which investigative journalism seeks to generate high profile news stories in order to supply 24/7 coverage of world events, corruption scandals offer a potent mix of newsworthiness and sensationalism. Moreover, the exponential growth of access to information and communication technologies (ICT) means that people can easily learn about the latest corruption scandals in all corners of the world (Thompson, 2000). Linked in some ways to these ICT developments, a third factor relates to the role of civil society and public awareness campaigns organized by NGOs to mobilize anticorruption sentiments. Civic advocacy has been partially responsible for making corruption a problem not just in corrupted countries, but also for those involved in corrupting them. In particular, the emergence of Transparency International (TI) as a highly visible international NGO dealing with corruption has significantly shaped the anti-corruption agenda. The publication of TI's annual Corruption

Perceptions Index (CPI) has become a significant international news event, which attracts considerable attention. Indeed, the CPI has become the standard reference point for assessing levels of corruption across the world.

Fourth, increased mobility and increasingly globalized markets have also contributed to corruption's greater visibility. In the words of Vito Tanzi (1998: 559),

> globalization has brought individuals from countries with little corruption into frequent contacts with those from countries where corruption is endemic. These contacts have increased the international attention paid to corruption, especially when some companies believed that they were cut out of some contracts because the winning company has paid a bribe.

This links in to the unexpectedly prominent role played by multinational corporations, which have moved from being viewed as major sources of corruption to posing as fighters against corruption. Multinational corporations have long used bribery to win contracts or favourable terms, especially for public sector construction works and the supply of military equipment. Indeed, until recently, bribery was seen as a normal business practice, which was even tax-deductible in states such as France, Germany, the Netherlands, and Norway.

In the 1960s and 1970s, foreign investors saw corruption as a useful way to open up and modernize the economies of developing countries. Corruption was used as an instrument to break the protectionist barriers that were imposed by the governments of postcolonial states, and could therefore even be seen positively. And multinational corporations were able to exert persuasive influence through their financial power, their value often dwarfing the GDP of those developing countries in which they sought to invest. However, two significant changes combined to alter the perspective of many multinational corporations. First, the US Foreign Corrupt Practices Act (FCPA) of 1977, designed to prevent corporate bribery of foreign officials, represented a significant (if flawed) step adopted in the wake of the Watergate investigations by the Security and Exchange Committee, which revealed widespread payments by US companies to foreign governments – notably the so-called Lockheed scandal, in which the US company bribed Japanese government officials to buy its aircraft. The FCPA made the issue of corporate corruption prominent, but it was not really until the anti-protectionist stance of the World Trade Organization (WTO) that the need to combat corruption in international business transactions was widely recognized by most developed countries.

Such anti-corruption sentiments were not inspired by any moral conversion on the part of multi-national corporations, nor arguably even by the WTO initiative and subsequent anti-bribery convention promoted by the OECD. Instead, as more developing and post-communist transition economies came to rely on IMF loans and foreign direct investment, so competition forced them to become more open and to abandon protectionism. However, compared with the more regulated markets in established democracies (themselves not immune to corruption), corrupted markets are characterized by the very high value of local knowledge. In order to corrupt public officials and win contracts, it is not enough simply to offer the biggest bribe. The market in corruption services is necessarily clandestine and closed, and in order to be competitive within it, players need to know when, to whom and how to give a bribe. Local businesses are much better positioned in this market because they are plugged into existing networks and possess local knowledge: thus, a corrupted business environment is much more favourable to local businesses than to foreign investors. Unlike the Lockheed scandal which prompted the FCPA, corruption scandals (especially in the transition economies) have often seen multinational corporations losing contracts or even seeing their property rights undermined – hence their support for stronger action against corruption.

Finally, there is increasing concern about the links between the spread of corruption and the rise of organized crime and, indeed, terrorism. For instance, an official report by the Russian secret services documented that widespread bribery in the Russian police made it possible for Chechen terrorists to smuggle in the explosives used in the 2002 attack on a Moscow theatre. Elsewhere across the world, various separatist and rebel organizations have imposed so-called 'revolutionary taxes' on local businesses, enforced via the threat of kidnap or assassination, whilst the Mafia (and national variants thereof) is believed to be responsible for much organized crime in a wide range of countries, but especially in Russia, Ukraine, and other transition economies in East-Central Europe. The link between corruption, crime, and terrorism is one which has generated major international concern since 9/11.

WHAT CAUSES CORRUPTION?

Not only is it difficult to define corruption, there has also been much debate about its causes. One kind of approach focuses on identifying incentives and opportunity structures. These can range from the level of an individual (for instance, venal public servants who abuse their position for personal financial gain) to a more structural level (for instance, the increasing cost of the political process generates incentives for political parties to find innovative ways to secure funds, and the readiness of corporate interests to buy access to the policy process provides the opportunity). This kind of analysis requires detailed process tracing of actual cases of corruption, usually based on exploring examples which have resulted in prosecution and conviction (for an outstanding example, see della Porta and Vannucci, 1999). Another approach seeks to develop testable hypotheses about the factors which lead to corruption, using existing indices and measures of corruption to inform various regression models based on factor analysis (for a recent overview, see Rose-Ackerman, 2006).

Such factors include religion (with individualist doctrines seen as less prone to corruption than hierarchical ones), culture (more homogeneous societies being seen as more likely to be corrupt), the geographical position of a country (in Europe, countries below 'the olive line' are seen as more corrupt, with southern hemisphere countries in general more corrupt than their northern counterparts), the level of economic development (poorer countries as more corrupt), the size of the public sector (the larger the sector, the more likely it is to be corrupt), the type of political regime (presidential systems being seen as more corrupt than parliamentary ones, federal states more corrupt than unitary ones), different types of legal codes (civil law being less adept at prosecuting corruption than non-hierarchical common law) as well as the quality of bureaucracy (linked in turn to the status of public officials and pride in holding office).

Most of these alleged determinants of corruption are contested. First, it is often unclear whether they cause or are in fact consequences of corruption (Lambsdorff, 2006). For instance, a low level of economic development has long been argued to produce higher levels of corruption (Huntington, 1968). Yet, international organizations also identify corruption as one of the main obstacles to economic development. Second, there is often a discrepancy between conventional wisdom and the findings of corruption research, for instance, low public sector wages are commonly associated with higher levels of corruption but research does not usually find a significant relationship between the two variables (Treisman, 2000).

Third, research on the causes of corruption, especially the impact of different 'patterns of democracy' (Lijphart, 1999), has produced contradictory results. Kunicova (2006), for instance, finds that presidential systems of government combined with proportional representation electoral systems and federalism are associated with highest levels of corruption. Yet, academic debate and international organizations such as the World Bank tend to praise decentralization of the state apparatus as a means to combat and reduce corruption (Klitgaard, 1988; Weingast, 1995).

Fourth, the dominant approach to analyzing the causes of corruption tends to test correlations between systemic, economic, and/or political input variables, on the one hand, and indices which rank perceptions of corruption on the other. These approaches develop causal mechanisms that connect factors such as the level of state decentralization with levels of corruption. Yet, they usually do not examine the causal mechanisms themselves nor do they investigate whether the conditions for the emergence of different mechanisms of corruption are present or not. However, given the nature of corruption, it is arguably very difficult to investigate causal mechanisms by tracing individual corrupt acts back to the presence or absence of institutional arrangements, the constellation of actors, and the incentives and identities of individuals. Ultimately – and consistent with the argument that there is no one definition of corruption – there is no single set of causal determinants to explain the emergence of corruption. We need to draw distinctions between macro-level factors and individual incentives, and accept that there are always likely to be a host of intervening variables in any given instance of corruption which makes it impossible to specify a casual chain with any precision. At best, we can highlight what appear to be some of key *risks* for corruption.

HOW MUCH CORRUPTION IS THERE?

As we have seen, there has been a significant growth in attempts to identify the causes of corruption through the use of statistical regression models. A key stimulus to that approach, as well as to various other attempts to measure the amount of corruption, has been Transparency International's Corruption Perceptions Index (CPI). First released in 1995 and published annually since then, the CPI has become established as the most widely cited indicator of levels of corruption across the world. The CPI is a composite index, calculated using data sources from a variety of other institutions which seek to measure 'the overall extent of corruption (frequency and/or size of bribes) in the public or political sectors' (Transparency International, 2007). The Transparency International website provides a detailed account of the various sources used (which vary from year to year) as well as the non-parametric statistics used to standardize these sources.

The CPI has become controversial. Although widely credited with playing a crucial role in focusing attention on the issue of corruption, the index has none the less been subject to many criticisms both on account of its methodology and the use to which it has been put (Andersson and Heywood, forthcoming). As is explicit in the title of the index, it measures *perceptions* rather than, for example, reported cases, prosecutions or proven incidences of corruption. This matters because perceptions can influence behaviour in significant ways: for instance, if we believe that all around us people are engaging in corrupt behaviour that may make us more likely to adopt such practices ourselves. Yet, research conducted by Miller et al. (2001) demonstrated that there can be a striking disjuncture between perceptions and personal experience of corruption: for instance, citizens in the Czech Republic are much less likely than those in Ukraine to have had direct involvement in corrupt exchanges with public officials, yet in both countries there is a widespread perception of corruption being rife. A recent detailed study of the relationship between the CPI and TI's Global Corruption Barometer, which seeks to capture the lived experience of corruption through the eyes of ordinary citizens, has also shown convincingly that experience is a poor predictor of perceptions and that 'the 'distance' between opinions and experiences vary haphazardly from country to country' (Weber Abramo, 2007: 6). Moreover, general perceptions cannot differentiate between various types of corruption, nor different sectors within countries. So, the question of whose perceptions, what their perceptions are of, and where those perceptions derive from is important.

Since the CPI is a composite index which draws upon a series of surveys mainly aimed at western business leaders and expert assessment, in practice the questions in many of the surveys relate specifically to business transactions (for instance, the need to pay bribes to secure contracts). Perceptions of corruption are likely to be seen primarily in terms of bribery, which cannot capture either the level of grand versus petty corruption, or indeed the impact of corruption (Kenny, 2006: 19; Knack, 2006: 2; Olken, 2005: 3). Moreover, the focus of questions is often on bribe-takers rather than bribe-givers: the implicit suggestion is that bribes are paid only when required by agents in the receiving country, rather than that they may be used proactively as a means to secure contracts.

A second problem relates to the question of how we can properly interpret what respondents to the various surveys understand by corruption. Each of the surveys operates with its own understanding of corruption (which may focus on different aspects, such as bribery of public officials, embezzlement, and so forth), and seeks to assess the 'extent' of corruption (Lambsdorff, 2005: 4). However, although the surveys often ask a panel of experts to rank corruption on a scale of low to high (or some variation thereof), we cannot know whether the experts share a common assessment of what constitutes any particular location on such a scale: what seems a 'low/modest' level of corruption to one person, may look high to another (cf. Knack, 2006: 18; Søreide, 2006: 6). In the absence of clear indicators, such rankings must be largely impressionistic. A third problem relates to the interval scales used in the CPI index, which ranks on a scale of 100 (1–10 to one decimal place). This suggests a high degree of accuracy can be achieved, and that a material difference can be identified between a country which scores, say, 7.0 and one which scores 6.9. That impression of accuracy is reinforced by the ranking being presented in a 'league table' format, with countries given a position within that table – although, since the number of countries included in each CPI varies, the position in the table can be influenced simply by the how many countries are covered in any year (see Knack, 2006: 20).

Although the CPI has been very important for research, there are other types of data, also based primarily on perceptions, that have been developed to some extent as a response to criticisms of the CPI. For example, Transparency International itself has published since 2003 the annual Global Corruption Barometer, based on a Gallup survey which seek to tap both into perceptions and lived experience of corruption, and the World Values Survey (approximately quinquennial since the early 1980s) includes questions on attitudes to corruption (e.g., Gatti et al., 2003). The World Bank's widely used Worldwide Governance Indicators (WGI) includes 'control of corruption' (identified as the exercise of public power for private gain) as one of six elements (Kaufmann et al., 2003; 2006) and is also a perception-based measure constructed through weighted averages and to some extent based on the same polls and surveys as the CPI (for examples, see Barbier et al., 2005; for a comprehensive critique of the WGI's construct validity, see Thomas, 2007). The World Bank Institute's diagnostic surveys provide in-depth surveys of countries by using both experience- and perception-based questions, whilst the EBRD-World Bank Business survey asks more than 10,000 firm managers to estimate unofficial payments to public officials as a share of annual sales in firms 'like theirs' (although it is arguable that these types of questions are not, as often claimed, indirectly experience based, since they ask how respondents perceive their surroundings rather than serving as an indirect way of reporting own experience – see Andvig, 2005). Finally, the International Crime Victim Survey asks respondents if government officials had solicited or expected bribes for service during the last year (see Svensson, 2005). So, since the mid-1990s, an increasing number of academic studies have begun to use these alternative measures of corruption either instead of or as a complement to the CPI. But many of these measures face the same problems of perception-based measures in general, and in the case of the widely used World Bank indicator 'control of corruption' the problems are very similar to those outlined above for the CPI (see Thomas, 2007).

COMBATING CORRUPTION

Since the increasing attention on corruption really began to take root in the 1990s, the issue of how best to combat it has become a core focus both of international organizations such as the World Bank, IMF, OECD, and various non-governmental organizations, especially Transparency International. Although there are successful examples of combating corruption, notably Hong Kong and Singapore, overall the results of the major efforts to fight corruption since the early 1990s have yielded rather meager results (see Bertucci and Armstrong, 2000; Cirtautas, 2001; DeWeaver, 2005; Doig and Marquette, 2004; Keuleers, 2005). Naturally, fighting corruption when it has already become established at a high level, and is also embedded within society, is not easy to accomplish. Moreover, since many anti-corruption campaigns take place in tandem with efforts to fight poverty in countries where corruption is often very widespread, we should perhaps not be surprised by poor results. Put simply, it is very difficult to break the vicious circle of corruption, since even if corruption is very obviously detrimental to economic and social development from a macro perspective, from the micro perspective of an individual facing a given situation it may still be the least bad alternative (Grødeland et al., 1988). Thus, although research has established a clear relationship between democracy and economic development, it has been argued that the relationship exists only when democracy has been an established feature for a very long time, or that it even disappears when controlling for other factors (see Lane and Ersson, 2000: 110–13; Sandholtz and Koetzle, 1998: 11; Treisman, 2000).

In developing mechanisms to combat corruption, the World Bank (and the World Bank Institute) as well as Transparency International, itself founded by former World Bank executives in 1993, have been very influential in formulating the dominant approaches. The prevailing view has been to focus on broad reforms, rather than to combat concrete cases of corruption and corrupt individuals (Krastev, 2003: 5). The aim has been to limit opportunities for corruption and the incentives involved. In the words of the World Bank (2004).

> Corruption prevails where there is ample opportunity for corruption at little cost. Incentive structures encourage corrupt behavior. Anticorruption strategies therefore aim at reducing the opportunities for corruption while increasing the expected cost, i.e. the risk of being caught and severely punished.

This has meant that, when the World Bank started to deal with corruption in the mid-1990s there was a strong focus on state deregulation, and on reducing opportunities for corruption. However, this approach has met with much criticism. First, it has been seen by some as having a damaging impact on the quality of public service and social welfare in general.

Second, the state downsizing argument in general seems generally unsupported by empirical examples of success. Third, the World Bank has often been criticized for not giving enough consideration to indirect means of reducing corruption, such as strengthening public institutions and improving public education and awareness. Moreover, the principal-agent framework that underpinned the approach partly hinges on the notion of the principal as always non-corrupt and committed to reform, which is obviously problematic in many countries. However, this has to some extent been taken into account by acknowledging the need for different policies in high-level and medium-level corrupt countries (Andvig and Fjeldstad, 2001: 105–6; Shah and Schacter, 2004). Fourth, the role of the private sector as a driver of corruption was insufficiently acknowledged, overlooking major forms of corruption such as the

purchase of influence and 'state capture' and their impact on reform measures (see Hellman et al., 2000: 1; Hellman and Kaufmann, 2001; Kaufmann, 2003: 21–22; see also Heywood and Krastev, 2006: 19).

Whilst much of the fundamental understanding of what causes corruption and how to combat it remains in place, some changes have been introduced in response to the criticisms, and the dominant approaches to combating corruption are moving away from directly targeting corruption towards broader and more inclusive measures. Transparency International has developed the National Integrity System approach which takes a holistic view of fighting corruption, pinpointing the pillars of integrity – key institutions, laws and practices that contribute to integrity, transparency, and accountability – to identify causes of corruption and the effectiveness of anti-corruption measures. It now dismisses the idea that a single ideal-type model can be implemented in any country, and it reflects a practitioner perspective on earlier failures (Doig and McIvor, 2003: 318–19; Transparency International, 2006). The revised emphasis of the World Bank is illustrated by Daniel Kaufmann, Director of Global Programs at the World Bank Institute (WBI) who states,

> A fallacy promoted by some in the field of anti-corruption, and at times also by the international community, is that the best way to fight corruption is by fighting corruption – that is, by means of yet another anti-corruption campaign, the creation of more anti-corruption commissions and ethics agencies, and the incessant drafting of new laws, decrees, and codes of conduct. (Kaufmann, 2005: 88)

So anti-corruption programmes are now beginning to look beyond just public administration and financial management reform to broader structural relationships, for example the internal organization of the political system, state-firms relationship, and the relationship between the state and civil society (World Bank, 2004).

More specifically, 'good governance' has become the keyword in fighting corruption and in development literature more generally, reflecting a high association between good governance and key development outcomes across countries (see Kaufmann, 2003: 17), although the direction is not always clear. International financial institutions and major donors are in turn increasingly making their aid and loans conditional on the undertaking of good governance reforms; recently, the World Bank has cancelled or suspended loans to India, Bangladesh, Argentina, and Kenya following evidence of corruption (The Economist, 2006).

This emphasis on good governance, which could be regarded as a result of a 'post-Washington consensus', suggests the need for states with a stronger regulatory capacity as a precondition for liberal markets, since deregulation in the absence of frameworks like competition policy may risk power transfer from state to private sector oligarchies. Such an approach is based on a particular understanding of politics that can serve to ground the economic reforms advocated by multilateral agencies such as the World Bank (Jayasuriya, 2002: 26–29). Governance, in general, is a broader concept than corruption but the two are increasingly treated as being directly linked – that is, environments characterized by bad governance offer more opportunities and incentives for corruption (see IMF, 2003; Kaufmann, 2003: 5). Essentially, governance is about the process of decision making and the process by which decisions are implemented. It can operate at various levels such as national, local, and international, and – depending on context and level – may include various actors such as the government, industry, associations, NGOs, religious leaders, finance institutions, political parties, and so forth. Good governance is described as participatory, accountable, transparent, responsive, consensus orientated, effective and efficient, equitable, and inclusive and follows the rule of law (see UNDP, 1997).

In general, good governance has implied a very broad approach to tackling corruption, focusing on improving political accountability, strengthening civil society, competitiveness in the private sector, institutional restraints on power, and public sector management. In a speech delivered in 2001, the Vice-President of Europe and Central Asia Region at the World Bank stated that because of the power of vested interest to resist change, 'Promoting good governance therefore, tends to require fundamental changes in the nature of incentives that are closely intertwined with the existing structure of political and economic power' (Linn, 2001: 1).

The results of efforts to improve governance are not conclusive, but overall it appears that there has been stagnation or deterioration in governance, as measured by the World Bank's governance indicators (Kaufmann, 2003: 10). However, the same research also shows that between 1996 and 2004 some countries did succeed in improving governance in a rather short time, notably in some of the transition countries that were promised membership of the European Union, whilst governance stagnated or deteriorated in those that were not offered membership (Kaufmann, 2005: 87–88).

So the contrast between the period before and after 1995 is stark. For example, the World Bank did not really engage in anti-corruption projects before 1995 as they were regarded as interfering in the politics of recipient countries, which according to its articles of agreement is not allowed. This led to criticism of the Bank for lending to corrupt regimes and regimes that violated human rights (Marquette, 2004: 413–14). The subsequent approach, with involvement in far-reaching anti-corruption programmes in recipient countries to improve governance, is mainly defended against allegations of political interference by the claim that action is undertaken only at the request of the recipient country. However, help is only provided with the proviso that programmes address not just corruption, but broader governance issues as well; one-off activities are discouraged. And earlier governance programmes did not pay as much attention to the regulatory capacity of the state and the creation of market order (Jayasuriya, 2002: 29).

The current approach naturally raises other questions. What are the risks with anti-corruption strategies which so overtly champion western democratic ideals or at least liberal democratic values (see Hindess, 2005: 1396)? In relation to East European transitions countries, Cirtautas (2001: 1) argues, 'It is clear that the heavily promoted, supposedly universal standards, derived mainly from idealized Western standards, are meant to supersede completely local customs and practices.' Even if good governance and anti-corruption are not the same, in practical terms anti-corruption programmes that fully address governance make the two look the same. Moreover, the broad approach and range of criteria might also undermine the credibility of sincere reformers if judged by standards that in many cases took decades to achieve elsewhere (see Linn, 2001). Credibility may be further undermined if anti-corruption approaches seem to reflect a double standard, such as membership conditions imposed by the EU, which the present members could probably not meet themselves, judging by recent profile corruption cases since the early 1990s (see Cirtautas, 2001: 3; EurActiv, 2003).

CONCLUSION

As has been shown, corruption remains a deeply contested concept. The grounds of contention relate to its very definition, its impact, its extent, its causes and how to combat it. What is really striking is that corruption has assumed such a prominent place in the discourse on development, and is also seen as a serious threat to the functioning of established democracies. One of the reasons for that is that corruption has come to be seen as both cause and explanation of a host of political difficulties facing developed and developing societies. That it can serve both roles is a reflection of the conceptual confusion which surrounds the term. In practice, the word 'corruption' is now so widely used that it risks losing any analytical purchase: as ever more activities are defined as corrupt, so there is ever more corruption to be discovered until we

reach a point in which all politics can come to be seen as corrupt.

At one level, that generates the risk of disillusionment and disaffection with the political process; at another level, however, it may inure citizens to corruption, making it ever harder to generate a sense of outrage or scandal over corrupt activity by politicians. There is evidence from recent elections in various parts of the world that citizens may 'discount' corruption as a factor influencing their voting choice. Indeed, some of the more apocalyptic claims about the dangers of corruption may become counter-productive, whilst the emphasis on 'good governance' as the best means to combat corruption risks placing insurmountable hurdles in the way of effective action. Ultimately, it is impossible to eliminate corruption and any attempts to do so are doomed to failure.

REFERENCES

Alatas, S.H. (1990) *Corruption: Its nature, causes and consequences.* Aldershot: Averbury.

Andersson, S. and Heywood, P.M. (forthcoming) 'The politics of perception: Use and abuse of Transparency International's approach to measuring corruption', *Political Studies,* DOI: 10.1111/j.1467–9248.2008.00758.x.

Andvig, J.C. (2005) *'A house of straw, sticks or bricks'? Some notes on corruption empirics.* (NUPI Working Paper No. 678)

Andvig, J.C. and Fjeldstad, O.-H. (2001) *Corruption: a review of contemporary research* (Report R 7, Development Studies and Human Rights) Chr. Michelsen Institute, Norway.

Barbier, E.B., Damania, R. and Leonard, D. (2005) 'Corruption, trade and resource conversion', *Journal of Environmental Economics and Management,* 50 (2): 229–446.

Bertucci, G. and Yi Armstrong, E. (2000, September) *Why anti-corruption crusades often fail to win lasting victories.* The anti-corruption summit, Arlington, Virginia, USA.

Cartier-Bresson, J. (2000) 'The economics of corruption', *OECD Observer.* Retrieved 10 March, 2008, from http://www.oecdobserver.org/

news/fullstory.php/aid/239/Economics_of_corruption.html

Cirtautas, A.M. (2001) 'Corruption and the new ethical infrastructure of capitalism', *East European Constitutional Review,* 10 (2/3): 79–84.

della Porta, D. (2000) 'Social capital, beliefs in government, and political corruption', in S.J. Pharr and R. Putnam (eds), *Disaffected democracies.* Princeton, NJ: Princeton University Press, pp. 202–28.

della Porta, D. and Vannucci, A. (1999) *Corrupt exchanges. actors, resources and mechanisms of political corruption.* New York: Aldine de Gruyter.

DeWeaver, M. (2005) 'Hidden motives in anti-corruption campaign', *Asia Times Online.* Retrieved 10 March, 2008, from http://www.atimes.com/atimes/China_Business/GJ29Cb05.html

Doig, A. and Marquette, H. (2004) 'Corruption and democratisation: the litmus test of international donor agency intentions?', *Futures,* 37: 199–213.

Doig, A. and McIvor, S. (2003) 'The national integrity system: Assessing corruption and reform', *Public Administration and Development,* 23: 317–32.

EurActiv (2003) *Good governance and corruption.* Retrieved 10 March, 2008, from www.euractiv.com/en/corruption

Ferejohn, J.A. (1974) *Pork-barrel politics: Rivers and harbors legislation, 1947–1968.* Stanford, CA: Stanford University Press.

Gatti, R., Paternostro, S. and Rigolini, J. (2003) *Individual attitudes toward corruption: Do social effects matter?* (World Bank Policy Research Working Paper No. 3122) Washington DC: World Bank.

Grødeland, A.B., Koshechkina, T.Y. and Miller, W.L. (1988) '"Foolish to give and yet more foolish not to take" – In-depth interviews with post-communist citizens on their everyday use of bribes and contacts', *Europe-Asia Studies,* 50 (4): 651–77.

Gupta, S., Davoodi, H. and Alonso-Terme, R. (1998) *Does corruption affect income inequality and poverty?* (IMF Working Paper No. 76) Washington, DC: International Monetary Fund.

Heidenheimer, A.J. (1970) *Political corruption: Readings in comparative analysis.* New Brunswick, NJ: Transaction.

Hellman, J. and Kaufmann, D. (2001) 'Confronting the challenge of state capture in transition economies', *Finance and Development,* 38 (3): 1–8.

Hellman, J.S., Jones, G. and Kaufmann, D. (2000) *'Seize the state, seize the day': State capture, corruption, and influence in transition* (Policy Research Working Paper 2444) Washington DC: World Bank.

Hellman, J.S., Jones, G. and Kaufmann, D. (2003) 'Seize the state, seize the day: State capture and influence in transition economies', *Journal of Comparative Economics,* 31 (4): 751–73.

Heywood, P.M. and Krastev, I. (2006) 'Political scandals and corruption', in P.M. Heywood, E. Jones, M. Rhodes and U. Sedelmeier (eds), *Developments in European politics.* Basingstoke: Palgrave Macmillan, pp. 157–77.

Hindess, B. (2005) 'Investigating international anti-corruption', *Third World Quarterly,* 26 (8): 1389–98.

Huntington, S. (1968) *Political order in changing societies.* New Haven, CT: Yale University Press.

IMF (2003) *The IMF and good governance. A factsheet – April 2003.* Retrieved 10 March, 2008, from http://www.imf.org/external/np/exr/facts/gov.htm

Jayasuriya, K. (2002) 'Governance, post-Washington consensus and the new anti-politics', in T. Lindsey and H. Dick (eds), *Corruption in Asia: Rethinking the governance paradigm.* Sydney: The Federation Press.

Johnston, M. (2005) *Syndromes of corruption: Wealth, power, and democracy.* Cambridge: Cambridge University Press.

Kaufmann, D. (2003) 'Rethinking governance: Empirical lessons challenge orthodoxy' (Discussion Draft 11 March) Retrieved 10 March, 2008, from http://www.worldbank.org/wbi/governance/pdf/rethink_gov_stanford.pdf

Kaufmann, D. (2005) 'Myths and realities of governance and corruption' In World Economic Forum, *The global competitiveness report 2005–2006: Policies underpinning rising prosperity* (Augusto Lopez–Claros, director; Klaus Schwab, Michael E. Porter, co-directors). New York: Palgrave Macmillan.

Kaufmann D., Kraay, A. and Mastruzzi, M. (2003) *Governance matters III: Governance indicators for 1996–2002* (World Bank Policy

Research Working Paper 3106) Washington DC: World Bank.

Kaufmann D., Kraay, A. and Mastruzzi, M. (2006) *Governance matters IV: Governance indicators for 1996–2005* (World Bank Paper) Washington DC: World Bank

Kenny, C. (2006) *Measuring and reducing the impact of corruption in infrastructure* (World Bank Working Paper No. 4099).

Keuleers, P. (2005, September) *Corruption, poverty and development.* Background paper (Plenary 2), ADB/OECD Anti-corruption initiative for Asia and the Pacific, 5th regional anti-corruption conference, Beijing, P. R. China.

Klitgaard, R. (1988) *Controlling corruption.* Berkeley, CA: University of California Press.

Knack, S. (2006) *Measuring corruption in Eastern Europe and Central Asia: A critique of the cross-country indicators* (World Bank Working Paper No. 3968).

Kopecký, P. and Mair, P. (2006, April) *Political parties and patronage.* Paper prepared for ECPR Joint Sessions of Workshops, Nicosia.

Krastev, I. (2003) *When 'should' does not imply 'can': the making of the Washington consensus on corruption.* Retrieved March 10, 2008, from http://www.colbud.hu/honesty-trust/krastev/pub01.PDF

Kunicova, J. (2006) 'Democratic institutions and corruption: Incentives and constraints in politics', in S. Rose-Ackerman (ed.), *International handbook on the economics of corruption.* Cheltenham: Edward Elgar, pp. 140–60.

Lambsdorff, J.G. (2005) *Consequences and causes of corruption – What do we know from a cross–section of countries.* Retrieved 10 March, 2008, from www.icgg.org/corruption.research_contributions.html

Lambsdorff, J.G. (2006) 'Measuring corruption – The validity and precision of subjective indicators (CPI)', in C. Sampford, A. Shacklock, C. Connors, and F. Galtung (eds), *Measuring corruption.* Aldershot: Ashgate, pp. 81–99.

Lane, J.-E. and Ersson, S. (2000) *The new institutional politics: Performance and outcomes.* London: Routledge.

Lijphart, A. (1999) *Patterns of democracy: Government forms and performance in thirty-six countries.* New Haven, CT: Yale University Press.

Linn, J.F. (2001) *Good governance and transparency in the transition countries.* Speech by the Vice President, Europe and Central Asia Region, the World Bank; OCSE conference on Good Governance and Transparency in the Transition Countries, Prague.

Marquette, H. (2004) 'The creeping politicisation of the World Bank: The case of corruption', *Political Studies,* 52: 413–30.

Miller, W.L., Grodeland, A.B. and Koshechkina, T.Y. (2001) *A culture of corruption: coping with government in post–communist Europe.* Budapest: CEU Press.

Olken, B.A. (2005) *Monitoring corruption: Evidence from a field experiment in Indonesia* (National Bureau of Economic Research Working Paper No. W11753).

Philip, M. (1997) 'Defining political corruption', in P. Heywood (ed.), *Political corruption.* Oxford: Blackwell, pp. 20–46.

Rose-Ackerman, S. (1999) *Corruption and government: Causes, consequences and reforms.* Cambridge: Cambridge University Press.

Rose-Ackerman, S. (2006) 'Introduction and overview', in S. Rose-Ackerman (ed.), *International handbook on the economics of corruption.* Cheltenham: Edward Elgar. pp. xiv–xxxviii.

Sandholtz, W. and Koetzle, W. (1998) *Accounting for corruption: Economic structure, democratic norms, and trade* (Center for the study of democracy, UC Irvine Research Papers).

Shah, A. and Schacter, M. (2004) 'Combating corruption: Look before you leap', *Finance and Development,* 41 (3): 40–3.

Shleifer, A. and Vishny, R. (1993) 'Corruption', *Quarterly Journal of Economics,* 108: 599–617.

Søreide, T. (2006) *Is it wrong to rank? A critical assessment of corruption indices* (Working paper 1) Chr. Michelsen Institute, Norway.

Svensson, J. (2005) 'Eight questions about corruption', *Journal of Economic Perspectives,* 19 (3): 19–42.

Tanzi, V. (1998) 'Corruption Around the World: Causes, Consequences, Scope, and Cures', *Staff Papers – International Monetary Fund,* 45 (4): 559–94.

Tanzi, V. and Davoodi, H. (1997) *Corruption, public investment, and growth* (IMF Working Paper No.139) Washington, DC: International Monetary Fund.

The Economist (2006) 'The World Bank. Just saying no: Paul Wolfowitz takes on graft', March, 378 (8467), 83.

Thomas, M. (2007) *What do the worldwide governance indicators measure?* SSRN. Retrieved 10 March, 2008, from http://ssrn.com/abstract=1007527

Thompson J.B. (2000) *Political scandal: Power and visibility in the media age.* Cambridge: Polity.

Transparency International (2006) *TI's national integrity system approach.* Retrieved 10 March, 2008, from www.transparency.org/policy_and_research/nis

Transparency International (2007) *Persistent corruption in low income countries requires global action.* Retrieved 10 March, 2008, from http://www.transparency.org/content/download/23972/358236

Transparency International (2008) *How do you define corruption?' – frequently asked questions.* Retrieved 10 March, 2008, from http://www.transparency.org/news_room/faq/corruption_faq

Treisman, D. (2000) 'The causes of corruption: A cross-national study', *Journal of Public Economics,* 76: 399–457.

Tullock, G. (1987) 'Rent seeking', in J. Eatwell, M. Milgate, P. Newman, R.H.I. Palgrave (eds), *The New Palgrave: A dictionary of economics.* London: Palgrave Macmillan. Vol. 4, pp.147–9.

UNDP (1997) *Governance for sustainable human development: A UNDP policy document.* United Nations Development Programme. Retrieved 10 March, 2008, from http://mirror.undp.org/magnet/policy/default.htm

Warburton, J. (2007) *The social nature of corrupt networks in the Queensland police force 1960–1987* (Unpublished PhD thesis, University of Sydney).

Weber Abramo, C. (2007) *How much do perceptions of corruption really tell us?* (Economics Discussion Papers 19) Retrieved 10 March, 2008, from www.economics-ejournal.org/economics/journalarticles

Weingast, B.R. (1995) 'The economic role of political institutions: Market-preserving federalism and economic development', *Journal of Law, Economics and Organization,* 11 (1): 1–31.

Wintour P. and Leigh, D. (2005) 'Bucking a legacy of corruption', *The Guardian,* 3 June.

World Bank (1997) *Helping countries combat corruption. The role of the World Bank.* Washington, DC: World Bank.

World Bank (2000) *Anti-corruption in transition. A contribution to the policy debate.* Washington: The World Bank.

World Bank (2004) *Multi-pronged strategies for combating corruption.* Retrieved 10 March, 2008 from http://go.worldbank.org/0U9HJ3QWP0

PART III

New and Emerging Issues in Comparative Politics

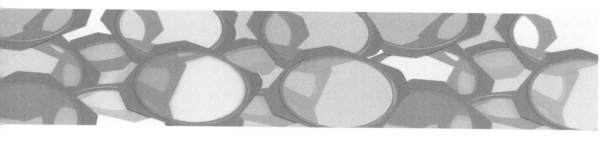

20

Electoral Authoritarianism

Andreas Schedler

INTRODUCTION

The literature on comparative democratization is turning into a misnomer. Instead of studying processes of democratic change it is more and more dedicated to the study of authoritarian regimes that prove resistant to the chants of transition, even while going through considerable theatrical efforts to *appear* as democratic, or at least as dutifully democratizing. A large number of political regimes in the contemporary world, ranging from Azerbaijan to Zimbabwe, from Russia to Singapore, from Belarus to Cameroon, from Egypt to Malaysia, have established the institutional facades of democracy, including regular multiparty elections for the chief executive, in order to conceal (and reproduce) harsh realities of authoritarian governance. In historical perspective, the authoritarian use of elections is nothing new; yet contemporary electoral authoritarian regimes take the time-honored practice of electoral manipulation to new heights. In response, an increasing number of comparative scholars, both in the case study and the statistical tradition, have been turning their attention to the study of these new forms of regimes that preach electoral democracy while they practice electoral authoritarianism.

After sketching the global rise of electoral authoritarianism, the present chapter provides an analytical overview over central conceptual, methodological, theoretical, and empirical themes the emerging literature on electoral authoritarian regimes has been revolving around: the strategies of electoral control authoritarian rulers have at their disposition; the contested line of demarcation that separates electoral authoritarian regimes from electoral democracies; the challenge of constructing valid and reliable databases for comparative research; the internal differentiation of electoral authoritarian regimes; the constitutive role of elections in the inner workings of electoral autocracies; and the tentative empirical generalizations we have been gathering regarding the dynamics and trajectories of these regimes.

THE RISE OF ELECTORAL AUTHORITARIANISM

Since the Portuguese Revolution of the Carnations in April 1974, the political drama that marked the official starting point of the 'third wave' of global democratization (Huntington, 1991), the number of democratic regimes worldwide has roughly doubled. Although different counts yield different pictures, the overall trend is quite clear.

For instance, the annual Freedom House report on political rights and civil liberties in the world identified 42 'free' countries in the year 1974. More than three decades later, in 2006, it judged 90 countries to be 'free' (out of a total of 123 countries it classified as 'electoral democracies').[1] Without doubt, these numbers are impressive. The breadth and resilience of the 'third wave' of democratic expansion is without precedents in the history of the international system. However, today the flurry of optimism sparked by the fall of the Berlin Wall in 1989 has subsided. Multiple experiences of state collapse and ethnic war, the terror unleashed inside advanced democracies by the transnational crime syndicate Al Qaeda, and more recently, the externally induced civil war in Iraq explain part of the new skepticism. Persisting realities of authoritarian rule explain the other part.

On the one hand, a significant number of old autocracies are surviving in different parts of the world, untouched by the stirs of regime crisis. This is true, for example, for the single-party regimes of Cuba, China, Laos, North Korea, Vietnam, Eritrea, Libya, and Syria, for the military regimes of Pakistan, Myanmar, and Sudan, and for the traditional monarchies of the Arab world. On the other hand, numerous transition processes, even if they led to an initial opening crowned by free and fair elections (as in many parts of Sub-Saharan Africa and the former Soviet Union), ended up establishing electoral authoritarian regimes, that is, new forms of authoritarianism behind electoral façades.

Electoral authoritarian regimes play the game of multiparty elections, as they hold regular elections for the chief executive and a national legislative assembly. Yet they violate the liberal-democratic principles of freedom and fairness so profoundly and systematically as to render elections instruments of authoritarian rule, rather then 'instruments of democracy' (Powell, 2000). Under electoral authoritarian rule, elections are broadly inclusive (they are held under universal suffrage) as well as minimally pluralistic (opposition parties are permitted to run), minimally competitive (opposition parties, while denied victory, are allowed to win votes and seats), and minimally open (opposition parties are not subject to massive repression, although they may experience repressive treatment in selective and intermittent ways). Overall, however, electoral contests are subject to state manipulation so severe, widespread, and systematic that they do not qualify as democratic.

Today, electoral authoritarian regimes probably (depending on definition) comprise the modal type of political regime in the developing world. An incomplete list of contemporary instances (as of early 2007) includes, in the post-soviet region, Armenia, Azerbaijan, Belarus, Kazakhstan, Kyrgyzstan, Russia, and Tajikistan; in Northern Africa and the Middle East, Algeria, Egypt, Tunisia, and Yemen; in Sub-Saharan Africa, Burkina-Faso, Cameroon, Chad, Congo (Kinshasa), Ethiopia, Gabon, Gambia, Guinea, Mauritania, Tanzania, Togo, and Zambia; and in South and East Asia, Cambodia, Malaysia, and Singapore.

STRATEGIES OF AUTHORITARIAN CONTROL

A widespread, two-fold consensus exists in the scholarly community regarding the role of elections for democratic governance. On the one hand, elections are essential ingredients of liberal democracy. No elections, no democracy. On the other hand, not any theatrical performance does the trick. To qualify as democratic, elections have to be competitive, free, and fair. Thus, while recognizing the centrality of elections, the current liberal-democratic mainstream is sensitive to the 'fallacy of electoralism' (Karl, 1995).

Electoral institutions are commonly considered to form part of a minimal, procedural definition of democracy. Yet, at close examination, it turns out that they involve a demanding set of normative conditions. In a previous essay (Schedler, 2002b), I stipulated that democratic elections are supposed to offer 'effective choice of political authorities among a community of free and equal citizens'. In order to meet this broad normative principle, I further claimed, building on Robert Dahl (1971), that elections must form a coherent 'chain of democratic choice.' They must comply with seven more specific normative demands that mold and restrain the entire electoral process, from its initial design to its final outcomes. Authoritarian rulers may break the chain at any link and thus deprive an election of its democratic character.

Access to power

Political elections are exercises of power. Voters do not take part in beauty contests or market surveys but in the binding selection of the 'most powerful collective decision makers' (Huntington, 1991: 7) in the political system. Authoritarian rulers may preempt potential threats emanating from popular elections by circumscribing either the scope or the jurisdiction of elective office. They may allow voters to fill subordinate positions of public authority, while keeping the 'high center' of power shut off from electoral pressures (reserved positions). Alternatively, they may keep elected officials from acquiring real power by removing crucial policy areas from their jurisdiction (reserved domains).

Freedom of supply

The notion of electing involves the availability of alternatives. Elections without choice (Hermet et al., 1978) do not qualify as democratic, nor do elections with choice confined to a narrow menu of state licensed options. Most transitional regimes do not count with anything resembling a consolidated party system. Authoritarian rulers may take opportunity of such fluid situations by manipulating the number and nature of nascent opposition actors. They may restrict the free formation of electoral alternatives by excluding opposition parties, fragmenting them, or controlling them from within.[2]

Freedom of demand

Democratic elections presuppose the free formation of voter preferences. Citizens who vote on the basis of induced preferences are no less constrained than those choosing from a manipulated set of alternatives. Unless parties and candidates enjoy free and fair access to the public space, the will of the people as expressed at the ballot box will mirror their structurally induced ignorance. To prevent voters from acquiring fair knowledge about available choices, incumbent parties may strive to prevent opposition forces from disseminating their campaign messages. They may try to shut them out of the public space by either denying them freedom of speech, assembly, and movement (repression) or by denying them reasonable access to media and campaign resources (unfairness).

Universal suffrage

In the contemporary world, democracy demands universal suffrage. The modern demos includes everybody, except those who are assumed to lack minimal capacities of rational decision-making (children and the mentally ill). Since the invention of representative governance, political actors have been tempted to control electoral outcomes by controlling the composition of the electorate, either by legal means (formal disenfranchisement) or bureaucratic practice (informal disenfranchisement).

The free expression of preferences

Once citizens have formed their preferences freely, they must be able to express them freely. The secrecy of the voting is designed to shield them from undue outside pressures. It pretends to insulate voters from the distorting force of violence, money, and social control. A regime that unleashes electoral competition and public debate may wish to put voters on chains the moment they express their preferences at the polls. Violence (voter intimidation) and money (vote buying) are common means to prevent citizens from voting their genuine preferences.

The fair aggregation of preferences

In democracy, once citizens have given free expression to their will at the polls, competent and neutral election management must have their votes weighed equally and counted honestly. Undemocratic distortions may result either from 'redistributive' practices (vote rigging) or from 'redistributive' rules of aggregation (self-serving institutions).

The decisiveness of results

As has been mentioned above, elections are only meaningful exercises of democratic governance when they endow elected officials with real power. Even if elections are decisive *ex ante*, with elected representatives enjoying full constitutional authority, they may fail to be decisive *ex post*. They may turn inconsequential, too, when undemocratic actors tie the hands of elected officials (authoritarian tutelage) or terminate the electoral regime by either preventing them from taking office or removing them from their positions (authoritarian abortion).

Compliance with democratic minimum norms is not, of course, a matter of reaching unattainable democratic ideals. All existing democracies deviate from ideal institutions and practices in manifold ways. No democracy is fully sovereign, no electoral system entirely neutral, no party system completely open, no electoral campaign absolutely fair (as democracy involves normative tensions and trade-offs, there is no such thing as an unequivocal democratic optimum anyway). Only if democratic norm violations are profound and systematic do they cancel the democratic quality of an electoral regime.

The idea of a multifaceted menu of electoral manipulation has found broad acceptance in the scholarly community. Numerous definitions of democracy more broadly, as well as numerous treatments of the democratic quality of elections more specifically, have been conceiving the *minima moralia* of liberal democracy in similar, multi-dimensional ways.[3] Scholarly disagreements concern less the normative foundations of democratic elections than the methodological possibility of clearing the 'gray zone' (Carothers, 2002) of 'ambiguous regimes' (Diamond, 2002) and drawing sharp qualitative distinctions between democratic and authoritarian elections.

ESSENTIALLY CONTESTED BOUNDARIES

Tracing the boundary between democratic and authoritarian elections is an essentially contested enterprise. Compelling political and methodological reasons conspire against consensual boundary settlements. Naturally, extreme cases of repression and electoral manipulation are easy to assess. Few observers would doubt, for instance, that contemporary Belarus, Egypt, and Zimbabwe pertain to the family of authoritarian regimes. The whole point of electoral authoritarianism, however, is to escape the category of easy cases. While all authoritarian regimes possess certain theatrical qualities, public simulation defines the very nature of electoral authoritarian regimes. Electoral autocracies are stage performances by definition. They practice 'democracy as deception' (Joseph, 1998: 59), displaying 'the trappings but not the substance of effective democratic participation' (Marshall and Jaggers, 2002: 12). For impartial efforts to assess the democratic (or authoritarian) quality of an election, the purposeful democratic masquerade of electoral autocracies poses two intricate methodological problems: factual opacity and normative ambiguity.

Obscure facts

Closed dictatorships want everyone to know who is in charge. They want to crush and control dissidence even before it arises. Carried out in broad daylight, their repression is remedial as much as preventive. They want everybody to see how much it costs rising up against the system. Electoral autocracies are different. Rather than publicizing their repressive capacities, they aspire to practice authoritarianism by stealth. They strive to control and distort opposition actors in indirect, oblique ways, with no one noticing. The very notion of electoral manipulation that is central for the idea of electoral authoritarianism hints at backstage activities hidden from the public eye. To a large extent, electoral manipulation is an undercover activity. Some things we can see, such as the enactment of discriminatory election laws, the repression of protest marches, or the exclusion of candidates from the ballot by administrative fiat. Such manipulative efforts take place in broad daylight, mobilize agents of the central state, and invoke the language of legality and public reason for their justification. By contrast, many other authoritarian strategies of electoral control, such as the alteration of electoral lists, the purchase and intimidation of voters, or the falsification of ballots on election day, constitute more decentralized activities that involve myriads of public and private agents trying to do their job without leaving public traces.

Normative ambiguities

Electoral autocracies are normatively ambiguous by design. They open up spaces of political contestation at the same time they strive to contain them through a broad variety of authoritarian measures – the more subtle, selective, and subterranean, the better. Preaching the virtues of modern democracy, and even establishing the formal institutions of modern democracy, while practicing the ancient art of manipulation, they are purposefully contradictory creatures.[4] The intended result is a pervasive lack of normative clarity. Less repressive than closed regimes, while less open than democratic systems, electoral autocracies put our judgment to test. They force us to reach inferences on the basis of pressing factual uncertainties; to weight and balance contradictory features of the political system; and to make sense of a conflicting chorus of voices trying to make sense of these uncertainties and ambiguities. If we add the fact that people may differ in their concrete definitions of democratic minimum standards, we can understand why the frontier between electoral democracy and electoral authoritarianism represents essentially contested terrain.

Passionate debates over the true nature of the system form an intrinsic element of electoral authoritarian regimes. But it is not just citizens and opposition parties who struggle with the structural ambiguities of manipulated elections. International election observers, too, have been wrestling with the empirical and normative complexities involved in evaluating flawed elections. Election monitoring agencies have become more and more methodologically sophisticated (as well as more and more demanding) in their assessments of political elections. They have broadened their presence and perspective much beyond election day; they have developed more precise and cautious vocabulary; they have written elaborate checklists, manuals, and codes of conduct; and they have made increasing use of statistical techniques of sampling, data processing, and inference. Overall, they have accepted the methodological challenge of catching up with electoral authoritarian rulers who incessantly innovate their toolset of authoritarian strategies.[5]

Given the blurred and controversial nature of the boundaries between electoral democracies and electoral authoritarian regimes, many authors have been treating the substandard electoral regimes that inhabit the contemporary world as genuine mid-points between democracy and authoritarianism. As these regimes combine democratic and authoritarian features, some scholars locate them at the very center of the conceptual spectrum and as a result consider them to be neither democratic nor authoritarian. Concepts such as 'hybrid regimes' (Diamond, 2002), 'semi-democracy' (Smith, 2005), 'semi-authoritarianism' (Ottaway, 2003), 'semi-dictatorship' (Brooker, 2000: 252), and 'the gray zone' (Carothers, 2002) express the idea of genuinely 'mixed regimes' situated in the messy middle ground between the poles of democracy and dictatorship.

The notion of electoral authoritarianism, by contrast, classifies these regimes as instances of non-democratic governance, and the same is true for akin concepts, such as 'pseudo-democracy' (Diamond et al., 1995: 8), 'disguised dictatorship' (Brooker, 2000: 228), and 'competitive authoritarianism' (Levitsky and Way, 2002). They all assume that the electoral regimes in question have crossed the contested threshold of democratic minima, despite their best efforts at maintaining the ambiguity of democratic facades.

THE CONSTRUCTION OF COMPARATIVE DATA

If country experts look at individual regimes, their fine-grained local knowledge may enable them to ascertain with reasonable confidence whether the regime under inspection complies, or fails to comply, with certain democratic standards. However, if we 'go comparative' and wish to study medium to large numbers of electoral regimes, measurement problems turn daunting. Leading datasets in comparative politics are not specifically designed to identify electoral autocracies. The two most commonly used historical time series of political regimes in the world, the Polity dataset and the annual Freedom House reports on civil liberties and political rights, do contain partial assessments of the democratic quality of national elections. Yet both are omnibus measures that include several additional dimensions that bear little relation with the electoral arena.

Besides, their measurement scales do not offer obvious cutting points for distinguishing democratic from authoritarian regimes.

Moreover, if much of electoral manipulation is not susceptible to public observation, how can we ever aspire to classify either historic or contemporary electoral authoritarian regimes in valid and reliable ways? Some authors are convinced that passing judgment on the authoritarian quality of elections is an impossible mission, as attempts 'to assess the degree of repression, intimidation, or fraud … cannot be made in a reliable way' (Przeworski et al., 2000: 24). They propose that we should instead rely on official election results, in particular the absence of alternation in power, a crucial non-event that may serve as objective indicator of authoritarian conditions.[6]

Nevertheless, over the past years, a growing number of comparative scholars have been accepting the challenge of constructing large-N datasets that do try to capture one of the core strategies of electoral control: electoral fraud. Most of them have been tracing reports on election fraud in international news sources and observer reports. To date, the most prominent measure of fraud has been a variable in the World Bank Database on Political Institutions (DPI). The DPI database includes a categorical measure that responds to the question of whether 'vote fraud or candidate intimidation were serious enough to affect the outcome of elections.' Even if a growing number of comparative studies have been using this variable (e.g., Hyde and Beaulieu, forthcoming; Simpser, 2004), it suffers from significant conceptual, methodological, and empirical flaws. Conceptually, it fuses two dimensions that should better be kept apart (electoral fraud and candidate intimidation). Methodologically, it violates basic requirements of transparency, as it does not reveal its definitions nor its operational decisions, coding rules, coding procedures, or sources.[7]

Empirically, the DPI variable contains numerous entries that raise serious doubts about their validity. It registers several instances of incisive fraud or intimidation that do not coincide with election dates. Most countries maintain their scores between elections. Yet, in some cases, scores change even though no national-level elections were held (as in Colombia in 1999). In others, registries of fraud and intimidation start one year after first elections took place (as in Nicaragua, Ghana, Kenya, and Senegal). The database also contains numerous false positives, that is, registries of decisive fraud and intimidation in cases that seemed fundamentally clean (like in Panama after 1990, Nicaragua after 1984, and Ghana in 1996). False negatives are frequent, too, that is, registries of electoral integrity in cases that seemed heavily contaminated by fraud and/or intimidation. Glaring examples are Mexico in 1988, Peru in 2000, communist Poland and Romania, the Soviet Union, Iran, Iraq, Syria, Ghana, and Kenya in 1992, Zimbabwe in the 1990s, Indonesia, Pakistan, and Singapore.

All in all, the DPI data on fraud and intimidation appear ill-conceived, methodologically opaque, and inconsistent with known facts. They are a sharp reminder of the fact that in the measurement of behavioral variables as opaque and controversial as the commission of electoral fraud, cheap shortcuts to high-quality data do not exist. Taking the quick and easy way in such complex fields of data construction may well lead right into the desert of measures drained of validity as well as reliability.

Other recently developed databases on the incidence of electoral fraud are of better quality, although limited in geographic, temporal, and substantive coverage. Jonathan Hartlyn, Jennifer McCoy, and Thomas Mustillo (2008) assess the integrity of presidential elections in Latin America since the 1990s. Daniela Donno (2006) works with an original dataset on 'electoral manipulation' (broadly conceived) in Eastern Europe, Latin America, and the Caribbean from 1990 through 2004. Michael Bratton and Nicolas van de Walle (1997) offer dichotomous evaluations of first or 'founding' presidential elections in Sub-Saharan Africa, extended by

Bratton (1998) to second elections. In a more comprehensive effort, Staffan Lindberg (2006b) traces the democratic quality of both presidential and legislative elections in Sub-Saharan Africa from 1989 through 2004. I myself have been constructing a dataset on electoral fraud in electoral autocracies worldwide, from 1980 to 2002 (see Schedler, 2006b). Overall, these parallel and partially overlapping efforts are setting the bases for empirical examinations of electoral authoritarian regimes that have been unavailable until very recently.

THE CONSTITUTIVE POWER OF ELECTIONS

Electoral authoritarian regimes set up the whole institutional landscape of representative democracy. They establish constitutions, elections, parliaments, courts, local governments, subnational legislatures, and even agencies of accountability. They also permit private media, interest groups, and civic associations. While none of these institutions are meant to constitute countervailing powers, all of them represent potential sites of dissidence and conflict. Without ignoring these multiple sites of contestation, the notion of electoral authoritarianism privileges one of them – the electoral arena. It assumes elections to constitute the central arena of struggle (see also Levitsky and Way, 2002: 54).[8]

Designating elections as the defining feature of a distinct category of non-democratic regimes makes sense only if they are more than mere adornments of authoritarian rule. Talking about electoral authoritarianism involves the claim that elections matter, and matter a lot, even in contexts of authoritarian manipulation. Still stronger, it involves the claim that it is the intrinsic 'power of elections' (Di Palma, 1993: 85), more than anything else, that drives the dynamic of stability and change in such regimes. In electoral authoritarian regimes, if they are to deserve their name, elections are more than rituals of acclamation. They are *constitutive* of the political game. Even if they are marred by repression, discrimination, exclusion, or fraud, they are constitutive of the playing field, the rules, the actors, their resources, and their available strategies.

While electoral authoritarian regimes establish multiparty elections as the official route of access to state power, they do not, as a matter of course, establish electoral competition as 'the only game in town.' At the same time they set up the electoral game (competition for votes), they introduce the meta-game of institutional change (struggle over rules). In addition to seeking popular support, ruling parties seek to control the substantive outcomes of electoral competition (electoral manipulation), while opposition parties seek to dismantle non-democratic restrictions that choke their struggle for votes (electoral reform). Authoritarian elections are no conventional 'games' in which players compete within a given institutional framework, known, accepted, and respected by all. They are fluid, adaptive, contested games whose basic rules players try to redefine as they play the game itself. In the language proposed by George Tsebelis, they form 'nested games' in which strategic interaction *within* rules goes hand in hand with strategic competition *over* rules (Tsebelis, 1990). Given formal institutions do not represent stable equilibria, but temporary truces. If the substantive outcomes of the game change, or if its underlying correlations of force change, actors will strive to alter its basic rules – either to prevent or to promote more democratic outcomes. The partisan struggle for votes is embedded in a partisan struggle over the fundamental conditions of voting (see also Schedler, 2002a). As authoritarian elections constitute the game of electoral competition, perpetually put into question by the meta-game of manipulation and reform, they are also constitutive of its component parts, in particular, its lead actors and their available strategies.

Citizens

By opening the peaks of state power to multiparty elections, electoral authoritarian regimes establish the primacy of democratic legitimation. They may feed themselves from various ideological sources of legitimacy: revolutionary (the creation of a new society), transcendental (divine inspiration), traditional (hereditary succession), communitarian (nation building, anti-imperialism, ethnic mobilization), charismatic (magical leadership), or substantive (material welfare, public integrity, law and order, external security). In the last instance, however, popular consent carries the day. Political elections recognize subjects as citizens. They endow them with 'the ultimate controlling power' (Mill, 1991: 97) over the occupation of the summit of the state. By establishing multiparty elections for highest office, electoral authoritarian regimes institute the *principle* of popular consent, even as they subvert it in *practice*.

The institutional concessions electoral authoritarian regimes make to the principle of popular sovereignty endow citizens with normative as well as institutional resources. Most importantly, elections open up avenues of collective protest. They provide 'focal points' that may create convergent social expectations and thus allow citizens to overcome problems of strategic coordination. Elections constitute citizens as individual carriers of political roles, but they also enable them to turn into collective actors, be it at the polls or on the streets. Authoritarian elections that do not open genuine venues for peaceful alternation in power may nevertheless allow discontent to crystallize into 'electoral revolutions.'[9]

Opposition parties

By admitting multiparty competition for positions of state power, electoral autocracies legitimate the principle of political opposition. They may still try to shape the field of opposition actors to their own liking. Some regimes create official opposition parties and even assign convenient ideological positions to them, as in Egypt under Anwar Sadat and Senegal under Léopold Senghor. Others exclude uncomfortable opposition parties and candidates at their convenience, which is a standard operating procedure in the post-soviet regimes of Eurasia. Yet they still have to live with opposition forces that enjoy at least minimal degrees of autonomy. By the simple fact of instituting multiparty politics, they abandon ideologies of collective harmony, accept the existence of societal cleavages, and give up their monopolistic hold on the definition of the common good. Subjecting the opposition to repressive treatment does not affect its basic legitimacy embodied in the formal institution of competitive elections. Quite to the contrary, once regimes recognize the principle of pluralism, silencing dissidence is likely to turn counterproductive; it is likely to augment the status of opposition forces, rather than diminishing it.

As electoral authoritarian regimes are systems in which opposition parties (are supposed to) lose elections, electoral contests are profoundly ambiguous affairs for opposition parties. To the extent that they serve to legitimate the system, demonstrate the power and popularity of the ruling party as well as the weakness of its opponents, elections tend to demoralize and demobilize opposition forces. To the extent that they allow opposition forces to get stronger and to demonstrate that the emperor is naked, that his cling on power is based on manipulation rather than popular consent, elections tend to reinvigorate opposition parties. In any case, authoritarian elections do not provide any of the normative reasons for accepting defeat losers have under democratic conditions. They fail to display the procedural fairness and substantive uncertainty that makes democratic elections normatively acceptable, and they fail to offer the prospects of a government *pro tempore* losers may hope to replace after the next round of elections. What remains is a calculus of protest in which opposition actors have to weigh the uncertain pros and cons of different strategic options both within and outside the electoral arena. Most importantly, as authoritarian rulers convoke elections, opposition forces have to decide whether to enter the game of unfree competition or to boo from the fences (participation versus boycott). Once the polls have closed

and official results are published, they have to decide whether to swallow the outcome or to take their complaints to the media, the courts, the streets, or the international arena (acceptance versus protest).[10]

Ruling parties

Electoral authoritarian regimes may display 'sultanistic tendencies,' with patrimonial rulers ratifying themselves in power through periodic multiparty elections. The organizational demands of authoritarian elections, however, limit the degree of personalism they can afford. Rulers who wish to govern through controlled multiparty elections need a party (as well as a subsidiary state) to mobilize voters, and they need a state (as well as a subsidiary party) to control elections.[11] Electoral authoritarian regimes do not rest upon single parties, but on parties they rest.

For the ruling party, elections are ambivalent tools, as they are for opposition parties. They create opportunities for distributing patronage, settling disputes, and reinforcing the ruling coalition, but they also mobilize threats of dissidence and scission. Like their opponents in the opposition camp, rulers have to take some key decisions regarding their strategic behavior in the electoral arena. Most importantly, they have to decide how to mix electoral manipulation and electoral persuasion in order to keep winning electoral contests. To what extent should they rely on authoritarian controls, and which strategies are they to pick from the variegated menu of electoral manipulation? And to what extent should they rely on the persuasion of voters, and which strategies are they to choose from the variegated menu of electoral mobilization?[12]

TRAJECTORIES OF ELECTORAL AUTHORITARIANISM

Authoritarian elections are *creative* institutions insofar as they constitute these three classes of actors (citizens, opposition, and ruling parties) and their respective bundles of core strategies. They are not *determinative*, however, insofar as the actual outcomes of the conflictive interaction between the three groups are open. The 'nested game' of authoritarian elections may facilitate gradual processes of 'democratization by elections,' as in Senegal or Mexico. It may lead to democracy through the sudden collapse of authoritarianism, as in Peru, Serbia, and Ukraine. It may provoke an authoritarian regression, with a breakdown of the electoral cycle through military intervention, as in Azerbaijan in 1993 and Côte d'Ivoire in 1999. Too, it may lead to extended periods of static warfare in which authoritarian incumbents prevail over opposition parties that neither succeed in gaining terrain nor accede to disband and abandon the unequal battle.

Under which conditions do authoritarian elections fulfill a 'stabilizing' role (Martin, 1978: 120) and when do they act as 'subversive' forces (Schedler, 2002a)? How do hegemonic regimes differ in their dynamics from competitive authoritarian regimes? Under which conditions do government and opposition forces succeed in maintaining their coherence and act as unitary actors? Under which conditions do rulers and opposition parties adopt which kind of strategies and to what effect? When are they successful and when do they fail? How do their strategic decisions in the conflictive game of authoritarian elections shape their correlations of strength? To what extent do the nature of actors and their choices respond to the endogenous dynamics of unfree competition and to what extent are they molded by structural conditions, institutional factors, and external actors?

The emerging comparative literature on electoral authoritarian regimes is beginning to provide tentative empirical answers to several of these questions (as political regimes are evolving creatures whose lead actors adapt and learn, there will never be *definitive* answers to any of them). For instance, despite the continuing 'paucity of comparative literature on opposition strategies' (Posusney,

2005: 109), we have been learning some things about the sources and consequences of opposition behavior. To begin with, when do opposition parties boycott an election? As it seems, they do so if the election is subject to severe manipulation, if they are strong enough to miss a turn in the electoral game, and if they are few enough to make an impact even if other opposition forces do not join them (Beaulieu, 2006; Lindberg, 2006a; Pripstein, 2005). Do election boycotts aid the process of democratization? They seem to augment the likelihood of posterior electoral reform, especially if all relevant opposition parties band together. They also appear to be effective in capturing the attention of international election observers. At the same time, they seem to strengthen ruling parties and to prolong the lifespan of the authoritarian regime (Beaulieu, 2006; Lindberg, 2006a; Pripstein, 2005).

When do opposition parties take to the streets to protest the outcome of an election? Again, the unfairness of the elections seems to be close to a necessary condition. Opposition actors acquiesce to many manipulated elections, and they protest some that look clean to outside observers. Yet, they almost invariably protest if ruling parties carry out incisive fraud. When they do engage in frivolous protest, they tend to desist within a couple of weeks (Hartlyn et al., 2008; Lindberg, 2006a; Schedler, 2006b). Are opposition protests effective means of pushing an authoritarian regime on a democratizing path? Although opposition protest tends to trigger 'liberalizing outcomes' (Howard and Roessler, 2006), it may well be that opposition acquiescence constitutes a more effective vehicle of incremental democratization (Lindberg, 2006b). When do opposition protests crystallize into an 'electoral revolution' that topples the authoritarian incumbent? Well, if the prevailing correlation of strength between civil society and the state permits the effective mobilization of the former as well as the effective paralysis of the latter, an electoral rebellion may well happen and happen to be successful (McFaul, 2005).

Naturally, even if our areas of ignorance are shrinking step by step, the concluding balance of an emerging field of inquiry cannot be otherwise than the sober recognition that much comparative research still needs to accomplished. Meanwhile, both authoritarian rulers and their democratic opponents will continue to play their complex game of strategic conflict, always open to learn and to ruin our incipient insights.

NOTES

1. The author counts on the basis of the Freedom House 1975 and 2007 Annual Report on Political Rights and Civil Liberties (www.freedomhouse.org). As the number of nation states augmented, in particular with the disintegration of the Soviet Empire in 1991, the proportions are somewhat less impressive.

2. The 'virtual politics' practiced in electoral authoritarian Russia and Ukraine (and lucidly described by Wilson, 2005) constitute breathtaking instances of comprehensive and profound manipulation of electoral realities, including the invention and simulation of opposition parties.

3. Illustrative syntheses of manifold strategies of authoritarian manipulation carried out in different contexts can be found, for example, in Case (2006), Conaghan (2005), Daniel and Southall (1999: 38–47), Ottaway (2003: 137–160), Pripstein (2005: 94–108), Schedler (2002b). Schaffer (2007) contains empirical analyses of one specific strategy, the purchase of votes, situated within the larger menu of manipulation.

4. I borrow the notion of manipulation as art-form from Riker (1986), even if his discussion focuses on the manipulation of voting processes in democratic contexts.

5. Bjornlund (2004) offers a fine overview of the evolution of international election monitoring. Munck (2006) gives testimony to the efforts by election monitors to tap academic knowledge about empirical research for their practical purposes. Elklit and Reynolds (2005) translate the common checklist approach into a framework for empirical research. Kelly (2006) provides a literature review on the relevance of international election observation and lays out the contours of an ambitious research program on international election monitoring.

6. For a more extensive discussion of the 'alternation rule,' see Schedler (2006a: 10).

7. For critical discussions of these datasets, see Munck and Verkuilen (2002), Schedler (2006a: 10–12; 2006b: 15–16).

8. The present section draws on Schedler (2006a: 12–15).

9. On the role of stolen elections in coordinating citizens and triggering protest movements, see Thompson and Kuntz (2004). On electoral revolutions, see McFaul (2005).

10. See also Schedler (2002a; 2006c). In his case study of Indonesia under Suharto, Edward Aspinall (2005) offers an insightful analysis of how the structural ambiguity of a regime produces structurally ambiguous opposition forces. In a similar vein, Ellen Lust-Okar (2005) shows how differential treatment of opposition forces by the electoral monarchies of Morocco and Jordan induces divisions within the opposition camp (between included and excluded actors).

11. As Richard Snyder states succinctly, 'in the absence of a state, there is no regime' (2006: 224). On the organizational demands of electoral fraud, see Way (2006).

12. Most empirical analyses of electoral authoritarian regimes stress the pursuit of electoral manipulation over efforts at electoral mobilization. Notable exceptions are Greene (2002), Langston and Morgenstern (2007), and Magaloni (2006).

REFERENCES

Aspinall, E. (2005) *Opposing Suharto: Compromise, resistance, and regime change in Indonesia.* Stanford University Press: Stanford.

Beaulieu, E. (2006) *Protesting the contest: Election boycotts around the world, 1990–2002.* (PhD Dissertation, San Diego, University of California).

Bjornlund, E.C. (2004) *Beyond free and fair: Monitoring elections and building democracy.* Washington, DC: Woodrow Wilson Center Press.

Bratton, M. (1998) 'Second elections in Africa', *Journal of Democracy,* 9 (3): 51–66.

Bratton, M. and van de Walle, N. (1997) *Democratic experiments in Africa: Regime transitions in comparative perspective.* Cambridge: Cambridge University Press.

Brooker, P. (2000) *Non-democratic regimes: Theory, government, and politics.* New York: St. Martin's Press.

Carothers, T. (2002) 'The end of the transition paradigm', *Journal of Democracy,* 13 (1): 5–21.

Case, W. (2006) 'Manipulative skills: How do rulers control the electoral arena?', in A. Schedler (ed.), *Electoral authoritarianism: The dynamics of unfree competition*. Boulder: Lynne Rienner Publishers. pp. 95–112.

Conaghan, C.M. (2005) *Fujimori's Peru: Deception in the public sphere*. Pittsburgh: University of Pittsburgh Press.

Dahl, R. (1971) *Polarchy*. Hew Haven: Yale University Press.

Daniel, J. and Southall, R. (1999) 'Electoral corruption and manipulation in Africa', in J. Daniel, R. Southall and M. Szeftel (eds), *Voting for democracy: Watershed elections in contemporary Anglophone Africa*. Aldershot: Ashgate, pp. 37–56.

Diamond, L. (2002) 'Elections without democracy: Thinking about hybrid regimes', *Journal of Democracy*, 13 (2): 21–35.

Diamond, L., Linz, J.J., and Lipset, S.M. (1995) 'Introduction: What makes for democracy?', in L. Diamond, J.J. Linz, and S.M. Lipset (eds), *Politics in developing countries: Comparing experiences with democracy*. Boulder: Lynne Rienner Publishers, pp. 1–66.

Di Palma, G. (1993) *To craft democracies: An essay on democratic transitions*. Berkeley, CA: University of California Press.

Donno, D. (2006) *Cheating pays: The impact of electoral manipulation on party systems*. Paper presented at the 102nd Annual Meeting of the American Political Science Association (APSA), Philadelphia.

Elklit, J. and Reynolds, A. (2005) 'A framework for the systematic study of election quality', *Democratization*, 12 (2): 147–62.

Greene, K.F. (2002) 'Opposition party strategy and spatial competition in dominant party regimes: A theory and the case of Mexico', *Comparative Political Studies*, 35 (7): 755–83.

Hartlyn, J., McCoy, J., and Mustillo, T.J. (2008) 'The "quality of elections" in contemporary Latin America: Issues in measurement and explanation', *Comparative Political Studies*, 41 (1): 73–98.

Hermet, G., Rouquié, A., and Linz, J.J. (1978) *Des élections pas comme les autres*. Paris: Presses de la Fondation nationale des sciences politiques.

Howard, M.M. and Roessler, P. (2006) 'Liberalizing electoral outcomes in competitive authoritarian regimes', *Journal of Politics*, 50 (2): 365–81.

Huntington, S.P. (1991) *The third wave: Democratization in the late twentieth century*. Norman and London: University of Oklahoma Press.

Hyde, S.D. and Beaulieu, E. (forthcoming) 'In the Shadow of Democracy Promotion: Strategic Manipulation, International Observers, and Election Boycotts', *Comparative Political Studies*.

Joseph, R. (1998) 'Is Ethiopia democratic? Oldspeak vs. newspeak', *Journal of Democracy*, 9 (4): 55–61.

Karl, T. L. (1995) 'The hybrid regimes of Central America', *Journal of Democracy*, 6 (3): 72–87.

Kelly, J. (2006) 'New wine in old wineskins: Promoting political reforms through the new European Neighborhood policy', *Journal of Common Market Studies*, 44 (1): 29–55.

Langston, J. and Morgenstern, S. (2007) *Campaigning in an electoral authoritarian regime: The case of Mexico*. Unpublished typescript. Mexico City and Pittsburgh: CIDE and University of Pittsburgh.

Levitsky, S. and Way, L.W. (2002) 'The rise of competitive authoritarianism', *Journal of Democracy*, 13 (2): 51–65.

Lindberg, S.I. (2006a) 'Tragic protest: Why do opposition parties boycott elections?', in A. Schedler (ed.), *Electoral authoritarianism: The dynamics of unfree competition*. Boulder: Lynne Rienner Publishers. pp. 149–163.

Lindberg, S.I. (2006b) *Democracy and elections in Africa*. Baltimore: Johns Hopkins University Press.

Lust-Okar, E. (2005) 'Opposition and economic crises in Jordan and Morocco', in M.P. Posusney and M.P. Angrist (eds), *Authoritarianism in the Middle East: Regimes and resistance*. Boulder: Lynne Rienner Publishers, pp. 143–68.

Magaloni, B. (2006) *Voting for autocracy: Hegemonic party survival and its demise in Mexico*. Cambridge: Cambridge University Press.

Marshall, M.G. and Jaggers, K. (2002) *Polity IV project: Political regime characteristics and transitions, 1800–2002: Dataset users' manual* (College Park, MD: Integrated Network for Societal Conflict Research,

Center for International Development and Conflict Management, University of Maryland) Retrieved March 14, 2008, from www.cidcm.umd.edu

Martin, D. (1978) 'The 1975 Tanzanian elections: The disturbing six per cent', in G. Hermet, R. Rose, and A. Rouquié (eds), *Elections without choice.* New York: Halsted Press, pp. 108–28.

McFaul, M. (2005) 'Transitions from postcommunism', *Journal of Democracy,* 16 (3): 5–19.

Mill, J.S. (1991) *Considerations on representative government.* Amherst, New York: Prometheus Books. (Original work published in 1861).

Munck, G.L. (2006) *Standards for evaluating electoral processes by OAS election observation Missions.* Unpublished typescript. Los Angeles, CA: University of Southern California.

Munck, G.L. and Verkuilen, J. (2002) 'Conceptualizing and measuring democracy: Evaluating alternative indices', *Comparative Political Studies,* 35: 5–34.

Ottaway, M. (2003) *Democracy challenged: The rise of semi-authoritarianism.* Washington, DC: Carnegie Endowment for International Peace.

Posusney, M.P. (2005) 'Multiparty elections in the Arab world: Election rules and opposition responses', in M.P. Posusney and M.P. Angrist (eds), *Authoritarianism in the Middle East: Regimes and resistance.* Boulder: Lynne Rienner Publishers, pp. 91–118.

Powell, B.G. (2000) *Elections as instruments of democracy: Majoritarian and proportional visions.* New Haven: Yale University Press.

Przeworski, A., Alvarez, M.E., Cheibub, J.A., and Limongi, F. (2000) *Democracy and development: Political institutions and well–being in the world, 1950–1990.* Cambridge, UK: Cambridge University Press.

Riker, W.H. (1986) *The art of political manipulation.* New Haven: Yale University Press.

Schaffer, F.C. (ed.) (2007) *Elections for sale: The causes and consequences of vote buying.* Boulder: Lynne Rienner Publishers.

Schedler, A. (2002a) 'The nested game of democratization by elections', *International Political Science Review,* 23 (1): 103–22.

Schedler, A. (2002b) 'Elections without democracy: The menu of manipulation', *Journal of Democracy,* 13 (2): 36–50.

Schedler, A. (2006a) 'The logic of electoral authoritarianism', in A. Schedler (ed.), *Electoral authoritarianism: The dynamics of unfree competition.* Boulder: Lynne Rienner Publishers, pp. 1–23.

Schedler, A. (2006b) *Patterns of repression and manipulation: Towards a topography of authoritarian elections.* Paper presented at the 20th World Congress of the International Political Science Association (IPSA). Fukuoka, Japan.

Schedler, A. (2006c) *When do losers protest? Opposition strategies under electoral authoritarianism.* Paper presented at the 102nd Annual Meeting of the American Political Science Association (APSA), Philadelphia.

Simpser, A. (2004) Making votes not count: Strategic incentives for electoral corruption (Working paper, Stanford University).

Smith, P. (2005) *Democracy in Latin America: Political change in comparative perspective.* Oxford: Oxford University Press.

Snyder, R. (2006) 'Beyond electoral authoritarianism: The spectrum of nondemocratic regimes', in A. Schedler (ed.), *Electoral authoritarianism: The dynamics of unfree competition.* Boulder: Lynne Rienner Publishers, pp. 219–31.

Thompson, M. and Kuntz, P. (2004) 'Stolen elections: The case of the Serbian October', *Journal of Democracy,* 15 (4): 159–72.

Tsebelis, G. (1990) *Nested games: Rational choice in comparative politics.* Berkeley: University of California Press.

Way, L. (2006) 'Authoritarian failure. How does state weakness strengthen electoral competition?', in A. Schedler (ed.), *Electoral authoritarianism: The dynamics of unfree competition.* Boulder: Lynne Rienner Publishers, pp. 224–41.

Wilson, A. (2005) *Virtual politics. Faking democracy in the post–Soviet world.* New Haven: Yale University Press.

21

Electoral Corruption

Sarah Birch

INTRODUCTION

Modern authoritarian and semi-authoritarian states hold elections; even text-book autocracies such as Saudi Arabia and China have recently begun experimenting on a small scale with electoral mechanisms for the choice of public officials. The prevalence of elections is not, however, associated with an equal prevalence of democracy, in the sense that this term is commonly understood in Western political science. The discrepancy between the institution of elections and the reality of democracy can be largely (though not exclusively) traced directly or indirectly to electoral corruption and manipulation.

The modern study of electoral corruption takes two principal forms: historical studies of corruption in unreformed electoral systems, and studies of electoral malpractice following (notional) democratization. The historical accounts of electoral corruption have in some cases been carried out by political scientists and in other cases by historians. They tend to be single country case studies employing either qualitative or quantitative techniques (see Lehoucq, 2003 for an overview). Work in this field has been undertaken fairly regularly since the nineteenth century, largely by country specialists. More recently, however, there has been an increased

interest in the topic of electoral corruption by students of the so-called third and fourth waves of democratization. Unlike the historical accounts, much of this work has an explicitly comparative focus, and it has led to the creation of a new sub-field of the comparative study of electoral corruption. Research in this emerging field includes practitioner guides to electoral best practice (e.g., Goodwin-Gill, 1994; 1998; IDEA, 2002), and a handful of short comparative analyses of the topic.[1]

This chapter reviews key developments and debates in the field of electoral corruption, with a particular emphasis on the more recent comparative studies of this phenomenon. It addresses the three topics that have, to date, received the most attention in this area: approaches to defining the concept of electoral integrity/corruption, the measurement of this phenomenon, and its explanation. It also provides an assessment of future directions for research in this field and an overview of the main tasks that confront it.

But first a word on the basic rationale for the study of electoral corruption. While the holding of high-quality elections is not a sufficient condition for a polity to be considered a democracy, it is nevertheless a necessary condition. Yet very often elections fail to embody the popular will, especially in the context of new, emerging and semi-democracies. This may be due to manipulation by incumbent elites or by others in the political process such as candidates, media outlets, voluntary organizations, and individual voters.

Most analyses of electoral behaviour in established liberal democracies rest on the twin assumptions that the values and evaluations of voters are primary determinants of vote choice, and that vote choices are the sole determinant of electoral outcomes (mediated, of course, by the electoral system). However, in many or even most parts of the world, neither of these assumptions holds; rather, leaders employ a variety of methods to shape vote options, vote choice, and vote counts such that genuinely-held values and evaluations play only a marginal role in determining the result of elections. Many of these practices fall under the rubric of electoral corruption, and they have a profound impact on the way the electoral process is understood and used, as well as the role of elections in the larger political process. With the increasing number of semi-democratic states in the world, this topic is of growing importance.

Electoral corruption has a number of serious consequences for democratic performance: it reduces the objective quality of representation, in that those elected in rigged elections may be less skilled at representing voters' genuine interests, and they will have less incentive to do so. Electoral malpractice also affects subjective evaluations of the quality of democracy in a polity and thereby compromises the legitimacy of the regime; in addition, it reduces levels of trust – both in political leaders by the general population and inter-personal trust between political actors. An additional consequence of electoral malfeasance is that it is likely to spawn corruption in other spheres, as those elected through illegitimate means will tend to use similar tactics to achieve their ends while in office. Moreover, poorly-conducted elections entail costs that go beyond democracy; not only are they likely to lead to allocative inefficiency in policy-making, but the misuse of state resources during the electoral period often results in a drain on the public purse.

Finally, electoral fraud and other forms of manipulation can, under certain circumstances, lead to violent protest, and can sometimes even spark civil unrest.

It is therefore not surprising that electoral corruption is fast coming to be seen as one of the main obstacles to the establishment of genuine and meaningful democracy in many post-transitional contexts (Elklit, 1999; Lehoucq, 2003; Mozaffar and Schedler, 2002; Pastor, 1999a; Schedler, 2002a, 2002b). Even in established democracies, there has been renewed interest in the topic of electoral corruption, following several high-profile scandals surrounding electronic and postal voting and vote counting technologies (e.g., Herron and Sekhon, 2003; Herron and Wand, 2007; Tomz and Van Houweling, 2003).

DEFINITIONS: THE CONCEPT OF ELECTORAL CORRUPTION

Drawing on common definitions of 'general' corruption as the abuse of public office for private gain,[2] electoral corruption can be defined at a basic level as the manipulation of electoral outcomes so as to substitute personal or partisan benefit for the public interest. It is possible to identify three main forms of electoral corruption: the manipulation of rules, the manipulation of voters, and the manipulation of votes. The manipulation of rules includes efforts to alter electoral laws and other administrative regulations to partisan advantage. The manipulation of voters includes systematic media bias and deceptive political communication during election campaigns, as well as the provision of particularistic incentives or sanctions (vote-buying, intimidation, coercion, and other forms of 'undue influence'). The manipulation of votes is a matter of maladministration and fraud: altering the implementation of the procedures governing elections so as to bias the outcome.

This basic conceptualization is relatively straightforward and uncontroversial, but the picture becomes more complicated when one attempts to define the concept in more precise operational terms. It is in this context that the principal debates have arisen over the definition of electoral corruption – and its obverse, electoral integrity. Four main approaches to specifying the quality of electoral conduct can be identified: definitions in terms of the laws of a given state, in terms of the perceptions of actors in a polity, inductively in terms of 'best practice', and deductively in terms of the normative principles of democracy. The first two approaches take as their framework a single social and legal context, while the last two are more general in scope.[3]

The legal approach

From a legalistic point of view, electoral malpractice can be defined as any act that violates the electoral and other laws of a given state. This is probably the most common practical approach to issues of electoral integrity, as discussions and debates within a state tend often to take the legal framework as their principal point of reference, and formal sanctions only apply to acts that violate the law. According to Lehoucq (2003: 235), 'A key advantage of the legalistic conception of fraud is that it permits assessing the location of the boundaries between acceptable and unacceptable political activity'). The main problem with the legal approach is that, as noted above, the laws themselves may be the object of manipulation by political leaders, who may well seek to alter the 'rules of the game' as a prerequisite to engaging in other forms of manipulation. While useful for the study of electoral fraud in the narrow sense, the legal approach is therefore not ideal when we want to assess the overall quality of elections.

The perceptual approach

In a 2002 article, Elklit and Reynolds 'conceptualise the quality of an election as the extent to which political actors see the entire process as legitimate and binding' (pp. 86–87). This approach has the advantage that it is relatively straightforward and it obviates the need for the researcher to make potentially arbitrary distinctions between legitimate and illegitimate practices, as these distinctions are attributed by the actors themselves. The problems with a purely perceptual definition of corruption are firstly, that defining electoral quality in terms of legitimacy precludes exploration of the complex relationship between the two concepts. It would, for example, be interesting to study how the accuracy of voters' perceptions of the extent of electoral fraud and other forms of malpractice affect their propensity to collude with politicians in perpetuating such practices. Definitions of corrupt practice in terms of perceptions also run up against the problem that populations may become inured to forms of behaviour that are indisputably corrupt by most common sense definitions (Philip, 1997). Thirdly, perceptions vary among groups within a state (a fact that Elklit and Reynolds acknowledge), leading to difficulties in knowing whose view is most relevant – ordinary citizens (who may not have an accurate view of the scale of malfeasance), those actively involved in politics (who are likely to have a clearer picture, but whose view may well be biased by their partisan affiliations), or those directly involved in running elections (who have the best view of what is really going on, but who cannot be assumed to be forthcoming when asked their opinion). This last point relates to a fourth problem with employing a perceptual definition: even if perceptions of electoral integrity are themselves accurate, the researcher may find it difficult to obtain an accurate picture of them, because those who are most likely to be in the know may also be least likely to tell the truth.

The inductive (best practice) approach

The assessment of electoral integrity according to international standards is commonly undertaken by those who are involved in practical electoral assistance and monitoring. Following W.J.M. Mackenzie's seminal work *Free Elections* (1958), many legal scholars and political scientists have also adopted this approach, whose aim is to establish standards of 'best practice' in the electoral realm on the basis of observed practice in states considered to be exemplary, and seek to identify the scope of 'legitimate' deviations from established norms (e.g., Beigbeder, 1994; Boda, 2005; Goodwin-Gill, 1994, 1998; López-Pintor, 2000; Pastor, 1999b). Malpractice can then be defined as acts of manipulation that fall without the acceptable range of electoral practice. This approach tends to focus largely on the many discrete processes that make up electoral administration (voter registration, boundary delimitation, campaign finance regulation, polling, etc.) and the norms appropriate to each.

International legal instruments that bear on elections are largely codified best practice as it has developed over time in the world's core democratic states. According to international law (the Universal Declaration of Human Rights, the International Covenant on Civil and Political Rights), elections must be held periodically; in addition they must meet five criteria to be considered free and fair: they must be held

1. by secret ballot;
2. under universal and equal suffrage;
3. in a non-discriminatory manner;
4. allowing direct choice; and
5. free expression (see Beigbeder, 1994; Goodwin-Gill, 1994, 1998; relevant extracts from these documents are presented in the Appendix).

As a result of debate and analysis undertaken by organizations such as the United Nations, Inter-Parliamentary Union, International IDEA, and regional bodies, there are currently many aspects of electoral procedures that have been recognized as 'best practice'.[4] Yet there are also areas on which the experts and practitioners involved in these deliberations have either failed to agree on what constitutes 'best practice' or

believe that a variety of different practices are acceptable (often with reference to the specific context in the state in question). As Goodwin-Gill (1994: 7) argues, the general principle behind international commitments to hold free and fair elections is one of 'obligation of result'; states are judged by the result of the electoral processes they implement, but they have a degree of choice in the means chosen to effect that result. Michael Boda (2005) elaborates on this concept and relates it to the related principle of 'obligation of conduct'.

While useful in practical situations, the international standards approach can be seen to suffer from the fact that it is so clearly embedded in political processes – the processes that have generated the international legal structure governing elections, and the historical processes within states that have resulted in the electoral practices of some states gaining more prestige than those of others.

The deductive (democratic theory) approach

The deductive approach based on normative democratic theory starts from the premise that to evaluate the quality of elections it is necessary to assess the extent to which a given electoral process is performing the function intended for it within the context of the democracy in question. Jorgen Elklit and colleagues have perhaps gone furthest in developing electoral assessment methodologies on the basis of the deductive approach (Elklit, 1994; Elklit and Reynolds, 2005a, 2005b; Elklit and Svensson, 1997; cf. Schedler, 2002a; 2002b). There are several common problems associated with this approach, however. As Richard Katz points out, there are many different normative models of democracy and a minimal threshold of democratic acceptability, understandings of electoral integrity and electoral corruption will depend on the democratic model adopted (Katz, 2005). Moreover, as Elklit and Svennson (1997) note, the terms 'free' and 'fair' are used in a variety of different ways, and they are not always clearly distinguished.

Whatever definitional approach is adopted, it is also necessary to bear in mind three key distinctions: firstly the distinction between the intentional manipulation of electoral processes for political and/or material ends (what is commonly termed electoral 'corruption'), and secondly unintentional malpractice arising from lack of experience, lack of resources, or sheer incompetence. In practice, of course, the distinction is often difficult to make; electoral administrators may be deprived of proper training and resources because incumbent power-holders perceive that this will be to their benefit; conversely, unintentional deficiencies in electoral administration are often interpreted as the result of intentional manipulation when the result benefits one group over another. Yet whatever the practical difficulty in distinguishing benign from maleficent misconduct, the theoretical distinction between the two is useful for analytic purposes.

The second distinction that needs to be borne in mind, within the category of intentional corruption, is the distinction between attempted and achieved malpractice. A political actor may, for example, make extensive but ultimately unsuccessful efforts to bribe voters; in this case there has been much effort but little result. A slightly different situation is that in which an actor is successful in altering the votes of a significant proportion of the electorate but not enough to alter the outcome of the election. We may therefore distinguish between attempted and achieved malfeasance, bearing in mind that 'achievement' can in this context itself be measured in a variety of ways – in terms of votes, seats (in a parliamentary election) or the overall result of the election (who wins).

A third distinction relates to the agent of corruption. We typically hold a state responsible for the quality of its elections. The state is understood as the main agent that maintains electoral integrity, by abstaining from engaging in violations and/or by providing safeguards that prevent other actors in society from committing acts of electoral violation. It is not entirely realistic to expect the state to bear all responsibility in this domain; meaningful elections are the result of efforts by state, citizens, and politicians alike. Yet it is worth bearing in mind that many practical assessments of elections are effectively assessments of the state's efforts to regulate the electoral process, which depends on a variety of factors that extend well beyond the electoral arena, on factors such as state capacity, rule of law, corruption in other spheres, resources, etc.

MEASUREMENT ISSUES AND DATA SOURCES

For comparative political scientists, evaluating the quality of elections has traditionally been viewed as fairly straightforward from a definitional point of view, yet fraught with measurement problems due to the fact that, like any form of corruption, electoral corruption is by definition extremely difficult, if not impossible, to observe directly. There are also obvious difficulties associated with obtaining reliable and comparable data for any reasonably large number of states. It is perhaps for this reason that studies of electoral malpractice have largely been case studies. But possibilities for data collection are improving, opening up opportunities for developing new measurement strategies.

Measurement

The measurement of electoral corruption can almost never be direct. As with any covert activity, those who perpetrate electoral malpractice have every incentive to cover their tracks, and it is rarely possible to obtain sufficiently comprehensive direct evidence of this sort of activity for valid measures to be made. The measurement of electoral corruption therefore relies on a variety of strategies designed to gauge the scale of improper activity in the electoral arena through indirect means. These strategies can be grouped into two principal approaches: (1) the use of perceptual data (reports of voters, election observers, and experts as well as legal complaints, charges and court rulings); and (2) the statistical analysis of patterns in electoral results. As these two approaches are closely linked to the types of data they employ, it is worth considering them in the context of data sources.

Data sources

Data sources can be divided into comparative and country-specific. Within each category we can distinguish between data sources based on official reports, those based on surveys, and other types of data. Report-based comparative datasets include Taylor and Hudson's coding of electoral irregularity in 112 states in the mid-1960s (Taylor and Hudson, 1972: 57); the 'fraud' indicator in the World Bank Database of Political Institution (Beck et al., 2001), Robert Pastor's database of 'flawed' elections (Pastor, 1999a), and the Freedom House Freedom in the World subcategory score for 'electoral process' (www.freedomhouse.org).

In addition, regional comparative databases that have been compiled on the basis of election observation reports (see, for example, Birch's dataset based on OSCE monitoring reports, as described in Birch, 2007, or the dataset compiled on post-communist and Latin American elections by Donno and Roussias, as described in Donno and Roussias, 2006). Such reports provide rich detail on the quality of the legislative framework governing elections, campaign practices (including media bias, the use of illegal campaign tactics and undue influence), and various aspects of the electoral process including electoral management body design, voter registration, candidate/party registration, polling arrangements, polling day activities, the count, vote tabulation, and reporting of results, and dispute adjudication.

The other main type of comparative data available for use in cross-national analysis of electoral corruption is perceptual data derived from mass surveys. Surveys that include questions on electoral quality include the Latinobarometer and Afrobarometer survey series, as well as Module I of the Comparative Study of Electoral Systems project and the 2004 International Social Survey Programme. In addition, the International Foundation for Electoral Systems has conducted a number of surveys in individual countries that ask similar, and in some cases identical, questions about electoral quality and electoral corruption. Such survey data have been used in several studies to probe the correlates of confidence in the electoral process (e.g., Anderson et al., 2005; Birch, 2005a, 2005b; Norris, 2002, 2004: 216–62; Zovatto and Payne, 2003).

Data available for analysis at the country level include the report-based and survey-based data mentioned above, as well as reports and surveys conducted in individual countries. Single country studies that have relied on report-based data include Cox and Koussner (1981); studies of electoral corruption that have employed survey-data at the country level include McCann and Dominguez (1998). Within a given state it is often also possible to rely on other types of data, including official criminal data on election-related crime, which has been used in several studies (e.g., Eisenstadt, 2002; Lehoucq and Molina, 2002; Molina and Lehouq, 1999). Official election results data themselves can also provide a rich source of data that, when suitably analyzed can lead to the discovery of anomalies consistent with certain forms of corruption and abuse; studies that have undertaken such analysis include Baum (1991); Berezkin et al. (1989); Christensen (2005); Elklit (1994); Herron and Johnson (2007); King (2001); Mayfield (1993); Oberst and Weilage (1990); and Powell (1989).

EXPLANATIONS: HOW AND WHY DO POLITICAL ACTORS ENGAGE IN ELECTORAL CORRUPTION?

Explanations of electoral corruption have typically been couched in terms of three main aims: to understand how actors manipulate elections,[5] to understand what accounts for the presence or absence of electoral corruption,[6] and to understand what causes the quality of elections to improve or deteriorate over time.[7]

Much of the literature on electoral corruption has been devoted to the first of these aims, to understanding the forms, prevalence, and mechanics of electoral corruption. This is particularly true of the historical literature, but it is also true of much writing on the electoral dynamics of developing countries.[8] We know, for example, that electoral corruption takes an almost infinite number of guises, depending on the opportunities available in the institutional architecture under which elections are conducted and the socio-economic structure of the polity in question. We also know that electoral abuse tends for the most part to be systemic, in the sense that it is deeply embedded in the political culture of the context in which it occurs, and it involves relatively stable electoral economies based on the exchange of votes for some form of benefit. Such economies may be based on clientelism of different types,[9] on systems of direct exchange,[10] on structures of intimidation and coercion,[11] on the abuse of state resources,[12] or on intra-party bargaining to divvy up the spoils of government.[13]

Whatever their basis, corrupt electoral economies often go undisturbed for extended periods. Yet gradual socio-economic change and exogenous shocks can and do disrupt such systems. This may be due to population increase and relatively minor changes in suffrage requirements that gradually make vote-buying too expensive, which then generates impetus for reform (Lehoucq and Molina, 2002; O'Gorman, 1996; O'Leary, 1962). Or governments may face such severe legitimacy crises that they are obliged to 'clean up' their electoral process to prevent mass disturbances, as happened in Argentina prior to the Sáenz Peña law of 1912 (Díaz, 1983). In other cases, incompetence and miscalculation may generate unacceptable levels of fraud and abuse, which lead to popular demands for reform. The 'electoral revolutions' in Yugoslavia (2000), Georgia (2003), and Ukraine (2004) are dramatic examples of this.

It is also worth mentioning that electoral corruption occurs in contexts that place it below the threshold of systematicity. It is well-known that a number of US states have long histories of dubious electoral practices that have not died out with the gradual sanitation of elections that has taken place in most other parts of the country. Other examples include revelations of fraud and abuse that have received prominent coverage in several European democracies in recent years, including the UK and France, not to mention the notoriously corrupt Italian system that is still, for all its faults, considered to be on the right side of democracy. As with the cases of 'systemic' corruption noted above, low-level and relatively isolated electoral abuse can often continue for long periods of time, until revelation and subsequent scandal puts pressure on the state to take measures to eliminate it.

There is thus considerable piecemeal knowledge of the context in which electoral corruption occurs, yet general explanatory accounts of variations in levels of electoral corruption across countries or over time have been relatively poorly developed in the existing literature. Fortunately this has begun to change in recent years, as scholars of electoral corruption have begun increasingly to investigate why malpractice occurs and what factors are associated with either increases or decreases in this phenomenon. Basic to the understanding of electoral corruption is the recognition that political elites face a trade-off between power and legitimacy (Birch, 2007; Schedler, 2002a; 2002b). Power-holders have a strong incentive to stay in power as long as they can, even if this involves manipulating electoral processes. At the same time the security of their tenure in power rests also on the legitimacy of their rule, and legitimacy has since pre-modern times been negotiated by means of elections (O'Gorman, 1996). Moreover, in a globalized world the international standing of leaders is increasingly important as a determinant of their ability to maintain power, and adverse reaction by the international community to evidence of electoral abuse virtually always has a negative impact on leaders' legitimacy in the international sphere. If leaders do not have sufficiently high levels of genuine popularity to keep them in power by means of fair elections, then they may find themselves tempted to engage in a variety of 'foul' means of maintaining power, electoral corruption being the most obvious and typically the most effective.

But not all forms of electoral corruption are equally appealing. The manipulation of legal framework governing elections is often costless to incumbent rulers, and if it is carried out within certain bounds, it often carries a limited risk to legitimacy. Other forms of manipulation such as vote-buying may also entail low risk to legitimacy in that such acts may often be tolerated or even welcomed by the domestic population, and they are difficult for the international community to monitor. Vote-buying has the added advantage for non-incumbents that no formal political power is required; it can be engaged in by anyone with sufficient funds. Vote-buying is costly, however, which may well be a potential deterrent to many actors. In the light of these considerations, it becomes clear that outright fraud, such as impersonation, ballot-box stuffing, and manipulation of the vote-counting process are unattractive. They carry a very high risk, as they are often detectable by local and international actors, and they can also carry high material costs, as all those who are complicit in such activity typically have to be compensated for their collusion, either directly or in terms of career rewards. We can therefore speculate that

political actors select manipulation strategies carefully, depending on their political and material endowments.

Further work needs to be done to examine the strategic considerations of those who participate in or are subject to electoral corruption. The factors that have to date been employed to account for the level or rate of change of electoral corruption can, for the sake of convenience, be divided into two main categories: institutional and contextual factors. On the institutional side, electoral management body independence is the institutional variable most clearly associated with electoral conduct (Lopez-Pintor, 2000). In the African context, independent electoral commissions (introduced in Burkina Faso, Bénin, Ghana, Mali, Niger, Nigeria, Sénégal, and Togo) have been linked to improved election quality (Mozaffar, 2002). Electoral commission independence has also been found to influence the quality of elections in Latin America (Hartlyn, 1994; McCoy and Hartlyn, 2006). Single member district electoral systems have also been found in some studies to be associated with higher levels of electoral corruption than more proportional systems (Birch, 2007; Lehoucq and Molina, 2002). Contextual factors that have been found to be associated with electoral malpractice include levels of socio-economic development (Akhter, 2001; Gosnell, 1968; Hartlyn, 1994; Lehoucq, 2003; McDonald, 1972; Scott, 1969), bureaucratic structure (Christensen, 2002; McCoy and Hartlyn, 2006), the presence of observers (McCoy and Hartlyn, 2006), the existence of other forms of corruption (Birch, 2007), and traditional culture (Beck, 1997; Callahan, 2000; McDonald, 1972; Schaffer and Schedler, 2005).

DIRECTIONS FOR FUTURE RESEARCH

As a relatively new field, the comparative study of electoral corruption offers a wide range of opportunities for further development. The paucity of existing research is partly the result of a lack of suitable cross-national databases, but it is also a product of the fact that most research on electoral corruption to date has taken a historical or ideographic approach, and has simply not sought to conceptualize the broad determinants and consequences of this phenomenon.

There is a pressing need in the study of electoral corruption for better cross-national databases. In this connection it is worth pointing to the dramatic increases in studies of 'general' corruption that was sparked by the creation and dissemination of the Transparency International's Corruption Perceptions Index, which includes annual cross-national data on a large number of countries. The development of a reliable comparative database of electoral corruption would undoubtedly significantly spur academic research in this field.

It would also be useful if surveys routinely incorporated questions on perceptions of electoral fairness into their questionnaires. It is striking that survey researchers have for decades asked respondents across the world about their attitudes toward and trust in a variety of institutions, but they have for the most part neglected to ask about the institution that is arguably most central to democracy – the electoral process. Most election studies fail to ask respondents about their views on the quality of electoral conduct, and the assumption of unmanipulated choice subtends most research in the field of electoral behaviour, even when circumstances would suggest that this in unlikely to be an accurate assumption.

There is also a need for better explanatory theories of electoral corruption. As noted above, most attention so far has been devoted to conceptualizing and describing this phenomenon, and relatively little effort has gone into explaining it. Political science would also benefit from a more detailed understanding of the impact of electoral corruption on other aspects of politics, including other aspects of corruption. In as much as elections are the lynchpin of democracy and the gateway to power in the vast majority of contemporary states, one can hypothesize that corruption of the electoral process has a knock-on effect on a wide range of political processes and outcomes, but little work has so far been done on delineating these impacts or assessing their magnitude. We do know that electoral corruption depresses turnout (Birch, 2005a; Bratton, 1998; Bratton and van de Walle, 1997: 206–10; McCann and Dominguez, 1998). We also know that anger about electoral corruption can result in popular unrest or even civil war. For example, the 1992 elections in Mauritania sparked bouts of violence (Wiseman, 1992), as did the 2000 elections on Zanzibar (Pottie, 2002). Some commentators have also linked the violence in the Congo (Brazzaville) in the mid-1990s to the questionable elections of 1993 (see Fleischhacker, 1999). Yet current knowledge about the impacts of electoral corruption is fragmentary at best.

In short, the comparative study of electoral corruption is an emerging field in which much remains to be done. With the recent rise of 'illiberal' or 'authoritarian' democracies (cf. chapter by Schedler, this volume), it is also a field that is of increasing relevance to contemporary politics. And as more and more authoritarian and semi-authoritarian leaders are pressed to legitimate their power through the ballot box, the 'demand' for electoral corruption is bound to increase. Likewise, as comparative datasets on elections increase in breadth to take in sets of states that are ever more diverse in political terms, electoral behaviouralists are going to be obliged to confront the possibility that the data on which they base their analyses do not reflect the free expression of the voters' will. There can thus be expected to be a commensurate increase in the 'demand' for a political science understanding of electoral corruption.

CONCLUSION

Political elites want to win elections. They may have other motives for becoming active in politics, but it can generally be assumed that in a polity where leaders are selected through electoral mechanisms, winning elections is a precondition for achieving most of the other aims of politicians. Any given member of the elite has a variety of different electoral strategies at his or her disposal. The vast majority of the previous research on electoral strategies has focused on legitimate strategies. Yet there are a large number of illegitimate and semi-legitimate strategies that are also potentially in the choice set considered by elites.

Preventing electoral corruption is key to maintaining and enhancing the seeds of electoral accountability in new and emerging democracies. Likewise, reducing electoral corruption in authoritarian states is in many cases the surest means of bringing about democratic change. It was small-scale electoral reform in 1989 in what was still a one-party state that opened the way for the collapse of communism in the Soviet Union and ultimately the collapse of the country itself. Likewise, it was the introduction of an independent electoral court in Mexico that is widely credited with bringing about the demise of the dominant Institutional Revolutionary Party in Mexico. Democratization is intimately associated with electoral reform, and electoral corruption is associated in an equally intimate manner with many forms of authoritarianism. The comparative study of electoral corruption is therefore central to understanding the difference between the two principal regimes types in the modern world; it also has substantial practical value to regimes that decide – for whatever reason – to clean up their elections; finally, the study of electoral corruption is of considerable relevance to decision-makers and aid workers from developed democracies seeking to improve the quality of democracy elsewhere.

APPENDIX: EXTRACTS FROM INTERNATIONAL AGREEMENTS RELATING TO ELECTIONS

UNIVERSAL DECLARATION ON HUMAN RIGHTS, GENERAL ASSEMBLY RESOLUTION 217 A (III) (10 DECEMBER 1948)

Article 21

1. Everyone has the right to take part in the government of his country, directly or through freely chosen representatives. ...
3. The will of the people shall be the basis of the authority of government; this will shall be expressed in periodic and genuine elections which shall be by universal and equal suffrage and shall be held by secret vote or by equivalent free voting procedures.

INTERNATIONAL COVENANT ON CIVIL AND POLITICAL RIGHTS, GENERAL ASSEMBLY RESOLUTION 2200A (XXI) (16 DECEMBER 1966)

Article 25

Every citizen shall have the right and the opportunity, without any of the distinctions mentioned in article 2 and without unreasonable restrictions:
(a) To take part in the conduct of public affairs, directly or through freely chosen representatives;
(b) To vote and to be elected at genuine periodic elections which shall be by universal and equal suffrage and shall be held by secret ballot, guaranteeing the free expression of the will of the electors; ...

NOTES

1. See, for example, Birch (2005a, 2005b, 2007); Boda (2005); Christensen (2005); Elklit (1999); Elklit and Reynolds (2002, 2005a, 2005b); Hartlyn and McCoy (2006); Lehoucq (2002); Mozaffar (2002); Mozaffar and Schedler (2002); Pastor (1999a); Posada-Carbó (2000); Schaffer (2002); Schedler (2002a, 2002b, 2004, 2006).

2. For an overview of different approaches to defining corruption, see Part I of the anthology on corruption compiled by Arnold Heidenheimer and Michael Johnston (Heidenheimer and Johnston, 2002).

3. It is not surprising, therefore, that the perceptual and legal approaches are employed more commonly in single case studies, whereas the more general inductive and deductive approaches are better suited to the comparative context.

4. See, for example, Council of Europe (2002); CSES (1990); International Institute for Democracy and Electoral Assistance (2002); Inter-Parliamentary Union (1994); Organization for American States (2001). See also the international documents referred to in the Appendix below.

5. For example, Beck (1997); Case (2006); Figueroa and Sives (2002); McDonald (1972); Mozaffar and Schedler (2002); Posada-Carbó (2000); Posusney (1998); Schedler (2002a, 2002b, 2006); Wilson (2005b).

6. Examples include Birch (2007); Gosnell (1968); Lehoucq (2003); McCoy and Hartlyn (2006); Scott (1969).

7. See, for instance, Eisenstadt (2002); Howard and Roessler (2006); Lehoucq (2000); Lehoucq and Molina (2002); McCoy and Hartlyn (2006); Molina and Lehoucq (1999); O'Leary (1962).

8. See, for example, the contributions to the edited volumes by Posado-Carbo (1996) and Hermet et al. (1978).

9. See, for example, Akhter (2001); Birch (1997); Dardé (1996); Gosnell (1968); Rouquié (1978); Scott (1969).

10. See Argersinger (1985/86); Brusco et al. (2004); Callahan (2000); Callahan and McCargo (1996); Cox and Thies (2000); Schaffer (2005; 2007); Schaffer and Schedler (2005).

11. See Baum (1991); Darden (2001); Figueroa and Sives (2002); Powell (1989); Pravda (1978).

12. See Argersinger (1985/86); Beck (1997); D'Anieri (2005); Dardé (1996); Deas (1996); McDonald (1972); Wilson (2005a: Chapter 4: 2005b).

13. See Eisenstadt (1999); Wilson, (2005b: 60–69).

REFERENCES

Akhter, M.Y. (2001) *Electoral corruption in Bangladesh*. Aldershot: Ashgate.

Anderson, C.J., Blais, A., Bowler, S., Donovan, T., and Listhaug, O. (2005) *Losers' consent: Elections and democratic legitimacy*. Oxford: Oxford University Press.

Argersinger, P.H. (1985/86) 'New perspectives on election fraud in the gilded age', *Political Science Quarterly*, 100 (4): 669–87.

Baum, D. (1991) 'Pinpointing apparent fraud in the 1861 Texas secession referendum', *Journal of Interdisciplinary History*, 22 (2): 201–21.

Beck, L.J. (1997) 'Senegal's 'patrimonial democrats': Incremental reform and the obstacles to the consolidation of democracy', *Canadian Journal of African Studies*, 31 (1): 1–31.

Beck, T., Clarke, G., Groff, A., Keefer, P., and Walsh, P. (2001) 'New tools and new tests in comparative political economy: The database of political institutions', *World Bank Economic Review*, 15 (1): 165–76.

Beigbeder, Y. (1994) *International monitoring of plebiscites, referenda and national elections: Self-determination and transition to democracy*. Dordrecht, Boston and London: Martinus Nijhoff.

Berezkin, A.V., Kolosov, V.A., Pavlovskaya, M.E., Petrov, N.V., and Smirnyagin, L.V. (1989) 'The geography of the 1989 elections of people's deputies of the USSR (Preliminary Results)', *Soviet Geography*, 30 (8): 607–34.

Birch, S. (1997) 'Nomenklatura democratization: Electoral clientelism in post-soviet Ukraine', *Democratization*, 4 (4): 40–62.

Birch, S. (2005a, September) *Perceptions of electoral fairness and voter turnout*. Paper presented at the Annual Meeting of the American Political Science Association. Washington, DC.

Birch, S. (2005b, September) *A cross-national analysis of confidence in the conduct of elections*. Elections, Public Opinion and Political Parties Conference, University of Essex.

Birch, S. (2007) 'Electoral systems and electoral misconduct', *Comparative Political Studies*, 40 (12): 1533–56.

Boda, M.D. (2005) 'Judging elections by public international law: A tentative framework', *Representation*, 41 (3): 208–29.

Bratton, M. (1998) 'Second elections in Africa', *Journal of Democracy*, 9 (3): 51–56.

Bratton, M. and van de Walle, N. (1997) *Democratic experiments in Africa: Regime transitions in comparative perspective*. Cambridge; Cambridge University Press.

Brusco, V., Nazareno, M., and Stokes, S.C. (2004) 'Vote-buying in Argentina', *Latin American Research Review*, 39 (2): 66–88.

Callahan, W.A. (2000) *Pollwatching, election and civil society in Southeast Asia*. Aldershot: Ashgate.

Callahan, W.A. and McCargo, D. (1996) 'Vote-buying in Thailand's Northeast', *Asian Survey*, 36 (4): 376–92.

Case, W. (2006) 'Manipulative sills: How do rulers control the electoral arena', in A. Schedler (ed.), *Electoral authoritarianism: The dynamics of unfree competition*. Boulder: Lynne Rienner, 95–112.

Christensen, R. (2002) *The drawing of electoral boundaries in Japan*. Paper presented at the annual meeting of the American Political Science Association, Boston, MA.

Christensen, R. (2005) *Stealing elections on election night: A comparison of statistical evidence from Japan, Canada, and the United States*. Paper presented at the annual meeting of the American Political Science Association, Washington, DC.

Council of Europe (2002) *Code of good practice in electoral matters*. Venice Commission. Retrieved March 20, 2008, from http://www.venice.coe.int/docs/2002/CDL–AD(2002)023rev–e.asp

Cox, G.W. and Kousser, J.M. (1981) 'Turnout and rural corruption: New York as a test case', *American Journal of Political Science*, 25 (4): 646–63.

Cox, G.W. and Thies, M.F. (2000) 'How much does money matter? "Buying" votes in Japan, 1967–1990', *Comparative Political Studies*, 33 (1): 37–57.

CSES (1990) *Copenhagen document*. Retrieved March 20, 2008, from http://www.osce.org/documents/mcs/1990/11/4045_en.pdf

Dahl, R. (1971) *Polyarchy: participation and opposition*. New Haven, CT: Yale University Press.

D'Anieri, P. (2005) 'The last hurrah: The 2004 Ukrainian presidential elections and the limits of machine politics', *Communist and Postcommunist Studies*, 38 (2): 231–49.

Dardé, C. (1996) 'Fraud and the passivity of the electorate in Spain, 1875–1923', in E. Posada-Carbó (ed.), *Elections before democracy: The history of elections in Europe and Latin America*. Basingstoke: Macmillan, pp. 201–21.

Darden, K.A. (2001) 'Blackmail as a tool of state domination: Ukraine under Kuchma', *East European Constitutional Review*, 10 (2/3): 67–71.

Deas, M. (1996) 'The role of the church, the army and the police in Colombian elections, c. 1850–1930', in E. Posada-Carbó (ed.), *Elections before democracy: The history of elections in Europe and Latin America*. Basingstoke: Macmillan, 163–80.

Díaz, H.A. (1983) *Ley Sáenz-Peña: Pro y contra*. Buenos Aires: Centro Editor de América Latina.

Donno, D. and Roussias, A. (2006, September) *Cheating pays: The impact of electoral manipulation on party systems*. Paper presented at the Annual Meeting of the American Political Science Association, Philadelphia.

Eisenstadt, T.A. (1999) 'Off the streets and into the courtrooms: Resolving postelectoral conflicts in Mexico', in A. Schedler, L. Diamond, and M.F. Plattner (eds), *The self-restraining state: Power and accountability in new democracies*. Boulder, CO: Lynne Rienner, pp. 83–103.

Eisenstadt, T.A. (2002) 'Measuring electoral court failure in democratizing Mexico', *International Political Science Review*, 23 (1): 47–68.

Elklit, J. (1994) 'Is the Degree of Electoral Democracy Measurable? Experiences from Bulgaria, Kenya, Latvia, Mongolia, and Nepal', in D. Beetham (ed.), *Defining and Measuring Democracy*. London: Sage, pp. 89–111.

Elklit, J. (1999) 'Electoral institutional change and democratization: You can lead a horse to water, but you can't make it drink', *Democratization*, 6 (4): 28–51.

Elklit, J. and Reynolds, A. (2002) 'The impact of election administration on the legitimacy of emerging democracies',

Common-wealth and Comparative Politics, 40 (2): 86–119.

Elklit, J. and Reynolds, A. (2005a) 'A framework for the systematic study of election quality', *Democratization*, 12 (2): 147–62.

Elklit, J. and Reynolds, A. (2005b) 'Judging elections and election management quality by process', *Representation*, 41 (3): 189–207.

Elklit, J. and Svensson, P. (1997) 'What makes elections free and fair?', *Journal of Democracy*, 8 (3): 32–45.

Figueroa, M. and Sives, A. (2002) 'Homogenous voting, electoral manipulation and the 'garrison' process in post-independence Jamaica', *Commonwealth and Comparative Politics*, 40 (1): 81–108.

Fleischhacker, H. (1999) 'Congo (Brazzaville)', in D. Nohlen, M. Krennerich and B. Thibaut (eds) *Elections in Africa: A data handbook.* Oxford: Oxford University Press, pp. 259–80.

Goodwin-Gill, G.S. (1994) *Free and fair elections*, Geneva: Inter-Parliamentary Union.

Goodwin-Gill, G.S. (1998) *Codes of conduct for elections.* Geneva; Inter-Parliamentary Union.

Gosnell, H.F. (1968) *Machine politics: Chicago model* (2nd edition) Chicago: University of Chicago Press.

Hartlyn, J. (1994) 'Crisis-ridden elections (again) in the Dominican Republic: Neopatrimonialism, presidentialism, and weak electoral oversight', *Journal of Interamerican Studies and World Affairs*, 36 (4): 91–144.

Hartlyn, J. and McCoy, J. (2006) 'Observer paradoxes; How to assess electoral manipulation', in A. Schedler (ed.), *Electoral authoritarianism: The dynamics of unfree competition.* Boulder: Lynne Rienner. pp. 41–54.

Heidenheimer, A.J. and Johnston, M. (eds) (2002) *Political corruption: Concepts and contexts* (3rd edition) New Brunswick: Transaction.

Hermet, G., Rose, R., and Rouquié, A. (eds) (1978) *Elections without choice.* London: Macmillan.

Herron, E.S. and Johnson, P.E. (2007) 'Fraud before the "revolution": Special precincts in Ukraine's 2002 parliamentary election', in I. Bredies, V. Yakushev, and A. Umland (eds), *Aspects of the Orange revolution III: elections in Post-Soviet Ukraine,* Stuttgart: Ibidem-Verlag.

Herron, M.C. and Sekhon, J.S. (2003) 'Overvoting and representation: An examination of overvoted presidential ballots in Broward and Miami-Dade counties', *Electoral Studies*, 22 (2): 21–48.

Herron, M.C. and Wand, J. (2007) 'Assessing partisan bias in voting technology: The case of the 2004 New Hampshire recount', *Electoral Studies*, 26 (1): 247–61.

Howard, M.M. and Roessler, P.G. (2006) 'Liberalizing electoral outcomes in competitive authoritarian regimes', *American Journal of Political Science*, 50 (2): 365–81.

International Institute for Democracy and Electoral Assistance (IDEA) (2002) *International Electoral Standards: Guidelines for Reviewing the Legal Framework of Elections*, Stockholm: International IDEA.

Inter-Parliamentary Union (1994) *Declaration on criteria for free and fair elections.* Retrieved March 20, 2008, from http://www.ipu.org/Cnl–e/154–free.htm

Katz, R.S. (2005) 'Democratic principles and judging "free and fair"', *Representation*, 41 (3): 161–79.

King, R.F. (2001) 'Counting the votes: South Carolina's stolen elections of 1876', *Journal of Interdisciplinary History*, 32 (2): 169–91.

Lehoucq, F.E. (2000) 'Institutionalizing democracy: Constraint and ambition in the politics of electoral reform', *Comparative Politics*, 32 (4): 459–77.

Lehoucq, F.E. (2002) 'Can parties police themselves? Electoral governance and democratization', *International Political Science Review*, 23 (4): 29–46.

Lehoucq, F.E. (2003) 'Electoral fraud: Causes, types, and consequences', *Annual Review of Political Science*, 6: 233–56.

Lehoucq, F.E. and Molina, I. (2002) *Stuffing the ballot-box: fraud, electoral reform, and democratization in Costa Rica.* Cambridge: Cambridge University Press.

López-Pintor, R. (2000) *Electoral management bodies as institutions of governance.* New York: United Nations Development Programme.

Mackenzie, W.J.M. (1958) *Free elections: An elementary textbook.* London: George Allen and Unwin.

Mayfield, L. (1993) 'Voting fraud in early twentieth-century Pittsburgh', *Journal of Interdisciplinary History*, 24 (1): 59–84.

McCann, J.A. and Domínguez, J.I. (1998) 'Mexicans react to political fraud and corruption: An assessment of public opinion and voting behavior', *Electoral Studies*, 17 (4): 483–503.

McCoy, J. and Hartlyn, J. (2006, August–September) *Election processes in Latin America: Historical legacies and proximate causes*. Paper delivered at the Annual Meeting of the America Political Science Association, Philadelphia.

McDonald, R.H. (1972) 'Electoral fraud and regime controls in Latin America', *Western Political Quarterly*, 25 (1): 81–93.

Molina, I. and Lehoucq, F. (1999) 'Political competition and electoral fraud: A Latin American case study', *Journal of Inter-Disciplinary History*, 30 (2): 199–234.

Mozaffar, S. (2002) 'Patterns of electoral governance in Africa's emerging democracies', *International Political Science Review*, 23 (1): 85–101.

Mozaffar, S. and Schedler, A. (2002) 'The comparative study of electoral governance – An introduction', *International Political Science Review*, 23 (2): 5–27.

Norris, P. (2002) 'Ballots not bullets: Testing consociational theories of ethnic conflict, electoral systems, and democratization', in A. Reynolds (ed.), *The architecture of democracy: Constitutional design, conflict management, and democracy*. Oxford: Oxford University Press, pp. 206–47.

Norris, P. (2004) *Electoral engineering: Voting rules and political behaviour*. Cambridge; Cambridge University Press.

Oberst, R.C. and Weilage, A. (1990) 'Quantitative tests of electoral fraud: The 1982 Sri Lankan referendum', *Corruption and Reform*, 5 (1): 49–62.

O'Gorman, F. (1996) 'The culture of elections in England: From the Glorious Revolution to the First World War, 1688–1914', in E. Posada-Carbó (ed.), *Elections before democracy: The history of elections in Europe and Latin America*. Basingstoke: Macmillan, pp. 17–31.

O'Leary, C. (1962) *The elimination of corrupt practices in British elections, 1868–1911*. Oxford: Clarendon Press.

Organization for American States (2001) *Inter-American democratic charter*. Retrieved March 20, 2008, from http://www.oas.org/OASpage/eng/Documents/Democractic_Charter.htm

Pastor, R.A. (1999a) 'The role of electoral administration in democratic transitions', *Democratization*, 6 (4): 1–27.

Pastor, R.A. (1999b) 'A third dimension of accountability: The international community in national elections', in A. Schedler, L. Diamond, and M. F. Plattner (eds), *The self-restraining state: Power and accountability in new democracies*. Boulder, CO: Lynne Rienner, pp. 123–42.

Philip, M. (1997) 'Defining political corruption', *Political Studies*, 45 (3): 436–62.

Posada-Carbó, E. (ed.) (1996) *Elections before democracy: The history of elections in Europe and Latin America*. Basingstoke: Macmillan.

Posada-Carbó, E. (2000) 'Electoral juggling: A comparative history of the corruption of suffrage in Latin America, 1830–1939', *Journal of Latin American Studies*, 32 (2): 611–44.

Posusney, M.P. (1998) 'Behind the ballot box: Electoral engineering in the Arab World', *Middle East Report*, 209: 12–15, 42.

Pottie, D. (2002) 'Party strife and political impasse in Zanzibar's October 2000 elections', *Representation*, 38 (4): 340–50.

Powell, L.N. (1989) 'Correcting for fraud: A quantitative reassessment of the Mississippi ratification election of 1868', *Journal of Southern History*, 55 (4): 633–58.

Pravda, A. (1978) 'Elections in communist party states', in G. Hermet, R. Rose, and A. Rouquié (eds), *Elections without choice*. London: Macmillan, pp. 169–95.

Rouquié, A. (1978) 'Clientelist control and authoritarian contexts', in G. Hermet, R. Rose, and A. Rouquié (eds), *Elections without choice*. London: Macmillan. pp. 9–35.

Schaffer, F.C. (2002) 'Might cleaning up elections keep people away from the polls? Historical and comparative perspectives', *International Political Science Review*, 23: 69–84.

Schaffer, F.C. (2005) *Clean elections and the great unwashed: Vote buying and voter education in the Philippines* (Occasional Paper No. 21) School of Social Science, Institute for Advanced Study, Princeton, NJ.

Schaffer, F.C. (ed.) (2007) *Elections for sale: The causes an consequences of vote buying.* Boulder: Lynne Rienner.

Schaffer F.C. and Schedler, A. (2005, November–December) *What Is vote buying? The limits of the market model.* Paper presented at the conference on Poverty, Democracy and Clientelism: The Political Economy of Vote Buying, Stanford University.

Schedler, A. (2002a) 'Elections without democracy: The menu of manipulation', *Journal of Democracy*, 13 (2): 36–50.

Schedler, A. (2002b) 'The nested game of democratization by elections', *International Political Science Review*, 23 (1): 103–22.

Schedler, A. (2004) *Degrees and patterns of party competition in electoral autocracies.* Paper presented at the Annual Meeting of the American Political Science Association, Chicago, IL.

Schedler, A. (2006) 'The logic of electoral authoritarianism', in A. Schedler (ed.), *Electoral authoritarianism: The dynamics of unfree competition.* Boulder: Lynne Rienner, pp. 1–23.

Scott, J.C. (1969) 'Corruption, machine politics and political change', *American Political Science Review*, 63 (4): 1142–58.

Taylor, C.L. and Hudson, M. (1972) *World handbook of political and social indicators.* New Haven: Yale University Press.

Tomz, M. and Van Houweling, R.P. (2003) 'How does voting equipment affect the racial gap in voided ballots?', *American Journal of Political Science*, 47 (1): 46–60.

Wilson, A. (2005a) *Virtual politics: Faking democracy in the post-Soviet world.* New Haven and London: Yale University Press.

Wilson, A. (2005b) *Ukraine's Orange Revolution.* New Haven: Yale University Press.

Wiseman, J.A. (1992) 'Early post-redemocratization elections in Africa', *Electoral Studies*, 11 (4): 279–91.

Zovatto, D. and Payne, M. (2003, October) *Trends in electoral participation in Latin America.* Paper prepared for the 2003 CSES Plenary Session, Stockholm.

22

Comparative Federalism

David McKay

INTRODUCTION

In relation to the study of other political institutions and processes in comparative government, scholarly work on federalism has always had uncertain status within political science. There are a number of reasons for this. First, students of federalism have long tended to conflate the normative and scientific by ascribing political desiderata such as freedom or democracy to the institution of federalism when this is patently not always the case. As a result many studies in the area have been dismissed as subjective and unscientific (Riker, 1964, Chapter 1). Second, because federalism involves the analysis of sub national government it has attracted scholars with interests in state and local government and in particular, American inter-governmental relations. Often, the resulting research has been largely descriptive or has limited implications beyond the limited world of US state and local politics. Third, the appeal of federal institutional arrangements has waxed and waned with changes in intellectual and political fashion. Having been popular among utopian thinkers prior to the Second World War and again among decolonizing powers in the post war period, federalism as a novel institutional device declined in popularity with the failure of so many post colonial federations during the 1950s and 1960s.[1] Within political science the study of federalism also waned – partly because practitioners of the new behavioural approach dismissed the normative assumptions adopted by so many of its proponents.

Most recently, the study of federalism in comparative context has experienced something of a renaissance as federal arrangements have been advanced both as possible solutions to inter-ethnic and religious conflicts in such places as Indonesia, Belgium and South Africa and as the basis for inter-state cooperation as in the case of the European Union (EU).

The purpose of this review is threefold. First, to catalogue the ways in which the comparative study of federalism has evolved over the last several decades; second, to evaluate the most recent scholarly trends in the subject area with a special emphasis on rational choice and comparative government approaches; third, to speculate on future developments in the study of comparative federalism.

COMPARATIVE FEDERALISM RESEARCH IN HISTORICAL PERSPECTIVE

Early approaches to the study of federalism including Althusius's seminal 1603 work

Politica stressed the idea of autonomous territorial units as part of broader political *communities*. Althusius argued for freedom for the City of Emden from both the regional Calvinist lord and the more distant Catholic emperor. To this end he propounded the idea of territorial hierarchies where each unit would have some autonomy in its rightfully assigned area (for a discussion, see Friedrich, 1968, chapter 2). Implicit in this scheme was the theme of effective state autonomy in the context of a larger community – in this case Christendom – a view that was later reinforced by the Kantian notion of a community of independent nation states each committed to perpetuating peaceful co-existence in a broader community of nations (Kant, 1784; in Reiss, 1970).

Thus early conceptions of federalism belonged more to the genus confederal rather than federal. Few argued for political arrangements involving constitutionally assigned powers between two levels of government. In other words, federal association was seen more as a voluntary arrangement than one that sealed relations between central and regional powers in a negotiated and permanent pact. Such arrangements could apply in the absence of democratic institutions that would be required to endorse the territorial division of power. All this was to change with the signing of the United States constitution in 1789 which enshrined the concept of citizens holding identities at two levels, the state and the federal. At the same time powers were assigned to the two tiers of government establishing the notion of *shared sovereignty*. So the US Constitution established a political authority where both governmental power and citizen identity were shared between different levels within a single polity. And this division of authority was legitimized through popular, democratic approval. This construct has become the standard measure of federalism ever since (see, for example, Wheare, 1964, Chapter 1).

From the outset both scholars and political practitioners understood that federal arrangements were appropriate only in certain types of polity. Intuitively it is obvious that federalism is most likely to work in the context of ethnically or culturally similar and contiguous collections of states that would reap some advantage from association with a larger entity. For this reason early political science studies of federalism strove to identify the likely necessary conditions for federation formation. Having observed the experience of the USA, Switzerland, Canada and other federations, most identified the existence of a 'common interest' as the spur to federation. Hence in 1957, Karl Deutsch named the 'essential' conditions of federation as:

1. mutual compatibility of main values;
2. a distinctive way of life;
3. expectation of stronger economic ties or gains;
4. marked increase in administrative capabilities of at least some participating units;
5. superior economic growth on the part of at least some participating units;
6. superior economic growth;
7. unbroken links of social communication both geographically between territories and sociologically between different social strata;
8. a broadening of the political elite;
9. mobility of persons at least among the politically relevant strata; and
10. a multiplicity of ranges of communications and transactions (Deutsch et al. 1957: 58).

Critics quickly noted that this list specified neither the necessary let alone sufficient conditions for federations, and in particular points 1, 2, 6, 8 and 10 were absent in many of the newer federations such as Malaysia and India (Birch, 1966). Moreover some groups of countries displayed most or all of these features (for example the Nordic states) but had not formed federations. Attempts to refine Deutsch's taxonomy by developing the 'common interest' condition failed to advance the argument much further (Wheare, 1964: 37–38; Watts, 1966: 42). One obvious problem related to the fact that federation as a political form emerged in a wide variety of historical, geographical and political settings. In some – for example, the Soviet Union and Yugoslavia, hegemonic political parties were the driving force behind federation among groups of states that had little in the way of common interest between them. In others, political parties exploited territorial entities inherited from colonial rule and forged new federal arrangements out of them. In some, these arrangements succeeded (India), in others they faltered and ended in civil war (Nigeria) and in others again they failed almost immediately after inception (the East African and West Indian federations).

The failure of federations raises the question of sustainability. After all, specifying the conditions for federation formation becomes a meaningful exercise only if the federation is sustained over a reasonable span of time. One of the first scholars to address this question was Thomas Franck in his edited 1968 collection *Why Federations Fail* where he argues that although common interest of some sort such as protection against an external threat or the need for economic growth may be a necessary condition for federation building, it is certainly not sufficient on its own. Instead, what is needed is an ideological commitment on the need for federation. This may come from elites or from the broader society, although in the case of post colonial states (the main focus of his study) federation building was likely to come from elites (Franck, 1968, Chapter 5). Although Franck suggests that an ideological commitment to federation is clearly linked to economic and political interest, he does not develop the relationship in ways that allow for causal inference. In other words why some elites favour federation while others do not and how this relates to territorial or national interests, is left unexplained, as is the longer term elite commitment to federation that Franck claims is needed to sustain polities over time.

As a result, it is not surprising that ideological explanations of federation formation are open to accusations of tautology, that is: that the existence of federal political institutions can be explained by the process of 'federalizing' (Riker, 1975: 131). This accusation has often been levelled at proponents of European integration who sometimes imply something inevitable about 'ever closer union.' As Noel Malcolm (1995) has noted federalist ideologues seem to subscribe to some 'kind of cartographic mysticism that intuits that certain large areas of the map are crying out to merge as single geographical units' (p. 53). This partiality is part of a long line of idealist views of supranational governance stretching all the way back to Emmanuel Kant and which gained particular currency during the latter half of the nineteenth century and between the two world wars. After 1945, realism rather than idealism dominated thinking on international cooperation, but in Europe at least many assumed that the drive towards functional integration might lead to federalist political arrangements on the Continent of Europe (see Duff et al., 1994, and sources cited). As will be developed later, the increasing powers of the EU led to fierce debate in the literature as to how to classify the EU political system, with many scholars believing that it was essentially *sui generis* and not amenable to comparison with other systems, while others viewed the EU as a nascent federal state.

As should be clear from this brief review, by the 1960s the study of federalism in comparative context had not advanced much beyond simple classifications and descriptions. In addition, many students of the subject were also proponents of federalism as a preferred political system, thus blurring the line between scientific inquiry and political advocacy. Over the subsequent three decades, however, all this was to change with the publication of theoretically more ambitious and empirically more sophisticated studies which we will now review.

Rational choice approaches

The first major theoretical breakthrough in the study of comparative federalism came with the publication of William Riker's *Federalism: Origins, Operation, Significance* in 1964 (Riker, 1964). Having surveyed the origins of all modern federations, Riker concluded that in all cases the decision to form a federation was a rational bargain between regional and national political elites both of whom saw some advantage in forming a larger association of states. Further, in all cases the bargain involved two conditions that Riker claimed must always be present before a successful bargain is struck. First, a desire on the part of those offering the bargain peacefully to expand territory by combining constituent governments into a new political entity in order to meet an external military threat or to prepare for diplomatic aggrandizement. Second, for those accepting the bargain some sacrifice of political control is exchanged for the promise of security provided by the new federal government. Both in his 1964 volume and a subsequent 1975 version, Riker is sure of the empirical validity of his theory. As he claims:

> In order to prove this hypothesis I have examined *all* instances of the creation of federalism since 1786 ... For those federalisms that have survived, I am able to show that the two conditions existed at the origin; and for those that failed, I am able to show that either the conditions never existed, or they existed only momentarily. Though such evidence does not constitute absolute proof of the hypothesis, it comes as close to a proof as a non-experimental science can offer (Riker, 1964: 10, see also Riker, 1975).

Riker later accepted that the threat might be internal (as in the case of Malaysia and Nigeria) as well as external (see Birch, 1966; Riker, 1975). Although Riker's theoretical insights represented a major advance it did not immediately spawn further research – although it did provoke criticism from established students of the subject (see Dikshit, 1971, 1975: 222–7; King, 1982). Instead, for much of the 1970s and 1980s federalism studies remained either country specific or were confined to theoretically-limited taxonomic approaches (Watts, 1996). Riker himself left the sub area and devoted most of the rest of his academic career to the application of rational choice theory to coalition building and to heresthetics or the manipulation of

the structure of issues for political advantage. However, Riker introduced a number of insights into the study of federalism that were later to result in important research. Apart from seeing federation formation as a rational bargain, Riker also understood the importance of political party structure and function in the *sustainability* of federations over time. Hence, inclusive political parties with appeals across diverse territories and social groups were more likely to sustain federation than territorially and socially exclusive parties. He also understood the importance of the relationship between parties and interests on the one hand and political institutions on the other. Hence federations were more likely to function effectively if diverse regional interests were represented at the national level in senates or second chambers. Indeed, drawing on the American experience, Riker realized that the entire constitutional structure needed to be constructed in ways that facilitated effective bargaining and coalition formation between regional and national interests (Riker, 1975).

It was not until the 1990s and beyond, however, that further empirical research using Riker's theoretical insights was forthcoming. Peter Ordeshook and his collaborators was one of the first to elaborate on the relationship between federalism and constitutional design by stressing the particular advantages that the United States enjoyed at its inception. A longstanding democratic and constitutional tradition, even as early as 1789, became the foundation of a democratic federalism. By way of contrast the task for emerging democratic federations such as post Soviet Russia was much more daunting. This opus came to full fruition with the publication of Filippov et al.'s *Designing Federalism: A Theory of Self Sustainable Federal Institutions* in 2004.

Drawing on the experience of a number of political systems and especially the ex-Communist states, the authors' main objective is to specify those design rules and modes of representation that would sustain federations over the longer term. With respect to federations, special rules should apply that have a specifically territorial dimension, namely:

1. 'A system of individual level incentives designed to ensure federal stability should apply not to individual citizens but to political elites, since it is they, even in a democracy, who lead society from one equilibrium to another' (Filippov et al., 2004: 163). Both regional and national elites must accept what Filippov et al. call Level 1 constraints, or an acceptance of the provisions of the constitutional settlement. Elites should also accept Level 2 constraints or the rules of the game and informal norms and procedures inherent in the constitutional settlement that govern day-to-day bargaining and negotiation.
2. The constitution should provide for 'effective co-ordination devices [that] must give local and regional political elites an incentive to uphold federative constraints even when their constituents prefer otherwise'. So, individual level incentives (what Filippov et al. call Level 3 rules) must operate in such a way as to legitimise the constraints inherent in federal arrangements (Filippov et al., 2004: 163).
3. In addition the federal constitution 'must create (office related) rewards for national [federal] elites that dissuade them from overstepping their constitutionally prescribed authority and to acquiesce in the legitimate authority of the regional governments' (Filippov et al., 2004: 163–4).
4. The final constitutional principle is 'federal stability requires that regional and national elites maintain some (possibly evolving) consensus over the definitions of "constitutionally prescribed" and "legitimate authority"' (Filippov et al., 2004: 164). This appears to suggest that acceptance of the basic design rules should persist through time and eventually be enshrined in custom and practice.

Filippov et al. also specify appropriate modes of representation that will facilitate cooperation bargaining rather than conflict and confrontation between the parties to the federal bargain. It is easy to infer which modes of representation are most likely to uphold these constitutional principles. They include *within* as opposed to *without* representation, or the formal incorporation of the states into decision making in upper houses; delegated rather than direct

representation because delegates are more likely to defer to regional interests rather than 'go national' and betray their regional base; and separation of powers rather than parliamentary arrangements because independent legislatures are more likely to check the centralizing tendencies of chief executives. As can easily be inferred from the above, Filippov et al. are actually contrasting 'favourable' US institutional arrangements with the 'unfavourable' institutional features of those of Canada and post Soviet Russia.

The same applies to their deliberations on how political parties interact with political institutions. Inclusive parties with little or no territorially specific base are preferred to territorially exclusive parties, and such devices as the separation of powers, proportional representation, power sharing and bicameralism, are more likely to encourage the growth of decentralized, inclusive parties.

As the authors readily admit their work owes a great intellectual debt to William Riker, but they develop Riker's perspectives radically by concentrating not on the origins of federation but on the conditions that sustain federations over time (Filippov et al., 2004, chapter 1). Working in the same tradition, Bednar, Eskridge and Ferejohn, argue that legal rules alone are insufficient to contain central governments intent on predatory judicial expansion of their powers (Bednar et al., 2001; see also Bednar et al., 1996). In addition structural constitutional constraints are required. Like Filippov et al., Bednar et al. are trying to solve the intellectual puzzle of what sort of constitutional architecture should be employed to ensure that state and federal governments stay within their legitimate spheres of activity. They too opt for devices that formally fragment central authority such as the separation of powers. However sophisticated the analyses, however, all of these efforts face a familiar problem: how, in diverse political and cultural contexts do you create 'appropriate' constitutional structures given inherited patterns of power and authority? Creating inclusive parties, for example, is highly problematical if existing historically determined patterns of power encourage territorially specific exclusive parties. Aware of this problem the authors construct a fourth analytical category, level '0' to characterize those features of political systems that are 'beyond design' (Filippov et al., 2004: 294–98). Included in this list are such features as the presence or absence of a democratic tradition, public access to decision making, the status of public office holders and the absence of ethnic, religious and linguistic cleavages with a history of redistributive conflict. In other words, they are aware of the fact that cultural and historical baggage cannot easily be manipulated merely by constitutional design. In the end the authors are forced to concede that 'one should not assume that an endogenously sustainable institutional equilibrium within the federal format is even *theoretically* attainable in every contiguous part of the world' (Filippov et al., 2004: 331, emphasis added).

A further problem with the more recent rational choice literature is a reluctance to be empirically inclusive. Typically, authors look for examples from the American experience or, as in the case of Filippov et al., from Communist and post Communist states that confirm their theoretical insights. As a result selection bias tends to confirm their general hypotheses. But evidence from two other federal systems – India and Switzerland – raises the greatest intellectual challenge. India is interesting because it seems to fail almost every institutional and constitutional design test, bar one – the existence of inclusive political parties. Yet it has survived, and even thrived for more than half a century. Switzerland is interesting for quite different reasons, namely its ability to hold together and maintain a national identity in the almost complete absence of central authority. It is for this reason that Switzerland has been cited as an exemplar for the nascent European Union federation. We will return to this point later.

Comparative politics approaches

The study of comparative politics has taken two distinct (and now converging) paths.

One, in the rational choice tradition, focussed on the relationship between the incentives of political actors and institutional environments. The method was deductive with empirical examples used to confirm or disconfirm theoretical insights. The second approach grew out of the traumas of the Second World War, with scholars searching for patterns of political development that might help reduce conflict and succour democracy (see in particular the work of Stein Rokkan, for a review see Flora, 1994). This approach was more inductive and taxonomic. By classifying diverse political systems students of comparative politics gradually built up a bank of knowledge in such areas as electoral and party systems, government structures and public opinion.

We have already referred to the post war federalism literature that attempted to make sense out of diverse patterns of federalization and thus identify general patterns and trends. We also noted the normative element to much of this literature with some writers conflating the process of federalizing with a preference for federal institutional arrangements. By the 1990s, however, a number of scholars were avoiding these pitfalls and were instead intent on more careful and comprehensive taxonomies of federal and federal like arrangements. Two of the most ambitious of these taxonomies was Daniel Elazar's *Federal Systems of the World: A Handbook of Federal, Confederal and Autonomy Arrangements* (1994), and Ronald Watts' *Comparing Federal Systems in the 1990s* (1996). Both of these authors are sensitive to the sheer complexity of federal-like arrangements, and also to the fact that some political systems, were very difficult to characterize. In some systems constitutional centralization was accompanied by *de facto* decentralization (Canada); in others the powers of the central authorities were greater than in many unitary systems (India); in others again a degree of administrative and cultural decentralization was paired with extreme political centralization (the Soviet Union). In addition, by the end of the twentieth century the world had acquired a large number of non-federal political systems ranging from the United Nations to functional economic associations including the EU, Mercosur and NAFTA. So apart from the obvious centralization/decentralization dimension, at least two others became obvious. One was the extent of coercive as opposed to consensual exercise of power among member states, and the other was the extent of mass public involvement, through democratic institutions, in decision making processes. While it is difficult to capture all of the possible arrangements in one diagram, Phillip Schmitter had made a reasonable attempt at it. Hence in Figure 22.1 'Coerced' federations such as in the Soviet Union, Yugoslavia and Imperial India would be placed in the top right hand box, while modern democratic federations would be placed in the bottom right hand box. The early EEC and most regional economic associations would be classified as functional associations with consensual decision rules and low exit costs for members.

The problem with such taxonomies, however, is that they tell you nothing about *why* regional associations take the shape that they do, nor do they explain the transition from one form of association to another. In fact, it is extremely rare for regional economic

associations and the like to develop into federations. Indeed the only plausible recent example is the transition of the EEC to the EU, and as we will see later, even this claim is disputed. In Figure 22.1, there is often movement between the top left hand and middle cells and some from imperial to federal but almost none from functional, confederal or condominial to federal.

In one important respect the taxonomic literature confirms Riker's assertion that what explains federations is the presence of an external or internal threat that is sufficiently serious for collectivities of states to cede power to a central authority capable of averting the threat. Absent the threat – or the mutual appreciation of the threat – and there is no incentive to form a federation, which strongly suggests that the causal dynamic behind other regional associations is quite different.

This accepted, Riker clearly oversimplified the nature of the threat. Using a crude realist perspective he lumped together cases as varied as the United States, the Soviet Union, Malaysia and India. All did experience external or internal threats of sorts, but in wildly different historical and geopolitical circumstances. Writing in 2001 Alfred Stepan used comparative method to refine

Cooperative	Low	Moderate	High
Unanimity	Symbolic	Status Conferring (Holy Roman Empire)	Imperial (British India USSR)
Consensus	Functional (early EEC, regional trade associations)	Confederal (later EC)	Consortial (Cold War NATO)
Majority	UN	Condominial (EU?)	FEDERAL (USA, Switzerland)

Integrative

Figure 22.1 Forms of regional cooperation and integration decision making rules x costs and benefits of membership
Source: Schmitter (2007) adapted from Figure 1

the Rikerian perspective by distinguishing between 'coming together', 'holding together' and 'putting together' federations. According to Stepan, in the first category which includes the USA, Switzerland and Australia, relatively autonomous states come together voluntarily and bargain between themselves on the best form of federal arrangements. In all these cases, security is the motivating force, so they conform nicely to the Rikerian imperative. Holding together federations are characterized by parliamentary decisions to create federal structures in order to placate ethnic, religious or linguistic differences. India, Spain and Switzerland are examples here. Finally 'putting together' federations are created by a coercive centralizing power intent on incorporating previously independent states. The USSR in 1922 is the exemplar case here (Stepan, 2001: 320–22).

Stepan further refined the Rikerian perspective by distinguishing between asymmetrical and symmetrical federalism which he defines both in terms of socio-economic and constitutional asymmetry. Thus some federations are multinational (Canada, Spain, Belgium) while others (USA, Germany) are not. Asymmetry holds important lessons for bargaining between groups and often results in constitutional asymmetry or special provisions designed to accommodate one or more sub group within the federation. India has many such provisions, while the United States has none (Stepan, 2001: 323–33). Stepan makes further distinctions including what he calls 'demos enabling' versus 'demos constraining' institutional structures. So while all federations are *ipso facto* centre constraining some (Russia) inhibit popular participation in decision making while others (Switzerland) facilitate it (pp. 333–37). Finally, with Riker, he accepts that the most important institutional feature for the adaptability and survival of federations is the nature of the party system and in particular whether or not political parties are territorially inclusive or exclusive (pp. 354–60).

While Stepan's work claims to advance our knowledge of federalism 'beyond Riker' it is essentially taxonomic in approach.

As such it fails to provide a theoretical framework that allows us to draw meaningful causal inferences from a universe of cases. Instead, we are provided with refinements and modifications of Riker's opus. Stepan's major theoretical claim is that federal institutions – that is, the detailed arrangements for the building of coalitions and exercise of territorially based vetoes – really do matter for public policy, something that he claims Riker denied (p. 337). Yet what Riker argued was that institutions are essentially expressions of political power that ultimately is rooted in culture and history. They are, if you like, intervening variables between culture and policy. Yet in his later work on coalitions and in the work of his intellectual heirs such as Shepsle and Weingast, the role of institutions is elevated to a new height. Often they help shape preferences and incentives rather then merely reflect them – something that Ordeshook and his collaborators were to refine with specific reference to the sustainability of federal systems of government.

The final strand in the comparative politics literature relates to the evolution of the European Union (EU) from a system based on limited functional integration to one with most of the hallmarks of federalism. For students of the subject the EU presents something of an intellectual challenge. It is the *only* system in recent history that has migrated to the bottom left hand cell from one of the others cells in Figure 22.1. Moreover, at precisely the time when the EU acquired the trappings of federalism, the external military threat from the Soviet bloc was declining rapidly, effectively to disappear by the early 1990s. Why then have so many European countries ceded important area of national sovereignty to what increasingly resembles a federal state? Until quite recently students of the European Union had great difficulty answering these questions. In particular, the 'second wave' of EU scholars (after the early integration theorists), who classified the EU as an international organization characterized by inter- and intra-state patterns of cooperation and conflict, simply lacked the analytical tools to make sense of its growing state like characteristics (for the most influential of these studies, see Moravscik, 1998). Nation states may conclude bargains with neighbours to accommodate domestic economic interests but why should they cede important aspects of their sovereignty to supranational political institutions with all the trappings of statehood, including citizenship and a common currency?

The answer was to be provided, at least in part, not from the international relations scholars but from students of comparative politics and especially those influenced by rational choice theory. In particular, David McKay (1999b) in *Federalism and European Union* attempts to explain the transformation of the EU from an international organization to a federal like state in Rikerian terms. He argues that the ceding of national sovereignty in monetary policy was motivated by a desire on most of the signatories at Maastricht to transfer the control of inflation to a European Central Bank, because of the inherent political problems of solving this problem domestically. German motives were somewhat different: they saw in Maastricht an opportunity for diplomatic aggrandizement that would result from playing a major part in a larger territorial entity. And in order to avoid inflationary recidivism on the part of past offenders such as Italy, they insisted, via the Convergence Criteria and the Stability and Growth Pact, that these countries be forced to adopt German standards of fiscal rectitude (McKay, 1999a). McKay specifically argues that the EU's federal status applies only to EMU members, for only these countries have ceded complete control of one of the main policy areas associated with statehood to a supranational institution (McKay, 1999b, Chapter 8). Clearly this perspective extends Riker's rationale for federalising to economic as well as traditional security threats.

Other scholars were quick to note that the new policy responsibilities of the EU combined with a constitutional architecture that looked for all intents and purposes like that of a nation state, justified classifying the EU as a nascent federation rather than a *sui generis*

variety of international organization. As a result, all the accumulated research in comparative politics from elections and voting to parties and regulation, could be utilized with specific application to the EU (see, for example, Hesse and Wright, 1996; Menon and Schain, 2006; Nicolaidis and Howse, 2001). With the coming of the new EU draft constitution, further comparisons were drawn from democratic and constitutional theory (Dobson and Follesdal, 2004). In effect, federalist theory and comparative politics replaced international relations as the main intellectual framework for the study of the European Union, with some scholars making systematic comparisons between the EU and other federations (see McKay, 2001; Treschel, 2006). In *Designing Europe: Comparative Lessons for the European Union*, McKay (2001) was one of the first specifically to use comparative method to place the EU in historical context. In particular, he links regional/national identities to the policy scope of the federal government in six federal systems and relates these outcomes to party structures and constitutional arrangements (McKay, 2001: Chapter 9). Like many other scholars working in the field he identifies the highly devolved Swiss system as holding the most lessons for the EU (Chap. 9; also Treschel, 2006).

Although the federal status of the EU can be exaggerated – especially given the limited membership of European Monetary Union (EMU), recent enlargements and the ratification failure of the draft constitution – there is no doubt that applying comparative method to Europe has given a considerable boost to research on federalism, although as we will discuss in the concluding section, serious research lacunae in the disciplinary sub area remain.

Comparative federalism: What we know, what we don't know and what we should know

As this brief review shows, early research on comparative federalism was bedevilled by the conflation of scientific inquiry with normative concerns. During the 1950s and 1960s most of the leading scholars in the area were also advocates of federalism as a system of government. In part this derived from the generally self-congratulary mood within American political science at the time and what was widely regarded as the success of US federalism. Riker's work transformed the scholarly landscape by demonstrating that federal arrangements were the result of hard fought bargains between state and central level politicians, whose need for external or internal security trumped all other considerations including economic advantage and other non-security common interests. It was not until the 1990s, however, that federalism studies progressed further, partly in response to the challenges of building democratic polities in post Communist states and partly in response to developments in the European Union. Valuable contributions both from rational choice theorists and from students of comparative politics advanced our understanding of federalism and in particular the relationship between institutional arrangements and the sustainability of federal systems of government. In sum, the most important advance is the addition of a territorial dimension to both the rational choice literature and to comparative politics approaches. With regard to the latter, for example, the seminal work by Lijphart and others (see in particular, Lijphart, 1977) on those consociational devices that can best sustain democracy in multi-cultural societies, has been developed and refined to include territoriality.[2] In this sense we are now much more sensitive to the problems inherent in holding multi-cultural states together. Long gone are the days when colonial administrators almost casually imposed federal arrangements in inappropriate contexts such as East Africa, the West Indies or (in its original form, at least) in Nigeria.

Another advance is in relation to the link between federalism and democratic preferences. Few, if any, democratic federations today would use coercion to maintain the territorial integrity of the whole, should a majority in one of the sub units wish to secede.

This is clearly the case with regard to Quebec, Scotland and both communities in Belgium. In all these cases novel institutional devices, including referenda, have been employed to maintain the integrity of states and policy makers in these and other examples such as South Africa and Northern Ireland have been quick to innovate on the basis of shared experience. Much more difficult are those cases where democratic processes are absent or are incomplete, such as in Indonesia and Russia where force has been used and local political preferences have been largely ignored.

More difficult again are those cases where an external power attempts to build democratic federalism in complex ethnic and cultural states with little in the way of a democratic tradition such as Iraq and Afghanistan. Here mistakes have been legion with, in the absence of a return to despotism, the prospects of eventual territorial disintegration, very high.

It is with respect to these latter groups of cases that our knowledge is most limited. For while millions of words have been written on the EU's slow transition to federalism and many more on the evolution of American federalism, we know relatively little about the precise dynamics of how, for example, Indian federalism works (but see Lijphart, 1996; Manor, 1998; Mitra, 2005).

Future research should, therefore, employ those methods and approaches drawn from the established federalism literature to further our understanding of the following:

1. *The Puzzle of Indian Federalism.* As previously noted, India's constitutional arrangements are hardly conducive to sustainable federation yet Indian federalism has not only survived, but has also thrived in an increasingly democratic context in recent years. Most commentators point to the party system as the major integrative force in the system, yet we know relatively little about the territorial dimension to Indian political parties.

2. *Would federalism help hold together multi-cultural states such as Indonesia that are making a transition to democracy.* After a long period of despotism, Indonesia is experimenting with devolution to accommodate its ethnic variety. Could asymmetric federal arrangements help legitimize the

Indonesian state among minorities? Even more challenging are cases such as Tibet in China and Chechnya in Russia where the transition to democracy has been halting or has yet to begin.

3. *Are federal arrangements appropriate in states such as Iraq and Afghanistan presently subject to military intervention by external powers?* Can the post intervention end game in these countries include federalism and if so of what variety? As with the Soviet Union, 'solution' might include secession *and* federalism for some part or parts of the remaining states.

4. *How might the federalism in such countries as Argentina, Brazil and Mexico evolve in rapidly changing political and economic contexts?* Hitherto, federalism in these countries has been viewed as ancillary to other patterns of political power, and especially the role of the military, hegemonic political parties and dominant political elites. With globalization and democratization, however, constitutional arrangements do provide the potential for the assertion of regional and provincial power organized as an oppositional force to central authority.

5. *What is the status of highly devolved regions such as the Spanish autonomous regions and Scotland?* In these and other cases the extent of devolution has led some commentators to assume that these areas are developing into federal like entities (on Spain, see Burgess and Gagnon, 1993; on Scotland, see McKay, 2006). Research on the changing entire of central/regional relations in devolved systems would show how the incentives of regional and national politicians are changing in ways that might lead to even grater autonomy or even independence.

6. *Can the EU continue on its 'federalizing' path given recent enlargements and problems with ratifying a new constitution?* Little of the literature on enlargement adopts a federalist approach, yet it is clear that the social and economic inequalities between new members and existing members are such that asymmetric arrangements in such areas as monetary policy and right to work will likely continue for the foreseeable future.

This is by no means an exhaustive list but in all cases the main challenge involves specifying the institutional conditions for sustaining federal arrangements and confronting the often intractable problem of reconciling the 'ideal' conditions with prevailing patterns of political power rooted in culture and history. It would, of course, be possible to produce another list

where many interesting questions remain but where the opportunity costs of further research are high. This would include using the US as a comparator case both for the EU and elsewhere when there are so many more pressing research cases where the American experience is of limited utility. It is also clear that the priority should be on countries making the transition to democracy or those emerging, very often in a highly untidy manner, from dictatorial regimes, for it is in these cases that federal institutional arrangements may be useful in reducing conflict and reconciling differences. But to echo Riker, there is nothing intrinsically meritorious about federalism. Whether it works or not is strictly a matter for empirical enquiry. Should unitary arrangements or secession be more appropriate, then so be it. What is essential is that scholars of the subject use comparative method in a theoretically informed manner when researching existing federations and making judgements as to the appropriateness of federal institutions in different geographical contexts.

NOTES

1. The list of post colonial federations that failed is quite long and includes the West Indies, East African Federation, The Federation of Rhodesia and Nyasaland, Malaysia (in part at least), Indonesia and Pakistan.

2. In many respects reconciling cultural difference is easier in those states where ethnic and other groups are territorially separated. In such instances the option of secession is usually available. Where groups are territorially mixed as in Northern Ireland, Brussels, the Baghdad region of Iraq and parts of South Africa, federal arrangements are of more limited utility, although it is possible to have federal-like institutions in combination with other consociational devices. Lijphart's work concentrated on these latter cases, rather then on federalism *per se*.

REFERENCES AND BIBLIOGRAPHY

Bednar, J., Eskridge, W.N. and Ferejohn, J. (2001) 'A political theory of federalism', in J. Ferejohn, J.N. Rakove and R. Riley (eds), *Constitutional culture and democratic rule.*

Cambridge: Cambridge University Press, pp. 223–67.

Bednar, J., Ferejohn, J. and Garrett, G. (1996) 'The politics of European federalism', *International Review of Law and Economics*, 16 (2): 279–94.

Birch, A.H. (1966) 'Approaches to the study of federalism', *Political Studies*, 14 (1): 15–33.

Burgess, M. (2000) *Federalism and European Union*. London: Routledge.

Burgess, M. and Gagnon, A.G. (eds) (1993) *Comparative federalism and federation: Competing traditions and future directions*. London: Harvester Wheatsheaf.

Deutsch, K., et al. (1957) *Political community in the North Atlantic area*. Princeton, NJ: Princeton University Press.

Dikshit, R.D. (1971) 'Military interpretations of federal constitutions: A critique', *Journal of Politics*, 33 (2): 180–9.

Dikshit, R.D. (1975) *The political geography of federalism: An enquiry into origins and stability*. New Delhi: Macmillan.

Dobson, L. and Follesdal, A. (2004) *Political theory and the European Constitution*. London: Routledge.

Duff, A., Pinder, J. and Pryce, R. (eds) (1994) *Maastricht and beyond: Building the European Union*. London: Routledge.

Dyson, K. (ed.) (2002) *European states and the euro: Europeanization, variation and convergence*. Oxford: Oxford University Press.

Elazar, D. (1987) *Exploring federalism*. Tuscaloosa: University of Alabama Press.

Elazar, D. (1994) *Federal systems of the world: A handbook of federal, confederal and autonomy arrangements*. Harlow, Essex: Longman.

Filippov, M., Ordeshook, P.C. and Shvetsova, O. (2004) *Designing federalism: a theory of self-sustainable federal institutions*. Cambridge: Cambridge University Press.

Flora, P. (ed.) (1994) *State formation, nation-building, and mass politics in Europe: The theory of Stein Rokkan*. Oxford: Oxford University Press.

Forsyth, M. (1981) *Union of states: The theory and practice of confederation*. Leicester: University of Leicester Press.

Franck, T.M. (1968) *Why federations fail: An enquiry into the requisites for successful federalism*. New York: New York University Press.

Friedrich, C.J. (1968) *Trend of federalism in theory and practice*. London: Pall Mall Press.

Hesse, J.J. and Wright, V. (eds) (1996) *Federalizing Europe: The costs, benefits and preconditions of federal political systems*. Oxford: Oxford University Press.

Kant, I. (1970/1784) 'Perpetual peace: A philosophical sketch', in H. Reiss (ed.), *Kant's political writings*. Cambridge: Cambridge University Press, pp. 93–130.

Karmis, D. and Norman, W. (eds) (2005) *Theories of federalism: A reader*. London: Palgrave.

King, P. (1982) *Federalism and federation*. London: Croom Helm.

Kymlicka, W. (2002) *Contemporary political philosophy: An introduction*. Oxford: Clarendon Press.

Lijphart, A. (1977) *Democracy in plural societies: A comparative exploration*. New Haven: Yale University Press.

Lijphart, A. (1996) 'The puzzle of Indian democracy: A consociational interpretation', *American Political Science Review*, 90 (2): 258–68.

Manor, J. (1998) 'Making federalism work', *Journal of Democracy*, 9 (3): 29–36.

Malcolm, N. (1995) 'The case against Europe', *Foreign Affairs*, March/April.

McKay, D. (1999a) 'The political sustainability of European Monetary Union', *British Journal of Political Science*, 29 (4): 463–85.

McKay, D. (1999b) *Federalism and European Union: A Political Economy Perspective*. Oxford: Oxford University Press.

McKay, D. (2001) *Designing Europe: Comparative lessons from the federal experience*. Oxford: Oxford University Press.

McKay, D. (2004) 'The EU as a self sustaining federation: Specifying the constitutional conditions', in L. Dobson and A. Follesdal (eds), *Political theory and the European Constitution*. London: Routledge.

McKay, D. (2004) 'William Riker on federalism: Sometimes wrong but more right than anyone else?', *Regional and Federal Studies*, 14 (2): 167–86.

Mckay, D. (2004) 'What is Scotland: Incentives ands Sustainability,' in Iain Cameron (ed), *Good Governance: Scottish and Swedish Perspectives*,' Uppsala, Uppsala University, Faculty of Law, 2004, 23–38.

Menon, A. and Schain, M.A. (2006) *Comparative federalism: The EU and the US in comparative perspective*. Oxford: Oxford University Press.

Mitra, S.K. (2005) *The puzzle of India's governance. Culture, context and comparative theory*. London: Routledge.

Moravcsik, A. (1998) *The choice for Europe: Social purpose and state power from Messina to Maastricht*. Ithaca, NY: Cornell University Press.

Nicolaidis, K. and Howse, R. (eds) (2001) *The federal vision: Legitimacy and levels of governance in the United States and the European Union*. Oxford: Oxford University Press.

Norman, W.J. (2006) *Negotiating nationalism: Nation-building, federalism and secession in multilateral states*. Oxford: Oxford University Press.

Ordeshook, P.C. and Shetsova, O. (1997) 'Federalism and constitutional design', *Journal of Democracy*, 8 (1): 27–42.

Rabushka, A. and Shepsle, K.A. (1972) *Politics in plural societies: A theory of democratic instability*. Columbus, OH: Bobbs Merrill.

Riker, W.H. (1955) 'The Senate and American federalism', *American Political Science Review*, 49 (2): 452–69.

Riker, W.H. (1964) *Federalism: Origins, operation, significance*. Boston: Little, Brown.

Riker, W.H. (1975) 'Federalism', in F.I. Greenstein and N. Polsby (eds), *The Handbook of political science*, Volume V: *Government institutions and processes*. Reading, MA: Addison Wesley, 93–172.

Riker, W.H. (1982) *Liberalism against populism: A confrontation between the theory of democracy and the theory of social choice*. IL: Waveland Press.

Riker, W.H. (1987) *The development of American federalism*. Boston: Kluwer.

Riker, W.H. (1996) 'European federation: Lessons of past experience', in J.J. Hesse and V. Wright (eds), *Federalizing Europe: The costs, benefits and preconditions of federal political systems*. Oxford: Oxford University Press, pp. 9–24.

Riker, W.H. and Lemco, J. (1987) 'The relation between structure and stability in federal governments', in W.H. Riker (1987), *The development of American federalism*. Boston: Kluwer, pp. 113–34.

Schmitter, P.C. (2007) *Regional cooperation and regional integration: Concepts, measurement and a bit of theory*. Unpublished manuscript. Fiesole, European University Institute.

Stepan, A. (1999) 'Federalism and democracy: Beyond the US model', *Journal of Democracy*, 10: 19–34.

Stepan, A. (2001) *Arguing comparative politics*. Oxford: Oxford University Press.

Treschel, A. (ed.) (2006) *Towards a federal Europe?* London: Routledge.

Watts, R.L. (1966) *New federations: Experiments in the Commonwealth*. Oxford: Oxford University Press.

Watts, R.L. (1996) *Comparing federal systems in the 1990s*. Ontario: Institute of Intergovernmental Relations, Queens University.

Wheare, K. (1964) *Federal government* (4th edition). Oxford: Oxford University Press.

23

Human Rights

Todd Landman

INTRODUCTION

The analysis of the relationship between the state and citizen has a long tradition in comparative politics dating back to Aristotle's evaluation of 'good' and 'corrupt' forms of government and has included many strands of research within the field, including constitutions and political institutions; political behaviour, choice, and agency; and subjective experiences, cultural orientations, and perceptions of the good life under different forms of government. Human rights, in their modern manifestation, are a collection of individual and group rights that establish certain entitlements for rights holders and corresponding legal obligations for duty bearers to uphold those rights, while the relationship between rights holders and duty bearers is meant to be one of constraint, tolerance, accountability, and respect. While human rights and the development of international and national systems for their protection are relatively new, the fuller notion of *rights* has a long history in normative political theory and the struggle for rights is grounded in the comparative political sociology of the modern state. The human rights movement has sought to make human rights universally applicable, indivisible, inter-related, and mutually reinforcing in ways that no modern state is free from the potential and

real constraints of international human rights law and practice.

The aspiration of the scholarly and practical community to establish a universal system for the promotion and protection of human rights provides an extraordinary set of challenges for empirical research in comparative politics. First, human rights are themselves the product of normative political theory and philosophy, which have attempted to establish the foundations for their existence and to make them universally applicable. Human rights are of deep moral concern and necessarily involve a particular set of value orientations to the kind of empirical research carried out by comparativists interested in researching human rights problems. Second, any comparison of human rights problems necessarily relies on some form of measurement, where the variation in a state's ability to respect, protect, and fulfil human rights serves as the main object of inquiry, and where the comparison variously includes large-N statistical analysis of many countries over time and space, small-N qualitative or quantitative analysis of 'most similar' or 'most different countries', or a single country study of human rights developments at the national or sub-national level (Landman, 2002, 2003, 2008). Third, the establishment and proliferation of international human rights norms and mechanisms that seek to constrain state behaviour in ways that lead to greater promotion and protection of human rights means that much comparative research in the field needs to take into account the international dimension. This dimension includes the theoretical insights and empirical realities of international relations and the precepts, assumptions, and analyses in the field of international law (Landman, 2005b; Slaughter Burley, 1993).

The comparative politics of human rights thus needs to overcome significant ontological, epistemological, and methodological challenges in order to provide valid, meaningful, and reliable inferences in this burgeoning sub-field of research. Ontologically, foundations for the existence of human rights have not been established and the core substantive content of many human rights remains contested, making the relative protection and/or enjoyment of human rights problematic for systematic comparative analysis. Epistemologically, there remains a tension between and among the normative origins of human rights, different empirical theories used to explain variation in their protection, and the use of rigorous comparative methods that draw on more positivistic elements within the philosophy of social science. Methodologically, the field has struggled with providing systematic measures of the variation in human rights protection over time and space, as well as standard problems associated with different comparative methods, such as indeterminate research designs, omitted variable bias, and problems associated with case selection.

This chapter examines the different ways in which the field of comparative politics has sought to overcome these challenges. First, the chapter examines the normative and empirical problems associated with human rights as an object of inquiry, and then examines how the field has concentrated on particular sets of human rights that have thus far been more tractable for systematic comparative analysis. Second, it outlines how large-N, small-N, and single case analysis have been

used to study human rights problems and how human rights measurement plays a major role in these efforts. Third, it reviews many of the key extant comparative studies on human rights, including global comparative quantitative studies, small-N quantitative and qualitative studies, and key single case studies that have made valuable contributions to the field. The fourth and final section looks to the future of comparative human rights analysis.

HUMAN RIGHTS AS AN OBJECT OF INQUIRY

Human rights are a modern set of individual and collective rights that have been formally promoted and protected through international and domestic law since the 1948 Universal Declaration of Human Rights. Since 1948, the international community has established a series of legally binding international treaties that have expanded both the scope and depth of those rights that ought to be protected, such that they now include civil, political, social, economic, and cultural rights. A comparative politics that seeks to make human rights its main object of inquiry must confront two significant challenges. The first involves the fact that normative political theory and philosophy have failed to establish any consensus on the grounds for the existence of human rights (Landman, 2005a; Mendus, 1995). The second involves the fundamental *moral* nature of human rights, which has led some to question whether the theories and methods of contemporary social science can be applied to their study especially those approaches that are more positivistic in their stance (see Freeman, 2001, 2002). In other words, can comparativists conduct systematic research on social phenomena for which there are no agreed philosophical foundations, and is such research appropriate for studying something that is fundamentally moral in character? A comparative politics of human rights needs to address these questions and it is apparent from the burgeoning comparative literature that scholars have begun to do so.

There are several answers to the problem concerning the absence of agreed philosophical foundations for the existence of human rights. First, there are many concepts and subjects of study in political science and the social sciences more generally for which there are no agreed philosophical foundations. One need only think of social class, the market, and/or democracy. And for some of these, such as democracy, there are no agreed definitions, making them what Gallie (1956) has called 'essentially contested concepts'. The absence of agreed foundations or definitions has not precluded vast amounts of research conducted on these and other such similar subjects. Second, efforts by political leaders, scholars, and practitioners have led to the construction of an increasingly global consensus about the main core content of human rights, as represented by the promulgation of international human rights treaties and the ever increasing numbers of state and non-state actors declaring the importance of human rights. Many have argued that this construction of rights is a sufficient demonstration of their importance if not their existence (see e.g., Donnelly, 1999). Freeman (1994: 493) celebrates the passion of human rights activism that has led to the generation of such consensus, but he questions the degree to which it has been achieved and warns that 'rights without reasons are vulnerable to denial and abuse'. But he does not appear to make a compelling case to preclude systematic analysis of the various levels of promotion and protection of human rights in the world. Rather, it seems that the opposite is true, describing, mapping, and explaining the variety of practices in the world that violate human integrity and human dignity may well help us find the kinds of reasons that Freeman demands.

Third, whatever their provenance, rights have proved to be useful 'tools' that have given subordinated groups throughout history a language to confront agents, structures, and conditions of power whose struggles have led to greater protection of rights (Barbalet, 1988; Foweraker and Landman, 1997; Marshall, 1963). While a large part of the political sociology and history of such struggles focuses on rights and citizenship rights, more recent comparative politics research has focused on the ways in which the struggle for *human* rights has led to state concessions and ultimately the development of more rights protective political regimes (see Hawkins, 2002; Risse et al., 1999). For some, human rights are the 'bulwarks against the permanent threat of human evil' (Mendus, 1995), while for others they are those sets of protections that guarantee human agency (Ignatieff, 2001), or are an important political lever for the realization of global justice (Falk, 2000). This more pragmatic approach suggests that in the absence of philosophical foundations, human rights can still be thought of as important catalysts for political and social transformation and as the kinds of protections against arbitrary state and non-state action that impinges on the lives of ordinary citizens. As above, this does not deny the need to continue to find the foundations for human rights, but rather shows how rights are used to improve the lives of ordinary people around the world.

Such a pragmatic approach suggests that systematic research on the conditions under which such protections are (or are not) made possible can help us understand how best to prevent human beings from doing their worst to one another, as well as how to overcome some of the structural barriers to achieving greater human dignity for a larger cross-section of humankind. Indeed, these arguments suggest that not only is a comparative politics of human rights possible, but it is also *essential* for explaining and understanding the conditions under which human beings forge their existence, assert their dignity, and seek protections for their different identities, pursuit of self-determination, and exercise of agency and autonomy. Like the study of markets, social classes, and democracy, the study of human rights reveals much about human nature, the ways in which structure and agency interact to create extraordinarily different life experiences across the globe, and provide valuable insights into the types of protections that need to be in place. To eschew comparative research on the basis that there are no agreed philosophical foundations for the phenomena under study would, in contrast to Freeman, be irresponsible, dangerous, and hugely short sighted.[1]

There are also several ways to address the problem of whether it is appropriate to use reputedly 'value free' techniques to carry out research on such a 'value-laden' concept as human rights. There are many public goods whose promotion, protection, and realization go well beyond the fulfilment of individual interests and needs, and that include an appeal to a distinct set of values that have been the subject of systematic research in comparative politics. Democracy is a value-laden subject. Environmental degradation and or environmental protection are laden with a particular set of value orientations. Economic development, in most modern definitions, includes dimensions of self-esteem in addition to raising living standards and increasing access to life-sustaining goods (e.g., Todaro, 1997). Finally, the study of post-material values themselves has been conducted using standard comparative analysis of survey data (Inglehart, 1977, 1990, 1997, 1998; Inglehart and Welzel, 2005). These examples are in line with the general position adopted by Max Weber that it is possible to carry out research on topics that have been *influenced* by values but that the research process itself should not have been so influenced. Such an approach to research is not to conflate the normative and the empirical, but to use the tools of the empirical analysis to research real-world problems that have significant normative importance (McCamant, 1981: 534). It is also entirely possible for those that are against human rights or highly sceptical of their realization and enforcement to use comparative analysis (see e.g., Watson, 1999).

MEASURING HUMAN RIGHTS

The comparative analysis of human rights problems is predicated on our ability as scholars to provide comparable measures of human rights practices either *within* states or *across* states. Such measures can be qualitative or quantitative and both types of measures provide some gauge of the degree to which human rights are being *respected, protected*, and *fulfilled* by states. The obligation to *respect* human rights requires the state and all its organs and agents to abstain from carrying out, sponsoring or tolerating any practice, policy or legal measure violating the integrity of individuals or impinging on their freedom to access resources to satisfy their needs. It also requires that legislative and administrative codes take account of guaranteed rights. The obligation to *protect* human rights obliges the state and its agents to prevent the violation of rights by other individuals or non-state actors. Where violations do occur the state must guarantee access to legal remedies. The obligation to *fulfil* human rights involves issues of advocacy, public expenditure, governmental regulation of the economy, the provision of basic services and related infrastructure and redistributive measures. The duty of fulfilment comprises those active measures necessary for guaranteeing opportunities to access entitlements (see UNDP, 2006).

The obligation to respect, protect, and fulfil applies to all categories of human rights found in the international law of human rights, including civil, political, economic, social, and cultural rights. The combination of these categories of human rights with the three dimensions of respect, protect, and fulfil provides a useful heuristic device for understanding what needs to be measured, which aspects of human rights can be measured, and which of those aspects have been measured to date. Figure 23.1 shows the matrix which results from combing the different categories of rights with their different dimensions. Such a matrix of rights and their

Dimensions of human rights

Categories of human rights		Respect No interference in the exercise of the right	Protect Prevent violations from third parties	Fulfil Provision of resources and the outcomes of policies
	Civil and Political	1 Torture, extra-judicial killings, disappearances, arbitrary detention, unfair trials, electoral intimidation, disenfranchisement	2 Measure to prevent non-state actors from committing violations, such as militias, uncivil movements, or private sector firms and organizations.	2 Investment in judiciaries, prisons, police forces, electoral authorities, and resource allocations to ability.
	Economic, Social and Cultural	4 Ethnic, racial, gender, or linguistic discrimination in health, education, and welfare, and resource allocations below ability.	5 Measures to prevent non-state actors from engaging in discriminatory behaviour that limits access to services and conditions.	6 Progressive realization Investment in health, education and welfare, and resource allocations to ability.

Figure 23.1   The categories and dimensions of human rights
Source: Adapted from UNDP (2006: 5)

different dimensions means that there are a variety of ways to measure human rights. Indicators for column 1 in the table on the respect for human rights measure the degree to which states are responsible for violating human rights (e.g., measures of incidences of torture, or acts of discrimination in public health authorities). Indicators for column 2 measure the degree to which non-state actors and other third parties violate human rights (e.g., incidences of third party deprivation of liberty or denial of access to private sector health provision). Indicators for column 3 measure the degree to which states provide the necessary resources and policies for realizing and promoting the protection of human rights (e.g., investment in police training on issues of torture and inhuman treatment or investment in the infrastructure for health, education, and welfare).

Traditionally, political science has been heavily influenced by liberal conceptions of the 'negative' rights of liberty and has therefore concentrated on the relative respect for civil and political rights (cell 1). This means that the attempt to operationalize these rights for comparative analysis has left out consideration of violations by non-state actors and state fulfilment of civil and political rights (cells 2 and 3), as well as the complete neglect of any consideration for economic, social, and cultural rights (cells 4, 5 and 6). For example, the global quantitative comparative analysis since the 1980s has been dominated by studies on the protection of civil and political rights, or 'personal integrity rights', (Davenport, 1999; Hafner-Burton and Tsutsi, 2005, 2007; Henderson, 1993; Landman, 2005a, 2005b; Mitchell and McCormick, 1988; Neumayer, 2005; Poe and Tate, 1994; Poe et al., 1999; Zanger, 2000a) while many qualitative studies have focused on that set of basic '"rights of the person" [that] have been most accepted as universal rights' (Risse and Sikkink, 1999: 2; see also Landman, 2005b: 52). Some of the quantitative studies have sought to analyze the relative protection of 'subsistence rights' but the measures that they use, such as the 'physical quality of life index' (PQLI) or the 'human development index' (HDI) are at best 'distant' proxy measures that are better understood as development measures than any kind of rights measure *per se* (see Landman and Häusermann, 2003; Milner et al., 1999). Only recently, have political scientists begun to assemble large data sets on some social and economic rights. For example, David Cingranelli and David Richards have developed a series of standards-based measures (i.e., interval scales derived from narrative reporting of rights conditions around the world) of worker rights and women's economic rights (www.humanrightsdata.com), and have developed a new measure of the effort of states to promote economic rights derived from regressing the PQLI on ratification of the International Covenant on Economic, Social, and Cultural Rights (as a measure of willingness) and per capita GDP (as a measure of capacity) (Cingranelli and Richards, 2007).

More progress on the measurement of social and economic rights has been made by the international development community, which has long worked on social exclusion indicators. In addition, work on patterns of discrimination has contributed to the measurement of some social and economic rights. For example, work carried out by the Bangladesh Rural Action Committee (BRAC), a large and well-funded non-governmental organization based in Dhaka has been able to show patterns of social exclusion for the 'ultra poor' across the country over time. Work carried out by the UK Department for International Development in Brazil has been able to show patterns of social exclusion in Brazil based on race. In a governmental impact assessment carried out in Australia, a Heckmann selection model was used to estimate patterns of discrimination in the labour market due to disability (Productivity Commission, 2004). These different examples suggest ways in which the disproportionality of access to service delivery or participation in the market can be measured. From a human rights perspective, such methods of estimation could be used to provide indicators for the *protect* dimension outlined above. Privatization

programmes in the health, education, and welfare sectors that result in vast sectors of the population being excluded from essential services could be understood as indicators for the ways in which a state is failing to uphold its international human rights obligations as laid out, for example, in the International Covenant on Social, Economic, and Cultural Rights.

But these efforts to track patterns of social exclusion and discrimination imply an agent that may be responsible for such patterns but do not adopt a 'violations' approach to the measurement of social and economic rights (see Chapman, 1996). Intensive case study analysis conducted by a combination of academics, official truth commissions, and non-governmental organizations has adopted a violations approach and has begun to collect large amounts of events-based data on violations, but the focus has thus far been on civil and political rights, and laterally, some cultural rights. These efforts collect data derived from a quantitative 'deconstruction' of human rights violation events using the 'who did what to whom' model (Ball et al., 2000) and in many cases, multiple sources of data. This model is explicit in identifying the agent of the violation, the type of violation, and the context in which it has happened. The most sophisticated studies to date that use this model include those carried out on the armed conflict in Guatemala from 1962 to 1996 (Ball, 2000; REMHI, 1999), Peru from 1980 to 2000 (Ball et al., 2003) and on the Indonesian occupation of East Timor from 1974 to 1999. Subsequent analysis of these data has also shown, particularly in the case of Guatemala and Peru that ethnic identity was a key category that explained the disproportionate pattern of violations in which indigenous groups suffered the brunt of political violence.

Attempts to apply this kind of model to social and economic rights have to date proved intractable (Chapman, 1996), although it is possible to conceive of specific agents who are responsible for the denial of access to certain social and economic entitlements, as well as specific instances in which social and economic rights have been violated that could be counted and or measured. Moreover, in a classic illustration of one of the main trade-offs that confronts all comparative research (see below), what these data gain in validity and reliability in measuring a particular set of human rights (i.e., civil rights and integrity rights) they lose in their ability to make empirical generalisations beyond the cases under scrutiny. They also tend to be collected for specific periods of heightened violence making their use for comparative research that seeks to compare across similar time periods problematic. Brockett's (2005) comparative study on mobilization and repression in Guatemala and El Salvador is a notable exception, since both countries experienced similar types of political violence during similar time periods.

To date, there are various sources of data on the *de jure* protection of human rights, their *de facto* realization, and socio-economic and administrative statistics on the different dimensions of respect, protect, and fulfil. Measures of *de jure* commitments of states code treaty signature, ratification, and reservations (see e.g., Keith, 1999; Hafner-Burton and Tsutsui, 2005, 2007; Hathaway, 2002; Landman, 2004, 2005a, 2005b; Neumayer, 2005), as well as national level legal frameworks (Keith and Poe, 2002; van Maarseveen and van der Tang 1978). Measures of *de facto* realization have relied on events-based, standards-based, and survey-based measures of human rights, where the tendency has been to focus on civil and political rights. For example, as mentioned above, the events-based data projects tend to cover a limited number of countries typically that have undergone periods of extreme political violence. The 'political terror scale', Oona Hathaway's (2002) torture scale, and Cingranelli and Richards (CIRI) data are interval scales of personal integrity rights and torture coded from the US State Department and Amnesty International country reports, although the CIRI data set has begun to focus on some social and economic rights. The World Values Surveys and various 'barometer' projects around the world (Europe, Latin America, Africa, and Asia) use mass surveys of representative national samples, while the work of organizations such as Physicians for Human Rights uses surveys collected from 'at risk' populations in countries such as Sierra Leone, Iraq, and Afghanistan (Physicians for Human Rights, 2002a, 2002b, 2002c, 2003).

COMPARING HUMAN RIGHTS

Despite the relative dearth of comparative measures across the different categories and dimensions of human rights outlined above, much comparative research has been carried out in an effort to explain and understand cross-national similarities and differences in the protection of human rights. There is now a large body of large-N quantitative studies, small-N qualitative and quantitative studies, as well as a vast array of single case studies that examine the causes, conditions, and consequences of human rights protection around the world. Extant global comparative studies on human rights protection have tended to focus on a narrow set of civil and political rights and carried out diachronic and synchronic analyses to estimate the effects of a series of important explanatory variables that account for their variation. Such explanatory variables have included economic development (Henderson, 1993; Mitchell and McCormick, 1988), population and population growth (Dixon and Moon, 1986; Poe and Tate, 1994; Poe et al., 1999), democracy and democratization (Davenport, 1999; Henderson, 1993; Poe and Tate, 1994; Poe et al., 1999; Zanger, 2000a), multi-national corporations (MNC) (Meyer, 1996, 1998, 1999a, 1999b), internal and external violent conflict (Poe and Tate, 1994; Poe et al., 1999; Zanger, 2000a), the end of the Cold War (Cingranelli and Richards, 1999), US and European foreign aid (Cingranelli and Pasquarello, 1985; Hofrenning, 1990; Poe, 1990; Poe and Sirirangsi, 1993, 1994; Regan, 1995; Stohl et al., 1984; Zanger, 2000b), domestic constitutional provisions

(Davenport, 1996, 1999), and religious differences and ethnic diversity (Park, 1987). Outside consideration of civil and political rights, other global comparative projects have focussed on discrimination, minorities, and conflict (Caprioli, 2000; Caprioli and Trumbore, 2003; Krain, 1997), US refugee policy (Gibney et al., 1992), and the provision of basic human needs (Dixon and Moon, 1986; Moon and Dixon, 1985).

The most recent area of interest has been the examination of the growth and effectiveness of the international human rights regime. The field of international law has examined the proliferation of international human rights norms and argued that the growth of the regime represents a consensus about the universality of human rights as well as a 'language of commitment' among states comprising the international system. Realists in international relations, on the other hand, have long claimed that international law reflects the distribution of power among states and that it is difficult to demonstrate how international law can have any independent effects on state behaviour (see Mearsheimer, 1994–1995). Interestingly, the field of comparative politics has begun to include international variables (Landman, 2008), and in the area of human rights, one such set of variables has become those that measure the international human rights regime. Moreover, since the international human rights regime represents one way in which inter-state relations can influence domestic state-citizen relations, large-N comparison has been one research design that has been adopted to analyse this important question.

Linda Camp Keith (1999) was the first to analyze the relationship between comparing the cross-national differences in ratification of the International Covenant on Civil and Political Rights to differences in human rights protection, while controlling for a variety of other variables such as economic development and democracy. While her bi-variate relationships proved to be significant, her multivariate analysis showed that ICCPR ratification made no difference for human rights protection.

Hathaway (2002) has had similar findings for a broader range of treaties and rights. Hafner-Burton and Tsutsiu (2005, 2007) and Neumayer (2005) added a layer of complexity to the relationship by specifying models that included an interaction effect between treaty ratification and democracy, which in turn has an effect on human rights protection. In similar fashion, Landman's (2005b) analysis includes both the level and timing of democratization, a feedback process between treaty ratification and human rights protection, as well as a weighted measure of treaty ratification that took into account the filing of reservations across the main international human rights treaties. While the earlier studies find little empirical support for a relationship between the regime and domestic rights protection, the later studies find support for a significant but limited effect of the regime, which is modelled as the product of changes occurring at the domestic and international levels, including democratization, economic development, and greater inter-state interdependence (see also Landman, 2006: 100–3).

Large-N comparative analysis has begun to illuminate a number of processes and factors at work that help account for cross-national variation in human rights protection. The key findings of this literature about which there is greatest consensus include the importance of economic development, democracy, and conflict resolution for better protection of human rights. There is certainly less consensus on the possible effects for foreign aid, direct foreign investment, and international human rights law itself. Moreover, as in many research areas in comparative politics, there are significant limitations to this mode of analysis. First, there is the absence of significant variables on the 'left hand' side of the regression equations, such as economic and social rights, as well as the absence of significant 'right hand' variables, such as poverty, income distribution, and human development. Further research is needed on testing the robustness of extant findings across a wider range of human rights as well as alongside additional independent variables. Are the tangible benefits for human rights from higher levels of wealth the same even if that wealth is differently distributed? What is the relationship between the distribution of land and human rights violations? Is there a significant interaction effect between development and democracy that will have an impact on human rights protection? Are countries with persistent problems in upholding social and economic rights more or less likely to receive foreign aid?

Second, there is a certain 'a-historical' quality to the large-N analysis. While the more recent analysis uses time-series cross-national data, the data sets tend to have highly restricted time periods that generally start in the 1970s and extend to 2003 or 2004. This 30-year period was, of course, highly influenced by a particular set of events, such as decolonization and the struggle for independence, the Cold War and its demise, and now the 'War on Terror'. While such events necessarily shaped the struggle for rights, it is only a very small fragment of world history to be using as a base for empirical generalizations. Analyses that go back before the 1948 Universal Declaration of Human Rights would help build a fuller picture of the possible dynamic process at work in which different rights protections were secured. The 30 year time period in the extant studies also reflects a certain structure of world politics, where there is a large collection of wealthy democracies, as well as countries in the core, semi-periphery, and periphery of the global economy. Greater attention should be given to the possible biases and effects that the inclusion of such countries in the absence of controls might have on any empirical generalizations that are being made.

Third, the studies remain thin on their use of empirical theories. With a few minor exceptions (e.g., Barratt, 2004; Hathaway, 2002; Landman, 2005b; Meyer, 1996; Poe, 2004), there has been little theoretical reflection about why certain variables have been selected for inclusion in these global analyses. In general, the variables that have been chosen reflect an orientation to economic structures and political institutions, with certain references to culture (e.g., British colonial experience). But to date there has been a dearth of integrated theoretical accounts from which a series of testable propositions have been derived, which is in part due to the fact that it is difficult to operationalize variables for 'agential' and 'cultural' accounts of human rights violations for large-N analysis. Even those studies that focus on structural explanations have tended to not look at *why* processes and dynamics of economic development would necessarily be related to human rights protection despite the statistical significance of such relationships, but focus more on the significant empirical relationships between such variables.

Finally, this particular research design is not appropriate for a series of issue areas that remain crucial for the field of human rights. For example, while the studies on multi-national capital test for the overall presence of multi-nationals in a country in terms of direct foreign investment, they do not examine the specific *practices* of multinational corporations (MNCs) nor do they capture the diverse forms of MNCs that operate in countries (i.e., export platform and manufacturing, mineral extraction, textiles, etc.), which may have different kinds of impact on different categories of human rights. Global comparative analysis cannot capture the intricacies of mobilization from human rights non-governmental organizations (NGOs) or other civil society organizations. While the number of international non-governmental organizations (INGOs) with registered offices in countries has featured in Landman's (2005b) analysis of the relationship between human rights norms and practices, such a variable will only every be a proxy measure for the freedom of association in civil society and/or the penetration of international civil society. Mitchell (2004) salutes the achievements of the global studies in establishing the broad parameters for understanding patterns in human rights violations, but in order to test the observable implications of his 'principal-agent' model, he adopts a small-N comparative research design (see below). Finally, such analyses are limited in their ability to map inter-subjective meanings and different cultural understandings of human rights, which may or may not have an effect on human rights practices. The cross-national work on 'values' and value change tends to employ survey data that collects relatively abstract and general attitudes about human rights rather than deeper identification with human rights that could be differentiated significantly across specific cultural contexts.

Analyses of human rights problems and puzzles that use a relatively small and intentional selection of countries address a number of common themes and adopt a wide range of comparative methods. The dominant themes in comparative politics include the struggle for rights and the relationship between social mobilization, political liberalization, and repression (Brockett, 2005; de Brito, 1997; Foweraker and Landman, 1997); the similarities and differences in the formation, function, outcomes and impact of truth commissions (De Brito et al., 2001; Hayner, 1994, 2002; Skaar, 1999; Skaar et al., 2005); the legacies of authoritarian rule (Hite and Cesarini, 2004; Roniger and Sznajder, 1999; see also Cesarini, this volume); non-state violence, 'uncivil' movements, and death squads (Campbell and Brenner, 2000; Payne, 2000); and the ways in which human rights norms have transcended state sovereignty through the use of 'transnational advocacy networks' that help form alliances and informational networks between domestic and international human rights organizations that are able to put pressure on rights violating states (Keck and Sikkink, 1998; Risse et al., 1999; Tarrow, 2005).

These various small-N studies have adopted a range of comparative cases, or 'focussed comparison' strategies, including most similar systems designs (MSSD) that compare different human rights related outcomes across similar cases (e.g., Brockett, 2005; Mitchell, 2004), most different systems designs (MDSD) that compare similar outcomes across different cases (Bob, 2005), the 'mirror image' of MSSD that compares similar variation across similar cases (Foweraker and Landman, 1997; Payne, 2000), and different

outcomes across different cases (e.g., Hayner, 1994, 2002; Risse et al., 1999). For example, Mitchell (2004) compares widely different levels of atrocity across three similar instances of civil war to support his model of the dynamic relationship between differently motivated 'principals' and the agents to whom they delegate authority to carry out their bidding. The focus on a smaller set of country cases allows for greater attention to processes, decision-making, historical dynamics, and more discrete causal mechanisms, but brings with it limits to the ability to draw larger inferences that extend far beyond the confines of the countries that feature in the comparison (see Landman, 2000, 2003, 2008).

Single country studies have long played an important part of comparative politics and social science more generally (Eckstein, 1975; George and Bennett, 2005). While some have dismissed them as providing 'evidence without inference' (Almond, 1996) or as having only comparative 'merit', others have been more robust in the contribution that single case studies can make to comparative politics and such a claim is certainly supported by the work being done in the field of human rights. Eckstein (1975) among others reminds us that single country studies are useful for description and classification, 'plausibility probes', generating and testing hypotheses, and as crucial cases (i.e., 'most likely' and 'least likely' examples) that can confirm, infirm, or disconfirm theories (see Landman, 2008: Chapter 5). The themes that are addressed in single country studies vary little from those that have featured in the large-N and small-N comparative studies, but as in the comparison of a few countries, single country analysis has allowed for much greater attention to process tracing and dynamic relationships between actors, conditions, and rights.

The work of Hawkins (2002) provides a good example of how process tracing provides deeper insight into causal mechanisms within a single county. In his study of authoritarianism in Chile and the response of the Pinochet regime to international human rights pressure, Hawkins (2002) examines thousands of internal communiqués within the Chilean military to show that there was a 'rule-oriented' faction within the regime that grew increasing wary of the possible delegitimizing power of international human rights pressure. This faction increasingly gained ground within the regime, which ultimately held a national plebiscite for the new constitution in 1980 and for President Pinochet himself in 1988. The defeat of Pinochet ushered in a relatively rapid transition to democracy. But the Hawkins (2002) analysis demonstrates several things that go far beyond the explanation of democratic transition in a particular country. First, he retains considerable leverage for the rationalist account of regime change that has been too easily dismissed by normative and constructive accounts. Second, he showed the discrete causal chains that lie between broader patterns of international human rights pressure and regime change by getting inside the factional tension within the regime itself. Third, he showed how the 'two-level' game (Putnam, 1988) originally devised to explain the behaviour of democratic regimes also applies to non-democratic regimes (see also Landman, 2005b). Finally, he extends his findings from the Chilean case to South Africa and Cuba to test the applicability of his explanation to contexts outside the focus of the study.

Increasingly, and in following the general methodological tenor of King et al. (1994) the inferential logic of large-N studies has begun to be applied to single country studies using sub-national divisions within individual countries, such as democracy and human rights in the federal systems of Mexico (Mitchell and Beer, 2004) and India (Beer and Mitchell, 2006), and democracy and political violence across the administrative districts of Nepal (Mitchell et al., 2006). In these studies, the use of states in a federal structure as the basic units of analysis allows for a large number of observations (or increased degrees of freedom) for the analysis of variation in human rights protection, while at the same time controlling for similarities, since these units are all from the same country. In this way, comparative research in federal systems is a form of most similar systems design (MSSD) and offers tremendous promise for research in the field of human rights.

THE FUTURE OF COMPARATIVE HUMAN RIGHTS RESEARCH

Systematic analysis of human rights problems is a burgeoning sub-field in comparative politics and in many ways is a natural place in the larger discipline of political science in which to locate such analysis. While the international human rights regime seeks to use the mechanism of international law to govern the ways in which states relate to their citizens, it is within states and it is across states that the promotion and protection of human rights varies. This variation, which makes reference to an ideal standard outlined within the many international human rights norms and instruments, is best analyzed through the various methods available to comparativists. These methods, which have developed through the analysis of many areas of research outside any concern for human rights, have served and will serve human rights well for the future.

But despite the many virtues of comparative analysis for human rights research, there are many challenges that remain in the field. Comparative politics does not have its own distinct theoretical tradition, but engages in rationalist, structuralist, and culturalist theorising in ways that can be developed more fully and fruitfully for human rights research. The attention to rationalism in Mitchell (2004) and Hawkins (2002) is laudable, especially since both afford an equally large role for ideational approaches. Mitchell's (2004) principals are motivated by material self interest, as well as ideology and it is precisely the differences in these motivations that help explain the differences in levels of atrocity that he observes. In similar fashion, the different factions in Hawkins' (2002) analysis of the military regime in Chile are motivated by the quest to maintain power, but also by a particular attachment to legal rules and standards both within and outside the Chilean constitutional order. It is precisely this kind of innovative development and testing of theories that is needed in future comparative research on human rights.

Finally, it is clear that more attention is needed on methodological issues. For questions of measurement, more attention is needed on the sources of human rights information, the procedures for coding human rights information, the development of measures of economic and social rights, and the provision of indicators that capture the many different dimensions of human rights outlined in Figure 23.1. These measurement issues are pertinent to all forms of comparative analysis from large-N studies to single country analysis. For studies that compare a few countries or a single country, more attention to the process of case selection is needed to avoid indeterminate research designs and severe forms of selection bias. 'Most similar' and 'most different' systems designs offer good first solutions for case selection, while greater attention to 'negative' cases (Goetz, 2006; Mahoney and Goetz, 2004) and 'crucial' cases (Eckstein, 1975; Gerring, 2004, 2006) is required to make the most of single country studies of particular human rights problems. Human rights research is a fascinating field and ought to be a central concern to comparative politics, since it has so many overlaps with other substantive topics in the discipline contained within this Handbook. But like these other fields, the standards for high quality and systematic rules of inquiry apply equally to this field.

NOTE

1. Freeman (1994: 493) contends that 'evading the task of finding the best grounding for human rights, in the face of philosophical sceptics and political opponents, demonstrates a lack of intellectual responsibility.'

REFERENCES

Almond, G. (1996) 'Political science: The history of the discipline', in R.E. Goodin and H. Klingemann (eds), *The new handbook of political science*. Oxford: Oxford University Press, pp. 50–96.

Ball, P.B. (2000) 'The Guatemalan commission for historical clarification: Generating analytical reports, inter-sample analysis', in P.B. Ball, H. F. Spirer and L. Spirer (eds), *Making the case: Investigating large scale human rights violations using information systems and data analysis*. Washington DC: American Association for the Advancement of Science, pp. 259–86.

Ball, P.B., Asher, J., Sulmont, D., and Manrique, D. (2003) *How many Peruvians have died?* Washington, DC: American Association for the Advancement of Science (AAAS) Retrieved March 26, 2008, from http://shr. aaas.org/peru/aaas_peru_5.pdf

Ball, P.B., Spirer, H.F., and Spirer, L. (eds) (2000) *Making the case: Investigating large scale human rights violations using information systems and data analysis*. Washington DC: American Association for the Advancement of Science.

Barbalet, J.M. (1988) *Citizenship: Rights, struggle and class inequality*. Milton Keynes: Open University Press.

Barratt, B. (2004) 'Aiding or abetting: British foreign aid decisions and recipient country human rights', in S.C. Carey and S.C. Poe (eds), *Understanding human rights violations: New systematic studies*. Aldershot: Ashgate, pp. 43–62.

Beer, C. and Mitchell, N. J. (2006) 'Comparing nations and states: Human rights and democracy in India', *Comparative Political Studies*, 39 (8): 996–1018.

Bob, C. (2005) *The marketing of rebellion: Insurgents, media, and international activism*. Cambridge: Cambridge University Press.

Brockett, C. (2005) *Political movements and violence in Central America*. Cambridge: Cambridge University Press.

Campbell, B.B. and Brenner, A.D. (eds) (2000) *Death squads in global perspective: Murder with deniability*. New York: St. Martin's Press.

Caprioli, M. (2000) 'Gendered conflict', *Journal of Peace Research*, 37 (1): 51–68.

Caprioli, M. and Trumbore, P. (2003) 'Ethnic discrimination and interstate violence: Testing the international impact of domestic behavior', *Journal of Peace Research*, 40 (1): 5–23.

Chapman, A. (1996) 'A "violations approach" for monitoring the International Covenant on Economic, Social, and Cultural Rights', *Human Rights Quarterly*, 18 (1): 23–66.

Cingranelli, D.L. and Pasquarello, T. (1985) 'Human rights practices and the distribution of U.S. foreign aid to Latin American countries', *American Journal of Political Science*, 29 (3): 539–63.

Cingranelli, D.L. and Richards, D.L. (1999) 'Measuring the level, pattern, and sequence of government respect for physical integrity rights', *International Studies Quarterly*, 43 (2): 407–17.

Cingranelli, D.L. and Richards, D.L. (2007) 'Measuring government effort to respect economic and social human rights: A peer benchmark', in S. Hertel and L. Minkler (eds), *Economic rights: Conceptual, measurement and policy issues*. Cambridge: Cambridge University Press, pp. 214–32.

Davenport, C. (1996) 'Constitutional promises and repressive reality', *Journal of Politics*, 58 (3): 627–54.

Davenport. C. (1999) 'Human rights and the democratic proposition', *Journal of Conflict Resolution*, 43 (1): 92–116.

De Brito, A.B. (1997) *Human rights and democratization in Latin America: Uruguay and Chile*. Oxford: Oxford University Press.

De Brito, A., González-Enríquez, C., and Aguilar, P. (2001) *The politics of memory: Transitional justice in democratizing societies*. Oxford: Oxford University Press.

Dixon, W. and Moon, B. (1986) 'Military burden and basic human rights needs', *Journal of Conflict Resolution*, 30 (4): 660–83.

Donnelly, J. (1999) 'The social construction of human rights', in T. Dunne and N. Wheeler (eds), *Human rights in global politics*. Cambridge: Cambridge University Press, pp. 71–102.

Eckstein, H. (1975) 'Case-study and theory in political science', in F.I. Greenstein and N.S. Polsby (eds), *Handbook of political science*, Vol. 7: *Strategies of inquiry*. Reading, MA: Addison-Wesley, pp. 79–137.

Falk, R. (2000) *Human rights horizons*. London: Routledge.

Foweraker, J. and Landman, T. (1997) *Citizenship rights and social movements: A comparative and statistical analysis*. Oxford: Oxford University Press.

Freeman, M. (1994) 'The philosophical foundations of human rights', *Human Rights Quarterly*, 16 (3): 491–514.

Freeman, M. (2001) 'Is a political science of human rights possible?', *The Netherlands Quarterly of Human Rights*, 19 (2): 121–37.

Freeman, M. (2002) *Human rights: An interdisciplinary approach*. Cambridge: Polity.

Gallie, W.B. (1956) 'Essentially contested concepts', *Proceedings of the Aristotelian Society*, 51 (2): 167–98.

George, A.L. and Bennett, A. (2005) *Case studies and theory development in the social sciences*. Cambridge: Cambridge University Press.

Gerring, J. (2004) 'What is a case study and what is it good for?', *American Political Science Review*, 98 (2): 341–54.

Gerring, J. (2006) *Case study research: Principles and practice*. Cambridge: Cambridge University Press.

Gibney, M., Dalton, V., and Vockell, M. (1992) 'USA refugee policy: A human rights analysis update', *Journal of Refugee Studies*, 5: 33–46.

Goetz, G. (2006) *Social science concepts: A user's guide*. Princeton: Princeton University Press.

Hafner-Burton, E.M. and Tsutsui, K. (2005) 'Human rights in a globalizing world: The paradox of empty promises', *American Journal of Sociology*, 110 (5): 1373–411.

Hafner-Burton, E.M. and Tsutsui, K. (2007) 'Justice lost! The failure of international human rights law to matter where needed most', *Journal of Peace Research*, 44 (4): 407–25.

Hathaway, O. (2002) 'Do treaties make a difference? Human rights treaties and the problem of compliance', *Yale Law Journal*, 111 (8): 1932–2042.

Hawkins, D. (2002) *International human rights and authoritarian rule in Chile*. Lincoln: University of Nebraska Press.

Hayner, P.B. (1994) 'Fifteen truth commissions – 1974–1994: A comparative study', *Human Rights Quarterly*, 16 (4): 597–655.

Hayner, P.B. (2002) *Unspeakable truths: Facing the challenge of truth commissions*. London: Routledge.

Henderson, C. (1993) 'Population pressures and political repression', *Social Science Quarterly*, 74 (3): 322–33.

Hite, K. and Cesarini, P. (eds) (2004) *Authoritarian legacies and democracy in Latin America and Southern Europe*. Notre Dame, IN: University of Notre Dame Press.

Hofrenning, D.J.B. (1990) 'Human rights and foreign aid: A comparison of the Reagan and Carter administrations', *American Political Quarterly*, 18 (4): 514–26.

Ignatieff, M. (2001) *Human rights as politics and idolatry*. Princeton: Princeton University Press.

Inglehart, R. (1977) *The silent revolution: Changing values and political styles among Western publics*. Princeton, NJ: Princeton University Press.

Inglehart, R. (1990) *Culture shift in advanced industrial societies*. Princeton, NJ: Princeton University Press.

Inglehart, R. (1997) *Modernization and post-modernization*. Princeton, NJ: Princeton University Press.

Inglehart, R. (1998) 'Political values', in J. W. van Deth (ed.), *Comparative politics: The problem of equivalence*. London: Routledge, pp. 61–85.

Inglehart, R. and Welzel, C. (2005) *Modernization, cultural change, and democracy: The human development sequence*. Cambridge: Cambridge University Press.

Keck, M. and Sikkink, K. (1998) *Activists beyond borders: Advocacy networks in international politics*. Ithaca, NY: Cornell University Press

Keith, L.C. (1999) 'The United Nations International Covenant on Civil and Political Rights: Does it make a difference in human rights behavior?', *Journal of Peace Research*, 36 (1): 95–118.

Keith, L.C. and Poe, S.C. (2002) *Personal integrity abuse during domestic crises: Exploring the relationships between constitutional protections, formal judicial independence, and executive constraint*. Paper presented at the Annual meeting of the American Political Science Association, Boston, MA.

King, G., Keohane, R.O., and Verba, S. (1994) *Designing social inquiry: Scientific inference in qualitative research*. Princeton, NJ: Princeton University Press.

Krain, M. (1997) 'State-sponsored mass murder: The onset and severity of genocides and politicides', *Journal of Conflict Resolution*, 41 (3): 331–60.

Landman, T. (2000) *Issues and methods in comparative politics: An introduction*. London: Routledge.

Landman, T. (2002) 'Comparative politics and human rights', *Human Rights Quarterly*, 24 (4): 890–923.

Landman, T. (2003) *Issues and methods in comparative politics: An introduction* (2nd edition) London: Routledge.

Landman, T. (2004) 'Measuring human rights: Principle, practice, and policy', *Human Rights Quarterly*, 26 (November): 906–931.

Landman, T. (2005a) 'Review article: The political science of human rights', *British Journal of Political Science*, 35 (3): 549–72.

Landman, T. (2005b) *Protecting human rights: A global comparative study*. Washington DC: Georgetown University Press.

Landman, T. (2006) *Studying human rights*. London: Routledge.

Landman, T. (2008) *Issues and methods in comparative politics: An introduction* (3rd edition) London: Routledge.

Landman, T. and Häusermann, J. (2003) *Map-making and analysis of the main international initiatives on developing indicators on democracy and good governance*. Report to the European Commission.

Mahoney, J. and Goertz, G. (2004) 'The possibility principle: Choosing negative cases in comparative research', *American Political Science Review*, 98 (4): 653–69.

Marshall, T.H. (1963) 'Citizenship and social class', in T.H. Marshall (ed.), *Sociology at the crossroads and other essays*. London: Heinemann.

McCamant, J.F. (1981) 'Social science and human rights', *International Organization*, 35 (3): 531–52.

Mearsheimer, J.J. (1994–1995) 'The false promise of international institutions', *International Security*, 19 (3): 5–49.

Mendus, S. (1995) 'Human rights in political theory', *Political Studies*, 43 (Special Issue): 10–24.

Meyer, W.H. (1996) 'Human rights and MNCs: Theory vs. quantitative evidence', *Human Rights Quarterly*, 18 (2): 368–97.

Meyer, W.H. (1998) *Human rights and international political economy in Third World nations: Multinational corporations, foreign aid, and repression*. Westport, CT: Praeger.

Meyer, W.H. (1999a) 'Confirming, infirming, and falsifying theories of human rights: Reflections on Smith, Bolyard, and Ippolito through the lens of Lakatos', *Human Rights Quarterly*, 21 (1): 220–28.

Meyer, W.H. (1999b) 'Human rights and international political economy in Third World nations: Multinational corporations, foreign aid, and repression', *Human Rights Quarterly*, 21 (3): 824–30.

Milner, W., Poe, S., and Leblang, D. (1999) 'Security rights, subsistence rights, and liberties: A theoretical survey of the empirical landscape', *Human Rights Quarterly*, 21 (2): 403–44.

Mitchell, N. (2004) *Agents of atrocity: Leaders, followers, and the violation of human rights in civil war*. London: Palgrave.

Mitchell, N. and Beer, C. (2004) 'Democracy and human rights in the Mexican states: Elections or social capital', *International Studies Quarterly*, 48 (2): 293–312.

Mitchell, N., Bohara, A., and Nepal, M. (2006). 'Opportunity, democracy and political violence: A sub–national analysis of conflict in Nepal', *Journal of Conflict Resolution*, 50 (1): 108–28.

Mitchell N.J. and McCormick, J.M. (1988) 'Economic and political explanations of human rights violations', *World Politics*, 40: 476–498.

Mitchell, C., Stohl, M., Carleton, D., and Lopez, G. (1986) 'State terrorism: Issues of concept and measurement', in M. Stohl and G. Lopez (eds), *Government violence and repression: An agenda for research*. New York, Greenwood Press, pp. 202–21.

Moon, B. and Dixon, W. (1985) 'Politics, the state, and basic human needs: A cross-national study', *Journal of Political Science*, 29 (4): 661–94.

Moon, B. and Dixon, W. (1992) 'Basic needs and growth: Welfare trade-offs', *International Studies Quarterly*, 36 (2): 191–212.

Neumayer, E. (2005) 'Do international human rights treaties improve respect for human rights?', *Journal of Conflict Resolution*, 49 (6): 925–53.

Park, H. (1987) 'Correlates of human rights: Global tendencies', *Human Rights Quarterly*, 9 (3): 405–13.

Payne, L. (2000) *Uncivil movements: The armed right wing and democracy in Latin America*. Baltimore: Johns Hopkins University Press.

Physicians for Human Rights (2002a) *Maternal mortality in Herat province, Afghanistan*. Boston MA and Washington, DC: Physicians for Human Rights.

Physicians for Human Rights (2002b) *War-related sexual violence in Sierra Leone: A population-based assessment*. Boston MA and Washington, DC: Physicians for Human Rights.

Physicians for Human Rights (2002c) *A survey of human rights abuses among new internally displaced persons Herat, Afghanistan, A briefing paper*. Boston MA and Washington, DC: Physicians for Human Rights.

Physicians for Human Rights (2003) *Southern Iraq: Reports of human rights abuses and views on justice, reconstruction and government, A briefing paper*. Boston MA and Washington, DC: Physicians for Human Rights.

Poe, S. (1990) 'Human rights and foreign aid: A review of quantitative studies and suggestions for future research', *Human Rights Quarterly*, 12 (4): 499–509.

Poe, S. (2004) 'The decision to repress: An integrative theoretical approach to research on human rights and repression', in S. Carey and S. Poe (eds), *Understanding human rights violations: New systematic studies*. Aldershot: Ashgate, pp. 16–42.

Poe, S. and Sirirangsi, R. (1993) 'Human rights and U.S. economic aid to Africa', *International Interactions*, 18 (4): 1–14.

Poe, S. and Sirirangsi, R. (1994) 'Human rights and us economic aid during the Reagan Years', *Social Science Quarterly*, 75 (3): 444–509.

Poe, S. and Tate, C.N. (1994) 'Repression of human rights to personal integrity in the 1980s: A global analysis', *American Political Science Review*, 88 (4): 853–72.

Poe, S.C., Tate, C.N., and Keith, L.C. (1999) 'Repression of the human right to personal integrity revisited: A global cross-national study covering the years 1976–1993', *International Studies Quarterly*, 43 (2): 291–313.

Productivity Commission (2004) *Review of the disability discrimination act 1992* (Report, no. 30) Melbourne: Commonwealth of Australia.

Putnam, R. (1988) 'Diplomacy and domestic politics: The logic of two-level games', *International Organization*, 42 (3): 427–60.

Recovery of Historical Memory Project (REMHI) (1999) *Guatemala never again! The official report of the human rights office, Archdiocese of Guatemala*, Mayknoll. New York: Orbis Books.

Regan, P.M. (1995) 'US economic aid and political repression', *Political Research Quarterly*, 48 (3): 613–28.

Risse, T. and Sikkink, K. (1999) 'The socialization of international human rights norms into domestic practices: Introduction', in T. Risse, S.C.Ropp and K. Sikkink (eds), *The power of human rights: International norms and domestic change*. Cambridge: Cambridge University Press, pp. 1–38.

Risse, T., Ropp, S.C., and Sikkink, K. (1999) *The power of human rights: International norms and domestic change*. Cambridge: Cambridge University Press.

Roniger, L. and Sznajder, M. (1999) *The legacy of human rights violations in the Southern Cone: Argentina, Chile, and Uruguay*. Oxford: Oxford University Press.

Skaar, E. (1999) 'Truth Commissions, trials – or nothing? Policy options in democratic transitions', *Third World Quarterly*, 20 (6): 1109–28.

Skaar, S., Gloppen, S., and Surhke, A. (eds) (2005) *Roads to reconciliation*. Lexington, MA: Lexington Books.

Slaughter Burley, A. (1993) 'International law and international relations theory: A dual agenda', *American Journal of International Law*, 87 (2): 205–39.

Stohl, M., Carleton, D., and Johnson, S. (1984) 'Human rights and U.S. foreign assistance', *Journal of Peace Research*, 21 (3): 215–226.

Tarrow, S. (2005) *The new transnational activism*. Cambridge: Cambridge University Press.

Todaro, M. (1997) *Economic development* (6th edition) London: Longman.

UNDP (2006) *Indicators for rights-based approaches to development programming: A user's guide*. Oslo: Oslo Governance Centre.

van Maarseveen H. and van der Tang, G. (1978) *Written constitutions: A computerized comparative study*. New York: Oceana Publications.

Watson, J.S. (1999) *Theory and reality in the international protection of human rights*. Ardsley, NY: Transnational Publishers.

Zanger, S.C. (2000a) 'A global analysis of the effect of regime changes on life integrity violations, 1977–1993', *Journal of Peace Research*, 37 (2): 213–33.

Zanger, S.C. (2000b) 'Good governance and European aid: the impact of political conditionality', *European Union Politics*, 1 (3): 293–317.

24

Governance

Philip Keefer

INTRODUCTION

A growing body of evidence points to governance failures as a root cause of slow and inequitable economic growth and as a defining characteristic of most poor countries. These findings justify placing governance high on any research agenda aimed at better understanding the political economy of economic development. Already, research into governance and development has had a notable impact: some dimensions of governance now sit at the center of academic and policy discussions of economic development. This chapter reviews the known effects of governance on development, the interrelationship among the different dimensions of governance, and the origins of 'good' governance. The review highlights where important questions remain to be answered, particularly with respect to the origins of good governance.

Although this chapter is a critical review of the governance literature, it turns out that most of that literature does not use the term 'governance.' Moreover, there is no agreed definition of governance that would provide a convenient device for organizing the literature. Finally, there are few research efforts that set out to analyze all dimensions or even most dimensions of governance jointly. For various, sometimes necessarily arbitrary reasons that

are explained below, the focus here is therefore on the literature that links economic development to secure property rights, voice and accountability, or the performance of the bureaucracy. Each of these seems to be at the core of all definitions of governance.

The basic conclusions of this review are threefold. First, further research on governance-related issues remains a high priority, but progress is likely to be fastest and most convincing when future work addresses the components of governance rather than aggregated concepts of governance. In many cases, the components of governance do not even bear the same causal relationship to development, nor is one component necessarily a good proxy for other components. The security of property rights, for example, can be considered a proximate contributor to economic development, in much the same way as macroeconomic or social policy. Voice and accountability, however, matter indirectly, through their influence on government decision making or the security of property rights. The review spells out the differences across governance indicators and their links to development.

The second conclusion of this review is that evidence and theory better support the influence of some components of governance on development than others. The security of property rights and the credibility of governments emerge as the components with the best documented and strongest influence on economic development. Causality problems cloud estimates of the influence of bureaucratic (or 'state') capacity and corruption on development. The most critical of these causality problems results from the omission from most analyses of political variables that are likely to influence both bureaucratic efficiency and integrity, and development outcomes. Finally, analyses of voice and accountability, or 'democracy', while the subject of substantial attention, have suffered from a lack of theoretical and empirical precision that clouds interpretation.

Third, future research that deepens our understanding of the determinants of good governance is likely to have the greatest payoff. Although progress has been made in identifying the political and social conditions that lead to more secure property rights, greater voice and accountability, or more efficient and honest bureaucracy, much remains unknown or puzzling. In addition, the governance literature has so far been isolated from much of the progress that has been made along these lines in the broader political economy literature. A growing literature outside the realm usually defined as governance describes the effects of voter information and political institutions on political incentives to seek rents; the tools and results of this literature have yet to be integrated into work on governance.

WHAT IS GOVERNANCE?

Whether in policy or academic settings, governance is among the more elastic concepts in the social science and development lexicons. Definitions tend to encompass one or both of the following: the extent to which governments are responsive to citizens and provide them with certain core services, such as secure property rights and, more generally, the rule of law; and the extent to which the institutions and processes of government give government decision makers an incentive to be responsive to citizens. Though similar, in fact the first are 'outcomes' while the second are 'causal' or more fundamental concepts. Corruption and bureaucratic quality are more direct indicators of lack of responsiveness, and only indirect indicators of government incentives; measures of democracy or voice and accountability, in contrast, directly capture the second more than the first.

In 2001, the Institute on Governance, in Canada, defined governance squarely in the second category, as comprising 'the traditions, institutions and processes that determine how power is exercised, how citizens are given a voice, and how decisions are made on issues of public concern'. Currently, it lists fundamental principles of good governance: legitimacy and voice, direction, performance, accountability and fairness. (IOG, 2008). The journal *Economics of Governance* essentially views governance as synonymous with governing, and encourages submissions that deal with all manner of problems that emerge in the way groups of individuals govern themselves in the public or private sectors. Its statement of aims and objectives, however, evades the tricky issue of how to define governance.

More common are definitions and realms of activity that straddle the outcome and institutional sides of governance. In 2002, the website of the OECD described governance as relating to 'institutions, policy making and participation of civil society. The Ford Foundation views governance as the extent to which government institutions are 'transparent, accountable and responsive'.[1] The US Agency for International Development focused on outcomes in defining good governance. In 2002, its website indicated that governance is present when governments can 'maintain social peace, guarantee law and order, promote or create conditions necessary for economic growth, and ensure a minimum level of social security'. However, underlying good governance are transparent and accountable government institutions, and USAID work on governance focuses explicitly on strengthening democratic institutions. In 2002, the

United Nations Development Program referred to 'democratic governance,' but its description of its goals implies that governance is the responsiveness of state institutions and processes to the needs of ordinary citizens (UNDP, 2008).

Perhaps not surprisingly, since their charters discourage engagement with countries on more overtly political issues, the least political definitions of governance can be found at the World Bank and International Monetary Fund. The World Bank (2008) introduces its work on governance and links it intrinsically to public sector reform, characterizing governance and public sector reform jointly as focused on 'building efficient and accountable public sector institutions'. Governance, then, is the extent to which public sector institutions are accountable and capable of sustaining development. The emphasis, however, is on the implementing or administrative agencies of government rather than the incentives of the political actors who sit atop them. Similarly, the International Monetary Fund views good governance as encompassing (but not necessarily exclusive to) the rule of law, the efficiency and accountability of the public sector, and corruption (IMF, 1997).

The various definitions of governance are evidently expansive. In fact, if the study of governance extends to all questions related to how groups of people govern themselves, as might be inferred from many of these definitions, then there are few subjects in all of political science and political economy that do not fall within the governance domain. Taken to this extreme, one might reasonably doubt whether the study of governance is at all novel or of independent analytic interest.

There are two responses to this. First, in one sense it does not really matter. As long as the literature labeled governance generates important findings about critical topics and does not ignore the broader research domain in which those topics may be nested, the label is irrelevant. Second, it is still possible to establish useful – if somewhat arbitrary – boundaries on governance as an independent sphere of inquiry. In both policy and academic circles

the term has acquired popularity only recently and with two particular concerns. Governance is first associated with establishing causal relationships between economic development and particular performance characteristics of developing countries to which earlier literature paid less attention. These characteristics include, especially, such phenomena as the security of property rights, the performance of bureaucracies and the predictability and credibility of government decision making. Second, governance is associated with establishing causal relationships between the underlying institutional characteristics of governments (typically, democracy or voice and accountability) and either the performance of governments (e.g., with respect to the rule of law) or economic development, or both.

The discussion below therefore takes these two lines of inquiry as comprising the study of governance. Although the literature does not always follow this division and often conflates the study of less and more fundamental notions of governance, in principle these are clearly two different and well-defined lines of inquiry that mark a literature that has grown in rigor and volume since the 1980s.

THE HAZARDS OF AGGREGATION IN GOVERNANCE RESEARCH

Policy and some academic discussions frequently refer to good governance, implicitly aggregating all of the underlying dimensions into a single concept. Kaufmann et al. (2002) reflect the breadth of this concept in their efforts to devise systematic measures of governance. They take 194 measures variously used in the literature as measures of governance, from 17 sources, and divide them into 6 categories: voice and accountability, political stability, government effectiveness, regulatory quality, rule of law and control of corruption. Theirs is a reasonable breakdown of governance concepts, and there are few analyses of governance, implicit or explicit, that do not fall into one or more of these categories. Aggregation of these concepts makes sense if all good things go together. In fact, they may not.

Kaufmann and Kraay (2002) highlight the difficulty of casually aggregating these governance components. They show that good performance on some of these dimensions does not imply good performance on others. Most countries in Latin America turn out to do better than other countries with similar per capita incomes with respect to voice and accountability, but worse with respect to government effectiveness, rule of law and corruption, and both better and worse with respect to political stability and regulatory quality. Recognizing this, in their substantive analysis of the effect of governance on growth they focus only on one of their indicators, the rule of law.

Studies of specific countries reveal how divergence among indicators might emerge. Figure 24.1 records the assessment by one political risk service of corruption perceptions in Indonesia. It shows clearly that corruption perceptions rose with the advent of democratic elections on June 7, 1999 and the demise of the Suharto autocracy. Voice and accountability therefore seem to have moved inversely with corruption perceptions. The paradox here is acute: the Suharto regime was widely regarded as among the most corrupt in the world, and no observer doubts that the absolute value of bribes going to the government has fallen precipitously, despite worsening corruption perceptions.

One explanation for this paradox is that corrupt transactions became less credible after Suharto's departure, suggesting that voice and accountability (at least as generated by new and imperfect democracies) may also diverge from government credibility. Under Suharto, businesses believed that if they paid a US $1,000,000 bribe they would get a high return on their investment because the underlying agreement was credible (or, in terms of the Kaufmann et al. variables, either the rule of law or political stability were high). They could be confident that they would, in fact, receive the rents conferred by the monopoly or regulatory privilege provided in exchange for the bribe. The political uncertainty of the post-Suharto era lowered the credibility of these transactions. Consequently, even if the bribe-price of entry or regulatory privileges fell since the end of the Suharto regime, the effective value of the privileges may have fallen by even more. Although total corrupt payments may have fallen, the perceived damage of corruption might have risen. The Indonesia case demonstrates that two components of governance – corruption and the credibility of government – may also move in opposite directions, at least as they are measured.

One final example of the potential divergence among typical dimensions of governance relates to the credibility of government

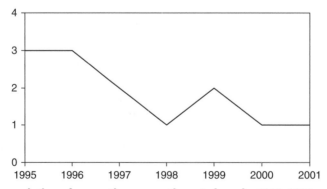

Figure 24.1   The evolution of corruption perceptions, Indonesia, 1995–2001
Note: Political Risk Services Corruption assessment, 0–6 scale, higher implies less corruption.

and bureaucratic quality. North and Weingast (1989) argue that credibility is a function of checks and balances among political decision makers. We can therefore imagine two governments, one exhibiting checks and balances, and one not. Which will have an easier time ensuring a high level of performance by civil servants? Keefer and Stasavage (2002) argue that independent central banks are much more likely to succeed in generating low inflation outcomes in the presence of checks and balances. This seems to suggest that credibility and bureaucratic quality might go together. However, problems of special interest capture of regulatory agencies are well-documented in many other contexts. To the extent that checks and balances insulate captured regulators from political interference, we might expect poor regulatory/bureaucratic performance to be greater when political institutions are associated with more credibility. Contributors to Libecap (1996) make exactly this point and Wallsten (2002) has documented worse outcomes in electricity regulation when regulators are fully independent of political authorities (when they cannot be removed from office and they have an independent source of financing).

AN ABRIDGED INTELLECTUAL HISTORY OF GOVERNANCE

The concerns motivating the governance literature have a distinct intellectual heritage. Broadly speaking, of course, analysis of the operation of bureaucracies and their honesty and efficiency dates back to Max Weber. The connection to economic development, a crucial component of the governance literature, is more recent. Similarly, though research on democracy and democratization goes back generations, it is only more recently that scholars have begun to ask systematic questions relating the incentives of government actors to outcomes in developing countries.

In the 1950s, the common wisdom in policy and academic circles characterized the

key obstacle to development as capital, so that economic development (or at least growth) depended on the transfer of capital to capital-starved poor countries. By the 1980s development thinking had shifted to concern with the economic policies of developing country governments, typically trade barriers, state ownership of industry, and loose management of the macro-economy. Experience and research then showed that reasonable economic policies were possibly a necessary but certainly not a sufficient condition for economic growth and development. This motivated a renewed look at other aspects of public sector performance. The work of North (1981; 1990) was particularly important in setting the intellectual stage for this new focus. He systematically linked country characteristics such as the security of property rights directly to the prosperity of nations. From this evolution, then, emerged one part of the governance research agenda: improved understanding of the effects of the non-policy characteristics of government performance on economic development.

The research stemming from this strand of the governance literature brought to the forefront the contribution to development of such previously under-examined phenomena as the security of property rights, the rule of law, expropriation, bureaucratic quality, red tape, and the quality of government regulation – concepts falling squarely under the rubric of governance. While these ideas flowered in the academic literature, they were also given great policy impetus by work not primarily intended for the research community, particularly the controversial, though influential contribution of de Soto (1989).

A second pillar of development wisdom in the 1950s – or, at least, an unexamined and implicit assumption – was that governments would, by and large, act in the general interests of society. Most explanations of underdevelopment ignored the incentives of the governments of developing countries and focused instead on exogenous or purely economic constraints on development or, in the political sphere, the role of industrialized countries in perpetuating underdevelopment. This was a reasonable focus for the times, since the colonial legacy was both recent and bitter in many developing areas.

Bates (1981) broke with this tradition by documenting how the political or economic self-interest of political actors could yield policies that were devastating for society at large, independent of external influence. He specifically showed that governments in the countries he considered sought the support of powerful interest groups and favored them at the expense of the unorganized or less threatening interest groups. This work inspired a new question: why did interest groups in the African countries that he examined have a more pernicious effect on outcomes than interest groups elsewhere – in Germany or the United States, for instance? Under what conditions, that is, do governments in some countries pursue socially beneficial policies while in other countries they do not? From these questions flows the second part of the governance research agenda: under what conditions do governments pursue the public interest and promote development in poor countries?

This overly – even unreasonably – condensed intellectual history of governance excludes some concepts and literature that others reasonably include within the governance domain. In particular, the inadequacy of development explanations rooted in capital inflows and economic policy choices led many researchers to focus not on self-interested political leaders but rather on broader characteristics of the state or the bureaucracy. This research has introduced concepts such as the rent-seeking state (Buchanan et al., 1980), embedded autonomy (Evans, 1995), and state capacity using analytical approaches that are useful to contrast with the more overtly political analyses spawned by Bates.

The literature on rent-seeking generally takes for granted that governments use the coercive power of the state for self-aggrandizement. It does not take into account the limits that political competition might impose on these efforts. Arguments about embedded autonomy and state capacity take a more benign view of the state than the rent-seeking literature. They emphasize the role of the administrative apparatus of the state in promoting development. Like the rent-seeking literature, however, this literature does not specify the conditions under which politicians support or demand high performance from the bureaucracy. In both cases, therefore, this work abstracts from the political considerations that are at the core of arguments such as those of Bates (1991).

The conclusion of Evans (1989), for example, suggests that politicians are but background or ancilliary actors in development: 'The comparative evidence suggests that the efficacy of the developmental state depends on a meritocratic bureaucracy with a strong sense of corporate identity and a dense set of institutionalized links to private elites.' This evidence could be persuasive if the politicians in the different countries confronted approximately the same electoral and institutional constraints on their actions. This may not be the case, however, since the conclusion rests on a comparison of Brazil, Japan, and Zaire. Evans (1989: 583) acknowledges some of these uncertainties, pointing out that despite evidence of the connection between development success and meritocratic bureaucracies working hand in hand with the private sector, '[t]he constraints that keep the inevitable clientelism and corruption from overwhelming the utility of ties to private capital are still not defined'.

At the same time, however, analyses such as those of Evans and, in a different tradition, those contained in Libecap (1996), suggest that it may also be problematic to ignore the independent role for the bureaucracy in public policy formation. The argument made below, however, is that the analysis of political incentives without taking into account bureaucratic capacity may be a more tenable strategy than the reverse.

GOVERNANCE AND ECONOMIC DEVELOPMENT: REVIEWING THE THEORY

The governance literature is largely empirical. The successes and failures on the empirical side of the literature, however, are related to the clarity and precision of its theoretical underpinnings. Clarity is of course inherently difficult to achieve with a concept as heterogeneous as governance. It helps to consider two sets of governance concepts separately, those related to government performance of its core functions and those related to the incentives of government officials to perform those functions.

The former is the most successful strand of the governance literature, making the argument that secure property rights, predictable and credible government, and honest and efficient bureaucracy have a significant impact on economic development. The second strand of the governance literature concerns the incentives of government actors to act in the public interest. This strand has confronted greater challenges and is the most promising and important for future research.

Within the first strand, the theoretical arguments are not equally strong or unambiguous. Least disputed and most clear is the theory linking insecure property rights to slow growth. Similarly, credible government is generally and unambiguously regarded as good for public policy. The frequent confusion of credibility with predictability undermines clarity, however, since the latter is not strongly related to development and the quality of public policy. However, as the foregoing brief references to embedded autonomy and state capacity suggest might be the case, the influence of an honest and efficient bureaucracy on economic development is most ambiguous of all. On the one hand, this influence depends, as a matter of logic, on what the bureaucracies are doing; on the other hand, what bureaucracies do is generally controlled by politicians. Each of these is considered separately in the sections that follow.

The second strand of the governance literature focuses on voice, accountability, and democracy and their effects on growth and development. It pays less attention to specific implications of different electoral and political institutions within democracies and to the dynamics of electoral competition, all of which vary across countries. In this sense, it is somewhat divorced from a sophisticated and rapidly growing literature exploring the political and electoral determinants of politician incentives to act in the public interest. Nevertheless, the introduction of notions of voice, accountability and democracy have been critical in pointing development research toward the question, 'Under what conditions do governments have the incentive to ensure the rule of law, secure property rights, and a well-functioning bureaucracy, and, more generally to serve the public interest?'

The security of property rights and economic growth

The theoretical case for secure property rights is simple: growth is a prerequisite for economic development (even if not a sufficient condition for it). Growth is not possible without investment. However, investors do not invest when they fear confiscation of their assets by government. North (1981) makes this point repeatedly, and a plethora of formal models explicitly chart the path from property rights insecurity to slow growth[2]. In its bare essentials, few propositions are less controversial than this argument. Still, there are objections to the theoretical case linking the security of property rights to growth. One relates to definitional confusion; the other to the effects of institutional influences that might explain both the security of property rights and economic growth.

Definitional confusion emerges because two important notions of property rights are often confused, the *allocation* of property rights and the *security* of property rights. The governance literature deals only with the latter: do property owners have protection from the arbitrary confiscation of their assets (either through expropriation, tax law changes, or through interpretations of existing regulation)?[3] Discussions of central planning, the transition from communism, and the costs and benefits of privatization address the other notion of property rights, their allocation. Przeworski and Limongi (1993) provide one example of the ease with which the two notions can be conflated. They point to arguments that democracy may render property rights less secure because the introduction of democracy creates opportunities for the poor to redistribute incomes away from the rich.[4] However, it is not democracy, *per se*, that creates insecurity, but the transition to democracy. In equilibrium, or once democracy is established, there is no reason to expect the distribution of property rights to change further. Property rights, after the initial *redistribution*, can therefore still be *secure*.[5] Similarly, Rodrik et al. (2002) argue that the success of countries such as China creates difficulty for the thesis that property rights matter for growth. Again, they are referring to the allocation of property rights rather than the security of the allocation.

As long as economic actors are confident that the rules will not change arbitrarily, even if the rules imply high tax rates, their rights are secure; it is when the rules are subject to arbitrary and significant alteration – regardless of whether they are initially favorable or not to the economic actors – that rights are insecure. There is ample evidence of this. Countries that have the highest scores on the security of property right measures, such as Australia, Germany, New Zealand, and the United States, collect taxes ranging from 18 per cent of national income (the US) to 36 per cent (Sweden). Tax collection in countries rated as posing high risks of contract repudiation or expropriation are often in the teens and rarely above 25 per cent of national income.[6]

The second objection that arises to the property rights arguments in the governance literature relates to causality. Arguments linking property rights to growth are sometimes asserted to be vulnerable to both of the usual causality flaws: either the association of secure property rights and economic growth is a reflection of reverse causality, from the second to the first, or, more difficult and interesting, the security of property rights and economic growth are both determined simultaneously by some third and omitted factor.

An important contribution of Acemoglu et al. (2001) to scholarship on property rights and growth is an ingenious econometric instrument that they discovered for the security of property rights (settler mortality rates in the eighteenth and nineteenth centuries). They use this variable as an econometric instrument for the property rights variable used in Knack and Keefer (1995), though they refer not to the security of property rights but to 'institutions'. They emphasize that their contribution is large because institutions are notoriously endogenous: 'It is quite likely that rich economies choose or can afford better institutions. Perhaps more important, economies that are different for a variety of reasons will differ both in their institutions and in their income per capita' (p. 1369).

Ironically, the theoretical (though not empirical) reasons to be concerned about whether secure property rights 'cause' economic growth are not particularly convincing.[7] If property rights are expensive to secure, for example, one might argue that rich countries are more likely than poor countries to secure them; fast-growing countries would therefore be more likely to improve property rights. However, to the extent that the security of property rights relates to the *absence* of expropriatory decisions by the state, there seem to be few financial costs to protecting property rights and little reason to argue that secure property rights should be sensitive to wealth. Even elaborate judicial systems are not particularly expensive.

Alternatively, it might be that citizens of rich countries prefer secure property rights more than citizens of poor countries. This is a more complex and interesting argument, but there is little evidence or support for any of its variants. For example, the citizens of poor countries, being poor, might discount the future more heavily and thus be more willing to incur the future costs of expropriation in return for the short-run benefits. While persuasive in principle, this argument is inconsistent with the observed willingness of the poor to take actions with distant payoffs and high current costs, such as investing heavily in the education of their children.

Poor countries might also exhibit higher income inequality, and therefore more policy volatility or willingness to expropriate (as, for example, Knack and Keefer, 1997a argue). However, it is well-known that income inequality and income exhibit an inverted *U*-shaped relationship: inequality is low at both low and high levels of income per capita, and higher over middle ranges. Such a relationship cannot generate a spurious correlation between growth and the security of property rights unless slow-growing countries are on average richer and fast-growing countries on average poorer. Evidence from the growth literature suggests that the reverse may be true, however.

A related literature argues that as countries grow wealthier, more effort and resources are spent to define and protect property rights. The insights of this literature are important in their own right, but they cannot be taken to support the argument that growth leads to secure property rights. The arguments here are simply that as countries grow, assets that previously held little value and were not worth protecting become more valuable, increasing the payoffs to defining ownership rights to them carefully.[8] The governance literature focuses on the insecurity of property rights to valuable assets.

Even if reverse causality is not an issue in the relationship between property rights security and economic growth, it is possible that other factors, omitted from most analyses, might simultaneously drive down the security of property rights and economic growth, yielding a spurious correlation between the latter two. Social polarization, political instability, the absence of political checks and balances, or unfortunate geographic location all might explain both insecure property rights and slow economic growth. However, for these omitted variables to create a problem of causality, it must also be the case that their effect on economic growth is largely through channels other than the security of property rights. This seems unlikely. If political instability or social polarization matter for growth, it is most reasonable to assume that they matter exactly because they drive down the

security of property rights. These are in fact the arguments in Acemoglu and Robinson (2001), Keefer and Knack (2002a) and Svensson (1998). Such omitted factors do not cause a spurious relationship between the security of property rights and growth. On the contrary, they precipitate the causal chain that runs from the first to the second.

Predictability and credibility

Some contributions to the governance literature refer not only to the security of property rights but to the closely related but somewhat broader concept of 'government credibility.' This is the case with Knack and Keefer (1995), for example. Only credible governments can assure investors that their assets are safe from expropriation. In addition, however, governments that are not credible cannot elicit any actions from citizens or investors in return for any future promise of government action. In times of fiscal crisis, for example, the non-credible government cannot offer future rewards to constituencies in exchange for current cutbacks. These governments cannot use any policy instrument to stimulate investment short of outright subsidies to investors that compensate them for their risk.

As in the case of property rights, an important definitional confusion arises in the area of credibility, particularly in empirical applications. Attempts to capture credibility issues in surveys tend to rely (as in many World Bank surveys, for example) on questions to respondents on their perceptions of the 'predictability of decision making'. At first glance, this seems a perfectly reasonable approach to governance: no one likes unpredictable decision making, and unpredictable and arbitrary decision making are surely pillars of bad governance. The problem is not that unpredictable decision making is good, however, but rather that it is not necessarily so bad and does not capture the sort of asymmetrical and unbounded threat that is implied by the lack of government credibility.

Strictly speaking, unpredictability is a 'mean-preserving' increase in the variance of future government policies. That is, unpredictability leaves the average or expected policy unchanged, but increases the range of potential policies that could emerge in the future. Predict-ability should have only a modest effect on economic outcomes (see Aizenman, 1995, for example). Assuming plausible parameters and an often-used functional form for investor utility, it is easy to show that a moderately risk-averse investor who would demand, say, a 10 per cent rate of return for a sure investment would demand just 11 to 12 per cent for an investment with a payoff that with 50 per cent probability returns 50 per cent less than the sure payoff, and with 50 per cent probability returns 50 per cent more. This sort of risk premium cannot explain the differential investment flows into Russia and Poland, or Zaire and Botswana. Credibility, on the other hand, is not mean-preserving: Instead, it is an asymmetric risk that emerges whenever investors or households make illiquid investments that governments can subsequently expropriate.[9]

Bureaucratic efficiency and honesty

A long line of research, stemming from Max Weber and extending to many current discussions of state capacity or the strength of states, such as Evans (1995), argues that the actions of bureaucracies have an independent effect on economic development. However, although it is well-known that bureaucratic quality is lower and corruption higher in poor countries, the inference that these phenomena cause poverty and slow growth is more difficult to draw. Of course, to the extent that government policies are ideal and government spending ideally allocated, then any bureaucratic breakdown must lower social welfare and, to the extent that the policies and spending are connected to economic growth, slow growth. What, however, if the policies and spending decisions are entirely deficient?

The classic conundrum is therefore the following: are societies better off when honest bureaucracies rigorously and predictably apply abusive regulations of firms and individuals or, given the existence of such laws and regulations, would citizens prefer that they be implemented by corrupt bureaucracies? In the context of corruption, Leff (1964) was the first of many to make the argument that corruption could be beneficial if it allowed citizens to circumvent welfare-reducing laws and regulations. More recent analyses have emphasized that arguments such as Leff's assume that bureaucracies have no influence on the content of the regulations that they implement. If they do, though, the potential for lucrative bribes would spur bureaucracies to generate abusive regulations that maximize bribes. Kaufmann and Wei (1999) have argued and provided evidence that in this more dynamic world, bureaucrats react to the opportunities for corruption by actually increasing red tape and reducing their (bribe-free) performance.

This later literature, in turn, relies on the assumption that bureaucracies enjoy significant discretionary authority. It is a characteristic of the governance literature that, although it gives apparently great weight to political processes in its emphasis on democracy, voice and accountability, it tends to analyze bureaucratic performance in isolation and to ignore the intimate relationship of bureaucrats and politicians. If one were sure that bureaucrats could exploit information and other advantages to act independently and even in opposition to the objectives of their political superiors, this assumption would be entirely appropriate. One could immediately begin to examine the effects of corruption or bureaucratic incompetence on outcomes. However, research into the delegation of authority by political actors to bureaucracies has made clear that politicians expend considerable effort to rein in deviant bureaucrats and to circumvent or compel recalcitrant ones.

Weingast and Moran (1983) and Keefer and Stasavage (2003) show systematic differences in the behavior of bureaucracies (the Federal Trade Commission and central banks, respectively) depending on the partisan control of government and the number of political checks and balances (respectively). Epstein and O'Halloran (1999) document how politicians limit the information advantages that bureaucrats have over them. McCubbins et al. (1987) have described in detail the constraints on bureaucratic discretion imposed by the US Congress through the Administrative Procedures Act and other vehicles. Kang (2002), while not relying on this literature himself, still demonstrates the intimate link between political imperatives and the nature of corruption in South Korea and the Philippines. In view of this literature, it seems likely that the observed effects of corruption or bureaucratic inefficiency on economic outcomes are more properly attributed to politician behavior that undermines both outcomes and bureaucratic performance, rather than to the specifics of bureaucratic organization.

This logic raises doubts about the causal relationship between growth or development and the characteristics of a country's bureaucracy. First, political incentives and politician actions are likely to generate both bad policies and a neglected, inefficient and/or corrupt bureaucracy. Second, it is likely that the bad policies, as much as or more than the characteristics of the bureaucracy, drive bad development outcomes, potentially giving rise to a spurious association between bureaucratic characteristics and development.

This is not to say that the bureaucracy is unimportant. Even if politicians substantially constrain bureaucratic discretion, residual discretion could nevertheless have meaningful economic consequences. However, there is substantial justification – not least of which are the numerous examples of well-oiled bureaucracies implementing catastrophic policies – to demand that any examination of this issue must be careful to control for the possibility that observed relationships between bureaucratic performance and economic growth or development might be spurious.

Voice and accountability as governance

A vast literature considers the importance of politics and political institutions in the process of economic development, covering topics ranging from regime type to political instability to clientelism to the institutions of electoral competition and political decision making. The subset of that literature that falls under the governance rubric centers on voice, accountability and democracy. This focus dates at least to Albert Hirschman (1970), who introduced 'voice' and 'exit' into the development lexicon.

The emphasis on voice and accountability rests on a natural and persuasive logic: governments that pay little attention to citizen concerns – because citizens are unable to voice them or are unable to sanction governments that ignore them – are less likely to pursue policies that further social welfare. Less clear are the specific attributes of political and social organization in a country that improve voice and accountability. The governance literature has explored systematically only one aspect of political organization that bears on voice and accountability, regime type, or democratic versus autocratic government. The presumption is that democracy is the only regime type that affords voice and accountability to citizens on a regular basis. Democracy should therefore promote economic development.

In fact, most of the research into democracy and economic growth is empirical and yields ambiguous results. Przeworski and Limongi (1993) underline the theoretical obstacles that might be responsible for this ambiguity. They begin by pointing out that much of the democracy literature argues that democracies raise growth rates by providing stronger guarantees for the security of property rights. But they argue that nothing about democratic decision making, seen as majority rule, makes expropriation more difficult, while long-lived dictatorships might provide even stronger protection for property rights.[10]

Their critique of the democracy and growth literature follows both the governance work on voice and accountability and the literature on democracy in treating the state as a unitary actor. Such analyses abstract from the substantial variation among polities in their political and electoral institutions, the dynamics of electoral competition, and differences in the constellations of interest groups across countries.[11] Integrating results and tools from the vast political economy literature that focuses on precisely these details is likely to provide fertile ground for assessing the underlying institutions that influence voice, accountability and, ultimately, economic development. The final section of this chapter discusses the significant payoffs to future research that bridges the governance literature with new developments in political economy.

EVIDENCE OF THE EFFECTS OF GOVERNANCE ON ECONOMIC DEVELOPMENT

Evidence from cross-country statistical research amply supports the importance of secure property rights, the rule of law, or the credibility of government for growth (Acemoglu et al., 2001; Knack and Keefer, 1995; Rodrik et al., 2002) or per capita incomes (Hall and Jones, 1999). However, large potential econometric problems emerge in this literature. For example, the empirical governance measures are usually subjective, introducing noise and, possibly, bias into the resulting estimates. Nevertheless, they represent a quantum leap in the ability to bring statistical analysis to bear on topics that were previously investigated only in theory or case studies, a leap that can be measured in terms of the sharp increase in research on governance-related topics that followed the introduction of these measures into the literature. Some of this literature is reviewed here.

Empirical tests of the effects of government credibility/secure property rights on development

With respect to the issue of property rights or the rule of law, fairly exhaustive attempts have been made to control for empirical difficulties ranging from endogeneity to measurement error. Results documenting the importance of secure property rights for growth have been robust to causality testing (Calderón and Chong, 2000), ingenious instruments and historical investigation (Acemoglu et al., 2001), and to the substitution of income for growth as the dependent variable (Hall and Jones, 1999). Although there is still room for skepticism, it is nevertheless true that the influence of secure property rights has withstood an unusually large amount of scrutiny.

The security of property rights has also been linked to development phenomena other than economic growth. Dollar and Kraay (2002) consider the impact of secure property rights on inequality, via growth. They find that the security of property rights raises the incomes of the rich and poor equally. Using beginning of period measures of property rights and later measures of inequality. In Knack (2002), secure property rights are actually progressive, raising the incomes of the poor faster than those of the rich. The security of property rights is also negatively related to rates of deforestation (Deacon, 1999).

The hypothesis that secure property rights accelerate economic development is supported by quantitative approaches other than those employing cross-country data, as well. Natural experiments involving property rights include work by Feder (1993) on the consequences of land titling for farmers in Thailand; Jiménez (1984) on the effects of titling on investment in and prices of homes in Manila; Alston et al. (1999) on the effects of property rights security on farm productivity and deforestation in the Brazilian Amazon; and O'Rourke (1999) on the effects of land tenure insecurity on the adoption of efficient butter production methods in Ireland contrasted with Denmark.

One caveat that is useful to recall in reviewing the empirical work on property rights and growth is that this work often contains broader statements about the importance of 'institutions' more generally. Knack and Keefer (1995), Acemoglu et al. (2001), and Rodrik et al. (2002) all argue for the dominant effect of 'institutions' on growth, but all use measures of the security of property rights as their measures of institutions. In the case of Knack and Keefer (1995), despite the use of the word 'institutions' in the title of the paper, both the hypotheses and the tests relate to the security of property rights and the rule of law. In other cases, however, the property rights variables are meant to stand for broader, less well-specified institutional concepts. The thrust of these papers is that 'institutions' matter, not that 'secure property rights' matter. This would be entirely benign if all of the institutional and governance forces that promote development were captured by measures of the security of property rights. This does not seem to be the case, however – nor would one expect it to be in view of the heterogeneity in the theoretical links between the different components of governance and economic outcomes.

Empirical research into corruption and bureaucratic quality

The conclusions from the empirical work on corruption and bureaucratic quality are broadly similar to the work on property rights. In the first and prototypical empirical contribution, Mauro (1995) shows that corruption reduces growth, though Li et al. (2000) show that taking inequality into account reduces the estimated effect of corruption. Gupta et al. (2002) present evidence that corruption exacerbates income inequality and poverty. Mo (2001) documents a causal chain linking higher corruption to lower growth through reduced investment in human and private capital. Rauch and Evans (2000) present quantitative evidence supportive of the 'embedded autonomy' hypothesis of Evans and, controlling for income, education and ethnic and linguistic diversity, find that some characteristics of an 'autonomous' bureaucracy (especially meritocratic recruitment) predict property rights security and bureaucratic quality.

It is, however, more difficult to draw firm conclusions about the effect of corruption and bureaucratic quality on economic development. On the one hand, in the cross-country work exemplified by Mauro (1995), the corruption variables exhibit considerable overlap with the measures used in the property rights literature. Mauro's variable is highly correlated, for example, with the property rights variable of Knack and Keefer, which is consistent with endogeneity problems to which the analysis of corruption is likely exposed.[12]

On the other hand, as the earlier discussion foreshadows, the more fundamental difficulty in drawing inferences about the impact of corruption and bureaucratic quality on development is their greater vulnerability to causality problems. Corruption in government is sensitive to the incentives of the political leadership, which are typically not controlled for in corruption work and are sure to have a significant independent effect on government performance and economic development. These causality problems emerge in at least two specific ways.

First, governments often put into place distortionary policies that directly slow economic development but also give rise to corruption. Broadman and Recanatini (2002) use evidence from surveys of businesspeople in transition countries regarding corruption and the effects of regulation to show that high regulatory barriers to entry and soft budget constraints on firms are both conducive to corruption. More optimistically, Cheng et al. (1998) argue that well-functioning bureaucracies in South Korea and Taiwan were the result of conscious decisions by political actors who, in turn, were motivated by a desire to avert past crises or to deter aggression by large neighbors.

Second, corruption can emerge from other governance problems that also directly limit development. Keefer and Knack (2007) present a model and evidence that if political decision makers find it difficult or costly to guarantee the security of property rights of private investors, they will change their policies accordingly. In particular, they will suppress productive public investment and increase rent-seeking or corruption. The evidence in this paper suggests that countries with less credible governments (countries with less secure property rights) spend 60 per cent more on public investment as a fraction of national income than countries with more secure property rights and that the difference is due the effect of insecure property rights on incentives to divert rents.[13] No investigations of the effect of corruption and bureaucratic quality on economic development take such endogeneity issues into account either at the level of theory or empirical testing.

Voice, accountability, and democracy: The evidence

There are no agreed indicators of the concepts 'voice' and 'accountability', either in theory or in the empirical literature. The literature employs proxies ranging from Freedom House indicators of political freedoms and civil liberties (found by Scully, 1988 to be predictors of growth), to structural indicators of democracy – whether there are competitive elections and the executive is constrained by a legislature. With respect to the Freedom House indicators, the empirical record is reasonably convincing that these variables are important for development. Like governance itself, they are also multidimensional. This makes it difficult to determine which concrete and objectively observable characteristics can be traced specifically to notions of voice and accountability, and to observed changes in development outcomes.

The democracy literature, relying on more structural and objective characteristics of polities, yields more ambiguous results. One source of confusion is that democratic countries are both richer and better performing. This naturally gives rise to the difficult question: are countries better performing because they are rich, or because they are democratic? For example, as we would expect, corruption and rent-seeking are higher in countries lacking fully competitive elections, as are the risks of expropriation.[14] However, countries with competitive elections are also substantially richer than other countries, even excluding the richest 20 democracies from the comparison (in 2000, excluding the richest 20, 97 countries with competitive elections had purchasing power parity adjusted per capita incomes of US $5,470, compared to US $3,121 for the countries that did not have fully competitive elections). In part because of this, a large literature that always controls for per capita incomes at the beginning of the period finds only an ambiguous relationship between democracy and growth. Many of the income gains that democracy generates may already be embedded in the higher initial per capita incomes of democratic countries.[15]

A number of investigations use more global indicators to test broader notions of governance or institutions on economic development. Easterly and Levine (2002), also engaging the debate on the role of institutions versus geography in economic development, use the global governance index of Kaufmann et al. (2002), rather than more narrow property rights and rule of law indicators. The broad governance index has the advantage of including more dimensions of a country's institutional performance. However, the aggregate measure exacerbates the problem of interpretation. Provided the coefficient estimates are significant, one can only say that some factors related to governance are positively associated with growth. One cannot say, however, which factors those are, nor even be sure that some other factors do not also have a negative impact on growth.

THE RESEARCH FRONTIER: IDENTIFYING THE DETERMINANTS OF GOOD GOVERNANCE

While governance research has made convincing contributions to the study of development, crucial questions remain. Some of these have to do with endogeneity issues raised by much of the governance literature. For example, does corruption suppress development or is corruption just symptomatic of a deeper problem in the political environment of a country? Understanding the determinants of good governance can help answer this question. However, regardless of the endogeneity and causality issues that are preoccupations of the governance literature, the determinants of good governance – of secure property rights, voice and accountability, or honest and efficient bureaucratic behavior – are key issues in their own right. Intellectually, they are some of the most challenging in the social sciences. From a policy perspective, they are essential to understand if one is to move forward in developing sustainable and effective reforms for countries suffering from, for example, insecure property rights.

There are two important political economy research efforts that relate to the sources of good governance. One relates the structure of political institutions and competition, including the information of voters, the credibility of political competitors, and the underpinnings of intra-party competition, to broad decisions of government, particularly related to fiscal allocations but extending to corruption. The second focuses more specifically on the conditions under which countries exhibit secure property rights.

The political economy of government spending and corruption

Recent important advances have brought great rigor to our understanding of the impact of political and electoral institutions, credibility and voter information on government incentives regarding fiscal policy, including rent-seeking (the textbook by Persson and Tabellini, 2000, provides a wide-ranging and complete summary). This literature focuses on the information of voters, the ability of governments to make credible pre-electoral promises to voters, and the details of the institutions of government decision making (parliamentary or presidential; if presidential, is it the president or the legislature that prepares the budget? What are the amendment powers of the respective entities?). The power of the analysis lies not so much in the accuracy of its assumptions about the political process, but rather in the coherent way in which the analysis marshals the many influences, ranging from institutions to information, that act on political decision makers' policy making incentives.

One particular emphasis in Persson and Tabellini (2000) is the role of political and electoral institutions on political incentives. For example, they predict that financing of public goods (those that benefit the whole population) relative to more targeted goods is higher in parliamentary democracies. In fact, among 24 parliamentary democracies for which data are available, the ratio of education (broad and relatively untargeted) to public investment spending (narrow and relatively targeted to specific voters) is about 20 percentage points higher than in 18 presidential democracies.[16] This has direct implications for governance work, which is concerned precisely with using government to efficiently improve the welfare of the average citizen – a goal that is more difficult to achieve when political institutions give policy makers incentives to provide inefficient targeted goods that benefit narrow slices of the population.

Models from this literature also predict that corruption (rent-seeking) should be higher under presidential systems and under non-proportional electoral systems with larger district magnitudes (legislative seats per electoral district). Empirical research has provided support for these predictions, as well.

Persson et al. (2002) find that electoral systems with non-proportional electoral rules and larger district magnitudes discourage corruption. Lederman et al. (2001) conclude that presidential systems are more corrupt.

The predictions regarding political and electoral institutions and their effects on policy outcomes or governance are sensitive to the underlying assumptions regarding how well-informed voters are, how ideologically divided they are, and how credible political promises to voters are prior to elections. Direct examination of these assumptions is a natural and important direction for future research. Already, however, research has provided early insights into the independent role of many of these assumptions on development outcomes.

Besley and Burgess (2001), for example, document the role of citizen information on political decision making. They show that in Indian states with greater literacy, electoral turnout and newspaper circulation (controlling for per capita incomes), state governments were more likely to respond to food shortages via the public distribution of food. Their work takes just one of many potential information problems as a point of departure. They leave aside the information issues prominent in Persson and Tabellini (2002), particularly the effects of voter and politician uncertainty about their respective ideological biases. They also apply their analysis to one particular policy problem, necessarily abstracting from, for example, the security of property rights.

Much of this work follows the 'rational choice' or 'new political economy' style of analysis – bringing more quantitative approaches to the study of individual actors and their incentives and largely ignoring historical or cultural differences that might influence outcomes. The comparative politics literature is full of valuable contributions that follow the reverse strategy, differentiating regime types by referring to historical and broad characteristics rather than to the incentives of the actors that run them. Remmer (1986) categorizes democracies as 'exclusionary' and inclusive, for example,

and Bratton and van de Walle (1994) argue that African democracies are different because they have their roots in neopatrimonial forms of government, where the executive maintains authority by dispensing personal patronage. In neither case are the authors explicit about the underlying characteristics of political competition or political institutions that permit elected officials to be exclusionary or neo-patrimonial. Whereas Bratton and van de Walle take as a characteristic feature of regimes the personal dispensation of targeted or private goods to individuals or small groups, the literature summarized in Persson and Tabellini (2000) seeks to *explain* the reliance on targeted public spending.

Efforts to bridge these two literatures can yield critical insights into the nature of economic development. For example, the new political economy literature regularly makes explicit and often different assumptions about the credibility of political promises, but it rarely analyzes variation in credibility across countries as a key determinant of differences in development outcomes. Keefer and Vlaicu (2008) makes an attempt in this direction, arguing that clientelism prevails when competing politicians can make credible pre-election promises to only a few people and dissipates when their promises are credible to the whole country. Lacking institutionalized bases for credibility (such as long-standing political parties with well-identified ideological platforms), political competitors can therefore only make credible promises to a small fraction of the population, leading to a preference for targeted, personalized and inefficient spending rather than efficient and broad-based public good provision.[17]

This argument is rooted in the detailed observations of clientelism (e.g., by Scott, 1972) and of the patterns of political recruitment in relatively clientelist democracies (e.g., the work of Krishna (n. d.) on candidate recruitment in India), but uses the tools summarized in Persson and Tabellini (2000) to explain why these patterns exist in some countries and not others and to sort out their policy implications. The value of the effort can be measured by its success in explaining important puzzling phenomena. There are two, in particular, to which the conclusions in Keefer and Vlaicu (2008) seem to apply.

First, to the extent that political actors in poor countries are less able to make credible promises to voters, they are more likely to spend on targeted and narrow constituencies, such as most public investments, than untargeted constituencies, as is the case with most education spending. In fact, in 1997, the ratio of education to public investment was 70 per cent higher in the 12 richest parliamentary democracies than in the 12 poorest (that is, holding institutions constant). At the same time, the 12 poorest parliamentary democracies allocated resources in almost the same way as 14 other countries that could not be considered functioning democracies at all (and for which data are available on education spending).

Second, as Bratton and van de Walle have argued, history seems to matter in the development of democracies. Bratton and van de Walle argue that there is a relationship between the nature of the pre-democratic regime and the subsequent possibilities for consolidating democracy, although they are less clear about the underlying causal relationship. Keefer and Vlaicu (2008) argues that the pre-democratic period determines whether political competitors in a democracy have credible policy stances on a wide range of issues. Evidence for this comes from the contrasting experience of British democracy after the massive expansion of the franchise in the early nineteenth century and the evolution of democracy in the Dominican Republic following the death of Rafael Trujillo. The first succeeded because of a history of political competition between relatively coherent and therefore credible political alternatives; the second has proceeded haltingly because of the absence or ruthless suppression of political competition prior to democracy.

The personalized relationships that characterize clientelism are found in other contexts as well. Heilbrunn's (2002) examination of much-publicized corruption episodes in France over the 1970s–1990s demonstrates the role of personal relationships – networks – among key decision makers. These informal networks circumvented or short-circuited apparently robust institutional checks and balances meant to control corrupt behavior. As a result, although one party was consistently associated with massive campaign spending scandals, including large procurement bribes associated with the purchase of warships by the Taiwanese and the diversion of money from the state oil company to party coffers and to the bank account of the chief judge of the Supreme Court, the other party refrained from pushing for prosecution.

Personal, cross-party ties – much as in many developing countries – seem to explain this. Heilbrunn (2002) argues that the circumstances that allowed these personalized ties to overwhelm the institutional checks and balances include members of the network controlling sufficient levers of power and network members being able to insure that the rewards of loyalty to other network members would exceed the potential costs of subverting the institutional checks and balances. The unraveling of these cases provides further evidence for the importance of networks: prosecution of these officials was eventually undertaken, but only at the initiative of a Norwegian-born female prosecutor, someone outside the networks documented by Heilbrunn.

In sum, the literature on the political roots of good governance offers promising directions for future research. The most promising seem to relate to the specific conditions of political decision making and electoral decision making, specifically to information, credibility and the nature of inter-personal relationships among politicians.

The political economy of secure property rights

The literature on the determinants of secure property rights emphasizes especially the role of political checks and balances, but also social characteristics such as polarization and social capital. Substantial puzzles remain, however. For example, property rights are insecure in many countries with formal institutional checks and balances, secure in others lacking them.

North and Weingast (1989) ask why the interest rates charged by Dutch lenders to the English Crown fell after the Glorious Revolution and argue that the introduction of checks and balances in government (a more powerful parliament) reduced the risk to lenders that the English Crown would renege on its contractual obligations. Stasavage (2003) and others have pointed out the substantial time lag (as much as 60 years) between the Revolution and the decline in interest rates, however. He argues that the introduction of additional institutional checks is insufficient to secure property rights. He shows that the time lag can be explained by the slow evolution of the preferences of the different actors who controlled the newly instituted checks and balances. To the extent that the preferences of at least one 'veto player' were aligned with those of lenders to the English Crown, checks and balances secured lender contractual rights; this did not occur, however, until some years after the institutional change took place.[18] Keefer and Stasavage (2002) also find that both preferences and institutional veto points matter in ensuring credibility with respect to monetary policy.

The literature is convincing that checks and balances are important to government credibility and secure property rights, but suggests as well that they are neither necessary nor sufficient. Essays in Boortz and Haber (2002), about the ability of the Mexican dictator Porfirio Diaz to entice considerable investment in the absence of institutional checks and balances, make it clear that checks and balances may not be necessary for government credibility or secure property rights. In cross-country comparisons, checks and balances have some effect on the security of property rights, but the effect is not robust to the presence of controls. There are straightforward

econometric difficulties that can explain the weak statistical relationship: the inevitable correlation of other explanatory variables, such as per capita income, with checks and balances and the fact that empirical variables used to represent checks and balances represent more accurately the number of institutional veto gates, but less accurately the preference alignments of the veto players who occupy those veto gates. However, beyond these difficulties, it is clear as well that the conditions under which non-democracies can establish credible commitments and some democracies cannot remains an open and important area of inquiry.

The work of Clague et al. (1996) deepens the property rights puzzle, highlighting the role of regime longevity. They find that long-lived autocrats offer as much or more protection to property rights than short-lived democracies, though long-lived democracies are the most secure of all. This conclusion reinforces the idea that the protection of property rights depends on more than formal institutional rules, but it also guides future research toward a more specific puzzle: what changes over time in democracies, such that older democracies provide more secure property rights than younger ones? Keefer and Vlaicu (2008) suggests that young democracies are more vulnerable to clientelism and, by implication, restricting to clients the fraction of investors to whom the government can make credible promises about the security of property rights. The literature has yet to rigorously link clientelism and the security of property rights, however.

Social explanations for the security of property rights also abound. Knack and Keefer (1997b) find that measures of social capital – essentially, measures of the extent to which people in different countries believe that others in their country are trustworthy – are positively associated with the security of property and contract rights. Naturally, causality problems emerge here: do people trust each other because their institutions make property rights and contractual commitments reliable, or the other way around? In either direction, however, there are important implications for development that have yet to be explored.

Polarization in society might also undermine property rights security – the argument being either that the more polarized are citizens, the less likely they are to respect the rights of others, or more in the vein of social choice, the more polarized are citizens, the more volatile is policy likely to be. Svensson (1998) has found inequality and property rights to be inversely associated, and offers econometric evidence that the effect is from the first to the second. Keefer and Knack (2002a) show that other forms of polarization – ethnic and linguistic – suppress the security of property rights, and it is in part through this channel that they affect growth. Acemoglu and Robinson (2001) argue that wealth inequality can increase political instability and, thereby, the insecurity of property rights. Keefer and Knack (2002a) find evidence that income inequality reduces insecurity, but no support for the role of political instability.

All of these contributions still leave up in the air the specific channels through which polarization undermines the security of property rights, however. Though following similar empirical strategies, for example, Svensson (1998) and Keefer and Knack (2002a) propose completely different channels: Svensson argues that property rights security are the result of investments by government – a fiscal decision – while Knack and Keefer model the security of property rights as the propensity of government decisions to change dramatically and unpredictably.

In sum, then, large questions about the determinants of property rights remain. There is evidence that long-running democracies promote property rights, broadly defined, but we do not know which characteristics of long-running democracies endow them with this characteristic. Nor do we have micro-level evidence that more systematically outlines the actions that are open to decision makers in short-lived democracies that are foreclosed to those in long-lived democracies. One might interpret the observation about clientelism as

implying that pre-democratic forms of political exchange survive the introduction of democratic institutions – but we do not know how or under what conditions they disappear. A promising line of research is surely to link these observations with the vast literature on the dynamics of political party evolution and the conditions under which political parties can make credible promises to voters.

CONCLUSION: HOW CAN WE IMPROVE GOVERNANCE?

Governance reform prospects and strategies depend significantly on whether one believes that flaws in the state apparatus (e.g., public administration) lie at the heart of governance failures, or whether one believes that they are more deeply embedded in the political and social dynamics of a country. If the former, significant opportunities for reform can open up. For example, corruption can be addressed by reforms to government financial management, procurement and audit systems. Voice and accountability can be addressed by requiring bureaucracies to open up the rule making process (the regulatory process) to more popular participation. Bureaucratic quality can be improved by boosting pay and strengthening meritocratic recruitment procedures.

If, on the other hand, governance failures are more deeply rooted in the incentives of political actors, these reforms may not translate into significant change in the way government operates – in the security of property rights, in the quality of regulation, or in the services provided by governments to citizens. This does not imply, however, that reform is impossible or that there is no role for outside assistance. Instead, it implies that reform must be structured to address or adapt to the underlying difficulties in the relationship between voters and politicians. Those outside the political process can potentially change the political equilibrium by providing relevant information about candidate performance to voters, verifying or debunking political claims of responsibility for good outcomes, and the mobilization of voters around service delivery issues (that is, making it more credible to politicians that voters whose apathy or support they took for granted might actually vote against them on the basis of service delivery or other dimensions of government performance that were not previously relevant). There is unlikely to be a generic blueprint good for all reforms in all countries. However, the literature is moving toward the identification of key, concrete political obstacles to good governance that, like the extent of voter information, are amenable to change.

DISCLAIMER

The contents and conclusions of this chapter are the author's own and are not intended to represent the views of the World Bank, its Executive Directors, or the countries they represent.

NOTES

1. http://www.fordfound.org/fields/governance/overview

2. Keefer and Knack (2002b), for example, show that whether property rights insecurity is the product of a general level of insecurity in a society that makes it costly for governments to protect property rights, or as the product of particularly short horizons of government leaders that makes it more likely for them to prefer expropriation over growth, property rights insecurity slows growth.

3. It should not go without saying that other, non-economic rights tend also to be insecure in these same countries.

4. They point to Marx's argument that capitalism and democracy are inherently incompatible, since democracy enables the poor to tax the rich, giving the rich an incentive to buy military intervention to overturn the democracy, an argument formalized by Acemoglu and Robinson (2001).

5. Acemoglu and Robinson (2001) develop a model in which, when the cost of coups by the rich against poor democracies and wealth inequality are in precisely the right combination, democracy is

chronically unstable. The insights they develop from this model are significant, but the empirical relevance of this particular case has not yet been established.

6. There is little evidence that redistribution – or more broadly, the *allocation* of property rights – is systematically associated with low growth. See, for example, Knack and Keefer (1997b).

7. There are, however, sound empirical reasons to be concerned about causality in the relationship between the security of property rights and economic growth. Among these, measurement error – observer bias that boosts assessments of the security of property rights in fast-growing countries – is the most important.

8. Rangeland in the American West had this characteristic – not so valuable prior to the arrival of the railroads, but very valuable and worth fencing after their arrival. Esther Boserup (1965) first argued that population pressure increases the value of land, leading to greater efforts to protect rights to land. Anderson and Hill (1990) show that the conditions under which investors (farmers, in this case) are allowed to establish property rights also has a significant effect on productivity. However, none of these studies show (nor are they intended to show) that growth makes insecure property rights secure. They demonstrate instead that growth makes it worthwhile to define previously worthless property rights. Worthless property rights are not, however, at the heart of the debate linking the security of property rights to economic development.

9. If there is a high correlation between the answer to the simple question ('how predictable is government decision making?') and the nuanced issues of credibility ('How easy would it be for a government official to make a decision or take some action that would reduce your profits by 50 per cent?'), then this strong theoretical distinction is less important for empirical work.

10. Przeworski, et al. (2000) introduce and provide substantial evidence for several novel variations on the theme of democracy and growth, showing in particular (though not explaining) that population growth is faster in dictatorships; controlling for this, per capita income growth is approximately the same in both dictatorships and democracies.

11. They summarize democratization as giving the median voter control over policy, leading to a shift in distribution towards the median voter and a consequent disruption, rather than reinforcement, of property rights.

12. Still, it is fair to point out that, among the variables that make up these risk guide indices, the lowest inter-variable correlation is with corruption, suggesting that the risk guide indicators are able to differentiate at least somewhat between corruption and other governance problems.

13. Political Risk Services generates the International Country Risk Guide, assessments of country risk

widely used by foreign investors. Two variables in the ICRG, bureaucratic quality and corruption, comprise the measure of 'bureaucratic performance' used in Keefer and Knack (2002b).

14. This comparison is between countries that have competitive legislative and executive elections (LIEC and EIEC equal to seven, from the Database on Political Institutions, Beck et al., 2001) and countries that do not.

15. Of course, Przeworski and Limongi (1993) would argue that there is in fact no theoretical case for arguing in favor of the superior economic or growth performance of democratic countries. Among the research documenting the empirical ambiguity are de Haan and Siermann (1998) and, especially, Przeworski et al. (2000). On the other hand, Quinn and Woolley (2001) argue that the effect of democracy is to make the economy less volatile, reflecting the preferences of citizens for lower risk (which, in democracies, they are better able to express).

16. Using political measures from the Database on Political Institutions, Beck et al. (2001).

17. Though the credibility approach to clientelism is arguably most consistent with the literature on clientelism and neo-patrimonialism, there are two important alternative theories. Robinson and Verdier (2002) argue that clientelism emerges when politicians can make no credible promises to anyone, but have a high regard for the welfare of some small group of citizens (e.g., members of the same tribe or citizens from the same region). Medina and Stokes (2002) assume politicians are always credible, but that clientelism emerges when some politicians have monopoly control over assets that voters value.

18. Keefer and Stasavage (2002) show, however, that policy stability and policy credibility are not the same. Policy can be stable (e.g., policy will always equal the median voter's preferred outcome in a one dimensional, simple model of policy making) but still not be credible (since, conditional on the response of citizens to the median voter's decision in the first period, the median voter may still gain from reneging or changing the policy, in the next period).

REFERENCES

Acemoglu, D. and Robinson, J. (2001) 'A theory of political transitions', *American Economic Review*, 91 (4): 938–63.

Acemoglu, D., Johnson, S., and Robinson, J. (2001) 'The colonial origins of comparative development: An empirical investigation', *American Economic Review*, 91: 1369–401.

Aizenman, J. (1995) 'Investment in new activities and the welfare cost of uncertainty', NBER Working Paper 5041 (February).

Alston, L., Libecap, G., and Mueller, B. (1999) *Titles, conflict and land use: The development of property rights and land reform on the Brazilian Amazon frontier*. Ann Arbor: University of Michigan Press.

Anderson, T.L. and Hill, P.J. (1990) 'Race for property rights', *Journal of Law and Economics*, 33 (April): 177–97.

Bates, R. (1981) *Markets and states in tropical Africa*. Berkeley: University of California Press.

Bates, R. (1991) 'The economics of the transition to democracy', *PS: Political Science and Politics*, 24 (1): 24–27.

Beck, T., Clarke, G., Groff, A., Keefer, P., and Walsh, P. (2001) 'New tools in comparative political economy: The database of political institutions', *World Bank Economic Review*, 15 (1): 165–76.

Besley, T. and Burgess, R. (2001) 'Political agency, government responsiveness and the role of the media', *European Economic Review*, 45 (4–6): 629–40.

Boortz, J.L. and Haber, S. (2002) *The Mexican economy, 1870–1930: Essays on the economic history of institutions, revolution and growth*. Stanford, CA: Stanford University Press.

Boserup, E. (1965) *The conditions of agricultural growth: The economics of agrarian change under population pressure*. New York: Aldine Publishing Co.

Bratton, M. and van de Walle, N. (1994) 'Neopatrimonial regimes and political transitions in Africa', *World Politics*, 46 (4): 453–89.

Broadman, H. and Recanatini, F. (2002) 'Corruption and policy: Back to the roots', *Journal of Policy Reform*, 5 (1): 37–49.

Buchanan, J.M., Tollison, R.D., and Tullock, G. (eds) (1980) *Toward a theory of the rent-seeking society*. College Station, TX: Texas A & M University Press.

Calderón, C. and Chong, A. (2000) 'Causality and feedback between institutional measures and economic growth', *Economics and Politics*, 12 (1): 69–81.

Cheng, T.J., Haggard, S., and Kang, D. (1998) 'Institutions and growth in Korea and

Taiwan: The bureaucracy', *Journal of Development Studies*, 34 (6): 87–111.

Clague, C., Keefer, P., Knack, S., and Olson, M. (1996) 'Property and contract rights under democracy and dictatorship', *The Journal of Economic Growth*, 1 (2): 243–76.

Deacon, R.T. (1999) 'Deforestation and ownership: Evidence from historical accounts and contemporary data', *Land Economics*, 75 (3): 341–59.

de Haan, J. and Siermann, C.L.J. (1998) 'Further evidence on the relationship between economic freedom and economic growth', *Public Choice*, 95 (3/4): 363–80.

de Soto, H. (1989) *The other path*. New York: Harper and Row.

Dollar, D. and Kraay, A. (2002) 'Growth is good for the poor', *Journal of Economic Growth*, 7 (3): 193–225.

Easterly, W. and Levine, R. (2002) *Tropics, germs and crops: How endowments affect economic development* (National Bureau of Economic Research Working Paper 9106)

Epstein, D. and O'Halloran, S. (1999) *Delegating powers: A transaction cost politics approach to policy making under separate powers*. New York: Cambridge University Press.

Evans, P. (1989) 'Predatory, developmental, and other apparatuses: A comparative political economy perspective', *Sociological Forum*, 4 (4): 561–87.

Evans, P. (1995) *Embedded autonomy: States and industrial transformation*. Princeton, NJ: Princeton University Press.

Feder, G. (1993) 'The economics of land and titling in Thailand', in K. Hoff, A. Braverman and J.E. Stiglitz (eds), *The economics of rural organization: Theory, practice, and policy*. New York: Oxford University Press, pp. 259–68.

Gupta, S., Davoodi, H., and Alonso-Terme, R. (2002) 'Does corruption affect income inequality and poverty', *Economics of Governance*, 3 (1): 23–45.

Hall, R.E. and Jones, C.I. (1999) 'Why do some countries produce so much more output per worker than others?', *Quarterly Journal of Economics*, 114 (1): 83–116.

Heilbrunn, J. (2002) *Oil and water? Elite politicians and corruption in France*. Mimeo, Colorado School of Mines.

Hirschman, A. (1970) *Exit, voice and loyalty: Responses to decline in firms, organizations and states*. Cambridge, MA: Harvard University Press.

IMF (1997) *Good governance: The IMF's role*. Retrieved March 31, 2008, from http://www.imf.org/external/pubs/ft/exrp/govern/govindex.htm

IOG (2008) *What we do*. Retrieved March 31, 2008, from http://www.iog.ca/about_us.asp?strTextSite=false

Jímenez, E. (1984) 'Tenure security and urban squatting', *Review of Economics and Statistics*, 66 (4): 556–67.

Kang, D. (2002) *Crony capitalism: Corruption and development in South Korea and the Philippines*. New York: Cambridge University Press.

Kaufmann, D. and Kraay, A. (2002) Growth without governance. *Economia*, 3 (1): 169–229.

Kaufmann, D., Kraay, A., and Zoído-Lobatón, P. (2002) *Governance matters III – Updated indicators for 2000/01* (World Bank Policy Research Department Working Paper No. 2772).

Kaufmann, D. and Wei, S.J. (1999) *Does 'grease money' speed up the wheels of commerce?* (National Bureau of Economic Research Working Paper 7093, April).

Keefer, P. and Vlaicu, R. (2008). "Democracy, Credibility and Clientelism." *Journal of Law, Economics and Organization* 24 (2): 371–406.

Keefer, P. and Knack, S. (2002a) 'Polarization, politics and property rights: Links between inequality and growth', *Public Choice*, 111 (1–2): 127–54.

Keefer, P. and Knack, S. (2007) 'Boondoggles, rent-seeking and political checks and balances: Public investment under unaccountable governments', *The Review of Economics and Statistics*, 89 (3): 566–72.

Keefer, P. and Stasavage, D. (2002) 'Checks and balances, private information, and the credibility of monetary commitments', *International Organization*, 56 (4): 751–74.

Keefer, P. and Stasavage, D. (2003) *The limits of delegation: Veto players, central bank independence and the credibility of monetary policy*. Mimeo: The World Bank.

Knack, S. (2002) 'Social capital, growth and poverty: A survey of cross-country evidence', in C. Grootaert and T. van Bastelaer, (eds), *The role of social capital in development: An empirical assessment*. 42–82. New York: Cambridge University Press.

Knack, S. and Keefer, P. (1995) 'Institutions and economic performance: Cross-country tests using alternative institutional measures', *Economics and Politics*, 7 (3): 207–28.

Knack, S. and Keefer, P. (1997a) 'Does inequality harm growth only in democracies? A replication and extension', *American Journal of Political Science*, 41 (1): 323–32.

Knack, S. and Keefer, P. (1997b) 'Does social capital have an economic payoff? A cross-country investigation', *Quarterly Journal of Economics*, 112: 1251–88.

Krishna, A. (n.d.) *Seizing the middle ground: New political entrepreneurs in India*. Mimeo, Sanford Institute for Public Policy, Duke University.

Lederman, D., Loayza, N., and Reis Soares, R. (2001) *Accountability and corruption: Political institutions matter*. (World Bank Policy Research Working Paper 2708, November).

Leff, N.H. (1964) 'Economic development through bureaucratic corruption', *The American Behavior Scientist*, 8 (2): 8–14.

Li, H., Xu, L.C., and Zou, H.-F. (2000) 'Corruption, income distribution and growth', *Economics and Politics*, 12 (2): 155–82.

Libecap, G.D. (ed.) (1996) *Reinventing government and the problem of bureaucracy*. Greenwich, CT: JAI Press.

Mauro, P. (1995) 'Corruption and growth', *The Quarterly Journal of Economics*, 110 (3): 681–712.

McCubbins, M., Noll, R. and Weingast, B. (1987) 'Administrative procedures as instruments of political control', *Journal of Law, Economics and Organization*, 3 (2): 243–77.

Medina, L.F. and Stokes, S. (2002) *Clientelism as political monopoly*. Mimeo. Department of Political Science, University of Chicago.

Mo, P.H. (2001) 'Corruption and economic growth', *Journal of Comparative Economics*, 29 (1): 66–79.

North, D. (1981) *Structure and change in economic history*. New York: W.W. Norton.

North, D. (1990) *Institutions, institutional change and economic performance*. Cambridge: Cambridge University Press.

North, D. and Weingast, B. (1989) 'Constitutions and commitment: The evolution of institutions governing public choice in seventeenth-century England', *Journal of Economic History*, 49 (4): 803–32.

O'Rourke, K.H. (1999) *Culture, politics and innovation: Creamery diffusion in late 19th century Denmark and Ireland*. Mimeo. Department of Economics, University College Dublin.

Persson, T. and Tabellini, G. (2000) *Political economics: Explaining public policy*. Cambridge, MA: The MIT Press.

Persson, T., Tabellini, G., and Trebbi, F. (2002) *Electoral rules and corruption*. Mimeo. Institute for International Economic Studies, Stockholm University.

Przeworski, A., Alvarez, M., Cheibub, J.A., and Limongi, F. (2000) *Democracy and development: Political institutions and well-being in the world, 1950–1990*. New York: Cambridge University Press.

Przeworski, A. and Limongi, F. (1993) 'Political regimes and economic growth', *The Journal of Economic Perspectives*, 7 (3): 51–69.

Quinn, D. and Woolley, J. (2001) 'Democracy and national economic performance: The preference for stability', *American Journal of Political Science*, 45 (July): 634–57.

Rauch, J. and Evans, P. (2000) 'Bureaucratic structure and bureaucratic performance in less developed countries', *Journal of Public Economics*, 75 (1): 49–71.

Remmer, K. (1986) 'Exclusionary democracy', *Studies in Comparative International Development*, 20 (4): 64–8.

Robinson, J. A. and Verdier, T. (2002) *The political economy of clientelism* (Center for Economic Policy Research Discussion Paper No. 3205, February).

Rodrik, D., Subramanian, A., and Trebbi, F. (2002) *Institutions rule: The primacy of institutions over geography and integration in economic development* (National Bureau of Economic Research Working Paper 9305, November).

Scott, J.C. (1972) 'Patron-client politics and political change in Southeast Asia', *American Political Science Review*, 66 (1): 91–113.

Scully, G.W. (1988) 'The institutional framework and economic development', *Journal of Political Economy*, 96 (31): 652–62.

Stasavage, D. (2003) *Public debt and the birth of the democratic state: France and Great Britain 1688–1789*. New York: Cambridge University Press.

Svensson, J. (1998) 'Investment, property rights and political instability: Theory and evidence', *European Economic Review*, 42 (7): 1317–41.

UNDP (2008) *Democratic governance*. Retrieved March 31, 2008, from http://www.undp.org/governance/

USAID (2005) *Promoting more transparent and accountable government institutions*. Retrieved March 31, 2008, from http:// www.usaid.gov/our_work/democracy_and_governance/technical_areas/governance/

Wallsten, S. (2002) *Of carts and horses: Regulation and privatization in telecommunications* (World Bank Policy Research Working Paper, October).

Weingast, B. and Moran, M. (1983) 'Bureaucratic discretion or congressional control? Regulatory policymaking by the federal trade commission', *Journal of Political Economy*, 91 (October): 765–800.

World Bank (2008) *Public sector governance: An overview*. Retrieved March 31, 2008, from http://www1.worldbank.org/publicsector/

25

Terrorism

Jennifer S. Holmes

INTRODUCTION

In the past, the study of terrorism has been divided into two competing paradigms, mirroring general fault lines in comparative politics between the qualitatively and quantitatively inclined scholars. This separation has postponed progress in clarifying continuing disputes in the field. In general, the study of terrorism is fragmented, conceptually muddled, handicapped by a lack of data, and troubled by political connotations. However, the challenge of understanding terrorism is urgent due to both its theoretical and substantive importance. Terrorism touches on many crucial areas of research, from violence and conflict, to issues of political stability and government response.

Within the last few years, a plethora of studies have been published dealing with terrorism. According to CSA Worldwide Political Science Abstracts, there were 1853 published works categorized with a variation of terror as a keyword from 1960 to 1989. This number increased to 1949 from 1990 to 2000, and ballooned to an astonishing 6564 works from 2001 to 2006. 'The widespread literature in this field … is neither sufficiently coordinated nor channeled so that it can build the cognitive and social structure of terrorism' (Gordon, 1999: 150). Despite the proliferation of publications within the last few years, little progress has been made to unify the subject matter or gain broad agreement about basic concepts or definitions.

FOUR FUNDAMENTAL DISPUTES

The field has progressed in a disjointed fashion due to four unresolved challenges about terrorism and its study: contested concepts, the division of the phenomenon, questions of perspective, and problems of quantification.

> Frequently neglected and often overlooked, the science of terror has been conducted in the cracks and crevices which lied between the large academic disciplines. There has been a chronic shortage of experienced researchers – a huge proportion of the literature is the work of fleeting visitors: individuals who are often poorly aware of what has already been done and naïve in their methods and conclusions (Silke, 2004a: 1).

This chapter will discuss the four fundamental disputes and propose possible solutions to create linkages among the different areas of research.

Disagreement about concepts

Defining terrorism has been a longstanding issue in the field, which hinders theory development, testing, and comparison. As Crenshaw

(2000) notes, 'the problem of defining terrorism has hindered analysis since the inception of studies in the early 1970s' (p. 406). It is doubtful that one definition of terrorism will be uniformly accepted as definitive and 'there appears to be a war-weariness among established researchers over definitional issues' (Silke, 2004c: 208). Despite the frustration with repeated efforts to create a broadly accepted definition, more progress is needed in coming to a consensus on at least a few definitions of terrorism.

> A more refined, integrated and cumulative theorizing, likely to allow the formulation of sound hypothesis, would undeniably contribute to expected major developments in the academic understanding of terrorism. Unfortunately though, there is still a persistent debate on the delimitation of this phenomenon and its analytical conceptualization (Reinares, 2003: 315).

Additionally, it is important to at least clarify meanings to facilitate the creation of sound policy. As Schmid earlier warned, a resistance to creating a clear definition is a 'dangerous attitude that plays into the hands of those experts from the operation antiterrorist camp who have a 'know-it-when-we-see-it' attitude that easily leads to double standards which produce bad science, and arguably, bad policies' (Schmid and Jongman, 1988: 1).

Many scholars view terrorism as an essentially contested concept. 'Agreement on definition, alas, does not exist, and there is no reason to assume that it will in the foreseeable future' (Laqueur, 1986: 88). The fear is that the term terrorism may not 'point to detectable phenomena that exhibit some degree of causal coherence' (Tilly, 2004: 8). Despite this, definitions of terrorism typically involve a version of 'a conspiratorial style of violence calculated to alter the attitudes and behavior of multiple audiences … terrorism is distinguished by its high symbolic and expressive value' (Crenshaw, 1995: 4). In addition to violence and intent, most definitions include requirements of victim and perpetrator (Enders and Sandler, 2006: 3).

Classic issues of conceptual validity are applicable to the study of terrorism as scholars attempt to generalize without falling into problems of concept stretching (Collier and Mahon, 1993; Sartori, 1970). What is clear is that terrorism is used for a political and rhetoric effect, suffers from 'border' and 'membership' problems, and 'suffers from 'stretching' and 'traveling' problems' (Weinberg et al., 2004: 778). In other words, it is difficult to differentiate terrorism from other types of violence. Additionally, the same acts tend to be labeled differently relative to the relationship or perspective of the observer. Finally, the meaning tends to be historically specific and unconducive to comparison, resulting in 'analytic vagueness as categories developed in one context are transported to another' (Weinberg et al., 2004: 779).

These well recognized problems pose unusual challenges that must be addressed. Scholars need to be aware and pragmatic about choice of concept. 'When such [conceptual] confusion arises, it is essential for scholars to engage in a self-conscious, critical evaluation that systematically appraises existing usage of concepts and seeks to channel it in more productive directions' (Collier, 1998a: 5). A good first step is to address the 'border and membership problems' by creating different divisions of the phenomenon with an architectonic view of diverse types of violence and governmental relations. Even scholars who may never agree with a general definition of terrorism can often agree to a less comprehensive definition of different types of terrorism.

Division of the phenomena

Questions of how to categorize terrorism or political violence are difficult. Mirroring the disagreement about how to define the concept, is a lively debate over how to subdivide different types of terrorism. Seemingly, the sole point of agreement is that the range is wide. The 'geographical, ideological, cultural, contextual and operational diversity of the problem cast doubt on the very justification for identifying terrorism as a fairly homogenous phenomenon' (Merari, 1991: 89). This multiformity of terrorism causes other problems, especially in terms of quantifying terrorism and comparability. 'Terrorism is an ambiguous variable not easily measured or quantified, in part because there are multiple forms of terrorism, and they are easily confused with other styles of violence' (Crenshaw, 1995: 6). Laqueur sternly warns scholars 'there is no such thing as terrorism pure and unadulterated, specific and unchanging, comparable to a chemical element; rather, there are a great many terrorisms' (Laqueur, 1986: 88). While the heterogeneity of the types of terrorism creates difficulty, it also adds richness to the field.

The variety of terrorism can make 'descriptive, explanatory and predictive generalizations, which are the ultimate products of scientific research, inherently questionable' (Merari, 1991: 89). Fortunately, progress can be made by clearly identifying and justifying comparisons. The creation of a typology is important. Schmid attempted to create a typology that would 'not subdivide terrorism – both state and non-state – in the political context between the forces of order and the forces of change, between power holders and power challengers, between the forces of social control and of social dissent' (Schmid and Jongman, 1988: 56). Instead, he listed divisions based upon actor, political orientation, and purpose, in addition to considering multidimensional categories. There are at least four different ways of dividing terrorism for analytical purposes: time, substance, strategy, and stages. However, it may be best for the field to remain flexible in terms of accepting multiple categorizations;

> Shifts in meaning … can push the analyst to adjust the corresponding domain of cases, and shifts in the domain of cases can necessitate an adjustment in the meaning, so as to maintain conceptual validity … Given that establishing the domain of relevant cases is an essential underpinning for addressing various methodological issues, it is productive to recognize that this initial fluidity in defining this domain does indeed occur in many studies (Collier, 1998a: 4).

In fact, this flexibility in classification may be productive by facilitating the broad perspective necessary to clarify the relevant domain of the concept, its subcategories, and its relationship to other types of political violence.

Chronological categories

In general, Crenshaw has advocated the recognition of the historical context of terrorism to identify the 'causal relationship between terrorism and its political, social and economic environment' and the 'impact of terrorism on this setting' (Crenshaw, 1995: 4). Scholars can turn to development studies for how to identify appropriate groupings;

> assuming that the time and place in which a structure or process appears make a difference to its character, that the sequence in which similar events occur has a substantial impact on their outcomes, and that the existing record of past structures and processes is problematic, requiring systematic investigation in its own right instead of lending itself immediately to social scientific syntheses (Tilly, 1984: 79).

In other words, careful scholars get 'the history right before generalizing, in order to be able to generalize soundly' (Tilly, 1984: 79). Specifically, in terms of studying terrorism, Rapoport (2001) has proposed dividing up terrorism into analytically distinct waves, which may have different causal factors. The first wave began with Russian rebellions against limited czarist reforms, in addition to Armenian, Balkan, anarchist violence that lasted from the late nineteenth century until the outbreak of World War I. The second wave lasted from the 1920s through the 1960s and was precipitated by movements of national self-determination. The third wave was motivated by the success of the Vietcong. It includes separatist, revolutionary, and international terrorism. The fourth wave of 'religious based separatist movements' began with the 1989 defeat of the Soviets in Afghanistan and the Iranian Islamic revolution of 1979. Conflating different waves can result in misleading results because groups within each wave are different both in terms of origin, but also in terms of action. Rapoport (2006) states: 'Modern terrorist organizations … learn from each other and from the experiences of groups that existed previously in the earlier modern waves. No matter when those organizations operated, groups in the pre-modern period did not learn or copy methods from each other' (pp. xxviii–xxix). However, Rapoport himself notes that the waves overlap to some extent. The implication is that scholars should be wary of combining groups and movements from one wave with another – without sufficient attention to the historical context or theoretical motivation in order to justify the comparison. Additionally, time is not the only possible way to create subcategories. To some extent, appropriate divisions will be determined by specific research questions.

Substantive categories

Typically, terrorism is divided by type, for example ideological terrorism (right or left wing), religious terrorism, nationalist terrorism, and so forth. However, a second proposed division is to analyze terrorism within a broader perspective of political violence;

> Where does terrorism stop and other forms of political violence begin, guerrilla warfare or urban warfare, for example? The same acts, such as air piracy or assassinations, may be considered terrorist acts on some occasions but not on others, usually based upon the assumed motivation of the perpetrators or the social standing of their victims (Weinberg et al., 2004: 778–9).

For example, when is an attack against noncombatant citizens terrorism? When is it a war crime? It may be useful to examine other types of political violence – 'collective attacks within a political community against a political regime' (Gurr, 1970: 3–4) including rebellion, revolution, extremism, insurgency and so forth, in order to gain insight into contemporary terrorism. For example, in the study of the Basque separatist group ETA, it is also useful to examine the politically motivated street violence committed by the MLNV (Basque National Liberation Movement) (Van den Broek, 2004). A broad

view is essential, especially given the conceptual confusion. For example, when studying a case of domestic terrorism, which literature is more useful, terrorism or counterinsurgency? A 'central characteristic of insurgency is the reliance on population for active support or at least passive acquiescence' (Long, 2006: 15). General principles about hearts and minds, holding territory, and so forth, can be analogous to maintaining support of the population, creating an effective government presence, and so forth. Moreover, classic questions of balance of response can be found in both literatures. Additionally, reflecting the confusion in the concept of terrorism, many of the cases previously categorized as insurgencies would now be called terrorism. Although much of the counterinsurgency literature is not theoretically driven, it contains rich case studies and policy oriented lessons learned (Long, 2006; O'Neill, 2001). These guiding principles may also provide a basis for questions regarding international terrorism, substituting international cooperation for domestic support or legitimacy. Similarly, the boundary between civil war and insurgency or terrorism is not always clear. Given that part of Crenshaw's 1995 definition of terrorism is size, the progression from being a terrorist movement to a party in a civil war may occur. Because of this, studies of civil war (Collier and Hoeffler, 2004), insurgency (Fearon and Laitin, 2003; Wood, 2004), extremism (Eatwell and Mudde, 2004; Mudde, 2005) or rebellion and revolution (Lichbach, 1994; Seligson, 1996; Wickham-Crowley, 1992) can be insightful. Similarly, studies of ethnic or religious conflict may also be instructive. For example, is a comparison of Algiers to Iraq appropriate, or Vietnam to Central America, or Spain to Northern Ireland, or lessons learned from cases of domestic terrorism to international terrorism? The boundaries of appropriate comparison are in dispute and in need of identification.

The contemporary civil war literature from economics revolves around greed versus grievance or motive versus opportunity or 'atypical grievance versus atypical opportunities' (Collier and Hoeffler, 2004: 564). A good overview to the debate can be found in Collier and Sambanis (2002). The general idea behind 'greed' driven conflicts is that economic resources can serve as a financial basis for insurgent groups. In general, Collier (2000) finds:

> The factors which account for this difference between failure and success are to be found not in the 'causes' which these two rebel organizations claim to espouse, but in their radically different opportunities to raise revenue ... the economic theory of conflict argues that the motivation of conflict is unimportant; what matters is whether the organization can sustain itself financially ... (p. 9).

This prominent theory focuses on lootable primary exports and the onset of conflict (See also Collier et al., 2003). Scholars such as Arbelaez et al. (2002: 42–3) find the onset of violence in areas 'related to the sudden development of primary products (gold, emeralds, oil, bananas, cocaine)' especially in the context of low state presence. Scholars have taken the theory beyond onset to explain magnitude and persistence of conflict:

> Conflicts ... which are sustained by marketable natural resources (diamonds, crude oil, coca) are difficult to bring to a conclusion. All too often, the perpetrators, both state actors and rebels, find the chaos of war conducive to the accumulation of personal wealth. Ongoing conflict provides opportunities for looting or the collection of protection money (Silberfein, 2003).

Another interesting focus on resources applies the development concept of 'resource curse' to the evolution of violent groups. How do resources influence 'character and conduct of rebel groups' (Weinstein, 2005: 598)? With initial resources, recruits 'are unwilling to make investments of time, energy, and resources without receiving the materials rewards they have been promised' (Weinstein, 2005: 621). Without initial resources, opportunistic types are kept out and the true believers 'sacrifices are a form of investment, with future rewards made credible by ties of social and political identity' (Weinstein, 2005: 622). This particular study incorporates both collective action models and case studies.

However, a general focus on the economic foundations of violent movements has been criticized. Kalyvas characterizes the greed literature as frighteningly ignorant of context. He states; 'ideological motivations are simply not always visible to observers looking for 'Western' patterns of allegiance and discourse? They also make the failed assumption that organizations using religious idioms and local cultural practices to mobilize people – rather than easily recognizable universalistic appeals – lack any ideology' (Kalyvas, 2001: 104–5). Instead, he advocates a microlevel approach that can identify relevant motivations. Some scholars, such as Crenshaw (1981), propose that grievance is mediated by elite actions:

> Terrorism per se is not usually a reflection of mass discontent or deep cleavages in society. More often it represents the disaffection of a fragment of the elite, who may take it upon themselves to act on the behalf of a majority unaware of its plight, unwilling to take action to remedy grievances, or unable to express dissent (p. 396).

Studies that apply the collective action approach to case studies are more immune to these types of criticism.

On the side of state actors, scholars have found the concept of state terrorism (Stohl and Lopez, 1984), human rights violations (Davenport, 1996), or repression (Moore, 1998; Poe and Tate, 1994) to be useful. The key is to be cognizant of the conceptual boundaries of different clusters. More studies on differentiating various types of violence are necessary to determine which types of violence are analogous to others in terms of causality. What lessons can we draw from other types of violence to terrorism? Considering the border and membership problems, this is a pragmatic approach to a perennial problem.

Strategic categories

Terrorism can also be divided up in terms of choice of different strategies or stages of conflict. Some concepts of terrorism define the phenomenon as a 'widely recurrent but imprecisely bounded political strategy' (Tilly, 2004: 5). Some scholars have found it productive to focus on particular actions that are recognized as terrorism, such as hijackings, suicide bombing and so forth. Recently, the suicide bombing literature has greatly expanded, as reflected by the works of Pape (2006), Bloom (2005), Hoffman and McCormick (2004), or Pedahzur (2006). Others have focused on the different choice of attacks, such as identified substitution effects in terms of attack mode, across countries, and inter-temporal, resulting from different responses (Enders and Sandler, 1993, 2004; Rosendorff and Sandler, 2004). Another cluster of research examines the relationship of organizations to terrorist groups and the choices of organizations to pursue terrorism (Pedahzur and Weinberg, 2003; Weinberg, 1991).

Stages of conflict

A particularly interesting focus could be on the stage of violence. The civil war literature differentiated among emergence/onset, duration, intensity (Collier and Hoeffler, 2004: 564), and to allow for the possibility that different factors influence separate stages differently. For example, in the case of the FARC, Daniel Pecaut (1997) and Sánchez et al. (2003) remind scholars that factors contributing to later growth can be independent of factors that encouraged its emergence. Reinares (2004) documents the changing demographic composition of ETA, suggesting that scholars take into consideration the life cycle of terrorist groups. In general, Crenshaw differentiated precondition 'factors that set the stage for terrorism in the long run' from precipitant 'specific events that immediately precede the occurrence of terrorism' (Crenshaw, 1981: 381).

Diverse clusters of terrorism are appropriate according to different research questions. More work directed at solving the 'border and membership problems' of terrorism will help to unify the subject matter, identify types of terrorism that share causal factors or consequences, and clarify the bounds of useful and valid comparisons.

Questions of perspective

Alex Schmid (1992) counsels to divide terrorism discussions into distinct areas, each with a separate purpose: academic area of study, state statements of terrorism and/or juridical definitions, public debate, and oppositional discourse. It is crucial to note the term terrorism is 'an organizing concept that both describes the phenomenon as it exists and offers a moral judgment' (Crenshaw, 1995: 9). Moreover, it is widely used in the media and by policy makers.

Because of the political and moral connotations of the term, it is essential to be aware 'of the perspective of researchers and research institutes in order to better understand the probable flaws and strengths of work coming from different sources' (Silke, 2004a: 16). In fact, some have charged that the vast majority of studies on terrorism are done from the perspective of the government, and therefore, have reduced the term terrorism to mean nothing more than violence against the West. 'The "private sector" of the industry is heavily interlocked with government intelligence, military and foreign policy agencies, and is funded by and serves both governments and corporate establishments' (Herman and O'Sullivan, 1990: 8). This potentially raises issues of objectivity when research projects or scholars are funded by separate sources. 'If a researcher obtains funding from an organization or government entity with a known bias or agenda then his/her role as an impartial observer or when engaging in participant observation may be jeopardized' (Schultz, 2004: 167). Even attempts to define terrorism according to international law change according to foreign policy objectives among states (Ganor, 2002). Dedeoglu (2003) finds a divergence of labeling groups as terrorist, even if they commit the same acts that are recognized as terrorist. The political and foreign policy implications often clearly determine the application of the term terrorist to particular groups:

> While the concepts defined as 'terrorist-terrorism-terrorist organization' have not been defined, lists

of 'terror criminals' have been published. States have taken a common position about a few terror crimes, yet could not come up with a consensus on such issues as the crime itself, penalization and all terror criminals ... This difference is based on the various interests of the states in the international system (Dedeoglu, 2003: 103).

Similarly, Silke (2004a) notes that 'despite the similarities in how both countries [US and UK] define terrorism, the lists they proscribed were quite different' (p. 5). Thus, a clear academic definition of terrorism is necessary to avoid the pitfalls found in the public domain.

Part of the problem relates to the fact that terrorists, especially when limited to non-state actors, are acting against the existing authority, most often with aims of replacing it. 'Violence is clearly an extremely complex phenomenon involving major ambiguity between the destruction and the creation of order' (Imbusch, 2003: 13). Scholars should embed the notion of terrorism within the context to identify the type of political order that is being challenged, instead of blindly accepting the status quo as legitimate (Holmes, 2001). This is essential given the political aspect of a terrorist conflict, in which legitimacy or support is often an aim at least – if not more – important than military objectives. Because of this, there is a battle of perception that must be accounted for 'as a political issue – the self-presentation of those who use terrorism and the construction governments and publics place on it' (Crenshaw, 1995: 7).

Problems of quantification

Many scholars are concerned by the lack of good data to study terrorism. In 1988, Ted Gurr described a 'disturbing lack of good empirically-grounded research' (Gurr, 1988: 115). Others have continued to note the problem, such as Merari (1991: 89). After the burst of scholarly activity following 2001, the problem is still noted: 'the overriding deficiency of this state of stagnation is a dearth of empirically-grounded research on

terrorism' (Schultz, 2004: 161). There are three reasons for this continued state of affairs.

First, the above mentioned contested concept of terrorism results in the creation of datasets that do not measure the same thing and are not comparable. The 'problems of conceptual fuzziness ... and the resulting problems with the operationalization and measurement of phenomena of violence should continue to have the highest priority' (Dollase and Ulbrich-Herrmann, 2003: 1233). This problem reflects the longstanding disagreements about concepts and definitions of terrorism. For example, back in 1981, Martha Crenshaw warned 'an initial obstacle to identification of propitious circumstances for terrorism is the absence of significant empirical studies of relevant cross-national factors' (Crenshaw, 1981: 381).

Second, the political connotations of the term create additional difficulties and may result in reporting bias both in terms of interviews and in terms of data creation. In terms of interviews and fieldwork, it is difficult to be perceived as an objective observer. Scholars can become directly or indirectly involved in events, regardless of intention: 'There is no 'observation' when people are at war and you arrive asking them about it. You are, whether you wish to be or not, a participant. When terror weaves its way through a community, words are no longer mere information – words become weapons' (Theidon, 2001: 20). In terms of statistics, the illegal status of the violence may lead to distortion:

These particular problems are to be found not only in surveys of individuals, but also in analyses of police crime statistics, insurance company accident statistics, and the like ... As a result, there is a particularly strong risk that data on violence and aggression from official statistics will give a distorted picture of reality ... the frequency of real violence and aggression vary quite considerably as a function of whether they are given from the offender, victim, or observer perspective. This is because each perspective tries to give a different definition of violence or aggression (Dollase and Ulbrich-Herrmann, 2003: 1221).

Because of this, it is a good idea to incorporate different sources of data. For example, Holmes et al. (2006) compare two identical models, but using different indicators, one using terrorism statistics from the Colombian government and another using human rights violations from a CINEP, a leading Colombian human rights organization. Especially in politically sensitive areas such as violence statistics, it is prudent to compare non-government and government numbers since different groups may have incentives to over or under report, respectively or use completely different standards for inclusion of an event.

Finally, some scholars doubt whether acts of terrorism can be extracted from the historical context: 'The common weakness of these quantitative methods when applied to terrorism is a reflection of the fact that this form of violent subversion erupts at various times in various places as the result of an often idiosyncratic combination of factors and conditions' (Hoffman and Morrison-Taw, 2000: 7). A richly detailed accounting of the conflict and context work to alleviate such concerns.

However, despite these difficulties, a few datasets have been created. Shellman (2006) provides an overview of leading events datasets. Although some scholars have criticized statistics drawn from media sources because of concerns such as accuracy, bias, and audience content (Silke, 2004b: 62–3), many others find them to be fairly reliable (Davenport and Ball, 2002; King and Lowe, 2003) and open to verification through comparison with other sources. Jongman (2001) provides an overview of internal conflict and human rights violations datasets. Despite the recent improvement of available data, lack of coverage and comparability remains a severe problem, especially for domestic terrorism. Although a database of international terrorism is available for purchase (ITERATE is available with coverage from 1968 to 2005, see, Mickolus, 1980, 1982 and Mickolus et al., 1989), few datasets of domestic terrorism exist or are accessible. An attempt to create a global dataset of domestic terrorism

(1998-present) is the MIPT dataset, which builds upon RAND's data. However, use and replication of these data is strictly limited by copyright (Shellman, 2006). Moreover, existing databases need to clearly identify their definition of terrorism and include sufficient information so that scholars may recode the database in order to be useful to others using a separate concept of terrorism. More comprehensive comparisons are necessary utilizing diverse data sources and providing transparent and detailed definitions of terrorism. ITERATE and Project Civil Strife (Asal et al., 2006) are good examples of projects that provide sufficiently detailed codebooks to enable scholars to recode the data to fit other uses and concepts.

INCORPORATING INSIGHTS FROM DIVERSE APPROACHES AND DISCIPLINES

Much of the literature on terrorism has been criticized according to basic research design principles. For example, Silke (2004a) states 'terrorism literature is composed mainly of studies which rely on relatively weak research methods … There is a heavy reliance on qualitative and journalistic approaches which lack the validity and reliability generally expected within mainstream social science research' (p. 11). However, many of these problems are the result of the muddled conceptual foundation of the subject. Despite this, progress can be made, especially in middle range theory and by the pragmatic, question driven incorporation of different approaches and methodologies.

The understanding of terrorism is greatly enhanced by an interdisciplinary approach, analogous to calls for an interdisciplinary approach to political science (Scott, 1995: 37). Insights from geography, history, economics, sociology, and psychology can all be useful to understand terrorism. Terrorism is a complex phenomenon. Because of this, it is particularly useful to incorporate a variety of tools, questions, and methods. The field desperately needs to avoid the type of situation, as described by Wickham-Crowley (1991), in regard to the study of revolutions:

> The former group [the quantitatively inclined] views with disdain the more 'impressionistic' research tools employed by the latter, and suspects them moreover of finding precisely whatever their ideological bent would desire ... The qualitatively inclined are not without their own profound suspicions, perhaps best exemplified by the more or less massive statisticophobia that prevails (p. 83)

Instead, consistent with the need of comparative politics in general, studies of terrorism need a dialogue between them. Moreover, the collaboration – or at least cross fertilization – between area specialists and generalists is essential to grapple with the challenges of studying the topic. Unfortunately, there is a 'troubling lack of cross-method communication' in studies of conflict (George and Bennett, 2004: 4). Recently, however, trends in articles published in the major terrorism journals, *Terrorism and Political Violence* and *Studies in Conflict and Terrorism* demonstrate an increasing openness to multiple styles of analysis. This is especially promising given the apparent multiple causal pathways and potentially probabilistic causation of terrorism. This situation, in general, calls for synergetic studies that integrate findings from works with different methodologies (Collier, 1998b: 4). For example, Gates (2002), uses a microfoundational approach to understanding rebellion/internal conflict, but also incorporates geography and ideology (Gates, 2002: 112). Holmes et al. (2006) incorporate geography and economics to understand conflict in Colombia.

Similarly, multiple levels of analysis are useful. Crenshaw notes that it is 'possible to integrate macro and micro levels of analysis in order to discover which elements in what situations encourage oppositions or states to turn to terrorist tactics' (Crenshaw, 1995: 5). In general, della Porta (2003: 388) calls for a multi-level analysis (macro, meso, and micro) because of the complex nature of the phenomenon of political violence. Moreover, scholars can delve into case studies both historically and statistically, by using a sub-national analysis (Holmes et al., 2006; Sambanis, 2004).

Scholars have noted a lack of both 'theoretically grounded case studies' (Schultz, 2004: 183–4) and 'comprehensive historical comparisons' (Rapoport, 2006: xxvii). Schultz calls for more historically grounded comparisons and stresses the need for researchers to 'become familiar with the history of terrorism' (Schultz, 2004: 183). More case studies need to be focused on what statistical analyses identify as deviant and representative cases to identify omitted variables and to more fully illustrate causal mechanisms. Moreover, insights from formal models can be explored in case studies, just as patterns identified in case studies can be formalized (George and Bennett, 2004: 34–5). Additionally, this collaboration can help to identify the boundaries among different types of terrorism and political violence that plagues the definition of terrorism. This is a best practice in comparative politics, where 'scholars routinely go back to a small number of cases to assess the validity of conceptualization and measurement, as well as to refine causal inferences (Collier, 1998a: 2). This type of collaboration is both helpful to clarify concepts and identify appropriate boundaries and typologies.

An example of the potential fruitfulness of the combination of approaches can be seen by some of the works focusing on collective action and terrorism. Many scholars have noted the importance of strategies and constraints on the choices of main actors to understand terrorism. For example, Crenshaw highlights the importance of 'interactions among political actors, primarily governments and oppositions, at specific points in history' (Crenshaw, 1995: 5). The study of strategic interactions naturally calls for insights of collective action. Oberschall (2004) identifies four dimensions of collective action appropriate to examine in terms of terrorism, including '(1) discontent; (2) ideology-feeding grievances; (3) capacity to organize; and (4) political opportunity' (p. 27). According to Sandler and Arce (2003), game theory illuminates strategic interactions 'between terrorists and a targeted government ... among rational actors ...' as a struggle to gain strategic advantage and maximize goals. This approach is also useful to analyze issues of asymmetric information and resources (Sandler, 2003: 780), common to conflicts between states and non-state actors, and choices of strategy, for example, substitution effects (Enders and Sandler, 2004). In general, game theory and formal theory can help us work through questions without the restrictions of data limitations, and can be tested with available cases and data. Three successful examples of game theory tested against real data include the following. First, Kydd and Walter (2002) use game theory to understand the use of terrorism to disrupt peace processes, based on a 'problem of trust between the moderate opposition group and a target government' (p. 265). The models are tested against data covering the Palestinian Israeli conflict from 1988 to 1998. Second, Sandler uses collective action to analyze international terrorism. The theories are tested against the ITERATE data of transnational terrorism to understand deterrence, substitutions, externalities of actions and so forth. Third, Azam and Hoeffler (2002) develop two models (with radically different policy prescriptions) and then test them against real data.

However, some scholars are concerned about the conceptualization of rationality in game theory or rational choice:

> Our underlying hypothesis is not that fundamentalists will never utilize a rational calculus in limited spheres but that they will demonstrate a particular perspective that differs in significant ways from nonfundamentalists' and, in particular, that this fundamentalist perspective will be one in which religious considerations will dominate over any rational calculus (Monroe and Kredie, 1997: 26).

However, critics must be careful not to equate rationality with objectives. Similarly, Crenshaw warns against ascribing a 'calculated rationality to past actions that is ultimately misleading' (Crenshaw, 1995: 5). These types of concerns may be alleviated by a rich understanding of rationality that includes norms, in the style of Ostrom (1998). To understand individual

behavior and choices, scholars may find a combination of historical work and collective action approaches useful.

One strength of the existing terrorism literature is that much of the work does cross disciplinary lines. Some of the unanswered questions of rationality can be probed in other studies of terrorism that use a psychological approach (Horgan, 2005; Kruglanski and Fishman, 2006; Victoroff, 2005). Others have focused on the group level, instead of examining individual level choices (Goodwin, 2001; Kalyvas, 2003; Pedahzur and Perliger, 2006; Tilly, 2003; Turk, 2004). Additionally, some have begun to look at network theory to understand group dynamics (Asal et al., 2007; Sageman, 2004). The field of terrorism should resist attempts to impose theoretical unity at the cost of gaining interdisciplinary insights.

CONCLUSION

Despite the fragmented nature of the study of terrorism, the pursuit of middle range theory and pragmatic, question driven research may offer concrete progress in clarifying the four areas of dispute. This more modest initial goal may be frustrating to some. Previously, the field was thought to be under-theorized. Now, there is a flood of different theoretical approaches. However, in the rush to promote theory development, the field should not be artificially narrowed. Middle range theory can be most useful to identify different categories of terrorism. It is also more likely to produce lessons learned from other case studies and to illuminate under which circumstances those lessons apply. 'Middle-range theories attempt to formulate well-specified conditional generalizations of more limited scope. These features make them more useful for policymaking' (George and Bennett, 2004: 266). Moreover, this approach is more likely to satisfy scholars who doubt whether general theories of terrorism are even possible:

> It would be wiser to proceed from the more prudent assumptions that, for civil violence as for other

things, what appears to be 'the same' effect may proceed from a variety of causes, and that 'the same' causal influences may yield a variety of different effects in different settings (della Porta, 2003: 395).

Above all, pragmatic, problem driven research is more likely to take advantage of the insights of research from different approaches and disciplines. Even progress on the concept of terrorism is possible given this inclusive approach:

> While recognizing that usage is shaped and constrained by the broader scholarly understanding of a concept's meaning, we hold that specific methodological choices are often best understood and justified in light of the theoretical framework, analytical goals, and context of research involved in any particular study. As theory, goals, and context evolve, choices about concepts likewise may evolve. (Collier and Adock, 1999: 539)

In an unsettled field such as terrorism, such a pragmatic approach may be particularly productive.

With a pragmatic and open approach, incremental progress can be made in the study of terrorism. The more modest aims of middle range theory, may clarify the currently troubled theoretical state of the field. Specifically, it may help to identify areas of productive comparison, alleviate the border and membership problems, clarify concepts, find insight in other disciplines, and facilitate data collection and usage.

ACKNOWLEDGEMENTS

Special thanks to Sheila Amin Gutíerrez de Piñeres, Victor Asal, Todd Sandler, Ami Pedahzur, and Steve Shellman for their constructive comments.

REFERENCES

Arbelaez, M.A., Echavarria, J.J., and Gaviria, A. (2002) *Colombian long run growth and the crisis of the 1990s*. Report submitted to Global Development Network/Interamerican Development Bank Project on 'Economic Growth in Latin America and the Caribbean.'

Asal, V., Nussbaum, B., and Harrington, W. (2007) 'Terrorist transnational terrorist networks', *Studies in Conflict and Terrorism*, 30: 15–39.

Asal, V.H., Shellman, S.M., and Meek, S. (2006, November) *How have you killed lately? A substitution model of domestic terrorism in India 1980–2005*. Paper presented at the Peace Science Society (International) annual meeting.

Azam, J.P. and Hoeffler, A. (2002) 'Violence against civilians in civil wars: looting or terror?', *Journal of Peace Research*, 39 (4): 461–85.

Bloom, M. (2005) *Dying to kill the allure of suicide terror*. New York: Columbia University Press.

Collier, D. (1998a) 'Comparative method in the 1990s', *APSA Comparative Politics Newsletter*, 9 (1): 1–5.

Collier, D. (1998b) 'Comparative historical analysis: Where do we stand?', *APSA Comparative Politics Newsletter*, 9 (2): 1–5.

Collier, D. and Adock, R. (1999) 'Democracy and dichotomies: A pragmatic approach to choices about concepts', *Annual Review of Political Science*, 2: 537–65.

Collier, D. and Mahon, J. (1993) 'Conceptual stretching revisited: Adapting categories in comparative analysis', *American Political Science Review*, 87 (4): 845–55.

Collier, P. (2000) *Economic causes of civil conflict and their implications for policy*. Washington, DC: World Bank.

Collier, P., Elliot, L., Hegre, H., Hoeffler, A., Reynal-Querol, M., and Sambanis, N. (2003) *Breaking the conflict trap: Civil war and development policy*. Washington, DC: World Bank Group.

Collier, P. and Hoeffler, A. (2004) 'Greed and grievance in civil war', *Oxford Economic Papers*, 56 (4): 663–95.

Collier, P. and Sambanis, N. (2002) 'Understanding civil war: A new agenda', *Journal of Conflict Resolution*, 46,: 3–12.

Crenshaw, M. (1981) 'The causes of terrorism', *Comparative Politics,* 13 (4): 379–99.

Crenshaw, M. (1995) 'Relating terrorism to historical contexts', in M. Crenshaw (ed.),

Terrorism in context edited. University Park, PA: Penn State Press, pp. 3–26.

Crenshaw, M. (2000) 'The psychology of terrorism: An agenda for the 21st century', *Political Psychology*, 21 (2): 405–20.

Davenport, C. (1996) 'The weight of the past: Exploring lagged determinants of political repression', *Political Research Quarterly*, 49 (2): 377–403.

Davenport, C. and Ball, P. (2002) 'Views to a kill: Exploring the implications of source selection in the case of Guatemalan state terror, 1977–1996', *Journal of Conflict Resolution*, 46 (3): 427–50.

Dedeoglu, B. (2003) 'Bermuda triangle: Comparing official definitions of terrorist activity', *Terrorism and Political Violence*, 15 (3): 81–110.

della Porta, D. (2003) 'Violence and the new Left', in W. Heitmeyer and J. Hagen (eds), *International handbook of violence research*. New York, NY: Kluwer Academic Publishers, pp. 382–98.

Dollase R. and Ulbrich–Herrmann, M. (2003) 'Strategies and problems in quantitative research on aggression and violence', in W. Heitmeyer and J. Hagen (eds), *International handbook of violence research*. New York: Kluwer Academic Publishers, pp. 1203–18.

Eatwell, R. and Mudde, C. (2004) *Western democracies and the new extreme right challenge.* New York: Routledge.

Enders, W. and Sandler, T. (1993) 'The effectiveness of antiterrorism policies: A vector-autoregression-intervention analysis', *American Political Science Review*, 87 (4): 829–44.

Enders, W. and Sandler, T. (2004) 'What do we know about the substitution effects in transnational terrorism?', in A. Silke and G. Ilardi (eds), *Researching terrorism trends, achievements, failures*. London: Frank Cass, pp. 99–137.

Enders, W. and Sandler, T. (2006) *The political economy of terrorism.* Cambridge: Cambridge University Press.

Fearon, J. and Laitin, D. (2003) 'Ethnicity, insurgency, and civil war', *American Political Science Review*, 97 (1): 75–90.

Ganor, B. (2002) 'Defining terrorism: Is one man's terrorist another man's freedom fighter', *Police Practice and Research*, 3 (4): 287–304.

Gates, S. (2002) 'Recruitment and allegiance: The microfoundations of rebellion', *Journal of Conflict Resolution,* 46 (1): 111–30.

George, A. and Bennett, A. (2004) *Case studies and theory development in the social sciences.* Cambridge, MA: MIT Press.

Goodwin, J. (2001) *No other way out: States and revolutionary movements, 1945–1991.* Cambridge: Cambridge University Press.

Gordon, A. (1999) 'The road less traveled: Trends in terrorism research', *Terrorism and Political Violence*, 11 (2): 141–50.

Gurr, T.R. (1970) *Why men rebel.* Princeton, NJ: Princeton University Press.

Gurr, T.R. (1988) 'Empirical research on political terrorism: The state of the art and how it might be improved', in R.O. Slater and M. Stohl (eds), *Current perspectives on international terrorism*. London: Macmillan Press, pp. 115–54.

Herman, E. and O'Sullivan, G. (1990) *The terrorism industry: The experts and institutions that shape our view of terror.* NY: Pantheon Books.

Hoffman, B. and McCormick, G. (2004) 'Terrorism, signaling, and suicide attack', *Studies in Conflict and Terrorism*, 27 (4): 243–81.

Hoffman, B. and Morrison-Taw, J. (2000) 'A strategic framework for countering terrorism', in F. Reinares (ed.), *European democracies against terrorism: governmental policies and intergovernmental cooperation.* UK: Ashgate Aldershot, pp. 3–29.

Holmes, J.S. (2001) *Terrorism and democratic stability. Perspectives on democratization.* Manchester: Manchester University Press.

Holmes, J.S., Amin Gutiérrez de Piñeres, S., and Curtin, K. (2006) 'Drugs, violence and development in Colombia: A department level analysis', *Latin American Politics and Society*, 48 (3): 157–84.

Horgan, J. (2005) *The psychology of terrorism.* New York: Routledge.

Imbusch, P. (2003) 'The concept of violence', in W. Heitmeyer and J. Hagen (eds), *International handbook of violence research.* New York: Kluwer Academic Publishers, pp. 13–39.

Jongman, A. (2001) 'Database section: Dimensions of contemporary conflict and human rights violations', *Terrorism and Political Violence*, 13 (2): 143–77.

Kalyvas, S. (2001) '"New" and "old" wars: A valid distinction?' *World Politics*, 54 (1): 99–118.

Kalyvas, S. (2003) 'The ontology of political violence: Action and identity in civil wars', *Perspectives on Politics*, 1 (3): 475–94.

King, G. and Lowe, W. (2003) 'An automated information extraction tool for international conflict data with performance as good as human coders: A rare events evaluation design', *International Organization*, 57 (3): 617–42.

Kruglanski, A. and Fishman, S. (2006) 'The psychology of terrorism: "Syndrome" versus "tool" perspectives', *Terrorism and Political Violence*, 18 (2): 193–215.

Kydd, A. and Walter, B. (2002) 'Sabotaging the peace: The politics of extremist violence', *International Organization*, 56 (2): 263–296.

Laqueur, W. (1986) 'Reflections on terrorism', *Foreign Affairs*, 65 (1): 86–100.

Lichbach, M. (1994) 'What makes rational peasants revolutionary: Dilemma, paradox, and irony in peasant rebellion', *World Politics*, 46 (3): 383–418.

Long, A. (2006) *On 'other war' lessons from five decades of RAND counterinsurgency research*. Santa Monica, CA: Rand.

Merari, A. (1991) 'Academic research and government policy on terrorism', *Terrorism and Political Violence*, 3 (1): 88–102.

Mickolus, E.F. (1980) *Transnational terrorism: A chronology of events 1968–1979*. Westport, CT: Greenwood Press.

Mickolus, E.F. (1982) *International terrorism: Attributes of terrorist events, 1968–1977* (ITERATE 2) ICPSR ed. Ann Arbor, MI: Interuniversity Consortium for Political and Social Research [producer and distributor].

Mickolus, E.F., Sandler, T., and Murdock, J.M. (1989) *International terrorism in the 1980s: A chronology of events* (2 volumes) Ames, IA: Iowa State University Press.

Monroe, K.R. and Kredie, L.H. (1997) 'The perspective of Islamic fundamentalists and the limits of rational choice theory', *Political Psychology*, 18 (1): 19–43.

Moore, W. (1998) 'Repression and dissent: Substitution, context and timing', *American Journal of Political Science*, 42 (3): 851–73.

Mudde, C. (2005) *Racist extremism in Central and Eastern Europe*. New York: Routledge.

Oberschall, A. (2004) 'Explaining Terrorism: The contribution of collective action theory', *Sociological Theory*, 22 (1): 26–37.

O'Neill, B.E. (2001) *Insurgency and Terrorism: Inside modern revolutionary warfare*. Potomac Books.

Ostrom, E. (1998) 'A behavioral approach to the rational choice theory of collective action', *American Political Science Review*, 92 (1): 1–22.

Pape, R.A. (2006) *Dying to win: The strategic logic of suicide terrorism*. Random House.

Pecaut, D. (1997) 'Presente, pasado y futuro de la violencia en Colombia', *Desarrollo Económico*, 36 (144): 891–930.

Pedahzur, A. (ed.) (2006) *The roots of suicide terrorism: The globalization of martyrdom*. London: Routledge.

Pedahzur, A. and Perliger, A. (2006) 'The changing nature of suicide attacks – A social network perspective', *Social Forces*, 84 (4): 1987–2008.

Pedahzur, A. and Weinberg, L. (2003) *Political parties and terrorist groups*. New York: Routledge.

Poe, S. and Tate C.N. (1994) 'Repression of human rights to personal integrity in the 1980s: A global analysis', *The American Political Science Review*, 88 (4): 853–72.

Rapoport, D.C. (2001) 'The fourth wave: September 11 in the history of terrorism', *Current History*, 100 (650): 419–424.

Rapoport, D.C. (2006) 'General introduction', in D.C. Rapoport (ed.), *Terrorism: Critical concepts in political science*. New York: Routledge, pp. xxvii–xxxvii.

Reinares, F. (2003) 'Terrorism', in W. Heitmeyer and J. Hagen (eds), *International handbook of violence research*. New York: Kluwer Academic Publishers, pp. 309–21.

Reinares, F. (2004) 'Who are the terrorists? Analyzing changes in sociological profile among members of ETA', *Studies in Conflict and Terrorism*, 27 (6): 465–88.

Rosendorff, B.P. and Sander, T. (2004) 'Too much of a good thing? The proactive response dilemma', *Journal of Conflict Resolution*, 48 (5): 657–71.

Sageman, M. (2004) *Understanding terror networks*. Philadelphia: University of Pennsylvania Press.

Sambanis, N. (2004) 'Expanding economic models of civil war using case studies', *Perspectives on Politics*, 2 (2): 259– 80.

Sánchez, F.J., Díaz, A.M., and Formisano, M. (2003) *Conflicto, violencia y actividad criminal en Colombia: Un análisis espacial* (Archivos de Economíia, Documento 219) Retrieved March 17, 2008, from http://www.dotec–colombia.org/index.php?option= com_contentandtask=viewandid=2185 andltemid=15

Sandler, T. (2003) 'Collective action and transnational terrorism', *World Economy*, 26 (6): 779–802.

Sandler, T. and Arce, D. (2003) 'Terrorism and game theory', *Simulation and Gaming*, 34 (3): 319–37.

Sartori, G. (1970) 'Concept misinformation in comparative politics', *American Political Science Review*, 14 (4): 1033–53.

Schmid, A., and Jongman, A. (1988) *Political terrorism: A new guide to actors, authors, concepts, data bases, theories, and literature*. New Brunswick: Transaction Books.

Schmid, A.P. (1992) 'Terrorism and democracy', *Terrorism and Political Violence*, 4 (4): 14–25.

Schultz, F. (2004) 'Breaking the cycle: Empirical research and postgraduate studies on terrorism', in A. Silke (ed.), *Research on terrorism: Trends, achievements and failures*. New York: Routledge, pp. 161–85.

Scott, J. C. (1995) 'The role of theory in comparative politics: A symposium', *World Politics*, 48 (1): 1–49.

Seligson, M. (1996) 'Agrarian inequality and the theory of peasant rebellion', *Latin American Research Review*, 31 (2): 140–57.

Shellman, S. (2006) Quantifying violence and nonviolence: Terrorism and political violence events datasets. *e–Extreme*, 7(4) Retrieved March 17, 2008, from http://webhost.ua.ac.be/extremismanddemocracy/newsletter/Article7_4.htm

Silberfein, M. (2003) 'Insurrections', in S. Cutter, D. Richardson and T. Wilbanks (eds), *The geographical dimensions of terrorism*. New York: Routledge, pp. 67–74.

Silke, A. (2004a) 'An introduction to terrorism research', in A. Silke (ed.), *Research on terrorism: Trends, achievements and failures*. New York: Routledge, pp. 1–29.

Silke, A. (2004b) 'The devil you know', in A. Silke (ed.), *Research on terrorism: Trends, achievements and failures*. New York: Routledge, pp. 57–71.

Silke, A. (2004c) 'The road less travelled: Recent trends in terrorism research', in A. Silke (ed.), *Research on terrorism: Trends, achievements and failures*. New York: Routledge, pp. 186–213.

Stohl, M. and Lopez, G. (1984) *State as terrorist*. Portsmouth, NH: Greenwood.

Theidon, K. (2001) 'Terror's talk: Fieldwork and war', *Dialectical Anthropology*, 26 (1): 19–35.

Tilly, C. (1984) *Big structures, large processes, huge comparisons*. New York: Russell Sage Foundation.

Tilly, C. (2003) *The politics of collective violence*. Cambridge: Cambridge University Press.

Tilly, C. (2004) 'Terror, terrorism, terrorists', *Sociological Theory*, 22 (1): 5–13.

Turk. A.T. (2004) 'Sociology of terrorism', *Annual Review of Sociology*, 30: 271–86.

Van den Broek, H. (2004) 'Borroka – The legitimation of street violence in the political discourse of radical Basque nationalists', *Terrorism and Political Violence*, 16 (4): 714–36.

Victoroff, J. (2005) 'The mind of the terrorist: A review and critique of psychological approaches', *Journal of Conflict Resolution*, 49 (1): 3–42.

Weinberg, L. (1991) 'Turning to terror. The conditions under which parties turn to terrorist activities', *Comparative Politics*, 23 (4): 423–38.

Weinberg, L., Pedahzur, A., and Hirsch–Hoefler, S. (2004) 'The challenges of conceptualizing terrorism', *Terrorism and Political Violence*, 16 (4): 777–94.

Weinstein, J. (2005) 'Resources and the information problem in rebel recruitment', *Journal of Conflict Resolution*, 49 (4): 598–624.

Wickham-Crowley, T. (1991) 'A qualitative comparative approach to Latin American revolutions', *International Journal of Comparative Sociology*, 32 (1 and 2): 82–109.

Wickham-Crowley, T. (1992) *Guerrillas and revolution in Latin America*. Princeton, NJ: Princeton University Press.

Wood, E. (2004) *Insurgent collective action and civil war in El Salvador*. Cambridge: Cambridge University Press.

26

Comparative Regional Integration and Regionalism

Fredrik Söderbaum

INTRODUCTION

Since the mid-1980s there has been an explosion of various forms of regionalist projects on a global scale. The widening and deepening of the European Union (EU) is the most pervasive example, but regionalism is also made visible through the revitalization or expansion of many other regional projects around the world, such as the Association of Southeast Asian Nations (ASEAN), the Economic Community of West African States (ECOWAS), the North American Free Trade Agreement (NAFTA), the Southern African Development Community (SADC), and the Southern Common Market (Mercosur).

Today's regionalism is closely linked with the shifting nature of global politics and the intensification of globalization. Regionalism is characterized by the involvement of almost all governments in the world, but it also involves a rich variety of non-state actors, resulting in multiplicities of formal and informal regional governance and regional networks in most issue areas. This pluralism and multidimensionality of contemporary regionalism gives rise to a number of new puzzles and challenges for comparative politics.

Cumulative knowledge has grown within the study of regionalism and regional integration during the last two decades, especially on aspects of European integration, the institutional design of regional organizations, the problems of collective action on the regional level, and the relationship between globalization and regionalism. However, the challenges and weaknesses in the study of regionalism and regional integration are primarily related to the fragmented nature of this research field, in particular the weak debate around comparative analysis.

Despite a growing number of specific comparisons of selected aspects of regionalism (especially regarding regional institutions and the role of power) in selected regions (particularly in the triad: Europe, East Asia, and North America), there is virtually no systematic debate regarding the fundamentals of comparison, such as 'what to compare', 'how to compare', or 'why compare'. Consequently, the purpose of this chapter is to contribute to the general discussion about 'the problem of comparison' in the study of regionalism and regional integration. It does not attempt a detailed empirical comparison of a set of pre-defined regions according to a fixed set of variables. The chapter will provide an overview of the state of comparative regional integration and regionalism, an outline of the main debates and controversies, and a discussion of the state of the research field and directions in which it ought to be moving.

This chapter is organized in four main sections. The first discusses the main concepts in the field, and the implications of this for comparative analysis. The second provides an overview of the development of the early and the more recent debates on regional integration and regionalism in terms of theoretical focus, empirical practices and the treatment of comparative analysis. The third and most extensive section provides an overview of the debates about regionalism in some of the most critical regions of the world in this regard (Europe, East Asia, the Americas, and Africa), highlighting in particular the tension between regional specialization and comparative analysis. The chapter concludes with suggestions for improving the comparative element in the study of regionalism and regional integration.

CONCEPTUALIZATIONS

It is natural to begin with the problem of definition, notwithstanding that such an exercise has often proved problematic, due to the fact that regional integration and regionalism are elusive and evolving concepts. Definitions are of course essential in comparative research, since the definition and choice of what is a comparable case will affect the ability to generalize. There have also been shifting and competing views regarding the dependent variable, which also results in problems in comparison.

The concept of 'region' derives from the Latin word 'regio', which means direction (Jönsson et al., 2000: 15). It also derives from the Latin verb 'regere': 'to rule' or 'to command'. Later in history the concept of region denoted border or a delimited space,

often a province. Historically, the concept of region has evolved primarily as a space between the national and the local within a particular state. These types of regions are here referred to as *micro-regions*. The concept of region can also refer to *macro-regions* (so-called world regions), which are larger territorial (as distinct from non-territorial) units or sub-systems, between the state level and the global system level.

The macro-region has been the most common object of analysis in international studies, while micro-regions have more commonly been considered in the realm of the study of domestic politics and economics. In current international affairs, with blurred distinctions between the domestic and the international, micro-regions have increasingly become cross-border in nature, precipitating an emerging debate about the relationship between macro-regionalism and micro-regionalism within the context of globalization (Perkmann and Sum, 2002; Söderbaum, 2005).

The minimum classical definition of a macro-region is 'a limited number of states linked together by a geographical relationship and by a degree of mutual interdependence' (Nye, 1971: vii). During the early debate about regional integration a large amount of research capacity was invested in trying to define regions scientifically (Cantori and Spiegel, 1970); a plethora of opinions were advanced regarding what mutual interdependencies mattered the most (such as economic, political and social variables, or historical, cultural and ethnic bonds). The results of this research were not compelling, however, and parsimonious attempts to define regions have essentially come to an end. Most scholars engaged in the contemporary debate agree that there are no natural or 'scientific' regions, and that definitions of a region vary according to the particular problem or question under investigation. This problem about how to define a region may pose certain challenges for comparative analysis, but many scholars solve the problem by concentrating on regional organizations and regional economic frameworks

(Acharya and Johnston, 2007; Fawcett and Hurrell, 1995), or security complexes/communities (Adler and Barnett, 1998; Buzan and Waever, 2003), which tend to make cases more 'comparable'.

The view that regions must not be taken for granted or be reduced to regional organizations is particularly emphasized in constructivist and post-structuralist scholarship. As Jessop (2003) points out, 'rather than seek an elusive objective ... criterion for defining a region, one should treat regions as emergent, socially constituted phenomena' (p. 183). From such a perspective, all regions are socially constructed and hence politically contested. Emphasis is placed on how political actors perceive and interpret the idea of a region and notions of 'regionness' (Hettne and Söderbaum, 2000). It is clear that such (inter) subjective understandings of regions pose certain challenges for systematic comparison.

Just as there are competing understandings about how to define a region, there are many contrasting and sometimes incompatible definitions of related concepts. One distinction is between regional cooperation and regional integration. Regional cooperation can be defined as an open-ended process, whereby individual states (or possibly other actors) within a given geographical area act together for mutual benefit, and in order to solve common tasks, in certain fields, such as infrastructure, water and energy, notwithstanding conflicting interests in other fields of activity. Regional integration refers to a deeper process, whereby the previously autonomous units are merged into a whole. A fruitful distinction is between political integration (the formation of a transnational political system), economic integration (the formation of a transnational economy), and social integration (the formation of a transnational society) (Nye, 1971: 26–7).

The concepts of regionalism and regionalization have entered the discussion during the recent debate.[1] 'Regionalism' represents the *policy and project*, whereby state and non-state actors cooperate and coordinate strategy within a particular region or as a type of world order. It is usually associated

with a formal programme, and often leads to institution building. 'Regionalization' refers to the *process* of cooperation, integration, cohesion, and identity creating a regional space (issue-specific or general):

> At its most basic it means no more than a concentration of activity – of trade, peoples, ideas, even conflict – at the regional level. This interaction may give rise to the formation of regions, and in turn to the emergence of regional actors, networks, and organisations (Fawcett, 2005: 25).

The majority of studies in this field of political science continue to focus on the policies of (formal and largely state-led) regionalism as opposed to the processes of regionalization (Fawcett and Hurrell, 1995; Gamble and Payne, 1996), although there is, as we should see below, an increasing amount of research on the relationship between regionalism and regionalization.

In summary, regions, regional cooperation, regional integration, regionalism, and regionalization are contested concepts that are used differently across disciplines, and frequently also within disciplines. Communication between different standpoints has been difficult because of the incomparability between different phenomena, resulting in problems of not only *what* to compare, *how* to compare, but also *why* to compare at all.

EARLY AND RECENT DEBATES ON REGIONALISM: CONTINUITIES AND DISCONTINUITIES

The phenomenon of regional integration/regionalism can be traced far back in history, as seen in the rich variety of geographically confined 'Staatenbünde', 'leagues', 'unions', 'pacts', and 'confederations' (Mattli, 1999: 1). The protectionist and neo-mercantilist trend of the 1930s is considered by some to have been the first main wave of regionalism. However, more often it is argued that voluntary and comprehensive regionalism is predominantly a post-World War II phenomenon, which therefore (according to some definitions) reduces the number of cases of regionalism. It is common to distinguish between an earlier wave of regionalism in the 1950s and 1960s (then often referred to as 'regional integration') and a more recent wave or generation of regionalism (often referred to as 'new regionalism') beginning in the latter half of the 1980s and now a prevalent phenomenon throughout the world. But after more than two decades of so-called 'new regionalism', the distinction between 'old' and 'new' has lost much of its original meaning (Hettne, 2003, 2005). It is arguably more appropriate to identify continuities and discontinuities between what can be understood as the early and the more recent debates.

The early debate[2]

The early or classical approaches to regional integration were foremost concerned with peace, and tended to view the nation-state as the problem rather than the solution. The most relevant theories were federalism, functionalism, neofunctionalism, and transactionalism (Rosamond, 2000). Federalism, which inspired the pioneers of European integration, was less a theory than a political programme; it was sceptical of the nation-state, although its project was in fact to create a new kind of 'state'. In Europe there was no obvious theorist associated with federalism, whereas, functionalism has been much strongly identified with David Mitrany (1966).

Functionalism was primarily a strategy (or a normative method) designed to build peace, constructed around the proposition that the provision of common needs and functions can unite people across state borders. Form, in the functionalist view, was supposed to follow function, whereas for federalists it was primarily form that mattered. Functional cooperation should concentrate on technical and basic functional programmes and projects within clearly defined sectors. Usually, the nation-state should be bypassed, and *international*

cooperation was preferred to *regional* cooperation. Mitrany criticized both federalism and neofunctionalism on the basis that both were primarily based on territory rather than function. He saw territoriality as part of the Westphalian logic, which was taken to imply conflict and war, although Mitrany considered the European Coal and Steel Community (ECSC) an acceptable organization.

Neofunctionalism enjoyed an enormous reputation during the 1960s. The central figure was Ernst Haas, who challenged the functionalists, and claimed a greater concern for the centres of power (Haas, 1958, 1964). Haas, in fact, theorized the 'community method' pioneered by Jean Monnet. Even if the outcome of this method could be a federation, it was not to be constructed through constitutional design. The basic mechanism in neofunctionalist theorizing was 'spillover', which referred to 'the way in which the creation and deepening of integration in one economic sector would create pressures for further economic integration within and beyond that sector, and greater authoritative capacity at the European level' (Rosamond, 2000: 60).

In the 1960s the neofunctional description (and prescription) became increasingly remote from the empirical world, now dominated by Charles de Gaulle's nationalism. Stanley Hoffman (1966) asserted that regional integration could not spread from 'low politics' (economics) to the sphere of 'high politics' (security), contrary to the stipulations of the (neo)functionalists. Perceptions of the role of the EC began to diverge. According to Alan Milward (1992) and the intergovernmentalist response, the EC should instead be seen as a 'rescue of the nation-state'.

Haas (1975) responded to critics by labelling the study of regional integration 'pretheory' (on the basis that there was no clear idea about dependent and independent variables), then referred to the field in terms of 'obsolescence', and ended up suggesting that the study of regional integration should cease to be a subject in its own right. Rather, it should be seen as an aspect of the study of interdependence (a concept popularized at that time by Robert Keohane and Joseph Nye). In retrospect it would appear that the neofunctionalists expected too much too quickly. They underestimated the anti-pluralist, centralist and nationalist orientations of their time, at the same time as the theory had relatively little regard for exogenous and extra-regional forces (Breslin and Higgott, 2000).

The early debate was always centred on Europe, and Europe was in many ways treated as a single case. Gradually the comparative element in the field grew stronger and some of the most respected (mainly neofunctionalist) theorists of their time also conducted comparisons. For instance, Ernst Haas, Philippe Schmitter, and Sydney Dell studied regional integration (or the lack of it) in Latin America (Dell, 1966; Haas, 1967; Haas and Schmitter, 1964; Schmitter, 1970). Amitai Etzioni compared the United Arab Republic, the Federation of West Indies, the Nordic Association, and the European Economic Community (Etzioni, 1965). Joseph Nye studied East Africa and conducted comparisons of the Arab League, the Organization of American States (OAS) and the Organization of African Unity (OAU) (Nye, 1970, 1971).

Even if many of these and other like-minded scholars were conscious of their own Eurocentrism, they searched above all for those 'background conditions', 'functional equivalents', and 'spill-over' effects that were derived from the study of Europe. As Breslin et al. (2002) point out, they 'used the European experience as a basis for the production of generalizations about the prospects for regional integration elsewhere' (p. 2). This resulted in difficulties in identifying comparable cases, or anything that corresponded to their definition of 'regional integration'. As will be discussed below, the treatment of European integration as the primary case or 'model' of regional integration still dominates many of the more recent studies of regionalism and regional integration, which is an important part of 'the problem of comparison' within this research area. Nonetheless, the rigour with which earlier theorists undertook comparative analysis can serve as an inspiration for the development of a more genuinely 'comparative' regionalism.

What can be broadly understood as a model for regionalism among developing countries emerged in response to the Europe-centred classical models in political science (particularly neofunctionalism) and economics (particularly neoclassical market integration) during the early debate. This model can be understood within the structuralist tradition of economic development, pioneered by Gunnar Myrdal, Arthur Lewis, and Raul Prebisch (Prebisch, 1963). From this perspective the rationale of regional cooperation and integration among less developed countries was not to be found in functional cooperation or marginal economic change within the existing structure, but rather, through the fostering of 'structural transformation' and the stimulation of productive capacities, whereby investment and trading opportunities were being created. This school thus shifted focus away from economic integration as a means of political unification to one of regional economic cooperation/integration as a means of economic development. Hence the dependent variable, as well as the underlying conditions for regionalism, was so different that it called for a different theory, according to which Europe and the developing world were not comparable cases (Axline, 1994a: 180).

The recent debate[3]

The 1970s was a period of 'Eurosclerosis' within the EC, but the 1985 White Paper on the internal market and the Single European Act resulted in a new dynamic process of European integration. This was also the start of what has often been referred to as the 'new regionalism' on a global scale. To some observers regionalism was 'new', mainly in the sense that it represented a revival of protectionism or neomercantilism (Bhagwati, 1993). But most observers highlighted the fact that closure of regions was not on the agenda; rather, the current regionalism was to be understood as 'open regionalism' (Anderson and Blackhurst, 1993; Cable and Henderson, 1994). Indeed, one of the characterizing features of the more recent debate on regionalism, especially within the field of international relations, is its focus on the conditions related to what has increasingly been called globalization, occurring in the context after the end of the Cold War. There are many ways in which globalization and regionalism interact and overlap, according to this type of scholarship (Bøås et al., 1999; Coleman and Underhill, 1998; Cooper et al., 2008; Farrell et al., 2005; Hettne et al., 1999; Schulz et al., 2001).

One prominent scholar of the recent debate, Björn Hettne, emphasizes that regionalism needs to be understood both from an *exogenous perspective* (according to which regionalization and globalization are intertwined articulations of global transformation) and from an *endogenous perspective* (according to which regionalization is shaped from within the region by a large number of different actors) (Hettne, 2002). As mentioned above, the exogenous perspective has primarily developed during the recent debate, whereas the endogenous perspective underlines the continuities back to functionalist and neofunctionalist theorizing about the integration of Europe, the role of agency and the long-term transformation of territorial identities. But in contrast with the time in which Haas and the early regional integration scholars were writing, today there are many regionalisms and thus a very different base for comparative studies. It is apparent that neither the object for study (ontology) nor the way of studying it (epistemology) has remained static. One indication of this is the emergence of a rich variety of theoretical frameworks for the study of regionalism and regional integration.[4] Indeed, current regionalism may be seen as a new political landscape in the making, characterized by an increasing set of actors (state and non-state) operating on the regional arena and across several interrelated dimensions (security, development, trade, environment, culture, and so on).

Historically the study of regional cooperation and integration has strongly emphasized states as actors, or political unification within (formal) regional organizations – although neofunctionalist, institutionalist, and especially transactionalist approaches certainly consider the underlying social fabric of non-state actors and interest groups. In contrast, many recent perspectives have placed additional emphasis on 'soft', *de facto*, or informal regionalism/regionalization, acknowledging the fact that a rich variety of non-state actors have begun to operate within as well as beyond state-led institutional frameworks. For instance, business interests and multinationals not only operate on the global sphere, but also tend to create regionalized patterns of economic activity (Rugman, 2005). Similarly, civil society is often neglected in the study of regionalism, notwithstanding that its impact is increasing, as evident in the transnational activist networks and processes of civil society regionalization emerging around the world (Acharya, 2003; Söderbaum, 2007; Warleigh, 2001).

As mentioned earlier, the distinction and causal relationship between formal and informal regionalism (or between state-led regionalism and non-state regionalization) has attracted considerable attention during the recent debate. Key issues in this debate are whether or not formal regionalism precedes informal regionalization, and the various ways in which state, market, and civil society actors relate and come together in different formal and informal coalitions, networks and modes of regional and multilevel governance (Bøås et al., 2005; Christiansen and Piattoni, 2004; Katzenstein and Shiraishi, 1997; Sandholtz and Stone-Sweet, 1998). According to Breslin et al. (2002) the distinction between formal and informal regionalism helps 'break out of the teleological shackles of the first wave and may help us to move our focus to different types of regional response [and] to more issue-specific questions' (p. 13). From a comparative perspective, the fundamental problem is that the current field of study is still fragmented, lacking communication between the many theoretical standpoints and various regional debates.

COMPARING DEBATES ON REGIONALISM IN EUROPE, EAST ASIA, THE AMERICAS, AND AFRICA

This section provides an overview and compares some of the main features of the debates about regionalism in Europe, East Asia, the Americas, and Africa. Worldwide regionalism is not, of course, restricted to these regions, but the 'sample' is broad enough to illustrate the pluralism of contemporary regionalism.

The ambition in this section is to describe and compare some of the general characteristics of each regional debate, rather than attempt to compare pre-defined regions or regional organizations according to a fixed and narrow set of variables (an exercise which would not be able to address the more general problem of comparison in this area of research). It should be stated that the analysis draws attention to the tension between regional specialization and comparative research. The main reason for this tension is that the majority of scholars tend to specialize in a particular region – regardless what discipline they come from (comparative politics, international relations, area studies). Sometimes comparisons are made within each region (for instance, comparing the different regionalisms in Asia), and an increasing number of scholars compare across regions as well. The fundamental problem is that many case studies and the vast majority of comparisons tend to use theoretical frameworks that are biased towards European integration theory and practice. Indeed, as this section will draw attention to, the comparative element is underdeveloped and European integration has become an obstacle for developing a comparative regionalism and regional integration.[5]

Debates about regionalism in Europe

Europe has a long history of integrative and disintegrative processes (Mattli, 1999). During recent decades the regionalization process has ultimately centred around one dominant project – what is today the EU – which has widened and deepened in scope, reach and ambition to a remarkable degree. Historically, an intense debate has swirled around varieties of realist/intergovernmental and functional/ liberal/institutional perspectives. These different approaches focus largely on different aspects of the integration process. For instance, realists and intergovernmentalists appear to have the most to say about the logic behind large Council meetings and treaty reforms such as Maastricht, Amsterdam, and Nice (Grieco, 1997; Moravcsik, 1998). Meanwhile, the functional/liberal/institutional approaches focus more on economic integration and other issue areas (especially under the first pillar) in which the EU's central institutions such as the Commission and the Court have a more prominent role (Pollack, 2003; Sandholtz and Stone-Sweet, 1998).

Other scholars emphasize other variables again, such as the fundamentally changed political landscape in Europe, blurring the distinction between international and domestic politics. One such perspective is 'multilevel governance', which posits that power and decision-making in Europe are not concentrated at one level (national or supranational), but are rather characterized by a complex web of relations between public and private actors nested in supranational, national and micro-regional levels (Hooghe and Marks, 2001).

In recent years social constructivism has gained a more prominent place in the study of European integration (Christiansen et al., 2001). This line of thinking has entered the discussion on European integration mainly as a spillover from the discipline of international relations, and as a means of transcending the rather introverted debates between the conventional and rationalist theories of

European integration referred to initially. The social constructivist approach emphasizes the mutual constitutiveness of structure and agency, and pays particular attention to the role of ideas, values, norms and identities in the social construction of Europe (rather than EU *per se*) (Christiansen et al., 2001). This theoretical approach has undoubtedly revitalized the study of European integration, but it makes its comparisons between Europe and *international* regimes rather than between Europe and other *regions*. There is therefore considerable scope for an increase in comparison of the social construction of various global regions.

The lack of communication and interaction between EU studies and regionalism in the rest of the world is stark, although some recent attempts have begun to remedy this lack (Laursen, 2003; Telo, 2007; Warleigh, 2004, 2006). Indeed, there has been a tendency within EU studies during the recent decade to consider the EU as a nascent, if unconventional, polity in its own right (the 'n=1' problem). This view holds that the EU should be studied as a political system rather than as a project of regional integration or regionalism (Caporaso and Keeler, 1995; Hix, 1994, 1999). The corollary is that established tools of political science and *comparative politics* should be used in EU studies and that *international studies and relations* are not equipped to deal with the complexity of the contemporary EU.[6] This view has also reinforced the notion that the EU is *sui generis*, thereby downplaying the similarities between the EU and other regionalist projects. According to Ben Rosamond, one prominent EU scholar, the parochialism inherent in this particular strand of EU studies has contributed little in deepening our understanding of the EU as a political system. He argues that EU studies should return to the broader ambitions of the comparative and classical regional integration theory (especially neofunctionalism), at least to the extent of developing generalizable and comparative conceptual and theoretical frameworks (Rosamond, 2005).

Debates about regionalism in East Asia

There exists no overall consensus for a definition of the Asian region or about the fundamental nature of regionalism in Asia. The meaning of regionalism has changed in relation to the question of what sub-regions to include and exclude, what dimensions of regionalism to investigate (such as security, economics, politics and identity) and over the particular theoretical perspectives employed. Conventionally Asia has been divided into the regions Central Asia, Northeast Asia, Southeast Asia and South Asia, with a blurred border towards the Middle East. Most literature in relation to regionalism has focused on East Asia, that is, Northeast Asia and Southeast Asia. Since East Asia is arguably the most interesting region, from a theoretical, empirical as well as comparative perspective, it is also the focus adopted here.

A considerable body of literature is concerned with the study of the Association of Southeast Asian Nations (ASEAN) (see Acharya, 2001). A major reason for this emphasis, at least historically, appears to be that ASEAN has been one of the few sustainable regional organizations in the larger East Asian region. During the Cold War the core of ASEAN cooperation was in its joint effort to consolidate the member nation states and to enhance stability. These goals were driven by a narrow political elite in what were, at that time, relatively fledgling and fragile state formations. Communism was the primary internal and external threat. The *raison d'être* of ASEAN – bulwarking against communist expansion – has of course been long absent from the political landscape; focus has shifted to achieving increased economic development and to ensuring security in a new context.

During recent decades an important part of the debate about regionalism in East Asia has focused on collective identity formation and informal or 'soft' regionalism (Acharya, 2001; Katzenstein, 2002). This scholarship seeks to account for the non-legalistic style of decision-making in this region, and the fact that there is no transfer of national sovereignty to a supranational authority. Nevertheless, there exists a dense network of informal gatherings, working groups and advisory groups, particularly within ASEAN, but also in the ASEAN Regional Forum, the Asia-Pacific Economic Cooperation forum (APEC), and more recently the Asia-Europe Meeting (ASEM) and ASEAN Plus Three (China, Japan and the Republic of Korea). This informal style of decision-making incorporates its own innate code of conduct that is often referred to as the 'ASEAN Way', which, in contrast with European-style formal bureaucratic structures and legalistic decision-making procedures, is built around discreetness, informality, pragmatism, consensus-building, and non-confrontational bargaining styles (Acharya, 1997: 329). Further, the ASEAN Way reflects to an extent the illiberal underpinnings of the 'Asian values' construct, which stresses a communitarian ethic ('society over the self') in explaining the region's economic dynamism (Acharya, 2002: 27–8).

The 1997/98 Asian financial crisis underlined not only the interdependence of Northeast and Southeast Asian countries, but, according to Higgott (2002: 2), also 'exposed the weakness of existing regional institutional economic arrangements'. This in turn appears also to have undermined the confidence in the soft institutionalism of the 'ASEAN Way' and underscored the need for deeper institutionalization and stronger commitments from countries. Following the region's recovery from the 1997/98 financial crisis the East Asian countries moved to institutionalize annual leaders' summits and ministerial dialogues through the ASEAN+3 (China, Japan and the Republic of Korea) framework. The most concrete project is the Chiang Mai Initiative (CMI), which was adopted in May 2000 in order to provide emergency foreign currency liquidity support in the event of a future financial crisis. But broader cooperation also exists across a range of areas such as small and medium-scale industry development, human resource development, agriculture, tourism, and information technology (Nesudurai, 2005: 167). It is too early to see what institutional structures will emerge, but as Higgott (2006: 32) points out, 'the range of interactions developing is unprecedented, with a considerable number of regular meetings across most policy domains, especially economics and finance, agriculture, forestry (and) tourism.' He also stresses that to 'see ASEAN+3 as but an exercise in extended conference diplomacy, reflecting weakness rather than strength, would be misleading' (Higgott, 2006: 32).

Most research concerning East Asian regionalism is based on case studies rather than comparisons. There are an increasing number of regional processes in East Asia, which provide a large base for comparison within the region. Generally speaking, studies on East Asian regionalism present a significant number of loose comparisons with, or sweeping references to, European integration theories and practices. The great majority of such references or comparisons with Europe characterize East Asian regionalism as looser and more informal, sometimes even as 'underdeveloped' (Choi and Caporaso, 2002: 485). It is problematic to regard EU-style institutionalization as an ideal model for regionalism. A particularly effective remedy for such misplaced comparison with European integration is the edited collection by Bertrand Fort and Douglas Webber (2006), *Regional Integration in East Asia and Europe: Convergence or Divergence?* Amitav Acharya (2006: 312–3), a leading scholar on East Asian regionalism and contributor to this book, points out that rather than elevating the European model over the Asian experience as a preferred model of regionalism, it is more productive to recognize that regional cooperation is a difficult and contested process that will throw up different, equally legitimate, outcomes. There is room for a more mutually reinforcing cross-fertilization in the study of European, East Asian, and also other regionalisms. There is, for instance, no reason to believe that soft institutionalism is a uniquely Asian phenomenon. Further, comparisons should not be limited to contemporary Asia and Europe, but would benefit from considering regionalism experience across various time periods.

Debates about regionalism in the Americas

Historically, the Americas have been divided and described according to North America, Latin America, and the Caribbean. Since the end of the Cold War this division has become increasingly inadequate for understanding regional processes on the American continent. There are strong convergences both within Latin America and between Latin America and North America. As Phillips (2005: 58) asserts;

> (t)he most profitable way of proceeding is therefore to abandon traditional categories in favour of a mode of analysis which seeks to advance an integrated understanding of the Americas *as a region*, the various parts of which are best disaggregated into ... distinctive but interlocking subregions (that is, Andean, Caribbean, Central America, North America and the Southern Cone).

An important aspect of the transformation of the Americas is linked to the changing strategy of the US and to the consolidation of, and resistance towards, neoliberal policies. Although there is a plethora of sub-regional projects across the Americas, most attention in the debate has focused on NAFTA in the north, and Mercosur in the south. These two projects are intriguing from a comparative perspective and they are therefore contrasted here.

The origins of NAFTA can be traced to the growing concerns of Canada and Mexico that protectionist US policies could potentially devastate their economies (Pastor, 2005: 220). NAFTA was preceded by a bilateral free trade agreement between Canada and the USA; when a similar agreement was proposed between Mexico and the US, Canada sought a tripartite agreement. Mexico's involvement is particularly intriguing. Mexico's tradition of a combined nationalism, protectionism, and

'anti-gringoism' is still evident, but the country's self-reliance based on an oil economy has now lost credibility. Mexico, which had earlier harboured the ambition of becoming a regional power, was the first Latin American country to conclude, in joining NAFTA in 1992, that a free trade policy was the path out of stagnation.

The North American integration process is characterized by a close cooperation between the US administration and American business interests. The NAFTA proposals were hotly debated in the US, where criticism focused particularly on the issues of migration, the relocation of manufacturing industries to Mexico and, to some extent, environment and labour issues. In Canada and Mexico, discussion concerning NAFTA predominantly related to the particular neoliberal character of the agreement and the dominant position of the US. It is hard to dispute that the NAFTA project is elite-driven and based on a neoliberal philosophy. Significantly, opposition to the project from civil society has taken a regional form. According to Marchand (2001: 210), the 'hyperliberal' NAFTA constitutes the worst of the new regionalism in North America, while the mobilization of a regionalized civil society constitutes the best of the new regionalism in North America.

NAFTA maintains a strong emphasis on trade and market liberalization in combination with a weak institutional structure and weak political ambitions, respecting the sovereignty of each member state, which contrasts sharply with the emphasis on deep and institutional integration of the EU. Although the NAFTA treaty is binding on its member states and involves certain dispute settlement mechanisms, these are *ad hoc* and NAFTA's objectives are limited to the regulation of trade and investment flows and the protection of property rights. 'The style of NAFTA's governance is laissez-faire, reactive, and legalistic: problems are defined by plaintiffs and settled by litigation' (Pastor, 2005: 220).

While NAFTA emerged more or less as a consequence of US bilateralism, Mercosur emerged both as a consequence of the democratic and economic reforms in Brazil and Argentina, and as a planned and intended regional venture. Mercosur has been described in terms of 'open regionalism' (*regionalismo abierto*) (ECLAC, 1994), pointing to that it is an outward-oriented regional response to the challenges of economic globalization and a mechanism for the governments to 'lock in' economic and political reform programmes. In this sense Mercosur represents a clear shift in the integration model in South America away from the inward-oriented model of the past. According to Alvaro Vasconcelos (2007: 166), the main motivation of the Mercosur lay in the desire to create a common market labelled on the European Community. In the 1990s Mercosur was widely considered a 'success' (Malamud, 2003), particularly because the participant countries agreed on far-reaching tariff liberalization, and because of the significant increase in the level of intra-regional trade, at least compared with previous failed projects, such as the Latin American Integration Association (LAIA). However the Mercosur of today faces serious problems, largely stemming from the crisis set off in 2002–3 in the context of Free Trade of the Americas (FTAA) negotiation, from which Mercosur has not fully emerged.

Mercosur has been a strongly statist project. Its formal institutions are weak and directly dependent on national administrations, which are responsible for the coordination and preparation of negotiations between the member governments. This can be understood as an intergovernmental negotiating structure, or as 'presidentialism', the latter should, according to Malamud (2003: 56), be seen as a 'functional equivalent' to regional institutions within the EU. The intergovernmental institutions exist alongside an embryonic legal doctrine in two areas: common trade regulations and a system for the resolution of disputes. The number of issues that inevitably require community level regulation has grown. However, the key member states (especially Brazil) appear to prefer 'political' and intergovernmental solutions in lieu of the 'legal' avenue through the supranational court of justice. Brazil's individualistic strategy implies weak central institutions and trade integration only. Conversely, Brazil favours a strengthened political role for Mercosur in the Americas, as a mechanism of resistance towards the US, including the FTAA. It appears that this emphasis on political counterweight has been emphasized with Venezuela's entry into the organization in 2006. In this sense Mercosur might represent a Latin alternative, resisting 'North Americanization', reminiscent of earlier models of regionalism in Latin America.

There is a rich base for comparative analysis in the Americas in time and space, due to the considerable number of old and more recent regional projects across the Americas. Empirically most of the comparisons conducted are between sub-regional frameworks within the Americas in general, or more specifically within Latin America. However, as far as theory and cross-regional comparison are concerned, the EU is by far the most salient point of reference or model, particularly when we are dealing with variations on the theme of the common market model rather than the free trade model. This implies that European integration theory and practice strongly influences the debate in and comparisons with Latin America, but not as much regarding NAFTA or the FTAA.[7]

Debates about regionalism in Africa

The ideological foundation of regional cooperation and integration in Africa is evidenced in the pan-African visions and series of treaties developed within the framework of the OAU and more recently the African Union (AU) and the New Partnership for Africa's Development (NEPAD) (Asante, 1997; Murithi, 2005; Taylor, 2005). While earlier strategies were built around state-led industrialization, import substitution and collective self-reliance, the dominant view today is that Africa 'must unite' in order to avoid marginalization in the global economy and instead exploit the opportunities provided by economic globalization. Indeed, an overarching market orientation in combination with EU-style institutionalization is the official strategy adopted by most of Africa's main regional cooperation and integration schemes, such as AU/NEPAD, the Common Market for Eastern and Southern Africa (COMESA), the Economic Community of West African States (ECOWAS), the Southern African Development Community (SADC), and the West African Economic and Monetary Union (UEMOA).

The academic debate about regionalism in Africa often focuses on state-led regional integration frameworks. Two partly overlapping schools of thought dominate the debate. The first line of thinking is mainly associated with institutionalist and liberal lines of thought, concentrating on formal inter-state frameworks and/or official trade and investment flows, commonly with reference to the EC/EU as a comparative marker or model (Fourutan, 1993; Holden, 2001; Jenkins and Thomas, 2001). What distinguish the second, 'pan-African', school of thought are synoptic overviews of African regional organizations and political-economic relationships, which are then coupled with demands for the strengthening of pan-African regional organizations and the so-called regional economic communities (RECs) of the envisioned African Economic Community (AEC) (Asante, 1997; Muchie, 2003). It is noteworthy that the pan-African line of thought often takes the EC/EU experience as inspiration and as a justification for the development of pan-African regionalism. Indeed, despite their foundational differences, the two strands of thought make implicit or explicit comparisons with the EU, and also come to a similar conclusion that, notwithstanding the 'failure' of regionalism in Africa hitherto, there is still great potential to build successful regionalism in the future.

A third and smaller group of scholars is more sceptical about whether the restructured regional organizations will be able to attain their goals of highly developed institutional frameworks – nearly always modelled on the EC/EU – with attendant economic and political integration. The scepticism of this group has generated a radically different interpretation of regionalism in Africa, associated with various approaches centring on critical political economy and new regionalism (Bach, 1999; Bøås et al., 2005; Grant and Söderbaum, 2003; Hentz and Bøås, 2003; Söderbaum, 2004). These approaches transcend the narrow focus on inter-state regional frameworks, and obviate the artificial separation, in the African context, of state and non-state actors, that are associated with traditional regional approaches.

An important argument within this rather loose school of thought is the claim that many ruling regimes and political leaders in Africa engage in symbolic and discursive activities – praising the goals of regionalism and regional organizations, signing cooperation treaties and agreements, and taking part in 'summitry regionalism' – while remaining uncommitted to, or unwilling to implement, jointly agreed policies. Regionalism is thus used as a discursive and image-boosting exercise: leaders demonstrate support and loyalty towards one another in order to raise the status, image and formal sovereignty of their often-authoritarian regimes, both domestically and internationally (Bøås, 2003; Clapham, 1996).

This type of 'regime-boosting' regionalism may be a goal in itself, but it may also be closely related to 'shadow regionalization'; what Bach refers to as 'trans-state regionalization' (Bach, 1999, 2005). Shadow regionalization draws attention to the potential for public officials and various actors within the state to be entrenched in informal market activities in order to promote either their political goals or their private economic interests. This particular type of regionalization grows from below and is built upon rent seeking or the stimulation of patron-client relationships. Bach claims, for instance, that regional organizations constitute a means for 'resource capture' and international patronage (Bach, 2005). It implies regionalization without regional integration or formal regionalism.

Many of the shadow networks are closely tied to the complex wars on the African continent. Taking the example of the Great Lakes region, Taylor and Williams argue that for well-placed elites and business people the war in this region offers potentially substantial resources for those able to exploit them. Foreign involvement is not only about preserving national security and defeating enemies, but also about securing access to resource-rich areas and establishing privatized accumulation networks that can emerge and prosper under conditions of war and anarchy (Taylor and Williams, 2001: 273).

In summary, both the mainstream and pan-African line of thought tend to elevate European integration theory and practice. Although the critical and new regionalism approaches are often cast within a general discussion about regionalism, there is little cross-fertilization and deep comparisons between Africa and regions in other parts of the world, including European integration. This is unfortunate, since it is unlikely that the phenomena highlighted through this scholarship are uniquely 'African'. Any particularity appears to be related to the nature of the African state-society complex and Africa's insertion in the global order. This specialization tends to reflect the tendency in the other regional debates, namely that many scholars tend to use specific contextual language to describe rather similar phenomena instead of applying general concepts and developing questions and hypotheses that can be transferred to cross-regional comparisons.

CONCLUSION

This chapter has highlighted deep divisions regarding the problem of comparison within the study of regionalism and regional integration. Contestations regarding what to compare, how to compare and sometimes even why to compare at all, arise predominantly as a consequence of the tension in the field between regional specialization (that is, in the form of case study or area study) and

comparative research. The ongoing development of comparative regionalism rests therefore upon finding a more mutually reinforcing relationship between these standpoints. This section begins with some conclusions regarding the problematic role of European integration theory and practice for comparative regionalism, before outlining a general way of thinking about comparison which will be able to facilitate dialogue in this fragmented field of study.

The problem of European integration theory and practice in comparative regionalism

This chapter reveals the tension between regional specialization and comparative research in the study of regionalism and regional integration. At least empirically, most scholars specialize in a particular region, which they will often consider 'special' or 'unique'. Even if intra-regional and cross-regional comparisons may be undertaken, there remains a strong bias towards European integration theory and practice in the field; most other regionalisms are compared – implicitly or explicitly – against the backdrop of European theory and practice.

Two broad attitudes towards comparative analysis within the field of regionalism are distinguishable, which revolve around two competing attitudes towards European integration theory and practice. One strand of thinking tends to elevate European integration theory and practice through comparative research, while the other is considerably less convinced of the advantages of comparative research and Europe-centred theories. The first perspective – especially variants of realist/intergovernmental and liberal/institutional scholarship – strongly emphasizes Europe-centred generalizations. This type of research has been dominated by a concern to explain variations from the 'standard' European case. Indeed, other modes of regionalism are, where they appear, characterized as loose and informal (such as Asia) or 'failed' (such as Africa), reflecting 'a teleological prejudice informed by the assumption that 'progress' in regional organization is defined in terms of EU-style institutionalization' (Breslin et al., 2002: 11). One reason for this bias lies in the ways the underlying assumptions and understandings about the nature of regionalism (which most often stem from a *particular* reading of European integration) influence perceptions about how regionalism in other parts of the world does (and should) look. As the authoritative scholar, Andrew Hurrell (2005), asserts, 'the study of comparative regionalism has been hindered by so-called theories of regionalism which turn out to be little more than the translation of a particular set of European experiences into a more abstract theoretical language' (p. 39).

Avoiding Europe-centredness has been an ongoing issue in the study of regionalism among developing countries and for critical scholarship in the field of international relations. There are persuasive reasons for taking stock of cumulative research on regional integration in the developing world and for being cautious regarding EU-style institutionalization inherent in most classical or mainstream perspectives or policies. Indeed, there have been a number of innovative efforts to develop a regional approach specifically aimed at the developing world (Axline, 1994c; Bøås et al., 1999). However even these perspectives tend to mirror the Europe-centred view, thus celebrating the differences in theory and practice between regionalism in Europe and in the developing word. According to Warleigh and Rosamond (2006), this has even resulted in a caricature of European integration or of classical regional integration theory, giving rise to unnecessary fragmentation within the field.

The barrier for achieving a nuanced comparative analysis is not European integration experience or theory *per se*, but rather the dominance of certain constructions and models of European integration. Conversely, discussions about regionalism in Africa or Asia have often reduced the EC/EU to the community method or a common market, or a simple point of reference, or to a model/anti-model. Further, many comparisons and generalizations, which depart from the European context, are skewed through a lack of sensitivity to the issues around comparing regions with different levels of development and holding unequal positions in the current world order.

A more advanced debate about regionalism will not be reached through simply celebrating differences from European integration theory and practice, but rather in going beyond dominant interpretations of European integration, and drawing more broadly upon alternative theories (Diez and Wiener, 2003; Rosamond, 2000). To neglect Europe is to miss the opportunity to take advantage of the richness of the EU project and laboratory. As Warleigh and Rosamond (2006) argue, comparative regionalism 'cannot afford to lock itself away from the most advanced instance of regionalism in world politics' (p. 2). The challenge for comparative regionalism is to both include and transcend European integration theory and practice. But this requires enhanced communication between various specializations and theoretical standpoints.

The future of comparative regionalism

Some of the most informative studies in the field of regionalism are case studies or studies situated in debates within a particular region, such as Europe, East Asia, the Americas, or Africa. Detailed case studies of regionalism are certainly necessary; these identify historical and contextual specificities and allow for a detailed and 'intensive' analysis of a single case (according to mono-, multi- or interdisciplinary studies). The disadvantage of case studies is, however, that a single case is a weak base for creating new generalization or invalidating existing generalizations (Axline, 1994b: 15).[8]

Comparative analysis has sometimes been heavily criticized by area specialists, post-modernists and others, who emphasize cultural relativism and the importance of a deep multidisciplinary knowledge of various contexts and people. Given that the comparative method is ultimately based on the same logic as 'the experimental method', it is reasonable that it should be used with care in the social sciences. But comparative analysis helps guard against ethnocentric bias and culture-bound interpretations that can arise when a specialization is over-contextualized or the area of study is too isolated.

The next step in the study of regionalism is to develop its comparative element, which will be crucial for enhancing cross-fertilization between various theoretical standpoints and regional specializations. For;

> when conducted properly, the comparative approach is an excellent tool … In particular, it is a key mechanism for bringing area studies and disciplinary studies together, and enhancing both. It provides new ways of thinking about the case studies whilst at the same time allowing for the theories to be tested, adapted and advanced (Breslin and Higgott, 2000: 341).

While doing comparative research, it is crucial to move beyond the 'false universalism' inherent in a selective reading of regionalism in the core, and in the EU in particular. As Hurrell (2005: 39) asserts, rather than trying to understand other regions through the distorting mirror of Europe, it is better to think in general theoretical terms and in ways that draw both on traditional international relations theory, comparative politics and on other areas of social thought. This will only be possible if the case of Europe is integrated within a larger and more general discourse of comparative regionalism, built around general concepts and theories, but that remains culturally sensitive.

This calls for a middle ground to be established between context and case/area studies on the one hand, and 'hard' social science as reflected in the use of 'laborative' comparisons on the other. This middle ground has been referred to as the 'eclectic center' of comparative studies (World Politics, 1995; also see Africa Today, 1997; Axline, 1994c; Payne, 1998).

Such a middle ground can avoid the equal interlopers of exaggerated contextualization on the one hand, and over-generalized (or irrelevant) theory on the other. Achieving this perspective on the eclectic centre of comparative studies will be inclusive rather than exclusive – even if it will be too 'social sciency' for some and too much of 'storytelling' for others (World Politics, 1995). There need not be any opposition between area studies and disciplinary studies/international studies, or between particularizing and universalizing studies. The eclectic centre perspective should enable area studies, comparative politics and international studies to engage in a more fruitful dialogue, and through that process overcome the fragmentation in the field of regionalism and regional integration. Such a perspective should be able to bridge divisions between earlier ('old') and more contemporary ('new') theories and experiences of regionalism and regional integration. It should also enable cross-fertilization between different regional debates and specializations. Finally, an eclectic centre perspective will highlight the richness of comparative analysis, and enhance a dialogue about the fundamentals of comparative analysis (for example, what constitute comparable cases, and the many different forms, methods and designs of comparative analysis). This chapter will have achieved its aim if it has contributed to furthering such a dialogue.

ACKNOWLEDGEMENTS

A great deal of the author's work on regionalism during the last decade has been carried out in liaison with Björn Hettne, and his contribution to this chapter has been invaluable. The author is also grateful for the helpful comments on an earlier version, especially by Ian Taylor, and also by Daniel Bach, Shaun Breslin, Todd Landman, Philippe de Lombaerde, Nicola Phillips, Rodrigo Tavares, Luk van Langenhove, and Alex Warleigh-Lack. The research funding from the Swedish International Development Cooperation Agency (Sida) is gratefully acknowledged.

NOTES

1. Hurrell (1995: 39–45) makes a more nuanced distinction between five different categories of regionalism: (1) social and economic regionalization; (2) regional awareness and identity; (3) regional inter-state cooperation; (4) state-promoted regional integration; and (5) regional cohesion.

2. Parts of this section draw on Hettne and Söderbaum (2008). See also Hettne (2005).

3. According to Axline (1994b: 1–5) the evolution of regional cooperation since the 1950s can be divided into four (rather than two) generations of regional cooperation: (1) traditional free trade areas; (2) regional import substitution; (3) collective self-reliance; and (4) regional cooperation in the new world order (that is, the 'recent debate').

4. The recent debate has seen the proliferation of a large number of theories and approaches to regional integration and regionalism. For instance, Mansfield and Milner's (1997) *The Political Economy of Regionalism* highlights neorealist and neoliberal institutional theories, new trade theories and the new institutionalism. *Theories of New Regionalism* by Söderbaum and Shaw (2003) draws attention to variants of liberalism institutionalism, security complex theory, to a variety of constructivist, critical and 'new regionalism' approaches, such as the world order approach (WOA), new regionalism approach (NRA) and region-building approach. Laursen's *Comparative Regional Integration* (2003) emphasizes a variety of governmentalist, power, constructivist, neofunctionalist and historical institutionalist perspectives, whereas Wiener and Diez (2005) is a coherent exposé of the richness of *European Integration Theory*, highlighting: federalism, neo-neo-functionalism, liberal intergovernmentalism, multi level governance, policy networks, new institutionalisms, social constructivism, integration through law, discursive approaches and gender perspectives.

5. At least three distinctions can be made regarding the impact of EU integration on other cases of regionalism: (1) EU as the paradigm of regionalism; (2) EU as a model of regionalism; and (3) the empirical relationship between EU and various world regions (which includes the EU's ideational and financial support of other regional organizations). These distinctions are analytically separate but rather difficult to keep completely apart.

6. See Rosamond (2000: Chapter 7) for a detailed discussion about the relationship between EU studies and international studies. Also see Warleigh (2004; 2006).

7. Thanks to Nicola Phillips for this point.

8. According to Axline (1994b: 15–16), case studies must be cast within a comparative context in order to contribute to general propositions. Drawing on Lijphart's work, Axline clarifies that six types of case studies can give a cumulative contribution to knowledge: (1) atheoretical case studies; (2) interpretative case studies; (3) hypothesis-generating case studies; (4) theory-confirming case studies; (5) theory-infirming case studies; and (6) deviant case studies. Atheoretical case studies have little utility for generalization in themselves, but may indirectly lead to theory-generation. Interpretative case studies may or may not include a theoretical element, and may or may not contribute to generalizations applicable to a number of different cases. The other four types of case studies do contribute to the building of generalizable knowledge through their contribution to theory building.

REFERENCES

Acharya, A. (1997) 'Ideas, identity and institution-building: from the "ASEAN way" to the "Asia-Pacific way"?' *The Pacific Review*, 10 (3): 319–46.

Acharya, A. (2001) *Constructing a security community in Southeast Asia: ASEAN and the problem of regional order*. London: Routledge.

Acharya, A. (2002) 'Regionalism and the emerging world order: sovereignty, autonomy, identity', in S. Breslin, C. Hughes, N. Phillips, and B. Rosamond (eds), *New regionalisms in the global political economy*. London: Routledge, pp. 20–32.

Acharya, A. (2003) 'Democratisation and the prospects for participatory regionalism in Southeast Asia', *Third World Quarterly*, 24 (2): 375–90.

Acharya, A. (2006) 'Europe and Asia: reflections on a tale of two regionalisms', in B. Fort and D. Webber (eds), *Regional integration in Europe and East Asia: Convergence or divergence?* London and New York: Routledge, pp. 312–21.

Acharya, A. and Johnston, A. (eds) (2007) *Crafting cooperation. Regional international institutions in comparative perspective*. London: Oxford University Press.

Adler, E. and Barnett, M. (eds.) (1998) *Security communities*. Cambridge: Cambridge University Press.

Africa Today (1997) Special issue: The future of regional studies, 44 (2): April–June, pp.111–93.

Anderson, K. and Blackhurst, R. (eds) (1993) *Regional integration and the global trading system*. Harvester: Wheatsheaf.

Asante, S.K.B. (1997) *Regionalism and Africa's development. Expectations, reality and challenges*. Basingstoke: Macmillan.

Axline, W.A. (1994a) 'Cross-regional comparison and the theory of regional cooperation: Lessons from Latin America, the Caribbean, South East Asia and the South Pacific', in W.A. Axline (ed.), *The political economy of regional cooperation. Comparative case studies*. London: Pinter Publishers, pp.178–224.

Axline, W.A. (1994b) 'Comparative case studies of regional cooperation among developing countries', in W.A. Axline (ed.), *The Political Economy of Regional Cooperation. Comparative case studies*. London: Pinter Publishers, pp. 7–33.

Axline, W.A. (ed.) (1994c) *The political economy of regional cooperation. Comparative case studies*. London: Pinter Publishers.

Bach, D.C. (1999) *Regionalisation in Africa. Integration and disintegration*. London: James Currey.

Bach, D.C. (2005) 'The global politics of regionalism: Africa', in M. Farrell, B. Hettne and L. van Langenhove (eds), *Global politics of regionalism. Theory and practice*. London: Pluto Press, pp. 171–86.

Bhagwati, J. (1993) *The world trading system at risk*. Princeton: Princeton University Press.

Bøås, M. (2003) 'Weak states, strong regimes: Towards a "real" political economy of African regionalization', in J. Andrew and F. Söderbaum (eds), *The new regionalism in Africa*. Aldershot: Ashgate, pp. 31–46.

Bøås, M., Marchand, M.H., and Shaw, T.M. (eds) (1999) 'New regionalisms in the new millennium', special issue of *Third World Quarterly*, 20 (5, October), pp. 897–1070.

Bøås, M., Marchand, M.H., and Shaw, T.M. (2005) *The political economy of regions and regionalism*. Basingstoke: Palgrave Macmillan.

Breslin, S. and Higgott, R. (2000) 'Studying regions: Learning from the old, constructing the new', *New Political Economy*, 5 (3): 333–52.

Breslin, S., Higgott, R., and Rosamond, B. (2002) 'Regions in comparative perspective', in S. Breslin, C. Hughes, N. Philips, and B. Rosamond (eds), *New regionalisms in the global political economy*. London: Routledge, pp. 1–19.

Buzan, B. and Waever, O. (2003) *Regions and powers: The structure of international security*. Cambridge: Cambridge University Press.

Cable, V. and Henderson, D. (eds) (1994) *Trade blocs? The future of regional integration*. London: Royal Institute of International Affairs.

Caporaso J.A. and Keeler, J. (1995) 'The European Union and regional integration theory', in S. Mazey and C. Rhodes (eds) *The state of the European Union Volume 3: Building a European polity?* Boulder, CO: Lynne Rienner, pp. 20–40.

Cantori, L.J. and Spiegel, S.L. (1970) *The international politics of regions: A comparative framework*. Englewood Cliffs, NJ: Prentice Hall.

Choi, Y.J. and Caporaso, J.A. (2002) 'Comparative regional integration', in Carlsnaes, W., T. Risse and B. Simmons (eds), *Handbook of international relations*. London: Sage. pp. 480–99.

Christiansen, T., Jørgensen, K.E. and Wiener, A. (eds) (2001) *The social construction of Europe*. London: SAGE.

Christiansen, T. and Piattoni, S. (eds) (2004) *Informal governance in the European Union*. Cheltenham: Edward Elgar.

Clapham, C. (1996) *Africa and the international system. The politics of state survival*. Cambridge: Cambridge University Press.

Coleman, W.D. and Underhill, G.R.D. (eds) (1998) *Regionalism and global economic integration. Europe, Asia and the Americas*. London: Routledge.

Cooper, A., Hughes, C., and de Lombaerde, P. (eds) (2008) *Regionalisation and Global Governance. The Taming of Globalisation*. London: Routledge.

Dell, S.S. (1966) *A Latin American common market?* New York: Oxford University Press.

Diez, T. and Wiener, A. (eds) (2003) *Theories of European integration*. Oxford: Oxford University Press.

ECLAC (1994) *Open regionalism in Latin America and the Caribbean: Economic integration as a contribution to changing production patterns with social equity*. Santiago: ECLAC.

Etzioni, A. (1965) *Political unification: A comparative study of leaders and forces*. New York: Holt, Rinehart and Winston.

Farrell, M., Hettne, B., and van Langenhove, L. (eds) (2005) *The global politics of regionalism. Theory and practice*. London: Pluto Press.

Fawcett, L. (2005) 'Regionalism from a historical perspective', in M. Farrell, B. Hettne, and L. van Langenhove (eds), *Global politics of regionalism. Theory and practice*. London: Pluto Press, pp. 21–37.

Fawcett, L. and Hurrell, A. (eds) (1995) *Regionalism in world politics. Regional organization and international order*. Oxford: Oxford University Press.

Fort, B. and Webber, D. (eds) (2006) *Regional integration in Europe and East Asia: Convergence or divergence?* London and New York: Routledge.

Fourutan, F. (1993) 'Regional integration in Sub-Saharan Africa: Past experience and future prospects', in J. de Melo and A. Panagariya (eds), *New dimensions in regional integration*. Cambridge: Cambridge University Press, pp. 234–76.

Gamble, A. and Payne, A. (eds) (1996) *Regionalism and global order*. Basingstoke: Macmillan.

Grant, A.J. and Söderbaum, F. (eds) (2003) *The new regionalism in Africa*. Aldershot: Ashgate.

Grieco, J.M. (1997) 'Systemic sources of variation in regional institutionalization in Western Europe, East Asia and the Americas', in E.D. Mansfield and H.V. Milner (eds), *The political economy of regionalism*. New York: Colombia University Press, pp. 164–87.

Haas, E.B. (1958) *The uniting of Europe: Political, social and economic forces 1950–1957*. Stanford: Stanford University Press.

Haas, E.B. (1964) *Beyond the nation-state*. Stanford: Stanford University Press.

Haas, E.B. (1967) 'The uniting of Europe and the uniting of Latin America', *Journal of Common Market Studies*, 5 (4): 315–45.

Haas, E.B. (1975) *The obsolescence of regional integration theory* (Working paper) Institute of International Studies: Berkeley, CA.

Haas, E.B. and Schmitter, P. (1964) 'Economics and differential patterns of integration: Projections about unity in Latin America', *International Organization*, 18 (4): 259–99.

Hentz, J.J. and Bøås, M. (eds) (2003) *New and critical security and regionalism: Beyond the nation state*. Aldershot: Ashgate.

Hettne, B. (2002) 'The Europeanization of Europe: Endogenous and exogenous dimensions', *Journal of European Integration*, 24 (4): 325–40.

Hettne, B. (2003) 'The new regionalism revisited', in F. Söderbaum and T.M. Shaw (eds), *Theories of new regionalism: A Palgrave reader*. Basingstoke: Palgrave, pp. 22–42.

Hettne, B. (2005) 'Beyond the 'new' regionalism', *New Political Economy*, 10 (4): 543–72.

Hettne, B., Inotai, A., and Sunkel, O. (eds) (1999) *Globalism and the new regionalism*. Basingstoke: Macmillan.

Hettne, B. and Söderbaum, F. (2000) 'Theorising the rise of regionness', *New Political Economy*, 5 (3): 457–74.

Hettne, B. and Söderbaum, F. (2008) 'The future of regionalism: Old divides, new frontiers', in A. Cooper, C. Hughes, and P. de Lombaerde (eds), *Regionalization and the taming of globalization*. London: Routledge, pp. 61–79.

Higgott, R. (2002) *From trade-led to monetary-led regionalism: Why Asia in the 21st century will be different to Europe in the 20th century* (UNU/CRIS e-Working Papers 2002/1) Bruges: UNU/CRIS.

Higgott, R. (2006) 'The theory and practice of region: the changing global context', in B. Fort and D. Webber (eds), *Regional integration in Europe and East Asia: Convergence or divergence?* London and New York: Routledge, pp. 17–38.

Hix, S. (1994) 'The study of the European Community: The challenge to comparative politics', *West European Politics*, 17 (1): 1–30.

Hix, S. (1999) *The political system of the European Union*. Basingstoke: Macmillan.

Hoffman, S. (1966) 'Obstinate or obsolete? The fate of the nation state and the case of Western Europe', *Daedalus*, 95 (3): 862–915.

Holden, M. (2001) 'Is a free trade agreement the answer for Southern Africa? Insights from development economic theory', in P. Vale, L. Swatuk and B. Odén (eds), *Theory, change and Southern Africa's future*. Basingstoke: Palgrave, pp. 148–65.

Hooghe, L. and Marks, G. (2001) *Multi-level governance and European integration*. Lanham: Rowman and Littlefield.

Hurrell, A. (1995) 'Regionalism in theoretical perspective', in L. Fawcett and A. Hurrell (eds) *Regionalism in world politics. Regional organization and international order*. Oxford: Oxford University Press, pp. 37–73.

Hurrell, A. (2005) 'The regional dimension in international relations theory', in M. Farrell, B. Hettne and L. van Langenhove (eds), *The global politics of regionalism. Theory and practice*. London: Pluto Press, pp. 38–53.

Jenkins, C. and Thomas, L. (2001) 'African regionalism and the SADC', in M. Telò (ed.), *European Union and new regionalism. Regional actors and global governance in a post-hegemonic era*. Aldershot: Ashgate, pp. 153–75.

Jessop, R. (2003) 'The political economy of scale and the construction of cross-border regions', in F. Söderbaum and T.M. Shaw (eds), *Theories of new regionalism. A Palgrave reader*. Basingstoke: Palgrave, pp. 179–196.

Jönsson, C., Tägil, S., and Törnqvist, G. (2000) *Organizing European space*. London: Sage.

Katzenstein, P.J. (2000) 'Regionalism and Asia', *New Political Economy*, 5 (3): 353–68.

Katzenstein, P.J. (2002) 'Regionalism and Asia', in C. W. Hughes, N. Phillip, and B. Rosamond (eds), *New regionalism in the global political economy*. London: Routledge. pp. 104–18.

Laursen, F. (ed.) (2003) *Comparative regional integration. Theoretical perspectives*. Aldershot: Ashgate.

Malamud, A. (2003) 'Presedentialism and Mercosur: A hidden cause for a successful experience', in F. Laursen (ed.), *Comparative regional integration. theoretical perspectives*. Aldershot: Ashgate, pp. 53–74.

Mansfield, E.D. and Milner, H.V. (eds) (1997) *The political economy of regionalism*. New York: Colombia University Press.

Marchand, M.H. (2001) 'North American regionalisms and regionalization in the 1990s', in M. Schulz, F. Söderbaum and J. Öjendal (eds), *Regionalization in a globalizing world. A comparative perspective on actors, forms and processes*. London: Zed Books, pp. 198–210.

Mattli, W. (1999) *The logic of regional integration. Europe and beyond*. Cambridge: Cambridge University Press.

Milward, A.S. (1992) *The European rescue of the nation state*. London: Routledge.

Mitrany, D. (1966) *A working peace system*. Chicago: Quardrangle Books. (1st edition 1946).

Moravcsik, A. (1998) *The choice for Europe: social purpose and state power from Messina to Maastricht*. Ithaca: Cornell University Press.

Muchie, M. (ed.) (2003) *The making of the Africa-nation: Pan-Africanism and the African renaissance*. London: Adonis and Abbey.

Murithi, T. (2005) *The African Union. Pan-Africanism, peace-building and development*. Aldershot: Ashgate.

Nesudurai, H.E.S. (2005) 'The global politics of regionalism: Asia and the Asia Pacific', in M. Farrell, B. Hettne, and L. van Langenhove (eds), *The global politics of regionalism. Theory and practice*. London: Pluto Press, pp. 155–70.

Nye, J.S., Jr. (1970) 'Comparing common markets: A revised neo-functionalist model', *International Organization*, 24 (4): 796–835.

Nye, J. (1971) *Peace in parts: Integration and conflict in regional organization*. Boston: Little, Brown and Company.

Pastor, R.A. (2005) 'North America and the Americas', in M. Farrell, B. Hettne, and L. van Langenhove (eds), *The global politics of regionalism. Theory and practice*. London: Pluto Press, pp. 202–21.

Payne, A. (1998) 'The new political economy of area studies', *Millennium: Journal of International Studies*, 27 (2): 253–73.

Perkmann, M., and Sum, N.L. (eds) (2002) *Globalization, regionalization and the building of cross-border regions*. Basingstoke: Palgrave.

Phillips, N. (2005) 'The Americas', in A. Payne (ed.), *The new regional politics of development*. Basingstoke: Palgrave, pp. 29–58.

Pollack, M.A. (2003) *The engines of European integration. Delegation, agency, and agenda setting in the EU*. Oxford: Oxford University Press.

Prebisch, R. (1963) *Towards a dynamic development policy for Latin America*. United Nations.

Rosamond, B. (2000) *Theories of European integration*. Basingstoke: Palgrave Macmillan.

Rosamond, B. (2005) 'The uniting of Europe and the foundation of EU studies: Revisiting the neofunctionalism of Ernst B. Haas', *Journal of European Public Policy*, 12 (2): April, 237–54.

Rugman, A.M. (2005) *The regional multinationals: MNEs and 'global' strategic management*. Cambridge: Cambridge University Press.

Sandholtz, W. and Stone–Sweet, A. (1998) *European integration and supranational governance*. Oxford: Oxford University Press.

Schmitter, P.C. (1970) 'A revised theory of regional integration', *International Organization*, 24 (4): 836–68.

Schulz, M., Söderbaum, F., and Öjendal, J. (eds) (2001) *Regionalization in a globalizing world. A comparative perspective on actors, forms and processes*. London: Zed Books.

Söderbaum, F. (2004) *The political economy of regionalism. The case of Southern Africa*. Basingstoke: Palgrave Macmillan.

Söderbaum, F. (2005) 'Exploring the links between micro-regionalism and macro-regionalism', in M. Farrell, B. Hettne, and L. van Langenhove (eds), *Global politics of regionalism. Theory and practice*. London: Pluto Press, pp. 87–103.

Söderbaum, F. (2007) 'Regionalisation and civil society: The case of Southern Africa', *New Political Economy*, 12 (3) September: 319–37.

Söderbaum, F. and Shaw, T.M. (eds) (2003) *Theories of new regionalism. A Palgrave reader*. Basingstoke: Palgrave.

Taylor, I. (2005) *NEPAD. Toward Africa's development or another false start?* Boulder: Lynne Rienner.

Taylor, I. and Williams, P. (2001) 'South African foreign policy and the Great Lakes crisis: African renaissance meets vagabonde politique', *African Affairs*, 100 (399): 265–86.

Telo, M. (2007) *European Union and new regionalism. Regional actors and global governance in a post-hegemonic era* (2nd edition) Aldershot: Ashgate.

Vasconcelos, À. (2007) 'European Union and MERCOSUR', in M. Telo (ed.), *European Union and new regionalism. Regional actors and global governance in a post-hegemonic era* (2nd edition) Aldershot: Ashgate, pp. 165–184.

Warleigh, A. (2001) 'Europeanizing civil society: NGOs as agents of political socialisation', *Journal of Common Market Studies*, 39 (4): 619–39.

Warleigh, A. (2004) 'In defence of intra-disciplinarity: "European Studies", the "new regionalism" and the issue of democratisation', *Cambridge Review of International Affairs*, 17 (2): 301–18.

Warleigh, A. and Rosamond, B. (2006) *Comparative regional integration: Towards a research agenda*. Description of Workshop for the ECPR Joint Sessions, Nicosia, Cyprus, 25–30 April 2006.

Warleigh-Lack, A. (2006) 'Towards a conceptual framework for regionalisation: bridging "new regionalism" and "integration theory"', *Review of International Political Economy*, 13 (5): 750–71.

Wiener, A. and Diez, T. (2005) *European integration theory*. Oxford: Oxford University Press.

World Politics (1995) The role of theory in comparative politics. *A Symposium,* 48(1), October, pp. 1–49.

27

Transitional Justice

Paola Cesarini

INTRODUCTION

Over the last three decades, close to eighty countries have experienced democratization and, in turn, the related challenges of dealing with previous authoritarian rulers and their crimes. In the face of this growing universe of cases, 'transitional justice' has rapidly grown from a minor area of investigation into a massive inter-disciplinary field[1] of study, full of promising avenues for academic research and practical experimentation. At the same time, the discipline of transitional justice is still in its adolescence – that is, eager to grow up, yet insecure about its core identity. And while most scholars and activists in the field concur that unresolved problems of transitional justice have a lasting impact on new democracies (Teitel, 2000: 9) significant disagreement remains on key conceptual and theoretical issues.

Transitional justice and comparative politics often intersect. Thus, for example, most theories in the field touch on political variables and adopt the comparative method. The discipline of transitional justice, however, is affected by a deplorable paradox: Despite its clear political content, it is rarely frequented by political scientists on account of its complex interdisciplinary nature, allegedly 'normative' qualities, and the many obstacles involved in formulating 'covering laws' and carrying out empirical testing. In contrast, it is enthusiastically embraced by scholars from other disciplines who – while focusing on the legal, social, moral, cultural, or psychological dimensions of transitional justice – often 'leave it up to the reader' to sort out the key political issues involved, or explore them with quite different theoretical ambitions and methodological tools than mainstream political scientists. This paradox unfortunately translates in to a body of scholarship that, while rather interesting, also frequently displays conceptual ambiguity, scarce appreciation for existing political constraints, limited theoretical claims, and lack of systematic empirical testing.

The potential for political scientists' contribution to the field of transitional justice is therefore considerable on many different levels. First, political scientists can help formulate a sound definition of transitional justice that captures its essential features, differentiates 'transitional' from other forms of justice, and readily leads to operationalization and testing. Second, they can provide a healthy dose of political realism to complement current normative approaches to transitional justice. Third, leaving aside the perhaps unrealistic goal of formulating covering laws, political scientists can contribute useful analyses 'of smaller-scale causal mechanisms [of transitional justice] that recur in different combinations with different aggregate consequences in varying historical settings' (McAdam et al., 2001: 24). Fourth, political scientists can shed light on the optimal combination and sequence of transitional justice choices. Finally, political scientists (and especially comparativists) can rigorously test existing theories of transitional justice against the available empirical evidence from several national transitional justice experiences around the world. Alas, to do all this political scientists also need to venture outside the confines of their own discipline, contemplate using more eclectic epistemologies, and vigorously challenge their more 'traditional' colleagues' skepticism about the scientific potential of a transitional justice research agenda.

In keeping with the Sage Handbook tradition, this chapter provides a detailed discussion of the main conceptual and theoretical debates on transitional justice, with a special focus on contributions by political scientists. In particular, it addresses questions such as: What is transitional justice? What determines a post-authoritarian society's transitional justice choices? Why do different countries adopt different transitional justice choices? What is the impact of different transitional justice choices on the future of new democracies? And which new areas of transitional justice research show promise for adding to our knowledge about how countries can deal with their past during difficult social and political transformation?

DEFINING TRANSITIONAL JUSTICE

Transitional justice is a broad – if not 'overstretched' – concept. According to a popular definition, it refers to all 'the choices made and quality of justice rendered when new leaders replace authoritarian predecessors presumed responsible for criminal acts' (Siegel, 1998)

Other definitions conceptualize transitional justice even more extensively. Thus, for example, in 2006 the International Center for Transitional Justice characterized it as: 'a range of approaches that societies undertake to reckon with legacies of widespread or systematic human rights abuse as they move from a period of violent conflict or oppression toward peace, democracy, the rule of law, and respect for individual and collective rights'.

These and other such broad conceptualizations[2] have led scholars to argue about quite different issues under the same 'transitional justice' label. Most frequently, transitional justice is used as a synonym for the *criminal prosecution* of former authoritarian rulers (and their agents) for alleged mass atrocities (i.e., war crimes, politically motivated disappearances, murder, torture, ethnic cleansing, genocide, and rape, etc.) Following World War II, transitional justice includes *domestic* as well as *international* criminal prosecutions (e.g., the Nuremberg and Tokyo trials, the International Courts for the former Yugoslavia and Rwanda; the International Criminal Court; etc.); *hybrid national/international courts* (e.g., Sierra Leone and Cambodia); and national courts operating under the doctrine of *universal jurisdiction*[3] (e.g., Spain and Belgium).

In practice, however, transitional justice goes well beyond criminal prosecution. As the most recent democratization 'wave' in Latin America, Eastern Europe and Africa shows, it may also involve a wide range of *extra-judicial efforts* – such as: official historical investigations of the authoritarian record,[4] purges,[5] reparations,[6] and traditional and community-based mechanisms of conflict resolution.[7]

Finally, many scholars and practitioners point out that carrying out *democratic* and even *socio-economic reforms* often provides the best guarantee of preventing future instances of authoritarianism and large-scale atrocities. These authors thus extend the concept of transitional justice well beyond *backward looking* measures, to include *forward looking* institutional, social and economic engineering. Such a 'holistic approach'

(Boraine, 2006) to transitional justice presents, of course, both benefits and costs. Benefits amount to coverage of a wider range of phenomena and greater richness of detail, while costs include conceptual ambiguity which, in turn, may discourage scientifically minded social scientists from pursuing research in the field of transitional justice.

It is thus paramount for comparative analysis that any useful conceptualization of transitional justice should strive to do two things: capture its essential features and differentiate 'transitional' from other forms of justice. To encapsulate its fundamental characteristics, a good definition of transitional justice should situate it exclusively in countries experiencing *democratic transition* (Teitel, 2000: 6), so that it would be impossible to speak of it in the context of other kinds of regime change (e.g., from totalitarianism to authoritarianism) or no regime change.[8] Second, transitional justice should address mainly the *problematic legacies* of the past, so that it would be difficult to speak of it in the absence of trauma and abuse at both the individual and societal level. Third, to differentiate transitional justice from other kinds of justice, a good definition should concentrate on a post-authoritarian society's *own democratically formulated choices.* In this fashion, transitional justice would be confused neither with 'victors' justice',[9] nor with 'wild' or 'people's' justice.[10] Finally, a good definition of transitional justice should take note of the latter's *positive purpose,* which usually goes beyond the mere sanction of past injustices to include both the pacification and democratization of formerly authoritarian societies.

In light of the above, this chapter argues that transitional justice should be parsimoniously defined as: the legitimate choices that post-authoritarian societies make with respect to the legacies of previous repressive rule[11] to build a future of enduring peace and democracy. Such choices are exquisitely *political,* in the sense that they go well beyond the judicial sphere; trigger intense confrontation among competing actors (e.g., former rulers, democratizing agents, victims, etc.) and, in the end, produce both winners and losers. They are also deeply *ethical,* because transitional justice is expected to redraw a firm boundary between good and evil in societies that experienced violent conflict (including civil war) and massive human rights abuse – principally, but not exclusively, at the hands of the state.[12] Finally, transitional justice choices are *historic,* as they ultimately determine whether or not a severely divided society embarks on a path toward pacification and, eventually, political reconciliation.

SUB-TYPES OF TRANSITIONAL JUSTICE

To make the concept more manageable, scholars have attempted to formulate various typologies of transitional justice. At a general level, the literature offers several *dichotomous classifications* of transitional justice choices. According to these, transitional justice can be *retributive* or *restorative* – with the former seeking the punishment of perpetrators of atrocities, and the latter the political, moral, and material rehabilitation of victims. It can be *retrospective* or *prospective* – with the former concentrating on past misdeeds, and the latter on future objectives. It can be *exclusive* or *inclusive* – with the former being led by a restricted and insulated circle of decision-makers, and the latter being carried out in close collaboration with victims and broad sectors of civil society. It can be *narrow* or *extensive* – with the former targeting only top-level crimes and/or perpetrators, and the latter seeking to go after everyone involved in carrying out atrocities. It can be *endogenous* or *exogenous* – with the former initiated by domestic actors, and the latter by external entities. It can be *top-down* or *bottom-up* – with the former instigated by political elites, and the latter by civil society. It can be *immediate* and *delayed* – with the former taking place right after regime change, and the latter many years (even decades) after democratization. It can be *bounded* or *open-ended* – with the former taking place within clearly defined temporal boundaries and the latter lasting over the course of several generations. It can be *confidential* or *public* – with the former taking place behind closed doors and the latter in open view (and with broad dissemination of outcomes.) Finally, transitional justice can focus either on *individuals* (perpetrators and victims) or *collectives* (groups of perpetrators and victims, and society as a whole).

While some of the classifications just mentioned are quite useful, others offer false dilemmas. In effect, 'transitional justice mechanisms are not a dichotomous choice but a continuum of options, and those countries that choose one option are more likely to choose others as well' (Sikkink and Walling, 2007: 442). In both Latin America and Europe, for example, transitional justice processes have often been (and still are) multilayered affairs, crafted so as to be simultaneously retributive and restorative, retrospective and prospective, confidential and public, etc.

Luckily, other more detailed classifications are also available. The one presented in Table 27.1 divides transitional justice into six different sub-types distinguished according to the different objectives and methods involved.

'Criminal' transitional justice

Criminal transitional justice refers to the prosecution by an official judiciary body (be it domestic, international or hybrid) of the previous authoritarian regime's individual leaders and agents allegedly responsible for human rights abuse. It is largely retrospective and generally focuses on crimes committed by single individuals. Its main purpose is retribution – that is, the punishment of individual perpetrators.

Criminal transitional justice continues to attract the greatest attention of scholars and activists, since public trials of former dictators often provide spectacular occasion of

Table 27.1   Sub-types of transitional justice

Sub-type	Objectives	Methods
Criminal	Retribution	Trials (domestic, international, hybrid, etc.)
Historical	Truth	Official bodies of inquiry with public disclosure of findings
Reparatory	Rehabilitation and reintegration of victims	Restitution, compensation, apology, and memorialization
Administrative	Marginalization of authoritarian elites and collaborators	Purges, lustration and vetting
Institutional	Democratization	Institutional reform, civil and political rights
Redistributive	Socio-economic justice	Socio-economic rights, redistribution, affirmative action

Source: With the exception of 'redistributive transitional justice', these categories are adapted from Teitel (2000).

collective 'rebirth' that – perhaps more than any other instance of transitional justice – effectively build 'a permanent, unmistakable wall between the new beginnings and the old tyranny' (Kirchheimer, 1961: 308). Criminal transitional justice, however, is also highly controversial. Supporters and opponents routinely confront each other over the appropriateness of criminal prosecution of former undemocratic rulers and their agents. What is more, even advocates of transitional justice often disagree on whether punishment should be more important than truth (or vice-versa), and on whether criminal transitional justice should be a purely domestic or an international affair.

In practice, however, criminal transitional justice choices are not always clear-cut. As Teitel points out, countries' experiences with criminal transitional justice often result in the so-called *'limited criminal sanction'* – that is, in 'prosecution processes [carried out by official judiciary bodies] that do not necessarily culminate in full punishment'

(Teitel, 2000: 47).[13] Furthermore, external intervention in national criminal transitional justice processes currently consists, not only of the establishment of international criminal courts *à la* Nuremberg, but also of hybrid national/international courts and/or financial and technical assistance to domestic prosecution efforts.

Supporters point to several positive features of criminal transitional justice. First, it supplies the most effective deterrent of mass atrocities,[14] because transitional criminal justice not only prevents established or would-be perpetrators from returning to positions of authority, but it also credibly threatens them with serious personal consequences in case they attempt to do so. Second, trials of former dictators often constitute victims' most pressing transitional justice demand. Thus, democratizing societies seeking to attend to victims' needs promote trials of former dictators and their agents as a way to restore dignity and respect to those who suffered at the hands of the former regime (Rothenberg, 2002). Third, criminal transitional justice often fulfills a state's international obligation under customary international law and international treaty – especially in case of mass atrocities (Orentlicher, 1991). In other words, through criminal transitional justice, democratizing societies effectively signal their adoption of universally recognized standards of human rights (Finnemore and Sikkink, 1998). Fourth, through 'secular rites of commemoration' (Osiel, 1997, 2000: 6), criminal transitional justice promotes the kind of behavioral change that is most conducive to democratic stability over time, and re-crafts post-authoritarian societies' political identity in a more democratic fashion (Sarat and Kearns, 1999: 2). Fifth, criminal transitional justice prevents impunity and, in so doing, promotes reconciliation. In contrast, 'allowing for impunity for those responsible [of mass atrocities ...] is not a good strategy of reconciliation because it rests upon an uncertain foundation. It is like a house built on shifting sand. Sooner or later, it will collapse because the [past] will return' (Rothenberg, 2002) to reignite conflict among old enemies.

Finally, criminal transitional justice highlights individual rather than collective blame. This, in turn, deters 'people's' justice; prevents destructive cycles of collective reprisals, and even eases the social divisions that led to mass atrocities in the first place (Boraine, 2006: 19; Teitel, 2000: 28–30).

Supporters of criminal transitional justice often debate the following question: should perpetrators be brought before the domestic courts of the nation where the atrocities were committed, or should they be prosecuted through international criminal justice? Those who privilege domestic criminal justice[15] point to several benefits that derive from holding public trials of perpetrators in and by the same country where the mass atrocities took place. First, domestic trials provide both a formal mechanism to confront past atrocities, and a means to rebuild a secure, just, and liberal new order (see Rothenberg, 2002; Teitel, 2000). In short, they help establish a new government's democratic credentials. Second, domestic trials advance the rule of law, since the latter requires that civilized societies carry out, 'within defined but principled limits, prosecution of especially atrocious crimes [... to unequivocally reaffirm] the authority of law itself' (Orentlicher, 1991). Third, domestic trials powerfully underscore a new democracy's break with the past. They constitute 'foundational and forward-looking affirmation that no group, including public officials and the armed forces, is above the law and that the new democracy will not tolerate such behavior' (Brody, 2001). Moreover, they provide 'a ritual of liberalizing states. [...] Through known, fixed processes, a line is drawn, liberating a past that allows the society to move forward' (Teitel, 2000: 67). Fourth, domestic trials ensure that control over transitional justice remains at home. Conversely, when trials take place abroad, ownership of the transitional justice process is effectively in the hands of foreign actors whose interests may diverge from those of the affected society. Finally, only domestic trials can effectively fulfill the 'national' pedagogical purpose exemplified by the motto 'never again'.

Supporters of international criminal justice counter with the following arguments. First, they point out how international criminal justice is relatively immune from domestic political pressure. Both international conventions and customary international law, in fact, effectively 'remove certain atrocious crimes from the provincial realm of a country's internal politics, and thereby place those crimes squarely within the scope of universal concern and the conscience of all civilized people' (Orentlicher, 1991).[16] Second, domestic legal systems in democratizing contexts are often either unwilling or unable to prosecute perpetrators of mass atrocities. When this is the case, international criminal justice can (and must) step in – with or without the agreement of the country in question. Third, international criminal justice is likely to offer wider guarantees of impartiality, equal protection under the law and due process for the accused than domestic courts in post-authoritarian contexts. Finally, international proceedings may bolster domestic criminal transitional justice efforts, by effectively urging national courts in post-authoritarian societies to take on litigation of previously barred cases (as it recently happened in Chile, Argentina, and Chad; see Dicker and Keppler, 2004).

Opponents of criminal transitional justice rely on several realist-type arguments. First and foremost, they argue that a transitional pact negating justice for the victims of past mass atrocities is often the necessary precursor of the political order required for successful democratization (see Snyder and Vinjamuri, 2003). In effect, to induce tyrants to relinquish power without making their people suffer further, new democratic governments have often been willing to negotiate a bargain with the 'devil'. These type of bargains usually provide former rulers with concrete guarantees ranging from impunity for past crimes (e.g., Spain), to continuing influence over the political, military and international affairs of the nation (e.g., Chile.) Second, opponents of criminal transitional justice often point out that institutional reform[17] often 'contributes

far more toward democratic transition than the punishment of prior leaders and their followers' (Siegel, 1998). Third, individual trials are 'ill suited to communal conflicts characterized by the targeting and terrorizing of civilian populations, neighbor attacking neighbor, and the breakdown of societal structures' (Gready, 2005: 6; see also Fletcher and Weinstein, 2002). Fourth, trials may rule out alternative measures of transitional justice and, in turn, reduce a country's flexibility in addressing the complexity of its post-authoritarian predicament. Thus, for example, when emerging democracies employ criminal trials as the principal tool to establish a historical record of the undemocratic experience, they risk sacrificing individual rights on the altar of society's need for an official interpretation of the past that may foster political stability. In short, 'trials run the risk of being perceived as political justice' (Teitel, 2000: 76) rather than as an honest search for the truth. Fifth, criminal transitional justice does not eliminate the problem of shared guilt. Thus, when both opposition groups and governmental forces committed mass atrocities (and many ordinary people served as indirect accomplices) 'a general amnesty for all provides a far stronger base for democracy than efforts to prosecute one side or the other' (Huntington, 1991: 214). Sixth, atrocities committed by a former authoritarian regime were often perfectly legal at the time they were perpetrated. Criminal trials, therefore, are often carried out on the questionable basis of *ex-post facto* law, which negates the very same principle of *nullo crime sine lege* (there's no crime without a previously established law) that a new democratic regime is supposed to uphold. Finally, since it is virtually impossible to indict all perpetrators of mass atrocities, criminal transitional justice is often reduced to selective prosecution of emblematic cases which often constitutes injustice (Brody, 2001) and – what is worse – undermines a new democracy's rule of law.

When international prosecution of perpetrators of mass atrocities is at stake, opponents rely on at least four additional arguments. First, by keeping the specter of prosecution alive (including for those alleged perpetrators who were granted amnesty at the national level) – international criminal justice unduly interferes with the legitimate political choice by democratically elected governments to forgive perpetrators of mass atrocities, rather than prosecute them (see Kissinger, 2001; Nino, 1991). It does so by effectively placing national politicians (including democratically elected ones) under the supervision of unelected foreign judges (Kissinger, 2001). Second, international prosecution undermines national extra-judicial reconciliation efforts carried out by a newly democratic society to deal with its questionable past (Kissinger, 2001). Third, where international tribunals have been created (e.g., former Yugoslavia or Rwanda,) they have proven highly ineffective in deterring subsequent human rights abuses (Snyder and Vinjamuri, 2003). Finally, international criminal justice predominantly reflect western values, with little or no concern for indigenous methods of conflict resolution.[18]

'Historical' transitional justice

In general, historical transitional justice refers to the efforts by a new democracy to officially pursue and publicize the truth about the former authoritarian/totalitarian regime, often after long periods of state-sponsored denial or amnesia. Historical transitional justice is restorative, in the sense that it seeks to establish the truth about the former regime, rather than the punishment of perpetrators. By focusing on the past, historical transitional justice is also largely retrospective. In contrast to trials, it represents a *non-adversarial process* that links 'historical judgment with a potential consensus [...] predicated on the truth's dissemination and acceptance in the public sphere' (Teitel, 2000: 81–83, emphasis added). Furthermore, it is designed to go beyond the objective or factual truth typical of trials, by pursuing not only the *personal truth* of victims, but also a *social truth* that may later provide the basis for a shared national collective memory. Finally, historical transitional justice is achieved through dialogue, transparency, and the participation of all interested

parties, rather than through courtroom confrontation. Its main goal is not to declare a winner, but to heal old wounds and prevent past patterns of conflict and atrocities from recurring in the future (Boraine, 2006: 20–21).

When it involves a government-sponsored official public body of inquiry – for example, a *'truth commission'* – historical transitional justice presents a few similarities with criminal trials. Like trials, in fact, truth commissions focus on past wrongdoings, and provide highly symbolic public rituals of political transformation. Unlike trials, however, truth commissions lack many of the powers associated with tribunals; include non-judiciary membership; investigate 'a pattern of abuses over a period of time (rather than a specific event)' (Hayner, 2002: 14); explore institutional or group responsibility (rather than just individual ones); refrain from meting out punishment; make a point of addressing victims' specific needs through public testimony; construct pedagogical narratives designed to promote democratization and national reconciliation; and are often empowered to recommend – not only amnesty for perpetrators – but also much needed reparations and/or memorialization for individual victims, as well as institutional and cultural reforms for the whole of society.

While trials and truth commissions are often portrayed in the literature as alternative to each other, they need not be. Indeed, criminal transitional justice and historical transitional justice mechanisms often operate simultaneously in the same country, in a fashion that is both complementary and cooperative. See, for example, the cases of Argentina (where the work of the CONADEP[19] was later used as a basis for criminal prosecution of military leaders) or South Africa (where the judiciary was mandated to prosecute individuals who refused to appear before the Truth and Reconciliation Commission.)

Supporters point to at least five advantages of historical transitional justice. First, historical transitional justice often constitutes the most effective means to uncover the truth about a country's difficult past. Thus, while 'the purpose of criminal trials is [...] to find out whether the criminal standard of proof has been satisfied on specific charges' (Hayner, 2002: 100–1), a truth commission's main task is instead to expose the factual truth. Moreover, historical transitional justice often provides the sole available tool to pursue the truth about the past, especially in countries where the democratic transition is the result of a 'pact' between authoritarian rulers and democratizing agents; the judiciary is compromised or in shambles; and the perpetrators are too many (Hayner, 2002: 12). Thus, where transitional criminal 'justice is not possible due to *force majeure* or other considerations, then the second best process is that of maximum discovery and dissemination of truth which gives authoritative testimony to crimes and violations of rights' (Siegel, 1998). Second, while trials generally aim to establish individual responsibility, historical transitional justice seeks to uncover systematic patterns of abuse, as well as clarify the role of state institutions – for example, the military, the police, the judiciary, and so forth – in committing or covering up mass atrocities. Historical transitional justice 'thus emerges as the leading mechanism to cope with the evil of the modern repressive state' (Teitel, 2000: 78). Third, unlike trials, historical transitional justice mechanisms (such as truth commissions) may be charged with broader and forward-looking tasks, such as: the elaboration of an official national narrative of the past; commemoration of and reparations to victims; recommendations for institutional and cultural reform, and 'non-judicial sanctions against named [perpetrators,] such as banning them from public positions of authority' (Hayner, 2002: 132). Fourth, especially in post-civil war situations, historical transitional justice is well suited to investigate all sides' atrocities simultaneously and – in so doing – promote a culture of evenhandedness that may, in the end, 'create the moral climate in which reconciliation and peace will flourish.'[20] Finally, historical transitional justice fundamentally promotes official acknowledgement of a country's difficult past through testimony by the heretofore oppressed (i.e., the former regime's surviving victims, and the families

of the deceased). In short, 'the report of a truth commission reclaims a country's history and opens it for public review' (Hayner, 2002: 25).

Opposition against historical transitional justice comes from several sources, including: champions of institutionalized amnesia; mental health experts; post-modernist scholars; victims and human rights activists. Supporters of institutionalized amnesia argue that 'forgetting' is also a legitimate – if not necessary – transitional justice choice. In effect, in many post-authoritarian countries[21] 'where collective political catastrophes have taken place, the institutional response has been to forget and to neutralize what happened' (Marques et al., 1997: 254–55). Moreover, amnesia may sometimes be necessary because as Nietzsche instructs us:

> it is altogether impossible to live at all without forgetting. [...] There is a degree of sleeplessness, of rumination, of the historical sense, which is harmful and ultimately fatal to the living thing, whether this [...] be a man or a people or a culture (Nietzsche, 1997: 62).

Mental health experts, on their part, caution that public testimony about their ordeal might re-traumatize victims of abuse, especially when the latter already suffer from post-traumatic stress disorder. 'When victims are asked to relate the details of their heart-wrenching story in one sitting, and are then given no follow-up support, the emotional and psychological impact can be great' (Hayner, 2002: 141). Post-modernist scholars claim that historical transitional justice's objective of uncovering the 'truth' is hopeless – when not misguided. This is because an 'official' truth is also inevitably a partial one. From this point of view, then, 'transitions are vivid instances of conscious historical production [...] in a heightened political context and driven by political purposes' (Teitel, 2000: 70) where not all voices are necessarily heard. Furthermore, certain key aspects of the truth – such as international complicity in *coups d'état* or in the state's persecution of political opponents – cannot be realistically unveiled by purely domestic historical transitional justice. In a similar vein, victims often criticize historical transitional justice's 'hidden' goal of 'reconciliation' as both misguided and immoral. In particular, they claim that historical transitional justice mechanisms that offer forgiveness to perpetrators without their explicit consent only deliver 'reconciliation without justice' (see Mamdani, 1996). On their part, legal scholars warn that (especially when they name perpetrators) truth commissions – to all intents and purposes – convict suspects without due process (José Maria Zalaquett, quoted in Heyner, 2002: 127–29). In other words, they illegitimately perform as judicial bodies, assigning guilt and distributing punishment without, however, giving alleged perpetrators a fair chance to defend themselves. Finally, human rights activists often criticize historical transitional justice as a stratagem to avoid trials for alleged perpetrators of mass atrocities. In this view, a government-sponsored truth commission search for 'truth' and 'reconciliation' only disguises a politically expedient amnesty.

'Reparatory' transitional justice

Reparatory transitional justice deals with the *moral* and *material rehabilitation* of specific individuals (or groups) singled out for persecution by the former authoritarian regime (see Elster, 1998). It is, therefore, *victim-centered* – in the sense that its main purpose is not the punishment of perpetrators, but the restoration of citizenship and dignity to the casualties of the dictatorship, so that they (and their families) may be fully reintegrated into the new political order. Reparatory transitional justice is retrospective, as it largely focuses on redressing past wrongs. It also generally involves accurately targeted acts of symbolic as well as material restitution, compensation and apology. *Restitution* 'strictly refers to the return of the specific actual belongings that were confiscated, seized, or stolen, such as [real estate], land, art, remains, and the like' (Barkan, 2002: xix). *Compensation* 'refers to

some form of material or symbolic recompense for that which cannot be returned, such as human life, culture, and identity' (Barkan, 2002). And *apology* refers 'to an admission of wrongdoing; a recognition of its effects; and – in some cases – an acceptance of responsibility for those effects and an obligation to its victims' (Barkan, 2002). Reparatory transitional justice also often entails *official public acts of rehabilitation and/or commemoration* of individual victims that greatly contribute to shaping the new political identity of the incoming democratic regime. Concrete examples of reparatory transitional justice thus range from financial payment, to the creation of memorials for those persecuted by the previous undemocratic regime; from reintegration of stolen property, to public and official admission of government wrongdoing; from the establishment of public holidays in honor of the dead, to a thorough revision of the contemporary history curriculum taught in public schools; and so forth.

The policy debate on reparatory transitional justice centers on the following issues: the identity and size of its target population (small number of individuals vs. entire victim groups); the forms of reparation (symbolic vs. material); and their magnitude (how much and for how long?) Thus, for example, while some countries have awarded substantial financial reparation to a restricted group of individual victims (e.g., Chile), others have opted for smaller monetary payments to a larger population (e.g., Argentina). And in at least one instance (e.g., Germany) a considerable sum was disbursed to a broad-based group of victims (of the Holocaust) Moreover, whereas some countries have opted for substantial financial compensation (Argentina), others (South Africa) have chosen more symbolic reparations on account of the large number of victims involved. Finally, while some countries have granted monetary payments exclusively to abuse victims, others have awarded a wide range of reparations (such as life-long pensions or even substantial welfare and educational benefits) not only to victims, but also to their descendants.

According to supporters, there are at least four reasons why reparatory transitional justice serves the public interest during democratic transition. First, it provides concrete evidence of a state's acknowledgement of responsibility for its past wrongdoing (Teitel, 2000: 127), which is often one of victims' most pressing demands of the new democratic government. Second, reparatory transitional justice has a direct and immediate impact on victims' lives, by providing 'a most tangible manifestation of the state's effort to remedy the harms they (or their loved ones) have suffered' (Boraine, 2006: 24). Moreover, reparatory transitional justice helps victims regain the reputation and resources needed to regain active citizenship in the new democracy. Third, reparatory transitional justice corrects the former regime's 'derogation from equal protection under the law' (Teitel, 2000: 126). In so doing, it also helps restore the collective faith in the rule of law that the dictatorship had previously shattered. Finally – especially when it takes the form of solemn public rituals, holidays, monuments, or memorials – reparatory transitional justice reshapes the national identity in a more democratic fashion. In this sense, it is an important component of the tool kit known as 'symbolic politics', whose importance in democratizing contexts is well established in the social science literature.

Reparatory transitional justice is likely to face opposition when it appears to be tied to *impunity* for perpetrators of mass atrocities and/or fails to be accompanied by any form of truth-telling. In other words, restitution, compensation, apologies, and memorialization are generally rejected by victims whenever such measures are perceived as a governmental payoff in exchange for their acquiescence to amnesty or national amnesia. Finally, reparatory transitional justice's targeted and one-off features raise eyebrows among those seeking broader and long-lasting socio-economic reforms of post-authoritarian societies.

'Administrative' transitional justice

Administrative transitional justice attempts to 'redefine the parameters of political membership, participation, and leadership that constitute the political community' in democratizing societies (Teitel, 2000: 8). In practice, it seeks to marginalize former ruling elites, so that they cannot exercise any influence over the new democracy in the future. It also seeks to penalize those employed in the public (and sometimes also in the private) sector who collaborated or compromised with the former undemocratic regime. Finally, administrative transitional justice seeks to reintegrate/rehabilitate those who had been 'purged' by the dictatorship on political grounds. Historically, administrative transitional justice has taken on different names. Post-World War II France and Italy carried out *'epuration'* and *'purghe'*, respectively, while post-communist Eastern European countries chose 'lustration' or 'vetting'. Purges refer first and foremost to the removal of all people associated with the earlier undemocratic regime from positions in government, politics, education, media, culture, business, and other sensitive professional sectors. *Lustration* (or *vetting*) refers instead to 'the procedures for screening persons seeking selected public positions for their involvement with the [previous undemocratic] regime' (Letki, 2002: 530–31), 'and/or for their 'integrity – including adherence to relevant human rights standards' (International Center for Transitional Justice, 2008).

Administrative transitional justice is strongly demanded by both victims and opponents of the previous dictatorship, as well as by dedicated supporters of democratic reform. 'Particularly in the security and justice sectors, [administrative transitional justice] is widely recognized as helpful in reestablishing civic trust and re-legitimizing abusive public institutions, disabling structures within which individuals carried out serious abuses, and removing obstacles to transitional reform' (International Center for Transitional Justice, 2008). Supporters point to several benefits of administrative transitional justice. First, it effectively restores public confidence in government institutions after a period of state-sponsored abuses. 'The public may reasonably be skeptical when told they will now be treated differently, if these institutions simply retain all their existing personnel. These, after all, are the same people who kept the engine of the repressive state operating' (Kritz, 1995). Second, renewing personnel in the public administration and other visible sectors of the state, business, media, and cultural establishments is one of the most effective tools to communicate to the public at large that a break with the past has finally occurred. Third, administrative transitional justice contributes to ease the democratic transition. This is because loyal employees from the previous undemocratic regime will be – at best – less than enthusiastic supporters of democratic reform and – at worse – active saboteurs of the new regime. Hence, their removal can only speed up democratic reform. Finally, it makes sense for the new democratic government to distribute key jobs in the public service, not only to those who supported the opposition struggle, but also to individuals who demonstrate a solid record of competence and professionalism.

Administrative transitional justice has many critics. First and foremost it is vehemently rejected by members and collaborators of the previous undemocratic regime – for obvious reasons. However, it is also frequently opposed by those who passively acquiesced to its policies and actions, especially when the dictatorship was widely popular and lasted for many years (as in the case of post-World War II Italy and Germany). Administrative transitional justice is criticized by scholars and practitioners on several additional grounds. First, excessively broad sweeps of administrative transitional justice often end up alienating the general population from the new democratic regime – especially when the previous undemocratic government involved a substantial proportion of citizens only guilty of minor wrongdoing (such as membership in the previously dominant political party.) Second, administrative transitional justice jeopardizes the smooth functioning of the state, especially during the pivotal transition period. This is not only because the targets of *epuration* often possess critical expertise to run the government, but also because some of them (e.g., judges) are hardly replaceable in the short run. Third, legal experts underscore that administrative transitional justice often consists of 'the imposition of punitive measures without full judicial process' (Teitel, 2000: 159). When this is the case, administrative transitional justice sends the wrong message – that is, that the new democracy will not shy away from undemocratic measures in order to settle accounts with the previous regime. Finally, administrative transitional justice can be – and in practice often is – abused for political motives (Kritz, 1995) – for example, to reward supporters or clients, eliminate unwanted competition for public office, or push through a particular set of policies that would not otherwise be implemented. When this is the case, the new democracy's practices will suspiciously resemble those of the previous undemocratic regime.

'Institutional' transitional justice

Institutional transitional justice endeavors to re-establish peace and order through behavioral change. More specifically, it creates institutions and procedures to 'engender a pattern of behavior which [...] ultimately reshapes political culture and common conceptions of justice, as actors bring their beliefs into harmony with their actions' (Sa'adah, 1998: 3). In practice, institutional transitional justice promotes democratic reform in key areas such as: the rule of law; separation of powers; checks and balances;

legal codes; access to the legal profession and the police; civil and political rights; and so forth. In contrast to other sub-types, institutional transitional justice is largely prospective,[22] and more concerned with the good of society as a whole, than with the fate of individual perpetrators and victims.

Supporters list the following benefits of institutional transitional justice. First, it is one of the most *effective* means to achieve regime change, because – since democracy is largely a matter of incentives – when 'domestic factors durably cripple the reproductive capacities of a fallen dictatorship and replace the dictatorship's institutions with democratic ones, then the dictatorship is finished' (Sa'adah, 1998: 280). Second, institutional transitional justice is *necessary*, because 'to achieve a just society, more than punishment is required. [...] Equally important is the need to begin transforming institutions: institutional structures must not impede the commitment to consolidating democracy and establishing a culture of human rights' (Boraine, 2006: 20). Third, institutional transitional justice is less contentious than other kinds of transitional justice, because it does not target any specific group or individual and is often perceived as part of the 'package deal' of democratization. Fourth, because it focuses on feasible short run objectives, institutional transitional justice is likely to register immediate results and, in turn, increase popular support for the new democratic regime.

Detractors point out several shortcomings of institutional transitional justice. First, it fails to affect victims' lives in any direct fashion, as it is only concerned with what is good for society as a whole. Second, it neglects to persuade new democracies to learn from their difficult past. Indeed, because it is largely forward-looking, institutional transitional justice spares former authoritarian societies the necessary introspection that may lead them to acknowledge past mistakes. Finally, to most human rights activists, institutional transitional justice is no justice at all, but rather a cunning attempt on the part of new pragmatic 'democratic' leaders to

contraband a set of institutional reforms they would have to adopt anyway as justice for the victims of earlier state repression.

Scholars concur that, 'from a transitional perspective, what is considered constitutionally just is contextual and contingent, relating to the attempt to transform legacies of past injustice' (Teitel, 2000: 196). In other words, 'constitutionalism' is often regarded as part and parcel of transitional justice because post-authoritarian reforms are also often motivated by a society's desire to redress the abuses of the previous regime. Others, however, reject this overlap between transitional justice and institutional reform as an unnecessary conceptual muddle, underscoring that – in the context of democratization – the notion of institutional transitional justice is often a clever spin to conceal a deliberate (albeit perfectly legitimate) political choice: that of foregoing transitional justice altogether.

Undoubtedly, the relationship between transitional justice and institutional reform is difficult to disentangle. On the one hand, transitional justice frequently requires key institutional changes to be implemented. What is more, in cases where former authoritarian elites maintain significant power, democratization must precede transitional justice. Few, in fact, would dispute that the trial of a former dictator serves transitional justice's purpose better if carried out by reformed courts and judicial procedures, rather than by the same judiciary institutions or personnel that actively collaborated with the previous authoritarian regime; or that a truth commission carries greater legitimacy if established by a democratically elected executive or legislative, rather than by the arbitrary fiat of an interim unelected administration or an external occupation force; or that financial or symbolic reparations to individual victims of the former regime acquire greater significance if inherited authoritarian patterns of systematic social and economic discrimination are also simultaneously eliminated. On the other hand, forward-looking institutional engineering stands to acquire greater popular legitimacy when complemented by sincere efforts to confront a traumatic authoritarian past. When all is said and done, then, it may be a good idea to keep transitional justice and constitutionalism conceptually separate while, at the same time, paying close attention to their close – and often necessary – connections.

'Redistributive' transitional justice

Redistributive transitional justice aims to 'redress not only the direct abuses perpetrated in conflict, but also their social and economic [...] consequences and ramifications' (Mani, 2005: 523), so as to grant fairness and equal opportunity to the broader array of victims of the dictatorship. To realize this goal, redistributive transitional justice systematically addresses the socio-economic exploitation carried out by the former authoritarian regime. In so doing, it goes beyond an exclusive focus on victims and perpetrators of political violence to include a broader range of actors – such as those who suffered from past socio-economic discrimination, as well as those who benefited from it. Redistributive transitional justice differs from the reparatory sub-type mentioned earlier, because it focuses more on the *collective* socio-economic dimension of authoritarian abuse. Thus, while on the one hand the state pursues reparatory justice to correct individual wrongs and – in turn – restores the dignity of victims, on the other it carries out redistributive justice to realize broader social objectives, such as: fairness, economic growth, political stability and even a new collective national identity.

In practice, redistributive transitional justice seeks to improve the opportunity structure of individuals (or groups) that were deprived in the past by eliminating – through reform – existing 'gross or unjustifiable inequalities in the distribution of, access to, and/or opportunities for socio-economic [...] power and their accruing benefits' (Mani, 2002: 127). Thus, concrete redistributive transitional justice measures range from the introduction of social

and economic rights (e.g., fiscal and welfare reform) to wide-ranging redistribution (e.g., nationalization of major economic and industrial sectors; land reform; etc.) and affirmative action programs. In its most radical form,[23] redistributive transitional justice aims to level the social and economic playing field so as to approximate equality.

Needless to say, redistributive transitional justice undermines the entrenched socio-economic interests of former ruling elites and privileged classes. Therefore;

> the challenge for transitional [redistributive] justice [...] is even more daunting than preventing revenge and forgetting, or promoting democratic accountability. It must grapple too with people's aspirations to reverse the legacy of socio-economic discrimination if it is to be meaningful to those most affected by past atrocities (Krieger, 2000: 65).

As a result, new democracies rarely choose to carry out redistributive transitional justice:

> This hesitation [...] stems from a complex mix of factors. They include: the risk of a backlash from elite groups and powerful institutions opposed to redistribution; the fear of alienating the business community and scaring off foreign investment; the desire to safeguard individual liberty even at the expense of equity; and the lack of resources to finance redistribution of assets or employment (Mani, 2002: 151).

Supporters list the following benefits of redistributive transitional justice. First, it is the only kind of transitional justice that directly addresses one of the most urgent demands of post-authoritarian societies – that of social justice. According to Mamdani (2000);

> when there has been a political community based on conquest and dispossession, the task is to create a political community based on consent and justice. [...] Only social justice that underlines the empathy within a community of survivors can lay the foundation of a new political community based on consent (pp. 182–83).

Second, by attending to victims' material needs – such as housing, health care, education, employment, and so forth – redistributive transitional justice is often 'more significant to their ability to lay the past to rest than testifying before truth commissions or at trials' (Fletcher, 2001: 434). Third, in directly addressing socio-economic disparity, redistributive transitional justice tackles one of the pre-eminent root causes of dictatorship and conflict. In so doing, it actively prevents the rise of authoritarianism in the future. Fourth, because redistributive transitional justice actively promotes structural change, it offers a more solid and long-lasting solution for preventing future abuse than other kinds of transitional justice. Finally, redistributive transitional justice contributes to economic growth, especially in those countries where the authoritarian regime was actively protecting a relatively small and indolent land-owning oligarchy. In such contexts, in fact, the right mix of redistribution and liberalization policies can create the kind of small property-owner class that has historically provided the backbone of democracy around the world.

Critics list at least four problems with redistributive transitional justice. First, it is likely to trigger a backlash from powerful elite groups opposed to redistribution. Thus, because democratic transition often impinges on the collaboration of such elites, redistributive transitional justice directly jeopardizes regime change. Second, even when domestic elites consent to it, redistributive transitional justice still alienates the international business and financial community and – in turn – discourages foreign investment. Thus, because a new democracy's longevity is often tied to its initial economic success, redistributive transitional justice weakens democratic stability by undermining the new regime's economic potential. Third, with its emphasis on equality, redistributive transitional justice sacrifices individual liberty on the altar of social justice. This, in turn, undermines the new regime's legitimacy in the eyes of many. Finally, redistributive transitional justice requires considerable investment to finance a redistribution of assets or employment (Mani, 2002: 151). Because post-authoritarian societies do not often possess a great amount of financial resources, redistributive transitional justice indirectly weakens democratization efforts in other areas.

Does including redistribution into the definition of transitional justice add to the conceptual muddle mentioned earlier?[24] If one believes that the more the concept of transitional justice embraces, the less analytically useful it becomes, the answer is yes. This chapter, however, argues in favor of including redistribution into the definition of transitional justice, not only so that the latter may embrace *fairness* (in addition to truth and retribution), but also because excluding it produces several relevant drawbacks. First, it drastically reduces the number of those who may legitimately claim victim status after the fall of a dictatorship. Second, it favors individual over group claims. And third, it conceives of democratization in minimalist or 'procedural' terms, privileging civil and political rights over economic, social and cultural ones. At the same time, one should keep in mind that equating transitional justice with redistribution alone presents negative consequences as well, because it discourages a new democratic society from confronting sources of tension unrelated to socio-economic factors, or promoting the full moral and political rehabilitation of individual victims of the former authoritarian regime.

EXPLAINING TRANSITIONAL JUSTICE

Transitional justice is potentially shaped by several factors – for example, the specific political circumstances surrounding a country's democratization; the political culture prevalent at the time; the unique legacies of injustice inherited from previous authoritarian regimes; the number and nature of the actors involved; and so forth.[25] Most scholars note that the wide array of causal variables and the marked 'context-dependence' of transitional justice provide insuperable obstacles to the formulation of covering laws (Elster, 2004: 77).[26] Consequently, there is also little consensus in the field both in terms of theory and policy. Disagreements notwithstanding, several arguments currently offer useful insights into the determinants of transitional justice, providing precious practical knowledge for those countries still hoping to settle accounts with their difficult past.

Political scientists usually seek to explain what determines a post-authoritarian society's transitional justice choices, why different countries adopt different paths of transitional justice, and why the same country may choose different transitional justice strategies at different times. They also often provide recommendations on which transitional justice measures are most effective in a particular case. Compared to other scholars', political scientists' work on transitional justice tends to be theoretically ambitious and empirically sound. However, also among political scientists, there is ample disagreement. The greatest divide is between 'realist' students of international relations and 'constructivist' human rights scholars. Realists insist that; 'in a world of failed states and weak institutions – a world where politics in fact often trumps law – prosecutors should show deference to responsible political leaders who have the skills and the mandate to make choices based on prudence and political consequences' (Snyder and Vinjamuri, 2006). Constructivists, in contrast, claim that transitional justice does not inadvertently promote atrocities, increase human rights violations, exacerbate conflict or threaten democracy (see Sikkink and Walling, 2007).

A first theory that holds both theoretical breadth and scholarly appeal among political scientists focuses on the nature of the democratic transition. Thus, when the latter is 'pacted' (as in the cases of Spain and Chile), transitional justice is more likely to be eschewed or consist exclusively of procedural democratic reforms (institutional transitional justice) and/or timid investigations of the past (historical transitional justice).

This is because 'pacted' transitions necessarily imply a compromise with former dictators, who often hold the upper hand during the negotiations. In contrast, when democratization results out of a 'collapse' of the authoritarian regime, dictators are severely weakened (by either vigorous internal opposition or external intervention) and, in turn, transitional justice is more likely to take place (see Huntington, 1968; O'Donnell et al., 1986). This theory is quite powerful in explaining why different democratizing countries make different transitional justice choices (including amnesia). It emphasizes the distribution of power between incoming and outgoing elites, while largely discounting the influence of civil society. It regards transitional justice essentially as a one-shot bargaining game between departing authoritarian rulers and new democratic leaders. And it claims that transitional justice merely reflects power relations and material interests, rather than universal moral principles.

While undoubtedly appealing, this theory can be challenged on several fronts. First and foremost, recent events in Spain and Chile show that even the most 'pacted' of transitions is – in the long turn – vulnerable to transitional justice, as both civil society and the international community resist institutionalized amnesia for very long periods of time. Conversely, in countries where the authoritarian regimes 'collapsed' as a result of military defeat and occupation, transitional justice has often been only timid or pro-forma (e.g., Japan and Austria). Second, the empirical evidence reveals, not only that most post-authoritarian countries have carried out some form of transitional justice, but also that citizens of recent democracies have often rejected 'pacts' at the polls on moral principle, by rewarding democratic leaders who promised to deliver – if not the end of injustice – at least the best available treatment for it (e.g., Argentina). Finally, several countries' experience bears witness to the fact that even a 'pacted' democratization is not merely a pragmatic, forward-looking agreement among old and new elites to rewrite the rules of the political game (see Przeworski, 1986).

It can also provide an ambitious social process of confronting and re-interpreting the past that heals a divided political community (e.g., South Africa). When it is all said and done, then, it would be more correct to say that 'pacted' transitions often dilute or delay transitional justice, rather than prevent it altogether.

A second, and largely alternative, theory underscores the role of universal principles, in general (and of international norms in particular), in instigating transitional justice. More specifically, it holds that, in this day and age, new democracies are far more likely to embrace transitional justice than in the past because punishing former rulers for human rights abuses is no longer just a moral imperative. Following the 'Pinochet effect'[27] and the establishment of the International Criminal Court, it is also an international legal obligation that not only implies serious 'limits on the immunity of government officials when hauled before national courts, accused of international crimes, [... but also mandates] that domestic laws enshrining unfair trials or shielding perpetrators [be] subject to outside scrutiny' (Roht-Arriaza, 2005: 197–8). Echoing Finnemore and Sikkink's (1998) 'Norm Life Cycle' thesis, this theory submits that – following the various democratization 'waves' of the twentieth century – the norm concerning 'crimes against humanity' (which first surfaced at the post-World War II Nuremberg Trials)[28] has now been embraced by a critical mass of states – that is, it has 'cascaded' (Lutz and Sikkink, 2001). It also implies that during the next and final phase of this norm's life cycle – that of 'internalization' – transitional justice will become 'the prevailing standard of appropriateness against which new norms emerge and compete for support' (Finnemore and Sikkink, 1998: 895). Finally, this theory explains differences among countries' transitional justice choices in light of the different degree of 'internalization' of the international norms concerning crimes against humanity. This theory is vigorously rejected, not only by 'realist' scholars who doubt the relevance of international regimes *tout court*, but also by

empirically minded social scientists who contend that it is virtually impossible to verify whether or not a norm has concretely 'cascaded' and – in turn – been 'internalized' on a global scale. It is nevertheless a powerful theory which 'allows us to treat our moral and legal values, including justice, as both historically situated constructs and powerful tools for bringing about social and political change' (Smiley, 2001: 1332).

Another set of theoretically ambitious – albeit widely divergent – arguments focuses on the historical and cultural contexts of transitional justice. Thus, while some authors find that 'the nature and extent of past abuses does not have any clear impact on transitional outcomes' (Sriram, 2005: 521), others argue that transitional justice is more likely to be carried out when the former authoritarian regime was particularly oppressive and short-lived (Elster, 2004: 75) (vs. relatively benign and long-lasting). Another group of scholars claims that institutional continuity with the previous regime provides a major obstacle to transitional justice (Cesarini, 2004). Thus, for example, when the same loyalists who faithfully served the dictatorship remain at their posts, or when established 'informal' rules of the game persist despite regime change, it is very difficult for a new democratic government to implement any measure mandated by the transitional justice process. On their part, students of political culture underscore the need for a significant evolution of the collective authoritarian mentality that facilitated injustice in the past. In this view, without an 'active and ongoing intellectual and emotional confrontation with the experience of dictatorship' (Sa'adah, 1998: 4) that transforms subjects into citizens; public diffidence into civic trust; and former enemies into legitimate political rivals, the same undemocratic culture that led to atrocities in the past is likely to undermine any future transitional justice effort.

Other theories focus on the influence of specific actors (such as: the state, civil society, political parties, international organizations, etc.) on transitional justice. Most scholars agree that the state is a key – if not 'the' key – actor of transitional justice. Only the state, in fact, can provide 'a process of public reinterpretation of past horrors to create a new national narrative about the past and help frame a new vision for the future of the community' (Fletcher, 2001: 436). And only the state can take responsibility for past atrocities, make amends to victims, and commit to prevent future human rights violations. Scholars, however, vigorously disagree on the relevance of civil society. Thus, most human rights experts and activists argue that state-led transitional justice processes with little or no involvement by civil society are either incomplete or doomed to failure. Other scholars, in contrast, claim that – on account of its excessive idealism and unrealistic expectations – civil society-led transitional justice is generally impractical or (even worse) counterproductive. Not in the least because it often sets in motion judicial processes that take on a life of their own. These, in turn, risk disrupting the fragile political balance that sustains democratization (see Kissinger, 2001; Nino, 1991).

Analyzing the role of political parties, Elster (2004) tentatively concludes that their influence on transitional justice 'can be decisive, but may also be limited by other political actors' (p. 245). Thus, traditional political parties are more likely to play a fundamental role in the democratic transition and, in turn, champion transitional justice when they actively opposed the former authoritarian regime and became a main target of the latter's repression. Political parties' support of transitional justice, however, can be (and often is) weakened by contingent political circumstances – such as: the residual power of outgoing authoritarian elites and/or the military; international influences; and the rise of new political organizations. Finally, there is little agreement among scholars regarding the influence of international actors on transitional justice. While some conclude that international actors help democratizing societies promote transitional justice (see Sriram, 2005), others find that the latter might be delayed or deterred altogether by what is often perceived as unwarranted external interference into delicate matters of national sovereignty.[29]

THE IMPACT OF TRANSITIONAL JUSTICE

According to several scholars, transitional justice is much more than the inert by-product of democratization: It plays an important transformative role in its own right. Transitional justice should thus be treated

> in the following ways: first, as part of institutional life, rather than as an ideal imposed from above; second, as infused with the practicalities of institutional life, rather than as tainted by them; third, as manifested differently at various stages of history and within distinct social and political institutions; and fourth, as a powerful tool for bringing about social and political change (Smiley, 2001: 1333).

This 'constructivist' notion of transitional justice (best exemplified by Ruti Teitel's work)[30] is unfortunately at odds with that espoused by most political scientists. Lamenting the 'scant evidence on the relationships between choices made concerning transitional justice and the outcomes sought' (Siegel, 1998), political scientists are quick to conclude that 'there is no strict causal link between measures of retroactive justice and the nature of a newly established democratic regime' (de Brito et al., 2001: 35). They also note that many countries have successfully achieved democratic consolidation despite taking very different transitional justice paths. Finally, they point out that, because numerous internal and external factors – other than transitional justice choices – shape long-term democratic development, it is almost impossible to pinpoint the direction of causality between transitional justice and democratization (see de Brito et al., 2001; Snyder and Vinjamuri, 2003).

These critiques are challenging indeed. Undeniably, the empirical evidence on the effects of transitional justice choices on new democracies is hard to come by. Nevertheless, old and new democratic leaders alike continue to agonize over transitional justice – in some cases, even several generations after the alleged mass atrocities took place. So, the question arises: Why do they do so, if they did not sincerely believe that transitional justice has a profound impact on their societies' future? As far as the assertion that democracies 'consolidate' despite making different transitional justice choices is concerned, it would indeed be a lethal criticism were it not for the fact that 'consolidation' is a vague and contested concept in its own right. Furthermore, only rarely do transitional justice's effects become apparent during the time horizon associated with 'consolidation'. Usually, much longer is needed, as many countries often revisit and revise their transitional justice over time (see Sikkink and Walling, 2007) – sometimes even several generations after the fact. Finally, very few scholars – including constructivist ones – would argue that democratization outcomes are entirely dependent on transitional justice choices. After all, good theories are less a matter of 'artificial choice between key factors', than a question of specifying 'how variables are joined together in specific historical instances' (Katznelson, 1997: 93; 99) – which is exactly what any good argument on the impact of transitional justice should attempt to do.

Several scholars have sought to establish whether transitional justice benefits or harms the democratization of post-authoritarian societies. Those who believe in the positive influence of transitional justice advance several interesting arguments. A first theory suggests that transitional justice benefits democracy by ending impunity. Transitional justice, in fact, eliminates undemocratic actors from the political stage and promotes legality and accountability at the highest levels of government. A second theory claims that transitional justice benefits democracy by providing the necessary precondition for the pacification between members of the former authoritarian regime and their victims. In effect, transitional justice not only eliminates potentially destabilizing sources

of future conflict (Rothenberg, 2002), but also creates a political environment that is conducive to both civility and pragmatism. A third theory argues that transitional justice benefits democracy by (re)creating the bonds of civic trust that authoritarianism dispensed with. In so doing, it adds to the legitimacy of the new democratic government, and promotes confidence in the new democratic institutions (see Cesarini, 2004; Orentlicher, 1991). Yet another theory underscores that transitional justice benefits democracy by fostering the renewal of a society's political identity. In effect, transitional justice is often associated with secular ceremonies that mark a definite break with the past, re-establish a lost sense of community; foster democratic attitudes; and celebrate regime change (see Osiel, 1997, 2000).

On the other hand, there are scholars who believe that transitional justice harms post-authoritarian democracies. Some claim that transitional justice undermines the political bargain struck between democratization's winners and losers. In so doing, it hurts democracy by creating a source of political instability that may lead to military coups or renewed civil war (Kissinger, 2001; Snyder and Vinjamuri, 2003). Others argue that transitional justice harms democratization by promoting indiscriminate collective punishment. In so doing, it subtracts precious human capital to the new regime, and may even produce dangerous backlash against democracy.[31] Yet another theory submits that transitional justice involves acts of political justice which are, by definition, unjust.[32] In so doing, it undermines democracy by weakening the very same basic principles of fairness that the new regime is supposed to uphold.

Unfortunately, to date only very few studies have focused on transitional justice's long-term implications. Of these, most do not even analyze transitional justice for its own sake. Rather, they do so incidentally, as part of an overall effort to study post-authoritarian societies' attempts to deal with their difficult past. It is also interesting to note that, while there are several theories on the causes of transitional justice and its short-term impact, only a handful of political scientists have ventured to formulate hypotheses about the long-term impact of transitional justice. In this context, four works deserve particular mention: Paloma Aguilar's *Memoria y Olvido de la Guerra Civil Espanola* (1996); Anne Sa'adah's *Germany's Second Chance* (1998); Consuelo Cruz's *Political Culture and Institutional Development in Costa Rica and Nicaragua* (2005); and David Art's *The Politics of the Nazi Past in Germany and Austria* (2005).

Paloma Aguilar's (1996) book analyzes the influence of the memory of the Civil War on Spain's democratic transition and beyond, and argues that the traumatic nature of the war's memory led Spain to choose amnesia over retribution and truth. Aguilar also shows that Spain's peculiar transitional justice choice – the *'pacto del olvido'*[33] – and its political ramifications have become so enshrined in the country's institutions that they continue to influence Spanish politics to the present day.

In her book, Anne Sa'adah (1998) compares the transitional justice processes in the Bonn Republic after the Third Reich with that of post-unification Germany after the (East) German Democratic Republic (GDR) experience. After thoughtful and detailed analyses of the different transitional justice strategies in question, Sa'adah argues that the limited success of the Bonn Republic's top-down institutional approach toward the Nazi past effectively set the stage for a remarkable political learning process. She also shows how, almost fifty years later, such learning process bore fruit, leading reunified Germany to adopt more extensive and culturally based transitional justice choices vis-à-vis the GDR.

On the basis of five centuries of political history in Costa Rica and Nicaragua, Consuelo Cruz's (2005) volume demonstrates that political culture – and, in particular, how countries rework their past experiences into practical lessons for building a 'better' future – configures economic development, institutional choices and political pacts in ways that directly affect democracy's chances and quality. Thus, different choices about their past led Costa Rica and Nicaragua to very different political outcomes, whereby the former is the most enduring democracy in Latin America, while the latter one of the most unstable.

After a careful comparative analysis of the different ways in which Austria and Germany dealt with the legacy of the Third Reich, David Art (2005) traces the long-term political consequences of such differences. He concludes that, while Germany's critical confrontation of its own Nazi past has prevented – thus far – far-right parties from becoming permanent political forces in this country, Austrians' stubborn denial of their active role in the Third Reich created an environment in which right-wing populist parties continue to meet significant electoral success. Different choices about the Nazi past, then, led to very different political outcomes, whereby Germany appears to enjoy a higher quality of democracy than Austria.

These excellent studies show that it is indeed feasible and productive to theorize about transitional justice's long-term implications. They also confirm that 'it is much more interesting to examine [...] what sequencing or judicious combination of transitional justice mechanisms can help build democracy and resolve conflicts' (Sikkink and Walling, 2007: 443), than focusing on the alleged short-term trade off between peace and justice. Finally, these studies illustrate how, in seeking to formulate broader theories (but not necessarily covering laws) of transitional justice, scholars should analyze the latter both as a key effect of a country's democratic transition, and as a relevant influence on its further democratic development. This, in turn, implies a two-stage approach to theory-building. In the first stage, scholars should study the specific transitional justice process(es) in question, and explain the latter's relationship with the democratic transition. In the second stage, scholars should formulate and test concrete hypotheses about the evolution and broader transformative role of transitional justice over time – a role that might well be quite different than the one originally envisaged at the time of democratic transition.

In my own work, I implement this two-stage approach to study transitional justice's role in shaping the quality of post-authoritarian democracies over time (Cesarini, 2009). To help separate the two analytical stages of my inquiry, I introduce the notion of *transitional justice 'regime'* – defined as a distinctive and enduring set of socially constructed principles, institutions and narratives that post-authoritarian actors commit to in order to carry out transitional justice over time. Thus, I first analyze the emergence of the transitional justice regimes of Italy, Portugal, and Argentina, and detail their main characteristics and short-term effects. Then, I illustrate how these transitional justice regimes evolved and became entrenched over time, eventually acquiring a key transformative role of their own: that of structuring Italy's, Portugal's, and Argentina's relationships with their authoritarian past, and the latter's influence on the present. Finally, I argue that the role of transitional justice in these countries was highly consequential, not only at the abstract level of their collective memories, but also on the more concrete plane of the design and practice of Italy's, Portugal's, and Argentina's institutions and, in turn, of the long-term quality of their democracies.

NEW AREAS OF TRANSITIONAL JUSTICE RESEARCH

The field of transitional justice is an interesting and thriving one. However, much work remains to be done. This last section identifies a select number of new areas for transitional justice research by political scientists in general – and comparativists in particular. These areas show great promise for adding to our knowledge about how countries deal with

their past during difficult social and political transformation.

Evolution and long-term effects

Recent research has finally put to rest the idea that choices about transitional justice are confined to the relative short time interval of the democratic transition, and that what matters most is transitional justice's short-term impact on democratic consolidation. The empirical evidence from 'historical' cases, in fact, unquestionably shows that transitional justice is a much more complex, nuanced, shifting, long-lasting, broad-based and consequential affair than most social scientists have thus far imagined. Scholars should therefore look at transitional justice as an ongoing process, and seek to find out more about the factors that prompt democratic societies to revisit their transitional justice choices even many decades after regime transition. Scholars also need to dedicate much more effort to evaluating the long-term impact of transitional justice. In particular, they need to formulate effective policy insights about which combination, sequence, and timing of available transitional justice sub-types (among those listed in Table 27.1) are most appropriate to promote the quality of a particular democratic society over time.

Redistributive transitional justice

The redistributive sub-type remains the most under-researched category of transitional justice. This is a consequence of the fact that, with very few exceptions, the debate on transitional justice has largely bypassed social and economic policies, while privileging judicial and institutional expedients. It also reflects the pre-eminence of civil and political rights in the current democratization discourse. However, as several scholars point out, while 'trials and conventional legal infrastructures [...] are important, [...] they are not enough, especially in countries characterized by poverty and illiteracy. [...] If justice is to contribute to peace and democracy [...], the imbalances within transitional justice need to be redressed' (Gready, 2005: 18–19), both in terms of academic research and concrete policy measures.

Constituencies of transitional justice

When is transitional justice more likely? When the state and civil society collaborate; when the state leads; or when civil society takes the initiative? Any research on effective constituencies of transitional justice should focus on the relationship between incoming democratic elites and organizations of civil society – especially human rights groups. It should treat transitional justice as a process that requires negotiation, not only among elites, but also between a country's leaders and its citizens. It should leave room for relevant actors to engage in political learning – not only from their own past, but also from other countries' experiences. It should seek to explain, not only why some societies may skip or backtrack from transitional justice, but also why they may re-embrace it several decades after democratic transition. Finally, this research should provide a solid empirical counterpoint to the more prevalent normative studies of transitional justice.

Epistemic communities of transitional justice

How and why did transitional justice become an international *cause celébre?* One possible answer to this question involves theorizing the rise of an *epistemic community* of transitional justice. According to Antoniades (2003), epistemic communities are *'thought communities* [...] made up of socially recognized knowledge-based networks, the members of which share a common understanding of a particular problem/issue or a common worldview and seek to translate their beliefs into dominant social discourse and social practices' (p. 26). There are at least two challenges for any research of this kind. The first is to establish the existence of a transitional justice epistemic community by identifying its membership and detailing its intellectual and advocacy activities over time. The second is to demonstrate that such epistemic community played (and continues to play) a critical role within the current international human rights regime in setting norms affecting transitional justice on a global scale.

Transitional justice and collective memory

While several good studies on the influence of the past on democratization are currently available,[34] much work remains to be done on the specific relationship between transitional justice and collective memory. This kind of research inevitably requires a major interdisciplinary effort – one that, unfortunately, only very few scholars are willing or able to undertake. Jon Elster is one of those few. After a careful analysis of the 'intricate interplay' between memory, emotions, democratization, and transitional justice, he concludes that the desire for transitional justice 'is blunted, if there is a long time interval between the wrongdoings and the transition, and also if there is a long delay between the transition and the trials' (Elster, 2004: 222). This is because the *memory* of even the more horrific of atrocities tends to decay over time, unless some mechanism intervenes to slow or arrest such decay.[35]

What Elster scarcely emphasizes, however, is that transitional justice choices shape collective memories well beyond the democratic transition. Thus, for example, a new democracy's initial choice to forget may render victims (or their families) subsequently more resolute in their refusal to let the memory of their beloved's plight fade. In contrast, the selection of a particular official narrative of the past may – over the years – influence selective collective amnesia. More research on the long-run feedback effects of transitional justice on collective memory is therefore in order. Such research necessarily requires a constructivist view of transitional justice – that is, as a process that is shaped by the recent authoritarian experience in the short run and, in turn, also shapes the collective memory of a post-authoritarian society over time.

Transitional justice and gender

Women have always been at the forefront of demands for transitional justice both as direct victims of crimes against humanity, and as relatives of the tortured, the murdered, and the disappeared. However, it was only after the 2001 sentence by the International Criminal Tribunal for the Former Yugoslavia that made rape a separate war crime (as well as an act of genocide), that transitional justice officially acquired a gender dimension. Since then, the international community has made significant progress in recognizing gender based war crimes – such as: rape, sexual slavery, forced pregnancy, enforced sterilization, and so forth (see Franke, 2006). In turn, women are gradually evolving from passive victims, into active participants of the transitional justice process.

While several interesting policy studies are emerging,[36] the gender dimension of transitional justice still needs more abstract theoretical work. Under-analyzed questions include the following: Are there gender-specific conceptions of transitional justice? (If yes, why? And what do they look like?); Do women have a key role in expanding the concept of transitional justice into the cultural and socio-economic realms?; Why does women's clout as protagonists of the opposition to authoritarian regimes so rarely transfer into decision-making power in matters of transitional justice?; Do women play a preponderant role in destabilizing transitional justice compromises? (If yes, why?)

NOTES

1. Transitional justice spans at least across six different disciplinary fields – that is, law, history, sociology, political science, anthropology, and psychology.

2. See also Bickford's definition of transitional justice as 'a field of activity and inquiry focused on how societies address legacies of past human rights abuses, mass atrocity, or other forms of severe social trauma, including genocide or civil war, in order to build a more democratic, just, or peaceful future' (Bickford, 2004: 1045–47).

3. The doctrine of universal jurisdiction allows countries to prosecute crimes against humanity in domestic courts, regardless of the nationality of victims and perpetrators, or the place where the atrocities were committed.

4. These include: truth commissions, historical research, compilation of victims' testimonials or oral histories, forensic anthropological research, and exhumation of victims' bodies. See Bickford (2004).

5. These include: wholesale dismissal of abusive, corrupt, or incompetent officials from the public administration, the police, the security services, the military, and the judiciary that served the previous regime.

6. These include: economic, rehabilitative and symbolic measures, such as: monetary compensation, health and education benefits, official apologies, memorials, etc.

7. See, for example, Rwanda's Gacaca courts.

8. It might be objected that such stringent criteria would leave important cases – such as Northern Ireland – outside the realm of transitional justice. This objection fails, however, to appreciate the fact that – for the most part – Northern Ireland's Catholics do not perceive British rule as 'democratic', since it equated for so long with Unionist supremacy. As seen from their point of view, then, the peace process also harbors regime change.

9. That is with military or international trials carried out by foreign powers in connection with interstate war crimes, whose primary goal is the punishment of aggression to global peace and security, rather than the democratization of the defeated country.

10. That is summary judgments carried out in time of war by kangaroo courts set up by particular factions whose main goal is revenge rather than justice.

11. Katherine Hite and Paola Cesarini (2004: 4) define 'authoritarian legacies' as 'those rules,

procedures, norms, patterns, practices, dispositions, relationships, and memories originating in well-defined authoritarian experiences of the past that, as a result of specific historical configurations and/or political struggles, survive democratic transition and intervene in the quality and practice of post-authoritarian democracies'.

12. In some cases – such as Peru – the bulk of human rights violations are committed by opposition forces.

13. 'In the limited sanction, the phases of ascertaining guilt and of ascribing penalty are differentiated. [...] Investigations may or may not lead to indictments, adjudication, and conviction. Moreover, convictions are commonly followed by light or no punishment' (Teitel, 2000: 47).

14. See Human Rights Watch official website at: http://hrw.org/justice/about.htm

15. Exemplified by the successful trials of the former members of the military juntas in 1975 Greece and 1983 Argentina.

16. The recent trial and execution of Saddam Hussein in Iraq under the aegis of a domestic tribunal convened under US watch, appear support this argument.

17. Such as putting the military under civilian control and creating an independent judiciary.

18. See, for example, Rwanda's Gacaca courts.

19. *Comisión Nacional de Investigación sobre la Desaparición de Personas* – National Investigative Commission on the Disappeared.

20. From Chile's President Patricio Aylwin's statement on public television in occasion of the presentation of the Report of the Chilean National Commission on Truth and Reconciliation.

21. See, for example, Spain, Mozambique, or Cambodia.

22. Except, of course, when it deliberately seeks to re-establish a democratic *status quo ante*.

23. Radical versions of redistributive transitional justice are usually supported by actors imbued with a communist or socialist ideology.

24. See under the previous section dedicated to institutional transitional justice.

25. See, among others, Teitel (2000) and Elster (2004).

26. For a similar conclusion, see de Brito et al. (2001).

27. This refers to the 1998 house arrest in England of General Augusto Pinochet – military dictator of Chile from 1973 to 1990 – for human rights abuses carried out under his rule. Pinochet's arrest was executed on the basis of the principle of universal jurisdiction following a request of extradition by Spanish judge Baltasar Garzón. The ensuing legal battle greatly emboldened activists worldwide and, according to many scholars, opened a new era in international human rights law.

28. The Nuremberg Charter defined 'crimes against humanity' as: 'murder, extermination, enslavement, deportation, and other inhumane acts committed against any civilian population, before or during the war, or persecutions on political, racial or religious grounds in execution of, or in connection with any crime within the jurisdiction of the Tribunal, whether or not in violation of the domestic law of the country where perpetrated'. See *Charter of the International Military Tribunal* (also known as Nuremberg Charter), art. 6(c).

29. Rwanda is a case in point.

30. See Teitel (2000) and Shapiro (1999).

31. See Germany after World War I.

32. Criminal prosecution of perpetrators of mass atrocities is often carried out on the basis of *ex-post facto* law or without proper guarantees of due process, equal protection and statutes of limitation for the accused. See Kirchheimer (1961) and Siegel (1998).

33. 'Agreement to forget'.

34. See, among others, Aguilar (1996); Booth (2001); Cruz (2005); de Brito et al. (2001); Mahoney (2002); Müller (2002); Osiel (1997, 2000); and Torpey (2003).

35. Such mechanisms include the following: 'communication among the victims of wrongdoing, codes of honor that keep memory alive until the desire for revenge has been satisfied, visible physical reminders of the wrongdoing, and perpetuation of the state of affairs caused by the wrongdoing' (Elster, 2004: 223).

36. See, for example, Rubio-Marín (2006).

REFERENCES

Aguilar Fernández, P. (1996) *La memoria histórica de la guerra civil española (1936–39): Un proceso de aprendizaje político*. Madrid: Alianza Editorial.

Antoniades, A. (2003) 'Epistemic communities, epistemes and the construction of (world) politics', *Global Society*, 17 (1): 21–38.

Art, D. (2005) *The politics of the Nazi past in Germany and Austria*. Cambridge: Cambridge University Press.

Barkan, E. (2002) *The guilt of nations: Restitution and negotiating historical injustices*. New York: Norton.

Bickford, L. (2004) 'Transitional justice', in D.L. Shelton (ed.), *The encyclopedia of genocide and crimes against humanity*. Macmillan Reference USA. Vol. 3, pp. 1045–47.

Booth, J. W. (2001) 'The unforgotten: Memories of justice', *American Political Science Review*, 95 (4): 777–92.

Boraine, A.L. (2006) 'Transitional justice: A holistic interpretation', *Journal of International Affairs*, 60 (1): 17–30.

Brody, R. (2001, April 20) 'Justice: The first casualty of truth?', *The Nation*, 25–31.

Cesarini, P. (2004) 'Authoritarian legacies and justice in Italy and Argentina', in Hite, K. and Cesarini, P. (eds), *Authoritarian legacies and democracy in Latin America and Southern Europe*. Notre Dame, IN: University of Notre Dame Press. pp. 159–90.

Cesarini, P. (2009) *Unforgettable justice: Transitional justice and the quality of democracy in post-authoritarian Italy, Portugal and Argentina* (unpublished PhD Dissertation).

Cruz, C. (2005) *Political culture and institutional development in Costa Rica and Nicaragua*. Cambridge: Cambridge University Press.

de Brito, A., Gonzales-Enriques, C., and Aquilar, P. (2001) *The politics of memory*. Oxford: Oxford University Press.

Diamond, L. and Morlino, L. (2004) 'The quality of democracy: An overview', *Journal of Democracy*, 15 (4): 20–31.

Dicker, R. and Keppler, E. (2004) Beyond The Hague: The challenges of international justice. *Human rights watch world report 2004*. Retrieved March 26, from, http://hrw.org/wr2k4/10.htm

Elster, J. (1998) 'Coming to terms with the past: A framework for the study of justice in the transition to democracy', *European Journal of Sociology*, 39: 7–48.

Elster, J. (2004) *Closing the books*. Cambridge: Cambridge University Press.

Finnemore, M. and Sikkink, K. (1998) 'International norm dynamics and political change', *International Organization*, 52 (4): 887–917.

Fletcher, L. (2001) 'Between vengeance and forgiveness: Facing history after genocide and mass violence (Book review)', *Berkeley Journal of International Law*, 19 (2): 428–42.

Fletcher, L.E. and Weinstein, H.M. (2002) 'Violence and social repair: Rethinking the contribution of justice to reconciliation', *Human Rights Quarterly*, 24 (3): 573–639.

Franke, K.M. (2006) 'Gendered subjects on Transitional Justice', *Columbia Journal of Gender and Law*, 15 (3): 813–27.

Gready, P. (2005) 'Reconceptualising transitional justice: Embedded and distanced justice', *Conflict, Security and Development*, 5 (1): 3–21.

Hayner, P. (2002) *Unspeakable truths: Facing the challenge of truth commissions*. New York and London: Routledge.

Hite, K. and Cesarini, P. (2004) *Authoritarian legacies and democracy in Latin America and Southern Europe*. Notre Dame, IN: University of Notre Dame Press

Huntington, S.P. (1968) *Political order in changing societies*. New Haven: Yale University Press.

Huntington, S.P. (1991) *The third wave: Democratization in the late twentieth century*. University of Oklahoma Press.

International Center for Transitional Justice (2006) *What is transitional justice?* Retrieved March 26, 2008, from http://www.ictj.org/en/tj/

International Center for Transitional Justice (2008) *Vetting research project*. Retrieved March 27, 2008, from http://www.ictj.org/en/research/projects/vetting/index.html

Katznelson, I. (1997) 'Structure and configuration in comparative politics', in M. Irving Lichbach and A.S. Zuckerman (eds), *Comparative politics: Rationality, culture, and structure*. Cambridge: Cambridge University Press. pp. 81–112.

Kirchheimer, O. (1961) *Political justice*. Westport, CT: Greenwood Press. Reprinted by arrangement with Princeton University Press.

Kissinger, H. (2001) 'The pitfalls of universal jurisdiction'. *Foreign Affairs*, 80 (4): 86–96.

Krasner, S. (ed.) (1983) *International regimes*. Ithaca: Cornell University Press.

Krieger, N. (2000) 'Transitional justice as socioeconomic rights', *Peace Review*, 12 (1): 59–65.

Kritz, N. (1995) 'The dilemmas of transitional justice', in N. Kritz (ed.), *Transitional justice: How emerging democracies reckon with former regimes*. USIP Press Books. Retrieved March 26, 2008, from http://www.usip.org/ruleoflaw/pubs/tjintro.html#non

Letki, N. (2002) 'Lustration and democratization in East-Central Europe', *Europe-Asia Studies*, 54 (4): 530–31.

Lutz, E. and Sikkink, K. (2001) 'The justice cascade: The evolution and impact of foreign human rights trials in Latin America', *Chicago Journal of International Law,* 2 (1): 1–33.

Mahoney, J. (2002) *The legacies of liberalism: Path dependence and political regimes in Central America.* Baltimore: The Johns Hopkins University Press.

Mamdani, M. (1996) 'Reconciliation without justice', *Southern African Review of Books,* 46 (November/December): 3–5.

Mamdani, M. (2000) 'The truth according to the TRC', in I. Amadiume and A. An-Naim (eds), *The politics of memory: Truth, healing and social justice.* London: Zed. pp. 182–83.

Mani, R. (2002) *Beyond retribution: Seeking justice in the shadows of war.* Cambridge, UK: Polity Press.

Mani, R. (2005) 'Rebuilding an inclusive political community after war', *Security Dialogue,* 36 (4): 511–26.

Marques, J., Paez, D., and Serra, A. (eds) (1997) *Collective memory of political events: Social psychological perspectives.* Mahwah, NJ: Lawrence Erlbaum Associates.

McAdam, D., Tilly, C., and Tarrow, S. (2001) *The dynamics of contention.* New York: Cambridge University Press.

Müller, J. W. (ed.) (2002) *Memory and power in post-war Europe.* Cambridge, UK: Cambridge University Press.

Nietzsche, F. (1997) 'On the uses and disadvantages of history for life', in Friedrich Nietzsche, Daniel Breazeale, and R.J. Hollingdale (eds) *Untimely Meditation.* (Cambridge Texts in the History of Philosophy). Cambridge: Cambridge University Press. pp. 57–124.

Nino, C. (1991) 'The duty to punish past abuses of human rights put into context: The case of Argentina', *Yale Law Journal,* 100 (8): 2619–40.

O'Donnell, G., Schmitter, P.C., and Whitehead, L. (eds) (1986) *Transitions from authoritarian rule.* Baltimore: Johns Hopkins University Press.

Orentlicher, D.F. (1991) 'Settling accounts: The duty to prosecute human rights violations of a prior regime', *Yale Law Journal,* 100 (8): 2537–615.

Osiel, M. (1997/2000) *Mass atrocity, collective memory and the law.* New Brunswick, NJ: Transaction Books.

Przeworski, A. (1986) 'Some problems in the study of transition to democracy', in G. O'Donnell, P. C. Schmitter and L. Whitehead (eds), *Transitions from authoritarian rule.* Baltimore: Johns Hopkins University Press. pp. 47–63.

Roht-Arriaza, N. (2005) *The Pinochet effect.* Philadelphia, PA: University of Pennsylvania Press.

Rothenberg, D. (2002) '"Let justice judge": An interview with Judge Baltasar Garzón and analysis of his ideas', *Human Rights Quarterly,* 24: 924–73.

Rubio-Marín, R. (ed) (2006) *What happened to the women? Gender and reparations for human rights violations.* New York: Social Science Research Council.

Sa'adah, A. (1998) *Germany's second chance: Trust, justice and democratization.* Cambridge, MA: Harvard University Press.

Sarat, A. and Kearns, T.R. (1999) *History, memory and the law.* Ann Arbor, MI: The University of Michigan Press.

Shapiro, I. (1999) *Democratic justice.* New Haven: Yale University Press.

Siegel, R.L. (1998) 'Transitional justice: A decade of debate and experience', *Human Rights Quarterly,* 20 (2): 431–54.

Sikkink, K. and Walling, C.B. (2007) 'The impact of human rights trials in Latin America', *Journal of Peace Research,* 44 (4): 427–45.

Smiley, M. (2001) 'Democratic justice in transition', *Michigan Law Review,* 99 (6): 1332–48.

Snyder, J. and Vinjamuri, L. (2003) 'Trials and errors: Principle and pragmatism in strategies of international justice', *International Security,* 28 (3): 5–44.

Snyder, J. and Vinjamuri, L. (2006, September 26) A midwife for peace. *International Herald Tribune.*

Sriram, C.L. (2005) 'Transitional justice comes of age: Enduring lessons and challenges', *Berkeley Journal of International Law,* 23 (2): 506–23.

Teitel, R.G. (2000) *Transitional justice.* New York: Oxford University Press.

Torpey, J. (ed) (2003) *Politics and the past.* Rowman and Littlefield Publishers.

28

The Globalization of Comparative Public Opinion Research

Pippa Norris

INTRODUCTION

One of the most dramatic recent developments, transforming the field of comparative politics during recent decades, has been the expanding range of survey resources facilitating the systematic cross-national analysis of public opinion around the globe. This process started more than four decades ago, with Gabriel Almond and Sidney Verba's path-breaking *The civic culture* (1963), which was immediately recognized and acclaimed by Philip Converse (1964) as 'an instant classic'. Previously a few other cross-national attitudinal studies had been deployed, notably, William Buchanan and Hadley Cantril's 9-country *How nations see each other* (1953), sponsored by UNESCO, sociological surveys of social stratification, and USIA surveys of attitudes toward international affairs.[1] The civic culture survey laid the foundation for the comparative study of public opinion and subsequent cross-national survey research as a distinctive sub-field in political science open to empirical investigation.

To explore the nature and evaluate the contribution of this sub-field, the first part of this

chapter examines the globalization of the study of cross-national public opinion over successive decades. The statistical revolution spurred the initial growth in survey research in Europe and the United States, emphasizing individual-level social-psychological variables and quantitative scientific methods. More recently the rise of the European Union (EU), international networks in the social sciences, the diffusion of the market research industry, and the expanding number of democratic states worldwide have all facilitated the growth and scope of data resources. This chapter compares and contrasts the major series of cross-national social survey datasets which are now available, summarized in Table 28.1, defined as those covering more than one independent nation-state which have established a regular series of surveys of social and political attitudes and behavior. This includes the Euro-barometer and related EU surveys (which started in 1970), the European Election Study (1979), the European Values Survey and the World Values Survey (1981), the International Social Survey Programme (1985), the Global Barometers (1990 and various), the Comparative National Elections Project (1990), the European Voter and the Comparative Study of Electoral Systems

Table 28.1 Key features of the cross-national series of surveys

Series	Series started (i)	Frequency	Total nations (latest survey) (ii)	Data downloadable (iii)	Coordinating organization	Online resources
Euro-barometer and related studies	1970	Bi-annual	27	Public archives	Directorate General Press and Comms, European Commission	Organizing and reports: http://europa.eu.int/comm/public_opinion/ Data and continuity guides from ZUMA, Cologne Archive: www.gesis.org/en/data_service/eurobarometer
European Values/ World Values Study- Study	1981–1983	Approx. 5 years	92	Public archives	Ronald Inglehart, Institute of Social Research, University of Michigan	Organizing and data; www.worldvaluessurvey.org/
International Social Survey Program (ISSP)	1985	Annual	38	Public archives	Secretariat: Bjørn Henrichsen, Norwegian Social Science Data Services (NSD), Bergen	Organizing: www.issp.org/ Data and continuity guide from the ZUMA Cologne Archive: www.gesis.org/en/data_service/issp/
Comparative Study of Electoral Systems (CES)	1996–2001	Module every 5 years	31	Public archives	Secretariat: David Howell, ISR, University of Michigan. Chair: Ian McAllister, ANU	Organizing and data: http://www.cses.org
Comparative National Election Study	1990	Irregular	19	Public archives	Richard Gunther, Ohio State University	Organizing and data: http://www.cnep.ics.ul.pt/
Global-barometers, including:						http://www.globalbarometer.net/_
New Europe Barometers	1991	Irregular	16		Richard Rose, CSPP, Aberdeen University	www.cspp.strath.ac.uk
Afrobarometer	1999	Annual	18	Public archives	Michael Bratton (Michigan State), Robert Mattes (IDASA, SA) and Dr E. Gyimah-Boadi (CDD Ghana)	www.afrobarometer.org
Latino-barometer	1995	Annual	18	Tables only	Marta Lagos, MORI, Santiago	www.latinobarometro.org

Continued

Continued

Table 28.1 Key features of the cross-national series of surveys

Series	Series started (i)	Frequency	Total nations (latest survey) (ii)	Data download-able (iii)	Coordinating organization	Online resources
Asian barometer	2001	Annual	17		Yun-han Chu, Taiwan	www.eastasiabarometer.org http://www.asianbarometer.org/
Arab Barometer	2005	Annual	5		Mark Tessler, University of Michigan	http://arabbarometer.org/
The European Social Survey (ESS)	2002	Biennial	21	Public archives	Roger JOWELL, Center for Comparative Social Surveys, City University	Organizing: http://www.europeansocialsurvey.org/ Data from the Norwegian archive: http://ess.nsd.uib.no.
Transatlantic Trends	2002	Annual	13	Public archives	German Marshall Fund of the United States and the Compagnia di San Paolo	http://www.transatlantictrends.org
The Pew Global Attitudes Survey	2002	Irregular	54	Via website	Andrew KOHUT, Director, The Pew Research Center for the People and the Press	http://pewglobal.org/
Gallup International *Voice of the People*	2002	Annual	60	Only tables released	Meril JAMES, Secretary General Gallup International	www.voice-of-the-people.net/

Notes: (i) In some cases there were often pilot studies and forerunners, such as the European Community Study, but this date is the recognizable start of the series in its present form. (ii) The number of countries included in each survey often varies by year. (iii) If not deposited in public archives or directly downloadable, access to some data may be available from the surveys organizers on request, but there might also be charges for access.

(1995), the European Social Survey (2002), the Transatlantic Trends survey (2002), the Pew Global Attitudes project (2002), and the Gallup World Poll (2005).

The final section of this chapter considers some of the perennial critiques of cross-national surveys, including issues about the quality of the data, the equivalence of concepts, and the need to understand public opinion within a broader structural context, and considers how far these raise valid concerns about the limits of this method. The conclusion argues that, despite important limitations, cross-national survey research is invaluable for establishing generalities about human behavior in a way that allows us to test regularities established in single-nation studies. The multiplicity of datasets which are now available for analysis strengthens replication, to ensure robust findings and generalizations. In particular, when large-scale multi-national surveys covering many societies are combined with systematic variations in institutional and societal contexts, this process is capable of providing powerful insights for the study of comparative politics.

THE EARLY EVOLUTION OF SURVEY RESEARCH

The earliest development of large-scale social surveys can be traced to the statistical movement in late-Victorian Britain (Bulmer et al., 1992). Surveys arose with the comprehensive street-by-street investigations into the conditions of poverty in London led by the business philanthropist Charles Booth (which started in 1886), building on Mayhew's more impressionistic observations thirty years earlier, and a similar social survey of working class living conditions which the social reformer and businessman Seebohm Rowntree conducted in York in 1897. Some of the earliest work on probability sampling was developed by the Norwegian statistician Kiaer around 1890, while estimates of the sources of error which influence

the precision of the results were developed at the LSE by the statistician Arthur L. Bowley (Bulmer, 1998). Bowley also devised and conducted sample surveys of working-class households in four English towns and presented the results in *Livelihood and poverty* (with A. R. Burnett-Hurst, 1915). The earliest social surveys in Britain called attention to issues of political reform to improve the living conditions for the urban poor.

Building on this work, in the United States the founders of the Chicago school, Harold Gosnell and Charles Merriam, had experimented with applying statistical and survey methods in pursuit of a new science of politics during the 1920s and 1930s (Bulmer, 1986). This approach was exemplified by Merriam and Gosnell, (1924), which employed sampling techniques and survey data. Prior to this, the Swedish social scientist, Herbert Tingsten (1937/1963), had employed aggregate data to understand political behavior, voting choice and turnout. The advantage of representative sample surveys is that these provided direct insights into the social and attitudinal characteristics of the electorate. Many of the leaders associated with the behavioral revolution were associated as faculty or graduates with the Chicago school, including Harold Lasswell, V. O. Key Jr., David Truman, Herbert Simon, and Gabriel Almond. Meanwhile the commercial applied uses of market survey research were also being developed. George Gallup experimented with using voting forms among a scientific sample of voters in each state in 1933, using this to predict the results of the 1934 Congressional races. He founded the American Institute of Public Opinion in 1935 and the British Institute of Public Opinion two years later. Straw polls and even large-scale house-to-house surveys based on self-selection had been used in many studies. The superiority of opinion surveys based on a small but scientifically selected random sample of the adult population came to public attention when Gallup used these techniques to predict successfully a Roosevelt victory in the 1936 presidential election, in marked contrast to the forecast of a Landon win based on the far larger but non-random poll published in the Literary Digest (Crossley, 1937).

The first issue of the journal *Public Opinion Quarterly* was published in 1937, seeking to document 'what public opinion is, how it generates, and how it acts' (Clinton Poole, 1937). A bibliography published in the first issue listed 5,000 titles on mass public opinion. Market research and public opinion surveys rapidly expanded in America in the next few years, including a wide range of polls conducted by George Gallup, Elmo Roper and Archibald Crossley (Geer, 2004). During World War II, many social psychologists, sociologists and economists also gained first-hand experience of opinion surveys while working in Washington DC for government agencies and bureaus, such as the Department of Agriculture's Division of Program Surveys studying attitudes among farmers and the Federal Reserve Board which analyzed economic behavior and consumer sentiment. The most well-known use of these techniques was exemplified by the American Soldier study, led by Samuel A. Stouffer for the War Department, examining the social psychology of the armed forces through over one hundred questionnaires administered to military personnel (Stouffer et al., 1949). Non-profit organizations also played an important role, notably the Rockefeller foundation which sponsored research on mass communications and the effects of radio.

Following these initiatives, academic survey institutions studying public opinion and social change became established in the US through pioneering work at the National Opinion Research Center (1941) which settled at the University of Chicago, Paul Lazarsfeld's Bureau for Applied Social Research (1944) at Columbia University, and the Survey Research Center (1946) at the University of Michigan. In particular, Lazarsfeld's Erie County, Ohio study used probability samples in a campaign panel survey during the Roosevelt-Wilkie presidential race, generating the landmark *The people' choice* (Lazarsfeld et al., 1944). During

the following decades, public opinion surveys based on scientific sampling techniques became more widely used by social science researchers and governments, reflecting the growth of the market research industry and the expansion in social science grants available from major agencies and foundations (Converse, 1987). The US was far from alone in this regard; many affluent postindustrial societies such as Britain saw the establishment of commercial market research companies, including Gallup, Harris, MORI, and Roper, and the spread of behavioral techniques in the social sciences in Scandinavia and many countries in Western Europe (Dahl, 1961). A strong international community of market research and survey researchers has long existed, exemplified by coverage of public opinion in different countries in the first issue of *Public Opinion Quarterly* and the establishment of the World Association of Public Opinion Research (WAPOR) in 1947.

DEMOCRATIC PARTICIPATION AND THE CIVIC CULTURE

Despite important transatlantic connections in the community of social scientists and market research organizations, the vast majority of political and social attitudinal surveys were based on samples of the population in each nation. The use of dedicated cross-national surveys using a single common instrument or battery of questions first arose with the 1948 study *How nations see each other* by Buchanan and Cantril, the USIA International Relations survey, the 1956 International Stratification survey by the sociologists Ganzeboom and Nieuwbeerta, the 1957 *Pattern of human concerns* survey also by Cantril, and the 1959 Civic culture study by Almond and Verba.

The focus of Almond and Verba's work reflected contemporary concern to understand the underlying causes of regime instability reflected in the rise of Nazi Germany and Italian fascism. The ground-breaking study presented an ambitious theory of cognitive and affective orientations among the mass population, developing concepts which remain central in the contemporary lexography of political science. The intellectual roots of the Civic culture, and the sociological and psychological explanation for political behavior, originated during the inter-war era with the Chicago school, notably Charles Merriam's study on *The making of citizens* (1931), as well as Harold Lasswell's *Psychopathology and politics* (1930). Harry Eckstein's (1961) work *A theory of stable democracy* was also highly influential. Building upon this foundation, Almond and Verba's theory emphasized that stable democracies required equilibrium with the mass public finely balanced between the dangers of either an excessively apathetic and disengaged citizenry, on the one hand, or an overly-agitated and heated engagement, on the other.[2] The idea that societies differed in their political culture was hardly novel; indeed it had been the subject of philosophical speculation for centuries, in classic works from Montesquieu to de Tocqueville. But one of the more radical aspects of the civic culture study was the way that empirical support for the theory was derived from a path-breaking cross-national opinion survey, demonstrating that citizen's orientations could be examined empirically among the mass publics in Mexico, Italy, Britain, France, and Germany.

This influential model established a quantum leap in the methods and concerns common in comparative political science. It was followed in 1963 by the 8-nation *Political Participation* study sponsored by the International Social Science Council, with Asher, Richardson and Weisberg et al. as the principle investigators. A few years later, Sidney Verba expanded upon his earlier work to develop the *Political Participation and Equality* survey in seven nations in 1966, with collaborators Norman Nie and Jae-On Kim. The eight-nation 1973 and 1981 *Political Action Surveys* by Klaus Allerbeck, Max Kaase, Hans-Dieter Klingemann, Samuel Barnes, Alan Marsh, and Ronald Inglehart shared similar concerns,

seeking to build upon this foundation and to expand the study of participation to understand 'unconventional' forms of protests and mass demonstrations which were widespread among the trilateral democracies during this decade (Barnes et al., 1979).

THE EXPANSION OF THE EU AND THE EURO-BAROMETER

Meanwhile in a parallel development, the use of survey methods in international affairs and by multilateral organizations saw important advances. The 1948 study *How nations see each other* sought to document attitudes and prejudices among the public and perceptions of foreign affairs. In Europe, in 1962 Jacques-Rene Rabier, in his role as Director General of Press and Information for the European Community, pioneered the first five-nation cross-national survey of mass attitudes toward European integration and institutions, as the fore-runner of the Euro-Barometer. In 1970, Rabier carried out a seven-nation survey to understand public support for and against European integration, including measures of Materialist/Post-Materialist values, with Ronald Inglehart serving as a consultant in the design and analysis. The results generated additional cross-national surveys in 1971 and 1973, leading to the launch of the Euro-barometer surveys in 1974. These studies have now been carried out every spring and fall since then, reflecting the steadily expanding borders of the European Union, now covering 27 countries. The program was later enlarged by small scale but topical Flash Euro-barometers and the Central and Eastern Euro-barometers; later replaced by the Candidate Countries Euro-barometers. The project was designed to be useful primarily for European Union officials and only secondarily for the research community.

Questions can be identified, trends for the standard items in the Euro-barometer series 1973–2004 can be generated interactively, and descriptive tables, graphs, or data down-loaded via the EB website.[3] Data were also integrated into the Mannheim Euro-barometer Trend File 1970–1999 and ZUMA also maintain the online Main Trends Documentation.[4] The data received from the principal investigator are checked, corrected, and formatted to archival standards by the Inter-university Consortium for Political and Social Research (ICPSR), in cooperation with ZUMA's Zentralarchiv at Cologne and the Swedish Social Science Data Service (SSD). ZUMA maintains a codebook and questionnaire continuity guide, which is an invaluable shortcut since around seventy separate surveys are available. Euro-barometer raw data and documentation (questionnaires and codebooks etc.) are stored at the ICPSR and at the Zentralarchiv and made available for research purposes by other social science Data Archives. Survey results are also regularly published in official reports issued by the Euro-barometer unit of the European Commission.[5] The Euro-barometer series has been commonly used in studies of the politics of the European Union, but, despite the richness of the accumulated datasets, the full potential of this series for comparative politics remains relatively under-utilized. The exemplification of its potential contribution includes Ingehart's *The silent revolution* (1977) as well as, more recently, the *Beliefs in Government* project headed by Max Kaase and Kenneth Newton (1995). The latter generated a five-volume book series, published in 1995 by Oxford University Press, exploring trends in a wide range of social and political orientations, patterns of political activism, and international attitudes.

GOING GLOBAL: THE WORLD VALUES SURVEY/EUROPEAN VALUES SURVEY

The Euro-Barometer also contributed directly toward the European Values Survey.[6] This project was launched in 1981 by a Belgian

Jesuit sociologist, Father Jan Kerkhofs, and a Dutch sociologist, Ruud de Moor, initially to understand why church attendance was falling sharply across Western Europe. The investigators were aware of the Euro-Barometer surveys and they contacted Jacques Rabier, who joined them in designing the surveys. Rabier persuaded them to do a broader study of values, on the basis that attitudes toward religion were linked to one's entire worldview. The European Values Survey based at the University of Tilburg was modeled on the Euro-barometer, with some of the same survey organizations and advisers.[7]

In 1990 the survey was replicated as the World Values Study (WVS) and Ronald Inglehart was charged with widening the geographic coverage, which doubled from 22 countries in 1981 to 41 in 1990–1991. The third wave of the WVS was carried out in 55 nations in 1995–1996. The fourth WVS wave, with 59 nation-states, took place in 1999–2001. The fifth WVS wave was carried out in 2005–2007.[8] The World Values Survey represents a worldwide investigation of socio-cultural and political change. This project has carried out representative national surveys of the basic values and beliefs of the publics in more than 90 independent countries, containing over 88 per cent of the world's population and covering all six inhabited continents. This project is carried out by an international network of social scientists, with local funding for each survey, although in some cases supplementary funds have been used from outside sources. In exchange for providing the data from interviews with a representative national sample of at least 1,000 people in their own society, each participating group gets access to the data from all of the other participating societies. The project is guided by the World Values Survey Association, representing all regions of the world. Coordination is managed by an executive steering committee and secretariat, chaired by Ronald Inglehart at the University of Michigan.

The World Values Study remains the only academic global public opinion survey with a standard instrument administered in countries in all world regions, including growing geographic coverage of societies in the Middle East, Asia, and Africa. Time-series analysis is hindered by the fact that country coverage and certain items vary across successive waves, and the 1981–1983 first wave focused on post-industrial societies. Nevertheless the WVS provides a benchmark for many developing societies, such as South Africa, where for many years it was the only widely available cross-national survey monitoring a wide range of social and political values. This study has given rise to numerous publications, in 16 languages.[9] The *Human beliefs and values* sourcebook (Inglehart et al., 2004) makes the data easily available. The WVS website facilitates the online generation of simple descriptive statistics, such as frequencies and cross-tabulations, as well as making available the questionnaires, technical details and the downloadable dataset.[10]

in 43 nations, including many industrial and post-industrial societies.[11] Each survey covers a representative sample of the national population. The focus is the inclusion of a thematic annual module with a battery of items carried in existing social national surveys, with the annual theme covering rotating issues in the social sciences, such as national identity, the role of government, religion, the environment, work orientations, and gender roles. Considerable attention is paid toward standardizing the social and demographic background information in the surveys. The ISSP has a more limited geographic scope than the World Values Survey, and a narrower thematic focus than the WVS or the Euro-Barometers. Nevertheless, the survey provides considerable depth on each thematic topic, with some comparisons over time where modules are repeated, and a rigorous focus on establishing the quality of cross-national survey methods. The ISSP has generated almost 3,000 publications, including various edited collections.[12]

THE INTERNATIONAL SOCIAL SURVEY PROGRAM

In 1972, in the University of Chicago, NORC started the General Social Survey, an annual (subsequently biennial) study of social and political attitudes. Other countries followed suit, including the Allgemeinen Bevolkerungsumfragen der Socialwissenschaften (ALLBUS) of the Zentrum für Umfragen, Methoden, und Analysen (ZUMA) in Mannheim, Germany in 1980 and the British Social Attitudes series conducted by Social and Community Planning Research (SCPR), London in 1983. The International Social Survey Program (ISSP) was established in 1985 to expand cross-national collaboration by bringing together pre-existing, social science projects. The ISSP coordinates research goals among the consortium, thereby adding a cross-national perspective to the individual, national studies. The ISSP started with just six countries but it has gradually grown to cover attitudes

THE COMPARATIVE STUDY OF ELECTORAL SYSTEMS

One of the most notable off-springs of the behavioral revolution were the programs of academic election surveys based on national probability samples of the electorate, which followed the establishment in 1948 of the American National Election Study series at the University of Michigan. Similar programs of national election studies were established in Sweden (1956), Germany (1961), Norway (1965), Britain (1963), and the Netherlands (1971). Often there were direct exports from the Michigan team, a process exemplified by the establishment of the British Election Study by Donald Stokes and David Butler, a series carried out by teams of scholars in each subsequent British general election. Stokes also collaborated with Don Aitkin in the first Australian national election study in 1967. Election studies shared many common intellectual roots, commonly using a similar (although not identical) survey research design and questions to monitor long-term patterns of social, partisan and ideological alignments, political and social values, attitudes toward specific election issues and government performance, and voting choice and participation. Nevertheless, at least until recently, important inconsistencies of methodology and questionnaire design even in the same series of elections within countries, as well as between nations, hampered comparative research efforts over time, as well as cross-nationally.

The launch of the Comparative Study of Electoral Systems in the mid-1990s strengthened collaborative links among national election studies in over 50 nation-states, by developing a common battery of questions to be carried in each country. The International Committee for Research into Elections and Representative Democracy (ICORE), founded at the 1989 ECPR Joint Workshops, played an important role in getting the project off the ground. The initial idea was to try to understand voting choices under varying conditions and institutional rules, suggesting the need to maximize the number of countries and types of national election under comparison.[13] The Comparative Study of Electoral Systems (CSES) brings together an international team of collaborators who have incorporated a special battery of survey questions into the national election studies, based on a representative sample of the electorate in each country. Data from each of the separate election studies is coordinated, integrated and cleaned by the Center for Political Studies, Institute for Social Research, at the University of Michigan. The dataset is designed to facilitate the comparison of macro and micro-level electoral data. Module 1 of the CSES (1996–2001) allows comparison of a representative cross-section of the electorate in 37 legislative and presidential national elections in 32 countries. The geographic coverage is remarkably diverse, ranging from Belarus and Ukraine to Canada, Australia, and Belgium. The focus on voters' choices, the cross-national integration, and above all the timing of the data collection

(within a year following each of the elections), provide a unique opportunity to compare voting behavior in a way that is not possible through other common sources of comparative data such as the World Values Survey. Fieldwork, data-collection, and integration of the third module are underway. Data for each wave is released for analysis as soon as it has been collected and deposited. The CSES facilitates cross-national electoral analysis although data analysis is complicated by the diverse range of global regions, regimes, and levels of democracy included in the study. This suggests adoption of a 'most different' comparative strategy, rather than the familiar regional/area approach. The integration of the data collected from each national election survey, for example the demographic and social coding, is also far more complicated than in a single-funded or single-instrument survey, such as the Euro-barometer. The main strength of the CSES is the capacity for multi-level analysis combining analysis of voting behavior and political participation within contrasting institutional contexts.

THE EUROPEAN VOTER, THE EUROPEAN ELECTION STUDY, THE COMPARATIVE NATIONAL ELECTIONS PROJECT

Resources for the comparative study of voting behavior are supplemented by the integration of six separate national election studies series, including those conducted over successive decades in Denmark, Sweden, Norway, the Netherlands, Germany, and Britain, into the European Voter dataset.[14] One important limitation concerns how far differences in wording and classification schemas used in separate questionnaires in the series of national election studies can be regarded as providing conceptual equivalence. This is important for reliable comparisons of basic background variables, such as social stratification and religiosity, as well as for analysis of ideological and issue positions. Where successive teams of researchers lead the research design, amendments to coding schemes, core topics, or question wording are often introduced over time into national election surveys. In such situations, it is difficult to establish if these discontinuities produced subtle but significant differences in responses, or whether public opinion has indeed altered. In addition, the comparative framework is limited to parts of Northern Europe; the dataset excludes available series such as the American National Election Study, as well as many European countries, such as France, Spain, and Ireland, which have not established an equivalent continuous series. The time-series is also irregular, with series starting in 1956 in Sweden but only in 1971 in the Netherlands and Denmark. Nevertheless, with these provisos, the integrated European Voter dataset has facilitated systematic cross-national time-series analysis for classic issues in voting behavior, such as whether social cleavages and partisan identification have gradually weakened their imprint on the electorate in successive elections across West European polities.

Since 1979, the quinquennial series of European Election Study (EES) has also explored voting choice, participation, and ideological issues in the direct elections to the European Parliament, as well as facilitating comparison of mass-elite attitudes, the evolution of the European community, and perceptions about the EU's performance.[15] The scope of the survey has expanded with EU membership. The EES has generated a series of books and articles, contributing to important methodological innovations as well as expanding our understanding of the conditions of voting choice and turnout in 'second-order' contests.[16]

The Comparative National Elections Project (CNEP) is another related study, coordinated by Richard Gunther, currently including two-dozen national election surveys conducted in 19 countries since 1990. It has evolved in three distinct phases: CNEP I, CNEP II, and CNEP III, which have steadily widened the global coverage. All share a concern with the processes of intermediation through which citizens receive information about policies, parties, candidates during the course of election campaigns, thus reviving the long neglected research perspective of the Columbia School established by Paul Lazarsfeld and his colleagues in the 1940s and 1950s. The study is particularly rich on questions about information flows via primary and secondary networks, as well as the role of the mass media.[17]

THE GLOBAL-BAROMETERS

Rather than a single entity, the global-barometer series consists of five separate regional projects, loosely coordinated, and originally inspired by the Eurobarometer model. These focus upon attitudes toward democracy, governance, economics, political participation, and national identity, with a special focus on newer democracies in developing nations. The *New Europe* series, coordinated by Richard Rose, has focused upon monitoring the process of cultural change in political and economic attitudes following the breakdown of communism. The annual survey has been conducted in selected Central and Eastern European countries and it has resulted in numerous papers and books. Under the leadership of Marta Lagos (MORI, Santiago), the *Latinobarometer* has conducted pioneering work monitoring annual trends in attitudes toward democracy. The series started with eight nations in 1995, initially funded by the EU, and it has subsequently expanded to cover representative samples of the publics in eighteen countries in the region. Founded as a private, non-profit institution, the survey has been less widely utilized by Latin Americanists than might be expected, given the topic and the quality of the data. Online interactive access to the questionnaire database is available.[18]

The *Afro-barometer* was pioneered by Michael Bratton et al. who developed networks of surveyors in many countries, such as Mali, Tanzania, and Zambia which have never had a series of social scientific surveys of political and social attitudes.[19] The Afrobarometer has conducted three rounds of national probability sample surveys covering 18 African countries in the most recent study. It also serves as a model of transparency by releasing full information about the work in progress, including questionnaires, publications, funding, and associates, as well as depositing all data through archives and its own dedicated website.[20]

The *East Asia Barometer* joined the network in 2002, sharing similar concerns to monitor public attitudes toward democratization and economic development, with eight nations coordinated in the survey by Yun-han Chu in Taiwan.[21] The study expanded in 2006 to become *the Asian Barometer* covering 17 nations (Japan, Mongolia, South Korea, Taiwan, Hong Kong, China, the Philippines, Thailand, Vietnam, Cambodia, Singapore, Indonesia, India, Pakistan, Bangladesh, Sri Lanka, and Nepal).[22] Lastly, under the leadership of Mark Tessler at the University of Michigan, in 2006 the *Arab Barometer* conducted surveys of economic and political attitudes in five Arab societies (the Palestinian Territories, Jordan, Morocco, Algeria, and Kuwait).[23]

Contemporary survey research is therefore now covering large parts of the developing world, such as Africa and the Middle East, which were previously neglected, thereby building up the infrastructure of experienced fieldwork teams, market and social science research organizations, and survey analysts that will pay dividends in future. The surveys facilitate cross-national networks among networks of collaborators, while also retaining the flexibility of regional autonomy to focus on specific themes of most interest to each area. The Global-barometer project is seeking to strengthen the collaborative linkages to use consistent question wording and methodologies.[24] An important challenge is to make sure that this data is not simply exported to the west but that it is available and utilized by the social science communities within each region, by equipping the next generation of graduate students with the necessary intellectual frameworks, skills, and infrastructure to exploit the data.

THE EUROPEAN SOCIAL SURVEY

The European Social Survey (the ESS), which started in 2002, is an academically-driven social survey designed to chart and explain the interaction between Europe's changing institutions and the attitudes, beliefs and behavior patterns of its diverse populations.[25] The survey covers two-dozen nations (in Western and Central Europe) and it uses rigorous methodologies. The survey contains a core battery of questions that is replicated every two years in addition to rotating thematic modules, allocated to teams of scholars on a competitive basis. Core funding comes from the European Commission's 5th Framework Programme, with supplementary funds from the European Science Foundation which also sponsored the development of the study over a number of years, while surveys in each country are funded by each national social science council. The project is directed by a Central Coordinating Team led by Roger Jowell at the Centre for Comparative Social Surveys, City University. The organization of the survey emphasizes transparency and employing high standards in sampling and fieldwork practices, and it is carefully standardizing the collection of social and demographic background data. The central coordination and funding of the ESS, the care in crafting and testing the questionnaire, and the development of additional contextual data, provides a model for cross-national survey research.

THE PEW GLOBAL ATTITUDES SURVEY

US-based survey organizations have also contributed toward the expansion of global resources. In response to the aftermath of 9/11, Afghanistan and Iraq, attention in the United States has turned increasingly toward understanding how the world (particularly Muslim societies) views America. 'Soft diplomacy' through the mass media has also spurred greater interest among the international relations and foreign policy community into issues of global cultural similarity and difference.

In response, in 2002 Andrew Kohut at the Pew Center for the People and the Press launched the *Pew Global Attitudes Survey*, an annual attempt to monitor public opinion in many countries, using market research. The project is a series of worldwide public opinion surveys, originally of more than 38,000 people in 44 countries in 2002, and expanded in 2003 with additional surveys to a total of nearly 75,000 people among the 50 populations surveyed (49 countries plus the Palestinian Authority). The initiative built on an earlier study, the *Pulse of Europe* (1991). The project encompasses a broad array of subjects ranging from people's assessments of their own lives to their views about the current state of the world and important issues of the day. The Pew Global Attitudes Project is chaired by former US Secretary of State Madeleine K. Albright. The project is funded by The Pew Charitable Trusts, with a supplemental grant from the William and Flora Hewlett Foundation. The published reports have attracted considerable media attention as well as interest in the State Department and in the broader policy community.

TRANSATLANTIC TRENDS

Similar factors prompted the launch of the *Transatlantic Trends* project in 2002, an annual public opinion survey examining American and European attitudes toward the transatlantic relationship.[26] Indeed this concern reflects some of the earliest surveys about how national publics regard each other,

and the role of public opinion in foreign policy. Sponsored by the German Marshall Fund of the United States and the Compagnia di San Paolo, with additional support from other foundations, the survey focuses upon attitudes in the United States and up to a dozen European countries. The study looks at a range of issues including the state of transatlantic relations; perceptions of international threats, such as terrorism, energy dependence, immigration, and global warming; attitudes toward the EU as a global actor in development, trade, peacekeeping, reconstruction, and combat; transatlantic cooperation on international challenges such as Afghanistan, Iran and Russia, and democracy promotion as a foreign policy goal. The surveys are designed primarily for journalists and policymakers, rather than for academic research.

GALLUP INTERNATIONAL
VOICE OF THE PEOPLE

The last survey under comparison, coordinated by Gallup International, is similar in orientation to the Pew survey but with a more commercial orientation. In 2002, Gallup International conducted a worldwide survey of 60 nations monitoring attitudes toward issues such as the environment, terrorism, global issues, governance and democracy. In 2003 this survey was conducted again covering Western Europe, the USA, and Canada but also Africa, the Middle East, Asia, Eastern Europe, and Latin America. Highlights of the results are published on their website but the published report (containing detailed cross-tabulations) and the electronic data are available only for commercial purchase. Gallup International offers the opportunity for clients to add items to the questionnaire, also at cost. Information about the quality of the detailed methodology, sampling, and fieldwork practices in countries where surveys are uncommon, such as in the Middle East and Africa, are available on Gallup's website.

Both Pew and Gallup are therefore breaking new ground by expanding their geographic coverage in ambitious attempts to monitor public opinion around the world. This contributes to the resources available for analysis although it remains too early to evaluate the quality and utility of these surveys.

THE GLOBALIZATION OF PUBLIC OPINION SURVEYS

What facilitated these developments? Many political and intellectual factors have contributed toward the internationalization of attitudinal and behavioral survey. As the world has become more interconnected through globalization, the social sciences have been tugged in its wake. The gradual expansion of the borders of the European Union played a direct role, as the European Commission has monitored public opinion on a regular basis since the early-1970s through the Euro-barometer and related surveys of mass and elite opinion. In turn, the existence of the Euro-barometer, including the fieldwork organizations and collaborators, served as a model shaping many other initiatives, such as the 1981 European Values Study and the 1979 European Elections Study. Regional and international associations of political scientists have strengthened professional networks and institutional linkages, notably the International Political Science Association and especially the European Consortium of Political Research, with regular workshops and conferences which strengthened intellectual and social networks among teams of collaborators. The growth of electoral democracies has also probably facilitated the study of public opinion, since this development facilitates freedom of expression for conducting independent social surveys and publishing the results of the analysis, also triggering the demand for commercial market research companies and non-profit social science institutes, free from political interference and overt state censorship. Many of the surveys, from the Civic culture study to the CSES

and global barometers, have been driven by the urge to understand the process of democracy and democratization. International development agencies, such as the UNDP, the World Bank, and Transparency International, have increasingly recognized that programs seeking to expand democracy and good governance need to monitor public opinion, as well as using the standard 'objective' developmental indicators.

Particular scholars in the field have had a decisive and enduring impact. Many colleagues have contributed to this process, including early pioneers such as Sidney Verba at Harvard University, Jacques-Rene Rabier in the European Union, Ronald Inglehart at the University of Michigan, Jaques Thomassen at the University of Twente, Richard Gunther at Ohio State University, Marta Lagos at MORI-Chile, and Roger Jowell at City University, all of whom played seminal roles, through initiating, managing, and sustaining major cross-national surveys which have had multiplier effects through funding public opinion institutes and training the next generation of field-work staff and survey analysts. The availability of training institutes has also contributed, such as the Michigan and Essex summer schools in social statistics, through strengthening skills in quantitative analysis among the younger generation of social scientists in many countries. Modern international communications, notably the ease of communicating among colleagues and distributing electronic datasets online through the standard social science archives and dedicated websites, have greatly facilitated awareness and use of these resources. Whether leading or following, intellectual fashions have also contributed toward this process, eroding interest in traditional approaches to area studies focused on specific countries, and encouraging the demand among the younger generation of researchers in Asia, Latin America, and Eastern Europe for more systematic cross-national comparison of political culture and behavior, conducted within varying institutional contexts.

The most recent spur has been the events of 9/11 and their aftermath in the Afghanistan and Iraq war, renewing American interest about public opinion in the rest of the world. In particular, this has stimulated new research in areas such as the Middle East where previously cross-national social science surveys have been non-existent or scarce. These developments have gradually transformed the geographic scope of coverage, with an exponential surge in the available survey resources occurring during the last decade, allowing comparativists to move 'from nations to categories', one of the key but elusive goals of the sub-discipline.

METHODOLOGICAL ISSUES ARISING FROM CROSS-NATIONAL SURVEYS

Nevertheless the expansion worldwide that has occurred has also raised critical challenges about ensuring the quality and comparability of the cross-national surveys (Jowell, 1998; Kuechler, 1987, 1998). Some of these concerns are far from novel; indeed concern dates back to the original Almond and Verba study (Verba, 1971). These concerns have arisen with greater urgency, however, with the growing spread of methods, techniques and theoretical frameworks in diverse cultures and contexts, including across varied developing societies (Park and Jowell, 1997).

The first issue which is often raised is about conceptual equivalence (van Deth, 1998; and in this volume). McIntyre (1973) voiced the concern whether core concepts such as national pride, used in the civic culture study, carried similar meanings in the context of societies such as Italy, Germany and Britain. This issue is a constant challenge for cross-national questionnaires which extends far beyond matters of linguistic translation. Languages are not just ways to communicate the same ideas and values; instead they may carry alternative ways of thinking and understanding. This problem is often encountered when ideas such as the left-right continuum or the liberal-conservative scale are interpreted quite differently in different societies; for example 'liberal' in the United States is usually understood as social liberalism located on the 'left' of the political spectrum, while 'liberal' in Europe is commonly regarded as 'economic' or 'free market' liberalism located on the center-right. The complexity of notions which are carried in social surveys, such as the concepts of 'democracy', 'corruption', 'religiosity', or 'nationalism', may well generate responses to the same words and phrases which are far from functionally-equivalent.

At the same time, while a particular challenge in interpreting the results of cross-national surveys, this problem is far from unique to these studies. Multilingual and plural societies face similar language issues, for example in India, as do cities and regions of the United States, such as California and New York, with a high proportion of immigrants and non-native speakers. Indeed the broader issue of whether the same wording generates the equivalent meaning also applies to interpreting any group differences in response within any society, for example whether there are shared understandings among social classes, regions, or sexes. The most appropriate, although not the perfect, standard way to try to ensure language equivalence uses processes of translation and then 'back' translation, which seeks to ensure linguistic consistency. The questionnaire designers should also provide supplementary notes for translators explaining the intended meaning of questions, to help identify functionally-equivalent phrases (Harkness, 2007). Rigorous tests should ideally also be employed, including piloting new questions prior to wholesale roll out and also checking by comparing the error structure for several items, and thus the reliability and validity of these questions in different languages.[27] In addition exploratory factor analysis can be used as a check on whether attitudinal and ideological scales have similar meaning in different societies.

Another major issue concerns the strict standards which should be used to evaluate the quality of any survey data and any systematic sources of error or bias. Even modest methodological differences in coding schemes, questionnaire design and item order, sampling processes, fieldwork and interview techniques, or cooperation and response rates can contribute toward misleading interpretations of the significance of any cross-national differences in attitudes and values (Heath et al., 2005; Kuechler, 1998). There are three main categories of cross-national datasets, and these differ substantially in how far they facilitate control of standards. *Centralized surveys* are administered and coordinated by a team of investigators, who raise and pool common core resources, with a single dedicated questionnaire instrument translated into different languages (exemplified by the Euro-barometers directed by the European Commission). *Collaborative surveys* are also centrally administered by a core team with a single common survey instrument, but fieldwork for each national survey is mainly funded from local sources (e.g., the World Values Survey). Lastly, *integrative projects* bring together locally administered and locally-funded surveys (e.g., The European Voter Study).

Common standards are easiest to maintain in the first category, and most difficult in the last. Making sure that methods and techniques are similar is a considerable challenge even with the same survey instrument, such as the European Social Survey, used by different fieldwork organizations. It is even more problematic in projects such as the Comparative Study of Electoral Systems and the European Voter, which seek to integrate standards used in independent parallel national surveys. The battery of items in the CSES, for example, can be carried in the main face-to-face questionnaire or it may be administered through a self-completion supplementary questionnaire. Standardization is as important for the background demographic and social variables, especially classifications based on social stratification, religious faith and ethnic identity, as it is for attitudinal and behavioral items, such as voting and party choice or ideological self-placement. Even modest variations in coding conventions, question order, fieldwork timing, or sampling procedures can seriously limit the comparability of the responses. Unfortunately demographic and social classifications, random probability or quota sampling methods, and forms of interviewing or non-response rates may be deeply institutionalized in the procedures used by each survey organization. Piggybacking a few questions into omnibus commercial or attitudinal surveys in each country is highly problematic, due to differences of sequencing and item order. Where there are common resources sponsoring the survey instrument and fieldwork, and a tight organizational and decision-making structure among teams of collaborators, as with the European Social Survey, this is most likely to ensure the most rigorous and consistent technical standards. Yet for many reasons, including lack of resources, most cross-national surveys do not have this framework. The best approach in these circumstances is to make sure that all procedures and technical matters are clearly documented and that this is available to researchers, who can then decide how best to handle any inconsistencies. In addition, the expansion in the availability of surveys in multiple countries facilitates replication of results, so that generalizations made on the basis of a few cases, or a single region, can be tested in other contexts and different conditions.

CONCLUSIONS

Opportunities for cross-national survey research have been transformed out of all recognition over the last decades. Until the early-1970s, most cross-national surveys of public opinion were largely focused upon affluent post-industrial societies, particularly Western Europe as a natural comparative laboratory, where market research organizations had become widely established, where there were dense networks of scholars and data archives, and where foundations and social science councils had the resources to support academic research. The 1985 launch and gradual expansion of the International Social Survey Program, accompanied by the transformation of the European Values Survey into the World Values Survey in 1990, represented the start of the globalization of public opinion research, a trend which continues today. Developing societies had most commonly used administrative and social surveys, as well as collecting census data, for information about social conditions. An example was the first national household survey, which was pioneered in India in 1950 (Bulmer, 1993). Mexico had also been included in some of the earliest surveys on political participation. But until the early-1990s, few cross-national surveys which systematically monitored social and political attitudes and behavior based on random samples of the general population were available covering a wide range of developing nations. The availability of cross-national datasets was transformed by the gradual expansion of successive waves of the World Values Survey since 1991 to over 90 nation-states, the network of national electoral studies brought together under the umbrella of the Comparative Study of Electoral Systems, the global barometer series covering a wide range of countries in Latin America, post-Communist states in the New Europe barometer, Africa, and Asia, as well as the 2002 European Social Survey, Transatlantic Trends, and the Pew and Gallup global surveys launched in recent years.

The multiplicity of surveys is to be welcomed by facilitating replication both across years and among nations. Some of the more commercial initiatives may fail, for example if America withdraws into itself and turns away from the world again, in its periodic cyclical fashion. Yet it seems likely that the underlying momentum will continue in subsequent decades, as younger generations of social scientists trained in survey methods and public opinion analysis are developing in each world region. Questions can be raised about the quality of sampling and fieldwork, especially for surveys conducted in developing nations which have not built

up experienced market research companies and established social science institutes. There are also issues about the reliability of conducting public opinion surveys in countries such as Belarus and China with repressive regimes which regularly suppress freedom of expression and opinion. Nevertheless the expansion of datasets has the important benefit of allowing replication across different surveys, thereby allowing independent cross-checks. Questions can be raised about the quality of questionnaire translations and the employment of equivalent standards across different nations – debates which have been with us ever since *The civic culture*. Yet in counterbalance there are certain distinct practical advantages associated with conducting surveys in developing nations, namely much lower refusal and non-response rates (currently approaching record levels for opinion polls conducted in the US), as well as relatively low budgets for fieldwork. Over time, as greater experience is gained, and as an institutional survey infrastructure is developed in the social sciences, these initiatives will gradually mature.

Therefore despite important limitations, cross-national survey research is invaluable for establishing generalities about human behavior, allowing us to test regularities arising from single-nation studies. The multiplicity of datasets which are now available for analysis in different societies strengthens replication, to ensure robust findings and generalizations, for example comparing trends in religiosity or class voting in the same countries using the Euro-Barometer, the World Values Survey and the European Voter study. Most importantly, the availability of many large-scale multi-national surveys covering many societies allows us to move from the analysis of countries to the study of public opinion under a wide variety of institutional and societal contexts, such as in developing and post-industrial economies, in predominately Muslim or Orthodox societies, in newer democracies in Mediterranean and Eastern Europe, or under democratic and autocratic regimes. Aggregating public opinion at societal level across multiple countries allows systematic tests of some of the core concerns in the discipline, such as whether underlying individual-level attitudes such as trust or political efficacy are conducive to the stability of democratic stability, as the civic culture study suggested. With a sufficiently large number of countries, the linkages between culture, social structure, and regime institutions can be examined. Through this process, the sub-field is gradually moving from the comparison of individuals and groups within countries as the core unit of analysis toward the comparison of people living under different types of societies and regimes, a development which is capable of providing powerful new insights for the study of comparative politics.

ACKNOWLEDGEMENTS

This chapter greatly benefited from detailed and invaluable comments and observations made to an earlier draft by Ronald Inglehart and Ian McAllister, including information about the historical evolution of the Euro-barometer and the European Values/World Values Surveys, as well as background to the CSES.

NOTES

1. A comprehensive chronological list of comparative survey research resources and datasets is available at http://www.gesis.org/en/data_service/eurobarometer/handbook/index.htm; see also Donsbach and Traugott (2008).

2. For the intellectual history of the origins of the civic culture study, see Almond (1996) and Munck and Snyder (2007).

3. EB website: http://ec.europa.eu/public_opinion/cf/index_en.cfm

4. Details can be found at: http://www.za.uni-koeln.de/

5. Details can be found at: http://europa.eu.int/en/comm/dg10/infcom/epo/eb.html.

6. I greatly appreciate the comments that Ronald Inglehart conveyed in personal communications about the historical evolution of the Euro-barometer and the European Values/World Values Surveys.

7. http://www.europeanvalues.nl

8. Full methodological details about the World Values Surveys, including the questionnaires, sampling procedures, fieldwork procedures, principle investigators, and organization can be found at: www.worldvaluessurvey.org.

9. Among the many publications emerging from this project, books include Inglehart and Norris (2003), Inglehart and Welzel (2005), Norris and Inglehart (2004).

10. www.worldvaluessurvey.org.

11. ISSP has grown to 43 nations, the founding four – Germany, the United States, Great Britain, and Australia – plus Austria, Ireland, Hungary, the Netherlands, Italy, Israel, Norway, the Philippines, New Zealand, Russia, Japan, Bulgaria, Canada, the Czech Republic, Slovenia, Poland, Sweden, Spain, Cyprus, France, Portugal, Slovakia, Latvia, Chile, Denmark, Brazil, South Africa, Switzerland, Venezuela, Belgium, Finland, Mexico, Taiwan, South Korea, Uruguay, Croatia, the Dominican Republic, Turkey, and China. In addition, East Germany was added to the German sample upon reunification.

12. For instance, Jowell et al. 1993, 1989, 1998.

13. For the use of the dataset for this purpose, see Norris (2004).

14. See Thomassen (2005). Data and methodological details are available from ZUMA (2008).

15. For details about the methodology, research design and questionnaire, see http://www.europeanelectionstudies.net/.

16. Book publication include, amongst others, Katz and Wessels (1999), Schmitt and Thomassen (2000), van der Brug and van der Eijk's (forthcoming), van der Eijk and Arbor (1996).

17. See Gunther et al. (2007), and http://www.cnep.ics.ul.pt.

18. http://www.latinobarometro.org/

19. Publications emerging from the Afrobarometer series include Bratton et al. (2004).

20. For information about the methodology and data, see http://www.afrobarometer.org.

21. See http://www.eastasiabarometer.org.

22. http://www.asianbarometer.org/; see also, Inoguchi et al. (2006).

23. http://arabbarometer.org/

24. http://www.globalbarometer.net/

25. For details, http://www.europeansocialsurvey.org/. See also Jowell et al. (2007).

26. http://www.transatlantictrends.org.

27. See the recommendations by Saris and Gallhofer (2007).

REFERENCES

Almond, G. (1996) *The civic culture: Prehistory, retrospect, and prospect* (Center for the Study of Democracy paper 96-01) University of California, Irvine. Retrieved March 27, 2008, from http://repositories.cdlib.org/csd/96–01

Almond, G. and Verba, S. (1963) *The civic culture*. Princeton, NJ: Princeton University Press.

Barnes, S., Kaase, M., and Allerbeck, K.R. (1979) *Political action: Mass participation in five Western democracies*. Beverley Hills, CA: Sage Publications.

Bowley, A.L. and Burnett-Hurst, A.R. (1915) *Livelihood and poverty: A study in the economic conditions of working-class households*. Bell.

Bratton, M., Mattes, R., and Gyimah-Boadi, E. (2004) *Learning about reform in Africa: Public opinion, democracy, and markets*. Cambridge: Cambridge University Press.

Buchanan, W. and Cantril, H. (1953) *How nations see each other: A study in public opinion*. Urbana: University of Illinois Press.

Bulmer, M. (1986) *The Chicago school of sociology: Institutionalization, diversity, and the rise of sociological research*. Chicago: University of Chicago Press.

Bulmer, M. (1993) *Social research in developing countries: Surveys and censuses in the Third World*. London: Routledge.

Bulmer, M. (1998) 'The problem of exporting social survey research', *The American Behavioral Scientist*, 42 (2): 153–67.

Bulmer, M., Bales, K., and Sklar, K.K. (eds.) (1992) *The social survey in historical perspective, 1880–1940*. Cambridge: Cambridge University Press.

Clinton Poole, D. (1937) 'Forward', *The Public Opinion Quarterly*, 1 (1): 3–5.

Converse, J.M. (1987) *Survey research in the United States: Roots and emergence 1890–1960*. Berkeley: University of California Press.

Converse, P.E. (1964) 'Review of Almond and Verba's "The civic culture: Political attitudes and democracy in five nations"', *Political Science Quarterly*, 79 (4): 591–93.

Crossley, A.M. (1937) 'Straw polls in 1936', *The Public Opinion Quarterly*, 1 (1): 24–35.

Dahl, R.A. (1961) 'The behavioral approach in political science: Epitaph for a monument to a successful protest', *The American Political Science Review*, 55 (4): 763–72.

Donsbach, W. and Traugott, M. (2008) *The SAGE handbook of public opinion research*. London: Sage.

Eckstein, H. (1961) *A theory of stable democracy*. Princeton, NJ: Princeton University Press.

Geer, J. (ed.) (2004) *Public opinion and polling around the world: A historical encyclopedia*. Santa Barbara, CA: ABC-Clio.

Gunther, R., Puhle, H.J., and Montero, J.R. (eds) (2007) *Democracy, intermediation, and voting on four continents*. Oxford: Oxford University Press.

Harkness, J.A. (2007) 'Improving the comparability of translations', in R. Jowell, C. Roberts, R. Fitzgerald, and G. Eva (eds), *Measuring attitudes cross-nationally: Lessons from the European Social Survey*. London: Sage Publications.

Heath, A., Fisher, S., and Smith, S. (2005) 'The globalization of public opinion research', *Annual Review of Political Studies*, 8: 297–333.

Inglehart, R. (1977) *The silent revolution*. Princeton, NJ: Princeton University Press.

Inglehart, R. and Norris, P. (2003) *Rising tide: Gender equality and cultural change worldwide*. Cambridge: Cambridge University Press.

Inglehart, R., Basàñez, M., Dìez-Medrano, J., Halman, L., and Luijkx, R. (eds) (2004) *Human beliefs and values: A cross-cultural sourcebook*. Mexico: Siglo XXI Editores.

Inglehart, R. and Welzel, C. (2005) *Modernization, cultural change and democracy: The human development sequence*. Cambridge: Cambridge University Press.

Inoguchi, T., Tanaka, A., Sonoda, S., and Dadabaev, T. (eds) (2006) *Human beliefs and values in striding Asia. East Asia in focus: Country profiles, thematic analysis, and sourcebook based on the AsiaBarometer Survey of 2004*. Japan: Akashi Shoten.

Jowell, R. (1998) 'How comparative is comparative research?', *American Behavioral Scientist*, 42: 168–77.

Jowell, R., Brook, L., Dowds, L., and Ahrendt, D. (eds) (1993) *International social attitudes: The 10th British social attitudes report*. Aldershot: Dartmouth.

Jowell, R., Curtice, J., Park, A., Brook, L., Thomson, K., and Bryson, C. (eds) (1998) *British – and European – social attitudes: The 15th BSA report*. Aldershot: Ashgate.

Jowell, R., Roberts, C., Fitzgerald, R., and Eva, G. (eds) (2007) *Measuring attitudes cross-nationally: Lessons from the European Social Survey*. London: Sage Publications.

Jowell, R., Witherspoon, S., and Brook, L. (eds) (1989) *British social attitudes: Special international report*. Aldershot: Gower.

Kaase, M. and Newton, K. (1995) *Beliefs in government*. Oxford: Oxford University Press.

Katz, R. and Wessels, B. (1999) *European parliament and European integration*. Oxford, Oxford University Press.

Kuechler, M. (1987) 'The utility of surveys for cross-national research', *Social Science Research*, 16: 229–44.

Kuechler, M. (1998) 'The survey method: An indispensable tool for social science research everywhere?', *American Behavioral Scientist*, 42 (2): 178–200.

McIntyre, A. (1973) 'Is a science of comparative politics possible?', in A. Ryan (ed.), *The Philosophy of social explanation*. Oxford: Oxford University Press.

Lasswell, H.D. (1930) *Psychopathology and politics*. Chicago: Chicago University Press.

Lazarsfeld, P.F., Gaudet, H., and Berelson, B. (1944) *The people's choice: How the voter makes up his mind in a presidential campaign*. New York: Duell, Sloan and Pearce.

Merriam, C.E. (1931) *The making of citizens: A comparative study of methods of civil training*. Chicago: University of Chicago Press.

Merriam, C.E. and Gosnell, H.F. (1924) *Non-voting, causes and methods of control*. Chicago: University of Chicago Press.

Munck, G.L. and Snyder, R. (2007) *Passion, craft, and method in comparative politics*. Johns Hopkins Press.

Norris, P. (2004) *Electoral engineering*. New York: Cambridge University Press.

Norris, P. and Inglehart, R. (2004) *Sacred and secular: Religion and politics worldwide*. Cambridge: Cambridge University Press.

Park, A. and Jowell, R. (1997) *Consistencies and differences in a cross-national survey*. London: SCPR.

Saris, W.E. and Gallhofer, I. (2007) 'Can questions travel successfully?', in R. Jowell, C. Roberts, R. Fitzgerald and G. Eva (eds), *Measuring attitudes cross-nationally: Lessons from the European Social Survey*. London: Sage Publications.

Schmitt, H. and Thomassen, J. (eds) (2000) *Political representation and legitimacy in the European Union*. Oxford: Oxford University Press.

Stouffer, S.A., et al. (1949) *The American soldier. Studies in social psychology in World War II* (Vol 1–2) Princeton, NJ: Princeton University Press.

Tingsten, H. (1937/1963) *Political behavior: Studies in election statistics*. Totowa, NJ: Bedminster Press.

Thomassen, J. (ed.) (2005) *The European voter*. Oxford: Oxford University Press.

van der Brug, W. and van der Eijk, C. (eds) (forthcoming) *European elections and domestic politics. Lessons from the past and scenarios for the future*. Southbend: University of Notre Dame Press.

van der Eijk, C. and Franklin, M. (eds) (1996) *Choosing Europe? The electorate and national politics in the face of union*. Ann Arbor: University of Michigan Press.

van Deth, J. (ed.) (1998) *Comparative politics: The problem of equivalence*. London: Routledge.

Verba, S. (1971) 'Cross-national survey research: the problem of credibility', in I. Vallier (ed.), *Comparative methods in sociology: Essays on trends and applications*. Berkeley: University of California Press.

ZUMA (2008) *The European Voter – database description*. Retrieved March 31, 2008, from https://info1.za.gesis.org/cei/evoter-db.asp

Index

(page references followed by f indicate a figurative illustration, t indicates a table)

Abbott, A., 80, 113, 115
Abdelal et al., 132
Abrams, D., 328
accountability and democracy, 439, 440, 441,
    442, 445, 448, 449–50, 452, 457
Acemoglu, D., 282, 283, 287, 290, 293, 294,
    295, 314, 336, 447, 457, 458
Acemoglu et al., 446, 450, 451
Acharya, A., 479, 482, 484, 485
Achen, C. H., 60
Ackerman, B., 254
activism, 305t, 309f, 311, 312, 313, 315
    see also social movements
Adams, J., 147, 156
Adams et al., 102, 108, 111
Adcock, R., 473
Adler, E., 479
Administrative Procedures Act, USA, 449
administrative transitional justice, 500t, 506–7
Adrian, C. R., 229
Afghanistan, 168, 320, 322, 323, 339, 419, 420,
    429, 465, 533, 535
Africa, 97, 105, 112, 165, 167, 171, 195, 248, 250,
    279, 290, 340, 382, 387, 444, 454, 478, 483,
    487–9, 490, 491, 498, 529, 532, 533, 537
African Economic Community (AEC), 488
African National Congress (ANC), 358
African Union (AU), 487, 488
'Afro-Asian', 166
Afrobarometer, 400, 429, 523t, 531–2, 538
Aguilar, P., 515, 519
Aitkin, D., 529
Aizenman, J., 448
Akhter, M. Y., 402, 405
Al Qaeda, 382
Alatas, S. H., 363, 364
Albright, M., 533
Albrow, M., 111
Alesina, A., 200
Alesina et al., 146
Alexander, J., 104, 111
Algeria, 382, 466, 532
Alker, H. R. Jr., 78
Allan, J. P., 218
ALLBUS, 529
Allen, M., 205
Allerbeck, K., 527
Almeida, P. D., 355, 356
Almond, G., 2, 3, 93, 94, 101, 267, 268, 269, 299, 300,
    302, 312, 432, 522, 525, 526, 527, 535, 538

Alston et al., 450
Alt, J. E., 200
Althusius, 410–11
Alvarez, R. M., 265
Alvarez et al., 37, 201, 280
American Institute of Public Opinion, 525
American National Election Study, 264, 529, 531
American Journal of Political Science, 1, 52
American Political Science Association on
    Comparative Politics, 1, 51, 160
    newsletter, 159
American Political Science Review (APSR), 1, 2,
    52, 250
Aminzade et al., 321, 331
Amnesty International, 74, 429
Amorim, N. O., 227
Amsterdam Treaty, 483
anarchy, 179, 180, 181, 465
Andersen, G. E., 207
Anderson, C. J., 270, 272, 303
Anderson, K., 482
Anderson, L., 279
Anderson, P., 107, 109
Anderson, T. L., 458
Anderson et al., 272, 400
Andersson, S., 370
Andrain, G. F., 112
Andvig, J. C., 371
Angola, 320
Antoniades, A., 517
Apter, D., 101, 112, 163, 164
Arab barometer, 524t, 532, 538
Arab League, 481
Arabian countries, 39, 251, 252, 481, 532
    see also United Arab Emirates
Arbelaez et al., 467
Arbor, A., 538
Arce, D., 471
area studies, role of, 159–74
    defining an area, 135–7
    institutional legacies, diffusion, and verstehen,
        167–70
    stereotypes, 161–5
Archer, M., 107
archival information, 53
Argentina, 60, 168, 198t, 373, 401, 420, 487,
    502, 505, 511, 516, 519
Argersinger, P. H., 405
Aristotle, 281, 300, 423
'aristocratic international' epoch, 183

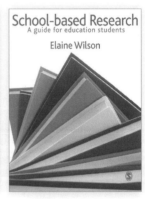

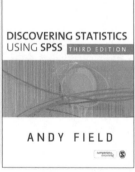
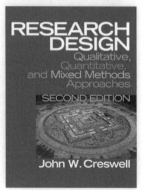

The Qualitative Research Kit

Edited by Uwe Flick

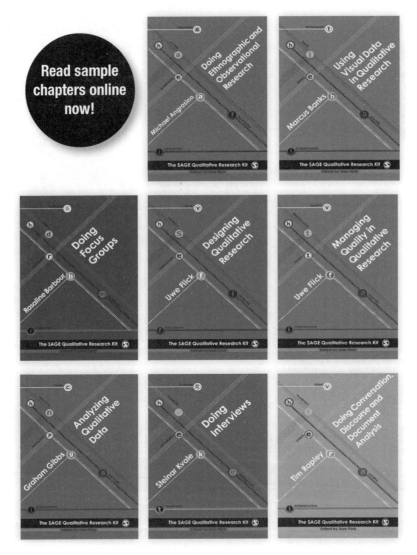

www.sagepub.co.uk